Guide to Psychological Assessment with Asians

Lorraine T. Benuto • Nicholas S. Thaler
Brian D. Leany
Editors

Guide to Psychological Assessment with Asians

Springer

Editors
Lorraine T. Benuto
Administrative Faculty
Department of Psychology
University of Nevada
Reno, NV, USA

Northcentral University
Graduate School Faculty
Prescott Valley, AZ, USA

Brian D. Leany
Lake's Crossing Center: Maximum Security Facility for Forensic Mental Health Services
Sparks, NV, USA

Northcentral University
Graduate School Faculty
Prescott Valley, AZ, USA

Nicholas S. Thaler
Department of Psychiatry and Biobehavioral Sciences
UCLA Semel Institute for Neuroscience and Human Behavior
Los Angeles, CA, USA

ISBN 978-1-4939-0795-3 ISBN 978-1-4939-0796-0 (eBook)
DOI 10.1007/978-1-4939-0796-0
Springer New York Heidelberg Dordrecht London

Library of Congress Control Number: 2014940287

Printed on acid-free paper

Springer is part of Springer Science+Business Media (www.springer.com)

To Counselor Yonesawa (also known as Amy Y), the biggest advocate for justice I know.

—L.T.B.

To my wife, Animikha.

—N.S.T.

To my phenomenal wife and rambunctious boys who provided me welcome distraction at just the right time throughout this process.

—B.D.L.

Contents

Contributors

Daniel N. Allen, Ph.D. Department of Psychology, University of Nevada, Las Vegas, NV, USA
daniel.allen@unlv.edu

Zoe Belcher-Timme Widener University, Chester, PA, USA

Lorraine T. Benuto, Ph.D. Administrative Faculty, Department of Psychology, University of Nevada, Reno, NV, USA

Graduate School Faculty, Northcentral University, Prescott Valley, AZ, USA
dr.benuto@gmail.com

Sopagna Eap Braje, Ph.D. Clinical Psychology Doctoral Program, California School of Professional Psychology, Alliant International University, San Diego, CA, USA
sbraje@alliant.edu

Lori A. Brotto, Ph.D. Department of Obstetrics/Gynaecology, University of British Columbia, Vancouver, BC, Canada
Lori.Brotto@vch.ca

Nancy M. Cha, Ph.D. Pacific Islands Division, Department of Veterans Affairs, National Center for PTSD, Honolulu, HI, USA
nancycha@gmail.com

Chin Pui Chau Widener University, Chester, PA, USA

Kelly Chau, M.S. Asian Americans for Community Involvement, San Jose, CA, USA

Michelle S. Chung, Psy.D. Department of Psychiatry, HEARTS: Healing Emotions and Achieving Resilience to Traumatic Stress, Beth Israel Medical Center, New York, NY, USA
drmichellechung@gmail.com

Olga Cirlugea, B.A. Department of Psychology, University of Nevada, Reno, NV, USA
olgacirlugea@gmail.com

Mary Comperini, Psy.D. California Department of Corrections and Rehabilitation, California Correctional Health Care Services, Manteca, CA, USA
Dr.Mary@Comperini.com

Anuradha S.K. Dutt, Ph.D. Psychological Studies Academic Group, National Institute of Education, Nanyang Technological University, Singapore, Singapore
anuradha.dutt@nie.edu.sg

Alice Fok-Trela, Psy.D. Shanghai Ocean University, Shanghai, China
dr.trela@yahoo.com

Daryl E.M. Fujii, Ph.D. ABPP-CN, Veterans Affairs, Pacific Island Health Care Services Community Living Center, Honolulu, HI, USA
dfujii07@gmail.com

Carolyn Ha Department of Psychology, University of Houston, Houston, TX, USA
carolynha22@gmail.com

Gordon C.N. Hall, Ph.D. Department of Psychology, University of Oregon, Eugene, OR, USA
gnhall@uoregon.edu

Diana Herva, Ph.D., M.A.O.B. Kaweah Delta Health Care District Graduate Medical Education, Visalia, CA, USA

State of California Department of Developmental Services, Porterville, CA, USA
dvangphd@gmail.com

Judy Ho, Ph.D. Pepperdine University Graduate School of Education and Psychology, Los Angeles, CA, USA
judy.ho@pepperdine.edu

Zornitsa Kalibatseva, M.A. Department of Psychology, Michigan State University, East Lansing, MI, USA
kalibats@msu.edu

Vidya Kamath, Ph.D. Neuropsychiatry Section, Department of Psychiatry, Perelman School of Medicine, University of Pennsylvania, Philadelphia, PA, USA
kamathv@mail.med.upenn.edu

Johanah Y. Kang, B.A. Department of Psychology, University of Nevada, Las Vegas, NV, USA

Sara Cho Kim, Ph.D. Department of Counseling and Human Development, Graduate School of Education and Human Development, George Washington University, Washington, DC, USA
schokim@gwu.edu

Hyun Kim, M.Sc. Department of Psychological and Brain Sciences, Boston University, Boston, MA
monhykim@bu.edu

Satoko Kimpara, Ph.D. Palo Alto University, Palo Alto, CA, USA

Alan J. Lee Widener University, Chester, PA, USA

Phey Ling Kit, Ph.D. Psychological Studies Academic Group, National Institute of Education, Nanyang Technological University, Singapore, Singapore
pheyling.kit@nie.edu.sg

Brian D. Leany, Ph.D. Lake's Crossing Center: Maximum Security Facility for Forensic Mental Health Services, Sparks, NV, USA

Northcentral University, Graduate School Faculty, Prescott Valley, AZ, USA
leanyb@gmail.com

Jungeun Lee, Ph.D. Geisel School of Medicine, Dartmouth College, Hanover, NH, USA
Jungeun.Lee@Dartmouth.edu

Frederick T.L. Leong, Ph.D. Department of Psychology, Michigan State University, East Lansing, MI, USA
fleong@msu.edu

Chieh Li, Ed.D., N.C.S.P. School Psychology Program, Department of Counseling & Applied Educational Psychology, Northeastern University, Boston, MA, USA
c.li@neu.edu

Ynez N. Lizarraga Department of Counseling Psychology, School of Education, University of San Francisco, San Francisco, CA, USA
ynezliz@gmail.com

Cara S. Maffini, M.A. Department of Counseling & Educational Psychology, Indiana University Bloomington, Bloomington, IN, USA
cmaffini@indiana.edu

Natalia Moss Department of Psychology, MSC03 2220, 1 University of New Mexico, Albuquerque, NM, USA

Jessica Murakami-Brundage, Ph.D. Department of Psychiatry, Aaron T. Beck Psychopathology Research Center, University of Pennsylvania, Philadelphia, PA, USA
jemuraka@mail.med.upenn.edu

Sanjay R. Nath, Ph.D. Institute for Graduate Clinical Psychology, Widener University, Chester, PA, USA
snath@widener.edu

William Nguyen, Ph.D. Department of Counseling Psychology, School of Education, University of San Francisco, San Francisco, CA, USA
WWNguyen@USFCA.edu

Stacy L. Reger, M.A. Department of Psychology, University of Nevada, Las Vegas, NV, USA

James G. Scott, Ph.D. Department of Psychiatry and Behavioral Sciences, University of Oklahoma Health Sciences Center, Oklahoma City, OK, USA
jim-scott@ouhsc.edu

Carla Sharp, Ph.D. Department of Psychology, University of Houston, Houston, TX, USA
csharp2@central.uh.edu

Rebekah Smart, Ph.D. Department of Counseling, California State University, Fullerton, CA, USA
rsmart@fullerton.edu

P. Song, M.D. Department of Neurology, Inje University Paik Hospital, Gyeonggi-do, Republic of Korea
songpama@hanmail.net

Sooyeon Suh, Ph.D., C.B.S.M. Sungshin Women's University, Department of Psychology, Sungshingwan, Seoul, Republic of Korea

Stanford University, Redwood City, CA, USA
alysuh@stanford.edu

Nicholas S. Thaler, Ph.D. Department of Psychiatry and Biobehavioral Sciences, Los Angeles Semel Institute for Neuroscience and Human Behavior, University of California, Los Angeles, CA, USA
nick.thaler@gmail.com

J.L. Tsai, Ph.D. Department of Psychology, Stanford University, Stanford, CA, USA
jltsai@stanford.edu

Yuying Tsong, Ph.D. Department of Human Services, California State University, Fullerton, Fullerton, CA, USA
ytsong@fullerton.edu

Vince Tsushima, Ph.D., J.D. Department of Psychology, Hawaii Pacific University, Honolulu, HI, USA
vtsushima@hpu.edu

Sally J. Vogel, M.A. Department of Psychology, University of Nevada, Las Vegas, NV, USA
sallyjvogel@live.com

Katherine A. Wainwright, M.A. Department of Psychology, University of Nevada-Reno, Reno, NV, USA
katherinewainwright@gmail.com

Zhengzheng Wang, M.S., N.C.S.P. Bilingual School Psychologist, Des Moines Public Schools, Des Moines, IA, USA
sophiawzz@gmail.com

Jorge Wong, Ph.D. Asian Americans for Community Involvement, San Jose, CA, USA

Palo Alto University, Palo Alto, CA, USA
Jorge.wong@aaci.org

Y. Joel Wong, Ph.D. Department of Counseling & Educational Psychology, Indiana University Bloomington, Bloomington, IN, USA
joelwong@indiana.edu

Jane S.T. Woo, M.A. Department of Psychology, University of British Columbia, Vancouver, BC, Canada
janewoo@psych.ubc.ca

Ivan H.C. Wu, M.A. Department of Psychology, Michigan State University, East Lansing, MI, USA
wuivan@msu.edu

Christine J. Yeh, Ph.D. Department of Counseling Psychology, School of Education, University of San Francisco, San Francisco, CA, USA
cjyeh@usfca.edu

May Yeh, Ph.D. Department of Psychology, College of Sciences, San Diego State University, San Diego, CA, USA
myeh@mail.sdsu.edu

Amy Yonesawa, J.D. Tramel Law Group, LV, NV, USA
ayonesawa@gmail.com

Y.L. Zhang, M.A. Department of Psychology, Stanford University, Stanford, CA, USA
ylzhang@stanford.edu

Guide to Psychological Assessment with Asians: An Introduction

1

Lorraine T. Benuto, Nicholas S. Thaler, and Brian D. Leany

Guide to Psychological Assessment with Asians: An Introduction

The American Psychological Association (APA, 2005) defines evidence-based practice in psychology (EBPP) as "the integration of the best available research with clinical expertise in the context of patient characteristics, culture, and preferences." This philosophy aligns well with both the goal and organization of this book. While some experts have questioned the use of EBPP with ethnic minority individuals due to the underrepresentation of such individuals in the scientific literature (Bernal & Scharró-del-Río, 2001) the extent to which EBPP applies to most ethnic groups has not been extensively researched. A review of the extant literature revealed that empirical evidence that contradicts the use of EBPP with ethnic minority clients is mostly absent (Benuto & O'Donohue, Submitted/Under Review). This text offers an overview of EBPP specific to psychological assessment with Asians in a US context. To this end, we identified experts from the field of psychology to write the chapters that together make-up this book. It was up to each individual author to determine the most commonly used and/or frequently researched assessment measures and as each author was selected based on their expertise on the topic in question, it was at their discretion to determine what measures to review.

The purpose of this book is to provide clinical psychologists with an understanding of the literature and best practices for working with Asian ethnic groups in the USA. Readers who regularly interact with Asian groups as well as those unfamiliar with cross-cultural guidelines with Asian minorities will find the information in these chapters helpful in delivering services to Asian-Americans. While the majority of the studies reviewed focus primarily on Asian-Americans, we also discuss relevant guidelines pertinent to recent immigrants to the USA and other Westernized countries, as well as cross-cultural guidelines from an international perspective. International research was examined particularly when there was an

L.T. Benuto, Ph.D. (✉)
Administrative Faculty, Department of Psychology MS0296, University of Nevada, Reno, NV 89557, USA

Northcentral University, Graduate School Faculty, 10000 E University Drive, Prescott Valley, AZ 86314, USA
e-mail: dr.benuto@gmail.com

N.S. Thaler, Ph.D.
Department of Psychiatry and Biobehavioral Sciences, Los Angeles Semel Institute for Neuroscience and Human Behavior, University of California, 760 Westwood Plaza, Los Angeles, CA 90024, USA
e-mail: nick.thaler@gmail.com

B.D. Leany, Ph.D.
Lake's Crossing Center: Maximum Security Facility for Forensic Mental Health Services, 500 Galletti Way, Sparks, NV 89504, USA

Northcentral University, Graduate School Faculty, 10000 E University Drive, Prescott Valley, AZ 86314, USA
e-mail: leanyb@gmail.com

L.T. Benuto et al. (eds.), *Guide to Psychological Assessment with Asians*,
DOI 10.1007/978-1-4939-0796-0_1, © Springer Science+Business Media New York 2014

Table 1.1 Asian-American Ethnicities as per the 2000 US Census Bureau

Ethnicity	Total (rounded to thousands)	Percentage
Asian Indian	1,899,000	15.5
Bangladeshi	57,000	<1.0
Burman	17,000	<1.0
Cambodian	207,000	1.6
Chinese	2,735,000	22.3
Filipino	2,365,000	19.3
Hmong	186,000	1.5
Indonesian	63,000	<1.0
Japanese	1,149,000	9.4
Korean	1,228,000	10.0
Laotian	198,000	1.6
Malaysian	19,000	<1.0
Nepalese	9,000	<1.0
Okinawan	11,000	<1.0
Pakistani	204,000	1.7
Singaporean	2,000	<1.0
Sri Lankan	25,000	<1.0
Taiwanese	145,000	1.2
Thai	150,000	1.2
Vietnamese	1,224,000	10.0
Other Asian	369,000	3.0

Note: Includes individuals reporting one or more ethnicities

absence of national research. The findings on international research also can be helpful in understanding the assessment differences and challenges when working first-generation immigrants.

In terms of organization, the first part of this book constitutes chapters on some of the cultural groups that make-up the Asian panoramic of the USA. We recognize that Asian-Americans are a diverse group that includes 24 ethnicities recognized by the US Census Bureau (2000; see Table 1.1). These chapters intend to provide cross-cultural recommendations pertinent to some ethnic groups subsumed with the Asian-American category including Japanese, Chinese, Korean, and Asian Indian Americans. We acknowledge that these chapters are inadequate in fully characterizing each of these groups and neglect to account for other Asian-American groups that are represented in the USA including Filipino, Vietnamese, Cambodian, Hmong, Pakistani, and Thai Americans, among others. The decision to focus on only a sample of Asian-American ethnicities was not an easy one to make, but was made based on the following: (1) the available EBPP literature predominantly focuses on these groups; (2) there was a desire to balance breadth and depth in this book by describing EBPP not just for specific ethnicities/nationalities, but also to do so across clinical populations in a variety of settings; and (3) where appropriate and possible best practices for other groups are provided.

The remainder of this book is structured such that there is a chapter specific to the types of tests psychologists administer (e.g., self-report, IQ); where appropriate chapters relevant to certain types of psychological assessment (e.g., forensic, neuropsychological, school-based); and chapters aligned with most of the major diagnostic categories (e.g., eating disorders, mood disorders etc.) in the Diagnostic and Statistical Manual of Mental Disorders IV-Text Revision (DSM-IV-TR: APA, 2000) are also included. It is important to note that as this book is being finalized (June, 2013) the DSM-V has come to press. While several authors inquired as to the extent to which they should align their chapters with the DSM-V, given that the updated criteria for each disorder is only just now (June, 2013) being released, psychological assessments that align with the new diagnostic criteria have not even been created making it difficult to discuss these measures, particularly as research on these measures and ethnic minorities is largely absent. Each chapter contains a general overview of cultural considerations that should be made when assessing the Asian-American client and then a specific exploration of the most commonly used and/or frequently researched assessment measures and the research that has been conducted on these measures with Asian-American participants. Conclusions are drawn and guidelines are provided.

Psychological Assessment

The purpose of assessment is to examine an individual across domains of psychosocial functioning and to describe his or her functioning within these specific domains. Typically there is a presenting problem that guides this assessment process, and the goal is to provide a holistic picture of the individual. The final evaluation should identify the level and pattern of functioning across domains, in order to identify a diagnosis (or in some cases to rule out diagnoses), and provide recommendations for intervention(s). In order to provide an accurate diagnosis, as well as corresponding prognostic and intervention recommendations, one must choose assessment measures that are appropriate for the presenting problem and have good validity and reliability.

The general question about what constitutes a "good" test is not as easy as it may seem. There has been much discussion about what constitutes such a test, with varying classification schemes that rely on the presence or absence of features considered to be necessary for a "good" test (e.g. cultural sensitivity and "suitability" including cost, and administration time; Bickman, Nurcombe, Twonsend, Belle, Schut, & Karver, 1999) as well as those that rely on classification by subject matter experts. Such experts rate the quality of a psychological test based on a "preponderance of the evidence" for psychometric properties as well as for more subjective criteria such as the ability to measure treatment effectiveness and clinical utility (Hunsley & Mash, 2008). Thus, determining selection criteria for a test is challenging. Wong and Fuji (2004) suggested that intra-individual consistency for test selection and interpretation is more important than inter-individual consistency, as the former would suggest that the individual professional is not taking a rational or scientifically informed approach (while this is specific to neuropsychological assessment there is general practical value in the global realm of assessment).

Thus challenges to providing a culturally appropriate assessment can occur at several different points, and in addition to the general psychometric considerations, an appropriate understanding of the referral question can be difficult due to specific cultural factors. Several chapters in this book describe the differential presentation that may occur within various ethnic groups, depending largely on the individual's acculturation. Additionally, each chapter in this edited book has identified language as a potential barrier for accurate assessment. Language can not only interfere with expected results but can frustrate the process of comprehending the presenting problem, as well as create challenges in selecting reliable and valid measures during the assessment process. A lack of available measures that are culturally appropriate does not necessarily preclude one from providing necessary assessment. Rather, the psychologist should initially make attempts to refer to a more appropriate provider (one who is specifically capable with regards to the presenting client). If such a referral is unavailable, the psychologist should seek appropriate consultation. The course of action is based not just on ethical guidelines, but also on the stake for the evaluation. This is to say that an assessment that is trying to establish a diagnosis for treatment is much less of a stake (although not unimportant) than an evaluation for the same client for criminal responsibility or competency. Thus, the stakes of the evaluation should play a prominent role in the heuristics of the decision to provide assessment services as well as the assessment selection and resulting interpretation.

The Cultural Sensitivity Movement (CSM) and EBPP

The Cultural Sensitivity Movement (CSM) is focused on the provision of "culturally sensitive" psychological services to cultural minorities. This movement is not new; the CSM surfaced in 1920s when Arthur (1926) attempted to construct a scale of individual performance tests that could differentiate ranges of intelligence irrespective of race, nationality, or culture. Since then, a plentitude of resources have been dedicated to this movement; positions specific for "diversity experts" in training programs and treatment facilities are plenty; government funds are allocated yearly in the form of grant monies to advance this movement; and researchers and academicians have made entire careers in this movement.

Specific to the cultural sensitivity movement are issues related to race and ethnicity; acculturation; socioeconomic status (SES); and language. These constructs are discussed in many of the chapters of this text (with a lesser focus on SES as this construct applies across cultures). As indicated at the outset of this chapter the APA (2005) defined EBPP as "the integration of the best available research with clinical expertise in the context of patient characteristics, culture, and preferences." Both parts of this definition fall in alignment with this book. First, our goal was to discuss at length the best available research in the field of psychological assessment that is specific to the cultural groups of interest in this book. We selected expert authors so that both clinical expertise and knowledge of relevant research could be combined within each chapter. In terms of the second component of the definition of EBPP—"patient characteristics, culture, and preferences," the APA (2005) asserted that psychological services are most effective when they are personalized to the individual client's problems, strengths, personality, sociocultural context, and preferences. The crux of this book is focused on socio*cultural* context and within each chapter ample discussion on the research available for the specific cultural group is included and specific and practical recommendations are made. Moreover, in the chapters that are specific to a disorder, there is most typically a discussion on cultural variations in how disorders can present, etiological considerations, and relevant epidemiological data. Last but not least, chapters specific to developmental status and life stage and how these factors can play into psychological assessment are also included. In sum, this book attempts to integrate the tenets of the CSM with the parameters of EPPP.

Trends and Themes in EPPP with Asians in a US Context

Through the editing (and authoring) process a number of trends and themes were observed. First, although the Asian population is one of the fastest growing minority groups in the United States, with a projected growth of 8 % of the US population by 2050 (US Census Bureau, 2004), the empirical literature is not representative of this prevalence. Identifying experts for many of the chapters was a challenge given the limited number of researchers and clinicians who specialize in working with this population. This was perhaps most evident when approaching authors to cover cross-cultural guidelines pertinent to Southeast Asian, Pacific Islander, and Pakistani clients. It is of particular concern that there were few experts available on cross-cultural issues with Filipino Americans, as this ethnicity as the second highest population in the USA following Chinese Americans. Moreover, as the reader will see, for many domains the research is very limited. In many studies Asians are not listed as participants (the elusive "other" category is often included but it is unknown to what extent Asians are included in this category) and when they are listed they constitute a small minority of the research samples. Studies that are exclusively focused on Asians are few and far in between. In addition, the Asian panoramic in the USA (and worldwide) is highly diverse though for the most part Asians are "lumped" together in a single category within both research studies and clinical practice guidelines.

Defining specific guidelines towards any minority group can be controversial. As experts who completed doctoral and post-doctoral training specific to cultural sensitivity, the editors were surprised by the degree to which our training on cross-cultural issues often relied on reductionist and overly simplistic heuristics that were designed to "capture" a group. For example, while it is true that many Asian-Americans have an emphasis on the family unit, deference to elders, and high values towards educational and occupational achievement, the prevailing attitude of these generalizations is to simply state these as essentialist truths and then move on. Experts have noted that there can iatrogenic effects when explicitly altering psychological services (e.g., directly referencing a client's ethnicity/race; Benuto & O'Donohue, Submitted/Under Review; Huey, 2014/Submitted) and therefore cultural considerations should not be solely focused on the applications of stereotypes. Clinicians and researchers should keep in mind that the term "diversity" can be infinitely expansive or minute depending on the user's intent of the word. In our view, diversity permeates all aspects of our field and each person, regardless of race, ethnicity, and other demographic background, has unique considerations that necessitate tailoring of treatment. Therefore, readers are urged to always take general cross-cultural guidelines with a grain of salt; while they have their place and can be educational and informative, they are simply what they claim to be—guidelines. Practitioners must avoid falling into the easy trap of using guidelines to shape stereotypes, and rather use them instead to shape hypotheses that then can be tested and, as is often the case, refuted.

In our experience, *ethnicity* is less of a determinant than *acculturation* is in influencing behavior. As all immigrants have varying degrees of acculturation to the USA and this, along with language proficiency, may be the most crucial issue in cross-cultural assessment with Asian populations. Therefore, while there may be tremendous variability in individual clients, ethnic subgroups, nationalities, and personal ethnic identity, the astute reader will find a common thread in the EBPP literature: level of acculturation is a key determinant in influencing the nature and degree of individual tailoring that may be required of a specific assessment/setting. This may be the best application of cross-cultural generalization; it is more likely that a recent Thai immigrant will face similar obstacles pertinent to assessment with recent Chinese, Hmong, Indian, and other minority immigrants than he or she would with a second-generation Thai youth.

Another relevant issue is the degree to which testing results should be altered, adapted or discounted with Asian-American individuals. As the literature in later chapters indicates, well-validated measures appear to generalize adequately when used cross-culturally as long as the method of administration is appropriate. Cross-cultural challenges such as language barriers, unfamiliarity with the testing setting, and limited Western education may limit comprehension, cooperation, and rapport and thereby call into question the appropriateness of some measures, but these issues must be considered on an individual basis. Chapters will not. Normative population standards of psychometric test data is a related issue, as many test batteries have norms that have limited inclusion of Asian-Americans. While we agree that interpretation of such scores is more difficult with individuals who are not represented in the standardization sample, we acknowledge the inherent difficulty of obtaining comprehensive norms that account for each individual variable that may influence test performance. We encourage the use of standard norms when no better ones are available, with the caveat that psychologists must be aware of the potential impact that culture and acculturation may have on performance. Lastly, as previously noted by Benuto (2013) there are instances in which cultural caveats are more important than in other instances. For example in a context where criminal proceedings are pending on a psychological evaluation or a person's capacity for financial decision-making is being questioned, cultural caveats could make a major difference in a person's life. Conversely in a context of assessing (e.g., using the Beck Depression Inventory) to track treatment progress the stakes are less and cultural caveats may require less emphasis.

The impetus for this work was an overarching sense (or concern) that an unintended consequence of the CSM, was that individuals were not being provided psychological services for fear of being perceived as culturally insensitive. As all three editors doctorial clinical training took place in a rural state and two of the three editors practice in rural communities, the concern is more prominent. This increased concern is not only due to the first hand experience with the challenges in a rural setting for finding providers as a whole, but the increased challenge for finding providers that have specific training with such a broad range of cultural groups. Thankfully through this process we have encountered research practitioners such as Tony Wong and Daryl Fuji (among many others) that seem to share this same concern. While specific to neuropsychological assessment (Wong & Fuji, 2004) they provide practical, common sense recommendations that can be applied to assessment in general and balance the APA's mandate for appropriate assessment practices with our obligation to provide services to those in need.

References

American Psychological Association. (2005). *American Psychological Association Statement Policy Statement on evidence-based practice in psychology*. Retrieved from: http://www.apa.org/practice/resources/evidence/evidence-based-statement.pdf

American Psychiatric Association. (2000). *Diagnostic and statistical manual of mental disorders (4th ed., text rev.)*. Washington, DC: American Psychiatric Association.

Arthur, G. G. (1926). A group point scale for the measurement of intelligence: A further study in method. *Journal of Applied Psychology, 10*(2), 228–244. doi:10.1037/h0073394.

Benuto, L. (2013). A guide to psychological assessment with Hispanics: An introduction. In L. Benuto (Ed.), *Guide to psychological assessment with Hispanics*. New York, NY: Springer.

Benuto, L. & O'Donohue, W. (Submitted/Under Review). Examining the substance of culturally sensitive psychotherapy for Hispanics: A status update of the cultural sensitivity movement. *Professional Psychology*.

Bernal, G., & Scharró-del-Río, M. R. (2001). Are empirically supported treatments valid for ethnic minorities? Toward an alternative approach for treatment research. *Cultural Diversity and Ethnic Minority Psychology, 7*(4), 328–342. doi:10.1037/1099-9809.7.4.328.

Bickman, L., Nurcombe, B., Twonsend, C., Belle, M., Schut, J., & Karver, M. (1999). *Consumer measurement mechanisms in child and adolescent health*. Canberra, ACT: Department of Health and Family Services.

Huey, S. J. (2014/Submitted). Do cultural adaptations enhance psychotherapy effects? A Meta-analysis of culturally tailored versus generic psychotherapies.

Hunsley, J., & Mash, E. J. (2008). Developing criteria for evidence-based assessment: An introduction to assessments that work. In J. Hunsely & E. J. Mash (Eds.), *A guide to assessments that work* (pp. 3–14). New York, NY: Oxford University Press.

U.S. Census Bureau. (2000). America's Asian population Demographic Patterns & Trends. Retrieved from: http://proximityone.com/asian_demographics.htm.

U.S. Census Bureau. (2004). Educational attainment in the United States: 2003. Retrieved May 6, 2013, from http://www.census.gov/prod/2004pubs/p20-550.pdf

Wong, T. M., & Fuji, D. E. (2004). Neuropsychological assessment of Asian Americans: Demographic Factors, cultural diversity, and practical guidelines. *Applied Neuropsychology, 11*(1), 23–36.

Cross-Cultural Considerations with Chinese American Clients: A Perspective on Psychological Assessment

2

Satoko Kimpara, Jorge Wong, and Kelly Chau

Cross-Cultural Considerations with Chinese-American Clients: A Perspective on Psychological Assessment

The US Census Bureau (2010) reports that Chinese Americans (3.8 million) are the largest Asian group in the United States, followed by Filipinos (3.4 million), Asian Indians (3.2 million), Vietnamese (1.7 million), Koreans (1.7 million), and Japanese (1.3 million). The majority of Chinese Americans are immigrants and descendants from Mainland China, Hong Kong, Macau, Taiwan, Malaysia, Singapore, Southeast Asia, with some Chinese Americans coming from countries in Latin America. The USA denotes Taiwanese (0.2 million) as a separate and unique subgroup of Chinese Americans. Chinese Americans constitute a rapidly growing population showing an increase of over one million since the 2000 Census, thus compromising 1.2 % of the US population, and 25.9 % of Asian-American populations. Approximately 36 % of Chinese Americans are US born and 64 % are foreign-born (University of Maryland, 2011; US Census Bureau, 2010).

S. Kimpara, Ph.D.
Palo Alto University, 1791 Arastradero Rd, Palo Alto, CA 94304, USA

J. Wong, Ph.D. (✉)
Asian Americans for Community Involvement, 2400 Moorpark Ave., Suite 300, San Jose, CA 95128-2680, USA

Palo Alto University, 1791 Arastradero Rd, Palo Alto, CA 94304, USA
e-mail: Jorge.wong@aaci.org

K. Chau, M.S.
Asian Americans for Community Involvement, 2400 Moorpark Ave., Suite 300, San Jose, CA 95128-2680, USA

Brief History of Chinese Americans in the USA

Historically, the first Chinese arrived to the USA in the 1820s. Between the two decades from 1840 to 1860, approximately 20,000 Chinese migrated to the USA due to excessive population growth or/and township battles in China, drawn to the Western US states due to the lure of the Gold Rush (Spector, 1996). Chinese miners and merchants contributed heavily to a large number of small mining towns by building productive irrigation and mining systems in Nevada and eastern Oregon, even while there existed high anti-Chinese sentiments throughout the country, especially in large European American-dominated mining towns (Chung, 2011). Asians, in particular the Chinese, worked well and contributed to building the Central Pacific Railroad as part of the transcontinental railroad, developing communities, and forming Chinatowns along the way. After the US economic recession in 1869, Chinese were victims of discrimination and faced labor and political assaults. In 1871, the Chinese were proclaimed ineligible for US citizenship.

L.T. Benuto et al. (eds.), *Guide to Psychological Assessment with Asians*,
DOI 10.1007/978-1-4939-0796-0_2, © Springer Science+Business Media New York 2014

Moreover, in 1882, the Chinese Exclusion Act prohibited future migration into the USA, forcing many Chinese to leave the country. Those who remained in the USA were recipients of institutional racism, violence, and loss of property (Chen & Yoo, 2010). This Chinese Exclusion Act was not abolished until 1943.

In 1965, the Immigration Reform Act was enacted and between 1965 and 1977, many Chinese immigrated from Hong Kong and Taiwan and developed the local Chinatowns in all major cities around the USA Approximately 50 % of these immigrants worked at labor-intensive and low-paying jobs such as making or selling garments, clothes, shoes, bags, and toys (Liu, 2001). In 1978, after diplomatic relations were restored between the USA and People's Republic of China, 20,000 immigrants entered the USA yearly from Taiwan, 20,000 more from mainland China, and an additional large number from Hong Kong who came on student visas. Many of them have stayed, worked, become citizens, and been educated while obtaining various professional degrees and jobs (Lee & Mock, 1996; Liu, 2001). Ethnic Chinese from war-ravaged countries, such as Vietnam, Laos, and Cambodia also immigrated to the USA and many of these war refugees survived starvation, rape, internment camps, forced relocation, and torture (Liu, 2001).

Language, Education, and Socioeconomic Status (SES)

Chinese Americans are vastly heterogeneous with regard to language, education, and socioeconomic status (American Community Survey, 2008–2010; Chen & Yoo, 2010). They predominately speak English and an array of Chinese languages and dialects including Mandarin Chinese, Yue Chinese (Cantonese, Taishanese), Hakka, Wu Chinese, and Min Chinese. The American Community Survey, 2008–2010 estimated that 84 % of first-generation Chinese immigrants speak more than one of the Chinese dialects, and 46 % speak English less than "very well." This demographic data points to the importance of appropriate language accessibility for services in Chinese American communities as just the linguistic heterogeneity within Chinese groups clearly poses a communication challenge. More functionally, Tsai, Simeonova, and Watanabe (2004) reported that Chinese Americans utilize somatic and contextually appropriate socially laden language to express their emotions rather than affectively laden, concretized, and descriptive verbal communication similar to Western European decent and North American individuals. Communication styles between Chinese Americans and European descent cultures are different. Chinese Americans express their emotions by using somatic and social languages (Tsai et al., 2004) and often rely on nonverbal communication styles such as facial expressions, gestures, voice tone, eye-contacts, and body-distance. Chinese also prefer to verbally communicate less, do so indirectly and allowing for direct and indirect actions to reinforce their oral communications. Sue and Sue (1987) indicated that Chinese Asians believe that silence is a sign of respect and the desire to continue speaking after having made a point during conversations is impolite and disrespectful.

Learning English can be a challenge for Chinese native speakers since English and Chinese belong to two different language families and have many significant linguistic differences. Language barriers have been commonly cited by Chinese American immigrants (Sung, 1985). However, acculturated immigrants are mostly bilingual and can be proficient at both English and their native Chinese dialects. Additionally, some American-born Chinese who grew up within a Chinese family with monolingual parents and grandparents are able to communicate with their family members in their Chinese language and dialect (Liu, 2001). As compared to oral communication, written Chinese uses the same pictographically developed writing across all Chinese cultural groups and language families. However, there are two primary styles that are used in the written Chinese language. The "traditional" text which is more pictographic and intricate is primarily used in Taiwan, Hong Kong, Singapore, and enclaves of Chinese who historically have viewed themselves separate and independent from the current government of the People's

Republic of China (PRC), while the "simplified" text developed by the PRC has become recognized as the official modernized writing for the country and all its affiliates.

Given the diversity in communication, one converging area for Chinese Americans is the pursuit of education. In the area of educational achievement, Chinese Americans are one of the most highly educated groups among all ethnic groups (University of Maryland, 2011), but there are significant differences based on age and gender. Among young Chinese Americans (25–35 years old) who were raised in the USA, 6.3 % have not completed a high school (HS) diploma and 71 % had more than college degrees while among senior Chinese Americans (>65 years old), 40 % have not completed a HS diploma and 30 % had more education beyond a 4-year college degree (US Census Bureau, 2010). It appears that when looking at education, no gender differences are found among young Chinese adults under 35 years old but significant gender difference have been found with older Chinese adults where males have more education than female Chinese older adults (US Census Bureau, 2010). This may reflect an immigration history and cohort effects for many of these individuals as newly arrived adults tend to pursue employment to sustain family needs and send their young children to school.

Socioeconomic success has often been tied to the Chinese as they have always been included in the Myth of the Model Minority (Takaki, 1998). Chinese Americans can be described as having a wide range of success and affluence (Barringer, Takeuchi, & Levin, 1995): some have achieved the highest desirable and attractive occupations to realize the American success story while others are invisible and concentrated in the lowest levels of society. Socioeconomic success has historically been peppered with residential geography and economic opportunities. Many Chinese enclaves have historically sprouted along the tracks of the intercontinental railways and large port cities originally being points of entry for the Chinese seeking the American dream (Takaki, 1998). Today more than half of Chinese Americans in the USA live in California and New York, followed by Texas, New Jersey, and Massachusetts. Poverty rates for Chinese Americans parallel those of other ethnic minorities as they were approximately 9.5 % for "all families" and among those with female head of households, the rate was 23 %. Ten percent of Chinese American children (under 18 years old), and 14.9 % of Chinese American older adults (over 65 years) live in poverty (US Census Bureau, 2010).

In addition to this brief introduction to the history and current status of Chinese Americans in the US, this chapter reviews: (1) family, language, acculturation, education, religion, and socioeconomic status (SES) in relationship to medical and mental health issues for Chinese American individuals; (2) "significant and practical" issues that should be considered when assessing and treating Chinese American clients while considering culture-bound syndromes and cultural symptom expressions; and (3) useful recommendations for assessing and treating Chinese American clients by highlighting these in a clinical case vignette.

Cultural Issues of Chinese American Clients

Chinese Custom and Values

Chinese customs, believes, values, and practices are structurally founded on Confucianism with emphases on harmony, duty, honor, and respect. Confucian philosophy guides the behaviors of many Chinese. They follow the principle of "Ren," which means goodness, benevolence, humanity, and kindheartedness. Along the same concept of "Ren," many Chinese Americans believe that having good virtues such as endurance and patience when faced with hardships will lead one to achieve one's goals in life (Nan, Yeung, & Nguyen, 2007). Additionally, the Chinese strive to achieve balance between the "yin" and "yang" so that the body or "chi" does not become disturbed and become susceptible to illnesses (Liu, 2001).

The traditional Chinese family has many unique characteristics. Respect for elders and filial piety are highly valued and the family is the most important social and economic unit of society among Chinese (Ho, 1996; Liu, 2001). Family interactions are defined by hierarchical roles, obligation, and duties. The Chinese family is patriarchal where males in the family have dominant roles, particularly the father and eldest son. Grandparents and extended family also significantly influence family life. Distinguished family dyads are observed in the Chinese family, where the spousal relationship is held secondary to the parent–child relationship, with the father–son dyad as the most elevated (Lee, 1997).

Immigration often brings changes to family roles and dynamics (Foner, 1997). General observations of contemporary Chinese Americans show that some traditional extended Chinese families have gradually moved towards a nuclear system and that husband and wife share equal familial decision-making roles and earning power. The husband-wife dyad often becomes more important than parent–child and father–son dyads (Lee, 1997). Although there have been shifts to the Chinese family systems due to economic, political changes, and acculturation, it is important to also recognize that there are contemporary Chinese Americans who still hold some traditional customs and values (Liu, 2001).

Attitudes and Beliefs Towards Mental Illness

Help seeking behaviors and attitudes toward seeking medical or mental health treatment are heavily influenced by how individuals perceive and understand their distress. Social stigma is one of the most well-researched barriers in obtaining professional treatment for mental health issues (Lee et al., 2007a; Lee, Tsang, Chui, Kwok & Cheung, 2007b; Leong & Lau, 2001; Parker, Gladstone & Chee, 2001). According to Givens, Houston, Van Voorhees, Ford, and Cooper (2007) Asian-Americans have the highest percentage of respondents that indicated they were concerned with many sources of stigma including employers, friends, and family as compared to other racial ethnic groups. Parker et al. (2001) indicated that negative attitudes and beliefs towards experiencing psychological distress may lead an individual to not fully disclose emotional distress to medical and mental health professionals, and thus be less likely to seek treatment for mental illness.

Additionally, mental illness is not positively perceived in Chinese communities and negative views are usually associated with a sense of shame (Nan et al., 2007). The family of the afflicted individual is implicated in the shame and loss of face due to the individual's mental health issues (Uba, 1994). Individuals with mental illness are considered shameful to the family and as a burden to society in general (Lee et al., 2007a; Nan et al., 2007; Parker et al., 2001). Mental illness can be seen as a disgrace that exposes the family to social criticism. Thus, it is not surprising that individuals with disabilities or mental illnesses are likely to be cared for by the family and these issues are discussed privately within the family (Lee, 1997). Generally it is only when family members can no longer cope with the symptoms of the individual that they seek treatment from a physician or professional (Lin, Inui, Kleinman, & Womack, 1982). When mental health services are sought outside the family, they tend to be for more severe issues as compared to European Americans who use similar services (Brown, Huang, Harris, & Stein, 1973; Duvasula & Sue, 1996; Zhang, Snowden, & Sue, 1998). This stigma related to social perception and judgmental views is barriers for seeking professional mental health treatment. However, younger Chinese Americans often have a better understanding of mental illness and are more accepting of those with mental illness than persons from older generations (Corrigan & Penn, 1999). Consequently, Liu (2001) purports that while older- and middle-generation Chinese Americans still maintain some traditional values and practices, younger generations of Chinese Americans have often tended to reject traditional conventions. Nan et al. (2007) state that younger and more acculturated Chinese American generations may have greater awareness and acceptance of mental illness since they have better access to health and mental health educational programs, outreach, and stigma reduction effort as compared to older generation of Chinese Americans.

The study by Abe-Kim et al. (2007) indicated generational differences in the help-seeking patterns and utilization rate of mental health services among Asian-Americans. Abe-Kim et al. (2007) explored the use of mental health-related services among immigrant and US-born Asian-Americans using archival data derived from the National Latino and Asian American Study (2002–2003) with the objectives to (1) examine rates of mental health service use among immigrant and US-born Asian-Americans during a 12-month period, (2) identify patterns of help-seeking as they varied by need and immigration-related characteristics, (3) explore perceptions of satisfaction with care and helpfulness, and (4) compare differences in patterns of mental health related service use among individuals who had a probable need for services and those who had no probable need for services. Findings from this study indicated that overall, Asian-Americans appear to have lower rates of mental health related service use compared with the general population. Of the total national sample of Asian-Americans ($N=2095$), 8.6 % sought any mental health services; 4.4 % sought help from general medical providers, 3.1 % sought help from mental health providers, and 34.1 % of individual who had a probable diagnosis sought any services. Rates of mental health-related services use, subjective satisfaction, and perceived helpfulness varied by birthplace and by generation. US-born Asian-Americans demonstrated higher rates of service use than did immigrants. Third-generation or later individuals who had a DSM-IV diagnosis during the 12 months sought help from any services at significantly higher rates (62.6 %) than individuals who were first- (30.4 %) or second- (28.8 %) generation Asian-Americans. Overall, the findings in this study indicate that important differences exist in service utilization between immigrants and US-born Asians. Interestingly, second generation Asians are more similar to their immigrant parents in their utilization of mental health services than to third generation Asians who were more similar in the pattern of mental health related service use to the general population sampled in this study.

Significant and Practical Issues When Assessing and Treating Chinese Americans

When assessing Chinese American clients, one needs to consider the heterogeneity inherent in each Chinese Americans' immigrant history, language, education, socioeconomic status, and acculturation levels, as these significant impact the clinical outcomes of each of these individuals. Acculturation and transgenerational struggles appear to have an especially large role in demonstrating differential impacts in individual and transgenerational distresses (Abe-Kim et al., 2007). When Chinese American individuals are the subject of cognitive testing, results often show their scores to be higher on the quantitative measures as compared with the verbal measures in relation to their levels of English language abilities and acculturation (Hsia & Peng, 1998). Okazaki and Sue (2000) addressed the issue of nonexisting or inadequate test reliability and validity of the Wechsler Adult Intelligent Scale-Third Edition (WAIS-III: Wechsler, 1997) when assessing nonnative English speaking individuals born in the USA. In particular, the degree and levels of acculturation, linguistic conceptualizations and expressions, and other culturally relevant factors such as disparate quality of educational access within the USA and country of origin, SES levels, and opportunities to interact with Western cultures and learn cultural values, geographic residence in the USA, and differential cultural exposure to American culture outside of ethnic enclaves tend to affect the overall results of cognitive testing for Chinese Americans.

While assessing acculturation with non-US-born Chinese Americans and recently arrived Chinese, examiners need to consider the Chinese values of maintaining harmony among family and social groups and respect toward authorities, in particular with individuals who come to reside in primary ethnic enclaves in various geographic locations in the USA. These cultural values significantly impact the depth of expression and communication of individual needs via minimization, preference toward controlling emotions in the sanctioned practice of maintaining "face," and unwillingness to seeking available mental health services until symptoms and conditions are more complex and deteriorated (Beach et al., 2006; Duvasula & Sue, 1996; Tseng & Wu, 1985). Thus, traditional Chinese Americans may not talk about or easily willing to share personal stories with mental health professionals as they are considered external to the family and kinship group and prefer to save such disclosures for family members, close friends, primary care providers (PCP), and traditional healers. PCP and traditional healers are recognized as physical health and traditional medicine professionals and therefore somatic focused health concerns are addressed even if their etiology may stem from psychological distress. Many recently immigrated individuals have never been exposed to mental or behavioral health services in their countries of origin and are often not accustomed to view behavioral health as part of the continuum of healthcare services practiced in the USA. However, once they are acculturated and more open to psychotherapy, Tseng, (2005) emphasized that Chinese American clients are more psychologically minded than originally perceived, as they understand very well about family and social dynamics, unspoken communication or high context communication, and work well with the insight or interpersonal oriented psychotherapists.

In accordance with these evidences, some Chinese American clients may prefer brief solution-focused therapies to limit expressing their emotional experience, to maintain them among family members and to achieve harmony (Chu, Huynh, & Aréan, 2011), though other Chinese American clients may prefer psychodynamic therapy to understand intra- and inter-psychological experiences and enact their past experiences well (Tung, 1991; Varvin & Gerlach, 2011).

Moreover, Okazaki, Okazaki, and Sue (2009) comprehensively summarized the status of clinical personality assessment for Asian-Americans. Although additional studies are needed to better understand and resolve issues of validity of concepts and assessment tools used to assess Chinese Americans, their comprehensive reviews showed that less acculturated Asian-Americans demonstrate slightly higher level of current symptoms on Scales F, 1, 2, 3, and 8 on the MMPI and the MMPI-2 studies when compared with acculturated Asian-Americans (e.g., Cheung & Song (1989), Cheung, Song, & Zhang (1996), Sue, Keefe, Enomoto, Durvasula, & Chao (1996), Tsai & Pike (2000)). This difference suggests that clinicians should assess levels and sources of current distress and to manage these stresses at the initial stages of treatment for less acculturated Chinese American clients in order to obtain a better overall treatment outcome. These research findings allow clinicians to understand some unique characteristics of symptoms expression from less acculturated Asian-Americans and consider the likelihood of culture-bounded syndrome expression for these clients.

Cognitive Test Assessment Problems

Cognitive tests have been utilized to assess processing and developmental matters at the educational systems, problem solving at health and mental health clinics, memory, and concentration problems at senior settings and so on in order to accommodate individual treatment needs based on testing results. Various forms of IQ tests such as Wechsler Intelligence Scales, Stanford-Binet, and nonverbal tests such as Raven's Progressive Matrices have been utilized in a variety of settings as standard measures with Asian-Americans. Based on these assessment strategies, Chinese American clients tend to perform well on quantitative measures as compared to verbal measures in relations to levels of English language proficiency and acculturation (Hsia & Peng, 1998). However, research suggests that interpretation of assessment results need to consider one major and importance issue, this being the influence of cultural cognitions on these performances.

Okazaki and Sue (2000) addressed the lack or inadequate test reliability and validity of these IQ measures for Chinese American clients. They examined the normative samples of WAIS-III and found no published data on the reliability and validity of these measures to Asian-Americans, especially since Asian Americans were categorized as part of the "Other" category grouped with other ethnic groups including the Native Americans and Pacific Islanders, which constituted under 2 % of population used for the standardization of the comparison groups. Moreover, two thirds of Chinese Americans in the sample were born in a foreign country of their origins, and these considerations were not represented in these sampling processes. Okazaki and Sue (2000) suggest collecting large normative data for Asian-Americans similar to the process utilized with African and Latino Americans for the standardization process, using test moderator variables, or starting collecting culturally relevant data (i.e., testing condition, demographic and cultural characteristics, reflecting community samples) as future test revision efforts to ensure the validity and reliability of test applicability and results interpretation with Asian-Americans.

Moreover, researchers and testers are becoming more aware of cultural cognitions in accordance with increasing cross-cultural studies. Nisbett (2003) has uniquely and technologically demonstrated cognitive differences between European and Asian-Americans by assessing basic cognitive processes such as categorization, learning, causal reasons, and attention/perception. He found that Asian-Americans, who have more collectivist cultures, tend to endorse group harmony and contextual understanding of situations holistically in contrast with European Americans who tend to be more analytic and attend to individual objects and categories. Lee, Hong, Cheong, and Oh (2008) also conducted and supported these cognitive differences when comparing Chinese, Korean, and European Americans. These findings regarding problem solving and conceptualization are consistent with results from psychotherapy research attending to differential coping styles between Asians and European Americans; coping styles were matched to clinical interventions in psychotherapy to optimize individuals' ability to cope effectively with their presenting treatment issues (Beutler & Clarkin, 1990, Tseng, 2005). Cultural cognitions are important factors to consider include and examine when developing standardized cognitive testing instruments for Chinese American clients.

Complexity and Chronicity of Psychological Problems

Traditional Chinese American clients place a high value on maintaining harmony among family members to whom they show filial piety to emphasize maintaining the family hierarchical structure; they follow well-ordered structures among groups, try to reduce individual needs, and may seek mental health treatments when symptoms are more chronic, complex, or severe (Beach et al., 2006; Duvasula & Sue, 1996). These clients most likely seek help and support for behavioral and emotional problems from close friends or family first. If this approach is ineffective, they seek treatment from their primary care providers for perceived accelerated cures. They may also use traditional healing methods for their familiar remedies for distress and holistic illnesses (e.g. Chinese herbal medicines, coining, cupping, acupuncture, religious and spiritual strategies, and traditional foods). They often practice these healthcare strategies as adjunctive treatments to on-going Western medicine rather than adhere strictly to biological treatments and explanations of the cause of mental illness from a Eurocentric perspective. Lin (1986) emphasizes that help seeking from a Western trained mental health professional may take as long at 10–20 years to engage as these problems are often kept within the family. In situations where stigma is a barrier to seek services, the provision of psychoeducation about mental health issues and the available treatment to Chinese American communities with linguistic and culturally competent providers is indispensable.

Beutler and Harwood (2002) described the importance of empirically support interventions to help patients with chronic and/or complex problems to achieve better treatment outcomes. Clinicians are first required to assess the degree of complexity the problem presents, understand the duration and chronicity of the condition, be knowledgeable of their relapse history, assess existing comorbidity of the client's presenting problems, and understand the broad disruption to interpersonal relationships in their micro, meso, and macro sociocultural systems.

During the evaluation process, clinicians must be able to estimate the degree to which client's problems impair specific areas of functioning (work, relationship, school, family, culture, etc.) and areas in which clients' strengths prevent them from developing more complex and/or chronic problems (Norcross & Beutler, 2011). As a result of this in-depth degree of these assessments, clinicians can utilize the client's own strengths and personal resources to deliver treatment modalities comprised of clinical interventions from a multi-therapy approach (e.g., pharmacotherapy, group or family therapy, social support, community engagement, etc.) and include individual therapy. Chu and Sue (2011) have emphasized these collaboratively working relationships between mental health providers and other support resources to induce fewer stigmas in the treatment process than solely providing professional mental health services. These multidisciplinary collaborations may include care provision from professionals as primary care providers, culturally sanctioned healers, preferred community leaders, and religious leaders. For instance, a treatment team comprised of a licensed mental health professional might team up with a Yue Chinese paraprofessional and cultural broker; if the licensed professional does not speak Yue or a dialect the client speaks to provide culturally sensitive and respectful support for Posttraumatic Stress Disorder to Yue Chinese speaking victims of domestic violence. A team approach is often better received in collectivistic cultures.

Levels of Loss of Face and Interpersonal Compliance

Chinese American clients may avoid situations and behaviors which are associated with *loss of face*, or in other words, with the need to maintain their own social dignity (Zane & Mak, 2003) when the relationship involves help-seeking for personal problems (Shon & Ja, 1982). Abe-Kim, Okazaki, and Goto (2001) conducted a study on relatively less acculturated (N=335) Asian American college students in order to assess levels of loss of face. Results showed that less acculturated Asian-Americans are more concerned about loss of face than more acculturated students. The fear of losing face appears to interfere with psychological interventions as well as compliance with treatment if clinicians provoke this perception. Although loss of face and its matching interventions require further studies, there may be something learning and applications from these studies on US majority populations in terms of motivational levels to engage in treatment as well as resistance to engage in treatment.

Norcross and Beutler (2011) recommend that clients with high resistance levels, expressed through therapeutic interventions, might best be treated by culturally competent and sensitive clinicians who understand their cultural backgrounds, adopt a stance that does not provoke resistance, and utilize indirect ways of communicating about difficult topics. Zane and Yeh (2002) emphasize that the importance of face is a key element to maintain interpersonal harmony, and provoking loss of face in self-disclosing for individuals or significant others interferes with the effectiveness of therapy if executed insensitively to the client's cultural values. Cultural competencies in understanding social dynamics and becoming sensitive to the client's loss of face in a cultural context are essential for clinicians treating Chinese American clients, particularly since Western therapies tend to emphasize individualistic rather than collectivist perspectives (Sue, 2006). Zane and Yeh (2002) also raise additional considerations in pointing out that extreme levels of loss of face may neglect the others' wellbeing and provoke domestic violence, child/dependent adult/senior abuse, interpersonal relationship, or financial issues among family members. In these cases, the clinician must be extra cautious in conducting clinical assessments to develop properly designed and culturally interventions while maintaining and respecting the client's confidentiality and self-integrity.

Norcross and Beutler (2011) emphasize that interpersonal compliance is a more productive stance for patients than resistance during therapy, and illustrate how the clinician's approach can provoke or reduce resistance in the client's behaviors. For example, in order for a Chinese client to feel safe, be willing to work toward solving problems, and to be open and willing to understand one's self and others, the Chinese client often must trust in those professionals who seem to have a greater professional authority than they have about themselves. Compliance with a treatment recommendation or even the decision to enter treatment requires three considerations by the client: (1) a level of interpersonal trust, (2) the ability to restrain one's impulses to protect themselves when others disagree with them; and (3) a readiness to comply with expert's suggestions while facing their own impulses of emotional avoidance. Assessing levels of resistance and rolling with them is an essential technique for therapists to enhance effectiveness of psychotherapy while considering clients' cultural understanding of the process and the context in which therapy is being conducted.

Levels of Subjective Distress

Okazaki et al. (2009) conducted comprehensive reviews of clinical personality assessments including significant studies using the Chinese versions of MMPI and the MMPI-2 from Hong Kong, Taiwan and mainland China, and compared findings to the USA. They found that significant response differences resulted from the examinees' perceived understanding of the contextual and cultural meaning attributed to each of the translated items on the MMPI/MMP-2, findings also supported previously in the literature (Cheung & Song, 1989; Cheung et al., 1996; Kwan, 2000; Stevens, Kwan, & Graybill, 1993; Sue et al., 1996). Less acculturated Asian-Americans demonstrated slightly higher levels on symptom scales for schizophrenia, somatization, depression, and neurotic disorders (e.g., Cheung et al. (1996), Cheung & Song (1989), Sue et al. (1996), Tsai & Pike (2000)). Thus, assessing levels of current distress and managing these stresses in their cultural contexts seem to be important at the beginning of any clinical interventions for Chinese American clients despite their acculturation levels.

Norcross and Beutler (2011) summarized results from clinical outcome studies of both inpatients and outpatients, totaling over 1,250 different psychological and health disorders and treatments, including both psychological and pharmacological interventions, and concluded that the levels of observed symptoms are influenced by clients' self-perception and motivation. For instance, Chinese American professionals in the mental health field who fail their attempt to pass their professional licensing exam, often due to language and cultural challenges posed by the test format, are able to manage their failed attempts and levels of stress effectively and retake the test until they are successful at passing it. These Chinese American professionals are able to perceive success as a matter of perseverance while understanding some of the cultural and linguistic limitations. Others who may subsequently avoid taking the exam and give up perceive their failed attempts as scripted by as fate. Mid-ranges of subjective distress seem to improve clients' performance: successful interventions leveraging this mid-level distress factor include those which (1) increase motivation by making a client aware his or her difficulties or (2) reduce the distress to manageable levels by teaching coping skills (Norcross & Beutler, 2011). These conceptual interventions are consistent with the *Stages of Change* (Prochaska & Norcross, 2001). When clients are on the Contemplation Stage, clinicians use *Motivational Interviewing*—a technique effective to raise aware of the client's own difficulties, especially for clients with addictive or unhealthy behaviors. In addition, Harwood and Beutler (2008, 2009) emphasized that to improve the effectiveness of psychotherapeutic outcomes, a clinician needs to consider both dimensions of the clients' functional levels. These levels include the objective (functional impairment and resources) and subjective (dysphoria, euthymia, and felt support) dimensions.

Coping Styles

Tseng and Wu (1985) pointed to traditional Chinese American values of achieving harmony and the social value given to acting in proper ways toward others and respecting authorities as being a dominant coping style. Zane and Yeh (2002) point to the importance of face as a key element in maintaining interpersonal harmony. Likewise, Tseng (2005) have concluded that Chinese American clients are more psychologically minded than European American individuals. It has also been posited that these Chinese American researchers better understand and is extremely more aware of indirect relationships, hierarchical positioning, and nonverbal communications between interacting social and family members, as well as, family and social group dynamics. The ability to understand these high context systemic communications, subtle culturally sensitive relationships and complex interactions requires special training in cultural competencies on the part of any treating clinicians (Sue, 2006). Some clients may choose to not self-disclose if they perceive the clinicians are not knowledgeable and respectful of their immigrant history, as well as of their client's cultural adaptations. Clinicians must be aware of the value their clients place on interpersonal harmony, loss of face, and social dynamics. Clinicians must be able skillfully deal with clients' presenting problems in both nonverbal and verbal contexts. For instance, they must be skillful to know when not to ask or when to ask emotionally laden questions to not offend and shame the clients. They must also be skillful to recognize when Chinese American clients are bending their expressions of personal preferences in ways that are designed to maintain interpersonal harmony, while at the same time clinically assessing the impairment associated with the clinical problems present for treatment and evaluate the personal and environmental resources needed to address these client presenting problems. This complex web of multirelational and multileveled understanding must be done without sacrificing clinician's understanding of their clients' perceptions of the problems that exist within the family, the social dynamics invoked to protect these perceptions, the therapeutic alliance, and the motivation needed to help the client therapeutically and respectfully.

While fostering clinicians' critical understanding of the Asian patient's cultural values, beliefs, and social dynamics, cultural competencies must include being aware of the differences that exist among culturally similar groups. A clinician must appreciate the vast heterogeneity that characterizes Chinese American clients. Beutler, Harwood, Kimpara, Verdirame, and Blau (2011) have described cultural and stylistic variations that exist across Asian individuals' *coping styles* (i.e., externalizing and internalizing) and the implications these stylistic variations suggest for matching best fit interventions to individual patients. Characteristically, people who have come from traditional Chinese cultures tend to rely heavily on internalizing coping styles to control their emotions. This internalizing coping style leads Chinese clients to confine their feelings and impulses while avoiding personal conflicts in order to achieve and maintain harmony. At the beginning of the treatment sessions, in order to achieve family or social harmony, brief solution focused interventions may be conducive to learning adaptive behaviors in these internalizing contexts. Traditional Chinese clients may be satisfied with these types of adaptive learning interventions since the solutions maintain one's social acceptability and social position with others (Tseng & Wu, 1985). However, if Chinese American clients are more acculturated and open to psychotherapy as a way of seeking and developing more solid relationships with others, the culturally competent therapists must be able to identify and determine these coping styles within their cultural contexts. Among these internalizing patients, interpersonal and insight oriented psychotherapy will provide more growth-producing therapeutic effects and a better match to coping styles of Chinese American clients (Beutler & Harwood, 2002).

In Western (individualistic) contexts or for more acculturated Chinese Americans in the USA, individuals with externalizing coping styles (those who tend to blame others and project their feelings onto others, as well as those who tend toward being undercontrolled) will be receptive to behavioral interventions to enhance healthy behavioral choices. This treatment approach contrasts the optimal intervention approach for individuals with internalizing coping styles (those who tend to blame themselves and remove themselves emotionally). It is a better fit with the use of interpersonal/insight oriented psychotherapy to increase understandings of their emotional experiences. In general, most individuals have both internalizing and externalizing characteristics to different degrees and it will require the culturally competent therapist to learn and match with relative reliance these strategies with corresponding balances between insight and behaviorally focused interventions to obtain optimal effects (Beutler & Clarkin, 1990; Beutler, Clarkin, & Bongar, 2000; Beutler & Harwood, 2002; Castonguay & Beutler, 2006).

Unique Characteristics of Symptoms for Chinese Americans

Somatic and Vegetative Symptoms and Depression/Anxiety

Unapparent causal links exist between a patient's coping style and the manifestation of depressive mood states. Culturally driven coping styles often determine how depression symptoms are expressed. Chinese American clients predominately express somatic/vegetative symptoms over simple depressive mood symptoms when compared to European Americans (Kleinman & Sung, 1979; Leong & Lau, 2001; Sue & Sue, 1974). Mak and Zane (2004) conducted analyses examining somatization for Chinese Americans by using a large and multistage household sample designs. They found that anxiety, depression, gender, age, education, psychosocial stressors, and social support were significantly linked to somatization but not acculturation or length of residence in the USA. They identified "a stress response" which is manifested with an increased distress, severity, and psychosocial stressors beyond those commonly expressed only though psychosomatic complains. This evidence supports the notion that degrees of social stressors and the levels of perceived worries (psychological stressors) are taken into consideration in the development for the treatments of somatization.

Cultural conceptualizations of depression for Chinese Americans include the identification of somatic symptoms with depression, which in turn express depression as expressions of poor physical health. Tseng and Wu (1985) highlighted reasons for this form of symptom transmigration: traditional Chinese medicines emphasize organ-oriented concepts of overall health to include mental health conditions (e.g., results of weak kidneys, hot intestines, and *qi* energy imbalances) while expression of somatic complains were considered more socially acceptable and much easily received than emotional complains without somatic anchors. The expression of emotions was considered as an interference with achieving harmony.

Culture-Bounded Syndromes for Chinese Americans

The Diagnostic and Statistical Manual of mental health disorders fourth edition (DSM-IV: APA, 2000) describes four different kinds of Chinese culturally-bounded syndromes including *Koro*, *Qi gong Psychotic Reaction*, *Shenjing Shuariro*, and *Shenkui* as systematically studied conditions. These aberrant behaviors with circumscribed somatic symptoms, unique development and onset, and elicited set of particular social responses are affected by specific indigenous factors and specific societal or cultural groups. Although these prescribed symptom specific behavioral set may be seen as unique to these conditions, similar DSM-IV symptomology and behaviors are seen throughout the world (APA, 2000).

Koro (*in Malaysia*) *Suk-yeong* (*in Cantonese Chinese*), *or suo-yang* (*Mandarin-speaking Chinese*) is a syndrome described by a complaint about genital retraction with a fear of impending death. Culturally specified beliefs (e.g., excessive intercourse, ghosts of the dead, and contaminated food) are also present. For examples, a person with *koro* may complain that his penis is shrinking and as a result this condition will kill him (Gaw, 1993). *Qigong Psychotic Reaction* is reported as dissociative paranoia, or other psychotic or nonpsychotic symptoms experienced acutely and in a time-limited fashion after practicing traditional Chinese practice of *Qigong* (exercise of *qi* energy). *Shenjing Shuariro or neurasthenia* is characterized by symptoms of physiological and mental fatigue, dizziness, headache, other pains, concentration difficulties, sleep disturbance, memory loss, gastrointestinal problems, sexual dysfunction, irritability, excitability, and various imbalances of autonomic nervous systems. These symptoms are diagnosed as *neurasthenia* in the People's Republic of China. *Shenkui* is described as anxiety or panic symptoms that occur concomitantly with somatic complains such as dizziness, backache, fatigability, general weakness, insomnia, frequent dreams, and complaints of sexual dysfunction. For instance, excessive loss of ejaculate is a manifest source of worry largely because it represents the concurrent belief that losing one's sexual potency represents the loss of one's essential core and therefore can be lethal.

Cultural Impacts on Alcoholism or Problem Gambling

Lin (1986) has described how, historically, alcoholism has not been considered a social or a psychiatric problem in Chinese societies. Social attitudes such as the traditional value of loss of face have been ascribed as protective factors from alcohol abuse and dependence. Chinese Americans overall show consistent low rates of alcohol abuse in treatment samples (Wong, 2002). However, when evaluating incidents of binge drinking, Asians Americans have been shown to have higher incident rates as compared to other ethnic groups (Wong, 2002) and Chinese Americans are often underrepresented in alcohol related research. Alcohol consumption is perceived favorably as a social activity culturally practiced in health and medicinal settings, cooking, significant social engagements, and religious purposes embedded into their everyday lives (Chu, 1972; Singer, 1974). Some studies support the findings that US-born or more acculturated Chinese Americans consume more alcohol than immigrant Americans or low acculturated Chinese Americans (Hendershot, Dillworth, Neighbors, & George, 2008, Huff & Kline, 1999; Sue, Zane, & Ito, 1979). However, Wong (2002) found that immigrant Asians tend to binge and consume alcohol at higher rates and volume during cultural festivities and celebrations (weddings and banquets) compared to more acculturated or US-born Asians who tended to consume higher amounts of alcohol more frequently over time (happy hours and regular social gatherings). Therefore, the findings about Asians and alcohol continue to be mixed in the literature. Moreover, rates of alcoholism for Chinese Americans have been correlated to one of the highest rates of Hepatitis B, liver cancer, and cirrhosis among US ethnic and racial populations. Studies by the Northern California Cancer Center (NCCC) have shown high associations among Hepatitis B, deterioration of liver functions, and excessive alcohol consumptions among Chinese Americans and require preventative education about the effects of Hepatitis B and C, and alcoholism on health (NCCC, 2007).

Culture impacts other addictive behaviors, such as problematic gambling, among Chinese Americans. Glionna (2006) postulates that Chinese Americans consider gambling to be an acceptable social and recreational activity, especially when conducted at home and during cultural celebrations (New Year's, holiday festivities, and weddings). Gambling can also facilitate long supernatural beliefs of improving luck, prosperity, and good fate. Chinese youths are often socialized to gamble for lucky money with their aunts, uncles, and their grandparents during extended family gatherings, or they may bet on events such as weather conditions with their peers at schools. Despite these cultural practices, the continued lack of prevalence studies of problem gambling for Chinese Americans is a concern. A large informal study in San Francisco's Chinatown by NICOS Chinese Health Coalition (1997), identified 70 % of 1,808 participants ranked gambling as the number 1 community problem and 21 % of those respondents met the criteria and were classified as pathological gamblers.

Fong et al. (2010) described problem gambling as associated with co-occurring substance use disorders, mood disorders, personality disorders, higher rates of suicidality, and domestic violence, in addition to increased financial, social, and interpersonal problems. In particular, their study points to Asian-Americans as one of most vulnerable populations to problem gambling. Several reasons were discussed in their study including, (1) major gambling industries began to target and satisfy Asian-Americans' preferences for food, gambling games, and preference for communal atmospheres; (2) social isolation resulting from immigration processes often separates families and makes gambling an appealing surrogate culturally accepted practice, especially when peers are betting or they are welcomed in their primary language; and (3) gambling itself is culturally accepted and approved as a nonstigmatizing social practice. These compounded factors and multilayered culturally accepted practices for Chinese and Chinese American gamblers should be considered when assessing and treating Chinese and Chinese American problem gamblers.

Case Description

Lam's wife Mei looked for a Chinese American male therapist who spoke Cantonese because her friends and family strongly recommended it. She found the therapist through 1-800-GAMBLER (California Council of Problem Gambling). Lam's wife called and talked to the therapist, noting that Lam has been addicted to gambling for more than 15 years. She also explained that she had discovered last year that their savings had evaporated and Lam had started borrowing money from family and friends to support his habit. Mei explained that they had been arguing incessantly and had talked to their friends and extended family to find someone who could help Lam stop gambling. While Lam had listened, he did so without taking any actions to improve his addictive behavior. Finally, Mei explained to the therapist that she had threatened to leave Lam if he does not seek help from a therapist.

Lam agreed to talk to the therapist via phone. From this conversation, the therapist learned that Lam was a 56 year-old Chinese American male with 14 years of education and has been married for about 28 years. He and Mei have one son who is 26 years old. Lam immigrated from Hong Kong in 1981 to the USA with his parents and some extended family members. He has been working as an electrician for over 20 years with the same company. Lam also reported he started having severe headaches 2–3 times a week beginning about 10 months ago, and recently they have become more frequent, especially when he feels overwhelmed. Lam also admitted that he was tired of telling lies to friends and family about his gambling because he had done so to the point that they do not trust him any longer. When asked to describe how much of a debt he has accumulated, he avoided conveying details and verbally distracted the conversation, though the therapist was able to deduce it was more than what he was willing to share at the moment.

Lam was 20 min late for the initial intake interview. The interview and subsequent interventions were conducted in Cantonese due to Lam's preference for his primary language. While greeting and escorting Lam to the therapy room, the therapist noticed that Lam responded with simple yes or no answers and was very guarded. The therapist started by describing his education and credentials, his cultural background, the practice of confidentiality, and the nature of psychotherapy. He continued to educate Lam about the typical behaviors associated with gambling addiction that have been found problematic and cause much family disruptions along with the interventions used at the clinic. The therapist also emphasized the roles each of them would take in treatment and how individual differences affect the therapeutic outcomes. Then, the therapist checked in with Lam as to whether he felt comfortable enough to answer more clinical inquires. Once the therapeutic process and the treatment expectations were explained, Lam was asked if he was willing to work with therapist now he was more informed as to what he had agreed to engage in. Lam responded, "Yes, I need to work on this since my wife threatens to leave me if I do not go to therapy," and appeared to show a reduction of tension in the session. As a final step during the initial session, the therapist took time to answer Lam's additional questions about psychotherapy and the clinic's procedures, an important and necessary psychoeducational step since Lam had no previous psychotherapy experience.

During this interview, the therapist learned that Lam was still gambling 2–3 times a month, but keeping it secret from his wife, family, and friends. Gambling was costing him over $1,000 per visit, and he had been borrowing money to pay these debts amounting to over $50,000 to local casinos, family, and friends. By his report, Lam started gambling 16 years ago. In the beginning, he just needed to go to a place to feel welcomed and normalized. However, in a short period, Lam started gambling regularly and developed an addiction that kept him going to the casinos regularly. The more Lam lost, the more he chased his losses, which would culminate him waging $1,000 within a couple of hours. Beginning 5 years ago, Lam started to withdraw money from his joint-savings account and would lie to Mei to cover this up. Lam lost all of their savings just last year. He started borrowing money secretly and shared with no one the actual amount of his debt to date. When asked to describe his readiness to change and engage in treatment, Lam stated he was ready to stop but he did not know how since he really wanted to improve his marital relationship and regain the trust of his wife. He did not want to divorce Mei.

Lam recalled that he had stopped gambling for 2 months after Mei initially found out their savings account had been depleted and after his family and extended friends had become involved in discussions about Lam owing them money. Lam further recalled that he had started gambling again because playing slot machines gave him a feeling of fulfillment. Playing slot machines was a familiar feel, like being with "close friends" where everyone knew each other and no one criticized anyone for their individual flaws. When asked if he actually had close friends, Lam indicated that he did not, but asserted that he sometimes called and talked to one cousin who is very supportive and lives 600 miles away. Based on this initial interview, Lam was diagnosed with severe pathological gambling as assessed by using the National Option Research Center DSM Screen for Problem Gambling (NODS) assessment with a Full Score of 10.

In addition to his pathological gambling, Lam reported an increasing number of headaches, 4–5 times a week, causing him to wake up early 2–3 times a week for nearly a year. He also disclosed that he currently was separately from Mei and living with his brother's family. Lam earned $45,000 annually and more than half of his salary was spent on gambling. Lam denied any substance abuse or preoccupation with death when asked but these latter ideations were persistent thoughts occurring 1–2 times a month. He told no one in his family about them but becoming tired of keeping these ideations secret. However, Lam maintained that because he wanted to save his marriage and was fearful of how his wife may view these suicidal thoughts. He described that these protective factors prevented him from any suicidal attempts or make plans.

Lam was raised by his biological parents and had an older brother and sister. His father and older brother did not get along. After moving to the USA, his brother committed suicide and since that time, Lam had become increasingly isolated from others. It was also following this event that Lam started gambling. Lam shared that his father drank almost every night until he was hospitalized due to chronic hepatitis and stopped drinking 10 years ago. When Lam was young, he often witnessed his father physically abusing his mother and brother. However, he does not remember if his father was abusive toward him as well. He attributed his lack of memory about any abuse by his father as being the result of having decided to emotionally ignore him.

Summaries and Case Formulation

- *Complexity and Chronicity of Psychological Problem*: Lam displayed a moderately high level of impairment as indicated by his chronic history of gambling addiction, symptoms of somatization, sleeping problems, interpersonal problems with his wife, family, and friends, feelings of isolation, and significant amounts of debts. A multi-faceted, intensive treatment strategy was recommended, consisting of weekly individual therapy to be conducted by a Cantonese-speaking therapist, and enrollment in a weekly Gambling Anonymous (GA) group. In addition, he was referred to the Self-Exclusion program at each of the casinos he frequented where he could voluntarily and be legally informed to exclude himself from the gambling premises for 1 year, 5, or indefinitely. A free financial counseling available online class was also recommended. The primary goals of therapy and the initial focus of treatment were to reduce Lam's self-destructive behaviors (i.e. gambling addiction and suicidal thoughts) by structuring his environment to reduce triggering cues to gambling and depression, and to increase his available social support in the community since family and friends were not providing sufficient support and trust.

- *Levels of Loss of Face and Interpersonal Compliance*: At the beginning of intake, Lam demonstrated a moderate level of *loss of face and resistance* as noted by his low level responsiveness in the waiting room. However, the therapist was knowledgeable and aware of the cultural issues that were likely to be at work and skillfully was able to deal with Lam's first psychotherapy experience, normalize gambling behaviors among Chinese Americans and to reflect Lam's expectation of treatment goals. Since Lam responded with a strong desire and commitment to stop gambling, the therapist was able to help forge a strong therapeutic alliance. This resulted in good treatment compliance and relatively little manifestation of resistance.
- *Levels of Subjective Distress*: Lam displayed a moderately high level of subjective distress as indicated by several symptoms of somatization, his report of feeling tired of misleading others about his depression and gambling, his estrangement, isolation, and distancing from others. The therapist emphasized that both objective (e.g., financial coaching, setting limitations to access gambling facilities, and social increased support from his cousin) and subjective (e.g., the therapist's positive regard, the encouragement of self-soothing behaviors, and his learning and controlling environmental triggers/alternative skills) were important to achieve improvement in psychotherapy.
- *Coping Styles*: Lam displayed a dominantly internalizing coping style as indicated by gambling activity with much guilt and anxiety. He had few interactions with others and had turned to gambling to feel validated. He also showed low self-esteem, deference to authority (his parents and extended family), but these internalizing processes were offset to some degree by externalizing coping styles. He had become argumentative with his wife and engaged in some externalized blaming. At the beginning of the interventions, the therapist helped the patient begin the processes of adapting a short solution-focused intervention including instructions for talking to his Mei with a softer voice, and improvement of his listening and conversational skills. After managing a level of subjective distress in this way, the therapist began to focus on the constructive use of insight oriented procedures to gain an understanding of how Lam had begun to develop gambling habits. The therapist also provided grief-oriented counselling and encouraged Lam to enact his desired image of self, examined his beliefs, explored his memories, and linked his emotions to his affective states. This therapeutic work drew the focus of therapy to reflect on the patient's relationship with his father.
- *Additional Considerations*: Since 20 % of pathological gamblers have made suicidal attempts, the therapist kept in mind the importance of conducting repeated suicidal assessments whenever Lam had increased suicide ideation and considering the self-statements of "he not wanting to live." As he became aware of the possibility that he may have been physical abused by his father, the therapist also kept an eye out for possible symptoms of dissociative behaviors and fragmented memories and other possible symptoms of Post

Traumatic Stress Disorder (PTSD). Sometimes, Lam did not want to talk about his financial debts or the other interpersonal problems, and whenever these omissions were noted, the therapist utilized available culturally sensitive resources to facilitate his own understanding of these relationship problems.

In accordance with these evidence-based principles (Beutler & Harwood, 2002; Castonguay & Beutler, 2006; Tseng, 2005), the therapist was aware that Chinese American clients are more "collectivistic" or "interpersonally" minded than European Americans, and they understand more complexly the interface between family and social dynamics at the same level of understanding as, European Americans understand self-reliance, critical thinking, and assertive communications. Sue (2006) emphasizes that these culturally sensitive and complex considerations require special cultural competencies on the part of clinicians. The clinician working with Lam found it helpful to have listened to a many past diverse narratives from Chinese Americans and it was important for the therapist to understand how these narratives provided by previous patients their diverse histories, experiences of discrimination, and *loss of face*. The therapist's increased understanding of Lam's language, cultural history, and clinical presentation led to an increased capacity to identify external objective resources that might be helpful to the patient, as well as to help reflect Lam's own emotional experiences accurately. The uses of narrative experiences and integrating them effectively with clients is challenging to learn and use effectively without becoming authoritative in the therapy session, but experienced clinicians appreciate all narratives from our diverse communities and utilize in combination with evidence-based principles to help clients gain their optimal coping abilities.

Summary and Conclusions

1. Chinese Americans are the largest Asian group in the United States coming from the most diverse countries of origin and with over 200 years of immigration history. Chinese Americans are vastly heterogeneous in terms of language, education, and social economic statuses. Clinicians should carefully recognize these varied issues within the Chinese American population as, reasonable accommodations on assessment approaches, case conceptualization, and treatment planning, need to account for different levels of acculturation. Functionally, first- and second-generation clients may utilize somatic and contextually appropriate socially laden language to express their emotions while acculturated clients use affectively laden, concretized, and descriptive verbal communication similar to Western European decent and North American individuals.
2. Chinese customs, beliefs, values, and practices are structurally founded on Confucianism. Confucian ideals emphasizes harmony, duty, honor, and respect. Therefore, the traditional Chinese family respect for elders, filial piety, and family have significant roles in social and economic units of society. However immigration often brings change to family roles and dynamics. While the contemporary family holds some traditional customs and values, the Chinese family has moved towards a new clearer system where the new structure includes the husband and wife sharing equal familial decision-making roles and having more equal earning potential.
3. Mental illness is not positively viewed in Chinese communities and negative views are generally associated with a sense of shame and loss of face. Chinese Americans tend to seek help from close friends or family members first and suppress their needs via minimization. They prefer controlling their emotions in the sanctioned practice of maintaining "face." Thus, when they seek mental health services outside the family, they tend to be for more complex and severe issues as compared to European Americans who use similar services for less severe and pathological conditions.
4. Chinese Americans clients may prefer brief solution-focused therapies to limit expressing their emotional experiences in order to maintain family harmony. However, more acculturated Chinese American clients tend to be more open and understand better family and social

dynamics, unspoken communication, high context communication, and work well with insight or interpersonal oriented psychotherapy.

5. Using cognitive assessments with Chinese American clients, the assessor needs to understand that this population will tend to perform very well on quantitative measures as compared to verbal measures, as a function related to levels of English language proficiency and levels of acculturation. Okazaki and Sue (2000) addressed the lack or inadequate test reliability and validity when utilizing these existing Intelligence Quotient (IQ) measures. Nisbett (2003) addressed cultural cognitions: Chinese Americans tend to endorse group harmony and contextual understanding of situations while European Americans tend to be more analytic and attend to individual objects and categories.
6. While considering levels of acculturations, one needs to be sensitive and understand tot diverse Chinese cultural customs, beliefs, values, and practices, evidence-based principles (Beutler & Clarkin, 1990; Beutler et al., 2000; Beutler & Harwood, 2002) such as complexity and chronicity of psychological problems, levels of loss of face and interpersonal compliance, levels of subjective distress, coping styles are addressed to enhance outcome of psychotherapy optimally by tailoring individual dispositional characteristic differences and matching interventions.
7. In addition, unique symptoms characteristics for Chinese Americans include culture-bound syndromes such as *Koro*, *Qi gong Psychotic Reaction*, *Shenjing Shuariro*, and *Shenkui*. These conditions share common cultural expressions favoring more somatic qualities over affective qualities. Chinese American clients predominately express somatic/vegetative symptoms more frequently than simple depressive mood symptoms when compared to European Americans. Chinese sociocultural practices also serve to maintain and reinforce less favorable behaviors such as alcoholism or problem gambling, as these activities are favorably perceived in social celebratory gatherings such as wedding, New Year, and holiday festivities. It is the behavioral or somatic component of the social activity which is the primary reinforcement to the clinical condition and/or syndrome.
8. In conclusion, the case study provided a clinical case to help clinicians work more culturally informed with Chinese American clients. Clinician's increased understanding of the client's culture (e.g., languages, immigration history, customs, values, experiences of discrimination, idioms of distress, etc.) leads to an increased capacity to identify external objective resources that may be helpful to the patient, as well as to help reflect the client's own emotional experiences more accurately. Therefore, these cultural competencies strengthen the therapeutic alliances and evidence-based principles guide clinicians to enhance the effectiveness of the psychotherapy process and experience.

References

Abe-Kim, J., Okazaki, S., & Goto, S. G. (2001). Unidimensional versus multidimensional approaches to the assessment of acculturation for Asian American populations. *Cultural Diversity and Ethnic Minority Psychology, 7*, 232–246.

Abe-Kim, J., Takeuchi, D. T., Hong, S., Zane, N., Sue, S., Spencer, M. S., et al. (2007). Use of mental health-related services among immigrant and US-born Asian Americans: results from the National Latino and Asian American Study. *American Journal of Public Health, 97*(10), 91–8.

American Community Survey. (2008–2010). American Community Survey 3-year estimates: B02006. *Selected population profile in the United States: Asia Population Group: Chinese alone*. Retrieved from http://factfinder2.census.gov/faces/nav/jsf/pages/index.xhtml

American Psychiatric Association. (2000). *Diagnostic and statistical manual of mental disorders* (4th ed.). Arlington, VA: Author.

Barringer, H., Takeuchi, D., & Levin, M. (1995). *Asians and Pacific Islanders in the United States*. New York, NY: Russell Sage Foundation.

Beach, M. C., Gary, T. L., Price, E. G., Robinson, K., Gozu, A., Palacio, A., et al. (2006). Improving health care quality for racial/ethnic minorities: a systematic review of the best evidence regarding provider and organization interventions. *BioMedCentral Public Health, 6*, 104.

Beutler, L. E., & Clarkin, J. F. (1990). *Systematic treatment selection: Toward targeted therapeutic intervention*. New York, NY: Brunner/Mazel.

Beutler, L. E., Clarkin, J. F., & Bongar, B. (2000). *Guide lines for the systematic treatment of the depressed patient*. New York, NY: Oxford University Press.

Beutler, L. E., & Harwood, T. M. (2002). *Prescriptive psychotherapy: A practical guide to systematic treatment selection*. New York, NY: Oxford University Press.

Beutler, L. E., Harwood, T. M., Kimpara, S., Verdirame, D., & Blau, K. (2011). Coping Style. In J. C. Norcross (Ed.), *Relationships that work: Therapist contributions and responsiveness to patient needs* (2nd ed.). New York, NY: Oxford University Press.

Brown, T. R., Huang, K. H., Harris, D. E., & Stein, K. M. (1973). Mental illness and the role of mental health facilities in Chinatown. In S. Sue & N. N. Wagner (Eds.), *Asian Americans: Psychological perspectives* (pp. 212–231). Palo Alto, CA: Science and Behavior Books.

Castonguay, L. G., & Beutler, L. E. (2006). *Principles of therapeutic change that work*. New York, NY: Oxford University Press.

Chen, W., & Yoo, G. Y. (2010). *Encyclopedia of Asian American issue today volume 1*. Santa Barbara, CA: Greenwood Press.

Cheung, F. M., & Song, W. (1989). A review on the clinical applications of the Chinese MMPI. *Psychological Assessment, 1*, 230–237.

Cheung, F. M., Song, W., & Zhang, J. (1996). The Chinese MMPI-2: Research and application in Hong Kong and the People's Republic of China. In J. N. Butcher (Ed.), *International adaptations of the MMPI-2* (pp. 137–161). Minneapolis, MN: University of Minnesota Press.

Chu, G. (1972). Drinking patterns and attitudes of rooming-house Chinese in San Francisco. *Quarterly Journal of Studies on Alcohol, 33*, 1–2.

Chu, J. P., Huynh, L. and Aréan, P. (2011). Cultural adaptation of evidence-based practice utilizing an iterative stakeholder process and theoretical framework: problem solving therapy for Chinese older adults. *International Journal of Geriatric Psychiatry, 27*(1), 97–106, January 2012. John Wiley & Sons, Ltd. doi: 10.1002/gps.2698

Chu, J. P. & Sue, S. (2011). Asian American Mental Health: what we know and what we don't know. *Online readings in psychology and culture, Unit 3*. Retrieved from http://scholarworks.gvsu.edu/orpc/vol3/iss1/4

Chung, S. F. (2011). *Pursuit of gold: Chinese American miners and merchants in the American West*. Urbana, IL: University of Illinois Press.

Corrigan, P. W., & Penn, D. L. (1999). Lessons from social psychology on discrediting psychiatric stigma. *American Psychologist, 54*, 765–776.

Duvasula, R., & Sue, S. (1996). Severity of disturbance among Asian American outpatients. *Cultural Diversity and Mental Health, 2*, 43–52.

Foner, N. (1997). The Immigrant Family: Cultural Legacies and Cultural Changes. *International Migration Review, 31*(4), 961–975.

Fong, T., Campos, M., Rosenthal, R., Brecht, M., Schwartz, B., Davis, A., et al. (2010). Problem Gambling Knowledge and Perceived Community Impact Among Asian-Pacific Islanders and Non Asian-Pacific Islanders. *Journal of Immigrant and Minority Health, 12*(2), 173–178.

Gaw, A. C. (1993). Psychiatric care of Chinese Americans. In A. C. Gaw (Ed.), *Culture, ethnicity and mental illness* (pp. 227–251). Washington, DC: American Psychiatric Press.

Givens, J. L., Houston, T. K., Van Voorhees, B. W., Ford, D. E., & Cooper, L. A. (2007). Ethnicity and preferences for depression treatment. *General Hospital Psychiatry, 29*, 182–191.

Glionna, J. M. (2006). *Gambling, addiction, and Asian culture Asian-Nation: The landscape of Asian America*. Retrieved October 20, 2012 from http://www.asian-nation.org/gambling.shtml

Harwood, T. M., & Beutler, L. E. (2008). EVTs, EBPs, ESRs, and RIPs: Inspecting the varieties of research based practices. In L. L'Abate (Ed.), *Toward a science of clinical psychology* (pp. 161–176). New York, NY: Nova Science Publishers.

Harwood, T. M., & Beutler, L. E. (2009). Assessment of Clients in pretreatment Planning. In J. N. Butcher (Ed.), *Handbook of personality assessment* (pp. 643–666). New York, NY: Oxford University Press.

Hendershot, C. S., Dillworth, T. M., Neighbors, C., & George, W. H. (2008). Differential effects of acculturation on drinking behavior in Chinese- and Korean-American college students. *Journal of Studies on Alcohol and Drugs, 69*, 121–128.

Hsia, J., & Peng, S. S. (1998). Academic achievement and performance. In L. C. Lee & N. W. S. Zane (Eds.), *Handbook of Asian American psychology* (pp. 325–357). Thousand Oaks, CA: Sage.

Ho, D. (1996). Filial piety and its psychological consequences. In M. D. Bond (Ed.), *Handbook of Chinese psychology* (pp. 155–165). Hong Kong: University of Hong Kong Press.

Huff, R., & Kline, M. (1999). *Promoting health in multicultural populations: A handbook for practitioners*. Thousand Oaks, CA: Sage.

Kleinman, A., & Sung, L. H. (1979). Why do indigenous practitioners successfully heal? *Social Science and Medicine, 13B*, 7–26.

Lee, E. (1997). *Working with Asian Americans: A guide for clinician*. New York, NY: The Guilford Press.

Lee, E., & Mock, M. R. (1996). Chinese Families. In M. McGoldrick, J. Giordano, & J. K. Pearce (Eds.), *Ethnicity and family therapy* (pp. 302–18). New York, NY: The Guilford Press.

Lee, K. S., Hong, C. H., Cheong, H. K., & Oh, B. H. (2009). Difference in nutritional risk between mild cognitive impairment group and normal cognitive function elderly group. *Archives of Gerontology and Geriatrics, 49*(1), 49–53.

Lee, S., Fung, S., Tsang, A., Zhang, M., Huang, Y., He, Y., et al. (2007). Delay in initial treatment contact after first onset of mental disorders in metropolitan China. *Acta Psychiatrica Scandinavica, 116*, 10–16.

Lee, S., Tsang, A., Chui, H., Kwok, K., & Cheung, E. (2007). A community epidemiological survey of generalized anxiety disorder in Hong Kong. *Community Mental Health Journal, 43*(4), 305–319.

Leong, F. T., & Lau, A. S. (2001). Barriers to providing effective mental health services to Asian Americans. *Mental Health Services Research, 3*(4), 201–14.

Lin, T. (1986). Psychiatry and Chinese culture. *Journal of Western journal of medicine, 139*, 862–867.

Lin, K., Inui, T., Kleinman, A., & Womack, W. (1982). Sociocultural determinants of the help-seeking behavior of patients with mental illness. *Journal of Nervous and Mental Disease, 170*(2), 78–85.

Liu, G. Z. (2001). *Chinese culture and disability: Information for US service providers*. Buffalo, NY: Center for International Rehabilitation Research Information and Exchange (CIRRIE).

Mak, W. W., & Zane, N. W. (2004). The phenomenon of somatization among community Chinese Americans. *Social Psychiatry and Psychiatric Epidemiology, 39*(12), 967–974.

Nan, Z., Yeung, T., & Nguyen, C. (2007). Perceptions of mental illness and rehabilitation services in Chinese and Vietnamese Americans. *Journal of Applied Rehabilitation Counseling, 38*(2), 14–23. 47–48.

NICOS. (1997). *Chinese community health study*. San Francisco, CA: NICHOS Chinese Health Coalition.

Nisbett, R. E. (2003). *The geography of thought: How Asians and Westerners think differently-and why*. New York, NY: Free Press.

Norcross, J. C., & Beutler, L. E. (2011). Integrative psychotherapy. In D. Wedding (Ed.), *Current psychotherapies casebook*. Belmont, CA: Brooks/Cole.

North California Cancer Center. (2007). *Highlight*. Fremont, CA: Newsletter.

Okazaki, S., Okazaki, M., & Sue, S. (2009). Clinical personality assessment with Asian Americans. In J. N. Butcher (Ed.), *Oxford handbook of personality assessment* (pp. 377–396). New York, NY: Oxford University Press.

Okazaki, S., & Sue, S. (2000). Implications of test revisions for assessment with Asian Americans. *Psychological Assessment, 12*(3), 272–280.

Parker, G., Gladstone, G., & Chee, K. T. (2001). Depression and the planet's largest ethnic group: The Chinese. *The American Journal of Psychiatry, 158*(6), 857–864.

Prochaska, J. O., & Norcross, J. C. (2001). Stages of change. *Psychotherapy, 38*(4), 443–448.

Singer, K. (1974). The choice of intoxicant among the Chinese. *British Journal of Addiction, 69*, 257–268.

Shon, S. P., & Ja, D. Y. (1982). Asian families. In M. McGoldrick, J. K. Pearce, & J. Giordano (Eds.), *Ethnicity and family therapy* (pp. 208–228). New York, NY: Guilford.

Spector, R. (1996). Health and illness in the Asian/Pacific Islander American community. In R. Spector (Ed.), *Cultural diversity in health and illness* (4th ed.). Stamford, CT: Appleton & Lange.

Stevens, M. J., Kwan, K. K., & Graybill, D. F. (1993). Comparison of MMPI-2 scores of foreign Chinese and Caucasian-American students. *Journal of Clinical Psychology, 49*, 23–27.

Sue, S. (2006). Cultural competency: From philosophy to research. *Journal of Community Psychology, 34*(2), 237–245.

Sue, S., Keefe, K., Enomoto, K., Durvasula, R. S., & Chao, R. (1996). Asian American and White college students' performance on the MMPI-2. In J. N. Butcher (Ed.), *International adaptations of the MMPI-2* (pp. 206–218). Minneapolis, MN: University of Minnesota Press.

Sue, D., & Sue, S. (1987). Cultural factors in the clinical assessment of Asian Americans. *Journal of Consulting and Clinical Psychology, 55*(4), 479–487.

Sue, S., & Sue, D. W. (1974). MMPI comparisons between Asian American and non-Asian students utilizing a student health psychiatric clinic. *Journal of Counseling Psychology, 21*, 423–427.

Sue, S., Zane, N., & Ito, J. (1979). Alcohol drinking patterns among Asian and Caucasian Americans. *Journal of Cross-Cultural Psychology, 10*, 41–56.

Sung, B. (1985). Bicultural conflicts in Chinese immigrant children. *Journal of Comparative Studies, 16*(2), 255–269.

Takaki, R. (1998). *Stranger from a different shore*. Boston, MA: Back Bay Books.

Tsai, D. C., & Pike, P. L. (2000). Effects of acculturation on the MMPI-2 scores of Asian American students. *Journal of Personality Assessment, 74*, 216–230.

Tsai, J. L., Simeonova, D. I., & Watanabe, J. T. (2004). Somatic and Social: Chinese Americans Talk About Emotions. *Personality and Social Psychology Bulletin, 30*(9), 1226–1238.

Tseng, W. (2005). Government dependence of Chinese and Vietnamese community organizations and fiscal politics of immigrant services. *Journal of Health and Social Policy, 20*(4), 51–74.

Tseng, W. S., & Wu, Y. H. (1985). *Chinese culture and mental health*. New York, NY: Academic Press.

Tung, M. (1991). Insight-oriented psychotherapy and the Chinese patient. *American Orthopsychiatric Association, 61*(2), 186–194.

Uba, L. (1994). *Asian Americans: Personality patterns, identity, and mental health*. New York, NY: Guildford Press.

University of Maryland. (2011). *A new profile of Chinese Americans in a new century*. Retrieved October 10, 2012 from http://www.aast.umd.edu

U. S. Census Bureau (2000). *Race reporting for the Asian population by selected categories*. Retrieved October 10, 2012 from https://www.census.gov/prod/2002pubs/c2kbr0116.pdf

U. S. Census Bureau. (2010). *Race reporting for the Asian population by selected categories*. Retrieved October 10, 2012, from http://factfinder2.census.gov/

faces/tableservices/jsf/pages/productview.xhtml?pid=DEC_10_SF1_QTP8&prodType=table

Varvin, S., & Gerlach, A. (2011). The development of psychodynamic psychotherapy and psychoanalysis in China. *International Journal of Applied Psychoanalytic Studies, 8*(3), 261–267.

Wechsler, D. (1997). *WAIS-III: Administration and scoring manual: Wechsler adult intelligence scale*. New York, NY: Psychological Corporation.

Wong, J. (2002). *Sentencing outcome comparison for first time alcohol-related felony DUI convicts among Asian, Latino and White Americans*. Unpublished doctoral dissertation, Pacific Graduate School of Psychology, Palo Alto University, Palo Alto, CA.

Zane, N., & Mak, W. (2003). Major approaches to the measurement of acculturation among ethnic minority populations: A content analysis and an alternative empirical strategy. In K. M. Chun, P. B. Organista, & G. Marin (Eds.), *Acculturation: Advances in theory, measurement, and applied research* (pp. 39–60). Washington, DC: American Psychological Association.

Zane, N., & Yeh, M. (2002). The use of culturally-based variables in assessment: Studies on loss of face. In K. S. Kurasaki, S. Okazaki, & S. Sue (Eds.), *Asian American mental health: Assessment theories and methods* (pp. 123–138). New York, NY: Kluwer.

Zhang, A. Y., Snowden, L. R., & Sue, S. (1998). Differences between Asian and White Americans' help seeking and utilization patterns in the Los Angeles Area. *Journal of Community Psychology, 26*, 317–326.

Cross-Cultural Considerations with Japanese American Clients: A Perspective on Psychological Assessment

3

Nicholas S. Thaler and Daryl E.M. Fujii

From the early migrants of the Hawaiian sugar plantations at the turn of the century to the 442 infantry heroes of World War II, to contemporary immigrants for business and education, Japanese have immigrated to and lived in the United States for over a hundred years. According to the U.S. Census Bureau (2010), there are now an estimated 1,304,000 individuals living in the United States who identify as Japanese American, with the majority living in California (395,000) and Hawaii (297,000). Although the Japanese have a relatively long tenure in the U.S., they have been misunderstood by many in the majority culture. Complicating this is the intra-ethnic diversity within the Japanese American community due to intergenerational and acculturation effects.

This chapter focuses on general cross-cultural considerations pertinent to the assessment of and psychotherapy with Japanese American clients. In addition, some of guidelines provided in this chapter pertain to Japanese nationals who have recently immigrated or temporarily moved to the United States. Both broad issues relevant to all immigrant groups, as well as specific culturally bound symptoms specific to Japanese Americans, are covered. First we review traditional Japanese customs and values, including attitudes towards mental illness. Next acculturation issues that can influence experience, expression, or internalization of values are described. Recommendations for assessment and treatment are then provided, followed by a section on the reasons for a myth of the model minority. The literature on several clinical disorders is reviewed. The chapter ends with a case sample and chapter summary. As with any set of guidelines developed to provide better understanding and treatment for a particular group of individuals, the following should only serve to provide initial direction. It is the responsibility of the psychologist to ascertain the relevance of applying these guidelines to his or her individual clients.

N.S. Thaler, Ph.D. (✉)
Department of Psychiatry and Biobehavioral Sciences, Los Angeles Semel Institute for Neuroscience and Human Behavior, University of California, 760 Westwood Plaza, Los Angeles, CA 90024, USA
e-mail: nick.thaler@gmail.com

D.E.M. Fujii, Ph.D.
ABPP-CN, Veterans Affairs, Pacific Island Health Care Services Community Living Center, 459 Patterson Road, Honolulu, HI 96819-1522, USA
e-mail: dfujii07@gmail.com

Traditional Japanese Customs and Values

In a traditional Japanese family, gender and family roles are hierarchical with the father serving as the leader and patriarch of the family. Outward displays of affection and emotion are not typically encouraged, especially among Japanese men, while women are traditionally viewed as

L.T. Benuto et al. (eds.), *Guide to Psychological Assessment with Asians*,
DOI 10.1007/978-1-4939-0796-0_3, © Springer Science+Business Media New York 2014

homemakers and nurturers. As with many individuals raised in a collectivist society, the emphasis is placed on the group and specifically the family unit (Kagawa-Singer & Chung, 2002). This loyalty extends beyond family to one's occupation, with many Japanese companies guaranteeing employment for life in exchange for unquestioned group loyalty, and to one's country (Roland, 1988). Children are extremely important in the family unit, with the oldest son generally treasured as the most privileged child. Young children are often showered with affection, even beyond what is expected in Western culture, but this affection diminishes for older children who are expected to be dutiful and obedient to the family unit (Matsuyoshi, 2001).

The collectivist emphasis in Japanese society manifests through indirect communication that endeavors to maintain interpersonal harmony within a group (Roland, 1988). Empathy and sensitivity to others' thoughts and feelings are encouraged, and cooperation is preferred over direct confrontation. When there is conflict, withdrawal and silence are generally encouraged over overt and aggressive behaviors. Individuals often keep personal thoughts to themselves, which is recognized in Japanese culture as a private and distinct aspect of the self that is not revealed to others (Doi, 1985). Japanese individuals are expected to experience and privately carry some degree of unhappiness and discomfort, and this is encouraged to be endured stoically and without complaint. Negative emotions such as sadness and anger are expected to be withheld, and therefore often manifest through somatic symptoms (Nakao, Yamanaka, & Kuboki, 2001).

Japanese customs and values are strongly influenced by Eastern philosophies and religions and should be understood within this context. Emphasis on interpersonal harmony can be traced to both Shintoism, the indigenous religion of Japan, and Zen Buddhism which emphasize both interdependence and harmony with nature. Japanese stoicism and endurance of unhappiness can be traced to Buddhism whose basic tenet states that life is suffering caused by desire. Thus the road to enlightenment entails absolving oneself of worldly desires. Confucian influence is evident in the hierarchal and structured nature of the family system, as well as the strong loyalty to the group or state. The latter is also echoed in Shinto beliefs of honoring the family and ancestors.

Attitudes Towards Mental Illness

There is a strong shame or stigma associated with mental illness in Japan (Desapriya & Nobutada, 2002) that is greater than other countries (Griffiths et al., 2006). This reaction is not surprising as Japanese are strongly motivated to avoid behaviors that would bring "hazukashii" or shame to the family name (Tanabe, n.d.). Other purported reasons for the stigma include the perception that mental illness is a loss over personal control in a culture where self-control is stressed (Munakata, 1986), and mentally ill deviate from the norm in a culture that values conformity (Griffiths et al., 2006).

Given the stigma associated with mental illness, it is not surprising that Japanese are less likely to seek treatment for mental illness in comparison to Westerners, and when they do seek treatment it is for more severe forms of mental illness (Kawakami et al., 2005; Uomoto & Gorsuch, 1984). This help seeking pattern is influenced by the shame associated with mental illness and also societal expectations that family care for the mentally ill, and therefore it is not a condition requiring professional treatment (Desapriya & Nobutada, 2002). Moderating variables for higher levels of seeking professional treatment include female gender, younger age, plans for moving to a different neighborhood (Yamawaki, Pulsipher, Moses, Rasmuse, & Ringger, 2011), and higher levels of education (Kawakami et al., 2005).

Characteristics Affecting Acculturation

The extent to which a Japanese American patient is influenced by traditional customs is highly dependent upon acculturation to American values. Characteristics that influence acculturation include generational status, the social environment, and English proficiency. Generational status is an important characteristic for Japanese, so much so that there are distinct labels assigned to the separate generations of Japanese Americans. Individuals who immigrated to the United States are referred as *Issei* (first generation), while their children are known as *Nissei* (second generation). Following the *Nissei* are the *Sansei* (third generation), then *Yonsei* and *Gosei* (fourth and fifth generations). Each generation represents a cohort of individuals who, overall, have within-group similarities in terms of age, education, proficiency of the English language, and other variables of acculturation that distinguish them from other generations (Tsushima, Tsushima, & Fujii, 2011).

English proficiency is another measure of acculturation. Japanese Americans on average demonstrate a higher level of familiarity with the English language compared to other Asian ethnic groups, with only an estimated 10 % reporting less-than-proficient competency (U.S. Census Bureau, 2010). The majority of this 10 % are most likely *Issei* Japanese American immigrants. Recent Japanese immigrants, as well as older Nisei, likely demonstrate different levels of bilingualism, whereas Sansei on average are fluent in English and less likely to be as proficient in Japanese.

Acculturation is also strongly affected by the social environment. For example, the Japanese have historically been one of the largest ethnic groups living in Hawaii (Hishinuma, Miyamoto, Nishimura, & Nahulu, 2000). As a majority population, Japanese Americans have had a large degree of social, cultural, and political influence in this state (Matsuyoshi, 2001). By contrast, Japanese living in the West Coast were and are a minority population that have historically faced discrimination, including the Johnson-Reed Act of 1924, and most famously Executive Order 9066, which relocated over 120,000 Japanese Americans to internment camps during the Pacific War. Many *Issei* and *Nissei* Japanese living today were directly impacted by this incident. Within this time period there were a group of Japanese men who refused to serve in the US army and forswore allegiance to the Japanese government, not due to pervading loyalty to Japan but generally to take a stand for their assumed rights within the USA. These "no-no" boys represent a small but culturally significant population of Japanese Americans.

Recommendations for Assessment

Providing a competent psychological evaluation for a client of Japanese heritage can be challenging if the psychologist is not aware of the cultural differences that can impact presentation and communication. The following are general recommendations for conducting a psychological evaluation.

As mentioned, mental illness carries much stigma in Japan as it is associated with shame for the family; thus if a Japanese client voluntarily seeks treatment or brings a family member for an assessment or treatment, he/she is likely experiencing a significant amount of stress (Fujii, Fukushima, & Yamamoto, 1996). Given the stoic nature observed in many traditional Japanese Americans, there may be a disconnect between the stress experienced and the client's presentation. Psychologists should be aware that many Japanese clients are more likely to communicate indirectly or tangentially due to a reluctance to disclose symptoms. At the same time, the family may seek to minimize or cover for the client given the combination of the social stigma of therapy and the emphasis on cohesiveness within the family unit. Thus any admission of suffering would likely reflect a "cry for help." The Japanese client may also express distress through nonverbal cues or through somatic complaints, so psychologists are encouraged to pay close attention to such cues.

When working with Japanese American clients, psychologists should be aware of their clients' generational identity and family background in the United States, which are moderating factors for acculturation and can guide initial assessment approaches. For example, *Issei* tend to be older and include Japanese wives of servicemen during the Allied occupation of World War II, or younger Japanese businessmen on temporary assignments in the USA for a finite period of time (Matsuyoshi, 2001). The former group, now an aging cohort, has been described as having an increased proclivity towards mental illness, perhaps due to additional stressors related to marrying during wartime (Marden, 1992). The latter group, while not "Japanese American" per se, may still be encountered by the practitioner and require a broader knowledge of Japanese cross-cultural issues to effectively treat.

Nisei and *Sansei* individuals typically are exposed to both cultures, and so discrepancies between generations grappling with traditional Japanese and western values may be a source of family conflict and distress (for a review see Suinn, 2010). Exposure of Japanese language within the household and bilingualism will vary. By contrast, those who are *Yonsei* or *Gosei* are more likely to be fully Americanized, speak primarily English, and identify minimally with their Japanese culture, though there is substantial variation across individuals. Suffice to say, English proficiency is a significant issue with both non-English speakers and bilinguals as it directly impacts a client's ability to comprehend and validly respond to psychological assessment tools including psychodiagnostic interviews, self-report forms, and neuropsychological tests (Artiola i Fortuny, 2004). When working with bilingual clients, psychologists should keep in mind that conversational fluency does not necessarily equate a full understanding of subtleties in context. Indeed, some bilingual individuals may struggle in fully understanding either Japanese or English (Yoshida, 1990), which may relate to an overall lower fund of vocabulary knowledge (Bialystok, Luk, Peets, & Yang, 2010). Interpreters should be used when necessary, though family members should not serve this role. Japanese individuals often have an academic knowledge of English and demonstrate reading and writing skills that extend beyond their verbal communication skills (Tsushima et al., 2011).

Many Japanese patients are socialized to be agreeable and avoid direct expression of opinions as to not offend (Honma-True, 1997). They may answer yes or nod if a question is not fully understood or even when in disagreement to avoid conflict (Kitano, 1993). Clients who are unfamiliar with mental health in general may also be wary of feedback and reluctant to request further clarification if something is misunderstood. Thus when providing feedback, psychologists should take care to ensure that their patients fully understand the implication of test results, their diagnoses and treatment plans even going beyond normal efforts of communication to ensure understanding.

Recommendations for Therapy

As with many Asian cultures, not only are Japanese reluctant to seek treatment for mental disorders due to shame and stigma, they are also more likely to terminate treatment early. It would not be uncommon for a psychologist to feel a session went well only to find that the Japanese client failed to return for the follow up session, as the client was too polite to directly communicate discomfort, unhappiness, or perplexity with the treatment. Chu and Sue (2011) cite several reasons for early termination in Asians including discomfort with emotional displays and personal disclosures that may be perceived as disloyalty to the family or a sign of personal weakness, unfamiliarity with western psychotherapy, lack of cultural understanding by the therapist, and language barriers. To overcome this tendency, psychotherapists should be aware of strategies to reduce shame, develop trust and rapport, and make psychotherapy more understandable and useful.

Establishing a therapeutic alliance is essential for any form of psychotherapy. For Japanese clients, addressing issues of shame is an important component for placing them at ease and developing rapport. Te Pou (2010) suggest the following strategies for reducing feelings of shame in Asian clients: (1) demonstrating acceptance through creation of a warm supportive atmosphere, (2) avoiding intense personal questioning during the initial session, (3) focusing on practical goals that do not focus on emotions, (4) normalizing problems by sharing instances where others have experienced the same situations, (5) reinforcing the confidentiality of therapy, (6) complimenting the client for their strength and concern for their family by seeking treatment, (7) positively reframing situations, 8) focusing on problems versus personal weaknesses, and (9) medicalizing problems by providing information on the biological basis of mental disorders.

Hwang (2006) provides additional strategies to make psychotherapy more comfortable for Asians clients within his Psychotherapy Adaptation and Modification Framework (PAMF). These strategies include orienting a client to therapy by explaining processes and expectations can reduce anxiety due to unfamiliarity with psychotherapy; asking about family background and migration history would be useful for developing rapport with Issei and Nisei clients; integrating cultural strengths such as emphasis on education and family involvement to make therapy more culturally relevant; and finally, being aware Asians often experience somatic symptoms when distressed facilitates communication and provides a focus for treatment relief.

Other suggestions for therapy include using humor, gently questioning attitudes or beliefs, and paying close attention to nonverbal communication as a guide towards successful treatment (Matsuyoshi, 2001). It can also be helpful to be mindful of the family dynamic during case conceptualization and treatment planning, and involving the family as feasibly as possible. In addition, a subset of Issei patients may have been exposed to Morita and Naikan therapies, which incorporate more introspection than traditional behavioral therapy. These techniques are accepted in Japanese society though there is limited scientific support for their efficacy (Isomura-Motoki & Mimura, 2011).

Myth of the Model Minority

Education and class are important factors to consider during a psychological assessment. In general, Japanese Americans are exposed to a relatively high quality of education compared to their peers, with an estimated 40.8 % holding at minimal a college degree and 4.6 % with an advanced degree (U.S. Census Bureau, 2010). This accomplishment is likely a reflection of the emphasis placed on education in Japanese culture, which promotes rigorous memorization of facts in preparation for entrance exams, an extended school calendar, and a focus on both academic and moral education, with the latter emphasizing the importance of putting forward maximum effort on all tasks (Cooke, 2005). Japanese Americans also enjoy a greater degree of occupational and financial success than the average US citizen, with a median family income of $61,630, in contrast to the median family income of $48,500 for Euro-Americans (U.S. Census Bureau, 2010).

Taken together, Japanese Americans as a whole enjoy a socioeconomic quality of life that is similar to that of Euro-Americans. This accomplishment is partially due to the fact that many Japanese American families have lived several generations in the USA, and are therefore more assimilated than recent immigrant groups, and also related to the emphasis placed on education ingrained within the Japanese culture.

The relative success of many Japanese Americans within the U.S. may in turn be responsible for the "model minority" myth, or that stereotype in which Japanese Americans, as well as many other Asian ethnicities, represent minorities who have "succeeded" in the United States. Japanese Americans experience the same challenges that other model minority labeled groups often face, as such individuals are often expected, both by their own group and by the others, to succeed academically and financially. Historically, the model minority myth once extended towards psychological well-being with the stereotype that Asian Americans exhibited little to no psychological distress, though this has since been discredited (Jung, 1985). It is now apparent that the implications associated with the model minority myth are inaccurate and inimical towards Japanese Americans and other minority groups (Chao, Chiu, Chan, Mendoza-Denton, & Kwok, 2013; Hurh & Kim, 1989; Yoshihama, 2001). Therefore, while Japanese Americans may have a quality of life equitable to that of Euro-Americans, when examined through the lens of socioeconomic status and education, there are additional risk factors in play which may contribute to psychological distress.

Clinical Disorders

Depression

To date, few studies have examined prevalence rates of major depressive disorder (MDD) in Japanese Americans, though rates for Asian Americans as a whole are at least as high as those of their Euro-American counterparts (Kuo, 1984). There is evidence that different generational cohorts experience depression in distinct ways (Yanagida & Marsella, 1978). For example, first-generation Japanese Americans are more likely to resemble Japanese nationals in their manifestation of depressive symptomatology while second-generation individuals may face psychosocial stressors affiliated with a dual cultural background. It is important to review Japanese concepts of depression and other forms of psychopathology that may be relevant for earlier generations and recent immigrants.

Underlying factors of depression, such as anhedonia, guilt, agitation, somatic symptoms, insomnia, and appetite changes are cross-culturally relevant for Japanese, European, and North American populations (Furukawa et al., 2005). From a diagnostic and treatment perspective, this finding provides support that several of the core diagnostic features of MDD as determined by the *Diagnostic and Statistical Manual, fourth Edition* (APA, 2000) are indeed generalizable across these cultures. Somatic symptoms appear to be particularly tied to the expression of depression in Japanese clients (Nakao et al., 2001; Waza, Graham, Zyzanski, & Inoue, 1999), as has been found with other Asian populations (Lee, Lei, & Sue, 2001). Both Japanese nationals and Japanese Americans report lower levels of positive affect compared to Euro-Americans (Kanazawa, White, & Hampson, 2007), though it is uncertain if this directly translates to increased prevalence of MDD. While self-esteem was found to equally predict emotional distress in Japanese and American college students, cohesion of the family unit accounted for more variance with the Japanese group, suggesting that the family unit may play a more important role in psychological functioning (Abe, 2004).

Linguistically, Japanese-nationals are also more likely to associate metaphorical or somatic terms with their depression (e.g. "rainy," "fatigue") compared to Japanese and Euro-Americans who are more likely to label internal mood states (e.g. "sad," "lonely") (Tanaka-Matsumi & Marsella, 1976). Japanese nationals with depression prefer a combination of psychotherapy and medication in treatment despite the increased costs (Okumura & Sakamoto, 2012), which may be related to ambiguous attitudes in Japan towards the practice of clinical psychology as a whole (Isomura-Motoki & Mimura, 2011).

Japanese Americans who identify strongly with their Japanese culture appear to have a resiliency towards depression, and this finding has been consistent for youth, adults, and geriatric groups (Harada et al., 2012; Iwamasa, 1997; Williams et al., 2005). In contrast, mixed-race Japanese American youth may experience additional stress due to additional conflicts with their identity formation (Williams et al., 2002). Geriatric Japanese Americans who are interdependent on their families for care are at an increased risk for depression (Shibusawa & Mui, 2001) and yet are more likely to underreport symptoms of functional decline (McCurry et al., 2002).

In summary, research indicates that depression is accepted as a real condition in Japanese culture, though individuals who are less acculturated to the United States may more frequently express their depression through somatic complaints, and may be less amenable to therapy. Resiliency factors such as self-identification towards the client's cultural heritage and the cohesion of his or her family unit should be evaluated. Treatment options should be reviewed with the client to determine attitudes towards psychotherapy and the client's preference for alternative treatments, including medication, should be factored in case conceptualization.

Anxiety Disorders

Some manifestations of anxiety in Japanese clients are distinct from that observed in American clients, as illustrated by the DSM-IV recognized culture-bound syndromes *taijin kyofusho* (Morita, 1974) and *hikikomori* (Saito, 1998). *Taijin kyofusho* is a form of social anxiety characterized by a marked fear of offending other people, often due to poor interpersonal skills or some perceived physical deformity, and is most typically found in younger men. Four subtypes of this disorder are recognized including *sekimen-kyofu*, or fear of blushing, *shubo-kyofu*, or fear of a deformed face or body, *jiko-shu-kyofu*, or a fear of one's own body odor, and *jiko-shisen-kyofu*, or fear of one's own glance towards others. As discussed by Iwata and colleagues (2011), the first two of these subtypes can be subsumed under DSM-IV diagnoses of social phobia and body dysmorphic disorder respectively, while the third subtype can be interpreted as a type of olfactory reference syndrome (Begum & McKenna, 2011), leaving *jiko-shisen-kyofu* as a relatively isolated East Asian culture-bound manifestation of anxiety. Regardless of their cross-cultural generalizability, these manifestations of social anxiety symptoms are more prevalent in Japanese than Western society.

Hikikomori is a separate culture-bound syndrome of anxiety characterized by severe social withdrawal, most typically found in adolescents and young adults (Saito, 1998). Although *hikikomori* can arguably be classified as a severe form of social phobia, it is most frequently found in Japanese culture and has been theorized to be linked to culture-specific anxiety regarding onc's presentation of his or her self in society (Teo & Gaw, 2010). Japanese, in comparison to Americans, appear more anxious in interpersonal relationships and more vigilant to disapproval (Ishii, Miyamoto, Mayama, & Niedenthal, 2011), providing additional support that social anxiety relating to interpersonal relationships is more prevalent in this population. It is uncertain how prevalent *hikikomori* and *taijin kyofusho* are in the United States, but as these two disorders are culturally linked with Japanese nationals and not Japanese Americans, they may be rarely if ever observed by Western practitioners. Psychologists are most likely to observe either of these disorders with recent and younger immigrants, in contrast to geriatric *Issei* clients or later generational cohorts given that both youth and a Japanese cultural background are primary risk factors for these conditions. If a psychologist does work with a client who is presenting with either of these disorders, he or she is encouraged to be particularly aware of the therapist-client relationship, given that the core features of these disorders focus on interpersonal relationships. Those who are unfamiliar with these disorders should seek outside consultation and review literature on treatment (e.g. Nagata et al., 2006; Saito, 2003).

As was found with depression, Japanese American youth in Hawaii who strongly identify with their cultural background are at less risk for experiencing anxiety compared to their counterparts who identify less so, including those who are of mixed-race (Williams et al., 2002), although Japanese American youth as a whole reported experiencing less anxiety than their Euro-American and Hawaiian counterparts (Hishinuma et al., 2000). Senior Japanese American adults were found to conceptualize anxiety to include depressive symptoms, and also reported more cognitive symptoms than somatic symptoms (Hilliard & Iwamasa, 2001). Additional research on the prevalence and manifestation of anxiety disorders within Japanese American populations is currently lacking.

Alcohol and Drug Use

Alcohol abuse is prevalent in Japanese society, with an estimated 22.7 % of men and 4.9 % of women reporting a regular pattern of heavy/binge drinking (World Health Organization, 2004). Japanese Americans exhibit the highest frequency of alcohol abuse among all Asian American groups (Iwamoto, Takamatsu, & Castellanos, 2012; Wong, Klingle, & Price, 2004), with prevalence rates comparable to Euro-Americans. Similarities to mainstream behaviors in the United States are not surprising, as Japanese Americans are on average more acculturated than other Asian minority groups. Supporting this the drinking patterns of Asian Americans in general are higher for those born in the U.S. compared to those who are foreign born (Makimoto, 1998). Acculturation to the U.S. is therefore a significant risk factor for increased alcohol consumption. Resiliency factors include an increased sense of ethnic identity and a genetic predisposition for an increased sensitivity to alcohol's effects (Iwamoto et al., 2012; Nakawatase, Yamamoto, & Sasao, 1993). Despite high levels of drinking behaviors, Japanese Americans are underrepresented in alcohol treatment centers, perhaps due to a reluctance to utilize such services (Zane & Huh-Kim, 1998).

Though drinking patterns may differ between Japanese Americans and Japanese nationals, there is also a positive cultural attitude towards drinking in Japanese society that psychologists may encounter when treating alcohol dependence. Japanese draw a distinction between work and leisure, and during periods of leisure, drinking is viewed as a positive and even obligated behavior among men. Japanese society tolerates public intoxication to a greater degree than Western society. These and other cultural aspects of drinking may bias Japanese nationals from seeking treatment for alcohol dependence (Matsuyoshi, 2001). Psychologists treating alcohol dependence are encouraged to assess their clients' attitudes towards their drinking behaviors and ascertain if there is a strong cultural tie to such behavior, whether expressed socially, occupationally, or otherwise. Motivational interviewing and other directive therapies that have demonstrated to effect change in other populations may prove useful when working with Japanese clients, though as of this publication there is a dearth of literature on the topic.

In contrast to alcohol use the prevalence rate of illicit and psychotropic drug use in Japan is lower than that of the USA and other countries (Tominaga et al., 2009). Regarding prevalence rates of Japanese Americans, it can be extrapolated from studies on alcohol consumption that individuals who are more acculturated to the United States are at an increased risk for substance abuse. Consistent with this hypothesis, it has been found Japanese Americans have the highest prevalence of marijuana and cocaine use among Asian American groups (Sasao, 1991). In addition, Japanese American adolescents, along with Korean American adolescents, exhibit the highest prevalence of smoking among all Asian American groups (Unger, Trinidad, Weiss, & Rohrbach, 2004). The stigma associated with drug use in Japan may be a preventive factor among Japanese nationals and Japanese Americans, though it is evident that this changes over generations. Psychologists must also be mindful of the increasing use of stimulant abuse on college campuses (Gomes, Song, Godwin, & Toriello, 2011). Although there has yet to be a specific link between Japanese American students and stimulant abuse, it is possible that certain youth may be at risk, particularly those who are more acculturated to the United States and are facing pressures to academically excel.

Major Psychiatric Illnesses

Major psychiatric illnesses including bipolar disorder and schizophrenia are popular areas of research among psychiatrists and psychologists in Japan (Kishi et al., 2011). It is likely that the neurobiological and genetic traits associated with these disorders and the necessity of pharmaceutical intervention make these conditions more readily recognized as a "medical" illness, thus more interesting to medical Japanese professionals. Despite the academic interest, schizophrenia is viewed very negatively by Japanese as it is perceived to result from a "weakness of character" (Nakane et al., 2005). Even mental health professionals frequently use derogatory terminology when describing persons with schizophrenia (Takei, Takagai, & Mori, 2005). The social stigma of general mental illness in Japan may be related to a cultural fear that MDD or anxiety disorders are similar in etiology and prognosis to these more severe disorders.

Schizophrenia and other psychiatric illnesses have a large impact on Japanese families, where care giving for dependents is a cultural expectation that is a dutiful burden one endures with resignation (Hanzawa et al., 2010). Interestingly, this expectation does not always apply to persons with schizophrenia, as Japan's institutionalized rate for patients with schizophrenia is the highest in the world (Hanzawa et al., 2010). This discrepancy between obligation and actual behavior is likely to cause distress within the family. Psychologists working with Japanese American patients with major mental illnesses should therefore be aware of the specific positive and negative impacts that the caregiver role has on such patients as well as their families.

Major mental illnesses have some unique presentations in Japanese culture with a few culture-bound syndromes. For example, studies on culture-bound psychosis in Japan found that compared to other groups, Japanese patients exhibit more delusions of reference such as being slandered, which may tie in with the strong emphasis on interpersonal relationships within Japanese culture (Tateyama, Asai, Kamisada, & Hashimoto, 1993). A unique presentation of conversion disorder is the Paris syndrome (Katada, 1998), a rare condition that affects approximately 20 Japanese tourists a year who experience mental breakdowns upon visiting Paris, France. Specific research on the cultural impact of a Japanese background on conversation disorders is currently lacking, but given the emphasis on restraint and avoidance of emotional expressivity within Japanese culture, along with increased rates of somatization in place of affective depression, it is certainly likely that such an impact does exist and can be quite significant for some individuals.

Eating Disorders

Eating disorders are particularly influenced by culture and societal pressures, and although anorexia and bulimia nervosa were once thought to be less common in Japan compared to the United States, it is becoming evident that their prevalence is on the rise, with an estimated sixfold increase over the past 25 years (Pike & Borovoy, 2004). This increase appears related to the dissemination of Western perceptions of ideal weight and beauty to other countries, including Japan. Japanese adolescent women are the most vulnerable to developing an eating disorder, although men and older women are also at risk. The current Japanese media focuses on an idealization of thinness that is unforgiving of any sort of weight gain and Japanese society celebrates thinness as beauty. Expectedly, there is an ever-increasing commercial demand for dietary and weight loss products that promises the individual can reach or maintain this ideal (Nakamura, 2011).

The value for thinness and strong society pressure for conformity can significantly impact how overweight persons are treated by their peers and family. For example, Japanese girls whose mothers frequently discuss food, weight, and dieting are at an increased risk of developing an eating disorder (Mukai, Crago, & Shisslak, 1994). As Japanese culture emphasizes the importance of the family unit, it is easy to understand how such critical attitudes may lead to eating disorders, along with other psychological problems. In a similar vein, Japanese society places an emphasis on cultural and physical homogenization, and so overweight individuals may particularly stand out and be vulnerable targets for ridicule.

Differences in dietary practices and ideal perceptions of beauty between Japan and the United States appear to affect the clinical presentation of anorexia and bulimia. For example, Japanese women with eating disorders appear to exhibit additional fears towards maturity that may be related to the traditional Japanese practice of living with one's parents well into the thirties (Pike & Mizushima, 2005). While perfectionism and thinness remain inherent issues for Japanese individuals with eating disorders, there is also evidence that their magnitude of severity is less than that than individuals living in the U.S. and Europe (Kayano et al., 2008; Pike & Mizushima, 2005). It may be that Japanese individuals with eating disorders do so for reasons that are somewhat distinct from their Western counterparts, such as a desire to remain "child-like" and youthful and to remain dependent on others for care, though the behavioral acts of restricting food intake and/or binging and purging appear similar.

To date, little research has examined the prevalence and manifestation of eating disorders among Japanese Americans, although Japanese Americans who were raised in the U.S. are at elevated risk for developing eating disorders at rates comparable to their Euro-American counterparts (Furukawa, 1994). As with other disorders, symptom presentation appears to resemble Euro-American symptom presentation as acculturation increases over generations. The stereotype that Japanese individuals have dietary and genetic resiliency factors towards eating disorders is erroneous. First, Japanese individuals who are thin are not exempt from developing eating disorders, as clearly demonstrated by extremely thin persons all over the world who still distort their body image. Second, as Japanese Americans become more acculturated to the United States, so do their dietary habits, and so consequent health and weight problems may manifest at comparable rates. Additional research is required to establish the prevalence, attitudes, and clinical presentation of Japanese Americans, particularly those whose acculturation levels are somewhat between Japanese nationals and fully acculturated individuals.

Case Sample

JH is a 23-year-old fourth-generation Japanese American male who was referred to a psychologist in Torrance, California, by his mother to assess for possible depression relating to recent career struggles. JH recently graduated college at UC Irvine with a 3.8 GPA in biology. He applied to several graduate programs in microbiology last year and received two offers, both out of the state. Although JH initially accepted an offer to a prestigious university in Michigan, he unexpectedly recanted his offer for reasons that are not well understood. Since declining, he has become somewhat reclusive at home, staying up at night playing video games and sleeping during the day. When he does go out, he spends time with a group of friends who mostly play basketball or video games at each other's houses. JH's father was reportedly livid when JH declined graduate school, and now refuses to speak to him. His mother tries to reach out to him, but JH is sullen and refuses to communicate. He replies "I don't know," when asked about his career goals. His older sister is an artist living in Los Angeles and he is close to her, though lately he's even been ignoring her phone calls. JH's mother took him to see his physician, who ruled out no medical problems. The physician referred JH to see a psychologist to rule out depression or another disorder.

JH and his mother arrived promptly on time. He presented as a well-groomed young man of below average height. Eye contact was variable and he spoke monosyllabically and without much affect to his tone. Rapport was slowly but gradually attained during the intake and the psychologist was able to elicit from JH that he was feeling somewhat down, and this was mostly related to the fact that he has no girlfriend. His mother, who is a third-generation Japanese American, was unsure what to do with her son but seemed willing to have him attend psychotherapy sessions. She related in a separate collateral interview that her husband, who is a first-generation Japanese immigrant, speaks English only somewhat well. She reported that he was accepting of his son attending therapy, because he wants him "cured" of whatever happened to him. She also reported that her husband and her son haven't gotten along for years, but it has worsened when JH declined graduate school.

JH scored only an eight on the BDI-II, indicating minimal depression. He did respond that he felt worthless and sad, but denied any somatic complaints, changes in sleep or appetite, or suicidal ideations. JH's State-Trait Anxiety score was higher and in the 98th percentile for State, and 85th percentile for Trait. Based on the interview and these initial scores, the psychologist made a tentative diagnosis of Adjustment Disorder with Mixed Depression and Anxiety and recommended that JH attend 12 sessions of cognitive-behavioral therapy to treat his condition. With JH's permission, his mother was present while the psychologist explicitly explained the basics of CBT to them. JH was fairly nonresponsive while listening to this, while his mother took careful notes. After the explanation, JH's mother profusely thanked the therapist and seemed very hopeful to the treatment outcome, while JH himself appeared nonchalant.

JH regularly attended sessions, with his mother calling ahead to cancel when they couldn't make it. He proved to be restrained and unforthcoming of information, other than he felt like a "loser" because he couldn't get a girlfriend. He also admitted insecurities with his height and anxiety about talking to girls. The psychologist sensed that there was more to the case than JH's initial complaints, as he observed that JH's father was never involved or mentioned in therapy, while his mother was perhaps too involved for a 23-year-old man. However, to maintain rapport he elected to focus on JH's initial problems. He challenged JH's negative beliefs about himself and attempted behavioral activation to encourage JH to spend less time on video games, and more time engaging in more healthy, alternative activities. While JH appeared willing to discount some of his black and white thinking about himself, he proved reluctant to complete homework and continued to play video games throughout the night. After four sessions, the psychologist shifted his strategy and played off JH's desire to date more. He encouraged JH to join a Japanese cultural group in Torrance, which JH started attending with some regularity. The group allowed him to get in touch with his heritage, which JH confessed at the sixth session to not really be aware of. JH related during this session that his father had never made Japan seem appealing to him and so he was never interested in exploring this side of his culture. However, he did enjoy the weekly activities and made a few acquaintances.

JH stated during the seventh session that he declined graduate school because he was questioning whether he wanted to pursue microbiology as a career. He added that his parents had always pressured him to go into medicine or medical research, but he himself was unsure if that was what he wanted to do. He also did not welcome the prospect of moving to Michigan, where he had no connections or friends. He didn't want to leave his family, particularly his sister, and friends behind. He added somewhat cautiously that he thinks his mother is overbearing and babies him too much, but he doesn't know how to stop it. He continued to shut down in therapy when asked about his father. The psychologist explored possible options for JH including moving out of his parents' home, and considering alternate career plans. By the ninth session, JH agreed that he needs to move out on his own, but is unsure how to do it. The psychologist and he worked on realistic ways to live on one's own, including joining a temp agency and applying for jobs that would fit his major. By the tenth session, JH appeared to have found his own solution—moving in temporarily with his sister. He stated that his mother is cautiously accepting of this idea. When asked about his father, JH shut down again. The psychologist decided to risk the alliance by broaching the subject of his father. Fortunately, JH was responsive to questions and readily admitted that his father has always been emotionally distant and was only approving of JH's academic achievements. Since declining graduate school, his father has become even more distant and when he speaks to JH, it is often accusatory of his "laziness." The psychologist gently challenged his father's statements about JH and worked with JH to ensure he was not turning these labels into his own cognitive distortions.

The last few sessions continued on this line, and by the twelfth session, JH reported that he was making plans to move in a few weeks to Los Angeles with his sister, and that his sister had several contacts in the city who might give him some initial work. He was still attending the cultural group, and though he hadn't started dating, there were three girls there who he liked. He also added that he was interested in perhaps visiting Japan, and the group regularly talked about saving up to go someday. He thanked the psychologist for working with him and seemed hopeful and somewhat optimistic about the future. His BDI-II was a six, essentially unchanged, though his State-Trait Anxiety scores dropped to the 66th and 73rd percentiles respectively. The psychologist lifted the Adjustment Disorder diagnosis and encouraged JH to contact his office anytime. Though JH promised he would, the psychologist did not hear him from him again. Unexpectedly, he received a call from JH's mother 2 weeks later. His mother was very optimistic and grateful over the phone and stated that JH was doing "great" living with his sister. She also asked several personal questions about JH's progress through therapy, which the psychologist politely declined to detail. He explained HIPAA guidelines to JH's mother, who appeared to understand and thanked the psychologist one last time.

The preceding case study details a relatively straightforward progression of how psychotherapy may treat a young man who is feeling somewhat lost in his early twenties. However, JH's cultural background does factor into play at key points. Unlike his parents, JH is highly acculturated to the United States, to the point that he does not strongly identify with his Japanese background. This appears to be a source of some of the tension between JH and his father, who is a first-generation immigrant. Though JH's relationship with his father was not explicitly addressed in therapy, the psychologist was able to address his self-esteem which was lowered by his father's cutting remarks. JH was also encouraged to partake in a Japanese cultural group, where he demonstrated a rapid interest in his heritage. This sense of community and belonging appeared beneficial to JH's self-esteem and was followed by some marked changes in his attitude and behavior. JH's mother also appeared to be quite involved with her son, which may stem from her own anxieties as well the Japanese cultural duty of keeping adult children within the home until they strike out on their own. JH's own closeness to his family may in part explain his reluctance to leave California for an unfamiliar place. This clashes with the expectation by his parents he would attend a graduate program in microbiology, which appears related to his withdrawal and anxiety. By addressing how these events impact JH's self-esteem, and by encouraging him to engage in activities such as his Japanese cultural group, the psychologist was able to effectively address some of this young man's problems.

Summary and Conclusions

1. Japanese have been immigrating to the USA for over a hundred years. Thus there is much generational heterogeneity with individuals ranging from first to fifth generation. Given the generational diversity, psychologists should be cognizant of their clients' generational cohort for assessment, case conceptualization, and treatment planning. First and second-generation clients will more closely resemble Japanese nationals in behavior, beliefs, and values, while later generations will more resemble their Euro-American peers. Psychologists should take care to use generational status as an initial guideline only, and pay attention to how their clients self-identify themselves.
2. Japanese Americans enjoy relatively high levels of SES and education compared to other Asian Americans. These accomplishments can have a positive impact on psychological assessment. For example, many Japanese Americans will score comparably to Euro-Americans on IQ and neuropsychological measures. However, equivalent performance does not mean that cross-cultural considerations in assessment do not exist.
3. Japanese culture emphasizes allegiance to the group and indirect communication, which can be unfamiliar behavior to some Western psychologists. Japanese clients may therefore not be particularly direct in assessment or therapy, nor may they be forthcoming about psychological issues. This is also related to the negative stigma associated with mental illness in Japanese society.
4. A strong emphasis is placed on the family unit, and so Japanese clients may wish to have their family involved in the therapeutic process. Psychologists should also be mindful of how intergenerational differences in values, experiences, and expectations may factor in to the presenting problems.
5. Depression may be presented through somatization rather than outward displays of affective sadness. Japanese individuals are taught to suppress and outwardly minimize any negative feelings of distress. Japanese men are particularly encouraged to behave stoically within and outside of the home. A connection to Japanese culture can be a strong resiliency factor against depression for Japanese Americans.
6. Anxiety disorders have culturally bound symptoms that are unique to Japan, as evidenced by disorders such as *hikikomori* and *taijin kyofusho*. These disorders appear related to the Japanese emphasis on preserving interpersonal harmony, working as a group, and saving individual face whenever possible.

These disorders are less prevalent amongst Japanese Americans, though psychologists should be aware of the importance placed on interpersonal interactions and how this may impact the therapist-client alliance.

7. Alcohol use is widely prevalent amongst Japanese nationals and Japanese Americans. Drinking alcohol is a culturally acceptable and encouraged behavior in Japan and so some Japanese nationals may see little need for change, even when faced with severe consequences. Japanese Americans appear to use alcohol and illicit drugs more as they become acculturated to the mainstream use within the United States.
8. Major mental illnesses such as schizophrenia are accepted as real medical disorders in Japan, but also have a large negative stigma. It is likely because to this stigma that other lesser clinical disorders are feared and denied. Japanese families are willing to care for members afflicted with major illnesses, though this is affiliated with great shame and burden.
9. Eating disorders are becoming increasingly prevalent in Japan, largely due to a spread of Western ideals for thinness and beauty. Japanese Americans who are acculturated to the USA appear to have similar symptom presentations of anorexia and bulimia as their Euro-American peers.

References

Abe, J. A. (2004). Self-esteem, perception of relationships, and emotional distress: A cross-cultural study. *Personal Relationships, 11*(2), 231–247. doi:10.1111/j.1475-6811.2004.00080.x.

American Psychiatric Association. (2000). *Diagnostic and statistical manual of mental disorders* (4th ed., text rev.). doi: 10.1176/appi.books.9780890423349.

Artiola i Fortuny, L. (2004). Perspectives in cross-cultural neuropsychology: Language, low education, and illiteracy. In J. H. Ricker (Ed.), *Differential diagnosis in adult neuropsychological assessment* (pp. 66–107). New York, NY: Springer.

Begum, M. M., & McKenna, P. J. (2011). Olfactory reference syndrome: A systematic review of the world literature. *Psychological Medicine, 41*(3), 453–461. doi:10.1017/S003329171000109l.

Bialystok, E., Luk, G., Peets, K. F., & Yang, S. (2010). Receptive vocabulary differences in monolingual and bilingual children. *Bilingualism: Language and Cognition, 13*(4), 525–531. doi:10.1017/S1366728909990423.

Chao, M., Chiu, C., Chan, W., Mendoza-Denton, R., & Kwok, C. (2013). The model minority as a shared reality and its implication for interracial perceptions. *Asian American Journal of Psychology, 4*(2), 84–92. doi:10.1037/a0028769.

Chu, J. & Sue, S. (2011). Asian American mental health: What we know and don't know. *Online Readings in Psychology and Culture, Unit 3*. Retrieved from http://scholarworks.gvsu.edu/orpc/vol3/iss1/4

Cooke, J. (2005, January/February). A comparison of Japanese and American education systems. *The Oregon Mathematics Teacher*, pp. 14–16.

Desapriya, E., & Nobutada, I. (2002). Stigma of mental illness in Japan. *Lancet, 359*(9320), 1866.

Doi, T. (1985). *The anatomy of the self*. Tokyo: Kodansha.

Fujii, J., Fukushima, S., & Yamamoto, J. (1996). Psychiatric care of Japanese Americans. In A. Gaw (Ed.), *Culture, ethnicity and mental illness* (pp. 304–345). Washington, DC: American Psychiatric Association.

Furukawa, T. (1994). Weight changes and eating attitudes of Japanese adolescents under acculturative stresses: A prospective study. *International Journal of Eating Disorders, 15*(1), 71–79. doi:10.1002/1098-108X(199401)15:1<71::AID-EAT2260150109>3.0.CO;2-R.

Furukawa, T. A., Streiner, D. L., Azuma, H. H., Higuchi, T. T., Kamijima, K. K., Kanba, S. S., & ... Miura, S. S. (2005). Cross-cultural equivalence in depression assessment: Japan-Europe-North American study. *Acta Psychiatrica Scandinavia, 112*(4), 279–285. doi:10.1111/j.1600-0447.2005.00587.x.

Gomes, J., Song, T., Godwin, L., & Toriello, P. J. (2011). Prescription stimulant abuse on university campuses. *Journal of Human Behavior in the Social Environment, 21*(7), 822–833. doi:10.1080/10911359.2011.615680.

Griffiths, K., Yoshibumi, N., Christensen, H., Yoshioka, K., Jorm, A., & Nakane, H. (2006). Stigma in response to mental disorders: A comparison of Australia and Japan. *BMC Psychiatry, 6*, 21. doi:10.1186/1471-244X-6-21.

Hanzawa, S., Bae, J., Tanaka, H., Bae, Y., Tanaka, G., Inadomi, H., & ... Ohta, Y. (2010). Caregiver burden and coping strategies for patients with schizophrenia: Comparison between Japan and Korea. *Psychiatry and Clinical Neurosciences, 64*(4), 377–386. doi:10.1111/j.1440-1819.2010.02104.x.

Harada, N., Takeshita, J., Ahmed, I., Chen, R., Petrovitch, H., ... Masaki, K. (2012). Does cultural assimilation influence prevalence and presentation of depressive symptoms in older Japanese American men? The Honolulu-Asia aging study. *The American Journal of Geriatric Psychiatry, 20*(4), 337–345. doi:10.1097/JGP.0b013e3182107e3b.

Hilliard, K. M., & Iwamasa, G. Y. (2001). The conceptualization of anxiety: An exploratory study of

Japanese American older adults. *Journal of Clinical Geropsychology, 7*(1), 53–65. doi:10.1023/A:1026416802568.

Hishinuma, E. S., Miyamoto, R. H., Nishimura, S. T., & Nahulu, L. B. (2000). Differences in state trait anxiety inventory scores for ethnically diverse adolescents in Hawaii. *Cultural Diversity and Ethnic Minority Psychology, 6*, 73–83.

Honma-True, R. (1997). Japanese American families. In E. Lee (Ed.), *Working with Asian Americans: A guide for clinicians* (pp. 114–124). New York, NY: Guilford Press.

Hurh, W., & Kim, K. (1989). The "success" image of Asian Americans: Its validity, and its practical and theoretical implications. *Ethnic and Racial Studies, 12*, 514–561.

Hwang, W. C. (2006). The psychotherapy adaptation and modification framework: Application to Asian Americans. *American Psychologist, 61*, 702–715. doi:10.1037/0003-066X.61.7.702.

Ishii, K., Miyamoto, Y., Mayama, K., & Niedenthal, P. M. (2011). When your smile fades away: Cultural differences in sensitivity to the disappearance of smiles. *Social Psychological and Personality Science, 2*(5), 516–522. doi:10.1177/1948550611399153.

Isomura-Motoki, A., & Mimura, M. (2011). Neuropsychology in Japan. In D. M. Fujii (Ed.), *The neuropsychology of Asian Americans* (pp. 237–245). New York, NY: Psychology Press.

Iwamasa, G. Y. (1997). Asian Americans. In S. Friedman (Ed.), *Cultural issues in the treatment of anxiety* (pp. 99–129). New York, NY: Guilford Press.

Iwamoto, D., Takamatsu, S., & Castellanos, J. (2012). Binge drinking and alcohol-related problems among U.S.-born Asian Americans. *Cultural Diversity and Ethnic Minority Psychology, 18*(3), 219–227. doi:10.1037/a0028422.

Iwata, Y., Suzuki, K., Takei, N., Toulopoulou, T., Tsuchiya, K. J., Matsumoto, K., & ... Mori, N. (2011). Jiko-shisen-kyofu (fear of one's own glance), but not taijin-kyofusho (fear of Interpersonal relations), is an east Asian culture-related specific syndrome. *Australian and New Zealand Journal of Psychiatry, 45*(2), 148–152. doi:10.3109/00048674.2010.534068.

Jung, J. (1985). The model minority? *Psyccritiques, 30*(11), 895–896. doi:10.1037/023340.

Kagawa-Singer, M., & Chung, R. (2002). Toward a new paradigm: A cultural systems approach. In K. S. Kurasaki, S. Okazaki, & S. Sue (Eds.), *Asian American mental health: Assessment theories and methods* (pp. 47–66). New York, NY: Kluwer Academic/Plenum Publishers.

Kanazawa, A., White, P. M., & Hampson, S. E. (2007). Ethnic variation in depressive symptoms in a community sample in Hawaii. *Cultural Diversity and Ethnic Minority Psychology, 13*(1), 35–44. doi:10.1037/1099-9809.13.1.35.

Katada, T. (1998). Reflections on a case of Paris syndrome. *Journal of the Nissei Hospital, 26*(2), 127–132.

Kawakami, N., Takeshima, T., Ono, Y., Uda, H., Hata, Y., Nakane, Y., ... Kikkawa, T. (2005). Twelve-month prevalence, severity, and treatment of common mental disorders in communities in Japan: Preliminary finding from the World Mental Health Japan survey 2002–2003. *Psychiatry and Clinical Neurosciences, 59*, 441–452.

Kayano, M., Yoshiuchi, K., Al-Adawi, S., Viernes, N., Dorvlo, A. S., Kumano, H., & ... Akabayashi, A. (2008). Eating attitudes and body dissatisfaction in adolescents: Cross-cultural study. *Psychiatry and Clinical Neurosciences, 62*(1), 17–25. doi:10.1111/j.1440-1819.2007.01772.x.

Kishi, T. T., Fukuo, Y. Y., Kitajima, T. T., Okochi, T. T., Yamanouchi, Y. Y., Kinoshita, Y. Y., & ... Iwata, N. N. (2011). SIRT1 gene, schizophrenia and bipolar disorder in the Japanese population: An association study. *Genes, Brain & Behavior, 10*(3), 257–263. doi:10.1111/j.1601-183X.2010.00661.x.

Kitano, H. (1993). *Generations and identity: The Japanese American*. Needham Heights, MA: Ginn Press.

Kuo, W. H. (1984). Prevalence of depression among Asian-Americans. *Journal of Nervous and Mental Disease, 172*(8), 449–457. doi:10.1097/00005053-198408000-00002.

Lee, J., Lei, A., & Sue, S. (2001). The current state of mental health research on Asian Americans. *Journal of Human Behavior in the Social Environment, 3*(3–4), 159–178. doi:10.1300/J137v03n03_11.

Makimoto, K. (1998). Drinking patterns and drinking problems among Asian-Americans and Pacific Islanders. *Alcohol Health & Research World, 22*(4), 270–275.

Marden, P. W. (1992). Japanese Americans. In C. F. Marden, G. Meyer, & M. Engel (Eds.), *Minorities in American society* (pp. 393–433). New York, NY: HarperCollins.

Matsuyoshi, J. (2001). Substance abuse interventions for Japanese and Japanese American clients. In S. Straussner (Ed.), *Ethnocultural factors in substance abuse treatment* (pp. 393–417). New York, NY: Guilford Press.

McCurry, S. M., Gibbons, L. E., Bond, G. E., Rice, M., Graves, A., Kukull, W. A., & ... Larson, E. B. (2002). Older adults and functional decline: A cross-cultural comparison. *International Psychogeriatrics, 14*(2), 161–179. doi:10.1017/S1041610202008360.

Morita, S. (1974). Phobia of blushing or taijin kyofusho and their treatment [Sekimen kyofusho matawa taijin kyofusho to sonoryoho]. In T. Kora (Ed.), *Shoma Morita collected works [Morita Shoma Zenshu]* (pp. 164–174). Tokyo: Hakuyosha (in Japanese).

Mukai, T., Crago, M., & Shisslak, C. M. (1994). Eating attitudes and weight preoccupation among female high school students in Japan. *Journal of Child Psychology and Psychiatry, 35*(4), 677–688. doi:10.1111/j.1469-7610.1994.tb01213.x.

Munakata, T. (1986). Japanese health perception. *Jurist, 44*, 30–35.

Nagata, T., van Vliet, I., Yamada, H., Kataoka, K., Iketani, T., & Kiriike, N. (2006). An open trial of paroxetine for the 'Offensive Subtype' of Taijin Kyofusho and social anxiety disorder. *Depression and Anxiety, 23*(3), 168–174. doi:10.1002/da.20153.

Nakamura, K. (2011). Struggles, commercialism, 'ideal' feminine images and internal oppression: Eating disorders and the pursuit of thinness in Japan. In R. A. Jones (Ed.), *Body, mind and healing after Jung: A space of questions* (pp. 160–173). New York, NY: Routledge.

Nakane, Y., Jorm, A., Yoshioka, K., Christensen, H., Nakane, H., & Griffiths, K. (2005). Public beliefs about causes and risk factors for mental disorders: A comparison of Japan and Australia. *BMC Psychiatry, 5*, 33. doi:10.1186/1471-244X-5-33.

Nakao, M., Yamanaka, G., & Kuboki, T. (2001). Major depression and somatic symptoms in a mind/body medicine clinic. *Psychopathology, 34*(5), 230–235. doi:10.1159/000049315.

Nakawatase, T. V., Yamamoto, J., & Sasao, T. (1993). The association between fast-flushing response and alcohol use among Japanese Americans. *Journal of Studies on Alcohol, 54*(1), 48–53.

Okumura, Y., & Sakamoto, S. (2012). Depression treatment preferences among Japanese undergraduates: Using conjoint analysis. *International Journal of Social Psychiatry, 58*(2), 195–203. doi:10.1177/0020764010390437.

Pike, K. M., & Borovoy, A. (2004). The rise of eating disorders in Japan: Issues of culture and limitations of the model of 'Westernization'. *Culture, Medicine and Psychiatry, 28*(4), 493–531. doi:10.1007/s11013-004-1066-6.

Pike, K. M., & Mizushima, H. (2005). The clinical presentation of Japanese women with anorexia nervosa and bulimia nervosa: A study of the eating disorders lnventory-2. *International Journal of Eating Disorders, 37*(1), 26–31. doi:10.1002/eat.20065.

Roland, A. (1988). *In search of self in India and Japan: Toward a cross-cultural psychology*. Princeton, NJ: Princeton University Press.

Saito, T. (1998). *Shakaiteki Hikikomori: Owaranai Shishunki (Social withdrawal: A never ending adolescence)*. Tokyo: PHP Kenkyujo.

Saito, T. (2003). Individual treatment and therapy for 'Hikikomori' cases. *Seishin Igaku (Clinical Psychiatry), 45*(3), 263–269.

Sasao, T. (1991). *Statewide Asian drug service needs assessment: A multimethod approach*. Sacramento, CA: California Department of Alcohol and Drug Programs.

Shibusawa, T., & Mui, A. C. (2001). Stress, coping, and depression among Japanese American elders. *Journal of Gerontological Social Work, 36*(1–2), 63–81. doi:10.1300/J083v36n01_05.

Suinn, R. (2010). Reviewing acculturation and Asian Americans: How acculturation affects health, adjustment school achievement, and counseling. *Asian American Journal of Psychology, 1*, 5–17.

Takei, N. N., Takagai, S. S., & Mori, N. N. (2005). Correspondence: Stigmatisation of people with schizophrenia in Japan. *The British Journal of Psychiatry, 187*(6), 589–590. doi:10.1192/bjp.187.6.589-a.

Tanabe, M. (n.d.). Health and healthcare of Japanese-American elders. Retrieved on October 2, 2012, from http://www.stanford.edu/group/ethnoger/japanese.html

Tanaka-Matsumi, J., & Marsella, A. J. (1976). Cross-cultural variations in the phenomenological experience of depression: I. Word association studies. *Journal of Cross-Cultural Psychology, 7*(4), 379–396. doi:10.1177/002202217674001.

Tateyama, M., Asai, M., Kamisada, M., & Hashimoto, M. (1993). Comparison of schizophrenic delusions between Japan and Germany. *Psychopathology, 26*(3–4), 151–158. doi:10.1159/000284815.

Te Pou. (2010). Talking therapies for Asian people: Best and promising practice guide for mental health and addiction services. Auckland: Te Pou o te Whakaaro Nui. Retrieved on October 2, 2012, from http://www.tepou.co.nz/library/tepou/talking-therapies-for-asian-people

Teo, A. R., & Gaw, A. C. (2010). Hikikomori, a Japanese culture-bound syndrome of social withdrawal? A proposal for DSM-5. *Journal of Nervous and Mental Disease, 198*(6), 444–449. doi:10.1097/NMD.0b013e3181e086b1.

Tominaga, M., Kawakami, N., Ono, Y., Nakane, Y., Nakamura, Y., Tachimori, H., & ... Kikkawa, T. (2009). Prevalence and correlates of illicit and non-medical use of psychotropic drugs in Japan: Findings from the World Mental Health Japan Survey 2002–2004. *Social Psychiatry and Psychiatric Epidemiology, 44*(9), 777–783. doi:10.1007/s00127-009-0499-1.

Tsushima, W. T., Tsushima, V. G., & Fujii, D. (2011). Neuropsychology of Japanese Americans. In D. M. Fujii (Ed.), *The neuropsychology of Asian Americans* (pp. 107–129). New York, NY: Psychology Press.

Unger, J. B., Trinidad, D. R., Weiss, J., & Rohrbach, L. (2004). Acculturation as a risk factor for smoking among Asian American adolescents: Is the association confounded by nationality? *Journal of Ethnicity in Substance Abuse, 3*(1), 65–79.

Uomoto, J. M., & Gorsuch, R. L. (1984). Japanese American response to psychological disorder: Referral patterns, attitudes, and subjective norms. *American Journal of Community Psychology, 12*(5), 537–550.

U.S. Census Bureau. (2010). *Current population survey, annual social and economic supplement*. Retrieved April 15, 2014, from http://www.census.gov/2010census/data/

Waza, K., Graham, A. V., Zyzanski, S. J., & Inoue, K. (1999). Comparison of symptoms in Japanese and American depressed primary care patients. *Family Practice, 16*(5), 528–533. doi:10.1093/fampra/16.5.528.

Williams, J., Else, N., Hishinuma, E. S., Goebert, D. A., Chang, J. Y., Andrade, N. N., & Nishimura, S. T. (2005). A confirmatory model for depression among Japanese

American and part-Japanese American adolescents. *Cultural Diversity and Ethnic Minority Psychology, 11*(1), 41–56. doi:10.1037/1099-9809.11.1.41.

Williams, J., Goebert, D., Hishinuma, E., Miyamoto, R., Anzai, N., Izutsu, S., & ... Baker, F. M. (2002). A conceptual model of cultural predictors of anxiety among Japanese American and part-Japanese American adolescents. *Cultural Diversity and Ethnic Minority Psychology, 8*(4), 320–333. doi:10.1037/1099-9809.8.4.321.

Wong, M. M., Klingle, R. S., & Price, R. K. (2004). Alcohol, tobacco, and other drug use among Asian American and Pacific Islander adolescents in California and Hawaii. *Addictive Behaviors, 29*, 127–141. doi:10.1016/S0306-4603(03)00079-0.

World Health Organization. (2004). *WHO global status report on alcohol.* Retrieved from http://www.who.int/substance_abuse/publications/en/japan.pdf

Yamawaki, N., Pulsipher, C., Moses, J., Rasmuse, K., & Ringger, K. (2011). Predictors of negative attitudes toward mental health services: A general population study in Japan. *European Journal of Psychiatry, 25*, 101–110.

Yanagida, E., & Marsella, A. J. (1978). The relationship between depression and self-concept discrepancy among different generations of Japanese-American women. *Journal of Clinical Psychology, 34*(3), 654–659. doi:10.1002/1097-4679(197807)34:3<654::AID-JCLP2270340314>3.0.CO;2-T.

Yoshida, K. (1990). Knowing vs behaving vs feeling: Studies on Japanese bilinguals. In L. A. Arena (Ed.), *Language proficiency: Defining, teaching, and testing* (pp. 19–40). New York, NY: Plenum Press.

Yoshihama, M. (2001). Model minority demystified: Emotional costs of multiple victimizations in the lives of women of Japanese descent. *Journal of Human Behavior in the Social Environment, 3*(3–4), 201–224. doi:10.1300/J137v03n03_13.

Zane, N. S., & Huh-Kim, J. (1998). Addictive behaviors. In L. C. Lee & N. S. Zane (Eds.), *Handbook of Asian American psychology* (pp. 527–554). Thousand Oaks, CA: Sage Publications.

Cross-Cultural Considerations with Korean American Clients: A Perspective on Psychological Assessment

4

Nancy M. Cha, Michelle S. Chung, and Sara Cho Kim

The Korean American population was the fastest growing of all Asian groups between 1990 and 2000, from 799,000 to 1,073,000 individuals, a 35 % increase (US Bureau of the Census, 2004). Persons of Korean descent compose over 10 % of the Asian Americans and Pacific Islanders (AAPIs) in the USA (US Bureau of the Census, 2004). Currently, Korean Americans rank among the largest AAPI subgroup in the USA (US Bureau of the Census, 2004). While other ethnic groups have been in the USA for several generations, more than two out of three Korean Americans are foreign-born, first generation immigrants (US Bureau of the Census, 2008). Given that Korean Americans have a relatively shorter immigration history compared to other ethnic groups, this may impact their familiarity with and assimilation into American culture. As such, greater research on immigration stress, discrimination, and psychological adjustment is needed for Korean American families.

The Sino-Japanese War, which took place in Korea, initiated Korea's first wave of immigration to the USA (Kitano & Daniels, 1995). Between 1903 and 1905, approximately 7,000 Koreans immigrated to Hawaii for better living conditions than that existed in Korea at the time (Hing, 1993) and the Japanese annexation in Korea brought Korean women as picture brides (Zia, 2000). On the islands of Hawaii, there was a need for laborers to work on the sugar plantations. However, during this time, the lower-class Korean Americans who made the initial move faced poverty and hardship in Hawaii (Hing, 1993). In the early twentieth century, Korean immigrants moved to the mainland to work on farms and railroads.

The second wave of Korean immigrants arrived in the USA after the Korean War in 1953. These immigrants were predominantly the wives of servicemen, war orphans, and a number of them were students and professionals. While many immigrants at this time were professionally skilled in medicine or engineering, language barriers and racial discrimination prevented many immigrants from obtaining professional positions (Hing, 1993). In order to make a living, many Korean immigrants instead chose to open

N.M. Cha, Ph.D. (✉)
Pacific Islands Division, Department of Veterans Affairs, National Center for PTSD, 3375 Koapaka Street, Suite I-560, Honolulu, HI 96819, USA
e-mail: nancycha@gmail.com

M.S. Chung, Psy.D.
Department of Psychiatry, HEARTS: Healing Emotions and Achieving Resilience to Traumatic Stress, Beth Israel Medical Center, First Avenue at 16th Street - 2 Bernstein, New York, NY 10003, USA
e-mail: drmichellechung@gmail.com

S.C. Kim, Ph.D.
Department of Counseling and Human Development, Graduate School of Education and Human Development, George Washington University, 2134 G. Street NW, Suite 317, Washington, DC 20052, USA
e-mail: schokim@gwu.edu

L.T. Benuto et al. (eds.), *Guide to Psychological Assessment with Asians*,
DOI 10.1007/978-1-4939-0796-0_4,

small businesses, such as groceries, dry cleaners, and restaurants. This downward shift from professionally skilled occupations to skilled labor jobs affected professional opportunities and financial livelihood, which in turn had psychological, physical, and inherently cultural effects on Koreans living in the USA.

Cross-Cultural Recommendations for Assessment and Therapy

Acculturation and Depression

Acculturation, the process of cultural adaptation by individuals, has been conceptualized as a central component in understanding the varied experience of ethnic and cultural minorities (Berry, 2005). It is a potentially stressful period, during which personal and interpersonal problems often arise in the process of attempting to resolve or minimize cultural differences between themselves and the host culture. Berry and Kim (1986) identified this as acculturative stress.

A review of the studies on Korean Americans and depression indicates that the prevalence of depression may vary according to acculturation levels. Assessing for acculturation levels may assist in establishing factors contributing to mood disorders (Jang, Kim, & Chiriboga, 2005). Given the high rates of immigration within the last 50 years, Korean Americans have to navigate a new host country and may be more prone to experiencing depressive symptoms (Takeuchi et al., 2007). In Jang et al.'s (2005) study, after controlling for the effects of demographic variables and chronic conditions, low acculturation levels remained a significant risk factor of high depressive symptoms for Korean Americans. Korean older adults in particular were found to manifest relatively more symptoms of depression.

Similarly, Oh, Koeske, and Sales (2002) reported that Korean participants who indicated abandonment of Korean traditions and values were more vulnerable to depressive symptoms. Furthermore, maintaining Korean traditions and adjusting to American culture adds a layer of psychological stress that nonimmigrant populations do not face (Aldwin & Greenberger, 1987; Oh et al., 2002).

The high rate of depression reported among Korean immigrants is strongly correlated specifically to increased rates of acculturative stress (Hurh & Kim, 1990; Kim & Rew, 1994; Oh et al., 2002). In a study examining the link between intergenerational acculturation conflict and depression symptoms, Kim (2011) found that increased depressive symptoms were related to incongruent cultural values. In fact, there is a positive correlation between depression and level of acculturative stress among Korean immigrants (Choi, 1997; Shin, 1994) suggesting that acculturated individuals may function better in the host culture and this contributes to their psychological well-being (Berry & Kim, 1986). However, longer residence in the USA and higher acculturation levels does not provide complete immunity from depression. Findings for the impact of acculturation levels (typically strong indicators of generational status) on psychological well-being have been inconsistent. The process of acculturation is a complex process for Asian immigrants with multiple factors influencing adjustment that could lead to increases in both levels of well-being and distress (Shin, Han, & Kim, 2007).

Social support plays an important role in adjusting to a new culture, decreasing acculturative stress, and reducing the risk of depression (Berry, Kim, Minde, & Mok, 1987; Choi, 1997; Kim, Han, Shin, Kim, & Lee, 2005; Shin, 1994). Family support and good family relations are associated with decreased levels of depression in Korean immigrants (Lee, Moon, & Knight, 2004; Mui, 2001). Similarly, Korean immigrants who are affiliated with a Korean church reported less depression (Hurh & Kim, 1990; Lee et al., 2004). Korean churches are an established social network, providing spiritual support, social services, counseling, cultural activities, and have become an important community for Korean immigrants in the USA (Hurh, 1998). Seventy percent of all Koreans living in America attend a Christian church. In some Christian-belief systems, mental illness is understood as a symbol of inherent evil (Kim-Goh, 1993). Korean clergy have reportedly advised church members not to seek professional help for mental health issues and instead recommend alternative treatments such as fasting, praying, or performing exorcisms. Outreach efforts have been made to educate Korean clergy members about mental health issues and to collaborate with them when working with Korean patients. As such, psychologists may want to consider working collaboratively with spiritual mentors and pastors in the client's life.

Acculturation and the Family Structure

Korean families value filial piety, clearly defined family roles (with the male as the head of the family), collectivism and interdependence, and education (Kitano & Daniels, 1988). A Confucian proverb known in the Korean culture demonstrates this mindset, the "law of the three obediences": obeying the father before marriage, obeying the husband following marriage, and obeying the oldest son after the husband's death (Kim-Goh, 1998). These values are largely intact in immigrant families; however as children of immigrant parents become acculturated into westernized society, family discord ensues. In Korean American families seeking mental health services, counselors may see a higher frequency of family conflict due to strain shifting family roles, communication difficulties, a gap in parent–child values, and parents' expectations in the areas of academic achievement, dating, and marriage.

For Korean immigrant males, there is oftentimes a shift of work related factors, as many immigrate as professionals and transition to occupations that require long hours spent at work in order to maintain an income. Among immigrant males, occupation, income and job satisfaction show the strongest correlation with mental well-being (Hurh, 1998). Many highly educated Korean males who are unable to find professional employment may develop substance abuse problems (Min, 2001). In addition, often becomes difficult to suppress feelings of anger and resentment given their social role shifts to a more egalitarian way of life and the difficulty in maintaining financial stability (Min, 2001).

Despite the fact that men are oftentimes the primary breadwinners in an immigrant household, Korean American women have had to work in the family businesses out of necessity (Kim & Kim, 1998). More than 75 % of Korean American women are employed full-time outside of the home (Hurh, 1998) and are also expected to perform all household and child-rearing tasks (Kim & Rew, 1994; Um & Dancy, 1999). This is contrary to life in Korea, where domestic responsibility belongs to women and fiscal responsibility belongs to men. Given the multiple roles women are required to fulfill and managing conflicts that arise at home and at work, they are subject to severe strain and stress (Kim & Rew, 1994). Considering this strain during the adjustment period following immigration, employed and married Korean immigrant women may also be at higher risk for depression and may face more barriers to seeking services due to cultural attitudes and expectations (Miller & Chandler, 2002; Noh & Avison, 1996; Shin, 1994). These financial, social-role, and legitimacy shifts for Korean immigrants are factors that create stress and psychological maladjustment for Korean American families, which may contribute to the high rate of domestic violence within the home (Rhee, 1997).

There are a number young children and adolescents who immigrated to the USA with their parents (the 1.5 generation). These youth often face similar challenges as American-born children of Korean immigrants, especially when faced with a conflicting set of demands. They are often encouraged by their middle-class parents toward upward mobility by attaining a better education and well-paying professions (Novas, Cao, & Silva, 2004). This orientation towards academic achievement creates a significant demand for success, and in turn a dynamic wrought in perfectionism in Korean American adolescents (Kim, 2005).

Research on Korean American children and their relationship with their parents is limited. Of the studies on Korean American children and their parents, a vast majority are with college age populations. Studies predominately focused on the gap that forms between parents and their children due to differential rates of acculturation and its effects on distress. In a study of examining the nature of parent–child conflicts and the use of coping strategies, a large majority of Korean American college students in the study reported having less adherence to cultural values than their parents (Ahn, Kim, & Park, 2008). As a result, when there was a greater parent–child values gap, there was a higher likelihood of parent–child conflict. When these conflicts occurred, Korean college students reported using problem solving as a coping strategy more frequently than social support. Conflicts that were most often cited included family expectations and conflicts regarding dating and marriage (Ahn et al., 2008).

With regard to parental strain, Choi, Dancy, Faan, and Lee (2012) found in a qualitative study that the main stresses that parents encountered while raising their adolescent children in the USA were inability to advocate for children, feeling uneasy and insecure about incompatible American culture, ambivalence towards children's ethnic identities, and feelings of alienation. Parents reported perceiving American culture to be liberal and individualized as opposed to Korean culture, which is perceived to be conservative and oriented towards familial, group, and community advancement, i.e. where the individual is subordinated in favor of the group. Parents felt that their children became more selfish and less respectful to adults the longer they lived in the USA (Choi et al., 2012). Due to living in two cultures, incongruent cultural values and conflicts between parents and children may increase over time and may place families at risk for mental health issues (Hwang, 2006).

Psychologists may want to consider addressing these aspects through a twofold approach considering the strains on both the parent(s) and the child as distinct but intertwined. Family therapy in particular can be a unique way for all parties to hear how the same strain has differing effects but result in distress nonetheless. Moreover there is oftentimes a third aspect and cultural value in a Korean American household, which includes the cultural practice as a caregiver to the elderly. The responsibility of caring for the elderly is often placed on adult children and can be an added stressor. As such, this burden is a risk factor for the mental health of the caretaker (Lee & Farran, 2004).

Korean Adoptees

The end of the Korean War in 1953 brought about the first Korean adoptees into the USA. Most Korean War orphans were adopted by US families (Kim, 1995b). Korean children adopted by American families accounted for approximately 20 % of all foreign adoptions in the 10-year period following the Korean War amounting to 4,163 children in the USA. By 1986, 6,150 Korean children were adopted, representing 59 % of all foreign children adopted in the USA, according to the annual report of the US Immigration and Naturalization Service (1992). There are now an estimated 110,000 children adopted by American families between 1953 and 2001 (Evan B. Donaldson Adoption Institute, 2007).

Several researchers (Lee, 2003; Lee & Quintana, 2005; Yoon, 2004) have noted that being adopted and ethnically different from other members of one's own family as well as from majority members of society can make the process of identity formation more complex for transracial adoptees. Although many Korean transracial adoptees have Caucasian family members, their racial features place them in the minority group. As such, they are forced to navigate the meanings of race and culture from two reference groups, the majority Euro-American group, and the Korean American group. A Korean adoptees' racial identity is also a challenging issue because they must both develop a sense of internal (family) identity while simultaneously attempting to come to some understanding of negotiating their external identity, as experienced by others (Randolph & Holtzman, 2010). In addition to racial identity, the development of a strong ethnic identity is also an important aspect of transracial adoptees' psychological well-being (Basow, Lilley, Bookwala, & McGillicuddy-Delisi, 2008).

However, research studies focusing on identity development and comfort with racial and ethnic identities present an inconsistent picture. In a longitudinal study with 366 transracially adopted Korean Americans in the 1970s in the Midwest, most adult adoptees were comfortable with their racial identity (Simon & Altstein, 2000). However, another study indicates that earlier generations of Korean adoptees did not identify strongly with their ethnic culture, viewing themselves as Caucasian or White children (Freundlich & Lieberthal, 2000). In situations where adoptees simply want to fit in with their majority Euro-American peers during childhood and adolescence, they may adopt a color-blind position by identifying more strongly with being "just a person" or American (Lee & Miller, 2009). In a similar vein, Johnson and Kim-Johnson (1998–1999) found that Korean transracially adoptees in Minnesota reported instances of "identity dissonance," experiences of indirect racism, and expressed the wish to be "just American." Kim, Suyemoto, and Turner (2010) explored the impact of sense of belonging and exclusion on racial and ethnic identity. They found that Korean transracially adoptees' individual identities are not solely choices made by individuals' internal decisions. Rather, social experiences with both White and the Korean American groups and responses from significant others and societies at large have influential roles in identity development (Kim et al., 2010).

Another important aspect to assess when examining psychological well-being in transracial adoptees is level of cultural socialization (Lee, 2003). In other words, it is important to consider the amount a Korean adoptee has been exposed to the cultural norms and expectations of one's birth culture and has internalized those cultural norms and expectations. Given that some Korean-born adoptees are raised by Caucasian families, they are exposed to and socialized into the dominant culture. Contact with other members of their racial group and/or exposure to an Asian ethnic culture may be minimal because of homogeneous neighborhoods, or because their family did not make an effort to expose them to their ethnic heritage (Lee, 2003). In particular, ethnic language knowledge is one of the most salient markers of cultural knowledge.

The role of adoptive parents is particularly crucial in the cultural socialization of their Korean adopted children. Parents make decisions regarding the degree to which they will, intentionally or unintentionally, affirm or discount the cultural and racial group memberships of their children and inherently influencing their child's identity formation process (Randolph & Holtzman, 2010). Korean "heritage" camps have been one approach to providing this experience. Generally, fostering an open environment that validates adoptees' racial experiences and educating adoptees about the possibility of encountering exclusion based on race and ethnicity is important.

Diagnoses, Treatment, and Assessment

Depression

Korean Americans have higher rates of depression when compared to Japanese Americans, Filipino Americans, and Chinese Americans. Depression is one of the most prevalent mental health issues among Korean Americans (Huang, Wong, Ronzio, & Yu, 2007; Kuo, 1984; Min, Moon, & Lubben, 2005; Shin, 2002; Yeh & Inose, 2002). Two particular studies report that 30–49 % of Korean Americans in their samples endorse depressive symptoms (Huang et al., 2007; Kim & Rew, 1994). This high rate of depression among Korean immigrants has continued for several decades (Hurh & Kim, 1990; Min et al., 2005; Shin, 1993). Despite the high prevalence of depression in the Korean American community, few speak about their depressive symptoms (Kim & Rew, 1994). Mental illness is viewed as stigmatizing and brings disgrace to the entire family (Kim, 1997). Wanting to "save face" on behalf of the family and a lack of culturally responsive treatments maintains a culture of underutilization of mental health services in the Korean American community (Shin, 2002).

In previous studies, depression was empirically linked to stressful life events (Choi, 1997;

Oh et al., 2002; Shin, 1994). In Korean Americans, depressive symptoms are linked to several factors, including aging, being female and changes in gender roles, divorce, or separation from family members, lower education level, low socioeconomic status, deficient social support, discrimination, rejecting acculturation, and language barriers (Choi, 1997; Im & Meleis, 2001; Kim, 1999; Koh, 1998).

A depression instrument was developed for use with Korean Americans: the Kim Depression Scale for Korean Americans (KDSKA). It captures the four domains of depression (affective, behavioral, cognitive, somatic) in a 25 item, four-point Likert-like scale. The questions were designed to be consistent with culturally salient descriptions of depression, such as "I cannot laugh with my whole heart." This instrument does have some clinical limitations that should be noted. The KDSKA is not intended to be a diagnostic tool because of its limited ability to delineate the severity of depression. It was designed as a screening tool based on the frequency of symptoms rather than severity. Additionally, this instrument does not have established norms or cutoff points and larger scale validation studies are required to establish these numbers (Kim, 2002).

Given the high rates of depression amongst Korean immigrants, it is alarming that this population rarely seeks the treatment they need (Kim & Rew, 1994). It has been reported that self-treatment for depression and other mental health issues results in increasing rates of alcohol abuse in Koreans (Duranceaux et al., 2008; Helzer et al., 1990). Untreated depression also affects the family unit making it a source of stress and nonsupport. Additionally, it has been found that depressive symptoms in parents negatively impact parenting (Lovejoy, Graxzyk, O'Hare, & Neuman, 2000). Depressed parents tend to be more hostile, coercive, less nurturing, less involved (Benner & Kim, 2010), and less supportive of their adolescents (Barrera & Garrison-Jones, 1992). However, despite the high rates of depression for Koreans, psychologists should first explore the way in which emotions and depressive symptoms are expressed and manifest.

Expression of Emotion and Depression

It has been found that Korean Americans experience, conceptualize, and express emotional problems differently than those in the dominant American culture (Kim, 1995a; McCollaum & Lester, 1997). In Korean culture, there is no differentiation between psychological and physical functioning. Based on classical Chinese beliefs and medicine, physical and emotional health are viewed in a holistic manner (Kim, 1995a). Emotional states and suffering are often interchangeable with physical sensations. Therefore, somatization is thought to be an important mode of expressing emotional problems for Korean Americans (Kim & Rew, 1994). Depressed Korean Americans often describe bodily sensation such as digestive distress, tightness in the chest, dizziness, constipation, back pain, and headaches. Studies have found that there is no clear distinction between body and mind; instead somatic metaphors are used to express affective states (Pang, 2000). For example, Pang (1998) found that Korean immigrants seemed to be describing somatic complaints when describing emotions, but instead were actually expressing emotional and psychological distress using somatic idioms or metaphors. Depression was described metaphorically using phrases like "My mind is wrapped with fog" (as cited in Pang, 1988, p. 105). Another notable difference in the expression of depression is using the color "black" rather than "blue" to depict negative emotions.

Furthermore, in the Korean dialect, there is no direct translation for "depression." The phrase that most closely describes the experience of depression is *woo-ul-jeuing* (Yi, 1990). This is a condition in which ones self is out of balance (Shin, 2010). Based on the Chinese philosophy of yin yang (the two forces in nature), the body, mind, and environment lacks balance or are not in harmony. When looking for "balance," it is difficult to differentiate and identify a single source of suffering, either through physical or mental illness (Choi, Stafford, Meininger, Roberts, & Smith, 2002; Shin, 2010).

Less acculturated Korean adults may adhere to more traditional Confucian values of modesty and for this reason, may be reluctant to express positive emotions such as happiness and satisfaction. In contrast, those who are more acculturated may be more accepting of Westernized ways of thinking and expression and are more likely to reveal and express themselves in a positive manner (Jang et al., 2005). A growing knowledge and exposure to Western culture may also be an indicator of successful coping or adaptability, which in turn has been linked to positive emotional states (Jang, Chiriboga, & Kim, 2006). Jang et al. (2005) questions whether reported depression symptoms are indicative of true emotional states or result from a cultural response style. In this way, a reluctance to express positive emotions may be more of an indication of cultural norms rather than symptoms of depression.

Korean culture also discourages expression of emotional problems, especially amongst Korean men. Koreans believe this is an important component of keeping harmony in a family unit or society and that a person's maturity is measured by the ability to control one's feelings (Kim, 1995a). Additionally, most Koreans believe that the acceptance of suffering is a way of life (Pang, 1998; Yamashiro & Matsuoka, 1997). Based on Taoist and Buddhist influences, Korean Americans attempt to overcome emotional distress by personal willpower and believe that emotional difficulties are situationally limited. To publicly express emotional suffering is a sign of weakness (Shin, 2010). Consequently, individuals hesitate to seek help from a mental health professional or member outside of their family (McCollaum & Lester, 1997). Physical complaints are socially accepted, but mental complaints are stigmatized (Cho & Kim, 1998; Pang, 1994). These cultural traits have been thought to influence the rate of somatization identified in East Asian individuals (Hsu & Folstein, 1997; Kleinman, 1982).

Substance Abuse in Korean Americans

In Korean culture, drinking alcohol is common, particularly during social gatherings, celebrations, and on holidays. Alcoholism and substance abuse were not viewed as social and legal problems in Korea until the last 20 years (Kwon-Ahn, 2011). Many Korean immigrants who arrived in the U. S. in the 1990s, may hold the same attitudes towards alcohol consumption and other substance use. As such, Korean Americans living in the USA may be unaware of the mental health consequences of alcoholism, cigarette smoking, and other substance use.

Social norms tend to dictate alcohol consumption (Cook, Hofstetter, Kang, Hovell, & Irvin, 2009). Based on the collectivist nature of Korean culture, when one is offered a drink, it is often considered rude not to accept it (Kwon-Ahn, 2011). Typically, the act is reciprocated until both or all those present in the same party have consumed a number of drinks. For women or deferential males, there is a different set of social norms. When they are in the presence of males or elders, they must turn away and consume their drink discreetly. Furthermore, it is disrespectful for women to smoke cigarettes in front of elders and males. For younger males, it is disrespectful to smoke in front of their elders. Gender differences may preclude women from having higher rates of alcohol and cigarette use. In the past, Korean males were reported to have higher rates of drinking than females (Lubben, Chi, & Kitano, 1989). Compared to other Asian subgroups, Korean Americans also have a higher rate of cigarette smoking. In particular, males tend to have a higher rate of cigarette use and addiction than females (Hahm, Lahiff, & Guterman, 2004).

Social norms may also influence the onset of first alcohol and cigarette use in Korean youth. There may be a greater potential for Korean American adolescents to experiment at an earlier age with alcohol, cigarettes, and illicit drugs with their same ethnic peers (Cook et al., 2009). Similar to other immigrant groups, peer influence is a significant factor associated with drinking behavior and other substance use in Korean American adolescents (Hahm et al., 2004). Studies have also examined acculturation levels as possible factors influencing early use of alcohol and cigarettes (Cook et al., 2009; Hendershot, Dillworth, Neighbors, & George, 2008; Unger, Trinidad, Weiss, & Rohrbach, 2004).

In the USA, there are few culturally appropriate counseling services to specifically treat Korean Americans with substance abuse. Several barriers exist in providing culturally appropriate substance abuse treatment to Korean Americans. One major obstacle is language barriers. Locating clinics that offer translation services, if necessary, may be more challenging. The second is in addressing cultural differences. For a culture that believes that hard work and willpower will overcome any addiction, psychoeducation for Korean Americans may be required to inform clients and their families that addiction may be related to biological, social, and/or environmental factors. For example, studies indicate that many Asian Americans and particularly Korean Americans lack the ALDH2*2 allele to metabolize alcohol resulting in difficulty breathing, redness of body and face, and skin irritation and itchiness (Hampton, 2006). Scientific studies and health information provided by physicians and leaders in the community may help to educate the Korean American community about the physiological differences of Asians as compared to others. Substance abuse counselors working with Korean Americans may need to be directive and make greater attempts to contact potential client than they typically would with non-Asian populations.

When assessing for alcohol and substance use, it is important to ask the client indirectly as a way of demonstrating respect. For example, direct or detailed questioning may appear disrespectful and elicit a defensive response. Asking the client to write down or give a written record of how much and how often they drink in a sitting may illicit greater responsiveness. If they are unwilling or are dismissive of your question, other options such as using a checklist or relating it to physical health concerns may be appropriate. It may also help at this point to remind them of confidentiality and their legal rights. Teaming up with local religious pastors or organizations may help to increase recruitment and retention of substance abusers and those with drinking problems.

Rates of Suicide and Suicidal Ideation

The rate of Koreans in America who commit suicide is increasing at an alarming rate. According to the Korean Consulate General, in 2009 the number of Korean citizens living in the USA who completed suicide has more than doubled from 7 to 15. This number does not account for Korean Americans that are citizens of the USA. The Korea Times, a Korean newspaper in the USA, reported that during 2010 at least 36 Koreans and Korea Americans in the New York region alone had taken their lives (Korean Beacon, 2010). Accurate data on the rates of mental health-related issues and suicides among first and second generation Korean Americans are difficult to ascertain. Part of this difficulty results from the data collection methods used by the Center for Disease Control (CDC). When the CDC reported on mental health statistics, all the East Asian ethnicities were lumped together as one category. Interestingly, this alarming increase in suicide rates of Koreans in the USA has mirrored the rise of suicides in South Korea. According to 2010 reports from the Organization for Economic Cooperation and Development (OECD), South Korea has the highest suicide rate among its 30 member nations, with 33.5 suicides per 10,000 people. Some experts trace the increase in the suicide rate, in part, to the nation's rapid transformation from an impoverished society to a booming industrial power (The Straits Times, September 10, 2012).

Critics of modern Korean culture report that the importance of traditional values has diminished and instead has been replaced with a sense of materialism. Money and achievement are emphasized starting from childhood. Failure to get into top colleges, perform well at school or climb the economic ladder can cause deep shame and embarrassment (BBC News Asia, Nov. 7, 2011). These recent changes continue to influence Korean immigrants in setting unreasonable expectations for achievements, furthering the rates of depression and suicidal ideations. Many community organizations are holding seminars and educational workshops on suicide risk factors and prevention. A report released by the Suicide Prevention Action Network USA and the Suicide Prevention Resource Center, concluded that Asian Americans are significantly less likely than Caucasians to mention suicidal thoughts or mental health concerns to a professional (4 % vs. 26 %) (n.d.). It is important to actively screen for suicidal risk when assessing a Korean American patient exhibiting distress.

Psychosis and Schizophrenia

There are very few published studies or epidemiological data collected on Korean Americans diagnosed with schizophrenia or psychotic disorders. Some attempts have been made to estimate prevalence rates of schizophrenia in Asian American groups by studying patients who received services in public treatment settings. The lifetime prevalence rate for schizophrenic disorders in Korean Americans is estimated to be 0.46 %. Those who sought out services exhibited a greater level of disturbance than others in the clinic population (Sue & Morishima, 1982). This finding may be related to the pattern of help-seeking behaviors found in Asian American communities. Asian patients are usually kept within the family for prolonged periods of time without proper mental health services, until the family can no longer care for the individual or the efforts are unsuccessful (Lin, Inui, Kleinman, & Womack, 1982; Lin, Tardiff, Donetz, & Goresky, 1978). Additionally, sociocultural and ethnic backgrounds unique to the Korean American experience may influence the expression, course, and treatment of schizophrenia (Hopper & Wanderling, 2000; Kirmayer, 1989; Kleinman, 1988; Lin & Kleinman, 1988; Weisman, 1997). For example, Asian families are more likely to accompany schizophrenic family members to clinic visits and are actively involved in treatment decisions (Lin, Miller, Poland, Nuccio, & Yamaguch, 1991).

Psychosocial differences were found in Korean American schizophrenic patients when compared to other minority groups (Bae & Brekke, 2002). These patients tend to live with their families, or if they live independently, their families maintain more parental contact and control. Many of the Korean American schizophrenic patients were employed at family owned businesses. Socially, these patients initiated less contact with people outside of their families. This can be interpreted as a way to go unnoticed in social interactions, to not call attention to themselves or to avoid undesirable behaviors (Abe & Zane, 1990). Furthermore, when compared to other ethnic groups, Korean American schizophrenic patients were significantly less satisfied with their social lives and had less general life satisfaction. Factors such as acculturative stress in addition to the complications of being diagnosed with a serious mental illness present additional challenges to this population.

Treatment and assessment of psychosis or schizophrenia in the Korean American population should incorporate cultural characteristics. Bae and Kung (2000) proposed that a culturally relevant family intervention model be used with Asian Americans with schizophrenia. Fostering a family bond and involving family members in a collaborative manner may be appropriate (Shon & Ja, 1982; Sue & Morishima, 1982). Additionally, when working to improve social functioning, the interventions should be culturally congruent. Social assertiveness or confrontations are likely to be rejected (Telles et al., 1995). A comprehensive psychosocial assessment should be conducted, including individual stressors and identifying factors that affect the individual's adjustment within the community.

Culture-Bound Syndromes Specific to Korean Americans

Hwa-Byung

The inability to express feelings may lead to a Korean culture-bound syndrome called "Hwa-byung" (anger illness or fire illness). Hwa-byung can be viewed as repressed negative emotions expressed through multiple physical symptoms, in response to emotional distress. It is believed to occur when women of Korean heritage suppress anger, frustration, hate, animosity, or other negative feelings toward their family or significant others. When these feelings are suppressed for a long time (even for as long as decades), a group of psychosomatic symptoms develop, including sensations of heat, pressure in the chest, nasal stuffiness, epigastric pressure, heart palpitations, headache, dry mouth, eating disturbances, insomnia, and heavy sighing. These physical symptoms are usually coupled with anxiety, hypervigilance and sadness (Min & Suh, 2010). In Western cultures, it is often misdiagnosed as depression or anxiety due to the similar symptom presentation and because they are highly correlated and at times comorbid (Park & Bernstein, 2008). Hwa-byung is diagnosed in approximately 4.0–11.9 %

of the population, mostly in middle-aged or older Korean immigrant women (Lin, 1983; Min, Namkoong, & Lee, 1990).

The unique features of Hwa-Byung that differentiate it from other mental illnesses are that patients usually acknowledge that they have Hwa-Byung. Often, these patients feel guilty for having it, have been submissive or obedient for long periods of time, have hidden their anger or negative feelings (at least 10 years), present with generalized anxiety, and yet show resilience and no suicidal ideation or attempts (Choi, 2006). The foremost method of assessing Hwa-byung is to explore the patient's social, cultural, and life history. When gathering demographic information from these patients, asking them to fill out a questionnaire before the interview is sometimes better than asking in person. During the interview, it is important to ask the patient directly if they think they have Hwa-Byung, to describe the symptoms, how it interferes with daily life, if they have sought out treatment from a doctor or alternative medicine, and if anything has helped elevate the symptoms (Choi & Yeom, 2011). Symptoms of Hwa-byung can be assessed using the Hwa-byung Scale (HB Scale) (Min et al., 2009). This assessment is offered in both English and Korean versions. It is known as a useful clinical tool to measure Hwa-Byung and has been found to have good validity and reliability (Choi, Phillips, Figueredo, Insel, & Min, 2008). Traditionally, Hwa-byung is treated holistically with psychosocial support from family, spiritual comfort, traditional Korean medicine, and biomedical treatments. Recent studies have shown that a combination of both pharmacological and nonpharmacological interventions improves symptoms of Hwa-byung (Choi & Yeom, 2011). Other interventions shown to be effective were psychotherapy, cognitive behavior therapy, social skills training, and working closely with the family. Additionally, facilitating support from the ethnic community can be a great assets and resources for the patient.

Shin-Byung

Shin-byung is a Korean culture-bound syndrome listed in the DSM-IV. Shin-byung is translated as "divine illness" or "god illness." It is characterized by anxiety and somatic complaints, followed by dissociation and possession by ancestral spirits.

According to Korean folklore, it is the initiatory process to become a shaman. In order to alleviate symptoms, the person must allow the foreign spirit, sometimes the spirit of an ancestor, to enter the body; however other shamans can dissuade the spirit from entering the body and halt the process and obligation of becoming a shaman (Yi, 2000).

There are three phases of Shin-byung: the prodromal phase, trance phase, and possession phase. The first phase, prodromal phase, is characterized by symptoms such as weakness, fatigue, dizziness, insomnia, digestion issues, depression, anxiety, fear of death, and conversion symptoms. These symptoms can last from several weeks to decades. Usually during this phase, patients will struggle to understand their symptoms, visiting various physicians. The symptoms will progress to the trance phase. This is when the patient suffers from unusual dreams, hallucinations, or illusions from spiritual beings, which suggest that they will enter the patient's body or that the patient becomes a shaman. This phase is often distressing for the patient and physicians, and so other shamans are often consulted for help. The trance phase can last from days to years. The last phase is called the possession phase. It is broken into two different subphases. The first is when the original spirit in the dreams or hallucinations coexists in the patient's body, creating multiple personalities. Soon after, full possession will occur, when the invading spirit dominates the patient's body, consciousness, and behaviors. Some accounts of full possession have included states of confusion, extreme excitement, and sometimes violence. It is believed that women living in chronically stressful family situations are vulnerable to developing Shin-byung. When perceived by a Western medical model, patients with Shin-byung are often diagnosed with schizophrenia, conversion disorder, and/or dissociative identity disorder. The treatment of Shin-byung is often a collaborative approach of therapy and the involvement of a shaman, although in modern Korean culture the help of a shaman is often the final option (Legerski, 2006).

Underutilization of MH Services

Although the Korean American population has grown, the number of Korean Americans represented in the US healthcare system remains minimal. Specific data on mental health utilization among Korean Americans has not been recorded, though a trend towards underutilization of mental health services has been found in Asian Americans in general. The Surgeon General found that only 17 % of the Asian Americans with a psychological problem sought assistance and less than 6 % did so from a mental health provider (US DHHS, 2001). When Asian Americans seek professional help, it is usually for psychotic, dangerous, or disruptive behaviors and less frequently for common personal problems or general emotional distress (Moon & Tashima, 1982; Tracey, Leong, & Glidden, 1986).

When Korean immigrants seek mental health services, it is usually on behalf of a family member suffering from a mental illness. The family member seeking help is often female. The underutilization of mental health services observed in the Korean American community may be attributed to many factors, including negative stigma, lack of knowledge regarding resources, unfamiliarly with treatment methods, pragmatic barrier to receiving treatment (such as financial resources, transportation, language, or access to insurance), as well as the failure of mental health services to provide culturally relevant interventions (Bernstein, 2007).

The negative stigma associated with mental illness among Korean immigrants has been deeply ingrained within the society for centuries (Leong & Lau, 2001). It is a common scenario that shame and denial over mental illness often encourage individuals and families to keep the illness secret. Having a family member who is different from the expected norms of society can be a source of shame for the whole family unit. In a culture where being able to control one's emotions and behaviors are respected and considered honorable, seeking professional mental help can be viewed as a sign of weakness, bringing further shame to the individual and family unit. In some cases, mental illness is perceived as a curse on the individual and family, bearing further shame and secrecy. When working with Korean American families, it is important to assure confidentiality and to address the shame and stigma. It can be helpful to reframe seeking help as a strength and a path to eventually maintain the family's dignity (Kim, 1985).

In some situations, economic limitations serve as a barrier to seeking healthcare. One out of every four elderly Korean immigrants lives below the poverty line, making access to health insurance and therefore, mental health services nearly impossible (Jang et al., 2006). When compared to other ethnic minority groups, Korean Americans rank among the lowest in having medical insurance (42 % without health insurance coverage, whether private, government-sponsored, Medicare/Medicaid). This lack of health insurance coverage is most likely related to their recent immigration history and reliance on income from small retail businesses, most of which are unable to afford private health insurance premiums (Lee, Hanner, Cho, Han, & Kim, 2008).

Another practical barrier to seeking treatment is language. Oftentimes, Korean immigrants are unaware of the services available to them. The number of Korean speaking clinicians may be limited and if none are available, dropping out of treatment due to language difficulties is probable (Donnelly, 2005). Additionally, certain culture-bound communication rules make talking about feelings to a clinician highly uncomfortable, such as avoiding eye contact and avoiding private topics (Beller, Pinker, Snapka, & Van Dusen, n.d.).

Typically, Korean American families first seek out traditional Eastern medicine, such as acupuncture or homeopathic care, to deal with everyday medical or mental health issues. Seeking mental health treatment is usually a last resort. Commonly, the assistance of family and friends, informal social networks, and community organizations such as the church are pursued first (Akutsu, Castillo, & Snowden, 2007). Mental Health professionals should inquire about the use of Eastern medicine or alternative supports and the willingness to accept Western-style practices (Jo & Dawson, 2010).

Public awareness and education efforts seem to have a positive influence on help-seeking behaviors of Korean Americans and reduce stigma (Shin & Lukens, 2004). Korean immigrants with higher levels of acculturation to Western society have more fluency in English, and those who have accomplished higher levels of educational status have been found to be more positive about seeking professional mental health services (Yi & Tidwell, 2005).

Case Example

Anna is a 38 year old single Korean American female. She is the oldest of two; her younger brother is 4 years younger. Anna's parents immigrated to the USA from Korea prior to her birth and owned a small laundry mat until her father recently retired. She recalls her parents fighting regularly and her father coming home late. She grew up in a Korean protestant church with strong Christian values. Her mother continues to attend church regularly, though her father no longer attends. The neighborhood in which she grew up in the Midwest was predominantly Caucasian, as were her primary and intermediate school demographics. Her parents were strict while she was growing up, emphasizing academics and the importance of education. She was rarely allowed to go out with friends in high school, and never allowed to attend sleepovers.

Anna graduated college from an Ivy League institution and received her law degree at a prestigious university. She distanced herself from most Asian Americans on campus and has only dated Euro-American men. She has had a series of relationships with men in the past, however, has been single for 2 years. She currently resides in an urban city on the east coast, while her parents and younger brother remain in the Midwest. She has been in her current position as an attorney in a law firm for the past 4 years.

Anna's mother recently attempted suicide for the second time. Anna states that her mother has a history of untreated depression and has attempted suicide shortly after divorcing her father when Anna was in college. Most recently, her father has shared that he will be remarrying. Anna has never shared with anyone that her mother has attempted suicide, nor has she ever spoken with her mother about either suicide attempts. Anna feared it would be disrespectful to ask her mother about her depression and only learned the details from her aunt. Anna believed a pastor was meeting with her mother regularly, providing pastoral counseling.

Anna is complaining of having difficulty sleeping and concentrating at work. Additionally, she's been going out to drink socially almost every weekend and sometimes blacks out and doesn't remember where she was before she woke up. Anna fears that she may also be susceptible to depression in the future and is seeking help to manage her feelings around her mother's suicide attempt.

Questions to consider in assessment or treatment with Anna:

1. How does the role of birth order and gender contribute to the family dynamic?
2. In what way are Anna's Christian values important in her case conceptualization?
3. What may be Anna's past and present stressors that inform her clinical presentation?
4. How might you understand her distancing herself from other Asian Americans and preference for dating Caucasian men?
5. In what way would you address Anna's understanding of her mother's SI?

Summary/Conclusions

1. Korean Americans have had a more recent immigration history compared to other Asian ethnic groups, which can impact their familiarity with and assimilation into American culture.
2. Given that most psychologists will be working with first or second generation Korean Americans, it is important to consider the effects of acculturative stress on the individual and/or the family. Low acculturation remains a significant risk factor of depressive symptoms for Korean Americans. First generation Korean women in particular may be at greater risk for depression given the shift in gender roles as well as multiple roles

they are required to fulfill and managing conflicts that arise at home and at work.

3. Acculturative stress for second generation Korean Americans often includes conflict over family expectations, perfectionism/ achievement, dating, and marriage.
4. It is important to consider the racial and ethnic identity development of Korean Americans in overall psychological well-being. For first generation Korean Americans, there often is a conflict between holding onto Korean cultural values in a western society and the strain of communicating with their more assimilated children. With respect to second generation Korean Americans, a strong racial and ethnic identity, and an awareness and acceptance of the roles of both cultures correlates with positive psychological health.
5. Korean adoptees are a unique but prevalent subpopulation in the Korean American community. Psychologists should consider the identity development, cultural socialization, and role of the adoptive parents in the identity formation of the Korean adoptee.
6. Depression is one of the most predominant mental health issues among Korean Americans. Depressive symptoms are linked to several factors including aging, changes in gender roles (particularly for females), divorce or separation from family members, lower education level, low socioeconomic status, lack of social support, discrimination, slower rate of acculturation, caring for elders, and language barriers.
7. Psychologists should take care in understanding the expression of emotion and how it impacts mood disorders like depression. In Korean culture there is no differentiation between psychological and physical functioning. Somatic complaints are often used when describing emotions and psychological distress for first generation Koreans in particular. Furthermore, there is no direct translation for "depression"; Koreans often translate the condition to being "out of balance" or harmony as a relatable experience.
8. Oftentimes less acculturated Korean Americans are reluctant to express positive emotions, as a cultural response style. As such, the absence of positive emotions should not be considered to be depressive mood symptoms, or indicative of true emotional states. Moreover, Korean Americans believe an important component is to keep harmony in the family and forbear one's burdens, accepting suffering as a way of life. Therefore depressive symptoms related to forbearing family burdens may appear to be causing distress, but the alternative; to think of and act as an individual separate from the collective family, in actuality may cause greater psychological distress.
9. Anxiety disorders and the expression of negative emotion have culture bound symptoms unique to Korea like *Hwa-byung* and *Shin-byung*. Hwa-byung is related to repressed negative emotions expressed through multiple physical symptoms, in response to emotional distress. On the other hand, Shin-byung is characterized by anxiety and somatic complaints, followed by dissociation and possession by ancestral spirits. Psychologists should be mindful of the expression of emotions and symptoms in this way, particularly for first generation Korean Americans.
10. There are stressors for Korean Americans including dynamics in the family that create pressure (perfectionism, acculturative stress, family role shifts). Psychologists should be aware of the patterns and way in which Korean Americans oftentimes respond to such pressures i.e. substance abuse, eating disorders, and in extreme cases suicide.
11. In Korean culture, drinking alcohol is common, particularly during social gatherings. For Korean Americans, these social norms often turn into abuse when alcohol becomes a coping mechanism to deal with distress and stressors.
12. For Korean Americans, mental illness is viewed as stigmatizing and brings shame to the family. The general underutilization and barriers to care observed in the Korean American community may be attributed to

many factors, including negative stigma, lack of knowledge regarding resources, unfamiliarity with treatment methods, pragmatic barrier to receiving treatment (such as financial resources, transportation, language, or access to insurance), as well as failure of mental health services to provide culturally relevant interventions.

13. The assistance of family, friends, and community organization such as church are the primary places Korean Americans turn to for social support. However, while a strong emphasis is placed on the family unit, a Korean American open to psychological assessment or treatment will not likely have shared with their family they are seeking such services.

References

Abe, J. S., & Zane, N. W. (1990). Psychological maladjustment among Asian and White American college students: Controlling for confounds. *Journal of Counseling Psychology, 37*(4), 437–444. doi:10.1037//0022-0167.37.4.437.

Ahn, A. J., Kim, B. S. K., & Park, Y. S. (2008). Asian cultural values gap, cognitive flexibility, coping strategies, and parent–child conflicts among Korean Americans. *Asian American Journal of Psychology, S*(1), 29–44.

Akutsu, P. D., Castillo, E. D., & Snowden, L. R. (2007). Differential referral patterns to ethnic-specific and mainstream mental health programs for four Asian American groups. *American Journal of Orthopsychiatry, 77*(1), 95–103. doi:10.1037/0002-9432.77.1.95.

Aldwin, C., & Greenberger, E. (1987). Cultural differences in the predictors of depression. *American Journal of Community Psychology, 15*, 789–813.

Bae, S. W., & Brekke, J. S. (2002). Characteristics of Korean-Americans with Schizophrenia: A Cross-ethnic comparison with African-Americans, Latinos, and Euro-Americans. *Schizophrenia Bulletin, 28*(4), 703–717.

Bae, S., & Kung, W. W. (2000). Family intervention for Asian Americans with a schizophrenic patient in the family. *American Journal of Orthopsychiatry, 70*(4), 532–541. doi:10.1037/h0087789.

Barrera, M., & Garrison-Jones, C. (1992). Family and peer social support as specific correlates of adolescent depressive symptoms. *Journal of Abnormal Child Psychology, 20*, 1–16.

Basow, S. A., Lilley, E., Bookwala, J., & McGillicuddy-Delisi, A. (2008). Identity development and psychological well-being in Korean-born adoptees in the U.S. *American Journal of Orthopsychiatry, 78*, 473–480.

BBC New Asia. (2011, November 7). Tackling South Korea's high suicide rates. Retrieved on January 30, 2012, from: http://www.bbc.co.uk/news/world-asia-pacific-15331921

Beller, T., Pinker, M., Snapka, S., & Van Dusen, D. (n.d.). Koreans. *Asian Health*. Retrieved on January 30, 2013, from https://bearspace.baylor.edu/Charles_Kemp/www/korean_health.htm

Benner, A. D., & Kim, S. Y. (2010). Understanding Chinese American adolescents' developmental outcomes: Insights from the family stress model. *Journal of Research on Adolescence, 20*(1), 1–12.

Bernstein, K. S. (2007). Mental health issues among urban Korean American immigrants. *Journal of Transcultural Nursing, 18*(2), 175–180. doi:10.1177/1043659606298610.

Berry, J. (2005). Acculturation: Living successfully in two cultures. *International Journal of Intercultural Relations, 29*, 697–712. doi:10.1016/j.ijintrel.2005.07.013.

Berry, J. K., & Kim, U. (1986). Acculturation and mental health. In P. R. Dasen, J. W. Berry, & N. Sartorius (Eds.), *Health and cross-cultural psychology: Toward applications* (pp. 207–236). Newbury Park, CA: Sage Publications.

Berry, J. K., Kim, U., Minde, T., & Mok, D. (1987). Comparative studies of acculturative stress. *International Migration Review, 21*(3), 491–511.

Census Bureau, U. S. (2004). *We the people: Asians in the United States. Census 2000 special reports*. Washington, DC: Author (Census 2000 Brief No. CENSR-17).

Census Bureau, U. S. (2008). *Statistical abstract of the United States: 2008*. Washington, DC: United States Department of Commerce.

Cho, M., & Kim, K. H. (1998). Use of the Center for Epidemiologic Studies Depression (CES-D) Scale in Korea. *Journal of Nervous & Mental Disease, 186*(5), 304–310.

Choi, G. (1997). Acculturative stress, social support, and depression in Korean-American families. In P. M. Brown & J. S. Shalett (Eds.), *Cross-cultural practice with couples and families* (pp. 81–91). New York, NY: Haworth Press.

Choi, Y. J. (2006). A transcultural model of Hwa-Byung: A grounded theory. *Journal of Korean Academy of Psychiatric and Mental Health Nursing, 15*(4), 508–512.

Choi, H., Dancy, B. L., Faan, R. N., & Lee, J. (2012). Raising children in America: Korean parents' experiences. *Journal of Psychiatric and Mental Health Nursing, 1*(2), 2–6.

Choi, M., Phillips, R. L., Figueredo, A. J., Insel, K., & Min, S. K. (2008). Construct validity of the Korean women's abuse intolerance scale. *Nursing Research, 57*, 40–50.

Choi, H., Stafford, L., Meininger, J. C., Roberts, R. E., & Smith, D. P. (2002). Psychometric properties of the Dsm Scale for Depression (Dsd) with Korean-American youths. *Issues in Mental Health Nursing, 23*(8), 735–756. doi:10.1080/01612840260433631.

Choi, M., & Yeom, H. (2011). Identifying and treating the culture-bound syndrome of Hwa-Byung among older Korean immigrant women: Recommendations for practitioners. *Journal of the American Academy of Nurse Practitioners, 23*(5), 226–232. doi:10.1111/j.1745-7599.2011.00607.x.

Cook, W. H., Hofstetter, C., Kang, M., Hovell, M. F., & Irvin, V. (2009). Rethinking acculturation: A study of alcohol use of Korean American adolescents in Southern California. *Contemporary Drug Problems, 36*(1/2), 217–244.

Donnelly, P. L. (2005). Mental health beliefs and help seeking behaviors of Korean American parents of adult children with schizophrenia. *Journal of Multicultural Nursing & Health, 11*(2), 23–34.

Duranceaux, N. C., Schuckit, M. A., Luczak, S. E., Eng, M. Y., Carr, L. G., & Wall, T. L. (2008). Ethnic differences in level of response to alcohol between Chinese Americans and Korean Americans. *Journal of Studies on Alcohol and Drugs, 69*(2), 227–234.

Evan B. Donaldson Adoption Institute. (2007). *International adoption facts*. Retrieved on June 22, 2007, from http://www.adoptioninstitute.org/FactOverview/international_print.html

Freundlich, M. & Lieberthal, J. K. (2000). The gather of the first generation of adult Korean adoptees: Adoptees' perceptions of International adoption. Retrieved on October 16, 2002, from http://www.adoptioninstitute.org/proed/korfindings.html

Hahm, H. C., Lahiff, M., & Guterman, N. B. (2004). Asian American adolescents' acculturation, binge drinking, and alcohol and tobacco-using peers. *Journal of Community Psychology, 32*(3), 295–308.

Hampton, T. (2006). Interplay of genes and environment found in adolescents' alcohol abuse. *JAMA: Journal of the American Medical Association, 295*(15), 1760.

Helzer, J. E., Canino, G. J., Yeh, E. K., Bland, R. C., Lee, C. K., Hwu, H. G., & Newman, S. (1990). Alcoholism-North America and Asia. A comparison of population surveys with the Diagnostic Interview Schedule. *Archives of General Psychiatry*, *47*(4), 313–319.

Hendershot, C. S., Dillworth, T. M., Neighbors, C., & George, W. H. (2008). Differential effects of acculturation on drinking behavior in Chinese- and Korean-American college students. *Journal of Studies on Alcohol & Drugs, 69*(1), 121–128.

Hing, B. O. (1993). *Making and remaking Asian American through immigration policy, 1850-1990*. Stanford, CA: Stanford University Press.

Hopper, K., & Wanderling, J. (2000). Revisiting the developed versus developing country distinction in course and outcome in schizophrenia: Results from ISoS, the WHO collaborative follow up project. *Schizophrenia Bulletin, 26*(4), 835–846.

Hsu, G., & Folstein, M. (1997). Somatoform disorders in Caucasian and Chinese Americans. *Journal of Nervous & Mental Disease, 185*(6), 382–387.

Huang, Z. J., Wong, F. Y., Ronzio, C. R., & Yu, S. M. (2007). Depressive symptomatology and mental health help-seeking patterns of U.S.- and foreign-born mothers. *Maternal and Child Health Journal, 11*(3), 257–267. doi:10.1007/s10995-006-0168-x.

Hurh, W. M. (1998). *The Korean Americans*. Westport, CT: Greenwood Press.

Hurh, W. M., & Kim, K. C. (1990). Correlates of Korean immigrant mental health. *The Journal of Nervous and Mental Disease, 178*(11), 703–711. doi:10.1097/00005053-199011000-00006.

Hwang, W. (2006). The psychotherapy adaptation and modification framework: Application to Asian Americans. *American Psychologist, 61*(7), 702–715.

Im, E., & Meleis, A. I. (2001). Women's work and symptoms during midlife: Korean immigrant women. *Women & Health, 33*(1/2), 83–103.

Jang, Y., Chiriboga, D. A., & Kim, G. (2006). Culture and depressive symptom reports. *Korean Gerontological Research, 15*, 51–73.

Jang, Y., Kim, G., & Chiriboga, D. (2005). Acculturation and manifestation of depressive symptoms among Korean-American older adults. *Aging & Mental Health, 9*(6), 500–507. doi:10.1080/13607860500193021.

Jo, M. Y., & Dawson, L. K. (2010). *The Neuropsychology of Asian Americans. Daryl E. M. Fujii (Ed.)*. New York, NY: Psychology Press.

Johnson, W. J. & Kim-Johnson, M. (1998–1999). Sometimes love isn't enough: The voices of some adult Korean adoptees in Minnesota. *Korean American Historical Society Occasional Papers, 4*, 99–109

Kim, S. C. (1985). Family therapy for Asian Americans: A strategic-structural framework. *Psychotherapy: Theory, Research, Practice, Training, 22*(2S), 342–348. doi:10.1037/h0085513.

Kim, M. T. (1995a). Cultural influences of depression experiences among Korean Americans. *Journal of Psychosocial Nursing, 33*(2), 13–18.

Kim, W. J. (1995b). International adoption: A case review of Korean children. *Child Psychiatry and Human Development, 25*(3), 141–154.

Kim, S. C. (1997). Korean-American families. In E. Lee (Ed.), *Working with Asian Americans: A guide for clinicians* (pp. 125–135). New York, NY: Guilford Press.

Kim, O. (1999). Predictors of loneliness in elderly Korean immigrant women living in the United States of America. *Journal of Advanced Nursing, 29*, 1082–1088.

Kim, M. T. (2002). Measuring depression in Korean Americans: Development of the Kim Depression Scale for Korean Americans. *Journal of Transcultural Nursing, 13*(2), 109–117.

Kim, J. M. (2005). *Culture-specific psychoeducational induction talk as an intervention to increase service utilization among minority populations: The case of Korean Americans*. Retrieved from http://counseling-outfitters.com/vistas/vistas05/Vistas05.art27.pdf.

Kim, E. (2011). Intergenerational acculturation conflict and Korean American parents' depression symptoms. *Issues in Mental Health Nursing, 32*, 687–695.

Kim, M., Han, H., Shin, H., Kim, K., & Lee, H. (2005). Factors associated with depression experience of Immigrant populations: A study of Korean immigrants.

Archives of Psychiatric Nursing, 19(5), 217–225. doi:10.1016/j.apnu.2005.07.004.

Kim, K. C., & Kim, S. (1998). Family and work roles in Korean immigrants in the United States. In H. I. McCubbin, E. A. Thompson, A. I. Thompson, & J. E. Fromer (Eds.), *Resiliency in Native American and immigrant families* (pp. 225–242). Thousand Oaks, CA: Sage.

Kim, S., & Rew, L. (1994). Ethnic identity, role integration, quality of life, and depression in Korean-American women. *Archives of Psychiatric Nursing, 6*(8), 348–356.

Kim, G. S., Suyemoto, K. L., & Turner, C. B. (2010). Sense of belonging, sense of exclusion, and racial and ethnic identities in Korean transracial adoptees. *Cultural Diversity & Ethnic Minority Psychology, 16*, 179–190.

Kim-Goh, M. (1993). Conceptualization of mental illness among Korean-American clergymen and implications for mental health service delivery. *Community Mental Health Journal, 29*(5), 405–412. doi:10.1007/BF00754408.

Kim-Goh, M. (1998). Korean women's Hwa Byung: Clinical issues and implications for treatment. In Y. I. Song & A. Moon (Eds.), *Korean American women: From tradition to modern feminism* (pp. 225–233). Westport, CT: Praeger.

Kirmayer, L. J. (1989). Cultural variations in the response to psychiatric disorders and emotional distress. *Social Science & Medicine, 29*(3), 327–339. doi:10.1016/0277-9536(89)90281-5.

Kitano, H. H., & Daniels, R. (1995). *Asian Americans: Emerging minorities*. Englewood Cliffs, NJ: Prentice Hall.

Kleinman, A. M. (1982). Neurasthenia and depression: A study of somatization and culture in China. *Cultural Medical Psychiatry, 6*, 117–190.

Kleinman, A. (1988). *Rethinking psychiatry: From cultural category to personal experience*. New York, NY: Free Press.

Koh, K. (1998). Perceived stress, psychopathology, and family support in Korean immigrants and non-immigrants. *Yonsei Medical Journal, 39*, 214–221.

Korean Beacon. (2010). Suicide among New York Koreans on the rise. Retrieved on January 30, 2012, from http://www.koreanbeacon.com/2010/01/06/suicide-among-new-york-koreans-on-the-rise/

Kuo, W. H. (1984). Prevalence of depression among Asian-Americans. *The Journal of Nervous and Mental Disease, 172*(8), 449–457. doi:10.1097/00005053-198408000-00002.

Kwon-Ahn, H. Y. (2011). Substance abuse among Korean Americans: A sociocultural perspective and framework for intervention. In S. L. A. Shulamith (Ed.), *Ethnocultural factors in substance abuse treatment* (pp. 418–435). New York, NY: The Guilford Press.

Lee, R. M. (2003). The transracial adoption paradox: History, research, and counseling implications of cultural socialization. *The Counseling Psychologist, 31*, 711–744.

Lee, E. E., & Farran, C. J. (2004). Depression among Korean, Korean American, and Caucasian American family caregivers. *Journal of Transcultural Nursing, 15*(1), 18–25.

Lee, H. B., Hanner, J. A., Cho, S., Han, H., & Kim, M. T. (2008). Improving access to mental health services for Korean American immigrants: Moving toward a community partnership between religious and mental health services. *Psychiatry Investigation, 5*(1), 14–20. doi:10.4306/pi.2008.5.1.14.

Lee, H., Moon, A., & Knight, B. G. (2004). Depression among elderly Korean immigrants: Exploring socio-cultural factors. *Journal of Ethnic & Cultural Diversity in Social Work, 13*(4), 1–26.

Lee, D. C., & Quintana, S. M. (2005). Benefits of cultural exposure and development of Korean perspective-taking ability for trasracially adopted Korean children. *Cultural Diversity & Ethnic Minority Psychology, 111*, 130–143.

Legerski, J. P. (2006). Culture-bound syndromes: Shin-Byung. In Y. Jackson (Ed.), *Encyclopedia of multicultural psychology*. Thousand Oaks, CA: SAGE Publications. doi:10.4135/9781412952668.n74.

Leong, F. T. L., & Lau, A. S. L. (2001). Barriers to providing effective mental health services to Asian Americans. *Mental Health Services Research, 3*(4), 201–214.

Lin, K. M. (1983). Hwa-byung: A Korean culture-bound syndrome? *American Journal of Psychiatry, 140*, 105–107.

Lin, K., Inui, T. S., Kleinman, A. M., & Womack, W. M. (1982). Sociocultural determinants of the help-seeking behavior of patients with mental illness. *The Journal of Nervous and Mental Disease, 170*(2), 78–85. doi:10.1097/00005053-198202000-00003.

Lin, K. M., & Kleinman, A. M. (1988). Psychopathology and clinical course of schizophrenia: A cross-cultural perspective. *Schizophrenia Bulletin, 14*(4), 555–567.

Lin, K., Miller, M. H., Poland, R. E., Nuccio, I., & Yamaguch, M. (1991). Ethnicity and family involvement in the treatment of schizophrenic patients. *The Journal of Nervous and Mental Disease, 179*(10), 631–633. doi:10.1097/00005053-199110000-00008.

Lin, T., Tardiff, K., Donetz, G., & Goresky, W. (1978). Ethnicity and patterns of help-seeking. *Culture, Medicine and Psychiatry, 2*(1), 3–13. doi:10.1007/BF00052447.

Lovejoy, M. C., Graxzyk, P. A., O'Hare, E., & Neuman, G. (2000). Maternal depression and parenting behavior: A meta-analytic review. *Clinical Psychology Review, 20*(5), 561–592.

Lubben, J. E., Chi, I., & Kitano, H. H. L. (1989). The relative influence of selected social factors on Korean drinking behavior in Los Angeles. *Advances in Alcohol & Substance Abuse, 8*, 1–17.

McCollaum, B., & Lester, D. (1997). Locus of control, depression and suicidality in Korean workers. *Psychological Reports, 80*, 1282.

Miller, A. M., & Chandler, P. (2002). Acculturation, resilience and depression in midlife women from the former Soviet Union. *Nursing Research, 51*(1), 26–32.

Min, P. G. (2001). Changes in Korean immigrants' gender role and social status, and their marital conflicts. *Sociological Forum, 16*(2), 301–320.

Min, J. W., Moon, A., & Lubben, J. E. (2005). Determinants of psychological distress over time among older Korean immigrants and Non-Hispanic White elders: Evidence from a two-wave panel study. *Aging & Mental Health, 9*(3), 210–222. doi:10.1080/13607860500090011.

Min, S. K., Namkoong, K., & Lee, H. Y. (1990). An epidemiological study of hwabyung. *Journal of the Korean Neuropsychiatry Association, 29*, 867–874.

Min, S. K., & Suh, S. (2010). The anger syndrome hwa-byung and its comorbidity. *Journal of Affective Disorders, 124*(1–2), 211–214. doi:10.1016/j.jad.2009.10.011.

Min, S. K., Suh, S. Y., Jon, D. I., Hong, H. J., Park, S. J., & Song, K. J. (2009). Effects of Paroxetine on symptoms of Hwa-Byung. *Korean Journal of Psychopharmacology, 20*, 90–97.

Moon, A., & Tashima, N. (1982). *Help-seeking behavior and attitudes of Southeast Asian refugees*. San Francisco, CA: Pacific Asian Mental Health Research Project.

Mui, A. C. (2001). Stress, coping, and depression among elderly Korean immigrants. *Journal of Human Behavior in the Social Environment, 33*, 281–299. doi:10.1300/J137v03n03_17.

Noh, S., & Avison, W. R. (1996). Asian immigrants and the stress process: A study of Koreans in Canada. *Journal of Health and Social Behavior, 37*, 192–206.

Novas, H., Cao, L., & Silva, R. (2004). *Everything you need to know about Asian-American history*. New York: Plume.

Oh, Y., Koeske, G., & Sales, E. (2002). Acculturation, stress, and depressive symptoms among Korean immigrants in the United States. *Journal of Social Psychology, 142*(4), 511–516.

Pang, K. C. (1994). Understanding depression among elderly Korean immigrants through their folk illnesses. *Medical Anthropology Quarterly, 8*(2), 209–216. doi:10.1525/maq.1994.8.2.02a00050.

Pang, K. Y. C. (1998). Symptoms of depression in elderly Korean immigrants: Narration and the healing process. *Culture, Medicine and Psychiatry, 22*, 93–122.

Pang, K. Y. C. (2000). Symptom expression and somatization among elderly Korean immigrants. *Journal of Clinical Geropsychology, 6*(3), 199–212.

Park, S., & Bernstein, K. (2008). Depression and Korean American immigrants. *Archives of Psychiatric Nursing, 22*(1), 12–19. doi:10.1016/j.apnu.2007.06.011.

Randolph, T. H., & Holtzman, M. (2010). The role of heritage camps in identity development among Korean transnational adoptees: A relational dialectics Approach. *Adoption Quarterly, 13*(2), 75–99.

Rhee, S. (1997). Domestic violence in the Korean immigrant family. *Journal of Sociology and Social Welfare, 24*, 63–77.

Shin, K. R. (1993). Factors predicting depression among Korean American women in New York. *International Journal of Nursing Studies, 30*(5), 415–423.

Shin, K. R. (1994). Psychosocial predictors of depressive symptoms in Korean-American women in New York City. *Women & Health, 21*(1), 73–82.

Shin, J. K. (2002). Help-seeking behaviors by Korean immigrants for depression. *Issues in Mental Health Nursing, 23*(5), 461–476. doi:10.1080/01612840290052640.

Shin, J. K. (2010). Understanding the experience and manifestation of depression among Korean immigrants in New York City. *Journal of Transcultural Nursing, 21*(1), 73–80.

Shin, H. S., Han, H.-R., & Kim, M. (2007). Predictors of psychological well-being amongst Korean immigrants to the United States. A structured interview study. *International Journal of Nursing Studies, 44*(3), 415–426 (03691).

Shin, S. K., & Lukens, E. P. (2004). Effects of culturally relevant psychoeducation for Korean American families of persons with chronic mental illness. *Research on Social Work Practice, 14*(4), 231–239. doi:10.1177/1049731503262130.

Shon, S., & Ja, D. Y. (1982). Asian families. In M. McGoldrick, J. Pearce, & J. Giordano (Eds.), *Ethnicity and family therapy* (pp. 208–229). New York, NY: Guilford Press.

Simon, R. J., & Altstein, H. (2000). *Adoption across borders: Serving the children in transracial and intercountry adoptions*. New York, NY: Rowman & Littlefield.

Sue, S., & Morishima, J. K. (1982). *The mental health of Asian Americans*. San Francisco, CA: Jossey-Bass.

Suicide Prevention Action Network USA and the Suicide Prevention Resource Center. (n.d.). *Suicide among Asian Americans/Pacific Islanders*. Retrieved from http://www.sprc.org/sites/sprc.org/files/library/asian.pi.facts.pdf

Takeuchi, D. T., Zane, N., Hong, S., Chae, D. H., Gong, F., Gee, G. C., ... Alegria, M. (2007). Immigration-related factors and mental disorders among Asian Americans. *American Journal of Public Health, 97*(1), 84–90. doi: 10.2105/AJPH.2006.088401

Telles, C., Karno, M., Mintz, J., Paz, G., Arias, M., Tucker, D., & Lopez, S. (1995). Immigrant families coping with schizophrenia: Behavioural family intervention versus case management with a low-income Spanish-speaking population. *British Journal of Psychiatry, 167*, 473–479.

The Straits Times. (2012, September 10). Suicide rate in S. Korea 2.6 times higher than OECD average. Retrieved on January 30, 2012, from: http://www.straitstimes.com/breaking-news/asia-news-network/story/suicide-rate-s-korea-26-times-higher-oecd-average-20120910

Tracey, T. J., Leong, F. T. L., & Glidden, C. (1986). Help seeking and problem perception among Asian-Americans. *Journal of Counseling Psychology, 33*, 331–336.

U.S. Census Bureau. (2000). *Census 2000*. Washington, DC: U.S. Census Bureau.

U.S. Department of Health and Human Services. (2001). *Mental health: Culture, race and ethnicity—A suppl. to mental health: A report of the Surgeon General.*

Rockville, MD: U.S. Department of Health and Human Services, Public Health Service, Office of Surgeon General.

Um, C. C., & Dancy, B. L. (1999). Relationship between coping strategies and depression among employed Korean immigrant wives. *Issues in Mental Health Nursing, 20*, 485–494.

Unger, J., Trinidad, D., Weiss, J., & Rohrbach, L. (2004). Acculturation as a risk factor for smoking among Asian American adolescents: Is the association confounded by nationality? *Journal of Ethnicity in Substance Abuse, 3*(1), 65–79.

Weisman, A. G. (1997). Understanding cross-cultural prognostic variability for schizophrenia. *Cultural Diversity & Mental Health, 3*(1), 23–35. doi:10.1037//1099-9809.3.1.23.

Yamashiro, G., & Matsuoka, K. (1997). Help-seeking among Asian and Pacific Americans: A multiperspective analysis. *Social Work, 42*(2), 176–186.

Yeh, C., & Inose, M. (2002). Difficulties and coping strategies of Chinese, Japanese, and Korean immigrant students. *Adolescence, 37*(145), 69–82.

Yi, K. (1990). *English-Korean, Korean-English dictionary*. Taegu-Si, South Korea: Samsong Munhwasa.

Yi, K. Y. (2000). Shin-byung (divine illness) in a Korean woman. *Culture, Medicine and Psychiatry, 24*(4), 471–486.

Yi, S. H., & Tidwell, R. (2005). Adult Korean Americans: Their attitudes toward seeking professional counseling services. *Community Mental Health Journal, 41*(5), 571–580. doi:10.1007/s10597-005-6362-2.

Yoon, D. P. (2004). Intercountry adoption: The importance of ethnic socialization and subjective well-being for Korean-born adopted children. *Journal of Ethnic & Cultural Diversity in Social work, 13*, 71–89.

Zia, H. (2000). *Asian American dreams: The emergence of an American people*. New York, NY: Farrar, Straus, and Giroux.

Cross-Cultural Considerations with Asian Indian American Clients: A Perspective on Psychological Assessment

5

Anuradha S.K. Dutt and Phey Ling Kit

According to the US Census Bureau (2010), Asian Indian Americans constitute the third largest Asian group in the USA with a population of 3.2 million (Hoeffel, Rastogi, Kim, & Shahid, 2010). In this chapter, we will use the term Asian Indian American to refer to those who are of family descent originating from the Indian subcontinent, currently living in the USA and have either been born or have become naturalized citizens of this country.

According to Chandrasekhar (1982), the earliest records of people arriving from the Indian subcontinent to the USA can be dated back to the late 1800s. Immigrants came in as Asian laborers but were not received well by the locals, as the USA was then considered a land for European Americans (Takaki, 1989). The Barred Zone Act in 1917 and later the Exclusion Act in 1924 were exclusionary policies prohibiting Indian immigrants from entering the USA, resulting in a decrease in this population (Chandrasekhar, 1982; Ninian, 2012). However, since the establishment of the US Immigration Act of 1965, an increase in the numbers of professional Asian Indian Americans and their families has been observed. These individuals were well-educated and middle-class urban professionals who sought to advance their career aspirations or seek higher education as graduate students (Farver, Narang, & Bhadha, 2002; Ninian, 2012; Ramisetty-Mikler, 1993). Currently, a large proportion of Asian Indian Americans consist of doctors, lawyers, engineers, scientists, academicians, and aspiring graduates in universities. Career advancement has always been a motivating factor to immigrate to the USA for many Indian professionals since the 1960s and continues to be a critical reason for the increase in population of Asian Indian Americans in the "land of opportunities" (Ramisetty-Mikler, 1993).

Considering the recent expanse of Asian Indian Americans as the third largest Asian community in the USA, this chapter focuses on informing practice within a multicultural context in relation to providing culturally sensitive psychological services to individuals of Asian Indian American heritage. A systematic search of articles published in peer-reviewed journals was conducted via PsycINFO, ERIC, and Proquest Databases during the previous three decades (1979–2012). Descriptors used to conduct this search included "Asian Indian Cultural Beliefs and Practices," "Asian Indian Attitudes towards Mental Health," "Asian Indian Americans cultural beliefs," "Asian Indian Americans and Religion," "Asian Indian Americans and Counseling issues," "Asian Indian Americans and psychological testing," and "Asian Indians and developmental issues." In addition, the references within the selected articles were searched for additional relevant sources. Based on the results of our literature search, broad areas

A.S.K. Dutt, Ph.D. (✉) • P.L. Kit, Ph.D.
Psychological Studies Academic Group, National Institute of Education, Nanyang Technological University, Block 2, Level 3, Room 109, 1 Nanyang Walk, Singapore 637616, Singapore
e-mail: anuradha.dutt@nie.edu.sg; pheyling.kit@nie.edu.sg

L.T. Benuto et al. (eds.), *Guide to Psychological Assessment with Asians*,
DOI 10.1007/978-1-4939-0796-0_5, © Springer Science+Business Media New York 2014

covered in this chapter include a review of the Asian Indian American cultural context and issues related to acculturation; attitudes towards mental health, disability, and help-seeking behaviors; and guidelines to inform practice when working with Asian Indian Americans.

Cultural Context and Understanding the Asian Indian American

To understand the ethnic identity of Asian Indian Americans, it is important to consider the cultural diversity within this minority group. India consists of multiple religions, languages, states, as well as different customs and traditional practices pertaining to each state. Eight main religions, which include Hinduism, Islam, Christianity, Sikhism, Judaism, Buddhism, Jainism, and Zoroastrianism, are found in India. Hinduism is the most widely practiced religion in India. In addition, India consists of 28 states, 7 union territories, and 22 languages with their own written scripts and 26 spoken dialects (Lai & Surood, 2008; Pattanayak, 1990). Despite the presence of many languages, it is common practice for professional, working-class Indians to be fluent in English (Pattanayak, 1990). In lieu of this diversity, it would not be surprising to find a similar diaspora of languages, religions, regional cultural variations, and differing traditional values and attitudes among Asian Indian Americans in the USA.

Issues Related to Ethnic Identity Formation and Acculturation

In addition to cultural variations, it is also important to consider that immigration of Asian Indian Americans is a relatively recent phenomenon that has picked up pace since the 1960s. Hence, understanding an individual's cultural background and its impact on his or her attitudes and behaviors should be taken in light of intergenerational influences and the level of acculturation attained among Asian Indian Americans. Acculturation is a group level phenomenon and is defined as the process of change that occurs within ethnic minority individuals when they adapt to the values, attitudes, and belief systems of the dominant culture (Berry, Kim, Power, Young, & Bujaki, 1989). Specifically, it is the extent to which these individuals retain the ethnic values, customs, beliefs, and traditions of their natal culture and the degree to which they identify with the host culture (Dasgupta, 1998; Farver, Narang, & Bhadha, 2002).

According to Berry's two dimensional acculturation model (1989), ethnic group members can adapt to the dominant culture in four different ways. Individuals can solely identify with the dominant culture while rejecting their natal culture through the process of assimilation. Alternatively, they can solely identify with their natal culture while severing ties with the dominant culture through the process of separation. They can also reject values and belief systems of the natal culture as well as the dominant culture via the process of marginalization or they can develop bicultural ethnic identities by maintaining characteristics from both cultural groups via the process of integration.

Broadly speaking, this minority group can be divided into first-generation and second-generation Asian Indian Americans. First generation Asian Indian Americans are those who moved to the USA in the mid 1960s in the pursuit of a better life, personally and professionally (Das & Kemp, 1997). This group of Asian Indian Americans generally have a strong affinity for traditional Indian roots and often attempt to recreate the same cultural milieu in a foreign land (Dasgupta, 1998; Farver, Xu, Bhadha, Narang & Lieber, 2007). In fact, first generation Asian Indian Americans are sometimes more "Indian" than the residents in India, as they struggle to retain the same sense of culture and tradition they had left with many decades ago despite changes that may have occurred since their departure from India (Farver, Narang, & Bhadha, 2002; Patel, Power, & Bhavnagri, 1996). In accordance to Berry's model (1989), this group of Asian Indian Americans would usually fall under the preferred acculturative mode of separation. In contrast, second-generation Asian Indian Americans are usually born on American soil and are socialized into two cultures. They are acculturated to both the traditional Indian culture of the family and the wider dominant culture of the American society (Das & Kemp, 1997; Farver et al., 2007). With reference to Berry's model, most members of this group attempt to develop a bicultural ethnic identity by integrating characteristics from both cultures.

The literature on acculturation suggests that higher levels of acculturative stress are associated with minority groups adhering either to the marginalization or the separation acculturation mode (Berry et al., 1989). Furthermore, a difference in the degree of acculturation not only has an impact on the difference in the development and maintenance of ethnic identity across the two generations but also contributes to a host of stressors that may be qualitatively different across both generation groups (Farver, Narang, & Bhadha, 2002). With Asian Indian American families, variations in attitudes and behaviors across the two generations may be observed in differences in perspectives towards gender roles, marriage, family structure and roles, child rearing practices, adherence to religious customs, social interactions and pro-social behaviors, and mental health issues (Ibrahim, Ohnishi, & Sandhu, 1997; Ramisetty-Mikler, 1993).

In addition to the stressors experienced by many Asian Indian Americans adapting to the values, attitudes, behavior, and belief systems of the dominant culture, another area of concern includes the acceptance of this minority population by other cultural groups in the USA. Asian Indian Americans who have different accents and sometimes lack fluency in the English language may experience problems with communication. In addition, their style of dressing (e.g., use of Indian attire), skin color, physical appearance, formal social behaviors, and mannerisms may result in other cultural groups perceiving them as being different or strange. Negative outcomes of such social situations may result in developing stereotypical perceptions of other cultural groups and feelings of isolation which could be considered as a potential source of adjustment stress (Sodowsky & Carey, 1987).

Issues Related to Family Structure, Role Expectations, and Child Rearing Practices

For Asian Indian Americans, family is the fundamental unit in one's society as well as a source of emotional and social support. First-generation Asian Indian Americans generally view the family structure as being formal and hierarchical with each member having a designated role. In traditional family units, the father is usually considered the head of the family, sole bread winner, enforcer of family rules, and decision maker whose authority should not be questioned. The mother is typically viewed as being nurturing and serving as the primary caretaker of the children's day-to-day needs. Children's compliance to parental demands and reverence for elders are considered essential family values. It is not uncommon for older generations to expect their children to care for them in their old age. It is also not uncommon to find married sons living with their families and parents in the same physical space. Furthermore, it is not unusual for traditional family units to place high expectations on their sons, as they would traditionally be responsible with carrying the family name for future generations (Ramisetty-Mikler, 1993).

In most Asian Indian American families, major decisions regarding education, occupation, scholastic and extracurricular activities, marriage, and social behaviors align with the approval of the elders or heads of the family. Attitudes, behaviors, and decisions that are in conflict with family values and rules are viewed in an extremely negative light. In such situations, guilt, shame, and moral obligation towards the family are instrumental in redirecting and governing behaviors and attitudes that conform to familial values and needs. Asian Indian American families usually follow an authoritarian parenting style and family needs are always placed before the needs of the individual members (Inman, Howard, Beaumont, & Walker, 2007; Ramisetty-Mikler, 1993). Professional achievement, academic success, and education are given paramount importance. Failure to achieve these goals could be considered a source of stress for many Asian

Indian American families (Ramisetty-Mikler, 1993; Rao, McHale, & Pearson, 2003). However, despite the rigidity in family structure, a few changes are being observed in family role expectations over the last few decades. For instance, immigrant families allow their children to enjoy more freedom and independence (Sinha, 1985) and immigrant mothers have become more authoritative in their parenting style (Ramisetty-Mikler, 1993).

Although flexibility in family role expectations has recently been observed, differential rates of acculturation across first-generation and second-generation family members may result in an increased risk for familial conflict. This usually occurs when second-generation adolescents or young adults have acculturated more rapidly with their host culture in the USA when compared to their first-generation parents. Common areas of familial conflict and family related stress are observed when second-generation adolescents or young adults desire more independence with decisions related to dating, career choices, and marriage (Farver, Narang, & Bhadha, 2002; Inman et al., 2007). In fact, research has indicated that less disparity in acculturation between generations in a family are associated with positive outcomes such as ethnic identity achievement, high self-esteem, lower familial conflict, and higher GPAs among Asian Indian American adolescents (Farver et al., 2007).

Issues Related to Gender Roles and Expectations

Educational level, social class, economic stability, and levels of acculturation are important factors that affect attitudes and behaviors towards gender roles and expectations among Asian Indian Americans. Gender identity may range from patriarchal to egalitarian. First-generation Asian Indian Americans often define gender roles as clearly demarcated and rigid in their definition. This group usually perceives men as being the bread winners and financial providers for the family while women manage the domestic domains of the home (Ibrahim et al., 1997). The eldest male member of the family is considered to be the head of the family and is responsible for taking all the major family decisions (Das & Kemp, 1997). First-generation Asian Indian American women usually tend to be more passive (Chowdhury, 2005; Prakash, 2003; Shaikh & Hatcher, 2004) and economically more dependent than their male counterparts as they are considered to be lower in status and power when compared to the male members of the family (Jejeebhoy & Sathar, 2001; Rani & Bonu, 2003). In fact, women in traditional Asian Indian American families are typically expected to place their family needs before their own (Arnold, Choe, & Roy, 1998; Narayan, Patel, Schafft, Rademacher, & Koch-Schulte, 2000).

An extremely traditional outlook towards gender roles entails males being viewed as more desirable compared to females as they are perceived to provide economic stability to the family. In addition, women are considered liabilities, in conservative, less educated, middle and lower class Indian families, as the Hindu custom of dowry for the female child may still be prevalent in some conservative Indian families (Das & Kemp, 1997). Furthermore, it is not uncommon for gender inequality to prevail within traditional Indian families (Choudhury, 2006), with both genders being discriminated against in different ways, thus threatening the security and well-being of family life (Choudhury & Carson, 2006).

In terms of gender role expression in psychological settings, women in traditional Indian families are perceived as more socially and emotionally dependent on other family members and therefore may be more comfortable with openly expressing their grievances in an emotional manner (Hussain & Cochrane, 2003). In contrast, men are expected to be aloof, tough, independent and non-expressive with their emotions. Therefore, it is more likely that men would avoid disclosing problems of an emotional nature (Agarwal, 1998; Kai, 1999; Mathuranath, George, Cherian, Matthew, & Sarma, 2005; Sudha, Suchindran, Mutran, Rajan, & Sanna, 2007).

With reference to marital practices and decisions in this area, a majority of the marriages among first-generation Asian Indian Americans are arranged and divorce rates are low. It is common practice for first-generation Asian Indian Americans to marry within their ethnic group, social caste, economic class, and religious denomination. Furthermore, it is expected that parents select potential mates for their children, especially daughters. This practice has usually led to the restriction or total prohibition of dating and/or expression of any form of sexuality for daughters of Asian Indian American families. For traditional Indian couples that have recently moved to the USA, new stressors may develop, especially if the husband is trying to establish a career and the wife is left alone at home with minimum contact with the outside world. This is a particularly important issue as extended Indian families in India often live together, and women tend to obtain a lot of support from other females in their families (Wasan, Neufeld, & Jayaram, 2009). Although this issue may be transitory in nature, it could have the potential to result in emotional distress, physical illness, and marital conflicts (Das & Kemp, 1997).

Despite the conservative perception in gender identity and roles amongst first-generation Asian Indian Americans, more flexible and egalitarian gender roles are observed across second-generation Asian Indian Americans. In recent years, arranged marriages are not necessarily the norm though marrying within the same culture and caste are still considered important (Khanna, McDowell, Perumbilly, & Titus, 2009). Marital decisions are made based on factors such as equality in educational levels, social class, and economic independence across both genders. In fact, dual income family providers are preferred over single income families among second-generation Asian Indian Americans as this typically ensures better economic stability and a higher quality of life. Furthermore, women are encouraged to participate in family decision making and more freedom in choice of career, dating practices, and marriage partners are observed in families that have assimilated to mainstream American culture (Das & Kemp, 1997).

Issues Related to Indian Customs, Values, and Belief Systems

When understanding Asian Indian Americans, whether first or second generation, it is important to consider the cultural values and belief systems that have been instilled within the family unit. Literature suggests that first-generation Asian Indian American immigrants continue to emphasize specific values and goals to their second-generation children—values that were instilled during their own upbringing (Inman et al., 2007). A few of the values that hold importance to Asian Indian Americans involve family interdependence, a strong sense of duty (or Dharma) towards the family, and protection of family honor. Individuality is encouraged within the confines and boundaries set by the family. Therefore, Asian Indian Americans are considered to be more allocentric in their predisposition as opposed to the egocentrism that is more common in Western cultures (Ibrahim et al., 1997; Das & Kemp, 1997). Asian Indian Americans believe in maintaining harmony in social interactions and therefore may be nonconfrontational and view silence as a virtue. Respect for the elderly and older individuals of the family (e.g., parents, older siblings etc.) are given much importance as Asian Indian Americans are taught to believe that "older means wiser" and one has much to learn from the advice given by the elderly because of wisdom the elderly have collected over the years. This respect is also extended to the larger community where sensitivity towards the social climate and formality in social interactions is emphasized (Das & Kemp, 1997).

In terms of intimate interpersonal relationships, modesty in sexual expression and affection in public settings is expected. Furthermore, emphasis is placed on Karma, or the law of cause and effect, especially among first-generation Asian Indian Americans who practice Hinduism, Jainism, or Buddhism. Karma posits that the type and quality of health and life one experiences in the present life is the direct result of one's deeds and actions in one's past lives. In the same vein, one's current behaviors can affect one's future lives (Lai & Surood, 2008). Hence, Karma is about retribution for one's past and future actions. Therefore, in the face of challenges, Asian Indian Americans are expected to be patient and endure this retribution to break the cycle of negativity, as this would ensure a better existence for their future lives. Attitudes and behaviors that are considered essential in character development and conform to the idea of Karma, include humility in one's actions, moderation in behavior, discipline and obedience, and a high regard for learning. Attitudes and behaviors that are in conflict with these values may be a source of stress for many Asian Indian Americans as they may fear "losing face" with their larger ethnic community (Das & Kemp, 1997; Ibrahim et al., 1997).

Attitudes Towards Mental Illness, Disability, and Help-Seeking Behaviors

Literature suggests that mental illness or disability among traditional Asian Indian Americans is considered an inherited defect borne of supernatural causes such as spirit possession or retribution for one's Karma or sins committed in past lives (Leung, Cheung, & Tsui, 2012; Parashar, Chan, & Leierer, 2008; Ramisetty-Mikler, 1993). In particular, traditional Asian Indian Americans hold higher superstitious causal beliefs towards mental illness rather than factoring in a biological or environmental basis to mental illness when compared to Western cultural groups (Soorkia, Rosemary, & Swami, 2011).

Keeping awareness of mental health challenges within the family is perceived as a necessary measure to avoid social stigma, maintain family honor, and reduce the chance of being rejected by the larger ethnic community as a whole (Leung et al., 2012; Parashar et al., 2008). Particularly, nondisclosure of psychiatric conditions such as depression and schizophrenia and disabilities such as intellectual disability are prevalent among Asian Indian Americans, because these are considered as least preferred disability types and are associated with the highest levels of stigmatization (Parashar et al., 2008). In fact, traditional Asian Indian American families are reticent about accessing psychological services, as this could potentially endanger the chances of marriage for other family members. Disclosure of a psychiatric illness or disability in the family may be suggestive of a genetic predisposition to mental illness or disability that could be passed on to future generations (Das & Kemp, 1997).

Furthermore, mental illnesses are often perceived as a character weakness rather than a treatable illness among traditional Asian Indian Americans. Therefore, traditional Asian Indian American families would prefer to turn to spiritual healers, occult practices and rituals, and complementary alternative medicine (CAM) such as Ayurveda (herbal medicines) or homeopathic remedies as a cure for these conditions (Ramisetty-Mikler, 1993). Of note, the use of CAM is much higher in Asian Indian American women and the elderly than Asian Indian American men (Misra, Balagopal, & Klatt, 2010). This could be due to the fact that the former two groups, particularly women and senior citizens that are new immigrants, tend to be domesticated, home-bound and have less contact with influences outside their home (Mathuranath et al., 2005; Sudha et al., 2007). Hence, they are more likely to seek support from their extended family, which would usually encourage the use of CAM and other traditional healing methods. Additionally, factors that result in a strong adherence to traditional Indian cultural values may contribute to the rejection of counseling or psychotherapeutic services (Soorkia et al., 2011). The first factor involves a preference towards sharing personal and intimate information with members of the family rather than a counselor, as seeking counseling could be perceived as a shameful practice by traditional Asian Indian American families (Das & Kemp, 1997; Soorkia et al., 2011). A second factor that may inhibit the need to seek mental health services includes the desire to maintain high standards of social and personal morality. In accordance with traditional Indian cultural values, excesses in any behavior or habit such as substance abuse or domestic violence are considered to be borne of poor emotional self-control. Therefore, disclosure of such sensitive information may suggest that the help-seeker is weak and has failed to maintain high standards of moral conduct. This perception could in turn affect the help-seeker's psychological well-being (Das & Kemp, 1997). A third factor that contributes to the underutilization of mental health services among Asian Indian Americans is the perception that counseling and psychotherapy are services required by individuals with severe psychological disorders and mental illness. The practice of seeking professional help to solve everyday problems does not exist, simply because it is usually taken care of by elders in the immediate and extended families. A fourth factor that results in the rejection of psychological services, particularly among Asian Indian American males, is the notion of maintaining a masculine exterior by denying vulnerabilities and concealing emotional and physical fragility that would not be possible within a counseling setting (Soorkia et al., 2011). Finally, as the mental health profession is dominated by Caucasian Americans, cultural mistrust towards this culture group is an important factor that can result in the underutilization of mental health services and negative attitudes towards psychological help-seeking behaviors among Asian Indian Americans (Soorkia et al., 2011).

Another notion prevalent among Asian Indian Americans is the preference for physical pathology over psychological distress, as physical symptoms to illness are perceived as a healthcare concern and therefore are considered treatable. Hence, it is not uncommon for Asian Indian Americans Americans to somatize psychological distress as it is viewed as culturally acceptable and less stigmatizing (Gilbert, 2002; Gilbert, Gilbert, & Sanghera, 2004). For instance, depression, the most common referral among Asian Indian Americans in Western countries (i.e., Canada, the USA, and the UK) and in India, is primarily presented with physical manifestations such as generalized aches (Bhugra & Mastrogianni, 2004; Bhui, Bhugra, & Goldberg, 2000; Bhui, Bhugra, Goldberg, Dunn, & Desai, 2001; Mukherji, 1995; Rait & Burns, 1997), loss of energy, sleep disorders, reduced libido (Wasan et al., 2009), and gastric pains (Ecks, 2004, 2005). Given the high rate of somatization of mental illness, it is therefore not surprising that research has found that Asian Indian Americans endorse the use of medications to treat mental illness that are associated with physical distress, as they believe that it would produce quicker and more satisfactory results. In addition, medication is viewed as more accessible, quicker, and affordable option than psychological treatments (Varghese, 2007).

Guidelines for Practice with Asian Indian Americans

The role of culture in clients' help-seeking attitudes cannot be stressed enough. Like many other Asian ethnicities, Asian Indian Americans who adhere strongly to traditional Indian values of family privacy and nonpublic expression of feelings are less likely to seek help from non-family members, particularly for mental health problems, which as discussed are considered a sign of weakness and which bring shame to the family (Khanna et al., 2009; Leung et al., 2012; Uba, 1994). Also, the underutilization of mental health services among Asian Indian Americans might occur because individual needs are met via other alternatives, such as through consulting with medical physicians, religious or spiritual leaders, herbal doctors or friends and family (Leung et al., 2012). Hence, mental health professionals should be aware of these beliefs, and be able to identify and acknowledge them when they arise so that they are able to work with, within and around these restrictions. Considering these findings, reframing mental health services to promote help-seeking behaviors and attitudes among Asian Indian Americans is required to better manage psychological issues (Leung et al., 2012).

Research suggests that anxiety and depression are prevalent among Asian Indian American because of stressors related to unemployment (Leung et al., 2012), immigration status (Khanna et al., 2009), familial and relationship conflicts associated with the acculturation gap between first-generation and second-generation Asian Indian Americans (Das & Kemp, 1997; Farver, Narang, & Bhadha, 2002), and adjustment issues with the dominant culture in the USA (Ramisetty-Mikler, 1993). The following guidelines are offered as a framework to make psychological services more accessible to Asian Indian Americans to meet their mental health needs. It is important to consider that most suggestions presented in this section should be implemented simultaneously rather than sequentially to better address the needs of the Asian Indian American clientele when providing culturally sensitive psychological services.

Reframing and Increasing Service Utilization by Customizing Service Delivery Methods

One of the reasons for the stigma and consequent high need for self-concealment of mental illness (Choi & Wynne, 2000) is that new Asian Indian American immigrants may not have been exposed to much information about the causes and interventions for mental health issues and therefore have different understandings of such issues (Choi & Wynne, 2000). Hence, to reduce the stigma associated with mental illness and increase help-seeking behaviors amongst Asian Indian Americans, it might be helpful for mental healthcare providers to promote mental well-being programs rather than curative programs. Mental well-being programs can focus on providing basic information about mental health issues, psychoeducational programs, and personal development counseling to enhance mental wellness (CHAT, 2010; Khanna et al., 2009; NIE Wellness Centre, 2012). Such alternatives may be more agreeable to Asian Indian American clients who are emotionally troubled, but are not ready to seek help for their psychological issues. These alternative could also help these clients learn more about their conditions and provide them with avenues to seek help that are less stigmatizing.

Alternatively, there may be some potential Asian Indian American clients who might recognize the need for help, but might not be ready to reveal their identities in a public venue. Research has suggested that counselors need to remember that like other Asian groups, Asian Indian Americans might be uncomfortable with individual face-to-face counseling in a structured time and place (Arthur, 1997; Fouad, 1991; Hayes & Lin, 1994; Siegel, 1991). Hence, the steps needed to access services could include help seekers to obtain a first consultation via non-face-to-face methods, such as telephone helplines or online chat rooms (Chang, Yeh, & Krumboltz, 2001), both of which provide relative anonymity. More importantly, such anonymous methods of communication allow mental health workers to respect Asian Indian American cultural beliefs about mental illness and cater to their need for self-concealment (Masuda & Boone, 2011). Once sufficient trust and rapport has been built between the therapist and the anonymous client on the phone or on-line, then it would be easier to move these sessions to a therapeutic counseling setting (Alife, 2013; Coman, Burrows, & Evans, 2001; Flynn, Taylor, & Pollard, 1992; Masuda & Boone, 2011; Pregnancy Crisis Service, 2012; Swinson, Fergus, Cox, & Wickwire, 1995).

Using Systems-Based Therapeutic Approaches

It is important to recognize the cultural variations that exist across individuals of this ethnic minority group within the broader context of acculturation (Khanna et al., 2009; Ramisetty-Mikler, 1993) in the USA. Literature on Asian Indian Americans suggest that first-generation and second-generation Asian Indian Americans may hold different perceptions on expected family roles, gender identity roles, and attitudes towards social conventions such as marriage, dating, interactions with other cultural groups and career choices (Das & Kemp, 1997; Dasgupta, 1998; Farver, Narang, & Bhadha, 2002: Khanna et al., 2009). Therefore it would be helpful for mental health professionals to understand the client's acculturation status (Garcia & Zea, 1997) using Berry's two dimensional acculturation model (1989) or Sue's model (1981) on minority identity development (Ramisetty-Mikler, 1993).

Although the literature suggests that first-generation Asian Indian Americans usually follow the acculturation mode of separation whereas second-generation Asian Indian Americans seem to be more bicultural in their ethic identification (Das & Kemp, 1997; Dasgupta, 1998; Farver, Narang, & Bhadha, 2002), our experience working with Asian Indian American families suggests that mental health professionals should directly ask the client their perceptions on various social and cultural issues. This assists mental health professionals to avoid making any inaccurate assumptions regarding the client's cultural worldview. In addition, direct questioning also aids in acquiring a comprehensive picture of the client's ethnic identity by understanding his/her multiple identifications in terms of age, gender, community, caste, religion, sexual orientation, and socio-economic status (Braun, Fine, Grief, & Devenny, 2010; Ibrahim et al., 1997). Furthermore, to gain a better understanding on the client's acculturation status, we find it most useful to ask the client questions on their perceptions on family and/or marital relationships, gender roles, religious/spiritual practices, cultural traditions, social conventions, and parenting practices (to name a few) to gain a better understanding of their acculturation status.

As most Asian Indian Americans have a culturally collectivistic orientation, it is important to understand the various social influences that may or may not have an impact on the client's attitudes and behaviors (Khanna et al., 2009). Bronfenbrenner's ecological model (1979) provides a comprehensive framework to examine the various social systems (such as the client's immediate and extended family, friends, religious groups, and larger community) and its influences (Ramisetty-Mikler, 1993). As family is the most prominent influence for many Asian Indian American clients, it is essential to understand the client's family structure, gender role expectations, class relationships, intergenerational relations, and expectations of filial duties (Khanna et al., 2009). Maybe more importantly, it is necessary to evaluate how the client's perceptions could be different or similar to the beliefs held by his/her immediate and extended family members. For some clients, the perceptions held by their friends, religious affiliations, and the larger community hold significance. Hence, when working with Asian Indian Americans who hold more traditional Asian Indian values, it is essential for the therapist to take into account these various contextual influences and the impact of both immediate and extended families on clients' decision making process and level of coping. (Leung et al., 2012).

Furthermore, the collectivistic nature of Asian Indian culture indicates that individuals in this culture often define themselves in relation to the people around them and the social situations they are in (Markus & Kitayama, 1998; Markus, Mullally, & Kitayama, 1997; Yeh & Hwang, 2000). Change can only take place with the help and in the context of the people whom the client interacts most with, i.e., his/her family, community, and social system (Yeh & Hwang, 2000). It may therefore be unrealistic for the therapists to expect their clients to make decisions that are independent of these systems—a concept that may be alien to the Western perspective of therapy. In such situations, the treatment dyad should therefore shift from "therapist-client" to "therapist-family," and the ethics of care should also shift from what's best for the client to what's best for the client in conjunction with the family (Wasan et al., 2009). Hence, it is important for therapists to engage the family in the therapeutic process and involve the family as the client's most important resource outside of therapy. For severely mentally ill clients, particularly those suffering from psychosis, the family may be key informants of the clients' medical history and therefore would play an important role in confirmation of diagnosis and medical management (Wasan et al., 2009). It is therefore recommended that the key focus of therapy is on enhancing the supportive aspects of the family system so as to maximize the family's ability to manage the care of the client. If family issues/stressors are the precipitating and perpetuating factors of the client's problem, then it might be helpful for the therapist to provide family therapy using a systemic approach.

Our experience with clients of Asian Indian American background supports that this minority group shows a strong preference towards psychological services that are more family based.

Therefore, assessment and treatment goals that are in conflict with the client's family and cultural values more often lead to poorer treatment outcomes such as noncompliance with treatment recommendations and/or premature termination of psychological services. Alternatively, treatment recommendations are perceived positively if they aim to facilitate family cooperation to allow flexibility in decision making instead of focusing on individualism that may affect the family structure. Our observations support the findings indicated in the literature on multicultural issues that need to be considered when working with Asian Indian Americans (Ibrahim et al., 1997; Khanna et al., 2009; Leung et al., 2012; Ramisetty-Mikler, 1993).

Using Directive Therapeutic Approaches

To successfully obtain the required information from the Asian Indian American client, therapists need to adopt counseling techniques or communication styles that are respectful and directive. Traditional Asian Indian Americans often assume that health care problems are usually beyond the control of patients, and therefore doctors have the responsibility of playing a very active role in identifying patient problems and providing solutions (Yeh, Hunter, Madan-Bahel, Chiang, & Arora, 2004). Contrary to Western forms of psychotherapy, this belief is also applied to therapists and mental health professionals who are expected to play a more active and "expert" role in problem identification and solution generation (Lee & Armstrong, 1995; Wasan et al., 2009). In fact, the literature indicates that client-centered therapy that involves extreme verbalization and self-disclosure of thinking processes and feelings may not meet the needs of this client population as it is in conflict with their cultural values of modesty in thought, action, and humility (Ibrahim et al., 1997; Ramisetty-Mikler, 1993). Instead, approaches that are more cognitively inclined such as psycho-education or collaborative decision making between the client and therapist are perceived as more useful in building a therapeutic alliance, as it allows the therapist to be more active in communication, self-disclosure, and advice giving (Khanna et al., 2009). In addition, the use of narratives (e.g., success and challenges faced by other Asian Indian Americans as examples), direct role playing techniques, and progress monitoring of skills have been considered instrumental in developing a comfortable therapeutic environment (Ramisetty-Mikler, 1993).

Finally, as the Asian Indian American client initially tends to be more passive in the therapeutic process, the communicative context is often saturated with nonverbal messages. In a few situations, the client's words may contradict his/her nonverbal behaviors. Hence under these circumstances, it would be helpful for therapists to be more sensitive to these nonverbal cues during the therapeutic process. Also, learning more about the nonverbal behaviors that are prevalent among Asian Indian American could help therapists gain a better understanding of the client's needs, attitude, and behaviors during the initial stages of therapy (Ibrahim et al., 1997; Khanna et al., 2009).

Allocating Counselors Based on Client Values and Gender Preferences

Considering the strict hierarchical nature of Indian society (Kakar & Kakar, 2009), mental health care providers must be aware that Asian Indian clients view people in terms of their positions/ranks relative to their own. For example, research in the USA has found that Asian American students, including Asian Indian Americans, tend to have greater respect for those whom they perceive as having more authority, knowledge, or expertise than them. Hence, they are more likely to develop positive relationships with "expert" counselors than "non-expert" ones (Shea & Yeh, 2008).

The patriarchal nature of Asian Indian American families also impacts Asian Indian American perceptions of gender-related authority. In the Indian Subcontinent, men are usually perceived as having more power and authority than women (Jejeebhoy & Sathar, 2001; Rani & Bonu, 2003).

Hence, more traditional Asian Indian Americans, as well as first-generation Asian Indian Americans, may prefer male therapists since these are perceived to have more authority than their female counterparts (Shea & Yeh, 2008).

Societal beliefs about male–female relationships could also have an impact on the gender of the therapist chosen to work with Asian Indian American clients (Rathod, Kingdon, Phiri, & Gobbi, 2010). For example, there may be objections to female therapists working with male clients or vice-versa, as public knowledge of this could put a strain on marital or familial relationships (Rathod et al., 2010). Therefore having the same gender treatment dyad may be helpful in facilitating the treatment process.

Given these cultural and societal beliefs, it is important for mental healthcare providers, particularly intake personnel, to check with potential clients about gender preferences for their therapist, and to respect and accede to their clients' choices. Doing so could potentially increase commitment to the therapeutic regime while reducing resistance towards building trust, rapport and disclosure during the therapeutic process.

Collaborating with Medical Professionals and Indigenous Healers

Literature suggests that Asian Indian Americans tend to be conservative and reserved with self-disclosure and often somatize their mental health issues (Leung et al., 2012). Therefore, given this high rate of somatization of mental illness amongst Asian Indian Americans (Gilbert, 2002; Gilbert et al., 2004), it is not uncommon for clients of this minority group to first seek assistance from primary health care providers. Considering this finding, it could be prudent for psychologists to collaborate with physicians to develop effective ways to assist Asian Indian Americans to become more accepting of receiving treatment. Treatment options in the form of allopathy and psychotherapy could be helpful in alleviating symptoms of depression and anxiety that are most prevalent in Asian Indian Americans (Leung et al., 2012).

The effectiveness of collaborating with indigenous healers (e.g., astrologers, yoga professionals, experts in Ayurveda etc.) in the therapeutic process has not been researched much in the multicultural literature. However it has been observed that some Asian Indian Americans may recruit alternative therapeutic and medicinal approaches to treat mental health issues (Misra et al., 2010). Therefore, if the Asian Indian American client appears to be more inclined towards seeking indigenous forms of healing, then it would be helpful for the therapist to acknowledge the participation of indigenous healers in the client's therapeutic process (Constantine, Myers, Kindaichi, & Moore, 2004; Khanna et al., 2009). For example, the therapist could collaborate with indigenous healers to create therapeutic formats that would fit within the client's understanding of mental illness or disabilities. However this could only be possible if the therapist and indigenous healer share similar collaborative attitudes and goals with the client. If direct collaboration is not possible, then we recommend that therapists at least other forms of help that the client would be comfortable using while undergoing Western-styled therapy (Highlen, 1996). This form of collaboration could be helpful for traditional Asian Indian Americans, especially if spiritual healing is part of their cultural worldview (Lee & Armstrong, 1995). Furthermore, collaboration of this nature could also aid to empower the client to gain insight into his own problems and create appropriate solutions that are compatible with their own cultural schema.

Conclusion

The immigration of Asian Indian Americans is a relatively recent phenomenon that has picked up pace since the 1960s. Currently, this minority population broadly consists of two generations—first- and second-generation immigrants. In addition, the Asian Indian American community consists of a diaspora of diverse languages, religions, class, education levels, and regional cultural variations. Despite this diversity, there exists commonly held beliefs, values, attitudes, and behaviors that may be considered when understanding the cultural context of this minority ethnic group. In addition to the cultural context, the degree of acculturation between first-generation and second-generation immigrants should also be considered when evaluating the needs of clientele from this ethnic group.

Stressors within this group could arise from issues related to unemployment, immigration status, familial and relationship conflicts associated with the acculturation gap between first-generation and second-generation Asian Indian Americans, and adjustment issues with the dominant culture in the USA. Furthermore, these stressors have resulted in the high prevalence of mental health issues such as anxiety and depression among Asian Indian Americans.

Despite the presence of mental health issues, psychological services are not being adequately used by Asian Indian Americans. Factors associated with the underutilization of mental health services include a strong adherence to traditional Indian values and practices, and the stigma associated with mental illness and psychological services. Solutions to make psychological services more accessible and acceptable for Asian Indian Americans include reframing mental services by using nonconventional forms of service delivery, collaborating with other professionals, and using system-based approaches to therapy.

References

Agarwal, B. (1998). Widows vs. daughters or widows as daughters. *Modern Asian Studies, 32*, 1–48.

Alife. (2013). Counselling Services. Retrieved from http://www.alife.org.sg/index.php?option=com_content&view=article&id=209

Arnold, F., Choe, M. K., & Roy, T. K. (1998). Son preference, the family-building process and child mortality in India. *Population Studies, 52*, 301–305. doi:10.1080/00324720310001 50486.

Arthur, N. (1997). Counselling issues with international students. *Canadian Journal of Counselling, 31*, 259–274.

Berry, J. W., Kim, U., Power, S., Young, M., & Bujaki, M. (1989). Acculturating attitudes in plural societies. *Applied Psychology, 38*, 185–206.

Bhugra, D., & Mastrogianni, A. (2004). Globalization and mental disorders: Overview with relation to depression. *British Journal of Psychiatry, 184*, 10–20. doi:10.1192/bjp.184.1.10.

Bhui, K., Bhugra, D., & Goldberg, D. (2000). Cross-cultural validity of Amritsar Depression Inventory and the General Health Questionnaire amongst Asian and Punjabi care attenders. *Social Psychiatry and Psychiatric Epidemiology, 35*, 248–254. doi:10.1007/s001270050235.

Bhui, K., Bhugra, D., Goldberg, D., Dunn, G., & Desai, M. (2001). Cultural influence on the prevalence of common mental disorder, general practitioners' assessments and help-seeking among Punjabi and Asian people visiting their general practitioner. *Psychological Medicine, 31*, 815–825. doi:10.1017/S0033291701003853.

Braun, F. K., Fine, E. S., Grief, D. C., & Devenny, J. M. (2010). Guidelines for multicultural assessment: An Asian Indian American case study. *Journal of Multicultural Counseling & Development, 38*, 130–141. doi:10.1002/j.2161-1912.2010.tb00121.x.

Bronfenbrenner, U. (1979). *The ecology of human development*. Cambridge, MA: Harvard University Press.

Chandrasekhar, S. (1982). A history of United States legislation with respect to immigration from India: Some statistics on Asian Indian immigration to the United States of America. In S. Chandrasekhar (Ed.), *From India to America: A brief history of immigration, problems of discrimination, admission and assimilation* (pp. 11–29). La Jolla, CA: Population Review.

Chang, T., Yeh, C., & Krumboltz, J. D. (2001). Process and outcome evaluation of an on-line support group for Asian American male college students. *Journal of Counseling Psychology, 48*, 319–329. doi:10.1037/0022-0167.48.3.319.

CHAT. (2010). Youth in mind. Retrieved from http://www.youthinmind.sg/

Choi, K., & Wynne, M. E. (2000). Providing services to Asian Americans with developmental disabilities and their families: Mainstream service providers' perspective. *Community Mental Health Journal, 36*, 589–595. doi:10.1023/A:1001934202450.

Choudhury, R. (2006). Understanding family life in India. In A. Chowdhury, D. K. Carson, & C. K. Carson (Eds.), *Family life education in India: Perspectives, challenges, and applications* (pp. 31–57). Jaipur: Rawat Publications.

Choudhury, A., & Carson, D. K. (2006). Developing resiliency in contemporary Indian families. In A. Chowdhury, D. K. Carson, & C. K. Carson (Eds.), *Family life education in India: Perspectives, challenges, and applications* (pp. 248–278). Jaipur: Rawat Publications.

Chowdhury, N. (2005). The assimilation of Bengali immigrants in the United States. Conference Papers-merican Sociological Association, 2005 Annual Meeting, Philadelphia, PA, pp. 1–20.

Coman, G. J., Burrows, G. D., & Evans, B. J. (2001). Telephone counselling in Australia: Applications and considerations for use. *British Journal Of Guidance & Counselling, 29*(2), 247–258. doi: 10.1080/03069880020047166.

Constantine, M. G., Myers, L. J., Kindaichi, M., & Moore, J. L., III. (2004). Exploring indigenous mental health practices: The roles of healers and helpers in promoting well-being in people of color. *Counseling and Values, 48*, 110–125. doi:10.1002/j.2161-007X.2004.tb00238.x.

Das, A. K., & Kemp, S. F. (1997). Between Two Worlds: Counseling South Asian Americans. *Journal of Multicultural Counseling & Development, 25*(1), 23–33. doi:10.1002/j.2161-1912.1997.tb00313.x.

Dasgupta, S. D. (1998). Gender roles and cultural continuity in the Asian Indian immigrant community in the U.S. *Sex Roles, 38*, 953–973.

Ecks, S. (2004). Bodily sovereignty as political sovereignty: 'Self-care' in Kolkata, India. *Anthropology and Medicine, 1*, 75–89. doi:10.1080/1364847042000204906.

Ecks, S. (2005). Pharmaceutical citizenship: Antidepressant marketing and the promise of demarginalization in India. *Anthropology and Medicine, 2*, 239–254. doi:10.1080/13648470500291360.

Farver, J. A., Narang, S. K., & Bhadha, B. R. (2002). East meets west: Ethnic identity, acculturation, and conflict in Asian Indian families. *Journal of Family Psychology, 16*(3), 338–350. doi:10.1037//0893-3200.16.3.338.

Farver, J. A., Xu, Y., Bhadha, B. R., Narang, S. K., & Lieber, E. (2007). Ethnic identity, acculturation, parenting beliefs, and adolescent adjustment: A comparison of Asian Indian and European American families. *Merrill-Palmer Quarterly, 53*, 184–215.

Flynn, T. M., Taylor, P., & Pollard, C. A. (1992). Use of mobile phones in the behavioral treatment of driving phobias. *Journal of Behaviour Therapy and Experimental Psychiatry, 23*(4), 299–302.

Fouad, N. A. (1991). Training counselors to counsel international students: Are we ready? *Counseling Psychologist, 19*, 66–71.

Garcia, G., & Zea, C. (Eds.). (1997). *Psychological interventions and research with Latino populations*. Boston, MA: Allyn and Bacon.

Gilbert, P. (2002). Body shame: Biopsychosocial conceptualization and overview, with treatment implications. In P. Gilbert & J. N. V. Miles (Eds.), *Body shame: Conceptualization. Assessment and intervention* (pp. 3–54). London: Routledge.

Gilbert, P., Gilbert, J., & Sanghera, J. (2004). A focus group of the impact of izzat, shame, subordination and entrapment on mental health and service use in South Asian women living in Derby. *Mental Health, Religion & Culture, 7*, 109–130. doi:10.1080/13674670310001602418.

Hayes, R. L., & Lin, H. (1994). Coming to America: Developing social support systems for international students. *Journal of Multicultural Counseling and Development, 22*, 7–16.

Highlen, P. S. (1996). MCT theory and implications for organizations/systems. In D. W. Sue, A. E. Ivey, & P. B. Pedersen (Eds.), *A theory of multicultural counseling and therapy* (pp. 65–85). Pacific Grove, CA: Brooks/Cole.

Hoeffel, E. M., Rastogi, S., Kim, M. O., & Shahid, H. (2010). The Asian population 2010: 2010 census briefs. Retrieved from https://www.census.gov/prod/cen2010/briefs/c2010br-11.pdf

Hussain, F. A., & Cochrane, R. (2003). Living with depression: Coping strategies used by South Asian women, living in the UK, suffering from depression. *Mental Health, Religion & Culture, 6*, 21–44. doi:10.1080/1367467021000014864.

Ibrahim, F., Ohnishi, H., & Sandhu, D. S. (1997). Asian American identity development: A culture specific model for South Asian Americans. *Journal of Multicultural Counseling & Development, 25*, 34–50. doi:10.1002/j.2161-1912.1997.tb00314.x.

Inman, A. G., Howard, E. E., Beaumont, R. L., & Walker, J. A. (2007). Cultural transmission: Influence of contextual factors in Asian Indian immigrant parents' experiences. *Journal of Counseling Psychology, 54*, 93–100. doi:10.1037/0022-0167.54.1.93.

Jejeebhoy, S. J., & Sathar, Z. A. (2001). Women's autonomy in India and Pakistan: The influence of region and religion. *Population and Development Review, 2*, 687–712. doi:10.1111/j.1728-4457.2001.00687.x.

Kai, J. (1999). Minority ethnic community participation in needs assessment and service development in primary care: Perceptions of Pakistani and Bangladeshi people about psychological distress. *Health Expectations, 2*, 7–20. doi:10.1046/j.1369-6513.1999.00033.x.

Kakar, S., & Kakar, K. (2009). *The Indians*. New Delhi: Penguin.

Khanna, A., McDowell, T., Perumbilly, S., & Titus, G. (2009). Working with Asian Indian American families: A Delphi study. *Journal of Systemic Therapies, 28*, 52–71.

Lai, D. W. L., & Surood, S. (2008). Predictors of depression in aging south Asian Canadians. *Journal of Cross-Cultural Gerontology, 23*, 57–75. doi:10.1007/s10823-007-9051-5.

Lee, C. C., & Armstrong, K. L. (1995). Indigenous models of mental health interventions: Lessons from traditional healers. In J. G. Ponterotto, J. M. Casas, L. A. Suzuki, & C. M. Alexander (Eds.), *Handbook of multicultural counseling* (pp. 441–456). Thousand Oaks, CA: Sage.

Leung, P., Cheung, M., & Tsui, V. (2012). Asian Indians and depressive symptoms: Reframing mental health help-seeking behavior. *International Social Work, 55*, 53–70. doi:10.1177/0020872811407940.

Markus, H. R., & Kitayama, S. (1998). The cultural psychology of personality. *Journal of Cross-Cultural Psychology, 29*, 63–87.

Markus, H. R., Mullally, P. R., & Kitayama, S. (1997). Selfways: Diversity in modes of cultural participation. In U. Neisser & D. A. Jopling (Eds.), *The conceptual self in context* (pp. 13–61). New York, NY: Cambridge University Press.

Masuda, A., & Boone, M. S. (2011). Mental health stigma, self-concealment, and help-seeking attitudes among Asian American and European American college students with no help-seeking experience. *International Journal for the Advancement of Counselling, 33*, 266–279. doi:10.1007/s10447-011-9129-1.

Mathuranath, P. S., George, A., Cherian, P. J., Matthew, R., & Sarma, P. S. (2005). Instrumental activities of daily living scale for dementia screening in elderly people. *International Psvchogeriatrics, 17*, 1–14. doi:10.1017/S1041610205001547.

Misra, R., Balagopal, P., & Klatt, M. (2010). Complementary and alternative medicine use among Asian Indians in the United States: A national study. *The Journal of Alternative and Complementary Medicine, 16*, 843–852. doi:10.1089/acm.2009.0517.

Mukherji, B. R. (1995). Cross-cultural issues in illness and wellness: Implications for depression. *Journal of Social Distress and the Homeless, 4*, 203–217. doi:10.1007/BF02088018.

Narayan, D., Patel, R., Schafft, K., Rademacher, A., & Koch-Schulte, S. (2000). Changing gender relations in the household. In *Voices of the poor: Can anyone hear us?* New York, NY: Oxford University Press. Retrieved from http://www.worldbank.org/poverty/ voices/ reports/canany/ch5.pdf

National Institute of Education. (2012). NIE Wellness Centre. Retrieved from http://www.ps.nie.edu.sg/ WELLNESS.htm

Ninian, A. (2012). The Indian and Pakistani Diaspora in the US. *Contemporary Review, 294*, 317–323.

Parashar, D., Chan, F., & Leierer, S. (2008). Factors influencing Asian Indian graduate students' attitudes toward people with disabilities: A conjoint analysis. *Rehabilitation Counseling Bulletin, 51*, 229–239.

Patel, N., Power, T. G., & Bhavnagri, N. P. (1996). Socialization values and practices of Indian immigrant parents: Correlates of modernity and acculturation. *Child Development, 67*, 302–313. doi:10.1111/1467-8624. ep9605280309.

Pattanayak, D. P. (Ed.). (1990). *Multilingulism in India*. Clevedon, Avon: Multilingual Matters.

Prakash, I. J. (2003). Aging, disability, and disabled older people in India. *Journal of Aging & Social Policy, 15*, 85–108. doi:10.1300/J031v15n02_06.

Pregnancy Crisis Service. (2012). About us. Retrieved from http://pregnancycrisis.sg/test/about-us/

Rait, G., & Burns, A. (1997). Appreciating background and culture: The South Asian elderly and mental health. *International Journal Geriatric Psychiatry, 12*, 973–977. doi:10.1002/(SICI)1099-1166(199710)12: 10<973::AID-GPS686>3.0.CO;2-M.

Ramisetty-Mikler, S. (1993). Asian Indian immigrants in America and sociocultural issues in counseling. *Journal of Multicultural Counseling & Development, 21*, 36–49. doi:10.1002/j.2161-1912.1993.tb00581.x.

Rani, M., & Bonu, S. (2003). Rural Indian women's care seeking behaviour and choice of provider gynecological symptoms. *Studies Family Planning, 34*, 173–185. doi:10.1111/j.1728-4465.2003.00173.x.

Rao, N., McHale, J. P., & Pearson, E. (2003). Links between socialization goals and child-rearing practices in Chinese and Indian mothers. *Infant and Child Development, 12*, 475–492. doi:10.1002/icd.341.

Rathod, S., Kingdon, D., Phiri, P., & Gobbi, M. (2010). Developing culturally sensitive cognitive behaviour therapy for psychosis for ethnic minority patients by exploration and incorporation of service users' and health professionals' views and opinions. *Behavioural and Cognitive Psychotherapy, 38*, 511–533. doi:10.1017/S1352465810000378.

Shaikh, B. T., & Hatcher, J. (2004). Health seeking behaviour and health service utilization in Pakistan: Challenging the policy makers. *Journal of Public Health, 27*, 49–54. doi:10.1093/pubmed/fdh207.

Shea, M. & Yeh, C. J. (2008). Asian American students' cultural values, stigma, and relational self-construal: Correlates of attitudes toward professional help seeking. *Journal of Mental Health Counseling, 30*, 157–172. Retrieved from http://search.proquest.com/docview/198671027?accountid=28158

Siegel, C. (1991). Counseling international students: A clinician's comments. *Counseling Psychologist, 19*, 72–75. doi:10.1177/0022002185016001003.

Sinha, S. R. (1985). Maternal strategies for regulating children's behavior. *Journal of Cross-Cultural Psychology, 16*, 27–40. doi:10.1177/0022002185016001003.

Sodowsky, G. R., & Carey, J. C. (1987). Asian Indian immigrants in America: Factors related to adjustment. *Journal of Multicultural Counseling & Development, 15*, 129–141. doi:10.1002/j.2161 1912.1988. tb00403.x.

Soorkia, R., Rosemary, S., & Swami, V. (2011). Factors influencing attitudes towards seeking professional psychological help among South Asian students in Britain. *Mental Health, Religion & Culture, 14*, 613–623. doi:10.1080/13674676.2010.494176.

Sudha, S., Suchindran, C., Mutran, E. J., Rajan, S. I., & Sanna, P. S. (2007). Marital status, family ties, and self-rated health among elders in South India. *Journal of Cross-Cultural Gerontology, 21*, 103–120. doi:10.1007/s10823-006-9027-x.

Sue, D. W. (1981). *Counseling the culturally different*. New York, NY: Wiley.

Swinson, R. P., Fergus, K. D., Cox, B. J., & Wickwire, K. (1995). Efficacy of telephone-administered behavioral therapy for panic disorder with agoraphobia. *Behavior Research and Therapy, 33*(4), 465–469.

Takaki, R. (1989). *Strangers from a different shore*. Boston, MA: Little, Brown and Company.

Uba, L. (1994). *Asian Americans: Personality patterns, identity, and mental health*. New York, NY: Guilford Press.

Varghese, S. T. (2007). Antipsychotic drug prescription in postgraduate psychiatry training programs in India: Time to reflect. *Indian Journal of Psychiatry, 49*, 225. doi:10.4103/0019-5545.37329.

Wasan, A. D., Neufeld, K., & Jayaram, G. (2009). Practice patterns and treatment choices among psychiatrists in New Delhi, India. *Social Psychiatry and Psychiatric Epidemiology, 44*, 109–119. doi:10.1007/ s00127-008-0408-z.

Yeh, C. J., Hunter, C. D., Madan-Bahel, A., Chiang, L., & Arora, A. K. (2004). Indigenous and interdependent perspectives of healing: Implications for counseling and research. *Journal of Counseling and Development, 82*, 410–419. doi:10.1002/j.1556-6678.2004.tb00328.x.

Yeh, C. J., & Hwang, M. Y. (2000). Interdependence in ethnic identity and self: Implications for theory and practice. *Journal of Counseling & Development, 78*, 420–429. doi:10.1002/j.1556-6676.2000.tb01925.x.

The Assessment of Acculturation, Enculturation, and Culture in Asian-American Samples

6

Y.L. Zhang and J.L. Tsai

Introduction

Based on the 2012 census, Asian-Americans are the fastest growing ethnic group in the USA—comprising 4.8 % of the US population, or 18.9 million individuals (US Census, 2013). Within this "Asian-American" group, however, exists tremendous variation. "Asian-Americans" not only vary in the specific countries they come from (e.g., China, Korea, Japan), but also in the length of time they have spent in the USA (e.g., 1 year vs. their entire lives), their generational status (e.g., first generation vs. third generation), their reasons for migrating to the USA (e.g., in search of occupational or educational opportunities vs. to flee persecution in their homelands), and in their views of the USA (e.g., as a temporary workplace vs. as a new home). In addition, there is tremendous variation in Asian-Americans' levels of engagement in American culture ("acculturation"), as well as their endorsement of specific Asian cultural ideas and practices ("enculturation"). Scientists and clinicians alike have long acknowledged the importance of measuring this variation, whether to answer scientific questions regarding how cultural ideas and practices shape psychological processes, or to assess the mental health needs of specific Asian-American communities. In this chapter, we review the different instruments that have been used to assess acculturation, enculturation, and culture in Asian-American populations.

Y.L. Zhang, M.A. (✉) • J.L. Tsai, Ph.D. (✉)
Department of Psychology, Stanford University, 450 Serra Mall Bldg 420, Jordan Hall, Stanford, CA 94305, USA
e-mail: ylzhang@stanford.edu; jltsai@stanford.edu

Measures of Acculturation and Enculturation

> ...[Being from another culture is] definitely an asset because we can mold ourselves to fit into our surroundings and it makes us more open to and accepting of other cultures that are hugely different from the American culture.—*Indian immigrant (Kim, Brenner, Liang, & Asay,* 2003*)*
>
> It is hard trying to fit into both worlds and cultures...my parents viewed some of my "American" behavior as not so good...there are [a] lot of benefits of being bicultural but it also means that you don't totally belong in one culture.—*Korean immigrant (Kim et al.,* 2003*)*

Almost 2/3 of Asian-Americans were born outside the USA. In addition, 60 % of Asian-American population growth in 2012 was due to international migration (US Census, 2013). What is it like to move to and live in a culture that is different from the one you were raised in? This process—adapting to a new culture—is what researchers refer to as "acculturation." Coming from a different culture may be an "asset," as described in the first quote, where individuals and the communities in which they live benefit from the ideas and practices of different cultures. However, as described in the second quote,

L.T. Benuto et al. (eds.), *Guide to Psychological Assessment with Asians*,
DOI 10.1007/978-1-4939-0796-0_6, © Springer Science+Business Media New York 2014

coming from another culture may also be "hard" because of the stresses of trying to integrate the conflicting values and practices of two (or more) different cultures (Berry, 2003). What factors determine whether Asian immigrants find adjusting to American culture easy or difficult? And what are the positive and negative consequences of adjusting to a new culture?

Defining Acculturation, Enculturation, and Cultural Orientation

The word *acculturation* was first used to describe the process of cultural change within a group due to contact with European settlers (Berry, 2003; Redfield, Linton, & Herskovits, 1936). Today, the term *acculturation* is used more broadly to refer to cultural change that occurs when individuals come in contact with a culture different from the one they were raised in (Suinn, 2010). Theoretically, two processes occur in parallel once cultural contact begins. At the individual level, immigrants may change their thoughts, attitudes, behaviors, and values following first-hand, prolonged contact with their host culture (*cultural adaptation* or *psychological acculturation*; Berry, 1990; Berry, Trimble, & Olmedo, 1986). Most research has focused on this level. However, at the cultural level, host cultures may also change in response to the ideas and practices that immigrants bring with them (Berry, 1990; Markus & Kitayama, 1991). Considerably fewer studies have investigated processes at this level. To refer to the process of maintaining one's culture of origin, researchers and clinicians use the term *enculturation* (Berry, 1994; Kim & Abreu, 2001).

Existing empirical evidence suggests that the processes of acculturation and enculturation are more complicated than previously thought. Lack of engagement with one's host culture (i.e., lower acculturation) has been linked to negative mental health outcomes, including heightened anxiety and depression, increased physiological symptoms, and lowered self-esteem (Suinn, 2010; Wang & Mallinckrodt, 2006; Yoon, Hacker, Hewitt, Abrams, & Cleary, 2012). This may be because many immigrants do not speak English, encounter discrimination, are poorly integrated socially, and/or live in poverty (Berry, 2003; Hwang & Ting, 2008; Ward, 1997). Lower acculturation is also associated with more negative attitudes towards mental health services in nondistressed Asian-American groups (Kim & Omizo, 2003), and lower rates of psychological help seeking and adherence to counseling recommendations in distressed ones (Kalibatseva & Leong, 2011; Ta, Holck, & Gee, 2010). At the same time, however, lower acculturation and higher enculturation (identification with Asian culture) have been associated with positive outcomes such as higher educational achievement and stronger work and family values among Asian-American immigrants (Huntsinger, Jose, Larson, Balsink Krieg, & Shaligram, 2000; Shin, 2004).

Researchers have also used the term *cultural orientation* to refer to how engaged individuals are in their different cultures. This term has been used for immigrant *and* nonimmigrant populations (Ying, 1995; Ying & Han, 2008). Unlike immigrants, nonimmigrant minorities (e.g., second-generation and above) are often exposed to multiple cultures simultaneously (e.g., Asian culture at home and American culture at school), and therefore, they may experience less cultural change. Thus, whereas acculturation and enculturation refer to processes that typically occur in immigrant groups, cultural orientation is an index of one's engagement in a culture at a particular moment in time, regardless of their place of birth (Tsai, Ying, & Lee, 2000). Moreover, while the term acculturation is often associated with contact with mainstream or Western culture, cultural orientation is used to describe engagement in any one or more cultures.

Models of Acculturation, Enculturation, and Cultural Orientation

Over the last few decades, two dominant models have emerged, the unidimensional (sometimes termed "unilinear" or "bipolar") and the bidimensional ("bilinear" or "multidimensional") models. Unidimensional models—dating back to 1921—assume that changes to one's values, behaviors, and attitudes occur on a single continuum (Flannery, Reise, & Yu, 2001), and typically view the acculturative process in terms of stages that ultimately result in assimilation to the dominant culture. For instance, in the context of food consumption, a unidimensional model assumes that eating more American food means eating less Asian food.

While the unidimensional approach may make sense for measuring certain domains, like media or food consumption, it may be less useful for more complex domains such as cultural identification, or the degree to which individuals feel a part of their ethnic or cultural groups. For example, one may feel strongly American *and* strongly Chinese at the same time. Unidimensional models are unable to account for this "bicultural" identification because they assume that once individuals strongly identify with their host cultures, they weakly identify with their cultures of origin.

Bidimensional models emerged with these drawbacks in mind. Bidimensional models allow for the possibility that immigrants' acculturative processes may be independent of their enculturative processes (Kim & Abreu, 2001; Phinney, 1990). More generally, bidimensional models assume that individuals (immigrant or nonimmigrant) can strongly identify with both their host and heritage cultures, weakly identify with both, or strongly identify with one and only weakly with the other. Berry (1990) first popularized the bidimensional model when he distinguished between *contact* with one's host culture and *maintenance* of one's culture of origin. According to Berry, these two dimensions yield four types of individuals: (1) integrated (high contact and high maintenance), (2) separated (low contact and high maintenance), (3) assimilated (high contact and low maintenance), and (4) marginalized (low contact and low maintenance).

For instance, an integrated Asian-American may participate in his culture of origin by joining Asian clubs and organizations, while simultaneously engaging in his host culture by voting and spending time with European American friends. On the other hand, a marginalized Asian-American may not participate in either culture. Assimilated Asian-Americans might sever ties with their local Asian community and completely embrace the values and behaviors of their American host culture, while separated Asian-Americans may avoid contact with European Americans and retain their Asian values and behaviors by living in segregated Chinatowns. Berry theorizes that integrated individuals fare the best psychologically because they experience the least amount of acculturative stress. In contrast, marginalized individuals fare the worst; indeed, they engage in deviant behaviors and experience more depressive symptoms than nonmarginalized individuals (Berry, 2003; Kim, Gonzales, Stroh, & Wang, 2006). Assimilated and separated individuals fall in between integrated and marginalized individuals (Berry, 2003).

Berry and colleagues used four distinct scales to measure these styles (Berry et al., 1986; Kang, 2006). However, empirical research on French and Hungarian immigrants in Canada show high correlations between integration and assimilation, as well as between assimilation and separation, which suggests that these types may overlap (Kang, 2006). Because of this drawback, Berry's scales are not often used for research and assessment with Asian-Americans. However, the bidimensional model still serves as the basis for many present-day assessments of acculturation and cultural orientation with Asian-American groups.

Despite the popularity of bidimensional models of acculturation, there is still some debate about whether the unidimensional or bidimensional model best captures the experiences of particular ethnic subgroups. Some believe unidimensional models are more economical and parsimonious (Flannery et al., 2001) even though empirical studies comparing the two models generally conclude that the bidimensional model is superior for in-depth examinations of acculturation, enculturation, and cultural orientation (Flannery et al., 2001; Yoon et al., 2012). It is also possible that different models apply to different subgroups. For instance, in one study (Tsai et al., 2000), we found that the unidimensional model applied more to Chinese Americans who immigrated to the US after adolescence, whereas the bidimensional model applied more to Chinese Americans who immigrated prior to adolescence.

Instruments

Early work in psychology used demographic information, like generational status and years of education in the USA, as a proxy for acculturation and enculturation (Berry, 2003). However, empirical evidence cautions against this practice, as cultural identification and cultural contact can be independent of variables like generational status. For example, a first generation immigrant would be categorized as low in acculturation using generational status alone. However, this classification does not consider individual variation, like one's motivation to acculturate, or the amount (i.e., time spent engaging in host culture) and degree of contact (i.e., depth of engagement in relationships, institutions, and products) with one's host culture. To accurately assess acculturation and enculturation in immigrants and cultural orientation in nonimmigrants, researchers recommend using instruments specifically designed to measure these constructs, particularly those that have been validated cross-culturally (Abe-Kim, Okazaki, & Goto, 2001).

Not surprisingly, the existing instruments used to measure acculturation, enculturation, and cultural orientation in Asian-American groups reflect either a unidimensional or a bidimensional approach. In unidimensional assessments, scales position the two cultures on opposite ends. For example, the original Suinn-Lew Asian Self-Identity Acculturation Scale (SL-ASIA) asks participants how they would rate themselves on a scale of 1 (Asian) to 5 (American). Researchers determine how bicultural an individual is by counting the number of items on which participants indicate equality between Asian and American cultures. For example, being "bicultural" would be a score of 3 (Asian-American) on the identification question (Abe-Kim et al., 2001). As mentioned above, however, these assessments do not allow researchers to distinguish between biculturals who are strongly Asian and strongly American from those who are weakly Asian and weakly American (Yoon et al., 2012).

Scales constructed to reflect bidimensional theories typically have two subscales that ask the same set of questions for each culture. For example, the General Ethnicity Questionnaire-American (GEQ-A) and the General Ethnicity Questionnaire-Chinese (GEQ-C) are used together to assess cultural orientation in Chinese Americans (the Chinese version may be revised to refer to different East Asian groups; see Tsai et al., 2000). Both assessments ask participants the degree to which they agree with statements like, "I was raised in a way that was American [Chinese]." Bidimensional scales like the GEQ allow for the possibility that one's level of involvement or identification with one culture is independent of their involvement or identification with another culture. Thus, one can score high on both subscales, low on both, or high on one and low on the other.

Other instruments probe more deeply into the processes of being bicultural. For instance, the Bicultural Identity Integration Scale (BIIS) assesses how individuals negotiate and navigate their multiple cultural identities, and is comprised of two orthogonal dimensions, harmony (vs. conflict) and compatibility (vs. distance). Participants are asked how much they agree with items like, "I keep Chinese and American cultures separate," (compatibility vs. distance), and "I don't feel trapped between the Chinese and American cultures," (harmony vs. conflict; Benet-Martinez & Haritatos, 2005; Benet-Martinez, Leu, Lee, & Morris, 2002).

Some researchers propose that more than two dimensions are needed to truly capture Asian-Americans' cultural orientation. For instance, Chung, Kim, and Abreu (2004) argue that Asian-Americans are not only oriented to American culture and their Asian culture of origin, but also to the pan-ethnic Asian-American culture in the USA. Therefore, they created the Asian-American Multidimensional Acculturation Scale (AAMAS), which includes three subscales: Culture of origin, European American, and Asian-American.

Table 6.1 lists in alphabetical order the most widely used measures of acculturation, enculturation, and cultural orientation developed for or used with Asian-Americans in general, as well as for specific ethnic Asian subgroups (i.e., Filipino Americans and Chinese Americans). In addition, we have listed whether the assessment is

Table 6.1 Assessments of acculturation

Acculturation assessment	Type	Language	Tested with	Items	Citations (as of 4/2014)	Validity	Reliability	Relevant research
A Short Acculturation Scale for Filipino Americans (ASASFA)	Unidimensional	English, Tagalog, and dual language	Filipino Americans and immigrant Filipinos	12	60	*Convergent*: Correlated with ethnic identity, age of arrival in the USA, family income, and educational level	0.85	Dela Cruz, Padilla, and Butts (1998); Also see: Dela Cruz, Padilla, and Agustin (2000)
Acculturation Rating Scale for Mexican Americans-II (ARSMA-II)	Bidimensional	English	Asian-Americans (Chinese, Filipino, Japanese, Korean, Vietnamese)	30	51	*Convergent*: Subscales correlated with generational status	0.75–0.88	Lee, Yoon, and Liu-Tom (2006); Also see: Farver, Narang, and Bhadha (2002); Lee, Choe, Kim, and Ngo (2000)
Acculturation Scale for Chinese Americans (ASCA)	Unidimensional	Not reported; likely English	First-generation Chinese immigrants	40	11	Conducted pilot study of factorial validity; Data not reported	0.58–0.75	Yao (1979)
Acculturation Scale for Southeast Asians (AS-SEA)	Unidimensional with bidimensional language subscale	English, Cambodian, Laotian, Vietnamese	Cambodian, Laotian, and Vietnamese	13	87	*Convergent*: Correlated with age, years in the USA, education, percentage of life in the USA, and age of immigration	0.76–0.98	Anderson et al. (1993)
Acculturation Scale for Vietnamese Adolescents (ASVA)	Bidimensional	English (oral translation for non-English speakers)	Vietnamese adolescents	50	65	*Convergent*: Correlated with language, years in the USA, and education	0.88–0.89	Nguyen and von Eye (2002)

(continued)

Table 6.1 (continued)

Acculturation assessment	Type	Language	Tested with	Items	Citations (as of 4/2014)	Validity	Reliability	Relevant research
Asian-American Acculturation Inventory (AAI)	Bidimensional	English	Chinese, Filipino, Korean, Vietnamese, and "Other" Asian students in U.S.	38	126	*Concurrent*: Correlated with SL-ASIA (0.66); *Predictive*: Predicted cultural knowledge, Asian preferences, etc., better than other scales used	0.73–0.76	Flannery, 1996; Also see: Flannery, Reise, and Yu (2001)*
Asian-American Multidimensional Acculturation Scale (AAMAS)	Tridimensional (culture of origin, European American, Asian-American)	English	Asian-American (Chinese, Filipino, Japanese, Korean, and Vietnamese)	45	159	*Concurrent*: Moderately correlated with SL-ASIA; *Convergent*: Correlated with generational status: *Discriminant*: Not correlated with Intergenerational Conflict Inventory	0.78–0.87	Chung, Kim, and Abreu (2004)
Asian Values Scale-Revised (AVS-R)	Unidimensional when used alone; bidimensional with EAVS-AA-R	English	Asia American (Cambodian, Chinese, Indian, Japanese, Korean, Laotian, Thai, Vietnamese, and "Other" Asian)	25	91	*Concurrent*: Original AVS correlated with value-oriented collectivism subscale of Individualism/ Collectivism Scale (see Table 6.3) *Discriminant*: Original AVS not related to behavioral acculturation (SL-ASIA)	Original AVS: 0.81–0.82 Test-retest = 0.83 AVS-R: 0.86–0.99	Kim and Hong (2004); Also see: Kim, Atkinson, and Yang (1999); Kim, Yang, Atkinson, Wolfe, and Hong (2001)
European American Values Scale for Asian-Americans Revised (EAVS-AA-R)	Unidimensional when used alone; bidimensional with AVS-R	English	Asian-Americans (Cambodian, Chinese, Filipino, Indian, Japanese, Korean, Vietnamese, and "Other Asian")	25	42	*Known groups validation*: Original EAVS-AA was compared to predicted generational differences; Validity not reported for revision	0.77–0.98	Hong, Kim, and Wolfe (2005); Also see: Wolfe, Yang, Wong, and Atkinson (2001)

Bicultural Identity Integration Scale-1 (BIIS-1)	Bidimensional	English	Chinese American	8	305	*Convergent*: Correlated with years in the U.S. and China, language use, and cultural identification	0.69 (Distance) to 0.74 (Conflict)	Benet-Martinez and Haritatos (2005); Also see: Benet-Martinez, Leu, Lee, and Morris (2002)
East Asian Acculturation Measure (EAAM)	Bidimensional	English	Asian-Americans (Chinese, Japanese, Korean)	29	55	*Convergent*: correlated with length of stay in USA; *Discriminant*: Interscale correlations	0.77–0.85	Barry (2001)
General Ethnicity Questionnaire-American (GEQ-A)	Unidimensional when used alone; Bidimensional when used with GEQC	English, Chinese, Korean	Chinese Americans and immigrant Chinese	37	296	*Convergent*: Moderately correlated with average cultural orientation, age of arrival, generational status, length of residence in the U.S.; *Known groups validation*: Compared to predicted generational differences	0.92; Test-retest = 0.62	Tsai, Ying, and Lee (2000)
General Ethnicity Questionnaire-Chinese (GEQ-C)	Unidimensional when used alone; Bidimensional when used with GEQA	English, Chinese, Korean	Chinese Americans and immigrant Chinese	37	296	*Convergent*: Moderately correlated with average cultural orientation, age of arrival, generational status, length of residence in the USA; *Known groups validation*: Compared to predicted generational differences	0.92; Test-retest = 0.57	Tsai, Ying, and Lee (2000)

(continued)

Table 6.1 (continued)

Acculturation assessment	Type	Language	Tested with	Items	Citations (as of 4/2014)	Validity	Reliability	Relevant research
Multicultural Acculturation Scale (MAS)	Bidimensional	English (oral translation for non-English speakers)	USA (ethnically diverse sample), Canadian, Southeast Asians (Vietnamese, Indochinese, Malaysian, Singaporean, Thai)	21	89	*Known groups validation*: Compared to predicted ethnic group differences	Not reported	Wong-Rieger and Quintana (1987)
Stephenson Multigroup Acculturation Scale (SMAS)	Bidimensional	English	USA (ethnically diverse sample) and Asian-Americans (Cambodian, Hong Kong Chinese, Mainland Chinese, Filipino, Indian, Japanese, Korean, Thai, Vietnamese)	32	206	*Concurrent*: Correlated with Acculturation Rating Scale for Mexican Americans-II (ARSMA-II); *Convergent*: Correlated with generational status	0.86	Stephenson (2000)
Suinn Lew Asian Self-Identity Acculturation Scale (SL-ASIA)	Unidimensional (can be scored as bidimensional)	English	USA (ethnically diverse sample)	21	577	*Convergent*: Correlated with generational status, length of residence in the USA, self-rating of ethnic identity	88	Suinn, Rickard-Figueroa, Lew, and Vigil (1987) Also: Ownbey and Horridge (1998)
Vancouver Index of acculturation (VIA)	Bidimensional	Not reported; likely English	Asian-Canadians (Chinese, Japanese, Korean, Vietnamese)	12	687	*Concurrent*: Correlated with SL-ASIA; *Convergent*: Moderately correlated with time living in the USA and % education in Western country	0.75 (Mainstream) to 0.79 (Heritage)	Ryder, Alden, and Paulhus (2000)

* Refers to Flannery, Reise, and Yu (2001); Flannery (1996) was unpublished

unidimensional, bidimensional, or tridimensional; the languages in which the scale has been translated the Asian-American groups the scale has been used with; and the number of total items (collapsed across subscales) contained in the scale. The popularity of the assessment is indicated by the number of times the original article has been cited, based on PsychInfo (gathered April, 2014), and therefore, does not include unpublished data or conference presentations. Reliability and validity for each acculturation assessment are also provided in Table 6.1. Note that validity—the degree to which a scale captures the construct it was intended to capture—is often assessed in different ways. Therefore, Table 6.1 specifies the type of validity assessed for each scale (i.e., concurrent validity, convergent validity, discriminant validity, or known groups validation).

Empirical evidence for the reliability and validity of these assessments can be found in the "Relevant Research" column in Table 6.1, which lists the first article to report the instrument's psychometrics (generally the first article published using the scale). One exception is the Asian Values Scale-Revised and European American Values Scale-Revised, for which articles that detail the construction of the revised scales are listed. In several cases, psychometrics are validated in multiple samples and mentioned in different articles. For these scales, we include a range of reliability values. In addition, we cite the original article for the validation of the scale and list other articles under "Also see." One limitation of Table 6.1 is that the data presented are limited to published data; it is likely that there are many instruments that have been translated into other languages and used in studies that have not yet been published.

Table 6.2 indicates the specific life domains that are represented by the instruments listed in Table 6.1. The domains are listed in order from most represented (left) to least represented (right). The specific domains include social relationships (i.e., romantic relationships, comfort with friends, interaction with associates), language (i.e., think, read, consume media, use with friends and family, preferred language), identity (i.e., identify with or feel part of culture of origin and host culture, have in common, feel at home), food consumption (i.e., eat at home, eat at restaurants, preferred food), media consumption (i.e., television, newspapers, movies, music), cultural knowledge and exposure (i.e., know about, have contact with, exposure to culture of origin or host culture), cultural activities and behaviors (i.e., dance, art, recreation, sports, everyday life), history and traditions (i.e., participation and knowledge of heritage, history, holidays; preservation of past), emotion (i.e., pride, shame, guilt), family (i.e., parental cultural identification, filial piety), cultural values (i.e., specific Asian cultural values like academic achievement; general beliefs in cultural values), and sociopolitical beliefs (i.e., views on gender norms and expectations, abortion, divorce). There are also less common domains, like religion and future life prospective, which are listed under "Other" in Table 6.2. Interestingly, only a few studies have actually examined whether acculturation varies by domain within the same individual, and whether domain-specific acculturation has an impact on mental health (Ying, 1995).

Which Instrument to Use?

Given the plethora of instruments available, which instrument should one choose? As with all instruments, the best ones should have acceptable *psychometrics* (i.e., reliability and validity) for the particular samples of interest (e.g., Chinese Americans vs. Asian-Americans more generally). For instance, a meta-analysis of three bidimensional acculturation scales—the SMAS, GEQ-A/GEQ-C, and VIA—highlights important considerations concerning the psychometrics of acculturation scales in general (Huynh, Howell, & Benet-Martínez, 2009). These authors compared 51 unique samples in which the three instruments were administered across the world, and found that while all three scales yielded acceptable reliability results (i.e., alpha above 0.8), there is cross-cultural variation. There were no significant differences in the reliabilities of measures of nondominant cultures, but there was considerable and significant variation on reliability scores for the dominant culture. In other words, the portion of the three assessments that

Table 6.2 Acculturation assessment domains

Assessment name	Domain: Social contact and relationships	Language	Identity	Media	Food	Cultural knowledge and exposure	Cultural activities and behaviors	History and traditions	Emotion	Family	Cultural values	Sociopolitical beliefs	Other
A Short Acculturation Scale for Filipino Americans (ASASFA)	✓	✓		✓									
Acculturation Rating Scale for Mexican Americans-II (ARSMA-II)	✓	✓	✓	✓	✓	✓				✓			
Acculturation Scale for Chinese Americans (ASCA)	✓						✓			✓		✓	Future prospective
Acculturation Scale for Southeast Asians (AS-SEA)	✓	✓			✓								
Acculturation Scale for Vietnamese Adolescents (ASVA)	✓	✓	✓	✓	✓		✓	✓		✓	✓		
Asian-American Acculturation Inventory (AAI)	✓	✓		✓	✓			✓					
Asian-American Multidimensional Acculturation Scale (AAMAS)		✓	✓	✓	✓			✓					
Asian Values Scale-Revised (AVS-R)						✓			✓	✓	✓	✓	
European American Values Scale for Asian-Americans (EAVS-AA-revised)	✓					✓			✓		✓	✓	

Bicultural Identity Integration Scale-1 (BIIS-1)			✓									Conflict; Integration
East Asian Acculturation Measure (EAAM)	✓	✓		✓								
General Ethnicity Questionnaire-American (GEQ-A)	✓	✓	✓	✓	✓	✓	✓	✓	✓			
General Ethnicity Questionnaire-Chinese (GEQ-C)	✓	✓	✓	✓	✓	✓	✓	✓	✓			
Multicultural Acculturation Scale (MAS)	✓	✓	✓				✓					Religion
Stephenson Multigroup Acculturation Scale (SMAS)	✓	✓	✓	✓	✓	✓		✓				
Suinn Lew Asian Self-Identity Acculturation Scale (SL-ASIA)	✓	✓	✓	✓	✓	✓		✓	✓	✓	✓	Gen. status
Vancouver Index of acculturation (VIA)	✓		✓	✓			✓	✓			✓	

asks about acculturation to the host or dominant culture was found to be inconsistent. The GEQ yielded slightly more reliable indicators of acculturation to the host culture than the other assessments.

But beyond this, the answer depends on what one is interested in and for what purpose one is using the instrument. For instance, if a researcher is interested in examining whether undimensional or bidimensional models best capture the acculturative process for a specific sample, then she should use a bidimensional instrument, which allows for unidimensionality. Indeed, several researchers have been interested in this for Asian-Americans in general, and have concluded that bidimensional models best capture the acculturation experience for Asian-Americans (Flannery et al., 2001; Ryder, Alden, & Paulhus, 2000). For example, in developing the bidimensional Vancouver Index of Acculturation (VIA), researchers tested the VIA in comparison with the unidimensional SL-ASIA. They find the VIA is superior to the SL-ASIA for multiple samples of first and second generation East Asians living in a Western country. They based these conclusions on the VIA outperforming the SL-ASIA on four criteria, including measurement reliability, concurrent and factorial validity, independence of the two dimensions, and correlations with personality, psychosocial adjustment, and self-identity.

Similarly, researchers and clinicians may choose instruments based on the specific domains represented in the instruments. Researchers and clinicians interested in deriving an overall assessment of acculturation, enculturation, or cultural orientation might choose an instrument that has the most domains represented, such as the SL-ASIA, which taps into ten different domains. However, other researchers and clinicians may be interested a specific domain, like family; in this case, the AVS would be a better instrument. Some instruments focus on behavioral acculturation, like the SL-ASIA, while other instruments focus on values acculturation, like the AVS/EAVS. Researchers suggest that behavioral acculturation is acquired more quickly and easily than values acculturation, and that the former may buffer against negative mental health outcomes while the latter may put Asian-Americans at risk for them (Miller, 2007; Oh, Koeske, & Sales, 2002; Suinn, 2010).

Clinicians in particular may be interested in the link between acculturation and specific mental health outcomes, and therefore, should choose the instrument that has demonstrated links to mental health (Yoon et al., 2012). For instance, the SL-ASIA has been used with various Asian-American groups, and has been linked to mental health outcomes like depression (Suinn, 2010). Specifically, increased behavioral acculturation (e.g., language use and social relationships) was linked to lower levels of acculturative stress and thus lower depression, whereas increased values acculturation to US culture (e.g., cultural identification) was linked to higher acculturative stress and higher levels of depression (Oh et al., 2002). Other studies support these findings (Hwang & Ting, 2008; Santos, 2006; Ward & Kennedy, 1994).

Additional Considerations

There are, of course, other issues to consider when assessing acculturation, enculturation, and cultural orientation. First, given increasing evidence that bicultural Asian-Americans are sensitive to the cultural cues of a particular situation, researchers and clinicians should consider how the setting in which Asian-American individuals are completing the instruments may influence their responses. Contextual variables like language, cultural cues, and situational identity may influence self-reports (Bond, 1983; Hong, Morris, Chiu, & Benet-Martínez, 2000; Yip, 2005). Second, it is important to consider how individuals' acculturation, enculturation, and cultural orientation may interact with different environmental factors, including socioeconomic status. For instance, being strongly oriented to American culture may manifest itself in different ways for a wealthy and highly educated Asian-American than for a poor and uneducated Asian-American (Sue & Sue, 1987). Moreover, socioeconomic status may contribute to individuals' motivation to retain or reject one's native culture (Berry, 1997).

Third, because most instruments assessing acculturation, enculturation, and cultural orientation are self-report, researchers and clinicians should take into consideration the degree to which response styles and self-presentation concerns might contribute to the validity of individuals' responses. For instance, when making ratings, members of Asian cultures tend to hover around the midpoint of Likert scales, reflecting the cultural emphasis on moderation (Chen, Lee, & Stevenson, 1995). To ensure that responses are not due to response style biases, researchers and clinicians may want to mean deviate or ipsatize scores (Fischer, 2004). Because Asian-Americans may be concerned about maintaining face, efforts should be made to reassure them that there is no correct or best answer.

Similarly, Heine and colleagues (2002) have referred to the "reference group effect," which suggests that people of different cultures may have different reference groups when completing the inventories. Thus, a Japanese American may score high on independence if she compares herself to her Japanese peers; however, she may score low on independence if she compares herself to her American peers. Similarly, researchers should be cautious when using the term "Asian-American" in place of "culture of origin" or vice versa, as the two terms have difference associations, and therefore, different reference points (Park, 2008).

Fourth, as with all self-report instruments, the validity of participants' responses depends in large part on how aware they are of their orientation to different cultures. Whereas some items such as food consumption should be easy to assess, items about cultural identification may be more difficult and require more insight. For instance, in the GEQ-Chinese version, one item requires individuals to reflect on how oriented they are to Chinese culture overall. The validity of participants' responses may depend on how individuals make this assessment (e.g., by thinking of specific parts of their lives, or just reporting their gut reaction).

Finally, although these instruments provide a general assessment of individuals' acculturation, enculturation, and cultural orientation, they do not indicate how much people engage in specific cultural practices or endorse specific cultural ideas and values. For instance, although the GEQ-C assesses how much Chinese Americans want to affiliate with other Chinese, it does not indicate whether Chinese Americans endorse relationship harmony, a value that has been associated with Chinese contexts. Thus, to assess more specific ideas and practices, researchers and clinicians should consult other instruments.

Measures of Specific Cultural Ideas and Practices

> I feel that I am far away from my own roots, like my culture, my roots...I had to start new and adjust because there's a big difference between Eastern and Western cultures.—*Chinese immigrant (Lieber, Chin, Nihira, & Mink,* 2001*)*

So far, we have discussed the ways in which individuals engage in their cultures of origin and in their host cultures. However, what specific cultural ideas and practices are Asian-Americans trying to reconcile? Of the 15 acculturation, enculturation, and cultural orientation measures we reviewed, only five assess endorsement of specific Asian cultural values (e.g., academic achievement, family obligation). And only one assessment, the EAVS-AA, includes specific values of American culture (e.g., individualism, freedom). In part, this is because many instruments were designed to be applicable to a wide range of Asian-American groups. However, significant research has demonstrated that even though specific ethnic Asian groups differ from each other in particular ideas and practices, in many important ways, they are more similar than different to each other when compared to American groups (LaFromboise, Coleman, & Gerton, 1993; Minoura, 1992; Park, Schwartz, Lee, & Kim, 2013). For instance, while Chinese and Japanese cultures differ in their orientation to authority versus peers (Dien, 1999), both are more oriented to others than North American culture. Using measures of these specific cultural ideas and practices to supplement assessments of acculturation, enculturation, and cultural orientation will add specificity and depth to how we understand the psychology of Asian-Americans.

Defining Culture

According to Kroeber and Kluckhohn (1952), culture refers to shared ideas that are socially transmitted across generations and that are instantiated in products (e.g., advertisements), rituals and practices, and institutions. In addition, Kroeber and Kluckhohn (1952) described these cultural ideas as products of human action and as producers of future human action. For instance, advertisements reflect the advertisers' values (and their knowledge of what their consumers value), and at the same time, advertisements teach those particular values to the people who are exposed to those advertisements.

For decades, ethnographers have provided rich descriptions of different practices, products and institutions in Western and Asian contexts (Ots, 1990; Potter, 1988; Weisz, Rothbaum, & Blackburn, 1984). Based in part on these ethnographies, starting in the 1970s and 1980s, psychologists began developing self-report instruments to capture some of these differences. These instruments have been used not only to demonstrate how Western and Asian contexts differ from each other, but also to examine variation within Western and Asian contexts.

Table 6.3 lists, in alphabetical order, 15 popular measures developed to capture different ideas and practices in Western and Asian contexts. We have categorized these measures into the domains of general values, individualism-collectivism, models of self, ways of thinking, and ways of feeling. As in Table 6.1, Table 6.3 indicates the languages in which the instruments have been translated, and the specific samples with which the instruments have been used. Popularity is based on the number of citations found on PsychInfo (generated April, 2014). Psychometrics are provided for the group(s) that the measures were validated with. The empirical articles associated with each instrument are also listed.

General Values

One approach to studying variation within and between cultures has been to examine a broad range of values. One popular instrument that has been used widely to study culture is the Schwartz Values Survey (SCS) (Schwartz, 1994). This survey assesses 57 values (e.g., equal opportunity for all, preservation of time-honored customs, stability of society) that have been categorized into ten types, which are defined by two general dimensions (openness to change vs. conservation and self-transcendence vs. self-enhancement). For instance, students from the USA ranked values of benevolence (e.g., responsibility and loyalty), achievement (e.g., ambition and success), and hedonism (e.g., pleasure and self-indulgence) as most important and values of stimulation (e.g., challenging and adventurous life), tradition (e.g., being humble and moderation), and power (e.g., wealth and authority) as least important. Singapore teachers, on the other hand, ranked security, benevolence, and conformity as most important and hedonism, stimulation, and power as least important (Schwartz & Bardi, 2001). While US students and Singapore teachers both ranked stimulation as low on their lists of important values, US students rated stimulation higher than the world-average while Singapore teachers rated it lower than the world-average—making these cultures distinct in the importance they place on having a varied and exciting life. These cultural differences in values have been replicated with other Western and East Asian samples.

Large-scale surveys, like the World Values Survey (WVS), have made great strides in tracking patterns of general cultural values. Since 1981, the WVS has collected data from samples representing 90 % of the world's population in order to identify changes in cultural values over time. For example, the WVS asks individuals what they want out of life (e.g., economic and social life) and what they believe (e.g., religion and politics). Findings from this project suggest that two dimensions of values (traditional vs. secular-relational, and survival vs. self-expression) explain over 70 % of the cultural variation in values (World Values Survey, 2008). Traditional societies emphasize parent-child ties and family values, deference to authority, and national pride; secular-rational societies move away from these values and are more tolerant of divorce, abortion,

Table 6.3 Assessments of culture

Cultural assessment	Domain	Language	Tested with	Items	Citations (as of 4/2014)	Validity	Reliability	Relevant research
Affect Valuation Index (AVI)	Ways of Feeling	English, Korean, Chinese	USA (European American and Chinese American), Hong Kong Chinese, Mainland Chinese	50	246	*Convergent*: Correlated with music preferences, leisure activities, and consumer products; *Discriminant*: Weak relationships with sensation seeking and regulatory focus	0.52–0.75	Tsai, Knutson, and Fung (2006); Also see: Tsai (2007); Tsai and Knutson (2006)
Analysis-Holism Scale (AHS)	Ways of Thinking	English, Korean	USA (ethnically diverse sample) and Korean	24	56	*Convergent*: Correlations with Attributional Complexity Scale, Inventory of Global Style, and Rahim Organizational Conflict Inventory; *Discriminant*: Not correlated with Individualism/ Collectivism Scale and Self-Construal Scale	0.74	Choi, Koo, and Choi (2007)
Dialectical Self Scale (DSS)	Ways of Thinking	English, Chinese	USA (European American and Asian-American), Mainland Chinese	32	132	*Convergent*: Negatively correlated with need for cognitive closure; positively correlated with dialectical self-esteem	0.67–0.86	Spencer-Rodgers, Srivastava, and Peng (2001); Also see: Spencer-Rodgers, Peng, Wang, and Hou (2004)*
Emotional Patterns Questionnaire (EPQ)	Ways of Feeling	English, Korean	USA (European American and Korean American)	37	9	*Convergent:* Positive correlations with acculturation proxies; (i.e., generational status); *Discriminant:* Not correlated with Vancouver Index of Acculturation	0.79–0.89	De Leersnyder, Mesquita, and Kim (2011)
Inclusion of Others in Self (IOS)	Models of Self	English, Chinese	USA (ethnically diverse sample), Mainland Chinese	1	605	*Convergent*: Correlations with Relationship Closeness Inventory, emotions about others, and self-deception scale; *Discriminant*: Not correlated with anger-sadness circles; *Predictive*: Predicted breakups in romantic relationships	0.93 Test-retest: 0.83	Aron, Aron, and Smollan (1992); Also see: Li (2002)

(continued)

Table 6.3 (continued)

Cultural assessment	Domain	Language	Tested with	Items	Citations (as of 4/2014)	Validity	Reliability	Relevant research
Independent and Interdependent Self-Construal Scale (IISC)	Models of Self	English, Chinese, Japanese, Korean	USA (ethnically diverse sample), Hong Kong Chinese, Japanese, Korean, Mainland Chinese	94	365	*Convergent*: Correlated with communication style and individualistic/collectivistic values; *Known groups validation*: Compare to predicted ethnic group differences	0.73–0.85	Gudykunst et al. (1996); Also see: Levine et al. (2003)
Individualism/Collectivism Scale (INDCOL)	Individualism & Collectivism	English, Chinese	USA (ethnically diverse sample), Hong Kong Chinese	63	343	*Convergent*: Correlations with Social Interest Scale, social desirability, obligation, and responsibility; Expert role-playing showed predicted trends *Discriminant*: Distinct from Locus of Control Scale, Achievement Motivation Questionnaire, and Tolerance of Ambiguity Scale	0.41–0.76	Hui (1988); Also see: Hui and Villareal (1989)
Independent and Interdependent Self Scale (IISS)	Models of Self	English, Chinese	British and Chinese	42	17	*Construct*: Compare to predicted independence/interdependence within groups; *Convergent*: Correlations with measures of self views and independence/collectivism	0.86–0.89	Lu and Gilmour (2007)
Individualism versus Collectivism Measure (unnamed)	Individualism & Collectivism	English, Chinese, Japanese, various others	USA (ethnically diverse sample), Hong Kong Chinese, Indian, Indonesian, Japanese, Mainland Chinese, others	21	523	*Construct*: Compare to predicted independence/interdependence between groups; *Convergent*: Correlations with Hofstede's (1980) individualism scores	Not reported	Triandis et al. (1986); Also see: Triandis et al. (1993)
Relational-Interdependent Self-Construal (RISC)	Models of Self	English	USA (ethnically diverse sample of citizens, noncitizens were excluded)	11	410	*Convergent*: Correlations with Communal Orientation Scale, Self-Construal Scale; *Known groups validation*: Compare to predicted gender differences	0.84–0.94; Test-retest= 0.63–0.73	Cross, Bacon, and Morris (2000); Also see: Cross, Gore, and Morris (2003); Cross, Morris, and Gore (2002)

Schwartz Values Survey (SVS)	General Values	Various	USA, Hong Kong Chinese, Indian, Indonesian, Japanese, Taiwanese, etc.	58	2,852	*Cross-cultural*: Values had consistent meanings across 83–90 % of samples in 20 countries	Not reported in original; average of 0.8 in other samples	Schwartz (1992, 1994); Also see: Brett and Okumura (1998)
Self-Construal Scale (SCS)	Models of Self	English, Chinese, various others	USA (ethnically diverse sample), Canadian, Hong Kong Chinese, Japanese, Taiwanese	24	1,261	*Construct*: Compare to predicted independence/interdependence between groups; *Predictive:* Predictive of attributions of situational influence	0.52–0.74	Singelis (1994); Also see: Levine et al. (2003); Lu et al. (2001)
Self-Construal Scale	Models of Self	English, Chinese	USA (ethnically diverse sample); Hong Kong Chinese	28	33	*Known groups validation*: Compare to predicted ethnic group differences; *Predictive:* Predicts response efficacy	0.79–0.90	Kim et al. (2000); Also see: Leung and Kim (1997)
Sixfold Self-Construal Scale	Models of Self	English and various others	U.K. (ethnically diverse sample), China, Jordan, Lebanon, Syria	30	28	*Convergent*: Correlated with self-construals, group identification, and Inclusion of Others in Self; *Discriminant*: Weaker relationships with subcategories of Schwartz Values Inventory	0.68–0.92	Harb and Smith (2008); Also see: Cross, Hardin, and Gercek-Swing (2011)
Twenty Statements Test (TST)	Models of Self	English, Chinese, Japanese, various others	USA (ethnically diverse sample); Japanese, Chinese	20	512	Compared to predicted frequencies of response categories	0.90; Test-retest = 0.85	Kuhn and McPartland (1954); Also see: Kanagawa, Cross, and Markus (2001); Hong, Ip, Chiu, Morris, & Menon (2001); Triandis, McCusker, and Hui (1990)

* Refers to Spencer-Rodgers, Peng, Wang and Hou (2004); Spencer-Rodgers, Srivastava, and Peng (2001) is unpublished

euthanasia, and suicide. While survival societies value economic and physical security, self-expression societies are often more concerned with subjective well-being and quality of life. Cultures also change over time, such that countries generally endorse traditional and survival values less. However, despite changes over time, cultural differences in values persist. For example, while Japan has become more self-expressive and rational-secular, and Canada has become more self-expressive from 1981 to 2007, Canada is still much lower on rational-secularism and much higher on self-expression than Japan (World Values Survey, 2008). Using data from the WVS, researchers generally show support for Asian-American values acculturation, such that Asian-Americans fall in between non Asian-Americans (who score high) and Asians (who score low) on self-reports of Western values like personal control (Sastry & Ross, 1998).

Individualism and Collectivism

Based on large survey studies, one major distinction between many East Asian and North American samples is the degree to which individuals endorse individualistic versus collectivistic values (Hostede, 1980; Triandis, 1995). Whereas individualistic cultures value uniqueness, autonomy, and a positive sense of self and personal success, collectivistic cultures value harmony, cooperation, and positive relationships with others (Markus & Kitayama, 1991; Oyserman, 1993; Triandis, 1995). Thus, individualism and collectivism, henceforth referred to as IND-COL, are often conceptualized as existing on a single continuum, where more individualism means less collectivism.

Researchers have designed several instruments to measure IND-COL, the most popular of which include the Individualism/Collectivism Scale (Hui, 1988) and the Individualism versus Collectivism Measure (Triandis et al., 1986). Participants are asked how much they agree with statements like, "I would rather struggle through a personal problem by myself than discuss it with my friends," (Hui, 1988); higher agreement with this item indicates greater individualism. Measures like these are used internationally to investigate cultural differences in levels of IND-COL. In a meta-analysis of 83 studies, with 27 different IND-COL measures, researchers find that European Americans are more individualistic and less collectivistic compared to 50 countries around the world (Oyserman, Coon, & Kemmelmeier, 2002). Chinese were found to be the most collectivistic and least individualistic. However, other East Asian countries (notably Japan and Korea) showed less consistent responses to the IND-COL.

Where do Asian-Americans fall on measures of IND-COL? The results are mixed. For instance, in an analysis of generational differences in IND-COL, researchers find that first generation (immigrant) Asian-Americans are higher on certain individualistic values, like self-reliance and competition, and lower on collectivistic values like sociability with neighbors than are American-born Asian-Americans (Abe-Kim et al., 2001). Other studies, however, find that Asian-Americans fall in-between Koreans and Europeans Americans on 10 out of 12 indices of IND-COL (Hui, 1988; Rhee, Uleman, & Lee, 1996). And a meta-analysis of 27 independent samples concludes that Asian-Americans do not significantly differ from European Americans in levels of IND-COL (Vargas & Kemmelmeier, 2013). Together, these findings demonstrate the considerable variability among Asian-Americans, and suggest that endorsement of specific cultural ideas may differ from what one would expect from levels of acculturation and cultural orientation alone. As we mentioned earlier, more acculturated Asian-Americans generally express more positive attitudes towards professional mental health services than do less acculturated Asian-Americans (Atkinson & Gim, 1989). However, Asian-Americans who endorsed individualistic values like self-reliance did not have a positive attitude towards professional help seeking when controlling for acculturation. In other words, among acculturated Asian-Americans, those who endorsed self-reliance were *less* likely to seek professional mental health services (Tata & Leong, 1994).

Regardless, individualistic and collectivistic values have been linked to differential outcomes among Asian-Americans. For instance, individualism is positively related to delinquency in Asian-American (Chinese, Cambodian, Laotian, and Vietnamese) youth, whereas collectivism is negatively related (Le & Stockdale, 2005). Thus, while individualism may put Asian-American youth at risk for maladaptive behavioral outcomes, collectivism and strong family ties may be a protective force against youth delinquency (Samaniego & Gonzales, 1999).

Models of Self

Differences in individualistic and collectivistic values have implications for individuals' models of self, with Western cultures viewing the self as bounded, stable, and distinct from others, and East Asian cultures viewing the self as fluid, contextual, and connected to others (Gudykunst et al., 1996; Markus & Kitayama, 1991; Singelis, 1994; Singelis, Bond, Sharkey, & Kriss, 1999). Various researchers have developed ways of measuring independent and interdependent models of self.

A popular free-response paradigm is the Twenty Statements Test (TST; Kuhn & McPartland, 1954), which asks participants to write 20 open-ended statements about themselves. The TST allows participants to describe themselves in their own words without imposing the constraints of Likert-scale instruments (McGuire & McGuire, 1988). Researchers like the TST because it reduces cultural bias in the construction of items, and reduces variation in the subjective interpretation of items (Kanagawa, Cross, & Markus, 2001). Another free-response scale is the Self-Focus Sentence Completion Scales (SFSCS; Exner, 1973), where participants complete stems like, "If only I could…" For both the TST and the SFSCS, responses are coded into categories like independent/interdependent or self/family to identify patterns of variation in responses (for coding guidelines, see Kanagawa et al., 2001 and Chentsova-Dutton & Tsai, 2010).

Likert scales are also used to measure models of self. A meta-analysis suggests that the Self-Construal Scale (SCS; Singelis, 1994), the Independent and Interdependent Self-Construal Scale (IISC; Gudykunst et al., 1996), and Kim and colleagues' Self-Construal Scale (2000; Leung & Kim, 1997) are the most common assessments of self (Levine et al., 2003) and have been validated cross-culturally with Western and Asian groups. These scales have two complementary subscales designed to measure independence and interdependence. For example, the SCS (Singelis, 1994) measures participants' agreement on independent items like, "I'd rather say 'No' directly, than risk being misunderstood," and interdependent items including, "It is important for me to maintain harmony within my group."

These self-report measures have been criticized for including overlapping items, including items that are theoretically different (i.e., not distinguishing between values and actual behavior), or having inconsistent psychometrics across cultures (Harb & Smith, 2008; Levine et al., 2003; Matsumoto, 1999; Park & Levine, 1999; van de Vijver & Leung, 1997). To address these issues, Harb and Smith (2008) constructed the Sixfold Self-Construal Scale, for which participants are asked to rate their agreement with items like "I think of myself as connected to _____" across six different dimensions (i.e., self, family, friends, social grouping, students at my university, political/government/religious institution). Cultural differences have been observed between Western and Middle Easter cultures, and the measure is currently being validated with Chinese samples. However, because this measure allows for more contextualized responses than other scales, researchers believe it is promising for future cross-cultural comparisons (Cross, Hardin, & Gercek-Swing, 2011).

An alternative to Likert-type scales for Asian-American samples is the Inclusion of Others in Self Scale (IOS; Aron, Aron, & Smollan, 1992), which uses Venn diagrams to illustrate overlap between oneself and others. Participants are asked to choose an option from a series of different diagrams that best captures their relationship with another person (i.e., mother, romantic partner, and sibling), ranging from almost completely overlapping to completely separate and distinct.

Much of the work on models of self has been devoted to mapping cultural differences in independence and independence, establishing the validity of the construct across cultures, and examining how models of self influence behaviors, ways of thinking, and ways of feeling (Cross et al., 2011; Markus & Conner, 2013; Markus & Kitayama, 2010; Oyserman et al., 2002; Spencer-Rodgers, Peng, Wang, & Hou, 2004; Stephens, Fryberg, Markus, Johnson, & Covarrubias, 2012; Tsai et al., 2006; Tsai, Miao, Seppala, Fung, & Yeung, 2007). Empirical work has also linked these models to important mental health outcomes. For example, independent patients (from Hawaii and mainland USA) demonstrated more willingness to be assertive during medical interviews than did interdependent patients (from Hong Kong; Kim et al., 2000).

Ways of Thinking

Another way in which Western and East Asian cultures differ is in their ways of thinking, specifically, the degree to which individuals engage in dialectical thinking (i.e., demonstrate a tolerance for change and contradiction, and an emphasis on holism; Spencer-Rodgers, Boucher, Mori, Wang, & Peng, 2009). Authors find that dialecticism is more prevalent in Asians than European Americans, and has consequences for how individuals attend to the visual field, solve problems, and interact with their environment (Nisbett, Peng, Choi, & Norenzayan, 2001; Peng & Nisbett, 1999). One way of assessing dialecticism is through content coding open-ended responses to the TST using a coding scheme (for coding guidelines, see Spencer-Rodgers et al., 2009) that categorizes statements that demonstrate contradiction, change, or holism. For example, "I am friendly, but shy," would be coded as a contradiction. Another way of assessing dialecticism is the Dialectical Self Scale (DSS; Spencer-Rodgers, Srivastava, & Peng, 2001), which asks participants to agree or disagree with items like, "I sometimes believe two things that contradict each other," and "I often find that my beliefs and attitudes will change under different contexts."

Empirical studies have demonstrated that dialectical thinking has psychological benefits and costs. For instance, individuals who engage in more dialectical thinking "bounce back" faster after negative events (Ji, Zhang, Usborne, & Guan, 2004). On the other hand, dialectical thinking has also been associated with lower global self-esteem and life satisfaction, increased anxiety and depression, and decreased self-enhancement (Spencer-Rodgers, Williams, & Peng, 2010), which are indicators of poor psychological health in American contexts (but may be less so in East Asian contexts).

Ways of Feeling

Decades of research have examined how culture shapes people's feelings, and much of this work has compared Western with East Asian cultural contexts. Indeed, most of the work from our lab has compared emotional processes in European American, Asian-American, and East Asian cultures. For instance, in our work, we distinguish the affective states that people ideally want to feel ("ideal affect") from those that people actually feel ("actual affect"). Using the Affect Valuation Index (AVI), which assesses both actual and ideal affect, we find that while European Americans and Hong Kong Chinese both want to feel positively, they differ in the specific types of positive states they want to feel. Whereas European Americans want to feel excited, enthusiastic, and other high arousal positive states more than Hong Kong Chinese, Hong Kong Chinese want to feel calm, relaxed, and other low arousal positive states more than European Americans (Tsai et al., 2006). These cultural differences in ideal affect emerge even after controlling for cultural differences in how much people actually feel these states. Moreover, these differences in ideal affect are reflected in various cultural products. For instance, children's storybooks, magazine advertisements, and Facebook pages in the USA have more excited and less calm content than those in Taiwan and Hong Kong (Chim, Tsai, Ang, & Fung, 2014; Huang & Park, 2012; Moon, Chim, Tsai, Ho, & Fung, 2011; Tsai, Louie, Chen, &

Uchida, 2007). Asian-Americans endorse both affective ideals: for instance, first and second generation Chinese Americans value excitement more than their European American counterparts but also value calm as much as their Hong Kong Chinese counterparts (Tsai et al., 2006). These findings have been replicated for East Asian-Americans in general (Tsai, Miao et al., 2007).

Individual and cultural differences in ideal affect have been linked to a whole host of behaviors, including what consumer products people choose, how they perceive other people, and even what physicians they prefer (Chim et al., 2014; Sims, Tsai, Koopmann-Holm, Thomas, & Goldstein, 2014; Tsai, Knutson, & Rothman, 2007). For instance, the more people value excitement and other high arousal positive states, the more they prefer a physician who promotes an "energetic lifestyle," whereas the more people value calm and other low arousal positive states, the more they prefer a physician who promotes "peace of mind" (Sims et al., 2014).

Discrepancies between actual and ideal affect have been linked to mental health for European American, Asian-Americans, and Hong Kong Chinese (Tsai et al., 2006). For European Americans, a greater discrepancy between actual and ideal *excitement* states (but not calm states) is associated with higher depression scores, whereas for Hong Kong Chinese, a greater discrepancy between actual and ideal *calm* states (but not excitement states) is associated with higher depression scores. For Chinese Americans, however, greater discrepancies between actual and ideal excitement states *and* calm states are associated with higher depression scores (Tsai et al., 2006), demonstrating that Asian-Americans internalize both the emotional values of their host culture and those of their heritage cultures (Tsai et al., 2006).

Researchers have also investigated emotional acculturation to host cultures using the Emotional Pattern Questionnaire (EPQ; De Leersnyder, Mesquita, & Kim, 2011), which first asks participants to recall a recent emotional situation that was positive or negative and was socially engaging or socially disengaging. Participants then rate the degree to which they experience 37 different emotions during the recalled situation. Participants' responses are averaged to generate profiles of emotional patterns unique to each of the four situations. Immigrants who better match the profile of the host culture are categorized as more emotionally acculturated. Researchers find that Korean Americans (second generation or later) show greater emotional acculturation than earlier generations. Interestingly, explicit measures of acculturation (i.e., VIA) do not predict emotional acculturation. Instead, desire for exposure to mainstream American culture predicts emotional acculturation for Korean immigrants (De Leersnyder et al., 2011), suggesting that emotional acculturation may be less conscious than other types of acculturation.

Which Instrument to Use?

As we mentioned earlier, measures of culture can add depth and specificity to our understanding of acculturation. Obviously, choosing a measure(s) depends on the goal of the investigation. Instruments that assess models of the self and cultural values can reveal how one relates to others, interprets their world, and makes decisions, as well as what drives behavior. Assessing ways of thinking can inform judgment and decision making processes, and inform mental health by assessing comfort with internal and external changes or contradictions. Instruments that assess ways of feeling may help clinicians base diagnoses of emotional distress on culturally relevant emotional indicators. Because much of Western mental health services are based on Western models of independence and consistency (Cross, Gore, & Morris, 2003), these instruments can help clinicians and practitioners tailor culturally sensitive treatment programs to Asian-American patients.

Additional Considerations

Measures of culture are particularly sensitive to external cues in the environment. For instance, Gardner and colleagues (1999) find that one can experimentally manipulate European American participants' model of self by having them circle all the "I" and "me" words in a passage (making the independent self more salient) or the "us" and "we" words (making the interdependent self more salient). Other researchers posit that because the interdependent self is more flexible, individuals with this model will be particularly sensitive to priming and experimental demand (Levine et al., 2003). Thus, researchers and practitioners must be careful to acknowledge and control for the potential environmental cues present at the time of assessment.

Current methods may not fully capture the theoretical distinctions mentioned above. Because most of the measures described above were developed in Western contexts, there may be an unconscious Western bias embedded in some of these instruments (Markus & Kitayama, 1998). For instance, free response paradigms have been criticized as culturally biased because they ask participants to report about themselves absent of context. For those with interdependent models of self, this task is both difficult and unrepresentative of their flexible self-constructs (Fiske, Kitayama, Markus, & Nisbett, 1998; Harb & Smith, 2008). Kanagawa and colleagues (2001) suggests that structured Likert-type questionnaires are no better, as they do not capture the dynamic nature of the interdependent, dialectical self. Thus, researchers may want to include a variety of measures that were derived in both Western and East Asian contexts in their assessments of Asian-Americans. Similarly, more behavioral assessments are needed to address some of the limitations of self-report methods described above.

Conclusions

How do we capture the tremendous variation that exists among Asian-Americans? One way is to examine the cultures to which they are exposed. Instruments assessing acculturation, enculturation, and cultural orientation are useful to examine how oriented individuals are to different cultures, and whether their cultural identities are in conflict or at peace with each other. Instruments assessing cultural ideas and practices are useful to examine the particular ways in which individuals are shaped by their cultures. As illustrated by some of the findings described above, general acculturation and cultural orientation levels may or may not be linked to endorsement of specific cultural ideas, and therefore, both types of instruments should be used. Used together, these instruments can help us achieve a better understanding of the cultural shaping of human experience and of the needs of today's Asian-Americans.

Acknowledgements We thank Michelle Peretz, Mallika Roy, and Angela Chou for their research assistance in preparation of this chapter, and the Stanford Culture and Emotion Laboratory for their valuable feedback on earlier versions of this chapter.

References

Abe-Kim, J., Okazaki, S., & Goto, S. G. (2001). Unidimensional versus multidimensional approaches to the assessment of acculturation for Asian American populations. *Cultural Diversity and Ethnic Minority Psychology, 7*(3), 232–246.

Anderson, J. J., Moeschberger, M. M., Chen, M. S., Kunn, P. P., Wewers, M. E., & Guthrie, R. R. (1993). An acculturation scale for Southeast Asians. *Social Psychiatry and Psychiatric Epidemiology, 28*(3), 134–141.

Aron, A., Aron, E. N., & Smollan, D. (1992). Inclusion of other in the self scale and the structure of interpersonal closeness. *Journal of Personality and Social Psychology, 63*(4), 596–612.

Atkinson, D. R., & Gim, R. H. (1989). Asian-American cultural identity and attitudes toward mental health services. *Journal of Counseling Psychology, 36*(2), 209–212.

Barry, D. T. (2001). Development of a new scale for measuring acculturation: The East Asian Acculturation Measure (EAAM). *Journal of Immigrant Health, 3*(4), 193–197.

Benet-Martinez, V., & Haritatos, J. (2005). Bicultural Identity Integration (BII): Components and antecedents. *Journal of Personality, 74*(4), 1015–1050.

Benet-Martinez, V., Leu, J., Lee, F., & Morris, M. W. (2002). Negotiating biculturalism: Cultural frame switching in biculturals with oppositional versus compatible cultural identities. *Journal of Cross-Cultural Psychology, 33*(5), 492–516.

Berry, J. W. (1990). Psychology of acculturation: Understanding individuals moving between cultures. In R. W. Brislin (Ed.), *Applied cross-cultural psychology* (pp. 232–253). Newbury Park, CA: Sage.

Berry, J. W. (1994). Acculturation and psychological adaptation: An over-view. In A. Bouvy, F. J. R. van de Vijver, P. Boski, & P. Schmitz (Eds.), *Journeys into cross-cultural psychology* (pp. 129–141). Berwyn, PA: Swets & Zeitlinger.

Berry, J. W. (1997). Immigration, acculturation, and adaptation. *Applied Psychology: An International Review, 46*(1), 5–34.

Berry, J. W. (2003). Conceptual approaches to acculturation. In K. M. Chun, P. Balls-Organista, & G. Marín (Eds.), *Acculturation: Advances in theory, measurement, and applied research* (pp. 17–37). Washington, DC: American Psychological Association.

Berry, J., Trimble, J., & Olmedo, E. (1986). Assessment of acculturation. In W. Lonner & J. Berry (Eds.), *Field methods in cross-cultural research* (pp. 291–324). Newbury Park, CA: Sage.

Bond, M. H. (1983). How language variation affects intercultural differentiation of values by Hong Kong bilinguals. *Journal of Language and Social Psychology, 2*(1), 57–66.

Brett, J. M., & Okumura, T. (1998). Inter- and intracultural negotiation: U.S. and Japanese negotiators. *Academy of Management Journal, 41*(5), 495–510.

Chen, C., Lee, S. Y., & Stevenson, H. W. (1995). Response style and cross-cultural comparisons of rating scales among East Asian and North American students. *Psychological Science, 6*(3), 170–175.

Chentsova-Dutton, Y. E., & Tsai, J. L. (2010). Self-focused attention and emotional reactivity: The role of culture. *Journal of Personality and Social Psychology, 98*(3), 507–519.

Chim, L., Tsai, J. L., Ang, J., & Fung, H. H. (2014). Cultural differences in perceptions of leadership: The role of ideal affect. Manuscript in preparation

Choi, I., Koo, M., & Choi, J. (2007). Individual differences in analytic versus holistic thinking. *Personality and Social Psychology Bulletin, 33*(5), 691–705.

Chung, R. H., Kim, B. K., & Abreu, J. M. (2004). Asian American multidimensional acculturation scale: Development, factor analysis, reliability, and validity. *Cultural Diversity and Ethnic Minority Psychology, 10*(1), 66–80.

Cross, S. E., Bacon, P. L., & Morris, M. L. (2000). The relational-interdependent self-construal and relationships. *Journal of Personality and Social Psychology, 78*(4), 791–808.

Cross, S. E., Gore, J. S., & Morris, M. L. (2003). The relational-interdependent self-construal, self-concept consistency, and well-being. *Journal of Personality and Social Psychology, 85*(5), 933–944.

Cross, S. E., Hardin, E. E., & Gercek-Swing, B. (2011). The what, how, why, and where of self-construal. *Personality and Social Psychology Review, 15*(2), 142–179.

Cross, S. E., Morris, M. L., & Gore, J. S. (2002). Thinking about oneself and others: The relational-interdependent self-construal and social cognition. *Journal of Personality and Social Psychology, 82*(3), 399–418.

De Leersnyder, J., Mesquita, B., & Kim, H. S. (2011). Where do my emotions belong? A study of immigrants' emotional acculturation. *Personality and Social Psychology Bulletin, 37*(4), 451–463.

Dela Cruz, F. A., Padilla, G. V., & Agustin, E. O. (2000). Adapting a measure of acculturation for cross-cultural research. *Journal of Transcultural Nursing, 11*(3), 191–198.

Dela Cruz, F. A., Padilla, G. V., & Butts, E. (1998). Validating a short acculturation scale for Filipino Americans. *Journal of American Academy of Nurse Practitioners, 10*(10), 453–460.

Dien, D. S. (1999). Chinese authority-directed orientation and Japanese peer-group related orientation: Questioning the notion of collectivism. *Review of General Psychology, 3*(4), 372–385.

Exner, J. E. (1973). The self-focus sentence completion: A study of egocentricity. *Journal of Personality Assessment, 37*(5), 437–455.

Farver, J., Narang, S., & Bhadha, B. (2002). East meets west: Ethnic identity, acculturation and conflict in Asian Indian families. *Journal of Family Psychology, 16*(3), 338–350.

Fischer, R. (2004). Standardization to account for cross-cultural response bias: A classification of score adjustment procedures and review of research in JCCP. *Journal of Cross-Cultural Psychology, 35*(3), 263–282.

Fiske, A., Kitayama, S., Markus, H., & Nisbett, R. E. (1998). The cultural matrix of social psychology. In D. T. Gilbert, S. T. Fiske, & G. Lindzey (Eds.), *The handbook of social psychology* (4th ed., Vol. 1 and 2, pp. 915–981). New York, NY: Oxford University Press.

Flannery, W. P. (1996). *Asian-American acculturation: An application of the culture diagnosticity method.* Unpublished doctoral dissertation, University of California, Riverside.

Flannery, W., Reise, S. P., & Yu, J. (2001). An empirical comparison of acculturation models. *Personality and Social Psychology Bulletin, 27*(8), 1035–1045.

Gardner, W. L., Gabriel, S., & Lee, A. Y. (1999). "I" value freedom, but "we" value relationships: Self-construal priming mirrors cultural difference in judgment. *Psychological Science, 10*(4), 321–326.

Gudykunst, W. B., Matsumoto, Y., Ting-Toomey, S., Nishida, T., Kim, K., & Heyman, S. (1996). The influence of cultural individualism-collectivism, self-construals, and individual values on communication styles across cultures. *Human Communication Research, 22*(4), 510–543.

Harb, C., & Smith, P. B. (2008). Self-construals across cultures: Beyond independence-interdependence. *Journal of Cross-Cultural Psychology, 39*(2), 178–197.

Heine, S. J., Lehman, D. R., Peng, K., & Greenholtz, J. (2002). What's wrong with cross-cultural comparisons of subjective Likert scales?: The reference-group effect. *Journal of Personality and Social Psychology, 82*(6), 903–918.

Hofstede, G. (1980). *Culture's consequences*. Beverly Hills, CA: Sage.

Hong, Y. Y., Ip, G., Chiu, C., Morris, M. W., & Menon, T. (2001). Cultural identity and dynamic construction of the self: Collective duties and individual rights in Chinese and American cultures. *Social Cognition, 19*(3), 251–268.

Hong, S., Kim, B. K., & Wolfe, M. M. (2005). A psychometric revision of the European American Values Scale for Asian Americans using the Rasch model. *Measurement and Evaluation in Counseling and Development, 37*(4), 194–207.

Hong, Y., Morris, M. W., Chiu, C., & Benet-Martínez, V. (2000). Multicultural minds: A dynamic constructivist approach to culture and cognition. *American Psychologist, 55*(7), 709–720.

Hostede, G. (1980). *Culture's consequences: International differences in work-related values*. Beverly Hills, CA: Sage.

Huang, C. M., & Park, D. (2012). Cultural influences on Facebook photographs. *International Journal of Psychology, 48*(3), 334–343.

Hui, C. (1988). Measurement of individualism-collectivism. *Journal of Research in Personality, 22*(1), 17–36.

Hui, C., & Villareal, M. J. (1989). Individualism-collectivism and psychological needs: Their relationships in two cultures. *Journal of Cross-Cultural Psychology, 20*(3), 310–323.

Huntsinger, C. S., Jose, P. E., Larson, S. L., Balsink Krieg, D., & Shaligram, C. (2000). Mathematics, vocabulary, and reading development in Chinese American and European American children over the primary school years. *Journal of Educational Psychology, 92*(4), 745–760.

Huynh, Q., Howell, R. T., & Benet-Martínez, V. (2009). Reliability of bidimensional acculturation scores: A meta-analysis. *Journal of Cross-Cultural Psychology, 40*(2), 256–274.

Hwang, W., & Ting, J. (2008). Disaggregating the effects of acculturation and acculturative stress on the mental health of Asian Americans. *Cultural Diversity & Ethnic Minority Psychology, 14*(2), 147–154.

Ji, L.-J., Zhang, Z., Usborne, E., & Guan, Y. (2004). Optimism across cultures: In response to the severe acute respiratory syndrome outbreak. *Asian Journal of Social Psychology, 7*, 25–34.

Kalibatseva, Z., & Leong, F. T. (2011). Depression among Asian Americans: Review and recommendations. *Depression Research and Treatment*. Retrieved from: http://dana.org/news/cerebrum/detail.aspx?id=31364

Kanagawa, C., Cross, S. E., & Markus, H. (2001). 'Who am I?' The cultural psychology of the conceptual self. *Personality and Social Psychology Bulletin, 27*(1), 90–103.

Kang, S. (2006). Measurement of acculturation, scale formats, and language competence: Their implications for adjustment. *Journal of Cross-Cultural Psychology, 37*(6), 669–693.

Kim, B. S. K., & Abreu, J. M. (2001). Acculturation measurement: Theory, current instruments, and future directions. In J. G. Ponterotto, J. M. Casa, L. Suzuki, & C. M. Alexander (Eds.), *Handbook of multicultural counseling* (2nd ed., pp. 394–424). Thousand Oaks, CA: Sage.

Kim, B. S. K., Atkinson, D. R., & Yang, P. H. (1999). The Asian Values Scale: Development, factor analysis, validation, and reliability. *Journal of Counseling Psychology, 46*(3), 342–352.

Kim, B. K., Brenner, B. R., Liang, C. H., & Asay, P. A. (2003). A qualitative study of adaptation experiences of 1.5-generation Asian Americans. *Cultural Diversity and Ethnic Minority Psychology, 9*(2), 156–170.

Kim, S., Gonzales, N. A., Stroh, K., & Wang, J. (2006). Parent-child cultural marginalization and depressive symptoms in Asian American family members. *Journal of Community Psychology, 34*(2), 167–182.

Kim, B. K., & Hong, S. (2004). A psychometric revision of the Asian Values Scale using the Rasch Model. *Measurement and Evaluation in Counseling and Development, 37*(1), 15–27.

Kim, M., Klingle, R., Sharkey, W. F., Park, H., Smith, D. H., & Cai, D. (2000). A test of a cultural model of patients' motivation for verbal communication in patient-doctor interactions. *Communication Monographs, 67*(3), 262–283.

Kim, B. K., & Omizo, M. M. (2003). Asian cultural values, attitudes toward seeking professional psychological help, and willingness to see a counselor. *The Counseling Psychologist, 31*(3), 343–361.

Kim, B. K., Yang, P. H., Atkinson, D. R., Wolfe, M. M., & Hong, S. (2001). Cultural value similarities and differences among Asian American ethnic groups. *Cultural Diversity and Ethnic Minority Psychology, 7*(4), 343–361.

Kroeber, A. L., & Kluckhohn, C. (1952). *Culture: A critical review of concepts and definitions. Harvard University Papers* (Vol. 47(1)). Cambridge, MA: Peabody Museum of Archaeology & Ethnology.

Kuhn, M. H., & McPartland, T. S. (1954). An empirical investigation of self-attitudes. *American Sociological Review, 19*, 68–76.

LaFromboise, T., Coleman, H. L., & Gerton, J. (1993). Psychological impact of biculturalism: Evidence and theory. *Psychological Bulletin, 114*(3), 395–412.

Le, T. N., & Stockdale, G. D. (2005). Individualism, collectivism, and delinquency in Asian American adolescents. *Journal of Clinical Child and Adolescent Psychology, 34*(4), 681–691.

Lee, R. M., Choe, J., Kim, G., & Ngo, V. (2000). Construction of the Asian American Family Conflicts Scale. *Journal of Counseling Psychology, 47*(2), 211–222.

Lee, R. M., Yoon, E., & Liu-Tom, H. (2006). Structure and measurement of acculturation/enculturation for Asian Americans using the ARSMA-II. *Measurement and Evaluation in Counseling and Development, 39*(1), 42–55.

Leung, T., & Kim, M. S. (1997). *A modified version of self-construal scale*. Honolulu, HI: University of Hawai'I at Manoa.

Levine, T. R., Bresnahan, M., Park, H., Lapinsky, M., Wittenbaum, G. M., Shearman, S., & Ohashi, R. (2003). Self-construal scales lack validity. *Human Communication Research, 29*(2), 210–252.

Li, H. Z. (2002). Culture, gender and self–close-other(s) connectedness in Canadian and Chinese samples.

European Journal of Social Psychology, 32(1), 93–104.

Lieber, E., Chin, D., Nihira, K., & Mink, I. (2001). Holding on and letting go: Identity and acculturation among Chinese immigrants. *Cultural Diversity and Ethnic Minority Psychology, 7*(3), 247–261.

Lu, L., & Gilmour, R. (2007). Developing a new measure of independent and interdependent views of the self. *Journal of Research in Personality, 41*(1), 249–257.

Lu, L., Gilmour, R., Kao, S., Weng, T., Hu, C., Chern, J., ... Shih, J. (2001). Two ways to achieve happiness: When the East meets the West. *Personality and Individual Differences, 30*(7), 1161–1174.

Markus, H. R., & Conner, A. (2013). *Clash! 8 cultural conflicts that make us who we are*. New York, NY: Penguin.

Markus, H. R., & Kitayama, S. (1991). Culture and the self: Implications for cognition, emotion, and motivation. *Psychological Review, 98*(2), 224–253.

Markus, H. R., & Kitayama, S. (1998). The cultural psychology of personality. *Journal of Cross-Cultural Psychology, 29*(1), 63–87.

Markus, H. R., & Kitayama, S. (2010). Cultures and selves: A cycle of mutual constitution. *Perspectives on Psychological Science, 5*(4), 420–430.

Matsumoto, D. (1999). Culture and self: An empirical assessment of Markus and Kitayama's theory of independent and interdependent self-construal. *Asian Journal of Social Psychology, 2*(3), 289–310.

McGuire, W. J., & McGuire, C. V. (1988). Content and process in the experience of the self. In L. Berkowitz (Ed.), *Advances in experimental social psychology* (Social psychological studies of the self: Perspectives and programs, Vol. 21, pp. 97–144). San Diego, CA: Academic.

Miller, M. J. (2007). A bilinear multidimensional measurement model of Asian American acculturation and enculturation: Implications for counseling interventions. *Journal of Counseling Psychology, 54*(2), 118–131.

Minoura, Y. (1992). A sensitive period for the incorporation of a cultural meaning system: A study of Japanese children growing up in the United States. *Ethos, 20*(3), 304–339.

Moon, A., Chim, L., Tsai, J., Ho, Y. W., & Fung, H. (January, 2011). The influence of cultural differences in ideal affect on self-presentation and other-perception of Facebook profiles. Poster presented at the 12th annual meeting of the Society for Personality and Social Psychology, San Antonio, TX, USA.

Nguyen, H. H., & von Eye, A. (2002). The Acculturation Scale for Vietnamese Adolescents (ASVA): A bidimensional perspective. *International Journal of Behavioral Development, 26*(3), 202–213.

Nisbett, R. E., Peng, K., Choi, I., & Norenzayan, A. (2001). Culture and systems of thought: Holistic versus analytic cognition. *Psychological Review, 108*(2), 291–310.

Oh, Y., Koeske, G. F., & Sales, E. (2002). Acculturation, stress and depressive symptoms among Korean immigrants in the United States. *The Journal of Social Psychology, 142*(4), 511–526.

Ots, T. (1990). The angry liver, the anxious heart, and the melancholy spleen. *Culture, Medicine and Psychiatry, 14*(1), 21–58.

Ownbey, S. F., & Horridge, P. E. (1998). The Suinn-Lew Asian Self-identity Acculturation Scale: Test with a Non-student, Asian-American sample. *Social Behavior and Personality, 26*(1), 57–68.

Oyserman, D. (1993). The lens of personhood: Viewing the self and others in a multicultural society. *Journal of Personality and Social Psychology, 65*(5), 993–1009.

Oyserman, D., Coon, H. M., & Kemmelmeier, M. (2002). Rethinking individualism and collectivism: Evaluation of theoretical assumptions and meta-analyses. *Psychological Bulletin, 128*(1), 3–72.

Park, J. Z. (2008). Second-generation Asian-American pan-ethnic identity: Pluralized meanings of a racial label. *Sociological Perspectives, 51*(3), 541–561.

Park, H., & Levine, T. R. (1999). The theory of reasoned action and self-construal: Evidence from three cultures. *Communication Monographs, 66*(3), 199–218.

Park, I. J. K., Schwartz, S. J., Lee, R. M., & Kim, M. (2013). Perceived racial/ethnic discrimination and antisocial behaviors among Asian American college students: Testing the moderating roles of ethnic and American identity. *Cultural Diversity and Ethnic Minority Psychology, 19*(2), 166–176.

Peng, K., & Nisbett, R. E. (1999). Culture, dialectics, and reasoning about contradiction. *American Psychologist, 54*(9), 741–754.

Phinney, J. S. (1990). Ethnic identity in adolescents and adults: Review of research. *Psychological Bulletin, 108*(3), 499–514.

Potter, S. H. (1988). The cultural construction of emotion in rural Chinese social life. *Ethos, 16*(2), 181–208.

Redfield, R., Linton, R., & Herskovits, M. J. (1936). Memorandum for the study of acculturation. *American Anthropologist, 38*(1), 149–152.

Rhee, E., Uleman, J. S., & Lee, H. K. (1996). Variations in collectivism and individualism by ingroup and culture: Confirmatory factor analysis. *Journal of Personality and Social Psychology, 71*(5), 1037.

Ryder, A. G., Alden, L. E., & Paulhus, D. L. (2000). Is acculturation unidimensional or bidimensional? A head-to-head comparison in the prediction of personality, self-identity, and adjustment. *Journal of Personality and Social Psychology, 79*(1), 49–65.

Samaniego, R. Y., & Gonzales, N. A. (1999). Multiple mediators of the effects of acculturation status on delinquency for Mexican American adolescents. *American Journal of Community Psychology, 27*(2), 189–210.

Santos, F. (2006). The relationship of stress and loss to the severity and duration of chronic depression in Southeast Asian refugees. *Dissertation Abstracts International: Section B: Sciences and Engineering, 67*(4), 2242.

Sastry, J., & Ross, C. E. (1998). Asian ethnicity and the sense of personal control. *Social Psychology Quarterly, 61*(2), 101–120.

Schwartz, S. H. (1992). Universals in the content and structure of values: Theoretical advances and empirical tests in 20 countries. In M. Zanna (Ed.), *Advances in experimental social psychology* (Vol. 25, pp. 1–65). Orlando, FL: Academic.

Schwartz, S. H. (1994). Beyond individualism/collectivism: New cultural dimension of values. In U. Kim, C. Triandis, C. Kagiticibasi, S. Choi, & G. Yoon (Eds.), *Individualism and collectivism: Theory, method and applications* (pp. 85–122). Thousand Oaks, CA: Sage.

Schwartz, S. H., & Bardi, A. (2001). Value hierarchies across cultures: Taking a similarities perspective. *Journal of Cross-Cultural Psychology, 32*(3), 268–290.

Shin, H. (2004). *Parental involvement and its influence of children's school performance: A comparative study between Asian (Chinese and Korean) Americans and Mexican-Americans*. Unpublished doctoral dissertation, Columbia University, New York, NY.

Sims, T. L., Tsai, J. L., Koopmann-Holm, B., Thomas, E. A. C., & Goldstein, M. K. (2014). Choosing a physician depends on how you want to feel: The role of ideal affect in health-related decision-making. *Emotion, 14*(1), 187–192.

Singelis, T. M. (1994). The measurement of independent and interdependent self-construals. *Personality and Social Psychology Bulletin, 20*(5), 580–591.

Singelis, T. M., Bond, M. H., Sharkey, W. F., & Kriss, S. Y. L. (1999). Unpacking culture's influence on self-esteem and embarassability: The role of self-construals. *Journal of Cross-Cultural Psychology, 30*, 315–341.

Spencer-Rodgers, J., Boucher, H. C., Mori, S. C., Wang, L., & Peng, K. (2009). The dialectical self-concept: Contradiction, change, and holism in East Asian cultures. *Personality and Social Psychology Bulletin, 35*(1), 29–44.

Spencer-Rodgers, J., Peng, K., Wang, L., & Hou, Y. (2004). Dialectical self-esteem and East-West differences in psychological well-being. *Personality and Social Psychology Bulletin, 30*(11), 1416–1432.

Spencer-Rodgers, J., Srivastava, S., & Peng, K. (2001). *The dialectical self scale*. Unpublished data.

Spencer-Rodgers, J., Williams, M. J., & Peng, K. (2010). Cultural differences in expectations of change and tolerance for contradictions: A decade of empirical research. *Personality and Social Psychology Review, 14*(3), 296–312.

Stephens, N. M., Fryberg, S. A., Markus, H. R., Johnson, C. S., & Covarrubias, R. (2012). Unseen disadvantage: How American universities' focus on independence undermines the academic performance of first-generation college students. *Journal of Personality and Social Psychology, 102*(6), 1178–1197.

Stephenson, M. (2000). Development and validation of the Stephenson Multigroup Acculturation Scale (SMAS). *Psychological Assessment, 12*(1), 77–88.

Sue, D., & Sue, D. (1987). Asian-Americans and Pacific Islanders. In P. Pedersen (Ed.), *Handbook of cross-cultural counseling and therapy* (pp. 141–146). New York, NY: Greenwood Press.

Suinn, R. M. (2010). Reviewing acculturation and Asian Americans: How acculturation affects health, adjustment, school achievement, and counseling. *Asian American Journal of Psychology, 1*(1), 5–17.

Suinn, R. M., Rickard-Figueroa, K., Lew, S., & Vigil, P. (1987). The Suinn-Lew Asian Self-Identity Acculturation Scale (SL-ASIA). *Educational and Psychological Measurement, 47*, 401–407.

Ta, V. M., Holck, P., & Gee, G. C. (2010). Generational status and family cohesion effects on the receipt of mental health services among Asian Americans: Findings from the national Latino and Asian American study. *American Journal of Public Health, 100*(1), 115–121.

Tata, S., & Leong, F. L. (1994). Individualism-collectivism, social-network orientation, and acculturation as predictors of attitudes toward seeking professional psychological help among Chinese Americans. *Journal of Counseling Psychology, 41*(3), 280–287.

Triandis, H. (1995). *Individualism and collectivism*. Boulder, CO: Westview Press.

Triandis, H. C., Bontempo, R., Betancourt, H., Bond, M., Leung, K., Brenes, A., … Montmollin, G. (1986). The measurement of the etic aspects of individualism and collectivism across cultures. *Australian Journal of Psychology, 38*(3), 257–267.

Triandis, H. C., McCusker, C., Betancourt, H., Iwao, S., Leung, K., Salazar, J., … Zaleski, Z. (1993). An etic-emic analysis of individualism and collectivism. *Journal of Cross-Cultural Psychology, 24*(3), 366–383.

Triandis, H. C., McCusker, C., & Hui, C. (1990). Multimethod probes of individualism and collectivism. *Journal of Personality and Social Psychology, 59*(5), 1006–1020.

Tsai, J. L. (2007). Ideal affect: Cultural causes and behavioral consequences. *Perspectives on Psychological Science, 2*(3), 242–259.

Tsai, J. L., & Knutson, B. (2006). *The affect valuation index: Reliability and validity*. Unpublished manuscript.

Tsai, J. L., Knutson, B., & Fung, H. H. (2006). Cultural variation in affect valuation. *Journal of Personality and Social Psychology, 90*(2), 288–307.

Tsai, J. L., Knutson, B., & Rothman, A. (2007). The pursuit of ideal affect: Variation in mood-producing behavior. Unpublished manuscript.

Tsai, J. L., Louie, J., Chen, E. E., & Uchida, Y. (2007). Learning what feelings to desire: Socialization of ideal affect through children's storybooks. *Personality and Social Psychology Bulletin, 33*(1), 17–30.

Tsai, J. L., Miao, F. F., Seppala, E., Fung, H. H., & Yeung, D. Y. (2007). Influence and adjustment goals: Sources of cultural differences in ideal affect. *Journal of Personality and Social Psychology, 92*(6), 1102–1117.

Tsai, J. L., Ying, Y., & Lee, P. A. (2000). The meaning of "being Chinese" and "being American": Variation among Chinese American young adults. *Journal of Cross-Cultural Psychology, 31*, 302–322.

U.S. Census. (2013). Asians fastest-growing race or ethnic group in 2012, Census bureau reports. Retrieved on July 31, 2013, from http://www.census.gov/newsroom/releases/archives/population/cb13-112.html

van de Vijver, F. J. R., & Leung, K. (1997). *Methods and data analysis of comparative research*. Boston, MA: Allyn & Bacon.

Vargas, J. H., & Kemmelmeier, M. (2013). Ethnicity and contemporary American culture a meta-analytic investigation of horizontal–vertical individualism–collectivism. *Journal of Cross-Cultural Psychology, 44*(2), 195–222.

Wang, C., & Mallinckrodt, B. (2006). Acculturation, attachment, and psychosocial adjustment of Chinese/Taiwanese international students. *Journal of Counseling Psychology, 53*(4), 422–433.

Ward, C. (1997). Culture learning, acculturative stress, and psychology: Three perspectives on acculturation. *Applied Psychology, 64*(1), 58–62.

Ward, C., & Kennedy, A. (1994). Acculturation strategies, psychological adjustment, and sociocultural competence during cross-cultural transitions. *International Journal of Intercultural Relations, 18*(3), 329–343.

Weisz, J. R., Rothbaum, F., & Blackburn, T. F. (1984). Standing out and standing in: The psychology of control in the U.S. and Japan. *American Psychologist, 39*(9), 955–969.

Wolfe, M. M., Yang, P. H., Wong, E. C., & Atkinson, D. R. (2001). Design and development of the European American values scale for Asian Americans. *Cultural Diversity and Ethnic Minority Psychology, 7*(3), 274–283.

Wong-Rieger, D., & Quintana, D. (1987). Comparative acculturation of Southeast Asian and Hispanic immigrants and sojourners. *Journal of Cross-Cultural Psychology, 18*(3), 345–362.

World Values Survey. (2008). Values change the world. Retrieved on August 9, 2013, from http://www.worldvaluessurvey.org/wvs/articles/folder_published/article_base_110/files/WVSbrochure6-2008_11.pdf

Yao, E. L. (1979). The assimilation of contemporary Chinese immigrants. *Journal of Psychology: Interdisciplinary and Applied, 101*(1), 107–113.

Ying, Y. (1995). Cultural orientation and psychological well-being in Chinese Americans. *American Journal of Community Psychology, 23*(6), 893–911.

Ying, Y., & Han, M. (2008). Cultural orientation in Southeast Asian American young adults. *Cultural Diversity and Ethnic Minority Psychology, 14*(1), 29–37.

Yip, T. (2005). Sources of situational variation in ethnic identity and psychological well-being: A palm pilot study of Chinese American students. *Personality and Social Psychology Bulletin, 31*(2), 1603–1616.

Yoon, E., Hacker, J., Hewitt, A., Abrams, M., & Cleary, S. (2012). Social connectedness, discrimination, and social status as mediators of acculturation/enculturation and well-being. *Journal of Counseling Psychology, 59*(1), 86–96.

The Assessment Interview: A Review of Structured and Semi-structured Clinical Interviews Available for Use Among Asian Clients

7

Diana Herva and Mary Comperini

Introduction

Of all the tools at a clinician's disposal, one of the most important is the assessment interview. Also known as the clinical interview, the assessment interview is a specialized technique that allows a clinician to glean accurate and often indispensable information regarding a client, including but not limited to the client's current condition, history, beliefs, and attitudes (Othmer & Othmer, 1994; Rogers, 2001). As such, it is important to understand the components critical for this process: building rapport, interview technique, assessment of mental status, and diagnostic needs. The purpose of the assessment interview, whether in psychological assessment or treatment, is to explain and/or classify the signs, symptoms, and behaviors that a client is exhibiting or reporting. For psychological assessments in particular, it is important for the clinician to blend the interpretation of evaluation results and the description of the symptoms (Othmer & Othmer, 1994; Rogers, 2001).

The art of the assessment interview lies in the clinician's ability to elicit essential information regarding the client. In order to do this, the clinician must have a clear idea of the evaluation's purpose and pay attention to not just content of the client's responses but also the facial expressions, tone of voice, and gestures. The assessment interview can also serve as a supportive role, which could improve rapport and help the clinician understand the client better (Othmer & Othmer, 1994; Rogers, 2001; The Department of Psychiatry Teaching Committee, 1973). Various interview styles are available and include unstructured, structured, and semi-structured interviews.

Unstructured Interviews

Traditionally, assessment interviews were unstructured. That is not to say that the clinician strides aimlessly through the assessment. Regardless of the interview style a clinician chooses to utilize, the clinician should have a clear idea of the ultimate goal (The Department of Psychiatry Teaching Committee, 1973). This understanding enables the clinician to guide the interview toward that goal. Without this guidance, the interview is unlikely to yield useful information. One of the draws of unstructured interviews is that this style is the most flexible

D. Herva, Ph.D., M.A.O.B. (✉)
Kaweah Delta Health Care District Graduate Medical Education, Visalia, CA USA

State of California Department of Developmental Services, Porterville, CA, USA
e-mail: drherva@gmail.com

M. Comperini, Psy.D.
California Department of Corrections and Rehabilitation, California Correctional Health Care Services, 1256 W Lathrop Road #351, Manteca, CA 95336, USA
e-mail: Dr.Mary@Comperini.com

L.T. Benuto et al. (eds.), *Guide to Psychological Assessment with Asians*,
DOI 10.1007/978-1-4939-0796-0_7, © Springer Science+Business Media New York 2014

due to its unrestricted nature, thereby allowing the clinician to build rapport with the client in a manner unhindered by the strict adherence to predetermined structure. However, the validity of the assessment is in question due to potential pitfalls, the most egregious of which is when a clinician prematurely terminates the interview. This can occur when the clinician comes to a conclusion regarding the client and the client's condition early on in the interview process which causes the clinician to overlook important information that could potentially disconfirm the clinician's initial opinion or that could identify additional diagnostic concerns (Othmer & Othmer, 1994; Rogers, 2001; The Department of Psychiatry Teaching Committee, 1973).

Structured Interviews

Since so many factors contribute to the validity and, thus, ultimate utility of the information obtained in an interview, structured interviews can be preferable in certain situations. Structured interviews have a predefined set of questions which provide for more reliable, quantifiable data. The structured approach has been designed rigorously to avoid biases in the line of questioning and allow for trained nonprofessionals to conduct the interview without missing important information (Rogers, 2001; Vatrapu & Perez-Quinones, n.d.). Standardized and systematic administration and scoring is clearly a major advantage of structured interviews. This comprehensive approach decreases the variability in interviewing and increases diagnostic accuracy. However, the drawback is its rigidity. Structured interviews do not allow for deviations from the language and sequence of the measurement. Therefore, a clinician cannot provide additional prompts and/or explanations without being concerned about the impact on the validity of the assessment. Even if a clinician adheres to the structure, there is still potential for validity concerns, especially if the clinician uses the structured interview in an unskilled manner. Strictly adhering to the protocol can lead to the unintended effects of missing important nonverbal information, damage of rapport due to the impersonal nature of the interview, and overwhelming the client with questioning (Rogers, 2001).

Semi-structured Interviews

Semi-structured interviews are a happy medium between the unstructured and structured interview styles. They blend the strengths of both styles: diagnostic accuracy and flexibility. Unfortunately, they also blend the weaknesses of both styles. Regardless, the use of semi-structured interviews may be more appealing when working with a minority population, especially non-English speakers as it allows much more flexibility in regards to the questions, optional prompts, and ability to explain or elaborate on particular points in the interview.

Recommendations

Regardless of the interview style that a clinician prefers, the clinician should keep in mind that establishing and maintaining rapport with the client is essential for obtaining relevant information. Additionally, the clinician should be careful not to miss important nonverbal cues, such as gestures, tone of voice, and hesitations. It could be beneficial to include screening measures in an assessment interview can help to identify individuals with severe mental illness as it could suggest the need for further assessment and treatment. Finally, the clinician should be flexible with his conclusions regarding diagnosis to avoid a confirmation bias. This can occur when the clinician simply seeks information to confirm the diagnosis rather than considering the possibility of alternative or additional diagnoses as well.

Cultural Considerations

Culturally sensitive interviews will take into consideration the client's characteristics and preferences as well as potential limitations. Skill and sensitivity are of utmost importance in this essential process of evaluation (Othmer & Othmer, 1994; Rogers, 2001; The Department of Psychiatry Teaching Committee, 1973). When working with diverse populations, it is critical that the clinician consider the stigma attached to mental health and mental health-related services in general. Sue and Sue (1987) explained that "the amount of stigma or shame associated with emotional difficulties is probably much greater among Asian-American groups. Mental illness in a family member is considered a failure of the family system itself" (p. 480). Even among Asian individuals of later generations, there is a low mental health utilization rate, often only seeking treatment for severe symptomology (Okazaki, 1998; Sue & Sue, 1987). Therefore, the clinician should consider the purpose of the evaluation and be aware that Asian-Americans may conceptualize mental health problems in different way, primarily via somatic complaints. The somatic manifestation of symptoms complicates the diagnostic process. For example, the DSM criteria for depression requires dysphoric mood as a primary symptom, which would exclude those Asian-Americans who express depression somatically (Sue & Sue, 1987). The different manifestations have often been discussed along with the prevalence of symptoms, symptom patterns, and disorders (Okazaki, 1998).

Another significant factor that clinicians should consider is the potential for language barriers. The APA's 1990 Guidelines for Providers of Psychological Services to Ethnic, Linguistic, and Culturally Diverse Populations recommends that the clinician interact with the client in the client's preferred language. If the clinician lacks this language skill, an appropriate referral or use of an interpreter should be considered. When using an interpreter, the clinician should ensure that the interpreter is knowledgeable about the culture, has appropriate professional background, and has no dual roles with the client. It is of particular importance that the clinician adheres to the latter as much as possible as it may affect the validity of the entire evaluation.

While research has shown that interpreter services improve overall health care experiences and outcomes, clients who required the use of interpreters were more likely to have questions that they wanted to ask but did not (Green et al., 2005), which could have significant implications regarding the client's level of understanding and ability to respond fully to questions asked of them. Clients also appear to engage more with individuals of the same culture than with someone of Anglo-American backgrounds (Vatrapu & Perez-Quinones, n.d.). Green et al. (2005) suggest that "[u]se of interpreters may also compromise rapport between patients and clinicians, and their presence may inhibit patients' questions, particularly about sensitive topics such as mental health" (p. 1054). Green et al. (2005) also found that clients who rated their interpreters highly were more likely to also rate overall care highly. Thus, the role of the interpreter is crucial to a client's access to health care, including mental health. It is important to keep in mind that when using an interpreter, the assessment may take more time or there may not be as much time for the client to ask for clarification. Clinicians who utilize interpreters should be cognizant of this and allow clients an opportunity to ask questions without feeling rushed. Clinicians should also be aware that there may not be corresponding words in the client's preferred language, which could reduce the effectiveness of the interview (Sue & Sue, 1987). Therefore, it is particularly important to refrain from using jargon and to speak in short, clear sentences in order to ensure understanding (Green et al., 2005). The clinician should also question overly simplistic responses as well as responses that fail to address the intended query as these could be indications that the client lacks adequate understanding of the question or that the question was inadequately translated.

The paucity of research on the Asian-American population is a barrier to the establishment of clear guidelines for culturally competent assessment and interpretation of assessment measures that are typical in a standard assessment battery. Partially, this is due to the sociodemographic shifts and within group differences (Okazaki, 1998; Sue & Sue, 1987). As such, it is critical that the clinician be culturally sensitive which means that the clinician has enough knowledge and understanding of a client's culture to adequately make distinctions between pathological and nonpathological symptomology (Okazaki, 1998). Despite the limited availability of structured and semi-structured interview instruments in Asian languages, they can nonetheless be useful. Brief measures, such as screening tools, appear to be well received by the Asian population (Veijola et al., 2003). In determining whether a measure would be appropriate to use with a particular population or subpopulation, however, the clinician must also consider the available psychometric properties of such measures.

Brief Review of Psychometric Properties

Psychometric properties such as reliability and validity are important in determining the usefulness of a measure. Reliability refers to the consistency of the results over time (test-retest reliability) and between different raters at the same point in time (interrater reliability). In regards to categorical constructs, such as psychiatric diagnoses as assessed on some psychological measures, is reported in terms of kappa, a statistic that corrects for chance agreement. Generally, kappa values above 0.70 are considered to reflect good agreement, kappa values between 0.50 and 0.70 are considered to be fair, and kappa values under 0.50 are considered to be poor.

Validity refers to the extent that a test measures what it claims to measure, particularly whether the test items cover what is being measured (content validity), whether the test is effective in predicting a construct (criterion-related validity), and whether the test is related to what it is meant to measure (construct validity). When psychometric properties are limited or absent, the clinician must make a decision whether to use such a measure or not by weighing the potential utility of the tool against the lack of data for its use with such a population. The validity of a diagnostic instrument is often measured by comparing agreement between diagnoses made by the instrument and diagnoses made via a "gold standard." It should be noted that the gold standard has yet to be definitively identified in regards to psychiatric diagnoses. Some studies use psychiatrist expert diagnoses while others use available comprehensive measures such as the Structured Clinical Interview for the DSM-IV Disorders (SCID) and World Health Organization (WHO) Composite International Diagnostic Interview (CIDI).

Structured and Semi-structured Assessment Measures

Given the complexities of an assessment interview, it would be beneficial to know what assessment measures are available. While there are many measures available for use with various populations, this chapter will focus on some of the more frequently used measures that are applicable to the assessment interview and is not meant to be a comprehensive or inclusive list of available measures. The included measures were selected based on their availability, accessibility, and utility for the purposes outlined in this chapter. Considering the diversity of the Asian-American culture and languages, these measures are not available in all languages and psychometric properties such as norms, reliability, and validity data are limited. Where available, these properties are discussed below.

In the event that such languages and norms are unavailable but a clinician chooses to utilize such measure, the clinician should be aware of the possible limitation of using such a measure on the desired population and have knowledge of the measure's reference population (APA, 2002). Any test results should be interpreted with caution while considering the client's cultural and linguistic characteristics. It is the clinician's responsibility to exercise critical judgment when deciding to use assessment measures not currently normed or linguistically available for a specific population.

At-a-glance summary table

Assessment name	Disorder assessed	Recommendation(s) and/or relevant research findings	May be used with	Available in
Structured Clinical Interview for DSM-IV Axis I Disorders (SCID-I)	Adjustment Disorders, Affective Disorders, Anxiety Disorders, Eating Disorders, Substance Use Disorders	Good for diagnosing schizophrenia and mood disorders in Chinese inpatients. Generally good reliability.	Chinese Americans, Korean Americans	Mandarin, Korean
Structured Clinical Interview for DSM-IV Axis II Disorders (SCID-II)	DSM-IV Personality Disorders	Reasonable validity with Cantonese-speaking and Japanese individuals. Excellent reliability in Thai population.	Japanese Americans, Korean Americans, Chinese Americans, Thai Americans	Japanese, Korean, Mandarin, Thai
Mini-Mental State Examination (MMSE-II)	Global Cognitive Status	Generally good psychometric properties. May not be appropriate for individuals with low education and/or literacy levels.	Chinese Americans, Indian Americans, Japanese, Americans, Korean Americans, Thai Americans, Vietnamese Americans	Bengali, Chinese (Cantonese and Mandarin), Gujarati, Hindi, Indian English, Japanese, Kannada, Korean, Malay, Malayalam, Marathi, Punjabi, Tamil, Telugu, Thai, Urdu, Vietnamese
Diagnostic Interview Schedule (DIS)	Affective Disorders, Anxiety Disorders, Antisocial Personality Disorder, Disruptive Behavior Disorders, Eating Disorders, Psychotic Disorders, Substance Use Disorders	Moderate concordance rates, but generally reliable.	Chinese Americans	Chinese
Hopkins Symptom Checklist-25 (HSCL-25)	Affective Disorders, Anxiety Disorders, Unspecified Distress	Use as a screening tool in traumatic contexts to measure unspecified distress. Well received by Southeast Asian population. Cutoff point = 1.75.	Southeast Asians (Cambodian, Hmong, Laotian, Vietnamese), Japanese Americans, Tibetans	Cambodian, Hmong, Japanese, Laotian, Tibetan, Vietnamese
Composite International Diagnostic Interview (CIDI)	Affective Disorders, Anxiety Disorders, Dissociative Disorders, Eating Disorders, Psychotic Disorders, Substance Use Disorders	Limited data on psychometric properties for translated versions. Identifies cases with fewer indictors.	Chinese Americans, Japanese Americans, ndian Americans	Chinese, Japanese, some Indian languages
Mini International Neuropsychiatric Interview (MINI)	Affective Disorders, Anxiety Disorders, Psychotic Disorders, Substance Use Disorders	Limited data on psychometric properties for translated versions.	Chinese Americans, Japanese Americans, Korean Americans, Malaysian Americans, Taiwanese Americans, Filipino Americans, Thai Americans	Cantonese, Japanese, Korean, Malay, Mandarin, Tagalog, Thai

Structured Clinical Interview for the DSM-IV Axis I and II Disorders (SCID-I and SCID-II)

The Structured Clinical Interview for the DSM-IV Axis I and II Disorders (SCID-I and SCID-II) are semi-structured interviews designed to diagnose major DSM-IV disorders (Biometrics Research Department, n.d.). The SCID-I has two main versions: a Clinical Version (SCID-CV) and several research versions. The SCID-CV was designed for efficient use in clinical settings while the research versions are more comprehensive. The primary difference in the SCID-CV and the SCID-I Research Version is the level of detail that is covered. Additionally, the SCID-I Research Version incorporates the following diagnoses, which are not included in the SCID-CV: Acute Stress Disorder, Minor Depressive Disorder, Mixed Anxiety Depressive Disorder, and Binge Eating Disorder. The SCID-I Research Versions include an extensive patient edition (SCID-I/P) for use with psychiatric patients and a shorter nonpatient edition (SCID-I/NP), abridged from the SCID-I/P, for use with subjects not identified as psychiatric patients. The SCID-II was designed to assess the 11 major Axis II personality disorders in the DSM-IV-TR, including Personality Disorder NOS, Depressive Personality Disorder, and Passive-Aggressive Personality Disorder (Biometrics Research Department, n.d.; Summerfeldt, Kloosterman, & Antony, 2010).

Validity, Reliability, and Utility

Biometrics Research Department (n.d.) reports reliability data from various sources indicating generally fair to good reliability and validity of the SCID-I and SCID-II. Interrater reliability kappa coefficients ranged from 0.48 to 0.98 and internal consistency coefficients were fair to good (0.71–0.94) (Biometrics Research Department, n.d.; Maffei et al., 1997). Available psychometric properties for versions adapted for use with Asian populations appear to demonstrate similar reliability and validity. The *Chinese-Bilingual SCID-I/P* (CB-SCID-I/P) demonstrated an overall kappa for interrater reliability of 0.84; specifically, the kappa for bipolar affective disorder was 0.84, mood disorder was 0.76, and schizophrenia was 0.75. The overall kappa value was 0.77 and the percentage of agreement was 89.6 %. The CB-SCID-I/P was determined to be a reliable instrument for diagnosing schizophrenia and mood disorders for inpatients (So et al., 2003). The *Borderline Personality Disorder Subscale (Chinese Version) of the SCID-II* was demonstrated to have internal consistency of 0.82 (Cronbach's alpha) with an agreement kappa of 0.82, sensitivity of 0.92, and specificity of 0.94. The SCID-II Borderline Personality Disorder Subscale (Chinese Version) was determined to have reasonable validity for use with Cantonese-speaking individuals (Wong & Chow, 2011). The *Japanese version* of the SCID-II personality questionnaire (SCID-II-PQ) has been demonstrated to have moderately good test-retest reliability, which increased to being very good following the SCID-II interview. The SCID-II was determined to be useful and reliable for the Japanese population. The overall kappa for the SCID-II-PQ was 0.56 and the overall kappa for the SCID-II was reported at 0.87 (Osone & Takahashi, 2003). The *Thai version* of the SCID-II has been shown to have good to excellent reliability with an interrater reliability for diagnoses ranging between 0.70 and 0.90 (Wongpakaran et al., 2012).

Although it is unclear if there is a Khmer translation available, Hinton, Ba, Peou, and Um (2000) reported that the Cambodian Panic Disorder Survey (CPDS) is a culturally valid adaptation of the SCID-panic module. Research provides for the prevalence and subtypes of panic disorders for this population (Hinton et al., 2000).

Interpretation

Normative data is not readily available. However, research conducted with translated versions of the SCID has shown it is generally a reliable measure (Osone & Takahashi, 2003; So et al., 2003; Wong & Chow, 2011; Wongpakaran et al., 2012). Research has shown that the SCID may be more conservative in identifying cases than screening measures although the SCID and screening measures tended to agree in regards to noncases (Silov et al., 2007).

Strengths and Limitations

As a comprehensive measure, the SCID instruments have clear advantages of being able to assess a broad scope of diagnoses in a hierarchical approach. These measures have good diagnostic reliability. Conversely, limitations in these measures include the length of assessment due to its comprehensive nature. Additionally, the focus on diagnosis can lead to insufficient attention to key symptoms. The SCID provides clinical and subclinical gradations, but may not be useful in evaluating changes in symptom severity.

Special Considerations

A SCID version has been developed for use in children (KID-SCID) with generally good reliability (Biometrics Research Department, n.d.; Summerfeldt et al., 2010). Unfortunately, research with this measure and its availability in other languages is limited.

Languages

The SCID-I is available in Korean and Mandarin while the SCID-II is available in Japanese, Korean, Mandarin, and Thai.

Specific Recommendations

The clinician should keep in mind cultural factors that may affect diagnoses, particularly as the SCID measures are based on the DSM-IV criteria. Additionally, with the recent release of the DSM-V, the clinician should be aware of changes to the diagnostic criteria that are not yet reflected in these measures.

Mini-Mental State Examination (MMSE)

No assessment interview is complete without a basic mental status examination. The MMSE is a structured measure that is commonly used to evaluate global cognitive status. The most current version, MMSE 2nd Edition (MMSE-2), is reported to be equivalent to the original MMSE and includes brief, standard, and expanded forms. The MMSE-2 expanded the MMSE to also be used with milder forms of cognitive impairment.

Validity, Reliability, and Utility

The *Japanese version* has been shown to have good reliability (Cronbach's coefficients exceeding 0.70) and three main factors (immediate memory, orientation and delayed recall, and working memory) that explain 44.6 % of the variance (Shigemori, Ohgi, Okuyama, Shimura, & Schneider, 2010). The Japanese version was determined to accurately reflect the cognitive profile of older Japanese adults and the question about orientation to time may be useful in the simplest assessment to identify cognitive dysfunction (Ideno, Takayama, Hayashi, Takagi, & Sugai, 2011; Shigemori et al., 2010). There are three *Korean versions*: full Korean MMSE (K-MMSE), MMSE optimized for screening dementia (MMSE-DS), and a short version of the MMSE-DS (SMMSE-DS) (Kim et al., 2010). The MMSE-DS was reportedly optimized for screening dementia. The SMMSE-DS was constructed from the MMSE-DS based on the diagnostic accuracy of items for dementia. The internal consistency (Cronbach's coefficient alpha = 0.826), interrater reliability (0.968), and test-retest reliability (0.825) were good. The MMSE-DS is reported to have significant correlation with the Clinical Dementia Rating and the K-MMSE. Research indicates that, as compared to the K-MMSE, the SMMSE-DS had increased sensitivity and specificity for dementia (Kim et al., 2010).

Interpretation

Although specific psychometric properties are not readily available on the *Cantonese version of the MMSE* (C-MMSE), research has been conducted on a telephone version of the C-MMSE (T-CMMSE) which suggests excellent inter- and intra-rater reliability (Wong & Fong, 2009). The agreement between the face-to-face MMSE and T-CMMSE was reported with a kappa of 0.60–0.80 for orientation, registration, and recall items. Wong and Fong (2009) suggested a cutoff score of 16 for the T-CMMSE for discrimination between clients with and without dementia.

In a study of Korean neurosurgical patients, the mean score on the *Korean version* (K-MMSE) was 22.3 with 62.1 % of scores below 23 (Kim et al., 2010). Based on the administration of the Mini-Mental State Examination from the Korean version of the Consortium to Establish a Registry for Alzheimer's Disease Assessment Packet (CERAD-K) Neuropsychological Assessment Packet (MMSE-KC), Kim et al. (2012) reported demographics-adjusted norms for the MMSE in elderly Koreans, suggesting that "clinicians need to take age, education, and gender into account for an accurate interpretation of the MMSE-KC total score" (p. 5). Please refer to Kim et al. (2012) for specific norms.

The mean score on the *Thai version* (MMSE-T) in general non-dementia Thai subjects was reported at 27.2 and ranged between 17 and 30; 7.44 % of the cases were reported to have MMSE-T scores above 23 (Wongchaisuwan, Sithinamsuwan, Udommongkol, & Wongmek, 2005). However, research suggests that the MMSE-T may not be appropriate as a screen for cognitive impairment in clients of lower literacy and education levels (Jitapunkul & Lailert, 1997; Wongchaisuwan et al., 2005).

PAR Publishers (2012) caution that users of non-English language versions of the MMSE-2 should base the clinical interpretation of the MMSE-2 scores upon locally collected standardization data and/or clinical patient data. The publishers indicate that they do not endorse the use of the U.S. population-based MMSE-2 norms for interpretation in the MMSE-2 scores of patients who do not match the demographic characteristics of the MMSE-2 standardization sample. "Clinical use of the raw sore cutoff ranges for the MMSE-2 should be based on the scientific literature on the MMSE/MMSE-2 in the native language in which it is being used" (PAR, 2012).

Strengths and Limitations

The obvious strength of this measure is its brief nature, which is likely part of the reason that it is so commonly used. However, the MMSE is a screening tool and does not provide diagnoses. Research has also shown that it may not be appropriate for all populations, especially in those with low education levels.

Special Considerations

The MMSE is generally used with adults and older adults as an assessment of global cognitive status. It is important to remember that this is a screening tool that should not be used independently for diagnostic purposes.

Languages

The MMSE-2 is available in simplified Chinese and Hindi. The original MMSE also has authorized translations in Bengali, Cantonese Chinese (for Hong Kong), Chinese, Chinese (for Hong Kong, Malaysia, Singapore, and Taiwan), Gujarati, Hindi, Indian English, Japanese, Kannada, Korean, Malay, Malayalam, Mandarin (also for China, Singapore, and Taiwan), Marathi, Punjabi, Tamil, Telugu, Thai, Urdu, and Vietnamese.

Specific Recommendations

If the MMSE is unavailable in the language necessary, other options may be to utilize select subtests from available translated versions of intelligence assessment measures such as the Wechsler Adult Intelligence Scales and Stanford-Binet (Zuckerman, 2005). Such subtests can include Information, Arithmetic, Comprehension, Similarities, and Digit Span. This method allows the clinician to assess a client's mental status while allowing for precise scoring and interpretation. However, the clinician should be cognizant of the fact that norming and validity may still be impacted due to the unstandardized manner of administering such intelligence tests (Zuckerman, 2005).

Diagnostic Interview Schedule (DIS)

The DIS is an extensive structured diagnostic interview that was designed to assess for current and lifetime diagnoses, which are organized into 19 diagnostic modules. Information obtained in the DIS includes onset, duration, and recency of symptoms. The DIS was originally designed for the purpose of determining the prevalence and incidence of certain diagnoses in the United Stated. Since its inception, the DIS has demonstrated its cross-cultural applications and utility in both clinical and research arenas. The structured nature of the DIS allows both professional and nonprofessional interviewers to administer it (Rogers, 2001).

Validity, Reliability, and Utility

The original Chinese version was reported to have a moderate concordance rate (kappa = 0.54). Studies generally indicate that the Chinese version is a reliable tool (Hwu & Chang, 1986; Hwu, Yeh, Chang, & Yeh, 1986).

Interpretation

Research with the Chinese version have found lower prevalence rates for certain disorders (Hwu et al., 1986; Hwu & Compton, 1994), which is reasonable considering that some psychiatric conditions are naturally less prevalent in Asian-Americans than in other populations.

Strengths and Limitations

Over the years, the DIS had been used as the gold standard due to its extensive and structured nature. It is easily administered by professionals and nonprofessionals alike. Additionally, the DIS has a self-administered version in two different formats (computer-assisted and paper-and-pencil), further simplifying the assessment process. However, like many assessment measures, the DIS is lacking in normative and validation data for translated versions, which can be significant considering cultural differences. Regardless, research has shown that the DIS is a good cross-cultural measure that has been widely used. In fact, the DIS so comprehensive and widely used that it was expanded into the WHO-CIDI by incorporating the International Classification of Diseases (ICD) diagnostic criteria.

Special Considerations

The DIS is meant for adults ages 18 and over. However, there is a Chinese version of the Diagnostic Interview Schedule for Children-Version 4 (DISC-IV). This version can be used on children and adolescents. Kappa coefficients ranged from 0.37 to 0.84 with three diagnoses falling under 0.50 (anxiety disorder, ADHD, and ODD). All three low kappa levels were found when the youth was the informant. Despite this, research indicates that the Chinese version had comparable test-retest reliability with the original English version (Ho et al., 2005).

Languages

The DIS is available in Chinese and Korean.

Specific Recommendations

As with any measure without specific norms or validation data, the DIS should be used with caution and the clinician should keep in mind the cultural differences that may affect diagnoses.

Hopkins Symptom Checklist-25 (HSCL-25)

The Hopkins Symptom Checklist (HSCL) is a semi-structured self-report screening instrument that was originally designed to measure change in a refugee client's clinical status, primarily unspecific distress. The HSCL-25 was developed for use in primary care settings from the 90-item Symptom Checklist (SCL-90), which was designed to assess patterns of current psychological symptoms (Mollica, Wyshak, de Marneffe, Khuon, & Lavelle, 1987; Ventevogel et al., 2007). It includes 10 items from the HSCL-58 anxiety cluster, 13 items from the depression cluster, and 2 additional somatic symptoms. The items are rated on a 4-point scale from "not at all" to "extremely." Depending on the purpose for using this measure, the entire measure or its subsections can be used separately. The HSCL-25 can also be administered by trained nonprofessionals.

The HSCL-25 was developed for use with the Southeast Asian population due to the lack of mental health care for refugees in the United States. In the 1980s, three versions were originally developed: Cambodian, Laotian, and Vietnamese. In 1995, a Hmong version became available (Mollica et al., 1987; Mounoutoua & Brown, 1995). The Japanese version was reportedly developed for use in the Kobe earthquake study (Mollica et al., 1987).

Validity, Reliability, and Utility

The original *Cambodian, Laotian, and Vietnamese versions* were validated together due to a small sample size for each language group alone (Mollica et al., 1987). Mollica et al. (1987) found that the HSCL-25 was sufficiently sensitive and specific for the presence of depression. The HSCL-25 was also found to be correlated with clients' self-assessments of clinical improvement. In regards to reliability, the "test-retest coefficients for the three language groups combined were 0.89 for the total score and 0.82 for anxiety and depression; the results for each language group separately were comparable. The interrater reliability for the total, anxiety, and depression scores for each of the three language groups was higher than 0.98" (Mollica et al., 1987, p. 499). Convergent reliability has been measured at 0.73–0.88 with measures of depression. Mollica et al. (1987) reported that these results were comparable to previous findings on the HSCL-25.

The *Hmong version* is reported to have "internal consistency of 0.97 and had a split-half coefficient of 0.92 and test-retest reliability of 0.90… The Hmong version of the HSCL-25 provided a sensitivity of 100 %, specificity of 78 % [resulting in a false positive rate of 22 %], and overall accuracy of 89 % [for distinguishing clinical and nonclinical groups], demonstrating that it is a useful screening tool for assessing general distress and anxiety problems in Hmong people" (abstract, p. 1). The Hmong version also used a cutoff score of 1.75 (Mounoutoua & Brown, 1995). The *Tibetan version* is reported to have coefficient alphas between 0.87 and 0.89 for the anxiety subscale and 0.85–0.92 for the depression subscale (Keller et al., 2006; Lhewa, Banu, Rosenfeld, & Keller, 2007). Results indicated good classification accuracy for anxiety (0.89), depression (0.92), and PTSD (0.83) (Lhewa et al., 2007). Research has reported prevalence rates for anxiety (25–77 %), depression (11.5–57 %), and PTSD (11–23 %) in Tibetan refugees (Mills et al., 2005). The *Japanese version* (J-HSCL-25) has been reported to have test-retest reliability coefficients of 0.75 for depression and 0.78 for anxiety with a cutoff score of 1.75. The Cronbach's alphas ranged from 0.90 to 0.91 for depression and 0.84–0.86 for anxiety (Mollica, McDonald, Massagli, & Silove, 2004; Sumi & Kanda, 2002).

Interpretation

For the original *Cambodian, Laotian, and Vietnamese versions*, a cutoff point of 1.75 was selected "for its consistency with data obtained from a random general population sample in California" (Mollica et al., 1987). Though most research studies have used 1.75 as the cutoff, Mollica et al. (1987) submit that there is no psychometric evidence to suggest that 1.75 is the ideal cutoff point. Research indicates that lower cutoff scores may be more sensitive and be able to accurately classify those individuals with PTSD (Keller et al., 2006). Regardless of the ambiguity surrounding the ideal cutoff point, these translated versions were found to be comparable to other HSCL-25 versions in regards to sensitivity, specificity, and reliability (Mollica et al., 1987; Mounoutoua & Brown, 1995; Sumi & Kanda, 2002).

Though the research for the available Asian language versions used cutoff scores of 1.75, other research suggests that the cutoff scores determined in one cultural group should be reconsidered in other groups (Ichikawa, Nakahara, & Wakai, 2006). Ichikawa et al. (2006) examined the use of the predetermined cutoff score of 1.75 on Afghan refugees in Japan. The results indicated that the use of this cutoff score overestimated the magnitude of mental health problems in this population. An algorithm method could improve classification accuracy as compared to using cutoff scores; however, its clinical validity remains unknown. Ichikawa et al. (2006) surmised that the overestimation in mental health problems as measured by the HSCL-25 may be due to the differences in response to the symptoms, causing noncases to be classified as cases. Therefore, considering the within group differences in the Asian population, the clinician should be cautious about applying the same cutoff score for subpopulations not yet represented in research. Nevertheless, as previously mentioned, research conducted with all the versions discussed above used a cutoff score of 1.75.

Strengths and Limitations

The HSCL-25 is a good screening measure for use with the Southeast Asian population. This is primarily due to its clinical utility, briefness, and economical nature (Sandanger et al., 1999). This measure has been shown to be readily accepted by Southeast Asians due to its similarity to medical tests (Mollica et al., 1987). Additionally, its linguistic simplicity allows clients of various educational levels to easily comprehend the items. The 4-point likert-type scale from "not at all" to "extremely" allows for measurement of clinical change in clients. Additionally, the HSCL-25 has been shown to have a sensitivity of 48 %, specificity of 87 %, and sensitivity of comorbid psychiatric disorders of 100 % for DSM-III-R psychiatric disorders; this suggests that it is a moderate instrument for screening (Veijola et al., 2003). Although studies on DSM-IV criteria are unavailable for review, this data suggests that this measure is adequate for screening purposes, particularly for cases that are sensitive to pain, distress, and impairment as well as for symptoms related to somatic illnesses (Sandanger et al., 1999). In fact, Silov et al. (2007) found that the HSCL-25 agreed with the SCID in identifying noncases and suggested that it may be more accurate in identifying cases in highly symptomatic clinic populations.

A limitation of this measure is that it does not provide a diagnosis. On the other hand, the clinician can gain useful information in regards to symptoms of anxiety and depression, which can help determine if deeper probing is warranted. Moreover, research has shown that the HCSL-25 can be helpful in evaluating victims of trauma, particularly for Southeast Asians who have experienced serious traumas. The design of this measure allows for the assessment of trauma in a nonthreatening manner that helps clients verbalize their symptoms.

Special Considerations

The HSCL-25 has been used primarily in traumatic contexts with adults and adolescents as young at 14 years of age.

Languages

The HSCL-25 is available in the Cambodian, Hmong, Japanese, Laotian, Tibetan, and Vietnamese languages.

Specific Recommendations

As with all screening tools, it is important to keep in mind that the purpose is to determine whether more in depth evaluation of such symptoms is warranted. Therefore, despite the potential limitations of this measure, it can provide the clinician with indications of areas for further exploration.

Composite International Diagnostic Interview (CIDI)

The CIDI is a structured measure that was developed in 1990 by the World Health Organization (WHO) as an expansion of the Diagnostic Interview Schedule (DIS). Its history can be traced back to the early 1980s when a WHO task force considered combining the DIS and Present State Examination (PSE) in a concerted international effort (WHO, n.d.; Wittchen, 1994). The CIDI expanded on the DIS by incorporating the International Classification of Disease (ICD) diagnostic system. The rationale was so that cross-national comparative research could be conducted without limitation to just mental disorders. In 1998, the CIDI was further expanded to include measurements for risk factors, consequences, treatment, etc. This measure evaluates lifetime and 12-month disorders (WHO, n.d.; Wittchen, 1994).

There are two versions of the CIDI available: the computer-assisted version (CAPI) and the paper and pencil version (PAPI). Both versions are modularized so the clinician can select any or all of the sections for administration as well as selecting the percentage of subjects who will randomly enter certain sections. The CAPI offers a user-friendly interface that simplifies the process of selecting sections (so that clinicians can choose which sections to assess as well as the percentage of subjects who will randomly enter certain sections). The PAPI formerly allowed for screening via the short form, which could be followed up by a long form. However, the WHO no longer supports the use of the CIDI short form as it has been determined to not be useful. The PAPI version also incorporates a reference card to assist the clinician in making decisions to skip or administer certain sections without having the clinician flip back and forth between pages for a client's previous responses (WHO, n.d.).

The CIDI Diagnostic Algorithms include: mood, anxiety, substance-related, and impulse control disorders. Included in mood disorders are: Major Depressive Disorder, Recurrent Brief Depression, Hypomania, and Mania. Anxiety disorders include: Agoraphobia, Generalized Anxiety Disorder, Panic Attack/Disorder, Social Phobia, Specific Phobia, Separation Anxiety Disorder, and Post Traumatic Stress Disorder (PTSD). Substance-relate disorders include: Alcohol Abuse/Dependence, Drug Abuse/Dependence, and Nicotine Dependence. Impulse Control Disorders include: Conduct Disorder, Intermittent Explosive Disorder, Anorexia Nervosa, Bulimia Nervosa, Pathological Gambling, Attention Deficit Disorder, Hyperkinetic Disorder, and Oppositional Defiant Disorder. The CIDI also include a diagnostic algorithm for Premenstrual Dysphoric Disorder (WHO, n.d.; Wittchen, 1994).

Validity, Reliability, and Utility

In general, the WHO-CIDI has been demonstrated to have "good to excellent Kappa coefficients for most diagnostic sections. In international multicenter studies as well as several smaller center studies the CIDI was judged to be acceptable for most subjects and was found to be appropriate for use in different kinds of settings and countries. There is however still a need for reliability studies in general population samples, the area the CIDI was primary [sic] intended for. Only a few selected aspects of validity have been examined so far, mostly in smaller selected clinical samples" (Wittchen, 1994, abstract). Test-retest kappa values ranged from 0.59 to 0.84 and interrater reliability kappa values ranged from 0.67 to 0.98 (Wittchen, 1994). Diagnostic concordance rates have been found to be relatively high (kappa values range between 0.73 and 0.83). However, these studies were involved small sample sizes; the CIDI lacks large-scale validation and no norms are available. Despite this, the CIDI has been widely translated and used in many countries. Part of its vast appeal is that the CIDI is based on both DSM and ICD diagnostic criteria, which allows for cross-national comparative research and utility. As such, the CIDI has been used for validation of other measures including the HSCL-25 and MINI (Lecrubier et al., 1997; Sandanger et al., 1999).

The Chinese version of the WHO-CIDI version 3.0 (CIDI-3.0) was reported to be an acceptably validated instrument for community survey on mental disorders (Huany et al., 2010). The screen section of the CIDI-3.0 had sensitivity values of 60.4–93.1 % and specificity values of 33.6–92.7 %. As for the different mental disorders, sensitivity values ranged from 33.3 to 70.3 % and specificity values ranged from 97.1 to 98.9 %. Consistency of any mental disorder was reported at 0.78 and test-retest reliability kappa values ranged from 0.74 to 1.00 (Huany et al., 2010).

Interpretation

Interpretation is simplified in that scoring algorithms for this measure are available to certified users and are computer-based, which minimizes user error. Despite the lack of large-scale validation and norms, this tool has been widely used and is determined to be useful for diagnostic purposes. The WHO has strict guidelines for the translation of this measure and translations are expected to be equivalent to the English version. Therefore, interpretation should be similar across cultures.

Strengths and Limitations

Copies of the CIDI are readily available at no charge. Formal training at an official TRC is required before the CIDI can be used. This training requires 30 h of at-home self-study followed by 3–5 days of in-person training and a certification assessment. The scoring algorithms are only available upon becoming a certified user. One of the strengths of this measure is that it can be administered by trained laypersons as well as clinicians.

Despite the comprehensiveness of this measure, one of the largest limitations is the extensive amount of time it takes to administer, especially if the entire measure is administered. As a result of the modularization, clinicians can significantly shorten the administration time if only specific sections are selected.

Special Considerations

The CIDI can be used with individuals ages 16 and older. Though there are no norms available, this measure has been widely translated and used. The WHO's strict translation requirements suggest that translated versions are equivalent to the English version. Additionally, since the CIDI is based on both DSM and ICD diagnostic criteria, this measure should, theoretically, be just as useful for translated versions.

Languages

The CIDI is available in Chinese, Japanese, and limited access in some Indian languages. However, the WHO cautions that many of the translated "versions were done for specific studies and are out of date" (WHO, n.d.).

Specific Recommendations

While this measure has been widely translated and used, the clinician should keep in mind the purpose of the evaluation. Research has indicated that the HSCL-25 and the CIDI identified the same amount of cases though the agreement of identified cases was only half (Sandanger et al., 1999). The cases identified by the HSCL-25 had significantly more illness indicators and the cases identified by just the CIDI had the least. Thus, the clinician must weigh the benefits of the measure against potential time constraints.

Mini-International Neuropsychiatric Interview (MINI)

The MINI is a short diagnostic structured interview developed by psychiatrists and clinicians in the United States and France. The primary purpose for its development was to create a short measure based on DSM. However, the current version (MINI 6.0) is based on both DSM-IV and ICD-10 criteria and screens for 17 Axis I disorders. This measure was designed in such a manner that it could be administered by nonspecialized interviewers in about 15 min. As such, this measure is widely used internationally for psychiatric evaluation and outcome tracking (Lecrubier et al., 1997; Medical Outcome Systems, n.d.; Sheehan et al., 1998).

Validity, Reliability, and Utility

The MINI has been validated against the SCID, CIDI, and expert opinions. It has been lauded as a fully validated and time-efficient measure that can be easily integrated into clinical interviews. In fact, research demonstrates that the MINI was better at diagnosing comorbid conditions. Additionally, it has been shown to be well accepted by clients (Medical Outcome Systems, n.d.; Pinninti, Madison, Musser, & Rissmiller, 2003; Sheehan et al., 1998). In general, sensitivity and specificity were considered to be "good" (sensitivity = 0.45–0.96, specificity = 0.86–1.00). Agreement between MINI diagnoses and experts was found in 85 % of cases. Test-retest reliability kappa values were between 0.35 and 1.00 with only Current Mania falling under 0.50, which is understandable considering that mania is a changing state. The interrater reliability kappa values were between 0.79 and 1.00 (Sheehan et al., 1998).

For the *Japanese version*, "[a]ll of the kappa values indicated excellent agreement (more than 0.75) except those for dysthymia (0.74) and generalized anxiety disorder (0.72)... Kappa values indicated excellent agreement (more than 0.75) for 3 of the 12 diagnoses (i.e. major depressive disorder, panic disorder, and generalized anxiety disorder), good agreement (0.60–0.74) for six diagnoses, and acceptable agreement (0.45–0.59) for two diagnoses. Only one kappa value (dysthymia) was less than 0.45" (Otsubo et al., 2005, p. 521). Otsubo et al. (2005) also found that in general, the MINI diagnoses had acceptable to excellent agreement with the SCID-P results (0.45 to more than 0.75); 3 of the 16 diagnoses were excluded because no subjects met the criteria for these diagnoses (PTSD, alcohol abuse, and drug abuse).

Additionally, there was poor concordance rate (<5 %) for the following diagnoses: mania, generalized anxiety disorder, drug dependence, and bulimia nervosa (Otsubo et al., 2005). Overall, these data appear similar to, if not better than, the validation data for the original MINI. Although data on reliability and validity are unavailable for the other translated versions of the MINI, it can be surmised that the translated versions would be equivalent to the English versions and, thus, retain similar psychometric properties.

Interpretation

Although widely used, this measure is lacking in adequate norms and validation for the translated versions. However, considering that it is based on both DSM and ICD criteria, there is a high likelihood that interpretation is similar across cultures.

Strengths and Limitations

For clinicians in private practice, this measure is available for a one-time fee and there is no per use fee. Additionally, there are paper and electronic versions available. The electronic version can be used directly from any browser. Clinicians can have clients complete the MINI at home prior to the in-office visit.

Clearly, the lack of norms and validation for translated versions of this measure are limitations that raise serious concerns about its applicability across cultures. However, as previously discussed, since it is based on both DSM and ICD diagnostic criteria, there is a high likelihood that the MINI would be just as useful diagnostically across cultures.

Special Considerations

This measure has a version (MINI-KID) developed specifically for use with children and adolescents. The MINI-KID version has a high concordance rate for mood disorders, anxiety disorders, substance use disorders, ADHD/behavioral disorders, and eating disorders (kappa values between 0.56 and 0.87) while results were more variable for psychotic disorders (kappa = 0.41). Sensitivity was between 0.61 and 1.00 and specificity was between 0.81 and 1.00. Test-retest and interrater reliability were deemed high (kappa values between 0.64 and 1.00). Overall, the MINI-KID appears to be reliable for use on children and adolescents. It should be noted that this version may not be widely available in other languages (Sheehan et al., 2010).

Languages

The MINI is available in Cantonese, Japanese, Korean, Malay, Mandarin Chinese for Taiwan, Tagalog, and Thai.

Specific Recommendations

The clinician should use caution when using this measure due to the lack of available norms and validation data. However, it could be a useful tool as it is based on both DSM and ICD criteria.

Summary/Conclusion

The assessment interview is essential to the evaluation process and allows a clinician to glean accurate and often indispensable information regarding a client, including but not limited to the client's current condition, history, beliefs, and attitudes (Othmer & Othmer, 1994; Rogers, 2001). Therefore, it is imperative that a clinician understand the components critical for this process: building rapport, interview technique, assessment of mental status, and diagnostic needs. The measure selected for use and interview style can greatly affect the validity and utility of data obtain from the interview itself. Screening measures can be used to help identify individuals with severe mental illness as it could suggest the need for further assessment and treatment while more comprehensive measures can assist with diagnostic needs.

Culturally sensitive interviews will take into consideration the client's characteristics and preferences as well as potential limitations. The paucity of research with the Asian population prevents the establishment of clear guidelines for culturally competent assessment and interpretation of assessment measures that are typical in a standard assessment battery. As such, it is critical that the clinician be culturally sensitive and have enough knowledge and understanding of a client's culture in order to adequately make distinctions between pathological and nonpathological symptomology (Okazaki, 1998). Clinicians should consider the purpose of the evaluation and be aware that Asian-Americans may conceptualize mental health problems in different way, namely somatic complaints, which further complicate the diagnostic process. Another significant factor that clinicians should consider is the potential for language barriers and the need for interpreter service as well as the possible complications that are involved.

The Asian-American population is so diverse that it is difficult to find, translate, or validate measures for all subpopulations. Even with the few that were identified and discussed in this chapter are limited linguistically and psychometrically. Therefore, it is inevitable that clinicians will require the use of psychological measures that have not been validated on the appropriate populations. In such an event, the clinician should be aware of the possible limitations of using such measures on the desired population and have knowledge of the measure's reference population (APA, 2002). The American Psychological Association's amended 2010 Ethical Principles of Psychologists and Code of Conduct specify that "[w]hen such validity or reliability [for the test population] has not been established, psychologists describe the strengths and limitations of test results and interpretation" (p. 12). In addition to this, test results should be interpreted with caution while considering the client's cultural and linguistic characteristics. Ultimately, it is the clinician's responsibility to exercise critical judgment when deciding to use assessment measures not currently normed or linguistically available for the specific population. In making this decision, the clinician should make an effort to seek consultation and proceed in a manner that is most in line with ethical standards. It is recommended that the clinician first attempt to identify alternative measures that may be appropriate for the intended purpose before attempting to modify existing measures for use. Clinicians should be aware that any modifications to the standardized administration of a measure may affect the test results; such limitations should be discussed and incorporated into the interpretation of the results.

References

American Psychiatric Association. (2000). *Diagnostic and statistical manual of mental disorders* (4th ed., text rev.). Washington, DC: American Psychiatric Association.

American Psychological Association. (2002, August). *Guidelines on multicultural education, training, research, practice, and organizational change for psychologists* [Publication]. Retrieved from http://www.apa.org/pi/oema/resources/policy/multicultural-guidelines.aspx

American Psychological Association. (2010, February). *Ethical principles of psychologists and code of conduct with the 2010 amendments*. Retrieved from http://www.apa.org/ethics/code/index.aspx

American Psychological Association, Office of Ethnic Minority Affairs. (1990, August). *Guidelines for providers of psychological services to ethnic, linguistic, and culturally diverse populations* [Publication]. Retrieved from http://www.apa.org/pi/oema/resources/policy/provider-guidelines.aspx

Biometrics Research Department. (n.d.). *Structured clinical interview for DSM disorders (SCID)*. Retrieved from http://www.scid4.org/index.html

Green, A. R., Ngo-Metzger, Q., Legedza, A. T. R., Massagli, M. P., Phillips, R. S., & Iezzoni, L. I. (2005). Interpreter services, language concordance, and health care quality experiences of Asian Americans with limited English proficiency. *Journal of General Internal Medicine, 20*, 1050–1056.

Hinton, D., Ba, P., Peou, S., & Um, K. (2000). Panic disorder among Cambodian refugees attending a psychiatric clinic. *General Hospital Psychiatry, 22*(6), 437–444.

Ho, T., Leung, P. W., Lee, C., Tang, C., Hung, S., Kwong, S., … Shaffer, D. (2005). Test-retest reliability of the Chinese version of the Diagnostic Interview Schedule for Children-Version 4 (DISC-IV). *Journal of Child Psychology and Psychiatry, 46*(10), 1135–1138.

Huany, Y., Shou-Fu, X., Jin, L., Jun-Ting, X., Wei-Min, D., Yi, L., … Rui, C. (2010). Community-based evaluation of the reliability and validity of Chinese version of Composite International Diagnostic Interview-3.0. *Chinese Mental Health Journal, 24*(1), 21–24.

Hwu, G. H., & Chang, L. Y. (1986). Chinese diagnostic interview schedule: I. Agreement with psychiatrist's diagnosis. *Acta Psychiatrica Scandinavica, 73*(3), 225–233.

Hwu, G. H., & Compton, W. M. (1994). Comparison of major epidemiological surveys using the Diagnostic Interview Schedule. *International Review of Psychiatry, 6*(4), 309–327.

Hwu, G. H., Yeh, E. K., Chang, L. Y., & Yeh, Y. L. (1986). Chinese diagnostic interview schedule, II. A validity study on estimation of lifetime prevalence. *Acta Psychiatrica Scandinavica, 73*, 348–357.

Ichikawa, M., Nakahara, S., & Wakai, S. (2006). Cross-cultural use of the predetermined scale cutoff points in refugee mental health research. *Social Psychiatry and Psychiatric Epidemiology, 41*, 248–250.

Ideno, Y., Takayama, M., Hayashi, K., Takagi, H., & Sugai, Y. (2011). Evaluation of a Japanese version of the Mini-Mental State Examination in elderly persons. *Geriatrics & Gerontology International, 12*(2), 310–316.

Jitapunkul, S., & Lailert, C. (1997). Mini-Mental Status Examination: Is it appropriate for screening in Thai elderly? *Journal of the Medical Association of Thailand, 80*(2), 116–120.

Keller, A., Lhewa, D., Rosenfeld, B., Sachs, E., Aladjem, A., Cohen, I., … Porterfield, K. (2006). Traumatic experiences and psychological distress in an urban refugee population seeking treatment services. *The Journal of Nervous and Mental Disease, 194*(3), 188–194.

Kim, T. H., Jhoo, J. H., Park, J. H., Kim, J. L, Ryu, S. H., Moon, S. W., … Kim, K. W. (2010). Korean version of Mini Mental Status Examination for Dementia Screening and its' [sic] short form. *Korean Neuropsychiatric Association, 7*(2), 102–108.

Kim, J. L., Park, J. H., Kim, B. J., Kim, M. D., Kim, S., Chi, Y. K., … Kim, K. W. (2012). Interactive influences of demographics on the Mini-Mental State Examination (MMSE) and the demographics-adjusted norms for MMSE in elderly Koreans. *International Psychogeriatrics, 24*(4), 642–650.

Lecrubier, Y., Sheehan, D. V., Weiller, E., Amorim, P., Bonora, I., Sheehan, K. H., …, Dunbar, G. C. (1997). The Mini International Neuropsychiatric Interview (MINI). A short diagnostic structured interview: Reliability and validity according to the CIDI. *European Psychiatry, 12*(5), 224–231.

Lhewa, D., Banu, S., Rosenfeld, B., & Keller, A. (2007). Validation of a Tibetan translation of the Hopkins Symptom Checklist 25 and the Harvard Trauma Questionnaire. *Assessment, 14*(3), 223–230.

Maffei, C., Fossati, A., Agostoni, I., Barraco, A., Bagnato, M., Deborah, D., … Petrachi, M. (1997). Interrater reliability and internal consistency of the structured clinical interview for DSM-IV axis II personality disorders (SCID-II), version 2.0. *Journal of Personality Disorders, 11*(3), 279–284.

Medical Outcome Systems. (n.d.). M.I.N.I. 6.0. *Medical Outcomes Systems: A diagnosis and treatment outcome tracking solutions company*. Retrieved from https://medical-outcomes.com/index/mini

Mills, E. J., Singh, S., Holtz, T. H., Chase, R. M., Dolma, S., Santa-Barbara, J., & Orbinski, J. J. (2005). Prevalence of mental disorders and torture among Tibetan refugees: A systematic review. *BMC International Health and Human Rights, 5*, 7.

Mollica, R. F., McDonald, L. S., Massagli, M. P., & Silove, D. M. (2004). *Measuring trauma, measuring torture: Instructions and guidance on the utilization of the Harvard Program in Refugee Trauma's versions of the Hopkins Symptom Checklist-25 (HSCL-25) and The Harvard Trauma Questionnaire (HTQ)*. Cambridge, MA: Harvard Program in Refugee Trauma.

Mollica, R. F., Wyshak, G., de Marneffe, D., Khuon, F., & Lavelle, J. (1987). Indochinese versions of the Hopkins Symptom Checklist-25: A screening instrument for the psychiatric care of refugees. *American Journal of Psychiatry, 144*(4), 497–500.

Mounoutoua, V. L., & Brown, L. G. (1995). Hopkins Symptom Checklist-25, Hmong Version: A screening instrument for psychological distress. *Journal of Personality Assessment, 64*(2), 376–383.

Okazaki, S. (1998). Psychological assessment of Asian Americans: Research agenda for cultural competency. *Journal of Personality Assessment, 70*(1), 54–70.

Osone, A., & Takahashi, S. (2003). Twelve month test-retest reliability of a Japanese version of the Structured Clinical Interview for DSM-IV Personality Disorders. *Psychiatry and Clinical Neurosciences, 57*(5), 532–538.

Othmer, E., & Othmer, S. C. (1994). *The clinical interview using DSM-IV Volume 1: Fundamentals*. Washington, DC: American Psychiatric Press.

Otsubo, T., Tanaka, K., Koda, R., Shinoda, J., Sano, N., Tanaka, S., … Kamijima, K. (2005). Reliability and validity of Japanese version of the Mini-International Neuropsychiatric Interview. *Psychiatry and Clinical Neurosciences, 59*, 517–526.

PAR. (2012). *Mini-Mental State Examination, 2nd Edition: Simplified Chinese (MMSE-2)*. Retrieved from http://www4.parinc.com/Products/Product.aspx?ProductID=MMSE-2:CHINESE

Pinninti, N., Madison, H., Musser, E., & Rissmiller, D. (2003). Mini International Neuropsychiatric Schedule: Clinical utility and patient acceptance. *European Psychiatry, 18*(7), 361–364.

Rettew, D. C., Lynch, A. D., Achenbach, T. M., Dumenci, L., & Ivanova, M. Y. (2009). Meta-analyses of agreement between diagnoses made from clinical evaluations and standardized diagnostic interviews. *International Journal of Methods in Psychiatric Research, 18*(3), 169–184.

Rogers, R. (2001). *Handbook of diagnostic and structured interviewing*. New York, NY: The Guilford Press.

Sandanger, I., Moum, T., Ingebrigtsen, G., Sorensen, T., Dalgard, O. S., & Bruusgaard, D. (1999). The meaning and significance of caseness: The Hopkins Symptom Checklist-25 and the Composite International Diagnostic Interview II. *Social Psychiatry and Psychiatric Epidemiology, 34*, 53–59.

Sheehan, D. V., Lecrubier, Y., Sheehan, K. H., Amorim, P., Janavs, J., Weiller, E., … Dunbar, G. C. (1998). The Mini-International Neuropsychiatric Interview (M.I.N.I.): The development and validation of a structured diagnostic psychiatric interview for DSM-IV and ICD-10. *Journal of Clinical Psychiatry, 59*(Suppl. 20), 22–33.

Sheehan, D. V., Sheehan, K. H., Shytle, R. D., Janavs, J., Bannon, Y., Rogers, J. E., … Wilkinson, B. (2010). Reliability and validity of the Mini International Neuropsychiatric Interview for Children and Adolescents (MINI-KID). *The Journal of Clinical Psychiatry, 71*(3), 313–326.

Shigemori, K., Ohgi, S., Okuyama, E., Shimura, T., & Schneider, E. (2010). The factorial structure of the Mini Mental State Examination (MMSE) in Japanese dementia patients. *BMC Geriatrics, 10*(36), 1–7.

Silov, D., Manicavasagar, V., Mollica, R., Thai, M., Khiek, D., Lavelle, J., & Tor, S. (2007). Screening for depression and PTSD in a Cambodian population unaffected by war: Comparing the Hopkins Symptom Checklist and Harvard Trauma Questionnaire with the structured clinical interview. *Journal of Nervous and Mental Disease, 195*(2), 152–157.

So, E., Kam, I., Leung, C. M., Chung, D., Liu, Z., & Fong, S. (2003). The Chinese-Bilingual SCID-I/P project: Stage 1-reliability for mood disorders and schizophrenia. *Hong Kong Journal of Psychiatry, 13*(1), 7–18.

Sue, E., & Sue, S. (1987). Cultural factors in the clinical assessment of Asian Americans. *Journal of Consulting and Clinical Psychology, 55*(4), 479–487.

Sumi, K., & Kanda, K. (2002). Relationship between neurotic perfectionism, depression, anxiety, and psychosomatic symptoms: A prospective study among Japanese men. *Personality and Individual Differences, 23*, 817–826.

Summerfeldt, L. J., Kloosterman, P. H., & Antony, M. M. (2010). Structured and semistructured diagnostic interviews. In M. M. Antony & D. H. Barlow (Eds.), *Handbook of assessment and treatment planning for psychological disorders* (2nd ed., pp. 95–140). New York, NY: The Guilford Press.

The Department of Psychiatry Teaching Committee. (1973). *Notes on eliciting and recording clinical information*. Oxford: Oxford University Press.

Vatrapu, R., & Perez-Quinones, M. A. (n.d.). Culture and international usability testing: The effects of culture in structured interviews [article]. Retrieved from http://arxiv.org/ftp/cs/papers/0405/0405045.pdf

Veijola, J., Jokelainen, J., Lasky, K., Kantojarvi, L., Kokkonen, P., Jarvelin, M., & Joukamaa, M. (2003). The Hopkins Symptom Checklist-25 in screening DSM-III-R axis I disorders. *Nordic Journal of Psychiatry, 57*(2), 119–123.

Ventevogel, P., Vries, G. D., Scholte, W. F., Shinwari, N. R., Faiz, H., Nassery, R., … Olff, M. (2007). Properties of the Hopkins Symptom Checklist-25 (HSCL-25) and the Self-Reporting Questionnaire (SRQ-20) as screening instruments used in primary care in Afghanistan. *Social Psychiatry and Psychiatric Epidemiology, 42*, 328–335.

Wittchen, H. (1994). Reliability and validity studies of the WHO-Composite International Diagnostic Interview (CIDI): A critical review. *Journal of Psychiatric Research, 28*(1), 57–84.

Wong, H. M., & Chow, L. Y. (2011). Borderline personality disorder subscale (Chinese version) of the structured clinical interview for DSM-IV axis II personality disorders: A validation study in Cantonese-speaking Hong Kong Chinese. *East Asian Archives of Psychiatry, 21*(2), 52–57.

Wong, S. S., & Fong, K. N. (2009). Reliability and validity of the telephone version of the Cantonese Mini-mental State Examination (T-CMMSE) when used with elderly patients with and without dementia in Hong Kong. *International Psychogeriatrics, 21*(2), 345–353.

Wongchaisuwan, T., Sithinamsuwan, P., Udommongkol, C., & Wongmek, W. (2005). Factors influencing MMSE-T score among Thai subjects. *Journal of the Medical Association of Thailand, 88*(S3), S155–S158.

Wongpakaran, T., Wongpakaran, N., Bookkamana, P., Boonyanaruthee, V., Pinyopornpanish, M., Likhitsathian, S., … Srisutadsanavong, U. (2012). Interrater reliability of Thai version of the Structured Clinical Interview for DSM-IV Axis II Personality Disorders (T-SCID II). *Journal of the Medical Association of Thailand, 95*(2), 264–269.

World Health Organization (WHO). (n.d.). About the WHO CIDI. *The World Mental Health Composite International Diagnostic Interview*. Retrieved from http://www.hcp.med.harvard.edu/wmhcidi/about.php#jump2

Zuckerman, E. L. (2005). *Clinician's thesaurus: The guide to conducting interviews and writing psychological reports*. New York, NY: The Guilford Press.

Projective Testing with Asian Clients

8

Sanjay R. Nath, Alan J. Lee, Zoe Belcher-Timme, and Chin Pui Chau

Introduction

The use of projective tests—now more typically labeled "performance-based" measures (Meyer & Kurtz, 2006)—has a long history in the psychological assessment of individuals, often associated informally with more subjective analysis of response content and psychoanalytic interpretation. The full history behind the projective hypothesis, the development of projective instruments, various interpretive systems that have existed throughout the second half of the twentieth century, the positioning of projective instruments vis-à-vis academic and applied clinical psychology, and details of the controversies regarding the reliability and validity of projective measures is beyond the scope of this chapter. Despite this complex and variegated history, the contemporary use of performance-based measures continues to play an important role in the context of personality assessment, diagnostic formulation, forensic assessment, and a number of referral situations where assessing socio-emotional functioning may play an important role in understanding individuals. Projective tests continue to be widely used in clinical settings in the USA, and projective assessment continues to have an important role in providing convergent personality data in the context of an assessment battery (McGrath, 2008).

Very few authors have explicitly discussed the relationship between cultural variables and projective instruments—one notable exception is Dana's *Handbook of Cross-cultural and Multicultural Personality* (2000) with two chapters on projective methods. This book, like much writing on cultural variables and assessment, tends to be broad in its approach, noting gender differences, racial/ethnic differences, and issues related to norms with projective methods. This chapter reflects an attempt to present an often disparate literature on Asians and Asian-Americans with regard to two primary projective testing methods: (1) the Rorschach Inkblot Method (RIM) and (2) story-telling assessment tasks, such as the Thematic Apperception Test (TAT; Murray, 1943). These methods continue to be some of the most widely utilized projective measures, and each also has a small but substantive literature for Asian populations both within the USA and internationally that has important implications for conducting assessment with Asian clients.

One might wonder why this chapter does not review information on projective drawings such as the house-tree-person or incomplete sentence blanks, also categorized as frequently used projective measures. They are omitted here because their use tends to be almost entirely idiographic as opposed to nomothetic (for example, compared to

S.R. Nath, Ph.D. (✉)
Institute for Graduate Clinical Psychology, Widener University, One University Place, Chester, PA 19013, USA
e-mail: snath@widener.edu

A.J. Lee • Z. Belcher-Timme • C.P. Chau
Widener University, Chester, PA, USA

L.T. Benuto et al. (eds.), *Guide to Psychological Assessment with Asians*,
DOI 10.1007/978-1-4939-0796-0_8, © Springer Science+Business Media New York 2014

the Rorschach where reliable manualized scoring and statistical normative comparison are an integral part of the method). Story-telling tasks, while also often analyzed idiographically, have also had a number of cultural variations produced (e.g., the Tell-Me-A-Story Test or TEMAS Test that features Asian, Hispanic, and African-American characters and urban settings). In addition, more research exists on cultural factors associated with story-telling tasks given the TAT's status as one of the oldest projective measures that has had a number of variations developed and has been studied extensively over the decades. Thus, while projective drawings and sentence blanks may be used with Asian clients, the literature on their general use is so scarce as to make a review of these tasks for Asian clients specifically quite limited or cursory in scope.

Given the limited recent literature on projective measures to begin with, this chapter will examine research from US-based samples as well as research data from international samples. While this broad focus is not ideal in that it addresses different Asian populations, international data may be more useful when assessing clients who have recently arrived in the USA or are less acculturated. Also, research that utilizes US-based samples often does not explicitly control for generational status or level of acculturation, so that a sharp divide between US-based studies and international studies may not be warranted. These issues related to sample origin are important (see Okazaki, 1988 for a discussion of this issue) but given the limited data available on such specific cultural factors, a broad approach (including both US and non-US sample data) is cautiously undertaken here, and caveats and limitations of the conclusions noted whenever possible. When research data is limited to specific Asian subgroups it is noted as well; Rorschach research on Asian populations has been conducted mostly in the nations of Japan, China, and India. Table 8.1 provides a summary of these measures, adaptations for cross-cultural use (primarily translation of instructions in the case of the Rorschach) and some salient references.

Rorschach Inkblot Method/ Rorschach Performance Assessment System

Given that the Rorschach utilizes a set of ten standard inkblots and has only a few sentences of instruction that might easily be translated or utilized with culturally diverse groups, one might imagine that the Rorschach is an instrument that is ripe for broad cross-cultural or multicultural adaptation. At the current time, there are two primary, viable systems of Rorschach scoring and interpretation in the USA—the Comprehensive System (CS) developed by Exner (2003) and the more recent update to this system known as the Rorschach—Performance Assessment System or R-PAS (Viglione, Blume-Marcovici, Miller, Giromini, & Meyer, 2012). The Rorschach CS has indeed been utilized in a number of international settings (see the special issue of *Journal of Personality Assessment, 89(S1)*, 2007 for international Rorschach CS data Israel, Spain, Greece, the Netherlands, Romania, Denmark, Italy, Argentina, Finland, Japan, Brazil, and Portugal). While some of this international research is focused on cross-cultural variations, some is driven by the desire to understand universal aspects of responding to the inkblots and to diversify the normative base.

At first blush one might consider the Rorschach an important instrument to use with Asians, being able to transcend cultural barriers given that the stimuli are easily administered and does not have items that need translation. However, since the results of the coding systems are heavily dependent on language and group norms (for example, the most frequently seen images, known as popular responses), it is also subject to difficulties related to cultural variation and how to best interpret the meaning of differences with Western samples. The current norms available for the Rorschach CS are based on gender and age (Exner, 2001). There is no systematic data in the CS normative tables that address the issue of different mean scores based on race, ethnicity, or national origin. As such, the normative database must be considered heavily US based and in line

Table 8.1 Summary of projective measures, adaptations, and salient references

Instrument	Adaptation	Salient references
Rorschach Performance Assessment System	*Stimuli*: Same (not culturally dependent since they are image-based inkblots) *Initial instructions*: "What might this be?" [In translation for various cultural adaptations; other aspects of administration (introduction to test, queries) also in translation; responses written down and scored verbatim in language of person assessed]	Meyer, G. J., Viglione, D. J., Mihura, J. L., Erard, R. E., & Erdberg, P. (2011). *Rorschach Performance Assessment System: Administration, coding, interpretation, and technical manual*. Toledo, OH: Rorschach Performance Assessment System. http://www.r-pas.org/ (online scoring and training Web site)
Rorschach Comprehensive System (Exner)	*Stimuli*: Same (not culturally dependent since they are image-based inkblots) *Initial instructions*: "What might this be?" [In translation for various cultural adaptations; other aspects of administration (introduction to test, queries) also in translation; responses written down and scored verbatim in language of person assessed]	Meyer, G. J., Erdberg, P., & Shaffer, T. W. (2007). Towards international normative reference data for the Comprehensive System. *Journal of Personality Assessment, 89*, S201–S216. doi:10.1080/00223890701629342. http://www.rorschachtraining.com/
Thematic Apperception Test	*Stimuli*: Tell-Me-A-Story-Test (TEMAS); images adapted for Puerto Ricans, other Hispanics, African-Americans, and non-Hispanic Whites; pilot version for Asians *Instructions/responses*: Responses recorded and interpreted in any language	Costantino, G., Dana, R. H., & Malgady, R. G. (2007). *TEMAS (Tell-Me-A-Story) assessment in multicultural societies*. Mahwah, NJ: Lawrence Erlbaum Associates.

with the sample drawn from various US subpopulations in the early 1990s (Exner, 2001). The normative sample from Exner's CS (2001) utilized 600 protocols and was intended to be updated, including data collection of 450 additional individuals (Exner, 2007), but this update was not completed after Exner's death.

This situation led to the development of the R-PAS, which was intended to develop the CS further by including variables with the strongest empirical evidence base (see Meyer & Eblin, 2012 for an overview). The R-PAS is relatively recent, and thus there is only a small literature base on it specifically, although the variables included are primarily from prior scoring systems. Its normative database ($N = 1{,}396$) is largely drawn from rescored CS protocols, including subsamples of the international data collected in 2007, but since its scoring system is online, and thus allows for expansion of the database as usage of the new scoring methodology grows. Unfortunately, there are no studies that yet examine Asians or Asian-Americans utilizing the R-PAS, but this undoubtedly may be a next step, especially since all included variables are *T*-scores and will provide for easier statistical comparison, especially in the cross-cultural realm. Again, as with Exner's CS, the norms for the R-PAS are adjusted only for age and gender, and thus do not make any type of adjustment for race, ethnicity, or national origin, although given its international dataset base, this may become more possible as the system evolves.

One issue with presenting research data on the Exner or R-PAS systems is that each protocol consists of several dozen variables, ratios, and indices, so that comparing Asian-based samples is difficult without a priori hypotheses about what differences might be expected. A number of studies tend to present descriptive data on Asian samples, but hypothesis testing comparisons to other groups or to general norms tables may or may not be included due to the likelihood of Type I errors given the number of comparisons possible within the coding systems. In addition, the scoring and interpretation of each protocol is quite time-consuming, and so many studies utilize small sample designs. Both of these issues make conclusions from such studies tentative at best.

A final difficulty with international data is that many researchers conduct and publish research in other languages and are more likely to have utilized older systems of Rorschach coding depending on what coding systems have been translated into other languages and when the research was conducted. In the heyday of projective testing in the USA (1940s to1970s) there were a number of cross-cultural studies conducted, but they tended to use older coding systems with less established reliability and validity compared to the current Exner CS or R-PAS. Thus, finding research data that is both methodologically sound and relies on more contemporary coding systems is a goal not easily attained. Meyer et al. make one such attempt with the development of international data for the Rorschach (Meyer, Erdberg, & Shaffer, 2007), but more with an eye to cross-cultural validity and convergence rather than guidelines on use for particular cultural groups. In their approach, cultural differences are a source of error and thus norms are strengthened by including data from disparate cultures.

Rorschach Data on Asians from Within the USA

There is quite limited published data that provides cross-cultural comparison of the Rorschach utilizing US-based samples. The existing information is limited to older studies from the 1950s to 1980s that are reviewed briefly here, as well as a few, more recent, unpublished doctoral dissertations. The results must be viewed with caution, particularly since this era was prior to the development of the more systematized CS system. While older systems of coding (e.g., Beck, Klopfer) often used in these studies do have variables that were carried forward to the CS and had a growing empirical base at the time, the methodology often employed, and typically small sample sizes, means that results such be viewed quite cautiously. It is also quite difficult to say whether studies that are now as much as 50 years old have relevance to current cross-cultural comparison given the generational changes that are likely to have occurred.

One of the oldest cross-cultural investigations of the Rorschach analyzed data collected in the 1940s as part of the Columbia University "Research in Contemporary Cultures" grant-funded project. The study, conducted by Abel and Hsu (1949), comparing a nonclinical China-born US-based sample ($n=27$) with a nonclinical American-born Chinese sample ($n=29$), and thus examined the effect of acculturation by utilizing birthplace as a proxy for level of acculturation. All subjects were between 20 and 30 years old. The investigation examined how individuals who were born in China and received their education there differed from their American-born counterparts on the Rorschach, and also undertook an examination of gender differences in the two groups on the Rorschach. The study was considered exploratory, and the system of Rorschach scoring was unspecified, although many of the results utilize what were to become Exner CS variables. The authors calculated ratios between the two samples on a number of variables, and conducted basic statistical tests on the ratios, reporting results at the $p=0.01$ level.

The results of this study suggested that China-born subjects tended to provide more whole responses (*W*), while American-born subjects provided more detail responses (*D*). China-born subjects also perceived whole human responses more frequently than American-born subjects, who tended to provide human detail responses more frequently. China-born groups also gave more FC than CF responses than American-born groups. When examining content, there were notable sex differences: American-born females described aggression or fear of aggression in 21 out of 87 responses, whereas China-born females described no aggression or fear of aggression. China-born females also provided more dependency content than American-born females. China-born females tended to describe their human responses in greater detail (age and sex characteristics), whereas American-born females describe seeing men or women (and more often, mythological people). China-born male participants tended to give "hard anatomy" responses (e.g., bony structures) while American-born male participants tended to give "soft anatomy" responses. The authors conclude that Chinese-born Americans fit "into this Chinese cultural pattern of controlling their impulses and maintaining a pliant but to some degree dissociated role in interpersonal relationships" (Abel & Hsu, 1949, p. 299) compared to American-born Chinese individuals who "less rigid control, more spontaneity, more overt expression of feeling" is apparent (p. 301). Nonetheless, these results must be taken in quite cautiously given the small sample size and the dated nature of the findings.

Hsu, Watrous, and Lord (1961) present a follow-up study describing differences between two groups of high school students—one a Hawaiian-based Chinese sample ($n=28$), the other an American, Chicago-based sample ($n=24$) based on Beck's normative adolescent data that was available at the time, with the samples matched for age. They utilize Beck's system of scoring. The Chinese sample produced a lower number of responses ($M=30.10$, SD=19.80) than the American sample ($M=41.35$, SD=15.00) on the protocols. The authors also note fewer vista responses (FV) and shading responses (C') among the Chinese sample, although the authors only conduct "a rough comparison" (p. 39). While most variables on the two samples do not appear to differ, the authors do note higher mean Hd responses in the Chicago group ($M=4.16$, SD=3.98 compared to the Chinese $M=2.25$, SD=3.18). What is most striking about their results is the level of similarity between the two samples despite the different subpopulations; the authors note that many Hawaiian-based Chinese are quite acculturated and may have resided in Hawaii for a number of generations.

A similar cross-cultural line of research was also developed for Japanese-Americans by De Vos (1954, 1955), a Fulbright fellow who spent time studying neuropsychiatry in Japan. The studies examine Japanese Americans in the Chicago area and in particular highlight differences between first and second generation Japanese immigrants. The studies utilized 140 Japanese American individuals ($n=50$ first generation, $n=60$ second generation, $n=30$ for a group that returned to Japan while growing up) and an American comparison group ($n=60$ normals, $n=50$ "neurotics", and $n=30$ individuals with schizophrenia). The Japanese American sample was randomly sampled from over 17,000 Japanese Americans living in the Chicago area, and was balanced for gender. The samples were also described in terms of class status and occupation in a detailed manner. The protocols were scored utilizing the Beck system (the American comparison group is data from Beck), and chi-square tests were used where appropriate to ascertain differences, as the authors note that many Rorschach variables are not easily compared on means due to the nonnormality of the distributions.

De Vos presents highly detailed results by Rorschach cluster, indicating differences in generational status, American-Japanese sample differences, and gender differences (1954); these results are summarized very briefly here. De Vos noted that Japanese Americans tended to produce shorter protocols (R), although the protocol length increased with generational status. In addition, Japanese Americans produced more W responses and fewer D responses and that the Japanese sample tended to have a greater organizational complexity (Z-scores) that is hypothesized to relate to intellectual striving in the Beck system. Additionally, Japanese protocols had higher number of color responses compared to Americans (C), and second generation Japanese Americans in particular had higher movement

(*M*) responses and shading responses (*Y*). In terms of content, the first-generation Japanese group evidenced significantly greater body preoccupation. De Vos also notes throughout that the second generation group more often resembles the American control, and that the first-generation group often differs from the second generation group, with the group that returned to Japan during childhood being intermediate. This suggests that the data do show a cultural difference that is attenuated by acculturation in a graded manner.

Takeuchi and Scott (1986), a number of years later, compared normal Japanese 5- and 6-year-olds ($n=20$) with their American counterparts based on the Exner CS norms for these age groups, with a particular interest in educational productivity of the Japanese educational system. The Japanese school-aged sample was Japan based and thus this was a truly cross-cultural (rather than immigrant-based) comparison. Japanese children produced nearly double the responses of their American counterparts and fewer whole (*W*), but more part (*D* and Dd) responses. This reverses the trend seen in the adult studies described above. Form quality scores (FQ) were also significantly lower for Japanese children, which might be expected since the answers would be less conventional or typical compared to US data and may reflect cultural variation.

Perhaps the most statistically rigorous study analyzing Exner CS Rorschach data involved an examination of Korean and American individuals conducted by Moon and Cundick (1983). The study utilized four groups: a monolingual group from Korea (non-English speaking) ($n=20$), a monolingual American college student group ($n=20$), a bilingual Korean immigrant group who had been in the USA more than 5 years ($n=20$), and a bilingual American group that had worked as missionaries in Korea for several years teaching Korean ($n=20$). The design allowed for Rorschach administration in Korean and English, and to compare not only Korean and American performance, but also the effect of monolingualism versus bilingualism. The study also limited exploration to 16 Exner CS variables and conducted ANOVAs to compare means. When comparing Korean and American monolinguals, six variables were statistically significant of the 16 (*R*, card rejection, *W*, *M*, *H*, and *X*+%). Korean participants had a lower number of total responses, higher card rejection, fewer whole and human responses, and less movement (*M*) and *X*+% scores. When comparing Korean and American bilinguals, five variables were again statistically significant—*W*, FC, CF+*C*, Sum *C*, and lambda. All of the variables had significantly lower means in the Korean sample except for lambda which was higher. The authors note that most variables were not statistically different. By contrasting the pattern of monolingual versus bilingual differences with the nationality differences, the authors concluded that the variables that were susceptible to cultural difference were those likely to be affected by acculturation rather than language. They state that, "in the main, it appears that the Rorschach test is perceived in many similar ways by individuals in Korean and American cultures and that the initial differences are reduced by acculturation" (p. 349).

Despite the numerous limitations of the methodologies and age of the studies reviewed here, there are a number of consistencies for the studies that utilized adult samples (this is not a surprise given the remarkable variation in children's Rorschach norms cross-culturally and even within the USA). Across the studies, there are a lower number of responses and more whole responses, less expression of affect and evidence of some affective constriction—while this may not represent the differences between the countries of origin where studies were presented, this nonetheless may fit with a "stereotypical" understanding of Asian emotion regulation and approach to testing circumstances. Such an approach, given the normative data presented here, should be considered strongly as part of the cultural makeup of individuals as opposed to psychopathology. Additionally, many of these variables were shown to have attenuated differences in the context of acculturation.

More recently, there have been two unpublished doctoral dissertations that examine the Rorschach and the effects of Asian ethnicity from within the USA from the last 10 years.

These documents must also be viewed quite cautiously given that they often employ small sample sizes and have never been peer-reviewed. Umina (2006) compared a sample of 42 East Asian college student's Rorschach scores to US norms employing Exner's CS and correlated results to acculturation level measured by self-report, examining nine selected variables. Finally, Chang (2011) compared Asian-American college students' performance on the Rorschach to European-American college students (in addition to other measures). These studies appear to corroborate aspects of the older studies, but further investigation is necessary.

Rorschach Data on Asians from Outside the USA (International Data)

Available international Rorschach data is primarily available from India, China, and Japan, with the bulk of published literature from Japan and India. In India, the *Journal of Projective Psychology and Mental Health* has been published by the Somatic Inkblot Society since 1994 (two issues a year) dedicated to projective testing that features numerous research studies on the Rorschach, including normative and clinical populations. Manickam and Dubey (2006) provide a historical review of the use of the Rorschach in India and various scoring systems employed, populations assessed, and the current status of the test. Sorai and Ohnuki (2008) provide a historical review of the Rorschach in Japan, beginning with initial interest in the Beck and Klopfer scoring systems, and then noting that many contemporary clinicians and researchers have adopted Exner's CS. China has the much lesser usage of the Rorschach, partially due to less interest in psychodynamic psychology, and also due to less contact with European/American psychology. There were a series of early studies in the 1960s but the test is not in the top 25 employed by Chinese psychologists (Cheung, 1996). Ryan, Dai, and Zheng (1994) provide an overview of the most popularly utilized assessment measures in China, and both the Rorschach and TAT were not commonly utilized.

The major issues in India for utilizing data towards understanding how to consider Rorschach profiles in the Asian-American context is the absence of standardized Indian norms and the lack of studies that compare Indian data to Western data for normative or clinical groups. There are a large number of studies that examine many clinical subpopulations within India and compare data within the Indian context, but this is less useful for Western assessment practitioners. However, there are a few larger scale published studies that assessors might turn to when examining a client of Indian origin. Shweta, Bajpai, Sengar, Singh, and Desai (2010) present data on 238 nonpatient Indian adults who were administered the Rorschach utilizing the Beck system, and focus on gender differences. They do present data (means and standard deviations) for the 238 person normative sample for 14 variables and eight content categories and also present gender differences on the available data. Chaudhury, Saldanha, et al. (2007) also provide data on 282 normal older Indians and compare them to 160 clinical patients in a number of categories (dementia, alcohol dependence, schizophrenia, mania, depression, and anxiety) utilizing the Rorschach and Klopfer's methods. They present detailed means for Rorschach variables of these individuals that would be quite useful in assessing an older Indian even in the US context if immigration was more recent; the authors conclude that using US norms with older Indians would be quite misleading given the pattern of data. Chaudhury, Sudarsanan, et al. (2007) also present data on extensive data on 313 children and adolescent patients broken down by diagnosis (schizophrenia, mania, depression, anxiety state, hysteria, nocturnal enuresis, head injury, epilepsy, and mental retardation).

In Japan, there is older Rorschach data on juvenile delinquents (De Vos, 1979; Taniguchi, De Vos, & Murakami, 1958) and aging adults facing terminal illness (Shimonaka & Nakazato, 1991), as well as more recent Exner CS data on Japanese children (Matsumoto, Nobuko, Shirai, & Nakabayashi, 2007), adolescents (Nakamura et al., 1992), adults (Nakamura, Fuchigami, & Tsugawa, 2007), and those suffering from chronic pain (Yamamoto et al., 2010). The child and adult normative data was published in the *Journal of Personality Assessment* supplement that detailed internationally compiled data discussed above and provides tables of data for use with recently immigrated Japanese individuals.

The childhood data reported descriptive Exner CS data from a series of studies with normal Japanese children (ages 5, 8, 9, 12, and 14; $n=346$). Of the sample, 32 had less than 10 responses, 112 had 10–14 responses, and the remainder averaged 18–20 responses, suggesting shorter protocols that may be affected by level of verbal expressiveness. The authors concluded that Japanese children had extremely high lambda (ranging from 4 to 8), low EA (ranging from 2 to 4), as well as high *X–%* and low *X+%* when compared to US-based norms. Adolescent data from the early 1990s (Nakamura et al., 1992) similarly suggested that lambda was higher than expected and that a very high percentage was positive for the hypervigilance index (35 % of adolescents). The adult normative sample (Nakamura et al., 2007) involved 240 Rorschach protocols with participants that had never received psychiatric treatment, including any form of psychotherapy. The sample consisted of 89 males and 151 females between the ages of 18 and 66. All participants spoke Japanese as their primary language and 78 % were middle-class, college/university graduates. The authors identified three main results: a mean lambda of 0.86, 40 % had an introversive style compared to 7 % extratensive, and 26 % of the sample were positive for the hypervigilance index (clothing response mean = 3.13, whole human content mean = 8.21, space response mean = 3.73, and Zf mean = 16.16).

Storytelling Projective Tests

As Ephraim (2000) has noted, there is a long history of a psychocultural approach to thematic concerns expressed by individuals in response to the ten Thematic Apperception Test (TAT; Murray, 1943) cards, the most widely utilized story-telling projective test and the main task for which data that pertains to Asians/Asian-Americans exists. Underlying this psychocultural interpretive approach is the idea that expressed projective themes (grouped as instrumental or expressive) are evident in all human relationships and that cultural context may impact the relative importance of such themes. Basic instrumental themes are achievement, control, cooperation-competition, competence and responsibility. Basic expressive themes are pleasure, nurturance, affiliation, appreciation, and harmony. Coding systems have emphasized some of identifying the presence of the ten themes themselves (e.g., the need for achievement; McClelland, Atkinson, Clark, & Lowell, 1976), activity versus passivity in relation to the themes (De Vos, 1973), horizontal or equal status relationships versus vertical or unequal status relationships, and descriptors such as positive/negative/unresolved (Ephraim, 2000).

Early approaches examined differences in response to specific TAT cards, such as the need for achievement as part of TAT card 1, depicting a boy with a violin. Such research (Caudill & De Vos, 1956; De Vos, 1996) compared responses to this card from Japanese immigrant to the USA, Japanese-Americans, and White Americans. For example, this study in particular noted cultural differences such as Japanese youth in high schools focusing on achievement and competence while White youth emphasized control issues of parental pressure and negative affiliation/nurturance.

There are also contemporary idiographic examples of TAT psychocultural interpretation for Asians in the clinical literature, including a sample interpretive protocol for a 49-year-old Fillipino male (in Dana, 2005). Ching et al. (1995) present TAT-based data on family values and roles among Japanese-Americans when comparing four Japanese-American families with seven European-American families, noting differences in views of the father (Card 2, viewed as more protective and nurturant by Japanese-Americans) younger woman (Card 3, viewed as more submissive by Japanese-Americans), and older woman (Card 3, happier in European-American stories). De Vos (1983) presents more detailed idiographic data by TAT card but also utilizes a larger sample and notes proportions of themes as well as cross-Asian comparative data. De Vos (1983) work includes a sample of 50 Korean individuals, 30 Japanese first generation immigrants, 40 Japanese second generation immigrants, and 60 Whites. Similarly, De Vos and Kim (2004) present data on 100 Koreans, 31 Japanese, and 50 Koreans residing in Los Angeles. These works have a tremendous amount of descriptive depth (include proportions of achievement motivation, authority, harmony/discord, and family/interpersonal relationships by Card and ethnic group) and are undoubtedly useful to anyone utilizing the Tat with Koreans or Japanese immigrants or second generation individuals.

In contrast to such rich idiographic data that is worth becoming familiar with when assessing Asians/Asian-Americans with storytelling projective tasks, there is also larger sample data that differences highlights differences to story-telling between US-based ethnic/cultural groups. In one large scale study ($n=323$) of ethnicity and imaginative story-telling (Pang & Schultheiss, 2005), US college undergraduates were administered images from the Picture Story Exercise (Koestner & McClelland, 1992) that assessed need for achievement, need for affiliation, and need for power. The authors found when comparing African Americans, Asians, and Whites (the largest ethnic group participants) that Asians affiliation strivings were higher than Whites but similar to African-Americans. The groups did not differ in needs for power, but African-Americans had slightly higher needs for achievement than Asians. Similarly, Salili (1996) examined achievement motivation in a large sample ($N=764$) British and Chinese students aged 13–55, noting results revealed age, sex, and cultural differences in the level of achievement motivation. Chinese high school students were more affiliative and had a higher need for achievement when compared to the British students. Yu (1980) also examined the need for achievement in 401 Taiwanese students, who evidenced strong collective identity rather than individualistic identity.

Additional Picture Tests

The Tell-Me-A-Story (TEMAS; Costantino, 1987) was developed for minority and nonminority children and adolescents (an updated narrative-based picture test analogous to the TAT) has produced a detailed research base and standardized norms for Puerto Ricans, other Hispanics, African-Americans, and non-Hispanic Whites. It has a very strong research base with Hispanic individuals where it has been utilized in English and Spanish with a reliable and valid scoring system and primarily urban-based norms. While there is a pilot form of the test with Asian-looking characters (to be utilized in English, Cantonese, Mandarin), there is not sufficient data to confirm its psychometric properties or to "justify reliable and valid clinical decision making with this version of the TEMAS test" (Costantino & Malgady, 2008, p. 567) at this time, although this is certainly a promising line for future research and clinical application.

In addition to some earlier Taiwanese data (Yang, Kuo, & Costantino, 2003), there is also pilot data on the TEMAS (Costantino, Dana, & Malgady, 2007) with 48 children from elementary schools in Taipei that utilized the Asian TEMAS cards and nonminority TEMAS cards in counterbalanced order, and attempted to correlate responses with paper-and-pencil adjustment measures. The two versions did not appear significantly different and did appear correlated to daily life adjustment, a measure of children's depression, and affective functioning; the Asian version also was more correlated with measures of aggression and interpersonal relationships on one self-report while the nonminority version appeared to have a stronger correlation with affective functioning.

Clinical Recommendations

In clinical practice, the use of projectives, and in particular the Rorschach and TAT, can add incrementally to the assessment findings. When faced with the assessment of an Asian or Asian-American, this information may be particularly valuable since stigma is often a factor in utilizing self-report data and these indirect performance-based measures may provide a valuable window into such clients' internal experiences. Clinicians are presented with Asians/Asian-American clients in the assessment context that may greatly benefit from the socio-emotional data that is gathered via projective assessment. Any such data must be utilized sensitively and cautiously. Assessing the level of acculturation of individuals is paramount before deciding to rely on any US-based norms at all; if less acculturated, it may very well make sense for clinicians, depending on the nationality of clients, to utilize data from many of the more recent studies described above where international data may suggest a path to interpretation. While there has been a tremendous amount of research on projective instruments, the authors truly lament the lack of greater focus on ethnic minority populations when considering the use of projective instruments.

It is particularly important to ascertain the examinee's comfort level with English in administering projective measures such as the TAT and Rorschach or to consider the issues involved with administering such tests in another language. One must be quite adept at understanding Asian/Asian-American clients in a holistic context and to gather such information during assessment intakes, including information on length of time in the US, level of acculturation of the household individuals grew up in, and the type of educational system individuals were exposed to. It is also important that clinicians develop a nuanced understanding of the experience of the client vis-à-vis the particular Asian culture of origin.

Perhaps most important initially is a consideration of the validity of projective data with a given individual Asian/Asian-American client. While the respective measures' standardized instructions are maintained, some modifications in the overall introduction to the assessment process may enhance utility of the data collected. From the authors' experience, the ambiguity and vagueness inherent in projective methods is often particularly difficult for many Asians to grasp. In a culture that often focuses on rational and emotionally detached thinking, the vagueness inherent in instructions such as "What might this be?" can be rather stymying. As such, some preliminary but thorough preparation in introducing the assessment procedures is particularly helpful. In particular, instructions and frank discussions that there are no "right" or "wrong" answers often helps allay some of the intrapsychic pressure to produce the "right" answer or responses on the task.

Especially given that shorter protocols have limited interpretive validity, and may be more culturally related, it is important that assessors be aware of the increased likelihood of short protocols with Asian and Asian-American clients and be prepared to understand such shortened protocols in context. In the R-PAS, the prompt part of the "prompt-pull" rule may help ensure a record of adequate length; in the CS it is important to attempt to elicit more than one response from Card I and promote a response set to provide more than one response per card. In the inquiry phase of the CS, the often verbal brevity among Asian examinees may limit elaboration in this phase. Nonetheless, shorter protocols are more likely among Asian/Asian-American clients, and this group-level finding must be considered carefully before over-interpreting a short protocol or questioning its validity prematurely.

In turn, the examiner's working familiarity with the coding system, and specifically ensuring that adequate inquiry and prompting (without over-inquiring) helps refine important coding distinctions such as form-dominance in color (FC-CF-*C*) or shading responses. Without sufficient prompting in inquiry, there runs a risk of excessive numbers of Form and Form-dominated determinants. Even so, the authors' experience has often been a preponderance of Form responses with Asian/Asian-American clients, contributing to a relatively high Lambda (*L*). While Lambda has been associated with different implications of situationally related response-style as well as trait issues, the authors have often been inclined to interpret high Lambda more as a product of the culture's emphasis on the rational and unemotional style (avoiding the use of affect and emotions). The heightened occurrence of mythological/

fictional human and animal may also reflect the culture's often belief in the same (e.g., the dragon or phoenix). Thus, these culture-based interpretive differences are both likely and especially important to adjust traditional interpretations of high Lambda.

It is fair to say that for the Rorschach, Asian/Asian-American clients are likely to produce shorter protocols that employ greater form, as well as produce protocols that suggest greater emotional constriction and less expressiveness. Many such protocols will have greater effort of putting together percepts into the whole blot, suggesting organizational energy and consolidation suggestive of hypervigilance. All content produced on Rorschach protocols must be interpreted in a limited fashion and considering cultural aspects of content, and in addition measures of reality-testing may be skewed due to the norms being grounded in Western cultural percepts. These protocols must be considered as normative and clinicians must be exceedingly cautious not to over-pathologize these results in clients, particularly by simply comparing them to US-based general norms and reaching grossly inaccurate and untenable conclusions. With these possibilities in mind, it is also not easy to say whether such differences are the result of differences in verbal expressiveness, attention to field rather than ground on inkblots, or due to differences in personality, so even interpreting what consistently appears different is a difficult given the complexity of cross-cultural research.

Story-telling tasks in Asians have often been particularly challenging, especially when the examinee is unfamiliar with the English language. There may be a dearth of detail or elaboration that often limits the seeming utility of story-telling tasks in identifying themes, conflicts, and core issues. With story-telling tasks, clinicians' own cultural biases and stereotypes may play into how such narrative data is summarized, utilized, and interpreted. It may be particularly important to consult references with additional cultural information and/or to consult with colleagues familiar with the Asian culture of origin to ensure a less biased approach.

Conclusion

As should be readily apparent from the above review, the literature on projective testing is itself in a period of decline in the last 20 years. There remains a very limited literature on either the Rorschach or TAT that is both recent and provides adequate data on US-based ethnic group differences, and in particular on Asians and Asian-Americans. In conclusion, these authors suggest that projective measures such as the TAT and Rorschach can be ethically, reliably, and validly utilized with Asian/Asian-American clients. Currently, a lot of the pressure to do so rests on the assessor; there are a number of roadblocks for that assessor to overcome in terms of knowledge, skills, and the art of how and when to adjust and accommodate interpretation based on ethnic group membership. These authors hope this chapter is an aid in clinicians faced with the need to use projective measures with Asian/Asian-Americans, and that it will be a useful resource as such clinicians, perhaps in consultation with others, attempts such an approach.

References

Abel, T. M., & Hsu, F. L. K. (1949). Chinese personality revealed by the Rorschach. *Journal of Personality Assessment, 13*, 285–301.

Caudill, W., & De Vos, G. A. (1956). Achievement, culture and personality: The case of the Japanese Americans. *American Anthropologist, 58*(6), 1102–1126.

Chang, J. (2011). Examining intra- and interpersonal variables involved in neuropsychological and personality assessment: Are Asian Americans the "model examinees"? (Order No. 3481953, University of California, Santa Barbara). *ProQuest Dissertations and Theses*, 169.

Chaudhury, S., Saldanha, D., Srivastava, K., Jyothi, S. G., Sundari, G. S., & Augustine, M. (2007). Rorschach responses of Indian children and adolescents with psychiatric disorders. *Somatic Inkblots Series Journal of Projective Psychology and Mental Health, 14*, 150–161.

Chaudhury, S., Sudarsanan, S. S., Seby, K. K., Salujha, S. K., Srivastava, K., Kundeyawala, S. M., & Rathee, S. P. (2007). Rorschach responses of older Indians. *Somatic Inkblots Journal of Projective Psychology & Mental Health, 14*(1), 30–43.

Cheung, F. M. (1996). The assessment of psychopathology in Chinese societies. In M. H. Bond (Ed.), *Handbook of Chinese psychology* (pp. 393–411). New York, NY: Oxford University Press.

Ching, J., McDermott, J. J., Fukunaga, C., Yanagida, E., Mann, E., & Waldron, J. (1995). Perceptions of family values and roles among Japanese Americans: Clinical considerations. *American Journal of Orthopsychiatry, 65*(2), 216–224.

Costantino, G. (1987). *TEMAS (tell-me-a-story): A multicultural thematic apperception test Picture Cards*. Los Angeles, CA: Western Psychological Services.

Costantino, G., Dana, R. H., & Malgady, R. G. (2007). *TEMAS (tell-me-a-story) assessment in multicultural societies*. Mahwah, NJ: Lawrence Erlbaum Associates.

Costantino, G., & Malgady, R. G. (2008). Tell-me-a-story (TEMAS). In S. Jenkins (Ed.), *A handbook of clinical scoring systems for thematic apperceptive techniques* (pp. 547–572). Mahwah, NJ: Lawrence Erlbaum Associates.

Dana, R. (2000). *Handbook of cross-cultural and multicultural personality assessment*. Mahwah, NJ: Lawrence Erlbaum Associates.

Dana, R. H. (2005). *Multicultural assessment: Principles, applications, and examples*. Mahwah, NJ: Lawrence Erlbaum Associates.

De Vos, G. A. (1954). A comparison of the personality differences in two generations of Japanese Americans by means of the Rorschach test. *Nagoya Journal of Medical Science, 17*, 153–265.

De Vos, G. A. (1955). A quantitative Rorschach assessment of maladjustment and rigidity in acculturating Japanese Americans. *Genetic Psychology Monographs, 52*, 51–87.

De Vos, G. A. (1973). *Socialization for achievement: Essays on the cultural psychology of the Japanese*. Berkeley, CA: University of California Press.

De Vos, G. A. (1979). A Rorschach comparison of delinquent and nondelinquent Japanese family members. *The Journal of Psychological Anthropology, 2*(4), 425–441.

De Vos, G. A. (1983). Achievement motivation and intra-family attitudes in immigrant Koreans. *The Journal of Psychoanalytic Anthropology, 6*(1), 25–71.

De Vos, G. A. (1996). Internalized achievement or external authority: Some cultural comparisons of responses to TAT card 1. *Rorschachiana, 21*(1), 91–126.

De Vos, G. A., & Kim, E.-Y. (2004). *Immigration and entrepreneurship: Culture, capital, and ethnic networks* (1st ed., pp. 205–241). New Brunswick, NJ: Transaction Publishers.

Ephraim, D. (2000). A psychocultural approach to TAT scoring and interpretation. In R. Dana (Ed.), *Handbook of cross-cultural and multicultural personality assessment* (pp. 427–445). Mahwah, NJ: Lawrence Erlbaum Associates.

Exner, J. (2001). *A Rorschach workbook for the comprehensive system* (5th ed.). Asheville, NC: Rorschach Workshops.

Exner, J. (2003). *The Rorschach: A comprehensive system* (Basic foundations 4th ed., Vol. 1). Hoboken, NJ: Wiley.

Exner, J. (2007). A new U.S. adult nonpatient sample. *Journal of Personality Assessment, 89*(S1), S154–S158.

Hsu, F. L. K., Watrous, B., & Lord, E. M. (1961). Culture pattern and adolescent behavior. *The International Journal of Social Psychiatry, 7*(1), 33–53.

Koestner, R., & McClelland, D. C. (1992). The affiliation motive. In C. P. Smith, J. W. Atkinson, D. C. McClelland, & J. Veroff (Eds.), *Motivation and personality: Handbook of thematic content analysis* (pp. 205–210). New York, NY: Cambridge University Press.

Manickam, L. S. S., & Dubey, B. L. (2006). Rorschach Inkblot Test in India: Historical review and perspectives for future action. *Somatic Inkblot Series Journal of Projective Psychology and Mental Health, 12*, 61–78.

Matsumoto, M., Nobuko, S., Shirai, H., & Nakabayashi, M. (2007). Rorschach comprehensive system data for a sample of 190 Japanese nonpatient children at five ages. *Journal of Personality Assessment, 89*(S1), S103–S112.

McClelland, D. C., Atkinson, J. W., Clark, R. A., & Lowell, E. L. (1976). *The achievement motive*. Oxford, England: Irvington.

McGrath, R. E. (2008). The Rorschach in the context of performance-based personality assessment. *Journal of Personality Assessment, 90*(5), 465–475.

Meyer, G. J., & Eblin, J. J. (2012). An overview of the Rorschach Performance Assessment System (R-PAS). *Psychological Injury and Law, 5*, 107–121.

Meyer, G. J., Erdberg, P., & Shaffer, T. W. (2007). Toward international normative reference data for the comprehensive system. *Journal of Personality Assessment, 89*, S201–S216.

Meyer, G. J., & Kurtz, J. E. (2006). Advancing personality assessment terminology: Time to retire 'objective' and 'projective' as Personality test descriptors. *Journal of Personality Assessment, 87*(3), 223–225. doi:10.1207/s15327752jpa8703_01.

Moon, T. I., & Cundick, B. P. (1983). Shifts and constancies in Rorschach responses as a function of culture and language. *Journal of Personality Assessment, 47*(4), 345–349.

Murray, H. A. (1943). *Thematic apperception test manual*. Cambridge, MA: Harvard University Press.

Nakamura, N., Fuchigami, Y., & Tsugawa, R. (2007). Rorschach comprehensive system data for a sample of 240 adult non-patients from Japan. *Journal of Personality Assessment, 89*(S1), S97–S102.

Nakamura, N., Sato, Y., Fujioka, J., Teramura, K., Kimura, N., & Kino, E. (1992). Japanese adolescents Rorschach nonpatient data by the comprehensive system. *Research-Aid Papers of the Yasuda Life Welfare Foundation, 28*(2), 70–75.

Okazaki, S. (1988). Psychological assessment of Asian Americans: Research agenda for cultural competency. *Journal of Personality Assessment, 70*(1), 54–70.

Pang, J., & Schultheiss, O. (2005). Assessing implicit motives in U.S. college students: Effects of picture type and position, gender and ethnicity, and cross-cultural comparisons. *Journal of Personality Assessment, 85*(3), 280–294.

Ryan, J. J., Dai, X.-Y., & Zheng, L. (1994). Psychological test usage in the People's Republic of China. *Journal of Psychoeducational Assessment, 12*, 324–330.

Salili, F. (1996). Achievement motivation: A cross-cultural comparison of British and Chinese students. *Educational Psychology, 16*(3), 271–279.

Shimonaka, Y., & Nakazato, K. (1991). Aging and terminal changes in Rorschach responses among the Japanese elderly. *Journal of Personality Assessment, 57*(1), 10–18.

Shweta, Bajpai, R. C., Sengar, K. S., Singh, A. R., & Desai, N. G. (2010). Rorschach profile of Indian adults. *SIS Journal of Projective Psychology & Mental Health, 17*(2), 180–186.

Sorai, K., & Ohnuki, K. (2008). The development of the Rorschach in Japan. *Rorschachiana, 29*, 38–63.

Takeuchi, M., & Scott, R. (1986). Educational productivity and Rorschach location responses of preschool Japanese and American children. *Psychology in the Schools, 23*, 368–373.

Taniguchi, M., De Vos, G., & Murakami, E. (1958). Identification of mother and father cards on the Rorschach by Japanese normal and delinquent adolescents. *Journal of Projective Techniques, 22*, 453–460.

Umina, T. F. (2006). The effect of acculturation on the Rorschach protocols of east Asian American college students (Order No. 3247317, Temple University). *ProQuest Dissertations and Theses*, 105.

Viglione, D. J., Blume-Marcovici, A. C., Miller, H. L., Giromini, L., & Meyer, G. (2012). An inter-rater reliability study for the Rorschach Performance Assessment System. *Journal of Personality Assessment, 94*(6), 607–612. doi:10.1080/00223891.2012.684118.

Yamamoto, K., Kanbara, K., Mutsuura, H., Ban, I., Mizuno, Y., Abe, T., … Fukunaga, M. (2010). Psychological characteristics of Japanese patients with chronic pain assessed by the Rorschach test. *BioPsychoSocial Medicine*, *4*(20), 1–13.

Yang, C., Kuo, L., & Costantino, G. (2003). *Validity of Asian TEMAS in Taiwanese children: Preliminary data*. Paper presented at the European Congress of Psychology, Vienna, Austria.

Yu, E. (1980). Chinese collective orientation and need for achievement. *The International Journal of Social Psychiatry, 26*(3), 184–189.

Assessing Personality Using Self-Report Measures with Asians and Asian Americans

9

Sopagna Eap Braje and Gordon C.N. Hall

Overview of Asians and Asian-Americans

Despite the fact that Asians comprise the majority of the world's inhabitants, the majority of the research in psychology has focused on WEIRD (Western, educated, industrial, rich, democratic) populations (Henrich, Heine, & Norenzayan, 2010). One of the challenges of studying Asians and Asian-Americans as a group is the breadth of diversity among the Asian subgroups. Individuals who identify as Asian-American come from over 43 different countries from the continent of Asia as well as the islands in the Pacific and Indian oceans (Liu, Murakami, Eap, & Hall, 2009). The linguistic, religious, and economic diversity represented among Asians contributes to the difficultly in generalizing between subgroups. Additionally, the various migration histories of different Asian-American subgroups suggest that each group have vastly different experiences living in the USA that in turn affects their psychological profiles. For instance, the major influx of Asians migrating to the USA took place in three waves under vastly different social and political circumstances. In contrast, the group known as Pacific Islanders include Hawaiians, Guamanians, and Samoans are automatically US citizens. Although most Americans either explicitly or implicitly perceive Asian-Americans as foreign (Devos & Banaji, 2005), those whose ancestries originate from one of the above US territories have a lineage that makes them nonnaturalized citizens. The circumstances related to citizenship and migration contributes to differences in economic and social standing that may lead to differences in psychological profiles.

Despite these differences, there are some cultural commonalities between Asian subgroups. Many countries in Asia are influenced by Buddhist and Confucian tenets. Buddhism began in India and spread to East and Southeast Asia. Values such as Filial Piety stem from Buddhist theology and may influence parent–child relationships in Asian cultures. Buddhist philosophy also promotes acceptance as a coping strategy, which has been shown to be utilized among Asian-Americans more frequently than among European Americans (Taylor et al., 2004). Moreover, Asian cultures, like many non-Western cultures, also tend to be collectivistic (Oyserman, Coon, & Kemmelmeier, 2002). This collectivistic orientation influences perceptions of the self and, by extension, socioemotional experiences and behavior. These traditionally Asian values may be held by many Asian subgroups, suggesting that, although Asians may

S.E. Braje, Ph.D. (✉)
Clinical Psychology Doctoral Program, California School of Professional Psychology, Alliant International University, 10455 Pomerado Road, San Diego, CA 92131-1799, USA
e-mail: sbraje@alliant.edu

G.C.N. Hall, Ph.D.
Department of Psychology, 1227 University of Oregon, Eugene, OR 97403-1227, USA
e-mail: gnhall@uoregon.edu

L.T. Benuto et al. (eds.), *Guide to Psychological Assessment with Asians*,
DOI 10.1007/978-1-4939-0796-0_9,

have very different historical experiences and cultural practices, there are similar underlying processes that justify examining Asians and Asian-Americans as a group.

Personality and Culture

The study of personality and culture has generated a large amount of debate. Triandis and Suh (2002) define personality as "a configuration of cognitions, emotions, and habits activated when situations stimulate their expression" (p. 136). The study of personality rests on the assumption that personality is predictable. There has been a long-standing debate between personality theorists on whether personality reflects an individual state or a trait. A personality state is transient and can change from situation to situation. A personality trait is more enduring, consistent, and is thought to reflect a genetic predisposition. Self-report measures of personality are based on trait models because it relies on behavioral consistencies.

Personality has been examined extensively cross-culturally, namely through self-reports (Heine & Buchtel, 2009). These efforts to study personality in different cultures have been driven by a desire to understand "national character," personality characteristics unique to each country (Terracciano et al., 2005). Early personality theorists believed that the number of distinct personality dimensions were universal because they were selected for as an adaptation to increase survival (e.g. Goldberg, 1981). Cross-cultural researchers, however, have challenged this assumption. Scholars make a distinction between an emic, or relativistic, and an etic, or constructivistic approach, towards measuring personality (Benet-Martínez & Oishi, 2008). An emic perspective assumes that conceptualization of personality can only be understood within a specific culture and that personality traits imposed by outside cultures are irrelevant when applied to diverse groups. An etic perspective postulates a universal conceptualization of personality. Cross-cultural researchers point out that the two different approaches yield different results.

Although both perspectives advocate seemingly contradictory approaches, there is evidence for both universal and culturally specific features relevant to personality among Asians and Asian-Americans. For this reason, Cheung, van de Vijver, and Leong (2011) advocate a third framework, which combines both an emic and etic approach for measuring and conceptualizing personality. They point out that emic and etic approaches each have limitations. According to Cheung et al., researchers identifying indigenous personality dimensions were not able to consistently establish reliable and valid measures, nor have they been able to establish appropriate norms. Personality researchers have also pointed out that traits identified as culturally specific might actually be universal. These findings underscore the weaknesses of an emic approach. An etic approach, however, tends to focus on traits important to Western cultures. Additionally, traits that have been purported to be universal have failed to yield strong coherence in non-Western cultures. One such example is the openness dimension from the Big Five theory of personality. A combined approach incorporates the strengths of an emic and etic perspective, while minimizing the limitations of both. This chapter will review the available research on personality assessment with self-reports with Asians and Asian-Americans.

Developing Self-Report Measures of Personality

There are several methods for developing a self-report measure of personality. Each of these methods has implications for its applicability to diverse populations. Many self-report measures of personality are developed through the lexical method. This process involves using words found in language that describe personality and then utilizing a statistical method called factor analysis to reduce the number down to the most important dimensions (Saucier & Goldberg, 1996). Factor analysis incorporates the statistical correlations between items to determine how many unique factors emerge from the data. For instance, the Big Five Model (FFM) of personality, discussed in more detail in the section below, was developed using the lexical method. English contains over 17,000 words to describe personality (Allport & Odbert, 1936). Because languages differ in the number of words that are available for a given concept, it is not surprising that applying a lexical approach with different languages also yields a different number of personality dimensions as well as different categories of personality. For instance, using words in the English language has consistently yielded five factors of personality, using words in Tagalog has yielded seven traits, five that are similar to the Big Five (Church, Reyes, Katigbak, & Grimm, 1997), and using Greek words has yielded six traits (Saucier, Georgiades, Tsaousis, & Goldberg, 2005). An emic approach utilizes words in the native language of a culture to understand personality. An etic approach, on the other hand, assumes that the personality structure that emerges in English is universal to all cultures.

Another method is an empirical (criterion) keying approach. The MMPI/MMPI-2 was derived using this method. This process involves identifying a criterion group and comparing that group to a noncriterion group. For instance, in order to differentiate between a group with antisocial personality disorder and a group without a researcher would compare the responses of the individuals from each group on a set of questions. Items that are responded to differently between the two groups would be included in the final measure to distinguish between people with antisocial personality tendencies and those who do not exhibit those tendencies.

Rationally or theoretically derived measures formulate scale items based on how theorists expect different people to respond based on their idea or conceptualization of the personality or based on a theory. The Myers-Briggs Type Indicator (MBTI; Briggs Myers, McCaulley, Quenk, & Hammer, 2003), which is loosely based on the Jungian model of personality is a theoretically derived model. Despite its popularity in the business sector, many call into question its validity (e.g., Arnau, Green, Rosen, Gleaves, & Melancon, 2003), suggesting that a theoretically derived approach may not be the most psychometrically valid way to develop a measure. Nonetheless, a meta-analysis from Capraro and Capraro (2002) of 210 studies has found reliability between 0.55 and 0.97 across different studies. However, only a small percentage of the available studies reported a measure of reliability on the MBTI. The study with the highest reliability coefficient (0.97) included over a 1,000 participants from six different continents. Additionally, Furnham, Moutafi, and Crump (2003) has found convergent validity between MBTI and the NEO-PI-R, replicating earlier results from McCrae and Costa (1989).

Given that the most commonly used and researched measures of personality were developed by people from the West, they have been criticized for not being applicable to diverse populations. Lexical models of personality can only include words that exist within any given language. Forcing one language structure onto another is problematic because some words do not have an equivalent word in a different language. Using an empirical method can also be inaccurate if a criterion group for one cultural group is then applied to a different cultural group. The criterion group for each cultural group may not share the same characteristics. Hence, the criterion group would be inappropriate to use. A measure based on theory may not reflect actual traits. Research has shown that intuition or perception about personality does not always accurately predict reality (Terracciano et al., 2005).

Personality is one of the most extensively researched topics cross-culturally. As such, there are a number of self-report measures of personality. While most of these measures have demonstrated strong psychometric properties in many different Asian groups, there are still caveats to using them. The next section will review the most common measures of personality. While the majority of these measures were derived from a universal framework (although some may argue they reflect a Western framework), there are a few indigenous or emic measures available for Asian or Asian-American populations.

Self-Report Measures of Personality for Asians/Asian-Americans

Self-report is the most widely used method of assessing personality differences among individuals (McCrae & Terracciano, 2005). There are a number of self-report measures for measuring personality that have been validated with an Asian or Asian-American sample. Although a more extensive review of the different self-report measures is beyond the scope of this chapter, this section will review a few of the most commonly used measures to assess personality. Some measures are utilized in clinical settings to assess for psychopathology. Other measures are utilized in applied and research settings to predict a wide range of behaviors in academic and occupational settings. Because acculturation has been shown to influence the expression of personality among Asian-Americans (e.g., Güngör et al., 2012), a few of the most commonly used acculturation and cultural measures will also be discussed.

Etic Measures

The MMPI-2 (Butcher, Dahlstrom, Graham, Tellegen, & Kaemmer, 1989) is widely used in clinical, occupational, and research settings. It is also commonly used in international settings, including many Asian countries such as China, Korea, Japan, Thailand, and the Philippines (see Butcher, Cheung, & Kim, 2003) for a more complete review). Due to the widespread utilization of the MMPI-2, it is subject to rigorous standards when adapted to cross-cultural populations. Many of the studies include a large sample size in order to establish appropriate norms. Translations of the MMPI-2 into different Asian languages have also undergone translation and back translation methods to ensure that items accurately capture the original meaning. In the U.S., however, there is a dearth of studies that utilize large samples of Asian-Americans. Indeed the MMPI-2 standardization sample included less than 1 % of the total sample (Butcher et al., 1989). Hall, Bansal, and Lopez's (1999) meta-analysis examining ethnic differences in the MMPI-2 did not discuss Asian-Americans due to the limited research that included an adequate number of Asian-American participants. Of the available studies, the evidence suggests that Asian-Americans do not have elevated validity scales (Tsushima & Tsushima, 2009) or clinical scales (Stevens, Kwan, & Graybill, 1993) relative to European Americans. These findings, however, may be misleading as extant literature suggests that MMPI-2 subscale scores are associated with acculturation, with low acculturated Asian-Americans having elevated scores relative to a European American norm and highly acculturated Asian-Americans (Sue, Keefe, Enomoto, Durvasula, & Chao, 1996; Tran, 1996; Tsai & Pike, 2000). Highly acculturated Asian-Americans scored similarly to European Americans. Despite its drawbacks, the MMPI-2 has the advantage of being available in several different Asian languages including Japanese, Korean, Chinese, Thai, Vietnamese, and Hmong (Okazaki & Sue, 2000). Test-retest reliability for the MMPI-2 among Asian-Americans ranges between 0.38 to 0.87 (Okazaki & Sue, 2000).

The Big Five personality traits have also been closely examined among Asian and Asian-American populations. Indeed, of all the self-report personality measures, the Big Five (BF) may be the most thoroughly culturally investigated model of personality. The Big Five theory of personality posits that there are five important personality dimensions; Extraversion, Neuroticism, Openness, Conscientiousness, and Agreeableness. The Big Five is commonly measured with the NEO-PI (McCrae, 2001) but can also be measured with the Big Five Inventory (BFI; John & Srivastava, 1999). Both the Neo-PI and the BFI have been validated among a wide range of Asian populations from countries such as Bangladesh, India, Indonesia, Malaysia, Philippines, Hong Kong, Japan, the Republic of Korea, and Taiwan (Schmitt, Allik, McCrae, & Benet-Martínez, 2007). The Big Five has shown cross-cultural robustness across different samples. Nonetheless, the data is weaker in some geographical regions. For instance, Schmitt et al. (2007) found that participants from South and Southeast Asia yielded a lower congruence coefficient for the factor structure of the BFI than other geographical regions, excluding South Africa. The congruence coefficient for these regions did not exceed 0.90, the value that would be considered robust. This lowered congruence was often due to a poor translation or a single item that did not seem to apply to the population. East Asia, however, did yield a robust factor structure. The difference observed between East Asian and South and Southeast Asian populations suggests that there are important cultural dissimilarities on personality between different groups in Asia. McCrae and Terracciano (2005) examined the NEO-PI-R in 50 different cultures using peer reports rather than self-reports and found very similar results. Only India (0.89) showed a lower overall congruence coefficient relative to the other Asian cultures, but the congruence is still high even though it is just shy of 0.90. It is also important to note that the majority of the participants in both studies were college students, which limits the generalizability of the results to the culture as a whole.

Despite the strong evidence for the total Big Five measure, some researchers have found that some of the big five dimensions are problematic in certain cultures and in some studies, only four out of the five dimensions emerged. Should be Schmitt et al. (2007) found that Agreeableness had a weaker internal reliability score (0.57) among South and Southeast Asians relative to other world regions. More commonly, it is the Openness dimension that has been problematic among an Asian or Asian-American sample (Triandis & Suh, 2002). In a study involving 50 countries, McCrae and Terracciano (2005) found that the Openness did not clearly emerge in developing Asian countries such as India (0.59), Malaysia (0.59), Thailand (0.75), and Indonesia (0.71). Cheung et al. (2008) were not able to identify an Openness dimension when combining an etic and emic approach to measuring personality.

Eap et al. (2008) has found that the coherence coefficient of the NEO-PI is affected by culture. Among an Asian-American male sample, they found that participants with lower scores on acculturation and higher scores on the Asian value of Loss of Face (LOF) had a lower factor coherence coefficient relative to European Americans. The LOF did not affect the factor structure for European Americans, suggesting that personality among Asian-Americans may be more strongly influenced by contextual or environmental factors than personality predisposition. Allik and McCrae (2004) found in a study on 36 different cultures that geographically proximal countries shared similar personality profiles. Because countries that are geographically close also tend to be culturally similar, their study lends further support to the role of culture in shaping personality.

Although generally the BF has a strong factor structure, studies have consistently found differences between people of Asian descent and European Americans on the five dimensions. People from Asian countries typically score lower on extraversion higher on neuroticism, higher on agreeableness, and lower on the openness dimensions relative to European Americans (McCrae, Yik, Trapnell, Bond, & Paulhus, 1998). These differences have also been replicated with Asian-Americans (e.g. Eap et al., 2008). Differences on the BF between Asians, Asian-Americans, and European Americans have been accounted for by levels of acculturation (Güngör et al., 2012); Asian-Americans that are highly acculturated have similar personality scores to European Americans. Nonetheless, the NEO-PI and the BFI are robust measures with strong reliability and validity. Interestingly, the correlation between NEO-PI and the BFI is not as strong as one would expect given that the two instruments purportedly measure the same construct (Schmitt et al., 2007). People utilizing this measure should be aware of some of the weaknesses that have been identified when the measure has been applied to diverse non-Western cultures.

The Eysenck Personality Questionnaire (EPQ; Eysenck & Eysenck, 1975) theorizes a four-factor structure of personality: Psychoticism, Extraversion, Neuroticism, and Social Desirability. The EPQ has been translated into Asian languages such as Chinese, Japanese, Korean, and Thai (Cheung, 2004). Barrett, Petrides, Eysenck, and Eysenck (1998) examined the validity of the EPQ among 34 different countries including Hong Kong, India,

Table 9.1 Summary of available indigenous measures of personality

Measure	Authors	Population/language	Scales	Cronbach alpha
Panukat ng Pagkataong Pilipino (PPP)	Carlota, 1985, as cited in Guanzon-Lapeña et al., 1998	Philippines/Tagalog	19 scales	0.52–0.87
Panukat ng Mga Katangian ng Personalidad (PKP)	Church et al. (1997), Katigbak et al. (2002)	Philippines/Tagalog	9 dimensions	0.81–0.90
Five-Factor Personality Questionnaire (*FFPQ*)	Tsuji (1998)	Japan/Japanese	5 supertraits	Unable to report

Adopted from Cheung, Cheung, Wada, and Zhang (2003)

Japan, Korea, Singapore, and Sri Lanka and found that the four factors were robust cross-culturally. However, they averaged responses across the different countries and did not report cross-cultural differences in their study. Van Hemert, van de Vijver, Poortinga, and Georgas (2002) found that the correlations between the four dimensions were different for the Asian countries China, India, and Japan, as well as Uganda. They also point out that for those countries, the psychological meaning of extraversion and neuroticism was similar between and within cultures, but that this was not found with Psychoticism and Social desirability. This supports the potential universality of the extroversion and neuroticism dimensions but call into question the cross-cultural validity of Psychoticism and Social Desirability.

The Myers-Briggs Type Indicator (MBTI; Briggs Myers, McCaulley, Quenk, & Hammer, 2003) is the most widely used personality instrument in the world. It is used in academic and occupational settings to predict performance and as a method of identifying the most appropriate careers for people seeking career counseling. Despite its common usage, there are few available empirical studies on its applicability to diverse populations. The MBTI is composed of four bipolar dimensions: Extroversion-Introversion (E-I), Sensing-Intuition (S-I), Thinking-Feeling (T-F), and Judging-Perceiving (J-P). These bipolar dimensions are combined, resulting in 16 possible personality profiles. Given the frequency in which the MBTI is used internationally, it is surprising that there is a dearth of available empirical research on Asian and Asian-American populations. There have been three published studies examining the MBTI among a Chinese population (Broer & McCarley, 1999; Jie & Xiaoqing, 2006; Sharp, 2008). These studies identified a high percentage of participants that were classified as sensing (S), which describes an individual that gathers information through the five senses and is drawn to a more methodological and concrete approach to decision making. Given that the majority of these studies utilized university samples, this finding may not be unexpected. Additionally, the S dimension corresponds with low scores on the openness dimension of the FFM, which is consistent with past research.

Emic Approaches

Cheung, Cheung, Wada, and Zhang (2003) reviewed several self-report personality measures from India, Korea, Japan, and the Philippines (see Table 9.1). They observed that many of the indigenous personality measures tend to emphasize relationships when describing conceptions of the self. One of the measures they describe is the *Panukat ng Pagkataong Pilipino* (PPP; Carlota, 1985, as cited in Guanzon-Lapeña, Church, Carlota, & Katigbak, 1998). The measure was developed by asking people from the local culture to generate a list of words to describe personality as well as by finding words through written text. Utilizing the lexical approach, Church et al. (1997) developed the *Panukat ng Mga Katangian ng Personalidad* (PKP), which identified seven personality dimensions: Conscientiousness, Concern for Others versus Egotism, Religiosity, Temperamentalness, Self-Assurance, Intellect, and

Gregariousness. Katigbak, Church, Guanzon-Lapeña, Carlota, and del (2002) later added Negative Valence and Positive Valence. The Five-Factor Personality Questionnaire (FFPQ; Tsuji, 1998 as cited in Cheung, Cheung, Leung, Ward, & Leong, 2003) was developed in Japan in an attempt to improve the structure fit of the FFM developed in the West. The FFPQ has the following supertraits: Introversion/extraversion, separateness/attachment, naturality/controlling, and unemotionality/emotionality, practicality/playfulness. Cheung et al. reported that the authors were able to find statistical coherence for their measure and were able to establish concurrent validity with the NEO-PI-R and the Big Five Scale.

Despite the availability of different indigenous self-report measures, some of the self-report instruments reviewed by Cheung et al. lacked psychometric data. Only the PPP and PKP have been included in English journals with published reliability and validity data.

Combined Etic and Emic Measure

The Chinese Personality Assessment Inventory and CPAI-2 (CPAI; Cheung et al., 1996) were developed as an alternative to the MMPI-2 and combine both an emic and etic approach to the assessment of personality. Cheung et al. searched for relevant personality constructs by examining contemporary Chinese literature, proverbs, asking professionals (e.g. nurses, social workers, teachers, and psychologists), and collecting statements of self-descriptors in an informal street survey. The CPAI-2 includes 28 scales not found in Western personality measures such as *harmony* (avoidance of conflict and achievement of inner peace), *face* (orientation describing a concern with bringing shame to one's in-group), and *Modernization* (attitude towards modernization versus tradition). These personality scales yield a total of four factors (*Social Potency/Expansiveness*, *Dependability*, *Accommodation*, and *Interpersonal Relatedness*) and the 12 clinical scales load onto two factors (*Emotional Problem* and *Behavioral Problem*) (Cheung et al., 2008). Initial test-retest reliability ranged between 0.56 and 0.94. Congruence coefficients ranged between 0.77 and 0.98. Cheung et al. (2001) has found that the CPAI was a better fit among a Chinese population relative to the NEO-PI-R (Costa & McCrae, 1992). The CPAI is also available in English and has obtained strong reliability and validity among a European American sample as well as an Asian-American sample (Cheung, 2009; Cheung, Cheung, Leung, et al., 2003). In addition to English and Chinese, the CPAI and CPAI-2 are also available in Korean, Japanese, and Vietnamese (Cheung et al., 2011). The CPAI-2 has been renamed the Cross-Cultural Chinese Personality Assessment Inventory.

An issue that has not been addressed in the CPAI studies is variability within China. China is a country of more than a billion people who vary along multiple dimensions such as ethnicity, class, and local culture that may influence personality. Similar to the criticisms of the measures above, it is unlikely that a single measure can capture all the personality diversity in China.

Acculturation and Measures of Culture

Because validity and reliability of different measures has been shown to be influenced by the degree of acculturation, measures of acculturation and other measures of culture may be appropriate to use with personality measures. Although there a variety to choose from, there are some specific to Asian-Americans including the Suinn-Lew Acculturation Scale (SL-ASIA; Suinn, Ahuna, & Khoo, 1992), and East Asian Acculturation Measure (EAAM; Barry, 2001). Aside from acculturation, there are other aspects of culture that can be measured. For instance, ethnic identity can be measured with the Multigroup Ethnic Identity Measure (Phinney, 1992); cultural values with the Asian Values Scale (Kim, Atkinson, & Yang, 1999); and face concerns with the Loss of Face Questionnaire (Zane & Mak, 2003). Ethnic identity and specific cultural values can yield valuable information about individual variables relevant to personality and other psychological constructs. For instance, Loss of Face has found to be associated with personality (Eap et al., 2008), sexual aggression (Hall, Teten, DeGarmo, Sue, & Stephens, 2005), and depression (Zane & Yeh, 2002) among Asian-Americans.

There is debate among personality researchers on whether personality traits are universal or culturally specific. In general, there are robust self-report measures of personality. However, there are limitations to their generalizability. The majority of validity studies with Asian participants are conducted in Asia initiated by Asian researchers overseas rather than in the U.S. When Asian-Americans are recruited for studies, they tend to be college students, fluent in English, and economically advantaged (Okazaki, Lee, & Sue, 2007). Likewise, studies conducted in Asia also typically recruit college students (Matsumoto, 2006). College students may be more Westernized than the rest of the Asian population, suggesting that measures of culture should accompany any comparison between cultures. Kinzie et al. (1982) contended it that may be inappropriate to apply any scale validated with one cultural group to another. Kinzie's perspective is influenced by an emic approach towards mental health assessment. Kinzie's views on adapting measures to different cultures may be extreme in light of the inefficiency associated with developing measures unique to each population. Additionally, some groups may not be culturally dissimilar enough to warrant different assessment measures. Clinicians and researchers interested in adapting one measure from one culture to another should keep in my mind some important factors that may compromise the validity of measures when used with Asian-Americans.

Problems Related to Self-Report Measures

Whenever self-report measures are developed and validated within one cultural group and then applied to another, there is the potential for bias. Leong and Chou (1997) suggest that this bias is likely the result of neglecting cultural variables (as cited in Leong & Lau, 2001). They recommend that researchers and clinicians should exercise diligence in maintaining the integrity of cultural validity, which would in turn strengthen psychometric validity. They identify that cultural validity can be compromised by a number of factors including language, conceptual disagreement, and response bias. The section below will review sources of bias related to self-report methods.

Response Bias

There is evidence that response styles are influenced by culture, underscoring the importance of validating with specific populations rather than generalizing from a European American population. One common issue is the tendency for people of Asian descent to resort to middle (Chen, Lee, & Stevenson, 1995) or acquiescent response styles (Johnson, Kulesa, Llc, Cho, & Shavitt, 2005) more frequently than non-Asian respondents. Moderate responding tends to be more pronounced when people from East Asia respond to measures in their native language rather than to a translated measure (Kuroda, Hayashi, & Suzuki, 1986). This type of response style is problematic as it may nullify results.

Researchers suspect that some of the cross-cultural differences observed on self-report measures of personality are attributed to response biases. One particularly problematic trait is the Conscientious trait from the FFM. Conscientiousness describes the tendency to be meticulous, responsible, and orderly. When different cultures are ranked on this trait based on national averages, Japan has been shown to score the lowest among 36 different countries (McCrae, 2002), a finding that is counterintuitive for an industrialized, highly educated, and wealthy country. These findings, as well as other counterintuitive findings, have led researchers to conclude that the responses may actually be due to response biases rather than reflecting real differences in personality.

The lower levels of extreme responding and tendency for moderate responding observed in East Asian cultures have been attributed to a dialectical thinking style. Hamamura, Heine, and Paulhus (2008) examined the relationship between thinking style and response patterns on the Big Five Inventory between European Canadians and East Asian Canadians. They calculated moderate responding by calculating the number of times an individual endorsed the midpoint choice for the 26 items that were not significantly different between the two groups. They found evidence that people of East Asian descent were more likely to endorse the midpoint more often and that this tendency was explained by the greater tendency towards dialectical thinking.

Uskul, Oyserman, Schwarz, Lee, and Xu (2013) also suggested that cultural orientations of collectivism, honor, and individualism can also affect survey responses by influencing question comprehension, recall, and response editing. They point out that features of a self-report, such as using a Likert scale that ranges from 0 to 10 versus one that ranges from −5 to 5, changes the meaning of a psychological construct even when the verbal anchors are the same between both scales. The former suggests a unipolar dimension (more or less of something) while the latter implies a bipolar dimension (where success and failure are both measured). People from collectivistic cultures may be more likely to give themselves low ratings due to concerns regarding modesty.

Some of these problems associated with moderate or acquiescent responding could be mitigated by employing certain strategies. Mõttus et al. (2012) suggest one possible method of investigating and correcting for response bias called anchoring vignettes. Participants were asked to rate themselves on conscientiousness before rating the conscientiousness of 30 hypothetical people from a set of brief vignettes. Because all responses were to the same vignettes, the authors reasoned that scores would reflect individual differences in response styles rather than real differences. They investigated this method with almost 3,000 people from 20 different countries, including China, Hong Kong, Japan, and South Korea, Malaysia, and the Philippines. They found that people from Hong Kong, Japan, and South Korea had the lowest scores on extreme responses, and countries such as mainland China, Malaysia, and the Philippines had the highest scores on extreme responses. Correcting for this response bias, Mõttus et al. (2012) demonstrated that this shifted national rankings on conscientiousness and reduced the problematic negative correlations with country Gross Domestic Product (GDP), but did not eliminate it completely.

McCrae, Herbst, and Costa (2001) contended that acquiescence bias can be statistically controlled for when comparing scores cross culturally. By calculating a score for acquiescence bias, McCrae and Terracciano (2005) demonstrated that acquiescence was significantly correlated with only the Openness dimension of the BF. Given the problematic nature of this factor in cross-cultural studies, their results provide an explanation for its relative psychometric weakness. Schmitt et al. (2007) controlled for acquiescence bias in their study by creating an acquiescence index, a score composed of an equal number positively and negatively keyed items which are scored in the same direction. They were able to improve convergent correlations after controlling for acquiescence bias.

Additionally, questionnaires can be created to eliminate the middle option of a Likert scale in order to deter moderate responding. Researchers can also choose items that are most likely to elicit strong responses. Another solution is to utilize Item Response Theory (IRT) to analyze responses on a self-report rather than looking at statistical norms such as means, reliability, or variance. IRT examines the degree to which items on a self-report measure fit the expected pattern of response for a given psychological construct between different groups. Moreover, IRT examines item characteristic curves (ICC) for different groups. ICCs that are shaped differently and do not correspond suggest the presence of measurement bias.

Culture may also influence memory bias, which can affect scores on self-reports. Thus, methods that rely on retrospective recall will likely result in differences that are not due to actual experiences. For instance, Oishi (2002) found that European Americans tend to report higher levels of mood and well-being retrospectively but did not differ from Asian-Americans in their daily reports. She found that these differences were due to the tendency for European Americans to weight their positive experiences more than Asian-Americans when retrospectively evaluating their week, whereas Asian-Americans weighted both equally. Lee, Okazaki, and Yoo (2006) demonstrated the same phenomenon with negative emotions. Despite experiencing the same number of events that elicit anxiety, Asian-Americans retrospectively reported higher scores on measures of anxiety. It is possible that self-reports developed and validated among Western cultures might also reflect this tendency towards what Oishi defines as the "optimism of memory," the tendency to feel more positive about events than was initially experienced.

Cross-Cultural Equivalence

When using self-report measurement scales between ethnic groups, one must also consider the degree of cross-cultural equivalence found between ethnic groups. Cross-cultural equivalence refers to the extent to which the responses obtained from members of one population are interpreted in the same way as the responses obtained from a different population. For instance, do elevated scores on the extraversion measure sociability and gregariousness in all cultures?

Marsella, Dubanoski, Hamada, and Morse (2000) have identified four conditions that must be satisfied in order to establish cross-cultural equivalence: conceptual equivalence, linguistic equivalence, metric equivalence, and normative equivalence. First, conceptual equivalence establishes that the meaning of a construct being measured is the same in different cultures. For instance, does the concept of *dependency* have the same connotations when used in different cultures? In cultures that value individualism, dependency is viewed more negatively than in collectivistic cultures. Secondly, researchers must establish linguistic equivalence. Linguistic equivalence describes the degree of similarity between translations of measured from one language to another. Translational accuracy is typically verified through translation and back translation of people who are fluent in both languages. Both conceptual and linguistic equivalences are particularly difficult to establish without inside cultural knowledge. The third condition has to do with metric equivalence establishes that participants are using the same scale when responding to an item. Metric equivalence can be determined by using factor analyses, comparing psychometric properties from different subgroups and cultures. Metric equivalence is compromised when people have different baselines for a behavior. This is known as the reference-group effect (RFE; Heine, Lehman, Peng, & Greenholtz, 2002). Because people have a tendency to respond to questions by comparing themselves to others, researchers examining mean differences between cultures may draw erroneous conclusions. For instance, if the average height is taller in the USA than it is in Thailand, a respondent who is 5 ft 7 in. tall may indicate that he is tall because he compares himself to the people around him. A person of the same height in the U.S. may respond that he is short. Objectively, they are the same height but subjectively, one feels taller than the other. As such, their metric scale is not the same. When applied to personality measures, participants responding to a question such as "I am a good public speaker" would require individuals to first decide how good others are and then decide how good he or she is compared to their perception of the others. The RFE is a problem whenever mean differences are compared between cultural groups that do not share the same context. Questions that require subjective interpretations are especially vulnerable to the reference group effect. Lastly, normative equivalence refers to the statistical norms obtained with a particular group. Norms taken from a European American group may not be appropriate to use with a different population. The MMPI utilizes different norms for people from Asian countries than among Americans (Cheung, 2004).

It is clear that the use of any self-report across ethnic or cultural group is problematic because of its susceptibility to response bias.

Any of the above measures may be compromised if individuals are unfamiliar with paper-and-pencil testing, or more common recently, Internet surveys. Cheung (2004) suggests that this type of testing is associated with evaluation in many Asian cultures, which may increase anxiety and cause people to respond in socially desirable ways.

Personality and Psychological Adjustment

Personality measures can be used to predict psychological adjustment among the general population. For instance, the scores on the Big Five dimensions are associated with positive affect. Low scores on Neuroticism and high scores on the Extraversion have been associated with high levels of subjective well-being (Steel, Schmidt, & Shultz, 2008). This relationship has been replicated with Asian samples from South Korea (Ha & Kim, 2013). Oishi, Diener, Suh, and Lucas (1999) suggested that the association between personality and well-being depends on individual values. For instance, they found that people who valued academic achievement incorporated academic achievement into their judgments of life satisfaction.

Matsumoto, Nakagawa, and Estrada (2009) investigated the mediating role of personality on explaining cross-cultural differences on psychological adjustment among American and Japanese participants and found that the Big Five traits significantly explained differences found on psychological adjustment. The psychological adjustment of the Japanese was lower than that of American participants, which was explained by higher scores on Neuroticism and lower scores on Extraversion reported among Japanese participants relative to Americans. They concluded that personality may be a more important explanation of cross-cultural differences than perceptions of the self. One of the problems related to Matsumoto's study was that the research variables were measured simultaneously rather than longitudinally, precluding a determination of causality.

The relationship between personality and psychological adjustment may be more complex than simply personality traits causing psychological vulnerabilities. Fulmer et al. (2010) proposed the person-culture match hypothesis to explain the relationship between personality and well-being among people from different cultures. Their theory predicts that when people possess a personality that is similar to the people in that culture, that match serves to enhance self-esteem and increase well-being. They found support for their theory for matching on individual level extraversion across 26 different countries. Despite personality differences observed among different cultures, Fulmer et al. (2010) found well-being, positive emotions, and life happiness were predicted based on country level similarity on extraversion. This suggests that Matsumoto's analysis may be simplistic and does not consider the context when evaluating psychological adjustment and personality variables.

Considering the context is important when evaluating the relationship between personality and psychological adjustment. For instance, the personality dimension extraversion may not have the same function among people from different cultures. Oishi, Krochik, Roth, and Sherman (2012) has found that extraversion served as a protective factor for European Americans against stress associated with residential mobility but did not buffer Asian-Americans or African-Americans. They suggest that one reason may be that European Americans are more likely to seek social support than Asian-Americans, which would be facilitated by an extroverted personality.

Personality has been shown in previous research to be associated with psychological adjustment. Low scores on extraversion and high scores on neuroticism, in particular, has been linked with depression (Steel, Smith, & Shultz, 2008). It has been suggested that cultural differences on personality traits reflect a biological predisposition toward negative affect (Matsumoto et al., 2009). However, there is evidence that the relationship between personality and psychological adjustment is better explained by the person-culture match hypothesis. Extraversion may not serve the same purpose among some cultural groups compared with European Americans.

Predictive Validity and Salience of Self-Report Measures

There is reason to believe that self-reports may not be as predictive of behavior for people from collectivistic cultures. People from Eastern cultures do not value self-consistency as highly as people from Western cultures. For instance, in East Asian cultures, it is common for emotional experiences to be minimized. People from Asian cultures might have emotional reactions similar to Americans in nonsocial situations, but suppress emotional responses in the presence of others, particularly in the presence of people they consider to be authority figures (Matsumoto & Kuppersbusch, 2001). People from Asian cultures may be less consistent across situations because they respond to contextual cues. People from individualistic cultures may be more likely to respond based on their own tendencies as opposed to people from collectivistic cultures, who are more likely to respond according to the situation.

This inconsistency may also influence the reliability of peer informants, which has also been utilized to assess personality (McCrae & Terracciano, 2005). Personality researchers have incorporated peer-informants in order to gather information from multiple perspectives. Using peer informants when it comes to Asians and Asian-Americans, however, may lead to conflicting information that might confuse rather than clarify. For instance, Suh (2002) compared Korean and American participants on peer and self-ratings of personality. She found lower correlations for Koreans than for Americans. This lack of agreement between self and others may also apply to Asian-Americans. Okazaki (2002) found that Asian-Americans and European Americans generally self-reported higher levels of depressive and anxiety symptoms than were reported for them by peers, but that peers tended to report fewer symptoms for Asian Americans than for European Americans. Although not directly measuring personality, Okazaki showed that peer report may be less concordant in an Asian-American population than in an European American population. These findings suggest that using multiple informants for Asian-Americans may not necessarily increase clarity.

Eastern and Western cultures have different views of the self which may influence definitions of personality. People from Eastern cultures do not value self-consistency as much as people from Western cultures (Suh, 2002). Indeed, people from Eastern cultures are more likely to view self as malleable and may be more accepting of self-contradictions within themselves (Boucher, Peng, Shi, & Wang, 2009). For instance, personality among people from Eastern cultures tends to be context dependent (Kanagawa, Cross, & Markus, 2001). Kanagawa et al. (2001) demonstrated that, compared with American participants, the self-descriptors given by Japanese participants depended on the testing conditions, whether they were alone, with a peer, or a professional. Consistent with this, Suh (2002) found that when Korean and American participants were asked to describe their personality with five different people as well as their general personality, Korean participants had much less consistency than American participants. English and Chen (2007) reported similar findings comparing Asian-Americans and European Americans. However, although Asian-Americans were less consistent relative to European Americans, they were consistent with their interactions within their social roles. This suggests that people of Asian descent are more likely shape their perception of their personality based on their roles and relationships whereas people from Western cultures are less likely to consider the situation when reflecting on their personality. This may be especially true for Asian-Americans who are bicultural. Mok and Morris (2009) demonstrated that bicultural Asian-Americans reported higher levels of Extraversion when primed with American images than when primed with images from Asia whereas Asian-Americans that were low on biculturalism demonstrated the opposite trend. People who are truly bicultural adapt their personality to different cultural contexts while those who are comfortable in one context may not truly show their personality because they don't feel as comfortable.

This tendency for explaining behavior in terms of the context rather than individual propensities among people of Asian descent is evidenced by the fact that Asians do not commit the fundamental attribution error (Choi, Nisbett, & Norenzayan, 1999). Church, Katigbak, Miramontes, del Prado, and Cabrera (2007) has found that people from individualistic cultures are more likely to endorse that personality is stable over time and important for predicting behavior. People from collectivistic cultures are more likely to believe that roles and obligations are important for predicting behavior.

As such, the construct of personality is likely to hold different meaning for people of Western versus Eastern cultures. This is illustrated in how people from Eastern cultures respond to feedback from personality tests. Spencer-Rodgers, Boucher, Peng, and Wang (2009) had Chinese, Asian-American, and non-Asian-American students take a series of personality tests and later gave them false feedback on the results of the personality tests. They found that non-Asians were more likely to respond to self-inconsistent feedback by resisting the information given to them whereas Chinese and Asian-American students responded to the feedback by changing their self-perceptions. Spencer-Rodgers et al. found that this was directly attributable to the tendency for dialectical thinking among people from East Asian cultures. Dialectical thinking is a cognitive style that recognizes the coexistence of contradictions whereas positive logical determinism assumes one truth (Peng & Nisbett, 1999). Eastern philosophy tends to reflect a more dialectical thinking pattern whereas Western philosophy is dominated by positive logical determinism. This difference in thinking styles may explain the cultural difference in the valuing of self-consistency.

Conclusions and Future Directions

The most commonly used self-report measures are well validated among Asian populations. However, Asian-Americans are typically underrepresented in the validation of personality self-report measures. There are few published studies that have empirically examined the MMPI/MMPI-2 among Asian-Americans and none that examined the MBTI.

Self-report measures are the most common way to measure personality. However, given the problems associated with bias, self-report is insufficient. Heine and Buchtel (2009) recommend that using multiple methods to assess personality is necessary for gathering evidence in support of observed differences or similarities between cultural groups. Interestingly, many well-validated self-report measures have failed to demonstrate convergent evidence when utilizing behavioral measures of personality in different cultures. For instance, people's perception of their country's level of conscientiousness was more strongly correlated to observed behaviors, such as the accuracy of clocks in public banks, and walking speed of the culture's citizens, than self-report responses on the NEO-PI-R and the BFI (Heine, Buchtel, & Norenzayan, 2008).

People from Eastern cultures have a different conceptualization of self than people from Western cultures. For instance, people from Eastern cultures are more likely to view the self as fluid rather than stable. Given that the assumption in personality research is that the self is stable and resistant to change, personality self-reports should be cognizant of the importance of social roles and context that shape conceptions of personality among people of Asian descent.

Based on the work of past researchers, we recommend the following with regard to measuring personality with self-report:

1. Include more Asian-Americans in personality self-report validation studies. Asians Americans are significantly underrepresented in personality research. There is more empirical work examining personality in Asia than there is in the U.S. Given the confounds that have been identified, including more Asian-Americans in personality research is essential for increasing the generalizability of commonly used self-report measures such as the MMPI/MMPI-2 and MBTI.
2. Evaluate levels of acculturation, ethnic identity, and cultural values. Because there is within group variability among Asians and

Asian-Americans, these measures may provide explanations for cross-cultural and multicultural differences. Research suggests that differences in personality are driven by culture. It is important to identify which aspects of culture are relevant to personality differences.

3. Consider the relevance of indigenous personality characteristics. There is evidence that personality traits have universal and culturally specific features. Research has shown that in some cases, combining indigenous measures with universal measures of personality may be a better model of personality for Asians than a purely universal conceptualization of personality (Cheung et al., 2001).
4. Measure personality in different contexts. There is evidence that people from Eastern cultures perceive themselves differently depending on their social roles (English & Chen, 2007). This flexibility in how people of Asian descent view themselves may decrease the saliency of self-report measures for people from Eastern cultures. As such, measuring personality in different contexts may increase the predictive validity of self-report measures for predicting behavior.
5. Include convergent evidence. The strongest evidence of validity is when multiple methods provide convergent validity. Researchers and clinicians should validate self-report measures with behavioral measures of personality. Relying on self-report measures can be problematic for a number of reasons. Given the relatively weak correlation between behavioral measures and self-report measures when measuring national character (Heine et al., 2008), it is imperative that personality researchers develop multiple methods to measures personality.

Asians and Asian-Americans are a heterogeneous group, which poses a significant challenge to generalizing research findings. Due to the diversity within the Asian and Asian-American groups, personality research should attempt to understand the social and cultural mechanisms that may influence ethnic differences rather than focus strictly on ethnic differences.

References

Allik, J., & McCrae, R. R. (2004). Toward a geography of personality traits patterns of profiles across 36 cultures. *Journal of Cross-Cultural Psychology, 35*, 13–28.

Allport, G. W., & Odbert, H. S. (1936). Trait-names: A psycho-lexical study. *Psychological Monographs, 47*(1 whole number No. 211), 1–171. doi:10.1037/h0093360.

Arnau, R. C., Green, B. A., Rosen, D. H., Gleaves, D. H., & Melancon, J. G. (2003). Are Jungian preferences really categorical? An empirical investigation using taxometric analysis. *Personality and Individual Differences, 34*, 233–251. doi:10.1016/S0191-8869(02)00040-5.

Barrett, P. T., Petrides, K. V., Eysenck, S. B. G., & Eysenck, H. J. (1998). The Eysenck Personality Questionnaire: An examination of the factorial similarity of P, E, N, and L across 34 countries. *Personality and Individual Differences, 25*, 805–819. doi:10.1016/S0191-8869(98)00026-9.

Barry, D. T. (2001). Development of a new scale for measuring acculturation: The East Asian Acculturation Measure (EAAM). *Journal of Immigrant Health, 3*, 193–197. doi:10.1023/A:1012227611547.

Benet-Martínez, V., & Oishi, S. (2008). Culture and personality. In O. P. John, R. W. Robins, & L. A. Pervin (Eds.), *Handbook of personality: Theory and research* (pp. 542–567). New York, NY: Guilford Press.

Boucher, H. C., Peng, K., Shi, J., & Wang, L. (2009). Culture and implicit self-esteem Chinese are "good" and "bad" at the same time. *Journal of Cross-Cultural Psychology, 40*, 24–45. doi:10.1177/0022022108326195.

Broer, E., & McCarley, N. G. (1999). Using and validating the Myers-Briggs Type Indicator in Mainland China. *Journal of Psychological Type, 51*, 5–21.

Butcher, J. N., Dahlstrom, W. G., Graham, J. R., Tellegen, A., & Kaemmer, B. (1989). *Manual for the restandardized Minnesota Multiphasic Personality Inventory: MMPI-2*. Minneapolis, MN: University of Minnesota Press.

Butcher, J. N., Cheung, F. M., & Kim, J. (2003). Use of the MMPI-2 with Asian populations. *Psychological Assessment, 15*, 248–256. doi:10.1037/1040-3590.15.3.248.

Capraro, R. M., & Capraro, M. M. (2002). Myers-Briggs Type Indicator score reliability across: Studies a meta-analytic reliability generalization study. *Educational and Psychological Measurement, 62*, 590–602. doi:10.1177/0013164402062004004.

Chen, C., Lee, S. Y., & Stevenson, H. W. (1995). Response style and cross-cultural comparisons of rating scales among East Asian and North American students. *Psychological Science, 6*, 170–175. doi:10.1111/j.1467-9280.1995.tb00327.x.

Cheung, F. M. (2004). Use of Western and indigenously developed personality tests in Asia. *Applied Psychology, 53*, 173–191. doi:10.1111/j.1464-0597.2004.00167.x.

Cheung, F. M. (2009). The cultural perspective in personality assessment. In J. N. Butcher (Ed.), *Oxford handbook of personality assessment* (pp. 44–56). New York, NY: Oxford University Press.

Cheung, F. M., Cheung, S. F., Leung, K., Ward, C., & Leong, F. (2003). The English version of the Chinese Personality Assessment Inventory. *Journal of Cross-Cultural Psychology, 34*, 433–452. doi:10.1177/0022022103034004004.

Cheung, F. M., Cheung, S. F., Wada, S., & Zhang, J. (2003). Indigenous measures of personality assessment in Asian Countries: A review. *Psychological Assessment, 15*, 280–289. doi:10.1037/1040-3590.15.3.280.

Cheung, F. M., Cheung, S. F., Zhang, J., Leung, K., Leong, F., & Huiyeh, K. (2008). Relevance of Openness as a personality dimension in Chinese culture: Aspects of its cultural relevance. *Journal of Cross-Cultural Psychology, 39*, 81–108. doi:10.1177/0022022107311968.

Cheung, F. M., Leung, K., Fan, R. M., Song, W.-Z., Zhang, J. X., & Zhang, J. P. (1996). Development of the Chinese Personality Assessment Inventory. *Journal of Cross-Cultural Psychology, 27*, 181–199. doi:10.1177/0022022196272003.

Cheung, F. M., Leung, K., Zhang, J. X., Sun, H. F., Gan, Y. Q., Song, W. Z., & Xie, D. (2001). Indigenous Chinese personality constructs: Is the Five-Factor Model complete? *Journal of Cross-Cultural Psychology, 32*, 407–433. doi:10.1177/0022022101032004003

Cheung, F. M., van de Vijver, F. J. R., & Leong, F. T. L. (2011). Toward a new approach to the study of personality in culture. *American Psychologist, 6*, 593–603. doi:10.1037/a0022389.

Choi, I., Nisbett, R. E., & Norenzayan, A. (1999). Causal attribution across cultures: Variation and universality. *Psychological Bulletin, 125*, 47–63. doi:10.1037/0033-2909.125.1.47.

Church, A. T., Katigbak, M. S., Miramontes, L. G., del Prado, A. M., & Cabrera, H. F. (2007). Culture and the behavioural manifestations of traits: An application of the act frequency approach. *European Journal of Personality, 21*, 389–417. doi:10.1002/per.631.

Church, A. T., Reyes, J. A. S., Katigbak, M. S., & Grimm, S. D. (1997). Filipino personality structure and the Big Five Model: A lexical approach. *Journal of Personality, 65*, 477–528. doi:10.1111/j.1467-6494.1997.tb00325.x.

Costa, P. T., & McCrae, R. R. (1992). Normal personality assessment in clinical practice: The NEO Personality Inventory. *Psychological Assessment, 4*, 5–13.

Devos, T., & Banaji, M. R. (2005). American = White? *Journal of Personality and Social Psychology, 88*, 447–466. doi:10.1037/0022-3514.88.3.447.

Eap, S., DeGarmo, D. S., Kawakami, A., Hara, S. N., Hall, G. C., & Teten, A. L. (2008). Culture and personality among European American and Asian American men. *Journal of Cross-Cultural Psychology, 39*, 630–643. doi:10.1177/0022022108321310.

English, T., & Chen, S. (2007). Culture and self-concept stability: Consistency across and within contexts among Asian Americans and European Americans. *Journal of Personality and Social Psychology, 93*, 478–490. doi:10.1037/0022-3514.93.3.478.

Eysenck, H. J., & Eysenck, S. B. G. (1975). *Eysenck Personality Questionnaire*. San Diego, CA: EdITS/Educational and Industrial Testing Service.

Fulmer, C. A., Gelfand, M. J., Kruglanski, A. W., Kim-Prieto, C., Diener, E., Pierro, A., & Higgins, E. T. (2010). On "feeling right" in cultural contexts: How person-culture match affects self-esteem and subjective well-being. *Psychological Science, 21*, 1563–1569. doi:10.1177/0956797610384742

Furnham, A., Moutafi, J., & Crump, J. (2003). The relationship between the revised NEO-Personality Inventory and the Myers-Briggs Type Indicator. *Social Behavior and Personality: An International Journal, 31*, 577–584. doi:10.2224/sbp.2003.31.6.577.

Goldberg, L. R. (1981). Language and individual differences: The search for universals in personality lexicons. *Review of Personality and Social Psychology, 2*, 141–165.

Guanzon-Lapeña, M. A., Church, A. T., Carlota, A. J., & Katigbak, M. S. (1998). Indigenous personality measures Philippine examples. *Journal of Cross-Cultural Psychology, 29*, 249–270. doi:10.1177/0022022198291013.

Güngör, D., Bornstein, M. H., Leersnyder, J. D., Cote, L., Ceulemans, E., & Mesquita, B. (2012). Acculturation of personality: A three-culture study of Japanese, Japanese Americans, and European Americans. *Journal of Cross-Cultural Psychology*. doi:10.1177/0022022112470749. Advanced online publication.

Ha, S. E., & Kim, S. (2013). Personality and subjective well-being: Evidence from South Korea. *Social Indicators Research, 111*, 341–359. doi:10.1007/s11205-012-0009-9.

Hall, G. C. N., Bansal, A., & Lopez, I. R. (1999). Ethnicity and psychopathology: A meta-analytic review of 31 years of comparative MMPI/MMPI-2 research. *Psychological Assessment, 11*, 186–197. doi:10.1037/1040-3590.11.2.186.

Hall, G. C. N., Teten, A. L., DeGarmo, D. S., Sue, S., & Stephens, K. A. (2005). Ethnicity, culture, and sexual aggression: Risk and protective factors. *Journal of Consulting and Clinical Psychology, 73*, 830–840. doi:10.1037/0022-006X.73.5.830.

Hamamura, T., Heine, S. J., & Paulhus, D. L. (2008). Cultural differences in response styles: The role of dialectical thinking. *Personality and Individual Differences, 44*, 932–942. doi:10.1016/j.paid.2007.10.034.

Heine, S. J., & Buchtel, E. E. (2009). Personality: The universal and the culturally specific. *Annual Review of Psychology, 60*, 369–394. doi:10.1146/annurev.psych.60.110707.163655.

Heine, S. J., Buchtel, E. E., & Norenzayan, A. (2008). What do cross-national comparisons of personality traits tell us? The case of Conscientiousness. *Psychological Science, 19*, 309–313. doi:10.1111/j.1467-9280.2008.02085.x.

Heine, S. J., Lehman, D. R., Peng, K., & Greenholtz, J. (2002). What's wrong with cross-cultural comparisons of subjective Likert scales? The reference-group effect. *Journal of Personality and Social Psychology, 82*, 903–918. doi:10.1037//0022-3514.82.6.903.

Henrich, J., Heine, S. J., & Norenzayan, A. (2010). Most people are not WEIRD. *Nature, 466*(7302), 29.

Jie, L., & Xiaoqing, Q. (2006). Language learning styles and learning strategies of tertiary-level English learners in China. *RELC Journal, 37*, 67–90. doi:10.1177/0033688206063475.

John, O. P., & Srivastava, S. (1999). The Big Five trait taxonomy: History, measurement, and theoretical perspectives. In L. A. Pervin & O. P. John (Eds.), *Handbook of personality: Theory and research* (2nd ed., pp. 102–138). New York, NY: Guilford Press.

Johnson, T., Kulesa, P., Llc, I., Cho, Y. I., & Shavitt, S. (2005). The relation between culture and response styles: Evidence from 19 countries. *Journal of Cross-Cultural Psychology, 36*, 264–277. doi:10.1177/0022022104272905.

Kanagawa, C., Cross, S. E., & Markus, H. R. (2001). "Who Am I?" The cultural psychology of the conceptual self. *Personality and Social Psychology Bulletin, 27*, 90–103. doi:10.1177/0146167201271008.

Katigbak, M. S., Church, A. T., Guanzon-Lapeña, M. A., Carlota, A. J., & del, P. (2002). Are indigenous personality dimensions culture specific? Philippine inventories and the five-factor model. *Journal of Personality and Social Psychology, 82*, 89–101.

Kim, B. S. K., Atkinson, D. R., & Yang, P. H. (1999). The Asian values scale: Development, factor analysis, validation, and reliability. *Journal of Counseling Psychology, 46*, 342–352.

Kinzie, J. D., Manson, S. M., Vinh, D. T., Tolan, N. T., Anh, B., & Pho, T. N. (1982). Development and validation of a Vietnamese-language depression rating scale. *The American Journal of Psychiatry, 139*, 1276–1281.

Kuroda, Y., Hayashi, C., & Suzuki, T. (1986). The role of language in cross-national surveys: American and Japanese respondents. *Applied Stochastic Models and Data Analysis, 2*(1–2), 43–59. doi:10.1002/asm.3150020105.

Lee, M. R., Okazaki, S., & Yoo, H. C. (2006). Frequency and intensity of social anxiety in Asian Americans and European Americans. *Cultural Diversity & Ethnic Minority Psychology, 12*, 291–305. doi:10.1037/1099-9809.12.2.291.

Leong, F. T. L., & Lau, A. S. L. (2001). Barriers to providing effective mental health services to Asian Americans. *Mental Health Services Research, 3*(4), 201–214. doi:10.1023/A:1013177014788.

Liu, C. H., Murakami, J., Eap, S., & Hall, G. C. N. (2009). Who are Asian Americans? An overview of history, immigration, and communities. In N. Tewari & A. Alvarez (Eds.), *Asian American psychology: Current perspectives* (pp. 1–30). New York, NY: Erlbaum.

Marsella, A. J., Dubanoski, J., Hamada, W. C., & Morse, H. (2000). The measurement of personality across cultures: Historical, conceptual, and methodological issues and considerations. *American Behavioral Scientist, 44*, 41–62. doi:10.1177/00027640021956080.

Matsumoto, D. (2006). Culture and cultural worldviews: Do verbal descriptions about culture reflect anything other than verbal descriptions of culture? *Culture & Psychology, 12*, 33–62. doi:10.1177/1354067X06061592.

Matsumoto, D., & Kuppersbusch, C. (2001). Idiocentric and allocentric in emotion expression, experience, and the coherence between expression and experience. *Asian Journal of Social Psychology, 4*, 113–131.

Matsumoto, D., Nakagawa, S., & Estrada, A. (2009). The role of dispositional traits in accounting for country and ethnic group differences on adjustment. *Journal of Personality, 77*, 177–212. doi:10.1111/j.1467-6494.2008.00542.x.

McCrae, R. R. (2001). Trait psychology and culture: Exploring intercultural comparisons. *Journal of Personality, 69*, 819–846.

McCrae, R. R. (2002). NEO-PI-R data from 36 cultures. In R. R. McCrae & J. Allik (Eds.), *The five-factor model of personality across cultures* (pp. 105–125). New York, NY: Kluwer Academic.

McCrae, R. R., & Costa, P. T. (1989). Reinterpreting the Myers-Briggs Type Indicator from the perspective of the five-factor model of personality. *Journal of Personality, 57*, 17–40. doi:10.1111/j.1467-6494.1989.tb00759.x.

McCrae, R. R., Herbst, J. H., & Costa, P. T., Jr. (2001). Effects of acquiescence on personality factors structures. In R. Riemann, F. M. Spinath, & F. Ostendorf (Eds.), *Personality and temperament: Genetics, evolution, and structure* (pp. 217–231). Berlin, Germany: Pabst Science Publishers.

McCrae, R. R., & Terracciano, A. (2005). Personality profiles of cultures: Aggregate personality traits. *Journal of Personality and Social Psychology, 89*, 407–425. doi:10.1037/0022-3514.89.3.407.

McCrae, R. R., Yik, M. S., Trapnell, P. D., Bond, M. H., & Paulhus, D. L. (1998). Interpreting personality profiles across cultures: Bilingual, acculturation, and peer rating studies of Chinese undergraduates. *Journal of Personality and Social Psychology, 74*, 1041–1055.

Mok, A., & Morris, M. W. (2009). Cultural chameleons and iconoclasts: Assimilation and reactance to cultural cues in biculturals' expressed personalities as a function of identity conflict. *Journal of Experimental Social Psychology, 45*, 884–889. doi:10.1016/j.jesp.2009.04.004.

Mõttus, R., Allik, J., Realo, A., Rossier, J., Zecca, G., Ah-Kion, J., … Johnson, W. (2012). The effect of response style on self-reported Conscientiousness across

20 countries. *Personality & Social Psychology Bulletin, 38*, 1423–1436. doi:10.1177/0146167212451275.

Myers, I. B., McCaulley, M. H., Quenk, N. L., & Hammer, A. L. (2003). *MBTI manual: A guide to the development and use of the Myers Briggs Type Indicator*. Palo Alto, CA: Consulting Psychologists Press.

Oishi, S. (2002). The experiencing and remembering of well-being: A cross-cultural analysis. *Personality and Social Psychology Bulletin, 28*, 1398–1406. doi:10.1177/014616702236871.

Oishi, S., Diener, E., Suh, E., & Lucas, R. E. (1999). Value as a moderator in subjective well-being. *Journal of Personality, 67*, 157–184. doi:10.1111/1467-6494.00051.

Oishi, S., Krochik, M., Roth, D., & Sherman, G. D. (2012). Residential mobility, personality, and subjective and physical well-being: An analysis of cortisol secretion. *Social Psychological and Personality Science, 3*, 153–161. doi:10.1177/1948550611412395.

Okazaki, S. (2002). Self-other agreement on affective distress scales in Asian Americans and White Americans. *Journal of Counseling Psychology, 49*, 428–437. doi:10.1037/0022-0167.49.4.428.

Okazaki, S., Lee, R. M., & Sue, S. (2007). Theoretical and conceptual models: Toward Asian Americanist psychology. In F. T. L. Leong, A. Ebreo, L. Kinoshita, A. G. Inman, L. H. Yang, & M. Fu (Eds.), *Handbook of Asian American psychology* (2nd ed., pp. 29–46). Thousand Oaks, CA: Sage Publications.

Okazaki, S., & Sue, S. (2000). Implications of test revisions for assessment with Asian Americans. *Psychological Assessment, 12*(3), 272. doi:10.1037/1040-3590.12.3.272.

Oyserman, D., Coon, H. M., & Kemmelmeier, M. (2002). Rethinking individualism and collectivism: Evaluation of theoretical assumptions and meta-analyses. *Psychological Bulletin, 128*, 3–72. doi:10.1037/0033-2909.128.1.3.

Peng, K., & Nisbett, R. E. (1999). Culture, dialectics, and reasoning about contradiction. *American Psychologist, 54*, 741–754. doi:10.1037/0003-066X.54.9.741.

Phinney, J. S. (1992). The Multigroup Ethnic Identity Measure: A new scale for use with diverse groups. *Journal of Adolescent Research, 7*, 156–176. doi:10.1177/074355489272003.

Saucier, G., Georgiades, S., Tsaousis, I., & Goldberg, L. R. (2005). The factor structure of Greek personality adjectives. *Journal of Personality and Social Psychology, 88*, 856–875. doi:10.1037/0022-3514.88.5.856.

Saucier, G., & Goldberg, L. R. (1996). The language of personality: Lexical perspectives on the five-factor model. In J. S. Wiggin (Ed.), *The five-factor model of personality: Theoretical perspectives* (pp. 21–50). New York, NY: Guildford.

Schmitt, D. P., Allik, J., McCrae, R. R., & Benet-Martínez, V. (2007). The Geographic Distribution of Big Five personality traits, patterns and profiles of human self-description across 56 nations. *Journal of Cross-Cultural Psychology, 38*, 173–212. doi:10.1177/0022022106297299.

Sharp, A. (2008). Personality and second language learning. *Asian Social Science, 4*(11), 17–25. doi:10.5539/ass.v4n11P17.

Spencer-Rodgers, J., Boucher, H. C., Peng, K., & Wang, L. (2009). Cultural differences in self-verification: The role of naïve dialecticism. *Journal of Experimental Social Psychology, 45*, 860–866. doi:10.1177/0146167208325772.

Steel, P., Schmidt, J., & Shultz, J. (2008). Refining the relationship between personality and subjective well-being. *Psychological Bulletin, 134*, 138–161. doi:10.1037/0033-2909.134.1.138.

Stevens, M. J., Kwan, K.-L., & Graybill, D. (1993). Comparison of MMPI-2 scores of foreign Chinese and Caucasian-American students. *Journal of Clinical Psychology, 49*, 23–27. doi:10.1002/1097-4679(199301)49:1<23::AID-JCLP2270490104>3.0.CO;2-O.

Sue, S., Keefe, K., Enomoto, K., Durvasula, R. S., & Chao, R. (1996). Asian American and White college students' performance on the MMPI-2. In J. N. Butcher (Ed.), *International adaptations of the MMPI-2* (pp. 206–218). Minneapolis, MN: University of Minnesota Press.

Suh, E. M. (2002). Culture, identity consistency, and subjective well-being. *Journal of Personality and Social Psychology, 83*, 1378–1391. doi:10.1037/0022-3514.83.6.1378.

Suinn, R. M., Ahuna, C., & Khoo, G. (1992). The Suinn-Lew Asian Self-Identity Acculturation Scale: Concurrent and factorial validation. *Educational and Psychological Measurement, 52*, 1041–1046. doi:10.1177/0013164492052004028.

Taylor, S. E., Jarcho, J., Takagi, K., Dunagan, M. S., Sherman, D. K., & Kim, H. S. (2004). Culture and social support: Who seeks it and why? *Journal of Personality and Social Psychology, 87*, 354–362. doi:10.1037/0022-3514.87.3.354.

Terracciano, A., Abdel-Khalek, A. M., Ádám, N., Adamovová, L., Ahn, C., Ahn, H., … Angleitner, A. (2005). National character does not reflect mean personality trait levels in 49 cultures. *Science, 310*(5745), 96–100. doi:10.1126/science.1117199

Tran, B. N. (1996). Vietnamese translation and adaptation of the MMPI-2. In J. N. Butcher (Ed.), *International adaptations of the MMPI-2* (pp. 175–193). Minneapolis, MN: University of Minnesota Press.

Triandis, H. C., & Suh, E. M. (2002). Cultural influences on personality. *Annual Review of Psychology, 53*, 133–160. doi:10.1146/annurev.psych.53.100901.135200.

Tsai, D. C., & Pike, P. L. (2000). Effects of acculturation on the MMPI-2 scores of Asian American students. *Journal of Personality Assessment, 74*, 216–230. doi:10.1207/S15327752JPA7402_4.

Tsushima, W. T., & Tsushima, V. G. (2009). Comparison of MMPI-2 validity scales among compensation-seeking Caucasian and Asian American medical patients. *Assessment, 16*, 159–164. doi:10.1177/1073191108327695.

Uskul, A. K., Oyserman, D., Schwarz, N., Lee, S. W. S., & Xu, A. J. (2013). How successful you have been in life depends on the response scale used: The role of cultural mindsets in pragmatic inferences drawn from question format. *Social Cognition, 31*, 222–236. doi:10.1521/soco.2013.31.2.222.

Van Hemert, D. A., van de Vijver, F. J., Poortinga, Y. H., & Georgas, J. (2002). Structural and functional equivalence of the Eysenck Personality Questionnaire within and between countries. *Personality and Individual Differences, 33*, 1229–1249. doi:10.1016/S0191-8869(02)00007-7.

Zane, N., & Mak, W. (2003). Major approaches to the measurement of acculturation among ethnic minority populations: A content analysis and an alternative empirical strategy. In K. M. Chun, P. B. Organista, & G. Marin (Eds.), *Acculturation: Advances in theory, measurement, and applied research* (pp. 39–60). Washington, DC: American Psychological Association.

Zane, N., & Yeh, M. (2002). The use of culturally-based variables in assessment: Studies on loss of face. In K. S. Kurasaki, S. Okazaki, & S. Sue (Eds.), *Asian American mental health* (pp. 123–138). New York, NY: Springer.

IQ Testing and the Asian-American Client

10

Nicholas S. Thaler, Johanah Y. Kang, and Stacy L. Reger

When working with a client from another ethnicity or culture, it is important to consider how cultural biases may impact performance. This is particularly crucial when assessing intellectual abilities, which are perceived by the general public as highly predictive of individuals' inherent aptitudes, and indeed their success in any current and future endeavors. Whereas Asian-Americans as a whole have been reported to exhibit IQ scores that are on average higher or equivalent to Euro-Americans (Lynn, 2010; Rushton, 2012), such generalizations neither account for the heterogeneous nature of the Asian-American label, nor provide any guidelines when assessing and interpreting intellectual functioning in Asian-American clients. Just as the lower mean IQ scores reported in other populations are ascribed to assessment biases and not to actual differences in true intellectual aptitude (Thaler & Jones-Forrester, 2012), the higher IQ scores observed in some Asian-American groups do not reflect true intellectual superiority in this population.

N.S. Thaler, Ph.D. (✉)
Department of Psychiatry and Biobehavioral Sciences, Los Angeles Semel Institute for Neuroscience and Human Behavior, University of California, 760 Westwood Plaza, Los Angeles, CA 90024, USA
e-mail: nick.thaler@gmail.com

J.Y. Kang, B.A. • S.L. Reger, M.A.
Department of Psychology, University of Nevada, 4505 S. Maryland Pkwy, Box 455030, Las Vegas, NV 89154-5030, USA

Test bias, whether advantageous or detrimental, is a consequence of numerous factors that impact testing performance on standardized intellectual assessments. Bias can be found in test content, although most well-constructed modern batteries are relatively content-neutral for minorities raised in the United States (Reynolds, 2000). However, biases can exist in many other forms including access to and years of education, class, early SES-related nutrition, access to medical care, and issues related to rapport with the examiner, such as stereotype threat and perceived discrimination (Brooks, Holdnack, & Iverson, 2011; Nisbett et al., 2012; Thames et al., 2013). Testing itself relies on a communication style that is primarily modeled in European cultures. These issues raise several questions; within a biased context, to what degree can IQ scores accurately reflect inherent aptitudes? In addition, how much of performance is influenced by the environment? The issue of testing bias also affects standardization samples that are stratified by socioeconomic status (SES). For example, when some underrepresented groups are compared to standardization samples, they are compared to the greater population who may have higher SES, and due to the educational and environmental benefits this affords better performance on tests.

The "Asian-American" label represents a heterogeneous group that ranges widely in educational attainment and income earnings. Asian-Americans are ethnically categorized by individual nationalities in the United States, which does address differences in culture and generational

L.T. Benuto et al. (eds.), *Guide to Psychological Assessment with Asians*,
DOI 10.1007/978-1-4939-0796-0_10, © Springer Science+Business Media New York 2014

immigration patterns that are often tied to national identity, but does not address subcultures present in many countries, such as in China or India. The 2000 US Census Bureau provides a detailed account of median educational attainment and household income. Briefly, Chinese, Filipino, Asian Indian, Korean, Japanese, Pakistani, and Thai Americans had, on average, higher educational attainment than the total US population, whereas Vietnamese, Cambodian, Hmong, and Laotian Americans had fewer-than-average years of education. This does not necessarily translate to household earnings; Chinese, Filipino, Asian Indian, and Japanese Americans overall enjoyed a higher median income than the general population, while Vietnamese, Korean, Pakistani, and Thai Americans approached the median general income. Cambodian, Hmong, and Laotian Americans earned significantly less than the median income, with an estimated 37.8 % of Hmong Americans living below the poverty rate in 1999. While these statistics warrant update, they do highlight the differences in SES and education that in turn impact performance on (and the relative bias of) IQ tests used in assessing Asian-Americans (Blair & Qian, 1998).

It is important to understand how significantly education influences IQ test performance. It is well established that children of the same age cohort differ on IQ tests depending on their grade level (Cahan & Cohen, 1989; Raven, Court, & Raven, 1975), which provides strong evidence indicating that opportunities to be exposed to additional information is predictive of IQ scores. Simply put, children in advanced grades have attained more knowledge than those in previous grades, and therefore outperform their same-age peers in lower grades. This fact is particularly relevant when considering Asian-American cultures, many of which place an emphasis on educational values within the home as a method for both social mobility and an adherence to Confucian beliefs emphasizing the importance of academic and occupational achievement (Caplan, Choy, & Whitmore, 1992; Dandy & Nettelbeck, 2002). Educational attainment is also linked to SES; individuals with higher occupational attainment are likely to raise their children with similar educational values, as well as expose their children to better academic environments and opportunities. Some minorities groups such as Hmong, Laotian, and Cambodian Americans are more likely to have come to the United States as refugees or rural farmers and represent lower SES cohorts (Fujii, 2011). Although there is limited information on IQ performance with these populations compared to standardization samples, clinicians are encouraged to be mindful of how differences in cultural emphasis on academic achievement and actual educational differences may influence test performance during assessment.

General assessment considerations pertaining to specific ethnicities are reviewed in detail in other chapters and will only be briefly mentioned here. Many Asian-American clients will work well in the testing environment, given the cultural emphasis on academic achievement that exists in some groups. In those cases, high effort and strong performance are likely (Mizokawa & Ryckman, 1990), though this should never become an expectation in practice. Culturally influenced perceptions of intelligence may also affect performance on IQ batteries. For example, there is evidence that Chinese nationals value nonverbal reasoning ability over verbal discussion and problem-solving, which may influence how individuals approach and adapt to testing (Suzuki, Mogami, & Kim, 2002). Older generations may be suspicious of Western psychological practice and reluctant to provide relevant clinical information during the interview, and some individuals from rural backgrounds may be unfamiliar with the testing environment (Fujii & Vang, 2011). Rapport with children may be more difficult to establish if the child perceives the examiner as a strong authority figure rather than a professional psychologist. Effort towards testing may also be unpredictable if the child or teenager fears failure to the point of giving up rather than attempting the task (Yeh & Yeh, 2002).

Language proficiency is important to ascertain when working with Asian-American clients. Asian-Americans in general demonstrate better quantitative than verbal abilities on US aptitude tests, which may reflect biases against individuals who learned English as a second language, or primarily do not speak it within the home (Kennedy & Park, 1994). While bilingualism has been associated with overall higher achievement and IQ scores (Bankston & Zhou, 1995; Hsieh & Tori, 1993), it also has been found to delay the acquisition of some verbal abilities in young children (Bialystok, 2002). This may be related to limited English usage within the home or the enrollment of English courses as a second language (Hsia & Peng, 1998). Regardless, psychologists should not equate English proficiency with fluency, as subtleties that may not be detected through conversational dialogue may nonetheless impact test performance. When working with clients who are non-native English speakers, it is important to employ proper translators or, if the psychologist does not deem this possible, refer out to appropriate sources.

The rest of this chapter reviews commonly used IQ batteries and their cross-cultural applicability to Asian-American populations. Several batteries normed for specific minority groups are also discussed. See Table 10.1 for a summary.

Table 10.1 IQ tests available for Asian-American populations

Measure	Languages	Notes/recommendations
Wechsler Adult Intelligence Scale—Third Edition	English	Asian-Americans were merged into an Other category with other minority groups. Clinicians should interpret results with caution, particularly with verbal subtests on individuals who do not speak English as a first language. Limited validity studies available for this population.
Wechsler Adult Intelligence Scale—Third Edition (translated editions)	Japanese, Korean, Taiwanese	Generally not available in the USA and should only be used by clinicians who are fluent in the translated battery's language. Some evidence of WAIS-III equivalent psychometric properties but clinical validity studies are limited.
Wechsler Adult Intelligence Scale—Fourth Edition	English	Asian-Americans comprise 3.3 % of the standardization sample, a narrower though still inadequate characterization of this ethnicity. Mean FSIQ of this subset was 106.1, which can likely be attributed to this group's overall higher education level. This likely does not represent Asian-Americans with lower educational attainment and SES, and the possibility of demographic-adjusted score biases should be investigated with independent replication studies.
Wechsler Abbreviated Scale of Intelligence	English	Little information regarding the proportion of minorities within the standardization sample. One independent study (Razani, et al., 2007) demonstrated that level of acculturation directly influenced WASI performance in a mixed minority sample that included Koreans. Limited to no published studies available for the updated WASI-II.
Wechsler Intelligence Scale for Children—Fourth Edition	English	Asian-American youth comprise 4.2 % of the standardization sample and have the highest mean FSIQ (106.5) and index scores. Particular advantages were observed for the PRI (107.3) and PSI (107.6) though even the VCI (102.3) and WMI (102.7) were higher than average. As with the WAIS-IV differences in educational attainment of the sample likely accounts for these discrepancies and may not accurately represent children from different backgrounds.
Wechsler Intelligence Scale for Children—Fourth Edition (translated editions)	Mandarin, Cantonese, Taiwanese	Used in China though less available in the USA. There are some reliability and validity studies supporting these measures' clinical application, though only clinicians who are fluent in the language of the battery should administer these tests.

(continued)

Table 10.1 (continued)

Measure	Languages	Notes/recommendations
National Adult Reading Test	English, Japanese	Premorbid estimates of intelligence should only be used when congruent with the patient's native language. A Japanese NART is available and has some evidence of clinical validity. The phonemic and grammatical structure of some languages (e.g., Korean) may limit the NART's translatability across some cultures.
Leiter International Performance Scale—Revised	English	Asian-Americans comprise 3.2 % of the standardization sample. No ethnic differences were found in the standardization sample. The Leiter-R appears to be an alternative to measuring nonverbal intellectual functioning in minority groups.
Universal Nonverbal Intelligence Test	English	Designed to have cross-cultural fairness, though information regarding the composition of Asian-Americans in the sample, as well as studies examining ethnic differences are limited at this time.

Wechsler Batteries

Wechsler Adult Intelligence Scale: Third Edition (WAIS-III; Wechsler, 1997)

The WAIS-III remains a widely used intelligence measure. Although the recent publication of the WAIS-IV (Wechsler, 2008a, 2008b) may depreciate the WAIS-III's future utility, the WAIS-III comes with a fund of published research that remains relevant across Wechsler batteries. Briefly, the WAIS-III was normed for adults between 16 and 89 years of age and standardized on 2,450 adults who were selected and stratified by sex, race, geographic region, and educational level to match 1995 US demographics. The four-factor Verbal Comprehension Index (VCI), Perceptual Organization Index (POI), the Freedom from Distractibility Index (FDI), and Processing Speed Index (PSI) are typically interpreted and are derived from 14 subtests.

Although the WAIS-III was stratified by race, Asian-Americans were merged with Native Americans and other minorities into an "Other" category. In addition, researchers have demonstrated that WAIS-III indexes do have cross-cultural biases. Acculturation variables including language preference, US experience, and US education were found to significantly predict both VCI and POI scores in minority immigrants above and beyond each participant's years of formal education (Harris, Tulsky, & Schultheis, 2003). Acculturation variables also predicted FFDI and PSI index scores. As might be expected, language preference was found to be a particularly strong predictor for VCI scores. Though this was a heterogeneous sample, this study is of relevance to Asian-Americans, many whom are immigrants and who speak English fluently but as a second language. Heaton and colleagues (2003) examined ethnicity effects on WAIS-III factor scores. As Asian-Americans were not separated in the WAIS-III standardization sample, they were unable to examine the influence of this label on scores, though differences observed in Hispanic and African American populations were present,

Translated versions of the WAIS-III are available in Japan (Fujita, Maekawa, Dairoku, & Yamanaka, 2006), Korea (Harris et al., 2003), and Taiwan (Wechsler, Chen, & Chen, 2002), while translated adaptations of earlier WAIS editions are available in Korea, India, and mainland China (Okazaki & Sue, 2000). However, these measures are unlikely to ever be widely available or used within the United States. There is also risk in interpreting patients on outdated norms for the older batteries (Flynn, 1999). Psychometric studies of these batteries generally confirm an equitable factor structure to the original WAIS-III in the standardization sample and some clinical samples (Chan, Lee, & Luk, 1999; Dai, Gong, & Zhong, 1990; Fujita et al., 2006; Ryan, Dai, Paolo, & Harrington, 1992; Wechsler et al., 2002). Validity studies remain scarce but those in existence provide psychometric scores among clinical populations that can guide psychologists administering these batteries (Chen & Yao, 2009; Izawa, Urakami, Kojima, & Ohama, 2009; Lin, Huang, Lin, & Pan, 2010; Srivastava & Shukla, 1988). Fewer studies exist for cultures that are not as Westernized, although there is evidence that verbal subtests rely more heavily on a westernized education than other subtests (Ogden & McFarlane-Nathan, 1997).

Wechsler Adult Intelligence Scale: Fourth Edition (WAIS-IV; Wechsler, 2008a)

The WAIS-IV is the most recent WAIS revision. It is notable for completely removing the Verbal and Performance IQ scores and relying on four factor indexes to produce a full-scale IQ score. To better reflect the constructs they purport to measure, the POI was renamed the Perceptual Reasoning Index (PRI) and the FDI was renamed the Working Memory Index (WMI). The WAIS-IV was standardized on an updated 2,200 individuals between 16 and 90 years of age and again stratified by ethnicity, geographic region, education level, and sex. There are some improvements to the WAIS-IV in its application towards Asian-American populations. Most notably, the label "Asian-American" was included as a separate ethnicity alongside White, African American, Hispanic, and Other groups, and represents approximately 3.3 % ($n=71$) of the standardization sample. However, Pacific Islanders remain separate from this label and are combined with Native American Indians and Alaskan Natives in the Other category. An advantage to the WAIS-IV is the availability of demographically adjusted norms, which can adjust scaled scores for sex, education, and ethnicity.

The mean FSIQ for Asian-Americans is 106.1 (SD = 15.0), the highest of all ethnic groups (Weiss, Saklofske, Coalson, & Raiford, 2010). This is likely related to the fact that the Asian-American group in the sample was the highest education group, with an estimated 74.6 % individuals having 13 or more years of education compared to 46.1 % of African Americans and 34.2 % of Hispanics (Sattler & Ryan, 2009). To date, no research has provided additional information on WAIS-IV performance in independent samples, including underrepresented minorities or Asian-American individuals with clinical disorders. Studies are important to establish if this higher IQ is replicated across more education equivalent individuals, or simply a phenomenon of the standardization sample. Such information is important to consider as a higher IQ bias may not represent the scores of Asian-Americans with lower years of education or other SES disadvantages.

Based on these updates, the WAIS-IV tentatively appears to be an acceptable measure of intellectual functioning in Asian-Americans who are acculturated to the United States and exposed to its educational system. The higher than average scores likely represent the higher educational attainment achieved by the subset of Asian-Americans included in the standardization sample. The individuals most at risk for assessment bias are those who are unfamiliar to Western standards of testing and measurement, such as recent immigrants to the USA. The WAIS-IV's stringent discontinue criteria for subtests may result in such individuals reaching a ceiling based on factors other than actual intellectual functioning, such as confusion with test instructions. Some new subtests such as the Visual Puzzles and Figure Weights require complex verbal instruction, which can further impede performance in individuals who did not fully comprehend the instructions. As method and comprehension of instruction can affect nonverbal reasoning tests (Knight, 2003), it is essential to ensure that proper communication has transpired before administering these subtests.

Wechsler Abbreviated Scale of Intelligence (WASI; Wechsler, 1999)

The WASI is a brief and reliable revision of the WAIS-III that consists of verbal and performance IQ indexes. While an attractive measure for brief cognitive assessment, the WASI did not stratify its standardization sample by ethnicity and the majority of the sample consisted of Euro-Americans. Razani and colleagues (2007) provided a detailed analysis on the relationship between acculturation and WASI test performance in a diverse sample of English fluent minorities that included Asian-Americans from Korea, Vietnam, and Indonesia. Results showed that the ethnically diverse group underperformed on the VIQ but not PIQ index, while level of acculturation significantly predicted performance on the Vocabulary test. While the proportion of minorities that were Asian-American were small and combined with Hispanic and Middle-Eastern individuals, these results do provide objective data that verbal Wechsler subtests are impacted by level of acculturation independent of language fluency (if not proficiency within a Westernized environment), and likely would generalize to similarly presented subtests on other batteries.

The WASI was recently updated (WASI-II; Wechsler, 2011). The WASI-II retains the WASI's two verbal and two nonverbal subtest structure along with a two-subtest or four-subtest FSIQ estimate. The battery was standardized on 2,300 children and adults from ages 6 to 90 years of age and items were revised to better correspond to the WAIS-IV and WISC-IV, as well as increase ceiling levels. As with the WASI, there is little information in regard to this measure's cross-cultural application though given the similar content of subtests, there are likely some biases for underrepresented groups.

Wechsler Intelligence Scale for Children: Fourth Edition (WISC-IV; Wechsler, 2003)

The WISC-IV is a commonly administered IQ battery normed on 2,200 children and adolescents between 6 and 16 years of age. This battery has ten core subtests and four supplemental subtests which form a VCI, PRI, WMI, and PSI as well as a FSIQ. The WISC-IV actually precedes the WAIS-IV in being the first Wechsler battery reconceptualized to allow for Catell-Horn-Caroll (CHC) theory interpretations of test scores, and there is factorial evidence that CHC models better explain subtest performance than the traditional Wechsler four-factor model across normative, cross-cultural, and clinical populations (Keith, Fine, Taub, Reynolds, & Kranzler, 2006; Lecerf, Rossier, Favez, Reverte, & Coleaux, 2010; Thaler et al., 2012). Available cross-cultural studies demonstrate the WISC-IV's equivalence and sensitivity to clinical dysfunction across different languages and nationalities (Grob et al., 2008; San Miguel Montes, Allen, Puente, & Neblina, 2010).

Asian-American children were included in the WISC-IV standardization sample proportional to the March, 2000 US Census Bureau and comprise 4.2 % ($n=92$) of the sample. Children from the standardization sample overall performed equitably to Euro-American children across the four indexes with a mean FSIQ of 106.5 (SD = 14.2). The PRI and PSI had the highest scores with means of 107.3 (SD = 12.8) and 107.6 (SD = 15.7) respectively, though even the VCI ($M=102.3$, SD = 15.7) and WMI ($M=102.7$, SD = 12.2) were approximately two points above the population mean. As discussed earlier, education levels and SES systematically vary among minority populations. Asian-Americans in general have above average academic achievement and SES, and thereby, above average score performance. The comparably lower scores on VCI and WMI may reflect the high verbal loading of the subtests in these indices which can detract from performance in children who do not speak English as a first language. Regardless, similar caution should be made when extrapolating these findings towards specific Asian-American groups, including recent immigrants and those of lower SES.

The WISC-IV has been adapted for use in China, Hong Kong, Macau, and Taiwan (Wechsler, 2007, 2008b, 2009, 2010) with samples matching recent census data for each region based on gender, parental education, and ethnicity. Each sample was also divided into balanced age groups between 6 and 16 years. Studies have reported that the original WISC-IV four-factor model is invariant across these normative samples (Chen, Keith, Weiss, Zhu, & Li, 2010) as well clinical samples (Chen & Zhu, 2012; Yang et al., 2013) providing support that the WISC-IV measures the same constructs across cultures and languages. Linguistically competent practitioners may also be interested in using translated versions of the WISC-III available in Japanese, Taiwanese, and Korean (Weiss, Saklofske, Prifitera, & Holdnack, 2006).

The WISC-IV appears to be a reliable estimate of intellectual functioning in Asian-American children, though as with the WAIS-IV, this must be considered in light of the socioeconomic and educational advantages that are availed some but not all Asian-American groups. Studies have generally indicated that translated versions of the WISC-IV are psychometrically reliable; however, clinical validity studies remain few and far between at this time. One study by Yang and colleagues (2013) reported that the Taiwanese WISC-IV has similar cognitive profiles as the original WISC-IV in children with ADHD, which is promising in characterizing a cross-cultural neurocognitive signature of this disorder. Additional studies examining clinical populations in this manner are warranted.

Premorbid Estimates of IQ

Premorbid IQ is often estimated with single-word reading tests. The National Adult Reading Test (NART; Nelson & McKenna, 1975) requires examinees to read 50 irregularly pronounced words. The NART was standardized in England on 120 inpatients ages 20–70, with a diagnosis of extracerebral disorder (Nelson, 1982). Blair and Spreen developed the North American Adult Reading Test (NAART; Spreen & Strauss, 1991)—a modification of the NART—for use with the North American population. The original standardization sample was limited to 66 participants ages 18–49; thus, age, gender, and education effects were not determined. More recently, Uttl (2002) administered the NAART to 351 participants ages 18–91. Ninety-eight percent of participants were native English speakers, and six participants were bilinguals with at least 10 years of English proficiency. No differences in NAART scores were observed between native English speakers and bilingual individuals. NAART scores increase with age and education but not gender. Asian-Americans were not separated in these studies, and this variable's influence on scores was not examined.

A Japanese version using 50 irregular kanji compound words is available and valid for estimated premorbid IQ in patients with Alzheimer's disease (Matsuoka, Uno, Kasai, Koyama, & Kim, 2006). Translations for some other Asian languages may be more difficult due to the inherent structure of the languages. For example, an analogous translation of an irregular pronunciation reading task is impossible in Korean language since it does not contain irregularly spelled words and silent letters (Fujii, 2011). For less acculturated examinees who do not have premorbid estimates readily available, best-practice involves obtaining a detailed demographic and clinical history that minimally includes: age, educational attainment, history of school performance, occupational history, and social class (Fujii, 2011; Uttl, 2002). This information can be used to estimate premorbid IQ levels.

Nonverbal IQ Tests

Leiter International Performance Scale: Revised (Leiter-R; Roid & Miller, 1997)

The Leiter-R is an efficient battery of 20 individually administered nonverbal cognitive subtests appropriate for children and young adults. The 20 subtests are equally divided into two groupings: (1) the Visualization and Reasoning (VR) Battery; and (2) the Attention and Memory (AM) Battery that can be administered separately or together depending on the referral question. There are two choices for the estimation of global intellectual ability: the Brief IQ comprised of four subtests, and the Full-Scale IQ comprised of six subtests.

The Leiter-R was standardized on a sample of 1,719 subjects ages 2–21 stratified on age, gender, ethnicity, geographic region, and parental education according to 1993 US Census data.

Asian-Americans comprised 3.2 % ($n = 55$) of the standardization sample and were separated from Caucasian, African American, Hispanic, and Native American groups also represented (McCallum, 2003). Fairness across gender, and Hispanic, African American, and Native American groups have been examined and no differences between groups have been identified (Blair, 1996; Roid, 1997; Roid, Nellis, & McLellan, 2003). Notably, the pantomime (nonverbal) administration procedures promote fairness across ethnic groups and are an attractive feature of the Leiter-R.

Universal Nonverbal Intelligence Test (UNIT; Bracken & McCallum, 1998)

The UNIT is a language-free measure of cognitive abilities that has become increasingly popular among practitioners assessing those who are from other cultures and cannot use English for communication, deaf (or hard of hearing), or have speech or language impairments. It is the only multidimensional assessment that offers a completely nonverbal administration and various response modes in order ensure fairness. The UNIT has six subtests that are grouped into Symbolic and Nonsymbolic subtests. The total test provides several scores including a Full-Scale score (FSIQ), Memory Quotient (MQ), Reasoning Quotient (RQ), Symbolic Quotient (SQ), and Nonsymbolic Quotient (NSQ).

The test was standardized on a sample of 2,100 children ages 5 through 17 who were stratified by US geographic regions, SES levels, ethnicity, community settings, classroom placements, special education services, and parental education attainment to match 1995 US demographics. Standardization data also included bilingual and ESL samples which accounted for 1.8 % and 2 % of the total sample, respectively; however, these proportions underrepresented the US population figures of 3.1 % and 4 %, respectively. The UNIT has not been standardized for use in foreign countries, nor does the manual address the issue of how to adapt UNIT administration in foreign countries when full-scale restandardization is not possible. These issues should be taken into consideration when administering the UNIT to Asian-Americans, despite the test authors' best efforts to ensure cross-cultural fairness (McCallum, 2003).

Summary and Recommendations

Assessment of intellectual functioning is integral to psychological testing across a wide variety of settings, including neuropsychological research and practice, assessment of cognitive disabilities, and assessments in school settings. Furthermore, IQ scores (for better or worse) are used by psychologists and the general populace as a lens through which to understand and predict numerous facets of an individual's functioning, including academic performance, career aspirations and skill development, and premorbid functioning in the case of brain injury. Because of the vast application and influence of IQ assessment, it is imperative that clinicians consider IQ in the context of cultural factors and bias that can heavily impact outcomes. In the case of Asian-Americans, there are four major considerations.

First, the categorical term "Asian-American" misleads by implying that Asian-Americans represent one homogenous cultural group. Research and census data make it clear that the label encompasses individuals of numerous cultural backgrounds, countries of origin, ethnicities, values, educational access, socioeconomic statuses, income levels, English proficiency levels, and immigrant statuses. Psychologists must be sensitive to the wide variety of clients and patients that may be represented as Asian-American. This issue can be addressed through the use of thorough intake and clinical interview practices that gather as complete a demographic profile as possible for each examinee.

The second major issue of concern in assessing intellectual functioning in Asian-American populations is the impact of education and SES. In many Asian-American cultures, academic performance is highly emphasized as a measure of success and social mobility (Blair & Qian, 1998; Dandy & Nettelbeck, 2002). In fact, Asian-Americans in general have higher educational achievement than other ethnic minority groups (US Census Bureau, 2004). Higher educational achievement is also often linked to higher SES and the numerous advantages that accompany it. Academic achievement is well known to affect performance on measures of intellectual functioning, thus, psychologists must consider that individuals of Asian-American backgrounds with higher educational attainment and higher SES are likely to perform better on measures of IQ. By the same token, care must be taken to avoid assuming higher education level and SES based on ethnic status, as some populations of Asian-Americans (particularly those from refugee backgrounds) are often less educated and of lower SES than average.

A third aspect of intellectual assessment important to Asian-American populations is the testing environment itself. Clinicians should be sensitive to the possible impact of their role as the authority figure in a testing setting (Yeh & Yeh, 2002), as well as generational (and acculturation-related) differences in beliefs about the value and validity of psychological testing (Fujii & Vang, 2011).

Finally, language proficiency is of particular concern in testing Asian-American clients, as numerous studies have shown that language abilities, bilingualism, and learning English as a second language influence testing outcomes (e.g., Bankston & Zhou, 1995; Bialystok, 2002; Hsia & Peng, 1998; Hsieh & Tori, 1993; Kennedy & Park, 1994). Again, a thorough clinical interview should clearly establish the context for an examinee's English proficiency, including whether it was his or her first language, what language is spoken in the home, and how long he or she has been speaking English. As always, assumptions about an individual's true fluency and comprehension should not be made based on conversational ability, length of residence in the US, or other superficial factors.

An examination of the extant normative data for Asian-Americans' performances on IQ measures reveals a wide variety of quality. In the past, Asian-Americans have been included in nonspecific (and thereby fairly uninformative) ethnic categories such as "Other" along with Native Americans and Pacific Islanders. More recent normative data improve upon this by including the (still-relatively-nonspecific, but somewhat narrowed) "Asian-American" category, though Asian-Americans often remain represented disproportionately less in normative testing data than in the actual US population. The data shows a potential language and education/SES bias in many cases, as Asian-Americans perform better on quantitative versus verbal measures, and have the highest IQ of any ethnicity on the well-used WAIS-IV. In fact the issue of language and translation of tests presents a particular problem in this group, as there are numerous languages spoken by those counted as Asian-Americans, and some languages (such as Korean) do not lend themselves readily to direct translation from English. One approach to these barriers is to become competent in administration of nonverbal intelligence tests that do not rely on language comprehension. In addition, continued inclusion of increasingly specific Asian-American populations in normative data and validity research is imperative to better understanding of the effect of test bias on these groups. The issues involved in testing intellectual functioning among Asian-Americans are complex, and present clinicians with the responsibility to educate themselves about each client's cultural background, education, acculturation, language ability, etc., in order to interpret test results cautiously within a well-understood context.

References

Bankston, C. L., & Zhou, M. (1995). Effects of minority-language literacy on the academic achievement of Vietnamese youths in New Orleans. *Society of Education, 68*(1), 1–17.

Bialystok, E. (2002). Acquisition of literacy in bilingual children: A framework for research. *Language Learning, 52*(1), 159–199. doi:10.1111/1467-9922.00180.

Blair, R. J. (1996). *Item bias analysis of the Leiter-R for English as a second language populations.* Unpublished doctoral dissertation, George Fox University, Mewberg, OR.

Blair, S., & Qian, Z. (1998). Family and Asian students' educational performance: A consideration of diversity. *Journal of Family Issues, 19*(4), 355–374. doi: 10.1177/019251398019004001.

Bracken, B. A., & McCallum, R. S. (1998). *Universal nonverbal intelligence test*. Austin, TX: PRO-ED.

Brooks, B. L., Holdnack, J. A., & Iverson, G. L. (2011). Advanced clinical interpretation of the WAIS-IV and WMS-IV: Prevalence of low scores varies by level of intelligence and years of education. *Assessment, 18*(2), 156–167. doi:10.1177/1073191110385316.

Cahan, S., & Cohen, N. (1989). Age versus schooling effects on intelligence development. *Child Development, 60*, 1239–1249.

Caplan, N., Choy, M. H., & Whitmore, J. K. (1992). Indochinese refugee families and academic achievement. *Scientific American, 266*, 18–24.

Chan, D. W., Lee, H. B., & Luk, C. (1999). Developing a Chinese vocabulary test as a WAIS-R subtest for adults in Hong Kong. *Psychologia, 42*(2), 89–100.

Chen, H., Keith, T. Z., Weiss, L., Zhu, J., & Li, Y. (2010). Testing for multigroup invariance of second-order WISC-IV structure across China, Hong Kong, Macau, and Taiwan. *Personality and Individual Differences, 49*(7), 677–682. doi:10.1016/j.paid.2010.06.004.

Chen, H., & Yao, S. (2009). A comparison between non-clinical and schizophrenia sample on the results measured by WAIS-III Chinese version. *Chinese Journal of Clinical Psychology, 17*(2), 157–160.

Chen, H., & Zhu, J. (2012). Measurement invariance of WISC-IV across normative and clinical samples. *Personality and Individual Differences, 52*(2), 161–166. doi:10.1016/j.paid.2011.10.006.

Dai, X., Gong, Y., & Zhong, L. (1990). Factor analysis of the mainland Chinese version of the Wechsler adult intelligence scale. *Psychological Assessment, 2*(1), 31–34. doi:10.1037/1040-3590.2.1.31.

Dandy, J., & Nettelbeck, T. (2002). The relationship between IQ, homework, aspirations and academic achievement for Chinese, Vietnamese and Anglo-Celtic Australian school children. *Educational Psychology, 22*(3), 267–276. doi:10.1080/01443410220138502.

Flynn, J. R. (1999). Searching for justice: The discovery of IQ gains over time. *American Psychologist, 54*, 5–20.

Fujii, D. M. (2011). *The neuropsychology of Asian Americans*. New York, NY: Psychology Press.

Fujii, D., & Vang, A. (2011). Neuropsychology of Hmong Americans. In D. M. Fujii (Ed.), *The neuropsychology of Asian Americans* (pp. 71–88). New York, NY: Psychology Press.

Fujita, K., Maekawa, H., Dairoku, K., & Yamanaka, K. (2006). *A Japanese version of the WAIS-III: Theoretical manual*. Tokyo, Japan: Nihon Bunka Kagakusha.

Grob, A., Petermann, F., Lipsius, M., Costan-Dorigon, J., Petermann, U., & Daseking, M. (2008). Differences in Swiss and German children's intelligence as measured by the HAWIK-IV. *Swiss Journal of Psychology, 67*(2), 113–118. doi:10.1024/1421-0185.67.2.113.

Harris, J. G., Tulsky, D. S., & Schultheis, M. T. (2003). Assessment of the non-native English speaker: Assimilating history and research findings to guide clinical practice. In D. S. Tulsky et al. (Eds.), *Clinical interpretation of the WAIS-III and WMS-III* (pp. 343–390). San Diego, CA: Academic Press. doi:10.1016/B978-012703570-3/50015-8.

Heaton, R. K., Taylor, M. J., & Manly, J. (2003). Demographic effects and use of demographically corrected norms with the WAIS-III and WMS-III. In D. S. Tulsky et al. (Eds.), *Clinical interpretation of the WAIS-III and WMS-III* (pp. 181–210). San Diego, CA: Academic Press. doi:10.1016/B978-012703570-3/50010-9.

Hsia, J., & Peng, S. S. (1998). Academic achievement and performance. In L. C. Lee & N. W. S. Zane (Eds.), *Handbook of Asian American psychology* (pp. 325–357). Thousand Oaks, CA: Sage.

Hsieh, S. L. J., & Tori, C. D. (1993). Neuropsychological and cognitive effects of Chinese language instruction. *Perceptual and Motor Skills, 77*(3f), 1071–1081.

Izawa, Y., Urakami, K., Kojima, T., & Ohama, E. (2009). Wechsler adult intelligence scale, 3rd edition (WAIS-III): Usefulness in the early detection of Alzheimer's disease. *Yonago Acta Medica, 52*, 11–20.

Keith, T. Z., Fine, J., Taub, G. E., Reynolds, M. R., & Kranzler, J. H. (2006). Higher order, multisample, confirmatory factor analysis of the Wechsler intelligence scale for Children—Fourth Edition: What does it measure? *School Psychology Review, 35*(1), 108–127.

Kennedy, E., & Park, H. S. (1994). Home language as a predictor of academic achievement: A comparative study of Mexican- and Asian-American youth. *Journal of Research and Development in Education, 27*(3), 188–194.

Knight, T. A. (2003). WAIS-III Matrix reasoning: Instruction effects on task perception and performance. *Psychological Reports, 93*(1), 66–68. doi: 10.2466/PR0.93.5.66-68.

Lecerf, T., Rossier, J., Favez, N., Reverte, I., & Coleaux, L. (2010). The four- vs. alternative six-factor structure of the French WISC-IV: Comparison using confirmatory factor analyses. *Swiss Journal of Psychology, 69*(4), 221–232. doi:10.1024/1421-0185/a000026.

Lin, S., Huang, M., Lin, H., & Pan, C. (2010). Deterioration of intelligence in methamphetamine-induced psychosis: Comparison with alcohol dependence on WAIS-III. *Psychiatry and Clinical Neurosciences, 64*(1), 4–9. doi:10.1111/j.1440-1819.2009.02035.x.

Lynn, R. (2010). High IQ is sufficient to explain the high achievements in math and science of the East Asian peoples. *Learning and Individual Differences, 20*(6), 567–568. doi:10.1016/j.lindif.2010.08.008.

Matsuoka, K., Uno, M., Kasai, K., Koyama, K., & Kim, Y. (2006). Estimation of premorbid IQ in individuals with Alzheimer's disease using Japanese ideographic script (Kanji) compound words: Japanese version of National Adult Reading Test. *Psychiatry and Clinical Neurosciences, 60*(3), 332–339. doi:10.1111/j.1440-1819.2006.01510.x.

McCallum, R. (2003). *Handbook of nonverbal assessment*. New York, NY: Kluwer Academic. doi:10.1007/978-1-4615-0153-4.

Mizokawa, D. T., & Ryckman, D. B. (1990). Attributions of academic success and failure: A comparison of six Asian-American ethnic groups. *Journal of Cross-Cultural Psychology, 21*(4), 434–451.

Nelson, H. E. (1982). *National adult reading test (NART): Test manual*. Berkshire, UK: NFER-NELSON.

Nelson, H. E., & McKenna, P. (1975). The use of current reading ability in the assessment of dementia. *British Journal of Social & Clinical Psychology, 14*(3), 259–267. doi:10.1111/j.2044-8260.1975.tb00178.x.

Nisbett, R. E., Aronson, J., Blair, C., Dickens, W., Flynn, J., Halpern, D. F., & Turkheimer, E. (2012). Intelligence: New findings and theoretical developments. *American Psychologist, 67*(2), 130–159. doi:10.1037/a0026699

Ogden, J. A., & McFarlane-Nathan, G. (1997). Cultural bias in the neuropsychological assessment of young Maori men. *New Zealand Journal of Psychology, 26*(2), 2–12.

Okazaki, S., & Sue, S. (2000). Implications of test revisions for assessment with Asian Americans. *Psychological Assessment, 12*(3), 272–280. doi:10.1037/1040-3590.12.3.272.

Raven, J. C., Court, J. H., & Raven, J. (1975). *Manual for Raven's progressive matrices and vocabulary scales*. London, UK: Lewis.

Razani, J., Murcia, G., Tabares, J., & Wong, J. (2007). The effects of culture on WASI test performance in ethnically diverse individuals. *The Clinical Neuropsychologist, 21*(5), 776–788. doi:10.1080/13854040701437481.

Reynolds, C. R. (2000). Why is psychometric research on bias in mental testing so often ignored? *Psychology, Public Policy, and Law, 6*(1), 144–150. doi:10.1037/1076-8971.6.1.144.

Roid, G. H. (1997). *Validity and fairness of prediction in the Leiter-R*. Paper presented at the meetings of the American Psychological Association, Chicago, August.

Roid, G. H., & Miller, L. J. (1997). *Leiter International Performance Scale-Revised (Leiter-R) manual*. Wood Dale, IL: Stoelting.

Roid, G. H., Nellis, L., & McLellan, M. (2003). Assessment with the Leiter International Performance Scale-Revised and the S-BIT. In R. McCAllum (Ed.), *Handbook of nonverbal assessment* (pp. 113–140). New York, NY: Kluwer Academic. doi:10.1007/978-1-4615-01534_6.

Rushton, J. (2012). Life history theory and race differences: An appreciation of Richard Lynn's contributions to science. *Personality and Individual Differences, 53*(2), 85–89. doi:10.1016/j.paid.2011.03.012.

Ryan, J. J., Dai, X., Paolo, A. M., & Harrington, R. G. (1992). Factor analysis of the Chinese WAIS with persons who have mental retardation. *American Journal on Mental Retardation, 97*(1), 111–114.

San Miguel Montes, L. E., Allen, D. N., Puente, A. E., & Neblina, C. (2010). Validity of the WISC-IV Spanish for a clinically referred sample of Hispanic children. *Psychological Assessment, 22*(2), 465–469. doi:10.1037/a0018895.

Sattler, J. M., & Ryan, J. J. (2009). *Assessment with the WAIS-IV*. San Diego, CA: Jerome M Sattler Publisher.

Spreen, O., & Strauss, E. (1991). *A compendium of neuropsychological tests. Administration, norms and commentary* (2nd ed.). New York, NY: Oxford University Press.

Srivastava, A., & Shukla, T. R. (1988). WAIS—R (Hindi, verbal) and WAPIS (Form-PR) in differential diagnosis of schizophrenia and organicity. *Indian Journal of Clinical Psychology, 15*(1), 42–44.

Suzuki, L. A., Mogami, T., & Kim, E. S. (2002). Interpreting cultural variations in cognitive profiles. In K. S. Kurasaki, S. Okazaki, & S. Sue (Eds.), *Asian American mental health: Assessment theories and methods* (pp. 159–171). New York, NY: Kluwer.

Thaler, N. S., Barchard, K. A., Parke, E., Jones, W. P., Etcoff, L. M., & Allen, D. N. (2012). Factor structure of the Wechsler Intelligence Scale for Children: Fourth Edition in children with ADHD. *Journal of Attention Disorders*. doi:10.1177/1087054712459952.

Thaler, N. S., & Jones-Forrester, S. (2012). IQ testing and the Hispanic client. In L. T. Benuto (Ed.), *Guide to psychological assessment with Hispanics* (pp. 81–98). New York, NY: Springer.

Thames, A. D., Hinkin, C. H., Byrd, D. A., Bilder, R. M., Duff, K. J., Mindt, M. R., …, Streiff, V. (2013). Effects of stereotype threat, perceived discrimination, and examiner race on neuropsychological performance: Simple as black and white? *Journal of the International Neuropsychological Society: JINS, 19*(5):583–593.

U.S. Census Bureau. (2004). *Educational attainment in the United States: 2003*. Retrieved May 6, 2013, from http://www.census.gov/prod/2004pubs/p20-550.pdf

Uttl, B. (2002). North American Adult Reading Test: Age norms, reliability, and validity. *Journal of Clinical and Experimental Neuropsychology, 24*(8), 1123–1137. doi:10.1076/jcen.24.8.1123.8375.

Wechsler, D. (1997). *Wechsler Adult Intelligence Scale—Third edition*. San Antonio, TX: Psychological Corporation.

Wechsler, D. (2003). *Wechsler intelligence scale for children* (4th ed.). San Antonio, TX: Psychological Corporation.

Wechsler, D. (1999). *Wechsler abbreviated scale of intelligence*. San Antonio, TX: The Psychological Corporation.

Wechsler, D. (2007). *Wechsler intelligence scale for children—Fourth edition, Taiwan Version*. Taipei, Taiwan: Chinese Behavioral Science Corporation.

Wechsler, D. (2008a). *Wechsler adult intelligence scale—Fourth edition*. San Antonio, TX: Pearson.

Wechsler, D. (2008b). *Wechsler intelligence scale for children—Fourth edition, Mainland China Version*. Zhuhai, Guangdong China: King-May Psychological Assessment Technology Development Limited Company.

Wechsler, D. (2009). *Wechsler intelligence scale for children—Fourth edition, Macau Version*. Zhuhai, Guangdong China: King-May Psychological Assessment Technology Development Limited Company.

Wechsler, D. (2010). *Wechsler intelligence scale for children—Fourth edition, Hong Kong Version*. Zhuhai, Guangdong China: King-May Psychological Assessment Technology Development Limited Company.

Wechsler, D. (2011). *Wechsler abbreviated scale of intelligence*. San Antonio, TX: Pearson.

Wechsler, D., Chen, Y. H., & Chen, X. Y. (2002). *WAIS-III Chinese version technical manual*. San Antonio, TX: Psychological Corporation.

Weiss, L. G., Saklofske, D. H., Coalson, D., & Raiford, S. E. (Eds.). (2010). *WAIS-IV clinical use and interpretation: Scientist-practitioner perspectives*. San Diego, CA: Academic Press.

Weiss, L. G., Saklofske, D. H., Prifitera, A., & Holdnack, J. A. (2006). *WISC-IV advanced clinical interpretation (Practical resources for the mental health professional)*. Burlington, MA: Academic Press.

Yang, P., Cheng, C. P., Chang, C. L., Liu, T. L., Hsu, H. Y., & Yen, C. F. (2013). Wechsler intelligence scale for children 4th edition—Chinese version index scores in Taiwanese children with attention-deficit/hyperactivity disorder. *Psychiatry and Clinical Neurosciences, 67*(2), 83–91.

Yeh, M., & Yeh, J. (2002). The clinical assessment of Asian American children. In K. S. Kurasaki, S. Okazaki, & S. Sue (Eds.), *Asian American mental health: Assessment theories and methods* (pp. 233–249). New York, NY: Kluwer.

Assessing Effort and Malingering with the Asian Client

11

Olga Cirlugea

What Is Malingering and Effort?

Malingering is defined as "the intentional production of false or grossly exaggerated physical or psychological symptoms, motivated by external incentives such as avoiding military duty, avoiding work, obtaining financial compensation, evading criminal prosecution, or obtaining drugs" by the DSM-IV-TR and recommendations for suspecting the presence of malingering are made in situations in which two or more of the following are observed: medicolegal context of presentation, marked discrepancy between self-reported stress or disability and objective findings, lack of cooperation during diagnostic evaluation or with prescribed treatment, or presence of antisocial personality disorder (American Psychiatric Association, 2000 p. 683). Rogers (1997) identified three models of malingering that map onto the APA's definition: pathogenic (underlying mental disorder), criminological (antisocial and oppositional motivation), and adaptational (cost–benefit analysis in response to adversarial circumstances). In order to study this construct, three primary approaches to assessing memory malingering have been developed: measures containing response style indices (e.g., MMPI-2), measures with a cutoff score indicative of memory malingering (e.g., Digit Span), and measures specifically designed for the assessment of memory malingering (e.g., Statement Validity Tests; Iverson & Binder, 2000). A number of problems in evaluating research on these measures with Asian populations have been raised: researchers often don't parse out the ethnic makeup of participants (e.g., Bowden, Shores, & Mathias, 2006), do not conduct analyses of ethno-racial factors, and fail to compare scores for different ethnic groups (e.g., O'Bryant, Engel, Kleiner, Vasterling, & Black, 2007; Temple, McBride, Horner, & Taylor, 2003).

Although the literature utilizes both "malingering" and "effort" as terms to describe a feigning of symptoms, in this chapter the term "malingering" is used as the majority of the assessment instruments discussed seek to determine whether symptoms are feigned and the term better captures the intentional production of symptoms that are motivated by an external incentive. By contrast, the term "effort" implies that motivation, which may arise from different sources (e.g., fatigue, boredom with the administration) plays a role in the examinee's performance and this doesn't adequately address the primary component of intentionality in malingering.

O. Cirlugea, B.A. (✉)
Department of Psychology, University of Nevada, Reno MS 0296, Reno, NV 89557, USA
e-mail: olgacirlugea@gmail.com

L.T. Benuto et al. (eds.), *Guide to Psychological Assessment with Asians*,
DOI 10.1007/978-1-4939-0796-0_11, © Springer Science+Business Media New York 2014

Why Assessment Is Important?

Accurate assessment of malingering is very important due to (a) the potential iatrogenic effects of an intervention delivered to someone who doesn't need it or of failing to deliver an intervention to someone who does need it and (b) the financial costs associated with malingering, which include both payments for unnecessary medical services but also cost associated with fraud (Garriga, 2007). Accurate assessment of malingering can be especially complicated with working with minorities such as Asians because the research is either scarce or nonexistent and because differences in performance may due to cultural differences when a measure has been applied to groups for whom it hasn't been validated. In line with the APA guidelines on working with ethnic, linguistic, and culturally diverse populations, clinicians should be able to justify the use of any measure for the detection malingering as well as to discuss any limitations in interpretations of results due to cultural and linguistic factors.

There are three types of research methodology used to study malingering: known-groups comparison, differential prevalence design, and simulation design, each with methodological advantages and limitations (Rogers, 1997). While simulation designs in which participants are given scenarios (e.g. you're a failing student, about to be expelled, but if you can convince the school that you have a mental disorder you may stay at the school) then instructed to fake symptoms in order to put on a convincing presentation of mental disorders are used most often and have high internal validity (and therefore will be the primary types of studies reviewed in this chapter), they have been criticized for their lack of external validity. In addition to the evaluation of measures for validity and reliability, measures such as malingering ones that seek to differentiate between those who feign symptoms and those who don't also must be tested for their sensitivity (identifying malingerers correctly) and specificity (identifying non-malingerers correctly).

Aims of the Chapter

Thus, the aim of this chapter is to explore the most commonly used and/or researched measures that strive to assess for malingering specifically in the context of their use with Asians and to generate evidence-based recommendations for the assessment of malingering with the Asian client. In addition to reviewing the research on these measures in-text below, Table 11.1 offers a summary of each measure and it's availability in relevant languages. Findings indicate that, for the most part, researchers aiming to validate malingering assessments have not specifically evaluated their psychometric properties with Asian populations, although Asians have not been completely excluded from such research studies. Asian versions of several instruments have been developed in foreign countries (e.g., China and Korea) and those have been demonstrated to be effective in discriminating malingerers from non-malingerers, though it should be noted that research conducted in other countries may not generalize to Asian-American clients. Clearly, further research on the use of malingering assessment instruments with Asian clients is warranted for many of the instruments described in this chapter. However, there is little evidence that cultural differences play a significant role in the way in which clients respond on such measures in a manner that reduces their accuracy in detecting malingering and therefore most of the instruments discussed below are acceptable for use with Asian clients.

Test of Memory Malingering (TOMM: Tombaugh, 1996)

The TOMM is a 50-item recognition test developed to distinguish exaggerated or faked memory impairment. Clients are administered two learning trials and an optional retention trial during which 50 line drawings of common figures are presented and have to be correctly identified in recognition panels which are subsequently shown to the client. The retention trial is only

Table 11.1 Malingering and effort tests

Test name	Original language	Available in Asian languages?[a]	Research conducted with Asians	Are cultural modifications necessary?
Test of Memory Malingering	English	Since this test is essentially a nonverbal test it can be utilized with Asian clients	Multiple studies have supported the use of this measure with Asians	No
The Medical Symptom Validity Test (1) and Nonverbal Medical Symptom Validity Test	English	No (1); Since the NVMSVT is a nonverbal test it can be administered in any language	Yes, limited research has been conducted	No
Digit Memory Test	English	Since this is a test employing numbers it can be utilized with Asian clients	Two studies have evaluated the DMT specifically with Asians	No
Rey 15 Items	English	No (letters and Roman numerals utilized are drawn from Latin alphabet)	One study evaluated the Rey 15 Items specifically with Asians	Yes—in the case of elderly clients; language issues may exist as well
Digit Span	English	Since this is a test employing numbers it can be utilized with Asian clients	One study evaluated the Digit Span specifically with Asians	No
MMPI, MMPI-II, and MMPI-2-RF	English	Chinese, Korean, Hmong (MMPI-2 only)	Extensive research has been conducted with Asian Samples	Yes—please see the section on the MMPI and MMPI-2 for specifics
The Structured Interview of Reported Symptoms	English	No	Yes, limited research has been conducted	Yes—in the case of evaluation of adolescents
Miller-Forensic Assessment of Symptoms Test (M-FAST)	English	No	Yes, limited research has been conducted	No

[a]These include, but are not limited to, Chinese, Japanese, Korean, and those spoken by Southeast Americans (e.g., Hmong, Filipino, Thai, Burman, and Laotian)

administered if individuals score lower than 45 on the second learning trial. Individuals who receive a score lower than 45 on the second trial are considered to have an invalid test performance. Research reveals that over half (55.6 %) of participants in nonclinical populations score 49 or 50 on the TOMM and only 8.4 % score lower than 45 (Tombaugh, 1996).

The TOMM has been researched specifically with Asians in a single international study conducted in Hong Kong. Chang (2006) developed an assessment battery for the detection of malingering that included two measures developed by Chang herself (a famous faces test and a subjective memory questionnaire), the TOMM, and indices in the Hong Kong List Learning Test (HKLLT, Chan & Kwok, 1999) indicative of memory malingering (i.e., Recognition Hits, Difference of Recall and Recognition, and False Alarm). Chang included the TOMM in her memory malingering battery of tests because the measure's stimuli "provided a cultural-free component" (p. 47). Two conditions were tested, simulated malingering (SM) and true effort (TE) in a sample of 57 community participants in Hong Kong. Significant differences between conditions were found for all four measures, and the battery assessment correctly classified 96 % of participants in the SM condition and 100 % of those in the TE condition. The TOMM cutoff score of 45 correctly identified 84 % of participants in the SM condition and 100 % of those in the TE condition.

Subsequent data analyses compared the scores of 57 community participants to those of a sample of depressed patients ($n=39$) in order to evaluate the effect of depression on memory malingering measures. Both groups were split into two the conditions described above, SM and TE; however, data from the simulated malingering Depression (SMD) group were dropped prior to analysis due to the failure of this group to comply with the feigning malingering instructions. Analysis of the remaining three groups, simulated malingering, true effort, and true effort depressed groups revealed significant differences between the SM and TE and SM and TED groups, and no significant differences between the two true effort groups on all measures of memory malingering except for on the HKLLT Recognition Hits index. The TOMM correctly identified 80 % of depressed patients and 100 % of normal controls.

A review of the extant literature on research of the TOMM in countries that have large immigrant populations (e.g., the USA, Canada) Asians have made up 0.008–40 % of the samples of studies where the TOMM was researched. For example, Moore and Donders (2004) examined the utility of the TOMM and the California Verbal Learning Test II (CLVT-II; Delis, Kramer, Kaplan, & Ober, 2000) in identifying invalid test performance in patients with Traumatic Brain Injury (TBI). The authors selected a sample of 132 patients, one of which was Asian-American who had suffered from a traumatic brain injury and had been seen at a Midwestern rehabilitation facility. Results indicated that the scores of 20 patients (15 %) were suggestive of invalid test performance (15 on the CLVT-II, 11 on the TOMM, and 6 on both measures). Further analysis of the data indicated that both financial compensation seeking and prior psychiatric history accounted for a large part of the invalid test performance.

Sollman, Ranseen, and Berry (2010) evaluated the ability of a battery of tests including ADHD self-report inventories, neuropsychological tests, Symptom Validity Tests (SVTs), and psychiatric malingering tests to detect feigning of ADHD symptoms in a sample 73 undergraduate students divided in three groups: an honest responding (clinically diagnosed) ADHD group (ADHD), a normal honest responding group (HON), and a normal feigning group (FGN). Three students, all in the FGN group, were Asian. SVT's included the TOMM, Digit Memory Test (DMT; Hiscock & Hiscock, 1989), Letter Memory Test, Card Version (LMT; Inman et al., 1998; Schipper, Berry, Coen, & Clark, 2008), and Nonverbal–Medical Symptom Validity Test (NV-MSVT; Green, 2006). Additionally, the Miller Forensic Assessment of Symptoms Test (M-FAST; Miller, 2001) was administered to screen for psychiatric response rather than for malingering and "few participants endorsed many of the questions" on this measure (p. 331). Significant Differences were found between the ADHD and FGN groups on all four measures of malingering. The TOMM was determined to be the most promising in detecting malingering, with trial one revealing high sensitivity and moderate specificity, while the second learning trial and retention trial both revealed moderate sensitivity and high specificity. The remaining SVTs (DMT, LMT, and NV-MSVT) all had moderate sensitivity and high specificity. When results on multiple measures were combined and the threshold of three or more failures was selected, positive predictive power (PPP) of feigning was 100 %, highlighting the importance of using multiple measures in the assessment of malingering.

Gervais, Wygant, Sellbom, and Ben-Porath (2011) evaluated the relationship between Symptom Validity Test (SVT) failure and exaggeration of psychological symptoms on the MMPI-2 Restructured Form validity and substantitative scales (Higher Order [H-O], Restructured Clinical [RC], Specific Problems [SP], and Interest scales, and revised versions of the PSY-5 scales; MMPI-2-RF; Ben-Porath &

Tellegen, 2008). Of the 1,003 Forensic Disability Claimant participants, 2.7 % were Asian. Participants were administered several SVTs including the TOMM, the Word Memory Test (Green, 2003), the Computerized Assessment of Response Bias (Allen, Conder, Green, & Cox, 1997), and the Medical Symptom Validity Test (MSVT; Green, 2004). Only participants who had completed at least three SVTs were included for analysis ($n=747$). Results indicated that a strong association existed between failure on the SVTs and overreporting of symptoms on the MMPY-2-RF as measured by the overreported psychological dysfunction (F-r), extreme psychopathology (Fp-r), somatic complaints (Fs), and noncredible reports of somatic or cognitive symptoms (FBS-r) scales.

Weinborn, Woods, Nulsen, and Leighton (2012) examined the effects of coaching on two Symptom Validity Tests, the MSVT (Green, 2004) and Nonverbal Medical Symptom Validity Test (NVMSVT; Green, 2007). Three conditions, symptom coached (SCG), test coaching (TCG), and combined symptom and test coaching (STCG), were compared to a control condition (best effort, BECG) in order to determine whether the original and nonverbal medical symptom validity tests were resistant to coaching interventions. These two STVs were then compared to a validated assessment instrument, the TOMM in a sample of 103 participants, which included 42 Asians (40.8 %). Specific to the TOMM, there was a statistically significant difference between SCG scores and TGC and STGC scores, with no significant difference emerging between the TGC and STGC conditions. Analyses of the MSVT found mixed results, with no statistical differences between TCG and SCG scores, statistically significant differences between STCG and TCG scores on four of the trials (Immediate Recall—IR, Delayed Recall—DR, Paired Associations—PA, and Free Recall—FR) and statistically significant differences between STCG and SCG scores on two of the trials (IR and FR). Lastly, results of the NVMSVT revealed no significant difference between TCG and SCG scores except for on the DRV and FR subtests, while there was a significant difference between STCG and SCG scores on IR, DR, Delayed Recognition-Associations (DRA), and Delayed-Recognition-Variations (DRV) trials but not on the Consistency (CNS) index. These findings indicate that the Best Effort Comparison Group's scores were "indicative of the highest levels of effort for all three SVT instruments, followed by the Symptom and Test Coached Group, then the Test Coached Group, with scores suggestive of the lowest levels of effort produced by the Symptom coached Group" (p. 839). Sensitivity scores were as follows: for the SCG, the TOMM and MSVT correctly identified 100 % of participants, while the NVMSVT correctly identified 96 %; for the TCG the TOMM 89 %, MSVT 92 %, NVMSVT 92 %; for the STCG the TOMM 83 %, 83 %, 88 %. These results indicate that both test and symptom coaching are required in order to produce better effort scores on the MSVT and NVMSVT, compared to just test coaching required for the TOMM.

With the exception of the international study conducted by Chang (2006), Asians have been largely excluded from research evaluating the TOMM. Additionally, given that the Chang (2006) study was conducted in Hong Kong, external validity issues may exist; the results may not generalize to Asians living in the USA; however, empirical evidence that suggests that the TOMM is not appropriate for use with Asians is absent. Therefore, the minimal research described above suggests that the TOMM is effective in detecting malingering and provides support for its use with Asian clients.

The MSVT (Green, 2004) and the NVMSVT (Green, 2007)

The MSVT is a shortened version of the Word Memory Test developed in order to assess effort. This measure contains three effort scales, Immediate Recall (IR), Delayed Recall (DR), and Consistency (CNS), and two memory scales, Paired Associates (PA) and Free Recall (FR). Effort is measured by the IR and DR scales by selecting between a correct and distracter word in a forced choice task, while the CNS scales measures the degree of consistency between the IR and DR scores. A score of 85 % or less on any of the three scales is indicative of poor effort demonstrated by the patient. However, a significantly lower performance on the memory scales than on the effort scales is indicative of a dementia profile. The NVMSVT is a forced choice test containing of 10 paired objects (e.g., a cartoon drawings) presented on a computer screen for a total of 20 objects. Green (2007) reported 72.5 % sensitivity in the simulators, 95 % specificity in dementia patients, and 100 % specificity in volunteers providing good effort in the development of the measure.

The MSVT has been evaluated utilizing Asian clients as research participants and their inclusion in research studies has ranged from 2.7 to 40.8 %. Armistead-Jehle (2010) administered the MSVT to a sample of 45 veterans who had scored positive on a traumatic brain injury (TBI) measure at the Veterans Health Administration. Demographic analyses indicated that 6.7 % of the veteran sample was Asian, 51.1 % Pacific Islander, 22.2 % Caucasian, 15.6 % African and 4.4 % Hispanic. Results revealed that 58 % of participants received a failing score of 85 % or lower on at least one of the easy subtests (IR, DR, and CNS). Of importance, no significant differences emerged between those who passed and those who failed the MSVT among the various ethnic groups. Additional studies evaluating the MSVT include Gervais et al. (2011), and Weinborn et al. (2012) and discussed in the section on the "TOMM" above. The NVMSVT has not been studied specifically with Asians; however, the Weinborn et al. (2012) and Sollman et al. (2010) studies discussed above in the section on the "TOMM" have included Asians in their sample. The limited research on the MSVT and NVMSVT with Asians highlights the need for further studies in order better determine the instruments' psychometric properties with this population. However, the outcome of the Armistead-Jehle (2010) study lends support for the recommendation to use this measure when evaluating malingering with the Asian client.

Digit Memory Test (DMT; Hiscock & Hiscock, 1989)

The DMT utilizes a forced-choice paradigm in which individuals are first exposed to a card containing a number for 5 s, and then are asked to select that card from a two-card presentation containing the correct card as well as a foil. The procedure is repeated with 10 and 25 s presentation times. Performance on the DMT at less than chance levels (i.e. at the $p < 0.05$ level) is indicative of malingering.

Two international studies have evaluated the utility of the DMT with Asian clients. Chiu and Lee (2002) enlisted 38 Chinese university freshmen in order to determine whether detection of malingering behavior changed based on the level of task difficulty of the DMT. Easy items were ones in which the foil and correct response were produced by a random table of numbers (e.g., 42719 and 81359) while difficult items included numbers with just a few digits that were different (e.g., 62866 and 62686). All participants were tested in the control and fake bad conditions. Results revealed significant differences between the control and malingering group, the latter group performing more poorly than the former. Additionally, malingering participants had lower scores at the higher level of difficulty on the DMT. Cutoff scores were established based on Hiscock and colleagues' (1994) suggestion of actual group performance on the test. This resulted in a cutoff score of 29.7 that correctly classified 76 % of malingering participants at the difficult level and 30 % at the easy level. Based on these findings, the authors recommended that a more stringent cutoff score be used when the easy level of the DMT is tested while keeping in mind the probability of getting false-positives and false-negatives.

Liu, Gao, Li, and Sheng (2001) also found significant differences on the DMT between simulating malingerers and controls in a college sample, providing further support for the use of the instrument in detecting feigning of memory deficits. A third study, Sollman et al. (2010), described in the section on the "TOMM," included

Fig. 11.1 Rey 15 items, Benuto (2013)

Asians in the sample although scores were not reported by ethnicity. Given the scarcity of research on the psychometric properties of the DMT with Asian clients, further studies should be conducted to evaluate the ability of the DMT to detect malingering in Asians. Additionally, two of the three studies described were conducted in China, and there is always the possibility that the results may not generalize to Chinese living in the USA, other Asians, etc. However, there is currently no evidence that the DMT may function differently for various ethnic groups; therefore, its use is recommended with the Asian client.

Rey 15-Item Memory Test (Rey, 1964) and Wechsler Digit Span (Wechsler, 1990)

Rey 15 Item

The Rey 15 Item requires individuals to memorize 15 printed items (see Fig. 11.1; Benuto, 2013) after being exposed to them visually for 10 s, and to draw them on a blank piece of paper. The score is the number of correctly reproduced items. Salazar et al. (2007) has advocated for lowering cutoffs (recall plus [recognition minus false positives <20]) on the Rey 15 Item in order to avoid excessive false positives that may emerge due to differences between bilinguals and monolingual non-English-speaking patients. The Rey 15 has been evaluated in an international study (see Yamaguchi, 2005 below).

Wechsler Digit Span

The Wechsler Digit Span includes two tasks, digit forward and digit backwards. In the digit forward task, the administrator reads a series of digits (beginning with 2 and ending at 9) at the rate of 1 per second and the client is instructed to repeat those digits back to the administrator in correct order. After failure on two consecutive trials of a series, the test is discontinued. Researchers found that the ability to repeat numbers back in correct order is retained for elderly patients, those with dementia, and TBI (e.g., Benton, Esligner, & Damasio, 1981, Storandt, Botwinick, Danziger, Berg, & Hughes, 1984). In the digit backward task, the client is instructed to repeat the digits backward; the same discontinuation criterion is applied. A score of less than five on the digit span forward and less than four on the digit span backward is deemed atypical even for those elderly individuals aged 85–89 (Wechsler, 1997).

Both Digit Span and the Rey 15 item have been assessed with an Asian population. Specifically, Yamaguchi (2005) evaluated the Rey 15-Item Memory Test and the Wechsler Digit Span subset of the WAIS-R (Wechsler, 1990) in detecting malingered memory impairment in a Japanese sample. Fifty-two participants, including healthy young and elderly controls, instructed malingering, and elderly nursing home individuals were utilized for the study. Fifteen participants were assigned to Group I and received standard instructions, 17 participants were assigned to Group II and were instructed to lie about head-trauma symptoms resulting from a car accident, 12 elderly participants were assigned to Group III and received standard instructions as well and group IV was comprised of 8 nursing home participants, 7 with dementia and 1 with psychiatric disorder. The Rey 15-Item Memory Test instructions were translated into Japanese by the researcher, after which they were back translated into English by ten bilingual volunteers to ensure the accuracy of the instructions. The Wechsler Digit Span subset was taken from the Japanese version of the WAIS-R (Wechsler, 1990). After the administration participants in the malingering group were asked to determine if they thought they had successfully lied about having a head injury. Two separate analyses were performed with the first including all participants in the malingering group while the second excluding participants who reported not being able to successfully malinger symptoms on both of the tests. Results for the Rey 15 Item revealed that the normal controls in group I performed similarly to the elderly in group III but significantly better than the malingerers in group II and the nursing home patients in group IV. Malingerers in group II and the elderly in group III both performed significantly better than the elderly in group IV. The most effective cutoffs were determined to be <9 for items and <2 for columns. Different sensitivity and specificity values were found for malingering based on which groups were used for comparison. Results of the Digit Span test indicated that normal controls in group I recalled significantly more items than malingerers in group II and nursing home elderly in group IV. There was no significant difference in number of items recalled between groups I and III, and groups II and IV. The most effective cutoffs were ≤8 digits for total digits, ≤4 and ≤5 digits for forward digit span, and ≤2 and ≤3 for backward digit span. Results were similar when the individuals who reported not successfully malingering were removed from the analyses. Effective cutoffs were ≤9 for items, and ≤1 and ≤2 for both columns and rows on the Rey 15 Item and ≤7 and ≤8 for total digit score, ≤4 for forward digit span and ≤2 and ≤3 for backward digit span. Taken together, these results provide most support for the utility of the Digit Span forward in identifying normal participants and discriminating them from the malingerers. The Rey 15 Item proved to be too difficult a task for the elderly nursing home residents with dementia. Because of this, the author recommended that the Digit Span be used when evaluating elderly impaired Japanese patients.

Neither the Rey 15 Item nor the Digit Span has been evaluated with Asians living in the USA. Therefore, the results of the Yamaguchi (2005) study may not generalize to those populations. However, there is no empirical evidence that ethnicity and culture significantly impact the ability of the Digit Span to detect malingering especially when items are drawn from a validated instrument (i.e., the Japanese version of the WAIS-R; Wechsler, 1990), and, therefore, its use is recommended with Asian clients. In the case of the Rey 15 Item there is some concern that the items, which include symbols derived from the Latin alphabet, may not function in the way they were expected for those who are only familiar with Asian alphabets. Further studies should be conducted to determine whether the Latin symbols are adequate for use with Asian populations or whether the Rey 15 Item should be revised to include Asian symbols. The potential issue of language and Yamaguchi's (2005) finding that assessment instrument was too difficult for elderly nursing home residents with dementia indicate that caution should be used when the Ray 15-Item is employed with Asian clients; additionally, evaluation procedures should make use of multiple measures to assess malingering.

Minnesota Multiphasic Personality Inventory (MMPI) and Its Variants

The MMPI is one of the most frequently used measures in psychology to assess for personality and psychopathology. Because a large portion of the personality assessment chapter was dedicated to the MMPI-2 and the Asian client, this section will only focus on the MMPI-2 and the Asian clients as the measure is associated with malingering. Several MMPI scales have been used to detect malingering. The Fake Bad Scale (FBS; Lees-Haley, English, & Glenn, 1991) is the primary scale used for this purpose as it was specifically developed to assess response bias (Larrabee, 1998). Research has indicated that the FBS possesses good discriminant validity in studies of traumatic brain injury litigants (Greiffenstein, Baker, Gola, Donders, & Miller, 2002; Larrabee, 2003; Martens, Donders, & Millis, 2001; Ross, Millis, Krukowski, Putnam, & Adams, 2004). Additional studies reported in the Berry, Baer, and Harris (1991) and Rogers, Sewell, and Salekin (1994) meta-analyses have found that other scales such as the F (Infrequency) Scale, the F-K (Infrequency minus Defensiveness) index, the Fb (Back Infrequency Scale) Scale, the revised Social Desirability Scale, and the obvious-subtle index were effective at detecting fake-bad profiles. Furthermore, the F and Fb scales and F-K index have been demonstrated to have good discriminate validity (Bagby, Nicholson, Buis, & Bacchiochi, 2000; Cramer, 1995; Lim & Butcher, 1996).

MMPI

With regard to the use of the MMPI and the Asian client, Sue and Sue (1974) compared the MMPI records of Chinese and Japanese students ($n=48$) to those of non-Asian controls ($n=120$) at a student clinic at a West Coast university and found that Asian students had elevated scores on the L and F scales. Results also revealed that the Asian students tended to underutilize mental health services, report a higher number of somatic complaints and to have higher familial discord. The authors hypothesized that the increased somatic complaints may be due to the acceptability of physical conditions over that of expression of mental problems in Asian families. Tsushima and Onorato (1982) conducted a similar study in which the medical records of white and Japanese-American patients at a private medical center in Hawaii were compared. Results indicated that there were no racial differences in scores on the different scales, and that other factors such as gender better accounted for any differences in responding. The authors noted that these results “imply that the MMPI interpretation rules based on white norms are applicable to certain Japanese-American medical patients” (p. 151) but that further research is needed in order for the results to generalize to other Asian-American population.

Wetter and colleagues (1992) attempted to determine whether validity scales on the MMPI-2 would be just as effective as the scales on its MMPI predecessor in differentiating random responses from malingering. In order to study the MMPI-2 scales, 151 college students, 7 % of which were Asian, were divided in four conditions: random responding, fake “moderate” group, fake “severe” group and control. Results indicated that the MMPI-2 scales were effective in differentiating between the two types of responding, especially the VRIN scale. Because the MMPI is in its second rendition, the research discussed above was conducted 20+ years ago below more recent research on the MMPI-2 is discussed.

MMPI-2

Researchers found that Asians tend to endorse more somatic symptoms than Caucasians on the MMPI-2, for example in the case of depression (e.g., Marsella, Kinzie, & Gordon, 1971, Ryder et al., 2008). Tsushima and Tsushima (2002) evaluated whether racial differences existed between the MMPI-2 scores of 130 white and 66 Japanese-American outpatients at a private medical center in Hawaii. The authors found no significant differences on any of the 13 scales. However, power for the study was low (0.50) and therefore these results can’t be interpreted to mean that Japanese-Americans score similarly to whites on the MMPI-2. A second study compared the scores of the outpatient sample to that of 32 “normals” that included two Japanese Americans, three Chinese Americans, one Korean American, and one Pacific Islander American. Specific to the validity scales, significant differences were found between the “normal” and outpatient sample, the latter scoring higher on scales F, K, and L. With regards to race, there were significant differences between Japanese-American Participants and “normals” on all scales with the exception of scale L and 5. Sue and colleagues (1996) evaluated differences in responding on the MMPI-2 among less acculturated Asians, highly acculturated Asians and Whites and the sample was 59.4 % Asian. The authors found no significant differences among the three groups on the Lie (L) and Defensiveness (K) scales, although there were significant gender differences on the L scale with females scoring higher than males. Differences were also significant on the Infrequency (F) scale, as less acculturated Asians scored significantly higher than their White counterparts. A pattern emerged among the three groups regardless of whether differences were significant or not, namely that the less acculturated Asians scored higher than the highly acculturated Asians, which in turn scored higher than the whites. This pattern was also observed in the profile validity of the three groups. In light of these findings, the authors suggest that cultural factors be taken into consideration when interpreting the profiles of Asian-American clients, especially when the level of acculturation is low.

Tsushima and Tsushima (2009) sought to determine whether differences existed between Asian-American and Caucasian patients seeking compensation or participating in personal injury litigation on the MMPI-2 validity scales. Scores of 48 Asian-American medical patients were compared to those of 109 Caucasian patients on the following scales: F scale, Back Infrequency Scale, Symptom Validity Scale, Infrequency-Psychopathology Scale, and Dissimulation Scale. Results revealed no significant differences between the two ethnic groups on performance on any of the five scales.

Barber-Rioja, Zottoli, Kucharski, and Duncan (2009) evaluated the utility of the newly developed Criminal Offender Infrequency scale (Fc scale; Megargee, 2004) derived from the MMPI-2 in detecting malingering in a forensic sample, of which less than 1 % was Asian. The Structured Interview of Reported Symptoms (SIRS; Rogers, 1986) was used to classify 140 male criminal defendants as either malingering (23 %) or honest responders (77 %) using the malingering criteria of "three or more SIRS scales in the probable range or one scale in the definite range" (p. 19). Results demonstrated that the F, Fc, Fb, and F(p) scales all had acceptable sensitivity and specificity, with the Fc scale having similar sensitivity and specificity as the F and Fb scales. These findings provide support for the predictive utility of the newly developed Fc scale in detecting malingering.

MMPI-2-RF

The MMPI-2-RF (Ben-Porath & Tellegen, 2008) was developed in order to provide a more current evaluation of the models of psychopathology and personality that are presently being used. Gervais, Ben-Porath, Wygant, and Sellbom (2010) evaluated the incremental validity of the MMPI-2-RF symptom overreporting scales (F, Back Infrequency (Fb), Infrequency-Psychopathology (Fp), and FBS scales) and the scale developed for the prediction of cognitive Symptom Validity Tests (SVT) scale, the Response Bias Scale (RBS; Gervais, Ben-Porath, Wygant, & Green, 2007) over the MMPI-2 in a sample of 1,187 non-TBI disability-related referrals and 2.7 % of them were Asian. Result indicated that the MMPI-2-RF scales had greater sensitivity in detecting memory complaints than their MMPI-2 counterparts. Building on the results of a previous study that demonstrated that elevated scores on the RBS were not associated with objective memory functioning (Gervais, Ben-Porath, Wygant, & Green, 2008), the authors point out that "subjective memory complaints in the context of elevated scores on RBS or the other MMPI-2-RF over-reporting scales are unlikely to indicate objective memory deficits, but rather suggest exaggerated memory or other cognitive complaints" (p. 281).

The Chinese MMPI

The Minnesota Multiphasic Personality Inventory (MMPI) was translated into Chinese in Hong Kong and China and the reliability of this version and its translation equivalence to the English version has been demonstrated in multiple studies (e.g., Boey, 1985; Cheung, 1985; National MMPI Coordinating Group, 1985). However, results have indicated that a number of scales including the F scale are elevated in Chinese populations (Cheung & Song, 1989). As a result, Cheung, Song, and Butcher (1991) developed two infrequency scales for the Chinese MMPI (ICH1 and ICH2) in response to the literature showing that Chinese American college students (Sue & Sue, 1974) and Chinese "normals" and psychiatric patients (Cheung, 1985, 1986; Cheung & Song, 1989; Cheung, Song, & Zhang, 1996; National MMPI Coordinating Group, 1982) all received elevated scores on the F scale on the original MMPI. Validation of the scales was conducted with a large sample including participants from Hong Kong (psychiatric patients, prisoners, and college students, some of whom were asked to fake good and some who were asked to fake bad) and China (convicted murderers, obsessive-compulsive, manic-depressive, and schizophrenic patients). Results indicated that the fake-bad group scored extremely high on the Chinese infrequency scales, and significant differences between that group and the patient and prisoner groups emerged. The fake group's scores were similar to those of the normative sample. Among the two infrequency scales, the ICH1, which included items that were endorsed by no more than 10 % of Chinese and Hong Kong samples, emerged as better discriminating between normals and patients within a valid range. The authors recommend the use of this scale with Chinese patients over the original F scale even when this scale is rescored using local norms given that such transformations ignore the norms on which the scale was originally developed and complicate interpretations of score elevations.

The Korean MMPI-2 and Korean MMPI-2-RF

The MMPI-2 (Butcher, Dahlstrom, Graham, Tellegen, & Kaemmer, 1989) was first translated into Korean by Han (1993, 1996) and subsequently underwent multiple translations and back-translations until items were deemed adequate for testing with a Korean population. Hahn (2005) explored the utility of the validation scales of the Korean MMPI-2 (Kim et al., 2005) in the detection of fake-bad and fake-good profiles. The F (infrequency), Fb (fake-bad), F–K, and F(p) scales were developed when the original US MMPI scales resulted in elevated scores (e.g., high scores on F scale reported by Cho, Park, Ahn, & Shin, 1990). A sample comprised of South Korean students and psychiatric patients ($n=219$) was utilized for the study. The students were assigned to one of three conditions (fake-bad, fake-good problem denial, and fake-good claiming extreme virtue). Participants in the fake-bad condition received higher scores on the F, Fb and F(p) scales, and lower scores on the K scale compared to the psychiatric sample. The scales correctly classified between 87 and 95 % of faking-bad and psychiatric participants, with the F scale being most useful in this classification. On the other hand, faking-good profiles were classified with less accuracy, and of the scales, the S scale was the most useful in the classification. Because of the differences in the endorsement of certain items between Americans and Koreans (e.g., #494—whether people should keep personal problems to themselves; #115—belief in after life; #20—satisfaction with sex life), the author recommended that instruments sensitive to a particular cultural context such as the Korean version of the MMPI-2 should be used. Dykhouse (2012) found that the Korean MMPI-2-RF validity scales developed from the Korean MMPI-2 item-pool correctly identified over or under-reporting honest participants in two conditions, uncoached and coached over (under)-report. Taken together, these results support the use of the Korean versions of the MMPI-2 and MMPI-2-RF. Further research is needed to determine whether these versions would be adequate for use with Koreans in the USA, particularly those who don't speak English or have a low level of acculturation.

The Structured Interview of Reported Symptoms (SIRS; Rogers et al. 1992)

The SIRS is the most widely used malingering measure in forensic practice (Archer, Buffington-Vollum, Stredny, & Handel, 2006). The second edition of the measure (SIRS-2; Rogers, Sewell, & Gillard, 2010) has been modified to prevent false-positive and false-negative classification errors (Rubenzer, 2010).

The SIRS has not been evaluated specifically with Asians; however, Asians have been part of the validation samples and their inclusion has ranged from 1 to 16.6 %. For example, Rogers, Gillis, Dickens, and Bagby (1991) evaluated the psychometric properties of the Structured Interview of Reported Symptoms (Rogers, 1986) in two studies. The first study evaluated the utility of the SIRS in differentiating simulators of malingering from two control groups, community and outpatient, and 7.4 % of the sample was defined as "Oriental." The second study evaluated potential differences in responding of suspected malingerers and psychiatric inpatients, of which 5.9 % were oriental. Responses on the SIRS were compared to results on the MMPI validity indicators and M Test. The authors found that in the first study the SIRS was effective in discriminating between the two groups with excellent interrater reliability, while the second study revealed that suspected malingerers only responded similar to psychiatric inpatients on four of the nine SIRS scales (DS, DA, OS, and SO). The findings of the first study provide support for the discriminant and concurrent validity of the SIRS. In another study, Rogers, Gillis, Bagby, and Monteiro (1991) evaluated the ability of the SIRS to discriminate between coached and uncoached simulators of malingering in a sample of university students, of which 16.6 % were Asian. Scores were compared to those of the psychiatric sample utilized in the Rogers, Gillis, Dickens, et al. (1991) study. Students in both conditions were given a scenario in which they were instructed to feign mental illness in order to avoid expulsion from the university for failing grades, with the coached group receiving additional information about feigning mental illness. Even though the coached simulators were successful in reducing their malingering scores, all but one of the SIRS scales effective in discriminating them from uncoached and psychiatric counterparts. The SIRS accurately identified 100 % of uncoached simulators and 96.7 % of coached simulators, providing further evidence for the discriminant validity of the measures.

Rogers, Hinds, and Sewell (1996) examined the validity of three assessment instruments for the detection of feigning, the SIRS, the Minnesota Mulitphasic Personality Inventory-Adolescent (MMPI-A; Butcher et al., 1992) and Screening Index of Malingered Symptoms (SIMS; Smith, 1992), for use with an adolescent population. Fifty-three adolescents participating in a residential treatment program were recruited for the study, and one of them was Asian. Two conditions were tested, honest and feigning, the latter requiring participants to simulate symptoms of one of three disorders, schizophrenia, major depression, and generalized anxiety disorder. The authors found that they had to apply different rules for classifying malingering from the ones utilized in studies of MMPI and MMPI-2 with adult populations as these were inadequate when implemented to detect adolescent feigning. Additionally, the SIRS demonstrated superior utility in classifying adolescents as either malingering or nonmalingering, with a smaller amount of false positives than the near one to one ratio found for the MMPI-A. These findings lent support for the clinical utility of the SIMS as a feigning screen for adolescents. Barber-Rioja et al. (2009) and Guy, Kwartner, and Miller (2006) have also utilized the measure in their studies, which can be found in the MMPI-2 section for the former and M-FAST section for the latter. Taken together, these results fail to reveal any evidence against using the SIRS with Asian clients; therefore, the use of the assessment instrument with this population is recommended.

Miller-Forensic Assessment of Symptoms Test (M-FAST; Miller, 2001)

The Miller-Forensic Assessment of Symptoms Test (M-FAST; Miller, 2001) is a 25-item structured interview developed to detect malingering of psychotic symptoms. Scales include Unusual Hallucinations, Reported Versus Observed, Rare Combinations, Extreme Symptomatology, Negative Image, Unusual Symptom Course, and Suggestibility and the measure can be scored in one of three ways: the total score evaluates likelihood of malingering psychopathology; the scale scores inform clinicians about how the responders attempt to feign symptoms (i.e., though the reporting of unusual hallucinations); and several scales reliably discriminate malingerers from honest responders. The M-FAST has been shown to have good psychometric properties (Miller, 2001, 2004).

Similar to the SIRS, the M-FAST has not validated specifically with Asian clients. Nevertheless, some studies evaluating the psychometric properties of the M-FAST have included Asians in their sample. Guy et al. (2006) evaluated the psychometric properties of the M-FAST using a sample comprised of undergraduate simulators and psychiatric patients, the latter group containing 1.4 % Asians. Simulators were instructed to feign one of four mental disorders (schizophrenia, major depressive disorder, bipolar disorder, and posttraumatic stress disorders), and malingering was identified using the SIRS and either the MMPI-2 or Personality Assessment Inventory (PAI; Morey, 1991). Results indicated that the M-FAST had excellent internal consistency but low mean interitem correlation. Additionally, the measure was effective in discriminating simulators from their psychiatric counterparts, with the rare combination scale and the remaining scales varying in this ability, and feigned schizophrenia being more easily distinguished from true schizophrenia than the other disorders.

Messer and Fremouw (2008) investigated the sensitivity of the M-FAST and Morel Emotional Numbing Test-Revised (MENT-R; Morel, 1998) in 169 students. The sample was comprised of honest responders, coached malingerers (feigning PTSD after a car accident in order to obtain monetary compensation), and clinical PTSD responders, and 1.4 % of participants were Asian. Results indicated that the coached malingering group scored significantly higher on the MENT-R and the M-FAST than the other two groups. Additionally, the MENT-R accurately identified 63 % of malingers, while the M-FAST correctly identified 78 % of malingerers, with a combined correct identification rate of 90 %. The authors note that only 4 of 41 malingering participants met criteria for successful malingering, which may have influenced these results. While further research on psychometric properties of this measure with Asian samples is recommended, we currently have no evidence for why the M-FAST should not be part of the assessment of malingering with the Asian client.

Summary and Recommendations

In this chapter some of the most commonly used and well-researched tests that aim to assess for malingering and/or effort have been reviewed and a summary of these measures with appropriate recommendations can be found in Table 11.1. This review has revealed that there are several measures for malingering that have been specifically evaluated with Asian clients. It is important to note that using a multi-method approach to the assessment of malingering as well as gathering collateral information will likely lead to increased accuracy of diagnoses that discern genuine psychological symptoms from symptoms of malingering. Additionally, limitations of the measures used, such as a lack of equivalency of a construct in the Asian client's native language, should be considered when administering a test that requires that results be interpreted with caution. In conclusion, clinicians should make use of the malingering assessment instruments described in this chapter in order to ensure that treatment is appropriately delivered and resources are not wasted on a client who does not in fact have a mental disorder.

References

Allen, L., Conder, R. L., Green, P., & Cox, D. R. (1997). *CARB '97 manual for the computerized assessment of response bias*. Durham, NC: CogniSyst.

American Psychiatric Association. (2000). *Diagnostic and statistical manual of mental disorders* (4th ed., text rev.). Washington, DC: Author.

Archer, R. P., Buffington-Vollum, J. K., Stredny, R. V., & Handel, R. W. (2006). A survey of psychological test use patterns among forensic psychologists. *Journal of Personality Assessment, 87*, 85–94.

Armistead-Jehle, P. (2010). Symptom validity test performance in U.S. veterans referred for evaluation of mild TBI. *Applied Neuropsychology, 17*(1), 52–59.

Bagby, R. M., Nicholson, R. A., Buis, T., & Bacchiochi, J. R. (2000). Can the MMIP-2 validity scales detect depression feigned by experts? *Assessment, 7*(1), 55–62.

Barber-Rioja, V., Zottoli, T., Kucharski, L., & Duncan, S. (2009). The utility of the MMPI-2 Criminal Offender Infrequency (Fc) Scale in the detection of malingering in criminal defendants. *International Journal of Forensic Mental Health, 8*(1), 16–24.

Ben-Porath, Y. S., & Tellegen, A. (2008). *MMPI-2-RF (Minnesota Multiphasic Personality Inventory-2-Restructured Form) manual for administration, scoring, and interpretation*. Minneapolis, MN: University of Minnesota Press.

Benton, A. L., Esligner, P. J., & Damasio, A. R. (1981). Normative observations on neuropsychological test performances in old age. *Journal of Clinical Neuropsychology, 3*, 33–42.

Benuto, L. (2013). Assessing effort & malingering with the Hispanic client. In L. Benuto (Ed.), *Guide to psychological assessment with Hispanics* (pp. 99–112). New York, NY: Springer.

Berry, D. T. R., Baer, R. A., & Harris, M. J. (1991). Detection of malingering on the MMPI: A meta-analysis. *Clinical Psychology Review, 11*(5), 585–598.

Boey, K. W. (1985). The MMPI response pattern of Singapore Chinese. *Acta Psychologica Sinica, 17*(4), 377–383.

Bowden, S. C., Shores, A. E., & Mathias, J. L. (2006). Does effort suppress cognition after traumatic brain injury: A re-examination of the evidence for the Word Memory Test. *The Clinical Neuropsychologist, 20*, 858–872.

Butcher, J. N., Dahlstrom, W. G., Graham, J. R., Tellegen, A. M., & Kaemmer, B. (1989). *MMPI-2: Manual for administration and scoring*. Minneapolis, MN: University of Minnesota Press.

Butcher, J. N., Williams, C. L., Grham, J. R., Archer, R., Tellegen, A. M., Ben-Porath, Y. S., & Kaemmer, B. (1992). *Minnesota Multiphasic Personality Inventory—Adolescent Version (MMPI-A)*. Minneapolis, MN: University of Minnesota Press.

Chan, A. S., & Kwok, I. (1999). *Hong Kong List Learning Test: Manual and preliminary norm*. Hong Kong: Chinese University of Hong Kong.

Chang, S. (2006). Development of a test battery for assessing memory malingering in Hong Kong and its application on depressed patients (China). *Dissertation Abstracts International, 68*.

Cheung, F. M. (1985). Cross-cultural considerations for the translation and adaptation of the Chinese MMPI in Hong Kong. In J. N. Butcher & C. D. Spielberger (Eds.), *Recent advances in personality assessment* (Vol. 8, pp. 131–158). Hillsdale, NJ: Lawrence Erlbaum Associates.

Cheung, F. M. (Ed.). (1986). *The Chinese Minnesota multiphasic personality inventory (MMPI): Research and applications* (Occasional Paper No. 12). Hong Kong: Centre for Hong Kong Studies, The Chinese University of Hong Kong.

Cheung, F. M., & Song, W. (1989). A review on the clinical applications of the Chinese MMPI. *Psychological Assessment: A Journal of Consulting and Clinical Psychology, 1*(3), 230–237. doi:10.1037/1040-3590.1.3.230.

Cheung, F. M., Song, W., & Butcher, J. N. (1991). An infrequency scale for the Chinese MMPI. *Journal of Consulting and Clinical Psychology, 3*, 648–653.

Cheung, F., Song, W., & Zhang, J. (1996). The Chinese MMPI–2: Research and applications in Hong Kong and the People's Republic of China. In J. N. Butcher (Ed.), *International adaptations of the MMPI–2: Research and clinical applications* (pp. 137–161). Minneapolis, MN: University of Minnesota Press.

Chiu, V. Y., & Lee, T. C. (2002). Detection of malingering behavior at different levels of task difficulty in Hong Kong Chinese. *Rehabilitation Psychology, 47*(2), 194–203.

Cho, S., Park, B., Ahn, C., & Shin, D. (1990). The effectiveness of random response set identification scale of MMPI profiles. *Korean Journal of Clinical Psychology, 9*, 184–191.

Cramer, K. M. (1995). Comparing three new MMPI-2 randomness indices in a novel procedure for random profile derivation. *Journal of Personality Assessment, 63*(3), 514.

Delis, D. C., Kramer, J. H., Kaplan, E., Ober, B. A., et al. (2000). *California Verbal Learning Test—second edition*. San Antonio, TX: The Psychological Corporation.

Dykhouse, A. S. (2012). *Examining sensitivity of Korean MMPI-2-RF validity scales to over-reporting and under-reporting of symptoms*. Retrieved from http://condor.cmich.edu/cdm/singleitem/collection/p1610-01coll1/id/3553/rec/7

Garriga, M. (2007). Malingering in the clinical setting. *Psychiatric Times, 24*(3), 1–4.

Gervais, R. O., Ben-Porath, Y. S., Wygant, D. B., & Green, P. (2007). Development and validation of a Response Bias Scale (RBS) for the MMPI-2. *Assessment, 14*, 196–208.

Gervais, R. O., Ben-Porath, Y. S., Wygant, D. B., & Green, P. (2008). Differential sensitivity of the Response Bias Scale (RBS) and MMPI-2 validity scales to memory complaints. *The Clinical Neuropsychologist, 22*, 1061–1079.

Gervais, R. O., Ben-Porath, Y. S., Wygant, D. B., & Sellbom, M. (2010). Incremental validity of the MMPI-2-RF over-reporting scales and RBS in assessing the veracity of memory complaints. *Archives of Clinical Neuropsychology, 25*(4), 274–284.

Gervais, R. O., Wygant, D. B., Sellbom, M., & Ben-Porath, Y. S. (2011). Associations between symptom validity test failure and scores on the MMPI-2-RF validity and substantive scales. *Journal of Personality Assessment, 93*(5), 508–517.

Green, P. (2003). *Green's Word Memory Test for Windows: Users manual*. Edmonton, AB: Author.

Green, P. (2004). *Green's Medical Symptom Validity Test (MSVT): User's manual*. Edmonton, AB: Author.

Green, P. (2006). *NV-MSVT for Windows, Version 1.3*. Edmonton, AB: Author.

Green, P. (2007). *Manual for the Nonverbal Medical Symptom Validity Test*. Edmonton, AB: Author.

Greiffenstein, M. F., Baker, W. J., Gola, T., Donders, J., & Miller, L. (2002). The fake bad scale in atypical and severe closed head injury litigants. *Journal of Clinical Psychology, 58*(12), 1591–1600.

Gualtieri, C., & Johnson, L. (2006). Reliability and validity of a computerized neurocognitive test battery, CNS Vital Signs. *Archives of Clinical Neuropsychology, 21*(7), 623–643.

Guy, L. S., Kwartner, P. P., & Miller, H. A. (2006). Investigating the M-FAST: Psychometric properties and utility to detect diagnostic specific malingering. *Behavioral Sciences and the Law, 24*(5), 687–702.

Hahn, J. (2005). Faking bad and faking good by college students on the Korean MMPI-2. *Journal of Personality Assessment, 85*, 65–73.

Han, K. (1993). The use of the MMPI–2 in Korea: Inventory adaptation, equivalence evaluation, and initial validation. *Dissertation Abstracts International, 54*.

Han, K. (1996). Adaptations in Asia and Southeast Asia. In J. N. Butcher (Ed.), *International adaptations of the MMPI-2: Research and clinical applications* (pp. 67–218). Minneapolis, MN: University of Minnesota Press.

Hiscock, C. K., Branham, J. D., & Hiscock, M. (1994). Detection of feigned cognitive impairment: The two-alternative forced choice method compared with selected conventional tests. *Journal of Psychopathology and Behavioural Assessment, 16*, 95–110.

Hiscock, M., & Hiscock, C. K. (1989). Refining the forced-choice method for the detection of malingering. *Journal of Clinical and Experimental Neuropsychology, 11*, 967–974.

Inman, T. H., Vickery, C. D., Berry, D. T. R., Lamb, D. G., Edwards, C. L., & Smith, G. T. (1998). Development and initial validation of a new procedure for evaluating adequacy of effort given during neuropsychological testing: The Letter Memory Test. *Psychological Assessment, 10*, 128–149.

Iverson, G., & Binder, L. (2000). Detecting exaggeration and malingering in neuropsychological assessment. *Journal of Head Trauma Rehabilitation, 15*, 829–858.

Kim, I. J., Han, K., Lim, J., Lee, J., Min, B., & Moon, K. (2005). *Korean MMPI-2 user manual*. Seoul, Korea: Maumsarang.

Larrabee, G. J. (1998). Somatic malingering on the MMPI and MMPI-2 in personal injury litigants. *The Clinical Neuropsychologist, 12*(2), 179–188.

Larrabee, G. (2003). Detection of malingering using atypical performance patterns on standard neuropsychological tests. *The Clinical Neuropsychologist, 17*(3), 410–425.

Lees-Haley, P. R., English, L. T., & Glenn, V. J. (1991). A fake bad scale on the MMPI-2 for personal injury claimants. *Psychological Reports, 68*, 203–210.

Lim, J., & Butcher, J. N. (1996). Detection of faking on the MMPI-2: Differentiation among faking-bad, denial, and claiming extreme virtue. *Journal of Personality Assessment, 67*(1), 1–25.

Liu, R., Gao, B., Li, Y., & Sheng, L. (2001). Simulated malingering: A preliminary trial on Hiscock's Forced-Choice Digit Memory Test. *Chinese Journal of Clinical Psychology, 9*(3), 173–175.

Marsella, A. J., Kinzie, D., & Gordon, P. (1971, March). *Depressive patterns among American college students of Caucasian, Chinese, and Japanese ancestry.* Paper presented at the Conference on Culture and Mental Health in Asia and the Pacific, Honolulu, Hawaii.

Martens, M., Donders, J., & Millis, S. R. (2001). Evaluation of invalid response sets after traumatic head injury. *Journal of Forensic Neuropsychology, 2*(1), 1–18.

Megargee, E. I. (2004, May). *Development and initial validation of an MMPI-2 infrequency scale (Fc) for use with criminal offenders*. Paper presented at the 39th Annual Symposium on Recent Developments on the MMPI-2/MMPI-A, Minneapolis, MN.

Messer, J., & Fremouw, W. (2008). Detecting malingered Posttraumatic Stress Disorder using the Morel Emotional Numbing Test-Revised (MENT-R) and the Miller Forensic Assessment of Symptoms Test (M-FAST). *Journal of Forensic Psychology Practice, 7*(3), 33–57.

Miller, H. A. (2001). *M-FAST: Miller Forensic Assessment of Symptoms Test*. Lutz, FL: Psychological Assessment Resources.

Miller, H. A. (2004). Examining the use of the M-Fast with criminal defendants incompetent to stand trial. *International Journal of Offender Therapy and Comparative Criminology, 48*, 268–280.

Moore, B. A., & Donders, J. (2004). Predictors of invalid neuropsychological test performance after traumatic brain injury. *Brain Injury, 18*(10), 975–984.

Morel, K. R. (1998). *Manual for the Morel Emotional Numbing Test for Posttraumatic Stress Disorder (MENT)*. Printed in USA.

Morey, L. C. (1991). *Personality Assessment Inventory: Professional manual*. Tampa, FL: Psychological Assessment Resources.

National MMPI Coordinating Group. (1982). The revision, employment and evaluation of MMPI in China. *Acta Psychologica Sinica, 14*, 449–458.

National MMPI Coordinating Group. (1985). Analysis of results of MMPI on normal Chinese subjects. *Acta Psychologica Sinica, 17*, 346–355.

O'Bryant, S. E., Engel, L. R., Kleiner, J. S., Vasterling, J. J., & Black, F. W. (2007). Test of Memory Malingering (TOMM) Trial 1 as a screening measure for insufficient effort. *Archives of Clinical Neuropsychology, 21*, 511–521.

Rey, A. (1964). *L'examen Clinique en Psychologie*. Paris: Presses Universitaires de France.

Rogers, R. (1986). *Structured interview of reported symptoms (SIRS)*. Clarke Institute of Psychiatry: Toronto, Unpublished scale.

Rogers, R. (1992). *Structured interview of reported symptoms*. Odessa, FL: Psychological Assessment Resources.

Rogers, R. (1997). Current status of clinical methods. In R. Rogers (Ed.), *Clinical assessment of malingering and deception* (2nd ed., pp. 373–379). New York, NY: Guilford Press.

Rogers, R., Gillis, J., Bagby, R., & Monteiro, E. (1991). Detection of malingering on the Structured Interview of Reported Symptoms (SIRS): A study of coached and uncoached simulators. *Psychological Assessment: A Journal of Consulting and Clinical Psychology, 3*(4), 673–677.

Rogers, R., Gillis, J., Dickens, S. E., & Bagby, R. (1991). Standardized assessment of malingering: Validation of the Structured Interview of Reported Symptoms. *Psychological Assessment: A Journal of Consulting and Clinical Psychology, 3*(1), 89–96.

Rogers, R., Hinds, J. D., & Sewell, K. W. (1996). Feigning psychopathology among adolescent offenders: Validation of the SIRS, MMPI-A, and SIMS. *Journal of Personality Assessment, 67*(2), 244.

Rogers, R., Sewell, K. W., & Salekin, R. T. (1994). A meta-analysis of malingering on the MMPI-2. *Assessment, 1*(3), 227–237.

Rogers, R., Sewell, K. W., & Gillard, N. D. (2010). *Structured interview of reported symptoms (SIRS)* (2nd Ed., professional manual). Lutz, FL: Psychological Assessment Resources.

Ross, S. R., Millis, S. R., Krukowski, R. A., Putnam, S. H., & Adams, K. M. (2004). Detecting incomplete effort on the MMPI-2: An examination of the Fake-Bad Scale in mild head injury. *Journal of Clinical & Experimental Neuropsychology, 26*(1), 115–124 & 10.

Rubenzer, S. (2010). Review of the structured interview of reported symptoms-2 (SIRS-2). *Open Access Journal of Forensic Psychology, 2*, 273–286.

Ryder, A. G., Jian, Y., Xiongzhao, Z., Shuqiao, Y., Jinyao, Y., Heine, S. J., & Bagby, R. (2008). The cultural shaping of depression: Somatic symptoms in China, psychological symptoms in North America? *Journal of Abnormal Psychology, 117*(2), 300–313.

Salazar, X. F., Lu, P. H., Wen, J., & Boone, K. B. (2007). The use of effort tests in ethnic minorities. In K. B. Boone (Ed.), *Assessment of feigned cognitive impairment: A neuropsychological perspective* (pp. 405–427). New York, NY: Guilford Press.

Schipper, L. J., Berry, D. T. R., Coen, E., & Clark, J. A. (2008). Cross validation of a manual form of the Letter Memory Test using a known groups methodology. *The Clinical Neuropsychologist, 22*, 345–349.

Smith, G. P. (1992). *Detection of malingering: A validation study of the SLAM test.* Unpublished dissertation, University of Missouri—St. Louis.

Sollman, M. J., Ranseen, J. D., & Berry, D. R. (2010). Detection of feigned ADHD in college students. *Psychological Assessment, 22*(2), 325–335.

Storandt, M., Botwinick, J., Danziger, W., Berg, L., & Hughes, C. P. (1984). Psychometric differentiation of mild senile dementia of the Alzheimer type. *Archives of Neurology, 41*, 497–499.

Sue, S., Keefe, K., Enomoto, K., Durvasula, R., & Chao, R. (1996). Asian American and White college students' performance on the MMPI-2. In J. N. Butcher (Ed.), *International adaptations of the MMPI-2: Research and clinical applications* (pp. 206–218). Minneapolis, MN: University of Minnesota Press.

Sue, S., & Sue, D. W. (1974). MMPI comparisons between Asian-American and Non-Asian students utilizing a student health psychiatric clinic. *Journal of Counseling Psychology, 21*(5), 423–427.

Temple, R. O., McBride, A. M., Horner, M. D., & Taylor, R. M. (2003). Personality characteristics of patients showing suboptimal cognitive effort. *The Clinical Neuropsychologist, 17*, 402–409.

Tombaugh, T. N. (1996). The Test of Memory Malingering (TOMM): Normative data from cognitively intact and cognitively impaired individuals. *Psychological Assessment, 9*, 260–268.

Tsushima, W. T., & Onorato, V. A. (1982). Comparison of MMPI scores of White and Japanese-American medical patients. *Journal of Consulting and Clinical Psychology, 50*(1), 150–151.

Tsushima, W. T., & Tsushima, V. G. (2002). Comparison of MMPI-2 scores of white and Japanese American medical patients. *Advances in Medical Psychotherapy and Psychodiagnosis, 11*, 1–8.

Tsushima, W. T., & Tsushima, V. G. (2009). Comparison of MMPI-2 validity scales among compensation-seeking Caucasian and Asian American medical patients. *Assessment, 6*, 159–164.

Wechsler, D. (1990). *Japanese Wechsler Adult Intelligence Scale-Revised: Manual* (F. Shinangawa, S. Kobayashi, K. Fujita, & H. Maekawa, Trans.). San Antonio, TX: Psychological Corporation.

Wechsler, D. (1997). *Wechsler Adult Intelligence Scale-III: Manual.* San Antonio, TX: Psychological Corporation.

Weinborn, M., Woods, S., Nulsen, C., & Leighton, A. (2012). The effects of coaching on the Verbal and Nonverbal Medical Symptom Validity Tests. *The Clinical Neuropsychologist, 26*(5), 832–849.

Wetter, M. W., Baer, R. A., Berry, D. R., Smith, G. T., & Larsen, L. H. (1992). Sensitivity of MMPI-2 validity scales to random responding and malingering. *Psychological Assessment, 4*(3), 369–374.

Yamaguchi, T. (2005). *Detecting malingered memory impairment using the Rey 15-Item Memory Test and the Wechsler Digit Span subtest in a Japanese population.* UMI Dissertation Services, ProQuest Information and Learning, Ann Arbor, MI.

Assessing Depression and Suicidality in Asian-Americans

12

Zornitsa Kalibatseva, Ivan H.C. Wu, and Frederick T.L. Leong

Major depression is one of the highest contributors to disability and the global burden of disease worldwide surpassing Alzheimer's and cancer (World Health Organization, 2008). Suicide is the 7th leading cause of death among men and the 15th leading cause of death among women in the USA (Heron, 2011). The serious consequences associated with depression and suicidality require increasing our understanding and familiarity with assessment tools that facilitate detection and inform appropriate intervention. The need for adequate assessment and intervention for depression and suicidality is particularly relevant for racial and ethnic minority populations in the USA given the existing mental health disparities (US Department of Health and Human Services, 2001).

The lifetime prevalence of depression among Asians and Asian-Americans varies (Kalibatseva & Leong, 2011). For example, the Chinese American Psychiatric Epidemiological Study (CAPES) indicated a 6.9 % lifetime prevalence rate of major depressive disorder among Chinese Americans (Takeuchi et al., 1998). Similarly, 9.1 % of Asian-Americans in the National Latino and Asian-American Study (Takeuchi, Hong, Gile, & Alegría, 2007) endorsed any affective disorder in comparison to 17.9 % of non-Latino Whites, 13.5 % of Hispanics, and 10.8 % of non-Hispanic Blacks in the National Comorbidity Study-Replication (NCS-R; Breslau et al., 2006). Although Asian-Americans reported significantly lower rates of depression than European Americans, their rates seem to be higher than their overseas Asian counterparts (Chang, 2002).

While depression is found cross culturally, the symptoms of major depression in the DSM-V (American Psychiatric Association, 2013) may not consistently and accurately capture experiences of depression across different racial/ethnic groups in the US (Kalibatseva & Leong, 2011; Ryder & Chentsova-Dutton, 2012). An important cultural consideration in the assessment of depression among Asian-Americans is the tendency to report somatic symptoms, whereas European Americans are more attuned to affective symptoms (Ryder et al., 2008). Additionally, symptoms may be presented differently as factor analytic studies have demonstrated support for fewer factors than the original solutions among ethnic minorities (e.g., Kim, DeCoster, Huang, & Chiriboga, 2011; Kuo, 1984).

Research on the assessment of depression among Asians and Asian-Americans primarily

Z. Kalibatseva, M.A. (✉)
Department of Psychology, Michigan State University, 316 Physics Road, Rm 127B, East Lansing, MI 48824, USA
e-mail: kalibats@msu.edu

I.H.C. Wu, M.A.
Department of Psychology, Michigan State University, 316 Physics Road, East Lansing, MI 48824, USA
e-mail: wuivan@msu.edu

F.T.L. Leong, Ph.D.
Department of Psychology, Michigan State University, 316 Physics Raod, Rm 136, East Lansing, MI 48824, USA
e-mail: fleong@msu.edu

L.T. Benuto et al. (eds.), *Guide to Psychological Assessment with Asians*,
DOI 10.1007/978-1-4939-0796-0_12, © Springer Science+Business Media New York 2014

uses self-report measures and structured or semi-structured clinical interviews (Kalibatseva & Leong, 2011). Leong, Okazaki, and Tak (2003) provided a detailed review of the literature examining self-report measures of depression in East Asia. While the authors found evidence for adequate psychometric properties of the translated Western depression questionnaires, they also questioned the practice of applying current Western ethnocentric conceptualizations of depression on other racial and ethnic groups as it may result in omissions of culture-specific expression of distress (Kalibatseva & Leong, 2011).

The goal of this chapter is to identify and review the most frequently used assessment measures of depression and suicidality among Asian-Americans. When research with Asian-Americans was not available, we reviewed research with Asian samples, which may be particularly relevant for first generation Asian-Americans. Along with providing information about the reliability, validity, and utility of each measure, we discuss their strengths and weaknesses and provide norms and cut-off scores when available. The measures that we identified based on a thorough review of the depression and suicide research literature with Asian-Americans include the Center for Epidemiological Studies—Depression, Beck Depression Inventory, Geriatric Depression Scale, Hamilton Rating Scale of Depression, Patient Health Questionnaire-9, and Zung Self-Rating Depression Scale (Table 12.1).

Assessment of Depression

Center for Epidemiological Studies: Depression

The Center for Epidemiological Studies—Depression scale (CES-D; Radloff, 1977) is one of the most widely used depression questionnaires in the US. It measures the frequency of 20 symptoms of depression over the past week using a four-point Likert scale from 0 (*rarely or none of the time*) to 3 (*most or all of the time*). The questionnaire was designed to measure depressive symptoms in the general population and validated with three White/European American samples (Radloff, 1977). Four factors emerged in these analyses, interpreted as depressed affect, positive affect, somatic symptoms, and interpersonal problems. An evaluation of the sensitivity and specificity of the CES-D suggested a cutoff of 16 to identify individuals at risk for clinical depression, although several authors recommended more stringent score cutoffs above 20 (McDowell, 2006). However, the majority of these studies recruited primarily White/European American samples and these cutoffs may differ across racial and ethnic groups.

The CES-D has been included in multiple studies with Asian and Asian-American samples although its reliability, validity, and diagnostic utility are still under research scrutiny with different Asian ethnic subgroups. One of the first studies to examine the prevalence of depression among Asian-Americans used the CES-D (Kuo, 1984). In a mixed sample of 484 Asian-Americans, the combined CES-D mean score ($M=9.38$, $SD=8.07$) was slightly higher than the mean of previously examined White/European samples (M ranges between 7.96 and 9.25). A principal component factor analysis revealed between two and three factors for each of the Asian subgroups, which differed from the four-factor solution Radloff (1977) proposed. Next, we review the CES-D research with Chinese, Japanese, Korean, and Southeast Asian-Americans to examine its validity, reliability, utility, strengths, and limitations.

Research with Chinese Samples

Ying (1988) administered the CES-D to a San Francisco community sample of 360 Chinese Americans over the phone. The measure was translated into Mandarin and Cantonese Chinese and administered in the language preferred by each participant. The mean CES-D score was 11.55 ($SD=8.23$), which was significantly higher than the Chinese American sample mean ($M=6.93$) in Kuo (1984) and the White/European sample means ($M=7.53$–8.58) in Radloff (1977). Ying (1988) found moderate reliability with an alpha coefficient of 0.77. Roughly one-fifth of the sample in Ying's study (24.2 %) and Kuo's study (19.1 %) scored above the suggested cutoff of 16.

Table 12.1 At-a-glance summary table

Assessment name	Condition assessed	Recommendation(s) and relevant research findings	Research conducted with:	Available in:
Beck Depression Inventory	Depression	Adequate psychometric properties	Chinese immigrants, inpatients, outpatients, and students, Asian-American college students, Asian Indian immigrants, Filipino community workers, Hmong refugees and outpatients, Japanese students, South Indian outpatients, and Thai community members	Chinese, Hmong, Korean, Japanese, Thai
Beck Depression Inventory II	Depression	Standardized Chinese version is available Adequate psychometric properties	Asian-American college students, Hong Kong students, Japanese patients and community members, Taiwanese students, and Thai police officers	Taiwanese, Chinese, Japanese, Thai
Center for Epidemiologic Studies—Depression	Depression	Mixed support for four-factor structure Bias of positive items Measurement equivalence studies are needed to assess the functional, conceptual, and metric equivalence of CES-D with various Asian groups	Chinese, Japanese, Korean, Filipino American, Vietnamese, Thai	Mandarin, Cantonese, Japanese, Korean, Vietnamese, Thai
College Student Reasons for Living Inventory	Suicidality		Asian-American college students	
Geriatric Depression Scale	Depression	Varying cut-off scores Use with caution in clinical settings Adequate psychometric properties	Chinese inpatients and outpatients, Singaporean outpatients, Japanese, Japanese Americans, and Koreans	Chinese, Japanese, Korean
Geriatric Suicide Ideation Scale	Suicidality	Adequate psychometric properties	Hong Kong Chinese	Chinese (Hong Kong)
Hamilton Rating Scale of Depression	Depression	Consistent five-factor structure Use with caution in clinical settings	Chinese outpatients and inpatients, and Japanese patients	Chinese, Japanese
Suicide Intent Scale	Suicidality	Adequate psychometric properties	Taiwanese	Chinese
Adult Suicide Ideation Questionnaire	Suicidality	Adequate psychometric properties, low positive predictive value (5.2 %)	Hong Kong Chinese adults	Chinese (Hong Kong)
Patient Health Questionnaire 9	Depression	High utility and adequate psychometric properties Questionable diagnostic ability	Chinese patients, Chinese American adults, Japanese outpatients, and Korean patients	Chinese, Japanese, Korean
Zung Self-Rating Depression Scale	Depression	Use with caution in clinical settings Adequate internal consistency and reliability Questionable factor structure	Chinese university students, Chinese elderly, and Japanese	Chinese, Japanese

Similar to Kuo's factor analysis, Ying did not replicate the four factors from Radloff's study. Instead, the Chinese Americans in both Kuo's and Ying's studies reported depressive symptoms that clustered in three factors: (1) depressed and somatic; (2) positive affect; and (3) interpersonal. This factor structure suggests that the Chinese Americans in both studies did not report somatic and affective symptoms separately.

The clustering of somatic and affective symptoms also occurred in a sample of Chinese American adolescents (Russell, Crocket, Shen, & Lee, 2008). This study examined cross-ethnic measurement invariance of the CES-D among Chinese, Filipino, and European American adolescents from the National Longitudinal Study of Adolescent Health (AddHealth). The results indicated that the four-factor solution did not fit well for the Chinese American sample. The alternative three-factor solution with 13 items offered in Ying (1988) provided a better fit of the data. Russell and colleagues (2008) concluded that Chinese American adolescents may experience distinct clusters of depressive symptoms than Filipino and European American youth. The findings suggest that the lack of differentiation between bodily and psychological depressive symptoms extends from first generation foreign-born Chinese Americans (Ying, 1988) to US-born Chinese American adolescents (Russell et al., 2008).

Li and Hicks (2010) examined the psychometric properties of the CES-D related to diagnostic validity, construct validity, internal reliability, and response bias in a probability sample of 167 Chinese American women. The CES-D revealed adequate reliability (Cronbach's $\alpha=0.86$) and 26 % of the sample had scores of 16 or above. The instrument revealed adequate construct validity as women with higher CES-D scores reported less social support, worse self-perceived general health, and more stressful life events. Moreover, women who met criteria for a current major depression diagnosis in an interview had higher CES-D scores than women who did not have a diagnosis (26.7 vs. 10.4, $p<0.001$). The study found that the CES-D cutoff of 16 or 17 ensured 100 % sensitivity (95 % CI: 44–100 %) and 76 % specificity. However, the positive predictive value (PPV) was low (3 % for a cutoff of 16), which suggests that CES-D score above the cutoff is unreliable in confirming a diagnosis of major depression. Additionally, Li and Hicks alerted to potential response bias, such that less acculturated Chinese American women were less likely to endorse positively worded CES-D items, which artificially increased their total CES-D scores compared to more acculturated Chinese American women.

In conclusion, the CES-D demonstrated low construct validity by mixed support for its factor structure, association between low acculturation and poor validity, and cultural response bias for positive items (Kuo, 1984; Russell et al., 2008; Wong et al., 2012; Ying, 1988). While the CES-D may be a useful screening tool for nondepressed Chinese Americans, it should be followed by a diagnostic interview to identify individuals with clinical depression. The potential lack for measurement equivalence of the CES-D suggests that clinicians need to apply increased caution when administering it to Chinese Americans.

Research with Japanese Samples

Several cross-cultural studies utilized the CES-D with Japanese Americans (e.g., Kanazawa, White, & Hampson, 2007) and Japanese university students, adult workers, and adolescents (Iwata & Buka, 2002; Iwata, Roberts, & Kawakami, 1995; Iwata, Saito, & Roberts, 1994). Across all studies, Japanese and Japanese American participants had lower scores on positively worded CES-D items than European Americans. Additionally, one study found that Japanese American college students in Hawaii reported more interpersonal problems than Chinese and European American college students (Marsella, Kinzie, & Gordon, 1973). There is scarcity of studies that examine the factor structure of the CES-D with both Japanese and Japanese American samples.

Whereas we did not locate a validation study of the CES-D with Japanese Americans, the questionnaire was translated into Japanese and validated in Japan and revealed adequate clinical validity (Shima et al., 1985 as cited in Iwata et al., 1994). Additionally, the CES-D demonstrated adequate reliability (Cronbach's α ranging from 0.76 to 0.81; Iwata et al., 1995) among Japanese samples. Kanazawa et al. (2007) also found adequate internal consistency (Cronbach's $\alpha=0.89$) for their Japanese American sample but it is important to note that these authors tested a 29-item measure as they added four items to the depressed affect factor and five items to the interpersonal problems factor. One study with Japanese workers in Japan established that 15.2 % of men and 10.6 % of women scored above 16 (Iwata, Okuyama, Kawakami, & Saito, 1989). These participants were more likely to be above age 50, never married/divorced, living alone, with bad conjugal and parental relationships, and high levels of perceived stress. We did not locate any studies that established reliable CES-D cutoffs with Japanese Americans.

Research with Korean Samples

The CES-D has been used consistently with Korean immigrants in North America. A Korean version of the CES-D was translated and validated by Noh, Avison, and Kasper (1992) with Korean immigrants in Canada. The version demonstrated content, construct, and concurrent validity and the factor structure resembled those found among American samples (Noh, Kasper, & Chen, 1998). However, several studies have suggested that Korean Americans may answer the positive items on the CES-D in a biased manner (Jang, Kim, & Chiriboga, 2005; Jang, Kwag, & Chiriboga, 2010; Oh, Koeske, & Sales, 2002). In particular, Koreans and Korean Americans were less likely to endorse the positive items, which resulted in higher overall depression scores. Since this cultural response bias has been consistently reported, some researchers have recommended calculating the total CES-D scores by excluding the positive items (Noh et al., 1998).

The reliability of the 20-item CES-D Korean version was high (Cronbach's $\alpha=0.89$) and it slightly improved in a 16-item CES-D version without the positive items ($\alpha=0.90$; Noh et al., 1998). When the positive items were reworded negatively, the reliability increased to 0.93. Additionally, the latter version demonstrated better construct validity as it correlated most highly with another depression questionnaire and a stressful life event inventory. Thus, the revised version with 20 negatively phrased items (CESD-K-R) revealed the best reliability and validity compared to the other two versions (Noh et al., 1998).

A few studies with Korean Americans pointed out the importance of assessing acculturation when assessing depression (Jang et al., 2005; Ji & Duan, 2006; Kim, Seo, & Cain, 2006). In particular, Korean Americans who were more acculturated to American mainstream culture had a higher likelihood of endorsing the positive CES-D items similarly to European Americans, which resulted in lower overall depression scores than less acculturated Korean Americans (Jang et al., 2005). However, when acculturation was examined as bi-dimensional construct, endorsement of Korean culture was not associated with biased responding (Kim et al., 2006). We did not find any studies that examined specific CES-D norms for Korean Americans but many studies reported higher overall scores of depression among Korean Americans compared to European Americans (e.g., Jang et al., 2005; Kim et al., 2006). As previously suggested, one possible explanation for these higher scores is the differential item functioning of the positive items. Therefore, removing those items or rewording them as negative items improves the reliability and validity of the CES-D with Korean Americans. This suggestion poses questions about the utility of the CES-D.

Research with Southeast Asians Samples

There is a dearth of studies that examined the CES-D with Southeast Asian-Americans (e.g., Vietnamese, Lao, Indonesian, Malaysian, Thai, and Cambodian). We had difficulty locating psychometric studies with specific South Asian or Southeast Asian groups in the USA. The only exception was a validation study of the CES-D with Filipino American adolescents in rural and small town Hawaii (Edman et al., 1999). The reliability for this sample was high (α = 0.89) but the factor analysis results suggested a potentially different conceptualization of depression. Fifteen of the 20 items loaded on one general factor that combined depressed affect, somatic symptoms, and interpersonal problems. The remaining four positive symptoms and the item "everything was an effort" loaded on a separate factor. Thus, although the CES-D demonstrated good reliability in this study, its factor structure with this sample of Filipino American adolescents differed from the four-factor solution.

Several studies conducted with populations from other countries included translated versions of the CES-D in Vietnam (Leggett, Zarit, Ngyuen, Hoang, & Nguyen, 2012) and Thailand (Trangkasombat & Nukhew, 1998 as cited in German et al., 2012). A cutoff of 22 was used with the Thai version to define significant level of depressive symptoms (German et al.). A cross-cultural study examined depressive symptoms using the CES-D in five Southeast Asian countries: Indonesia, North Korea, Myanmar, Sri Lanka, and Thailand (Mackinnon, McCallum, Andrews, & Anderson, 1998). There was evidence that one general depression factor fits the data better than the initially proposed four-factor solution for all samples, similar to the previously reported findings with other Asian-American samples.

Overall, the CES-D has consistently demonstrated adequate reliability and has been used successfully with community samples. Yet, researchers and clinicians need to be careful when using it with specific Asian-American populations because the proposed four-factor structure has not been replicated in a number of studies. Additionally, a substantial number of studies revealed that the positive items function differently and may need to be removed or reworded in a negative way.

Beck Depression Inventory

The Beck Depression Inventory (BDI) is a commonly used depression scale that consists of 21 symptoms and attitudes rated on intensity from 0 to 3 (Beck, Steer, & Carbin, 1988). Constructed based on a predominantly White/European American sample, the cut-off score for minimal depression is 9, mild to moderate depression is 18, moderate to severe depression is 29, and severe depression is >30 (Beck & Beamesderfer, 1974). In the past, the English version of the BDI has been administered to Asian samples such as South Indian women in India (Chandra, Satyanarayana, & Carey, 2009), Japanese American university students ($\alpha=0.84$; Abe, 2004), Filipino Americans ($\alpha=0.87$; Napholz & Mo, 2010), and mixed samples of Asian-Americans ($\alpha=0.86$; Norasakkunkit & Kalik, 2002). The use of the BDI has expanded into studies of Asians in various countries including USA, India, China, Taiwan, Japan, Korea, and Thailand as well as various types of samples including outpatient and inpatient samples, college students, adolescents, and immigrants.

Research with Chinese Samples

In our review, we identified few standardized Chinese versions of the BDI. According to Chan (1991), the BDI has been translated into Chinese by various researchers and clinicians. These various measures appear to demonstrate adequate validity and reliability. For example, Chinese versions of the BDI have been related to posttraumatic stress disorder among Chinese workers in America (de Bocanegra & Brickman, 2004; de Bocanegra, Moskalenko, & Chan, 2005), poor self-rated health among Chinese adolescents in China (Xu et al., 2011), loneliness among Chinese university students in Taiwan (Hsu, Hailey, & Range, 1987), and hopelessness among Chinese patients (Chiles et al., 1989).

One particular version has recently undergone significant psychometric scrutiny. While Zheng, Wei, Lianggue, Guochen, and Chenggue (1988) developed a version of the BDI that yielded acceptable reliability estimates (i.e., Cronbach's $\alpha = 0.85$) and concurrent validity (i.e., moderate correlation with the Chinese Hamilton Depression Rating Scale), closer examination of the factor structure revealed three of six factors that were uninterpretable and one particularly problematic item (i.e., Item 21: libido loss). Further examining the utility of this particular version of the BDI Yeung et al. (2002) administered the questionnaire to 503 outpatient Chinese Americans (age 18+). The investigators found that the measure's optimal sensitivity and specificity was at the cutoff score of 13 and the area under the Receiver Operating Characteristic (ROC) curve was 0.94

indicating high accuracy for screening depression in their sample. Later studies conducted among this research group continued to find adequate reliability of the measure (Yeung et al., 2004, 2005; Yeung, Chang, Gresham, Nierenberg, & Fava, 2004).

Other Chinese versions of the BDI also appear to demonstrate adequate reliability. Among a group of researchers studying Chinese immigrants in the USA, reliability estimates of one translation ranged from 0.87 to 0.93 (de Bocanegra et al., 2005; de Bocanegra & Brickman, 2004; de Bocanegra, Moskalenko, & Kramer, 2006). Yet another translation revealed an overall internal reliability estimate of 0.86 and a split-half reliability of 0.77 among 2,150 Chinese adolescents in Hong Kong (Shek, 1990).

There are limited directions in guiding the interpretation of the unstandardized Chinese versions of the BDI. In fact, different cut-off scores are used depending on the study. For instance, one study of 251 Chinese inpatients in China used the cut-off scores of 13, 24, and 25 to describe normal, mild-moderate, and moderate-severe depression, respectively (Yang, Zuo, Su, & Eaton, 1987). The study found that the cut-off score of 14 in their sample best discriminated between depressed and nondepressed patients. A later study of 331 students and psychiatric inpatients in Hong Kong found the cut-off scores of 10, 19, and 30 in their Chinese version of the BDI had adequate sensitivity and specificity for determining normal, mild-moderate, and moderate-severe categories of depression, respectively, while the cut-off scores of 9, 18, and 29 in the English version of the BDI had adequate sensitivity and specificity. In both versions of the BDI, they noted that the cut-off scores for mild-moderate and moderate-severe categories had higher sensitivity and specificity than the cut-off score for the normal category (Chan, 1991).

These studies show a number of strengths and limitations among Chinese versions of the BDI. A clear strength is the strong internal consistency throughout the studies. The findings suggest that Chinese versions of the BDI, although unstandardized, demonstrate adequate reliability in screening for depression among a wide range of samples. A notable strength of the reviewed studies is the large sample sizes. However, a number of limitations are worth noting. The lack of agreement in cut-off scores is problematic, as this limits the clinical utility of the measure. While Chan (1991) offered cut-off scores based on item analyses, further research is recommended to validate these cut-off scores. Another limitation is the lack of psychometric studies. For instance, our review did not yield any studies that conducted item response analyses or measurement equivalency for the Chinese versions of the BDI.

In summary, the studies reviewed demonstrate adequate reliability and validity for unstandardized Chinese versions of the BDI. With any unstandardized measure, however, we recommend clinicians to interpret results using Chinese versions of the BDI with caution. There lacks an agreed upon set of cut-off scores for categorizing severity, which limits the interpretability of Chinese versions of the BDI. In view of these limitations, Chinese versions of the BDI may serve as reliable supplementary assessments of depression.

Research with Hmong Samples

A Hmong version that has demonstrated adequate reliability and validity is available. The Hmong Adaptation of the Beck Depression Inventory (HABDI) made a number of changes to increase cultural sensitivity and simplicity (Mouanoutoua, Brown, Cappelletty, & Levine, 1991). The HABDI consists of 22 items rated on a three-point frequency scale rather than a severity scale found in the original BDI. An extra item was added due to translation difficulties for Item 2 (i.e., "I feel like the future is hopeless and cannot improve"). After administering the adapted version to 50 depressed and 73 nondepressed Hmong (18–66 years old) living in the US, the measure yielded a Cronbach's α of 0.93 and a 2-week test–retest reliability of 0.92. Results indicated that the depressed group scored significantly higher than the nondepressed group and a cut-off score of 46 was recommended. This cut-off score demonstrated adequate sensitivity and specificity, 94 % and 78 %, respectively.

A number of limitations are warranted in consideration of using the HABDI. First, items are rated on a frequency scale rather than a severity scale. While the BDI has traditionally been considered a severity scale for depression, the HABDI assesses the presence or absence of symptoms limiting the ability for clinicians to determine severity. Therefore, it is recommended that the HABDI be used to supplement decisions regarding presence or absence of depression and not for severity. Second, the second item of the BDI was transformed into two items due to difficulties in translation. For instance, "I feel like the future is hopeless and cannot improve" became "I feel like the future is hopeless" and "I feel like things cannot improve." Although seen as a solution to the double-barreled item, the item analyses indicated that many endorsed the pessimism item (i.e. "I feel like the future is hopeless").

In summary, the HABDI appears to be a clinically useful tool to discriminate between depressed and nondepressed patients. However, due to the lack of empirical studies that further examine the psychometric properties of the measure, it is difficult to ascertain the degree to which this measure is reliable across the Hmong population. Thus, clinicians and researchers should interpret the findings with caution.

Research with Korean Samples

A Korean version of the BDI that has demonstrated adequate reliability is available. The BDI-K was administered to 279 Korean university students (17–37 years old) and subjected to a Rasch rating scale modeling procedure to assess the psychometric properties of the instrument (Hong & Wong, 2005). In particular, principle component analyses did not indicate any higher order factor structures despite Items 19 (i.e., weight loss) and 21 (i.e., libido loss) demonstrating low correlations with the rest of the scale. The mean score for their sample was 11.56 compared to a mean of 25.18 found in a sample of clinically depressed Koreans (Shin, Kim, & Park, 1993, as cited in Hong & Wong, 2005). The investigators further noted that the somatic items yielded greater difficulty, potentially due to the lower levels of severity in their sample. In summary, the BDI-K appears to be a reliable measure of depression among Korean university students and clinically depressed samples.

Research with Japanese Samples

A Japanese version of the BDI was translated and found to have adequate reliability among a sample of 79 female Japanese university students (Arnault, Sakamoto, & Moriwaki, 2005). The investigators found that BDI scores ranged from 0 to 39 with a mean of 12.66. Further, their scale yielded a Cronbach's α of 0.79. In a later study of 50 Japanese university women, BDI scores were significantly related to somatic distress ($r=0.57$), which explained 31 % of the variance in depression scores (Arnault, Sakamoto, & Moriwaki, 2006). In both studies, the Japanese samples had higher mean scores than the American comparative sample. Although this version consistently demonstrated adequate reliability across the two studies, further studies that examine the psychometric properties of the measure are required.

Research with Thai Samples

A Thai version of the BDI was translated and administered to a sample of community participants ($n=3{,}133$) in Thailand (Thavichachart et al., 2009). In an effort to examine the prevalence rates of PTSD and depression, the investigators found that their version of the BDI yielded low reliability (split-half reliability = 0.74). Notably, they found that 14.3 % suffered from depression, 33.6 % from PTSD, and 11.3 % from both.

Beck Depression Inventory-II

The BDI-II (Beck, Steer, & Brown, 1996) is a revision of the earlier BDI. The BDI-II consists of 21-items that are rated based on four statements of increasing symptom severity. Distinct from the BDI, the BDI-II includes four new symptoms (i.e., agitation, worthlessness, concentration difficulty, and loss of energy) to better match the DSM-IV criteria, and a different set of cut-off scores. The cut-off scores for minimal depression is 0–13, mild depression is 14–19, moderate depression is 20–28, and severe depression is 29–63. The BDI-II is positively correlated with the Hamilton Depression Rating Scale ($r=0.71$), demonstrates high internal consistency ($\alpha=0.91$), and high 1-week test–retest reliability ($r=0.93$).

Research with Chinese Samples

Unlike the BDI, a standardized Chinese version of the BDI-II (BDI-II-C) was developed by the Chinese Behavioral Science Corporation in 2000. Previous studies find adequate internal consistency. For instance, two studies calculated Cronbach's α of 0.86 (Chang, 2005) and 0.94 (Lu, Che, Chang, & Shen, 2002) in samples of college students and outpatients, respectively. Supporting these findings, recent psychometric evaluations find that the BDI-II-C possesses strong reliability and construct validity.

Focused efforts to examine the psychometric properties support the use of the BDI-II-C in Asian samples. Using a Rasch model to examine the factorial structure of the BDI-II-C revealed two dimensions (i.e., somatic and cognitive-affective items) in a sample of 2,095 Taiwanese high school students (14–18 years old) (Wu & Chang, 2008). Similarly, a later study found that person heterogeneity did not impact the two-factor structure among a sample of 810 Taiwanese college students and found internal consistency coefficients ranging from 0.82 to 0.89 in their sample (Wu & Huang, 2010). These findings support the two-factor structure found in a sample of predominantly Caucasian university students (Storch, Roberti, & Roth, 2004). Further bolstering the psychometric properties of the BDI-II-C, a recent study of 2,922 Taiwanese adolescents (13–18.5 years old) found that overall raw scores of the two subscales were not influenced by differential item functioning across genders suggesting the use of total raw scores (Wu, 2010). Another study found that BDI-II-C items were invariant across Hong Kong and American adolescents (Byrne, Stewart, Kennard, & Lee, 2007). The investigators also found an internal consistency coefficient of 0.83 in their Hong Kong sample.

Research with Other Asian Samples

Translated into other languages, the BDI-II continued to demonstrate adequate reliability. For instance, in one study of 3,000 Thai police officers, the investigators found an internal consistency coefficient of 0.93 despite adding an extra item assessing eating habit (Chongruksa, Parinyapol, Sawatsri, & Pansomboon, 2012). A different study translating the BDI-II into Japanese found strong internal consistency ($\alpha=0.87$) and concurrent validity ($r=0.69$ with the CES-D) among Japanese outpatients (Kojima et al., 2002). A principal component analysis also revealed a two-factor structure (i.e., somatic and cognitive-affective items) similar to previous studies in other samples and appropriate use of cut-off scores provided by Beck et al. (1996). In a later study using the same translation as Kojima et al. (2002) among a sample of outpatients, the BDI-II correlated strongly with the DSM-IV depression severity index ($r=0.77$) (Hiroe et al., 2005). The investigators recommended that a change in 5 points be considered minimal, 10–19 points be considered moderate, and >20 points be considered large clinically significant changes. Similar to the previous study, the cut-off scores provided by Beck et al. (1996) were found to be appropriate in their sample.

In summary, the reviewed studies suggest strong psychometric properties of translated versions of the BDI-II among Taiwanese, Chinese, Japanese, and Thai samples. This is consistent with one study that found adequate reliability of an English version of the BDI-II among a sample of Asian-American college students ($\alpha>0.89$) (Hambrick et al., 2010). Despite these findings, clinicians and researchers should interpret the measure with caution. Wu and Chang (2008) discovered two items that provided inadequate fit to the overall measure (i.e., Item 10—crying and Item 21—libido loss).

Geriatric Depression Scale

The Geriatric Depression Scale (GDS) is a 30-item self-report or orally administered measure that assesses behavioral and affective symptoms of depression rated on a yes/no scale. Increasing ease of administration, shorter versions of the GDS have been developed including a 15-, 12-, 10-, 5-, 4-, and 1-item version (Straus, Sherman, & Spreen, 2006). The GDS has been translated into numerous languages although its validity is questioned due to potential cultural differences in expression of depression (Jang, Small, & Haley, 2001).

Research with Chinese Samples

Existing validation studies with Chinese populations find acceptable internal reliability and validity. An early study found that the Chinese 30-item version significantly correlated with the original ($r=0.94$) and modified ($r=0.91$) 15-item version of the GDS (Liu, Lu, Yu, & Yang, 1998). The investigators also found adequate internal consistency for the original ($\alpha=0.77$) and modified form ($\alpha=0.81$). Similarly, among a sample of 461 psychiatric outpatients in Hong Kong, the Chinese version of 30-item version demonstrated adequate internal consistency ($\alpha=0.89$) and 2-week test–retest reliability ($r=0.89$) (Chan, 1996). The measure significantly correlated with the CES-D ($r=0.96$) as well as DSM-III-R diagnosis of Major Depressive Disorder ($r=0.95$).

Closer examination of the GDS, however, reveals varying cut-off scores. A study of Singaporean psychiatric outpatients suffering from dementia recommended the cut-off score of 9/10 for patients with mild dementia (sensitivity = 66.7 %, specificity = 95.0 %), and 11/12 for patients with severe dementia (sensitivity = 40 %, specificity = 100 %) (Lam et al., 2004). Another study suggested the cut-off score of 4 or above (sensitivity = 84 %, specificity = 85.7 %) among a community sample in Singapore (Lim et al., 2000). Yet, another study found that the cut-off score of 7/8 yielded high sensitivity (96 %) and specificity (88 %) among a community sample of depressed inpatients and outpatients (60–87 years old) in Hong Kong (Lee, Chiu, Kowk, & Leung, 1993). The varying cut-off scores are likely due to a severity effect or differences in samples. Therefore, clinicians and researchers using short form Chinese versions of the GDS are recommended to interpret cut-off scores with caution. Further, clinicians and researchers should also be wary of using the full form as a diagnostic tool (Chan, 1996).

Research with Japanese Samples

We identified one translation commonly used in the literature developed by Niino, Imaizumi, and Kawakami (1991). A recent study in Japan orally interviewed 111 elderly Japanese using the Niino et al. translation and recommended the cut-off score of 6 based on high sensitivity (97 %) and specificity (96 %), and notable false positive (89 %) and false negative (0 %) rates (Schreiner, Hayakawa, Morimoto, & Kakuma, 2003). Supporting these findings, a different study with a community sample elderly Japanese Americans found that the cut-off score of 5 identified 20.6 % of their sample as suffering from moderate to severe depression (Mui & Shibusawa, 2003). The investigators also found a Cronbach's α of 0.86 and a split-half reliability coefficient of 0.78. The findings support the use of this measure among Japanese samples to screen for depression.

Research with Korean Samples

An early translation of the GDS short form was conducted by Jang et al. (2001) among a community sample of elderly Koreans living in metropolitan areas of Korea. The internal consistency was 0.85 and split-half reliability was 0.77. The factor structure of the Korean version of the GDS revealed the following three dimensions: (1) internal perceptions, (2) external aspects, (3) staying at home and problems with memory. While this version seemed to be reasonably useful, a later translation revealed stronger psychometric properties.

A Korean translation of the GDS developed by Bae and Cho (2004) is available and demonstrates strong psychometric properties. In this study, the full (GDS-K) and short form (SGDS-K) of the GDS was translated into Korean and administered to 154 elderly psychiatric patients in Korea. Findings of the study revealed strong correlations between the GDS-K, the SGDS-K, the Hamilton Rating Scale for Depression, and the CES-D. Further analyses indicated adequate internal reliability for the GDS-K ($\alpha=0.91$) and the SGDS-K ($\alpha=0.86$). Principal component analyses revealed the following three dimensions in the SGDS-K: (1) negative judgment about the past, present, and future, (2) lowered affect, and (3) cognitive inefficiency and lack of motivation. Overall, the researchers recommended the cut-off score of 18 for the GDS-K (sensitivity = 84 %, specificity = 82 %) and 10 for the SGDS-K (sensitivity = 86 %, specificity = 86 %).

Hamilton Rating Scale of Depression

The Hamilton Rating Scale of Depression (HRSD) is a 17-item scale that taps into various problems and symptoms of depression rated on a three- or five-point scale (Hamilton, 1960). Despite the commonly used cut-off score of 7 in clinical trials, few studies empirically examine the sensitivity and specificity of this criterion. Zimmerman, Posternak, and Chelminski (2005) found high sensitivity (97.0 %) and acceptable specificity (90.5 %) using the broad definition of DSM-IV remission in a sample of 303 psychiatric outpatients. Our review yielded few studies that sought to examine the psychometric properties of the HRSD in Asian populations.

Research with Chinese Samples

An early translation of the HRSD was conducted by Zheng, Zhao, et al. (1988) that demonstrated low reliability ($\alpha=0.71$) among a sample of outpatient and inpatients adults. Further, the scale moderately correlated with the Global Assessment Scale (GAS) ($r=-0.49$). Principal component analyses revealed the following five factors: (1) anxiety, somatization, weight-loss, (2) agitation, insight, (3) depressed mood, suicide, genital-symptoms, (4) guilt, psychomotor-retardation, and (5) sleep disturbance. A later study found that the cut-off score of 12/13 provided adequate sensitivity (88 %) and specificity (86 %) (Leung, Wing, Kwong, & Shum, 1999).

Research with Japanese Samples

A recent study conducted a cross-cultural equivalence study on the HRSD among a sample of Japanese, North American, and European patients (>18 years old) (Furukawa et al., 2005). Results indicated a somewhat consistent factor structure across the three samples. In particular, the following five factors were revealed: (1) anhedonia/retardation, (2) guilt/agitation, (3) bodily symptoms, (4) insomnia, and (5) appetite. The findings suggest an underlying factor structure across the three samples suggesting potential in cross-cultural comparisons using the HRSD.

Patient Health Questionnaire

The Patient Health Questionnaire-9 (PHQ-9) is a 9-item self-report questionnaire based on nine symptoms of depression in the DSM-IV. Each item is rated on a four-point scale indicating frequency of each symptom in the past 2 weeks. Scores ranging between 10 and 14 suggest moderate levels of depression, 15–19 suggest moderate to severe level of depression, and scores above 20 suggest severe depression (Kroenke, Spitzer, & Williams, 2001). Studies suggest that the PHQ-9 serves as an easy and short assessment for depression among Asian populations.

Research with Chinese Samples

Past studies indicate that the Chinese version of the PHQ-9 demonstrates strong psychometric properties. For instance, one study of 364 elderly Chinese patients (>60 years old) revealed high internal reliability ($\alpha=0.91$) and strong utility (7.5 min administration) (Chen et al., 2010). Further analyses indicated that the optimal cut-off of 8/9 yielded adequate sensitivity (86 %) specificity (85 %). Similarly, another study of 3,417 Chinese American adults (18–87 years old) found that 4.1 % of their sample suffered from significant depression using the cut-off score of 9/10 (Chen, Huang, Chang, & Chung, 2006). Using a higher cut-off score, a different study of 1,940 Chinese American adults (>18 years old) found high internal consistency ($\alpha=0.91$) and the cut-off score of 15 yielded moderate sensitivity (81 %) and high specificity (98 %) (Yeung et al., 2008). The authors indicated that the high cut-off score was chosen to screen for depression severity requiring psychological intervention.

Research with Japanese Samples

A study using a Japanese version of the PH-9 with a sample of 153 psychiatric outpatients identified the cut-off of 13/14 as demonstrating high sensitivity (86 %) and low specificity (67 %) for screening current major depressive episodes (Inoue et al., 2012). Further, total scores were moderately correlated with the HDRS ($r=0.55$) and the GAF ($r=-0.59$). In sum, the investigators supported the use of the PHQ-9 for screening, but argued against the use of the scale for diagnostic purposes in their sample.

Research with Korean Samples

A Korean version of the PHQ-9 was developed by Han et al. (2008) with a sample of 1,060 elderly Korean patients (>60 years old). The investigators found that their measure demonstrated adequate internal consistency ($\alpha=0.86$) and low 3 week test–retest reliability ($r=0.79$). Further analyses indicated that the cut-off score of 4/5 yielded adequate sensitivity (80 %) and specificity (78 %) for depressive disorders. Their translation of the measure also was significantly correlated with the GDS ($r=0.74$) and the CES-D ($r=0.66$). Overall, although the Korean version of the PHQ-9 demonstrated strong criterion validity, its ability as a diagnostic tool for depression is questionable.

Zung Self-Rating Depression Scale

The Zung Self-Rating Depression Scale (SDS) is a 20-item measure that taps into characteristics of depression (Zung, Richards, & Short, 1965). Items are rated on a four-point scale based on the extent to which each item applies to the person at the time of the test. Half of the items are symptomatically positive and the other half are symptomatically negative. While the SDS has been predominantly used in White/European American samples, translations in Japanese and Chinese exist.

Research with Chinese Samples

An early study by Lee (1990) sought to examine the psychometric properties of a Chinese version of the SDS in a sample of 265 undergraduate students in Hong Kong (17–26 years old). The scale demonstrated adequate internal reliability ($\alpha=0.80$) and criterion validity evidenced by moderate correlations with the BDI ($r=0.63$), General Health Questionnaire ($r=0.58$), and the Chinese Minnesota Multiphasic Personality Inventory D-scale ($r=0.59$). Interestingly, further analyses suggested that the scale is difficult to "fake good," yet relatively easy to "fake bad." To this end, the investigators cautioned the use of the SDS in clinical settings.

A later study examining the psychometric properties of the SDS among a sample of elderly Chinese in Hong Kong also found adequate reliability (Lee et al., 1994). In this sample, the SDS demonstrated strong internal consistency ($\alpha=0.91$) and split-half reliability ($r=0.89$). Furthermore, the SDS was strongly related to the GDS ($r=0.88$) and the Chinese HDRS ($r=0.86$). Overall, the cut-off score of 42/43 yielded the highest sensitivity (92.3 %) and specificity (87.5 %).

Research with Japanese Samples

A recent study of 7,136 residents in Japan (20–79 years old) were administered a Japanese version of the SDS (Chida, Okayama, Nishi, & Sakai, 2004). The investigators used the following cut-off scores: 20–39 indicated no or insignificant symptomology, 40–47 indicated mild depression, 48–55 indicated moderate depression, and >56 indicated severe depression. Results showed that 13.7 % of the sample scored within the moderate to severe range with more females (16.3 %) than males (10.6 %) in this range. Factor analyses revealed a two factor structure that only retained 12 of the 20 items in the overall sample. The researchers recommended against the use of this scale among depressed individuals reporting mainly somatic symptoms as many of these items were dropped from the factor analysis. To this end, other rating scales of depression are recommended among Japanese individuals.

Assessment of Suicidality

Suicide was the eighth leading cause of death among Asian-Americans in 2007 and the second leading cause of death for Asian-Americans in the 15–34 age group (Heron, 2011). Asian-American adults reported a lifetime prevalence of suicide ideation of 8.6 % and suicide attempts of 2.5 % (Duldulao, Takeuchi, & Hong, 2009). Choi, Rogers, and Werth (2009) provided a thorough review of issues that may arise during the suicide risk assessment process when working with Asian-American college students. The authors recommended paying attention to issues such as self-disclosure, acculturation, intergenerational conflict, collectivistic values, the model minority myth, and perfectionism when conducting a risk assessment with Asian-American clients (Choi et al., 2009).

We found only few studies with Asian-Americans that examined the psychometric properties of suicide measures. The validity of the College Student Reasons for Living Inventory was examined with Asian-American college students (Choi & Rogers, 2010). Five of the original six factors were replicated and the reliability for each scale varied from moderate to high. The scale still explained 8 % of the variance in suicidal behavior after depression and hopelessness were already accounted for. Thus, the CSRLI seems to be a valid and reliable measure of assessing suicide risk among Asian-American college students (Choi & Rogers, 2010).

Several other measures were translated and validated with Chinese samples. The Geriatric Suicide Ideation Scale-Chinese (GSIS-C; Chou, Jun, & Chi, 2005) demonstrated adequate psychometric properties with Hong Kong older adults. Similarly, the Suicide Intent Scale had acceptable psychometric properties in a large community sample of Taiwanese respondents who committed deliberate self-harm (Gau, Chen, Lee, Chang, & Cheng, 2009). The Chinese version of the Adult Suicide Ideation Questionnaire measures the severity of suicidal ideation and also displayed appropriate psychometric properties with Hong Kong adults (Fu, Liu, & Yip, 2007). The questionnaire correctly classified 25 out of 33 people with suicidality (75 %) but had a low positive predictive value (5.2 %; cutoff score = 1). The few studies that we examined reveal that a large amount of the research in this area has been conducted in the last decade and there is a need to accumulate a body of research before determining the strengths and weaknesses of specific suicidality measures.

Conclusions and Recommendations

This chapter reviewed the most commonly used assessment measures of depression and suicidality in Asian-Americans. Based on the reviewed studies, we provide a summary of our findings and suggest that future research needs to evaluate instruments' internal and external validity (Leong, 1997).

Our review is consistent with Leong et al.'s (2003) observation that a select few measures dominate the area of depression. Specifically, the BDI and the CES-D continue to receive significant psychometric scrutiny. While this increases our psychometric understanding of these measures, less attention is directed to other promising measures.

Moreover, in order to compare depression and suicidality across groups, it is necessary to demonstrate "an underlying *universal* or by searching for *equivalences*" (Berry, 1980, p. 8, italics in the original). Despite recommendations for specific procedures in the translating and adaptation of tests (International Test Commission, 2010), few studies demonstrated the measurement equivalence of each instrument. The internal validity or measurement equivalence requires that the words' meanings in another language are preserved (linguistic equivalence), the construct serve the same function across groups (functional equivalence), the conceptual frame is preserved (conceptual equivalence), and the measure's psychometric properties are transportable and generalizable to other groups (metric equivalence; Leong, Kalibatseva, & Park, 2013).

Recent research also indicated the emphasis on identifying cut-off scores and establishing the sensitivity and specificity of the used instruments. Cut-off scores and sensitivity/specificity information are especially helpful for clinicians using self-report questionnaires as supplementary diagnostic tools. Thus, instruments with adequate external validity will be able to detect correctly individuals with below clinical (i.e., specificity) and clinical levels of depression and suicidality (i.e., sensitivity). Studies, however, have largely depended on small sample sizes or convenience samples to examine cut-off scores. Although criteria may be established for specific groups, researchers and clinicians need to use cut-off scores with caution and supplement their diagnostic decisions with data from other sources.

The increase in attention towards understanding the psychometric properties of existing measures is encouraging. This signals greater interest in validating existing measures. Yet, we noticed that it was a small pool of researchers who were conducting these validity studies. Therefore, future recommendations include establishing the measurement equivalence and specificity/sensitivity for various depression measures other than the CES-D and BDI, building on current findings and encouraging collaborations across research teams.

References

Abe, J. A. A. (2004). Self-esteem, perception of relationships, and emotional distress: A cross-cultural study. *Personal Relationships, 11*(2), 231–247.

American Psychiatric Association. (2013). *Diagnostic and statistical manual of mental disorders* (4th ed.). Washington, DC: Author.

Arnault, D. S., Sakamoto, S., & Moriwaki, A. (2005). The association between negative self-descriptions and depressive symptomatology: Does culture make a difference? *Archives of Psychiatric Nursing, 19*(2), 93–100.

Arnault, D. S., Sakamoto, S., & Moriwaki, A. (2006). Somatic and depressive symptoms in female Japanese and American students: A preliminary investigation. *Transcultural Psychiatry, 43*(2), 275–286.

Bae, J. N., & Cho, M. J. (2004). Development of the Korean version of the Geriatric Depression Scale and its short form among elderly psychiatric patients. *Journal of Psychosomatic Research, 57*(3), 297.

Beck, A., & Beamesderfer, A. (1974). Assessment of depression: The depression inventory. In P. Pichot (Ed.), *Psychological measurements in psychopharmacology: Modern problems in pharmacopsychiatry* (Vol. 7, pp. 151–169). Oxford: Karger.

Beck, A. T., Steer, R. A., & Brown, G. K. (1996). *Manual for the Beck Depression Inventory-II*. San Antonio, TX: Psychological Corporation.

Beck, A. T., Steer, R. A., & Carbin, M. G. (1988). Psychometric properties of the Beck Depression Inventory: Twenty-five years of evaluation. *Clinical Psychology Review, 8*(1), 77–100.

Berry, J. W. (1980). Introduction to methodology. In H. Triandis & J. Berry (Eds.), *Handbook of cross-cultural psychology* (Methodology, Vol. 2, pp. 1–28). Boston, MA: Allyn and Bacon.

Breslau, J., Aguilar-Gaxiola, S., Kendler, K. S., Su, M., Williams, D., & Kessler, R. C. (2006). Specifying race-ethnic differences in risk for psychiatric disorders in a USA national sample. *Psychological Medicine: A Journal of Research in Psychiatry and the Allied Sciences, 36*, 57–68.

Byrne, B. M., Stewart, S. M., Kennard, B. D., & Lee, P. W. H. (2007). The Beck Depression Inventory-II: Testing for measurement equivalence and factor mean differences across Hong Kong and American adolescents. *International Journal of Testing, 7*(3), 293–309.

Chan, D. W. (1991). The Beck Depression Inventory: What difference does the Chinese version make? *Psychological Assessment: A Journal of Consulting and Clinical Psychology, 3*(4), 616.

Chan, A. C. (1996). Clinical validation of the Geriatric depression scale (GDS). *Journal of Aging and Health, 8*(2), 238–253.

Chandra, P. S., Satyanarayana, V. A., & Carey, M. P. (2009). Women reporting intimate partner violence in India: Associations with PTSD and depressive symptoms. *Archives of Women's Mental Health, 12*(4), 203–209.

Chang, D. F. (2002). Understanding the rates and distribution of mental disorders. In K. S. Kurasaki, S. Okazaki, & S. Sue (Eds.), *Asian American mental health: Assessment theories and methods* (pp. 9–27). New York, NY: Kluwer Academic/Plenum Publishers.

Chang, H. (2005). Dimensions of the Chinese Beck Depression Inventory-II in a university sample. *Individual Differences Research, 3*(3), 193–199.

Chen, S., Chiu, H., Xu, B., Ma, Y., Jin, T., Wu, M., & Conwell, Y. (2010). Reliability and validity of the PHQ-9 for screening late-life depression in Chinese primary care. *International Journal of Geriatric Psychiatry, 25*(11), 1127–1133.

Chen, T. M., Huang, F. Y., Chang, C., & Chung, H. (2006). Using the PHQ-9 for depression screening and treatment monitoring for Chinese Americans in primary care. *Psychiatric Services, 57*(7), 976–981.

Chida, F., Okayama, A., Nishi, N., & Sakai, A. (2004). Factor analysis of Zung Scale scores in a Japanese general population. *Psychiatry and Clinical Neurosciences, 58*(4), 420–426.

Chiles, J. A., Strosahl, K. D., Ping, Z. Y., Michael, M. C., Hall, K., Jemelka, R., … Reto, C. (1989). Depression, hopelessness, and suicidal behavior in Chinese and American psychiatric patients. *American Journal of Psychiatry, 146*(3), 339–344.

Chinese Behavioral Sciences Society (ed.). (2000). *The Chinese version of the Beck Depression Inventory* (2nd ed., Licensed Chinese translation, The Psychological Corporation). Hacourt Brace: New York; 2000.

Choi, J. L., & Rogers, J. R. (2010). Exploring the validity of the College Student Reasons for Living Inventory among Asian American college students. *Archives of Suicide Research, 14*, 222–235.

Choi, J. L., Rogers, J. R., & Werth, J. L. (2009). Suicide risk assessment with Asian American college students: A culturally informed perspective. *The Counseling Psychologist, 37*, 186–218.

Chongruksa, D., Parinyapol, P., Sawatsri, S., & Pansomboon, C. (2012). "Efficacy of eclectic group counseling in addressing stress among Thai police officers in terrorist situations": Corrigendum. *Counselling Psychology Quarterly, 25*(3), 343.

Chou, K.-L., Jun, L. W., & Chi, I. (2005). Assessing Chinese older adults' suicidal ideation: Chinese version of the Geriatric Suicide Ideation Scale. *Aging & Mental Health, 9*, 167–171.

de Bocanegra, H. T., & Brickman, E. (2004). Mental health impact of the World Trade Center attacks on displaced Chinese workers. *Journal of Traumatic Stress, 17*(1), 55–62.

de Bocanegra, H. T., Moskalenko, S., & Chan, P. (2005). PTSD and depression among displaced Chinese workers after the world trade center attack: A follow-up study. *Journal of Urban Health: Bulletin of the New York Academy of Medicine, 82*(3), 364–369.

de Bocanegra, H. T., Moskalenko, S., & Kramer, E. J. (2006). PTSD, depression, prescription drug use, and health care utilization of Chinese workers affected by the WTC attacks. *Journal of Immigrant and Minority Health, 8*(3), 203–210.

Duldulao, A. A., Takeuchi, D. T., & Hong, S. (2009). Correlates of suicidal behaviors among Asian Americans. *Archives of Suicide Research, 13*, 277–290.

Edman, J. L., Danko, G. P., Andrade, N., McArdle, J. J., Foster, J., & Glipa, J. (1999). Factor structure of the CES-D (Center for Epidemiologic Studies Depression Scale) among Filipino-American adolescents. *Social Psychiatry and Psychiatric Epidemiology, 34*, 211–215.

Fu, K., Liu, K. Y., & Yip, P. S. F. (2007). Predictive validity of the Chinese version of the Adult Suicidal Ideation Questionnaire: Psychometric properties and its short version. *Psychological Assessment, 19*, 422–429.

Furukawa, T. A., Streiner, D. L., Azuma, H., Higuchi, T., Kamijima, K., Kanba, S., … Miura, S. (2005). Cross-cultural equivalence in depression assessment: Japan–Europe–North American study. *Acta Psychiatrica Scandinavica, 112*(4), 279–285.

German, D., Sutcliffe, C. G., Sirirojn, B., Sherman, S. G., Latkin, C. A., Aramrattana, A., et al. (2012). Unanticipated effect of a randomized peer network intervention on depressive symptoms among young metamphetamine users in Thailand. *Journal of Community Psychology, 40*, 799–813.

Gau, S. S. F., Chen, C. H., Lee, C. T. C., Chang, J. C., & Cheng, A. T. A. (2009). Development of a Chinese version of the Suicide Intent Scale. *Suicide and Life-Threatening Behavior, 39*, 332–342.

Hambrick, J. P., Rodebaugh, T. L., Balsis, S., Woods, C. M., Mendez, J. L., & Heimberg, R. G. (2010). Cross-ethnic measurement equivalence of measures of depression, social anxiety, and worry. *Assessment, 17*(2), 155–171.

Hamilton, M. (1960). A rating scale for depression. *Journal of Neurology, Neurosurgery, and Psychiatry, 23*(1), 56.

Han, C., Jo, S. A., Kwak, J. H., Pae, C. U., Steffens, D., Jo, I., & Park, M. H. (2008). Validation of the Patient Health Questionnaire-9 Korean version in the elderly population: The Ansan Geriatric study. *Comprehensive Psychiatry, 49*(2), 218–223.

Heron, M. (2011). Deaths: Leading causes for 2007. *National Vital Statistics Reports, 59*, 8.

Hong, S., & Wong, E. C. (2005). Rasch rating scale modeling of the Korean version of the beck depression inventory. *Educational and Psychological Measurement, 65*(1), 124–139.

Hiroe, T., Kojima, M., Yamamoto, I., Nojima, S., Kinoshita, Y., Hashimoto, N., ... & Furukawa, T. A. (2005). Gradations of clinical severity and sensitivity to change assessed with the Beck Depression Inventory-II in Japanese patients with depression. *Psychiatry Research, 135*(3), 229–235.

Hsu, L. R., Hailey, B. J., & Range, L. M. (1987). Cultural and emotional components of loneliness and depression. *The Journal of Psychology, 121*(1), 61–70.

Inoue, T., Tanaka, T., Nakagawa, S., Nakato, Y., Kameyama, R., Boku, S., … Koyama, T. (2012). Utility and limitations of PHQ-9 in a clinic specializing in psychiatric care. *BMC Psychiatry, 12*(1), 1–6.

International Test Commission. (2010). *ITC guidelines for translating and adapting tests*. Accessed online on June 3, 2013, from http://www.intestcom.org/upload/sitefiles/40.pdf

Iwata, N., & Buka, S. (2002). Race/ethnicity and depressive symptoms: A cross-cultural/ethnic comparison among university students in East Asia, North, and South America. *Social Science & Medicine, 55*, 2243–2252.

Iwata, N., Okuyama, Y., Kawakami, Y., & Saito, K. (1989). Prevalence of depressive symptoms in a Japanese occupational setting: A preliminary study. *American Journal of Public Health, 79*, 1486–1489.

Iwata, N., Roberts, C. R., & Kawakami, N. (1995). Japan–US comparison of responses to depression scale items among adult workers. *Psychiatry Research, 58*, 237–245.

Iwata, N., Saito, K., & Roberts, R. E. (1994). Responses to a self-administered depression scale among younger adolescents in Japan. *Psychiatry Research, 53*, 275–287.

Jang, Y., Kim, G., & Chiriboga, D. A. (2005). Acculturation and manifestation of depressive symptoms among Korean-American elder adults. *Aging & Mental Health, 9*, 500–507.

Jang, Y., Kwag, K. H., & Chiriboga, D. A. (2010). Not saying I am happy does not mean I am not: Cultural influences on responses to positive affect items in the CES-D. *Journal of Gerontology: Psychological Sciences, 65B*(6), 684–690.

Jang, Y., Small, B. J., & Haley, W. E. (2001). Cross-cultural comparability of the Geriatric Depression Scale: Comparison between older Koreans and older Americans. *Aging & Mental Health, 5*(1), 31–37.

Ji, P., & Duan, C. (2006). The relationship among acculturation, acculturation stress, and depression for a

Korean and a Korean-American sample. *Asian Journal of Counselling, 13*, 235–270.

Kalibatseva, Z., & Leong, F. T. L. (2011). Depression among Asian Americans: Review and Recommendations. *Depression Research and Treatment*, Article ID: 320902. doi: 10.1155/2011/320902

Kanazawa, A., White, P. M., & Hampson, S. E. (2007). Ethnic variation in depressive symptoms in a community sample in Hawaii. *Cultural Diversity and Ethnic Minority Psychology, 13*, 35–44.

Kim, G., DeCoster, J., Huang, C., & Chiriboga, D. A. (2011). Race/ethnicity and the factor structure of the Center for Epidemiologic Studies Depression Scale: A meta-analysis. *Cultural Diversity and Ethnic Minority Psychology, 17*, 381–396.

Kim, E., Seo, K., & Cain, K. C. (2006). Bi-dimensional acculturation and cultural response set in CES-D among Korean immigrants. *Issues in Mental Health Nursing, 31*, 576–583.

Kojima, M., Furukawa, T. A., Takahashi, H., Kawai, M., Nagaya, T., & Tokudome, S. (2002). Cross-cultural validation of the beck depression inventory-II in Japan. *Psychiatry Research, 110*(3), 291–299.

Kroenke, K., Spitzer, R. L., & Williams, J. B. (2001). The PHQ-9. *Journal of General Internal Medicine, 16*(9), 606–613.

Kuo, W. H. (1984). Prevalence of depression among Asian-Americans. *Journal of Nervous and Mental Disease, 172*, 449–457.

Lam, C. K., Lim, J., Ping, P. I., Low, B. L., Ng, L. L., Chiam, P. C., & Sahadevan, S. (2004). Depression in dementia: A comparative and validation study of four brief scales in the elderly Chinese. *International Journal of Geriatric Psychiatry, 19*(5), 422–428.

Lee, H. C. B. (1990). Reliability, validity and fakability of the Zung Self-rating Depression Scale. *Bulletin of the Hong Kong Psychological Society, 24*, 5–15.

Lee, H. C. B., Chiu, H. F. K., Kowk, W. Y., & Leung, C. M. (1993). Chinese elderly and the GDS short form: A preliminary study. *Clinical Gerontologist: The Journal of Aging and Mental Health, 14*(2), 37–42.

Lee, H. C. B., Chiu, H. F. K., Wing, Y. K., Leung, C. M., Kwong, P. K., & Chung, D. W. S. (1994). The Zung self-rating depression scale: Screening for depression among the Hong Kong Chinese elderly. *Journal of Geriatric Psychiatry and Neurology, 7*(4), 216–220.

Leggett, A., Zarit, S. H., Ngyuen, N. H., Hoang, C. N., & Nguyen, H. T. (2012). The influence of social factors and health on depressive symptoms and worry: A study of older Vietnamese adults. *Aging & Mental Health, 16*, 780–786.

Leong, F. T. L. (1997). Cross-cultural career psychology: Comment on Fouad, Harmon, and Borgen (1997) and Tracey, Watanabe, and Schneider (1997). *Journal of Counseling Psychology, 44*, 355–359.

Leong, F. T. L., Kalibatseva, Z., & Park, Y. S. (2013). Evaluating measurement equivalence in cross-cultural stress research. In P. Genkova, T. Ringeisen, & F. T. L. Leong (Eds.), *Handbook stress and culture: Intercultural and cross-cultural perspectives* (pp. 173–188). Wiesbaden, Germany: Springer Fachmedien.

Leong, F. T. L., Okazaki, S., & Tak, J. (2003). Assessment of depression and anxiety in East Asia. *Psychological Assessment, 15*, 290–305.

Leung, C. M., Wing, Y. K., Kwong, P. K., & Shum, A. L. K. (1999). Validation of the Chinese - Cantonese version of the Hospital Anxiety and Depression Scale and comparison with the Hamilton Rating Scale of Depression. *Acta Psychiatrica Scandinavica, 100*(6), 456–461.

Li, Z., & Hicks, M. H. (2010). The CES-D in Chinese American women: Construct validity, diagnostic validity for major depression, and cultural response bias. *Psychiatry Research, 175*, 227–232.

Lim, P. P. J., Ng, L. L., Chiam, P. C., Ong, P. S., Ngui, F. T., & Sahadevan, S. (2000). Validation and comparison of three brief depression scales in an elderly Chinese population. *International Journal of Geriatric Psychiatry, 15*(9), 824–830.

Liu, C., Lu, C., Yu, S., & Yang, Y. (1998). Correlations between scores on Chinese versions of long and short forms of the geriatric depression scale among elderly Chinese. *Psychological Reports, 82*(1), 211–214.

Lu, M. L., Che, H. H., Chang, S. W., & Shen, W. W. (2002). Reliability and validity of the Chinese version of the Beck Depression Inventory-II. *Taiwanese Journal of Psychiatry, 16*, 301–310.

Mackinnon, A., McCallum, J., Andrews, G., & Anderson, I. (1998). The Center for Epidemiological Studies Depression Scale in older community samples in Indonesia, North Korea, Myanmar, Sri Lanka, and Thailand. *Journal of Gerontology: Psychological Sciences, 53*, 343–352.

Marsella, A. J., Kinzie, D., & Gordon, P. (1973). Ethnic variations in the expression of depression. *Journal of Cross-Cultural Psychology, 4*, 435–458.

McDowell, I. (2006). *Measuring health: A guide to rating scales and questionnaires* (3rd ed.). New York, NY: Oxford University Press.

Mouanoutoua, V. L., Brown, L. G., Cappelletty, G. G., & Levine, R. V. (1991). A hmong adaptation of the beck depression inventory. *Journal of Personality Assessment, 57*(2), 309–322.

Mui, A. C., & Shibusawa, T. (2003). Japanese American elders and the Geriatric Depression Scale. *Clinical Gerontologist, 26*(3–4), 91–104.

Napholz, L., & Mo, W. (2010). Attribution of importance to life roles and their implications for mental health among Filipino American working women. *Health Care for Women International, 31*(2), 179–196.

Niino, N., Imaizumi, T., & Kawakami, N. (1991). A Japanese translation of the Geriatric Depression Scale. *Clinical Gerontologist, 10*, 85–87.

Noh, S., Avison, W. R., & Kasper, V. (1992). Depressive symptoms among Korean immigrants: Assessment of a translation of the Center for Epidemiologic Studies-Depression Scale. *Psychological Assessment, 4*, 84–91.

Noh, S., Kasper, V., & Chen, X. (1998). Measuring depression in Korean immigrants: Assessing validity of the translated Korean version of CES-D Scale. *Cross-Cultural Research, 32*, 358–377.

Norasakkunkit, V., & Kalik, M. S. (2002). Culture, ethnicity, and emotional distress measures. *Journal of Cross-Cultural Psychology, 33*, 56–70.

Oh, Y., Koeske, G., & Sales, E. (2002). Acculturation, stress, and depressive symptoms among Korean immigrants in the United States. *Journal of Social Psychology, 142*, 511–516.

Radloff, L. (1977). The CES-D Scale: A self-report depression scale for research in the general population. *Applied Psychological Measurement, 1*, 385–401.

Russell, S. T., Crocket, L. J., Shen, Y., & Lee, S. (2008). Cross-ethnic invariance of self-esteem and depression measures for Chinese, Filipino, and European American adolescents. *Journal of Youth and Adolescence, 37*, 50–61.

Ryder, A. G., & Chentsova-Dutton, Y. E. (2012). Depression in cultural context: "Chinese somatization", revisited. *Psychiatric Clinics of North America, 35*, 15–36.

Ryder, A. G., Yang, J., Zhu, X., Yao, S., Yi, J., Heine, S., & Bagby, R. M. (2008). The cultural shaping of depression: Somatic symptoms in China, psychological symptoms in North America? *Journal of Abnormal Psychology, 117*, 300–313.

Schreiner, A. S., Hayakawa, H., Morimoto, T., & Kakuma, T. (2003). Screening for late life depression: Cut-off scores for the Geriatric Depression Scale and the Cornell Scale for Depression in Dementia among Japanese subjects. *International Journal of Geriatric Psychiatry, 18*(6), 498–505.

Shek, D. T. L. (1990). Reliability and factorial structure of the Chinese version of the Beck Depression Inventory. *Journal of Clinical Psychology, 46*(1), 35–43.

Shima, S., Shikano, T., Kitamura, T., & Asai, M. (1985). New self-rating scale for depression. [In Japanese] *Clinical Psychiatry, 27*, 717–723.

Shin, M. S., Kim, Z. S., & Park, K. B. (1993). The cut-off score for the Korean version of Beck Depression Inventory. *Korean J Clin Psychol, 12*(1), 71–81.

Storch, E. A., Roberti, J. W., & Roth, D. A. (2004). Factor structure, concurrent validity, and internal consistency of the beck depression inventory-second edition in a sample of college students. *Depression and Anxiety, 19*(3), 187–189.

Straus, E., Sherman, E. M. S., & Spreen, O. (2006). *A compendium of neuropsychological tests: Administration, norms, and commentary*. New York, NY: Oxford University Press.

Takeuchi, D. T., Chung, R. C. Y., Lin, K. M., Shen, H., Kurasaki, K., ChinChun, C., … Sue, S. (1998). Lifetime and twelve-month prevalence rates of major depressive episodes and dysthymia among Chinese Americans in Los Angeles. *American Journal of Psychiatry, 155*(10), 1407–1414.

Takeuchi, D. T., Hong, S., Gile, K., & Alegría, M. (2007). Developmental contexts and mental disorders among Asian Americans. *Research in Human Development, 4*, 49–69.

Trangkasombat, U., & Nukhew, O. (1998). Psychopathology of suicidal adolescents. *Journal of the Psychiatric Association of Thailand, 43*, 22–38.

Thavichachart, N., Tangwongchai, S., Worakul, P., Kanchanatawan, B., Suppapitiporn, S., Pattalung, A. S., … Chareonsook, O. (2009). Posttraumatic mental health establishment of the tsunami survivors in Thailand. *Clinical Practice and Epidemiology in Mental Health, 5*, Article 11.

U.S. Department of Health and Human Services. (2001). *Mental health: Culture, race, and ethnicity—a supplement to mental health: A report of the Surgeon General*. Rockville, MD: U.S. Department of Health and Human Services, Substance Abuse and Mental Health Services Administration, Center for Mental Health Services.

World Health Organization (2008). The Global Burden of Disease 2004 update. Accessed online on April 28, 2013, from http://www.who.int/healthinfo/global_burden_disease/GBD_report_2004update_full.pdf

Wong, R., Wu, R., Guo, C., Lam, J. K., & Snowden, L. R. (2012). Culturally sensitive depression assessment for Chinese American immigrants: Development of a comprehensive measure and a screening scale using an item response approach. *Asian American Journal of Psychology, 3*, 230–253.

Wu, P. (2010). Differential functioning of the Chinese version of Beck Depression Inventory-II in adolescent gender groups: Use of a multiple-group mean and covariance structure model. *Social Indicators Research, 96*(3), 535–550.

Wu, P., & Chang, L. (2008). Psychometric properties of the Chinese version of the Beck Depression Inventory-II using the Rasch model. *Measurement and Evaluation in Counseling and Development, 41*(1), 13.

Wu, P., & Huang, T. (2010). Person heterogeneity of the BDI-II-C and its effects on dimensionality and construct validity: Using mixture item response models. *Measurement and Evaluation in Counseling and Development, 43*(3), 155–167.

Xu, Z., Su, H., Zou, Y., Chen, J., Wu, J., & Chang, W. (2011). Self-rated health of Chinese adolescents: Distribution and its associated factors. *Scandinavian Journal of Caring Sciences, 25*(4), 780–786.

Yang, L., Zuo, C., Su, L., & Eaton, M. T. (1987). Depression in Chinese medical inpatients. *The American Journal of Psychiatry, 144*(2), 226–228.

Yeung, A., Chan, R., Mischoulon, D., Sonawalla, S., Wong, E., Nierenberg, A. A., & Fava, M. (2004). Prevalence of major depressive disorder among Chinese-Americans in primary care. *General Hospital Psychiatry, 26*(1), 24–30.

Yeung, A., Chang, D., Gresham, R. L., Jr., Nierenberg, A. A., & Fava, M. (2004). Illness beliefs of depressed Chinese American patients in primary care. *The Journal of Nervous and Mental Disease, 192*(4), 324–327.

Yeung, A., Fung, F., Yu, S. C., Vorono, S., Ly, M., Wu, S., & Fava, M. (2008). Validation of the Patient Health Questionnaire-9 for depression screening among

Chinese Americans. *Comprehensive Psychiatry, 49*(2), 211–217.

Yeung, A., Kung, W. W., Murakami, J. L., Mischoulon, D., Alpert, J. E., Nierenberg, A. A., & Fava, M. (2005). Outcomes of recognizing depressed Chinese American patients in primary care. *The International Journal of Psychiatry in Medicine, 35*(3), 213–224.

Yeung, A., Neault, N., Sonawalla, S., Howarth, S., Fava, M., & Nierenberg, A. A. (2002). Screening for major depression in Asian Americans: A comparison of the Beck and the Chinese Depression Inventory. *Acta Psychiatrica Scandinavica, 105*(4), 252–257.

Ying, Y. (1988). Depressive symptomatology among Chinese-Americans as measured by the CES-D. *Journal of Clinical Psychology, 44*, 739–746.

Zheng, Y., Wei, L., Lianggue, G., Guochen, Z., & Chenggue, W. (1988). Applicability of the Chinese beck depression inventory. *Comprehensive Psychiatry, 29*(5), 484–489.

Zheng, Y. P., Zhao, J. P., Phillips, M., Liu, J. B., Cai, M. F., Sun, S. Q., & Huang, M. F. (1988). Validity and reliability of the Chinese Hamilton Depression Rating Scale. *The British Journal of Psychiatry, 152*(5), 660–664.

Zimmerman, M., Posternak, M. A., & Chelminski, I. (2005). Is the cutoff to define remission on the Hamilton Rating Scale for Depression too high? *The Journal of nervous and mental disease, 193*(3), 170–175.

Zung, W. W., Richards, C. B., & Short, M. J. (1965). Self-rating depression scale in an outpatient clinic: further validation of the SDS. *Archives of General Psychiatry, 13*(6), 508.

Assessment of Anxiety with Asians 13

Jungeun Lee

Assessment of Anxiety with Asian Clients

Anxiety and the Asian Client

The Asian population in the USA has rapidly grown to 12 million (US Department of Homeland Security, 2010) and Asian-born immigrants are the country's second-largest population behind those from Latin America (US Census Bureau, 2011). In 2009, their share increased to 28 % of the foreign-born population, up from 5 % in 1960 (US Census Bureau, 2011). In addition, the composition of the Asian population is constantly changing. The Asian-American population today is primarily born overseas, contrary to the situation three decades ago (Lee, Lei & Sue, 2000). Furthermore, the Asian population in the USA is extremely diverse and includes Indians, Chinese, Filipinos, Japanese, Koreans, Thai, Vietnamese, Pacific Islander Americans, and people from other heritages (Lee et al., 2000). Thus, it is important to be aware of the composition of Asian-Americans and their heterogeneity in the USA in order to understand them better and not simply group them as "Asians."

The prevalence of anxiety disorders among Asian-Americans has risen from 5.75 % (Gee, Spencer, Chen, & Takeuchi, 2007) to 11.8 % (Gonzalez et al., 2010). Asian-Americans are less likely to meet the diagnostic criteria for generalized anxiety disorder, posttraumatic stress disorder, social anxiety disorder, and panic disorder than other ethnic groups (e.g., Hispanics White Americans; Asnaani, Richey, Dimaite, Hinton, & Hofmans, 2010). The specific prevalence rate for social anxiety disorder is 5.3 %, generalized anxiety disorder is 2.4 %, and panic disorder is 2.1 % among an Asian sample consisting of Chinese, Filipino, Vietnamese, or other Asian ancestry (Asnaani et al., 2010). These rates are lower than those of White Americans, whose rates are 12.6 % for social anxiety disorder, 8.6 % for generalized anxiety disorder, and 5.1 % for Panic Disorder (Asnaani et al., 2010). The lifetime prevalence of posttraumatic stress disorder (PTSD) was also lowest among Asians (4.0 %) compared to African Americans (8.7 %), Hispanics (7.0 %), and White Americans (7.4 %) (Roberts, Gilman, Breslau, Breslau, & Koenen, 2010). However, Asian immigrants in the USA report a higher rate of mental health problems compared with individuals in their native countries, although this is less studied (Tiwari & Wang, 2006). For example, the 12-month prevalence rate of social anxiety disorder based on East Asian surveys is much lower in the native countries compared to Asian-Americans in the USA, in the range of 0.4 % in Taiwan (Hsu & Alden, 2008), 0.2–0.6 % in Korea (Kung & Lu, 2008), 0.2 % in China (Roy-Byrne et al., 2005), and 0.8 % in Japan (Matsunaga, Kiriike, & Matsui, 2001).

J. Lee, Ph.D. (✉)
Geisel School of Medicine, Dartmouth College, Hanover, NH 03755, USA
e-mail: Jungeun.Lee@Dartmouth.edu

L.T. Benuto et al. (eds.), *Guide to Psychological Assessment with Asians*,
DOI 10.1007/978-1-4939-0796-0_13,

Considering that immigrants tend to have better health compared to those who remain in their home country, the higher prevalence of anxiety disorders in foreign-born Asian immigrants supports the hypothesis that acculturation and adjustment issues may contribute to acculturative stress, which has been associated with depression, anxiety, and other health outcomes (Woodward et al., 2011).

Cultural Sensitivity

There has been a growing concern among psychologists for awareness of cross-cultural variation in psychopathology. Even though anxiety disorders have been found to exist across cultures (Good & Kleinman, 1985), the symptoms vary considerably cross-culturally (Barlow, 2002). As mentioned above, Asian-Americans are typically less likely to endorse and report symptoms of anxiety disorders than other racial groups including Caucasians, Latinos, and African Americans (Asnaani et al., 2010). Experts hypothesized that this is because language differences may impact the degree to which diagnostic instruments capture the meaning of anxiety symptoms among Asian-Americans (Alegria et al., 2004). Another explanation for the lower prevalence rate is related to culture. In terms of a collectivistic worldview, an emphasis on the importance of maintaining harmonious relationships with other people and overall well-being may explain the lower rate of anxiety symptoms identified among Asian populations (Asnaani et al., 2010). There are, however, some notable exceptions. In fact social anxiety is exceptionally high among this group. Collectivistic countries (e.g., Japan, Korea, and Spain) showed higher levels of social anxiety and more positive attitudes toward socially avoidant behaviors than individualistic countries (e.g., Australia, Canada, Germany, the Netherlands, and the USA; Heinrichs, Rapee, & Alden, 2006). For Asian populations, the strict social norms of collectivist cultures that ensure group harmony (including being submissive and quiet) may increase social anxiety due to the negative consequences when those norms are violated (Rapee & Spence, 2004). When Asians move to the USA, they might be more conscious of other people's feelings and try to avoid situations where they might hurt other people's feelings based on their cultural values (Kleinknecht, Dinnel, & Kleinknecht, 1997). Thus, when assessing Asian clients, researchers and clinicians need to be aware whether culture/heritage-specific issues are influencing their endorsement and report of anxiety symptoms.

This Chapter

This chapter will identify (1) which measures are most commonly used to assess anxiety in English-speaking populations, (2) assessment measures for generalized anxiety disorder, panic disorder, specific phobias (e.g., social phobia and social anxiety), PTSD, and their reliability and validity, (3) different types and symptoms of anxiety disorders and their respective measures depending on each nation and culture (Indian, Chinese, Japanese, Korean, Southeast Asian), and (4) the availability of measures in different languages. In addition, this chapter emphasizes the importance of administrating assessments for somatic symptoms of anxiety as researchers identified that Asians often express mental health symptoms through somatization, and this is a critical cultural consideration when assessing anxiety disorders (Table 13.1).

Assessment of Anxiety as a Domain

Generalized Anxiety Disorder

The *Generalized Anxiety Disorder Questionnaire-IV* (GADQ-IV; Newman et al., 2002) is a nine-item self-report measure that assesses DSM-IV criteria for Generalized Anxiety Disorder (GAD), such as the presence and interference of worry and related physical symptoms. The measure assesses the presence, frequency, and controllability of excessive worry, the number of endorsed worry themes and physical symptoms (e.g., restlessness, irritability, being easily fatigued, difficulty concentrating, muscle tension), and the interference and distress

Table 13.1 Anxiety disorder assessment measures with Asians

Measure	Disorder assessed	Relevant research findings	Available in
Generalized Anxiety Disorder Questionnaire for DSM-IV	Generalized anxiety disorder	1. Good sensitivity and specificity in distinguishing individuals with GAD from those with other anxiety diagnoses 2. A single factor across different racial groups	Japanese
Penn State Worry Questionnaires	Generalized anxiety disorder	1. Good internal consistency when examined for different ethnic groups (Caucasian, Hispanic, Asian)	Chinese, Japanese, Korean
State-Trait Anxiety Inventory	Examines two dimensions of anxiety: state and trait anxiety	1. Most widely used self-report measure in the USA 2. High validity and reliability among Asian-Americans	Chinese, Hong Kong, Japanese, Korean
Beck Anxiety Inventory	Panic disorder	1. Few/no studies for Asian-Americans 2. Excellent reliability and validity among Asians	Chinese, Japanese, Korean
Panic Disorder Severity Scale	Panic disorder	1. Few/no studies for Asian-Americans 2. Validated in different Asian languages	Chinese, Japanese, Korean
Social Phobia and Anxiety Inventory	Social phobia	1. Empirically derived from somatic, cognitive, and behavioral responses to social fears 2. One study reported high reliability for Asian Americans	Chinese, Japanese, Korean
Social Avoidance and Distress Scale	Social anxiety	1. One study published for Chinese Americans 2. High reliability and validity for Japanese and Koreans	Japanese, Korean
Social Interaction Anxiety Scale	Social anxiety	1. Few/no studies for Asian Americans 2. High reliability and validity for different Asian languages	Chinese, Japanese, Korean
Traumatic Life Events Questionnaire	Posttraumatic stress disorder	1. Few/no studies for Asian Americans 2. High reliability and validity for Chinese	Chinese
PTSD Checklist-Civilian version	Posttraumatic stress disorder	1. Few/no studies for Asian Americans 2. Excellent reliability for Cambodian refugees	Chinese

caused by worry and its symptoms. It has good psychometric properties being sensitive and specific for distinguishing individuals with GAD from those with other anxiety disorders (Newman et al., 2002). A recent factor analytic study has supported a one-factor model of the GADQ-IV (Rodebaugh, Holaway, & Heimberg, 2008). Based on this factor analysis, there is a single factor across all racial groups including African American, Caucasian, Hispanic/Latino, and Asian groups, and this result was consistent with a previous factor analysis conducted on a primarily Caucasian sample (Robinson et al., 2010). Another study found out that Asian-Americans do not have the variations in intensity of worry depending on the circumstances while Caucasians and African Americans do (Scott, Winnie, & Heimberg, 2002). Other than those two studies, there are little/no recent studies published regarding this measure for Asian-Americans in English-language journals for the past 5 years. However, it has been translated and used in China (e.g., Wang, Wang, & Jiang, 2007) and Japan (e.g., Takebayasi, Koki, & Thugiura, 2012) and it appears this is appropriate for individuals of Chinese and Japanese origin.

The *Penn State Worry Questionnaire* (PSWQ; Meyer, Miller, Metzger, & Borkovec, 1990) is a 16-item self-report questionnaire that measures an individual's tendency toward excessive worry. Each item is rated on a 1 ("not at all typical of me") to 5 ("very typical of me") Likert-type scale.

Eleven items ask individuals to endorse worry items, with higher numbers meaning more worry (e.g., "My worries overwhelm me"; "I worry all the time"). Five items include items asking respondents to rate a lack of worry (e.g., "I find it easy to dismiss worrisome thoughts"; "I never worry about anything") and the items are reverse-scored before computing the total score. The questionnaire has strong psychometric properties with clinical populations (Brown, Antony, & Barlow, 1992) and has been shown to distinguish patients with GAD from those with other anxiety disorders and healthy controls (Brown et al., 1992). The PSWQ has excellent psychometric characteristics and there are studies comparing those characteristics across diverse groups of ethnic backgrounds. The directly worded items demonstrated good reliability when examined collectively or separately by different ethnic groups including Caucasian, Hispanic, and Asian groups in a community sample (all Cronbach's as >0.90; Gillis, Haaga, & Ford, 1995). In addition, the PSWQ has been translated into Chinese (e.g., Zhong, Wang, Li, & Liu, 2009), Japanese (e.g., Matsumi, 2009), and Korean (e.g., Lim, Kim, Lee, & Kwon, 2008) and used pervasively in Asia.

The *State-Trait Anxiety inventory* (STAI; Spielberger, Gorsuch, Lushene, Vagg, & Jacobs, 1983) is a self-report measure with 40 items that assesses two dimensions of anxiety: state and trait anxiety (Virella, Arbona, & Novy, 1994). State anxiety refers to nervousness or worry that is highly relevant to situational factors. Trait anxiety is considered to be more stable and dispositional anxiety. The STAI is one of the most commonly used measures of anxiety in the USA. It has been used in clinical settings to diagnose anxiety and to distinguish it from depressive symptoms. The STAI-X is a previous form of the STAI-Y. The STAI-Y uses 20 items to assess trait anxiety and 20 items to evaluate state anxiety. State anxiety items (how one feels at a particular moment in time) include "I am tense; I am worried; I feel calm; I feel secure." Trait anxiety items (how the individual generally feels over an indefinite period of time) include "I worry too much over something that really doesn't matter," "I am content," "I am a steady person." The responses are on a four-point Likert scale, such that higher scores indicate greater anxiety. The scale has high internal consistency from 0.86 to 0.95 (Spielberger et al., 1983).

There is one study that validated the STAI for Asian/Pacific-Islander adolescents in the USA, and it showed that the scale had high reliability and concurrent validity (Hishinuma et al., 2001). Although there are few/no other studies published using the STAI with Asian-American populations, a lot of efforts were made to translate it into Asian languages, and there are several studies published in English-language journals. Shek (1988) conducted a number of studies to validate the Chinese translation of the STAI–X. He reported that the translated scale was valid and could be a reliable assessment instrument to measure anxiety in Chinese populations. Lee and Oei (1994) used a Chinese version of the revised STAI–Y in their research for 226 college students in Hong Kong. The Cronbach's alpha for the STAI-Y Chinese was 0.90 in that study. Psychometric data on the Japanese version of the STAI suggest that it has satisfactory reliability and validity for assessing anxiety in Japanese populations (Iwata et al., 1998). In one cross-cultural study for Koreans, Youn, Knight, Jeong, and Benton (1999) translated the STAI–Y into Korean and then back-translated it into English. Cronbach's alpha for the Korean translation was 0.94 in that study, which suggests that this measure is appropriate for individuals with Chinese, Japanese, and Korean origin.

Panic Disorder

The *Beck Anxiety Inventory* (BAI; Beck, Epstein, Brown, & Steer, 1988) is a reliable 21-item self-report measure useful in the assessment of panic symptomatology rather than for anxiety, and it has been shown to discriminate the construct of anxiety from depression (Beck et al., 1988). It is one of the most frequently used measures to assess the current level of various anxiety symptoms. Among the 21 items, 14 reflect somatic symptoms (e.g., numbness or tingling, feeling hot, dizzy or lightheaded) and the remaining seven items refer to specific aspects of cognition related to anxiety and panic symptoms (e.g., fear of the worst happening, fear of losing control, and fear of dying). The BAI asks individuals to endorse their symptoms during the past week by using a four-point severity scale with responses ranging from "Not at all" to "Severely-I could barely stand it" (Steer, Ranieri, Beck, & Clark, 1993). The BAI has demonstrated excellent reliability and validity in clinical samples (Creamer, Foran, & Bell, 1995). Unfortunately, there are few/no studies published in English-language journals regarding the psychometric properties of the BAI for Asian-Americans. There is one study on using the BAI for outpatients attending the Neuroscience Psychiatric Clinic at a tertiary referral hospital in Singapore, which was published in an English-language journal (Luo, Fones, Thumboo, & Li, 2003). The participants were fluent in either English or Chinese, and they used identical English or Chinese questionnaires according to each individual's preference. However, the study did not report on the reliability and validity of the Chinese BAI. Other Asian countries have been pervasively using the BAI, but the resulting studies have not been published in English journals. An examination of Chinese (e.g., Li et al., 2008) and Korean (e.g., Han, Cho, Park, Kim, & Kim, 2003) translations of the BAI in Asian journals, revealed numerous studies using these translated measures strong psychometric properties of the translated measures. From these results, it appears that translated BAI version is appropriate for individuals with Asian origins (e.g., Chinese and Korean) or who are not fluent in English. At the same time, original English version of BAI is fine for Asian-Americans who prefer English.

The *Panic Disorder Severity Scale* (PDSS; Houch, Spiegel, Shear, & Rucci, 2002) is a self-report measure with seven items assessing the overall severity of panic disorder. It evaluates the frequency of panic disorder, perceived distress, social and occupational interference, anticipatory anxiety, and avoidance of agoraphobic situations as interoceptive cues (e.g., (1) how many panic and limited symptoms attacks did you have during the week, (2) during the past week, how much have you worried or felt anxious about when your next panic attack would occur or about fears related to the attacks?). Respondents rate each question from 0 to 4 on a five-point Likert scale, and the total score ranges from 0 to 28. The scale has comparative reliability and validity when the measure is used for panic disorder patients, and it is sensitive to change with treatment (Houch et al., 2002). Thus, the PDSS is a useful tool in clinical and research settings. There are few/no studies published using this measure for Asian-Americans in the English journals. However, it has been translated and used pervasively in Asian countries including China (e.g., Hu, Cui, & Li, 2012), Japan (e.g., Dakasi et al., 2004), and Korea (e.g., Lim, Yu, & Kim, 2007) to measure panic disorder symptoms.

Specific Phobias

The *Social Phobia and Anxiety Inventory* (SPAI; Turner, Beidel, Dancu, & Stanley, 1989) is a self-report measure with 45 items assessing social anxiety and fear. It evaluates specific somatic and affective symptoms, cognitions, and behaviors due to potentially fear-producing situations (e.g., with authority figures, with strangers). The measure was developed on an empirical basis and it has high test–retest reliability and good internal consistency (Turner et al., 1989). The SPAI is known to be an ideal screening tool for social phobia and anxiety in various settings including inpatient and outpatient clinics, residential treatment facilities, prisons, schools, and employment settings (Turner et al., 1989). In addition, the SPAI score has been shown to be sensitive to the distinction between socially anxious and nonsocially anxious populations (Beidel, Turner, Stanley, & Dancu, 1989) and it also distinguishes participants with social phobia and those with panic disorder with or without agoraphobia (Turner et al., 1989). There is one study using the SPAI to understand cultural differences between European Americans and Asian-Americans regarding social anxiety in anxiety-provoking situations. Asian-Americans reported higher average number on negative emotions in social situations than European Americans. The Cronbach's alpha coefficient for Asian-Americans was 0.97 in that study (Lee, Okazaki, & Yoo, 2006). Although there are few studies regarding the SPAI in English-language journals, the measure has been translated and used frequently in Asian countries including China (e.g., Chin & Zhang, 2010), Japan (e.g., Okajima, Yoshihiro, & Sasagawa, 2008), and Korea (e.g., Kim, 2004). Studies on its use in these countries have been published in Asian journals in the respective languages. Thus, it is appropriate to use a translated version of measure for individuals of Asian origin who do not speak English or prefers their native languages (i.e., China, Japan, and Korea).

The *Social Avoidance and Distress Scale* (SADS; Watson & Friend, 1969) is a self-report measure with 28 items evaluating the affective and behavioral components of social anxiety including distress, discomfort, fear, anxiety, and the avoidance of social situations. Half of the items assess social avoidance (i.e., the behavioral component of social anxiety) and the other 14 assesses social anxiety (i.e., the affective component of social anxiety). The items include "I feel relaxed even in unfamiliar social situations," "I try to avoid situations which force me to be very sociable," and "It is easy for me to relax when I am with strangers." Respondents answer with either true or false. The SADS has high reliability, with an internal consistency of 0.94 and a test-reliability ranging from 0.68 (Watson & Friend, 1969). There is one study on Chinese Americans using the SADS to examine passivity and nonassertiveness (Sue, Sue, & Ino, 2001). However, the study did not report psychometric properties. Another study using the SADS for Japanese Americans reported high internal reliability, with Cronbach's alpha at 0.91 (Norasakkunkit & Kalick, 2009). The SADS was translated into Chinese (e.g., Peng, Fan, & Li, 2003) and Korean (e.g., Lee & Choi, 1997) and has been used frequently by researchers and clinicians.

The *Social Interaction Anxiety Scale* (SIAS; Mattick & Clarke, 1998) is a self-report measure with 20 items, reflecting anxiety in social interaction situations such as fear of being boring and unclear, or not knowing what to say. The items include anxiety-associated reactions to a variety of social interaction situations, such as "I get nervous if I have to speak to someone in authority" and "When mixing socially I am uncomfortable." Respondents are asked to indicate to what extent the statements describe themselves on a five-point Likert scale ("not at all" to "extremely"). It has good internal consistency and well-established validity in clinical and nonclinical samples (Mattick & Clarke, 1998). There have been few to no studies on the reliability or validity of the SIAS for Asian-Americans. However, the SIAS has been translated into Chinese (e.g., Ye, Qian, Liu, & Chen, 2007) and Japanese (e.g., Ochiai & Matsui, 2009), and it has been used pervasively to measure anxiety in social situations.

Posttraumatic Stress Disorder

The *Traumatic Life Events Questionnaire* (TLEF; Kubany et al., 2000) is a self-report measure evaluating the various types of traumatic events that a respondent has experienced during his or her lifetime with 23 items. Categories of trauma include natural disasters, exposure to warfare, interpersonal violence such as domestic abuse, sexual assault, and child abuse, and robbery involving a weapon. Respondents provide the number of times they experienced such events, ranging from "never" to "more than five times." The TLEQ also assesses whether respondents experienced helplessness, fear, or horror in response to the endorsed trauma exposure with a yes or no response (Kubany et al., 2000). There is one study examining the relationship of PTSD and related perinatal behavioral risk factors among Caucasian, Asian, and Pacific Islander women. However, the study did not report the psychometric properties of the measure (Onoye, Goebert, Morland, Matsu, & Wright, 2009). In Chinese journals, it was observed that the TLEQ has been translated into Chinese (e.g., Huang, Zhang, Liu, & Wei, 2008). The other Asian countries such as Japan and Korea appear to have developed their own measures and use them instead of a translated TLEQ.

The *PTSD Checklist-Civilian version* (PCL-C; Weathers, Litz, Herman, Huska, & Keane,

1993) assesses lifetime and current PTSD symptoms in clients who were exposed to trauma with 17 items through self-report. The PCL-C includes items (re-experiencing, avoidance, arousal) based on the Diagnostic and Statistical Manual of Mental Disorders-IV (American Psychological Association, 1994) criteria for determining PTSD diagnoses. Each item corresponds to 1 of 17 DSM-IV PTSD symptoms on a 1–5 Likert scale from "Not at all" to "Extremely" (Weathers et al., 1993). Example items are "Repeated, disturbing memories, thoughts, or images of a stressful experience from the past," "Feeling very upset when something reminded you of a stressful experience from the past," and "Avoid thinking about or talking about a stressful experience from the past or avoid having feelings related to it." The measure has high internal consistency (alpha = 0.85–0.98) (Wilkins, Lang, & Norman, 2011). There is one study published in an English-language journal on Cambodian refugees with PTSD that uses this measure (Hinton, Rasmussen, & Nou, 2009). The Cambodian version of the PTSD-C has excellent test–retest (at 1 week) and inter-rater reliability ($r = 0.91$ and 0.95, respectively) (Hinton et al., 2009). In Chinese journals, we observe that the PCL-C has been translated into Chinese and used pervasively (e.g., Wang, Sui, Li, & Jie, 2010). However, this measure is not translated into other Asian languages. The other Asian countries such as Japan and Korea have developed their own measures.

Culture/Nation Specific Anxiety Disorder and Symptoms

Asian-Americans tend to report anxiety in terms of physical symptoms (irrespective of the trigger) rather than psychological symptoms, which does not show up very often in Americans. For example, Asian-Americans may express concerns about throwing up or fainting when they are anxious (Gordon & Teachman, 2008). Specifically, there are so-called culture-bound syndromes of Asian populations. For example, Koreans experience *hwabyung*, which literally means fire disease or anger disease. Japanese have been applied the diagnosis of *shinkeishitsu* (indicating a nervous character) and *taijin kyofusho* (meaning fear of interpersonal relations). In Khmer, there is a syndrome of *kyol goeu*, meaning wind overload. There has been debate whether these are cultural variations of Western anxiety disorders (e.g., Hinton, Um, & Ba, 2001; Lin, 1983). Although multiple functional somatic symptoms are common anxiety presentations, there are culture-specific syndromes for each Asian nation with particular cognitions about anxiety-type somatic and psychological symptoms. For clinicians and researchers, it is important to be aware of those race/nation specific syndromes and symptoms when assessing and measuring anxiety symptoms.

North East Asia

China. In China, patients with anxiety often complain of "neurasthenia" or "weak nerves" (Shen, Zhang, & Huang, 2006); the Western diagnosis of "neurasthenia" was adopted in China at the beginning of the twentieth century. Key features of "weak nerves" include excessive worry, headache, and fatigue. The patient is concerned that worry drains his or her mind and body and results in further fatigue, damaging the soul and the body (Shen et al., 2006). In China, it is believed that neurasthenia produces catastrophic thoughts, and these contribute to the severity and frequency of generalized anxiety disorder and panic disorder. In addition, dizziness is a common complaint among Chinese patients with panic disorder (Park & Hinton, 2002). Due to the influence of traditional Chinese medicine, anxiety states are often attributed to organ dysfunction, especially to a "weak kidney" or a "weak heart" (Park & Hinton, 2002). In China, medical doctors used to attribute panic symptoms to such organ failure. Western doctors may have to be aware of the traditional approaches the Chinese used to have and intervene correctly when Chinese Americans report certain catastrophic cognitions and hypervigilance for certain somatic symptoms.

Japanese. In Japan, as in China, "neurasthenia" refers to common anxiety disorder symptoms (Kitanishi & Kondo, 1994). Neurasthenia is a term that captures various mental health disorders ranging from social phobia to schizophrenia. Anxiety states in Japan are often diagnosed as "neurocirculatory asthenia" and typical symptoms include palpitations, fatigue, and orthostatically induced dizziness (Hinton et al., 2007). The syndrome of "orthostatic dysregulation" is a common manifestation of panic disorder. Patients with panic disorder have orthostasis-induced symptoms and appear to have various phobias, especially social phobia, which is presented as a syndrome called *taijin kyofusho*, which means literally "fear of people" (Maeda & Nathan, 1999). Patients with *taijin kyofusho* avoid social relationships and social settings due to fears of blushing, being observed, having offensive odors, making inappropriate facial expressions, and offending other people (Kirmayer, 1991). However, *taijin kyofusho* differs from social phobia because there is a greater emphasis on fear of offending others instead of embarrassing oneself (Nagata et al., 2003). *Tajin kyofusho* has been frequently considered as a Japanese culture-specific expression of social anxiety disorder.

Korean. Hwabyung, literally indicating "fire sickness," is a common syndrome in Korea that has also been reported among Koreans in the USA (Lin, 1983). *Hwabyung* occurs in middle-aged Korean women of low socioeconomic status, with symptoms including generalized anxiety, panic, depression, aggression, and persistent sadness. They also report somatic symptoms such as digestive problems, abdominal pain, hot or cold flashes, and sleeplessness. Researchers have remarked that *hwabyung* may result in panic attacks and may also be a presentation of generalized anxiety disorder (Lin et al., 1992).

Indian Americans (Indian, Pakistani, and Bangladeshi). Semen-loss syndrome is a well-known and common presentation of anxiety among Indian Americans (Perme, Ranjith, Mohan, & Chandrasekaran, 2005). Semen-loss anxiety involves fears of risky bodily depletion. A sufferer of semen-loss attributes multiple somatic symptoms (weakness, palpitations, aches, and pains) and psychological symptoms (anxiety, fear) to an excessive loss of semen through urination, nocturnal emissions, or excessive masturbation. Semen loss syndrome usually starts with an acute onset characterized by intense anxiety symptoms consisting of high arousal, fatigue, somatic symptoms, and sexual dysfunction (Sumathipala, Siribaddana, & Bhugra, 2004).

Southeast Americans

Cambodia. As in China and Japan, the Western diagnostic category of neurasthenia has been adopted in Cambodia (Hinton, Hinton, Um, Chea, & Sak, 2002). Cambodians have several functional somatic syndromes that overlap with anxiety. Weakness is a common complaint among Cambodians who suffer from anxiety. Based on Cambodian belief, body weakness may result in various anxiety type symptoms including worry, frequent fear, tinnitus, shortness of breath, and a feeling of lightness in the body. Cambodians have a great fear of heart weakness, too (Hinton et al., 2002). Especially among Cambodian refugees, "weak heart" syndrome is a common presentation of generalized anxiety disorder, panic disorder, and PTSD. Specific anxiety symptoms such as palpitations, orthostatic dizziness, cold extremities, and even shortness of breath are attributed to a weak heart. In addition, Cambodian refugees commonly report neck-focused distress often associated with panic attacks, and those panic attacks frequently combine with both panic disorder features (e.g., catastrophic cognitions) and PTSD symptoms (e.g., trauma associations).

Thailand. In northeastern Thailand (where most of the population is Laotian speaking), patients with anxiety, especially panic disorder and PTSD, complain of having a weak heart (Hinton, 2000). They also report an "abdominal wind" syndrome, which is a frequent anxiety presentation (Hinton, 2000). Both Cambodians and northeastern Thais have ethnophysiology-caused catastrophic cognitions resulting in hypervigilance of somatic symptoms (e.g., particularly cardiac and gastrointestinal symptoms). Interestingly, the concept of "abdominal wind" that exists in northeastern Thailand is not reported by people in central Thailand. In addition, the rates of gastrointestinal-focused panic are much lower in central and Southern Thailand (Hinton et al., 2007).

Vietnam. During French colonial rule, the "neurasthenia" and "cardiac neurasthenia" theories were adopted in Vietnam. As in Cambodia, common symptoms of anxiety disorder including generalized anxiety disorder, panic disorder, and PTSD were viewed as "weakness" and "heart weakness" in Vietnam (Chung & Singer, 1995). In addition, the Chinese diagnosis of "weak kidney" was adopted in Vietnam, which resulted in the fear that weakness may lead to "kidney weakness." Cautious of disordered kidneys, Vietnamese are hypervigilant to back sensations and sometimes experience urination-induced panic attacks. They worry that semen can be lost in the urine (Hinton, Nguyen, Tran, & Quinn, 2005). Vietnamese frequently report headache-focused panic, indicating that a headache to them means serious physiological abnormalities including overly tense nerve fibers that may snap and cause death, insanity, or permanent loss of intelligence (Hinton, Chau, et al., 2001).

Non-English Measures Available to Each of Group

There have been attempts to translate English assessment measures into Asian languages in Asian countries. In the process, those items considered inappropriate were eliminated or revised in accordance with the tester's opinion. Unfortunately, studies on the full array of validated instruments and measures used for Asian-Americans in the USA cannot be found in English-language journals. However, there are lots of instruments that have been translated, validated, and made available in Asian countries, and increasing numbers of publications concerning psychological assessment are appearing in Asian journals. Nevertheless, they are only published in Asian language journals that limit international access to the contents of those articles, and it is difficult to see the psychometric properties of each measure. Some of the Asian countries have developed their own culture-sensitive measures, but these also have limited access for international researchers.

Conclusion

It has been particularly problematic and difficult to conduct valid assessment research due to cultural differences in self-disclosure tendencies and stigma around mental health illness among Asian populations. Culturally, Asians come from an orientation with strong family ties (Fong, 1973) and there is a strong tradition of controlling emotional expression (Lai & Linden, 1993). This makes it hard for researchers to believe the prevalence rates and self-reporting among Asian-Americans. Another major issue in the anxiety assessment of Asian-Americans concerns the adaptation and translation of inventories. The most important question is whether the content of the measure is relevant to Asian-Americans, which is content validity. Another question is whether the test actually predicts the relevant behavior in Asian-Americans, predictive validity.

In this chapter, many measures that are viable for use with Asian populations are presented. In addition, culture-specific anxiety syndromes and symptoms are introduced. It is crucial for clinicians and researchers to keep in mind that psychological symptoms of anxiety may be defined and manifested differently in various countries and cultures. Clinicians and researchers need to be mindful of those culture-bound differences regarding anxiety and utilize those measures carefully when evaluating the presence of an anxiety disorder with Asians. This is to develop correct treatment planning and implementation of high-quality health care based on accurate assessments and understanding.

References

Alegria, M., Takeuchi, D., Canino, G., Duan, N., Shrout, P., Meng, X., & Gong, F. (2004). Considering context, place and culture: The National Latino and Asian American Study. *International Journal of Methods in Psychiatric Research, 13*, 208–220.

American Psychological Association. (1994). *Diagnostic and statistical manual of mental disorders* (4th ed.). Washington, DC: Author.

Asnaani, A., Richey, A., Dimaite, R., Hinton, E. E., & Hofmans, S. G. (2010). A cross-ethnic comparison of lifetime prevalence rates of anxiety disorders. *Journal of Nervous and Mental Disease, 198*, 551–555.

Barlow, D. H. (2002). *Anxiety and its disorders* (2nd ed.). New York, NY: Guilford Press.

Beck, A. T., Epstein, N., Brown, G., & Steer, R, A., (1998). An inventory for measuring clinical anxiety: Psychometric properties. *Journal of Consulting and Clinicial Psychology, 56*, 893–897.

Beidel, D. C., Turner, S. M., Stanley, M. A., & Dancu, C. V. (1989). The social phobia and anxiety inventory: Concurrent and external validity. *Behavior Therapy, 20*, 417–427.

Brown, T. A., Antony, M. M., & Barlow, D. H. (1992). Psychometric properties of the Penn State Worry Questionnaire in a clinical anxiety disorders sample. *Behaviour Research and Therapy, 30*, 33–37.

Chin, P., & Zhang, Y. (2010). The reliability and validity of the Chinese version of Social Phobia Inventory. *West China Medical Journal, 26*(2), 477–479.

Chung, R. C., & Singer, K. M. (1995). Interpretation of symptom presentation and distress: A Southeast Asian refugee example. *Journal of Nervous and Mental Disease, 183*, 639–648.

Creamer, M., Foran, J., & Bell, R. (1995). The Beck Anxiety Inventory in a non-clinical sample. *Behaviour Research and Therapy, 33*, 477–485.

Dakasi, O., OOTS, B., Danaka, K., Aoya, M., Ikawa, H., Yosida, Y., & Hurukawa, H. (2004). Examination of validity of Panic Disorder Severity Scale in Japanese (PDSS-J). *Clinical Psychopharmacology, 7*, 1155–1168.

Fong, S. L. (1973). Assimilation and changing social roles of Chinese Americans. *Journal of Social Issues, 29*, 115–128.

Gee, G. C., Spencer, M., Chen, J., & Takeuchi, Y. T. (2007). The association between self-reported racial discrimination and 12-month DSM-IV mental disorders among Asian Americans nationwide. *Social Science & Medicine, 64*, 1984–1996.

Gillis, M. M., Haaga, D. A. F., & Ford, G. T. (1995). Normative values for the Beck Anxiety Inventory, Fear Questionnaire, Penn State Worry Questionnaire, and Social Phobia and Anxiety Inventory. *Psychological Assessment, 7*, 450–455.

Gonzalez, H. M., Tarraf, W., West, B. T., Chan, D., Miranda, P. Y., & Leong, F. T. (2010). Antidepressant use among Asians in the United States. *Depression and Anxiety, 27*, 46–55.

Good, B. J., & Kleinman, A. M. (1985). Culture and anxiety: Cross-cultural evidence for the patterning of anxiety disorders. In A. H. Tuma & J. D. Maser (Eds.), *Anxiety and anxiety disorders* (pp. 297–323). Hillsdale, NJ: Erlbaum.

Gordon, T. L., & Teachman, B. A. (2008). Ethnic group differences in affective, behavioral, and cognitive markers of anxiety. *Journal of Cross-Cultural Psychology, 39*(4), 424–446.

Han, E., Cho, Y., Park, S., Kim, H., & Kim, S. (2003). An application of confirmatory factor analysis in psychiatric patients. Factor structure of the Korean version of the Beck Anxiety Inventory. *Korean Journal of Clinical Psychology, 22*(1), 261–270.

Heinrichs, N., Rapee, R. M., & Alden, L. A. (2006). Cultural differences in perceived social norms and social anxiety. *Behavior Research and Therapy, 44*, 1187–1197.

Hinton, D. E. (2000). Musical healing and cultural syndromes in Iran: Landscape, conceptual metaphor, and embodiment. (Doctoral dissertation, Harvard University, 2000). *Dissertation Abstracts International, 60*(2553), 1–899.

Hinton, D. E, Chau, H., Nguyen, L., Nguyen, M., Pham, T., Quinn, S., & Tran, M. (2001). Panic disorder among Vietnamese refugees attending a psychiatric clinic: Prevalence and subtypes. *General Hospital Psychiatry, 23*, 337–344.

Hinton, D. E., Hinton, L., Tran, M., Nguyen, M., Nguyen, L., Hsia, C., & Pollack, M. H. (2007). Orthostatic panic attacks among Vietnamese refugees. *Transcultural Psychiatry, 44*, 515–544.

Hinton, D. E., Hinton, S., Um, K., Chea, A., & Sak, S. (2002). The Khmer "weak heart" syndrome: Fear of death from palpitations. *Transcultural Psychiatry, 39*, 323–344.

Hinton, D. E., Nguyen, L., Tran, M., & Quinn, S. (2005). Weak kidney and panic attacks in a traumatized Vietnamese male: Clinical history. *Culture, Medicine and Psychiatry, 29*, 125–135.

Hinton, D. E., Rasmussen, A., & Nou, L. (2009). Anger, PTSD, and the nuclear family: A study of Cambodian refugees. *Social Science and Medicine, 69*, 1387–1394.

Hinton, D., Um, K., & Ba, P. (2001). *Kyol goeu* (wind overload): I. A cultural syndrome of orthostatic panic among Khmer refugees. *Transcultural Psychiatry, 38*, 403–432.

Hishinuma, E. S., Miyamoto, R. H., Nishimura, S. T., Goebert, D. A., Noelle, Y. C., Yuen, G., … Carlton, B. S. (2001). Prediction of anxiety disorders using the State–Trait Anxiety Inventory for multiethnic adolescents. *Anxiety Disorders, 15*, 511–533.

Houch, P. R., Spiegel, D. A., Shear, M. K., & Rucci, P. (2002). Reliability of the self-report version of the Panic Disorder Severity Scale. *Depression and Anxiety, 15*(4), 183–185.

Hsu, L., & Alden, L. E. (2008). Cultural influences on willingness to seek treatment for social anxiety in Chinese- and European-heritage students. *Cultural Diversity and Ethnic Minority Psychology, 14*(3), 215–223.

Hu, Q., Cui, H., & Li, C. (2012). Systematic review of studies of BDNF levels in the peripheral blood of patients with panic disorder. *Journal of Psychiatric Medicine, 25*(1), 11–14.

Huang, G., Zhang, Y., Liu, N., & Wei, M. (2008). Characteristics of traumas and PTSD symptom among perpetrators of domestic violence. *Chinese Journal of Behavioral Medical Science, 17*(8), 724–726.

Iwata, N., Mishima, N., Shimizu, T., Mizoue, T., Fukuhara, M., Hidano, T., & Spielberger, C. D. (1998). Positive and negative affect in the factor structure of the State–Trait Anxiety Inventory for Japanese workers. *Psychological Reports, 82*, 651–656.

Kim, N. J. (2004). Validation of the Korean version of the Social Phobia and Anxiety Inventory. *The Korean Journal of Clinical Psychology, 23*(4), 1011–1027.

Kirmayer, L. (1991). The place of culture in psychiatric nosology: *Taijin kyofusho* and DSM-III-R. *Journal of Nervous and Mental Disease, 179*, 19–28.

Kitanishi, K., & Kondo, K. (1994). The rise and fall of neurasthenia in Japanese psychiatry. *Transcultural Psychiatric Research Review, 31*, 137–152.

Kleinknecht, R. A., Dinnel, D. L., & Kleinknecht, E. E. (1997). Cultural factors in social anxiety: A comparison of social phobia symptoms and *Taijin Kyofusho. Journal of Anxiety Disorder, 11*, 157–177.

Kubany, E. S., Haynes, S. N., Leisen, M. B., Owens, J. A., Kaplan, A. S., & Watson, S. B. (2000). Development and preliminary validation of a brief broad-spectrum measure of trauma exposure: The Traumatic Life Events Questionnaire. *Psychological Assessment, 12*(2), 210–224.

Kung, W. W., & Lu, P. C. (2008). How symptom manifestations affect help seeking for mental health problems among Chinese Americans. *Journal of Nervous and Mental Disease, 196*, 46–54.

Lai, J., & Linden, W. (1993). The smile of Asia: Acculturation effects on symptom reporting. *Canadian Journal of Behavioural Science, 25*(2), 303–313.

Lee, J., & Choi, C. (1997). A study of the reliability and the validity of the Korean versions of social phobia and scales (K-SAD, K-FNE). *The Korean Journal of Clinical Psychology, 16*(2), 251–264.

Lee, J., Lei, A., & Sue, S. (2000). The current state of mental health research on Asian Americans. *Journal of Human Behavior in the Social Environment, 3*(3–4), 159–178.

Lee, H. B., & Oei, T. P. S. (1994). Factor structure, validity, and reliability of the fear questionnaire in a Hong Kong Chinese population. *Journal of Psychopathology and Behavioral Assessment, 16*, 189–199.

Lee, M. R., Okazaki, S., & Yoo, H. C. (2006). Frequency and intensity of social anxiety in Asian Americans and European Americans. *Cultural Diversity and Ethnic Minority Psychology, 12*, 291–351.

Li, Z., Ma, T., Zhang, R., Long, X., Song, L., Li, B., … Tang, X. (2008). The study of the various characteristic in recruits anxiety mood and influencing factors in different training phase. *Chinese Journal of Health Care and Medicine, 10*(5), 350–352.

Lim, Y. J., Kim, Y. H., Lee, E. H., & Kwon, S. M. (2008). The Penn State Worry Questionnaire: Psychometric properties of the Korean version. *Depression and Anxiety, 25*(10), E97–E103.

Lim, Y. J., Yu, B. H., & Kim, J. H. (2007). Korean panic disorder severity scale: Construct validity by confirmatory factor analysis. *Depression and Anxiety, 24*(2), 95–102.

Lin, K. M. (1983). *Hwa-Byung*: A Korean culture-bound syndrome. *American Journal of Psychiatry, 140*, 105–107.

Lin, K. M., Lau, J., Yamamoto, J., Zheng, Y. P., Kim, H. S., Cho, K. H., & Nakasaki, G. (1992). *Hwa-byung:* A community study of Korean Americans. *Journal of Nervous and Mental Disease, 180*, 386–391.

Luo, N., Fones, C. S. L., Thumboo, J., & Li, S. C. (2003). Factors influencing health-related quality of life of Asians with anxiety disorders in Singapore. *Quality of Life Research, 13*, 557–565.

Maeda, F., & Nathan, J. (1999). Understanding *taijin kyofusho* through its treatment, Morita therapy. *Journal of Psychosomatic Research, 46*, 525–530.

Matsumi, J. (2009). Examination of the reliability and validity of the Japanese version (PSWQ) Penn State Worry Questionnaire—self-assessment questionnaire of worry. *Counseling Study, 42*(3), 247–255.

Matsunaga, H., Kiriike, N., & Matsui, T. (2001). Taijin kyofusho: A form of social anxiety that responds to serotonin reuptake inhibitors? *The International Journal of Neuropsychopharmacology, 4*, 231–237.

Mattick, R. P., & Clarke, J. C. (1998). Development and validation of measures of social phobia scrutiny fear and social interaction anxiety. *Behaviour Research and Therapy, 36*, 455–470.

Meyer, T. J., Miller, M. L., Metzger, R. L., & Borkovec, T. D. (1990). Development and validation of the Penn State Worry Questionnaire. *Behaviour Research and Therapy, 28*, 487–495.

Nagata, T., Oshima, J., Wada, A., Yamada, H., Iketani, T., & Kiriike, N. (2003). Open trial for *taijin-kyofusho* in Japanese patients with social anxiety disorder. *International Journal of Psychiatry in Clinical Practice, 7*, 107–112.

Newman, M. G., Zuellig, A. R., Kachin, K. E., Constantino, M. J., Przeworski, A., Erickson, T., & Cashman-McGrath, L. (2002). Preliminary reliability and validity of the GAD-Q-IV: A revised self-report diagnostic measure of generalized anxiety disorder. *Behavior Therapy, 33*, 215–233.

Norasakkunkit, V., & Kalick, S. M. (2009). Experimentally detecting how cultural differences on social anxiety measures misrepresent cultural differences in emotional well-being. *Journal of Happiness Studies, 10*(3), 313–327.

Ochiai, M., & Matsui, Y. (2009). How high social anxiety individuals recognize changing facial expressions. *Research in Social and Interpersonal Psychology, 9*, 46–54.

Okajima, I., Yoshihiro, K., & Sasagawa, S. (2008). Revised Social Phobia and Anxiety Inventory in Japanese. *Association of Behavior Therapy, 34*(3), 297–309.

Onoye, J. M., Goebert, D., Morland, L., Matsu, C., & Wright, T. (2009). PTSD and postpartum mental health in a sample of Caucasian, Asian, and Pacific Islander women. *Archives of Women's Mental Health, 12*, 393–400.

Park, L., & Hinton, D. (2002). Dizziness and panic in China: Associated sensations of Zang Fu organ disequilibrium. *Culture, Medicine and Psychiatry, 26*, 225–257.

Peng, C., Fan, X., & Li, L. (2003). The validity and reliability of Social Avoidance and Distress Scale in Chinese students. *Chinese Journal of Clinical Psychology, 17*(5), 279–281.

Perme, B., Ranjith, G., Mohan, R., & Chandrasekaran, R. (2005). *Dhat* (semen loss) syndrome: A functional somatic syndrome of the Indian subcontinent. *General Hospital Psychiatry, 27*, 215–217.

Rapee, R. M., & Spence, S. H. (2004). The etiology of social phobia: Empirical evidence and an initial model. *Clinical Psychology Review, 24*, 737–767.

Roberts, A. L., Gilman, S. E., Breslau, J., Breslau, N., & Koenen, K. C. (2010). Race/ethnic differences in exposure to traumatic events, development of post-traumatic stress disorder, and treatment-seeking for post-traumatic stress disorder in the United States. *Psychological Medicine, 41*, 71–83.

Robinson, C. M., Klenck, S. C., & Norton, P. J. (2010). Psychometric properties of the generalized anxiety disorder questionnaire for DSM-IV among four racial groups. *Cognitive Behavioral Therapy, 39*(4), 251–261.

Rodebaugh, T. L., Holaway, R. M., & Heimberg, R. G. (2008). The factor structure and dimensional scoring of the Generalized Anxiety Disorder Questionnaire for DSM-IV. *Assessment, 15*, 343–350.

Roy-Byrne, P. P., Craske, M. G., Stein, M., Sullivan, G., Bystritsky, A., Katon, W., … Sherbourne, C. D. (2005). A randomized effectiveness trial of cognitive-behavioral therapy and medication for primary care panic disorder. *Archives of General Psychiatry, 62*(3), 290–298.

Scott, E. L., Winnie, E., & Heimberg, R. (2002). Ethnic differences in worry in a nonclinical population. *Depression & Anxiety, 15*(2), 79–82.

Shek, D. T. L. (1988). Reliability and factorial structure of the Chinese version of the State–Trait Anxiety Inventory. *Journal of Psychopathology and Behavioral Assessment, 10*, 303–317.

Shen, Y. C., Zhang, M. Y., & Huang, Y. Q. (2006). Twelve-month prevalence, severity, and unmet need for treatment of mental disorders in metropolitan China. *Psychological Medicine, 36*, 257–267.

Spielberger, C. D., Gorsuch, R. L., Lushene, R., Vagg, P. R., & Jacobs, G. A. (1983). *Manual for the state-trait anxiety inventory*. Palo Alto, CA: Consulting Psychologists Press.

Steer, R., Ranieri, W., Beck, A., & Clark, D. (1993). Further evidence for the validity of the anxiety inventory with psychiatric outpatients. *Journal of Anxiety Disorders, 7*, 195–205.

Sue, D., Sue, D. M., & Ino, S. (2001). Assertiveness and Social Anxiety Chinese-American Women. *The Journal of Psychology, 124*(2), 155–163.

Sumathipala, A., Siribaddana, S., & Bhugra, D. (2004). Culture-bound syndromes: The story of dhat syndrome. *British Journal of Psychiatry, 184*, 200–209.

Takebayasi, Y., Koki, T., & Thugiura, N. (2012). Development of Generalized Anxiety Disorder Questionnaire for DSM-IV (GAD-Q-IV) in Japanese. *Legal Capacity and Psychiatric Diagnostics, 5*, 89–98.

Tiwari, S. K., & Wang, J. (2006). The epidemiology of mental and substance use-related disorders among White, Chinese, and other Asian populations in Canada. *Canadian Journal of Psychiatry, 51*, 904–912.

Turner, S. M., Beidel, D. C., Dancu, C. V., & Stanley, M. A. (1989). An empirically derived inventory to measure social fears and anxiety: The Social Phobia and Anxiety Inventory. *Psychological Assessment, 1*, 35–40.

U.S. Census Bureau. (2011). *Asian/Pacific American Heritage Month: May 2010*. Retrieved from http://www.census.gov/newsroom/relases/archives/facts_for_features_special_editions/cb10-ff07.html

U.S. Department of Homeland Security. (2010). *2010 Yearbook of Immigration Statistics*. Washington, DC: Office of Immigration Statistics.

Virella, B., Arbona, C., & Novy, D. (1994). Psychometric properties and factor structure of the Spanish version of the state-trait anxiety inventory. *Journal of Personality Assessment, 63*(3), 401–412.

Wang, M., Sui, D., Li, G., & Jie, H. (2010). Psychometric properties of the PTSD checklist-civilian version among junior school students from earthquake-hit region. *Chinese Journal of Behavioral Medicine and Brain Science, 19*(6), 566–568.

Wang, Z., Wang, X., & Jiang, K. (2007). Analysis of the clinical characters of first episode generalized anxiety disorder. *Shanghai Archives of Psychiatry, 19*(3), 133–135.

Watson, D., & Friend, R. (1969). Measurement of social-evaluation anxiety. *Journal of Consulting and Clinical Psychology, 33*, 448–457.

Weathers, F., Litz, B., Herman, D., Huska, J., & Keane, T. (1993). *The PTSD Checklist (PCL): Reliability, validity, and diagnostic utility*. Paper presented at the Annual Meeting of International Society for Posttraumatic Stress Studies.

Wilkins, K. C., Lang, A. J., & Norman, S. B. (2011). Synthesis of the psychometric properties of the PTSD checklist (PCL) military, civilian, and specific versions. *Depression & Anxiety, 28*(7), 596–606.

Woodward, A. T., Taylor, R. J., McKeever, K. B., Aranda, M. P., Lincoln, K. D., & Chatters, L. M. (2011). Prevalence of lifetime DSM-IV affective disorders among older African Americans, Black Caribbeans, Latinos, Asians and Non-Hispanic White people. *International Journal of Geriatric Psychiatry, 27*, 816–827.

Ye, D., Qian, M., Liu, X., & Chen, X. (2007). Revision of Social Interaction Anxiety Scale and Social Phobia Scale. *Chinese Journal of Clinical Psychology, 15*(2), 115–117.

Youn, G., Knight, B. G., Jeong, H. S., & Benton, D. (1999). Differences in familism values and caregiving outcomes among Korean, Korean American, and White American dementia caregivers. *Psychology and Aging, 14*, 355–364.

Zhong, J., Wang, C., Li, J., & Liu, J. (2009). Penn State Worry Questionnaire: structure and psychometric properties of the Chinese version. *Journal of Zhejiang University. Science. B, 10*(3), R749–B846.

Assessing Substance-Related Disorders in Asian Americans

14

Sally J. Vogel and Daniel N. Allen

Introduction

It is estimated that 17.3 million Asian-Americans live in the USA, according to the 2010 US Census bureau (Hoeffel, Rastogi, Kim, & Shahid, 2012). The majority identified as Asian alone, 14.7 million, while the remaining 2.6 million identified as Asian in combination with one or more ethnic groups. Asian is a diverse group, being defined as "a person having origins in any of the original peoples of the Far East, Southeast Asia, or the Indian subcontinent, including, for example, Cambodia, China, India, Japan, Korea, Malaysia, Pakistan, the Philippine Islands, Thailand, and Vietnam" by the US Census Bureau (Hoeffel et al., 2012, p. 2). The largest Asian-American groups, alone or in any combination, were Chinese, Filipino, Asian Indian, Vietnamese, Korean, and Japanese. Asian-Americans were also found to be the fastest growing racial group from 2000 to 2010, growing by 43 % as compared to 9.7 % for the total population. The assessment and treatment of health and behavioral problems within this large and growing population within the USA is an important consideration.

A once common theory regarding health and behavioral problems in Asian-American populations was that of the model minority (Choi & Lahey, 2006; Evans, Pierce, Li, Rawson, & Hser, 2012; Fong & Tsuang, 2007). The model minority theory suggests that Asian-Americans have lower levels of health problems, are higher achieving, and maintain more self-sufficient family units than other ethnic groups (Choi & Lahey, 2006). Research has been mixed with regard to this theory, however, with some studies finding equal or higher rates of health and behavioral problems in Asian-Americans compared to other ethnic groups and others finding lower rates. Choi and Lahey (2006) found that Asian American Pacific Islanders (AAPI) in grades 7–12 were less likely to smoke, consume alcohol, get drunk, or use substances than White youth. They did find some effect for immigration factors, such that first-generation immigrant children reported less problem behaviors than second-generation or nonimmigrant children. The differences found in substance use behavior between White and Asian Pacific Islander youth were greater for immigrant than nonimmigrant children. This highlights the fact that immigration status and acculturation may be a factor in the differing results of health problems in Asian-American populations. AAPI may experience more tension between their culture of origin and Western cultural values, particularly when the acculturation level between themselves and their families is discrepant. This tension, as well as desire for acceptance by peer groups, may

S.J. Vogel, M.A. (✉) • D.N. Allen, Ph.D.
Psychology Department, University of Nevada,
4505 S Maryland Pkwy MS5030,
Las Vegas, NV 89154, USA
e-mail: sallyjvogel@live.com; daniel.allen@unlv.edu

L.T. Benuto et al. (eds.), *Guide to Psychological Assessment with Asians*,
DOI 10.1007/978-1-4939-0796-0_14,

increase the propensity for drug use as a coping mechanism (Rastogi & Wadhwa, 2006). Biracial Asian-American individuals likely feel similar tension between multiple cultural identities (Clark, Doyle, & Clincy, 2013). Clark and colleagues (2013) found biracial White-Asian-American children to begin drinking alcohol and smoking marijuana at earlier ages than White children and to use all substances at earlier ages than Asian-American children. Another factor that may account for differing results in health and problem behaviors is the use of different Asian subpopulations considering there are approximately 50 subgroups of AAPIs (Office of Minority and National Affairs, 2010). The National Survey on Drug Health and Use (NSDUH, 2011) found lower levels of alcohol, cigarette, and marijuana use in the past month in Asian-American youth ages 12–17 as compared to the national average. When specific subgroups were compared they found a high of 9.7 % in Filipino youth for past month alcohol use and a low of 5.1 % among Asian Indians. With regard to past month marijuana use, a high of 5.2 % in Korean youth and a low of 1.0 % among Asian Indians was found. Similar to Choi and Lahey (2006), there was an effect for immigration status, such that Asian-American youth born in the USA had higher rates of past month alcohol use than foreign-born Asian-American youth; however, foreign-born Asian-Americans had slightly higher rates of nonmedical prescription drug use.

Regardless of differences in prevalence rates among ethnic groups, substance abuse and dependence in Asian American Pacific Islanders does occur and warrants attention to ensure accurate assessment and treatment. Research has found that Asian-American populations may be underutilizing mental health and addiction treatment services (Fong & Tsuang, 2007; Office of Minority and National Affairs, 2010). This may be due to shame associated with or unwillingness to disclose one's problems (Fong & Tsuang, 2007; Office of Minority and National Affairs, 2010), particularly outside of the family (Rastogi & Wadhwa, 2006). This fact may also contribute to the lower levels of mental health problems found in AAPI. Additionally, AAPI individuals that do seek or present for treatment tend to have more severe mental health problems, which may be a result of delayed treatment seeking (Fong & Tsuang, 2007; Office of Minority and National Affairs, 2010). AAPIs also tend to manifest mental health problems through physical symptoms (Office of Minority and National Affairs, 2010).

Additional cultural considerations when assessing AAPI clients include considerations of language, cultural values, and religion. It is estimated that one-third of Asian-Americans speak English "less than well" (Office of Minority and National Affairs, 2010). Cultural or religious values may increase the prevalence of substance use and clash with disclosure of and treatment seeking for mental health problems. For example, women tend to have fewer freedoms and to be disciplined more sternly (Rastogi & Wadhwa, 2006). This may increase the tendency to use substances or inhibit the afflicted person or her family from seeking resolution outside the family.

When working with AAPI subgroups, the availability of culturally specific assessment measures is an important consideration. Research, particularly for some Asian-American subgroups may be lacking. This chapter will focus on cultural considerations when assessing Asian-American clients and will describe substance use assessment instruments available for use (Table 14.1). In this chapter, substance use disorder assessment instruments will be reviewed. This chapter is divided into two primary sections. The first section discusses general alcohol and substance abuse and dependence measures that have evidence for their effective use in AAPIs. Some measures assess only one drug class while others assess general drug and alcohol misuse. The second section reviews alcohol abuse and dependence assessment measures that have been researched for use in AAPI subgroups. The psychometric evidence of each assessment instrument will be discussed when available in addition to specific AAPI subgroups and ages the instruments have support in. For psychometric evidence, published reports often include estimates of reliability/precision (e.g., internal consistency, test–retest reliability), as well as sensitivity (the true positive classification rate) and specificity

Table 14.1 Substance-related assessment instruments for use in Asian-Americans

Instrument	Type of assessment	Age range	Languages
Addiction Severity Index (ASI)	• Semi-structured interview • Computer administration	Adults	Chinese, Japanese, Korean
Drug Abuse Screening Test (DAST)	• Self-report • Structured interview	Adults	India—exact language unknown
Drug Abuse Screening Test-Adolescent (DAST-A)	• Self-report • Structured interview	Adolescents: (13–17)	None
Severity of Dependence Scale (SDS)	• Self-report • Interview	Adults	Chinese, Japanese
CRAFFT	• Self-report	Adolescents and young adults: (16–26)	Chinese
Alcohol Use Disorders Identification Test (AUDIT)	• Interview • Self-report • Computer-assisted	Adults	Chinese, Hindi, Japanese, Nepali, Vietnamese
Michigan Alcoholism Screening Test (MAST)	• Self-report • Structured interview	Adults	Chinese, India, Korean
CAGE Questionnaire	• Self-report	Adults	Chinese, Korean

(the true negative classification rate) estimates. A number of studies have also used receiver operating characteristics (ROC) analyses, to determine sensitivity, specificity and a variety of other psychometric properties of the substance abuse instruments. Briefly, in ROC analyses, the area under the ROC curve (AUC) indicates the ability of a test score to distinguish between two groups, for example substance use and nonsubstance use groups. An AUC of 1.00 indicates perfect classification while and AUC of 0.50 indicates classification rate at chance levels. AUCs between 0.80 and 0.90 indicate good classification accuracy (Hosmer & Lemeshow, 2000).

General Substance Use Assessment Instruments

Addiction Severity Index (ASI)

The Addiction Severity Index (ASI; McLellan, Luborsky, Woody, & O'Brien, 1980) is a semi-structured interview that assesses alcohol and substance use problems. The interview takes approximately 50 min to 1 h to complete and assesses both current (within the last 30 days) and lifetime alcohol and substance use. The ASI assesses not only actual extent of alcohol and substance use, but areas typically affected by substance use and treatment considerations. The seven areas commonly affected by substance use that are assessed by the ASI are: alcohol use, drug use, medical, psychological, legal, family/social, and employment/support (Denis, Cacciola, & Alterman, 2013; McLellan et al., 1980). A composite score (CS) and a severity rating (SR) are calculated for each problem area. The ASI underwent slight changes since 1980 with the most significant revision occurring in its sixth edition (Denis et al., 2013; McLellan, Cacciola, Alterman, Rikoon, & Carise, 2006). By its sixth edition, the ASI had been translated into 20 different languages (McLellan et al., 2006) and may be the most widely used addiction assessment in different settings and populations (Denis et al., 2013). Manuals and some paper-and-pencil versions of the ASI are freely accessible online at http://triweb.tresearch.org/index.php/tools/download-asi-instruments-manuals/, although at this time the Web site contains only the fifth version and does not contain AAPI-relevant versions.

AAPI-Relevant Versions of the ASI

The ASI has been translated into Chinese, Japanese, and Korean. The following is a review of the available research on those translations.

Chinese

A Chinese version, based on the fifth version of the ASI, has been assessed in Chinese patients in methadone maintenance treatment (Luo, Wu, & Wei, 2010). Luo and colleagues (2010) found acceptable internal consistency for six of the seven problem areas, with Cronbach's alphas ranging from 0.63 to 0.79. The legal area, however, had a Cronbach's alpha of 0.44. Notably, the authors deleted two questions in the legal scale for sociocultural reasons, which may have negatively impacted the internal consistency of the legal portion. One-week test–retest reliability for the composite scores was good, with significant correlations ranging from 0.68 to 0.84. The psychiatric and family/social areas showed good criterion validity, significantly correlating with the SCL-90 and the Family Adaptability and Cohesion Evaluation Scale α-Chinese Version (FACES α-CV), respectively.

Japanese

A Japanese version, modeled after the fifth version of the ASI, has been assessed in Japanese substance users (ASI-J; Senoo et al., 2006). Senoo and colleagues (2006) found the inter-rater reliability in each area to range from 0.68 to 0.99. Cronbach's alpha for each composite score ranged from 0.57 to 0.86, supporting the reliability of most areas with the exception of the drug use and employment/support areas. Also, the composite scores were significantly correlated with drug craving levels, length of abstinence, mental health, and/or relapse, supporting their concurrent and predictive validity.

The same Japanese version has also been evaluated in male inpatients with a history of alcohol use disorders (Haraguchi et al., 2009). Haraguchi and colleagues (2009) found the internal consistency of six of the seven problem areas to be acceptable with Cronbach's alphas ranging from 0.67 to 0.84. The family/social scale, however, had the lowest Cronbach's alpha at 0.53. The family/social CS was significantly higher in individuals that relapsed than those that remained abstinence, however, suggesting this scale may provide some relapse predictive validity. The alcohol use composite scale and severity rating were also significantly correlated with some biochemical markers, such as glutamic-oxaloacetic transaminase, a measure of liver function.

Korean

A Korean version has also been developed and assessed in patients with alcoholism (Lee et al., 1997). This article is also not available in English, so the summary information is provided here. Lee and colleagues (1997) found significant inter-rater reliability. A "reasonable level" of item consistency was found in the medical, alcohol, family/social and psychiatric sections. Correlations between composite scores and severity ratings of corresponding section were significant for all sections. The severity ratings in the psychiatric section were significantly correlated with the Michigan Alcohol Screening Test (MAST) and Symptom Checklist-90-Revised (SCL-90-R), supporting concurrent validity.

Summary

The original ASI authors have encouraged the modification of the ASI for specific interests or populations. They recommend clinicians maintain the original questions within the versions of the ASI, as eliminating or modifying some questions may alter the reliability and validity research has established (McLellan et al., 1992). However, an entire section, or problem area, can be eliminated if it is not considered necessary. Also, additional questions addressing special interest, such as culturally specific questions, can be added to the interview (McLellan et al., 1992) as deemed appropriate.

The research on the ASI in Asian populations just discussed has all been conducted in their respective countries. This may limit the generalizability of the instrument to Asian-Americans as they may be omitting important considerations unique to Asian-Americans, such as acculturation issues. Also, the populations examined are limited. For example, Haraguchi examined only male inmates. A clinician using the ASI or an Asian population-specific ASI should consider adding culturally relevant questions or assessment measures, such as the impact acculturation stress, traumas, or gender roles may have on substance use.

Application with Younger Populations

Four versions of the ASI have been adapted from the adult version to be used with younger populations (McLellan et al., 1992). These versions are the Teen Addiction Severity Index (T-ASI; Kaminer, Bukstein, & Tarter, 1991), The Adolescent Drug Abuse Diagnosis (ADAD; Friedman & Utada, 1989), Adolescent Problem Severity Index (APSI; Metzger, Kushner, & McLellan, 1991), and the Comprehensive Addiction Severity Index for Adolescents (CASI-A; Meyers, McLellan, Jaeger, & Pettinati, 1995).

Of the adolescent versions of the ASI, the T-ASI has been researched the most extensively. The T-ASI has been translated into multiple languages and its psychometric properties have been assessed in a number of populations (Kaminer, 2008); however, the languages and populations covered to date do not include Asian subgroups.

Drug Abuse Screening Test (DAST)

The Drug Abuse Screening Test (DAST; Skinner, 1982) is a brief abuse and dependence screening measure for a wide variety of substances. The DAST can be found in 28- 20- and 10-item versions (Yudko, Lozhkina, & Fouts, 2007). The DAST was modeled after the Michigan Alcohol Screening Test (MAST, discussed below).

AAPI-Relevant Versions

The short version of the Drug Abuse Screening Test (DAST-10) was evaluated in psychiatric inpatients in India (Carey, Carey, & Chandra, 2003). The items were completed in interview format "using the language most comfortable for the patient" (p. 3). Exploratory factor analyses of the DAST-10 determined one factor to be the best fit for all items. Internal consistency was excellent, with a Cronbach's alpha of 0.94. Of the patients that were discharged with a drug use disorder diagnosis, 6 (35 %) had not exceeded the DAST-10 cut score of ≥3. Notably, these six patients had lifetime use but had not used in the past year. Because the DAST assesses drug use during the past year these patients were not detected. Of those patients that exceeded the same cut-score and were considered high-risk, 16 (59 %) did not receive a diagnosis of a drug use disorder at discharge. There was no significant difference in DAST-10 scores between the high-risk patients that did and did not receive a discharge diagnosis of a drug use disorder.

Application with Younger Populations

The Drug Abuse Screening Test for Adolescents (DAST-A; Martino, Grilo, & Fehon, 2000) is a 27-item self-report measure modeled after the adult version. It takes approximately 5 min to administer and results in scores ranging from 0 to 27. Martino and colleagues (2000) found the scale to have excellent internal consistency (0.91), and good 1-week test–retest reliability ($r = 0.89$) in a sample of 15–19 year-olds. A cut-off score of ≥6 was considered optimal to indicate a drug-related disorder. The DAST-A has not been evaluated in Asian subgroups.

Severity of Dependence Scale

The Severity of Dependence Scale (SDS; Gossop et al., 1995) is a five-item screening measure assessing psychological components of dependence. It can be used to assess dependence in different kinds of drugs, and its use has been examined with respect to some drug categories. The five-items are rated on a scale of 0–3 with regard to frequency and the last item referring to difficulty, resulting in a total score ranging from 0 to 15. In its general version, the SDS does not name any specific drug, but instead inserts [named drug] when necessary in the questions. The SDS can be modified for any specific drug class and the name of the drug class of interest inserted as appropriate (Gossop et al., 1995).

AAPI-Relevant Versions

Chinese

A Chinese version of the SDS has been evaluated in non-institutionalized heroin users in China (Gu et al., 2008). Gu and colleagues (2008) found a two-factor structure for the Chinese version, accounting for 69.59 % of the variance. The first factor consisted of items 1, 2, and 5 and was named the "Impact" factor, while items 3 and 4 loaded on a separate "Perception." Item-total correlations ranged from 0.36 to 0.75, with items 4 and 3 having the lowest correlations, respectively. The authors recommend a shortened three-item version of the SDS consisting of the first factor items (SDS-R). Internal consistency for the SDS was 0.61, while the SDS-R had a Cronbach's alpha of 0.78. The two versions had comparable test–retest reliability (0.63 and 0.64). The SDS was also significantly correlated with the Opiate Addiction Severity Index and the Quality of Life-Drug Addiction. The SDS-R was more highly correlated with these measures.

The Chinese version has also been evaluated in heroin users in Taiwan (Chen et al., 2008). A single factor was found for the five-items, accounting for 50.2 % of the variance. Internal consistency was 0.75 and test–retest reliability was 0.88 for the total score. For individual items, test–retest reliability ranged from 0.59 to 0.93 with items 4 and 3 having the lowest correlations (0.59 and 0.66, respectively). While they did not find a second factor for these two items, results are consistent with the previous study (Gu et al., 2008) finding lower reliability for items 3 and 4.

Japanese

A Japanese version has also been evaluated in a nationwide mental hospital survey (Ozaki & Wada, 2005). The article is written in Japanese so the following information is based upon the English abstract. The SDS-J was found to have a Cronbach's alpha of 0.76. A single factor was found for the five-items, accounting for 50.8 % of the variance. Item-total correlations ranged from 0.68 to 0.76.

Application with Younger Populations

The SDS has been evaluated with regard to cannabis use in adolescents ages 14–18 (Martin, Copeland, Gates, & Gilmour, 2006). They found an internal consistency of 0.83 and a test–retest reliability of 0.88. A single factor was found, accounting for 60 % of the variance. Using ROC analysis a cut-off score of 4 was found to be the best at determining cannabis dependence with a sensitivity of 65.1 and a specificity of 94.3. The SDS has not been evaluated in AAPI adolescent populations.

CRAFFT

The CRAFFT is a six-item alcohol and other drug screening instrument developed for use in adolescents (Knight et al., 1999). Its name is an acronym to represent the questions that are contained within the measure. The acronym represents the problem areas car, relax, alone, forget, and family/friends (Knight et al., 1999). The CRAFFT has been found to have a sensitivity of 92.3 and specificity of 82.1 using a cut-off score of ≥2 in adolescents ages 14–18 (Knight et al., 1999). It has also been found to have sensitivity ranging from 0.76 to 0.92 and specificity from 0.80 to 0.94 in identifying problem use, abuse, or dependence using a cut-off score of ≥2 (Knight, Sherritt, Shrier, Harris, & Chang, 2002).

Applications with Asian Populations

The CRAFFT has been evaluated in a multiethnic Asian population of adolescents and young adults ages 16–26 years in Singapore (Subramaniam, Cheok, Verma, Wong, & Chong, 2010). The internal consistency was acceptable at 0.73. The optimal cut-off score for drug or alcohol abuse or dependence was ≥1.

Alcohol Use Assessment Instruments

Alcohol Use Disorders Identification Test (AUDIT)

The Alcohol Use Disorders Identification Test (AUDIT; Babor, de la Fuente, Saunders, & Marcus, 1992; Babor, Higgins-Biddle, Saunders, & Monteiro, 2001) is a ten-item screening instrument for alcohol-related problems consistent with International Statistical Classification of Diseases and Related Health Problems revision 10 (ICD-10) diagnostic criteria. The first eight items address alcohol use in the last year, with scores ranging from 0 to 4 based on amount consumed or frequency of problem behaviors, while the last two items address lifetime alcohol use, with higher scores given to occurrences in the last year. The AUDIT takes approximately 2–4 min to complete and can be administered as an interview, self-report, or computer assisted (Babor et al., 2001). The AUDIT is intended to identify drinking patterns that qualify as "hazardous," drinking that is at risk to become harmful; "harmful," drinking that results in negative consequences; and "dependence," drinking resulting in behavioral, cognitive, and physiological problems (Babor et al., 2001). Briefer versions of the AUDIT have been used and both the original and briefer versions have been researched extensively (Reinert & Allen, 2007).

AAPI-Relevant Versions

AAPI-relevant translations of the AUDIT include Chinese, Japanese, Hindi (Babor et al., 2001), Nepali (Pradhan et al., 2012), and Vietnamese (Giang, Spak, Dzung, & Allebeck, 2005) versions. Most of these translated versions can be obtained by writing to the Department of Mental Health and Substance Dependence, World Health Organization. Babor and colleagues (2001) also suggest contacting the World Health Organization to inquire about more recent translations or the procedure of translating before attempting to do so.

Chinese

Li and colleagues (2011) reviewed articles from 1980 to 2009 referring to Chinese versions of the AUDIT published in both English and Chinese. They found 21 relevant articles, 9 of which examined the psychometric properties of Chinese versions of the AUDIT and the remaining used Chinese versions of the AUDIT for clinical purposes. With regard to the 9 psychometric studies, translations include Mandarin, Cantonese, and Tibetan, and versions include the full AUDIT, AUDIT-C (items 1–3), AUDIT-4 (items 1–3 and 10), and AUDIT-3 (item 3). The Cantonese translation resulted in an 18-item measure that addresses culturally relevant drinking practices. Overall, all versions and translations demonstrated good sensitivity and specificity, ranging from 0.88 to 0.997 and 0.71 to 0.93, respectively. However, lower specificity for alcohol dependence was found among Min-Nan Taiwanese at 0.58.

India

The AUDIT was evaluated in 297 individuals recruited from treatment centers in North India in interview format (Pal, Jena, & Yadav, 2004). There are 845 major languages spoken in India, with Hindi being the official language and English being the associate official language (Ramanathan, 2008). A Hindi AUDIT has been created (Babor et al., 2001), however, the authors did not indicate a translation process or specific language used so it seems the English version was used in this study. They found the AUDIT to have good internal consistency, with a Cronbach's alpha of 0.92. Using the traditional cut-off of ≥8, receiver operating characteristic (ROC) analyses found a sensitivity of 93.0 and specificity of 66.7 in identifying individuals qualifying for harmful use or alcohol dependence based on ICD-10 criteria. Using a cut-off of ≥16, the sensitivity was 85.3 and specificity 89.4. ROC analyses were also conducted to determine the sensitivity and specificity of distinguishing ICD-10 harmful users and alcohol dependence. The cut-off score and corresponding sensitivity and specificity were as follows: ≥8, 96.2, 28.6; ≥10, 95.2, 42.9; ≥24, 81.0, 85.7.

Carey and colleagues (2003) also examined the AUDIT in psychiatric inpatients in India in interview format "using the language most comfortable for the patient" (p. 3). This study was mentioned previously for the DAST-10. Exploratory factor analyses of the AUDIT determined one factor to be the best fit for all ten items. Internal consistency was excellent, with a Cronbach's alpha of 0.94. Of the patients that were discharged with an alcohol use disorder diagnosis, 2 (10 %) had not exceeded the AUDIT cut score of ≥8. Of those patients that exceeded the same cut-score and were considered high-risk, 65 (77 %) did not receive a diagnosis of alcohol use disorder at discharge. Because no standard diagnostic interview was used, these individuals may represent false positives or actual alcohol abusers that were not detected by standard psychiatric interview.

Japanese

The AUDIT has been translated to Japanese using a method approved by the World Health Organization. Cut scores ≥11 have been found to indicate substance abuse in Japan (Hiro & Shima, 1996). Using the same cut-score, the reliability of the Japanese version was evaluated in 113 male workers in a car manufacturing company in Japan (Kawada, Inagaki, & Kuratomi, 2011). The internal consistency was 0.67 for the full version of the AUDIT and 0.51 for the AUDIT-C.

Gender difference for the AUDIT were evaluated by national surveys in 15 countries as part of the Gender, Alcohol, and Culture: An International Study (GACAIS; Peng, Wilsnack, Kristjanson, Benson, & Wilsnack, 2012). Japan is the only AAPI-relevant country surveyed. Cronbach's alpha was calculated for the total score and each subscale. The total score had the highest internal consistency at 0.68 for men and 0.70 for woman. Confirmatory factor analysis was conducted for men and women in each country. Both two- and three-factor models were a good fit in Japanese men. None of the models were good fit for Japanese women. For the pooled sample of all countries data, AUDIT total scores and subscale scores were significantly correlated with measures of alcohol-related problems, withdrawal, intoxication, expectancy, and intimacy.

Korean

The AUDIT and briefer versions have been evaluated in several Korean samples (Kim et al., 2013; Kwon et al., 2013; Ryou, Kim, Jung, Kim, & Choi, 2012; So & Sung, 2013). In Korean men 65 years and older, the AUDIT had better sensitivity and specificity than a four-item alcohol screening instrument (CAGE, reviewed later in this chapter) and a geriatric version of the MAST (MAST-G) in detecting at-risk drinking and alcohol use disorders (Ryou et al., 2012). The optimal AUDIT cut-off for at-risk drinking was ≥7, and ≥11 for alcohol use disorders.

The AUDIT, AUDIT-C, and CAGE were compared in Korean college students (Kwon et al., 2013). The area under the receiver operating characteristic curve (AUC) was the largest for the AUDIT-C in detecting at-risk drinking, but not significantly different than the AUDIT. The AUC was largest for the AUDIT in detecting alcohol use disorders, but again not significantly different from the AUDIT-C. Both AUDIT and AUDIT-C had significantly larger AUC than the CAGE in detecting at-risk drinking and alcohol use disorders. The optimal AUDIT cut-off score for at-risk drinking was ≥8 for males and ≥5 for females and ≥10 for alcohol use disorders in males and ≥8 in females. The optimal AUDIT-C cut-off score for at-risk drinking was ≥6 for males and ≥4 for females and ≥7 for alcohol use disorders in males and ≥6 in females.

So and Sung (2013) derived a brief AUDIT, consisting of items 3, 4, 5 and 9, using factor analysis in Korean males in an outpatient hospital and psychiatric ward. The brief AUDIT was then compared to the CAGE and the National Alcoholism Screening Test (NAST). They found good internal consistency for the AUDIT and the brief AUDIT, at 0.87 and 0.82, respectively, which was equivalent to the NAST and superior to the CAGE. Using ROC analysis, the optimal brief AUDIT cut-off score for alcohol use disorders was ≥5 and ≥10 for alcohol dependence. The authors' chose to maximize sensitivity, resulting in recommended cut-off scores of ≥6 for alcohol use disorders and ≥9 for alcohol dependence. Additionally, the brief AUDIT had greater AUC than the NAST and CAGE for alcohol abuse (0.87) and dependence (0.97).

Finally, Kim and colleagues (2013) developed the five-item AUDIT (AUDIT-5) consisting of items 2, 4, 5, 9, and 10 using regression analysis. This version was then compared to other brief versions of the AUDIT and the CAGE. They found good internal consistency for all AUDIT versions evaluated, ranging from 0.82 to 0.92, with the AUDIT being the highest and the AUDIT-5 the lowest. AUC for problem drinking screening for all versions of the AUDIT ranged from 0.94 to 0.99, with the AUDIT-5, AUDIT-C, and AUDIT having the highest values. The AUDIT, AUDIT-5, AUDIT-PC, and CAGE had high AUCs, ranging from 0.91 to 0.95 for alcohol use disorder screening. The same measures had high AUCs, ranging from 0.92 to 0.96 for alcohol dependence screening.

Nepali

Pradhan and colleagues (2012) translated the AUDIT to Nepali and examined its validity in 1,068 hospital outpatients in Nepal. They found good internal consistency with a Cronbach's alpha of 0.82. They examined the diagnostic validity using DSM-IV (APA, 2000) alcohol abuse and dependence criteria. ROC curves indicated optimal cut-off scores ≥11 for alcohol dependence in men and women, cut-off scores ≥9 for both alcohol dependence and abuse in men and women, and cut-off scores ≥5 for men and ≥4 for women to indicate hazardous drinking.

Vietnamese

Giang and colleagues (2005) translated the AUDIT to Vietnamese and evaluated it in a rural district in Vietnam. Due to the low occurrence of alcohol problems found in female in the study, analyses were conducted with only male data. They found an optimal cut-off score of 7/8 for at-risk screenings in the general population. At this cut-off the sensitivity was 81.8 and specificity 76.1 for detecting at-risk drinking. Using ICD-10 criteria, for Harmful Use the sensitivity was 100 and specificity 69.9 and for alcohol dependence the sensitivity was 93.8 and specificity 87.4. The AUC was 0.91 for Harmful Use and 0.84 for alcohol dependence.

Application with Younger Populations

The AUDIT has been found to be superior to other alcohol screening measures at identify alcohol use problems in adolescents using a cut-off score of ≥10 (Kelly, Donovan, Chung, Cook, & Delbridge, 2004) and ≥9 (Cook, Chung, Kelly, & Clark, 2005). The AUDIT has not been evaluated in adolescent Asian subgroups.

Michigan Alcoholism Screening Test (MAST)

Another commonly used and extensively researched alcohol screening instrument is the Michigan Alcoholism Screening Test (MAST; Selzer, 1971). The MAST is 25-items, with briefer versions available, such as the 10-item brief MAST (B-MAST; Pokorny, Miller, & Kaplan, 1972), and the 13-item short MAST (SMAST; Selzer, Vinokur, & Rooijen, 1975).

AAPI-Relevant Versions

Chinese

A Mandarin Chinese version of the short MAST (SMAST) has been evaluated in hospitalized patients in Taiwan (Wu et al., 2008). The AUC was 0.87 for the entire sample and 0.81 for men only. The AUDIT and three briefer versions were significantly better than the SMAST, while the SMAST was equivalent to the CAGE.

India

The SMAST was evaluated in the same study mentioned previously for the AUDIT in North India (Pal et al., 2004). The internal consistency was 0.80. Using the cut-off of ≥4, ROC analyses found a sensitivity of 87.4 and specificity of 83.3 in identifying individuals qualifying for harmful use or alcohol dependence based on ICD-10 criteria. Using a cut-off of ≥6, the sensitivity was 85.7 and specificity 87.9. ROC analyses were also conducted to determine the sensitivity and specificity of distinguishing ICD-10 harmful users and alcohol dependence. The cut-off score and corresponding sensitivity and specificity were as follows: ≥5, 91.9, 66.7; ≥10, 81.0, 90.5.

Korean

The geriatric version of the MAST (MAST-G) was evaluated in Korean men aged 65 years and older in the same study discussed previously for the AUDIT (Ryou et al., 2012). The AUDIT was found to have greater sensitivity and specificity than the MAST-G and CAGE. The optimal MAST-G cut-off for at-risk drinking was ≥2, and ≥4 for alcohol use disorders.

Cutting Down, Annoyed, Guilty, Eye-Opener (CAGE)

The CAGE is a four-item alcohol screening instrument (Mayfield, McLeod, & Hall, 1974). Its name is an acronym for the four questions contained in the measure, specifically the patients' need to cut down on drinking, becoming annoyed by criticism, feeling guilty about drinking and taking a drink as an eye-opener first thing in the morning. Each question has a value of one point, with scores ≥2 indicative of alcoholism.

AAPI-Relevant Versions

Much of the research conducted in Asian subgroups on the CAGE has been in the examination of the psychometric properties of another screening instrument. The results of those studies are summarized below.

Chinese

A Mandarin Chinese version of the CAGE has been evaluated in hospitalized patients in Taiwan (Wu et al., 2008). The AUC was 0.85 for the entire sample and 0.78 for men only. The AUDIT and three briefer versions were significantly better than the CAGE, while the CAGE was equivalent to the SMAST.

Korean

The CAGE was evaluated in several studies previously mentioned in the AUDIT (Kwon et al., 2013; Ryou et al., 2012; So & Sung, 2013). In Korean men aged 65 years and older the AUDIT was found to have greater sensitivity and specificity than the CAGE and MAST-G, with no significant differences found between CAGE and MAST-G (Ryou et al., 2012). The optimal CAGE cut-off for at-risk drinking and alcohol use disorders was ≥2.

The AUDIT and AUDIT-C were found to be superior to the CAGE in detecting both at-risk drinking and alcohol abuse disorders in Korean college students (Kwon et al., 2013). The optimal cut-off scores for at-risk drinking and alcohol use disorders in both males and females was ≥1. In Korean males in an outpatient hospital and psychiatric ward the internal consistency of the CAGE was found to be 0.69 (So & Sung, 2013). The AUC was 0.76 ± 0.05 for alcohol abuse and 0.93 ± 0.03 for alcohol dependence. Kim and colleagues (2012) found the internal consistency of the CAGE to be 0.70. The AUC for problem drinking was 0.76, 0.91 for alcohol use disorders, and 0.92 for alcohol dependence. Four versions of the AUDIT were found to be superior in screening for problem drinking, however, the CAGE was found to be superior to two brief versions of the AUDIT (AUDIT-3 and AUDIT-C) in screening for alcohol use disorders and alcohol dependence.

Application with Younger Populations

ROC analyses were conducted on the CAGE and other screening measures in adolescents in the USA (Cook et al., 2005; Kelly et al., 2004). Kelly and colleagues (2004) found the AUC to be 0.68, which was the lowest of the screening measures assessed. Cook and colleagues (2005) found an AUC of 0.70, which was also the lowest of the screening measures assessed. Both studies found ≥1 to be the optimal cut-off score. An additional study found a sensitivity of 0.37 and specificity of 0.96 (Knight, Sherritt, Harris, Gates, & Chang, 2003). The CAGE has not been evaluated in adolescent Asian subgroups.

Summary and Recommendations

Assessment measures for alcohol and substance use disorders have received some attention in the literature in Asian American Pacific Islander (AAPI) populations. Many of the cultural considerations discussed in this chapter are general guidelines. As mentioned, there are more than 50 subgroups of AAPIs and adequate coverage of each group's cultural considerations is beyond the scope of this chapter. It is important for a health professional working with a specific Asian-American population to familiarize him/herself with the cultural and religious beliefs of that group, and how those beliefs may promote or inhibit disclosure and treatment of problem behaviors.

Much of the AAPI research on psychometric properties of alcohol and drug assessment measures just discussed has been conducted in their respective countries. Modifications were made to some instruments in some languages to address sociocultural and dialectical differences. However, the modifications do not address important considerations unique to Asian-Americans, such as acculturation issues. Clinician should consider adding culturally relevant questions or additional assessment measures to address these missing items, such as the impact acculturation stress, traumas, or gender roles may have on substance use. Another consideration is that the same instrument may have been translated to a specific language by separate research groups, making its comparability across studies difficult. Finally, the samples were limited, with research into these instruments conducted primarily in males and in hospital settings. Further research into additional Asian subgroups, females, and adolescents are warranted.

References

APA. (2000). *Diagnostic and Statistical Manual of Mental Disorders* (4th ed., Text Rev., Vol. 285). Washington, DC: Author.

Babor, T. F., de la Fuente, J. R., Saunders, J. B., & Marcus, G. (1992). *The Alcohol Use Disorders Identification Test: Guidelines for use in primary health care*. Geneva: World Health Organization.

Babor, T. F., Higgins-Biddle, J. C., Saunders, J. B., & Monteiro, M. G. (2001). *The Alcohol Use Disorders Identification Test: Guidelines for use in primary care* (2nd ed.). Geneva: World Health Organization.

Carey, K. B., Carey, M. P., & Chandra, P. S. (2003). Psychometric evaluation of the alcohol use disorders identification test and short drug abuse screening test with psychiatric patients in India. *Journal of Clinical Psychiatry, 64*(7), 767–774.

Chen, V. C.-H., Chen, H., Lin, T.-Y., Chou, H.-H., Lai, T.-J., Ferri, C. P., & Gossop, M. (2008). Severity of heroin dependence in Taiwan: Reliability and validity of the Chinese version of the Severity of Dependence Scale (SDS[Ch]). *Addictive Behaviors, 33*(12), 1590–1593. doi:10.1016/j.addbeh.2008.06.001

Choi, Y., & Lahey, B. B. (2006). Testing the model minority stereotype: Youth behaviors across racial and ethnic groups. *Social Service Review, 80*(3), 419–452. doi:10.1086/505288.

Clark, T. T., Doyle, O., & Clincy, A. (2013). Age of first cigarette, alcohol, and marijuana use among U.S. biracial/ethnic youth: A population-based study. *Addictive Behaviors, 38*(9), 2450–2454. doi:10.1016/j.addbeh.2013.04.005.

Cook, R. L., Chung, T., Kelly, T. M., & Clark, D. B. (2005). Alcohol screening in young persons attending a sexually transmitted disease clinic. Comparison of AUDIT, CRAFFT, and CAGE instruments. *Journal of General Internal Medicine, 20*(1), 1–6. doi:10.1111/j.1525-1497.2005.40052.x.

Denis, C. M., Cacciola, J. S., & Alterman, A. I. (2013). Addiction Severity Index (ASI) summary scores: Comparison of the recent status scores of the ASI-6 and the composite scores of the ASI-5. *Journal of Substance Abuse Treatment*, 6–12. doi:10.1016/j.jsat.2013.06.003

Evans, E., Pierce, J., Li, L., Rawson, R., & Hser, Y. (2012). More alike than different: Health needs, services utilization, and outcomes of Asian American and Pacific Islander (AAPI) populations treated for substance use disorders. *Journal of Ethnicity in Substance Abuse, 11*(4), 318–338. doi:10.1080/15332640.2012.735172.

Fong, T. W., & Tsuang, J. (2007). Asian-Americans, addictions, and barriers to treatment. *Psychiatry, 4*(11), 51–58.

Friedman, A. S., & Utada, A. (1989). A method for diagnosing and planning the treatment of adolescent drug abusers: The Adolescent Drug Abuse Diagnosis [ADAD] instrument. *Journal of Drug Education, 19*(4), 285–312.

Giang, K. B., Spak, F., Dzung, T. V., & Allebeck, P. (2005). The use of AUDIT to assess level of alcohol problems in rural Vietnam. *Alcohol and Alcoholism, 40*(6), 578–583. doi:10.1093/alcalc/agh198.

Gossop, M., Darke, S., Griffiths, P., Hando, J., Powis, B., Hall, W., & Strang, J. (1995). The Severity of Dependence Scale (SDS): Psychometric properties of the SDS in English and Australian samples of heroin, cocaine and amphetamine users. *Addiction (Abingdon, England), 90*(5), 607–614.

Gu, J., Lau, J. T. F., Chen, H., Liu, Z., Lei, Z., Li, Z., … Wang, T. (2008). Validation of the Chinese version of the Opiate Addiction Severity Inventory (OASI) and the Severity of Dependence Scale (SDS) in non-institutionalized heroin users in China. *Addictive behaviors, 33*(5), 725–41. doi:10.1016/j.addbeh.2007.12.009

Haraguchi, A., Ogai, Y., Senoo, E., Saito, S., Suzuki, Y., Yoshino, A., … Ikeda, K. (2009). Verification of the addiction severity index Japanese version (ASI-J) as a treatment-customization, prediction, and comparison tool for alcohol-dependent individuals. *International Journal of Environmental Research and Public Health, 6*(8), 2205–2225. doi:10.3390/ijerph6082205

Hiro, H., & Shima, S. (1996). Availability of the Alcohol Use Disorders Identification Test (AUDIT) for a complete health examination in Japan. *Nihon Arukōru Yakubutsu Igakkai Zasshi, 31*(5), 437–450.

Hoeffel, E. M., Rastogi, S., Kim, M. O., & Shahid, H. (2012). *The Asian population: 2010 Census Briefs*. Washington, DC: U.S. Census Bureau.

Hosmer, D. W., & Lemeshow, S. (2000). *Applied logistic regression* (2nd ed.). New York, NY: John Wiley & Sons.

Kaminer, Y. (2008). The Teen Addiction Severity Index around the globe: The Tower of Babel revisited. *Substance Abuse, 29*(3), 89–94. doi:10.1080/08897070802219230.

Kaminer, Y., Bukstein, O., & Tarter, R. E. (1991). The Teen-Addiction Severity Index: Rationale and reliability. *International Journal of the Addictions, 26*(2), 219–226.

Kawada, T., Inagaki, H., & Kuratomi, Y. (2011). The alcohol use disorders identification test: Reliability study of the Japanese version. *Alcohol, 45*, 205–207. doi:10.1016/j.alcohol.2010.08.012.

Kelly, T. M., Donovan, J. E., Chung, T., Cook, R. L., & Delbridge, T. R. (2004). Alcohol use disorders among emergency department-treated older adolescents: A new brief screen (RUFT-Cut) using the AUDIT, CAGE, CRAFFT, and RAPS-QF. *Alcoholism: Clinical and Experimental Research, 28*(5), 746–753. doi:10.1097/01.ALC.0000125346.37075.85.

Kim, J. W., Lee, B. C., Lee, D. Y., Seo, C. H., Kim, S., Kang, T.-C., & Choi, I.-G. (2013). The 5-item Alcohol Use Disorders Identification Test (AUDIT-5): An effective brief screening test for problem drinking, alcohol use disorders and alcohol dependence. *Alcohol and Alcoholism, 48*(1), 68–73. doi:10.1093/alcalc/ags082

Knight, J. R., Sherritt, L., Harris, S. K., Gates, E. C., & Chang, G. (2003). Validity of brief alcohol screening tests among adolescents: a comparison of the AUDIT, POSIT, CAGE, and CRAFFT. *Alcoholism: Clinical and Experimental Research, 27*(1), 67–73. doi:10.1097/01.ALC.0000046598.59317.3A.

Knight, J. R., Sherritt, L., Shrier, L. A., Harris, S. K., & Chang, G. (2002). Validity of the CRAFFT substance abuse screening test among adolescent clinic patients. *Archives of Pediatrics & Adolescent Medicine, 156*(6), 607–614.

Knight, J. R., Shrier, L. A., Bravender, T. D., Farrell, M., Vander Bilt, J., & Shaffer, H. J. (1999). A new brief screen for adolescent substance abuse. *Archives of Pediatrics & Adolescent Medicine, 153*(6), 591–596.

Kwon, U. S., Kim, J. S., Kim, S. S., Jung, J. G., Yoon, S.-J., & Kim, S. G. (2013). Utility of the alcohol consumption questions in the Alcohol Use Disorders Identification Test for screening at-risk drinking and alcohol use disorders among Korean college students. *Korean Journal of Family Medicine, 34*(4), 272–280. doi:10.4082/kjfm.2013.34.4.272.

Lee, D. K., Jang, W. S., Seol, S. G., Youn, S. J., Cho, J. S., & Byun, W. T. (1997). The validity and reliability of Addiction Severity Index in alcoholic patients. *Journal of Korean Neuropsychiatric Association, 36*(6), 1033–1040.

Li, Q., Babor, T. F., Hao, W., & Chen, X. (2011). The Chinese translations of alcohol use disorders identification test (AUDIT) in China: A systematic review. *Alcohol and Alcoholism, 46*(4), 416–423. doi:0.1093/alcalc/agr012.

Luo, W., Wu, Z., & Wei, X. (2010). Reliability and validity of the Chinese version of the Addiction Severity Index. *Journal of Acquired Immune Deficiency Syndromes, 53*(Suppl 1), 1–14. doi:10.1097/QAI.0b013e3181c7dfca.Reliability.

Martin, G., Copeland, J., Gates, P., & Gilmour, S. (2006). The Severity of Dependence Scale (SDS) in an adolescent population of cannabis users: Reliability, validity and diagnostic cut-off. *Drug and Alcohol Dependence, 83*(1), 90–93.

Martino, S., Grilo, C. M., & Fehon, D. C. (2000). Development of the Drug Abuse Screening Test for Adolescents (DAST-A). *Addictive Behaviors, 25*(1), 57–70.

Mayfield, D., McLeod, G., & Hall, P. (1974). The CAGE questionnaire: Validation of a new alcoholism screening instrument. *American Journal of Psychiatry, 131*(10), 1121–1123.

McLellan, A. T., Cacciola, J. C., Alterman, A. I., Rikoon, S. H., & Carise, D. (2006). The Addiction Severity Index at 25: Origins, contributions and transitions. *The American Journal on Addictions, 15*(3), 113–124. doi:10.1080/10550490500528316.

McLellan, A. T., Kushner, H., Metzger, D., Peters, R., Smith, I., Grissom, G., … Argeriou, M. (1992). The fifth edition of the Addiction Severity Index. *Journal of Substance Abuse Treatment, 9*(3), 199–213.

McLellan, A. T., Luborsky, L., Woody, G. E., & O'Brien, C. P. (1980). An improved diagnostic evaluation instrument for substance abuse patients: The Addiction Severity Index. *The Journal of Nervous and Mental Disease, 168*(1), 26–33.

Metzger, D. S., Kushner, H., & McLellan, A. T. (1991). *Adolescent Problem Severity Index. Administration manual*. Philadelphia, PA: Biomedical Computer Research Institute.

Meyers, K., McLellan, A. T., Jaeger, J. L., & Pettinati, H. M. (1995). Development of the Comprehensive Addiction Severity Index for Adolescents (CASI-A): An interview for assessing multiple problems of adolescents. *Journal of Substance Abuse Treatment, 12*(3), 181–193.

NSDUH. (2011). *NSDUH report: Substance use among Asian adolescents*. Retrieved from http://oas.samhsa.gov/2k11/006/WEB_SR_006_HTML.pdf

Office of Minority and National Affairs. (2010). *Fact Sheet: Mental health disparities: Asian Americans*. Retrieved from www.psychiatry.org/File Library/…/Fact-Sheet---Asian-Americans.pdf

Ozaki, S., & Wada, K. (2005). A validation of the applicability of the Severity of Dependence Scale (SDS) in a nationwide mental hospital survey on substance-related psychiatric disorders (Japanese). *Nihon Arukōru Yakubutsu Igakkai Zasshi, 40*(2), 126–136.

Pal, H. R., Jena, R., & Yadav, D. (2004). Validation of the Alcohol Use Disorders Identification Test (AUDIT) in urban community outreach and de-addiction center samples in North India. *Journal of Studies on Alcohol, 65*, 794–800.

Peng, C., Wilsnack, R. W., Kristjanson, A. F., Benson, P., & Wilsnack, S. C. (2012). Gender differences in the factor structure of the Alcohol Use Disorders Identification Test in multinational general population surveys. *Drug and Alcohol Dependence, 124*(1–2), 50–56. doi:10.1016/j.drugalcdep.2011.12.002.Gender.

Pokorny, A. D., Miller, B. A., & Kaplan, H. B. (1972). The brief MAST: A shortened version of the Michigan Alcoholism Screening Test. *The American Journal of Psychiatry, 129*(3), 342–345.

Pradhan, B., Chappuis, F., Baral, D., Karki, P., Rijal, S., Hadengue, A., & Gache, P. (2012). The alcohol use disorders identification test (AUDIT): Validation of a

Nepali version for the detection of alcohol use disorders and hazardous drinking in medical settings. *Substance Abuse Treatment, Prevention, and Policy, 7*(42). doi:10.1186/1747-597X-7-42

Ramanathan, H. (2008). Testing of English in India: A developing concept. *Language Testing, 25*(1), 111–126. doi:10.1177/0265532207083747.

Rastogi, M., & Wadhwa, S. (2006). Substance Abuse among Asian Indians in the United States: A consideration of cultural factors. *Substance Use & Misuse, 41*, 1239–1249. doi:10.1080/10826080600754470.

Reinert, D. F., & Allen, J. P. (2007). The alcohol use disorders identification test: An update of research findings. *Alcoholism: Clinical and Experimental Research, 31*(2), 185–199. doi:10.1111/j.1530-0277.2006.00295.x.

Ryou, Y. I., Kim, J. S., Jung, J. G., Kim, S. S., & Choi, D. H. (2012). Usefulness of alcohol-screening instruments in detecting problem drinking among elderly male drinkers. *Korean Journal of Family Medicine, 33*(3), 126–133. doi:10.4082/kjfm.2012.33.3.126.

Selzer, M. L. (1971). The Michigan Alcoholism Screening Test: The quest for a new diagnostic instrument. *The American Journal of Psychiatry, 127*(12), 1653–1658.

Selzer, M. L., Vinokur, A., & Rooijen, L. V. (1975). A self-administered Short Michigan Alcoholism Screening Test (SMAST). *Journal of Studies on Alcohol, 36*(1), 117–126.

Senoo, E., Ogai, Y., Haraguchi, A., Kondo, A., Ishibashi, Y., Umeno, M., … Ikeda, K. (2006). Reliability and validity of the Japanese version of the Addiction Severity Index (ASI-J). *Nihon Arukoru Yakubutsu Igakkai Zasshi (Japan), 41*(4), 368–379.

Skinner, H. A. (1982). The Drug Abuse Screening Test. *Addictive Behaviors, 7*(4), 363–371.

So, K., & Sung, E. (2013). A validation study of the Brief Alcohol Use Disorder Identification Test (AUDIT): A brief screening tool derived from the AUDIT. *Korean Journal of Family Medicine, 34*(1), 11–18. doi:10.4082/kjfm.2013.34.1.11.

Subramaniam, M., Cheok, C., Verma, S., Wong, J., & Chong, S. A. (2010). Validity of a brief screening instrument-CRAFFT in a multiethnic Asian population. *Addictive Behaviors, 35*(12), 1102–1104. doi:10.1016/j.addbeh.2010.08.004.

Wu, S.-I., Huang, H.-C., Liu, S.-I., Huang, C.-R., Sun, F.-J., Chang, T.-Y., … Jeng, K.-S. (2008). Validation and comparison of alcohol-screening instruments for identifying hazardous drinking in hospitalized patients in Taiwan. *Alcohol and Alcoholism, 43*(5), 577–582. doi:10.1093/alcalc/agn036

Yudko, E., Lozhkina, O., & Fouts, A. (2007). A comprehensive review of the psychometric properties of the Drug Abuse Screening Test. *Journal of Substance Abuse Treatment, 32*(2), 189–198. doi:10.1016/j.jsat.2006.08.002.

Assessing Sexual Dysfunction in Asian Clients

15

Jane S.T. Woo, Alice Fok-Trela, and Lori A. Brotto

The seminal work of Masters and Johnson (1966) posited that the human sexual response cycle consisted of four stages—excitement, plateau, orgasm, and resolution. About a decade later, Kaplan (1977, 1979) and Lief (1977) expanded this model to recognize the important role of sexual desire as a separate phase of the sexual response cycle that precedes excitement. This triphasic model of desire—desire, excitement, and orgasm—served as the basis of the categorization of the sexual disorders from the third edition of the Diagnostic and Statistical Manual of Mental Disorders (DSM-III; American Psychiatric Association, 1980) onwards: the Sexual Desire Disorders, Sexual Arousal Disorders, and Orgasmic Disorders correspond to the first three stages of the sexual response cycle. The Sexual Pain Disorders were added as a fourth category of sexual dysfunction although the empirical research supporting their inclusion suggested that they were better placed within the Pain Disorders section of the DSM (Binik, 2010a, 2010b).

In the decades since the triphasic model of the sexual response cycle was introduced, a growing body of research has revealed greater complexity in the sexual response cycle as well as multifarious factors that are implicated in the aetiology and maintenance of sexual dysfunctions. Among these factors, the influence of culture on sexuality has received little empirical attention, with a review of published sexuality articles over a 25-year period finding that only 26 % described the cultural characteristics of the sample and just 7 % studied ethnicity as a variable of interest (Wiederman, Maynard, & Fretz, 1996). Of the research that has examined ethnic influences on sexuality, significant differences in sexual function have been found among ethnic groups, and Asians are no exception. For example, Cain et al. (2003) found that Euro-American women reported sexual desire and arousal more frequently than Chinese- and Japanese-American women, and pain during intercourse less frequently than Chinese- and Japanese-American women. While these comparative studies have provided valuable insights into culture-linked differences in sexuality, one of the issues with this research, especially in studies that were conducted in the west, is the propensity to use measures that were developed and validated in largely European American samples and to assume that the measures are equally valid when used in ethnic minority groups. Interpretation of between-group

J.S.T. Woo, M.A. (✉)
Department of Psychology, University of British Columbia, Vancouver, 2136 West Mall, Vancouver, BC, Canada V6T 1Z4
e-mail: janewoo@psych.ubc.ca

A. Fok-Trela, Psy.D.
Shanghai Ocean University, Shanghai, 999 Hucheng Ring Road, Lingang New City, Pudong New District, Shanghai 201306, China
e-mail: dr.trela@yahoo.com

L.A. Brotto, Ph.D.
Department of Obstetrics/Gynaecology, University of British Columbia, Vancouver, 2775 Laurel Street, 6th Floor, Vancouver, BC, Canada V5Z 1M9
e-mail: Lori.Brotto@vch.ca

L.T. Benuto et al. (eds.), *Guide to Psychological Assessment with Asians*,
DOI 10.1007/978-1-4939-0796-0_15,

differences is therefore problematic as they may be artefacts of the way that members of different cultures respond to the measures. Furthermore, few measures of sexual function have been developed and validated in Asian languages and populations, and of the few English language sexual function measures that have been translated into Asian languages, only a subset have been empirically validated in the relevant populations.

The purpose of this chapter is to promote the assessment of sexual dysfunction in Asian individuals by offering the best options that are currently available in the absence of validated instruments. We will begin by presenting a brief overview of the DSM-IV diagnostic criteria for the sexual dysfunctions and the likely upcoming changes in the next revision of the DSM, followed by estimates on their prevalence among individuals of Asian descent. We will then review cultural issues that may arise in the assessment of sexual dysfunction among Asian Americans and conclude with the best available tools for assessing sexual dysfunction in this population.

The Sexual Dysfunctions

According to the fourth edition with text revision of the Diagnostic and Statistical Manual of Mental Disorders (DSM-IV-TR; American Psychiatric Association, 2000), a sexual dysfunction is "characterized by a disturbance in the processes that characterize the sexual response cycle or by pain associated with sexual intercourse" (p. 535). The diagnostic criteria comprise (1) recurrent or persistent symptoms relating to one of the phases of the sexual response cycle, or pain with sexual intercourse, (2) marked distress or interpersonal difficulty, and (3) the disturbance is not better accounted for by another Axis I disorder and is not due solely to the physiological effects of a substance or a general medical condition. Within the DSM-IV-TR, the sexual dysfunctions that affect the desire phase are Hypoactive Sexual Desire Disorder and Sexual Aversion Disorder; those affecting the excitement phase are Female Sexual Arousal Disorder and Male Erectile Disorder; and those that affect the orgasm phase are Female Orgasmic Disorder, Male Orgasmic Disorder, and Premature Ejaculation. The sexual pain disorders are Dyspareunia and Vaginismus, with dyspareunia occurring in both men and women, and vaginismus occurring only in women. It is important to note that like other Axis I disorders, there is high comorbidity among the sexual dysfunctions.

The DSM-5: Merging and Deletion

A brief summary of the changes in the DSM-5 will be presented here as they reflect the current research on sexual dysfunctions.

DSM-5 reflects a major change in the number of female sexual dysfunctions. A new diagnostic category of Sexual Interest/Arousal Disorder with an expanded list of specifiers has replaced DSM-IV-TR's Hypoactive Sexual Desire Disorder and Female Sexual Arousal Disorder. Sexual Aversion Disorder has been dropped from DSM-5. Each disorder is also accompanied by a list of biopsychosocial factors that affect sexual function (Brotto, 2010; Graham, 2010). This proposed change reflects the rarity of Sexual Aversion Disorder and the clinical difficulty in distinguishing between Hypoactive Sexual Desire Disorder and Female Sexual Arousal Disorder, as well as women's difficulties in differentiating sexual desire from subjective sexual arousal (Brotto, Heiman, & Tolman, 2009; Graham, Sanders, Milhausen, & McBride, 2004; Hartmann, Heiser, Ruffer-Hesse, & Kloth, 2002). Similarly, the previous diagnostic categories of Dyspareunia and Vaginismus have been replaced by a single category, Genito-Pelvic Pain/Penetration Disorder (Binik, 2010a, 2010b). The major reasons for this proposal are (1) there is currently no evidence that suggests that Vaginismus and Dyspareunia can be reliably differentiated, and (2) there is evidence that suggests that Dyspareunia may be more appropriately considered a pain disorder than a sexual one. In summary, the proposed changes will result in three female sexual dysfunctions in the DSM-5: Sexual Interest/Arousal Disorder, Female Orgasmic Disorder, and Genito-Pelvic Pain/Penetration Disorder.

With regard to the male sexual dysfunctions, most changes are relatively minor, but include additional specifiers (as was done for the female sexual dysfunctions), as well as changes to the names of the dysfunctions. Delayed Ejaculation has been suggested as an alternative to Male Orgasmic Disorder and Early Ejaculation has been proposed as an alternative to Premature Ejaculation (Segraves, 2010a, 2010b, 2010c). No name changes have been proposed for Hypoactive Sexual Desire Disorder except the inclusion of "Male" before the name of this disorder to distinguish it from Sexual Interest/Arousal Disorder in women.

Prevalence of Sexual Difficulties in Asian Individuals

In the largest study of sexuality-related attitudes, beliefs, behaviours, and satisfaction in middle-aged and older adults that has been conducted to date, 13,882 women and 13,618 men aged 40–80 years in 29 countries were assessed for the presence of sexual difficulties in the Global Study of Sexual Attitudes and Behaviors (GSSAB; Laumann et al., 2005). Participants were asked whether they had experienced lack of interest in having sex, difficulty in reaching orgasm, reaching orgasm too quickly, physical pain during sexual intercourse, lack of pleasure with sex, difficulty achieving or maintaining an erection (men only), or difficulty becoming sufficiently lubricated (women only) during the previous 12 months. A follow-up question regarding frequency (occasionally, sometimes, or frequently) was asked of participants who endorsed the presence of sexual problems, with frequency of the problem serving as a proxy for severity. Laumann and colleagues (2005) found that the prevalence of sexual problems was almost always higher in East Asia (defined as China, Hong Kong, Japan, Korea, and Taiwan) and Southeast Asia (defined as Indonesia, Malaysia, Philippines, Singapore, and Thailand) compared to other regions in the world. Among women, the incidence of lack of sexual interest, inability to reach orgasm, reaching orgasm too quickly, pain during sex, finding sex not pleasurable, and lubrication difficulties was higher in East Asia and Southeast Asia than in Europe and North America. Similarly, among men, the incidence of lack of sexual interest, inability to reach orgasm, early ejaculation, pain during sex, finding sex not pleasurable, and erectile difficulties was higher in East Asia and Southeast Asia than in the west. Studies of individuals of Asian and European descent conducted in North America have yielded similar findings, and results have been consistent across diverse populations ranging from university and community samples to population-based studies (e.g., Avis et al., 2005; Brotto, Chik, Ryder, Gorzalka, & Seal, 2005; Brotto, Woo, & Gorzalka, 2012; Cain et al., 2003; Woo, Brotto, & Gorzalka, 2011).

In addition to the well-documented ethnic differences in sexual function, more recent research findings indicate that acculturation within ethnic groups, which has been defined as changes that occur in the self-identity of individuals who move from one culture to another, also influences self-reported sexual functioning. Specifically, greater acculturation to western culture among Asian individuals has been linked to higher sexual desire, arousal, and satisfaction (e.g., Brotto et al., 2005; Woo, Brotto, & Gorzalka, 2009) and higher affiliation with the culture of origin has been associated with more sexual avoidance and more sexual complaints (Brotto et al., 2005; Woo & Brotto, 2008).

Cultural Considerations in the Assessment of Sexual Dysfunction in Asian Americans

Sex Guilt

What are the mechanisms by which culture influences sexuality? Recent research suggests that among Chinese, Japanese, and Korean men and women, sex guilt may play an important role in sexual functioning. Sex guilt may be understood as guilty feelings in relation to sexual behaviour or sexual situations. The results of three studies that examined sex guilt and sexual desire among

Chinese Canadian, Japanese Canadian, Korean Canadian, and European Canadian university men and women revealed that Asian ethnicity was associated with higher self-reported sex guilt, which in turn was associated with lower self-reported sexual desire (Brotto et al., 2012; Woo et al., 2011; Woo, Brotto, & Gorzalka, 2012). Although it is not possible to empirically demonstrate a causal relationship between sex guilt and sexual dysfunction, there is a small but growing body of evidence that indicates an association between the two. In addition to the studies cited above, Nobre and Pinto-Gouveia (2006) found that sex guilt was one of the best discriminants between women with and without sexual dysfunction, and Nobre and Pinto-Gouveia (2003) found that sex guilt was negatively correlated with sexual desire and sexual satisfaction, such that higher sex guilt was associated with lower sexual desire and sexual satisfaction.

These findings have important clinical implications for the assessment of sexual dysfunction in Chinese, Japanese, and Korean American individuals. Specifically, they suggest that participation in the assessment of sexual functioning may be difficult for these individuals as guilty feelings may be elicited through the discussion of sexual material. Individuals from these cultures may thus choose not to present for the assessment and treatment of sexual difficulties, a speculation that appears reasonable based on anecdotal observations that individuals from these cultures are underrepresented in treatment settings in a metropolitan Canadian city with a large Asian population. Furthermore, and consistent with their higher levels of sex guilt, individuals from these cultures are more likely to view sex as procreative than recreative (e.g., Cain et al., 2003) and may seek treatment only when their sexual difficulties interfere with fertility. When an individual presents for assessment, it may therefore be especially important for the assessor to be mindful of the potential for culture-linked discomfort with sexuality. It may be helpful to discuss the client's discomfort and to normalize it. While it is generally important for questions about sexuality to be asked in a serious manner in professional settings (e.g., doctor's office, psychologist's clinic) and for the clinician to demonstrate comfort with the topic, a serious demeanour, comfort with discussing sexuality, and the ability to put clients at ease may be especially important when assessing sexual dysfunction among Chinese, Japanese, and Korean American clients. Unfortunately, as similar research has not been conducted among other Asian American groups, the extent to which these findings and implications generalize to Indian Americans and Southeast Asian American individuals is unknown.

Sexual Communication in Asian Individuals

The research that has considered sexual communication among Asian individuals suggests that undergoing an assessment of sexual dysfunction is likely to elicit considerable discomfort. Cross-cultural quantitative research suggests that Asian Americans talk to their friends less frequently about sex compared to European Americans (Chan, 1997; Moore & Erickson, 1985). This pattern is also seen within families (Kim & Ward, 2007) and is consistent with the cultural belief that sexuality is a private topic that is inappropriate for discussion with others (Okazaki, 2002). This belief may pose an additional barrier to presenting for an assessment of sexual dysfunction for Asian Americans.

If this barrier is overcome and the client presents for assessment, another feature of communication in Asian cultures becomes salient. Despite the observation that individuals in Asian cultures *talk about* or *discuss* sex less frequently than their western counterparts, qualitative research on Asian sexual communication reveals that much is communicated about sex through nonverbal or indirect means. Asian cultures have been described as "high-context" cultures in that speakers convey messages in indirect and implicit ways, and listeners use contextual cues to discern the meaning of the verbal portion of the message. Asian parents have been documented to convey their disapproval of premarital sex through the use of statements such as "romance is for marriage, and not before" (Kim & Ward, 2007) and Chinese Canadian women participating in focus groups about Pap testing and sexuality were observed to discuss these topics in depth with minimal use of the terms "sex" and "Pap testing" (Chang, Woo, Yau, Gorzalka, & Brotto, 2013). In both of these instances, the speakers' meaning was clearly understood without the need to resort to explicit statements.

In the clinical setting, Asian Americans are therefore more likely than their Euro-American counterparts to refer to sexuality-related issues such as genitalia, sexual difficulties, and sexual activities in what may appear to be vague terms. Clinical sensitivity will be required to establish and maintain a balance between the clinician's need to gather specific information to inform the diagnosis and treatment, and the client's preference for avoiding the use of explicit statements. It may be especially important to allow the client to begin by describing the problem in their own words. This would provide the clinician with the opportunity to observe the client's style of communication and degree of comfort with discussing sexual issues. It may also be helpful for the clinician to preface requests for greater specificity with a brief rationale for the requests.

Assessment Tools

Clinical Interview

The clinical interview represents the primary source of information about the client's sexual functioning and is the most important tool at the clinician's disposal. It is also likely to yield information on culturally relevant influences on the client's sexual functioning. Whereas standardized structured or semi-structured interviews are available for the assessment of other Axis I disorders, there is as yet no similar instrument for the assessment of sexual dysfunctions. However, guidelines for the comprehensive clinical evaluation of sexual dysfunction have been proposed by a number of experts in the field (e.g., Derogatis & Balon, 2009; Pukall, Meana, & Fernandez, 2010) and these are summarized here.

The clinical interview usually begins with open-ended questioning, allowing the client to describe their sexual difficulties in their own words. Using the client's characterization as a starting point, the clinician can follow the client's cues and gradually ask more specific questions about the difficulties. Increasing specificity in questioning may be especially important in the assessment of Asian American clients as research on East Asian learning styles suggests that East Asians dislike ambiguity and uncertainty, both of which are inherent elements of open-ended questions. With regard to the content of the interview, it is essential to ascertain the phase or phases in the sexual response cycle at which the difficulties occur, the course of the difficulties, as well as the biological, psychological, social, and cultural influences that may underlie the sexual problems. Because sexual dysfunctions can arise from multiple etiological factors, and because these factors often interact with and reinforce one another, careful and thorough examination is required to enable the clinician to construct an accurate case conceptualization.

Biological factors that may influence sexual functioning include age, body mass index, physical illness (e.g., diabetes mellitus, cardiovascular disease, sexually transmitted infections), chronic pain, hormone levels, and lifestyle (e.g., exercise, diet). A wide array of medications such as selective serotonin re-uptake inhibitor antidepressants, antipsychotics, and antihypertensives have the potential to affect normal functioning at multiple stages of the sexual response cycle and it is important to inquire about the temporal relationship between the commencement of medication use and the onset of sexual problems. It may be necessary to make a medical referral for the assessment of some of these factors.

During the interview, it is also important to assess psychological factors, including stress and mental illness such as anxiety and depression as the latter are frequently associated with sexual dysfunction. For example, it has been estimated that about 40–50 % of individuals diagnosed with major depressive disorder also have sexual dysfunction (Bonierbale, Lancon, & Tignol, 2003). Other psychological factors that have been implicated in sexual functioning include body image, self-esteem, and difficulties with mindfulness (i.e., staying in the moment) during sexual activity. Fear of disease or pregnancy may also disrupt the sexual response cycle and should be asked about. As discussed earlier, high sex guilt has been associated with poorer sexual function; as such, it is important for the clinician to explore the potential presence of guilty feelings surrounding sexuality.

Social or relational issues also need to be assessed in the interview. Examples of issues relating to the current relationship that are important to assess include discrepancies in sexual desire and preferences (e.g., preferences for position, techniques, frequency, timing), the effectiveness of communication, and the quality of the relationship (e.g., amount of conflict). The availability of both partners for assessment, either separately or together, is helpful as sexual dysfunction in the partner is common, and this can be assessed directly if the partner is willing to be interviewed. The clinician should also ask about affairs outside the relationship and whether the sexual dysfunction occurs or has occurred in other sexual relationships.

Finally, it is important to explore cultural and religious attitudes and beliefs about sexuality and their impact on the client's sexual functioning. For instance, is sex viewed as an enjoyable activity with the partner or as serving a purely procreative role? Does the client see sex as something shameful or as an integral part of human nature? What messages did the client receive about sexuality from their family of origin? Sexuality-related beliefs and attitudes can be influential in the development and perpetuation of sexual difficulties and need to be respected for successful treatment of the client.

It is important to note that compared to the assessment of other psychological difficulties, the assessment of sexual dysfunction may be especially influenced by the clinician's characteristics. One reason for this, as discussed earlier, is the absence of a standardized structured or semi-structured interview for assessing sexual dysfunction, which leaves clinicians to their own devices in terms of deciding what questions to ask. A related issue is that sexuality, arguably more so than other psychological difficulties, is a topic that is value-laden and the clinician's personal values and beliefs, as well as their views of Asians and sexuality, may affect the questions they ask and the conclusions that they draw. The effective assessment and treatment of sexual dysfunction in the Asian American client therefore requires that clinicians be aware of their personal biases that may influence their clinical judgment.

Self-Report Measures of Sexual Dysfunction

In this section, information on the most frequently used psychometric measures that were developed to assess the quality of an individual's sexual functioning will be presented, with an indication of which are available in languages that are relevant to the cultural groups that are the focus of this book (Table 15.1). While there are a large number of measures that have been developed to assess sexual dysfunction, there is a relatively small handful of widely used measures. Moreover, the vast majority of these measures were created and validated in the west, with norms and cutoff scores that were developed based primarily on research conducted in western samples. An additional caveat on the use of psychometric measures is that formal diagnosis of a sexual dysfunction cannot occur on the basis of these measures alone, even though diagnostic-like domain labels may suggest otherwise; the clinical interview is an integral component of the diagnostic process.

In addition to measures of sexual dysfunction, we have also included the Female Sexual Distress Scale (FSDS; Derogatis, Rosen, Leiblum, Burnett, & Heiman, 2002). The FSDS is a self-report measure of sexually related personal distress in women and is included here because the presence of sexuality-related distress is required before a DSM-IV-TR diagnosis of a sexual dysfunction can be made and because the FSDS has

Table 15.1 Tools for assessing sexual dysfunction with Asian clients

Measure	Languages	Notes/recommendations
Measures applicable to men and women		
Arizona Sexual Experience Scale (McGahuey et al., 2000)	English, Chinese. However, the Chinese version does not appear to have been published	Measures sexual drive, arousal, penile erection/vaginal lubrication, ability to reach orgasm and satisfaction from orgasm in men and women
Changes in Sexual Functioning Questionnaire (Clayton et al., 1997)	English, Chinese (traditional)	Measures sexual desire, frequency, pleasure, arousal, and orgasm in men and women
Derogatis Interview for Sexual Functioning (Derogatis, 1997)	English	Measures sexual cognition/fantasy, arousal, sexual behaviour/experience, orgasm, sexual drive/relationship in men and women
Golombok-Rust Inventory of Sexual Satisfaction (Rust & Golombok, 1986)	English	Subscales in the male version are labelled Impotence, Premature Ejaculation, Non-sensuality, Avoidance, Dissatisfaction, Infrequency, and Noncommunication. Subscales in the female version are labelled Vaginismus, Anorgasmia, Non-sensuality, Avoidance, Dissatisfaction, Infrequency, and Noncommunication
Nagoya Sexual Function Questionnaire (Kikuchi et al., 2011)	Japanese	Male version measures the frequency of pulsating sensations in the mammary area, galactorrhea, interest in women, sexual interest, sexual self-confidence, erectile dysfunction, and ejaculatory difficulties. Female version measures the frequency of menstrual irregularity, pulsating sensations in the mammary area, galactorrhea, interest in men, sexual interest, sexual self-confidence, and sexual arousal
Measures applicable to women		
Brief Index of Sexual Functioning for Women (Taylor et al., 1994)	English	Measures sexual thoughts/desire, arousal, frequency of sexual activity, receptivity/initiation, pleasure/orgasm, relationship satisfaction, and problems affecting sexual function
Female Sexual Distress Scale (Derogatis et al., 2002)	English, Korean	Measures sexually related personal distress
Female Sexual Function Index (Rosen et al., 2000)	English, Chinese (traditional and simplified), Japanese, Malay, Tamil	Measures sexual desire, arousal, lubrication, orgasm, sexual satisfaction, and pain with intercourse
McCoy Female Sexuality Questionnaire (McCoy & Matyas, 1998)	English	Measures sexual enjoyment, sexual arousal, sexual interest, satisfaction with partner, feelings of attractiveness, frequency of sexual intercourse, frequency of orgasm, pleasure from orgasm, lubrication, pain with sexual intercourse, and impact of partner's potential erectile difficulties
Profile of Female Sexual Function (Derogatis et al., 2004)	English	Measures sexual desire, arousal, orgasm, sexual pleasure, sexual concerns, sexual responsiveness, and sexual self-image
Sexual Interest and Desire Inventory (Clayton et al., 2006; Sills et al., 2005)	English	Measures sexual satisfaction, sexual receptivity, sexual initiation, frequency of desire, affection, satisfaction with level of desire, distress regarding level of desire, positive thoughts about sex, interest in erotica, frequency of arousal, ease of arousal, continuation of arousal and orgasm

(continued)

Table 15.1 (continued)

Measure	Languages	Notes/recommendations
Short Personal Experiences Questionnaire (Dennerstein et al., 2001)	English	Measures feelings for partner, sexual responsivity, sexual frequency, libido, partner problems in sexual performance, and vaginal dryness/dyspareunia
Measures applicable to men		
Brief Sexual Function Inventory—(O'Leary et al., 1995)	English	Measures sexual drive, erection, ejaculation, perceptions of problems in each area, and overall sexual satisfaction
Chinese Index of Premature Ejaculation (Yuan et al., 2004)	Chinese (simplified)	Measures degree of sexual interest, frequency of erections hard enough for sexual intercourse, frequency of maintenance of erections until the completion of sexual intercourse, intravaginal ejaculatory latency, difficulty in prolonging sexual intercourse, sexual satisfaction, partner's sexual satisfaction, frequency of partner reaching orgasm, confidence in being able to complete sexual activity, and frequency of feelings of anxiety, depression, or stress during sexual activity
Index of Premature Ejaculation (Althof et al., 2006)	English	Measures ejaculatory control, sexual satisfaction, and distress
International Index of Erectile Function (Rosen et al., 1997)	English, Chinese, Japanese, Korean, Malay	Measures erectile function, orgasmic function, sexual desire, intercourse satisfaction, and overall satisfaction
Male Sexual Health Questionnaire (Rosen et al., 2004)	English, Korean	Measures ejaculation, erection, and sexual satisfaction

become a benchmark in the psychometric measurement of sexual distress in women.

Measures applicable to both men and women. The *Arizona Sexual Experience Scale* (ASEX; McGahuey et al., 2000) is a self-report measure that was designed to assess sexual functioning in men and women being administered psychotropic drugs. The ASEX consists of five single-item domains—drive, arousal, penile erection/vaginal lubrication, ability to reach orgasm, and satisfaction from orgasm—that are assessed on a 6-point Likert scale. Total scores may range from 5 to 30, with higher scores being indicative of more sexual dysfunction. The ASEX demonstrated excellent internal consistency (Cronbach's $\alpha=0.91$) and strong test–retest reliability (ranging from 0.80 for patients to 0.89 for controls) in the validation sample.

Although the ASEX has been translated into Chinese and there are references to validation studies of the Chinese version (e.g., Jenkins et al., 2011; Lin, Juang, Wen, Liu, & Hung, 2012), these validation studies appear to have not been published and authors wishing to use the ASEX in Chinese-literate populations have conducted their own translations of the original English version (e.g., Chen, Lin, Wang, & Shuai, 2011).

The *Changes in Sexual Functioning Questionnaire* (CSFQ; Clayton, McGarvey, & Clavet, 1997) is designed to assess illness- and medication-related changes in sexual functioning and may be clinician-administered as a structured interview or self-administered as a questionnaire. The CSFQ consists of 35 items in the female version and 36 items in the male version that fall into five domains of sexual functioning—sexual desire, frequency, sexual pleasure, sexual arousal, and orgasm—and also provides a total score that indicates overall sexual functioning, with lower scores reflecting poorer sexual functioning. The CSFQ was originally standardized on a sample of American medical students and psychiatry residents and was found to possess high test–retest reliability. The CSFQ has also been abbreviated into the CSFQ-14, a 14-item self-administered version of the measure which yields scores for the five domains of the original CSFQ as well as a score for overall sexual functioning (Keller, McGarvey, & Clayton, 2006).

The CSFQ-14 has been translated into Chinese and validated in a number of studies of sexual dysfunction in Taiwan (e.g., Chen et al., 2008, 2009). The Chinese version of the CSFQ-14 has good internal consistency (Cronbach's $\alpha=0.86$ in the Chinese validation sample). The cutoff score for women is 32 and that for men is 42, with scores below these thresholds indicating the potential presence of a sexual dysfunction that should be thoroughly evaluated through a clinical interview.

The *Derogatis Interview for Sexual Functioning* (DISF/DISF-SR; Derogatis, 1997) is similar to the CSFQ in that it may be either clinician administered as an interview (DISF) or self-administered as a gender-keyed questionnaire (DISF-SR). Both versions of the DISF consist of 25 items that are responded to on four-point Likert scales and assess overall sexual functioning in addition to five specific domains: sexual cognition/fantasy, sexual arousal, sexual behaviour/experience, orgasm, and sexual drive/relationship. Higher scores on the DISF/DISF-SR indicate better sexual functioning. Test–retest reliability ranged from 0.80 to 0.90, and internal consistency ranged from 0.74 for the sexual drive/relationship domain to 0.80 for the orgasm domain. To date, there are no published studies that have described the use of the DISF/DISF-SR or its validation in Asian Americans.

The *Golombok-Rust Inventory of Sexual Satisfaction* (GRISS; Rust & Golombok, 1986) is a self-report inventory with gender-specific versions that measure the existence and degree of sexual dysfunction. Both versions contain 28 items with a five-point Likert response format that comprise seven subscales. Higher scores on the GRISS indicate lower sexual functioning. The subscales in the male version are labelled Impotence, Premature Ejaculation, Non-sensuality, Avoidance, Dissatisfaction, Infrequency, and Noncommunication. The subscales in the female version are labelled Vaginismus, Anorgasmia, Non-sensuality, Avoidance, Dissatisfaction, Infrequency, and Noncommunication. Split-half reliability for the overall male GRISS in the standardization is 0.87 and test–retest reliability is 0.76. Internal consistency of the subscales ranges from 0.61 for Noncommunication to 0.78 for Impotence and Premature Ejaculation, and test–retest reliability ranges from 0.52 for Noncommunication to 0.84 for Premature Ejaculation. Standardization data for the overall female GRISS indicate that split-half reliability is 0.94 and test–retest reliability is 0.65. Internal consistency of the subscales ranges from 0.61 for Noncommunication to 0.83 for Anorgasmia and test–retest reliability ranges from 0.47 for Female Dissatisfaction to 0.82 for Vaginismus. Both versions of the GRISS effectively discriminate between individuals with and without sexual dysfunction in research settings.

There are no published studies that reference versions of the GRISS that have been translated into Asian languages. However, the English version of the GRISS has been used in the study of the effects of acculturation on the sexual functioning of Asian (Chinese, Southeast Asian, Korean, Japanese, Vietnamese) Canadian men and women (e.g., Brotto, Woo, & Ryder, 2007; Woo & Brotto, 2008).

The *Nagoya Sexual Function Questionnaire* (NSFQ; Kikuchi et al., 2011) is a self-administered, gender-specific questionnaire that was created by researchers in Nagoya, Japan, who aimed to develop and validate a Japanese measure of sexual functioning for patients with schizophrenia taking antipsychotic medications. The NSFQ consists of seven items that are responded to on a five-point adjectival scale. Higher scores on the NSFQ indicate lower sexual functioning. The male version contains items that inquire about the frequency of pulsating sensations in the mammary area, galactorrhea, interest in women, sexual interest, sexual self-confidence, erectile dysfunction, and ejaculatory difficulties. The female version contains items that inquire about the frequency of menstrual irregularity, pulsating sensations in the mammary area, galactorrhea, interest in men, sexual interest, sexual self-confidence, and sexual arousal. The NSFQ demonstrated acceptable internal consistency (0.76 for men and 0.79 for women) and excellent test–retest reliability (0.92 for both men and women) and has been used in a study of the prevalence of sexual dysfunction in patients with schizophrenia (Kikuchi et al., 2012).

Measures applicable to women. The *Brief Index of Sexual Functioning for Women* (BISF-W; Taylor, Rosen, & Leiblum, 1994) is a self-report questionnaire that consists of 22 items that yield an overall score for sexual function and assess the dimensions of thoughts/desire, arousal, frequency of sexual activity, receptivity/initiation, pleasure/orgasm, relationship satisfaction, and problems affecting sexual function. Responses are given in a variety of formats. A principal components analysis identified three factors which were labelled as Sexual Interest/Desire, Sexual Activity, and Sexual Satisfaction. Internal consistency of the factors ranged from 0.39 for Sexual Interest/Desire to 0.83 for Sexual Activity, and test–retest reliability ranged from 0.68 for Sexual Satisfaction to 0.78 for Sexual Activity.

The BISF-W has been used in the study of sexual function in married women in North India (Avasthi et al., 2008). Unfortunately, data on reliability and validity in this sample are unavailable.

The *Female Sexual Distress Scale* (FSDS; Derogatis et al., 2002) is a 12-item self-report inventory that measures sexually related personal distress in women. Items are responded to on four-point adjectival scales and higher scores on the FSDS indicate higher levels of sex-related distress. The scale was initially validated on a total of about 500 women, of whom 340 had been diagnosed with a sexual dysfunction at the time of their evaluation. The FSDS demonstrated high internal consistency and test–retest reliability across all of the three initial validation studies, in addition to demonstrating a strong ability to distinguish between women with and without sexual dysfunction.

The FSDS has been translated into Korean and validated in a sample of married Korean women (FSDS-K; Bae et al., 2006). The FSDS-K consists of 20 items and showed excellent internal consistency (0.96) and test–retest reliability (0.99). The FSDS-K also effectively discriminated between women with and without subjective distress related to sexual dysfunction. The FSDS was also used in a study of the efficacy and safety of a topical cream for the treatment of female sexual arousal disorder in Chinese women (Liao et al., 2008) although no published studies have reported on the validation of this measure in Chinese populations.

The *Female Sexual Function Index* (FSFI; Rosen et al., 2000) is the most widely used self-report measure of overall sexual functioning in women. It contains 19 items with five- or six-point adjectival scales that inquire about sexual function in the previous 4 weeks. The FSFI yields an overall score for sexual functioning as well as scores for the domains of sexual desire, arousal, lubrication, orgasm, sexual satisfaction, and pain with intercourse. Higher scores on the FSFI indicate better sexual functioning. In the original validation sample, test–retest reliability was high, ranging from 0.79 for the pain domain to 0.86 for the lubrication domain, and internal consistency was also high and ranged from 0.89 for the satisfaction domain to 0.96 for the lubrication domain.

The FSFI has been translated into and psychometrically validated in a number of Asian languages, and these versions of the FSFI will be described here in turn. The Malay version of the FSFI (MVFSFI; Sidi, Abdullah, Puteh, & Midin, 2007) was validated in a sample of married women who presented at a primary care clinic in Kuala Lumpur, Malaysia. Like the FSFI, the MVFSFI contains 19 items that are responded to on five- or six-point adjectival scales and covers the same six domains of sexual functioning. Test–retest reliability of the MVFSFI was high and ranged from 0.77 for the arousal domain to 0.97 for the orgasm domain. Internal consistency was also high and ranged from 0.87 for the desire domain to 0.95 for the satisfaction domain.

There is also a Japanese version of the FSFI (FSFI-J; Takahashi, Inokuchi, Watanabe, Saito,

& Kai, 2011) that was validated in Japanese women who were in partnered relationships. Some instructions from the FSFI were modified in the FSFI-J in an attempt to reduce the occurrence of missing data. For instance, pilot testing revealed that women who had not engaged in sexual activity in the previous 3 months were more likely to skip questions about their satisfaction with the sexual relationship with their partner. To address this issue, "all of the following questions can be answered even if you do not have a partner or sexual activity" was added at the beginning of the FSFI-J. Exploratory factor analysis of the FSFI-J revealed five principal factors (compared to six for the FSFI): desire/arousal, lubrication, orgasm, satisfaction, and pain. Internal consistency of the FSFI-J was excellent and ranged from 0.84 for the satisfaction domain to 0.97 for the lubrication domain.

There are two validated Chinese language versions of the FSFI—one in traditional Chinese which was developed in Taiwan (Chang, Chang, Chen, & Lin, 2009), and one in simplified Chinese which was developed in China (Sun, Li, Jin, Fan, & Wang, 2011). The former was developed to measure the sexual concerns of pregnant women in Taiwan and demonstrated adequate test–retest reliability (0.69) and excellent internal consistency (0.96) in a random sample of pregnant who presented for prenatal examinations at a medical centre in Taipei, Taiwan. The latter, the Chinese version of the FSFI (CVFSFI; Sun et al., 2011), was validated in women who presented at the obstetrics and gynaecology outpatient department of a teaching hospital in Beijing, China. Principal component analysis revealed the same six-factor structure as the original FSFI. Test–retest reliability was good and ranged from 0.82 for the desire domain to 0.92 for the arousal domain. Similarly, internal consistency was good and ranged from 0.86 for the desire and orgasm domains to 0.94 for the pain domain.

The FSFI has also been used in Indian women (e.g., Grover, Shah, Dutt, & Avasthi, 2012; Singh, Tharyan, Kekre, Singh, & Gopalakrishnan, 2009) and has been translated into Tamil (Singh et al., 2009). Although the Tamil version of the FSFI was pilot-tested for linguistic accuracy and cultural appropriateness, no published study has reported on its psychometric properties.

The *McCoy Female Sexuality Questionnaire* (MFSQ; McCoy & Matyas, 1998) is a 19-item self-report measure that assesses a woman's sexual experience over the previous 4 weeks and was designed to assess aspects of female sexuality that are likely to be affected by changing levels of sex hormones during the menopausal transition period. Items are responded to on a seven-point adjectival scale and inquire about overall sexual enjoyment, sexual arousal, sexual interest, satisfaction with partner, feelings of attractiveness, frequency of sexual intercourse, enjoyment of sexual intercourse, frequency of orgasm, pleasure from orgasm, lubrication, pain with sexual intercourse, and the impact of partner's potential erectile difficulties. Establishing the reliability and validity of the MFSQ has been challenging as researchers who have used the MSFQ have tended to omit some items due to cultural sensitivity, researchers' discomfort with specific questions, and the need for brevity (McCoy, 2001). As a result, no data exist on the psychometric properties of the complete MFSQ, although studies that have used abbreviated versions suggest that those versions demonstrate acceptable reliability, good face and content validity, and evidence of construct validity. No published studies have described the use of the MFSQ or its validation in Asian Americans.

The *Profile of Female Sexual Function* (PFSP; Derogatis et al., 2004; McHorney et al., 2004) is a self-administered questionnaire that was developed for the assessment of loss of sexual desire and other sexuality-related symptoms in menopausal women with hypoactive sexual desire disorder. The PFSP consists of 37 items that cover seven domains of sexual functioning—sexual desire, arousal, orgasm, sexual pleasure, sexual concerns, sexual responsiveness, and sexual self-image. Higher scores on the PFSP indicate higher sexual function. The PFSP was translated into seven languages from the original English version and initially validated in about 500 oophorectomized women with low sexual desire in North America, Europe (Germany, UK, Italy, and France), and Australia. Test–retest reliability ranged from 0.57 to 0.91, and internal consistency ranged from 0.74 to 0.95 for the seven domain scores (Derogatis et al., 2004). No published studies have described the use of the PFSP or its validation in Asian Americans.

The *Sexual Interest and Desire Inventory* (SIDI-F; Clayton et al., 2006; Sills et al., 2005) is a clinician-administered instrument that was created to assess the severity of Hypoactive Sexual Desire Disorder, or changes in the severity of Hypoactive Sexual Desire Disorder in response to treatment, among premenopausal women. It also has a broader conceptualization of sexual desire compared to the FSFI's narrow focus on desire frequency and intensity. The SIDI-F consists of 13 items that assess the domains of sexual satisfaction, sexual receptivity, sexual initiation, frequency of desire, affection, satisfaction with level of desire, distress regarding level of desire, positive thoughts about sex, interest in erotica, frequency of arousal, ease of arousal, continuation of arousal, and orgasm. Higher scores on the SIDI-F indicate higher sexual function. The SIDI-F demonstrated excellent internal consistency (0.90). No published studies have described the use of the SIDI-F or its validation in Asian Americans.

The *Short Personal Experiences Questionnaire* (SPEQ; Dennerstein, Lehert, & Dudley, 2001) consists of nine items and was designed to measure sexual functioning among middle-aged women. The SPEQ was adapted from the MSFQ (McCoy & Matyas, 1998). Items are responded to in a variety of formats and assess the domains of feelings for partner, sexual responsivity, sexual frequency, libido, partner problems in sexual performance, and vaginal dryness/dyspareunia. No published studies have described the use of the SPEQ or its validation in Asian Americans.

Measures applicable to men. The *Brief Sexual Function Inventory-M* (BSFI-M; O'Leary et al., 1995) is a self-report measure that consists of 11 items that cover the domains of sexual drive, erection, ejaculation, perceptions of problems in each area, and overall sexual satisfaction. Response options consist of 5-point adjectival scales, with higher scores indicating better sexual functioning. There are no published studies that have used Asian language translations of the BSFI-M.

The *Chinese Index of Premature Ejaculation* (CIPE; Yuan et al., 2004) was developed in China and is a ten-item Chinese language measure designed to assess the sexual functioning of men with premature ejaculation. Items are responded to on a five-point adjectival scale, with higher scores on the measure indicating better sexual function. The CIPE includes questions about the degree of sexual interest, the frequency of erections hard enough for sexual intercourse, the frequency of maintenance of erections until the completion of sexual intercourse, intravaginal ejaculatory latency, difficulty in prolonging sexual intercourse, sexual satisfaction, partner's sexual satisfaction, frequency of partner reaching orgasm, confidence in being able to complete sexual activity, and frequency of feelings of anxiety, depression or stress during sexual activity. Receiver operating characteristic analysis suggests that a cutoff score of 35 on the CIPE results in 97.6 % sensitivity, 94.7 % specificity, 96.4 % positive predictive value, and 95.6 % negative predictive value. Data on the reliability and validity of the CIPE are not available.

The *Index of Premature Ejaculation* (IPE; Althof et al., 2006) is a ten-item self-report measure that assesses three subjective aspects of premature ejaculation—ejaculatory control, sexual satisfaction, and distress. Items are responded to on five- to six-point adjectival scales. Internal consistency ranges from 0.74 for the control domain to 0.91 for the distress domain and test–retest reliability ranges from 0.70 for the distress domain to 0.90 for both the sexual satisfaction and control domains. There has been no published research on the use of Asian language translations of the IPE.

The *International Index of Erectile Function* (IIEF; Rosen et al., 1997) is a self-report questionnaire that consists of 15 items and covers five domains of sexual function—erectile function, orgasmic function, sexual desire, intercourse satisfaction, and overall satisfaction. Items are responded to on five- or six-point adjectival scales with reference to sexual functioning in the previous 4 weeks. Higher scores on the IIEF indicate better sexual function. There is also a shorter version of the IIEF, the IIEF-5 (Rosen, Cappelleri, Smith, Lipsky, & Pena, 1999), which consists of five items from the IIEF that assess erectile function and intercourse satisfaction.

The IIEF has been translated and linguistically validated in over 30 languages, including Japanese, Korean, Malay, and Chinese, although not all of these translations have been psychometrically validated (e.g., Chinese). The Japanese version of the IIEF was validated in Japan (Shirai et al., 1999). Based on the English-language abstract, test–retest reliability of the Japanese version of the IIEF ranged from 0.51 to 0.79 for patients with erectile dysfunction, and from 0.63 to 0.80 for controls. Unfortunately, as the original article is in Japanese, it was not possible to ascertain whether the authors assessed the internal consistency of their instrument.

The Korean version of the IIEF was validated in a sample of men who presented at an andrology clinic with erectile difficulties and age-matched controls who presented at the department of family medicine at an academic medical centre in Seoul, Korea (Chung et al., 1999). Test–retest reliability ranged from 0.67 for the orgasmic function domain to 0.88 for the overall satisfaction domain and internal consistency ranged from 0.70 for the sexual desire domain to 0.96 for the overall satisfaction domain. The Korean version of the IIEF-5 (Ahn, Lee, Kang, Hong, & Kim, 2001) was validated in men who presented at an andrology clinic in Seoul, and was found to possess high sensitivity (91.3 %) and specificity (86.3 %). Data on reliability were not made available, but this version of the IIEF-5 has been used in a number of studies on the sexual function of Korean men (e.g., Ahn et al., 2007; Choi, Song, & Son, 2012).

There are two Malay versions of the IIEF that were independently developed (Lim et al., 2003; Quek, Low, Razack, Chua, & Loh, 2002). One version (Mal-IIEF) was validated in patients who had lower urinary tract symptoms (Quek et al., 2002). Test–retest reliability was good and ranged from 0.75 for the orgasmic function domain to 0.87 for the sexual drive domain. Internal consistency was also good and ranged from 0.74 for the orgasmic function domain to 0.87 for the sexual drive domain. The other version was validated in two separate studies: one enrolled healthy volunteers from the community and patients presenting at primary care clinics, and the other enrolled patients who had been diagnosed with erectile dysfunction and who were going to undergo a trial of sildenafil therapy (Lim et al., 2003). Both test–retest reliability and internal consistency were high. Test–rest reliability ranged from 0.82 for the orgasmic function and sexual desire domains to 0.89 for the intercourse satisfaction domain and internal consistency ranged from 0.80 for the sexual desire domain to 0.96 for the overall satisfaction domain.

The *Male Sexual Health Questionnaire* (MSHQ; Rosen et al., 2004) is a 25-item self-report questionnaire that assesses the domains of ejaculation, erection, and sexual satisfaction in aging men who have urogenital health concerns. Higher scores on the MSHQ indicate higher sexual function. Internal consistency for all three domains was high in the validation sample, ranging from 0.81 for the ejaculation domain to 0.90 for the erection and satisfaction domains. Test–retest reliability was also high and ranged from 0.86 for the ejaculation domain to 0.88 for the satisfaction domain.

The MSHQ has been translated into Korean and validated in a Korean population (Oh, Lee, & Chung, 2005). The Korean version of the MSFQ was found to have high internal consistency (0.95, 0.90, and 0.93 for the ejaculation, erection, and satisfaction domains, respectively) and high test–retest reliability (0.89, 0.81, and 0.87 for the ejaculation, erection, and satisfaction domains, respectively) and has been used in the assessment of sexual functioning in Korean men with benign prostatic hyperplasia (Lee et al., 2009) and those who have undergone urethrotomy (Choi, Song, Kim, & Moon, 2013).

Conclusion

Like the assessment of most psychological problems in any population, the cornerstone of the assessment of sexual dysfunction in Asian

Americans is the clinical interview, which can be supplemented by self-report measures. However, although a handful of self-report measures of sexual function have been translated into Asian languages and validated in specific Asian populations (most frequently Chinese, Japanese, and Korean), the interpretation of these measures as used in Asian Americans needs to be done with particular caution as overall, empirically validated translations remain lacking. In assessing sexual dysfunction in Asian Americans, it is important for clinicians to bear in mind the general reluctance of Asians to discuss sexual issues and the use of indirect and nonverbal communication in discussing sexuality in Asian cultures. Furthermore, it is important for clinicians to recognize that the assessment may arouse significant discomfort and potential feelings of guilt in the client, and to utilize their clinical judgment to guide the assessment process.

References

Ahn, T. Y., Lee, D. S., Kang, W., Hong, J. H., & Kim, Y. S. (2001). Validation of an abridged Korean version of the international index of erectile function (IIEF-5) as a diagnostic tool for erectile dysfunction. *Korean Journal of Andrology, 42*, 535–540.

Ahn, T. Y., Park, J. K., Lee, S. W., Hong, J. H., Park, N. C., Kim, J. J., … Hyun, J. S. (2007). Prevalence and risk factors for erectile dysfunction in Korean men: Results of an epidemiological study. *Journal of Sexual Medicine, 4*, 1269–1276.

Althof, S., Rosen, R., Symonds, T., Mundayat, R., May, K., & Abraham, L. (2006). Development and validation of a new questionnaire to assess sexual satisfaction, control, and distress associated with premature ejaculation. *Journal of Sexual Medicine, 3*, 465–475.

American Psychiatric Association. (1980). *Diagnostic and statistical manual of mental disorders* (3rd ed.). Washington, DC: Author.

American Psychiatric Association. (2000). *Diagnostic and statistical manual of mental disorders* (4th ed.). Washington, DC: Author.

Avasthi, A., Kaur, R., Prakash, O., Banerjee, A., Kumar, L., & Kulhara, P. (2008). Sexual behavior of married young women: A preliminary study from North India. *Indian Journal of Community Medicine, 33*, 163–167.

Avis, N. E., Zhao, X., Johannes, C. B., Ory, M., Brockwell, S., & Greendale, G. A. (2005). Correlates of sexual function among multi-ethnic middle-aged women: Results from the study of women's health across the nation (SWAN). *Menopause: The Journal of the North American Menopause Society, 12*, 385–398.

Bae, J. H., Han, C. S., Kang, S. H., Shim, K. S., Kim, J. J., & Moon, D. G. (2006). Development of a Korean version of the female sexual distress scale. *Journal of Sexual Medicine, 3*, 1013–1017.

Binik, Y. M. (2010a). The DSM diagnostic criteria for vaginismus. *Archives of Sexual Behavior, 39*, 278–291.

Binik, Y. M. (2010b). The DSM diagnostic criteria for dyspareunia. *Archives of Sexual Behavior, 39*, 292–303.

Bonierbale, M., Lancon, C., & Tignol, J. (2003). The ELIXIR study: Evaluation of sexual dysfunction in 4557 depressed patients in France. *Current Medical Research and Opinion, 19*, 114–124.

Brotto, L. A. (2010). The DSM diagnostic criteria for hypoactive sexual desire disorder in women. *Archives of Sexual Behavior, 39*, 221–239.

Brotto, L. A., Chik, H. M., Ryder, A. G., Gorzalka, B. B., & Seal, B. N. (2005). Acculturation and sexual function in Asian women. *Archives of Sexual Behavior, 34*, 613–626.

Brotto, L. A., Heiman, J. R., & Tolman, D. L. (2009). Narratives of desire in mid-age women with and without arousal difficulties. *Journal of Sex Research, 46*, 387–398.

Brotto, L. A., Woo, J. S. T., & Gorzalka, B. B. (2012). Differences in sexual guilt and desire in east Asian and Euro-Canadian men. *Journal of Sex Research, 49*, 594–602.

Brotto, L. A., Woo, J. S. T., & Ryder, A. G. (2007). Acculturation and sexual function in Canadian East Asian men. *Journal of Sexual Medicine, 4*, 72–82.

Cain, V. S., Johannes, C. B., Avis, N. E., Mohr, B., Schocken, M., Skurnick, J., & Ory, M. (2003). Sexual functioning and practices in a multi-ethnic study of midlife women: Baseline results from SWAN. *Journal of Sex Research, 40*, 266–276.

Chan, C. (1997). Attitudes toward sexuality and sexual behaviors of Asian American adolescents: Implications for risk of HIV infection. In R. D. Taylor & M. C. Wang (Eds.), *Social and emotional adjustment and family relations in ethnic minority families* (pp. 133–144). Mahwah, NJ: Lawrence Erlbaum.

Chang, S. R., Chang, T. C., Chen, K. H., & Lin, H. H. (2009). Developing and validating a Taiwan version of the female sexual function index for pregnant women. *Journal of Sexual Medicine, 6*, 1609–1616.

Chang, S. C., Woo, J. S. T., Yau, V., Gorzalka, B. B., & Brotto, L. A. (2013). Cervical cancer screening and Chinese women: Insights from focus groups. *Frontiers in Psychology, 4*, 48.

Chen, C. Y., Lin, T. Y., Wang, C. C., & Shuai, H. A. (2011). Improvement of serum prolactin and sexual function after switching to aripiprazole from risperidone in schizophrenia: A case series. *Psychiatry and Clinical Neurosciences, 65*, 95–97.

Chen, K. C., Yang, Y. K., Lee, I. H., Yeh, T. L., Lu, R. B., & Chen, P. S. (2008). Sexual dysfunction and physician's perception in medicated patients with major depression in Taiwan. *Depression and Anxiety, 35*, E56–E62.

Chen, K. C., Yeh, T. L., Lee, I. H., Chen, P. S., Huang, H. C., Yang, Y. K., & Lu, R. B. (2009). Age, gender, depression, and sexual dysfunction in Taiwan. *Journal of Sexual Medicine, 6*, 3056–3062.

Choi, J. W., Song, P. H., Kim, H. T., & Moon, K. H. (2013). Impact of visual internal urethrotomy on sexual function in patients with urethral stricture. *Journal of Endourology, 27*, 214–219.

Choi, W. S., Song, S. H., & Son, H. (2012). Epidemiological study of complementary and alternative medicine (CAM) use for the improvement of sexual function in young Korean men: The Korean internet sexuality survey (KISS), Part II. *Journal of Sexual Medicine, 9*, 2238–2247.

Chung, T. G., Lee, T. K., Chung, S., Lee, M. S., Kim, Y. S., & Ahn, T. Y. (1999). The Korean version of the international index of erectile function (IIEF): Reliability and validation study. *Korean Journal of Urology, 40*, 1334–1343.

Clayton, A. H., McGarvey, E. L., & Clavet, G. J. (1997). The Changes in Sexual Functioning Questionnaire (CSFQ): Development, reliability, and validity. *Psychopharmacology Bulletin, 33*, 731–745.

Clayton, A. H., Segraves, R. T., Leiblum, S., Basson, R., Pyke, R., Cotton, D., … Wunderlich, G. R. (2006). Reliability and validity of the sexual interest and desire inventory-female (SIDI-F), a scale designed to measure severity of female hypoactive sexual desire disorder. *Journal of Sex & Marital Therapy, 32*, 115–135.

Dennerstein, L., Lehert, P., & Dudley, E. (2001). Short scale to measure female sexuality: Adapted from McCoy female sexuality questionnaire. *Journal of Sex & Marital Therapy, 27*, 339–351.

Derogatis, L. R. (1997). The Derogatis interview for sexual functioning (DISF/DISF-SR): An introductory report. *Journal of Sex & Marital Therapy, 23*, 291–304.

Derogatis, L. R., & Balon, R. (2009). Clinical evaluation of sexual dysfunctions. In R. Balon & R. T. Segraves (Eds.), *Clinical manual of sexual disorders* (pp. 23–57). Washington, DC: American Psychiatric Publishing.

Derogatis, L. R., Rosen, R., Leiblum, S., Burnett, A., & Heiman, J. (2002). The Female Sexual Distress Scale (FSDS): Initial validation of a standardized scale for assessment of sexually related personal distress in women. *Journal of Sex & Marital Therapy, 28*, 317–330.

Derogatis, L. R., Rust, J., Golombok, S., Bouchard, C., Nachtigall, L., Rodenberg, C., … McHorney, C. A. (2004). Validation of the profile of female sexual function (PFSF) in surgically and naturally menopausal women. *Journal of Sex & Marital Therapy, 30*, 25–36.

Graham, C. A. (2010). The DSM diagnostic criteria for female sexual arousal disorder. *Archives of Sexual Behavior, 39*, 240–255.

Graham, C. A., Sanders, S. A., Milhausen, R. R., & McBride, K. R. (2004). Turning on and turning off: A focus group study of the factors that affect women's sexual arousal. *Archives of Sexual Behavior, 33*, 527–538.

Grover, S., Shah, R., Dutt, A., & Avasthi, A. (2012). Prevalence and pattern of sexual dysfunction in married females receiving antidepressants: An exploratory study. *Journal of Pharmacology and Pharmacotherapeutics, 3*, 259–265.

Hartmann, U., Heiser, K., Ruffer-Hesse, C., & Kloth, G. (2002). Female sexual desire disorders: Subtypes, classification, personality factors and new directions for treatment. *World Journal of Urology, 20*, 79–88.

Jenkins, T. A., Reynolds, G. P., Yuan, Y. G., Zhang, X. R., Zhang, Z. J., & Zhu, R. X. (2011). Sexual dysfunction in male schizophrenia: Influence of antipsychotic drugs, prolactin and polymorphisms of the dopamine D2 receptor genes. *Pharmacogenomics, 12*, 1127–1136.

Kaplan, H. S. (1977). Hypoactive sexual desire. *Journal of Sex & Marital Therapy, 3*, 3–9.

Kaplan, H. S. (1979). *Disorders of sexual desire*. New York, NY: Brunner/Mazel.

Keller, A., McGarvey, E. L., & Clayton, A. H. (2006). Reliability and construct validity of the changes in sexual functioning questionnaire short-form (CSFQ-14). *Journal of Sex & Marital Therapy, 32*, 43–52.

Kikuchi, T., Iwamoto, K., Sasada, K., Aleksic, B., Yoshida, K., & Ozaki, N. (2011). Reliability and validity of a new sexual function questionnaire (Nagoya sexual function questionnaire) for schizophrenic patients taking antipsychotics. *Human Psychopharmacology, 26*, 300–306.

Kikuchi, T., Iwamoto, K., Sasada, K., Aleksic, B., Yoshida, K., & Ozaki, N. (2012). Sexual dysfunction and hyperprolactinemia in Japanese schizophrenic patients taking antipsychotics. *Progress in Neuro-Psychopharmacology & Biological Psychiatry, 37*, 26–32.

Kim, J. L., & Ward, L. M. (2007). Silence speaks volumes: Parental sexual communication among Asian American emerging adults. *Journal of Adolescent Research, 22*, 3–31.

Laumann, E. O., Nicolosi, A., Glasser, D. B., Paik, A., Gingell, C., Moreira, E., & Wang, T. (2005). Sexual problems among women and men aged 40-80y: Prevalence and correlates identified in the global study of sexual attitudes and behaviors. *International Journal of Impotence Research, 17*, 39–57.

Lee, S. H., Kim, J. C., Lee, J. Y., Kim, J. H., Oh, C. Y., Lee, S. W., … Chung, B. H. (2009). Effects of components of metabolic syndrome on sexual function in Korean BPH/LUTS patients. *Journal of Sexual Medicine, 6*, 2292–2298.

Liao, Q., Zhang, M., Geng, L., Wang, X., Song, X., Xia, P., … Liu, V. (2008). Efficacy and safety of Alprostadil cream for the treatment of female sexual arousal disorder: A double-blind, placebo-controlled study in Chinese Population. *Journal of Sexual Medicine, 5*, 1923–1931.

Lief, H. I. (1977). Inhibited sexual desire. *Medical Aspects of Human Sexuality, 7*, 94–95.

Lim, T. O., Das, A., Rampal, S., Zaki, M., Sahabudin, R. M., Rohan, M. J., & Isaacs, S. (2003). Cross-cultural adaptation and validation of the English version of the international index of erectile function (IIEF) for use in Malaysia. *International Journal of Impotence Research, 15,* 329–226.

Lin, C. F., Juang, Y. Y., Wen, J. K., Liu, C. Y., & Hung, C. I. (2012). Correlations between sexual dysfunction, depression, anxiety, and somatic symptoms among patients with major depressive disorder. *Chang Gung Medical Journal, 35,* 323–331.

Masters, W. H., & Johnson, V. E. (1966). *Human sexual response*. Boston, MA: Little, Brown.

McCoy, N. L. (2001). The McCoy female sexuality questionnaire. *Quality of Life Research, 9,* 739–745.

McCoy, N. L., & Matyas, J. R. (1998). McCoy female sexuality questionnaire. In C. M. Davis, W. L. Yarber, R. Bauserman, G. Schreer, & S. L. Davis (Eds.), *Handbook of sexuality related measures* (pp. 249–251). Thousand Oaks, CA: Sage Publications.

McGahuey, C. A., Gelenberg, A. J., Laukes, C. A., Moreno, F. A., Delgado, P. L., McKnight, K. M., & Manber, R. (2000). The Arizona sexual experience scale (ASEX): Reliability and validity. *Journal of Sex & Marital Therapy, 26,* 25–40.

McHorney, C. A., Rust, J., Golombok, S., Davis, S., Bouchard, C., Brown, C., ... Derogatis, L. (2004). Profile of female sexual function: A patient-based, international, psychometric instrument for the assessment of hypoactive sexual desire in oophorectomized women. *Menopause, 11,* 474–483.

Moore, D. S., & Erickson, P. I. (1985). Age, gender, and ethnic differences in sexual and contraceptive knowledge, attitudes, and behaviors. *Family and Community Health, 8,* 38–51.

Nobre, P. J., & Pinto-Gouveia, J. (2003). Sexual modes questionnaire: Measure to assess the interaction among cognitions, emotions, and sexual response. *The Journal of Sex Research, 40,* 368–382.

Nobre, P. J., & Pinto-Gouveia, J. (2006). Emotions during sexual activity: Differences between sexually functional and dysfunctional men and women. *Archives of Sexual Behavior, 35,* 491–499.

O'Leary, M. P., Fowler, F. J., Lenderking, W. R., Barber, B., Sagnier, P. P., Guess, H. A., & Barry, M. J. (1995). A brief male sexual function inventory for urology. *Urology, 46,* 697–706.

Oh, C. Y., Lee, J. S., & Chung, B. H. (2005). A validation and reliability study for the Korean version of the male sexual health questionnaire. *Korean Journal of Urology, 46,* 1308–1326.

Okazaki, S. (2002). Influences of culture on Asian American sexuality. *Journal of Sex Research, 39,* 34–41.

Pukall, C., Meana, M., & Fernandez, Y. (2010). Sexual dysfunctions and deviations. In D. L. Segal & M. Hersen (Eds.), *Diagnostic interviewing* (4th ed., pp. 283–314). New York, NY: Springer.

Quek, K. F., Low, W. Y., Razack, A. H., Chua, C. B., & Loh, C. S. (2002). Reliability and validity of the Malay version of the international index of erectile function (IIEF-15) in the Malaysian population. *International Journal of Impotence Research, 14,* 310–315.

Rosen, R., Brown, C., Heiman, J., Leiblum, S., Meston, C. M., Shabsigh, R., ... D'Agostino, R. (2000). The female sexual function index (FSFI): A multidimensional self-report instrument for the assessment of female sexual function. *Journal of Sex & Marital Therapy, 26,* 191–208.

Rosen, R. C., Cappelleri, J. C., Smith, M. D., Lipsky, J., & Pena, B. M. (1999). Development and evaluation of an abridged, 5-item version of the international index of erectile function (IIEF-5) as a diagnostic tool for erectile dysfunction. *International Journal of Impotence Research, 11,* 319–326.

Rosen, R. C., Catania, J., Pollack, L., Althof, S., O'Leary, M., & Seftel, A. D. (2004). Male Sexual Health Questionnaire (MSHQ): Scale development and psychometric validation. *Urology, 64,* 777–782.

Rosen, R. C., Riley, A., Wagner, G., Osterloh, I. H., Kirkpatrick, J., & Mishra, A. (1997). The International Index of Erectile Function (IIEF): A multidimensional scale for assessment of erectile dysfunction. *Urology, 49,* 822–830.

Rust, J., & Golombok, S. (1986). The GRISS: A psychometric instrument for the assessment of sexual dysfunction. *Archives of Sexual Behavior, 15,* 157–165.

Segraves, R. T. (2010a). Considerations for diagnostic criteria for erectile dysfunction in DSM-V. *Journal of Sexual Medicine, 7,* 654–660.

Segraves, R. T. (2010b). Considerations for a better definition of Male Orgasmic Disorder in DSM-V. *Journal of Sexual Medicine, 7,* 690–695.

Segraves, R. T. (2010c). Considerations for an evidence-based definition of premature ejaculation in the DSM-V. *Journal of Sexual Medicine, 7,* 672–679.

Shirai, M., Ishii, N., Takanami, M., Nagao, K., Suzuki, M., Oishi, M., ... Hosoe, H., (1999). Japanese validation of the international index of erectile function (IIEF). *Impotence, 14,* 1–28.

Sidi, H., Abdullah, N., Puteh, S. E. W., & Midin, M. (2007). The female sexual function index (FSFI): Validation of the Malay version. *Journal of Sexual Medicine, 4,* 1642–1654.

Sills, T., Wunderlich, G., Pyke, R., Segraves, R. T., Leiblum, S., Clayton, A, ... Evans, K. (2005). The sexual interest and desire inventory – female (SIDI-F): Item response analyses of data from women diagnosed with hypoactive sexual desire disorder. *Journal of Sexual Medicine, 2,* 801–818.

Singh, J. C., Tharyan, P., Kekre, N. S., Singh, G., & Gopalakrishnan, G. (2009). Prevalence and risk factors for female sexual dysfunction in women attending a medical clinic in south India. *Journal of Postgraduate Medicine, 55,* 113–120.

Sun, X., Li, C., Jin, L., Fan, Y., & Wang, D. (2011). Development and validation of Chinese version of female sexual function index in a Chinese population - A pilot study. *Journal of Sexual Medicine, 8,* 1101–1111.

Takahashi, M., Inokuchi, T., Watanabe, C., Saito, T., & Kai, I. (2011). The female sexual function index (FSFI): Development of a Japanese version. *Journal of Sexual Medicine, 8*, 2246–2254.

Taylor, J. F., Rosen, R. C., & Leiblum, S. R. (1994). Self-report assessment of female sexual function: Psychometric evaluation of the brief index of sexual functioning for women. *Archives of Sexual Behavior, 23*, 627–643.

Wiederman, M. W., Maynard, C., & Fretz, A. (1996). Ethnicity in 25 years of published sexuality research: 1971-1995. *Journal of Sex Research, 33*, 339–342.

Woo, J. S. T., & Brotto, L. A. (2008). Age of first sexual intercourse and acculturation: Effects on adult sexual responding. *Journal of Sexual Medicine, 5*, 571–582.

Woo, J. S. T., Brotto, L. A., & Gorzalka, B. B. (2009). The role of sexuality in cervical cancer screening among Chinese women. *Health Psychology, 28*, 598–604.

Woo, J. S. T., Brotto, L. A., & Gorzalka, B. B. (2011). The role of sex guilt in the relationship between culture and women's sexual desire. *Archives of Sexual Behavior, 40*, 385–394.

Woo, J. S. T., Brotto, L. A., & Gorzalka, B. B. (2012). The relationship between sex guilt and sexual desire in a community sample of Chinese and Euro-Canadian women. *Journal of Sex Research, 49*, 290–298.

Yuan, Y. M., Xin, Z. C., Jiang, H., Guo, Y. J., Liu, W. J., Tian, L., & Zhu, J. C. (2004). Sexual function of premature ejaculation patients assayed with Chinese index of premature ejaculation. *Asian Journal of Andrology, 6*, 121–126.

Assessing Eating Pathology in Asian Americans

16

Yuying Tsong and Rebekah Smart

Overview of Cultural Considerations

Relatively little research has been conducted on eating disorders (EDs) among Asian and Asian American (AA) women. In recent years, some researchers have found that Asians and AAs have equal or greater rates of disturbed eating (Wildes, Emery, & Simons, 2001), and body dissatisfaction (Grabe & Hyde, 2006) as do Whites, and that AAs may be more concerned with shape or body parts than with weight (Mintz & Kashubeck, 1999).

Much of the existing ED research with Asian women in Asia or AA (or Asian British) women consists of survey research on attitudes, behaviors, and risk factors for ED with nonclinical convenience samples, using different measures and criteria, leading to contradictory results (Cummins, Simmons, & Zane, 2005). Furthermore, researchers found that clinicians were less likely to give ED diagnoses or referrals to ethnic minorities (Becker, Franko, Speck, & Herzog, 2003; Franko, Becker, Thomas, & Herzog, 2007). In a qualitative study, therapists working with this population reported that subclinical and atypical EDs were more common in their practices and clients often had a mix of subclinical features, and that EDs were not always the presenting issue (Smart, Tsong, Mejía, Hayashino, & Braaten, 2011).

An additional population that is relevant to this chapter is Asian Pacific Islander (API) Americans who comprise approximately 4.8 % of the U.S. population (Humes, Jones, & Ramirez, 2011). Over 48 different ethnic groups fall under the "Asian" racial group and there are large differences in language, religion, and values (Sandhu, 1997). In fact, more than half of Pacific Islanders endorsed multiple races and over 2.5 million additional census respondents checked Asian and one other ethnic group. Complicating things further, more than 60 % of AAs are immigrants, with more than two thirds speaking a non-English language at home and about 40 % not speaking English "very well" (U.S. Census Bureau, 2012). The diversity in ethnic cultures and the within-in group differences (acculturation levels, immigration experiences, SES, family structure, degree of adherence to country of origin values, religious beliefs, and more) further compound the difficulties in assessing and working with this population based on any over-generalization of the "Asian American" stereotypes, and miss the possible important distinctions between different Asian ethnic group eating disorder patterns, as well as risk and protective factors.

Y. Tsong, Ph.D. (✉)
Department of Human Services, California State University, 800 N. State College Blvd, EC-405, Fullerton, CA 92834, USA
e-mail: ytsong@fullerton.edu

R. Smart, Ph.D.
Department of Counseling, California State University, 800 N. State College Blvd, EC-405, Fullerton, CA 92834, USA
e-mail: rsmart@fullerton.edu

L.T. Benuto et al. (eds.), *Guide to Psychological Assessment with Asians*,
DOI 10.1007/978-1-4939-0796-0_16,

It is also unclear if the current ED assessment measures are culturally appropriate for Asian Pacific American women of different religious practices, dieting, and family traditions. Current assessment measures originally developed for Western populations may not, for example, accurately distinguish between culturally appropriate fasting behaviors and ED behaviors (Ahmad, Waller, & Verduyn, 1994b). Data resulting from Western measures could be reflecting issues such as the willingness to disclose, cultural definitions of thinness or attractiveness, or cultural differences in eating behaviors (Lucero, Hicks, Bramlette, Brassington, & Welter, 1992). In addition, the stereotype that API women are well adjusted and naturally petite may lead mental health professionals to be less likely to assess for an ED. Further, it may be more culturally acceptable for some API women to have their ED symptoms manifest more somatically (e.g., indigestion and stomachaches), which can further confuse diagnosis (H.-Y. Lee & Lock, 2007; Ting & Hwang, 2007). Controversy exists as well regarding the commonly used DSM-IV criteria for anorexia because the required "fear of fat" criterion may not occur or present differently in Asian women (H.-Y. Lee & Lock, 2007; S. Lee & Katzman, 2002) (Table 16.1).

Assessment Measures

Eating Disorder Examination (EDE)

The EDE (Fairburn & Cooper, 1993) is a 62-item semi-structured interview designed to assess the specific psychopathology of EDs and correct for some of the inherent difficulties of self-report questionnaires. The advantage of the EDE is that the interviewer can provide specific explanations of the complex behaviors in question and obtain more detail from participants. The EDE is one of the most widely used semi-structured interviews for the assessment of specific ED behaviors; it can be used to provide a diagnosis and track treatment outcomes (Kashubeck-West & Mintz, 2001). It has four subscales: *dietary restraint, eating concern, shape concern*, and *weight concern*. The global EDE score is obtained by taking the average of the four subscales. Most items are rated on a 7-point scale (ranging 0–6) to assess either frequency (0 = absence of the feature, 6 = presence to an extreme degree) or severity (Anderson, De Young, & Walker, 2009). The EDE assesses frequency over the previous 4 weeks and arrives at the diagnosis of AN, BN, and BED measuring behaviors over the past 3–6 months. The internal consistency reliability ranges from 0.67 to 0.96 (Cooper, Cooper, & Fairburn, 1989; Stice & Fairburn, 2003) in overall populations.

Research with Asian Americans. Specific reliability and validity data for AAs are not available. However, a number of researchers have used the EDE with AA girls and women. One study found that AA adolescent girls (12–18 year olds) scored significantly lower on the *Restraint* subscale ($M = 1.48$) and the *Weight Concerns* subscale ($M = 1.35$) than did their non-Asian peers (H.-Y. Lee & Lock, 2007). In another study comparing AA, Hispanic, and White adolescent girls and young women (13–20 years), it was found that all three groups had similar ED symptom scores in a Cognitive Dissonance-based program ($M = 15.45$, $SD = 14.92$) (Rodriguez, Marchand, Ng, & Stice, 2008). When comparing AA female undergraduate students with their White counterparts, it was found that AA women reported more *Shape Concerns* ($M = 16.62$, $SD = 11.6$) (Haudek, Rorty, & Henker, 1999). Shaw, Ramirez, Trost, Randall, and Stice (2004) used the EDE to compare multiple ethnic groups, both adolescents and young adults across four data sets (8 % AA), and found no statistical difference in ED symptoms across groups.

Languages available. A Cantonese-Chinese version for the Eating Disorder Examination (CC-EDEI) was validated by Lau and her colleagues (Lau, Lee, Lee, & Wong, 2006) with young women at a university-affiliated psychiatric clinic in Hong Kong. They found satisfactory and comparable internal reliability for both the global scales and the subscales: 0.81 (*restraint*), 0.89 (*eating concern*), 0.95 (*shape concern*), and

Table 16.1 At-a-glance summary of measures

Assessment name	Disorder assessed	Administration	Has been used with	Format and languages available in
Eating Disorder Examination (EDE)	Specific ED psychopathology (*restraint, eating concern, shape concern*, and *weight concern)*	Semi-structured interviews (30–60 min)	AA Adolescent girls. Cantonese-Chinese version validated for AN psychiatric patients	Cantonese-Chinese
Eating Disorder Examination Questionnaire (EDE-Q)	Core pathology of EDs (*Dietary Restraint, Eating Concern, Weight Concern, and Shape Concern*)	Self-report version of the EDE	AA college students, Singaporean women. Chinese secondary school students in Hong Kong	Chinese (Hong Kong)
Eating Attitudes Test (EAT): EAT-40, EAT-26	Attitudes, thoughts, and behaviors associated with AN (*Dieting, bulimia,* and *oral control/food preoccupation)*	Questionnaire	AA college students, South Asian U.S. women, South Asian British women, Asian Australian girls	Chinese, Japanese, Korean, Pakistan
Eating Disorder Inventory (EDI, EDI-2, EDI-3)	Psychological, behavioral, and cognitive behaviors and symptoms common to AN and BN	Self-report measure	Asian Australian young women, South Korean and Chinese female college students, South Korean and Chinese early adolescent boys and girls	Japanese, Chinese, Korean
SCOFF	ED screening	Screening instrument for nonspecialists	AA graduate students, Japanese women currently in treatment, Chinese secondary school students	Japanese and Chinese
Yale Brown Cornell Eating Disorder Scale (YBC-EDS)	Process-oriented approach for measuring the presence, type, and severity of ED-related preoccupations and rituals	Semi-structured clinician-administered interview	AA adolescent girls	
Bulimic Investigatory Test, Edinburgh (BITE)	Attitudes and behaviors associated w BN	Self-report questionnaire	South Asian adolescents in U.K. Chinese. Taiwanese women clinical patients	Mandarin Chinese
Dieting Peer Competitiveness Scale (DPC)	The degree to which individuals compare themselves to their peers in relation to their physical appearance and eating habits, especially in social situations	Questionnaire	Australian adolescent girls. Chinese, Chinese Australian	Chinese
Restrained Eating Scale (RES)/Dutch Eating Behavior Questionnaire (DEBQ)	Evaluate *restrained, emotional* (in response to diffuse emotions, and in response to clearly labeled emotions), and *external eating behaviors*	Self-assessment scale	AA adolescents, nonclinical female Korean adults	Korean

0.81 (*weight concern*) compared to the other studies conducted (e.g., Cooper et al., 1989). The CC-EDEI also provides good discriminant validity for BN and AN (Lau et al., 2006) using the global scale and three out of the four subscales (i.e., all except weight concern).

Special considerations. Because the EDE uses a semi-structured interview protocol and allows the interviewer to follow up and also rate the reported experiences, some suggest that the EDE may be less susceptible to self-report biases than questionnaires or other self-report assessment tools. However, it also has been suggested that shame, social desirability, and other factors may prevent individuals from fully disclosing their psychopathology and disordered eating behaviors (Anderson, Simmons, Milnes, & Earleywine, 2007). For AAs, the tendency to minimize pathology to avoid the danger of "loss of face" may be even more salient (B. S. K. Kim, Brenner, Liang, & Asay, 2003), particularly for those who adhere to more traditional values of avoidance of shame and embarrassment. Lee and Lock's (2007) study, mentioned earlier, may be a case in point: the AA adolescents with anorexia had lower scores on the EDE, even though their illnesses were just as severe as those of their non-AA counterparts, possibly due to less fat phobia, denial, or a presentation influenced by cultural factors. This may indicate a disadvantage to using the EDE with AAs; however, given that the gold standard for ED diagnosis remains a clinical interview and the paucity of interview data with AAs, it is strongly recommended that more research is done in this area. Researchers who are trained in cultural competency, aware of the cultural context of ED behaviors, and aware of some of the cultural differences in ED presentation and symptoms, could likely make good use of the EDE and its interpretations. For example, in their cross-cultural validation study of the EDE in Cantonese, Lau et al. (2006) took note of people who met all the DSM IV criteria for anorexia, except for fat phobia. The EDE also requires the administrator to have training and it is noted by the authors that training is essential if it is to be used for research purposes (Fairburn, 2008). In conjunction with the relatively lengthy administration (30–60 min), it may be less practical than self-report measures for many clinicians and researchers.

Eating Disorder Examination Questionnaire (EDE-Q)

The EDE-Q (Fairburn, 2008; Fairburn & Bèglin, 1994) is a self-report version of the interview-based EDE. It has thirty-six 7-point (0–6) Likert-scale items and measures ED pathology in the past 28 days, with scores of 4 or higher considered to be in the clinical range (Anderson et al., 2009). It assesses the core pathology of EDs using four subscales (*Dietary Restraint, Eating Concern, Weight Concern, and Shape Concern*), produces a global score, and ED diagnoses can be generated from the participants' ratings.

The four subscales and the global score have been found to have acceptable internal consistency reliability with 0.70, 0.73, 0.72, 0.83, and 0.90 respectively in the overall population (Peterson et al., 2007). The sixth edition was published in 2008 (Fairburn, 2008), and a modified form for adolescents along with normative data was published in 2001 (J. C. Carter, Stewart, & Fairburn, 2001). Numerous studies have demonstrated good agreement between the EDE and the EDE-Q; however, the EDE-Q, like other self-report measures, struggles to adequately capture behaviors that are left open to interpretation, such as binging (Anderson et al., 2009). There is some indication that the EDE-Q results in higher levels of pathology than does the EDE and it may be better used as a screening measure rather than a diagnostic one (Kashubeck-West & Mintz, 2001).

Research with Asian Americans. No studies on the psychometric properties of the EDE-Q with Asian Americans, to the best of our knowledge, have been conducted. However, the EDE-Q has been used to compare AA and non-AA students (Akan & Grilo, 1995; Shaw et al., 2004; Tomiyama & Mann, 2008). High internal consistency was reported with AAs as part of the sample with α of 0.95 (Tomiyama & Mann, 2008). One study found that AA female college students had lower scores on *dietary restraint* and *eating concerns* subscales and a lower global score than their White peers (Akan & Grilo, 1995). Normative means for the four subscales and the global score were 0.80 for *dietary restraint*, 0.54 for *eating concern*, 1.66 for *shape concern*, 1.47 for *weight concern*, and 1.14 for the global score (Akan & Grilo, 1995).

International Research. A comparative study examining ED behavior between Australian and Singaporean young women (18–20 years old) found that there were no differences on their EDE-Q subscales (Mond, Chen, & Kumar, 2010). However, at the item analysis level, Singaporean women had more fear regarding weight gain and loss of control over eating. Normative data for the four subscales and the global score were 0.96 (SD = 1.07) for *dietary restraint*, 1.06 (SD = 1.03) for *eating concern*, 2.31 (SD = 1.44) for *shape concern*, 1.96 (SD = 1.36) for *weight concern*, and 1.57 (SD = 1.07) for the global score. Internal consistency reliability α were 0.72, 0.67, 0.86, 0.77, and 0.92 respectively for the Australian and Singaporean young women population.

In another study examining ethnically Asian women in Australia and Singapore, after controls, Singaporean Chinese had more ED symptomatology than did European Australian, East Asian Australian, or European women living in Singapore (Soh et al., 2007).

Languages available. It has been translated into Chinese and validated with secondary school students in Hong Kong with good internal consistency reliability (0.69–0.89), and normative descriptive data for females and males separately have been provided (Leung et al., 2009).

Special considerations. A modified form of the EDE-Q for adolescents with normative data for the age group has been published by Carter and her colleagues (J. C. Carter et al., 2001). In addition, a modified version of the EDE-Q with instructions (EDE-Q-I) is available to improve its validity for assessing binge-eating behaviors, which provides definitions and examples of "unusually large amount of food" and "sense of loss of control" (Goldfein, Devlin, & Kamenetz, 2005). Since there is preliminary evidence that the EDE-Q and EDE were equally appropriate across a cross-cultural sample (see Shaw et al., 2004), this measure may have promise for use with AAs. However, only small samples of AAs have been included in just a handful of studies, with no interviews to back up the results. Reliability and validity studies with AAs and specific subgroups of AAs are sorely needed.

Eating Attitudes Test (EAT)

The EAT (Garner & Garfinkel, 1979), considered the first self-report questionnaire developed to assess ED symptoms, is a 40-item questionnaire (EAT-40) with 6-point Likert scales (1 = never, 6 = always). It was originally designed to measure attitudes, thoughts, and behaviors associated with anorexia nervosa. A shortened 26-item version (EAT-26) was developed later (Garner, Olmsted, Bohr, & Garfinkel, 1982) and assesses three factors: restrictive attitudes and behaviors (*dieting*), bulimic attitudes and behaviors (*bulimia*), and social and practical control over intake (*oral control/food preoccupation*). Both versions are used widely. They are scored by summing scores of each item from 3 points (most extreme response) to 0 point (the three least extreme responses). A cutoff score of 30 on the EAT or 20 on EAT-26 is used to indicate the presence of clinically significant eating pathology (Garfinkel & Newman, 2001). However, it has been suggested that EAT-26 is best used as a continuous score (Kashubeck-West & Mintz, 2001).

The EAT has satisfactory internal consistency of 0.79 (Garner et al., 1982) and good test–retest reliability ($r = 0.84$) (P. I. Carter & Moss, 1984). When used as a measure of symptom severity, the EAT-26 has been shown to correspond to full-threshold, subthreshold, symptomatic, and asymptomatic diagnoses (Mintz & O'Halloran, 2000). Garner and his colleagues published norms for the EAT-26 (Garner et al., 1982) based on early definitions of the disorder, which is different from the current diagnostic criteria in DSM-IV-TR or DSM 5 (American Psychiatric

Association, 2000). Norms for women in the community (e.g., Dolan, Evans, & Lacey, 1992; Dolan, Lacey, & Evans, 1990) have been found to be between 11 and 15, and typically 10–15 % of women screened with EAT report above the cutoff EAT score (Garfinkel & Newman, 2001).

Research with Asian Americans. There are no studies on the psychometric properties of the EAT with Asian Americans, to our knowledge. Even though the EAT has been widely used around the world and has been used in numerous U.S. studies comparing European Americans and African Americans, relatively few (e.g., Akan & Grilo, 1995; Bisaga et al., 2005; Iyer & Haslam, 2003) have used the EAT in studies that included AAs.

Akan and Grilo (1995) found that AA female college students had lower scores on the EAT than did their White peers but were similar to African American female college students. The normative mean for AA female college students found in this study was 53.62 (SD = 15.35). In a study on South Asian American female college students (Iyer & Haslam, 2003), history of hurtful racial teasing was found to be associated with disturbed eating behaviors, even after controlling for body mass. The EAT-26 had satisfactory Cronbach's alpha value of 0.91 in this study.

The EAT has been used with other Western populations of Asian descent, notably in Britain and Australia. For example, Asian British women were compared with Afro-Caribbean and White women living in London (Dolan et al., 1990), and South Asian female adolescents living in the U.K. were compared with their White counterparts (Furnham & Patel, 1994).

Jennings, Forbes, McDermott, and Hulse (2006) found no differences between Asian and Caucasian Australian young women (18–24 years old) in their EAT-26 scores, which had Cronbach's alpha of 0.87. However, in adolescent girls (14–17 years old), Asian Australian girls reported significantly higher eating psychopathology in the Dieting subscale ($M = 27$) of the EAT-26, but not other areas (Jennings, Forbes, McDermott, Juniper, & Hulse, 2005).

Languages available. The EAT has also been used as a measure of disordered eating in non-Western populations. It has been translated into Chinese (S. Lee, 1993), Japanese (Mukai, Crago, & Shisslak, 1994; Ujiie, Kono, Eisler, & Dare, 1990), and Korean (Ko & Cohen, 1998), as well as Urdu, Hebrew, Turkish, Arabic, and numerous European languages (Anderson et al., 2009).

Its Chinese version exhibited good reliability and validity among undergraduates (S. Lee, 1993), and high school students in Hong Kong (A. M. Lee & Lee, 1996). S. Lee (1993) modified several of the items to better provide cultural equivalents. For example, "cut my food into small pieces" was used instead of "eat very slowly" because Chinese people use chopsticks; "aware of how much weight the food that I eat will cause me to put on" was used instead of "aware of the calorie content of foods that I eat" because it was uncommon for people to count calories in Hong Kong. And as "diet food" was not a popular Chinese term, examples ("diet coke and artificial sweeteners") were given for eat diet foods (A. M. Lee & Lee, 1996, p. 178). Lee (1993) also reported a similar factor structure using data from bilingual Chinese university students in Hong Kong.

The Japanese version showed acceptable internal reliability (0.79) and validity (Mukai et al., 1994) with the mean total scores of 16.66 (SD = 7.76) in a nonclinical sample of Japanese high school female students.

The Korean version (K-EAT-26) was adapted and translated from the EAT-26 for Korean-speaking populations. It has a suggested clinical cutoff of 21 in the Korean population, slightly higher than the English North American version (Jackson, Keel, & Lee, 2006). Previous studies have supported the cross-cultural validity of the scale (Rhee, Go, Lee, Whang, & Lee, 2001), with reported Cronbach's internal consistency of 0.81 (Rhee et al., 1998). In a study comparing eating attitudes between Native Koreans and Korean American women, it was suggested that Native Koreans had more disordered eating attitudes (Jackson et al., 2006).

It was translated into Urdu for school girls in Mirpur, Pakistan (Choudry & Mumford, 1992). The factor structure of the EAT in Mirpur differed substantially from those obtained in studies among Western populations (Garner et al., 1982) and from Asian Pakistani school girls living in Bradford and Lahore in the U.K. (Mumford, Whitehouse, & Choudry, 1992; Mumford, Whitehouse, & Platts, 1991) suggesting that the eating disordered beliefs, attitudes, and behaviors may present and cluster differently for Pakistani girls (whether living in Pakistan or the U.K.) than their Western counterparts.

Special considerations. It has been used with adolescents, and the Children's Eating Attitudes Test (ChEAT) was developed for Children (Maloney, McGuire, & Daniels, 1988) to assess four factors: (a) *dieting, (b) overconcern with eating, (c) social pressure to increase body weight, and (d) extreme weight control practices*.

In a study (Stark-Wroblewski, Yanico, & Lupe, 2005) with international students studying in the United States from Taiwan, People's Republic of China, Hong Kong, and Japan, participants indicated that the translation would not be particularly helpful. However, they did find some items to be confusing in the English version (e.g., "preoccupied with"). This may suggest that if no adequate translated versions are available, researchers and clinicians should provide additional explanations or synonyms to terminologies or phrases in the questionnaire.

Although the EAT has been translated into numerous languages and has demonstrated various degrees of reliability and validity across cultures, many researchers have reported difficulty with the wording and cultural misunderstandings, so we believe it is best to check whether norms have been created for the measure in that specific country and to conduct pilot studies using alternative wording. Given that symptom presentation can differ across cultural groups and total scores may obscure the subtleties, it is suggested that researchers examine the separate factors (subscales) when possible.

The advantage of the EAT is that it is the most widely used self-report measure in the field, it is easy to use, and it has been used across cultures. It is best used as a screening tool for EDs in general (but not to differentiate among EDs or predict them) or as a continuous measure of problematic eating for European American women (Kashubeck-West & Mintz, 2001). Since small samples of AAs have been included in studies that used the EAT, it can provide a point of comparison for future studies and may be a good self-report option for researchers. However, reliability and validity studies with AAs, and specific subgroups of AAs, are greatly needed; at this point, it is not clear whether the EAT is valid and reliable for AAs.

Eating Disorder Inventory (EDI)

The EDI (Garner, Olmsted, & Polivy, 1983) is a self-report measure developed to assess psychological, behavioral, and cognitive characteristics and symptoms common to AN and BN. The first EDI had 64 6-point items and eight subscales: *Drive for Thinness, Bulimia, Body Dissatisfaction, Ineffectiveness, Perfection, Interpersonal Distrust, Interoceptive Awareness, and Maturity Fears*. The items scores range from "always," "usually," to "never." The revised EDI, or the EDI-2 (Garner, 1991), added three additional subscales (*Asceticism, Impulse Regulation*, and *Social Insecurity*). The second revision, the EDI-3 (Garner, 2004) increased from 11 subscales to 12 scales, and added six composite scores and three response style indicators. There are three eating disorder-specific scales (*Drive for Thinness, Bulimia, Body Dissatisfaction*) and nine general psychological scales (*Low Self-Esteem, Personal Alienation, Interpersonal Insecurity, Interpersonal Alienation, Interoceptive Deficits, Emotional Dysregulation, Perfectionism, Asceticism, and Maturity Fears*). Out of the six composite scores, one is ED specific (*Eating Disorder Risk*), and the other five are general psychological constructs (*Ineffectiveness, Interpersonal Problems, Affective Problems, Overcontrol, General psychological maladjustment*). The three response-style indicators to gauge response style and profile validity are *Inconsistency, Infrequency*, and *Negative Impression*. Internal consistency reliabilities are high (over 0.80) for all the scales and composite score for U.S. adults, international adults, and U.S. adolescent samples (Anderson et al., 2009).

Research with Asian Americans. To our knowledge, there are no studies that have examined the psychometric properties of the EDI with AAs specifically, even though, similar to the EAT, the EDI has been used across numerous populations. Using EDI-2, a prevalence rate of 0.78 % for BN ($M=41$, $SD=26$) was found with AA female college students (Tsai & Gray, 2000), which is similar to the rates of 1.10 % in China (Chun, Mitchell, Li, & Yu, 1992) and 0.46 % in Hong Kong (S. Lee, 1993). However, Ting and Hwang (2007) noted that if only three of the four criteria for BN in DSM-IV were used (rather than all the diagnostic criteria), 5.10 % of the AA women in this study would be characterized as bulimic, suggesting that prevalence rates among AA women may be higher than we currently think, if we consider the subclinical nature of this group. In another study comparing AA female undergraduate students with their White counterparts, AA women reported more *Body Dissatisfaction* ($M=35.08$, $SD=8.63$) and *Drive for Thinness* ($M=23.12$, $SD=8.19$) (Haudek et al., 1999).

The EDI has also been used with other Western groups of Asian descent. No differences were found between Asian and Caucasian Australian young women (18–24 years old) in their EDI-2 scores, which had Cronbach's alpha of 0.93 (Jennings et al., 2006). However, in adolescent girls (14–17 years old), Asian Australian girls reported significantly higher EDI-2 scores ($M=26.9$) than did their Caucasian counterparts, as well as in *Interpersonal Distrust, Maturity Fears, Impulse Regulation, and Social Insecurity* subscales (Jennings et al., 2005).

Languages available. The EDI has been translated into Japanese and back translation was used to obtain item equivalence (Ujiie et al., 1990). The EDI-2 was also used in a study comparing clinical and nonclinical groups of Japanese women in Japan and clinical and nonclinical groups of North American women (Pike & Mizushima, 2005) that provided descriptive data of the EDI-2 and a profile of eating pathology for both Japanese women with and without DSM-IV EDs.

The EDI was also translated into Chinese to examine the prevalence of AN and BN among college students in China (Chun et al., 1992), and while no case of AN was found in this study, the "fear of being fat" was very common (78.1 %) in these female college students, which may suggest that the EDI may not be very useful in identifying Asian women with EDs because the "fear of being fat" is prevalent in nonclinical populations, while it is often not found in AN patients in Asia (e.g., S. Lee, 1994; S. Lee, Ho, & Hsu, 1993). More discussion on the phenomenon of "fear of fat" can be found at the end of this chapter. Another Mandarin Chinese version of the EDI was developed and validated with a Taiwanese ED clinical patient sample (Tseng & Hu, 2012) that demonstrated internal consistency reliabilities above 0.70 for all scales.

The *Drive for Thinness Scale* (EDI-DTFS) and the *Bulimia Scale* (EDI-BS) of the EDI were translated into Korean to compare the eating pathology of female college students in South Korea with those in the United States (Jung & Forbes, 2006), and it was found that South Korean college women reported more disordered eating on the EDI *Bulimic* scale, but no differences were found on the *Drive for Thinness* scale. Cronbach's alpha coefficients for the Korean sample were 0.86 for EDI-DFTS and 0.82 for EDI-BS, with normative descriptive data of a mean of 22.70 ($SD=6.36$) and 18.66 ($SD=5.78$) respectively. When comparing these South Korean college women to those in China and the United States using the same two scales in the EDI (*Drive for Thinness* and *Bulimia*), alpha coefficients were found to be similar (0.91 and 0.85 for the EDI-DT China and U.S. samples, and 0.75 and 0.82 for the EDI-B China and United States samples) (Jung & Forbes, 2007). The authors found that the Korean and Chinese female college women had more eating disordered behaviors than those in the United States. Similarly, when comparing early adolescents in

South Korea and the United States (Jung, Forbes, & Lee, 2009), South Korean girls reported the most disordered eating, followed by South Korean boys, then girls in the United States, and then boys in the United States.

Special considerations. The *Bulimia* subscale of the EDI is not a diagnostic tool, but rather measures the behavioral and cognitive features of the disorder, and can be used as a screening instrument. In fact, many researchers only use specific subscales of the EDI. The advantages to the EDI and its revisions are that they are easy to administer and score, and take only approximately 20 min to administer. Its usefulness is as a screening tool in nonclinical populations and to track treatment progress; however, it remains unclear as to whether this usefulness applies to AAs. Although the EDI, like the EAT, is widely used in other countries and has been translated into other languages, no research exists examining the validity and reliability of the measure with AAs. Given this, although using specific subscales is potentially useful, it is recommended that researchers utilize multiple measures (ideally with pilot studies or interviews as a second step) and keep in mind that culture may influence factors such as *perfectionism* and *drive for thinness.*

SCOFF

The purpose of the SCOFF (Morgan, Reid, & Lacey, 1999) is typically to serve as a quick and simple screening instrument for EDs used in medical settings by nonspecialists. There are five Yes/No questions that can be administered orally or in written format (Perry et al., 2002). Scores of two or greater (answering "yes" to two or more questions) were originally suggested as the cutoff scores for detecting AN and BN. However, it was suggested later that a cutoff of 3 was the "best compromise between sensitivity and specificity" (Siervo, Boschi, Papa, Bellini, & Falconi, 2005, 81). The original SCOFF used words that were specific to the U.K. (e.g., "lost more than one stone in a 3-month period," vs. "14 founds"), but adaptations have been made to the U.S. version (Morgan et al., 1999).

Test–retest reliability was found to be high in a sample of previously undiagnosed ED patients over a 2-week interval. Normative data for both adult patients with EDs as well as for nonclinical community samples can be found in a summary by Anderson and his colleagues (Anderson et al., 2009).

Research with Asian Americans. The SCOFF was validated as a "moderately effective" (p. 105) screening tool with a graduate student sample that included 19.2 % AAs as participants (Parker, Lyons, & Bonner, 2005). Other than that, we know of no research that provides psychometric data on the use of the SCOFF with AAs.

Language available. The SCOFF has been translated into Japanese and was found to be correlated with EAT-26; the detection rates for AN or BN and EDNOS (not otherwise specified) were 96.2 % and 48.1 % respectively (Noma et al., 2006) of the patients receiving treatment in Japan. It was translated into Chinese and validated with secondary school students in Hong Kong with acceptable internal consistency reliability (0.44–0.57), and normative descriptive data was provided for females and males separately (Leung et al., 2009).

Special considerations. It is important to keep the purpose of the SCOFF in mind: With only five questions, it is very easy to administer and is moderately useful in adult primary care environments as a screening tool. Given that medical complications are common with EDs, it is potentially quite important; however, this cannot replace the need for additional questions and follow-up. It is not clear whether it reliably screens AAs with EDs. However, researchers are encouraged to conduct reliability and validity studies of the measure with AAs because there is some evidence that it is culturally more acceptable for some AAs to seek help for physical symptoms (rather than psychological issues) and indeed that ED symptoms may manifest physically (e.g., stomach aches, nausea) in some AAs (Ting & Hwang, 2007).

Yale Brown Cornell Eating Disorder Scale (YBC-EDS)

The YBC-EDS (Mazure, Halmi, Sunday, Romano, & Einhorn, 1994) is a semi-structured clinician-administered interview that provides a process-oriented approach (e.g., "How much of your time is occupied by these symptoms?" p. 426) for measuring the preoccupations and rituals common to people with EDs in those who have already been diagnosed. The first part consists of 65 items associated with *preoccupations* with food, eating, appearance, and more, as well as *rituals* associated with eating, bingeing, purging, exercise, and more. The second part rates those symptoms on a 0–4 Likert scale, and the third part assesses for *Time Occupied, Interference, Distress*, and *Degree of Control* regarding the preoccupations and rituals.

The YBC-EDS takes approximately 45–60 min to administer. A self-report version has been developed (Bellace et al., 2012). The Yale-Brown-Cornell Eating Disorder Scale Self-Report Questionnaire (YBC-EDS-SRQ) provides a *Preoccupation* Subtotal, *Rituals* Subtotal, and *Total* score; takes only 20–25 min to complete; and it provides good test–retest reliability and strong convergent validity between the YBC-EDS interview and the YBC-EDS-SRQ (Bellace et al., 2012).

Research with Asian Americans. H.-Y Lee and Lock (2007) reported on the YBC-ED descriptive data of AA adolescent girls (12–18 year olds) diagnosed with AN and found the AAs in their study resembled the non-Asians in demographic and clinical presentation. However, most studies using the UBC-ED have either not reported the ethnicity of their participants or have not included AAs.

Languages available. No other language is available.

Special considerations. The YBC-ED and YBC-EDS-SRQ are relatively newer assessment tools for ED pathology. The unique advantage of them is that they assess the nature and severity of people's preoccupations and rituals related to their ED, and so are potentially quite useful in measuring response to treatment and nature of recovery. It is suggested that the YBC-EDS can effectively distinguish healthy eating controls from restrained eating dieters and ED patients who had recovered for at least 6 months (Sunday & Halmi, 2000) and the ED preoccupations and rituals may help in understanding the onset and maintenance of ED.

AAs, as discussed earlier, may feel more comfortable disclosing their problematic symptoms and less likely to minimize them by completing a questionnaire independently, rather than talking to an interviewer, and so the questionnaire version may be more helpful in this case. However, there are no data available on the psychometric properties of these measures with AAs. Nevertheless, more research using these instruments with AAs is encouraged, importantly to ascertain whether they are reliable and valid, but then also to further the state of research regarding EDs in AAs beyond prevalence and correlational data and into examining the expression and severity of ED symptomatology, as well as treatment response.

Bulimic Investigatory Test, Edinburgh (BITE)

The BITE (Henderson & Freeman, 1987) is a 33-item self-report questionnaire used to measure attitudes, behaviors, and severity of binging, purging, and dieting in the previous 3 months. It consists of a *Symptom* subscale with a maximum score of 30 and a *Severity* subscale that uses frequency to measure the severity of disordered eating behavior with a maximum score of 39. A cutoff score of 20 or more on the Symptom scale indicates a likely BN diagnosis (using DSM III criteria); and a cutoff score of 5 on the Severity scale and a total score of 25 suggest symptoms that are clinically important.

The internal consistency for the *Symptom* subscale is very good (0.96), and for the *Severity* subscale it is moderately good (0.62) (Henderson & Freeman, 1987). A copy of the instrument and other psychometric information can be found in the original article (Henderson & Freeman, 1987). Norms can be found in a review by Anderson and his colleagues (Anderson et al., 2009).

Research with Asian Americans. Although the BITE has been used across different countries (e.g., Turkey, India, Spain, Taiwan), we are not aware of any studies that have utilized it with AAs. The BITE has been used with South Asian (Indian, Bangladeshi, Pakistani, and Sri Lankan) adolescent students (age 13–15) in East London, U.K. (Bhugra & Bhui, 2003), and it was found that these students, compared to their Anglo and African-Caribbean peers, were more likely to fast and eat compulsively. It was unclear whether the fasting behaviors were related to religious practices, only one example of how difficult it is to discern ED behavior from normal cultural practices in a questionnaire.

Languages available. The Mandarin Chinese version of the BITE had good internal consistency (0.95 for the Symptom Scale and 0.77 for the Severity Scale) in a Taiwanese women clinical patient sample (Tseng & Hu, 2012). No normative descriptive data are available.

Special considerations. The BITE can be administered by untrained individuals for assessing the clinical significance and severity of the symptoms and provide a screening for BN. The advantage is that it more specifically targets binge and purge behaviors than do most other measures. However, as has been discussed earlier, the subjectivity and personal interpretations of questions regarding binging make accurate assessment notoriously difficult. Because there are no psychometric data available for use with AAs and few studies, if any, that have used it with AA samples, there is very little basis on which to recommend it. Reliability and validity studies are greatly needed; in the meantime, if researchers specifically want to screen for bulimic behavior, it is recommended that they perform pilot studies, or use additional measures, such as the bulimia subscale of the EDI, and ideally follow up with interviews.

Additional Diet-Related Assessments

Dieting Peer Competitiveness Scale (DPC)

The DPC (Huon, Piira, Hayne, & Strong, 2002) focuses on the degree to which girls compare themselves to other girls regarding their bodies, appearance, and eating habits, particularly as those manifest in social situations. It is also useful in distinguishing between serious and nonserious dieters. There are nine items and they are on a 5-point Likert scale ("not at all like me" to "extremely like me"). Although the instrument has not, to our knowledge, been validated with U.S. populations, it has been validated with Australian girls 12–17 years old (Huon, Piira et al., 2002) and has been used with Asian and Asian Australian groups (Huon et al., 2002). Its internal consistency (above 0.76), test–retest reliability (above 0.70), and split-half reliability (above 0.70) were all high (Huon, Piira et al., 2002). Higher scores indicate that the individual is competitive with her peers about weight control issues.

Languages available. A Chinese version was developed to compare peer competitiveness in dieting between Chinese, Chinese Australian, and non-Chinese Australian girls (12–16 years old), and found that Chinese girls ($M=24.01$, $SD=5.77$) were significantly more competitive than were the Chinese Australian girls regarding their dieting behavior ($M=21.40$, $SD=5.46$) (Gunewardene, Huon, & Zheng, 2001).

Dutch Restrained Eating Scale (DRES)/Dutch Eating Behavior Questionnaire (DEBQ)

The DRES is from the Dutch Eating Behavior Questionnaire (DEBQ) (Van Strien, Frijters, Bergers, & Defares, 1986). The DEBQ is a 33-item, self-assessment scale developed to evaluate *restrained* eating (ten items which ascertain people's attempts to deliberately control their weight), *emotional* (13 items which ascertain people's eating in response to negative emotions), and *external eating behaviors* (ten items which ascertain people's susceptibility to environmental cues that increase eating) (Lowe & Thomas, 2009). It has been shown to have reliability in early adolescent and ethnically diverse samples (Stice, 1998; Weiss, Merrill, & Gritz, 2007). The DRES is one of the three most commonly used restraint measures and has excellent internal consistency and is reliable both for people who are considered normal weight or obese (Lowe & Thomas, 2009). Restraint is of interest to some ED researchers because dieting behavior can be a precursor to binge eating and bulimia (Kashubeck-West & Mintz, 2001) or it can be separate from EDs but range in its severity and impact. Items are measured on a 5-point Likert scale (1 = never, 5 = very often), with items like, "Do you try to eat less at mealtimes than you would like to eat?" and "Do you deliberately eat foods that are slimming?" (Van Strien, Frijters, Van Staveren, Defares, & Deurenberg, 1986, p. 752).

Research with Asian Americans. A study with eighth and ninth graders used a modified version of the DRES to assess weight concerns and found that AA adolescents reported the lowest weight concerns compared to their African American, White, and Hispanic counterparts (Weiss et al., 2007). The DEBQ was used to assess restraint, emotional eating, and external eating in a large-scale study of Korean American adult twins and their families (Sung, Lee, Song, Lee, & Lee, 2010). Internal consistency reliabilities with this AA sample were 0.92 for the Restrained Eating subscale, 0.94 for the Emotional Eating subscale, and 0.86 for the External Eating subscale.

Languages available. A translated Korean version of the DEBQ (H.-J. Kim, Lee, & Kim, 1996) was developed with nonclinical female Korean adults (average age 19.3 years).

Special considerations. This measure shows preliminary promise for use with AAs, given that it has been used in a couple of studies that included an AA sample. However, given that specific reliability and validity data are not available, it is not clear whether cultural factors regarding eating, overall restraint, or response bias (particularly the desire to present as having restraint) may impact use of this measure with AAs. As with all the other measures, more research is needed.

Additional Assessment Considerations

It should be noted that while some of the assessments and measures discussed above have been translated into different Asian languages and validated using Asian populations it does not mean that they are valid for AAs. For example, the definition of "excessive" regarding exercise food consumption may be different for Asians and AAs (Adkins & Keel, 2005). There is also evidence suggesting that the manifestation of EDs may vary with cultural context. Lee's work with Hong Kong's Chinese population has suggested that while "fat phobia" has been an essential criterion in diagnosing AN in the United States in DSM-IV, it only presents in a minority of AN inpatient participants in Hong Kong (S. Lee et al., 1993), and a similar phenomenon has been observed in India, Malaysia, Singapore, and Japan (S. Lee, 1994).

One major limitation in the current ED literature on AAs is the definition and interpretation of "Asian American" samples. As described above, more than 48 distinct ethnic groups with different language, histories, cultural practices, and physical features are included in the group of "Asian American." Eating disordered presentations and levels of severity cannot be assumed to be the same for this broad category of "Asian heritage." For example, South Asian British young girls were found to report eating problems seven times more likely than East and South East Asian American college students (Dolan et al., 1990; Lucero et al., 1992; Mumford et al., 1991). Other contextual factors, such as age, place of residence, experiences with discrimination, adherence of traditional Asian or family cultural values or practices, must also be taken into consideration when making assessment and planning treatments with this population.

Comparing results from international research on ethnically Asian individuals is particularly problematic because the same "Asian" category is given to individuals with varied immigration histories, food and diet practices, etc. For example, most of the individuals given the "Asian" category in the ED research from the U.K. are South Asian (e.g., Indian, Pakistani), while the individuals in the "Asian" category in the United States are usually East Asians (e.g., Japanese, Korean, Chinese) and sometimes South East Asian (e.g., Vietnamese).

Sociocultural Factors

Discrimination. APIA women experience both sexism ("beauty" for women is considered to be more important than for men, within the API community) and racism (many standards of beauty are racially based, e.g., eyes, breast size, skin color, etc.) and may be more vulnerable to body image distortion and disordered eating behaviors (Hall, 1995).

Research found that ethnic minority women who have endured racist and oppressive aggressions can experience lowered self-esteem, helplessness, and a loss of the sense of control (Fernando, 1984). Teasing based on racially and ethnically distinctive attributes (e.g., being shorter, single-fold eyelid, low nose bridges) may exacerbate the struggles that some API women already encounter as they navigate the process of integration into the dominant culture, and may contribute to eating and body image disturbances, as found in a study on South Asian American women (Iyer & Haslam, 2003).

Acculturation. Acculturation is a complex process in which immigrants adopt and adapt, to varying degrees, the values and customs of the host culture. Research has examined the role of acculturation with EDs, hypothesizing that higher levels of acculturation to Western values and behaviors are associated with more incidences of EDs. However, the results have been inconclusive (Cummins et al., 2005). In addition, the traditional Asian Confucian values, such as an emphasis on self-restraint and conforming to the norm, may provide their own thinness ethic and standards (Jackson et al., 2006), and the standard of thinness may be even higher than that of Caucasian women (Smart et al., 2011). In a study in the United States examining Pakistani immigrant girls, those who were classified as being more traditional also reported a greater risk of eating disordered behaviors (Mumford et al., 1991). Similarly, when comparing U.S.-born non-Korean-speaking Korean American female college students with native Koreans female college students, women in South Korea reported more disordered eating behaviors in both dieting and bulimia, even after controlling for their BMI (Ko & Cohen, 1998). Nevertheless, some studies have compared rates of disordered eating among adolescents and young women residing in their country of origin with those who have recently immigrated, and found that immigration to a Western society was a risk factor for ED. For example, female South Asian immigrants to the U.K. were found to have more disordered eating attitudes than their counterparts who were not immigrants (Mumford et al., 1991, 1992).

Role of Family

Several familial factors (e.g., parental bonding, family history) have been found to be associated with EDs. For AA women, parental control and overprotection also have been found to be associated with EDs (Ahmad, Waller, & Verduyn, 1994a; Furukawa, 1994). Therapists who worked with API women with EDs believed family dynamics as a relevant factor to their clients' EDs, such as parents' sense of self being linked to the children's achievement, using traditional Asian authoritarian parenting styles with more U.S. acculturated daughters, and the blunt expressions commenting on the clients' physical appearance and need for improvement (Smart et al., 2011), even though the implicit understanding was that these comments came from love and care.

Individual Factors

Perfectionism. Perfectionistic tendencies have been found in people with AN (Hewitt & Flett, 1991) and body dissatisfaction (Kiemle, Slade, & Dewey, 1987). Therapists who have worked with

API women with EDs observed their clients were often under extraordinary pressure to achieve in academics, career, and appearance (Smart et al., 2011). It was hypothesized that AA women may be more vulnerable to EDs due to their adherence to collectivism and may feel a heavy burden to correct the negative image of their culture in the United States, and work to become the "perfect Asian Woman" in behaviors, image, and appearance (Hall, 1995; Root, 1990).

Fear of fatness/Desire for Thinness. Intense fear of fatness, a central criterion in the DSM-IV diagnosis of AN, has been questioned in its usefulness in assessing Asian and AAs and indeed, criteria in DSM-V are now more flexible. Several studies in Asia (e.g., Hong Kong, Japan, Singapore, and India) found that many AN patients engage in strict dieting without self-reporting "fat phobia" (Khandelwal, Sharan, & Saxena, 1995; S. Lee, 1991, 1995, 2001; Pike & Mizushima, 2005). However, nonclinical studies found a high prevalence (78 %) of "fear of fat" among Chinese female college students (Chun et al., 1992), greater "fear of fat" amongst AA female college students within healthy BMI limits compared to their White counterparts (Sanders & Heiss, 1998), and high prevalence of weight concerns and dieting practices in a nonclinical sample of Japanese high school girls (Mukai et al., 1994).

S. Lee and his colleagues (S. Lee, Lee, Ngai, Lee, & Wing, 2001) suggested that AN patients may switch to nonfat-phobic rationales because they are not as challengeable as fat-phobia rationales as these patients are visibly emaciated. The high prevalence of "fear of fat" in nonclinical samples may also be explained by other cultural-specific factors, such as the pursuit of thinness in Japan being linked to the "culture of cute"(Pike & Borovoy, 2004) or as cultural practices of conforming to the norm of a higher standards of thinness (Smart et al., 2011).

Summary

This chapter provided clinicians and researchers with a brief overview of some of the issues pertinent to the assessment of EDs for AAs, and an examination of the most frequently used eating pathology assessments that have been validated with AA samples. The chapter reviewed research conducted in the United States on AAs, ethnically Asian individuals in other western counties (e.g., U.K., Australia), and also Asians living in Asian countries. Finally, the chapter provided additional considerations when assessing ED or eating disordered behaviors.

References

Adkins, E. C., & Keel, P. K. (2005). Does 'Excessive' or 'Compulsive' best describe exercise as a symptom of bulimia nervosa? *International Journal of Eating Disorders, 38*(1), 24–29. doi:10.1002/eat.20140.

Ahmad, S., Waller, G., & Verduyn, C. (1994a). Eating attitudes among Asian schoolgirls: The role of perceived parental control. *International Journal of Eating Disorders, 15*(1), 91–97. doi:10.1002/1098-108X(199401)15:1<91::AID-EAT2260150111>3.0.CO;2-7.

Ahmad, S., Waller, G., & Verduyn, C. (1994b). Eating attitudes and body satisfaction among Asian and Caucasian adolescents. *Journal of Adolescence, 17*(5), 461–470. doi:10.1006/jado.1994.1039.

Akan, G. E., & Grilo, C. M. (1995). Sociocultural influences on eating attitudes and behaviors, body image, and psychological functioning: A comparison of African-American, Asian-American, and Caucasian college women. *International Journal of Eating Disorders, 18*(2), 181–187. doi:10.1002/1098-108X(199509)18:2<181::AID-EAT2260180211>3.0.CO;2-M.

American Psychiatric Association. (2000). *Diagnostic and statistical manual of mental disorders - Text revision*. Washington D.C: Author.

Anderson, D. A., De Young, K. P., & Walker, D. C. (2009). Assessment of eating disordered thoughts, feelings, and behaviors. In D. B. Allison (Ed.), *Handbook of assessment methods for eating behaviors and weight-related problems: Measures, theory, and research* (2nd ed., pp. 397–446). Thousand Oaks, CA: Sage Publications.

Anderson, D. A., Simmons, A. M., Milnes, S. M., & Earleywine, M. (2007). Effect of response format on endorsement of eating disordered attitudes and behaviors. *International Journal of Eating Disorders, 40*(1), 90–93. doi:10.1002/eat.20342.

Becker, A. E., Franko, D. L., Speck, A., & Herzog, D. B. (2003). Ethnicity and differential access to care for eating disorder symptoms. *International Journal of Eating Disorders, 33*, 205–212.

Bellace, D. L., Tesser, R., Berthod, S., Wisotzke, K., Crosby, R. D., Crow, S. J., … Halmi, K. A. (2012). The Yale-Brown-Cornell Eating Disorders Scale Self-Report Questionnaire: A new, efficient tool for clinicians and researchers. *International Journal of Eating Disorders, 45*(7), 856–860. doi: 10.1002/eat.22023

Bhugra, D., & Bhui, K. (2003). Eating disorders in teenagers in East London: A survey. *European Eating Disorders Review, 11*(1), 46–57. doi:10.1002/erv.486.

Bisaga, K., Whitaker, A., Davies, M., Chuang, S., Feldman, J., & Walsh, B. T. (2005). Eating disorder and depressive symptoms in urban high school girls from different ethnic backgrounds. *Journal of Developmental & Behavioral Pediatrics, 26*(4), 257–266.

Carter, P. I., & Moss, R. A. (1984). Screening for anorexia and bulimia nervosa in a college population: Problems and limitations. *Addictive Behaviors, 9*(4), 417–419. doi:10.1016/0306-4603(84)90045-5.

Carter, J. C., Stewart, D. A., & Fairburn, C. G. (2001). Eating disorder examination questionnaire: Norms for young adolescent girls. *Behaviour Research and Therapy, 39*(5), 625–632. doi:10.1016/S0005-7967(00)00033-4.

Choudry, I. Y., & Mumford, D. B. (1992). A pilot study of eating disorders in Mirpur (Pakistan) using an Urdu version of the eating attitudes test. *International Journal of Eating Disorders, 11*(3), 243–251.

Chun, Z. F., Mitchell, J. E., Li, K., & Yu, W. M. (1992). The prevalence of anorexia nervosa and bulimia nervosa among freshman medical college students in China. *International Journal of Eating Disorders, 12*(2), 209–214.

Cooper, Z., Cooper, P. J., & Fairburn, C. G. (1989). The validity of the Eating Disorder Examination and its subscales. *The British Journal of Psychiatry, 154*, 807–812. doi:10.1192/bjp.154.6.807.

Cummins, L. H., Simmons, A. M., & Zane, N. W. S. (2005). Eating disorders in Asian populations: A critique of current approaches to the study of culture, ethnicity, and eating disorders. *American Journal of Orthopsychiatry, 75*, 553–574.

Dolan, B. M., Evans, C., & Lacey, J. H. (1992). The natural history of disordered eating behavior and attitudes in adult women. *International Journal of Eating Disorders, 12*(3), 241–248.

Dolan, B. M., Lacey, J. H., & Evans, C. (1990). Eating behaviour and attitudes to weight and shape in British women from three ethnic groups. *The British Journal of Psychiatry, 157*, 523–528. doi:10.1192/bjp.157.4.523.

Fairburn, C. G. (2008). *Cognitive behavior therapy and eating disorders*. New York, NY: Guilford Press.

Fairburn, C. G., & Bèglin, S. J. (1994). Assessment of eating disorders: Interview or self-report questionnaire? *International Journal of Eating Disorders, 16*(4), 363–370.

Fairburn, C. G., & Cooper, Z. (1993). The eating disorder examination (12th edition). In C. G. Fairburn & G. T. Wilson (Eds.), *Binge eating: Nature, assessment, and treatment* (pp. 317–360). New York, NY: Guilford Press.

Fernando, S. (1984). Racism as a cause of depression. *International Journal of Social Psychiatry, 30*(1–2), 41–49. doi:10.1177/002076408403000107.

Franko, D. L., Becker, A. E., Thomas, J. J., & Herzog, D. B. (2007). Cross-ethnic differences in eating disorder symptoms and related distress. *International Journal of Eating Disorders, 40*(2), 156–164. doi:10.1002/eat.20341.

Furnham, A., & Patel, R. (1994). The eating attitudes and behaviours of Asian and British schoolgirls: A pilot study. *International Journal of Social Psychiatry, 40*(3), 214–226. doi:10.1177/002076409404000307.

Furukawa, T. (1994). Weight changes and eating attitudes of Japanese adolescents under acculturative stresses: A prospective study. *International Journal of Eating Disorders, 15*(1), 71–79. doi:10.1002/1098-108X(199401)15:1<71::AID-EAT2260150109>3.0.CO;2-R.

Garfinkel, P. E., & Newman, A. (2001). The eating attitudes test: Twenty-five years later. *Eating and Weight Disorders, 6*(1), 1–24.

Garner, D. M. (1991). *Eating Disorder Inventory-2 professional manual*. Odessa, TX: Psychological Assessment Resources.

Garner, D. M. (2004). *Eating Disorder Inventory-3. professional manual*. Lutz, FL: Psychological Assessment Resources.

Garner, D. M., & Garfinkel, P. E. (1979). The eating attitudes test: An index of the symptoms of anorexia nervosa. *Psychological Medicine: A Journal of Research in Psychiatry and the Allied Sciences, 9*(2), 273–279. doi:10.1017/s0033291700030762.

Garner, D. M., Olmsted, M. P., Bohr, Y., & Garfinkel, P. E. (1982). The eating attitudes test: Psychometric features and clinical correlates. *Psychological Medicine, 12*, 871–878.

Garner, D. M., Olmsted, M. P., & Polivy, J. (1983). The eating disorder inventory: A measure of cognitive behavioral dimensions of anorexia and bulimia. In P. L. Darby, P. Garfinkel, D. M. Garner, & D. V. Coscina (Eds.), *Anorexia nervosa: Recent developments* (pp. 173–184). New York, NY: Alan R. Liss.

Goldfein, J. A., Devlin, M. J., & Kamenetz, C. (2005). Eating Disorder Examination-Questionnaire with and without instruction to assess binge eating in patients with binge eating disorder. *International Journal of Eating Disorders, 37*(2), 107–111. doi:10.1002/eat.20075.

Grabe, S., & Hyde, J. S. (2006). Ethnicity and body dissatisfaction among women in the United States: A meta-analysis. *Psychological Bulletin, 132*, 622–640.

Gunewardene, A., Huon, G. F., & Zheng, R. (2001). Exposure to Westernization and dieting: A cross-cultural study. *International Journal of Eating Disorders, 29*(3), 289–293. doi:10.1002/eat.1020.

Hall, C. C. (1995). Asian eyes: Body image and eating disorders of Asian and Asian American women. *Eating Disorders: The Journal of Treatment & Prevention, 3*, 8–19.

Haudek, C., Rorty, M., & Henker, B. (1999). The role of ethnicity and parental bonding in the eating and weight concerns of Asian-American and Caucasian college women. *International Journal of Eating Disorders, 25*, 425–433.

Henderson, M., & Freeman, C. P. (1987). A self-rating scale for bulimia: The 'BITE'. *The British Journal of Psychiatry, 150*, 18–24. doi:10.1192/bjp.150.1.18.

Hewitt, P. L., & Flett, G. L. (1991). Perfectionism in the self and social contexts: Conceptualization, assessment, and association with psychopathology. *Journal of Personality and Social Psychology, 60*(3), 456–470. doi:10.1037/0022-3514.60.3.456.

Humes, K., Jones, N., & Ramirez, R. (2011). Overview of race and hispanic origin: 2010, 2010 Census Briefs. Retrieved on October, 2011, from http://www.census.gov/prod/cen2010/briefs/c2010br-02.pdf

Huon, G. F., Gunewardene, A., Hayne, A., Sankey, M., Lim, J., Piira, T., & Walton, C. (2002). Empirical support for a model of dieting: Findings from structural equations modeling. *International Journal of Eating Disorders, 31*(2), 210–219. doi: 10.1002/eat.10023

Huon, G. F., Piira, T., Hayne, A., & Strong, K. G. (2002). Assessing body and eating peer-focused comparisons: The dieting peer competitiveness (DPC) Scale. *European Eating Disorders Review, 10*(6), 428–446. doi:10.1002/erv.439.

Iyer, D. S., & Haslam, N. (2003). Body image and eating disturbance among South Asian-American women: The role of racial teasing. *International Journal of Eating Disorders, 34*(1), 142–147. doi:10.1002/eat.10170.

Jackson, S. C., Keel, P. K., & Lee, Y. H. (2006). Transcultural comparison of disordered eating in Korean Women. *International Journal of Eating Disorders, 39*(6), 498–502. doi:10.1002/eat.20270.

Jennings, P. S., Forbes, D., McDermott, B., & Hulse, G. (2006). Acculturation and eating disorders in Asian and Caucasian Australian university students. *Eating Behaviors, 7*(3), 214–219. doi:10.1016/j.eatbeh.2005.08.006.

Jennings, P. S., Forbes, D., McDermott, B., Juniper, S., & Hulse, G. (2005). Acculturation and eating disorders in Asian and Caucasian Australian adolescent girls. *Psychiatry and Clinical Neurosciences, 59*(1), 56–61. doi:10.1111/j.1440-1819.2005.01332.x.

Jung, J., & Forbes, G. B. (2006). Multidimensional assessment of body dissatisfaction and disordered eating in Korean and US college women: A comparative study. *Sex Roles, 55*(1–2), 39–50. doi:10.1007/s11199-006-9058-3.

Jung, J., & Forbes, G. B. (2007). Body dissatisfaction and disordered eating among college women in China, South Korea, and the United States: Contrasting predictions from sociocultural and feminist theories. *Psychology of Women Quarterly, 31*(4), 381–393. doi:10.1111/j.1471-6402.2007.00387.x.

Jung, J., Forbes, G. B., & Lee, Y.-j. (2009). Body dissatisfaction and disordered eating among early adolescents from Korea and the US. *Sex Roles, 61*(1–2), 42–54.

Kashubeck-West, S., & Mintz, L. (2001). Eating disorders in women: Etiology, assessment, and treatment. *The Counseling Psychologist, 29*, 627–634.

Khandelwal, S. K., Sharan, P., & Saxena, S. (1995). Eating disorders: An Indian perspective. *International Journal of Social Psychiatry, 41*, 132–146. doi:10.1177/002076409504100206.

Kiemle, G., Slade, P. D., & Dewey, M. E. (1987). Factors associated with abnormal eating attitudes and behaviors: Screening individuals at risk of developing an eating disorder. *International Journal of Eating Disorders, 6*(6), 713–724. doi:10.1002/1098-108X(198711)6:6<713::AID-EAT2260060604>3.0.CO;2-5.

Kim, B. S. K., Brenner, B. R., Liang, C. T. H., & Asay, P. A. (2003). A qualitative study of adaptation experiences of 1.5-generation Asian Americans. *Cultural Diversity and Ethnic Minority Psychology, 9*(2), 156–170. doi:10.1037/1099-9809.9.2.156.

Kim, H.-J., Lee, I.-S., & Kim, J.-H. (1996). A study of the reliability and validity of the Korean version of the Eating Behavior Questionnaire. *Korean Journal of Clinical Psychology, 15*(1), 141–150.

Ko, C., & Cohen, H. (1998). Intraethnic comparison of eating attitudes in Native Koreans and Korean Americans using a Korean translation of the Eating Attitudes Test. *Journal of Nervous and Mental Disease, 186*(10), 631–636. doi:10.1097/00005053-199810000-00007.

Lau, L. L. S., Lee, S., Lee, E., & Wong, W. (2006). Cross-cultural validity of the eating disorder examination: A study of Chinese Outpatients with eating disorders in Hong Kong. *Hong Kong Journal of Psychiatry, 16*(4), 132–136.

Lee, S. (1991). Anorexia nervosa in Hong Kong: A Chinese perspective. *Psychological Medicine, 21*(3), 703–711. doi:10.1017/S0033291700022340.

Lee, S. (1993). How abnormal is the desire for slimness? A survey of eating attitudes and behaviour among Chinese undergraduates in Hong Kong. *Psychological Medicine, 23*(2), 437–451. doi:10.1017/S0033291700028531.

Lee, S. (1994). The diagnostic interview schedule and anorexia nervosa in Hong Kong. *Archives of General Psychiatry, 51*(3), 251–252. doi:10.1001/archpsyc.1994.03950030087010.

Lee, S. (1995). Self-starvation in context: Towards a culturally sensitive understanding of anorexia nervosa. *Social Science & Medicine, 41*(1), 25–36. doi:10.1016/0277-9536(94)00305-D.

Lee, S. (2001). Fat phobia in anorexia nervosa: Whose obsession is it? In M. Nasser, M. A. Katzman, & R. A. Gordon (Eds.), *Eating disorders and cultures in transition* (p40–54). New York, NY: Taylor & Francis.

Lee, S., Ho, T. P., & Hsu, L. K. (1993). Fat phobic and non-fat phobic anorexia nervosa: A comparative study of 70 Chinese patients in Hong Kong. *Psychological Medicine, 23*(4), 999–1017. doi:10.1017/S0033291700026465.

Lee, S., & Katzman, M. (2002). *Cross-cultural perspectives on eating disorders. Eating disorders and obesity: A comprehensive handbook* (p260–264). New York, NY: Guilford Press.

Lee, A. M., & Lee, S. (1996). Disordered eating and its psychosocial correlates among Chinese adolescent females in Hong Kong. *International Journal of*

Eating Disorders, 20(2), 177–183. doi:10.1002/(SICI)1098-108X(199609)20:2<177::AID-EAT8>3.0.CO;2-D.

Lee, S., Lee, A. M., Ngai, E., Lee, D. T. S., & Wing, Y. K. (2001). Rationales for food refusal in Chinese patients with anorexia nervosa. *International Journal of Eating Disorders, 29*(2), 224–229.

Lee, H.-Y., & Lock, J. (2007). Anorexia nervosa in Asian-American adolescents: Do they differ from their non-Asian peers. *International Journal of Eating Disorders, 40*(3), 227–231. doi:10.1002/eat.20364.

Leung, S. F., Lee, K. L., Lee, S. M., Leung, S. C., Hung, W. S., Lee, W. L., … Wong, Y. N. (2009). Psychometric properties of the SCOFF questionnaire (Chinese version) for screening eating disorders in Hong Kong secondary school students: A cross-sectional study. *International Journal of Nursing Studies, 46*(2), 239–247. doi: 10.1016/j.ijnurstu.2008.09.004

Lowe, M. R., & Thomas, J. F. (2009). Measures of restrained eating:Conceptual evolution and psychometric update. In D. B. Allison (Ed.), *Handbook of assessment methods for eating behaviors and weight-related problems: Measures, theory, and research* (p137–186). Thousand Oaks, CA: Sage Publications.

Lucero, K., Hicks, R. A., Bramlette, J., Brassington, G. S., & Welter, M. G. (1992). Frequency of eating problems among Asian and Caucasian college women. *Psychological Reports, 71*, 255–258.

Maloney, M. J., McGuire, J. B., & Daniels, S. R. (1988). Reliability testing of a children's version of the Eating Attitude Test. *Journal of the American Academy of Child & Adolescent Psychiatry, 27*(5), 541–543. doi:10.1097/00004583-198809000-00004.

Mazure, C. M., Halmi, K. A., Sunday, S. R., Romano, S. J., & Einhorn, A. M. (1994). The Yale-Brown-Cornell Eating Disorder Scale: Development, use, reliability and validity. *Journal of Psychiatric Research, 28*(5), 425–445. doi:10.1016/0022-3956(94)90002-7.

Mintz, L. B., & Kashubeck, S. (1999). Body image and disordered eating among Asian American and Caucasian college students: An examination of race and gender differences. *Psychology of Women Quarterly, 23*, 781–796.

Mintz, L. B., & O'Halloran, M. S. (2000). The eating attitudes test: Validation with DSM-IV eating disorder criteria. *Journal of Personality Assessment, 74*(3), 489–503. doi:10.1207/s15327752jpa7403_11.

Mond, J. M., Chen, A., & Kumar, R. (2010). Eating-disordered behavior in Australian and Singaporean women: A comparative study. *International Journal of Eating Disorders, 43*(8), 717–723. doi:10.1002/eat.20771.

Morgan, J. F., Reid, F., & Lacey, H. (1999). The SCOFF questionnaire: Assessment of a new screening tool for eating disorders. *British Medical Journal, 319*, 1467–1468.

Mukai, T., Crago, M., & Shisslak, C. M. (1994). Eating attitudes and weight preoccupation among female high school students in Japan. *Journal of Child Psychology & Psychiatry & Allied Disciplines, 35*, 677–688. doi:10.1111/j.1469-7610.1994.tb01213.x.

Mumford, D. B., Whitehouse, A. M., & Choudry, I. Y. (1992). Survey of eating disorders in English-medium schools in Lahore, Pakistan. *International Journal of Eating Disorders, 11*(2), 173–184.

Mumford, D. B., Whitehouse, A. M., & Platts, M. (1991). Sociocultural correlates of eating disorders among Asian school girls in Bradford. *British Journal of Psychiatry, 158*, 222–228.

Noma, S. i., Nakai, Y., Hamagaki, S., Uehara, M., Hayashi, A., & Hayashi, T. (2006). Comparison between the SCOFF Questionnaire and the Eating Attitudes Test in patients with eating disorders. *International Journal of Psychiatry in Clinical Practice, 10*(1), 27–32. doi:10.1080/13651500500305275.

Parker, S. C., Lyons, J., & Bonner, J. (2005). Eating disorders in graduate students: Exploring the SCOFF questionnaire as a simple screening tool. *Journal of American College Health, 54*(2), 103–107. doi:10.3200/JACH.54.2.103-107.

Perry, L., Morgan, J., Reid, F., Brunton, J., O'Brien, A., Luck, A., & Lacey, H. (2002). Screening for symptoms of eating disorders: Reliability of the SCOFF screening tool with written compared to oral use. *International Journal of Eating Disorders, 32*, 466–472.

Peterson, C. B., Crosby, R. D., Wonderlich, S. A., Joiner, T., Crow, S. J., Mitchell, J. E., … le Grange, D. (2007). Psychometric properties of the eating disorder examination-questionnaire: Factor structure and internal consistency. *International Journal of Eating Disorders, 40*(4), 386–389. doi: 10.1002/eat.20373

Pike, K. M., & Borovoy, A. (2004). The rise of eating disorders in Japan: Issues of culture and limitations of the model of "Westernization". *Culture, Medicine and Psychiatry, 28*, 493–531.

Pike, K. M., & Mizushima, H. (2005). The Clinical Presentation of Japanese Women with Anorexia Nervosa and Bulimia Nervosa: A Study of the Eating Disorders Inventory-2. *International Journal of Eating Disorders, 37*(1), 26–31. doi:10.1002/eat.20065.

Rhee, M. K., Go, Y. T., Lee, H. K., Whang, E. J., & Lee, Y. H. (2001). A validation of the Korean version of Eating Attitudes Test-26. *Korean Journal of Psychosomatic Medicine, 9*, 153–163.

Rhee, M. K., Lee, Y. H., Park, S. H., Sohn, C. H., Chung, Y. C., Hong, S. K., … Yoon, A. R. (1998). A standardization study of the Eating Attitudes Test-26: Korean version (K-EAT-26): Reliability and factor analysis. *Korean Journal of Psychosomatic Medicine, 6*, 155-175.

Rodriguez, R., Marchand, E., Ng, J., & Stice, E. (2008). Effects of a cognitive dissonance-based eating disorder prevention program are similar for Asian American, Hispanic, and White participants. *International Journal of Eating Disorders, 41*(7), 618–625. doi:10.1002/eat.20532.

Root, M. P. P. (1990). Disordered eating in women of color. *Sex Roles, 22*, 525–535.

Sanders, N. M., & Heiss, C. J. (1998). Eating attitudes and body image of Asian and Caucasian college women. *Eating Disorders: The Journal of Treatment & Prevention, 6*(1), 15–27. doi:10.1080/10640269808249244.

Sandhu, D. S. (1997). Psychocultural profiles of Asian and Pacific Islander Americans: Implications for counseling and psychotherapy. *Journal of Multicultural Counseling and Development, 25*(1), 7–22. doi:10.1002/j.2161-1912.1997.tb00312.x.

Shaw, H. E., Ramirez, L., Trost, A., Randall, P., & Stice, E. (2004). Body image and eating disturbances across ethnic groups: More similarities than differences. *Psychology of Addictive Behaviors, 18*(1), 12–18.

Siervo, M., Boschi, V., Papa, A., Bellini, O., & Falconi, C. (2005). Application of the SCOFF, Eating Attitude Test 26 (EAT 26) and Eating Inventory (TFEQ) questionnaires in young women seeking diet-therapy. *Eating and Weight Disorders, 10*(2), 76–82.

Smart, R., Tsong, Y., Mejía, O. L., Hayashino, D., & Braaten, M. E. T. (2011). Therapists' experiences treating Asian American women with eating disorders. *Professional Psychology: Research and Practice, 42*(4), 308–315. doi:10.1037/a0024179.

Soh, N. L.-W., Touyz, S., Dobbins, T. A., Surgenor, L. J., Clarke, S., Kohn, M. R., … Walter, G. (2007). Restraint and eating concern in North European and East Asian women with and without eating disorders in Australia and Singapore. *Australian and New Zealand Journal of Psychiatry, 41*(6), 536–545. doi: 10.1080/00048670701332318

Stark-Wroblewski, K., Yanico, B. J., & Lupe, S. (2005). Acculturation, internalization of western apperance norms, and eating pathology among Japanese and Chinese international student women. *Psychology of Women Quarterly, 29*, 38–46.

Stice, E. (1998). Prospective relation of dieting behaviors to weight change in a community sample of adolescents. *Behavior Therapy, 29*(2), 277–297. doi:10.1016/S0005-7894(98)80007-5.

Stice, E., & Fairburn, C. G. (2003). Dietary and dietary-depressive subtypes of bulimia nervosa show differential symptom presentation, social impairment, comorbidity, and course of illness. *Journal of Consulting and Clinical Psychology, 71*(6), 1090–1094. doi:10.1037/0022-006X.71.6.1090.

Sunday, S. R., & Halmi, K. A. (2000). Comparison of the Yale-Brown-Cornell Eating Disorder Scale in recovered eating disorder patients, restrained dieters, and nondieting controls. *International Journal of Eating Disorders, 28*(4), 455–459. doi:10.1002/1098-108X(200012)28:4<455::AID-EAT15>3.0.CO;2-B.

Sung, J., Lee, K., Song, Y.-M., Lee, M. K., & Lee, D.-H. (2010). Heritability of eating behavior assessed using the DEBQ (Dutch Eating Behavior Questionnaire) and weight-related traits: The Healthy Twin study. *Obesity, 18*(5), 1000–1005. doi:10.1038/oby.2009.389.

Ting, J. Y., & Hwang, W. (2007). Eating disorders in Asian American women: Integrating multiculturalism and feminism. *Women & Therapy, 30*, 145–160.

Tomiyama, A. J., & Mann, T. (2008). Cultural factors in collegiate eating disorder pathology: When family culture clashes with individual culture. *Journal of American College Health, 57*(3), 309–313. doi:10.3200/JACH.57.3.309-314.

Tsai, G., & Gray, J. (2000). The eating disorders inventory among Asian-American college women. *The Journal of Social Psychology, 140*(4), 527–529. doi:10.1080/00224540009600490.

Tseng, M.-C. M., & Hu, F.-C. (2012). Latent class analysis of eating and impulsive behavioral symptoms in Taiwanese women with bulimia nervosa. *Journal of Psychosomatic Research, 72*(1), 65–72. doi:10.1016/j.jpsychores.2011.06.003.

U.S. Census Bureau. (2012). Facts for features: Asian American heritage month. Retrieved from http://www.census.gov/newsroom/releases/archives/facts_for_features_special_editions/cb12-ff09.html

Ujiie, T., Kono, M., Eisler, I., & Dare, C. (1990). *Eating attitudes test and eating disorders inventory in Japan: Clinical utility and epidemiological use for eating disorders in a population of female students*. Paper presented at the 12th International Congress of International Association for Child and Adolescent Psychiatry and Allied Professionals, Kyoto, Japan.

Van Strien, T., Frijters, J. E., Bergers, G. P., & Defares, P. B. (1986). The Dutch Eating Behavior Questionnaire (DEBQ) for assessment of restrained, emotional, and external eating behavior. *International Journal of Eating Disorders, 5*(2), 295–315. doi:10.1002/1098-108X(198602)5:2<295::AID-EAT2260050209>3.0.CO;2-T.

Van Strien, T., Frijters, J. E., Van Staveren, W. A., Defares, P. B., & Deurenberg, P. (1986). The predictive validity of the Dutch Restrained Eating Scale. *International Journal of Eating Disorders, 5*(4), 747–755. doi:10.1002/1098-108X(198605)5:4<747::AID-EAT2260050413>3.0.CO;2-6.

Weiss, J. W., Merrill, V., & Gritz, E. R. (2007). Ethnic variation in the association between weight concern and adolescent smoking. *Addictive Behaviors, 32*(10), 2311–2316. doi:10.1016/j.addbeh.2007.01.020.

Wildes, J. E., Emery, R. E., & Simons, A. D. (2001). The roles of ethnicity and culture in the development of eating disturbance and body dissatisfaction: A meta-analytic review. *Clinical Psychology Review, 21*, 521–551.

Personality Disorder Assessment in Asian Americans

17

Carolyn Ha and Carla Sharp

Introduction

Clinical assessments afford clinicians and researchers insight into various forms of psychopathology, and allow for more precise diagnosis and treatment of individuals. An important area of assessment is in personality disorders. Personality disorders were placed on a separate axis to distinguish it from Axis I disorders beginning with the third revision of the *Diagnostic Statistical Manual of Mental Disorders* (DSM-III; APA, 1980) to encourage diagnosis of maladaptive personality traits and stimulate research. The DSM-IV-TR defines personality disorders as "an enduring pattern of inner experience and behavior that deviates markedly from the expectations of the individual's culture..." (APA, 2000). This emphasizes the importance of cultural experiences in shaping personality traits. Furthermore, personality disorders "should not be confused with problems associated with acculturation following immigration or with the expression of habits, customs, or religious and political values professed by the individual's culture of origin" (APA, 2000). Therefore, culturally sensitive assessments are central to adequately distinguish maladaptive personality traits in ethnic minorities who may come from various cultural backgrounds with different levels of acculturation, religious, and cultural values. Lack of attention to cultural sensitivity of personality disorder instruments, and clinician bias in administering and interpreting these assessments can lead to inaccurate diagnoses and ineffective treatments for personality disorders in ethnic minority populations.

One of the fastest growing ethnic populations in the United States is Asian Americans, with a 46 % increase in the population between 2000 and 2010 (U.S. Census Bureau, 2010). However, there continue to be few empirical studies examining personality pathology and its assessment in this population. The goal of this chapter is to first provide an overview of the Asian American population and sociocultural factors that influence personality traits in this ethnic group. Next, available personality disorder assessment tools for this population will be discussed, with suggestions and recommendations for interpretation and use of these assessments in Asian American clients. A summary of available measures along with research findings on psychometric properties and norms for Asian Americans is outlined in Table 17.1.

Demographics of Asian American population in the United States

The Asian population in the United States covers a diverse range of cultures encompassing individuals from Chinese, Japanese, Korean, Vietnamese,

C. Ha • C. Sharp, Ph.D. (✉)
Department of Psychology, University of Houston, 126 Heyne Building, Houston, TX 77204, USA
e-mail: carolynha22@gmail.com; csharp2@central.uh.edu

L.T. Benuto et al. (eds.), *Guide to Psychological Assessment with Asians*,
DOI 10.1007/978-1-4939-0796-0_17, © Springer Science+Business Media New York 2014

Table 17.1 At-a-glance summary of personality disorder assessments for Asian Americans

Assessment	Recommendations/research findings	May be used with these Asian American subgroups	Translations
MMPI	Chinese MMPI (Cheung, 1995) • Recommendations to use both the U.S. and Chinese norms. • Elevations have been found on the F scales, on scale 2 (Depression), and scale 8 (Schizophrenia) when using the U.S. norms (Cheung & Song, 1989). • When the Chinese norms are used, the profiles for psychiatric samples are moderately elevated; therefore it is recommended that a *T*-score of 60 be used as a cutoff for Chinese psychiatric patients (Butcher et al., 2003; Cheung, 1995; Cheung & Song, 1989).	Chinese	Chinese
MMPI-2	Chinese MMPI-2: (Bullock, 1995; Cheung et al., 1996; Tsai, 1996) • Elevations on Social Introversion (0), Depression (2), and Schizophrenia (8) scales		
	Vietnamese MMPI-2 (Dong & Church, 2003; Tran, 1996) • Validity was supported for the Vietnamese MMPI-2, but interpret with caution. • Elevated MMPI-2 profiles were found for older age groups, less acculturation, veteran status, and immigration traumas. • Moderate elevations on Scales F (Infrequency), L (Lie), 1 (somatic complaints), 2 (depression), 7 (anxiety), and 8 (social alienation) • These elevations are interpreted as normative for Vietnamese refugees given their experiences.	Vietnamese	Vietnamese
	Hmong translation (Dienard, Butcher, Thao, Moua Vang, & Hang, 1996) • Reliability has been established (Tran, 1996). • An audiotaped version of the MMPI2 is available for use with Hmong individuals who are illiterate.	Hmong	Hmong
	Japanese translation (Shiota et al., 1996 • U.S. norms are appropriate for use with Japanese Americans, although more studies need to be conducted with Japanese Americans.	Japanese	Japanese
	Korean (Chung, Weed, & Han, 2006; Han, 1996) • Mean elevations on F (Infrequency), 2 (Depression), 8 (Schizophrenia) scales. • Support for use of Korean version of the MMPI-2 in Korean Americans with support for cross-cultural equivalence.	Korean	Korean
	Thai translation (Pongpanich, 1996) • U.S. norms found to be valid with Thai translation, although more validity studies need to be conducted with Thai Americans.	Thai	Thai
	Filipinos (for a review see Butcher et al., 2003) • English version of MMPI adequate for use in Filipinos, with U.S. norms.	Filipinos	No translation
MMPI-A	• Elevation on Scale 2 (Depression). • Recommendations to compare both raw scores and standardized *T*-scores obtained with U.S. norms, with Chinese norms (Cheung & Ho, 1997).	Chinese	Chinese

CPAI	• Level of acculturation accounted for some differences in the Extraversion scale (Lin & Church, 2004) – Less acculturated Chinese Americans scored lower in Leadership and Adventurousness, and higher in Meticulousness, logical orientation, and introversion. • Less acculturated Chinese Americans scored significantly higher on the Interpersonal Relatedness total score while highly acculturated Chinese Americans were not significantly different from European Americans (Lin & Church, 2004). • It is recommended to assess for level of acculturation in Chinese Americans when using this scale, to aid in the interpretation of scores. • More research into the validity of the English version of the CPAI for use in Chinese Americans is needed as the one study found modest overall reliabilities (Lin & Church, 2004). Future studies should also examine the Mandarin version of the CPAI in Chinese American samples.	Chinese	Chinese English
MCMI-III	Mandarin translation (So, 2005) • Only one study has examined the use of the translated MCMI-III in Chinese populations, and reliability for the scales ranged from moderate ($\alpha=0.75$) to high ($\alpha=0.94$). • Until further reliability and validity are reported in Chinese Americans, results from use of this translated scale should be interpreted with caution.	Chinese	Chinese
	English version with Korean Americans (Gunsalus & Kelly, 2001) • Koreans differed from Americans in 7 out of 11 scales on the MCMI-III. • Koreans score higher on Dependent scale, Schizoid, Avoidant, Depressive, Aggressive, and Self-defeating scales. Koreans scored significantly lower than Americans on the Histrionic scales. • Recommendations are to be cautious in interpretation of the results in Korean Americans, and to take cultural considerations of collectivism and passivity into account. • Future validity studies are needed in Korean Americans.	Korean	No translation
PDQ-4	• The Chinese translation has only been validated for use in Chinese populations (Yang et al., 2002, 2000; Yang, Shen, Wang, & Yang, 2002). • It is recommended that the PDQ-4 be used as a screening instrument, prior to administering a semi-structured interview to identify personality pathology (i.e., PDI-IV or SCID-II). • More studies are needed to examine the utility of the translated PDQ-4 in Chinese Americans.	Chinese	Mandarin
PDI-IV	• The Chinese translation has only been validated for use in Chinese populations (Yang et al., 2002, 2000). • Validity has been supported (Yang et al., 2002), with clinical utility for psychiatric populations in China. • Studies are needed to examine the utility of the translated PDI-IV in Chinese Americans.	Chinese	Mandarin
SCID-II	• A Chinese translation of the SCID-II has been validated for use with Chinese populations (Dai & Xiao, 2006; Dai et al., 2006; Zhang et al., 2012). • Studies are needed to examine the utility of the translated measure in Chinese Americans.	Chinese	Chinese

Asian Indian, and Filipino descents. According to the U.S. 2010 Census, Asians comprise 5.6 % of the general population (U.S. Census Bureau, 2010). Chinese Americans comprise the largest Asian population in the United States with Filipinos following, then Asian Indians, Vietnamese, Korean, and Japanese (U.S. Census Bureau, 2010). As can be seen from the U.S. Census data, Asian Americans comprise a heterogeneous group of individuals with diverse cultural and linguistic influences.

Asian Americans are often referred to as the "model minority" as they are often perceived as a successful ethnic minority group with high rates of educational and occupational achievement. Fifty percent of Asian Americans have a bachelor's degree or higher education compared to 28 % of all Americans, and 20 % of Asian Americans have a graduate or professional degree, compared to 10 % of all Americans (U.S. Census Bureau, 2010). The median household income for Asian Americans in 2010 was $67,022, but this varied by Asian groups (U.S. Census Bureau, 2010). This stereotype of Asian Americans being a "model minority" has led to the problematic perception that these individuals experience few mental health problems (Sue & Morishima, 1982).

Barriers to Mental Health Use in Asian Americans and Risk Factors

Several sociocultural factors influence help-seeking behaviors in Asian Americans. Research has shown that Asian Americans tend to underutilize mental health services and prematurely terminate treatment compared to other ethnic minority groups (Leong & Lau, 2001; Sue & Sue, 1987; Uba, 1994). Many factors contribute to this underutilization of mental health services in Asian Americans, including problems with stigma, language barriers, lack of knowledge of available resources, lack of financial resources, and a lack of culturally sensitive or ethnic matched counselors (Sue & Sue, 1987; Uba, 1994). Less acculturated Asian Americans often have more concerns over stigma associated with mental health problems (Atkinson & Gim, 1989), stemming from traditional views that help-seeking is a sign of weakness or shame associated with having a mental disorder.

Being a collectivistic culture, Asian Americans tend to seek help from within their own family and ethnic community in dealing with emotional or psychological problems (Leong & Lau, 2001; Uba, 1994). Studies examining cultural factors that influence psychopathology in Asian Americans have consistently found that Asian Americans tend to somaticize their symptoms (Kleinman & Sung, 1979; Leong & Lau, 2001; Lin, Carter, & Kleinman, 1985; Sue & Morishima, 1982; Sue & Sue, 1987) as this is more culturally acceptable than expressing emotional complaints. Therefore, Asian Americans may be more likely to seek help from a medical professional for mental health problems. This somatization of symptoms is important to note as Asian Americans may over-endorse somatic symptoms on self-report instruments assessing for personality pathology. Cultural factors are important to take into consideration when conducting assessments with Asian Americans, in order to avoid underpathologizing or overpathologizing symptoms that are related to cultural influences. It is also important to be aware of barriers to mental health usage in Asian Americans, as these clients may not seek treatment until symptoms are severely impairing.

Sociocultural Influences in Asian Americans

Given that Asian Americans consist of heterogeneous groups, it is important to take into consideration various sociocultural influences including level of acculturation, immigration status, socioeconomic status, cultural belief systems and values (e.g., collectivism), language, and other cultural factors that influence personality traits in Asian Americans. Below, we discuss several of these issues as they are crucial in the assessment of the Asian American client.

First, several studies have found a relation between level of acculturation and personality, with clinical scales of the MMPI being more sensitive to level of acculturation than normal personality traits (Cuellar & Parniagua, 2000; Stevens, Kwan, & Graybill, 1993; Tsai & Pike, 2000). Therefore, level of acculturation should be assessed alongside personality disorder. Several acculturation measures have been developed and are discussed elsewhere in this handbook.

Second, traditional Asian cultural values including collectivism, deference to authority, filial piety, controlled emotional expression, and an emphasis on academic and occupational achievement (Kim, Atkinson, & Yang, 1999; Sue & Sue, 1999; Uba, 1994) have been shown to influence personality traits. Collectivism, an important cultural value for Asian Americans, places an emphasis on group harmony and group goals, which has implications for concepts of personality and self (Mulder, 2012; Oyserman, Coon, & Kemmelmeier, 2002). A meta-analysis reported that among Asian Americans, Chinese Americans are more collectivistic than Caucasian Americans, but that Caucasian Americans were not more collectivist than Japanese or Korean Americans (Oyserman et al., 2002). This illustrates the within-group differences and heterogeneity within Asian Americans, and the differential emphasis certain Asian groups place on cultural values like collectivism. It is important for clinicians to be aware of these differences in interpretation and administration of personality disorder assessments to various Asian American populations, as not all Asian Americans place similar emphasis on collectivistic values.

Other cultural values that may also impact personality traits in Asian Americans include the emphasis on indirect forms of communication in families, with less verbal communication, more indirect expression of emotions, and an emphasis on conformity and cohesion (Uba, 1994). Asian cultural values should be taken into consideration during selection, administration, and interpretation of personality disorder assessments with Asian Americans to minimize risk of overpathologizing or underpathologizing clients. Also of importance is the recognition that Asian Americans comprise a heterogeneous group, and these cultural values are mostly researched in Chinese, Japanese, Korean, Filipino, and Vietnamese Americans, with very little research including Asian Indians, although this is the third largest Asian American group.

Cross-Cultural Assessment, Bias, and Test Equivalence

Test equivalence helps to minimize test and interpretation biases in the assessment of personality disorders in Asian Americans, as some of the most popular personality disorder assessments have been translated into several Asian languages for international use. Three important types of equivalence that have been proposed in cross-cultural assessment include linguistic, conceptual, and psychometric equivalence (Allen & Walsh, 2000; Brislin, 1993; Cheung, 2009; Marsella, Dubanoski, Hamada, & Morse, 2000; Nichols, Padilla, & Gomez-Maqueo, 2000).

Linguistic equivalence refers to the accurate translation and adaptation of the assessment instrument. Guidelines have been established for translations of assessment instruments to ensure accurate translation of items, starting with an initial translation of the instrument, then a back translation, and a comparison of the two translations (Brislin, 1993; Geisinger, 1994). Additionally, Geisinger (1994) has outlined steps for determining reliability and validity of translated measurement scores. Conceptual equivalence refers to the process of ensuring that the meaning of the psychological construct remains consistent across cultures. Psychometric equivalence refers to whether the assessment scores can demonstrate similar reliability and validity across cultures. Statistical methods including factor analyses, regression analyses, and item response theory (IRT) have been employed to examine the cross-cultural validity of personality assessment instruments (for a review, see Allen & Walsh, 2000).

It is important to ensure adequate test equivalence so that an objective and unbiased assessment can provide an accurate diagnosis, and aid in treatment planning with Asian Americans. While all three methods described above are useful for determining equivalence, IRT is especially promising.

Through the use of Differential Item Functioning (DIF), it is possible to determine whether groups differ at the level of the item or trait. These differences can then be related to mean differences on the test scores (Sharp, Goodyer, & Croudace, 2006). It is therefore possible to determine whether true differences exist for instance between American Chinese and other groups, or whether these differences are due to measurement inequivalence.

Personality Disorders in Asian Americans

The DSM-IV-TR broadly defines personality disorder as an enduring pattern of internal and external experiences that distinctly deviate from the expectations of an individual's culture, and is characterized by dysfunction in two or more areas including cognition (i.e., perception of self, other, and events), affectivity (i.e., appropriateness of emotional response), interpersonal functioning, or impulse control (APA, 2000). The dysfunction has to be "inflexible and pervasive across a broad range of personal and social situations," and "its onset can be traced back at least to adolescence or early adulthood" (APA, 2000). Personality disorders are classified into three broad clusters based on similar characteristics, with the odd or eccentric disorders classified into Cluster A; dramatic, emotional, or erratic classified into Cluster B; and anxious or fearful personalities classified into Cluster C (APA, 2000). Cluster A includes Paranoid, Schizoid, and Schizotypal personality disorders, while Cluster B includes Antisocial, Borderline, Histrionic, and Narcissistic Personality Disorders, and Cluster C includes the Avoidant, Dependent, and Obsessive-Compulsive Personality Disorders (APA, 2000).

While the DSM-IV-TR uses a categorical approach to diagnosing personality disorders, there have been many arguments made for use of a dimensional approach to diagnosis which was proposed in the newest revision of the manual, the DSM 5. While changes to the hybrid dimensional-categorical approach were not accepted for the main body of the DSM 5 (published in May 2013), it was included in Section III of the DSM 5 which is the section for suggestions for future research. As we will argue throughout this chapter, the dimensional approach to assessing personality disorder holds great promise for the future of personality disorder in clinical and research practice in general, but specifically also for cross-cultural research since cross-cultural studies of personality pathology have supported the use of a dimensional trait approach to examine cross-cultural variations of maladaptive personality (Widiger & Boyd, 2009).

Much of the cross-cultural studies examining personality, personality traits, and disorders have argued that personality disorder is a construct derived from Western views of the self that do not fit with other culture's views of self, yet there is emerging evidence for the universality of personality traits across various cultures (Mulder, 2012). In particular, individualistic and collectivistic values shape different perspectives on the self and personality in various cultures (Mulder, 2012). While studies on the interactions of personality with culture are scarce, a hypothesis has been proposed to explain the interaction, suggesting that this clash between personality and culture places individuals at risk for developing personality disorders (Mulder, 2012). There is emerging data in support of a "goodness of fit" model (Mulder, 2012), where individuals may develop maladaptive patterns if they are placed in a society or culture that is not supportive of their own cultural values. This has major implications for Asian Americans, in particular in immigrants or in less acculturated individuals, as traditional cultural values of collectivism may interact with personality traits in ways that place individuals at risk for development of personality pathology as they attempt to navigate and assimilate to their new social and cultural environment, which emphasize values very different from their own.

Currently, there are no epidemiological studies investigating the prevalence of personality disorders in Asian Americans. Mulder (2012) provided a review on cross-cultural studies of personality traits which support the universality of personality traits across cultures, using the Five Factor Model (Costa & McCrae, 1990). There is evidence that antisocial personality disorder (ASPD) is universal across cultures, although the prevalence rates may vary depending on location and sociocultural factors (Mulder, 2012). For example, Asian countries like Taiwan has a much lower prevalence of ASPD in community samples, compared to the United States with rates ranging from 0.10 to 0.22 % in Taiwan compared to 1.49–5.66 % in the United States (Compton et al., 1991). In Japan, a rate of 5.8 % was found for a sample of patients from a general medical clinic. A higher rate of ASPD was reported for South Korea (2.1 %) which was similar to rates found in the United States (Lee, Kavoc, & Rhee, 1987). Furthermore, the community prevalence of personality disorders in China was found to be very low at 0.13 %, although the author acknowledged that the low rates may have been attributed to underreporting as there is much stigma surrounding having mental health problems (Cheung, 1991). In clinical settings, a prevalence study of personality disorders in psychiatric outpatients conducted in Shanghai, China reported a rate of 31.9 % for any personality disorder diagnosis (Zhang et al., 2012).

These findings in Asian countries provide evidence that maladaptive personality patterns do exist in Asian cultures. Additionally, there is supporting evidence that the DSM-IV criteria in diagnosis of personality disorders are relevant for Chinese individuals (Zhang et al., 2012). Therefore, it is important to assess for personality pathology in Asian Americans, as many recent immigrants are first generation Americans.

Assessment Instruments for Personality Disorders in Asian Americans

Accurate assessment of personality disorders can be a complex task, as there are many factors to take into account, including the consideration of boundaries between adaptive and maladaptive personality traits, boundaries with other Axis I and Axis II psychopathology, and gender and cultural factors that may play a role in shaping these personality traits (Widiger & Boyd, 2009). Therefore, researchers have recommended that a multi-method approach be taken, through use of semi-structured interviews, self-reports, and reports from significant others such as close friends or spouses (Widiger & Chaynes, 2003; Widiger & Samuel, 2005). Specifically, Widiger (2002) has recommended a two-step procedure in obtaining an evidence-based assessment of personality disorders, beginning with the use of a self-report instrument to detect the presence of personality pathology, and then to follow-up with a semi-structured interview to confirm the presence of these maladaptive traits (Widiger & Samuel, 2005). Cross-cultural researchers have also recommended the use of multi-method assessments, including measures of acculturation, use of an ethnic consultant, and translated instruments when appropriate (Okazaki, Okazaki, & Sue, 2009).

There continues to be a lack of culturally sensitive assessment tools for examining personality disorders in Asian Americans. However, many Asian countries have used translated versions of some well-known personality assessments including the Minnesota Multiphasic Personality Inventory (MMPI; Butcher, 1996; Butcher, Lim, & Nezami, 1998), the Millon Clinical Multiaxial Inventory-III (MCMI-III; Millon, Millon, Davis, & Grossman, 2009), as well as developed their own measures of personality assessment (Cheung, 2004). One measure developed and normed in Chinese populations, the Chinese Personality Assessment Inventory (CPAI; Cheung et al., 1996) has been used in cross-cultural research on personality disorders, with preliminary evidence supporting its use with Chinese American samples (Cheung, Cheung, Leung, Ward, & Leong, 2003; Lin & Church, 2004). Most of the research in Asian American personality assessment has been with Chinese Americans, and there continues to be a lack of research in other Asian American subgroups, in particular with Asian Indians.

Other personality disorder assessments that have been translated for use in China include the Personality Diagnostic Questionnaire (PDQ-4; Bagby & Farvolden, 2004), Personality Disorder Interview (PDI-IV; Widiger, Mangine, Corbitt, Ellis, & Thomas, 1995), and the Structured Clinical Interview for DSM-IV Axis II Disorders (SCID-II; First, Gibbon, Spitzer, Williams, & Benjamin, 1997). These instruments have shown reliability and validity in assessment of Chinese psychiatric patients, but there remains no research on their use in Asian Americans. Therefore, these assessments will only be briefly summarized in this chapter, as their applicability for assessment of Chinese Americans remains uncertain.

This section will first focus on research examining the use of the MMPI and MMPI-2, in Asian Americans, with a review of research evidence for the utility of the Chinese translations of the MMPI and MMPI-2. Findings from the cross-cultural research on the utility of the CPAI (Cheung et al., 1996) will also be discussed in terms of its development for use in China and the research conducted on the English translation for use with Chinese Americans. Then, research findings from Chinese translated versions of the PDQ-4, PDI-IV, and SCID-II will be briefly reviewed, and implications for use with Asian Americans will be discussed. Since there continues to be a paucity of research on personality disorder assessments in Asian Americans, translated assessments and their use in Asia will be reviewed, with implications for the potential use of these assessments in Asian Americans discussed. Finally, a brief discussion on personality disorder assessment in adolescents will be provided along with evidence in support of a translated version of the MMPI-A for use with Chinese adolescents. A summary of available assessment tools for Asian Americans is provided in Table 17.1 along with normative data and recommendation for interpretation.

Minnesota Multiphasic Personality Inventory (MMPI and MMPI-2)

One of the most frequently used tools for personality assessment includes the MMPI and MMPI-2, which have gained popularity with international clinicians and researchers. The first MMPI was published in 1943 (Hathaway & McKinkey, 1943), with ten clinical scales and several validity scales. The restandardization of the MMPI involved updating the normative sample and revision of items, which began in 1982, leading to an updated version of the MMPI. The MMPI-2 contains 567 items with a true or false response option (Butcher, Dahlstrom, Graham, Tellegen, & Kaemmer, 1989). The MMPI-2 consists of 10 clinical scales, 9 validity scales, and 15 content scales. The clinical scales of the MMPI-2 are identified by assigned scale numbers as follows: (1) Hypochondriasis, (2) Depression, (3) Hysteria, (4) Psychopathic Deviance, (5) Masculinity/Femininity, (6) Paranoia, (7) Psychasthenia, (8) Schizophrenia, (9) Hypomania, and (0) Social Introversion. Validity scales include Cannot Say, Variable Response Inconsistency (VRIN), True Response Inconsistency (TRIN), Infrequency (F), Back Infrequency (Fb), Infrequency-Psychopathology (Fp), Lie (L), Correction (K), Superlative Self-Presentation (S). Interpretations for scales can be found in several manuals and handbooks (Butcher, 2006; Butcher et al., 1989; Cox, Weed, & Butcher, 2009; Graham, 2006).

Both the MMPI and MMPI-2 continue to be widely used nationally and internationally with translations in over 22 languages. Specific guidelines have been established for its adaptation and translation, and a breadth of cross-cultural investigations has reported on the psychometric properties of the translated versions (Butcher, 2004; Butcher et al., 1998). A review of cross-cultural studies using the MMPI-2 translations has supported the use of U.S. established norms in several countries, except with the Korean translation (Butcher et al., 1998). Additionally, countries have collected their own norms and the raw scores have been found to be very similar to U.S. established norms (Butcher et al., 1998). While adaptations of the MMPI and MMPI-2 currently exist in Asian countries with translations in Chinese, Japanese, Korean, Filipino, Vietnamese, Hmong, and Thai languages (Butcher, Cheung, & Lim, 2003; Butcher et al., 1998; Okazaki et al., 2009), few empirical studies have been conducted with Asian Americans using these assessments. Existing studies have been primarily conducted in middle class and educated Asian American college student samples, limiting the generalizability of these findings to other Asian American populations including clinical samples.

The Chinese MMPI was translated and standardized in Hong Kong by Fanny M. Cheung

(1985, 1995) using structured methods to assess for linguistic equivalence. It has been used in clinical settings in both mainland China and Hong Kong, with several research studies conducted in clinical populations (Butcher et al., 2003). It is recommended that both the U.S. and Chinese norms are used for interpretation of scores on the Chinese MMPI (Cheung, 1995), as Chinese respondents have been shown to be elevated on the F scales, on scale 2 (Depression), and scale 8 (Schizophrenia) when using the U.S. norms (Cheung & Song, 1989). The profiles for psychiatric samples are moderately elevated when using the Chinese norms; therefore the researchers have suggested that a T-score of 60 be used as a cutoff for Chinese psychiatric patients (Butcher et al., 2003; Cheung, 1995; Cheung & Song, 1989). The Chinese MMPI-2 has also been extensively investigated for equivalence and validity (Cheung, Song, & Zhang, 1996; Cheung, Zhang, & Song, 2003) in Chinese samples. Okazaki and colleagues (2009) recently reviewed the literature on the MMPI and MMPI-2 in Asian Americans and their use overseas in Asia.

In the United States, both the MMPI and MMPI-2 have been investigated in several studies with Asian Americans (Kwan, 1999; Stevens et al., 1993; Tsai & Pike, 2000). These studies revealed that significant differences exist between Asian Americans and Caucasian nonclinical samples on certain scales of the MMPI, with Asian Americans receiving elevated scores on scales 0 (Social Introversion), 2 (Depression), and 8 (Schizophrenia: Bullock, 1995; Kwan, 1999; Tsai, 1996). Similarly, in the few studies conducted on the MMPI and MMPI-2 with Asian American clinical samples, it has been found that compared to Caucasian samples, Asian American patients were more elevated on several scales (Kwan, 1999). In general, findings from these studies have supported the reliability and validity of the translated MMPI-2 for use with Asian Americans (Vietnamese and Hmong translations of the MMPI-2). The Japanese translation of the MMPI-2 (Shiota, Krauss, & Clark, 1996), and Korean (Han, 1996) and Thai (Pongpanich, 1996) translations have also demonstrated adequate psychometric properties (Okazaki et al., 2009). It is important to note that studies have found that the level of acculturation influences discrepant scores on the MMPI-2 between both groups, with highly acculturated Asian Americans scoring similar to Caucasians, and less acculturated Asian Americans demonstrating significant elevations (Sue, Keefe, Enomoto, Durvasula, & Chao, 1996; Tran, 1996; Tsai, 1996; Tsai & Pike, 2000). Therefore, it is suggested to use acculturation measures in conjunction with the MMPI or MMPI-2 in interpretation of the clinical profiles (Kwan, 1999) and to take a more conservative approach in the interpretation of results for less acculturated clients whose scores may be different from the U.S.-based norms (Okazaki et al., 2009; Okazaki & Sue, 1995).

Depending on the client's acculturation level and linguistic proficiency in English, it may be appropriate to use a translated version of the MMPI-2 and compare the client's profile scores to both U.S. norms and norms developed in Asian countries. Velásquez and colleagues (2002) provided eight basic guidelines for clinicians to consider in the administration and interpretation of the MMPI-2 with ethnic minorities. In summary, these are to: (1) consider whether the MMPI-2 is the most appropriate measure for your client, along with considering the client's linguistic and ethnic background; (2) follow standardized procedures for administering the MMPI-2; (3) employ caution in using computerized interpretive reports generated by software programs; (4) consider use of supplementary scales; (5) consider the appropriateness of using a translated adaptation of the MMPI-2 for clients whose native language may not be English; (6) consider acculturation factors; (7) consider the language in which feedback is given to clients; and (8) seek consultation as needed.

Chinese Personality Assessment Inventory (CPAI)

The CPAI (Cheung et al., 1996) was initially developed as an indigenous assessment of personality for use in China and Hong Kong to address the limitations of using imported or translated personality assessments (Cheung, 2004).

The development of the CPAI followed a similar structure to the MMPI-2, with both personality and clinical scales, and has been validated, normed, and standardized for use with Chinese populations (Cheung, Kwong, & Zhang, 2003). The CPAI consists of 510 self-report items using a true-false response format, with 22 personality scales, 12 clinical scales, and 3 validity scales (Cheung et al., 1996). The CPAI has demonstrated adequate convergent validity with the MMPI-2 in a sample of Chinese students from Hong Kong and Southern China (Cheung, Cheung, & Zhang, 2004). Four personality factors were derived from factor analyses of the CPAI, including Dependability, Interpersonal Relatedness, Social Potency, and Individualism (Cheung et al., 2001). The Interpersonal Relatedness factor was found to be unique to Chinese individuals compared to a non-Chinese sample of Hawaiian undergraduate students, emphasizing collectivistic values such as maintaining harmony, avoidance of conflict, saving face, and adherence to norms and reciprocity in social interactions (Cheung et al., 2001). An English version of the CPAI has been adapted using structured back-translation guidelines similar to what has been used in translating Western developed instruments, with psychometric properties investigated in Caucasian and Chinese American samples (Cheung et al., 2003; Lin & Church, 2004).

Several studies have reviewed the development and validation of the CPAI across different populations (Cheung, 2004; Cheung et al., 2004; Okazaki et al., 2009). There is evidence in support of its clinical utility in forensic and psychiatric populations and in discriminating clinical and nonclinical samples in Hong Kong and China (Cheung et al., 2003). Similar factor structures were found for a sample from Singapore and Caucasian Americans, using Chinese norms (Cheung et al., 2003).

Currently, only one study has investigated the use of the English version of the CPAI with a community sample of Chinese Americans (Lin & Church, 2004). Results from this study confirmed the four factor structure found with Chinese normative samples for Chinese Americans. Significant differences were found between less acculturated Chinese Americans and Caucasian Americans in the Interpersonal Relatedness scale, supporting the concurrent validity of the CPAI (Lin & Church, 2004). However, overall reliability was modest with alphas ranging from 0.43 to 0.81 (Lin & Church, 2004). This study supports the potential use of the CPAI with Chinese American samples, although future studies should investigate the psychometric properties of the assessment in clinical populations. While the CPAI appears to be a promising assessment of personality pathology, in particular with less acculturated Chinese Americans, it should be used in conjunction with other methods of assessment and interpreted with caution, as normative data may not fit well for highly acculturated Chinese Americans.

Millon Clinical Multiaxial Inventory-III (MCMI-III)

The MCMI-III is a self-report instrument for the assessment of DSM-IV-TR personality disorders, developed and standardized for use with clinical populations. The inventory consists of 175 items with a true-false response format, and provides a profile containing 14 personality disorder scales, 10 clinical scales, and 2 validity scales (Millon et al., 2009). Extensive research has been conducted with this measure and it's one of the most popular self-report measures for assessing personality pathology (Widiger & Boyd, 2009).

While the MCMI-III is a valid and reliable self-report inventory for assessment of personality disorders, there are no studies reporting its use with Asian Americans. It has, however, been translated and adapted for use in China, but only one study has reported on its use in a Chinese sample of substance abusers (So, 2005). The study reported a high prevalence of Axis II comorbidity, with ASPD being the most prevalent in the sample (So, 2005). However, the study does not report on the validity or reliability of the translated MCMI-III. While the translated version of the MCMI-III may be of use for Chinese American immigrants with limited fluency in English, it should be used in conjunction with other assessments and interpreted with caution as it is unknown how Chinese Americans may perform on these scales using the standard American norms. Future studies should investigate the psychometric properties of the translated MCMI-III and establish its clinical utility in Chinese American samples. Additionally, future research should evaluate the use of the MCMI-III in other Asian American populations, and consider translations in other Asian languages.

Another study conducted in a Korean sample was conducted using the English version of the MCMI-III. In this study, college students in Seoul, Korea were selected only if they majored in English, as English fluency was required to complete the MCMI-III (Gunsalus & Kelly, 2001). A sample of American college students (Gunsalus & Kelly, 2001) was also selected for participation in the study as a comparison group. The study demonstrated significant differences on 7 out of 11 scales on the MCMI-III profiles, with Koreans scoring higher on Schizoid, Avoidant, Depressive, Aggressive, and Self-defeating scales of the MCMI-III (Gunsalus & Kelly, 2001). Again, conclusions of this study pointed to the importance of multi-method assessments for personality disorder in Korean Americans and emphasize the need for therapists to consider cultural values of collectivism and orientation toward others that should be taken into consideration as cultural influences that may elevate scores on the MCMI-III as opposed to actual personality pathology (Gunsalus & Kelly, 2001). It should be noted that findings from this study have limited generalizability to Korean Americans as the sample consisted of a specific group of Korean college students majoring in English. Future research should examine the clinical utility of the MCMI-III in Korean American and other Asian American samples.

Other Assessments of Personality Disorder in Asians

The SCID-II (First et al., 1997) is one of the most widely used semi-structured interviews for the assessment of DSM-IV personality disorders. Interviewers rate symptom criteria for each of the 10 DSM-IV personality disorders as absent or false (1), subthreshold criteria (2), or as threshold criteria or true (3) based on the interviewer's clinical judgment and the interviewee's responses (First et al., 1997). There is a short screening 119-item screening tool for the SCID-II rated by self-report to shorten administration time (First et al., 1997). A Chinese translation of the SCID-II has been developed, and its psychometric properties have been supported (Dai & Xiao, 2006; Dai, Xiao, Wang, Zhang, & Chen, 2006). Most recently, it has been used in examination of the prevalence of personality disorders using the DSM-IV Axis II criteria in an outpatient psychiatric sample from Shanghai, China (Zhang et al., 2012). Support was demonstrated for use of the DSM-IV classification system for identifying personality disorders in a Chinese clinical sample (Zhang et al., 2012).

The Personality Disorders Questionnaire for DSM-IV (PDQ-4; Bagby & Farvolden, 2004; Hyler, 1994) and the Personality Disorder Interview-IV (PDI-IV; Widiger et al., 1995) were adapted and translated into Chinese for use with clinical samples in China (Yang, Bagby, Costa, Ryder, & Herbst, 2002; Yang et al., 2000). The PDQ-4 is a self-report instrument consisting of 99 items with a true-false response format. Seven of the original items on the PDQ-4 were replaced with more culturally appropriate items, and an additional eight items were added to substitute for items that were culturally irrelevant (Yang et al., 2000). The Chinese translation consists of 107 items. Adequate reliability and validity of the PDQ-4 has been reported for use with Chinese psychiatric patients and in a community sample of Chinese college students (Ling, Qian, & Yang, 2010; Yang, Shen, Wang, & Yang, 2002). The PDQ-4 has also been used to assess for prevalence of personality disorders in a sample of psychiatric outpatients in China (Zhang et al., 2012) and similar to studies in U.S. populations, the self-report instrument was found to overdiagnose PDs in Chinese samples. It is recommended that the PDQ-4 be used as a screening instrument, prior to administering a semi-structured interview to identify personality pathology. However, the PDQ-4 has not been validated for use in

Chinese American populations, so it remains unclear whether this instrument would be an effective screener for personality disorders in this population.

The PDI-IV (Widiger et al., 1995) is a semi-structured interview of DSM-IV personality disorders, but it is the least used of existing measures to assess for personality pathology (Widiger & Boyd, 2009). The interviewer rates responses using a 3-point scale, with 0 indicating absence of the symptom, 1 indicating present, and 2 indicating present to a severe or substantial degree. The Chinese adaptation moved the Antisocial Personality disorder module to the end of the interview as opposed to the beginning, and 31 new culturally relevant questions were added to the interview (Yang et al., 2002). There is evidence for its utility in assessment of personality pathology in Chinese clinical populations (Yang et al., 2002, 2000).

Research studies using these measurements have supported the diagnosis of almost all of the personality disorders as defined by the DSM-IV in Chinese psychiatric samples, except for Schizotypal Personality Disorder (Yang et al., 2000). While these are promising findings and have demonstrated clinical utility in Chinese psychiatric samples, it is unclear whether these translated instruments would be adequate for use in Asian American populations as there are no research studies examining the psychometric properties of these measures in America.

Personality Disorder Assessment in Asian American Youths

It is important to note that although there has been significant advances in the assessment of PD in children and adolescents over the last decade (Sharp, Ha, Michonski, Venta, & Carbonne, 2012; Sharp & Kine, 2008), there remains some controversy and hesitation over diagnosis of personality disorders in adolescence (Adshead, Broderick, Preston, & Deshpande, 2012). One of the major arguments has been over the stability and continuity of personality disorders from childhood and adolescence into adulthood (Adshead et al. 2012). However, emerging evidence in the area of personality disorder research has supported the stability of personality disorder diagnoses into adulthood (Bondurant, Greenfield, & Tse, 2004; Cohen, Crawford, Johnson, & Kasen, 2005; Sharp & Romero, 2007). There is also extensive evidence for the validity of personality disorder diagnoses in adolescence (Bernstein et al., 1993; Levy et al., 1999; Miller, Muehlenkamp, & Jacobson, 2008; Sharp et al., 2012). Prevalence studies of personality disorders in youths have reported high rates in the community from 15 % (Kasen, Cohen, Skodol, Johnson, & Brook, 1999) to 31 % (Bernstein et al., 1993). Given the wealth of evidence in support of a personality disorder diagnosis in adolescence, it is important to adequately assess youths so that early intervention may afford positive outcomes. However, there continues to be a paucity of research on personality disorder diagnoses in Asian American youths. In addition, assessments tools are lacking for this ethnic minority population, with only one instrument available for Chinese adolescents, the MMPI-A. Findings from the validation study conducted on the MMPI-A may inform future research and clinical use with Chinese Americans; therefore its development and validity findings are reported below.

The MMPI-A was adapted for assessment of adolescents ages 14–18, with 478 items, and 10 clinical scales, 6 validity scales, and 3 social introversion subscales (Butcher et al., 1992). Currently, only one study has been conducted in examining the psychometric properties of the translated MMPI-A in a sample of Chinese adolescents from Hong Kong (Chueng & Ho, 1997). The study reported findings of moderate elevations on several clinical and content scales for Chinese adolescents when using U.S. norms, with a notable elevation on the Depression scale, in which Chinese adolescents scored one standard deviation above the mean (Chueng & Ho, 1997; Okazaki et al., 2009). However, these results are similar to those found in adult studies using U.S. norms for Chinese adults on the Chinese MMPI and MMPI-2 (Cheung et al., 1996) and none of the elevations exceeded the clinical cutoff (*T*-score = 65). The authors suggested that this may be more reflective of cultural differences between U.S. and Chinese adolescents rather than actual psychopathology in Chinese youths (Chueng & Ho, 1997). Suggestions for interpretation of Chinese adolescent MMPI-A profiles include comparing both raw scores and standardized *T*-scores obtained with U.S. norms, with means obtained for the sample of Hong Kong adolescents (Cheung & Ho, 1997).

While the study established norms for Chinese adolescents, no studies have examined the clinical utility of the MMPI-A in Chinese American adolescents. The availability of a Chinese version of the MMPI-A may be useful for researchers and clinicians in assessment of personality pathology in Chinese American adolescents, in particular with less acculturated adolescents or those who have recently immigrated from China or Hong Kong and may not be proficient in English. When conducting personality disorder assessment in Asian American youths, similar standards and guidelines as outlined for adults should be taken into consideration (Velásquez et al., 2000) as well as extra caution not to misdiagnose the disorder in youths, due to concerns over stigmatizing youths with a lifelong disorder which may hinder their access to appropriate clinical services (Adshead et al. 2012). In assessment of personality disorders in youths, it is integral to take a multi-method assessment approach and incorporate multiple perspectives, including parent- and teacher-reported symptoms to provide a comprehensive assessment and aid in formulation of an accurate diagnosis. Consultation with an expert in adolescent personality disorders is also highly recommended.

Conclusion

There continues to be a dearth of research on personality disorder assessment with Asian Americans, examining the equivalence, validity, and reliability of personality disorder instruments for use in Asian American samples. While this presents a significant ethical dilemma, as psychologists are required to use appropriate assessments that have been adapted for target populations (APA, 2003), there are challenges to adapting measures appropriate for use with Asian Americans as they represent a diverse group with heterogeneity in terms of background, language, and level of acculturation. In terms of Chinese Americans alone, the largest Asian American population, it would be impractical to have standardized assessment tools available in every Chinese dialect, as there are several dialects spoken by Chinese immigrants.

While some psychometric research has been conducted for Chinese Americans, clearly more research is warranted. Moreover, this review also clearly points to an urgent need for psychometric studies with other Asian American populations, including Asian Indians. The best studied evidence-based assessment of personality pathology is with the MMPI and MMPI-2 in Asian Americans, with translations in several Asian languages and recommendations on scale interpretations. There is increasing research being conducted in China in using measures specifically developed for personality disorders, including an indigenous measure of personality pathology in China. The availability of translated measures assists with cross-cultural evaluations of personality disorder, and helps to identify which underlying personality constructs are universal, and which are culture-specific. While it may be appropriate to use some of the measures for which Asian norms have been established in China, it is recommended that clinicians do so with caution in interpreting the results, as there continues to be a lack of evidence of the reliability and validity of these norms for use in Asian Americans (Okazaki & Sue, 2000).

As suggested throughout this chapter, it is essential that personality disorder assessment include a multi-method approach, including assessing for linguistic proficiency, level of acculturation, and use of both self-report and interview-based assessments. However, clinicians must be aware of test bias, and take caution in interpretation of the assessment results, as there continues to be limited research available on the reliability and validity of these instruments with the diverse Asian American population. Whenever appropriate, it may be useful to seek out an ethnic consultant in assisting with administering and interpretation of the assessment data.

References

Adshead, G., Brodrick, P., Preston, J., & Deshpande, M. (2012). Personality disorder in adolescence. *Advances in Psychiatric Treatment, 18*, 109–118.

Allen, J., & Walsh, J. A. (2000). A construct-based approach to equivalence methodologies for cross-cultural/multicultural personality assessment research. In R. H. Dana (Ed.), *Handbook of cross-cultural and multicultural personality assessment* (pp. 63–85). Hillsdale, NJ: Erlbaum.

American Psychiatric Association. (1980). *Diagnostic and statistical manual of mental disorders* (3rd ed.). Washington, DC: American Psychiatric Press.

American Psychiatric Association. (2000). *Diagnostic and statistical manual of mental disorders* (4th ed.). Washington, DC: APA (DSM-IV-TR). Text revision.

American Psychological Association. (2003). Guidelines on multicultural education, training, research, practice, and organizational change for psychologists. *American Psychologist, 58*(5), 377–402.

Atkinson, D. R., & Gim, R. H. (1989). Asian-American cultural identity and attitudes toward mental health services. *Journal of Counseling Psychology, 36*(2), 209–212.

Bagby, R., & Farvolden, P. (2004). The Personality Diagnostic Questionnaire-4 (PDQ-4). In M. J. Hilsenroth & D. L. Segal (Eds.), *Comprehensive handbook of psychological assessment* (Personality assessment, Vol. 2, pp. 122–133). Hoboken, NJ: John Wiley & Sons.

Bernstein, D. P., Cohen, P., Velez, C. N., Schwab-Stone, M., Siever, L. J., & Shinasto, L. (1993). Prevalence and stability of the DSM-II-R personality disorders in a community-based survey of adolescents. *The American Journal of Psychiatry, 150*(8), 1237–1243.

Bondurant, H., Greenfield, B., & Tse, S. M. (2004). Construct validity of the adolescent borderline personality disorder: A review. *The Canadian Child and Adolescent Psychiatry Review, 13*(3), 53–57.

Brislin, R. W. (1993). *Understanding culture's influence on behavior*. New York, NY: Harcourt Brace.

Bullock, S. L. (1995). *Comparison of MMPI-2 scores of Asian and Caucasian college students*. (Doctoral dissertation). Biola University. *Dissertation Abstracts International, 57*(04), 2857B.

Butcher, J. N. (Ed.). (1996). *International adaptations of the MMPI-2: Research and clinical applications*. Minneapolis, MN: University of Minnesota Press.

Butcher, J. N. (2004). Personality assessment without borders: Adaptation of the MMPI-2 across cultures. *Journal of Personality Assessment, 83*, 90–104.

Butcher, J. N. (2006). Assessment in clinical psychology: A perspective on the past, present challenges, and future prospects. *Clinical Psychology: Science and Practice, 13*, 205–209.

Butcher, J. N., Cheung, F. M., & Lim, J. (2003). Use of the MMPI-2 with Asian populations. *Psychological Assessment, 15*, 248–256.

Butcher, J. N., Dahlstrom, W. G., Graham, J. R., Tellegen, A., & Kaemmer, B. (1989). *Minnesota Multiphasic Personality Inventory (MMPI-2): Manual for administration, scoring and interpretation* (Revisedth ed.). Minneapolis, MN: University of Minnesota Press.

Butcher, J. N., Lim, J., & Nezami, E. (1998). Objective study of abnormal personality in cross-cultural settings: The Minnesota Multiphasic Personality Inventory (MMPI-2). *Journal of Cross-Cultural Psychology, 29*(1), 189–211.

Butcher, J. N., Williams, C. L., Graham, J. R., Archer, R. P., Tellegen, A., Ben-Porath, Y. S., et al. (1992). *Minnesota Multiphasic Personality Inventory-Adolescent (MMPI-A): Manual for administration, scoring, and interpretation*. Minneapolis, MN: University of Minnesota Press.

Cheung, F. M. (1985). Cross-cultural considerations for the translation and adaptation of the Chinese MMPI in Hong Kong. In J. N. Butcher & C. D. Spielberger (Eds.), *Advances in personality assessment, Vol. 4* (pp. 131–158). Hillsdale, NJ: Lawrence Erlbaum Associates.

Cheung, P. (1991). Adult psychiatric epidemiology in China in the 80s. *Culture, Medicine and Psychiatry, 15*(4), 479–496.

Cheung, F. M. (1995). *Administration manual of the Minnesota Multiphasic Personality Inventory (MMPI)* (Chineseth ed.). Hong Kong: The Chinese University Press.

Cheung, F. M. (2004). Use of western and indigenously developed personality tests in Asia. *Applied Psychology: An International Review, 53*(2), 173–191.

Cheung, F. M. (2009). The cultural perspective in personality assessment. In J. N. Butcher (Ed.), *Oxford handbook of personality assessment* (pp. 44–56). New York, NY: Oxford University Press.

Cheung, F. M., Cheung, S., Leung, K., Ward, C., & Leong, F. (2003). The English version of the Chinese Personality Assessment Inventory. *Journal of Cross-Cultural Psychology, 34*(4), 433–452.

Cheung, F. M., Cheung, S., & Zhang, J. (2004). Convergent validity of the Chinese Personality Assessment Inventory and the Minnesota Multiphasic Personality Inventory-2: Preliminary findings with a normative sample. *Journal of Personality Assessment, 82*(1), 92–103.

Cheung, F. M., & Ho, R. M. (1997). Standardization of the Chinese MMPI-A in Hong Kong: A preliminary study. *Psychological Assessment, 9*, 499–502.

Cheung, F. M., Kwong, J. Y. Y., & Zhang, J. (2003). Clinical validation of the Chinese Personality Assessment Inventory. *Psychological Assessment, 15*, 89–100.

Cheung, F. M., Leung, K., Fan, R. M., Song, W. Z., Zhang, J. X., & Zhang, J. P. (1996). Development of the Chinese Personality Assessment Inventory. *Journal of Cross-Cultural Psychology, 27*, 143–164.

Cheung, F. M., Leung, K., Zhang, J. X., Sun, H. F., Gan, Y. G., Song, W. Z., et al. (2001). Indigenous Chinese personality constructs: Is the five-factor model complete? *Journal of Cross-Cultural Psychology, 32*, 407–433.

Cheung, F. M., & Song, W. Z. (1989). A review on the clinical applications of the Chinese MMPI. *Psychological Assessment, 1*, 230–237.

Cheung, F. M., Song, W. Z., & Zhang, J. X. (1996). The Chinese MMPI-2: Research and applications in Hong Kong and the People's Republic of China. In J. N. Butcher (Ed.), *International adaptations of the MMPI-2: A handbook of research and applications* (pp. 137–161). Minneapolis, MN: University of Minnesota Press.

Cheung, F. M., Zhang, J. X., & Song, W. Z. (2003). *The Chinese Minnesota Multiphasic Personality Inventory (MMPI-2)*. Hong Kong: The Chinese University Press.

Chung, J. J., Weed, N. C., & Han, K. (2006). Evaluating cross-cultural equivalence of the Korean MMPI-2 via bilingual test-retest. *International Journal of Intercultural Relations, 30*, 531–543.

Cohen, P., Crawford, T. N., Johnson, J. G., & Kasen, S. (2005). The children in the community study of developmental course of personality disorder. *Journal of Personality Disorders, 19*(5), 466–486.

Compton, W. M., Helzer, J. E., Hwu, H., Yeh, E., McEvoy, L., Tipp, J. E., et al. (1991). New methods in cross-cultural psychiatry: Psychiatric illness in Taiwan and the United States. *The American Journal of Psychiatry, 148*, 1697–1704.

Costa, P. T., & McCrae, R. R. (1990). Personality disorders and the five-factor model of personality. *Journal of Personality Disorders, 4*(4), 362–371.

Cox, A. C., Weed, N. C., & Butcher, J. N. (2009). The MMPI-2: History, interpretation, and clinical Issues. In J. N. Butcher (Ed.), *Oxford handbook of personality assessment* (pp. 250–276). New York, NY: Oxford University Press.

Cuéllar, I., & Paniagua, F. A. (2000). *Handbook of multicultural mental health*. San Diego, CA: Academic Press.

Dai, Y. F., & Xiao, Z. P. (2006). A survey on the comorbidity of personality disorders in patients counseling in a mental hospital. *Chinese Mental Health Journal, 18*, 5–7.

Dai, Y. F., Xiao, Z. P., Wang, Z., Zhang, H. Y., & Chen, J. (2006). The reliability and validity of a Chinese version of the Structured Clinical Interview for DSM-IV personality disorders. *Shanghai Arch Psychiatry, 18*, 1–4.

Dienard, A. S., Butcher, J. N., Thao, U. D., Moua Vang, S. H., & Hang, K. (1996). Development of a Hmong translation of the MMPI-2. In J. N. Butcher (Ed.), *International adaptation of the MMPI-2* (pp. 194–205). Minneapolis, MN: University of Minnesota Press.

Dong, Y. T., & Church, A. (2003). Cross-cultural equivalence and validity of the Vietnamese MMPI-2: Assessing psychological adjustment of Vietnamese refugees. *Psychological Assessment, 15*(3), 370–377.

First, M. B., Gibbon, M., Spitzer, R. L., Williams, J. B. W., & Benjamin, L. S. (1997). *User's guide for the structured clinical interview for DSM-IV axis II personality disorders*. Washington, DC: American Psychiatric Press.

Geisinger, K. F. (1994). Cross-cultural normative assessment: Translation and adaptation issues influencing the normative interpretation of assessment instruments. *Psychological Assessment, 6*(4), 304–312.

Graham, J. R. (2006). *MMPI-2: Assessing personality and psychopathology* (4th ed.). New York, NY: Oxford University Press.

Gunsalus, A., & Kelly, K. R. (2001). Korean cultural influences on the Millon Clinical Multiaxial Inventory III. *Journal of Mental Health Counseling, 23*(2), 151–161.

Han, K. (1996). The Korean MMPI-2. In J. N. Butcher (Ed.), *International adaptation of the MMPI-2* (pp. 88–136). Minneapolis, MN: University of Minnesota Press.

Hathaway, S., & McKinley, J. (1943). *The Minnesota multiphasic personality inventory*. Minneapolis, MN: University of Minnesota Press.

Hyler, S. E. (1994). *PDQ-4+ Personality Questionnaire*. New York, NY: Author.

Kasen, S., Cohen, P., Skodol, A., Johnson, J. G., & Brook, J. S. (1999). The influence of childhood psychiatric disorders on more persistent forms of psychopathology in young adulthood. *American Journal of Psychiatry, 156*(10), 1529–1535.

Kim, B. K., Atkinson, D. R., & Yang, P. H. (1999). The Asian Values Scale: Development, factor analysis, validation, and reliability. *Journal of Counseling Psychology, 46*(3), 342–352.

Kleinman, A., & Sung, L. H. (1979). Why do indigenous practitioners successfully heal? *Social, Science & Medicine, 13B*(1), 7–26.

Kwan, K.-L. K. (1999). MMPI and MMPI-2 performance of the Chinese: Cross-cultural applicability. *Professional Psychology: Research and Practice, 30*, 260–268.

Lee, K. C., Kavoc, Y. S., & Rhee, H. (1987). The National Epidemiological Study of mental disorders in Korea. *Journal of Korean Medical Science, 2*, 19–34.

Leong, F. L., & Lau, A. L. (2001). Barriers to providing effective mental health services to Asian Americans. *Mental Health Services Research, 3*(4), 201–214.

Levy, K. N., Becker, D. F., Grilo, C. M., Mattanah, J. J., Garnet, K. E., Quinlan, D. M., et al. (1999). Concurrent and predictive validity of the personality disorder diagnosis in adolescent inpatients. *American Journal of Psychiatry, 156*(10), 1522–1528.

Lin, E. H. B., Carter, W. B., & Kleinman, A. M. (1985). An exploration of somatization among Asian refugees and immigrants in primary care. *American Journal of Public Health, 75*(9), 1080–1084.

Lin, E. J. L., & Church, A. T. (2004). Are indigenous Chinese personality dimensions culture-specific? An investigation of the Chinese Personality Assessment Inventory in Chinese American and European American samples. *Journal of Cross-Cultural Psychology, 35*, 586–605.

Ling, H., Qian, M., & Yang, B. (2010). Reliability and validity of the Chinese version of the Personality Diagnostic Questionnaire-4+: A study with Chinese college students. *Social Behavior and Personality, 38*(3), 311–320.

Marsella, A. J., Dubanoski, J., Hamada, W. C., & Morse, H. (2000). The measurement of personality across cultures: Historical conceptual, and methodological issues and considerations. *American Behavioral Scientist, 44*(1), 41–62.

Miller, A. L., Muehlenkamp, J. J., & Jacobson, C. M. (2008). Fact or fiction: Diagnosing borderline personality disorder in adolescents. *Clinical Psychology Review, 28*, 969–981.

Millon, T., Millon, C., Davis, R., & Grossman, S. (2009). *MCMI-III manual* (4th ed.). Minneapolis, MN: Pearson Assessments.

Mulder, R. T. (2012). Cultural aspects of personality disorder. In T. A. Widiger (Ed.), *The Oxford handbook of personality disorders* (pp. 260–274). New York, NY: Oxford University Press.

Nichols, D. S., Padilla, J., & Gomez-Maqueo, E. L. (2000). Issues in the cross-cultural adaptation and use of the MMPI-2. In R. H. Dana (Ed.), *Handbook of cross-cultural and multicultural personality assessment* (pp. 247–266). Hillsdale, NJ: Erlbaum.

Okazaki, S., Okazaki, M., & Sue, S. (2009). Clinical personality assessment with Asian Americans. In J. N. Butcher (Ed.), *Oxford handbook of personality assessment* (pp. 377–395). New York, NY: Oxford University Press.

Okazaki, S., & Sue, S. (1995). Methodological issues in assessment research with ethnic minorities. *Psychological Assessment, 7*(3), 367–375. doi:10.1037/1040-3590.7.3.367.

Okazaki, S., & Sue, S. (2000). Implications of test revisions for assessment with Asian Americans. *Psychological Assessment, 12*(3), 272–280.

Oyserman, D., Coon, H. M., & Kemmelmeier, M. (2002). Rethinking individualism and collectivism: Evaluation of theoretical assumptions and meta-analyses. *Psychological Bulletin, 128*(1), 3–72.

Pongpanich, L. (1996). Use of the MMPI-2 in Thailand. In J. N. Butcher (Ed.), *International adaptations of the MMPI-2* (pp. 162–174). Minneapolis, MN: University of Minnesota Press.

Sharp, C., Goodyer, I. M., & Croudace, T. J. (2006). The Short Mood and Feelings Questionnaire (SMFQ): A unidimensional item response theory and categorical data factor analysis of self-report ratings from a community sample of 7-through 11-year-old children. *Journal of Abnormal Child Psychology, 34*(3), 379–391.

Sharp, C., Ha, C., Michonski, J., Venta, A., & Carbonne, C. (2012). The diagnosis of Borderline Personality Disorder in adolescents: Evidence in support of the CI-BPD in a sample of adolescent inpatients. *Comprehensive Psychiatry, 53*(6), 765–774.

Sharp, C., & Kine, S. (2008). The assessment of juvenile psychopathy: Strengths and weaknesses of currently used questionnaire measures. *Child and Adolescent Mental Health, 13*(2), 85–95.

Sharp, C., & Romero, C. (2007). Borderline personality disorder: A comparison between children and adults. *Bulletin of the Menninger Clinic, 71*(2), 85–114.

Shiota, N. K., Krauss, S. S., & Clark, L. A. (1996). Adaptation and validation of the Japanese MMPI-2. In J. N. Butcher (Ed.), *International adaptations of the MMPI-2: A handbook of research and applications* (pp. 67–87). Minneapolis, MN: University of Minnesota Press.

So, H. W. (2005). Substance abuse and psychiatric comorbidity: Millon clinical multiaxial inventory-III profiles of Chinese substance abusers. *Hong Kong Journal of Psychiatry, 15*(3), 89–96.

Stevens, M. J., Kwan, K., & Graybill, D. F. (1993). Comparison of MMPI-2 scores of foreign Chinese and Caucasian-American students. *Journal of Clinical Psychology, 49*(1), 23–27.

Sue, S., Keefe, K., Enomoto, K., Durvasula, R. S., & Chao, R. (1996). Asian American and White college students' performance on the MMPI-2. In J. N. Butcher (Ed.), *International adaptations of the MMPI-2* (pp. 206–228). Minneapolis, MN: University of Minnesota Press.

Sue, S., & Morishima, J. K. (1982). *The mental health of Asian Americans*. San Francisco, CA: Jossey-Bass.

Sue, D., & Sue, S. (1987). Cultural factors in the clinical assessment of Asian Americans. *Journal of Consulting and Clinical Psychology, 55*(4), 479–487.

Sue, D., & Sue, D. (1999). *Counseling the culturally different: Theory and practice* (3rd ed.). Hoboken, NJ: John Wiley & Sons.

Tran, B. N. (1996). Vietnamese translation and adaptation of the MMPI-2. In J. N. Butcher (Ed.), *International adaptation of the MMPI-2* (pp. 175–193). Minneapolis, MN: University of Minnesota Press.

Tsai, D. C. (1996). Asian American acculturation and the MMPI-2 (Doctoral dissertation, Rosemead School of Psychology, 1996). *Dissertation Abstracts International, 57*, 6598B.

Tsai, D. C., & Pike, P. L. (2000). Effects of acculturation on the MMPI-2 scores of Asian American students. *Journal of Personality Assessment, 74*(2), 216–230.

Uba, L. (1994). *Asian Americans: Personality patterns, identity, and mental health*. New York, NY: Guilford Press.

U.S. Census Bureau. (2010). The Asian Population: 2010. Retrieved from http://www.census.gov/prod/cen2010/briefs/c2010br-11.pdf

Velásquez, R. J., Mendoza, S., Nezami, E., Castillo-Canez, I., Pace, T., Choney, S. K., et al. (2000). Culturally competent use of the Minnesota Multiphasic Personality Inventory-2 with minorities. In I. Cuéllar & F. A. Paniagua (Eds.), *Handbook of multicultural mental health* (pp. 389–417). San Diego, CA: Academic Press.

Widiger, T. A. (2002). Personality disorders. In M. M. Antony & D. H. Barlow (Eds.), *Handbook of assessment, treatment planning, and outcome for psychological disorders* (pp. 453–480). New York, NY: Guilford Press.

Widiger, T. A., & Boyd, S. E. (2009). Personality disorders assessment instruments. In J. N. Butcher (Ed.), *Oxford handbook of personality assessment* (pp. 336–363). New York, NY: Oxford University Press.

Widiger, T. A., & Chaynes, K. (2003). Current issues in the assessment of personality disorders. *Current Psychiatry Reports, 5*, 28–35.

Widiger, T. A., Mangine, S., Corbittt, E. M., Ellis, C. G., & Thomas, G. V. (1995). *Personality disorder interview-IV: A semistructured interview for the assessment of personality disorders* (p. 1995). Odessa, FL: Psychological Assessment Resources.

Widiger, T. A., & Samuel, D. B. (2005). Evidence-based assessment of personality disorders. *Psychological Assessment, 17*(3), 278–287.

Yang, J., Bagby, M., Costa, P. T., Ryder, A. G., & Herbst, J. H. (2002). Assessing the DSM-IV structure of Personality Disorder with a sample of Chinese psychiatric patients. *Journal of Personality Disorders, 16*(4), 317–331.

Yang, J., McCrae, R. R., Costa, P. T., Yao, S., Dai, X., Cai, T., et al. (2000). The cross-cultural generalizability of Axis-II constructs: An evaluation of two personality disorder assessment instruments in the People's Republic of China. *Journal of Personality Disorders, 14*(3), 249–263.

Yang, Y., Shen, D., Wang, J., & Yang, J. (2002). The reliability and validity of the Personality Diagnostic Questionnaire (PDQ-4+) in China. *Chinese Journal of Clinical Psychology, 10*(3), 165–168.

Zhang, T., Wang, L., Good, M. D., Good, B. J., Chow, A., Dai, Y., et al. (2012). Prevalence of personality disorders using two diagnostic systems in psychiatric outpatients in Shanghai, China: A comparison of uni-axial and multi-axial formulation. *Social Psychiatry And Psychiatric Epidemiology, 47*(9), 1409–1417.

Assessing Culture-Bound Syndromes Among Asian-Americans

18

Christine J. Yeh, William Nguyen, and Ynez N. Lizarraga

Assessing Culture-Bound Syndromes Among Asian-Americans

In 2010, Asians surpassed Hispanics as the largest immigrant group in the United States (Pew Research Center, 2012) with more than 17 million Asian-Americans residing in the country, or 5.6 % of the US. population (Pew Research Center; US Bureau of the Census, 2011). Despite the model minority stereotype, many Asian-Americans (including immigrants) experience psychological and physical problems, posing complex challenges for practitioners and medical services (Yeh, Kim, Pituc, & Atkins, 2008). In this chapter, we discuss different types of Asian culture-bound syndromes and their diagnosis, assessment, and treatment.

At some point in their career, many medical and mental health practitioners will work with an Asian client who may not be easy to diagnose with traditional Western assessment methods. These practitioners may encounter problems that are experienced emotionally, physically (chest pains, trouble sleeping, etc.), or a combination of both. In fact, different cultural groups have their own unique conceptualizations of psychiatric disorders. *Culture-bound syndromes* (or culture-specific syndromes) are a combination of somatic and psychiatric symptoms that are specific to a cultural group or setting (American Psychiatric Association, 2000). A description of some of the more common culture-bound syndromes are listed in the DSM-IV-TR (American Psychiatric Association, 2000); however, the notion of cultural syndromes is still not widely accepted and training in this area remains at its infancy. Due to large numbers of Asian-Americans living in the United States, it is imperative that practitioners be familiar with and competent in assessing culture-bound syndromes.

History and Evolution of Diagnosis of Culture-Bound Syndromes

The history of the classification and diagnosis of culture-bound syndromes is representative of their marginal status in the US psychiatric community with little clarity and professional attention. According to the literature, cultural syndromes were first described as "peculiar, atypical, or exotic psychiatric disorders" (Tseng, 2006, p. 555) and "peculiar to certain cultures" by Yap (1951, p. 313). This was later changed to the term "atypical, culture-bound, psychogenic psychosis," (Yap, 1962, p. 163) and then offered "culture-bound reactive syndrome" (Yap, 1965, p. 172), which eventually was changed to "culture-bound syndrome." Hence, from 1970 to

C.J. Yeh, Ph.D (✉) • W. Nguyen, Ph.D • Y.N. Lizarraga
Department of Counseling Psychology, School of Education, University of San Francisco, 2130 Fulton Street, San Francisco, CA 94117, USA
e-mail: cjyeh@usfca.edu; WWNguyen@USFCA.edu; ynezliz@gmail.com

L.T. Benuto et al. (eds.), *Guide to Psychological Assessment with Asians*,
DOI 10.1007/978-1-4939-0796-0_18, © Springer Science+Business Media New York 2014

1980, the term "culture-bound syndrome" was used. However, Western psychiatrists continued to use terms such as "exotic," "rare," "uncommon," "extraordinary," and "unclassifiable" mental disorders (Tseng, 2006).

In the past few decades, research has indicated that culture-bound syndromes were not necessarily confined to just one culture (Tseng, 2006). In fact, there were many commonalities in symptoms that spanned across cultures. For example, *latah* in Malaysia had similarities to *imu* in Japan and *taijin-kyofusho*has found in both Korea and Japan (Kleinknecht, Dinnel, Kleinknecht, Hiruma, & Harada, 1997). Due to the overlap in cultural-bound syndromes across different countries, the term "culture-related specific syndromes" appeared (Tseng, 2006). Moreover, many culture-bound syndromes evolve and change over time with some decreasing in occurrence while new syndromes are also emerging as societies and cultural dynamics shift.

Description of Different Asian Culture-Bound Syndromes

Identifying, classifying, and describing all the different Asian culture-bound syndromes is an ambitious task. In fact, Hughes (1996) contends that it is impossible to create a definitive list of this group of diagnostic entities because it is not clear what should be included. For example, should behaviors from different countries be lumped together or split apart? In addition, are phenomena such as possessions and trances with local names considered culture-bound syndromes? It is also not clear what the difference is between an illness and a cultural view of a person's physical or emotional, mental, and spiritual state. These questions pose complex issues relating to the categorization and definitions of cultural syndromes.

Various professionals have made attempts to compile a complete list of culture-bound syndromes. From 1890 to 1970, the first recognizable disorders were described including *latah*, *amok*, *koro*, *mali-mali*, *imu*, *dhat*, and *frigophobia*. These were followed by additional syndromes that were reported around the world, such as *anthrophobia*, *phi pob*, *hwa-byung*, and *susto* (Tseng, 2006). Simons (2001) created a list of almost 200 folk illnesses that have at one time been considered culture-bound syndromes. Simons asserted that some of the syndromes (such as *latah*) are indeed syndromes while others are not. There are also culture-bound experiences that are not mentioned in the DSM-IV category. For example, the syndrome, *lanti* in the Philippines, refers to the combination of several illnesses (i.e., a fever, stomachache, shouting during sleep, incessant crying, various skin ailments). In this chapter, we focus on the most common syndromes and their symptoms and have found that many syndromes can be organized based on commonalities. Table 18.1 includes a listing of common Asian cultural syndromes, their regions, case examples, and groupings based on similar symptoms.

Mind and Body Connection

From a cultural perspective, Asian culture-bound syndromes often represent a strong mind and body connection. In fact, many culture-bound syndromes can be described with both psychological and physical characteristics. For example, different Asian cultures have some variation of *dhat*. *Dhat* originates from India and refers to strong anxiety and hypochondriacal beliefs associated with the discharge of semen (American Psychiatric Association, 2000). This syndrome emerges from a culture where many men in general believe that semen loss is harmful (Malhotra & Wig, 1975). Similarly, in China, semen is viewed as the essence of energy or chi, so a loss of chi is considered to be sign of weakness (Sumathipala, Siribaddana, & Bhugra, 2004). *Dhat* also resembles other syndromes in which anxiety is associated with the malfunction of a man's penis or genitalia. These disorders are referred to as *rok-joo* in Thailand, *jiryan* in India, *sukra prameha* in Sri Lanka, *shenkui* in China, and *koro* in Malaysia. Specifically, koro is a sudden episode and powerful fear that one's reproductive organs are shrinking and will disappear into the body and in some cases cause death.

Table 18.1 Common CBS: Diagnostic criteria and interviewing

Syndrome	Criteria	Assessment
Taijin kyofusho	Something about one's physical appearance offending the public	1. Inquire about their anxiety or fears: Does it have an origin/trigger? 2. Have them describe their symptoms of social anxiety/social phobia more concretely. 3. Encourage them to explore what about being in public is so distressing. 4. Inquire about how they perceive others to see them. Then follow up with why they have this belief or why they believe that this is true. Example: How do people treat you? What do people think of you? Do you think that people want to socialize with you? Example: Why do you think people treat you that way? Why do you think people avoid you? How do you know that people are avoiding you? Assessment tool: Taijin-Kyofusho Scale (Kleinknecht et al., 1997).
Koro	Fear that one's reproductive organ is diminishing in size	1. Inquire about the physical malformation in question. Encourage the patient to be as specific as possible. (This may be a delicate matter and proper development of rapport is crucial.) 2. Explore the concerns with the patient. Get additional information about when it started for them, precipitating events, and determine if there are any medical conditions that would better explain or account for this experience.
Dhat	Anxiety over one's perceived semen loss	Similar inquiries as koro.
Amok	Unexpected aggressive and violent outburst, can be homicidal in nature	1. It is important to gather information from the patient and family/significant others. Inquire about the conditions that prompted the violence (was there a period of brooding, was the violent unexpected or predictable).
Latah	A startle response that puts one into a trancelike state in which movements/speech are repetitive in nature	1. Individuals diagnosed with latah are usually self-diagnosed and can identify this disturbance. Inquiries can be made about what happens when the patient is startled, do they recall what just occurred, and do they recall being startled. Inquiries should also be made of family members and significant others to determine if this is an appropriate diagnosis.
Hikikomori	Disorder in which one completely withdraws from society and family and shuts themselves in a room for at least 6 months	1. Due to the clear and dramatic behaviors of these patients, the family and patient can clearly identify if the individual is suffering from hikikomori. Inquiries should be made in regard to the withdrawing behaviors observed that include silence, not leaving the room, disengagement in social functions and activities, and a difficulty leaving the room. 2. In some cases in Japan, patients suffering from hikikomori will not leave their rooms to eat and must be brought their food (often parents/loved ones will leave food at the door of the room). Assessment tool: Hikikomori Behavioral Checklist (Sakai, 2004).
Hwa-byung	Disorder in which one's suppressed anger (usually women) is sublimated into various physical symptoms; this disorder is typically self-diagnosed by patient. Patients often feel a lot of guilt in regard to having these symptoms and may often feel like a burden upon their family	1. Assess for current symptoms, and discuss with patient if the emergence of symptoms followed a traumatic or a difficult family event. 2. Inquire about any environmental factors that may have contributed to the current disorder: shifts in family dynamics, familial discord, conflicts with in-laws, or death of a spouse or a loved one. 3. A defining characteristic of HB is that patients will acknowledge that they have HB and/or family members will note that the patient has HB. 4. Despite having HB (and various manifestations of depressive symptoms) the patient will appear quite resilient and typically does not have thoughts of suicide or self-harm. Make inquiries about the patient's resiliency and what they are able to do despite these symptoms. Assessment tool: Korean MMPI-II and Hwa-Byung Scale (Ketterer et al., 2010; Roberts, Han, & Weed, 2006).

During the assessment process, be sure to note the patients' cultural heritage before attempting to diagnose a cultural bound syndrome. The cultural bound syndrome must match their identified cultural heritage. The context of the symptoms is critical in determining the presence or the absence of a cultural bound syndrome

Koro has differing variations found in China, Thailand, and India (Haque, 2008; Roy et al., 2011; Yeh & Kwong, 2008).

Sumathipala et al. (2004) performed an extensive literature search on *dhat* syndrome to better understand the prevalence rates, treatment, and cultural attitudes toward semen loss. For example, in a previous research study by Malhotra and Wig (1975), 175 males in India (aged 30–50 years) were asked about their attitudes toward semen loss. They were also inquired about causes and the management of semen loss. Researchers found that a significant number of respondents believed that semen loss was harmful and 30 % favored no intervention for its occurrence. In addition, 22.5 % of participants advocated for the psychological and behavioral persuasion by relatives and friends to avoid negative influences, masturbation, and erotic literature. A small number of men suggested dietary intervention, and 6 % recommended marriage as a treatment option.

Semen loss may also cause anxiety in China as semen is seen as the essence of energy (chi), so it is thought that its excretion produces weakness. Hence, people who experience semen loss may fear that they will lose their strength and energy. Moreover, in this review, Sumathipala et al. (2004) also found historical evidence, indicating that *dhat* syndrome was prevalent in Europe, Asia, and Australia mainly in the nineteenth century, but is not as prevalent in the Western world today. The authors argued that with industrialization and urbanization, anxiety about semen loss in the West has diminished and that the same is likely to occur in southern parts of Asia. They also believe that the category "culture-bound syndromes" should be abandoned and that a focus on multiaxial systems, which include cultural factors in aetiology and management, be implemented.

Somatization and Emotional Suppression

Other Asian culture-bound syndromes underscore somatization over emotional expressions. For example, neurasthenia (also known as *shenjing shuairuo*) is perceived as a Chinese version of major depressive disorder but the main focus is on the physical versus the psychological symptoms such as weakness, fatigue, chest pain, and intense heartbeat that may be irregular (palpitations, tachycardia); cold and clammy hands and feet; abnormally rapid breathing (hyperventilation); dizziness or faintness; periodic sighing; and/or sweating for no apparent reason, yet triggered by anxiety and depression (Kleinman, 1977).

Asian culture-bound syndromes also underscore the cultural emphasis on restraining one's emotions. Specifically, *hwa-byung* or *wool-hwa-bung* in Korea (known as *anger syndrome*) is believed to emerge from the suppression of anger. Symptoms from this syndrome include insomnia, panic, fear of impending death, indigestion, palpitations, generalized aches and pains, and a feeling of a mass in the epigastrium (Glossary of Culture-Bound Syndromes, 2001; Min & Lee, 1989). *Hwa-byung* has been reported to occur in 4–11.9 % of women of Korean descent. This is more common in older women who are from South Korea, and the symptoms continue even when they immigrate to the United States. According to Korean culture, women with mental illnesses are seen as social deviants. Hence, they tend to avoid seeking professional help for fear of bringing shame onto themselves and their families (Myunghan & Hye-A, 2011). Myunghan and Hye-A (2011) shared specific ideas for how practitioners can assess for *hwa-byung*, diagnose it, and manage its symptoms. They also provided a case study of a 61-year-old first-generation South Korean immigrant who came to the United States 37 years ago and continues to have *hwa-byung*. This case helps to describe the difference between *hwa-byung* and depressive disorder.

Haque (2008) described the main culture-bound syndromes in Malay and Chinese cultures that relate to fear, anger, and violence. In particular, *amok* is a brief and sudden outburst of unrestrained violence, typically of a homicidal nature, that precedes a period of brooding and exhaustion. While the DSM-IV recognizes *amok*, it fails to acknowledge the more common syndrome, *beramok*, which is related to personal loss and is preceded by depression. *Amok* is also connected to feelings of rage and the possibility of violent attacks.

The second disorder described by Haque (2008) is *latah. Latah* is a trance syndrome exemplified by a severe response to startling stimuli and an intense hypersensitivity to sudden fright. *Latah* is frequently associated with echopraxia, echolalia, and dissociative or trancelike behaviors (Haque, 2008). *Latah* is a condition in which a person is often startled or surprised and reacts by yelling out obscene utterances or in some instances imitate words, gestures, or actions or automatically obeys commands that would not normally be followed (Winzeler, 1995). *Latah* affects some individuals more than others. Moreover, people often report that they have no memory of an episode of *latah*. The examples provided by Winzeler (1995) emerge from his own observation and from stories shared by Malaysian individuals. He contends that *latah* is well known in Malaysia and is often depicted in the mass media and discussed during government trials. He also shares a brief history of culture-bound syndromes and the different perspectives related to the terminology used to describe them.

Spiritual and Ancestral Worlds

Asian culture-bound syndromes also often prioritize connections to the spiritual and ancestral world. In Taiwan, there is a syndrome known as *hsieh-ping* which is exemplified by a brief period of disorientation during which one is overwhelmed by an ancestral ghost, who tries to communicate to one's family members. Symptoms of *hsieh-ping* often include a daze-like state, tremors, and visual or auditory hallucinations. Likewise, in Korea, there is a syndrome known as *shin-byung*, which refers to feelings of anxiety and a series of physical reactions such as faintness, appetite loss, insomnia, and gastrointestinal problems. People with *shin-byung* also often experience dissociation and possession by ancestral spirits (Burnhill, Park, & Yeh, 2008).

Interdependence

In addition to a cultural emphasis on the spiritual and ancestral world, many Asian cultures highlight the importance of interdependence, and this cultural value is embedded in notions of cultural syndromes. In fact, many Asian cultural syndromes include intense social reactions and feelings. An especially unique culture-bound syndrome, *hikikomori*, is from Japan. *Hikikomori* describes the phenomenon of youth and young adults (typically male) who unexpectedly withdraw from society by locking themselves in their bedroom or another room in their home for a minimum of 6 months (Jones, 2006; Teo, 2009). Many experts believe that this type of confinement and alienation often emerges from the experience of intense social pressures, relationships, family problems, and a lack of interest in social relations. One expert estimates that the number of hikikomori are close to one million in Japan, but others believe that the number is significantly lower (roughly 20 % of all male youth in Japan). The majority of *hikikomori* cases are with the oldest son in the family, perhaps because of the intense familial pressure to be successful (Jones, 2006). There have also been cases reported in South Korea, Taiwan, Hong Kong, and among Asian immigrants in the United States.

Two additional examples of culture-bound syndrome that illuminate interpersonal and emotional issues in Asian cultures are *jiko-shisen-kyofu* (fear of one's own glance) and *taijin-kyofusho* (fear of interpersonal relations), both found primarily in Japan (Iwata et al., 2011). Iwata and colleagues (2011) describe four cases that illuminate the unique cultural aspects of these syndromes. In the first case, a 27-year-old male first fears his own glance at the age of 16 and eventually withdraws from societal interactions because of his extreme worry that his glance causes others discomfort. He was admitted to a hospital and advised to receive Morita therapy, which was developed in Japan in the 1920s as a type of cognitive-behavioral therapy, proven effective in the treatment of *taijin-kyofusho*. However, the patient declined the offer. In the second case, a 21-year-old female that has *jiko-shisen-kyofu* was abused by her father throughout her childhood. She was treated with alprazolam and risperidone to reduce her anxiety, agitation, labile affect, and suicidal ideation but not given any medicine to treat her fear of offending others with her glance. During an intervention, her father was warned against seeing her, which greatly reduced her worries about her own glance. In the third case, a 50-year-old male taxi driver had *jiko-shisen-kyofu* since he was 20 years old. At 22, he was treated with an antidepressant, but it did not alleviate the fear of his own glance. Later he was treated with pimozide but still continued to have *jiko-shisen-kyofu*. In the fourth case, a 52-year-old female with fear of her glance responded well to a combination of 30 mg/day of maprotiline and 6 mg/day of bromazepam. After the treatment, she reported only rare feelings of embarrassment due to the problem.

Iwata et al.'s (2011) main point is that unlike the other subtypes of *taijin-kyofusho*, *jiko-shisen-kyofu* is the only true culture-bound syndrome. All cases have been reported in Japan, with the exception of one case that has been reported in Korea. The other subtypes of *taijin-kyofusho* have related syndromes that can be found in Western countries. For example, a fear of blushing is common among people with social phobia in the West. Additionally, the fear of a deformed face or body fulfills the criteria for body dysmorphic disorder under the DSM-IV. Although phobia of one's own foul body odor cannot be assigned to any of the diagnoses in the DSM-IV, a similar condition (olfactory reference syndrome) exists in the West.

Cultural Considerations in Assessing Asian Culture-Bound Syndromes

Asian culture-bound syndromes have still not been adequately recognized in the Western diagnostic system. Specifically, the DSM-IV primarily holds a Western worldview of mental health and normalcy and does not fully consider other cultural world views. Haque (2010) contends that in order to assess and treat Asian culture-bound syndromes, it is important to have a strong appreciation and knowledge of mental health, conceptions of illness, and treatment based on Hinduism, Buddhism, Chinese beliefs, and Islam. Haque (2010)offers specific practical guidelines relating to assessing clients. These include assessing the client's holistic cultural identity, seeking to understand his/her perspective of illness, the role of one's culture in his/her life, and the role and need for a language interpreter.

As described in the previous sections, Asian culture-bound syndromes tend to emphasize mind and body connection, spiritual and ancestral worlds, somatization and emotional suppression, and interdependence. These cultural priorities underscore critical values and aspects of Asian culture that must be considered in the assessment and treatment of Asian culture-bound syndromes. For Asian-Americans and immigrants living in the United States, there are many additional factors that may influence the expression of Asian culture-bound syndromes: cultural orientation, ethnic identity, acculturation, cultural explanations for illness, available social support systems, religion, and kin networks. In particular, a critical problem with the Western medical model of psychology and psychiatry is that many cultural groups do not share this conceptualization of mental health and disease and in fact have a considerably unique and shared cultural view of health. It follows that assessment and treatment plans should be consonant with indigenous perceptions and beliefs about disease and health.

Haque (2008) provided a description of mental health concepts in Malay and Chinese cultures as well as cultural practices in healing. For example, in Malay culture, there is a strong belief in the spiritual world and that humans are made of both body and soul. While the body needs and desires physical pleasure there may be a tendency to overstep its boundaries. In these cases, the soul of a person intervenes and strikes a balance in the individual. Moreover, in Chinese culture, emotion is a critical element in the body's basic functions and is managed by the circulation of chi (air or breath). Emotions that are abnormal impact the functions of chi. In this regard, excessive, unbalanced, or undisciplined emotions are the basis for most types of illnesses.

It is important to recognize that approaches to healing reflect deeply embedded cultural belief systems. For example, Malays rely on a local healer (known as *bomoh*) for the treatment of their culture-bound syndromes. This healer may in fact be someone in the family. There are many different kinds of *bomoh* based on the different types of illnesses. *Bomoh* often treat illnesses through specific ceremonies that entail reading from the Quran, using magical charms, calling upon spirits, or food preparation. In Chinese culture, there is a reliance on *shen*, who are spiritual beings who also behave as mediums during traces and communicate with the deities. *Shen* also use various traditional practices such as acupuncture, herbal medicine, special diets, and exercises to clear a blocked chi (Haque, 2008).

As another example, the treatment of *hikikomori* also reflects some specific Asian cultural values in Japan. In particular, most families who have a child with *hikikomori* leave them alone in hopes that they will get out of this phase or grow out of it. Many families do not discuss the syndrome with anyone, including close friends and family. In order to hide their secret, many families create elaborate stories. While there are different programs emerging in Japan to address *hikikomori*, families are slow to react and engage. While from an American perspective many parents may assertively respond to the social confinement, in Japan, such an approach may be harmful to social harmony. Furthermore, many Japanese families may wish to keep the *hikikomori* a secret in order to save face and maintain social relations (Jones, 2006).

The typical Japanese responses for dealing with *hikikomori* reflect important cultural orientations and values that exist for other culture-bound syndromes as well. For example, in treating various syndromes such as neurasthenia, the most common method is to treat the physical symptoms only with herbal remedies, acupuncture, or other forms of traditional Chinese medicine. Similarly, when treating syndromes that have a spiritual component, it is common to use prayer, ancestral worship, and communication with spirits (Inman, Yeh, Madan-Bahel, & Nath, 2007). Hence, treatment for Asian culture-bound syndromes must be considered in the context of a culture's understanding and conceptualization of disease and health in addition to cultural orientation and ethnic identity. Cultural specific responses to disease or stress may not always involve a specific treatment plan or indigenous healer and may also refer to an individual's culturally responsive coping strategies (Yeh, Arora, & Wu, 2006).

Assessing and Treating Asian Culture-Bound Syndromes

The assessment of cultural bound syndromes can be a difficult process especially when the practitioner is unfamiliar with the differential diagnoses and/or has never been exposed to the specific syndrome. In this section, we present a general assessment process to help clarify the presence of a potential cultural bound syndrome. We discuss cultural consideration, ecological and systemic perspectives, and conducting a clinical interview. We focus on diagnostic criteria for specific cultural bound syndromes of interest and provide sample questions and inquiries when conducting a clinical interview. Finally, we also offer assessment tools and measures to consider to use during the assessment process.

In all assessment processes, it is important for the practitioner to develop a good working rapport with the patient. Working collaboratively with the patient and encouraging the patient to describe the disturbance in behavioral, affective, and/or cognitive ways will increase the likelihood of determining the appropriate diagnosis. Moreover, a strong connection with the patient will positively impact the effectiveness of treatment. In previous literature (Choi, 2006; Choi & Lee, 2007; Kim, Kim, & Kelly, 2006; Mezzich, Kleinman, Fabrega, & Parron, 2002), the practitioner is advised to help the patient to funnel his or her symptoms or disturbances from vague and general disturbances to very specific and discrete symptoms.

For instance, if the patient describes "being sad" as a symptom, inquiries should clarify what the patient means by the words "being sad." This may include asking questions such as the following: "What does your sadness look like?" "How often does your sadness appear?" "How long does your sadness last?" "What specifically triggers your being sad?" "What happens when you are sad?" "What do you typically do when you are sad?" Practitioners need to create spaces that allow patients to indicate in how these symptoms have manifested, the progression of each symptom, and how it has impacted their day-to-day living experience. In giving patients permission to describe their symptoms and experiences in their own language, it allows them to feel much more comfortable and supported by the practitioner (Mezzich et al., 2002).

Asian cultural conceptions of health should also be considered when conducting an assessment. For many Asian cultures, there is a strong mind and body connection, which contributes to how symptoms are experienced and expressed (Yeh, 2000). In fact, expressing emotional concerns is considered to be stigmatizing and a sign of weakness. Hence, physical symptoms may be reported more frequently than psychological ones (Haque, 2008). With this cultural context in mind, it is important for the practitioner to differentiate actual physical symptoms with medical origins versus physical symptoms with psychological origins (Beale, 2009; Bybee et al., 2004; Choi, 2006; Haque, 2008; Penas-Lado, Barriales-Villa, & Goicolea, 2003; Tsuchihashi et al., 2001). A medical evaluation may be warranted to rule out a diagnosable medical disorder, if the patient presents with very specific physical symptoms.

Another cultural consideration that must be made during the assessment process is that many Asian cultures prefer not to make direct eye contact with the practitioner. This can often be confused as avoidance, anxiety, or social awkwardness, but in fact for many Asian cultures, this is a sign of respect (Yeh, 2012). Additionally, the practitioner should not immediately start asking about the patient's family, financial stability, martial satisfaction, sex, or other similar "sensitive" topics. In Asian cultures, talking with a stranger about personal problems is inappropriate and reflects poorly on the family name. Since personal information is often guarded as private, the patient may be unwilling to immediately disclose the information without getting to know the process, the experience, or the practitioner a little better (Yeh, Hunter, Madan-Bahel, Chiang, & Kwong, 2004).

Once the practitioner has a much more developed sense of the presenting symptoms, it is important to understand the symptoms within a specific context (Choi & Yeom, 2009; Mezzich et al., 2002; Min, 2004). The context of the presenting symptoms will enable the practitioner to determine if a cultural bound syndrome may be present (Flaskerud, 2009). In developing the context, the practitioner is advised to make inquiries about the history of the disturbance and how their culture has viewed these and/or similar symptoms in their homeland and to also assess the patient and family's level of acculturation to the United States (Flaskerud, 2009; Mezzich et al., 2002).

Ecological and Systemic Perspectives in Assessment

In fact, practitioners are instruments in the assessment process and are prone to threats of reliability and validity (Yeh & Kwan, 2010). They can be unreliable and invalid tools when their questions do not represent the client's main issues, when client data are interpreted out of context, and when a culturally inappropriate approach is applied to understand client's concerns. It is critical for practitioners to envision the individual as embedded in a larger set of familial, political, social, and cultural systems and structures.

An ecological perspective (Bronfenbrenner, 1979) is a helpful approach to assessment on different levels: the microsystem (e.g., families), the mesosystem (e.g., communities), and the macrosystem (e.g., policies and structures). Practitioners must learn to effectively conduct assessments as embedded in a larger social and cultural context; investigate the influence of political history, acculturation, immigration, community, and family; and examine language, translation issues, and preferred indigenous coping strategies (Yeh & Kwan, 2010).

Specifically, it is necessary to adopt an ecological approach when assessing for cultural bound syndromes. In addition to focusing on the individual, practitioners may also identify systemic forces that influence clients' presenting symptoms. An ecological assessment schema offers significant contextual information during a clinical interview that may help rule out inaccurate or culturally inappropriate diagnoses. The ability to place clients' psychological and behavioral problems in the correct sociopolitical context is also an issue of cultural competence and ethical practice.

Conducting a Clinical Interview

It is essential for the practitioner to complete a thorough interview in regard to how the patient's culture is or is not related to the presenting symptoms in order to make a proper diagnosis of a cultural bound syndrome (Blease, 2010; Haque, 2008; Min, 2004). The difference between how Western cultures and Asian cultures define, understand, treat, and accept specific symptoms is vital in determining if a cultural bound syndrome exists (Flaskerud, 2009; Haque, 2008). Without the proper cultural context, the practitioner is likely to misdiagnose the disorder as being a DSM-IV diagnosable disorder, such as a somatoform disorder, dissociative disorder, anxiety, depression, impulse control disorder, and/or an eating disorder, as opposed to being an actual cultural bound syndrome (Chang, 1997; Choi & Yeom, 2009; Clarvit, Schneier, & Liebowitz, 1996; Flaskerud, 2009; Ketterer, Han, & Weed, 2010; Kim, Rapee, & Gaston, 2008; McNally, Cassiday, & Calamari, 1990; Min, 2004; Park & Bernstein, 2008; Tanaka-Matsumi, 1979).

In addition to assessing the patient, the practitioner is advised to get additional information from spouses, family members, and other significant individuals about the context of the disturbance (Ketterer et al., 2010; Mezzich et al., 2002; Min, 2004). In interviewing the family members and close relations, similar interviewing techniques should be employed to assist in clarifying the diagnosis and to determine if a strong enough cultural context exists that explains for the presenting symptoms. Family involvement allows clients to tell their story and history and incorporates critical dimensions of the clients' social and cultural world (Yeh, 2012).

In developing a collaborative relationship with the patient and the family/significant others, the practitioner will find that all parties involved will be much more candid and open to the interventions and support of the practitioner. Once the practitioner has clearly identified that a potential cultural bound syndrome exists, Table 18.1 can assist the practitioner in determining what cultural bound syndrome can best describe the symptoms presented by the patient.

Future Directions for Assessing Asian Culture-Bound Syndromes

The assessment and diagnosis of Asian culture-bound syndromes are still in a beginning phase. Clearly there needs to be more research in regard to the development of structured and unstructured interviews and assessment protocols that assess for specific cultural bound syndromes (Tseng, Min, Nakamura, & Katsuragawa, 2012). Additionally, these assessments need to be created in the appropriate languages and translated into English, as these disorders are increasingly appearing in the United States and culturally appropriate instrumentation needs to be available to practitioners in the United States.

Additional research studies also need to empirically validate the efficacies of pharmacological and therapeutic treatments for culture-bound syndromes. Specially, a guide book or manual can aid the well-informed practitioner in regard to how best to treat patients suffering from the various cultural bound syndromes. This type of manual should incorporate the perspectives of practitioners and healers from these native countries.

We also suggest that comparative samples and research studies should be conducted between individuals living in the United States that are diagnosed with a cultural bound syndrome and should be compared to others with the same cultural bound syndrome in their country of origin in order to determine if any differences exist in the progression, manifestation, and treatment of the syndrome across countries. Currently, there are very few studies that even focus on the prevalence of Asian culture-bound syndromes in the

United States, so developing culturally responsive treatment plans is quite challenging for practitioners.

We also advocate for the development of diagnostic criteria that clearly and accurately reflect the defining characteristics of the cultural bound syndrome. We also believe that it is important to have specific strategies outlined so that practitioners can more effectively differentiate between the cultural bound syndrome and different types of DSM-IV diagnoses. Furthermore, Simons (2001) believes that it is essential for the diagnoses to be coherent and accurate because individuals are often very conscious of the way they are labeled and may try to change their behavior and self-conceptions in response to their classification.

This chapter centered on the assessment of culture-bound syndromes among Asian-Americans. Given the increasing numbers of immigrants coming to the United States from various Asian countries, we believe that it is urgent for practitioners, researchers, and educators to better understand the unique history and background of these syndromes. We offered many examples of different syndromes in an attempt to better explain the importance of cultural considerations and the need for an unbiased cultural approach when working with Asian-American clients and patients who may present with Asian culture-bound syndromes. Additionally, we offered some specific recommendations for the assessment and treatment of Asian-American individuals who appear to have Asian culture-bound syndromes. We underscored the importance of incorporating cultural values in working with clients who present with such concerns. Finally, we provide some suggestions and ideas for future efforts in research and practice as they relate to Asian culture-bound syndromes.

References

American Psychiatric Association. (2000). *Diagnostic and statistical manual of mental disorders-IV-TR* (4th ed.). Washington, DC: American Psychiatric Press.

Beale, A. (2009). Stress-induced cardiomyopathy in women. *Advance for Nurse Practitioners, 17*(11), 33–36.

Blease, C. (2010). Scientific progress and the prospects for culture-bound syndromes. *Studies in History and Philosophy of Biological and Biomedical Sciences, 41*(4), 333–339.

Bronfenbrenner, U. (1979). *The ecology of human development: Experiments by nature and design*. Cambridge, MA: Harvard University Press.

Burnhill, D. A., Park, J., & Yeh, C. J. (2008). Indigenous models of healing: Implications for counseling. In C. C. Lee, D. A. Burnhill, A. L. Butler, C. P. Hipolito-Delgado, & M. Humphrey (Eds.), *Elements of culture in counseling* (pp. 105–126). Allyn & Bacon/Longman: Boston, MA.

Bybee, K. A., Kara, T., Prasad, A., Lerman, A., Barsness, G. W., Wright, R. S., et al. (2004). Systematic review: Transient left ventricular apical ballooning: A syndrome that mimics ST-segment elevation myocardial infarction. *Annals of Internal Medicine, 141*(11), 858–865.

Chang, S. C. (1997). Social anxiety (phobia) and East Asian culture. *Depress Anxiety, 5*, 115–120.

Choi, Y. J. (2006). A transcultural model of Hwa-Byung: A grounded theory. *Journal of Korean Academy of Psychiatric and Mental Health Nursing, 15*(4), 508–512.

Choi, Y., & Lee, K. (2007). Evidence-based nursing: Effects of a structured nursing program for the health promotion of Korean women with Hwa-Byung. *Archives of Psychiatric Nursing, 21*, 12–16.

Choi, M., & Yeom, H.-A. (2009). Identifying and treating the culture-bound syndrome of Hwa-Byung among older Korean immigrant women: Recommendations for practitioners. *Journal of the American Academy of Nurse Practitioners, 23*, 226–232.

Clarvit, S. R., Schneier, F. R., & Liebowitz, M. R. (1996). The offensive subtype of Taijin-Kyofu-Sho in New York City: The phenomenology and treatment of a social anxiety disorder. *Journal of Clinical Psychiatry, 57*, 523–527.

Flaskerud, J. H. (2009). What do we need to know about the culture-bound syndromes? *Issues in Mental Health Nursing, 30*, 406–407.

Glossary of Culture-Bound Syndromes (2001). Retrieved on May 7, 2006 from http://weber.ucsd.edu/~thall/cbs_glos.html.

Haque, A. (2008). Culture-bound syndromes and healing practices in Malaysia. *Mental Health, Religion and Culture, 11*(7), 685–696.

Haque, A. (2010). Mental health concepts in Southeast Asia: Diagnostic considerations and treatment implications. *Psychology, Health & Medicine, 15*(2), 127–134. doi:10.1080/13548501003615266.

Hughes, C. C. (1996). The culture bound syndromes and psychiatric diagnosis. In J. E. Mezzich, D. L. Parron, & A. Kleinman (Eds.), *Culture and psychiatric diagnosis: A DSM-IV perspective* (pp. 298–308). Washington, DC: APA.

Inman, A. G., Yeh, C. J., Madan-Bahel, A., & Nath, S. (2007). South Asian families: bereavement and coping post-9/11. *Journal of Multicultural Counseling and Development, 35*, 101–115.

Iwata, Y., Suzuki, K., Takei, N., Toulopoulou, T., Tsuchiya, K. J., Matsumoto, K., … Mori, N. (2011). Jiko-shisen-kyofu (fear of one's own glance), but not taijin-kyofusho (fear of interpersonal relations), is an east Asian culture-related specific syndrome. *Australian and New Zealand Journal of Psychiatry, 45*(2), 148–152.

Jones, M. (2006). Shutting themselves in. *New York Times Magazine, 155*(53460), 15.

Ketterer, H., Han, K., & Weed, N. C. (2010). Validation of a Korean MMPI-2 Hwa-Byung Scale using a Korean normative sample. *Cultural Diversity and Ethnic Minority Psychology, 16*(3), 379–385.

Kim, I. J., Kim, L. I. C., & Kelly, J. G. (2006). Developing cultural competence in working with Korean immigrant families. *Journal of Community Psychology, 34*(2), 149–165.

Kim, J., Rapee, R. M., & Gaston, J. E. (2008). Symptoms of offensive type Taijin-Kyofusho among Australian social phobics. *Depression and Anxiety, 25*, 601–608.

Kleinknecht, R. A., Dinnel, D. L., Kleinknecht, E. E., Hiruma, N., & Harada, N. (1997). Cultural factors in social anxiety: A comparison of social phobia symptoms and Taijin Kyofusho. *Journal of Anxiety Disorders, 11*, 157–177.

Kleinman, A. M. (1977). Depression, somatization, and the "new cross-cultural psychiatry". *Social Sciences & Medicine, 11*, 3–9. doi:10.1016/0037- 7856(77)90138-X.

Malhotra, H. K., & Wig, N. N. (1975). Dhat syndrome: a culture-bound sex neurosis of the Orient. *Archives of Sexual Behavior, 4*(5), 519–528.

McNally, R. J., Cassiday, K. L., & Calamari, J. E. (1990). Taijin-kyofu-sho in a black American woman: Behavioral treatment of a "Culture-bound" anxiety disorder. *Journal of Anxiety Disorders, 4*, 83–87.

Mezzich, J. E., Kleinman, A. M., Fabrega, H., Jr., & Parron, D. (Eds.). (2002). *Culture and psychiatric diagnosis, a DSM-IV perspective*. Washington, DC: American Psychiatric Association.

Min, S. K. (2004). Treatment and prognosis of Hwabyung. *Psychiatry Investigation, 1*, 29–36.

Min, S., & Lee, H. (1989). A clinical study of Hwa-Byung. *Transcultural Psychiatry, 26*, 137–147.

Myunghan, C., & Hye-A, Y. (2011). Identifying and treating the culture-bound syndrome of Hwa-Byung among older Korean immigrant women: Recommendations for practitioners. *Journal of the American Academy of Nurse Practitioners, 23*(5), 226–232. doi:10.1111/j.1745-7599.2011.00607.x.

Park, S., & Bernstein, K. S. (2008). Depression and Korean American immigrants. *Archives of Psychiatric Nursing, 22*(1), 12–19.

Penas-Lado, M., Barriales-Villa, R., & Goicolea, J. (2003). Transient left ventricular apical ballooning and outflow tract obstruction. *Journal of the American College of Cardiology, 42*, 1143–1144.

Pew Research Center. (2012). The rise of Asian Americans. *Pew social & demographic trends.* Retrieved from July 7, 2012. http://www.pewsocialtrends.org/files/2012/06/SDT-The-Rise-of-Asian-Americans-Full-Report.pdf.

Roberts, M. E., Han, K., & Weed, N. C. (2006). Development of a scale to assess Hwa-byung, a Korean culture-bound syndrome, using the MMPI-2. *Transcultural Psychiatry, 43*, 383–400.

Roy, D., Hazarika, S., Bhattacharya, A., Das, S., Nath, K., & Saddichha, S. (2011). Correspondence: Koro: culture bound or mass hysteria? *The Royal Australian and New Zealand College of Psychiatrists, 45*(8), 683.

Sakai, M. (2004). Development of hikikomori behavioral checklist (HBCL) and examination of its reliability and validity. *Japanese Journal of Counseling Science, 37*, 3.

Simons, R. C. (2001). Introduction to culture-bound syndromes. *Psychiatric Times, 18*(11), 1–4.

Sumathipala, A., Siribaddana, S. H., & Bhugra, D. (2004). Culture-bound syndromes: The story of dhat syndrome. *The British Journal of Psychiatry, 184*(3), 200–209. doi:10.1192/bjp.184.3.200.

Tanaka-Matsumi, J. (1979). Taijin Kyofusho: Diagnostic and cultural issues in Japanese psychiatry. *Culture, Medicine, and Psychiatry, 3*, 231–245.

Teo, A. (2009). A new form of social withdrawal in Japan: A review of Hikikomori. *International Journal of Social Psychiatry, 56*(2), 178–185. doi:10.1177/0020764008100629.

Tseng, W. (2006). From peculiar psychiatric disorders through culture-bound syndromes to culture-related specific syndromes. *Transcultural Psychiatry, 43*(4), 554–576. doi:10.1177/1363461506070781.

Tseng, W., Min, S. K., Nakamura, K., & Katsuragawa, S. (2012). Culture-related specific psychiatric syndromes observed in Asia. In E. C. Chang (Ed.), *Handbook of adult psychopathology in Asians: Theory, diagnosis and treatment* (pp. 393–413). New York, NY: Oxford University Press.

Tsuchihashi, K., Ueshima, K., Uchida, T., Oh-mura, N., Kimura, K., Yoshiyama, M., … Morii, I. (2001). Transient left ventricular apical ballooning without coronary artery stenosis: A novel heart syndrome mimicking acute myocardial infarction. *Journal of the American College of Cardiology, 38(1)*, 11–18.

U.S. Bureau of the Census. (2011). Asian/Pacific American Heritage Month: May 2011. *Facts for features.* Retrieved from July 7, 2012. http://www.census.gov/Press-Release/www/releases/archives/facts_for_features_special_editions/004522.html.

Winzeler, R. L. (1995). *Latah in Southeast Asia: The history and ethnography of a culture-bound syndrome*. New York: Cambridge University Press.

Yap, P. M. (1951). Mental diseases peculiar to certain cultures: A survey of comparative psychiatry. *Journal of Mental Science, 97*, 313–327.

Yap, P. M. (1962). Words and things in comparative psychiatry, with special reference to the exotic psychoses. *Acta Psyciatrica Scandinavica, 38*, 163–169.

Yap, P. M. (1965). Koro: A culture-bound depersonalization syndrome. *The British Journal of Psychiatry, 111*, 43–50.

Yeh, C. J. (2000). Depathologizing Asian-American perspectives of health and healing. *Asian American and Pacific Islander Journal of Health, 8*, 138–149.

Yeh, C. J. (2012). Working with Asian American and Pacific Islander clients: Interdependent and indigenous approaches to counseling. In M. E. Gallardo, C. J. Yeh, T. A. Parham, & J. Trimble (Eds.), *Culturally adaptive counseling: Demonstrations of evidence-based practices*. Thousand Oaks, CA: Sage Publications.

Yeh, C. J., Arora, A. K., & Wu, K. (2006). A new theoretical model of collectivistic coping. In P. T. P. Wong & C. J. Wong (Eds.), *Handbook of multicultural perspectives on stress and coping* (pp. 55–72). New York: Springer.

Yeh, C. J., Hunter, C. D., Madan-Bahel, A., Chiang, L., & Kwong, A. (2004). Indigenous and interdependent perspectives of healing: Implications for counseling and research. *Journal of Counseling and Development, 82*, 410–419.

Yeh, C. J., Kim, A. B., Pituc, S. T., & Atkins, M. (2008). Poverty, loss, and resilience: The story of Asian immigrant youth. *Journal of Counseling Psychology, 55*, 34–48.

Yeh, C. J., & Kwan, K.-L. K. (2010). Advances in multicultural assessment and counseling with adolescents: Community, ecological, and social justice approaches. In J. G. Ponterroto, J. M. Casas, L. A. Suzuki, & C. M. Alexander (Eds.), *Handbook of multicultural counseling* (3rd ed., pp. 637–647). Thousand Oaks, CA: Sage Publications Inc.

Yeh, C. J., & Kwong, A. K. (2008). Asian American indigenous healing (Invited book chapter). In A. Alvarez & N. Tewari (Eds.), *Asian American psychology* (pp. 561–575). New York: Taylor & Francis.

Assessment of Dementia: Screening for Cognitive Decline with Asian Clients

19

Lorraine T. Benuto, Katherine A. Wainwright, and Brian D. Leany

In our review of the extant literature on cognitive decline and dementia in Asian elders we made several key observations. First, the literature on the assessment of cognitive decline in Asian elders in a US context is extraordinarily limited. In fact, the vast majority of relevant research has been internationally conducted, possibly limiting the generalizability of norms and cutoffs to Asian elders residing in the USA. Second, many Asian cultures possess a great deal of stigma towards with cognitive decline, making assessment more difficult. For example, the Chinese word for dementia is 痴呆 Chīdāi; the first character means "imbecile" or "silly" and the second means "foolish" or "stupid" (Dementia, 2013).

Unfortunately, dementia is present in Asian elders with an estimated prevalence rate of 9 % in primacy care settings. While this is lower than the 16 % prevalence rate observed in Caucasian individuals in primary care settings (Chen, Foo, & Ury, 2002), it is clear from these numbers that a substantial number of Asian elders are impacted by cognitive impairment. Complicating things further is the broad range of diversity that constitutes the Asian culture; 24 ethnicities make up the Asian American panoramic in the USA (U.S. Census Bureau, 2000), and each of these ethnic groups has its own language, customs, and challenges in assessment. Finally, our review of the literature also revealed numerous sources that emphasized the importance of considering literacy and educational attainment when assessing for cognitive decline with Asian elders.

In addition to the observations we made in our review of the literature, Dick and colleagues (2006) outlined the challenges in assessing dementia in Asian elders which include perceiving memory problems as a normal part of aging and misattributing cognitive impairment to the stress of immigration and acculturation, an imbalance of yin and yang, mental illness, or punishment for past actions. Dick and colleagues also noted the complexities of language that result in difficulty translating and adopting existing tests. As a result, a number of experts have proposed alternatives for words when words or phrases either do not exist in another language or the translation itself creates nuanced problems. For example, in the Shanghai version of the MMSE

L.T. Benuto, Ph.D. (✉)
Administrative Faculty, Department of Psychology MS0296, University of Nevada, Reno, NV 89557, USA

Northcentral University, Graduate School Faculty, 10000 E University Drive, Prescott Valley, AZ 86314, USA
e-mail: dr.benuto@gmail.com

K.A. Wainwright, M.A.
Department of Psychology, University of Nevada-Reno, Reno, NV 89557, USA
e-mail: katherinewainwright@gmail.com

B.D. Leany, Ph.D.
Lake's Crossing Center: Maximum Security Facility for Forensic Mental Health Services, 500 Galletti Way, Sparks, NV 89504, USA

Northcentral University, Graduate School Faculty, 10000 E University Drive, Prescott Valley, AZ 86314, USA
e-mail: leanyb@gmail.com

L.T. Benuto et al. (eds.), *Guide to Psychological Assessment with Asians*,
DOI 10.1007/978-1-4939-0796-0_19,

"please close your eyes" was replaced with "please raise your hands" as "please close your eyes" has a death connotation in Shanghai (Zhang et al., 1990). Moreover, differential linguistic performance has been demonstrated for tasks that involve recall where the number of syllables varies across languages. For example, Hispanic individuals completing digit span tend to perform poorer on digit span as the numbers in Spanish produce a greater number of syllables whereas Vietnamese and Chinese speaking individuals score higher on these same tests (Dick et al., 2006).

Dick and colleagues (2006) also discussed the relevance of timed tasks with Asian clients, emphasizing that many Western psychological tests place a premium on efficiency. Specifically, they discussed how Spreen and Strauss (1998) found that Asian individuals took longer to complete Part A of the Trail Making Test than their Caucasian peers even when educational differences were accounted for. Others have also cited the fast pace as a Western and particularly US cultural characteristic. Indeed, researchers have found that even when education is controlled for, Chinese individuals take longer on timed tests than Caucasians (Spreen & Strauss, 1998). Therefore the test administrator may take this into account particularly in instances where performance is poor on time measures only.

Given the limited research available on this population, we choose to limit the scope of this chapter to assessment measures that function as screens for cognitive impairment and to assessments that are specific to Asian cultural groups. We also took care to limit our discussion of the measures that are the most applicable to Asians who are residing in the USA as the focus in this book is mostly within that context, although when necessary we extended beyond research conducted in a US context and ventured abroad for resources to provide the most salient recommendations for assessment possible.

The American Psychological Association (2011) created guidelines for the evaluation of dementia and age-related cognitive decline, emphasizing the importance of the clinical interview and the administration of standardized psychological and neuropsychological tests. The guidelines call for the use of a brief mental status examination and for comprehensive neuropsychological evaluations for dementia and cognitive change including tests that assess multiple cognitive domains including memory, attention, perceptual and motor skills, language, visual-spatial abilities, reasoning, and executive functions (and in certain instances measures of mood and personality). Because the neuropsychological assessment chapter in this book covers a range of tests that are specific for the evaluation of the above domains, we refer the reader to that chapter for specifics regarding the appropriate use of these tests in Asian American populations.

Mini-Mental Status Examination

The Mini-Mental Status Examination (MMSE; Folstein, Folstein, & McHugh, 1975) is a 30-item measure assessing seven cognitive domains including orientation to time, orientation to place, registration, attention and calculation, recall, language, and visual construction. For the standard English version of the MMSE the cutoff is 24 out of 30, with a score of 23 or less indicating cognitive impairment.

There are several versions of the MMSE that are applicable to Asian individuals although the bulk of the research on these measures was conducted abroad and therefore their generalizability should be taken into consideration. For example, the Chinese Mini-Mental Status Examination (C-MMSE) was initially developed by Katzman et al. (1988) and since then a series of cultural and linguistic modifications of MMSE for C-MMSE have been recommended (see Table 19.1 for details). In addition to cultural and linguistic modifications, our review of the literature revealed varying cutoff scores with corresponding sensitivity and specificity levels (see Table 19.2 for details). Moreover, adjustments based on literacy and educational attainment have been developed. For example Cui and colleagues (2011) reported that the Institute of Mental Health of Peking University recommends using the following cutoff scores: 14/15 for individuals who are illiterate and 19/20 for individuals who are non-illiterate. In terms of educational adjustments, Cui et al. reported that the Shanghai Mental Health Center

Table 19.1 Cultural and linguistic modifications for Chinese versions of the MMSE

Measure	Item	Revised item	Source
CMMSE	Orientation (place, floor, city, county, state)	Province, district, street, place, floor	Katzman et al., 1988 as cited in Zhang et al., 1990
	Repetition ("no if, ands, or buts")	"Forty-four stone lions"	Katzman et al., 1988 as cited in Zhang et al., 1990
	Following commands ("close your eyes")	"Please raise your hands"	Katzman et al., 1988 as cited in Zhang et al., 1990
	Sentence construction ("write a sentence")	"Say a sentence" to account for lack of education	Chiu et al., 1998
	Attention (spell "world" backwards)	Reversal of five digits	Chiu et al., 1998
	Registration (apple, table, penny)	National flag, tree, rubber ball	Xu, Meyer, Huang, & Du, 2003
CAMSE	Registration (apple, table, penny)	Apple, table, ax	Xu et al., 2003
	Attention (spell "world" backwards)	"JIN MU SHUI HUO TU" (metal, wood, water, fire, earth) backwards	Xu et al., 2003
	Naming (pencil, watch)	Button, watch	Xu et al., 2003
	Following commands ("close your eyes")	Observing and imitating the posture shown by a cartoon of a man crossing his arms across his chest	Xu et al., 2003
	Sentence construction ("write a sentence")	Ask: "If you did not know my name how would you find out my name?"	Xu et al., 2003

CMMSE Chinese Mini-Mental Status Examination, *CAMSE* Chinese Adapted Mini-Mental Status Examination

Table 19.2 Cutoff scores and sensitivity and specificity levels for the Chinese versions of the MMSE

Measure	Source	Cutoffs	Specificity (%)	Sensitivity (%)	Notes
CAMSE	Xu et al., 2003	22	86.44	81.67	For literate participants
	Xu et al., 2003	20	73.17	84.85	For illiterate participants
CMMSE	Wong et al., 2013	23/24	84	58	
	Sahadevan, Lim, Tan, & Chan, 2000	20/21	93	94	Aged 60–74 with 0–6 years of education
	Sahadevan et al., 2000	23/24	87	93	Aged 60–74 with more than 6 years of education
	Sahadevan et al., 2000	18/19	92	94	Aged 75 and older with 0–6 years of education
	Sahadevan et al., 2000	22/23	88	100	Aged 75 and older with more than 6 years of education
	Zhang et al., 1990	17/18	92.7	85.2	No formal education
	Zhang et al., 1990	20/21	92.7	85.2	1–6 years of education
	Zhang et al., 1990	24/25	92.7	85.2	More than 6 years of education
	Hu et al., 2013	26	53	85	For detecting MCI
	Hu et al., 2013	26	95	94	For detecting AD

CMMSE Chinese Mini-Mental Status Examination, *CAMSE* Chinese Adapted Mini-Mental Status Examination

recommends 17/18 for those without formal education, 20/21 for those with 1–6 years of education (primary school), and 24/25 for participants with more than 6 years of education (middle school or higher). Similarly, the Beijing Union Medical College recommends the following cutoff scores: 19/20 for those without formal education, 22/23 for those with 1–6 years of education (primary school), and 26/27 for participants with more than 6 years of education (middle school or

Table 19.3 Cultural and linguistic modifications for Indian version of the Hindi Mini-Mental Status Examination (H-MMSE; Ganguli, Ratcliff, Chandra, Sharma, & Gilby, 1995)

Item	Revised item
Orientation (day, date, month, year, season)	Time of day, day of week, date, month, season
Orientation (place, floor, city, county, state)	District, postal district, village, block, "whose house is this?"
Registration (apple, table, penny)	Mango, chair, coin
Attention (spell "world" backwards)	Name the days of the week backwards
Naming (pencil, watch)	Pen, watch
Repetition (repeat "no if, ands, or buts")	"Neither this nor that"
Following commands ("close your eyes")	If illiterate, told "look at me and do exactly what I do" and then the examiner closes his or her own eyes
Sentence construction ("write a sentence")	Ask "tell me something about your house"
Copy intersecting pentagons	Copy a diamond within a square

higher). If an individual scores below these cutoffs cognitive impairment is suspected and further assessment is required. In additional to the C-MMSE, other renditions of the MMSE that are specific to varying cultural groups also exist. Tables 19.3 and 19.4 summarize linguistic and cultural modifications to various renditions of the MMSE, and Table 19.5 summarizes recommended cutoff scores and sensitivity and specificity levels for the same measures.

In our review we noted a few important findings that merit a discussion here. First, Tse and colleagues (2013) noted that enhancement of older adults' performance on some C-MMSE items, including attention and orientation to time and place, highlights the role of attention as an early marker for dementia. While not specific to Asians, Tse et al. also reported that it is likely that education enhances performance in some C-MMSE components because the tasks involved reflect typical routine tasks learned in school. In light of the findings described above some experts focused on adapting the MMSE for those who are illiterate or minimally educated (Xu et al., 2003). For example, as shown in Table 19.1, the CAMSE asks participants to respond to the question "If you did not know my name how would you find out my name?" rather than "write a sentence" to account for educational differences.

Montreal Cognitive Assessment

The Montreal Cognitive Assessment (MoCA) is used to assess for mild cognitive impairment (MCI) and covers several domains including attention, orientation, language, verbal memory, visual-spatial ability, and executive function. A score of ≥ 26 (out of a possible 30 points) is indicative of normal cognitive functioning with a 1-point education correction for those individuals who have less than 12 years of education (Nasreddine, Phillips, Bedirian, et al., 2011). It is freely available in multiple languages on the Internet (http://www.mocatest.org/) with available references regarding its use related to a broad spectrum of cognitive disorders (e.g., Parkinson's, Alzheimer's dementia, HIV-related dementia) as well as a bibliography detailing the research that has been conducted on this measure. This measure has been demonstrated to be reliable, valid, specific, and sensitive (e.g., Nasreddine et al., 2011; Luis, Keegan, & Mullan, 2009). For example, Smith, Gildeh, and Holmes (2007) administered the MoCA and the MMSE to 32 individuals with dementia, 23 individuals with MCI, and 12 controls at baseline and at 6-month follow-up. They found that the MoCA was effective in identifying those at risk of developing dementia at 6-month follow-up.

A review of the extant literature revealed that the MoCA may effectively be used with Taiwanese (Tsai et al., 2012), Japanese (Fujiwara et al., 2010), Korean (Lee et al., 2008), Chinese (Hu et al., 2013; Lu et al., 2011; Wong, Lam et al., 2013; Zhang & Liu, 2008), Thai (Tangwongchai et al., 2009), and Sri Lankan individuals (Karunaratne, Hanwella, & de Silva, 2011). Moreover, research on this measure with Chinese individuals revealed that it is a useful and psychometrically valid tool for the assessment of gross cognitive function in patients who have experienced a traumatic brain

Table 19.4 Cultural and linguistic modifications for Korean, Taiwanese, and Thai versions of the MMSE

Group	Measure	Item	Revised item	Source
Korean MMSE	K-mMMSE	Registration (apple, table, penny)	Airplane, pine tree, sincerity	Seul-Ki, Ki-Hyun, & Jae-Min, 2004
	MMSE-K	Following commands ("close your eyes")	Ask: "Why do people wash their clothes?"	Park & Kwon, 1990
	MMSE-K	Sentence construction ("write a sentence")	Ask: "How can you give an ID card back to the owner if you find it on the street?"	Park & Kwon, 1990
	MMSE-K	Repetition (repeat "no if, ands, or buts")	In Korean, "all Korea, beautiful"	Park & Kwon, 1990
	K-MMSE	Repetition (repeat "no if, ands, or buts")	In Korean, "seeing is believing"	Han et al., 2008
	K-MMSE	Three-stage command ("take this paper in your right hand, fold it in half, and put it on the floor")	"Turn the paper over, fold it in half, and give it to me"	Han et al., 2008
Taiwanese MMSE	CMMSE	Orientation (place, floor, city, county, state)	City, district, street, floor, room	Shyu & Yip, 2001
		Registration (apple, table, penny)	Bicycle, happy, red	Shyu & Yip, 2001
		Repetition (repeat "no if, ands, or buts")	"Black words are truly written on white paper"	Shyu & Yip, 2001
Thai MMSE		Repetition (repeat "no if, ands, or buts")	"Today is a good day"	Phanthumchinda, Jitapunkul, Sitthi-Amorn, Bunnag, & Ebrahim, 1991
		Attention (spell "world" backwards)	Spell "Bangkok" backwards (in Thai)	Phanthumchinda et al., 1991

Given the limited existent data for the Japanese MMSE there are no suggested cultural and linguistic modifications

injury (Wong et al., 2013) and for individuals with cerebral small vessel disease (Wong et al., 2009). The usefulness of this measure is not only specific to Chinese individuals but also with elderly individuals from other Asian backgrounds and can be used effectively to screen for MCI (Lee et al., 2008). Table 19.6 summarizes the research on the MoCA with various Asian groups.

Despite the ample body of research that supports the use of this measure with individuals of various Asian backgrounds, Lu and colleagues (2011) highlighted that the generalizability of the MoCA's validity to large general (non-clinical) populations (as it had mostly been researched in clinical settings) was questionable. In light of this, Lu et al. examined the use of the MoCA with cognitively normal individuals, individuals with MCI, and individuals with dementia in mainland China. They established that the MoCA is in fact a valid screen for cognitive impairment.

Similar to the MMSE, several authors recommended cultural and linguistic modifications of MoCA for the different Asian populations. For example, even among those with the highest level of education, the words "watch" and "ruler" in the abstract thinking task were only correctly identified 50 % of the time in the Chinese population (Hu et al., 2013). Table 19.6 summarizes linguistic and cultural modifications that are recommended, and Table 19.7 summarizes available recommended cutoff scores and sensitivity and specificity levels. It is important to note that much of the research described above has been conducted abroad and therefore when using the MoCA with individuals residing in the USA, results may need to be interpreted with caution.

Table 19.5 Cutoff scores and sensitivity and specificity levels for the Indian, Japanese, Korean, Taiwanese, and Thai versions of the MMSE

Group	Measure	Source	Cutoffs	Spec. (%)	Sens. (%)	Recommendations
Indian MMSE	MMSE	Ng, Niti, Chiam, & Kua, 2007	23/24	75.6	97.5	This study included Chinese, Malay, and Indian participants
Japanese MMSE	Japanese MMSE	Konagaya et al., 2007	26	95.3	91.8	
	Japanese MMSE	Fujiwara et al., 2010	28/29	97	89	Participants in study limited to mild AD
Korean MMSE	K-mMMSE	Seul-Ki et al., 2004	69/70	79	86	For detecting MCI; authors used an expanded scoring (0–100) to allow for finer discrimination
	K-mMMSE	Seul-Ki et al., 2004	59/60	78	91	For detecting AD; authors used an expanded scoring (0–100) to allow for finer discrimination
	MMSE-K	Park, Park, & Ko, 1991	23/24	91.5	92	
	K-MMSE	Heo, Lee, Park, Ahn, & Kim, 2012	23/24	80	82	For detecting AD
	K-MMSE	Heo et al., 2012	26/27	65	62	For detecting MCI
Taiwanese MMSE	MMSE-short	Lou, Dai, Huang, & Yu, 2007	11 (out of 16)	97.4	100	16-item measure assessing orientation, recall, and attention and calculation
Thai MMSE	MMSE-Thai 2002	Limpawattana et al., 2012	24	66.3	78.7	
	MMSE-Thai 2002	Limpawattana et al., 2012	24	76.8	35.4	Illiterate participants; suggested cutoff is 14
	MMSE-Thai 2002	Limpawattana et al., 2012	24	88.9	56.6	Participants with 0–6 years of education; suggested cutoff is 17
	MMSE-Thai 2002	Limpawattana et al., 2012	24	91.2	92	Participants with more than 6 years of education; suggested cutoff is 22
	Thai MMSE	Phanthumchinda et al., 1991	18	75	78	

Hasegawa Dementia Scale

The original Hasegawa Dementia Scale (HDS; Hasegawa, Inoue, & Moria, 1974) consisted of 11 items, took 10 min to administer, was predominantly used in East Asian countries, and was characterized by eastern social and cultural backgrounds. Since then the HDS has been revised (HDS-R) and shortened to nine items that assess for orientation to age, time, and date; orientation to place; memory of three words; calculation; recall of numbers in reverse order; delayed recall of three words; memory of five objects; and verbal fluency. A score of 20 or less (out of 30) indicates cognitive impairment

Table 19.6 Cultural and linguistic modifications for the MoCA

Group	Measure	Item	Revised item	Source
Chinese	MoCA-C; BJ-MoCA	Alternating Trail Making (Roman alphabets)	Chinese character sequences 甲/乙/丙/丁/戊	Hu et al., 2013; Lu et al., 2011; Nie et al., 2012; Yu, Li, & Huang, 2012
	MoCA-C; BJ-MoCA	Attention-Auditory Vigilance (English alphabet)	Arabic numerals	Hu et al., 2013; Lu et al., 2011; Nie et al., 2012; Yu et al., 2012
	MoCA-C	Language—Sentence repetition	Names were changed to more common Chinese names	Hu et al., 2013
	MoCA-C; BJ-MoCA	Language—Verbal fluency (phonemic letter fluency)	Animal category fluency	Hu et al., 2013; Lu et al., 2011; Nie et al., 2012; Yu et al., 2012
	MoCA-C	Alternating Trail Making (character sequence)	Suggested change: Color changes	Hu et al., 2013
	MoCA-C	Naming Test ("rhinoceros" and "camel")	Suggested change: Replace with "tiger" and "panda"	Hu et al., 2013
	MoCA-C	Word memory test ("velvet" and "church")	Suggested change: Replace with "silk" and "temple"	Hu et al., 2013
	BJ-MoCA	Word memory test ("velvet" and "daisy")	"Silk" and "chrysanthemum"	Yu et al., 2012; Lu et al., 2011
Korean	MoCA-K	Word memory test ("velvet" and "daisy")	"Silk" and "azalea"	Lee et al., 2008
	MoCA-K	Language—Verbal fluency (phonemic letter fluency)	Objects bought in a market fluency	Lee et al., 2008
	MoCA-K	Alternating Trail Making (Roman alphabets)	Korean character sequences	Lee et al., 2008
Sinhalese	MoCA-S	Alternating Trail Making (Roman alphabets)	Sinhala alphabet	Karunaratne et al., 2011
		Naming Test ("rhinoceros" and "camel")	"Rabbit" and "elephant"	Karunaratne et al., 2011
		Word memory test ("velvet," "church," and "daisy")	"Cotton," "temple," "Araliya" (a flower)	Karunaratne et al., 2011
		Language—Sentence repetition (the name "John")	The name "Nimal"	Karunaratne et al., 2011
		Verbal fluency (words beginning with "F")	Words beginning with "S"	Karunaratne et al., 2011

(Katoh et al. as cited in Tsuboi et al., 2009). The HDS-R is more focused on memory and verbal fluency than the MMSE and therefore may be more sensitive and specific regarding screening for Alzheimer's disease than the MMSE (Kim et al., 2005; Tsukamoto et al., 2009). The HDS and the HDS-R have both been fairly well researched with a focus in Japan and China (e.g., Mu et al., 2000). Our review of the literature also revealed a Korean version of the HDS-R, which has been demonstrated to be more robust to demographic influences than the MMSE (Jeong et al., 2007) and better suited as a screening instrument for Alzheimer's disease than the MMSE (Kim et al., 2005). Some additional observations that we made as we were reviewing the literature include that older age, lower education, and being male can impact the performance of the HDS-R (Jeong et al., 2007; Mu et al., 2000) and therefore adjustments to cutoff scores based on these factors may be necessary. Specifically Jeong et al. (2007) found that these factors were associated with lowered performance on the HDS-R. Despite these caveats the HDS-R has been demonstrated to be a valid means to screen for cognitive impairment (Kim et al., 2005;

Table 19.7 Cutoff scores and sensitivity and specificity levels for the MoCA

Group	Measure	Source	Cutoffs	Specificity (%)	Sensitivity (%)	Recommendations
Chinese	MoCA-C	Hu et al., 2013	26	85	92	For detecting MCI
	MoCA-C	Hu et al., 2013	26	96	92	For detecting AD
	BJ-MoCA	Lu et al., 2011	13/14	83.2	80.9	No formal education
	BJ-MoCA	Lu et al., 2011	19/20	82.5	83.8	1–6 years of education
	BJ-MoCA	Lu et al., 2011	24/25	81.5	89.9	More than 6 years of education
	BJ-MoCA	Yu et al., 2012; Lu et al., 2011	22	63.9	68.7	
Japanese	MoCA-J	Fujiwara et al., 2010	25/26	87	93	For detecting MCI
	MoCA-J	Fujiwara et al., 2010	25/26	89	100	For detecting AD
Korean	MoCA-K	Lee et al., 2008	22/23	84	89	For detecting MCI
	MoCA-K	Lee et al., 2008	22/23	84	98	For detecting AD
Sinhalese	MoCA-S	Karunaratne et al., 2011	24	79.6	98.1	
Taiwan	MoCA-T	Tsai et al., 2012	23/24	78	92	
Thailand	Moca-Thai	Tangwongchai et al., 2009	24	80	80	

Table 19.8 Cutoff scores and sensitivity and specificity levels for the HDS-R

Group	Measure	Source	Cutoffs	Specificity (%)	Sensitivity (%)	Recommendations
Chinese	HDS-R	Mu et al., 2000	17	97.7	95.1	
Japan	HDS-R	Fujiwara et al., 2010	26/27	97	97	Participants in study limited to mild AD
Korea	HDS-R	Kim et al., 2005	18/19	89	88.6	For detecting MDI
	HDS-R	Kim et al., 2005	17/18	92.7	90.2	For detecting AD

Yamamoto et al., 2012) and has been used frequently in epidemiological research studies (e.g., Shiba et al., 1999). Table 19.8 summarizes the limited available data for recommended cutoff scores and sensitivity and specificity levels.

Cognitive Abilities Screening Instrument

The Cognitive Abilities Screening Instrument (CASI) is a 40-item measure of global cognitive functioning that combines items from the MMSE and HDS-R to assess attention, concentration, orientation, short-term memory, long-term memory, language abilities, visual construction, list-generating fluency, abstraction, and judgment (Teng et al., 1994). Originally designed for use in Japan, scores range from 0 to 100 with Teng and colleagues finding the original cutoff to range between 70 and 76 in Japan.

Dick and colleagues (2006) summarized the research on the CASI and indicated that valid versions of the CASI exist for English-speaking individuals in Guam; Chinese elders in Kimmen and Taiwan; Japanese elders in Seattle, Honolulu, and Japan; and individuals in Vietnam. They also reported that both education and age-related norms exist for the Chinese and Taiwanese versions of this measure. Some experts have indicated that the (Chinese) CASI has superior specificity and similar sensitivity to the MMSE (Rong, Zhuming, & Xiehe, 2000), at least when used in international settings. Our review of the literature revealed that the CASI has been used extensively in a variety of areas, including examining cognitive decline in mild Alzheimer's disease (Huang et al., 2013), depression (Chen,

Table 19.9 Cutoff scores and sensitivity and specificity levels for the CASI

Group	Measure	Source	Cutoffs	Specificity (%)	Sensitivity (%)	Recommendations
Chinese	CASI C-2.0	Lin et al., 2002	49/50	85	83	No education
	CASI C-2.0	Lin et al., 2002	67/68	91	83	1–5 years of education
	CASI C-2.0	Lin et al., 2002	79/80	90	89	More than 6 years of education
	CASI C-2.0	Tsai, Lin, Wu, & Liu, 2004	78.5	97.1	91.9	
Osaka, Japan	CASI	Teng et al., 1994	70/71	94	95	
Tokyo, Japan	CASI	Teng et al., 1994	75/76	93	93	

Yeh, & Tsai, 2012), and white matter lesions (Inaba et al., 2011).

We identified only a single study that examined the psychometric properties of the CASI. Gibbons and colleagues (2009) reported that while the CASI had been designed for use in cross-cultural studies in Japanese and Japanese-American elderly in Japan and the USA, the equivalence of the Japanese and English-language version of this measure had not been investigated. Using an impressive sample of Japanese-American elderly they found that the CASI measures cognitive function equivalently in Japanese and English. Recommended cutoff scores and sensitivity and specificity levels are reported in Table 19.9.

The Seoul Neuropsychological Screening Battery

The Seoul Neuropsychological Screening Battery (SNSB; Kang & Na, 2003) assesses traditional domains of language, visual-spatial abilities, as well as attention, memory, and executive functioning that are common in most neuropsychological evaluations. This battery is being described here as it has been adapted to include a dementia-specific screen (SNSB-D; Ahn, Kim, Saxton, & Kim, 2007) that has good overall convergent validity with the MMSE ($r=0.876$) as well as moderate-to-good convergent validity for the general cognitive functioning score and the subdomains of the SNSB-D (attention $r=0.629$, language and related function $r=0.848$, visual-spatial function $r=0.779$, memory $r=0.945$, frontal/executive function $r=0.919$). Further, the SNSB-D was able to differentiate among a sample of Korean patients with MCI, Koreans with Alzheimer's dementia, and normal controls, with a high degree of test–retest reliability (0.960 for normal controls, 0.999 for MCI, and 0.918 for Alzheimer's dementia). With the exception of the subtest that is used to measure frontal lobe/executive functioning ($p<0.072$), the discriminant validity of this measure is good (being able to discriminate normal controls from cognitively impaired individuals). Despite the apparent strong psychometric properties of this measure, it was developed and designed for use in Korea. Thus, it presents several challenges for the clinician who is not fluent in Korean and who practices in the USA. It was introduced here mainly to support the initial assertion that there are universal constructs across cultures as evidenced by the inclusion of the aforementioned domains of neuropsychological functioning.

Clinical Dementia Rating Scale

The Clinical Dementia Rating (CDR) is a semi-structured, informant-based interview designed to examine a person's memory, orientation, judgment and problem solving, community affairs, home and hobbies, and personal care. The person is assigned a score (on a 5-point spectrum) ranging from "none" to "severe." Scores in each of these are combined to obtain a composite score that ranges from 0 through 3 (Morris, 1993). The CDR is relevant here as it has been described as a global clinical scale, has established diagnostic, severity-ranking utility, and has been amply researched with Asian individuals (Lim, Chong, & Sahadevan, 2007). In a review of the extant literature on the CDR and Asian individuals Lim, Chong, and Sahadevan concluded that clinicians who use the CDR with Asian individuals should be mindful of the influence of cultural factors on premorbid lifestyle, informant reliability, and performance in certain CDR test items (specifically judgment and problem solving, community, and home and hobbies).

Generally speaking there is support that this measure can be useful with Asian clients who are suspected of having dementia. For example, Lim and colleagues (2005) conducted a retrospective review of 329 multiracial Asian patients who attended their clinic from 1994 to 1999. They found substantial evidence for the validity of the CDR's overall ability to stage dementia severity. Specifically the CDR showed convergent validity when compared against clinical features, mental status, and psychometric test scores and DSM III-R measures of dementia severity. More recently Lam and colleagues (2010) explored the applicability of a combined cognitive and clinical approach to identify older Chinese adults at risk of cognitive decline. Community-dwelling participants (aged 60 or over; $N=740$) were assessed at baseline and 2 years with CDR and a cognitive battery. They conducted that a combined approach may be more practical in screening for MCI participants with diverse educational and cultural background highlighting the importance of collateral contacts when cognitive decline is suspected. Therefore in addition to cognitive batteries, measures such as the CDR should be used to assess for the presence of cognitive decline. In addition to the above, the CDR has been effectively used in validity and reliability studies of other measures to assess Alzheimer's disease in Korean patients (Ahn et al., 2007).

Recommendations

In this chapter we reviewed several screening instruments that can be used with Asian elders to screen for cognitive impairment as well as other relevant measures that can be useful when cognitive decline associated with dementia is suspected. Our review of the literature revealed several themes, which resulted in the following recommendations.

The Asian cultural panoramic in the USA is broad, and clinicians are likely to encounter individuals with varying levels of acculturation as well as individuals who were born in the USA; individuals who immigrated to the USA during childhood; and individuals who immigrated to the USA as adults. Our first recommendation is that the clinician assess the client's level of acculturation as well as his or her level of fluency in English (which again can range broadly—some clients will be native English speakers whereas others may not be able to speak English at all). Based on the client's level of acculturation and level of English proficiency, the clinician should determine the client's optimal language for testing (this is typically the person's native language) as researchers found an inverse relationship between years spent in one's native country during school age and cognitive performance in late life (Yano et al., 2000).

The clinician should be aware that the client may not come forth with concerns about cognitive decline because of the stigma associated with dementia and also with the possible misattributions of memory impairments that have been documented in the literature (Dick et al., 2006). Therefore it is important that when cognitive decline is suspected (particularly cognitive decline that is associated with dementia) measures such as the CDR be used and/or that the clinician make contact with collaterals. Moreover, the clinician should not assume that multilingualism may act as a protective factor against the development of dementia. For example, researchers have found that for Japanese individuals, multilingualism did not act as a protective factor against the development of cognitive decline in later life (Crane et al., 2010). Screening for cognitive impairment is important, and thus our second recommendation is that screening for cognitive impairment occur at routine appointments, as researchers found that Asians are not as likely to seek mental health services as other ethnic groups (Meyers, 2006).

Our third recommendation is that clinicians consider the various adjustments discussed within this chapter. Adjustments to scores may be necessary based on the client's education (e.g., Tse et al., 2013) and age. We also encountered an abundance of literature that emphasized the importance for considering literacy and for the MMSE adjustments based on whether or not the person can read does exist (Xu et al., 2003). Moreover, the presence of agraphia may not in and of itself be an indicator of cognitive impairment despite literacy levels as individuals who do not practice writing characters regularly may be prone to committing errors due to lack of practice rather than cognitive impairment (Akanuma et al., 2010).

In this chapter we covered the following measures: MMSE, MoCA, HDS, CASI, SEOL, and CDR. Each of these measures comes with its own strengths and weaknesses, and the utility of each of these measures varies in terms of the client's educational attainment, literacy, and native language. These factors should all be considered for selecting the ideal screening instrument for a particular client or homogenous group of individuals. Ultimately each of these measures offers a reasonable means for screening for cognitive impairment, and if concerns arise, the clinician should refer the client for further testing. The neuropsychological assessment chapter in this book provides a detailed overview of the specific domains that should be tested when cognitive impairment is suspected and details recommendations for specific measures that assess said domains.

References

Ahn, I., Kim, J., Saxton, J., & Kim, D. (2007). Reliability and validity of a short form of the Severe Impairment Battery in Korean Alzheimer's disease patients. *International Journal of Geriatric Psychiatry, 22*(7), 682–687. doi:10.1002/gps.1731.

Akanuma, K., Meguro, K., Meguro, M., Chubaci, R. Y. S., Caramelli, P., & Nitrini, R. (2010). Kanji and Kana agraphia in mild cognitive impairment and dementia: A trans-cultural comparison of elderly Japanese subjects living in Japan and Brazil. *Dementia & Neuropsychologia, 4*(4), 300–305.

American Psychological Association. (2011). *Guidelines for the evaluation of dementia and age-related cognitive decline*. Retrieved from http://www.apa.org/practice/guidelines/dementia.aspx.

Chen, H., Foo, S., & Ury, W. (2002). Recognizing dementia. *Western Journal of Medicine, 176*(4), 267–270.

Chen, H. H., Yeh, H. L., & Tsai, S. J. (2012). Association of lower hemoglobin levels with depression, though not with cognitive performance, in healthy elderly men. *Psychiatry and Clinical Neurosciences, 66*(4), 367–369. doi:10.1111/j.1440-1819.2012.02347.x.

Chiu, H.F., Lam, L.C., Chi, I., Leung, T., Li, S.W., Law, W. T., … Lau, J. (1998). Prevalence of dementia in Chinese elderly in Hong Kong. *Neurology*, 50, 1002–1009.

Crane, P. K., Gruhl, J. C., Erosheva, E. A., Gibbons, L. E., McCurry, S. M., Rhoads, K., … White, L. (2010). Use of spoken and written Japanese did not protect Japanese-American men from cognitive decline in late life. *The Journals of Gerontology: Series B: Psychological Sciences and Social Sciences, 65B*(6), 654–666. doi: 10.1093/geronb/gbq046

Cui, G. H., Yao, Y. H., Xu, R. F., Tang, H. D., Jiang, G. X., Wang, Y. Y., … Cheng, Q. Q. (2011). Cognitive impairment using education-based cutoff points for CMMSE scores in elderly Chinese people of agricultural and rural Shanghai China. *Acta Neurologica Scandinavica, 124*(6), 361–367.

Dementia. (2013). In *MDBG Chinese-English dictionary*. Retrieved on August 27, 2013, from http://www.mdbg.net/chindict/chindict.php

Dick, M. B., Dick-Muehlke, C., & Teng, E. L. (2006). Assessment of cognitive status in Asians. In G. Yeo & D. Gallagher-Thompson (Eds.), *Ethnicity and the dementias* (2nd ed., pp. 55–69). New York, NY: Routledge.

Folstein, M. F., Folstein, S. E., & McHugh, P. R. (1975). "Mini-mental state": A practical method for grading the cognitive state of patients for the clinician. *Journal of Psychiatric Research, 12*, 189–198.

Fujiwara, Y., Suzuki, H., Yasunaga, M., Sugiyama, M., Ijuin, M., Sakuma, N., … Shinkai, S. (2010). Brief screening tool for mild cognitive impairment in older Japanese: Validation of the Japanese version of the Montreal Cognitive Assessment. *Geriatrics & Gerontology International, 10*(3), 225–232. doi: 10.1111/j.1447-0594.2010.00585.x

Ganguli, M., Ratcliff, G., Chandra, V., Sharma, S., & Gilby, J. (1995). Hindi version of the MMSE: The development of a cognitive screening instrument for a largely illiterate rural elderly population in India. *International Journal of Geriatric Psychiatry, 10*(5), 367–377.

Gibbons, L. E., McCurry, S., Rhoads, K., Masaki, K., White, L., Borenstein, A. R., … Crane, P. K. (2009). Japanese-English language equivalence of the Cognitive Abilities Screening Instrument among Japanese-Americans. *International Psychogeriatrics, 21*(1), 129–137. doi: 10.1017/S1041610208007862

Han, C., Jo, S., Jo, I., Kim, E., Park, M., & Kang, Y. (2008). An adaptation of the Korean mini-mental state examination (K-MMSE) in elderly Koreans: Demographic influence and population-based norms (the AGE study). *Archives of Gerontology and Geriatrics, 47*(3), 302–310.

Hasegawa, K., Inoue, K., & Moria, K. (1974). The study on the brief intelligence scale for the demented elderly. *Psychiatry, 16*, 965–969.

Heo, J., Lee, K., Park, T., Ahn, J., & Kim, M. (2012). Validation of the Korean Addenbrooke's cognitive examination for diagnosing Alzheimer's dementia and mild cognitive impairment in the Korean elderly. *Applied Neuropsychology: Adult, 19*(2), 127–131.

Hu, J., Zhou, W., Hu, S., Huang, M., Wei, N., Qi, H., … Xu, Y. (2013). Cross-cultural difference and validation of the Chinese version of Montreal Cognitive Assessment in older adults residing in Eastern China: Preliminary findings. *Archives of Gerontology and Geriatrics, 56*(1), 38–43. doi:10.1016/j.archger.2012.05.008

Huang, C. W., Chang, W. N., Huang, S. H., Lui, C. C., Chen, N. C., Chang, Y. T., … Chang, A. Y. W. (2013). Impact of homocysteine on cortical perfusion and cognitive decline in mild Alzheimer's dementia. *European Journal of Neurology, 20*(8), 1191–1197. doi: 10.1111/ene.12159

Inaba, M., White, L., Bell, C., Chen, R., Petrovitch, H., Launer, L., … Masaki, K. (2011). White matter lesions on brain magnetic resonance imaging scan and 5-year cognitive decline: The Honolulu-Asia Aging Study. *Journal of the American Geriatrics Society, 59*(8), 1484–1489. doi: 10.1111/j.1532-5415.2011.03490.x

Jeong, J. W., Kim, K. W., Lee, D. Y., Lee, S. B., Park, J. H., Choi, E. A., … Woo, J. I. (2007). A normative study of the Revised Hasegawa Dementia Scale: Comparison of demographic influences between the Revised Hasegawa Dementia Scale and the Mini-Mental Status Examination. *Dementia and Geriatric Cognitive Disorders, 24*(4), 288–293. doi: 10.1159/000107592

Kang, Y., & Na, D. L. (2003). *Seoul neuropsychological screening battery*. Incheon: Human Brain Research & Consulting.

Karunaratne, S., Hanwella, R., & de Silva, V. (2011). Validation of the Sinhala version of the Montreal Cognitive Assessment in screening for dementia. *Ceylon Medical Journal, 56*(4), 147–153.

Katzman, R., Zhang, M., Qu, O., Wang, Z., Liu, W. T., Yu, E., et al. (1988). A Chinese version of the mini-mental state examination: Impact of illiteracy in a Shanghai dementia survey. *Journal of Clinical Epidemiology, 41*, 971–978.

Kim, K. W., Lee, D. Y., Jhoo, J. H., Youn, J. C., Suh, Y. J., Jun, Y. H., … Woo, J. -I. (2005). Diagnostic accuracy of mini-mental status examination and revised Hasegawa dementia scale for Alzheimer's disease. *Dementia and Geriatric Cognitive Disorders, 19*(5–6), 324–330. doi: 10.1159/000084558

Konagaya, Y., Washimi, Y., Hatoori, H., Takeda, A., Watanabe, T., & Ohta, T. (2007). Validation of the Telephone Interview for Cognitive Status (TICS) in Japanese. *International Journal of Geriatric Psychiatry, 22*(7), 695–700.

Lam, L. W., Tam, C. C., Leung, G. Y., Lui, V. C., Fung, A. T., Chiu, H. K., … Chan, W. M. (2010). Combined clinical and cognitive criteria to identify mild cognitive impairment in a Southern Chinese community. *Alzheimer Disease and Associated Disorders, 24*(4), 343–347. doi:10.1097/WAD.0b013e3181eb2f42

Lee, J., Lee, D., Cho, S., Na, D. L., Jeon, H., Kim, S., … Cho, M. (2008). Brief screening for mild cognitive impairment in elderly outpatient clinic: Validation of the Korean version of the montreal cognitive assessment. *Journal of Geriatric Psychiatry and Neurology, 21*(2), 104–110.

Lim, W., Chin, J., Lam, C., Lim, P., & Sahadevan, S. (2005). Clinical dementia rating: Experience of a multi-racial Asian population. *Alzheimer Disease and Associated Disorders, 19*(3), 135–142. doi:10.1097/01.wad.0000174991.60709.36.

Lim, W. S., Chong, M., & Sahadevan, S. (2007). Utility of the clinical dementia rating in Asian populations. *Clinical Medicine and Research, 5*(1), 61–70.

Limpawattana, P., Tiamkao, S., Sawanyawisuth, K., & Thinkhamrop, B. (2012). Can Rowland Universal Dementia Assessment Scale (RUDAS) Replace Mini-Mental State Examination (MMSE) for Dementia Screening in a Thai Geriatric Outpatient Setting? *American Journal of Alzheimer's Disease & Other Dementias, 27*(4), 254–259.

Lin, K.-N., Wang, P.-N., Liu, C.-Y., Chen, W.-T., Lee, Y.-C., & Liu, H.-C. (2002). Cutoff scores of the Cognitive Abilities Screening Instrument, Chinese version in screening of dementia. *Dementia and Geriatric Cognitive Disorders, 14*(4), 176–182. doi:10.1159/000066024.

Lou, M., Dai, Y., Huang, G., & Yu, P. (2007). Identifying the most efficient items from the Mini-Mental State Examination for cognitive function assessment in older Taiwanese patients. *Journal of Clinical Nursing, 16*(3), 502–508.

Lu, R., Luo, Z., & Liu, X. (2000). Reliability and validity of the Cognitive Abilities Screening Instrument C-2.0 (CASI) used in elderly people in Chengdu, China. *Chinese Journal of Clinical Psychology, 8*(2), 70–71, 69.

Lu, J., Li, D., Li, F., Zhou, A., Wang, F., Zuo, X., … Jia, J. (2011). Montreal Cognitive Assessment in detecting cognitive impairment in Chinese elderly individuals: A population-based study. *Journal of Geriatric Psychiatry and Neurology, 24*(4), 184–190. doi:10.1177/0891988711422528

Luis, C. A., Keegan, A. P., & Mullan, M. (2009). Cross validation of the Montreal Cognitive Assessment in community dwelling older adults residing in the Southeastern US. *International Journal of Geriatric Psychiatry, 24*(2), 197–201.

Meyers, L. (2006). Asian-American mental health. *APA Monitor on Psychology, 37*(2), 44.

Morris, J. C. (1993). The Clinical Dementia Rating (CDR): Current version and scoring rules. *Neurology, 43*(11), 2412–2414.

Mu, N., Lu, Y., Feng, R., Fang, S., Zhou, W., & Jiang, M. (2000). Application of the revised Hasagawa's Dementia Scale (HDS-R) in screening senile dementia in coastal rural areas of Guangdong province. *Chinese Mental Health Journal, 14*(3), 164–166.

Nasreddine, Z. S., Phillips, N. A., Bedirian, V. V., Charbonneau, S. S., Whitehead, V. V., Collin, I. I., … EBRSR Research, G. P. (2011). *Montreal cognitive assessment*. Retrieved from Www.Ebrsr.Com.

Ng, T., Niti, M., Chiam, P., & Kua, E. (2007). Ethnic and educational differences in cognitive test performance on mini-mental state examination in Asians. *The American Journal of Geriatric Psychiatry, 15*(2), 130–139.

Nie, K., Zhang, Y., Wang, L., Zhao, J., Huang, Z., Gan, R., … Wang, L. (2012). A pilot study of psychometric properties of the Beijing version of Montreal Cognitive Assessment in patients with idiopathic Parkinson's disease in China. *Journal of Clinical Neuroscience, 19*(11), 1497–1500

Park, J., & Kwon, Y. (1990). Modification of the mini-mental state examination for use in the elderly in a non-western society: Part I. Development of Korean version of mini-mental state examination. *International Journal of Geriatric Psychiatry, 5*(6), 381–387.

Park, J., Park, Y., & Ko, H. N. (1991). Modification of the mini-mental state examination for use in the elderly in a non-western society: Part II. Cutoff points and their diagnostic validities. *International Journal of Geriatric Psychiatry, 6*(12), 875–882.

Phanthumchinda, K., Jitapunkul, S., Sitthi-Amorn, C., Bunnag, S. C., & Ebrahim, S. (1991). Prevalence of dementia in an urban slum population in Thailand: Validity of screening methods. *International Journal of Geriatric Psychiatry, 6*(9), 639–646.

Sahadevan, S., Lim, P., Tan, N., & Chan, S. (2000). Diagnostic performance of two mental status tests in the older Chinese: Influence of education and age on cut-off values. *International Journal of Geriatric Psychiatry, 15*(3), 234–241.

Seul-Ki, J., Ki-Hyun, C., & Jae-Min, K. (2004). The usefulness of the Korean version of modified Mini-Mental State Examination (K-mMMSE) for dementia screening in community dwelling elderly people. *BMC Public Health, 4*, 31–37.

Shiba, M., Shimogaito, J., Kose, A., Fujiuchi, S., Nishiyama, H., Yoshimasu, F., … Rocca, W. A. (1999). Prevalence of dementia in the rural village of Hanazono-mura, Japan. *Neuroepidemiology, 18*(1), 32–36.

Shyu, Y. I., & Yip, P. K. (2001). Factor structure and explanatory variables of the Mini-Mental State Examination (MMSE) for elderly persons in Taiwan. *Journal of Formosa Medical Association, 100*, 676–683.

Smith, T., Gildeh, N., & Holmes, C. (2007). The montreal cognitive assessment: Validity and utility in a memory clinic setting. *Canadian Journal of Psychiatry, 52*(5), 329–332.

Spreen, O., & Strauss, E. (1998). *A compendium of neuropsychological tests: Administration, norms, and commentary* (2nd ed.). New York, NY: Oxford University Press.

Tangwongchai, S., Charernboon, T., Phanasathit, M., Akkayagorn, L., Hemrungrojn, S., Phanthumchinda, K., Nasreddine, Z. S. The Validity of Thai version of the Montreal Cognitive Assessment (MoCA-T), Presented at the International Psychogeriatric Association Conference, Sept. 2009, Montreal, QC, Canada

Teng, E. L., Hasegawa, K., Homma, A., Imai, Y., Larson, E., Graves, A., … White, L. R. (1994). The Cognitive Abilities Screening Instrument (CASI): A practical test for cross-cultural epidemiological studies of dementia. *International Psychogeriatrics, 6(1)*, 45–58.

Tsai, C.-F., Lee, W.-J., Wang, S.-J., Shia, B.-C., Nasreddine, Z., & Fuh, J.-L. (2012). Psychometrics of the Montreal Cognitive Assessment (MoCA) and its subscales: Validation of the Taiwanese version of the MoCA and an item response theory analysis. *International Psychogeriatrics, 24*(4), 651–658. doi:10.1017/S1041610211002298.

Tsai, R.-C., Lin, K.-N., Wu, K.-Y., & Liu, H.-C. (2004). Improving the screening power of the Cognitive Abilities Screening Instrument, Chinese version. *Dementia and Geriatric Cognitive Disorders, 18*(3–4), 314–320. doi:10.1159/000080125.

Tse, C. S., Chang, J. F., Leung, G. Y., Fung, A. T., Hau, K. T., Chiu, H. K., et al. (2013). Effects of education on very mild dementia among Chinese people in Hong Kong: Potential mediators in the Cantonese Mini-Mental State Examination tasks. *Aging & Mental Health, 17*(3), 310–318.

Tsuboi, K., Harada, T., Ishii, T., Ishizaki, F., Nitta, Y., & Nitta, K. (2009). Evaluation of correlations between a simple touch panel method and conventional methods for dementia screening in the elderly. *International Medical Journal, 16*(3), 175–179.

Tsukamoto, R., Akisaki, T., Kuranaga, M., Takata, T., Yokono, K., & Sakurai, T. (2009). Hasegawa Dementia Scale – Revised, for screening of early Alzheimer's disease in the elderly with type 2 diabetes. *Geriatrics & Gerontology International, 9*(2), 213–215. doi:10.1111/j.1447-0594.2009.00524.x.

U.S. Census Bureau. (2000). *Profiles of general demographic characteristics*. Retrieved from http://www2.census.gov/census_2000/datasets/demographic_profile/0_United_States/2kh00.pdf

Wong, G., Lam, S., Wong, A., Ngai, K., Poon, W., & Mok, V. (2013). Comparison of Montreal cognitive assessment and mini-mental state examination in evaluating cognitive domain deficit following aneurysmal subarachnoid haemorrhage. *PLoS One, 8*(4), 1–7.

Wong, G., Ngai, K., Lam, S., Wong, A., Mok, V., & Poon, W. (2013). Validity of the Montreal Cognitive Assessment for traumatic brain injury patients with intracranial haemorrhage. *Brain Injury, 27*(4), 394–398. doi:10.3109/02699052.2012.750746.

Wong, A., Xiong, Y. Y., Kwan, P. L., Chan, A. Y., Lam, W. M., Wang, K., ... Mok, V. T. (2009). The validity, reliability and clinical utility of the Hong Kong Montreal Cognitive Assessment (HK-MoCA) in patients with cerebral small vessel disease. *Dementia and Geriatric Cognitive Disorders*, *28*(1), 81–87. doi:10.1159/000232589

Xu, G., Meyer, J., Huang, Y., & Du, F. (2003). Adapting Mini-Mental State Examination for dementia screening among illiterate or minimally educated elderly Chinese. *International Journal of Geriatric Psychiatry, 18*(7), 609–616.

Yamamoto, N., Ishizawa, K., Ishikawa, M., Yamanaka, G., Yamanaka, T., Murakami, S., ... Otsuka, K. (2012). Cognitive function with subclinical hypothyroidism in elderly people without dementia: One year follow up. *Geriatrics & Gerontology International, 12*(1), 164–165. doi: 10.1111/j.1447-0594.2011.00727.x

Yano, K., Grove, J. S., Masaki, K. H., White, L. R., Petrovitch, H., Chen, R., ... Curb, J. D. (2000). The effects of childhood residence in Japan and testing language on cognitive performance in late life among Japanese American men in Hawaii. *Journal of the American Geriatrics Society, 48*(2), 199–204.

Yu, J., Li, J., & Huang, X. (2012). The Beijing version of the Montreal cognitive assessment as a brief screening tool for mild cognitive impairment: A community-based study. *BMC Psychiatry, 12*(1), 156–163.

Zhang, M., Katzman, R., Salmon, D. P., Jin, H., Cai, G., Wang, Z., ... Liu, W. T. (1990). The prevalence of dementia and Alzheimer's disease in Shanghai, China: Impact of age, gender, and education. *Annals of Neurology*, *27*(4), 428–437.

Zhang, L., & Liu, X. (2008). Determination of the cut-off point of the Chinese version of the Montreal Cognitive Assessment among Chinese elderly in Guangzhou. *Chinese Mental Health Journal, 22*(2), 123–125.

Assessing for Schizophrenia in Asian Americans

20

Daryl E.M. Fujii, Vince Tsushima, Jessica Murakami-Brundage, and Vidya Kamath

Introduction

Schizophrenia is a severe and persistent mental illness afflicting approximately 1 % of the population. It is characterized by positive symptoms such as hallucination, delusions, and disorganized thinking; negative symptoms such as avolition and affect flattening (American Psychiatric Association, 2000); and cognitive deficits most prominent for memory, attention, and executive functioning (Heinrichs & Zakzanis, 1998). The general course of schizophrenia includes a prodrome phase that lasts between 2 and 5 years before the onset of a full-blown presentation of symptoms (Häfner, Riecher-Rössler, Maurer, Fätkenheuer, & Löffler, 1992). Treatment for schizophrenia involves both antipsychotic medications and psychosocial interventions that target improving insight into illness, developing skills for independent living, minimizing negative symptoms, maximizing cognitive and social functioning, educating family, and providing support with an overall goal of maximizing quality of life and restoring functioning (Tandon, Nasrallah, & Keshavan, 2010).

Assessment and formal testing are important for diagnosis, monitoring symptoms, and treatment planning. Schizophrenia is typically diagnosed through clinical interview using Diagnostic and Statistical Manual-IV (DSM-IV; American Psychiatric Association, 2000) or International Statistical Classification of Diseases and Related Health Problems (ICD-10; World Health Organization, 2010) criteria. However, other formal tools such as the Structured Clinical Interview for DSM-IV (SCID; First, Spitzer, Gibbon, & Williams, 2002), Structured Interview for Prodrome Symptoms (Miller et al., 2002), Positive and Negative Symptom Scale (PANSS; Kay, Fiszbein, & Opler, 1987), and Brief Psychotic Rating Scale (BPRS; Overall & Gorham, 1962) are also utilized for research purposes, tracking the course of illness, and measuring treatment effectiveness. Other assessment tools measuring moderating factors such as insight into illness (McEvoy et al., 1989), neurocognition, violence risk (Webster, Douglas, Eaves, & Hart, 1997), and

D.E.M. Fujii, Ph.D (✉)
ABPP-CN, Veterans Affairs, Pacific Island Health Care Services Community Living Center, 459 Patterson Road, Honolulu, HI 96819-1522, USA
e-mail: dfujii07@gmail.com

V. Tsushima, Ph.D., J.D.
Department of Psychology, Hawaii Pacific University, Honolulu, HI 96813, USA
e-mail: vtsushima@hpu.edu

J. Murakami-Brundage, Ph.D.
Department of Psychiatry, Aaron T. Beck Psychopathology Research Center, University of Pennsylvania, 3535 Market St., Rm 3063, Philadelphia, PA 19107, USA
e-mail: jemuraka@mail.med.upenn.edu

V. Kamath, Ph.D
Neuropsychiatry Section, Department of Psychiatry, Perelman School of Medicine, University of Pennsylvania, 3400 Spruce Street, 10 Gates Pavilion, Philadelphia, PA 19104, USA
e-mail: kamathv@mail.med.upenn.edu

L.T. Benuto et al. (eds.), *Guide to Psychological Assessment with Asians*,
DOI 10.1007/978-1-4939-0796-0_20,

quality of life (Frisch, Cornell, Villanueva, & Retzlaff, 1992) are also useful for providing information for targeting specific symptoms to improve functional outcome.

Assessing Asian Americans with schizophrenia (AAS) can be very challenging. First, there is limited research on cultural factors specific to Asian Americans on assessment measures. Translating measures is also not a straightforward process. Asian languages have different grammatical structures from European languages, which can considerably alter how questions are interpreted (Ertan & Eker, 2000). In addition, certain cultures do not use medical terminology to describe mental states which can prevent accurate assessment of the patient's symptoms (Aggarwal, 2007).

Second, cultural factors are complicated by the diversity within the Asian American population. For example, the US Census Bureau recognizes over 20 different ethnicities as Asian (Hoeffel, Rastogi, Kim, & Shahid, 2012). AAS differ in acculturation and generation in the United States as well as English proficiency (Reeves & Bennett, 2004). Factors such as educational level, migration history, traumatic history, socioeconomic status, and access to care also differ between Asian groups within the United States. Each of these factors can impact the assessment and treatment of schizophrenia. Recent migration, for example, is associated with mental health problems (Lauber & Rossler, 2007), and an increased risk of schizophrenia has been found among first- and second-generation immigrants (Weiser et al., 2008).

In addition, the expression of emotions varies across cultures (Abu-Lughod & Lutz, 1990). Emotional restraint tends to be highly valued in Asian cultures (Sue & Sue, 1999). This is particularly relevant to diagnostic assessments for schizophrenia in which clinicians often use behavioral observation to rate factors such as emotional expression, insight, and agitation levels. It has also been noted that the doctor–patient relationship varies across cultures and can impact self-report; endorsement of symptomatology could be impacted in Asian cultures, where patients are expected to obey their families and physicians (Tsai, 2001). Finally, the assessment of schizophrenia has proved to be challenging in Asian American populations due to the stigma of mental illness within Asian American families.

The purpose of this chapter is to identify and describe cultural issues related to assessment of AAS and to make recommendations for testing. Specifically, we focus on diagnosis, presentation, and moderating variables known to have predictive validity for outcome and quality of life. This chapter is organized in the following sections: (1) presentation of schizophrenia in Asians and Asian Americans, (2) diagnostic assessment issues for treatment with a focus on test validity, and (3) assessment recommendations. We conclude with an illustrative case study. Within each section, we attempt to review the literature on Asian Americans and Asians and parse out diversity issues with individual ethnicities. Given the number of Asian ethnicities, our focus will be on the most common Asian ethnicities in the United States including Chinese, Filipino, Asian Indian, Vietnamese, and other Southeast Asians, Korean, and Japanese.

Presentation of Schizophrenia

Research has consistently demonstrated that early intervention leads to a better prognosis in schizophrenia, which appears to apply to AAS (Yamazawa et al., 2008). Unfortunately, many AAS delay seeking treatment (Lin & Cheung, 1999), thus entering into mental health treatment only after a substantial duration of untreated psychosis. Lin, Inui, and Kleinman (1982) reported that Asians sought mental health services for schizophrenia an average of 3 years after the onset of psychotic symptoms. This duration of untreated psychosis was about three times longer than Whites and twice as long as for Blacks. Given delays, it is not surprising that on average, AAS present with more severe symptoms that require longer hospitalizations (Lin & Cheung, 1999). In line with this, emergency rooms are often the first point of contact in the pathway to mental healthcare (Archie et al., 2010).

Not all AAS, however, delay treatment. Okazaki (2000) found that AAS who sought treatment within 6 months of the onset of symptoms demonstrated more violent and suicidal behaviors and also had families reporting lower levels of shame and stigma. Once Asian Americans present for their initial evaluation, it is reasonable to assess them for schizophrenia using our current diagnostic system.

Although it is not clear whether and how individual diagnostic criteria may be relevant to Asian populations (Krishnadas, Moore, Nayak, & Patel, 2007; Lin, Hwu, & Tsuang, 2012), the DSM conceptualization of schizophrenia appears to be relevant for these groups. A study by Flaskerud and Hu (1992) examined the relationship among White, Black, Latino, and Asian clients of the Los Angeles County mental health system. In a large sample of adult inpatient and outpatient clients seen in county mental health facilities between January 1983 and August 1988, they found that ethnicity had a significant and consistent relationship with diagnosis, with Black and Asian clients receiving more diagnoses of schizophrenia and other psychoses than Whites and Latinos receiving fewer of these diagnoses than Whites. Filipinos, Koreans, and Southeast Asians had particularly high percentages of psychotic diagnoses. It is unclear whether Asians were overdiagnosed with psychotic disorders or whether Asians were more likely to meet the criteria for psychotic disorders in this sample. However, it is reasonable to assume that Asians are being diagnosed with schizophrenia and other similar disorders in the United States at rates comparable to other racial groups using our current diagnostic system.

Cross-Cultural Similarities and Differences in Schizophrenia Symptoms

The current presumption is that the schizophrenia symptom profile for Asians is similar to Western populations. However, delusional content, context, and significance vary across ethnic/cultural groups (Bhavsar & Bhugra, 2008; Lin et al., 2012), and cross-cultural factors play a role in the development and threshold of hallucinations (Al-Issa, 1995; Lin et al., 2012). Kim et al. (1993) conducted a transcultural study of schizophrenic delusions among Koreans in Seoul, Korea, and Korean-Chinese and Chinese in Yanbian, China. They found significant differences in delusional themes among the three cultural groups, which could be explained by sociocultural and political factors. For example, delusions about "family" and "love affairs" were most frequent in Koreans, and this may be related to strong family ties among Koreans and the recent liberation from traditional sexual rigidity and suppression. Meanwhile, delusions of "political themes" were most frequent in Korean-Chinese, and these may be related to their being dominated culturally by North Korea's communist regime and politically by China's communist government. This study illustrates how a person's cultural context may influence the manifestation of their psychotic experiences.

Another study conducted by Lee, Chong, Chan, and Sathyadevan (2004) examined the nature of the command hallucinations among Asian schizophrenia inpatients in Singapore and found rates of compliance (62 %) similar to rates found in Western samples. Patients experiencing violent command hallucinations were less likely to comply in contrast to those experiencing nonviolent command hallucinations. The participants who were able to ignore command hallucinations used various coping methods, especially prayer. In addition to assessing the content of command hallucinations, this study illustrates the importance of assessing beliefs about voices and coping strategies, which may be particularly significant for AAS with strong religious backgrounds; religious beliefs can both increase or decrease a person's willingness to comply with his/her auditory hallucinations.

Further research is needed to identify how Asian cultures influence the development and maintenance of delusions and hallucinations. For example, are AAS more likely to experience somatic delusions? Additionally, research is needed to determine how Asian cultures influence the development and maintenance of negative symptoms and disorganization in schizophrenia. Research is also needed to understand how Asian cultural values (e.g., deference to authority) influence the interpretation of these symptoms and a person's relationship with their symptoms (e.g., auditory hallucinations).

Cross-Cultural Similarities and Differences in Neurocognition

Studies indicate that neurocognition accounts for between 20 and 60 % of the variance in outcome of persons with schizophrenia (for a review see Kurtz, 2012); thus, this is an important area for evaluation. In general, neurocognitive deficits appear to be similar in Asian and non-Asian samples. However, the impact of these deficits varies by culture. In a study of Indian patients with schizophrenia, Krishnadas et al. (2007) found significant deficits on tests of attention, concentration, verbal and visual memory, and tests of frontal lobe/executive functions compared to matched controls, which is similar to what has been found in Western studies. However, they did not find a statistically significant relationship between cognitive function and scores on a disability scale, in contrast to studies of Western samples. Sociocultural factors, such as family assumption of patient care, may lessen the impact of these deficits on a person's daily life. However, neurocognitive deficits have been associated with poorer quality of life in Japanese and Singaporeans with schizophrenia (Matsui, Sumiyoshi, Arai, Higuchi, & Kurachi, 2008; Woon, Chia, Chan, & Sim, 2010), medication adherence in Japanese with schizophrenia (Maeda et al., 2006), and social functioning in Chinese with schizophrenia (Zhu et al., 2007).

Further, neuropsychological deficits may also contribute to worse social disability for some AAS (Yang et al., 2012). Western-language patients with schizophrenia demonstrate tonal deficits; however, language processing is minimally affected. Meanwhile, Mandarin-speaking patients use syllables, which are voiced in different tones, with word meaning varying accordingly. Yang et al. (2012) investigated whether schizophrenia tonal deficits would impair Mandarin language performance in patients with schizophrenia compared to healthy controls. Results showed that the patient group was significantly lower on tone-matching and distorted tunes as well as word discrimination and word identification. Moreover, tonally impaired patients had "lower status" jobs overall when compared with tonally intact patients. This study illustrates how common symptoms of schizophrenia can interact with unique characteristics of specific Asian cultures to moderate levels of disability.

Cross-Cultural Similarities and Differences in Substance Abuse and Suicide

In addition to assessing the core symptoms of schizophrenia in AAS, it is also important to be aware of cultural differences in problems frequently associated with schizophrenia, specifically for substance abuse and suicide. Studies with Western patients with schizophrenia typically show a strong relationship between schizophrenia and substance use, which may be less pronounced in Asians. Thara et al. (2009) examined the clinical characteristics of a diagnostically and ethnically homogenous schizophrenia sample from Tamil Nadu, India. The investigators found that none of the affected participants had used illicit drugs such as cannabis, amphetamine, and cocaine; only 1.1 % reported alcohol abuse/dependence, and only 12.4 % had ever smoked. These findings may have been due to the fact that an overwhelming majority of affected individuals lived with family members, which may reduce financial autonomy and the freedom to purchase and use substances. Similar studies have demonstrated a lower rate of substance abuse in Asians diagnosed with schizophrenia compared to white samples (McLean et al., 2012; Verma, Subramaniam, Chong, & Kua, 2002).

Research has also found some possible differences in the relationship between schizophrenia and suicide among Asian patients. Unlike almost every other country, the prevalence of schizophrenia and suicide in China is higher in women than in men, which may be due to the overall lower rates of substance abuse in China (Phillips, Yang, Li, & Li, 2004). Other risk factors for suicide in Western samples with psychosis, such as a history of depression or a diagnosis of schizophrenia, were not found to be related to suicide in an Indian sample with schizophrenia (Bhatia et al., 2006). In another study, Xiang, Weng, Leung, Tang, and Ungvari (2007) found that the lifetime prevalence of suicide attempts in Chinese outpatients with schizophrenia differed between Hong Kong and Beijing samples, 20 % and 33.6 %, respectively. The authors noted that Hong Kong is a cosmopolitan city with a Western social structure and mental health system, while Beijing demonstrates more traditional Chinese values with a less well-developed mental health system.

Overall, when assessing AAS, it is important to assess for suicidality, even in the absence of the usual risk factors, such as substance abuse. Although the symptom profile of AASs may be generally similar to Western schizophrenia patients, there may be substantial differences in the development, interpretation, and consequences of specific symptoms.

Further Areas of Assessment

Besides symptoms and neurocognition, Asian culture influences a number of other important areas for assessment in AAS, including—but not limited to—treatment-seeking behavior/engagement, etiological models of illness, family dynamics and involvement, treatment preferences (e.g., the use of complementary and alternative medicine), stigma (including self-stigma), and religious beliefs, which impact not only the content of hallucinations and delusions but also the ways in which AAS interpret and respond to their unusual experiences. We highlight three of these areas below: etiological models, family involvement, and the use of complementary and alternative medicine.

Etiological Models

AAS' explanations for their unusual experiences impact whether or not they seek treatment and from whom. When AAS encounter the mental health system, whether voluntarily or involuntarily, their illness explanations influence their treatment engagement. For example, a genetic and biological explanation of illness may increase a patient's willingness to take medications. Conversely, it may also increase the patient's hopelessness if they do not respond to medication and may make it less likely that they will engage in psychosocial treatments. Because etiological explanations of illness directly impact a patient's behavior (e.g., treatment adherence, willingness to comply with voices), it is important to assess how persons explain the cause of their unusual experiences and their strength of conviction in their explanations. Research in Asian countries offers some clues as to the etiological models that AAS may hold, especially those who recently emigrated from these countries.

Saravanan et al. (2007) examined the explanatory models among first episode patients with schizophrenia in South India. Their findings demonstrated that the majority of patients (70 %) considered spiritual and mystical factors as the cause of their schizophrenia, and 22 % had multiple models of illness. Other studies of non-patient samples have not found such high rates of spiritual or mystical explanations of illness. For example, Furnham and Chan (2004) compared British and Chinese young people's beliefs about the manifestations, causes, and cures of schizophrenia. Chinese participants endorsed more negative attitudes and beliefs about schizophrenia than the British. Also, the Chinese tended to use a sociological model to explain the etiology of schizophrenia. There were no group differences in the endorsement of superstitious beliefs to explain schizophrenia symptoms. The lack of group differences regarding superstitious beliefs may have been due to the younger age of the sample and the fact that the Chinese participants came from Hong Kong, which is less traditional than mainland China.

Similarly, Swami, Furnham, Kannan, and Sinniah (2008) examined the beliefs about causation and treatment of schizophrenia among Malay, Chinese, and Kadazan-Dusun participants in Kota Kinabalu, Malaysia. Their results showed that Malaysians tended to favor social-environmental explanations of schizophrenia.

Specifically, Malay participants more strongly endorsed that schizophrenia has a social cause and that treatment should be focused on changes on a societal level. However, they also endorsed a belief in the effectiveness of mental hospitals. The authors speculated that these results were due to recent government initiatives to improve mental healthcare in Malaysia, which, among other things, has combated the once prevalent view that schizophrenia is due to supernatural forces.

Interestingly, Asian American caregivers may demonstrate different beliefs about schizophrenia than Asians from Asia. Kung (2004) interviewed Chinese American caregivers in Los Angeles who cared for relatives suffering from schizophrenia and found that they endorsed biological and stress explanations for schizophrenia. Of those who cited to stress-related causes, over half referenced familial stressors, reflecting the sociocentric culture and centrality of family. Supernatural causes were subscribed to the least. Higher acculturation was also found to be positively associated with biological attributions of the illness. Caregivers with this attribution are more in line with the beliefs of service providers, which increased the likelihood of mental health service utilization. Another study found that Chinese Americans were more likely than European Americans to attribute genetic explanations for mental illness (WonPat-Borja, Yang, Link, & Phelan, 2012). Of note, genetic attribution actually appeared to be destigmatizing among Chinese Americans while it increased stigma or made no difference among European Americans.

Due to the diversity of beliefs within Asian populations, it is misleading to generalize AAS' etiological models of illness based on a few studies. What these studies illustrate is the need to evaluate each patient's explanations of illness and to explore the consequences of these beliefs with each patient. It is not accurate to assume that AAS will endorse superstitious explanations of their illness. Once the patient's explanations are elicited, it is possible to use this information to guide treatment decisions. For example, patients who endorse a socio-environmental explanation of their illness (e.g., family stress) may particularly benefit from family interventions.

Family Involvement/Issues

A thorough assessment of AAS includes questions related to family involvement and dynamics. Although one study found that Chinese relatives of individuals with schizophrenia expressed fewer critical comments and less emotional over-involvement (i.e., expressed emotion) in comparison to Western family members (Ran, Leff, Hou, Xiang, & Chan, 2003), family stress may be particularly distressing for some AAS who value maintaining harmony and avoidance of loss of face (i.e., social shame). Whenever possible (e.g., during family visits in inpatient settings), it is helpful to observe family dynamics and to inquire about patient's interactions with their family members. For example, one AAS inpatient reported that his voices became more aggressive after his visits with family members, and he appeared more agitated for days afterward. The patient subsequently reported that he believed that his family members had been replaced with "imposters." Since the patient lived with his parents, it was necessary to address these beliefs in order for him to return home.

Assessment of family dynamics is also helpful with treatment planning. Bae and Brekke (2002) suggested that interventions designed to foster family relationships and involve families in a collaborative effort may be more appropriate for Asian Americans because of the interdependent nature of their family dynamics (*see* Lin & Cheung, 1999). They also argued that it is imperative that the cultural congruence of interventions to improve social functioning be assessed before they are applied to Asian groups. In support of family involvement in treatment, Kennedy, Schepp, and Rangruangkonkit (2008) conducted a qualitative study with a Chinese, Korean, and Lao family, in the United States, who had a child with schizophrenia in a community-based, family-centered, self-management intervention program, and found that Asian American parents valued participating in the group intervention and realizing their similarities with non-Asian American families with a mentally ill youth.

In general, the research shows that Asian schizophrenia patients and their families prefer to have the families involved in treatment, particularly in residential treatment. This suggests that treatment issues, such as discussion of the patient's diagnosis, medication, and treatment goals and objectives, should incorporate the family members and take into account the context of the family dwelling, neighborhood, and family-related practices (e.g., worship, recreation). Even when caregiver burden is high, Asians may still prefer the care of family members to non-family members (Hanzawa et al., 2010). Family involvement may be considered as a strength of AAS. The finding that outcomes for schizophrenia in developing countries, including China and India, tend to be better than for that in developed countries (Cohen, Patel, Thara, & Gureje, 2008; Hopper & Wanderling, 2000; Sartorius, Gulbinat, Harrison, Laska, & Siegel, 1996) has been attributed the greater tolerance for and acceptance of individuals with schizophrenia by family and community members in developing countries (Leff, Sartorius, Jablensky, Korten, & Ernberg, 1992) as well as lower rates of expressed emotions from family members (Leff et al., 1990).

Complementary and Alternative Medicine

Finally, it is important to assess for the use of complementary and alternative medicine, especially in less acculturated AAS and recent immigrants. Wong and Xuesong (2011) examined schizophrenia-related knowledge and preferences about professional help, medication, and treatment among Chinese living in Shanghai, China, as compared to Chinese living in Melbourne, Australia, and Hong Kong. Although a far lower percentage of Shanghai Chinese endorsed the use of counseling professionals, a much higher percentage endorsed the use of Chinese medical doctors and herbal medication. However, a higher percentage of Shanghai Chinese endorsed the use of psychiatric treatment and the traditional Chinese practices of nutritious diet and supplements than the other two groups of Chinese. The authors noted that mainland Chinese do not see traditional Chinese medicine and Western medicine as incompatible, and it is not uncommon to adopt both types of medical approaches in treating illnesses. However, they tend to believe that Chinese medicine is useful in maintaining health and preventing illness from occurring.

Cultural factors may also direct Asian schizophrenia patients towards initially utilizing traditional and culturally based remedies. Tang, Sevigny, Mao, Jiang, and Cai (2007) found that a majority of inpatients with schizophrenia in Beijing sought help from at least one type of non-psychiatric facility (NPF), including acupuncturists and "qigong" masters or other folk healers. Among the reasons for seeking treatment from NPFs, the most common ones included feeling shameful or stigmatized about going to psychiatric hospitals, inaccessibility to or unavailability of psychiatric hospitals, and fear of being incarcerated or receiving electric shock treatment. Similar studies have also found that the use of traditional medicine is perceived as less stigmatizing than Western mental health treatment (Higgins, Dey-Ghatak, & Davey, 2007; Raguram, Raghu, Vounatsou, & Weiss, 2004).

While the use of complementary and alternative medicine is not contraindicated for schizophrenia—indeed, there is some evidence that the use of Chinese herbal medicine is beneficial when combined with antipsychotic medication (Rathbone et al., 2007)—it is important for medical professionals to be aware of any supplements that may interfere or provide a catalyst for antipsychotic medications. Also, patients may choose to discontinue Western treatments in favor of traditional treatments without informing their providers, and this may be harmful to patients, especially if tapering of medication does not occur.

Summary

On the matter of the presentation of schizophrenia in Asians or Asian Americans, current research indicates that Asian schizophrenia patients may differ in terms of delusions/hallucinations, neuropsychological functioning, substance abuse, suicide, and outcome.

Cultural factors also affect beliefs about schizophrenia, treatment seeking and engagement, family engagement, and utilization of traditional remedies. The aforesaid clearly have ramifications for the assessment of Asian schizophrenia patients and the particular tests and measurements which may be used to evaluate Asians suffering from schizophrenia.

Assessment Measures

Diagnosis

Clinical Interviews. There is significant heterogeneity in the presentation of schizophrenia with some individuals showing predominantly positive symptoms, predominantly negative symptoms, or a mixture of both positive and negative symptoms. Several semi-structured clinical interviews have been developed to assess whether an individual meets diagnostic criteria for schizophrenia in Asian populations. The Structured Clinical Interview for DSM-IV-R, the Composite International Diagnostic Interview for ICD-10 (CIDI), Schedules for Clinical Assessment in Neuropsychiatry (SCAN), and the Schedule for Affective Disorders and Schizophrenia (SADS) are the most widely used structured clinical interview assessment tools. The most popular among these measures is the Structured Clinical Interview for DSM-IV Axis I Disorders (SCID-I), which bases its questions off the diagnostic criteria in the Diagnostic and Statistical Manual of Mental Disorders, Fourth Edition, Text Revision (DSM-IV-TR; American Psychiatric Association, 2000). The SCID-I has been shown to be both a reliable measure for determining if an individual meets the criteria for an Axis I DSM-IV-TR diagnosis when compared with the "gold standard" of consensus diagnosis (Ventura et al., 1998). The SCID has been translated into several languages for use with Asian American populations, including Chinese (So et al. 2003), Japanese (Osone & Takahashi, 2003), and Korean (Hahn et al., 2000). The SCAN also has a Chinese equivalent (Cheng et al., 2001).

The Diagnostic Interview for Genetic Studies (DIGS) is another structured clinical interview that was developed in 1994 by the National Institute of Mental Health (NIMH). The DIGS allows the clinician to extract multiple psychiatric diagnoses according to different diagnostic systems. Furthermore, the DIGS was designed for comprehensive assessment of illness course, chronology, and comorbidity. It is particularly useful when assessing families because the same assessment tool can be used across families allowing for greater reliability and standardization in the assessment process. The DIGS has been translated into Hindi (Deshpande et al., 1998), Japanese, Chinese, and Korean (Joo et al. 2004), with studies indicating good reliability and validity between the DIGS and its translations.

Other structured interviews include the Early Signs Scale (Birchwood et al. 1989), which has been translated into Japanese (Koichi & Miyamoto, 2011), and the Composite Diagnostic Interview (CIDI) Schedule which was used in the National Latino and Asian American Study (NLAAS), an epidemiological study evaluating for mental health service utilization in the United States, although results for psychotic illness were not reported (Takeuchi et al., 2007). The CIDI has been translated into more than 25 languages, including Arabic, Japanese, Cantonese, Chinese, Hindi, Italian, Japanese, Korean, Mandarin, and Nepali. The Schedule for Affective Disorders and Schizophrenia was developed by Endicott and Spitzer (1978) based on research diagnostic criteria outlined in Spitzer, Endicott, and Robins (1978). The authors can be contacted for available versions in over ten languages.

It is notable that several of these interviews contain hundreds of questions and often require 1–2 h to conduct. This can prove to be difficult with patients that have attention problems or are experiencing agitation or when clinicians have limited time for assessment. The Mini-International Neuropsychiatric Interview (MINI) is one alternative that has been developed which allows for briefer assessment of psychiatric diagnosis (Sheehan et al., 1998). This measure has been translated to over 50 languages including

Japanese (Otsubo et al., 2005), Arabic (Kadri et al., 2005), Korean (Yoo et al., 2006), Punjabi, Tamil, Telugu, Bengali, Gujarati, Hindi, Kannada, Malayalam, Marathi, Urdu, and Chinese.

Prodromal Measures. Interventions early in the course of the illness can have a profound impact on public health costs and functional disability associated with the development of schizophrenia. This is not possible without valid and reliable methods to identify young people who are at risk for conversion to psychosis. The "ultrahigh" risk strategy (McGorry, Yung, & Phillips, 2003; Phillips, Yung, & McGorry, 2000) is one method that helps determine youths with sub-psychotic or "prodromal" symptoms that are severe enough to prompt clinical referral and have a relatively high rate of conversion to psychosis (Cannon et al., 2008). Structured interview measures (akin to the SCID and DIGS) were developed to diagnose youths at risk for psychosis. For example, the Comprehensive Assessment of At-Risk Mental States (CAARMS) and the Structured Interview for Prodromal Syndromes (SIPS) are two face-to-face clinical interviews that can be used with at-risk populations. The SIPS has been translated to Korean (Jung et al., 2010).

Screening questionnaires are another alternative that can be preferable because they allow for rapid and efficient delineation of those who need further assessment via clinical interview. They also allow for a community-based screening approach where large cohorts can be screened quickly. The PRIME Screen questionnaire for prodromal symptoms (PS-R) was developed to screen for prodromal symptomatology using items derived from the SIPS. However, translated versions of these scales are available for use in individuals speaking Japanese (Kobayashi et al., 2008). A Chinese version of the Prodromal Questionnaire is also available (Chiu, Hwu, Shiau, Yao, & Hsieh, 2010).

Presentation

Schizophrenia Symptoms. The Positive and Negative Symptom Scale is a 30-item rating instrument to assess negative and positive symptoms in schizophrenia and measure treatment response (von Knorring & Lindstrom, 1995), level of daily functioning (Llorca, Blanc, Samalin, Bosia, & Cavallaro, 2012), and insight (Monteiro, Silva, & Louza, 2008). The PANSS contains four subscales: positive symptoms, negative symptoms, general psychopathology, and a composite scale (Kay, Opler, & Fiszbein, 1992). The PANSS also includes five additional scores for clusters of symptoms including anergia, thought disturbance, activation, paranoid/belligerence, and depression. Each dimension has distinct criteria in order to rate all levels of symptom severity. Each of the 30 items of the PANSS has a specific definition, and each of these definitions is accompanied by detailed anchor criteria for the seven-point rating scale. Reliability assessments of the PANSS have shown that each item correlated strongly with the appropriate scale total (Kay et al., 1987). Assessments of validity have shown strong discriminate, convergent, criterion, predictive, and concurrent validity (Kay et al., 1992).

The PANSS was first published in 1987 and since then has been translated into many languages including Japanese (Igarashi et al., 1998), Thai (Nilchaikovit, Uneanong, Kessawai, & Thomyangkoon, 2000), and Chinese (Phillips et al., 1991). The Chinese translation of the PANSS was part of a four-center study which confirmed its internal consistency and both test–retest and interrater reliability. Other versions of the PANSS and its application in Chinese populations have been developed as well (He & Zhang, 1997). Studies comparing PANSS scores between psychiatric patients in China to the United States have noted significant differences in the profile of symptoms (Aggarwal et al., 2011). Chinese inpatients endorsed greater hostility and disturbance of volition with poorer insight and impulse control, which the authors attributed to cross-cultural differences in how patients related to their doctors.

Other instruments have been developed to characterize the clinical and emotional status of schizophrenia patients including the Scales for the Assessment of Negative Symptoms (SANS; Andreasen, 1983) and Positive Symptoms (SAPS; Andreasen, 1984), which are available in Chinese. The Brief Psychiatric Rating Scale has also been used with Chinese psychiatric inpatients, but its psychometric properties have not been evaluated in other Asian populations or in Chinese schizophrenia patients (Chan & Lai, 1993).

General Psychiatric Symptoms. General psychiatric measures are also available including the Peters et al. Delusion Inventory for use in a Taiwanese population (Kao et al., 2012) and the Arabic self-reporting questionnaire (SRQ) which was developed by the World Health Organization for use as a psychiatric screening instrument in a Saudi medical patient sample (Ghubash, Daradkeh, El-Rufaie, & Abou-Saleh, 2001). In addition, the Arabic General Health Questionnaire (AGHQ) was also developed for use with this population and both were revealed to be useful in screening for psychiatric morbidity (Al-Subaie, Mohammed, & Al-Malik, 1998).

Depressive Symptoms. The Beck Depression Inventory and the 21-item Hamilton Rating Scale for Depression (HAM-D; Hamilton, 1960) are well-known measures of depressive symptomatology and contain a question regarding suicidality as well. There are Chinese versions of the Beck Depression Inventory (CBDI) (Yeung et al., 2002; Zheng & Lin, 1991) and Chinese clinician and self-report versions of the Quick Inventory of Depressive Symptomatology (Liu et al., 2013).

Moderating variables

Insight. Insight is a multidimensional construct that can be helpful to assess as studies have shown that it is not independent of cultural experiences and can impact assessment, treatment, and prognosis. Insight involves awareness of psychiatric symptoms, the consequences of having those symptoms, and an understanding of the need for treatment. To date, few studies have examined insight in Asian populations. Nevertheless, one study reported reduced insight in over 75 % of stable Chinese patients with schizophrenia (Wang et al., 2011). Assessment at follow-up 1 year later only showed a 5 % improvement suggesting that psychiatric care does not heavily impact the level of insight in Chinese schizophrenia patients. In contrast, a study conducted in patients in South India found comparable levels of insight reported in patients from Western populations. However, the authors noted that there is potentially poor agreement in categorizing patient's indigenous illness attributions (e.g., black magic, evil spirits) as poor or good based on locally accepted explanatory frameworks (Saravanan et al., 2007).

Violence Risk. Although most persons with schizophrenia are not violent, violence risk assessment is important particularly for forensic psychiatric inpatients where discharge is contingent upon confidently predicting safe behaviors within the community and developing discharge plans to maintain nonaggressive behaviors. Despite its clinical importance, only a handful of studies have assessed predictors of violence in Asians with schizophrenia. In a study of state hospital inpatients using the Historical Clinical Risk Management 20 (HCR-20; Webster et al., 1997) as a predictor of institutional violence, Asian American persons with schizophrenia were compared with persons of Euro-American and Native Hawaiian heritages. There were no differences in the percentage of participants demonstrating violent behaviors between the groups; however, the AAS group had significantly lower total HCR-20 scores as well as historical predictors associated with violent behaviors. There also existed differences in predictors for violent behaviors between the ethnic groups. For Asian Americans, current emotional lability (HCR-20: Impulsivity) predicted violence, as compared to Euro-Americans for whom violence was predicted by young age at the first incidence of violence.

In a study of Singaporeans with schizophrenia, the PANSS was found to be useful in discriminating patients with a history of violence versus those with no history (Verma, Poon, Subramaniam, & Chong, 2005). Violent patients demonstrated elevated PANSS scores for hostility, poor impulse control, lack of insight, judgment, and somatic concern. They were also found to have a significantly longer duration of untreated psychosis.

Only one violence scale has been developed specifically for assessing aggressive behaviors for Asians with schizophrenia, the Chinese version of the Violence Scale which was adapted from Morrison's Violence Scale (Chen & Hwu, 2009).

Quality of Life. While controlling and reducing symptoms is the immediate focus in the treatment of schizophrenia, enhancement of patient's quality of life, including one's passions, values, and life goals, can impact long-term prognosis and perceived stigma. In Chinese populations, spirituality has been reported to be of potential benefit to Chinese patients with severe mental illness. In particular, tranquility, resistance to disorientation, and resilience were associated with improved quality of life (Young, 2010). Measures for assessment of quality of life in Asian populations include the Chinese version of the Schizophrenia Quality of Life Scale Revision 4 (SQLS-R4), which was evaluated in Taiwanese schizophrenia patients (Kuo et al., 2007) and the Schizophrenia Quality of Life Scale, which was validated in a Japanese population (Kaneda, Imakura, Fujii, & Ohmori, 2002).

Neurocognition

Neuropsychological assessment with AAS can be highly challenging. Given that about 69 % of Asian Americans are immigrants (Reeves & Bennett, 2004), English proficiency and acculturation are important issues that can significantly impact test performance in this population (Fujii, 2010). Unfortunately, there is a paucity of translated tests or norms for the majority of Asian ethnicities with most translated into Chinese, Korean, Japanese, and primary Asian Indian languages. The only schizophrenia-specific cognitive battery translated into an Asian language is the Brief Assessment of Cognition in Schizophrenia (BACS) that has been translated and validated in Japanese (Kaneda et al., 2007). In addition, many Southeast Asians suffer from undiagnosed post-traumatic stress disorder (PTSD), a mental disorder that can present similarly to schizophrenia (Morrison, Frame, & Larkin, 2003) and is also associated with cognitive deficits, particularly memory problems (Bremner, 2006). Thus, when testing neurocognition in AAS, the psychologist will be faced with several decisions including determining the need for an interpreter, selecting appropriate tests, interpreting findings, and determining diagnostic accuracy.

Fujii (2012) provides guidelines for performing neuropsychological testing with Asian Americans which are summarized here. The first step is to evaluate for English proficiency and acculturation to the United States. AAS who are born, raised, and educated in the United States can be assumed to be English proficient. For first-generation AAS, age at immigration, whether the primary language is spoken at home, past placement in English as a Second Language (ESL) programs, and general ability to converse and answer open-ended questions are important considerations for determining proficiency. Command of English can also be determined quantitatively through measures such as the Bilingual Verbal Abilities Test that compares verbal skills in English versus a person's native language (Munoz-Sandoval, Cummins, Alvarado, & Ruef, 1998). Acculturation can also be determined formally through measures such as the Asian American Multidimensional Acculturation Scale (Gim-Chung, Kim, & Abreu, 2004) or informally by asking questions concerning cultural practices such as typical foods eaten, ethnicity of friends, and frequency of participation in cultural activities.

Tests should be administered in English if a person is born in the United States, English is the primary language spoken at home, or the person is an immigrant but attending a university. For AAS who were educated in Asia, and those with partial education in the United States who speak their native language at home, and/or are less acculturated, it is recommended that tests that are translated and normed in the AAS native language be administered through an interpreter. All first-generation AAS should be asked whether they would prefer an interpreter. Psychologists can refer to the American Academy of Clinical Neuropsychology (AACN) Multicultural Reference (Fujii, 2007) or *The Neuropsychology of Asian Americans* (Fujii, 2010) for a list of translated tests.

If normed tests are not available, Fujii (2010) recommends translating tests demonstrating cross-cultural validity, such as Color Trails,

Digit Span, and the Rey Auditory Verbal Learning Test (RAVLT), administered in the World Health Organization (WHO) studies (Maj et al., 1994), or the shopping list memory test (Lim et al., 2009). Although discouraged by many, "spot" translations can provide useful information, particularly if the person scores within the normal range as this type of performance would rule out impairment. Use of test translation guidelines is useful for reducing biases and identifying other potential problems (International Test Commission, 2010).

When interpreting test performances for AAS who come from ethnicities without norms, "ball park" test expectation can be determined by IQ scores attained by persons in that country (see Lynn, 2006). Using these IQ scores as an initial base, AAS functioning can be estimated by adjusting for background information which would provide clues for functioning in comparison with the ethnic peer group. For example, persons with higher levels of education than the countries' average might be estimated to score higher while those below the average lower. Current performances can be interpreted by comparing scores to expectations for premorbid abilities. When writing reports, the non-standardized nature of the evaluation and test materials should be described and caveats for test interpretation emphasized.

Finally, PTSD should always be assessed for Southeast Asian immigrants to determine the accuracy of schizophrenia diagnosis. Psychologists can screen for trauma by asking AAS to describe in detail their experience of immigrating to the United States. Alternatively, family members can be asked if the AAS is unable to provide this information. Inquiries can then be made about past or current PTSD symptoms using DSM-IV criteria.

Summary

Studies validating assessment measures for schizophrenia on entirely Asian American samples are almost nonexistent. There is much variability in the validation and translation of assessment tools evaluating the presentation of and moderating variables associated with schizophrenia for different Asian ethnicities. Widely used tools measuring general symptoms of schizophrenia are more likely to be validated than more specified measures, for example, prodromal symptoms, insight, violence risk, or quality of life. The most widely translated test, however, is a brief assessment for neuropsychiatric diagnosis. Tests are most likely to be translated in the more resource-rich Asian countries including China, India, Japan, and South Korea. Assessing neurocognition can be challenging, particularly for ethnicities where there are no translated tests or norms. Fujii (2010) provides general recommendations for assessing neurocognition of Asian Americans.

Recommendations

Given the relatively small but emerging literature on assessment for AAS, and heterogeneity of the AA population, the following recommendations for assessing AAS are provided:

1. Clinicians should be familiar with the general culture of the specific ethnicity of the AAS to provide a context for interpreting behaviors, facilitating rapport and communication, diagnosing, and making culturally relevant treatment recommendations.
2. If the clinician is not familiar with the culture of an AAS, referring to or consulting with a knowledgeable colleague or collaborating with a cultural broker is recommended to facilitate communication and understanding by contextualizing behaviors. For example, many Asian ethnicities nod their heads or respond "yes" to statements made by clinicians to indicate that they are listening and paying attention versus actual agreement. Also the stoicism and tendency of many Asians to hold in emotions may be mistaken for negative symptoms.
3. Clinicians should be familiar with the AAS literature but be aware of the heterogeneity of AA, such that findings from one specific ethnicity may not apply to another.

Generation in United States and acculturation are also important moderating variables whereby the more acculturated an individual is to Western values, the less likely the findings from his/her country of origin will apply.

4. Assess for acculturation, informally by asking questions about language spoken at home, neighborhood, ethnicity of friends, and food eaten or formally through measures such as the Suinn–Lew Asian Self-Identity Scale (Suinn, Richard-Figueroa, Lew, & Vigil, 1987). Generation and level of acculturation can provide clues to beliefs about severe mental illness and treatment approaches.
5. Assessment tools for symptoms and moderating variables associated with schizophrenia have not been validated or normed with pure AA samples; thus, these tools should be interpreted with caution. For example, Asians do not demonstrate a self-enhancement bias and thus may score worse on depression measures, may respond with a central tendency bias, and may be less likely to endorse suicidal ideation on intake questionnaires (for a review see Chu & Sue, 2011).
6. Vietnamese, Cambodian, and Laotian immigrants who lived through the aftermath of the Vietnam War and/or were housed in refugee camps should be screened for PTSD which can present with hallucinations and paranoid ideation similar to schizophrenia.
7. Explore shame and stigmatization associated with mental illness and impact on family. If salient, attempt to normalize through education about biological models of schizophrenia and instill hope. In addition Tepou (2010) recommends the following to reduce shame: pay respect to the client; demonstrate acceptance by creating a warm, open, and supportive atmosphere; avoid intense personal questioning in the initial session; focus on practical help that does not emphasize emotional disclosures; and normalize problems by sharing instances where others have experienced similar problems and improved.
8. Be aware that many Asians experience somatic symptoms when distressed. Thus AAS who also suffer from depression may not complain of mood symptoms but instead present with multiple somatic complaints. In addition, for AAS who are first or second generation, consider differences in intergenerational expectations and acculturation issues, for example high parental expectations, shame, intergenerational conflicts, perfectionism, or problem-solving deficiencies, as potential sources of depression or suicidal ideation (Barongan, 2008).
9. Also explore attribution of causes of mental illness that can help to direct treatment that is congruent with belief system to maximize cooperation. For example, AAS with spiritual models of etiologies may benefit from involvement of church or cultural spiritual leaders, while AAS who report sociological attributions may benefit from family interventions.
10. Similarly, inquire about the use of CAM which can be a useful adjunct to help empower through bolstering cultural identity and improve quality of life. If herbs are used, evaluate the impact on or interaction with psychotropic medications and make appropriate recommendations. Asking about duration CAM can be used to assist in identifying the onset and duration of untreated psychosis.
11. AAS often have close-knit families who are highly involved in care. Thus it would be important to involve family in treatment through discussing diagnoses, medications, treatment goals and objectives, and psychosocial interventions. Be sure to obtain consent from the client before involving the family. Evaluation of family dynamics would also be important.

Case Study

Brief Overview and Reason for Testing

Peter is a 48-year-old, married Filipino veteran with a long history of inpatient psychiatric treatment for paranoid schizophrenia. He survived one suicide attempt in his early 40s, in which he jumped from a bridge into traffic.

Although he survived, Peter became paralyzed and suffered a traumatic brain injury from his fall, requiring 24-h care in a residential facility. He was referred for testing by his psychiatrist to determine his current level of cognitive functioning and suicidality and to provide psychosocial treatment recommendations based on his assessment results.

Testing Considerations

Peter spoke fluent English and requested that the assessment occur in English. However, his first language was Filipino, thus raising the possibility of unfamiliar terms and concepts during testing. Further testing considerations included the following: 1) the lack of norms for the majority of neuropsychological tests and symptom measures with a Filipino American sample; 2) concern regarding the veteran's desire to please authority figures and its potential to influence the veteran's responses; and 3) fatigue caused by the veteran's medication regiment, which consisted of three antipsychotics, two mood stabilizers, an antidepressant, and oral medications for high blood pressure and diabetes. Despite these concerns, Peter's willingness to participate in assessment and his motivation to perform well on neurocognitive tests made it possible to assess him and draw preliminary conclusions based on these assessments.

Presentation

Peter agreed to meet with a psychologist for evaluation at the request of his psychiatrist. Initially, attempts were made to engage the veteran in the initial clinical interview through the use of self-disclosure. For example, Peter was asked about his children and informed by the interviewer that she also had a child. How difficult it is to be apart from his children was reflected. Attempts to put the veteran at ease were also made through the use of small talk about lighter topics (e.g., the food at the hospital) and by identifying shared interests (e.g., love of animals; he kept a picture of his dog near his bed).

Peter's mood appeared to be sad and did not match his self-descriptions. For example, when asked how he was feeling, he replied, "Wonderful, fantastic, magnificent ...." He avoided eye contact, which was judged to be reduced even within the context of his Filipino background. He was also very respectful and spoke in a deferential manner (e.g., "Yes, doctor ... thank you, doctor."). Although Peter reported that he heard voices in the recent past, he did not appear to be responding to internal stimulation during the assessment. He did, however, have some trouble focusing on conversation, and questions had to be repeated to him and simplified.

Also of interest, Peter's room was decorated with crosses and he kept a Bible nearby. His room was clean, and he appeared adequately groomed; according to hospital staffs, his wife assisted him with his activities of daily living and brought in new clothes for him every day. She was able to participate in one of the meetings and provided corroborative information and her own perspective. She also became an important part of Peter's treatment plan, which is described below.

Relevant History

Peter grew up in Manila until the age of 13, when he moved to the United States with his mother to live with his older brother and sister-in-law, directly following the sudden death of his father, who had been killed in a motor vehicle accident. He described his childhood as "happy, wonderful, marvelous ...." However, he reported one instance of forced sexual contact with an older male as an early teenager.

After graduating from high school where he received mostly Bs and Cs, he decided to join the military in order to become a naturalized citizen. This appeared to be of great importance to Peter, who emphasized his status as a US citizen several times during the interview. For 2 years, the veteran worked in artillery in the army. His military career ended unexpectedly when he started hearing voices, which resulted in psychiatric hospitalization and a medical discharge. He could not recall a history of mental illness in his family, although it is possible that illness existed and went undiagnosed.

After being diagnosed with paranoid schizophrenia and in-between multiple hospitalizations, the veteran married a woman from the Philippines and brought her to the United States in his mid-20s. They had two children together before the marriage ended due to the veteran's violent behavior, and he was not able to remain in contact with his children. He remarried a woman from the Philippines, and they had a child together shortly afterward. Peter supported his family through his military disability benefits and was able to bring his mother-in-law over to the United States, who also visited him on occasion.

Illness Beliefs

Peter stated that his problems are called "schizophrenia." When asked what does schizophrenia mean, he replied, "It means I need to take medication." He reported that he took medication for his voices and because he sees scary faces. Further questioning revealed that he believed he developed schizophrenia after receiving an alcoholic beverage at a party at the age of 15. He explained that he was "infected" with the virus of schizophrenia at that time, which reflected a poor understanding of schizophrenia and a literal interpretation of schizophrenia as an illness. He reported that he believed he heard the voice of God, reflecting a spiritual interpretation of his auditory hallucinations and, perhaps, vacillating interpretations of his experiences (to assess for a person's explanatory model of illness, see Kleinman's 1978 guidelines). He also reported that having schizophrenia means that he is a "killer," and "un-American," reflecting internalized stigma and conflict with his cultural identity.

Peter also reported that he believed he had dementia, since he had memory difficulties. He was not sure how old he was but suspected that he was 81 years old (though this number also varied over the course of meeting with him). He identified medication as the only way to improve his problems and endorsed the belief that his problems would never improve because "medications make me sleepy."

Neuropsychological Tests

Peter was administered the COGNISTAT, which tests language, construction, memory, calculations, and reasoning. Attention, level of consciousness, and orientation are also assessed. He was also administered the Trail Making Test A and B to assess attention and executive functioning and the Adult North American Reading Test (ANART), which is designed to estimate a person's verbal IQ. Despite English being his second language, his verbal IQ appeared to be in the average range.

Testing indicated that Peter's cognitive strengths included his ability to orient himself to time and place, perform simple mathematical calculations without the aid of pen and paper, and make appropriate judgments for minor, everyday problems and situations (e.g., what to do if he is running late for an appointment). Additionally, he demonstrated an average reading ability. Although he showed significant deficits of attention across testing measures, he was able to learn new words with a number of repetitions and was able to recall or recognize these words with interference and time delay, indicating potential for new learning with repetition.

Overall, testing revealed a number of moderate–severe cognitive deficits in the areas of memory, language, and construction, with evidence of perseverating thoughts and behaviors. Peter performed very poorly in a test of abstraction, which is consistent with behavioral observations of concrete thinking and poor abstract reasoning. For example, when a staff member showed him a ladybug and said that she had brought with her a "friend" from the outside, he corrected the staff member and stated, "That is not a friend—that is an insect." He also had difficulty holding more than two–three words in his working memory. Although he was able to follow one-step commands, he was not able to follow two- and three-step commands. Similarly, he could not repeat back phrases longer than three syllables.

Peter also had difficulty integrating different pieces of information. When presented with a picture of a situation, he could not tell a coherent story and instead focused on different parts of the picture. He also could not identify the emotion of the boy in the picture, and it is likely that further testing would have revealed deficits in emotion recognition, both of self and others.

Symptom Measures and Suicidal Risk Assessment

Positive and Negative Syndrome Scale. Peter endorsed a number of positive and negative symptoms on the PANSS, including visual and auditory hallucinations and delusions. He reported seeing scary faces, hearing a voice calling his name, and interpreting this voice to be the voice of God. He also believed that he had died when he jumped off the bridge and had been brought back to life by God because he was too young to die at the time. He displayed a number of negative symptoms, as well (blunted affect, emotional withdrawal, alogia, amotivation, and stereotyped thinking), disorganized thought content, depression, and guilt for being a "playboy" in his past and, therefore, "unclean."

Beck Depression Inventory. Although Peter reported feeling "wonderful, fantastic, magnificent …," he scored a 26 on this measure of depressive symptoms, which is in the moderate range. He reported suicidal ideation, but no intent. Upon further questioning, Peter said that he believes that Jesus has been calling him and that he is going to die soon. However, he believes that he does not need to die to go to heaven and that God will take him while he is alive. If God does not come for him right away (within the next year), then he said that he is okay with waiting. It became clear from talking with him, however, that he was very depressed and understandably so, given his circumstances and lack of meaningful activity. Besides visits from his wife, mother-in-law, and child, he engaged very little with other residents and staff members. In fact, he rarely left his room, even for meals, which were brought to him, with the exception of attending the facility's church service. His quality of life was poor, and his behavior (staying in bed most of the time) reflected his attitude of waiting to die.

Goals and Strengths

Peter identified his treatment goals as, being able to walk again, elimination of his auditory and visual hallucinations and going home. With prompting, he identified the importance of his role as a father to his youngest daughter and wanted to see her grow up to be successful. He also was a devout Roman Catholic and sought out a close relationship with God through prayer and reading the Bible. Peter also reported that he wanted to be "like God," become a doctor (or President), and help others.

In addition to these goals, the involvement and devotion of his wife were considered a particular strength of Peter's. Although nursing staff members were available to bathe Peter and help him to the bathroom, the veteran's wife took on these responsibilities on a daily basis. She expressed a willingness to be involved in Peter's treatment plan, specifically a token economy.

Treatment Considerations/ Recommendations

Taking all of this information into account, a number of recommendations were made to Peter's treatment team. Foremost, it was important for Peter to spend more time outside of his room, as isolation and perseverative thinking, in addition to his interpretations of his auditory hallucinations as God wanting him to die/leave the world, were worsening his depression. There had initially been some concern about Peter eating with other residents due to his history of violent and aggressive behavior. However, he had not engaged in such behavior in years, and his desire to be "good" for God and for his treatment team suggested that it was unlikely for him to act out in such a way. Therefore, it was recommended that Peter eat his meals with the other residents, and he was encouraged to interact with them.

Peter also rarely left the treatment facility, which also contributed to his depression. His wife expressed concern that Peter would hurt himself again, since he has talked about joining God for several years. However, the veteran promised that he would not hurt himself or others and seemed excited at the idea of going out to eat at restaurants that he had enjoyed in the past. In order to reward Peter for engaging in new activities (e.g., helping wipe down tables in the dining room), a token economy was started for Peter with his wife's help. Due to his short-term memory and attention problems, it was necessary for staffs to spend a lot of time initially helping the veteran with the task and reminding him what to do. However, eventually he was able to remember to help out on his own, earning poker chips every time he engaged in cleaning tables. He was able to exchange these chips to eat at his favorite restaurant. This served several functions, including building up a sense of mastery in Peter, thereby decreasing his depression, and also building up confidence in his wife that he would not hurt himself when she took him outside of the facility.

It was also recommended that Peter receive individual therapy, focusing on his feelings of guilt for being a "playboy" and shame about his early unwanted sexual contact with an older male, exploring alternative interpretations to the belief that his voices were God calling him from this world, and providing him with coping strategies for when he saw scary faces, which were interpreted to mean that the devil was terrorizing him. It was also suggested that therapy should focus on repetition of simple and meaningful ideas, such as "Your children need you." Peter's reasons for living included seeing his children grow up and be successful. The meaning of what it means to be diagnosed with schizophrenia was another important area to explore in therapy, especially since it related to Peter's mixed feelings about his cultural identity and beliefs that he was less than American because he was born in the Philippines. It was emphasized to the veteran how brave he was for joining the military and fighting for the United States and that being a Filipino American did not make him any less American than being a European American or a Japanese American, etc.

Cognitive remediation was also recommended in order to strengthen the veteran's cognitive abilities, specifically his ability to pay attention and concentrate. The veteran initially began memorizing the different states of the United States, which was important to him and helped him to feel a greater sense of connection to his country. Throughout Peter's course of individual therapy, which lasted for 6 months, his wife occasionally participated in the sessions despite her limited English-speaking abilities. She provided validation to Peter that he was important to her and that she did not want him to die. Peter's mood continued to improve over the course of treatment, and he started to engage in physical activities such as pull-ups as well. Staff members were encouraged to continue praising the veteran for his hard work and friendliness to other people. The ultimate goal of treatment was to help Peter feel part of the community at the residential facility and closer to his family, so that he felt a sense of purpose and spent less time perseverating about dying.

References

Abu-Lughod, L., & Lutz, C. A. (1990). Introduction: Emotion, discourse, and the politics of everyday life. In C. Lutz & L. Abu-Lughod (Eds.), *Language and the politics of emotion* (pp. 1–23). Cambridge: Cambridge University Press.

Aggarwal, N. K. (2007). Exploring identity, culture, and suffering with a Kashmiri Sikh refugee. *Social Science Medicine., 65*, 1654–1665.

Aggarwal, N. K., Tao, H., Xu, K., Stefanovics, E., Zhening, L., & Rosenheck, R. A. (2011). Comparing the PANSS in Chinese and American inpatients: cross-cultural psychiatric analyses of instrument translation and implementation. *Schizophrenia Research, 132*(2–3), 146–152.

Al-Issa, I. (1995). The illusion of reality or the reality of illusion: Hallucinations and culture. *British Journal of Psychiatry, 166*, 368–373.

Al-Subaie, A. S., Mohammed, K., & Al-Malik, T. (1998). The Arabic self-reporting questionnaire (SRQ) as a psychiatric screening instrument in medical patients. *Annals of Saudi Medicine, 18*, 308–310.

American Psychiatric Association. (2000). *Diagnostic and Statistical Manual 4th Ed.* Washington DC: Text Revision. Author.

Andreasen, N. C. (1983). *The Scale for the Assessment of Negative Symptoms (SANS).* Iowa City, IA: The University of Iowa.

Andreasen, N. C. (1984). *The Scale for the Assessment of Positive Symptoms (SAPS).* Iowa City, IA: The University of Iowa.

Archie, S., Akhtar-Danesh, N., Norman, R., Malla, A., Roy, P., & Zipursky, R. B. (2010). Ethnic diversity and pathways to care for a first episode of psychosis in Ontario. *Schizophrenia Bulletin, 36*, 688–701. doi:10.1093/schbul/sbn137.

Bae, S.-W., & Brekke, J. S. (2002). Characteristics of Korean-Americans with schizophrenia: A cross-ethnic comparison with African-Americans, Latinos, and Euro-Americans. *Schizophrenia Bulletin, 28*, 703–717.

Barongan, C. (2008). *December). Suicide prevention in Asian American college students*. Boston, MA: Poster presented at the annual meeting of the Asian American Psychological Association.

Bhatia, T., Thomas, P., Semwal, P., Thelma, B. K., Nimgaonkar, V. L., & Deshpande, S. N. (2006). Differing correlates for suicide attempts among patients with schizophrenia or schizoaffective disorder in India and USA. *Schizophrenia Research, 86*, 208–214. doi:10.1016/j.schres.2006.04.015.

Bhavsar, V., & Bhugra, D. (2008). Religious delusions: Finding meanings in psychosis. *Psychopathology, 41*, 165–172.

Birchwood, M., Smith, J., Macmillan, F., Hogg, B., Prasad, R., Harvey, C., et al. (1989). Predicting relapse in schizophrenia: The development and implementation of an early signs monitoring system using patients and families as observers, a preliminary investigation. *Psychological Medicine, 19*(3), 649–656.

Bremner, J. (2006). The relationship between cognitive and brain changes in posttraumatic stress disorder. *Annals of the New York Academy of Science, 107*, 80–86.

Cannon, T. D., Cadenhead, K. S., Cornblatt, B., Woods, S. W., Addington, J., Walker, J., … , Heinssen R. (2008). Prediction of psychosis in youth at high clinical risk: a multisite longitudinal study in North America. *Archives of General Psychiatry, 65*, 28–37.

Chan, D. W., & Lai, B. (1993). Assessing psychopathology in Chinese psychiatric patients in Hong Kong using the brief psychiatric rating scale. *Acta Psychiatrica Scandinavica, 87*(1), 37–44.

Chen, S. C., & Hwu, H. G. (2009). Psychometric evaluation of Chinese version of Violence Scale for objective rating among inpatients with schizophrenia. *Journal of Clinical Nursing, 18*, 1889–1896.

Cheng, A. T. A., Tien, A. Y., Chang, C. J., Brugha, T. S., Cooper, J. E., Lee, C. S., … Chen, H. M. (2001). Cross-cultural implementation of a Chinese version of the Schedules for Clinical Assessment in Neuropsychiatry (SCAN) in Taiwan. *The British Journal of Psychiatry, 178*(6), 567–572.

Chiu, S. C., Hwu, H. G., Shiau, S. J., Yao, G., & Hsieh, Y. S. (2010). Applicability of the Chinese version of the Prodromal Questionnaire. *Journal of the Formosan Medical Association, 109*, 647–655.

Chu, J. P., & Sue, S. (2011). Asian American mental health: What we know and what we don't know. *Online Readings in Psychology and Culture, 3*(1), 4.

Cohen, A., Patel, V., Thara, R., & Gureje, O. (2008). Questioning an axiom: Better prognosis for schizophrenia in the developing world? *Schizophrenia Bulletin, 34*, 229–244. doi:10.1093/schbul/sbm105.

Deshpande, S. N., Mathur, M. N., Das, S. K., Bhatia, T., Sharma, S., & Nimgaonkar, V. L. (1998). A hindi version of the diagnostic interview for genetic studies. *Schizophrenia Bulletin, 24*(3), 489–493.

Endicott, J., & Spitzer, R. L. (1978). A diagnostic interview: The schedule for affective disorders and schizophrenia. *Archives of General Psychiatry, 35*(7), 837.

Ertan, T., & Eker, E. (2000). Reliability, validity, and factor structure of the geriatric depression scale in Turkish elderly: Are there different factor structures for different cultures? *International Psychogeriatrics, 12*, 163–172.

First, M., Spitzer, R., Gibbon, M., & Williams, J. (2002). *Structured clinical interview for DSM-IV-TR axis I disorders, research version, patient edition (SCID--I/P)*. New York: Biometrics Research, New York State Psychiatric Institute.

Flaskerud, J. H., & Hu, L.-T. (1992). Relationship of ethnicity to psychiatric diagnosis. *The Journal of Nervous and Mental Diseases, 180*, 296–303.

Frisch, M., Cornell, J., Villanueva, M., & Retzlaff, P. (1992). Clinical validation of the Quality of Life Inventory. A measure of life satisfaction for use in treatment planning and outcome assessment. *Psychological Assessment, 4*, 92–101.

Fujii, D. (2007). *Multicultural references*. Retrieved on July 21, 2010 from http://www.theaacn.org/position_papers/.

Fujii, D. (2010). Introduction. In D. Fujii (Ed.), *The neuropsychology of Asian-Americans* (pp. 1–10). New York, NY: Psychology Press.

Fujii, D. (2012). Cultural issues. In B. Marcopulos & M. Kurtz (Eds.), *Clinical Neuropsychological Foundations of Schizophrenia* (pp. 103–118). New York: Psychology Press.

Furnham, A., & Chan, E. (2004). Lay theories of schizophrenia: A cross-cultural comparison of British and Hong Kong Chinese attitudes, attributions and beliefs. *Social Psychiatry Psychiatric Epidemiology, 39*, 543–552. doi:10.1007/s00127-004-0787-8.

Ghubash, R., Daradkeh, T., El-Rufaie, O. F., & Abou-Saleh, M. T. (2001). A comparison of the validity of two psychiatric screening questionnaires: the Arabic General Health Questionnaire (AGHQ) and Self-Reporting Questionnaire (SRQ-20) in UAE, using Receiver Operating Characteristic (ROC) analysis. *European Psychiatry, 16*(2), 122–126.

Gim-Chung, R., Kim, B., & Abreu, J. (2004). Asian American multidimensional acculturation scale: Development, factor analysis reliability, and validity. *Cultural Diversity and Ethnic Minority Psychology, 10*, 66–80.

Häfner, H., Riecher-Rössler, A., Maurer, K., Fätkenheuer, B., & Löffler, W. (1992). First onset and early symptomatology of schizophrenia. A chapter of epidemiological and neurobiological research into age and sex differences. *European Archives of Psychiatry and Clinical Neuroscience, 242*, 109–118.

Hahn, O. S., Ahn, J. H., Song, S. H., Cho, M. J., Kim, J. K., Bae, J. N., … Hong, J. P. (2000). Development of Korean version of structured clinical interview schedule for DSM-IV axis I disorder: Interrater reliability.

Journal of Korean Neuropsychiatric Association, 39(2), 362–372.

Hamilton, M. (1960). A rating scale for depression. *Journal of Neurology, Neurosurgery, and Psychiatry, 23*, 56–62.

Hanzawa, S., Bae, J. K., Tanaka, H., Bae, Y. J., Tanaka, G., Inadomi, H., … Ohta, Y. (2010). Caregiver burden and coping strategies for patients with schizophrenia: Comparison between Japan and Korea. *Psychiatry and Clinical Neurosciences, 64*(4), 377–386.

He, Y. L., & Zhang, M. Y. (1997). The Positive and Negative Syndrome Scale (PANSS) and its application (in Chinese). *Journal of Clinical Psychiatry, 7*, 353–5.

Heinrichs, R., & Zakzanis, K. (1998). Neurocognitive deficit in schizophrenia: A quantitative review of the evidence. *Neuropsychology, 12*, 426–445.

Higgins, L., Dey-Ghatak, D., & Davey, G. (2007). Mental health nurses' experiences of schizophrenia rehabilitation in China and India: A preliminary study. *International Journal of Mental Health Nursing, 16*, 22–27. doi:10.1111/j.1447-0349.2006.00440.x.

Hoeffel, E., Rastogi, S., Kim, M., & Shahid, H. (2012). *The Asian population: 2012 census briefs*. Retrieved August 23, 2012 from http://www.census.gov/prod/cen2010/briefs/c2010br-11.pdf.

Hopper, K., & Wanderling, J. (2000). Revisiting the developed versus developing country distinction in course and outcome in schizophrenia: Results from ISoS, the WHO collaborative follow-up project. *Schizophrenia Bulletin, 26*, 835–846.

Igarashi, Y., Hayashi, N., Yamashina, M., Otsuka, N., Kurokil, N., Anzai, N., et al. (1998). Interrater reliability of the Japanese version of the Positive and Negative Syndrome Scale and the appraisal of its training effect. *Psychiatry and Clinical Neurosciences, 52*(5), 467–470.

International Test Commission. (2010). *International test commission guidelines for translating and adapting tests*. Retrieved August 2, 2012 from http://www.intestcom.org.

Joo, E. J., Joo, Y. H., Hong, J. P., Hwang, S., Maeng, S. J., Han, J. H., … Kim, Y. S. (2004). Korean version of the diagnostic interview for genetic studies: Validity and reliability. *Comprehensive Psychiatry, 45*(3), 225–229.

Jung, M. H., Jang, J. H., Kang, D. H., Choi, J. S., Shin, N. Y., Kim, H. S., … Kwon, J. S. (2010). The reliability and validity of the Korean version of the structured interview for prodromal syndrome. *Psychiatry Investigation, 7*, 257–263.

Kadri, N., Agoub, M., El Gnaoui, S., Alami Kh, M., Hergueta, T., & Moussaoui, D. (2005). Moroccan colloquial Arabic version of the Mini International Neuropsychiatric Interview (MINI): qualitative and quantitative validation. *European Psychiatry: The Journal of the Association of European Psychiatrists, 20*, 193–195.

Kaneda, Y., Imakura, A., Fujii, A., & Ohmori, T. (2002). Schizophrenia quality of life scale: validation of the Japanese version. *Psychiatry Research, 113*(1–2), 107–113.

Kaneda, Y., Sumiyoshi, T., Keefe, R., Ishimoto, Y., Numata, S., & Ohmori, T. (2007). Brief assessment of cognition in schizophrenia: Validation of the Japanese version. *Psychiatry and Clinical Neurosciences, 61*, 602–609.

Kao, Y. C., Wang, T. S., Lu, C. W., Cheng, T. H., & Liu, Y. P. (2012). The psychometric properties of the Peters et al. Delusions Inventory (PDI) in Taiwan: Reliability, validity, and utility. *Social Psychiatry and Psychiatric Epidemiology, 47*(8), 1221–1234.

Kay, S., Fiszbein, A., & Opler, L. (1987). The positive and negative syndrome scale (PANSS) for schizophrenia. *Schizophrenia Bulletin, 13*, 261–76.

Kay, S. R., Opler, L. A., & Fiszbein, A. (1992). *The Structured Clinical Interview for the Positive and Negative syndromes of Schizophrenia*. New York: Multi-Health Systems.

Kennedy, M. G., Schepp, K. G., & Rangruangkonkit, S. (2008). Experiences of Asian American parents in a group intervention for youth with schizophrenia. *Journal of Child and Adolescent Psychiatric Nursing, 21*, 220–227.

Kim, K. -I., Li, D., Jiang, Z., Cui, X., Lin, L., Kang, J. J., … Kim, C. K. (1993). Schizophrenic delusions among Koreans, Korean-Chinese and Chinese: A transcultural study. *The International Journal of Social Psychiatry, 39*, 190–199.

Kleinman, A. (1978). Concepts and a model for the comparison of medical systems as cultural systems. *Social Science & Medicine. Part B: Medical Anthropology, 12*, 85–93.

Kobayashi, H., Nemoto, T., Koshikawa, H., Osono, Y., Yamazawa, R., Murakami, M., … Mizuno, M. (2008). A self-reported instrument for prodromal symptoms of psychosis: Testing the clinical validity of the PRIME Screen-Revised (PS-R) in a Japanese population. *Schizophrenia Research, 106*(2–3), 356–362.

Koichi, R., & Miyamoto, Y. (2011). Reliability and validity of the Japanese semistructured interview version of the Early Signs Scale (ESS-JI) for outpatients with schizophrenia (study 1). *International Journal of Mental Health Nursing, 20*(2), 144–151.

Krishnadas, R., Moore, B. P., Nayak, A., & Patel, R. R. (2007). Relationship of cognitive function in patients with schizophrenia in remission to disability: A cross-sectional study in an Indian sample. *Annals of General Psychiatry, 6*, 19–27. doi:10.1186/1744-859X-6-19.

Kung, W. W. (2004). Causal attributions of schizophrenia by Chinese American caregivers. *Journal of Ethics and Cultural Diversity in Social Work, 13*, 37–57. doi:10.1300/J051v13n01_03.

Kuo, P. J., Chen-Sea, M. J., Lu, R. B., Chung, M. S., Kuo, C. C., & Huang, W. C. (2007). Validation of the Chinese version of the Schizophrenia Quality of Life Scale Revision 4 (SQLS-R4) in Taiwanese patients with schizophrenia. *Quality of Life Research: An International Journal of Quality of Life Aspects of Treatment, Care and Rehabilitation, 16*, 1533–1538.

Kurtz, M. (2012). Neurocognition and functional outcome in schizophrenia. In B. Marcopulos & M. Kurtz (Eds.), *Clinical Neuropsychological Foundations of*

Schizophrenia (pp. 81–102). New York: Psychology Press.

Lauber, C., & Rossler, W. (2007). Stigma towards people with mental illness in developing countries in Asia. *International Review of Psychiatry, 19*, 157–178. doi:10.1080/09540260701278903.

Lee, T. M. Y., Chong, S. A., Chan, Y. H., & Sathyadevan, G. (2004). Command hallucinations among Asian patients with schizophrenia. *Canadian Journal of Psychiatry, 49*, 838–842. Retrieved from http://web.ebscohost.com.ezproxy.hpu.edu/ehost/resultsadvanced?sid=bf5560ab-4513-43c8-9984-7b40f83ff561%40sessionmgr13&vid=3&hid=12&bquery=TI(command+AND+hallucinations+AND+among+AND+asian)&bdata=JmRiPXBiaCZ0eXBlPTEmc2l0ZT1laG9zdC1saXZl.

Leff, J., Sartorius, N., Jablensky, A., Korten, A., & Ernberg, G. (1992). The international pilot study of schizophrenia: Five-year follow-up findings. *Psychological Medicine, 22*, 131–145.

Lim, Y. Y., Prang, K. H., Cysique, L., Pietrzak, R., Snyder, P., & Maruff, P. (2009). A method for cross-cultural adaptation of a verbal memory assessment. *Behavior Research Methods, 41*, 1190–1200.

Lin, K.-M., & Cheung, F. (1999). Mental health issues for Asian Americans. *Psychiatric Services, 50*, 774–780.

Lin, K. M., Hwu, H.-G., & Tsuang, M. T. (2012). Schizophrenia and other psychosis in Asians and Asian Americans. In E. C. Chang (Ed.), *Handbook of adult psychopathology in Asians* (pp. 83–107). New York: Oxford University Press.

Lin, K. M., Inui, T., & Kleinman, A. (1982). Sociocultural determinants of help-seeking behavior of patients with mental illness. *Journal of Nervous and Mental Disease, 170*, 78–85.

Liu, J., Xiang, Y. T., Wang, G., Zhu, X. Z., Ungvari, G. S., Kilbourne, A. M., … Chiu, H. F. (2013). Psychometric properties of the Chinese versions of the Quick Inventory of Depressive Symptomatology–Clinician Rating (C-QIDS-C) and Self-Report (C-QIDS-SR). *Journal of Affective Disorders, 147*(1), 421–424.

Llorca, P. M., Blanc, O., Samalin, L., Bosia, M., & Cavallaro, R. (2012). Factors involved in the level of functioning of patients with schizophrenia according to latent variable modeling. *European Psychiatry, 27*, 396–400.

Lynn, E. (2006). *Race differences in intelligence: An evolutionary analysis*. Augusta, GA: Washington Summit Publishers.

Maeda, K., Kasai, K., Watanabe, A., Henomatsu, K., Rogers, M., & Kato, N. (2006). Effects of subjective reasoning and neurocognition on medication adherence for persons with schizophrenia. *Psychiatric Services, 57*, 1203–1205.

Maj, M., Satz, P., Janssen, R., Zudig, M., Starace, F., D'Elia, L., Sughondhabirom, B. (1994). WHO neuropsychiatric AIDS study, cross-sectional phase II: Neuropsychological and neurological findings. *Archives of General Psychiatry, 51*, 51–61.

Matsui, M., Sumiyoshi, T., Arai, H., Higuchi, Y., & Kurachi, M. (2008). Cognitive functioning related to quality of life in schizophrenia. *Progress in Neuro-Psychopharmacology and Biological Psychiatry, 32*, 280–287.

McEvoy, J., Apperson, L., Appelbaum, P., Ortlip, P., Brecosky, J., Hammill, K., … Roth, L. (1989). Insight n schizophrenia. Its relationship to acute psychopathology. *Journal of Nervous and Mental Disease, 177*, 43–47.

McGorry, P. D., Yung, A. R., & Phillips, L. J. (2003). The "close-in" or ultra high-risk model: a safe and effective strategy for research and clinical intervention in prepsychotic mental disorder. *Schizophrenia Bulletin, 29*, 771–790.

McLean, D., John, S., Barrett, R., McGrath, J., Loa, P., Thara, R., et al. (2012). Refining clinical phenotypes by contrasting ethnically different populations with schizophrenia from Australia, India and Sarawak. *Psychiatry Research, 196*, 194–200. doi:10.1016/j.psychres.2011.12.027.

Miller, T., McGlashan, T., Rosen, J., Somjee, L., Markovich, P., Stein, K., et al. (2002). Prospective diagnosis of the initial prodrome for schizophrenia based on the Structured interview for prodromal syndromes: Preliminary evidence of interrater reliability and predictive validity. *American Journal of Psychiatry, 159*, 863–865.

Monteiro, L. C., Silva, V. A., & Louza, M. R. (2008). Insight, cognitive dysfunction and symptomatology in schizophrenia. *European Archives of Psychiatry and Clinical Neuroscience, 258*, 402–405.

Morrison, A., Frame, L., & Larkin, W. (2003). Relationships between trauma and psychosis: A review and integration. *British Journal of Clinical Psychology, 42*, 331–353.

Munoz-Sandoval, A., Cummins, J., Alvarado, C., & Ruef, M. (1998). *Bilingual verbal abilities tests*. Itasca, IL: Riverside Publishing.

Nilchaikovit, T., Uneanong, S., Kessawai, D., & Thomyangkoon, P. (2000). The Thai version of the Positive and Negative Syndrome Scale (PANSS) for schizophrenia: Criterion validity and interrater reliability. *Journal of the Medical Association of Thailand., 83*, 646–651.

Okazaki, S. (2000). Treatment delay among Asian-American patients with severe mental illness. *American Journal of Orthopsychiatry, 70*, 58–64.

Osone, A., & Takahashi, S. (2003). Twelve month test–retest reliability of a Japanese version of the Structured Clinical Interview for DSM-IV Personality Disorders. *Psychiatry and Clinical Neurosciences, 57*(5), 532–538.

Otsubo, T., Tanaka, K., Koda, R., Shinoda, J., Sano, N., Tanaka, S., … Kamijima, K. (2005). Reliability and validity of Japanese version of the Mini-International Neuropsychiatric Interview. *Psychiatry and Clinical Neurosciences, 59*(5), 517–526.

Overall, J., & Gorham, D. (1962). The brief psychiatric rating scale. *Psychological Reports, 10*, 799–812.

Phillips, M. R., Xiong, W., Wang, R. W., Gao, Y. H., Wang, X. Q., & Zhang, N. P. (1991). Reliability and validity of the Chinese versions of the scales for assessment of positive and negative symptoms. *Acta Psychiatrica Scandinavica., 84*, 364–370.

Phillips, M. R., Yang, G., Li, S., & Li, Y. (2004). Suicide and the unique prevalence pattern of schizophrenia in mainland China: A retrospective observational study. *The Lancet, 364*, 1062–1068. http://web.ebscohost.com.ezproxy.hpu.edu/ehost/resultsadvanced?sid=46c1fb45-d237-4798-98d0-d4c8fdceea86%40sessionmgr15&vid=2&hid=17&bquery=TI+(suicide+AND+the+AND+unique+AND+prevalence+AND+pattern)&bdata=JmRiPXBiaCZ0eXBlPTEmc2l0ZT1laG9zdC1saXZl.

Phillips, L. J., Yung, A. R., & McGorry, P. D. (2000). Identification of young people at risk of psychosis: Validation of personal assessment and crisis evaluation clinic intake criteria. *Australian and New Zealand Journal of Psychiatry, 34*, 164–169.

Raguram, R., Raghu, T. M., Vounatsou, P., & Weiss, M. G. (2004). Schizophrenia and the cultural epidemiology of stigma in Bangalore, India. *The Journal of Nervous and Mental Disease, 192*, 734–744. doi:10.1097/01.nmd.0000144692.24993.1b.

Ran, M.-S., Leff, J., Hou, Z.-J., Xiang, M.-Z., & Chan, C. L.-W. (2003). The characteristics of expressed emotion among relatives of patients with schizophrenia in Chengdu, China. *Culture, Medicine and Psychiatry, 27*, 95–106. http://web.ebscohost.com.ezproxy.hpu.edu/ehost/pdfviewer/pdfviewer?vid=3&hid=7&sid=85701d6f-006d-4116-bcfc-9a998e571294%40sessionmgr13.

Rathbone, J., Zhang, L., Zhang, M., Xia, J., Liu, X., Yang, Y., et al. (2007). Chinese herbal medicine for schizophrenia Cochrane systematic review of randomised trials. *The British Journal of Psychiatry, 190*(5), 379–384.

Reeves, T. J., & Bennett, C. E. (2004). *We the people: Asians in the United States*. Washington, DC: U.S. Census Bureau.

Saravanan, B., Jacob, K. S., Johnson, S., Prince, M., Bhugra, D., & David, A. S. (2007). Beliefs models in first episode schizophrenia in South India. *Social Psychiatry Psychiatric Epidemiology, 42*, 446–451. doi:10.1107/s00127-007-0186-z.

Sartorius, N., Gulbinat, W., Harrison, G., Laska, E., & Siegel, C. (1996). Long-term follow-up of schizophrenia in 16 countries: A description of the international study of schizophrenia conducted by the World Health Organization. *Social Psychiatry Psychiatric Epidemiology, 31*, 249–258.

Sheehan, D. V., Lecrubier, Y., Sheehan, K. H., Amorim, P., Janavs, J., Weiller, E., … Dunbar, G. C. (1998). The mini-international neuropsychiatric interview (M.I.N.I.): The development and validation of a structured diagnostic psychiatric interview for DSM-IV and ICD-10. *The Journal of Clinical Psychiatry, 59* (Suppl 20), 22–33: quiz 34–57.

So, E., Kam, I., Leung, C. M., Chung, D., Liu, Z., & Fong, S. (2003). The Chinese-bilingual SCID-I/P project: Stage 1-reliability for mood disorders and schizophrenia. *Hong Kong Journal of Psychiatry, 13*(1), 7–18.

Spitzer, R. L., Endicott, J., & Robins, E. (1978). Research diagnostic criteria: Rationale and reliability. *Archives of General Psychiatry, 35*(6), 773.

Sue, D. W., & Sue, D. (1999). *Counseling the culturally diverse: Theory and practice* (3rd ed.). New York: Wiley.

Suinn, R. M., Richard-Figueroa, K., Lew, S., & Vigil, P. (1987). The Suinn-Lew Asian self-identity acculturation scale: An initial report. *Educational and Psychological Measurement, 47*, 401–407.

Swami, V., Furnham, A., Kannan, K., & Sinniah, D. (2008). Beliefs about schizophrenia and its treatment in Kotga Kinabalu, Malaysia. *International Journal of Social Psychiatry, 54*, 164–179. doi:10.1177/0020764007084665.

Takeuchi, D. T., Zane, N., Hong, S., Chae, D. H., Gong, F., Gee, G. C., et al. (2007). Immigration-related factors and mental disorders among Asian Americans. *American Journal of Public Health, 97*, 84–90.

Tandon, R., Nasrallah, H., & Keshavan, M. (2010). Schizophrenia, "just the facts" 5. Treatment and prevention. Past, present, and future. *Schizophrenia Research, 122*, 1–23.

Tang, Y.-L., Sevigny, R., Mao, P.-X., Jiang, F., & Cai, Z. (2007). Help-seeking behaviors of Chinese patients with schizophrenia admitted to a psychiatric hospital. *Administration and Policy in Mental Health and Mental Health Services Research, 34*, 101–107. doi:10.1007/s10488-006-0084-9.

Tepou. (2010). *Talking therapies for Asian peoples: Best and promising practice guide for mental health and addiction services*. Auckland: Te Pou o te Whakaaro Nui. Retrieved on April 24, 2013 from http://www.tepou.co.nz/library/tepou/talking-therapies-for-asian-people.

Thara, R., Srinivasan, T., John, S., Nancarrow, D., Chant, D., Holliday, E., et al. (2009). Design and clinical characteristics of a homogeneous schizophrenia pedigree sample from Tamil Nadu, India. *Australian and New Zealand Journal of Psychiatry, 43*, 561–570. http://web.ebscohost.com.ezproxy.hpu.edu/ehost/pdfviewer/pdfviewer?vid=3&hid=12&sid=e97e00a7-1c6d-4f2c-939a-fb847017554c%40sessionmgr10.

Tsai, D. F. (2001). How should doctors approach patients? A Confucian reflection on personhood. *Journal of Medical Ethics., 27*, 44–50.

Ventura, J., Liberman, R. P., Green, M. F., Shaner, A., & Mintz, J. (1998). Training and quality assurance with the Structured Clinical Interview for DSM-IV (SCID-I/P). *Psychiatry Research, 79*(2), 163–173.

Verma, S., Poon, L. Y., Subramaniam, M., & Chong, S. (2005). Aggression in Asian patients with first-episode psychosis. *International Journal of Social Psychiatry, 51*, 365–371.

Verma, S. W., Subramaniam, M., Chong, S.-A., & Kua, E. H. (2002). Substance abuse in schizophrenia: A Singapore perspective. *Social Psychiatry and Psychiatric Epidemiology, 37*, 326–328. doi:10.1007/s00127-002-0553-8.

von Knorring, L., & Lindstrom, E. (1995). Principal components and further possibilities with the PANSS. *Acta Psychiatrica Scandinavica, 388*(Suppl), 5–10.

Wang, Y., Xiang, Y. T., Wang, C. Y., Chiu, H. F., Zhao, J. P., Chen, Q., … Ungvari, G. S. (2011). Insight in Chinese schizophrenia patients: a 12-month follow-up. *Journal of Psychiatric and Mental Health Nursing, 18*(9), 751–757.

Webster, C., Douglas, K., Eaves, D., & Hart, S. (1997). *HCR-20: Assessing the Risk for Violence (Version 2).* Vancouver: Mental Health, Law, and Policy Institute, Simon Fraser University.

Weiser, M., Werbeloff, N., Vishna, T., Yoffe, R., Lubin, G., Shmushkevitch, M., et al. (2008). Elaboration on immigration and risk for schizophrenia. *Psychological Medicine, 38*, 1113–1119. doi:10.1017/S003329170700205X.

Wong, D. F. K., & Xuesong, H. (2011). Schizophrenia literacy among Chinese in Shanghai, China: A comparison with Chinese-speaking Australians in Melbourne and Chinese in Hong Kong. *Australian and New Zealand Journal of Psychiatry, 45*, 524–531. doi:10.3109/00048674.2011.585604.

WonPat-Borja, A. J., Yang, L. H., Link, B. G., & Phelan, J. C. (2012). Eugenics, genetics, and mental illness stigma in Chinese Americans. *Social Psychiatry and Psychiatric Epidemiology, 47*, 145–156. doi:10.1007/s00127-010-0319-7.

Woon, P. S., Chia, M. Y., Chan, W. Y., & Sim, K. (2010). Neurocognitive, clinical and functional correlates of subjective quality of life in Asian outpatients with schizophrenia. *Progress in Neuro-Psychopharmacology and Biological Psychiatry, 34*, 463–468.

World Health Organization. (2010). *International classification of diseases (ICD-10).* Retrieved August 23, 2012 from http://www.who.int/classifications/icd/en/.

Xiang, Y. T., Weng, Y. Z., Leung, C. M., Tang, W. K., & Ungvari, G. S. (2007). Clinical and social determinants of antipsychotic polypharmacy for Chinese patients with schizophrenia. *Pharmacopsychiatry, 40*(02), 47–52.

Yamazawa, R., Nemoto, T., Kobayashi, H., Chino, B., Kashima, H., & Mizuno, M. (2008). Association between duration of untreated psychosis, premorbid functioning, and cognitive performance and the outcome of first-episode schizophrenia in Japanese patients: Prospective study. *Australian and New Zealand Journal of Psychiatry, 42*, 159–165. http://web.ebscohost.com.ezproxy.hpu.edu/ehost/pdfviewer/pdfviewer?vid=5&hid=16&sid=6a77f814-7ea0-4ef5-b6ee-f3130f522e4c%40sessionmgr15.

Yang, L., Chen, S., Chen, C.-M., Khan, F., Forchelli, G., & Javitt, D. C. (2012). Schizophrenia, culture and neuropsychology: Sensory deficits, language impairments and social functioning in Chinese-speaking schizophrenia patients. *Psychological Medicine, 42*, 1485–1494. doi:10.1017/S003329171002224.

Yeung, A., Howarth, S., Chan, R., Sonawalla, S., Nierenberg, A. A., & Fava, M. (2002). Use of the Chinese version of the Beck Depression Inventory for screening depression in primary care. *Journal of Nervous and Mental Disease, 190*, 94–99.

Yoo, S. W., Kim, Y. S., Noh, J. S., Oh, K. S., Kim, C. H., Nam, K. K., … Kim, S. J. (2006). Validity of Korean Version of the MINI international neuropsychiatric interview. *Anxiety and Mood, 2*, 50–55.

Young, K. W. (2010). Spirituality and Quality of Life for Chinese People with Severe Mental Illness. *Journal of Religion and Spirituality in Social Work: Social Thought, 29*, 1–13.

Zheng, Y. P., & Lin, K. M. (1991). Comparison of the Chinese Depression Inventory and the Chinese version of the Beck Depression Inventory. *Acta Psychiatrica Scandinavica, 84*, 531–536.

Zhu, C. Y., Lee, T. M., Li, X. S., Jing, S. C., Wang, Y. G., & Wang, K. (2007). Impairments of social cues recognition and social functioning in Chinese people with schizophrenia. *Psychiatric Clinics in Neurosciences, 61*, 149–158.

Assessing Sleep Disorders in the Asian Client

21

Sooyeon Suh, P. Song, and Hyun Kim

Introduction

Sleep disorders are highly prevalent, affecting approximately one-third of the population based on epidemiology studies (Partinen & Hublin, 2011). Sleep disorders are commonly seen in various health-care settings, such as primary care, sleep clinics, and mental health facilities. Proper diagnosis of sleep disorders can help guide clinical care, especially as effective treatments for sleep disorders become more widely available. Additionally, considering that sleep disorders are often comorbid with other physical and mental disorders, implementing adjunctive sleep treatment may enhance treatment for a comorbid physical or psychiatric illness.

The most widely studied sleep disorders that are comorbid with psychiatric disorders include insomnia, obstructive sleep apnea (OSA), and narcolepsy. While Asian-Americans are one of the fastest-growing minority groups in the USA, there have been very few studies examining sleep disorders specifically in Asian-American populations. Thus, the main objective of this chapter is to provide a comprehensive overview of various sleep disorders, provide prevalence rates in Asian-Americans if available, introduce subjective and objective assessment tools in diagnosing sleep disorders, and discuss cultural considerations associated with Asian-Americans for various sleep disorders.

Among the different sleep disorders, the current chapter focuses primarily on insomnia, OSA, and narcolepsy. Because very few studies have investigated sleep disorders with Asian-American populations, studies that have been conducted in the countries of origin are also discussed to provide a wider framework of understanding.

Insomnia

Description and Prevalence

Insomnia is the most common sleep disorder that psychologists encounter and diagnose. Insomnia is characterized by a combination of nocturnal and diurnal symptoms and is recognized as an independent disorder in all diagnostic classification systems. The two most widely used diagnostic classification systems are the

S. Suh, Ph.D., C.B.S.M. (✉)
Sungshin Women's University, Department of Psychology, Sungbuk-gu Dongsun-dong 3 ga, 249-1, Sungshingwan #920, Seoul, Republic of Korea

Stanford University, 450 Broadway Street, M/C 5704, Redwood City, CA, USA
e-mail: alysuh@stanford.edu

P. Song, M.D.
Department of Neurology, Inje University Paik Hospital, Juhwa-ro 170, Ilsanseo-gu, Goyang-si, Gyeonggi-do, Republic of Korea
e-mail: songpama@hanmail.net

H. Kim, M.Sc.
Department of Psychological and Brain Sciences Boston University, 648 Beacon Street, 2nd floor, Boston, MA 02215
e-mail: monhykim@bu.edu

L.T. Benuto et al. (eds.), *Guide to Psychological Assessment with Asians*,
DOI 10.1007/978-1-4939-0796-0_21, © Springer Science+Business Media New York 2014

International Classification of Sleep Disorders, 2nd edition (ICSD) and Diagnostic and Statistical Manual for Mental Disorders, 4th edition (DSM-IV). Both classification systems include diagnostic criteria of insomnia as having both nocturnal symptoms (i.e., difficulty initiating or maintaining sleep, early morning awakenings, or nonrestorative sleep) and diurnal symptoms characterized by impairment of daytime functioning (i.e., difficulties with memory or concentration that are related to sleep difficulty) as well as marked distress due to sleep disturbance.

The Diagnostic and Statistical Manual for Mental Disorders, 5th edition (DSM-5) is scheduled to be published in 2012, and the DSM-5 sleep advisory committee on sleep nosology has proposed changing primary insomnia disorder to a single diagnosis of insomnia disorder with use of specifiers for clinical comorbidities (see Table 21.1). This moves away from more established notions of "secondary" versus "primary" insomnia and also moves away from causal attribution. The proposed diagnosis of insomnia disorder based on the new DSM-5 criteria also includes the presence of sleep disturbance for at least 3 nights a week, for at least 3 months

Epidemiologic studies indicate that the prevalence of insomnia disorder in the USA is between 6 and 10 % (Ford & Kamerow, 1989; Ohayon, 2002) and based on population surveys, approximately 30 % of Americans report experiencing at least one insomnia symptom (Ancoli-Israel & Roth, 1999). In Asian countries, insomnia symptoms have been shown to be present in approximately 17 % of the Korean population, with 5 % meeting criteria for insomnia disorder, which is comparable with Western countries (Ohayon & Hong, 2002).

Table 21.1 Proposed changes for diagnosing insomnia in DSM-5

(A)	The predominant complaint is dissatisfaction with sleep quantity or quality. In children or the elderly, the complaint may be made by a caregiver or family member.
(B)	Report of one or more of the following symptoms:
	1. Difficulty initiating sleep. In children, this may be manifested as difficulty initiating sleep without caregiver intervention.
	2. Difficulty maintaining sleep, characterized by frequent awakenings or problems returning to sleep after awakenings. In children this may be manifested as difficulty returning to sleep without caregiver intervention.
	3. Early-morning awakening with inability to return to sleep.
	4. Non-restorative sleep.
	5. In children, prolonged resistance to going to bed and/or bedtime struggles.
(C)	The sleep complaint is accompanied by significant distress or impairment in daytime functioning as indicated by the report of at least one of the following:
	1. Fatigue or low energy.
	2. Cognitive impairment (e.g., attention, concentration, memory).
	3. Mood disturbance (e.g., irritability, dysphoria).
	4. Behavioral problems (e.g., hyperactivity, impulsivity, aggression).
	5. Impaired occupational or academic functioning.
	6. Impaired interpersonal/social functioning.
	7. Negative impact on caregiver or family functioning (e.g., fatigue, sleepiness)
(D)	The sleep difficulty occurs at least 3 nights per week.
(E)	The sleep difficulty is present for at least 3 months.
(F)	The sleep difficulty occurs despite adequate opportunity for sleep.

Risk Factors and Psychiatric Comorbidity

Risk factors for insomnia can be divided into static risk factors and modifiable risk factors. Static risk factors include gender, age, ethnicity, and genetics. Women are far more likely to be diagnosed with insomnia than men. This has been attributed to fluctuating hormone levels that may predispose women to have a higher prevalence of mental disorders than men (Seeman, 1997). Additionally, women report higher incidence during certain junctures in life, especially during pregnancy and when entering menopause (Kravitz et al., 2008; Mindell & Jacobson, 2000; NIH, 2005; Seron-Ferre, Ducsay, & Valenzuela, 1993; Steiger, 2007). Other psychological factors, such as difference in coping styles, higher likelihood of rumination, and more frequent exposure to stressful events may predispose or perpetuate insomnia in women.

Age has also been shown to be a significant risk factor for insomnia. One meta-analysis (Lichstein, Durrence, Ridel, & Bush, 2004; Lichstein, Taylor, McCrae, & Ruiter, 2011) indicated that over 60 % of studies found heightened risk of insomnia with older age. However, other studies have found that after controlling for comorbid factors such as physical illness, age no longer remains a significant risk. Both ethnicity and genetics have been indicated to be a risk factor for insomnia. There has been scarce research on genetics, but heritability estimates range from 20 to 40 % based on twin studies (Lichstein et al., 2011).

Modifiable risk factors for insomnia include hyperarousal, stress and life events, medical comorbidities, and psychiatric comorbidities. Many of the modifiable risk factors are targets for behavioral treatment of insomnia. Insomnia has long been considered to be associated with hyperarousal states, and studies have suggested that activation of the hypothalamic–pituitary–adrenal axis may contribute to the development of insomnia (Richardson, 2007). Additionally, the combination of having a predisposition towards hyperarousal (i.e., anxiety) and stressful life events increases the likelihood of developing a sleep disturbance after a stressful event.

Both medical and psychiatric illnesses increase risk of developing insomnia. Medical conditions such as chronic pain, cancer, and HIV status have a twofold to threefold risk of subsequently developing insomnia (Blazer, Hays, & Foley, 1995). Among psychiatric disorders, depression has been shown to be a stable risk factor for insomnia, with odds ratios ranging from 1.4 to 8.6 (Foley, Monjan, Izmirlian, Hays, & Blazer, 1999; Foley, Monjan, Simonsick, Wallace, & Blazer, 1999). While there have not been many longitudinal studies investigating the bidirectional relationship between insomnia and other psychiatric disorders, considering that insomnia is a symptom of most psychiatric disorders, it raises the possibility that these disorders may also be risk factors for developing insomnia.

Assessment Tools

1. The Clinical Interview

The first step to diagnosing insomnia usually starts with a clinical interview. The clinical interview should provide comprehensive information about nighttime symptoms (e.g., current sleep patterns, difficulty initiating or maintaining sleep), daytime symptoms (i.e., impact of sleep disturbance on daytime functioning), and etiological or comorbid conditions that contribute to the sleep disturbance. A clinical interview typically covers three broad domains: (a) the patient's current sleep patterns and daytime functioning, (b) history and developmental course, and (c) comorbid psychiatric or medical conditions.

Current sleep patterns and daytime functioning: A review of the patient's current sleep patterns typically involves the patient recalling his/her sleep schedule for the past 1–2 weeks. Completing sleep diaries prior to the initial clinical interview may help the clinician analyze the patient's current sleep patterns and derive sleep indices (i.e., average total sleep time, sleep onset latency) that are frequent targets for behavioral treatments for insomnia. At the minimum, the clinician should inquire about average total sleep time, time spent in bed, sleep onset latency, time spent awake in the middle of the night, and early morning awakenings. Additionally, some patients will report night-to-night variability in insomnia symptoms, as well as weekday–weekend variability in sleep schedules, so it is important to obtain at a minimum 1 week of sleep schedule data.

In addition to sleep patterns, the impact of sleep disturbance on daytime functioning should also be assessed. This can include irritability, changes in mood, difficulties with attention or concentration, reduction in social or physical activities, and preoccupation with sleep-related cognitions. Other compensatory behaviors, such as taking sleep medication, excessive caffeine intake, or taking prolonged daytime naps should also be assessed.

History and developmental course: Obtaining a history of insomnia can be helpful in understanding etiological features, as well as the presence of comorbid conditions, and making differential diagnosis. The 3-P model introduced by Spielman and Glovinsky (1991) provides a diathesis-stress framework for understanding the insomnia patient's history. This model proposes that predisposing, precipitating, and perpetuating factors are involved in the development and maintenance of insomnia disorder.

Predisposing factors include familial vulnerability to insomnia, or proneness to anxiety that increase one's risk of developing insomnia. A predisposing factor that is often overlooked in the assessment of insomnia is the patient's chronotype. A person's chronotype is determined by the patient's circadian rhythm, defined by oscillations of some indicator (such as core body temperature or blood pressure), with one complete oscillation occurring approximately every 24 h. A person's chronotype determines when a person's sleep propensity is the strongest. The terms *morningness* and *eveningness* are used to distinguish people who endorse extreme diurnal preferences. *Morningness* refers to those who show preferences for daytime activity. Individuals with strong morningness tendencies report peak performance and alertness in the early-morning hours. The opposite is true for those who show *eveningness*, or preferences for nighttime activities. Those with strong eveningness tendency report heightened alertness and peak performance during the evening hours.

Chronotype varies for each individual, and it is common for individuals with strong morning or evening tendency to develop insomnia, due to a misalignment in their circadian rhythm and imposed sleep–wake schedule due to social restraints. A patient's chronotype can be determined by asking a patient about their preferred sleep–wake schedules on an unrestrained schedule without work or social obligations.

Predisposing factors alone do not cause insomnia, and precipitating factors such as stressful life events (e.g., losing a job or death in the family) may cause acute insomnia. The sleep disturbance in acute insomnia is usually a normal response to a stressor. In response to acute insomnia, perpetuating factors may contribute to the maintenance of insomnia. These include cognitive and behavioral reactions to the sleep disturbance, such as preoccupation with the need for sleep, increasing time spent in bed, rumination about the consequences of poor sleep, using alcohol as a sleep aid, and misuse of sleep medication.

Comorbid sleep, psychiatric or medical conditions: An assessment of comorbid conditions is necessary in understanding the relationship between insomnia and the comorbid disorder. Comorbid sleep disorders, or other psychiatric and/or medical illnesses, may contribute to the development and severity of insomnia. Common comorbid sleep disorders with insomnia include OSA, restless leg syndrome, periodic limb movement disorder, and narcolepsy. It is also important to review the presence of medical disorders and medications that the patient is currently taking. Common medical disorders that are associated with insomnia include chronic pain, hyperthyroidism, cancer, and HIV. Medications such as steroids, stimulants, and beta-agonist drugs may also contribute to insomnia.

Assessment of psychiatric disorders is also important, considering that insomnia is a symptom of many psychiatric disorders including unipolar depression, bipolar disorder, generalized anxiety disorder, and post-traumatic stress disorder (PTSD). Among all the psychiatric disorders, depression has been shown to be the most strongly associated with insomnia, with early morning awakenings frequently being a sign of the onset of depression. Sleep disturbance has also been found to be associated with suicidal ideation, and thus, a thorough suicide risk assessment is necessary if a patient is severely depressed and reporting suicidal ideation (Bernert, Joiner, Cukrowicz, Schmidt, & Krakow, 2005; Bjorngaard, Bjerkeset, Romundstad, & Gunnell, 2011; Singareddy & Balon, 2001).

2. Self-report Questionnaires

The most commonly used measures for diagnosing insomnia include the Insomnia Severity Index (ISI; Bastien, Vallieres, & Morin, 2001) and the Pittsburgh Sleep Quality Index (PSQI; Buysse, Reynolds, Monk, Berman, & Kupfer, 1989). The ISI consists of seven items that assesses the degree of subjective symptoms of insomnia during the past 2 weeks on a five-point Likert scale, with scores ranging from 0 to 28. A higher score reflects greater insomnia severity. Guidelines for interpreting the total scores are as follows: Scores 0–7 reflect no significant insomnia, scores 8–14 reflect subthreshold insomnia, scores 15–21 reflect moderate insomnia, and scores 22–28 reflect severe insomnia. Scores higher than 14 are consistent with insomnia disorder. The ISI is used widely in both research and clinical settings, and is brief and easy to administer.

The PSQI is a self-report questionnaire assessing sleep quality and disturbances over the past month. The scale yields a total score that ranges from 0 to 21, with higher scores indicating more difficulties with sleep. The scale has good diagnostic sensitivity and specificity, and a score greater than 5 has been established as an optimal cutoff point to differentiate poor sleepers from good sleepers (Backhaus, Junghanns, Broocks, Riemann, & Hohagen, 2002). The questionnaire also has seven subscales including subjective sleep quality, sleep latency, sleep duration, habitual sleep efficiency, sleep disturbances, use of sleeping medications, and daytime dysfunction.

Other supplementary questionnaires are frequently used to assess features of insomnia, such as levels of hyperarousal, maladaptive beliefs about sleep, circadian preference, and sleep hygiene. Hyperarousal is common in insomnia patients, defined as heightened or conditioned arousal state in association with sleep (i.e., worrying about sleep, having intrusive thoughts at bedtime). The most frequently used questionnaires to assess for hyperarousal levels is the Hyperarousal Scale (HS; Pavlova et al., 2001) and Presleep arousal scale (PSAS; Nicassio, Mendlowitz, Fussell, & Petras, 1985). The HS consists of 26 items that assess the level of hyperarousal in individuals. The HAS can identify those with high levels of hyperarousal using an extreme score (number of items checked "extremely") and an introspective score (sum of six scores measuring introspectiveness) and a react score (sum of three items measuring reactivity). The PSAS consists of 16 items assessing both cognitive ("worrying about falling asleep") and somatic ("heart racing") arousal of insomnia patients. Patients are asked to rate symptoms reflecting hyperarousal during the time prior to sleeping on a five-point Likert scale. It is common to use the PSAS daily with a sleep diary to monitor hyperarousal states. There are currently no known cutoff scores for identifying pathological levels of hyperarousal in insomnia patients.

Another common feature of insomnia patients are maladaptive beliefs about sleep. The Dysfunctional Beliefs and Attitudes Scale (DBAS; Morin, Stone, Trinkle, Mercer, & Remsberg, 1993) consists of 30 items reflecting common dysfunctional beliefs about sleep. Higher scores on this scale reflect higher levels of maladaptive beliefs about sleep, and are later targeted during cognitive therapy to treat insomnia. The original version of the questionnaire consists of five subscales: (1) dysfunctional beliefs about the consequences of insomnia; (2) beliefs that sleep is unpredictable and uncontrollable; (3) unrealistic sleep expectations; (4) misconceptions about the causes of insomnia; and (5) erroneous beliefs about sleep-promoting habits. Recently, there have been two abbreviated versions with 10 items (DBAS-10) and 16 items (DBAS-16), and both have been reported to have adequate psychometric properties (Edinger & Wohlgemuth, 2001; Espie, Inglis, Harvey, & Tessier, 2000).

Chronotypes or circadian rhythms influence an individual's sleep schedule, and often a misalignment of work schedules and natural circadian rhythms may be an etiological feature of insomnia. The Horne–Östberg Morningness–Eveningness Questionnaire (MEQ; Horne & Ostberg, 1976) consists of 19 items reflecting questions about circadian preference, including daytime and nighttime activities, sleep exercise, mental activity, and alertness. The MEQ produces scores on a morningness–eveningness continuum (scores ranging from 16 to 86). Individuals can be classified into morning types (M-type; scores 59–86), neither type (N-type; scores

42–58), and evening types (E-type; scores 16–41). The MEQ demonstrates high correlations with physiological measurements of circadian rhythms (Kerkhof & Van Dongen, 1996; Lack & Bailey, 1994).

3. Polysomnography

An overnight polysomnography (PSG) is not necessary in the diagnosis of insomnia, but is often used to rule out other sleep disorders, especially sleep-disordered breathing (Kushida et al., 2005). Traditionally, diagnostic PSG is conducted in a sleep laboratory, but studies have found night-to-night variability of sleep recordings and first-night effects that produce sleep disturbance may interfere with obtaining an accurate recording of the patient's sleep. Recently, portable home monitoring PSG has been developed to avoid the first-night effect (Edinger et al., 1997).

A subgroup of insomnia patients have a tendency towards sleep misperception, which is often called paradoxical insomnia. Specifically, these patients have a discrepancy between their subjectively perceived sleep and objective sleep (typically measured by PSG). Past studies have indicated that many insomnia patients have the propensity to underestimate the amount of sleep they got, and research has also linked this to neurobiological dysfunction, including elevated levels of global cerebral metabolism during sleep, cortical arousal, and cerebral response to increasing task demands (Drummond, Meloy, Yanagi, Orff, & Brown, 2005; Nofzinger et al., 2004; Perlis, Giles, Mendelson, Bootzin, & Wyatt, 1997). If a patient consistently reports very little sleep each night without accompanied daytime impairment, it may be useful for the patient to undergo PSG to assess for sleep misperception.

4. Sleep Diaries

Sleep diaries are the essential self-reporting tool for diagnosing insomnia, and are considered the gold standard for the subjective assessment of insomnia (Carney et al., 2012). It is recommended that at least 2 weeks of sleep diary information is obtained for a baseline assessment of insomnia. The content of the sleep diaries should include the following sleep parameters: sleep onset latency (SOL), amount of time spent awake after sleep onset (WASO), total time actual spent in bed (TIB), early morning awakenings, lights on/off, and total amount of actual sleep (TST). Sleep efficiency (SE), often used as a treatment outcome indicator, can be calculated as TST/TIB × 100. Information on the type and timing of sleep medication can also be included in the sleep diary, in addition to subjective ratings of sleep quality, and daytime sleepiness and fatigue levels. There is also often a section for notes and comments that can be used to elaborate on unusual circumstances that affected the patient's sleep schedule.

Information derived from the sleep diary can also be helpful in identifying night-to-night variability in a patient's sleep patterns, such as weekday–weekend variability. Some patients may exaggerate the severity of sleep disturbance across the week based on a few nights of poor sleep. Sleep diaries can also help guide treatment by challenging the patient's beliefs about sleep in thinking that a bad night of sleep will directly affect the patient's daytime consequences.

5. Actigraphy

Actigraphy is a wristwatch size device that contains an accelerometer which monitors the degree of motion to differentiate between wakefulness and sleep. Compared to PSG, which is based on multiple channels of information (EEG, EMG, EOG), actigraphy determines sleep and wakefulness states solely based on the occurrence and degree of motion. Research has indicated that there is acceptable agreement between actigraphy-derived estimates of sleep parameters and PSG (Tryon, 2004). Actigraphy is also frequently used to detect change in sleep for a patient who is in treatment. The main advantage of actigraphy-based measures is that it allows recording of sleep–wake data for long periods of time in the patient's natural sleep environment. While actigraphy is not recommended for diagnosing insomnia, it is often useful for evaluating specific aspects of insomnia, and also used along with sleep diaries for accurate sleep schedule information.

Cultural Considerations

A common feature in Asian cultures, especially Korean and Chinese, is the somatization of emotional distress. In many Asian cultures, negative emotions such as anxiety, depression, or other psychological problems are rarely expressed, and mental illness is usually stigmatized (Kim & Rhi, 1976). This is rooted in traditional Chinese medicine, which is characterized by an "unwillingness to differentiate between psychological and physiologic functions" (Lin, 1980). Thus, it is common for a patient who is suffering from emotional distress to express his/her difficulties through physical complaints. It has been suggested that people from Asian cultures who conceptualize their health based on solely their physical health are less likely to express their psychological states and have very poor skills in communicating their emotional states (Kleinman, 1980).

Several culture-bound syndromes that are indicated in the DSM-IV-TR highlight this issue, and sleep disturbance or insomnia is a frequent physical complaint of these conditions. One example is *hwa-byung*, a culture-bound syndrome found specifically in the Korean culture, especially in Korean women who are brought up to suppress their emotions and be submissive based on traditional Confucian values. The direct translation of *hwa-byung* is "fire-illness" or "anger syndrome" and it is associated with suppressed anger manifesting in psychosomatic symptoms. Insomnia is known to be one of the main symptoms of *hwa-byung* and also provides a way of conceptualizing and resolving emotional distress through somatic complaints in Korean elderly immigrant women (Pang, 1990). It is common for Koreans to have physical complaints rather than psychological or mental complaints when they are expressing emotional distress (Kleinman, 1980; Lock, 1980).

Another culture-bound syndrome that is frequently seen in China is called *shenjing shuairuo* ("neurasthenia" or "weakness of nerves"). *Shenjing shuairuo* is characterized by various somatic and psychological complaints including fatigue or weakness, poor concentration, memory loss, irritability, and sleep disturbance. Studies on *shenjing shuairuo* and its similarities to diagnoses in the ICD-10 highlight that it is most similar to both somatoform and anxiety disorders. Similarly, *Shen-k'uei* (Taiwan) or *Shenkui* (China) is also a culture-bound syndrome that is characterized by somatic complaints such as dizziness, fatigue, general weakness, and insomnia, for which no physical cause can be found. *Shen-k'uei* is usually accompanied by marked anxiety or panic symptoms, and patients with this syndrome attribute their symptoms to excessive semen loss, which is feared to drain one of their vital essence and is perceived as being life-threatening.

Thus, when seeing an Asian-American patient who is complaining of insomnia,, especially from Korean or Chinese cultures, it may be important to assess for deeper underlying issues of emotional distress and suppressed anger, and thus, a more thorough evaluation of comorbid psychological illnesses is important.

Another issue relevant to Asian-Americans in the assessment of insomnia is comorbid PTSD, especially in Southeast Asian refugees who have immigrated to the USA to escape political turmoil. The impact of traumatic events tend to be lifelong in these refugees, and it puts them at high risk for a wide variety of mental illnesses, especially PTSD. For example, research has shown that over 90 % of Cambodian refugees who immigrated to the USA who experienced traumatic events during the 4 years of Pol Pot's regime prior to coming to America were found to meet criteria for PTSD (Rhee, 2009). It is important to assess for comorbid PTSD among Southeast Asian immigrants who were refugees prior to coming to the USA, as sleep disturbance is a common symptom of PTSD and is often characterized by vivid nightmares in PTSD patients. Implementing adjunctive psychological treatment with treatment for insomnia or nightmares (imagery rehearsal therapy) may increase the effectiveness in the treatment of the underlying illness.

Obstructive Sleep Apnea

Description and Prevalence

OSA is a disorder characterized by repeated episodes of partial or complete upper airway obstruction during sleep. Individuals diagnosed

Table 21.2 Characteristics of obstructive sleep apnea (OSA)

1. Overnight polysomnography (PSG) (Recommended by the AASM guideline[a]) (A) Apnea severity is observed by the *apnea–hypopnea index (AHI)*, the count of apneas and hypopneas per hour of sleep • *Apnea*: complete or near cessation of airflow for at least 10 s with or without the presence of associated oxygen desaturation or sleep fragmentation • *Hypopnea*: at least 30 % reduction in airflow reduction from the baseline that is accompanied by at least a 4 % drop in oxygen saturation (SaO2). – (Alternatively) at least 50 % reduction in oronasal airflow associated with a decreased oxyhemoglobin saturation or an EEG arousal. (B) Classification of OSA Severity: • AHI <5 ("No OSA"), • 5≤AHI<15 ("Mild OSA"), • 15≤AHI<30 ("Moderate OSA"), • AHI≥30 ("Severe OSA")
2. Physical examination / symptoms: (A) Nighttime symptoms: • Prominent snoring • Witnessed apneas or gasping (B) Daytime symptoms: • Daytime sleepiness • Mood or affective disturbance

[a]American Academy of Sleep Medicine Task Force, 2007

with OSA often experience loud snoring, witnessed breathing interruptions, awakenings resulting from gasping or choking, and excessive daytime sleepiness (EDS). As part of sleep-disordered breathing (SDB), OSA is among the most common class of disorders diagnosed in the sleep centers all across the USA, and is known to account for about 70 % of all patients evaluated in sleep clinics (Punjabi et al., 2000) (Table 21.2).

OSA is known to be prevalent in 24 % of men and 9 % of women in the general population, when defined by the diagnostic criteria of an Apnea–Hypopnea Index (AHI)>5. When distinguished further by accompanying symptoms, such as daytime sleepiness, 4 % of men and 2 % of women are presented with OSA (Cao & Kushida 2011). Only one previous study has looked at OSA prevalence in Asian-Americans, reporting that OSA was prevalent in 3.81 % of the Asian-American population, a rate lower compared to other races (Stein et al., 2011). However, the rate of snoring was found to be similar between Asian-Americans and Caucasians (O'Connor et al. 2003). On the other hand, large prevalence studies focused on the Asian countries (i.e., Hong Kong, Korea, and India) reported the prevalence of OSA is comparable to those of Caucasian studies using similar methodological designs and definitions (Bixler et al., 2001; Duran et al., 2001; Gislason et al., 1988; Ip et al., 2001; Kim et al., 2004; Udwadia et al., 2004).

Risk factors and Psychiatric Comorbidity: There are several well-known risk factors of OSA which may provide critical evidence for the presence of the disease. One of the strongest risk factors is old age (age 65 and older). The prevalence of OSA increases with age in Asian populations, similar to Western countries (Ong & Clerk, 1988). Male gender is also a well-known risk factor for OSA. The fact that android-type obesity (fat deposition mainly in the neck and abdomen) is more dominantly seen in men may explain this gender predominance for OSA. Women are at greater risk for OSA in presence of obesity during the postmenopausal state. Craniofacial structural factors are established risk factors for OSA, and it has been reported that Asians are predisposed to a higher severity of OSA due to craniofacial skeletal features that contribute to development of OSA (Li et al., 2000; Ong & Clerk, 1988). Abnormal cranial features may be good indicators for detecting OSA in nonobese Asian patients (Lam et al. 2007).

Body-mass index (BMI) is a good indicator for obesity, and also has good sensitivity and specificity for predicting OSA (Tsai et al., 2003). A positive correlation between BMI and OSA has been also reported in the population-based studies of Asian countries, but when comparing Asian patients to Caucasian patients, obesity is suggested to be a less significant risk factor for OSA in the Asian race. There seems to be a notable difference between the percentage of obesity in Asian and Caucasian OSA patients (Li et al., 2000), and BMI is significantly lower in this group compared to Caucasian patients when age, sex, and disease severity were controlled (Genta et al., 2008; Li et al., 2000)

Psychiatric symptoms or disorders are commonly presented with OSA, and they may be controlled with treatment of OSA (Millman et al., 1989). Research has shown that more than half of OSA patients have comorbid psychiatric symptoms such as depression (21.8 %), anxiety (16.7 %), and bipolar disorder (3.3 %), and female patients had higher prevalence of psychiatric problems than male patients (DeZee et al., 2005; Dursunoglu et al., 2009; Uyar et al., 2011). This association may be explained by common neurobiological risk factors share by OSA and affective disorders, especially on the neurotransmitter level; for example, serotonin reuptake inhibitors (SSRI), commonly prescribed as a medication for depression, is suggested to improve OSA (Schroder & O'Hara, 2005). Sleep fragmentation and hypoxemia in OSA could also cause metabolic impairment and result in depressive symptoms (Kamba et al., 1997). The relationship between OSA and depression is complex, and thus, information on a patient's sleep schedule should be evaluated when assessing for depressive disorders.

Assessment Tools

1. Clinical Interview

While an overnight PSG study is required to confirm the diagnosis of OSA, it is typical for the clinician (physician or clinical psychologist) to conduct a clinical interview and physical examination to assess for risk factors and symptoms suspicious of OSA prior to the overnight sleep study. Patients are often not aware of their symptoms, and thus, it is important to obtain this information from someone who has observed the patient's sleep habits.

Nighttime Symptoms: A typical characteristic of OSA is loud snoring or brief gasps alternating with nocturnal snorting and gasping. Loud and disruptive snoring accompanied by apneic events or choking is commonly observed by bed partners of OSA patients (Guilleminault et al., 1976; Hoffstein & Szalai, 1993; Kales et al., 1985), but most OSA patients are unaware of their symptoms, and the absence of this symptom does not exclude the possibility of having the disorder. Dry mouth and thirst upon waking up in the morning are reported by a majority of patients with OSA (Kales et al., 1985).

Daytime Symptoms: Sleep fragmentation and poor sleep quality are well-known consequences of abnormal breathing events in OSA, and they are often presented as EDS and fatigue (Hoffstein & Szalai, 1993; Kales et al., 1985; Marin et al., 2005). Patients with OSA commonly report drowsiness or napping during the daytime, and these symptoms can result in catastrophic consequences such as motor vehicle accidents (George et al., 1987; Ip et al., 2001; Tufik et al., 2010). It is essential to inquire about the presence and level of sleepiness while driving a motor vehicle or operating machines if a clinician suspects a patient has OSA.

Research has shown that cognitive dysfunction is a common consequence of OSA, and many complaints of problems in concentration, attention, memory, or judgment (Redline et al., 1997). Specific neurocognitive tests that involve the prefrontal cortex have been shown to be impaired in OSA patients, which may be a result of sleepiness. Studies of the psychomotor vigilance task (PVT), a task sensitive to sleep loss and sleepiness, also revealed that OSA patients showed slower reaction time and more lapses as compared to individuals without OSA (Kim et al., 2007). Most patients appear to show improved performance with treatment (e.g., nasal continuous positive airway pressure (CPAP) treatment), but it has been suggested that there may be specific genetic susceptibilities (i.e., ApoE-e4 gene) that could contribute to persistent neurobehavioral deficits in OSA (O'Hara et al., 2005).

During the clinical interview, information on a decreased sex drive, change in mood, nocturnal heartburn, and a history of hypertension should also be noted, because these are symptoms commonly related with OSA. Craniofacial structures, such as having a short, thick neck, a short lower jaw, or receding chin, and a large tongue, may also indicate that the patient is vulnerable to developing OSA (Cartwright, 2001).

2. Self-report Questionnaires

The Berlin questionnaire is a simple questionnaire that consists of three categories measuring the risk of having OSA (Netzer et al., 1999). The patient can be categorized into High Risk or Low Risk depending on their responses to questions related to (1) snoring behavior, (2) daytime sleepiness, and (3) obesity and hypertension, and positive responses to at least two categories indicate a high likelihood of exhibiting OSA. This questionnaire has been demonstrated to predict a RDI > 5 with sensitivity of 0.86 and specificity of 0.77 and is widely used in primary care settings (Heistand et al., 2006).

Another self-report questionnaire that is frequently used in detecting EDS is the Epworth Sleepiness Scale (ESS; see Narcolepsy section below for detailed description). In the OSA population, the ESS cutoff is greater than 10 for detecting EDS (Johns, 1991).

3. Polysomnography

According to the International Classification of Sleep Disorders (ICSD), a diagnosis of OSA requires evidence-based data from a PSG study (AASM). The scoring guidelines provided by the American Academy of Sleep Medicine (AASM) recommends scoring obstructive hypopneas based on the number of abnormal breathing events during nocturnal sleep, namely, an AHI, which reflects the count of apneas and hypopneas per hour of sleep. Clinically, OSA is defined by the presence of at least five obstructive respiratory events per hour of sleep (Cao et al., 2011). The severity of OSA is usually defined by AHI <5 (no OSA), $5 \leq \text{AHI} < 15$ (mild OSA), $15 \leq \text{AHI} < 30$ (moderate OSA), and AHI ≥ 30 (severe OSA), but respiratory disturbance index (RDI; the count of apneas and hypopneas) plus respiratory effort-related arousals (RERAs) per hour of sleep, can also be used interchangeably due to the variability of measurement outcome (Cao et al., 2011). AHI is also most commonly used to evaluate OSA in children, and OSA is defined as AHI >1, according to the criteria of the AASM (AASM, 2005).

Pediatric OSA

Diagnosis of OSA in children is made on the basis of a thorough evaluation of sleep history, physical examination, and PSG data (AASM, 2005). Parental complaint about their children's sleep is a critical factor of identifying OSA, and hyperactivity or attention deficits are also notable clinical features of OSA in children. Displays of EDS or frequent napping could also provide major evidence for detecting sleep problems in older children.

Cultural Considerations in OSA patients

In the Asian-American population, a higher level of acculturation is known to be associated with higher BMI and elevated rates of obesity (Frisbie et al., 2001), which reflects adoption of an American lifestyle such as physical inactivity and diet consisting of high-fat and calorie-dense food (Cho & Juon, 2006; Kandula & Lauderdale, 2005). This trend in obesity indicates the possibility of increased risk of OSA in Asians who were born in the USA or immigrants who resided in the USA for a long duration, although no previous study has focused on this particular topic.

Previously, OSA has been reported to be under-recognized in Asian-American communities, with low BMI being one factor that most strongly associated with low rate of recognition (Kapur et al., 2002). Considering that Asian patients have lower BMI compared to other ethnic groups, it is possible that OSA in Asian-Americans is largely under-recognized in comparison to other ethnicities; most patients presented in sleep clinics are obese, but this may be due to high rate of suspicion for having OSA. Likewise, one study reported that the risk of OSA related to high BMI is greatly under-recognized in Japanese descendants as compared with Caucasian descendants (Genta et al., 2008). The fact that sleep medicine is relatively underdeveloped in many Asian countries may also affect Asian-American immigrants' awareness of OSA (Lam et al., 2007).

Narcolepsy

Description and Prevalence

Narcolepsy is characterized by the following symptoms: (a) *EDS*: It is characterized by pathological or inappropriate somnolence, and has been defined in the International Classification of Sleep Disorders, 2nd Edition (ICSD-2) as "the inability to stay awake and alert during the major waking episodes of the day, resulting in unintended lapses into drowsiness and sleep (American Academy of Sleep Medicine). Daytime sleepiness is the most disabling and frequent cause for consultation (Dauvilliers et al., 2001; Guilleminault et al., 1974; Overeem et al., 2001; Scammell, 2003). These sleep attacks are typically short, but refreshing. However, a single sleep attack is not enough to eliminate sleepiness in these patients. (b) *Cataplexy*: It is characterized by a reversible sudden drop of muscle tone triggered by emotional factors, most often by positive emotions such as laughter, pleasant surprise, or anger, but almost never by stress, fear, or physical effort (Overeem et al., 2001; Scammell, 2003; Thorpy, 2006). Awareness is preserved throughout the attacks. Although the attacks are abrupt, they usually take several seconds to reach their maximum, and lasts from several seconds to several minutes. Cataplexy is pathognomonic of narcolepsy, and found in 60–70 % of narcoleptic patients (Bassetti et al., 2003; Poirier, Montplaisir, Decary, Momege, & Lebrun, 1986). (c) *Hypnagogic or Hypnopompic Hallucinations*: Both hypnagogic and hypnopompic hallucinations are vivid dreamlike experiences that occur during the transition between wakefulness and sleep. Some patients report difficulty in differentiating dreams from reality and are occasionally misdiagnosed as schizophrenic. (d) *Sleep paralysis*: Sleep paralysis is the inability to move during the onset of sleep or on awakening, while patients are subjectively awake and conscious. It is usually of short duration but can at times last several minutes. (e) *Disrupted nocturnal sleep*: Approximately one-third of narcolepsy patients indicate they have no difficulty initiating sleep, but have more difficulty maintaining sleep after sleep onset (Table 21.3).

Table 21.3 Diagnostic criteria for narcolepsy with and without cataplexy

Criteria for narcolepsy
1. Excessive daytime sleepiness (EDS) occurring almost daily for at least 3 months.
2a. [*For Narcolepsy with cataplexy*] Definite history of cataplexy, defined as sudden and transient (less than 2 min) episodes of loss of muscle tone, generally bilateral, triggered by emotions (usually laughing and joking).
2b. [*For Narcolepsy without cataplexy*] Typical cataplexy is not present, although doubtful or atypical cataplexy-like episodes may be reported.
3. Diagnosis should, whenever possible, be confirmed by nocturnal PSG (with a minimum of 6 h sleep) followed by a daytime MSLT:
(a) Mean daytime sleep latency 8 min or shorter, with two or more sleep onset in REM periods (the time from sleep onset to REM sleep should be less than 15 min in at least two naps).
(b) Alternatively, hypocretin-1 concentrations in the cerebrospinal fluid 110 ng/mL or lower, or a third of mean control values.
4. Hypersomnia is not better explained by another sleep disorder, medical or neurological disorders, mental disorder, medication use, or substance use disorder.

PSG polysomnography, *MSLT* multiple sleep latency test, *REM* rapid eye movement

The prevalence of narcolepsy is usually about 25–50 per 100,000 (Longstreth, Koepsell, Ton, Hendrickson, & van Belle, 2007). According to the previous general population studies, prevalence rates of narcolepsy were 0.02–0.05 % in the US (Longstreth et al., 2009; Silber, Krahn, Olson, & Pankratz, 2002). Currently, there are no studies investigating the prevalence of narcolepsy in Asian-Americans, but population-based prevalence studies consisting of racially diverse ethnic groups suggest that Asian-Americans have lower prevalence of narcolepsy compared to African-Americans or Caucasians (Longstreth et al., 2009). However, prevalence in certain racial or ethnic groups requires further research.

Risk Factors and Psychiatric Comorbidity: Pathophysiological studies have shown that narcolepsy is caused by the early loss of neurons in the hypothalamus that produce hypocretin, a wakefulness-associated neurotransmitter present in cerebrospinal fluid (CSF). The cause of neural loss could be autoimmune in nature since most patients have the HLA DQB1*0602 allele that predisposes individuals to the disorder (Dauvilliers, Arnulf, & Mignot, 2007).

Narcolepsy is highly comorbid with psychiatric disorders, especially depression and anxiety. The prevalence of depression in narcolepsy has been reported to be as high as 20–37 %, which has been attributed to be caused by the reaction to the disorder and its effects (Kales et al., 1982; Krishnan, 1984; Mosko, 1989; Sours, 1963; Vandeputte, 2003) However, a recent study has found that narcolepsy does not increase frequency of diagnosable depressive disorders when overlapping symptoms of narcolepsy and depression (i.e., sleep, fatigue) are excluded (Vourdas et al., 2002). Another study reported there may be higher frequency of depressive symptoms such as depressed mood, pathological guilt, crying, and anhedonia (Fortuyn, 2010).

High levels of anxiety have also been reported in narcolepsy patients, with 35 % of patients meeting criteria for anxiety disorder, compared to 3 % in the general population (Fortuyn, 2010). Elevated anxiety symptoms can partially be explained by perceived loss of self-control associated with the narcolepsy symptoms and vivid memories of daytime hallucinations.

Narcolepsy patients are often misdiagnosed as having schizophrenia, usually due to experiencing hypnagogic and hypnopompic hallucinations, which are observed in 30 % of narcolepsy patients. However, hallucinations in schizophrenic patients are distinctly different from hypnagogic and hypnopompic hallucinations observed in narcolepsy patients. Schizophrenic hallucinations are typically auditory, while hallucinations in narcolepsy patients are usually a combination of visual, auditory, as well as tactile experiences (Dahmen, Kasten, Mittag, & Muller, 2002).

Assessment Tools

1. Clinical Interview

A diagnosis of narcolepsy is based primarily on clinical symptoms, which are usually obtained during a diagnostic interview. Narcolepsy with cataplexy is based on EDS occurring daily for at least 3 months, and a history of cataplexy. The diagnosis of narcolepsy without cataplexy has the same criteria without typical cataplexy, although doubtful or atypical cataplexy-like episodes may be reported (AASM, 2005).

The most common causes of EDS can be differentiated by the sleep related histories. It is important to enquire about the patient's general sleep hygiene and other lifestyle issues that may have irregular sleep patterns and sleep deprivation. A sleep diary can also be helpful in making differential diagnoses.

2. Self-report Questionnaires

The subjective severity of daytime sleepiness can be quantified using scales such as the ESS and Stanford Sleepiness Scale (SSS) (Hoddes & Zarcone, 1972; Johns, 1991). The ESS is an 8-item questionnaire that measures the degree of sleepiness during the daytime (Johns, 1991) and is commonly used to evaluate the level of daytime sleepiness in narcolepsy patients. The ESS questionnaire requires subjects to rate the likelihood that they might doze off or fall asleep in eight different everyday situations. The sleepiness is scored from 0 to 3 points, where 3 represents a high likelihood of dozing or falling asleep. ESS scores of ≥15 are common in untreated narcolepsy patients (Johns, 1991) (Table 21.4).

The SSS was developed to quantify the subjective sleepiness of patients throughout the day. It is a 1–7 rating scale, and the patients are asked to pick one that best represents how they are feeling. While the ESS has been validated for narcolepsy, the SSS is not specific for narcolepsy.

The Pediatric Daytime Sleepiness Scale (PDSS), a validated scale, is more appropriate for use in children and teenagers between ages of 11 and 15 years (Drake et al., 2003). This is useful when considering largest incidence of narcolepsy is around 15 years. It was created to determine the relationship between daytime sleepiness and school performance, and now used as sleepiness measures, and score of 16 or higher is likely to be associated with a negative impact on daily functioning.

The Ullanlinna Narcolepsy Scale (UNS) consists of 11 narcolepsy and cataplexy related

Table 21.4 Self-report questionnaires for sleep disorders

Assessment name	Disorder assessed	Recommendation(s) and/or relevant research findings	May be used with	Available in
Insomnia Severity Index	Insomnia	Scores 0–7: no insomnia Scores 8–14: subthreshold Scores 15–21: moderate Scores 22–28: severe Cutoff score >14 found to be optimum cutoff for insomnia as a clinical disorder	Adults, adolescents	Korean Chinese Japanese
Pittsburgh Sleep Quality Index	Insomnia	Score >5 represents clinical insomnia Includes seven subscales: sleep latency, subjective sleep quality, sleep duration, habitual sleep efficiency, sleep disturbances, use of sleeping medications, daytime dysfunction	Adults	Korean Chinese Japanese Taiwanese Hindi
Dysfunctional Beliefs and Attitudes Scale	Insomnia	Short versions with 10 items (DBAS-10) and 16 items (DBAS-16) available	Adults	Korean Chinese Malaysian
Hyperarousal Scale	Insomnia	No known cutoff scores	All	None validated in Asian languages
Presleep Arousal Scale	Insomnia	No known cutoff scores	Adults	None validated in Asian languages
Horne Östberg Morningness–Eveningness Questionnaire	Insomnia	Evening type (Scores 16–41) Neither type (Scores 42–58) Morning type (Scores 59–86)	Adults	Korean Chinese Japanese Hindi
Berlin Questionnaire	OSA	"Snoring" is present with ≥2 positive responses to Q's 2–6 "Daytime sleepiness" is present with ≥2 positive responses to Q's 7–9 "Hypertension and/or obesity" is determined with ≥1 positive responses and/or a BMI >30 Presence of two out of the three symptoms indicates a high likelihood of sleep disordered breathing	Adults	Korean Japanese Chinese Hindi Filipino
Ullanlinna Narcolepsy Scale (UNS)	Narcolepsy	Score >14 consistent with narcolepsy	All	Korean Chinese
Epworth Sleepiness Scale (ESS)	Daytime sleepiness in Insomnia, OSA and Narcolepsy	Scores >10 consistent with EDS in the general population and OSA patients; Scores ≥ 15 used for untreated narcolepsy patients.	All	Korean Chinese Japanese Filipino
Stanford Sleepiness Scale (SSS)	Daytime sleepiness in OSA and Narcolepsy	Cutoff scores not reported	All	Korean Japan
Pediatric Daytime Sleepiness Scale	Daytime sleepiness in adolescents with narcolepsy	Score ≥16 reflecting EDS	Adolescents ages 11–15	

questions. Each question is rated from 0 to 4 which indicate how frequently individuals experience those symptoms. Total scores range from 0 to 44, and cutoff scores of 14 or more have high sensitivity and specificity for narcolepsy (Hublin et al., 1994). This scale has been translated in Korean and Chinese (Shin et al., 2008; Wing et al., 2000).

3. Polysomnography

An overnight PSG is not essential in the diagnostic workup, yet it remains an important part of the evaluation process and usually done the night before the Multiple Sleep Latency Test (MSLT; see below). The main purpose of the PSG is to exclude other conditions related to daytime sleepiness, such as OSA, periodic limb movement disorder, or behaviorally induced voluntary sleep restriction. In a PSG study, a short sleep latency of less than 10 min and a sleep-onset REM (SOREM) sleep are frequent findings in narcolepsy patients. SOREM during nocturnal sleep is observed in 25–50 % of cases of narcolepsy with cataplexy and is a highly specific finding.

4. MSLT and MWT

The MSLT consists of five 30-min trial naps every 2 h (from 9 a.m. to 6 p.m.) in a dark room (Carskadon et al., 1986). The mean sleep latency (mean time to fall asleep) and number of sleep-onset REM sleep (SOREM: REM sleep appearing within 15 min after sleep onset) are documented. Mean daytime sleep latency of 8 min or shorter, with two or more SOREM, are needed for the diagnosis of narcolepsy.

The MWT is similar to MSLT. Patients remain awake in a comfortable sitting position in a dark room for five 20-min trials given at 10 a.m., noon, and 2, 4, and 6 p.m. (Mitler, Walsleben, Sangal, & Hirshkowitz, 1998). The purpose of the MWT is to test the patient's ability to stay awake. This measurement is not used for diagnosis, but rather to assess treatment effects of psychostimulant alertness, and risk of falling asleep associated with specific jobs or activities.

5. Hypocretin Concentration

Hypocretin is a deficient neurotransmitter in narcolepsy. CSF measurement of hypocretin-1 level is low in narcolepsy, and the absolute value for diagnosis is defined as CSF hypocretin-1 concentration lower than 110 ng/mL or lower, or a third of mean control values. Although deficient hypocretin is a genuine disease entity of narcolepsy cataplexy, the specificity is still to be determined (Mignot et al., 2002).

6. Genetic Testing

Narcolepsy occurs sporadically in 99 % of patients, but genetic factors may play a role in which environmental factors act on. Genetic testing has been used to aid the clinical diagnosis of narcolepsy. The HLA DQB1*0602 is the most specific genetic marker for narcolepsy across all ethnic groups, including Asians, and is found in 95 % of narcoleptic patients with cataplexy (Mignot, Hayduk, Black, Grumet, & Guilleminault, 1997).

Cultural Considerations in Narcolepsy Patients

One cultural aspect to consider in Asian-American populations, especially adolescents, is EDS following chronic sleep deprivation. Many Asian-American adolescents are under tremendous pressure and carry enormous social and psychological importance in academic success. This may lead many Asian-American students to stay awake late at night to complete their academic loads. As a result, insufficient sleep and irregular sleep patterns in Asian students can lead to EDS and may manifest as symptoms similar of narcolepsy. For example, the mean school night total sleep times for Korean high school students were 6.02 h, 5.62 h, and 4.86 h for 10th, 11th, and 12th graders, respectively, and amount of sleep deprivation correlated with daytime sleepiness (Yang, Kim, Patel, & Lee, 2005). The academic demands/stress and early school start time are the important contributing factors for sleep deprivation among Korean adolescents (Yang et al., 2005). Similarly, total sleep time in Japanese adolescents were 6–7 h, and 7.5 h in Chinese adolescents (Fukuda & Ishihara, 2001; Liu & Zhou, 2002). This is comparably shorter than American peers of 7–8 h (Wolfson & Carskadon, 1998).

In Asian-Americans, experiencing hypnagogic or hypnopompic hallucinations in narcoleptic patients may hold beliefs of being possessed by evil spirits. For instance, some Korean narcoleptic patients may be mistaken for *shin-byung* or "a culture-bound syndrome specific to Koreans, characterized by sleep disturbance and various psychosomatic symptoms, developing into waking-state hallucinations," before proper diagnosis.

Summary and Conclusions

1. The essential tools for the assessment of insomnia includes a clinical interview and sleep diaries. Self-report questionnaires such as the Insomnia Severity Index and the Pittsburgh Sleep Quality index, along with actigraphy, can be used as adjunctive measures to aid assessment. Polysomnography is not indicated, but can help rule out other sleep disorders.
2. When assessing for insomnia in Asian-Americans, it is common for individuals from Asian cultures to express their emotional distress through somatization, as mental illness is usually stigmatized, and thus, it is important to be sensitive to underlying emotional distress. Asian-Americans may be more likely to conceptualize their health based only on their physical health and may have poor skills in communicating their emotional distress. Complaining of insomnia may be one way to express underlying negative emotions, and thus, a more thorough evaluation of comorbid psychological disorders is important.
3. While an overnight PSG study is required to confirm the diagnosis of OSA, presence of snoring, daytime sleepiness, hypertension, or obesity may be used as strong indicators of OSA.
4. Considering that Asian OSA patients have lower BMI compared to Caucasian patients, it is possible that OSA is largely under-recognized in the Asian-American population. Nonetheless, adoption of the American lifestyle (e.g., high-calorie intake, physical inactivity) in Asian-Americans with high acculturation often leads to increase in BMI, which may result in increased risk of OSA in the Asian-American population.
5. Narcolepsy is characterized by EDS, cataplexy, hypnagogic or hypnopompic hallucinations, sleep paralysis, and disrupted nocturnal sleep. A diagnosis of narcolepsy is confirmed by nocturnal polysomnography followed by an MSLT. Questionnaires such as the ESS and SSS can indicate EDS, regardless of etiology of the symptom; such as OSA and narcolepsy. The Ullanlinna Narcolepsy Scale (UNS) is a questionnaire which includes symptoms of narcolepsy specific EDS and cataplexia. EDS, the most common presenting symptom of narcolepsy, should be considered with individual's sleep schedule in the assessment of insomnia.
6. Many Asian-American adolescents are under tremendous pressure to perform well in school. This may lead many Asian-American adolescents to be sleep deprived because of academic work during the night, which in turn may present as EDS symptoms, a symptom that is often mistaken for narcolepsy.
7. Symptoms of hypnagogic or hypnopompic hallucinations in narcolepsy can be misdiagnosed as schizophrenia, or cultural bound syndromes such as *"shin-byung"* in Korean-Americans.

References

American Academy of Sleep Medicine. (2005). The international classification of sleep disorders: Diagnostic and coding manual (2nd ed.), Chicago, IL: AASM.

Ancoli-Israel, S., & Roth, T. (1999). Characteristics of insomnia in the United States: Results of the 1991 National Sleep Foundation Survey. I. [Research Support, Non-U.S. Gov't Research Support, U.S. Gov't, Non-P.H.S. Research Support, U.S. Gov't, P.H.S.]. *Sleep, 22* (Suppl 2), S347–S353.

Backhaus, J., Junghanns, K., Broocks, A., Riemann, D., & Hohagen, F. (2002). Test-retest reliability and validity of the Pittsburgh Sleep Quality Index in primary insomnia [Validation Studies]. *Journal of Psychosomatic Research, 53*(3), 737–740.

Bassetti, C., Gugger, M., Bischof, M., Mathis, J., Sturzenegger, C., Werth, E., … Mignot, E. (2003). The narcoleptic borderland: A multimodal diagnostic approach including cerebrospinal fluid levels of hypocretin-1 (orexin A) [Comparative Study]. *Sleep Medicine, 4*(1), 7–12.

Bastien, C. H., Vallieres, A., & Morin, C. M. (2001). Validation of the Insomnia Severity Index as an outcome measure for insomnia research. *Sleep Medicine, 2*(4), 297–307.

Bernert, R. A., Joiner, T. E., Jr., Cukrowicz, K. C., Schmidt, N. B., & Krakow, B. (2005). Suicidality and sleep disturbances [Research Support, Non-U.S. Gov't]. *Sleep, 28*(9), 1135–1141.

Bixler, E. O., Vgontzas, A. N., Lin, H. M., Ten Have, T., Rein, J., Vela-Bueno, A., et al. (2001). Prevalence of sleep-disordered breathing in women: Effects of gender. *American Journal of Respiratory and Critical Care Medicine, 163*(3 Pt 1), 608–613.

Bjorngaard, J. H., Bjerkeset, O., Romundstad, P., & Gunnell, D. (2011). Sleeping problems and suicide in 75,000 Norwegian adults: A 20 year follow-up of the HUNT I study. *Sleep, 34*(9), 1155–1159. doi:10.5665/SLEEP.1228.

Blazer, D. G., Hays, J. C., & Foley, D. J. (1995). Sleep complaints in older adults: A racial comparison [Comparative Study Research Support, U.S. Gov't, P.H.S.]. *The Journals of Gerontology Series A, Biological Sciences and Medical Sciences, 50*(5), M280–M284.

Buysse, D. J., Reynolds, C. F., 3rd, Monk, T. H., Berman, S. R., & Kupfer, D. J. (1989). The Pittsburgh Sleep Quality Index: A new instrument for psychiatric practice and research [Research Support, U.S. Gov't, P.H.S.]. *Psychiatry Research, 28*(2), 193–213.

Cao, M. T., & Kushida, C. (2011). Clinical features and evaluation of obstructive sleep apnea and upper airway resistance syndrome. In M. H. Kryger, T. Roth, & W. C. Dement (Eds.), *Principles and practice of sleep medicine* (5th ed.). St. Louis, MO: Elsevier Saunders.

Carney, C. E., Buysse, D. J., Ancoli-Israel, S., Edinger, J. D., Krystal, A. D., Lichstein, K. L., et al. (2012). The consensus sleep diary: Standardizing prospective sleep self-monitoring [Research Support, N.I.H., Extramural Research Support, Non-U.S. Gov't Research Support, U.S. Gov't, Non-P.H.S.]. *Sleep, 35*(2), 287–302. doi:10.5665/sleep.1642.

Carskadon, M. A., Dement, W. C., Mitler, M. M., Roth, T., Westbrook, P. R., & Keenan, S. (1986). Guidelines for the multiple sleep latency test (MSLT): A standard measure of sleepiness. *Sleep, 9*(4), 519–524.

Cartwright, R. (2001). What's new in oral appliances or snoring and sleep apnea: An update. *Sleep Medicine Review, 5*(1), 25–32.

Cho, J., & Juon, H. S. (2006). Assessing overweight and obesity risk among Korean Americans in California using World Health Organization body mass index criteria for Asians. *Preventing Chronic Disease, 3*(3), A79.

Dahmen, N., Kasten, M., Mittag, K., & Muller, M. J. (2002). Narcoleptic and schizophrenic hallucinations. Implications for differential diagnosis and pathophysiology. *European Journal of Health and Economy, 3*(Suppl 2), S94–98. doi:10.1007/s10198-002-0113-x.

Dauvilliers, Y., Arnulf, I., & Mignot, E. (2007). Narcolepsy with cataplexy [Review]. *Lancet, 369*(9560), 499–511. doi:10.1016/S0140-6736(07)60237-2.

Dauvilliers, Y., Montplaisir, J., Molinari, N., Carlander, B., Ondze, B., Besset, A., et al. (2001). Age at onset of narcolepsy in two large populations of patients in France and Quebec. *Neurology, 57*(11), 2029–2033.

DeZee, K. J., Hatzigeorgiou, C., Kristo, D., & Jackson, J. L. (2005). Prevalence of and screening for mental disorders in a sleep clinic. *Journal of Clinical Sleep Medicine, 1*(2), 136–142.

Drake, C., Nickel, C., Burduvali, E., Roth, T., Jefferson, C., & Pietro, B. (2003). The pediatric daytime sleepiness scale (PDSS): Sleep habits and school outcomes in middle-school children [Validation Studies]. *Sleep, 26*(4), 455–458.

Drummond, S. P., Meloy, M. J., Yanagi, M. A., Orff, H. J., & Brown, G. G. (2005). Compensatory recruitment after sleep deprivation and the relationship with performance [Research Support, N.I.H., Extramural Research Support, Non-U.S. Gov't]. *Psychiatry Research, 140*(3), 211–223. doi:10.1016/j.pscychresns.2005.06.007.

Duran, J., Esnaola, S., Rubio, R., & Iztueta, A. (2001). Obstructive sleep apnea-hypopnea and related clinical features in a population-based sample of subjects aged 30 to 70 yr. *American Journal of Respiratory and Critical Care Medicine, 163*(3 Pt 1), 685–689.

Dursunoglu, N., Ozkurt, S., & Sarikaya, S. (2009). Is the clinical presentation different between men and women admitting to the sleep laboratory? *Sleep & Breathing, 13*(3), 295–298.

Edinger, J. D., Fins, A. I., Sullivan, R. J., Jr., et al. (1997). Sleep in the laboratory and sleep at home: Comparisons of older insomniacs and normal sleepers. *Sleep, 27*(1), 158–165.

Edinger, J. D., & Wohlgemuth, W. K. (2001). Psychometric comparisons of the standard and abbreviated DBAS-10 versions of the dysfunctional beliefs and attitudes about sleep questionnaire. *Sleep Medicine, 2*(6), 493–500.

Espie, C. A., Inglis, S. J., Harvey, L., & Tessier, S. (2000). Insomniacs' attributions. psychometric properties of the dysfunctional beliefs and attitudes about sleep scale and the sleep disturbance questionnaire [Research Support, Non-U.S. Gov't]. *Journal of Psychosomatic Research, 48*(2), 141–148.

Foley, D. J., Monjan, A. A., Izmirlian, G., Hays, J. C., & Blazer, D. G. (1999). Incidence and remission of insomnia among elderly adults in a biracial cohort [Research Support, U.S. Gov't, P.H.S.]. *Sleep, 22*(Suppl. 2), S373–S378.

Foley, D. J., Monjan, A., Simonsick, E. M., Wallace, R. B., & Blazer, D. G. (1999). Incidence and remission of insomnia among elderly adults: An epidemiologic study of 6,800 persons over three years. *Sleep, 22*(Suppl 2), S366–372.

Ford, D. E., & Kamerow, D. B. (1989). Epidemiologic study of sleep disturbances and psychiatric disorders.

An opportunity for prevention? [Research Support, U.S. Gov't, P.H.S.]. *JAMA: The Journal of the American Medical Association, 262*(11), 1479–1484.

Fortuyn, H. A., Lappenschaar, M. A., Furer, J. W., Hodiamont, P. P., Rijnders, C. A., Renier, W. O., et al. (2010). Anxiety and mood disorders in narcolepsy: A case–control study. *General Hospital Psychiatry, 32*(1), 49–56.

Frisbie, W. P., Cho, Y., & Hummer, R. A. (2001). Immigration and the health of Asian and Pacific Islander adults in the United States. *American Journal of Epidemiology, 153*(4), 372–380.

Fukuda, K., & Ishihara, K. (2001). Age-related changes of sleeping pattern during adolescence [Research Support, Non-U.S. Gov't]. *Psychiatry and Clinical Neurosciences, 55*(3), 231–232. doi:10.1046/j.1440-1819.2001.00837.x.

Genta, P. R., Marcondes, B. F., Danzi, N. J., & Lorenzi-Filho, G. (2008). Ethnicity as a risk factor for obstructive sleep apnea: Comparison of Japanese descendants and white males in Sao Paulo, Brazil. *Brazilian Journal of Medical and Biological Research, 41*(8), 728–733.

George, C. F., Nickerson, P. W., Hanly, P. J., Millar, T. W., & Kryger, M. H. (1987). Sleep apnoea patients have more automobile accidents. *Lancet, 2*(8556), 447.

Gislason, T., Almqvist, M., Eriksson, G., Taube, A., & Boman, G. (1988). Prevalence of sleep apnea syndrome among Swedish men—An epidemiological study. *Journal of Clinical Epidemiology, 41*(6), 571–576.

Guilleminault, C., Wilson, R. A., & Dement, W. C. (1974). A study on cataplexy. *Archives of Neurology, 31*(4), 255–261.

Guilleminault, C., Tilkian, A., & Dement, W. C. (1976). The sleep apnea syndromes. *Annual Review of Medicine, 27*, 465–484.

Hiestand, D. M., Britz, P., Goldman, M., & Phillips, B. (2006). Prevalence of symptoms and risk of sleep apnea in the US population: Results from the national sleep foundation sleep in America 2005 poll. *Chest, 130*(3), 780–786.

Hoddes, E. D. W., & Zarcone, V. (1972). The development and use of the Stanford Sleepiness Scale (SSS). *Psychophysiology, 9*, 150.

Hoffstein, V., & Szalai, J. P. (1993). Predictive value of clinical features in diagnosing obstructive sleep apnea. *Sleep, 16*(2), 118–122.

Horne, J. A., & Ostberg, O. (1976). A self-assessment questionnaire to determine morningness-eveningness in human circadian rhythms. *International Journal of Chronobiology, 4*(2), 97–110.

Hublin, C., Kaprio, J., Partinen, M., Koskenvuo, M., Heikkila, K., Koskimies, S., et al. (1994). The prevalence of narcolepsy: An epidemiological study of the Finnish Twin Cohort [Comparative Study Research Support, U.S. Gov't, P.H.S.]. *Annals of Neurology, 35*(6), 709–716. doi:10.1002/ana.410350612.

Ip, M., Lam, B., Lauder, I. J., Tsang, K. W., Chung, K. F., Mok, Y. W., et al. (2001). A community study of sleep-disordered breathing in middle-aged Chinese men in Hong Kong. *Chest, 119*(1), 62–69.

Johns, M. W. (1991). A new method for measuring daytime sleepiness: The Epworth sleepiness scale. *Sleep, 14*(6), 540–545.

Kales, A., Soldatos, C. R., Bixler, E. O., Caldwell, A., Cadieux, R. J., Verrechio, J. M., et al. (1982). Narcolepsy-cataplexy. II. Psychosocial consequences and associated psychopathology. *Archives of Neurology, 39*(3), 169–171.

Kales, A., Cadieux, R. J., Bixler, E. O., Soldatos, C. R., Vela-Bueno, A., Misoul, C. A., et al. (1985). Severe obstructive sleep apnea—I: Onset, clinical course, and characteristics. *Journal of Chronic Diseases, 38*(5), 419–425.

Kamba, M., Suto, Y., Ohta, Y., Inoue, Y., & Matsuda, E. (1997). Cerebral metabolism in sleep apnea. Evaluation by magnetic resonance spectroscopy. *American Journal of Respiratory and Critical Care Medicine, 156*(1), 296–298.

Kandula, N. R., & Lauderdale, D. S. (2005). Leisure time, non-leisure time, and occupational physical activity in Asian Americans. *Annals of Epidemiology, 15*(4), 257–265.

Kapur, V., Strohl, K. P., Redline, S., Iber, C., O'Connor, G., & Nieto, J. (2002). *Sleep & Breathing, 6*(2), 49–54.

Kerkhof, G. A., & Van Dongen, H. P. (1996). Morning-type and evening-type individuals differ in the phase position of their endogenous circadian oscillator [Research Support, Non-U.S. Gov't]. *Neuroscience Letters, 218*(3), 153–156.

Kim, K. I., & Rhi, B. Y. (1976). A review of Korean cultural psychiatry. *Transcultural Psychiatric Research, 13*, 101–114.

Kim, J., In, K., Kim, J., You, S., Kang, K., Shim, J., et al. (1998). Comparison of the severity of sleep-disordered breathing in Asian and Caucasian patients seen at a sleep disorders center. *Respiratory Medicine, 92*(6), 843–848.

Kim, H., Dinges, D. F., & Young, T. (2007). Sleep-disordered breathing and psychomotor vigilance in a community-based sample. *Sleep, 30*(10), 1309–1316.

Kleinman, A. (1980). *Patients and Healers in the context of culture. An exploration of the Borderland between anthropology, medicine, and psychiatry*. Berkeley, CA: University of California Press.

Kravitz, H. M., Zhao, X., Bromberger, J. T., Gold, E. B., Hall, M. H., Matthews, K. A., et al. (2008). Sleep disturbance during the menopausal transition in a multi-ethnic community sample of women [Comparative Study Multicenter Study Research Support, N.I.H., Extramural]. *Sleep, 31*(7), 979–990.

Krishnan, R. R., Volow, M. R., Miller, P. P., & Carwile, S. T. (1984). Narcolepsy: Preliminary retrospective study of psychiatric and psychosocial aspects. *The American Journal of Psychiatry, 141*(3), 428–431.

Kushida, C. A., Littner, M. R., Morgenthaler, T., Alessi, C. A., Bailey, D., Coleman, J., Jr., … Wise, M. (2005). Practice parameters for the indications for polysomnography and related procedures: An update for 2005 [Practice Guideline Research Support, Non-U.S. Gov't Review]. *Sleep, 28*(4), 499–521.

Lack, L. C., & Bailey, M. (1994). Endogenous circadian rhythms of evening and morning types. *Sleep Research, 23*, 501.

Lam, B., Lam, D. C., & Ip, M. S. (2007). Obstructive sleep apnoea in Asia. *Internal Journal of Tuberculosis and Lung Disease, 11*(1), 2–11.

Li, K. K., Kushida, C., Powell, N. B., Riley, R. W., & Guilleminault, C. (2000). Obstructive sleep apnea syndrome: A comparison between Far-East Asian and white men. *Laryngoscope, 110*(10 Pt 1), 1689–1693.

Lichstein, K. L., Durrence, H. H., Ridel, B. W., & Bush, A. J. (2004). *Epidemiology of sleep: Age, gender, and ethnicity*. Mahwah, NJ: Erlbaum.

Lichstein, K. L., Taylor, D. J., McCrae, C. S., & Ruiter, M. E. (1999). Insomnia: Epidemiology and risk factors. In M. H. Kryger, T. Roth, & W. C. Dement (Eds.), *Principles and practice of sleep medicine* (pp. 827–837). St. Louis, MO: Elsevier.

Lin, K. M. (1980). Traditional Chinese medical beliefs and their relevance for mental illness and psychiatry. In A. Kleinman & Y. Y. Lin (Eds.), *Normal and abnormal behavior in Chinese culture* (pp. 95–111). Boston, MA: D. Reidel.

Liu, X., & Zhou, H. (2002). Sleep duration, insomnia and behavior problems among Chinese adolescents. *Psychiatry Research, 111*(1), 75–85.

Lock, M. (1980). *East Asian medicine in urban Japan. Comparative studies of health systems and medical care*. Berkeley, CA: University of California Press.

Longstreth, W. T., Jr., Koepsell, T. D., Ton, T. G., Hendrickson, A. F., & van Belle, G. (2007). The epidemiology of narcolepsy [Research Support, N.I.H., Extramural Review]. *Sleep, 30*(1), 13–26.

Longstreth, W. T., Jr., Ton, T. G., Koepsell, T., Gersuk, V. H., Hendrickson, A., & Velde, S. (2009). Prevalence of narcolepsy in King County, Washington, USA. *Sleep Medicine, 10*(4), 422–426. doi:10.1016/j.sleep.2008.05.009.

Marin, J. M., Carrizo, S. J., Vicente, E., & Agusti, A. G. (2005). Long-term cardiovascular outcomes in men with obstructive sleep apnoea-hypopnoea with or without treatment with continuous positive airway pressure: An observational study. *Lancet, 365*(9464), 1046–1053.

Mignot, E., Hayduk, R., Black, J., Grumet, F. C., & Guilleminault, C. (1997). HLA DQB1*0602 is associated with cataplexy in 509 narcoleptic patients [Clinical Trial Multicenter Study Research Support, Non-U.S. Gov't Research Support, U.S. Gov't, P.H.S.]. *Sleep, 20*(11), 1012–1020.

Mignot, E., Lammers, G. J., Ripley, B., Okun, M., Nevsimalova, S., Overeem, S., … Nishino, S. (2002). The role of cerebrospinal fluid hypocretin measurement in the diagnosis of narcolepsy and other hypersomnias [Research Support, Non-U.S. Gov't Research Support, U.S. Gov't, P.H.S.]. *Archives of Neurology, 59*(10), 1553–1562.

Mindell, J. A., & Jacobson, B. J. (2000). Sleep disturbances during pregnancy. *Journal of Obstetric, Gynecologic, and Neonatal Nursing: JOGNN/NAACOG, 29*(6), 590–597.

Mitler, M. M., Walsleben, J., Sangal, R. B., & Hirshkowitz, M. (1998). Sleep latency on the maintenance of wakefulness test (MWT) for 530 patients with narcolepsy while free of psychoactive drugs [Clinical Trial Multicenter Study]. *Electroencephalography and Clinical Neurophysiology, 107*(1), 33–38.

Millman, R. P., Fogel, B. S., McNamara, M. E., & Carlisle, C. C. (1989). Depression as a manifestation of obstructive sleep apnea: Reversal with nasal continuous positive airway pressure. *Journal of Clinical Psychiatry, 50*(9), 348–351.

Morin, C. M., Stone, J., Trinkle, D., Mercer, J., & Remsberg, S. (1993). Dysfunctional beliefs and attitudes about sleep among older adults with and without insomnia complaints. *Psychology and Aging, 8*, 463–467.

Mosko, S., Zetin, M., Glen, S., Garber, D., DeAntonio, M., Sassin, J., et al. (1989). Self-reported depressive symptomatology, mood ratings, and treatment outcome in sleep disorders patients. *Journal of Clinical Psychology, 45*(1), 51–60.

National Institutes of Health State-of-the-Science Conference Statement: Management of Menopause-Related Symptoms. (2005). Consensus development conference consensus development conference, NIH Review. *Annals of Internal Medicine, 142*(12 Pt 1), 1003–1013.

Netzer, N. C., Stoohs, R. A., Netzer, C. M., Clark, K., & Strohl, K. P. (1999). Using the Berlin Questionnaire to identify patients at risk for the sleep apnea syndrome. *Annals of Internal Medicine, 131*(7), 485–491.

Nicassio, P. M., Mendlowitz, D. R., Fussell, J. J., & Petras, L. (1985). The phenomenology of the pre-sleep state: The development of the pre-sleep arousal scale. *Behaviour Research and Therapy, 23*(3), 263–271.

Nofzinger, E. A., Buysse, D. J., Germain, A., Price, J. C., Miewald, J. M., & Kupfer, D. J. (2004). Functional neuroimaging evidence for hyperarousal in insomnia [Comparative Study Research Support, U.S. Gov't, P.H.S.]. *The American Journal of Psychiatry, 161*(11), 2126–2128. doi:10.1176/appi.ajp.161.11.2126.

O'Connor, G. T., Lind, B. K., Lee, E. T., Nieto, F. J., Redline, S., Samet, J. M., et al. (2003). Variation in symptoms of sleep-disrodered breathing with race and ethnicity. *Sleep, 26*(1), 74–79.

O'Hara, R. (2005). The role of hypoxia in apolipoprotein E4-associated cognitive impairment: Implications for neurodegeneration and sleep-disordered breathing. *Sleep, 28*(11), 1355–1357.

Ohayon, M. M., & Hong, S. C. (2002). Prevalence of insomnia and associated factors in South Korea [Research Support, Non-U.S. Gov't]. *Journal of Psychosomatic Research, 53*(1), 593–600.

Ong, K. C., & Clerk, A. A. (1998). Comparison of the severity of sleep-disordered breathing in Asian and Caucasian patients seen at a sleep disorders center. *Respiratory Medicine, 92*(6):843–848.

Overeem, S., Mignot, E., van Dijk, J. G., & Lammers, G. J. (2001). Narcolepsy: Clinical features, new pathophysiologic insights, and future perspectives [Research Support, Non-U.S. Gov't Research Support, U.S. Gov't, P.H.S. Review]. *Journal of Clinical Neurophysiology, 18*(2), 78–105.

Pang, K. Y. C. (1990). Hwabyung: The construction of a Korean popular illness among Korean elderly immigrant women in the United States. *Culture, Medicine, and Psychiatry, 14*, 495–512.

Partinen, M., & Hublin, C. (2011). Epidemiology of sleep disorders. In T. Roth, W. C. Dement, & M. H. Kryger (Eds.), *Principles and practice of sleep medicine* (pp. 694–715). St. Louis, MO: Elsevier.

Pavlova, M., Berg, O., Gleason, R., Walker, F., Robers, S., & Regestein, Q. (2001). Self-reported hyperarousal traits among insomnia patients. *Journal of Psychosomatic Research, 51*(2), 435–441.

Perlis, M. L., Giles, D. E., Mendelson, W. B., Bootzin, R. R., & Wyatt, J. K. (1997). Psychophysiological insomnia: The behavioural model and a neurocognitive perspective [Review]. *Journal of Sleep Research, 6*(3), 179–188.

Poirier, G., Montplaisir, J., Decary, F., Momege, D., & Lebrun, A. (1986). HLA antigens in narcolepsy and idiopathic central nervous system hypersomnolence [Research Support, Non-U.S. Gov't]. *Sleep, 9*(1 Pt 2), 153–158.

Punjabi, N. M., Welch, D., & Strohl, K. (2000). Sleep disorders in regional sleep centers: A national cooperative study. Coleman II Study Investigators. *Sleep, 23*(4), 471–480.

Redline, S., Strauss, M. E., Adams, N., Winters, M., Roebuck, T., Spry, K., et al. (1997). Neuropsychological function in mild sleep-disordered breathing. *Sleep, 20*(2), 160–167.

Rhee, S. (2009). The impact of immigration and acculturation on the mental health of Asian Americans: Overview of Epidemiology and Clinical Implications. In N. H. Trinh et al. (Eds.), *Handbook of Mental Health and Acculturation in Asian American families*. New York, NY: Humana Press.

Richardson, G. S. (2007). Human physiological models of insomnia [Research Support, N.I.H., Extramural Research Support, Non-U.S. Gov't Review]. *Sleep Medicine, 8*(Suppl. 4), S9–S14. doi:10.1016/S1389-9457(08)70003-0.

Scammell, T. E. (2003). The neurobiology, diagnosis, and treatment of narcolepsy [Research Support, U.S. Gov't, P.H.S. Review]. *Annals of Neurology, 53*(2), 154–166. doi:10.1002/ana.10444.

Schroder, C. M., & O'Hara, R. (2005). Depression and obstructive sleep apnea (OSA). *Annals of General Psychiatry, 4*, 13.

Seeman, M. V. (1997). Psychopathology in women and men: Focus on female hormones [Review]. *The American Journal of Psychiatry, 154*(12), 1641–1647.

Seron-Ferre, M., Ducsay, C. A., & Valenzuela, G. J. (1993). Circadian rhythms during pregnancy [Research Support, Non-U.S. Gov't Research Support, U.S. Gov't, P.H.S. Review]. *Endocrine Reviews, 14*(5), 594–609.

Shin, Y. K., Yoon, I. Y., Han, E. K., No, Y. M., Hong, M. C., Yun, Y. D., ... Hong, S. C. (2008). Prevalence of narcolepsy-cataplexy in Korean adolescents. *Acta Neurologica Scandinavica, 117*(4), 273-278. doi: 10.1111/j.1600-0404.2007.00930.x

Silber, M. H., Krahn, L. E., Olson, E. J., & Pankratz, V. S. (2002). The epidemiology of narcolepsy in Olmsted County, Minnesota: A population-based study [Case Reports Research Support, Non-U.S. Gov't]. *Sleep, 25*(2), 197–202.

Singareddy, R. K., & Balon, R. (2001). Sleep and suicide in psychiatric patients [Review]. *Annals of Clinical Psychiatry: Official Journal of the American Academy of Clinical Psychiatrists, 13*(2), 93–101.

Sours, J. A. (1963). Narcolepsy and other disturbances in the sleep-waking rhythm: A study of 115 cases with review of the literature [Review]. *The Journal of Nervous and Mental Disease, 137*, 525–542.

Spielman, A. J., & Glovinsky, P. (1991). The varied nature of insomnia. In P. J. Hauri (Ed.), *Case studies in insomnia* (pp. 1–15). New York, NY: Plenum Press.

Steiger, A. (2007). Neurochemical regulation of sleep [Research Support, Non-U.S. Gov't Review]. *Journal of Psychiatric Research, 41*(7), 537–552. doi:10.1016/j.jpsychires.2006.04.007.

Stein, J. D., Kim, D. S., Mundy, K. M., Talwar, N., Nan, B., Chervin, R. D., et al. (2011). The association between glaucomatous and other causes of optic neuropathy and sleep apnea. *American Journal of Ophthalmology, 152*(6), 989–998.

Thorpy, M. J. (2006). Cataplexy associated with narcolepsy: Epidemiology, pathophysiology and management [Review]. *CNS Drugs, 20*(1), 43–50.

Tryon, W. W. (2004). Issues of validity in actigraphic sleep assessment. *Sleep, 27*(1), 158–165.

Tsai, W. H., Remmers, J. E., Brant, R., Flemons, W. W., Davies, J., & Macarthur, C. (2003). A decision rule for diagnostic testing in obstructive sleep apnea. *American Journal of Respiratory and Critical Care Medicine, 167*(10), 1427–1432.

Tufik, S., Santos-Silva, R., Taddei, J. A., & Bittencourt, L. R. (2010). Obstructive sleep apnea syndrome in the Sao Paulo Epidemiologic Sleep Study. *Sleep Medicine, 11*(5), 441–446.

Uyar, M., Vrt, O., Bayram, N., Elbek, O., Savas, E., Altindag, A., et al. (2011). Gender differences with respect to psychiatric comorbidity in obstructive sleep apnea syndrome. *Southern Medical Journal, 104*(7), 495–498.

Vandeputte, M., & de Weerd, A. (2003). Sleep disorders and depressive feelings: A global survey with the Beck depression scale. *Sleep Medicine, 4*(4), 343–345.

Vourdas, A., Shneerson, J. M., Gregory, C. A., Smith, I. E., King, M. A., Morrish, E., et al. (2002). Narcolepsy and psychopathology: Is there an association? *Sleep Medicine, 3*(4), 353–360.

Wing, Y. K., Li, R. H., Ho, C. K., Fong, S. Y., Chow, L. Y., & Leung, T. (2000). A validity study of Ullanlinna Narcolepsy Scale in Hong Kong Chinese [Research

Support, Non-U.S. Gov't Validation Studies]. *Journal of Psychosomatic Research, 49*(5), 355–361.
Wolfson, A. R., & Carskadon, M. A. (1998). Sleep schedules and daytime functioning in adolescents [Research Support, U.S. Gov't, P.H.S.]. *Child Development, 69*(4), 875–887.
Yang, C. K., Kim, J. K., Patel, S. R., & Lee, J. H. (2005). Age-related changes in sleep/wake patterns among Korean teenagers [Research Support, Non-U.S. Gov't]. *Pediatrics, 115*(1 Suppl), 250–256. doi:10.1542/peds.2004-0815G.

Assessing Somatization with Asian American Clients

22

Cara S. Maffini and Y. Joel Wong

An older male from Afghanistan presents with stomach, head, and joint aches, difficulty falling asleep, restless sleep, fatigue, and ritualized behaviors. His family took him to countless medical doctors seeking an answer as to what was wrong. Finally, a physician recommended that he speak with a mental health provider. During the first two sessions, the client and his family shared that he had survived multiple wars with bombings outside his home. He moved to the USA 5 years ago, but only has a small network of friends that speak Dari, and has limited communication with friends and family still in Afghanistan. He once prided himself for his independence and his role as the provider for his family. He now feels dependent on his progeny due to language barriers. He spends much of his day worrying about the care of his son with congenital physical impairments who still resides in Afghanistan and has experienced physical abuse by previous caretakers.

The preceding vignette illustrates a common symptom presentation among Asian-American clients. Experiences of physical symptoms may lead Asian-Americans to seek medical attention only to find no diagnosis that explains or encapsulates all of their symptoms. When considering a holistic conceptualization of their experiences, it may become evident that their symptoms are physical indicators of emotional distress. Somatization refers to the experiences of emotional, social, or psychological distress that manifest in physical complaints though there is no organic basis for their symptoms (Lin, Carter, & Kleinman, 1985). Research has shown that experiences of somatic symptoms are cross-culturally ubiquitous though prevalence, symptoms, and conceptualizations may vary across cultures (Isaac et al., 1995; Isaac, Janca, & Orley, 1996; Kirmayer & Young, 1998). Asian-Americans are more likely to somaticize than other ethnic groups (US DHHS, 2001).

Asian-Americans comprise 5 % of the US population and include more than 25 different ethnic groups (US Census, 2010). According to the Pew Research Center (2012), 74 % of Asian-Americans are first generation immigrants. The heterogeneity within Asian-Americans indicates the need to better understand the diverse cultures of origin, experiences of acculturation and enculturation in the USA, and how these varied experiences of health and mental health intersect with Western treatments, philosophies, values, and beliefs.

The purpose of this chapter is to synthesize the extant literature on somatization focusing specifically on Asian-Americans. Due to the limited research on somatization among this population, we will focus on Asian-Americans in general, and provide specific examples of ethnic group differences when possible; however, readers are encouraged to consider both between

C.S. Maffini, M.A. (✉) • Y.J. Wong, Ph.D.
Department of Counseling & Educational Psychology, Indiana University Bloomington, Bloomington, IN 47405, USA
e-mail: cmaffini@indiana.edu; joelwong@indiana.edu

L.T. Benuto et al. (eds.), *Guide to Psychological Assessment with Asians*,
DOI 10.1007/978-1-4939-0796-0_22, © Springer Science+Business Media New York 2014

group differences (e.g., comparing Asian and White Americans) and within group differences (e.g., comparing Chinese and Filipino Americans) when working with this population. In this chapter, we will examine *what* somatization is, *why* it occurs with Asian-American clients, and *how* clinicians can effectively assess these clinical presentations. We will begin by reviewing three clusters of somatization: somatoform disorders, culturally bound somatic syndromes, and somatic symptoms. We will then examine cultural factors that may influence the clinical presentations of somatization. We will review assessments of somatization created for Asian-Americans or measures normed on Asian-Americans. Finally, we will provide implications for future research and suggestions for clinical assessment with Asian-American clients who may present with somatization.

Somatization Among Asian-American Clients

Somatization refers to somatoform disorders, culturally bound somatic syndromes, and somatic symptoms, all of which can be indicators of psychological distress. Somatoform disorders and somatic culturally bound syndromes have diagnostic criteria outlined in the DSM-IV-TR, whereas somatic symptoms may be classified with other diagnoses. Even if clients do not meet criteria for a somatoform disorder or culturally bound syndrome, they still may exhibit somatic symptoms as a marker of distress. In the following section, we will review three types of somatization examining research, prevalence, and within-group differences among Asian-American clients.

Somatoform Disorders

According to the DSM-IV-TR, somatoform disorders refer to a cluster of somatic symptoms that cannot otherwise be explained by a medical diagnosis (APA, 2000). Symptoms fall into four broad domains. Pain symptoms may occur throughout the body including the head, back, joints, extremities, chest, or during biological processes such as menstruation, intercourse, or urination. Gastrointestinal symptoms include nausea, vomiting, or diarrhea. Sexual symptoms include erectile dysfunction or vomiting throughout pregnancy. Finally, pseudoneurological symptoms pertain to the brain and include impaired coordination or balance, hallucinations, double vision, dizziness, blindness and seizures. These symptoms are rooted in stress rather than in an organic neurological etiology and are referred to as psychogenic (Reuber & Elger, 2003). For example, psychogenic non-epileptic seizures (PNES) is a medical term used to refer to patients who experience seizures when they experience stress, though there is no organic basis for the seizures. As with all diagnoses, these symptoms must present a clinically significant level of impairment in functioning in order to meet criteria (APA, 2000). There are seven somatoform disorders according to the DSM-IV-TR:

(a) Somatization disorder: symptoms from each of the four clusters: gastrointestinal, sexual, pseudoneurological, and pain symptoms with symptoms persistent for years and onset before the age of 30.
(b) Undifferentiated somatoform: a cluster of somatic symptoms below the threshold of somatization disorder lasting a minimum of 6 months.
(c) Conversion disorder: symptoms that impair motor or sensory functioning.
(d) Pain disorder: ongoing experience of pain unexplained by a medical disorder; endurance and severity are influenced by psychological distress.
(e) Hypochondriasis: preoccupation with the fear of developing a serious illness.
(f) Body dysmorphic disorder: preoccupation with distorted perceptions of the body focusing on slight imperfections.
(g) Somatoform disorder not otherwise specified: somatic symptoms not otherwise explained by another somatoform disorder (NOS; APA, 2000).

Somatoform disorders were introduced in the DSM-III (Mayou, Kirmayer, Simon, Kroenke, &

Sharpe, 2005) as a label for a cluster of symptoms that are otherwise unexplainable using medical diagnoses. Extant research has shown that more stringently defined somatoform disorders as defined by the DSM-IV-TR are rare, whereas those that are more broad such as undifferentiated somatoform or somatoform disorder NOS are more commonly seen (Mayou et al., 2005). Prevalence of several of the disorders is hard to estimate because people may not meet thresholds or all the criteria outlined in the DSM-IV-TR to qualify for a diagnosis or their reported symptoms may change over time (Mayou et al., 2005). One study examined cases of "medically unexplained symptoms" and found that depression and anxiety diagnoses better explained the clinical presentation than somatoform disorders (Smith et al., 2005). Diagnostic labels, criteria, and inclusion of somatoform disorders continue to evolve, and changes in this category of disorders are seen in the DSM-5. Further research should examine the prevalence, applicability and relevance of the new classifications among Asian-American clients.

The extant literature on somatoform disorders among Asian-Americans is scarce. A study by Hsu and Folstein (1997) found that somatization was significantly more common among Chinese American patients referred for psychiatric consultation than among their Caucasian American counterparts. Additionally, somatoform disorders manifested differently among Chinese Americans than they did among Caucasians. Chinese Americans presented with symptoms of the heart, lung, and balance, whereas Caucasian patients demonstrated symptoms congruent with the four domains of somatoform symptoms outlined in the DSM-IV-TR. Interestingly, in both the Caucasian and Chinese American groups, most participants with these somatic complaints also met criteria for Major Depressive Disorder. Another study examined somatization disorder in older Korean immigrants and found that one third of participants who were depressed also met criteria for somatization disorder as outlined in the DSM-III-TR (Pang & Lee, 1994). That number jumped to 41 % when they used culturally specific somatic symptoms such as "hot face" and "lumps in gastrointestinal tract" (p. 156).

Somatoform disorders are difficult to study particularly among Asian-Americans because many clients may not meet criteria for a specific somatoform disorder. Alternatively, their symptoms may strongly intersect with an anxiety or depressive disorder (Lee & Kleinman, 2007) or they experience culturally specific symptoms such as in the Pang and Lee (1994) study. Some Asian-Americans, particularly those who adhere to more traditional beliefs and worldviews, may meet criteria for a somatic culturally bound syndrome which may be a more appropriate conceptualization than a diagnosis based in a Western framework. Lee (1997) stated that somatoform disorders capture the dualistic mind–body conceptualization seen in Western culture, whereas Chinese cultures have a more holistic view integrating mind and body evident throughout diagnoses. He cited the absence of a separate section on somatoform disorders in the Chinese Classification of Mental Disorders, Second Edition (CCMD-2). Interestingly, that section was added in the CCMD-3 (Mak, Cheung, & Leung, 2012). Next, we turn our attention to somatic culturally bound syndromes among Asian-Americans.

Culturally Bound Somatic Syndromes

There are many syndromes influenced by cultural considerations that include somatic symptom presentations along with a dimension of psychological distress. Just as the DSM is written from a Western framework, each of these syndromes reflects differing cultural conceptualizations of health, values, and beliefs. Each also reflects a holistic notion of mind–body integration.

In India, *dhat* and *jiryan*, and in Sri Lanka *sukra pramea* are diagnoses which refer to symptoms including severe anxiety, weakness, exhaustion, and hypochondriasis related to ejaculation. Similarly, in Taiwan *shen-k'uei* and in China *shenkui* includes dizziness, backache, weakness, insomnia, and sexual dysfunction. People with this syndrome fear that they have lost too much semen, which is believed to be essential to vitality. Excessive loss is thought to be life threatening (APA, 2000). *Koro* is seen in many South and East Asian cultures and includes an intense fear that one's sexual organs will recede into the body and cause death (APA, 2000; Tseng, 2006).

A fear-based syndrome in Japan is called *taijin kyofusho* and includes intense concerns that one's body parts are perceived to be offensive to others in appearance and smell including facial expressions and physical movements (APA, 2000). In Korean culture, *shin-byung* is a fear-based syndrome that includes anxiety coupled with somatic symptoms such as weakness, dizziness, anorexia, insomnia, gastrointestinal difficulties, dissociation, and possession by ancestral spirits (Yi, 2000).

Congruent with a value of emotional control to promote interpersonal harmony in Korean culture, *hwa-byung* or "anger syndrome" (Kim, 2011) is a suppression of negative emotions that leads to physical symptom expression, which is arguably more socially acceptable. Symptoms may include but are not limited to heart palpations, shortness of breath, poor appetite, epigastric pain, diarrhea, constipation, muscle and joint aches, feeling cold, insomnia, dysphoria, and fear of death (Leong & Lau, 2001; Lin, 1983; Pang, 1990). Researchers examined experiences of somatization disorder among Korean older adults and found culturally specific symptoms that make their experience of the disorder a bit different than a Western sample (Pang & Lee, 1994). They found that somatic symptoms commonly seen among Korean older adults includes "indigestion, lumps in gastrointestinal tract, white coated tongue, dry mouth, tight chest, hot face, pushed chest, body chills and hotness, sighs, numbness, heavy and pressured headaches, lays down because of fatigue, edema and sweating in extremities" (Pang & Lee, 1994, p. 158).

Kyol goeu which translates to "wind overload" is a fainting syndrome seen among Cambodian refugees (Hinton, Um, & Ba, 2001). In response to trauma, many Cambodian refugees experienced heightened concerns regarding symptoms of their autonomic nervous system such as dizziness, nausea, trembling, coldness in extremities, and increased heart rate. Many of the words used to describe these symptoms reflect cultural conceptualizations of the mental health such as "shaking of the chest" and "wind shooting from … ears" (Hinton et al., 2001, p. 406). Hinton, Ba, Peou, and Um (2000) studied panic disorder among Cambodian refugees and found culturally specific criteria that more accurately reflects the experiences among this population. The symptoms are as follows: "sore neck, orthostatic panic, gastrointestinal distress, effort-induced dysphoria, olfactory-triggered distress, sudden 'while-sitting dizziness,' hunger-induced dysphoria, and 'bouts of increasing bodily wind'" (pp. 438–439).

Arguably the most well-known psychological syndrome among Chinese people, *shenjing shuairuo* or neurasthenia ("weakness of the nerves"; Chang et al., 2005) is conceptualized slightly differently by Chinese and Chinese Americans than the DSM. Chinese characterize the disorder as a cluster of symptoms that include nervous pain, sleep disturbance, excitement, weakness, and emotional symptoms (Lee & Kleinman, 2007). Through a slightly different lens, the DSM-IV-TR places a strong focus on mental and physical fatigue with additional symptoms that include dizziness, headaches, irritability, muscle aches and pain, gastrointestinal difficulties, and difficulties with sleep and relaxation (APA, 2000; Lee & Kleinman, 2007; Stewart, Lee, & Tao, 2010). Clients may be mislabeled with "undifferentiated somatoform disorder" when neurasthenia is not considered as a diagnosis (Zheng et al., 1997). Neurasthenia also overlaps with anxiety and depressive disorders, though there are unique qualities that support the notion that it is a separate disorder (Schwartz, 2002; Zheng et al., 1997). A study of 1,747 Chinese Americans residing in Los Angeles found that 6.4 % of the sample met criteria for neurasthenia as defined by the ICD-10. Almost 5 % of the sample met criteria for "pure" neurasthenia meaning they did meet criteria for another disorder listed in the DSM-III at the time of the study. The lifetime prevalence of neurasthenia was 3.61 % in that sample (Zheng et al., 1997).

Neurasthenia is also seen in Japan and is called *shinkeisuijaku* which means "nervousness or nervous disposition" (Tsung, 1989).

To summarize, both researchers and clinicians would benefit from greater awareness and understanding of culturally bound somatic syndromes that may impact Asian-American clients and may better capture their experiences than Western classifications of somatoform disorders. Conceptualization and experience of emotional distress and somatization varies across cultures (Simon, VonKorff, Piccinelli, Fullerton, & Ormel, 1999) giving credence to culturally bound somatic symptoms (e.g., Hinton et al., 2000; Pang & Lee, 1994). These symptoms and syndromes may be more relevant and applicable with clients who closely align with Asian traditions, beliefs, and worldviews (Kim, 2011).

Somatic Symptoms

Somatic symptoms refer to physical experiences associated with psychological distress and may include weakness, difficulty breathing, or numbness, as well as memory and concentration impairment, sleep difficulties, nightmares, irritability, social isolation, suicidal ideation, and self-harming behaviors (Collier, Munger, & Moua, 2012; Sue & Sue, 2008; Westermeyer & Her, 2007). Somatic symptoms are more prevalent than somatoform disorders and culturally bound somatic syndromes as clients do not need to meet particular criteria. Many disorders in the DSM-IV-TR use physical symptoms in the criteria. For example, depressive and anxiety disorders include physical markers such as sleep, fatigue/energy, appetite, concentration, and aches (APA, 2000). Research has demonstrated a strong relationship between distress and somatic symptoms, with previous studies demonstrating a high comorbidity of somatic symptoms and anxiety and depression among Asian-Americans (Mak & Zane, 2004; Sue, Sue, Sue, & Takeuchi, 1995). For example, Iu Mien and Cambodian Americans who presented with depression also endorsed somatic symptoms and suicidality (Akutsu & Chu, 2006).

Ample research has shown that Asian-Americans convey distress through somatic symptoms (Akutsu & Chu, 2006; Kroll et al., 1989; Nishio & Bilmes, 1987). Examining group differences, Iu Mien Americans were more likely to report somatic symptoms than other Asian counterparts, followed by Cambodian and Vietnamese then Japanese, Filipino, Chinese, and Korean Americans (Akutsu & Chu, 2006). A study of a Hmong community in the USA found more severe symptom presentations among adolescent males and older adults than others in the community (Collier et al., 2012). Mak and Zane (2004) found that in a sample of Chinese Americans, somatic symptoms were more prevalent in men than women. Though limited, the extant research conveys heterogeneity among Asian-Americans. In the following section, we examine factors that influence the experience of somatic symptoms.

Acculturation/enculturation. Cultural adjustment and identification influences the experience of somatic symptoms among Asian-Americans. Acculturation refers to the process of adjusting to the mainstream culture, whereas enculturation refers to the preservation of one's heritage culture amidst a new mainstream setting (Kim, 2007). The findings related to somatic symptoms and acculturation/enculturation are mixed.

Previous research has indicated that somatic symptom presentations are more common among recent immigrants and refugees who have had less influence from Western cultures (Akutsu, 1997; Westermeyer, Bouafuely, Neider, & Callies, 1989). Researchers examined a sample of Asian immigrants and refugees who sought medical attention and found that refugees were more likely to present with somatic complaints and receive a somatization diagnosis and less likely to receive a diagnosis of another physical disorder than their immigrant counterparts (Lin et al., 1985). Koh (1998) found that Korean immigrants had higher reports of somatization than US-born Koreans. Given extensive support that newer immigrants and refugees are more likely to endorse somatic symptoms, many argue that Asian-Americans who are more highly enculturated are more likely to somaticize than those who are more acculturated (Kim, 2011).

In contrast, using generation status as a proxy for acculturation, Willgerodt and Thompson (2006) found that third-generation Chinese youth had greater reports of somatic symptoms than their first and second-generation counterparts. Conversely, second generation Filipino adolescents reported greater levels of somatic symptoms than first or third generation peers. Finally, Mak and Zane (2004) found no relationship between acculturation (assessed by length of time in the USA) and somatization. Overall, these findings may speak to the need for different measures to capture the complexities of acculturation/enculturation beyond length of time in the USA and generational status (Willgerodt & Thompson, 2006). The mixed findings parallel other findings related to acculturation/enculturation (Wong, Maffini, & Shin, 2014). Individual differences, ethnic group differences, and measurement of acculturation/enculturation influence these discrepant results.

Protective factors. Using somatic symptoms as a marker of psychological distress, studies have examined protective factors to reduce negative outcomes. One study found that Chinese Americans who had who provided instrumental support such as lending tools or shelter and providing transportation reported reduced somatic symptoms following negative life events (Mak & Zane, 2004). Similarly, another study found that among Asian-American adolescents, greater emotional connections with fathers were associated with decreased experiences of somatic symptoms, while engaging in more activities with mothers was linked to reduced somatic symptoms following experiences of victimization (Maffini, Wong, & Shin, 2011). Overall, the extant research demonstrates the role of social support in reducing somatic symptoms among Asian-Americans.

Having reviewed three domains of somatization, including somatoform disorders, somatic culturally bound somatization, and somatic symptoms, we shift our focus to factors that may explain why Asian-Americans are more likely than other racial groups to have this clinical presentation.

Cultural Factors That Influence Somatization

Three prevailing themes emerge in the literature providing insight into somatization among Asian-Americans: (a) an integration of mind and body, (b) stigma associated with mental health, and (c) culturally sanctioned values regarding emotional expression.

Mind and Body Integration

Somatic experiences of mental health are grounded in a conceptualization of the mind and body being integrated, a belief held in many non-Western cultures including Asian cultures (Lee & Kleinman, 2007; Tsui & Schultz, 1985). With mental and physical health intertwined, problems in one domain affect the other (Wong, Tran, Kim, Van Horn Kerne, & Calfa, 2010). Thus, experiences of distress or anxiety may manifest as a change of mood (e.g., psychological symptom) or nausea, aches, and fatigue (e.g., physical symptoms). Because the two domains are integrated, it is culturally intuitive to attend to one's corporal needs in an effort to treat one's psychological needs (Nishio & Bilmes, 1987). This conceptualization can be contrasted with a dualistic categorization of mind versus body seen in Western culture. The ascription of mind and body as integrated is one reason that Asian-Americans may experiences somatic symptoms as markers of emotional distress (Hwang, 2006). A study examining the experiences of Korean older adults illustrates the prevailing conceptualization of the mind and body as interconnected. Results showed that these older adults communicated their experiences of cultural, social, and familial stress distress associated with immigration through somatic symptoms (Pang, 2000). Providing support for a mind–body integrated conceptualization of depression, Ying's (1988) factor analysis of the Center for Epidemiological Studies-Depression Scale revealed that affective and somatic items loaded on the same factor in a community sample of Chinese Americans. Considering this holistic approach integrating mind and body, it is counterintuitive to see two separate providers for mental and physical health. Thus, many Asian-Americans who believe in the integration of mental and physical health seek help from a medical doctor or a holistic healer (Ma, Shea, & Yeh, 2012).

Stigma

In addition to the mind–body integration, a strong stigma around mental health among many Asian-Americans influences how clients experience and express distress (Hwang, 2006). Physical experiences of distress and medical diagnoses are more widely condoned than psychological disorders (Kleinman & Kleinman, 1985; Lee, Le, & Sue, 2001; Leong & Lau, 2001), thus making it more acceptable for Asian-Americans to attend to one's physical needs than psychological needs (Sue & Sue, 2008). Researchers have discussed the importance of avoiding interpersonal shame and saving face in not seeking mental health help. One study interviewed 29 Chinese Americans who reported being depressed, yet only one of them reported seeking help from a mental health provider (Yeung, Chang, Gresham, Nierenberg, & Fava, 2004). In a qualitative study examining the mental health needs among Hmong Americans, participants discussed the strong stigma around being labeled as having mental health difficulties and the inclination to wait until symptoms feel severe before seeking help (Collier et al., 2012). In contrast, it might be less stigmatizing for Asian-Americans to seek professional help for somatization. To illustrate, Wong et al. (2010) found that among Asian-Americans who strongly adhered to Asian cultural values, belief that depression would result in somatic consequences (e.g., a poor appetite) was associated with increased likelihood of seeking professional help.

Emotional Expression

A third common attribution for somatization among Asian-American clients is cultural values surrounding emotional expression. In many Asian cultures, excessive displays of emotions are considered to be a sign of weakness, lack of control, or immaturity (Sue & Sue, 2008; Tsui & Schultz, 1985). In suppressing emotions, clients may begin to experience distress in other parts of their bodies, which is more culturally acceptable (Lee, 1997). However, when Asian-American clients feel safe or are directly asked about their affective experiences, they may be willing to admit their emotional distress (Kroll et al., 1989; Xu, 1994) speaking to the importance of a strong therapeutic relationship and appropriate assessment. Yeung and colleagues (2004) conducted a study examining the clinical presentations of 40 Chinese Americans who spoke at least one Chinese dialect. They found that 76 % of Chinese American participants reported somatic symptoms including fatigue, insomnia, and headaches while only 14 % discussed psychological symptoms such as feeling depressed or irritable. However, though they did not report emotional distress at the outset, when they were asked about the experiences specifically, 93 % of the participants endorsed having a depressed mood. These studies call attention to the need for a strong therapeutic relationship and appropriate and explicit questions specifically about somatic symptoms.

Mind–body integration, stigma about mental health, and culturally sanctioned displays of emotion and distress contextualize the prevalence of somatization among Asian-Americans. Now that we have addressed what somatization is and why it are more commonly seen among Asian-Americans, we shift our attention to how clinicians can assess it.

Measures Used to Assess Somatization with Asian America Clients

After reviewing what somatization is, and why somatization is prevalent among Asian-Americans, we now focus on how clinicians can assess these symptoms with Asian-American clients. A multitude of measures assessing somatic

Table 22.1 Measures used to assess somatization with Asian-American clients

Measures	Languages	Recommendations
Phan Vietnamese Psychiatric Scale (PVPS)	Vietnamese, English	Culturally appropriate idioms Focus on behavioral symptoms versus emotions
Vietnamese Depression Scale (VDS)	Vietnamese, English	Culturally appropriate expression of distress More appropriate for highly enculturated Vietnamese Americans
Korean Diagnostic Interview Schedule (KDIS)	Korean, English	Culturally specific symptoms More appropriate with highly enculturated Korean immigrants
Southeast Asian Symptom Checklist	Hmong, Cambodian, Laotian, Vietnamese, English	Developed primarily for Hmong; may be less appropriate for other Southeast Asian groups Not well validated
Symptom Checklist (SCL-90-R)	Chinese, Korean, Japanese, Vietnamese, English, etc.	Used to examine neurasthenia and psychopathology
Hopkin's Symptom Checklist (HSCL)	Cambodian, Hmong, Laotian, Vietnamese, English	Culturally congruent idioms and phrases
Somatic Symptom Index		Used to examine somatization among Chinese Americans
Composite International Diagnostic Interview (CIDI)		Used to examine prevalence of psychopathology and neurasthenia among Chinese Americans
AddHealth dataset Somatic Symptoms	English	National dataset Primarily sampled Chinese and Filipino adolescents

symptoms exist; however, most are normed on White populations. In this section, we review measures developed specifically for Asian-Americans as well as those normed on Asian-American populations (Table 22.1).

Phan Vietnamese Psychiatric Scale (PVPS)

Phan, Steel, and Silove (2004) created a measure that captures dimensions and experiences specific to Vietnamese culture. The Phan Vietnamese Psychiatric Scale (PVPS) includes three subscales: depression (26 items), anxiety (13 items), and somatization (14 items). Phan and colleagues' concerns with previous measures were that they fail to incorporate indigenous symptoms and conceptualizations of mental health. The authors utilized idioms and cultural conceptualizations of distress in the PVPS. For example, somatization was described as "disturbed mental and physical balance" (Phan et al., 2004, p. 204). The items are provided in both Vietnamese and English and seem congruent with somatic symptoms described on other measures inquiring about aches, pain, fatigue, indigestion, and nausea.

The authors provide the measure in both languages, which may make it more accessible to first generation immigrants and refugees. They also considered indigenous conceptualizations and used culturally appropriate idioms, which may be lost if one does a direct translation from one language to another. Even items on the anxiety and depression inventory include behavioral markers and focus less on emotions. The benefit of this measure is that it may be more accessible to Vietnamese immigrants and refugees. However, this measure may be less relevant to US-born Vietnamese Americans who have low levels of enculturation.

Vietnamese Depression Scale (VDS)

The Vietnamese Depression Scale (VDS) was created as a culturally relevant measure of depression for use with Vietnamese refugees (Kinzie et al., 1982). The VDS is a 15-item scale with a maximum score of 34 and a cut-off of 13 points to qualify as depression. Sample items include "downhearted and low spirited," "shameful and dishonored," and "exhausted" (Kinzie et al., p. 1279). After little use in the decades following its creation, Dinh, Yamada, and Yee (2009) conducted analyses to determine the factor structure of the scale. They found three factors: somatic symptoms, cultural-specific symptoms, and depressed affect. Similar to the PVPS, it is available in both Vietnamese and English, includes culturally appropriate expressions of distress, and may be more appropriate with more highly enculturated Vietnamese Americans.

Korean Diagnostic Interview Schedule (KDIS)

The Diagnostic Interview Schedule (DIS) was created to facilitate diagnoses based on the DSM-III and DSM-III-R (Robins, Helzer, Croughan, & Ratcliff, 1981). The Korean version utilizes the original DIS and incorporates an additional twelve items assessing culturally specific symptoms; it has also been well-validated (Lee et al., 1986). Pang and Lee (1994) used this measure with Korean older adults and examined disorders laid out in the DSM-III as well as culturally specific somatic symptoms. Strengths of the KDIS include it being based on a well-validated measure with additional culturally specific items. Similar to the PVPS and VDS, this measure may be more appropriate with clients who are more highly enculturated such as first generation immigrants.

Southeast Asian Symptom Checklist

With no existing inventory of somatic symptoms specific to Southeast Asian refugees at the time, Kroll and colleagues (1989) created their own. The Southeast Asian Symptom Checklist is a 19-item measure created in English, and translated by interpreters into the four respective languages of their sample—Hmong, Cambodian, Laotian, and Vietnamese. Limitations of the measure are that it was not validated, is not widely used, and may lack cultural validity. Researchers developed the measure by primarily considering the needs of the Hmong, the largest Southeast Asian ethnic group in the area. Therefore, Hmong participants had higher endorsement of symptoms than their Cambodian and Laotian counterparts indicating that the measure may not be as culturally appropriate for those groups.

Symptom Checklist (SCL-90-R)

The Symptom Checklist is comprised of 90 items spanning nine subscales including somatization, obsessive-compulsive, interpersonal sensitivity, depression, anxiety, hostility, phobic anxiety, paranoid ideation, and psychoticism. The measure also includes three indices: Global Severity Index conveys the level of overall psychological distress; the Positive Symptom Distress Index (PSDI) refers to the intensity of symptoms, and the Positive Symptom Total (PST) is the number of self-reported symptoms.

Benefits of the SCL-90-R are that it can be answered fairly quickly, which can be useful in reducing burnout, yet it still covers a wide-variety of symptoms to provide a more holistic view of a client's presentation. Additionally, because the measure is so widely used, it has been translated into many languages including Korean, Chinese, Japanese, and Vietnamese (Derogatis & Unger, 2010), which makes it more accessible. Several studies have applied the SCL-90-R to Asian-American populations. Koh (1998) used this measure to examine somatization among immigrant and non-immigrant Korean Americans. Several studies have used the SCL-90-R with Chinese Americans. Mak and Zane (2004) used it to examine somatization and found a strong reliability coefficient of 0.82 in their sample of Chinese Americans. Zheng and colleagues

(1997) administered the measure in either Chinese or English to a sample of Chinese adults living in Los Angeles to examine the prevalence of neurasthenia. Finally, Sue and colleagues (1995) used the SCL-90-R to examine psychopathology among Chinese Americans.

Preceding the SCL-90-R was the Hopkin's Symptom Checklist (HSCL), which was modified to meet the needs of refugees from Southeast Asia. Different versions focusing entirely on somatic symptoms were created and validated for use with Cambodian, Laotian, Vietnamese (Mollica, Wyshak, de Marneffe, Khuon, & Lavelle, 1987), and Hmong American populations (Mouanoutoua & Brown, 1995). Items were created in English and translated into different languages using culturally congruent idioms and phrases. For example, in the Hmong version, "nervousness or shakiness inside" was translated to "unstable heart or shaky heart" (Mouanoutoua & Brown, 1995, p. 379).

Other Measures

Due to the limited measures created for or normed on Asian-American samples, researchers have used existing measures and applied them to this population, particularly Chinese American samples. For example, Mak and Zane (2004) used the Somatic Symptom Index to examine somatization among Chinese Americans. Other studies used the Composite International Diagnostic Interview (CIDI) with Chinese Americans. One study examined the prevalence of psychopathology among Chinese Americans (Sue et al., 1995) and another study examined the prevalence of neurasthenia using the structured interview (Zheng et al., 1997).

Other studies have utilized less formal measures of somatic symptoms to assess mental well-being among Asian-Americans. For example, studies have utilized 14 items assessing somatic symptoms in the AddHealth dataset. Previous research has found a positive association between this measure and depression among Chinese and Filipino adolescents indicating appropriate validity (Willgerodt & Thompson, 2006). Reliability for these scales was found to be 0.83 in the first wave of data collection and 0.81 in the second wave (Maffini et al., 2011).

Implications for Practice and Research

Implications for Practice

There are several important considerations for clinicians assessing somatization among Asian-American clients. First, as with all clients who initially present with somatic concerns, it is important to coordinate care and ensure clients are evaluated by a physician to rule out medical etiology of symptoms. Emotional distress may also exacerbate physical symptoms; therefore, even if symptoms may be medically explained, counseling may still be beneficial.

Second, it is important for clinicians to be aware of their biases and values regarding mental illness and psychological well-being. Specifically, clinicians should guard against pathologizing the expression of somatic complaints and the implicit assumption that expressing one's affective experiences is psychologically healthier (Ryder et al., 2008). Ryder et al. argued that some clients are able to experience and express emotions but may simply choose to express their concerns somatically because emotions are not central to their lives. Indeed, some scholars have turned the issue of somatization on its head by questioning whether researchers have focused too much on Asians' tendency to somaticize and arguing that Westerners may be overemphasizing the affective aspects of psychopathology (Kalibatseva & Leong, 2011; Ryder et al., 2008).

Third, once in counseling, as several studies have shown, a focus on building rapport is essential in working with Asian-Americans. Building a relationship may take longer with Asian-American clients and may involve explaining the structure of counseling, the roles and expectations of the counselor and client, emphasizing confidentiality, and giving clients "gifts" or strategies to help manage their symptoms (Sue, 2006). For Asian-American clients who report somatic symptoms, one tangible expression of therapeutic gift giving is providing practical strategies to relieve somatic symptoms (e.g., deep breathing exercises for clients who have difficulty sleeping). It is important to gather information about clients' worldviews and values to contextualize their experiences and facilitate rapport. With a strong therapeutic relationship, clinicians may be able to gather more information and clarify symptoms and diagnoses (Hwang, 2006; Tsui & Schultz, 1985). It may be helpful for clinicians to attempt to articulate the affective experience the somatization is trying to convey. For example, articulating how distressed the client feels and is experiencing in their body helps capture both somatic and affective experiences. Additionally, it may be helpful to use idioms or vernacular congruent with the client's conceptualizations of mental health. Clients may feel most comfortable using their primary language to explain their symptoms and may utilize cultural idioms, words, or phrases. Using the same somatic metaphors clients use to describe their affective experiences can facilitate therapeutic rapport. For example, if a client uses the term "feeling prickly in my back" to mean feeling frustrated, the therapist can use the same phrase in her or his questions or interventions (e.g., *In what situations do you feel prickly in your back?*).

Fourth, clinicians should be mindful of the possibility that Asian-Americans' clinical presentation of somatization and affective experiences may vary depending on the assessment method (Yang & Wonpat-Borja, 2007). Some Asian-Americans may report somatic complaints in response to open-ended questions but are be more willing to report affective symptoms in response to a structured screening tool (Yeung et al., 2004). Therefore, when assessing Asian-Americans, clinicians could include explicit questions about physical and emotional experiences even if they are not reported by the client. Clients may still endorse affective symptoms when asked (Yeung et al., 2004).

Fifth, clinicians who are able to incorporate their Asian-American clients' somatic concerns into a treatment plan are more likely to have successful therapeutic outcomes. For instance, Lau and Kinoshita (2006) described the case of AC, a Chinese American older adult who was referred to therapy by his primary care physician because of somatic complaints. AC told his therapist that his physical problems were a result of an imbalance in his energy force. Instead of disputing this explanation, the therapist incorporated aspects of this perceived etiology into her treatment plan. In another example, Hinton, Pich, Chhean, Safren, and Pollack (2006) reported the effectiveness of a culturally modified cognitive behavioral intervention for post-traumatic stress disorder in Cambodian refugees that addressed their somatic symptoms (e.g., the experience of neck-focused panic).

Finally, if clinicians use standardized measures to assess a client's somatization, the therapist should be aware of the client's preference and be cognizant of the items in the measure. For clients who are more highly enculturated, a measure with culturally specific symptoms using idioms they connect with (e.g., using the PVPS with highly enculturated Vietnamese Americans) may provide more insight than a Western measure. Conversely, others may feel more comfortable with a Western measure.

Implications for Research

Overall, the research on somatization among Asian-Americans, particularly somatoform disorders and culturally bound somatic syndromes, is scarce. Chen (2010) called for a need to use more culturally appropriate measures of mental health when sampling Asian-Americans. Though Asian-Americans are more likely to somaticize than other groups (US DHHS, 2001), it is important for researchers and practitioners to integrate both somatic and affective symptoms in work with this population (Yeung et al., 2004).

Much of the research on somatization among Asian-Americans was done in the 1980s and 1990s, with much less information done in the past decade. Researchers and clinicians would benefit from research that more accurately reflects the Asian-American population today. With such a high number of first generation immigrants in the USA (Pew Research Center, 2012), the intersection between Eastern and Western beliefs will continue to shift with second and third generation Asian-Americans. More information will be needed as to how growing numbers of US-born Asian-Americans experience and conceptualize mental health including the role of somatic symptoms.

Furthermore, many studies used the DSM-III. With the DSM-5 released in May 2013, more research is needed to better understand the appropriateness of criteria and prevalence of somatoform disorders among Asian-Americans using the new criteria and diagnostic labels. Additionally, more information is needed about common somatic symptoms and prevalence of culturally specific symptoms so as to further inform culturally appropriate assessments of mental health.

Finally, as earlier mentioned, there are over 25 Asian ethnic groups living in the USA, yet much of the existing research uses samples of larger groups such as Chinese-Americans. Researchers and clinicians would benefit from more research about different ethnic groups as well as variations by age, gender, acculturation and other variables to provide a more nuanced understanding of this heterogeneous group. Further development of research surrounding somatoform disorders, somatic culturally specific disorders, and somatic symptoms can be used to better inform assessment and treatment interventions with Asian-Americans.

References

Akutsu, P. D. (1997). Mental health care delivery to Asian Americans: Review of the literature. In E. Lee (Ed.), *Working with Asian Americans: A guide for clinicians* (pp. 464–476). New York, NY: Guilford Press.

Akutsu, P. D., & Chu, J. P. (2006). Clinical problems that initiate professional help-seeking behaviors from Asian Americans. *Professional Psychology: Research and Practice, 37*, 407–415. doi:10.1037/0735-7028.37.4.407.

American Psychiatric Association. (2000). *Diagnostic and statistical manual of mental disorders (4th ed., text rev.)*. Washington, DC: American Psychiatric Association.

Chang, D. F., Myers, H. F., Yeung, A., Zhang, Y., Zhao, J., & Yu, S. (2005). Shenjing shuairuo and the DSM-IV: Diagnosis, distress, and disability in a Chinese primary care setting. *Transcultural Psychiatry, 42*, 204–218. doi:10.1177/1363461505052660.

Chen, W.-Y. (2010). Exposure to community violence and adolescents' internalizing behaviors among African American and Asian American adolescents. *Journal of Youth Adolescence, 39*, 403–413. doi:10.1007/s10964-009-9427-7.

Collier, A. F., Munger, M., & Moua, Y. K. (2012). Hmong mental health needs assessment: A community-based partnership in a small Mid-Western community. *American Journal of Community Psychology, 49*, 73–86. doi:10.1007/s10464-011-9436-z.

Derogatis, L. R., & Unger, R. (2010). *Symptom checklist-90-revised. Corsini encyclopedia of psychology (Vol. 1–2)*. Hoboken, NJ: John Wiley.

Dinh, T. Q., Yamada, A. M., & Yee, B. W. K. (2009). A culturally relevant conceptualization of depression: An empirical examination of the factorial structure of the Vietnamese Depression Scale. *International Journal of Social Psychiatry, 55*, 496–505.

Hinton, D., Ba, P., Peou, S., & Um, K. (2000). Panic disorder among Cambodian refugees attending a psychiatric clinic: Prevalence and subtypes. *General Hospital Psychiatry, 22*, 437–444.

Hinton, D. E., Pich, V., Chhean, D., Safren, S. A., & Pollack, M. H. (2006). Somatic-focused therapy for traumatized refugees: Treating posttraumatic stress disorder and comorbid neck-focused panic attacks among Cambodian refugees. *Psychotherapy: Theory, Research, Practice, Training, 43*, 491–505.

Hinton, D., Um, K., & Ba, P. (2001). *Kyol goeu* ('wind overload') Part I: A cultural syndrome of orthostatic panic among Khmer refugees. *Transcultural Psychiatry, 38*, 403–432. doi:10.1177/136346150103800401.

Hsu, L. K. G., & Folstein, M. (1997). Somatoform disorders in Caucasian and Chinese Americans. *The Journal of Nervous & Mental Disease, 185*, 382–387. doi:10.1097/00005053-199706000-00004.

Hwang, W.-C. (2006). The psychotherapy adaption and modification framework: Application to Asian Americans. *American Psychologist, 61*, 702–715. doi:10.1037/0003-066X.61.7.702.

Isaac, M., Janca, A., Burke, K. C., Costa e Silva, J. A., Acuda, S. W., Altamura, A. C., … Tacchini, G. (1995). Medically unexplained somatic symptoms in different cultures: A preliminary report from phase I of the World Health Organization International Study of Somatoform Disorders. *Psychotherapy and Psychosomatics, 64*, 88–93.

Isaac, M., Janca, A., & Orley, J. (1996). Somatization—A culture-bound or universal syndrome? *Journal of Mental Health, 5*, 219–222.

Kalibatseva, Z., & Leong, F. T. (2011). Depression among Asian Americans: Review and recommendations. *Depression Research and Treatment, 2011*, 9. doi:10.1155/2011/320902.

Kim, B. S. K. (2007). Acculturation and enculturation. In F. T. L. Leong et al. (Eds.), *Handbook of Asian*

American psychology (pp. 141–158). Thousand Oaks, CA: Sage.

Kim, B. S. K. (2011). *Counseling & diversity: Counseling Asian Americans*. Belmont, CA: Brooks/Cole.

Kinzie, D., Manson, S. M., Vinh, D. T., Tolan, N. T., Anh, B., & Pho, T. N. (1982). Development and validation of a Vietnamese-language depression rating scale. *American Journal of Psychiatry, 139*, 1276–1281.

Kirmayer, L. J., & Young, A. (1998). Culture and somatization: Clinical, epidemiological, and ethnographic perspectives. *Psychosomatic Medicine, 60*, 420–430.

Kleinman, A., & Kleinman, J. (1985). Somatization: The interconnections in Chinese society among culture, depressive experiences, and the meanings of pain. In A. Kleinman & B. J. Good (Eds.), *Culture and depression: Studies in the anthropology and cross-cultural psychiatry of affect and disorder* (pp. 429–490). Berkeley, CA: University of California Press.

Koh, K. B. (1998). Perceived stress, psychopathology, and family support in Korean immigrants and nonimmigrants. *Yonsei Medical Journal, 39*, 214–221.

Kroll, J., Habenicht, M., Mackenzie, T., Yang, M., Chan, S., Vang, T., … Cabugao, R. (1989). Depression and posttraumatic stress disorder in Southeast Asian refugees. *American Journal of Psychiatry, 146*, 1592–1597.

Lau, A. W., & Kinoshita, L. M. (2006). Cognitive–behavioral therapy with culturally diverse older adults. In P. A. Hays & G. Y. Iwamasa (Eds.), *Culturally responsive cognitive–behavioral therapy: Assessment, practice, and supervision* (pp. 179–198). Washington, DC: American Psychological Association.

Lee, S. (1997). A Chinese perspective of somatoform disorders. *Journal of Psychosomatic Research, 43*, 115–119. doi:10.1016/S0022-3999(97)00037-8.

Lee, S., & Kleinman, A. (2007). Are somatoform disorders changing with time? The case of neurasthenia in China. *Psychosomatic Medicine, 69*, 846–849. doi:10.1097/PSY.0b013e31815b0092.

Lee, M. H., Lee, H. Y., Min, S. K., Kim, K. H., Kim, S. Y., Song, D. H., et al. (1986). Development of Korean version of the NIMH diagnostic interview schedule and its validity test—Kangwha psychiatric epidemiological survey. *Neuropsychiatry, 25*, 300–313.

Lee, J., Lei, A., & Sue, S. (2001). The current state of mental health research on Asian Americans. *Journal of Human Behavior in the Social Environment, 3*, 159–178.

Leong, F. T. L., & Lau, A. S. L. (2001). Barriers to providing effective mental health services to Asian Americans. *Mental Health Services Research, 3*, 201–214. doi:10.1023/A:1013177014788.

Lin, K.-M. (1983). Hwa-byung: A Korean culture-bound syndrome? *American Journal of Psychiatry, 140*, 105–107.

Lin, E. H. B., Carter, W. B., & Kleinman, A. M. (1985). An exploration of somatization among Asian refugees and immigrants in primary care. *American Journal of Public Health, 75*, 1080–1084.

Ma, P.-W. W., Shea, M., & Yeh, C. J. (2012). Promoting mental health in Asian immigrants. In E. Vera (Ed.), *The Oxford handbook of prevention in counseling psychology* (pp. 439–454). New York, NY: Oxford University Press.

Maffini, C. S., Wong, Y. J., & Shin, M. (2011). The potential impact of violent victimization on somatic symptoms among Asian American adolescents: A national longitudinal study. *Asian American Journal of Psychology, 2*, 157–167. doi:10.1037/a0024920.

Mak, W. W. S., Cheung, F. M., & Leung, F. (2012). Somatoform disorders in Asians. In E. C. Chang (Ed.), *Handbook of adult psychopathology in Asians: Theory, diagnosis, and treatment* (pp. 179–202). New York, NY: Oxford University Press.

Mak, W. W. S., & Zane, N. W. S. (2004). The phenomenon of somatization among community Chinese Americans. *Social Psychiatry & Psychiatric Epidemiology, 39*, 967–974. doi:10.1007/s00127-004-0827-4.

Mayou, R., Kirmayer, L. J., Simon, G., Kroenke, K., & Sharpe, M. (2005). Somatoform disorders: Time for a new approach in DSM-V. *American Journal of Psychiatry, 162*, 847–855. doi:10.1176/appi.ajp.162.5.847.

Mollica, R. F., Wyshak, G., de Marneffe, D., Khuon, F., & Lavelle, J. (1987). Indochinese versions of the Hopikins Symptom Checklist-25: A screening instrument for the psychiatric care of refugees. *American Journal of Psychiatry, 144*, 497–500.

Mouanoutoua, V. L., & Brown, L. G. (1995). Hopkins Symptom Checklist—25, Hmong Version: A screening instrument for psychological distress. *Journal of Personality Assessment, 64*, 376–383.

Nishio, K., & Bilmes, M. (1987). Psychotherapy with Southeast Asian Americans clients. *Professional Psychology: Research and Practice, 18*, 342–346.

Pang, K. Y. C. (1990). Hwabyung: The construction of a Korean popular illness among Korean elderly immigrant women in the United States. *Culture, Medicine and Psychiatry, 14*, 495–512.

Pang, K. Y. C. (2000). Symptom expression and somatization among elderly Korean immigrants. *Journal of Clinical Geropsychology, 6*, 199–212. doi:10.1023/A:1009541200013.

Pang, K. Y., & Lee, M. H. (1994). Prevalence of depression and somatic symptoms among Korean elderly immigrants. *Yonsei Medical Journal, 35*, 155–161.

Pew Research Center. (2012). *The rise of Asian Americans*. Retrieved from http://www.pewsocialtrends.org/2012/06/19/the-rise-of-asian-americans/

Phan, T., Steel, Z., & Silove, D. (2004). An ethnographically derived measure of anxiety, depression, and somatization: The Phan Vietnamese Psychiatric Scale. *Transcultural Psychiatry, 41*, 200–232. doi:10.1177/1363461504043565.

Reuber, M., & Elger, C. E. (2003). Psychogenic nonepileptic seizures: Review and update. *Epilepsy & Behavior, 4*, 205–216. doi:10.1016/S1525-5050(03)00104-5.

Robins, L. N., Helzer, J. E., Croughan, J., & Ratcliff, K. S. (1981). The NIMH Diagnostic Interview Schedule: Its history, characteristics, and validity. *Archives of General Psychiatry, 38*, 381–389. doi:10.1001/archpsyc.1981.01780290015001.

Ryder, A. G., Yang, J., Zhu, X., Yao, S., Yi, J., Heine, S. J., et al. (2008). The cultural shaping of depression: Somatic symptoms in China, psychological symptoms in North America? *Journal of Abnormal Psychology, 117*, 300–313. doi:10.1037/0021-843X.117.2.300.

Schwartz, P. Y. (2002). Why is neurasthenia important in Asian cultures? *Western Journal of Medicine, 176*, 257–258.

Simon, G. E., VonKorff, M., Piccinelli, M., Fullerton, C., & Ormel, J. (1999). An international study of the relation between somatic symptoms and depression. *The New England Journal of Medicine, 341*, 1329–1335.

Smith, R. C., Gardiner, J. C., Lyles, J. S., Sirbu, C., Dwamena, F. C., Hodges, A., … Goddeeris, J. (2005). Exploration of DSM-IV criteria in primary care patients with medically unexplained symptoms. *Psychosomatic Medicine, 67*, 123–129. doi:10.1097/01.psy.0000149279.10978.3e

Stewart, S. M., Lee, P. W. H., & Tao, R. (2010). Psychiatric disorders in the Chinese. In M. H. Bond (Ed.), *Oxford handbook of Chinese psychology*. New York, NY: Oxford University Press.

Sue, S. (2006). Cultural competency: From philosophy to research and practice. *Journal of Community Psychology, 34*, 237–245.

Sue, D. W., & Sue, D. (2008). *Counseling the culturally diverse: Theory and practice* (5th ed.). Hoboken, NJ: John Wiley & Sons.

Sue, S., Sue, D. W., Sue, L., & Takeuchi, D. T. (1995). Psychopathology among Asian Americans: A model minority? *Cultural Diversity and Mental Health, 1*, 39–51.

Tseng, W.-S. (2006). From peculiar psychiatric disorders through culture-bound syndromes to culture-related specific syndromes. *Transcultural Psychiatry, 43*, 554–576. doi:10.1177/1363461506070781.

Tsui, P., & Schultz, G. L. (1985). Failure of rapport: Why psychotherapeutic engagement fails in the treatment of Asian clients. *American Journal of Orthopsychiatry, 55*, 561–569.

Tsung, Y. L. (1989). Neurasthenia revisited: Its place in modern psychiatry. *Culture, Medicine and Psychiatry, 13*, 105–129.

U.S. Census Bureau. (2010). *The Asian populations: 2010*. Retrieved from http://www.census.gov/prod/cen2010/briefs/c2010br-11.pdf

U.S. Department of Health and Human Services. (2001). *Mental health: Culture, race and ethnicity—A supplement to mental health: A report of the surgeon general*. Rockville, MD: U.S. Department of Health and Human Services, Public Health Service, Office of Surgeon General.

Westermeyer, J., Bouafuely, M., Neider, J., & Callies, A. (1989). Somatization among refugees: An epidemiologic study. *Psychosomatics, 30*, 34–43.

Westermeyer, J., & Her, C. (2007). Western psychiatry and difficulty: Understanding and treating Hmong refugees. In J. P. Wilson & C. C. S.-K. Tang (Eds.), *Cross-cultural assessment of psychological trauma and PTSD* (pp. 371–393). New York, NY: Springer Science.

Willgerodt, M. A., & Thompson, E. A. (2006). Ethnic and generational influences on emotional distress and risk behaviors among Chinese and Filipino American adolescents. *Research in Nursing & Health, 29*, 311–324.

Wong, Y. J., Maffini, C. S., & Shin, M. (2014). The racial-cultural framework: A framework for addressing suicide-related outcomes in communities of color. *The Counseling Psychologist, 42*, 15–34. doi:10.1177/0011000012470568.

Wong, Y. J., Tran, K. K., Kim, S. H., Van Horn Kerne, V., & Calfa, N. A. (2010). Asian Americans lay beliefs about depression. *Journal of Clinical Psychology, 66*, 317–332.

Xu, Y. X. (1994). About ICD-10. *Journal of Clinical Psychology in Medical Settings, 4*, 224–226 (in Chinese).

Yang, L. H., & WonPat-Boria, A. J. (2007). Psychopathology among Asian-Americans. In F. T. L. Leong, A. G. Inman, A. Ebreo, L. H. Yang, L. M. Kinoshita, & M. Fu (Eds.), *Handbook of Asian American psychology* (2nd ed., pp. 379–405). Thousand Oaks, CA: Sage.

Yeung, A., Chang, D., Gresham, R. L., Nierenberg, A. A., & Fava, M. (2004). Illness beliefs of depressed Chinese American patients in primary care. *The Journal of Nervous and Mental Disease, 192*, 324–327.

Yi, K. Y. (2000). Shin-byung (divine illness) in a Korean woman. *Culture, Medicine and Psychiatry, 24*, 471–486.

Ying, Y. W. (1988). Depressive symptomatology among Chinese-Americans as measured by the CES-D. *Journal of Clinical Psychology, 44*, 739–746.

Zheng, Y.-P., Lin, K.-M., Takeuchi, D., Kurasaki, K. S., Wang, Y., & Cheung, F. (1997). An epidemiological study of neurasthenia in Chinese-Americans in Los Angeles. *Comprehensive Psychiatry, 38*, 249–259.

Assessing the Asian Child and Adolescent: Special Considerations

23

Judy Ho, Natalia Moss, and May Yeh

Considerations for Assessing Asian-American Youth

Asian-American youth in the USA are a heterogeneous group originating from approximately 52 different Asian countries from the Asia continent, Southeast Asia, and the Indian subcontinent, with over 100 spoken languages and dialects. These youth originate from different social classes, speak different languages with varying degrees of fluency, practice different religions, and adhere to diverse cultural values (Huang, 1994). One of the fastest growing ethnic/racial minorities in the USA, the Asian-American population has increased at a higher rate than all other race groups in the country, growing by 46 % from 11.9 million in 2000 to 17.3 million in 2010 (Hoeffel, Rastogi, Kim, & Shahid, 2012). Extant research has contradicted earlier notions of Asian-Americans as the "model minority," and literature has documented various social, educational, health and mental health disparities among this population along with comparable mental health illness and psychological distress prevalence rates to the general population (see Lee, Lei, & Sue, 2001 for a review). Over 12 % of Asian-Americans live in poverty, higher than the 9.9 % rate of poverty among non-Hispanic whites (US Census, 2010), and the illiteracy rates of Asian-Americans is 5.3 times that of non-Hispanic whites (Le, 2013). Southeast Asians have the highest high school dropout rates in the country, 33 % of Asian-American students in public high schools drop out or do not graduate on time, and 24 % of Asian-Americans over the age of 25 do not have a high school degree equivalent (Le, 2013). Relatively little is known about the mental health status and needs of Asian-American youth, but existing research suggests that there are higher rates of depression, anxiety, and suicide among this group. Thirty percent of Asian-American girls in grades 5 through 12 reported depressive symptoms, higher than the rates reported in White girls (22 %), Latino girls (27 %), and African-American girls (17 %) (Schoen et al., 1997). Seventeen percent of Asian-American boys in grades 5 through 12 reported physical abuse, as compared to 8 % among White boys (Schoen et al., 1997). Further, generational differences and conflict regarding family values and beliefs may cause additional strain, stress, anxiety problems, and behavioral difficulties for these youth. Equally concerning is the evidence that Asian-American families tend

J. Ho, Ph.D. (✉)
Pepperdine University Graduate School of Education and Psychology, 6100 Center Drive, Los Angeles, CA 90045, USA
e-mail: judy.ho@pepperdine.edu

N. Moss
Department of Psychology, MSC03 2220, 1 University of New Mexico, Albuquerque, NM 87131, USA

M. Yeh, Ph.D.
Department of Psychology, College of Sciences, San Diego State University, 6363 Alvarado Court, Ste. 103/10, San Diego, CA 92120-4913, USA
e-mail: myeh@mail.sdsu.edu

L.T. Benuto et al. (eds.), *Guide to Psychological Assessment with Asians*,
DOI 10.1007/978-1-4939-0796-0_23, © Springer Science+Business Media New York 2014

to delay professional service seeking even when clinical problems arise (USDHHS, 2001), and Asian-American youth have consistently demonstrated a higher level of unmet mental health needs and lower levels of mental health service engagement than non-Hispanic White youth (Li & Seidman, 2010).

In order to address Asian-American youths' emotional/behavioral problems, accurate appraisal of their mental health status is essential to identifying those who could benefit from psychological intervention and to designing effective treatment plans. There are numerous assessments that exist for the evaluation of youth emotional and behavioral problems in the USA. However, many of these have not been explicitly validated on Asian-American youth populations. Most existing assessments have demonstrated their psychometric properties on predominantly non-Hispanic white samples, and their results may not be readily generalized to Asian-American youth due to varying cultural factors that are salient to the psychological development of youth from different cultures. Some measures have been translated for use with indigenous populations, but it is not always clear from existing psychometric studies whether these translated versions have achieved cross-cultural equivalence at the individual test item level and/or at the construct level. In addition, there is a lack of psychometric information regarding how these translated versions of assessments that have originated from Asian countries might be used with Asian-American populations.

For example, one cannot assume that a questionnaire that is developed and normed on one cultural group can be used to assess the same construct in another cultural group (Arnold & Matus, 2000). When administering any instrument as part of a clinical assessment, one must consider how the respondent may interpret the items. This is particularly important if the respondents are immigrants, nonnative English speakers, or originate from a culture different from the one in which the instrument was developed and validated (Gee, 2004). Individuals from varying cultural groups may ascribe different meanings to symptoms than were intended by the authors of the original instrument. For example, symptom expression has been shown to vary in different Asian-American ethnic groups (USDHHS, 2001; Paniagua, 2000), and several culture-bound syndromes have been documented in different Asian populations in the DSM-IV-TR (APA, 2000). For instance, Vietnamese Americans have been shown to endorse symptoms of depression that include somatic complaints (e.g., pains, poor appetite) as well as other symptoms that could not be readily translated into an English language equivalent (Kinzie et al., 1982). For Asian-American youth, symptoms of anxiety may also consist of somatic complaints, along with sleep disturbance, and poor school performance (Huang, 1997). Lack of awareness or attention to these potential cultural differences is likely to lead to misclassification or underdiagnosis of emotional/behavioral disorders in Asian-American youth.

Another important issue to consider that bears implications for cross-cultural equivalence is the use of multiple informants in the assessment of psychopathology in Asian-American youth. Weisz, McCarty, Eastman, Chaiyasit, and Suwanlert (1997) asserted that the study of youth emotional/behavioral problems "is inevitably the study of two phenomena: the behavior of the child, and the lens through which adults view child behavior" (p. 569). The use of several reporters for youth psychopathology assessment is common for many existing evaluation tools (evidenced by the availability of different informant forms for the same questionnaire), and the information gained in this way is highly valuable. However, reports from youth, parents, and teachers have consistently shown low cross-informant agreement (Achenbach, McConaughy, & Howell, 1987), and the research base suggests that inter-informant discrepancies may vary systematically by race/ethnicity (Lau et al., 2004). These racial/ethnic differences suggest that there may be problems in meeting one or more of the conditions set forth by Marsella and Kameoka (1989) when evaluating cross-cultural equivalence and interrater reliability: (1) Linguistic equivalence and conceptual equivalence require that raters have a shared understanding of the characteristic being rated, and an understanding of the range of behaviors that are representative of that characteristic; (2) Metric equivalence requires that raters have a shared metric so that they may accurately scale behaviors that are related to the characteristic being rated; and (3) Normative equivalence requires that raters can determine the presence and absence of behaviors relevant to the characteristic being rated.

Closer examination suggests that youth–teacher and parent–teacher disagreements may be explained in part by cultural differences and/or racial ethnic biases (Lau et al., 2004). There is evidence that culture may influence adults' attitudes toward youth behaviors and the determination of whether an observed behavior constitutes a problem necessitating professional intervention (Lau et al., 2004). For example, consistent with traditional Buddhist values, Thai parents rated both undercontrolled problems (e.g., disobedience, fighting) and overcontrolled problems (e.g., shyness, fear) as less serious, less worrisome, and more likely to improve with time compared to American parents (Weisz et al., 1988). Another example utilizes two traditional Chinese concepts emerged from Confucian thought: (1) "Chiao Shun," which refers to the Chinese youth behaving in ways consistent to his or her training (i.e., teaching the child appropriate conduct by exposing him/her to explicit examples of proper behavior and restricting exposure to undesirable behavior in the context of a supportive, highly involved, and physically close parent–child relationship), and (2) "Guan," which equates parental care, concern, and involvement with firm control and governance of the child (Chao, 1994, 2000). Traditional parents may not view some internalizing behaviors on Western assessment scales such as passivity, obedience without question, and lack of assertiveness as clinical problems but rather desired behaviors in their child consistent with the concepts of "Chiao Shun" and "Guan." Similarly, differing views of desired attachment styles in traditional Japanese families may lead Japanese mothers to view some internalizing behaviors as normative and expected in their children. For example, the indigenous Japanese concept of "Amae" which refers to relationships that involve both attachment and dependence (Doi, 1989; Emde, 1992) have been shown in research to translate to more expressed feelings of sadness due to separation between Japanese mothers and children than between American mothers and children (Mizuta, Zahn-Waxler, Cole, & Hiruma, 1996). These findings suggest that concepts of sadness and loss have different meanings to parents and children in Japan than in the USA, and can potentially significantly affect assessment and intervention of attachment and youth emotional problems (Rothbaum, Weisz, Pott, Miyake, & Morelli, 2000).

Complicating the multi-informant assessment picture are linguistic challenges when assessing families in which parents may speak only one language (from their country of origin) proficiently, and in which the youth may speak only English proficiently or are bilingual. In 2011, the foreign born from Asia represented over one-fourth of the total foreign-born population in the USA (Gryn & Gambino, 2012), which suggests that a substantial amount of these foreign-born Asian-Americans are not native English speakers. For these individuals, issues regarding acculturation status and relatedly, linguistic considerations, must be considered when conducting a multi-informant assessment. For example, when translated versions are available, is it appropriate to administer the scale in one language to the parent, and in another language to the youth? When administered in different languages, how can we ensure that the raters have a shared, or culturally equivalent, understanding of the characteristic being rated? If there are intergenerational differences between the parent and youth regarding level of acculturation to the mainstream American culture, these cultural differences may affect the determination by the parent and youth of whether a behavior constitutes a problem necessitating professional intervention. Specifically, parents who are less acculturated to mainstream American culture compared to their child may rate a particular behavior as non-problematic, whereas their child may rate a particular behavior as problematic, or vice versa, leading to larger parent–youth disagreement on an assessment. Further, if only and English version of an assessment is available, would it be appropriate to request the youth to serve as an interpreter? If so, how might this affect the validity of the parent's report of the youth's emotional/behavioral problems provided that the youth is hearing these responses and also doing the written transcribing when it is a written measure? The existing literature is limited in providing guidelines on how to handle the above outlined issues, particularly with multi-informant assessments with children, and the field would benefit from more research in this area.

The perceptions of adult observers who are not part of the nuclear family may be particularly subject to the influence of race-related beliefs about base rates of youth psychopathology (Lau et al., 2004). Teacher expectancies for student achievement and classroom behaviors have been related to student race (Dusek & Joseph, 1983). Teachers may have the tendency to view Asian-American youth as model students who are diligent and respectful, yet passive with low assertiveness and poor social competence (Bannai & Cohen, 1985; Schneider & Lee, 1990). Similarly, teachers may rate overcontrolled behaviors such as worry and shyness as more representative of Asian students than students of other ethnicities (Chang & Sue, 2003). Intergenerational differences may also affect youths' perception of their own behaviors. For example, youth from immigrant families may adopt dominant American cultural values, norms, and behaviors more easily than their parents (Szapocznik & Truss, 1978), leading to more pronounced parent–youth disagreements about youth emotional/behavioral problems (Lau et al., 2004).

Another crucial issue to contemplate is whether syndromes of child psychopathology in the USA readily translate to those of various Asian cultures. Syndromes, groups of emotional/behavioral problems that co-occur, often are the bases for clinical assessment, yet may not be similar across cultures. For example, the Achenbach scales (e.g., Achenbach, 1991, 1995) utilize syndromes as organizational units for its subscales. Although information on youth psychopathology has grown quickly in recent decades, most studies have been conducted in Western countries. This restricted range of cultures sampled in empirical research may limit our cross-cultural understanding of psychopathology as findings from Western countries may not generalize to other cultures (Weisz, Weiss, Suwanlert, & Chaiyasit, 2003). Weisz and colleagues (2003) found that some child psychopathology syndromes may not match up very well between Thai and US children. For example, the narrowband syndromes did not show strong concordance, and only two of the eight broadband comparisons showed substantial or almost perfect agreement. Research is limited in this area, but if child psychopathology syndromes differ systematically across cultures, this would undermine efforts to develop a common classification system to be used for all cultures. Relatedly, the construct validity of assessment tools developed using syndromes from a common classification system as a basis may be questionable when applied to different cultures. The appropriateness of clinical assessments conducted in Asian cultures using scoring categories developed from US samples may also be called in to question. Thus, it may be wise to assess syndromal similarity across cultures before applying the syndrome-based categories of one culture to another.

Without an accurate assessment of the clinical picture, motivating and engaging the youth and his/her family for professional services and designing and implementing effective treatment plans become even more of a challenge for this already underserved population.

Recommendations

Many Asian cultural groups prefer more indirect ways of communication that involve a combination of verbal, explicit, nonverbal, and implicit responses. For example, traditional Chinese groups tend to rely on indirect, more complex methods of communication like indefinite comments while Westerners tend to adopt direct and simple methods (Su, Wang, Fan, Su, & Gao, 2008). These differences in communication and response style may render direct responses to face-valid surveys (the majority of most emotional/behavioral assessment tools) more difficult for Asians compared to their American counterparts. Further, many Asian groups both in the USA and internationally tend to avoid mental health services because of their fear and rejection of mental health disorders (USDHHS, 2001). Thus, the adoption of a more indirect communication style coupled with the stigma against mental illness may significantly influence how Asian groups respond to items on a face-valid mental health assessment. They may be more likely to underreport symptoms and this has been demonstrated consistently in the literature (USDHHS, 2001). Misunderstandings may also ensue as symptom expression is often different for various Asian groups (e.g., the tendency to somaticize symptoms for many Asian groups; USDHHS, 2001).

The way the items on an instrument are constructed may also alter response patterns for different Asian groups. For example, many Asian languages bear linguistic structure differences to English. In Korean, the verb comes at the end of the sentence, as do positive and negative valence words. Therefore, Korean respondents may give more attention to the last portions of sentences. In English, the verb does not always come at the end of the sentence. Therefore, the way in which an item question is structured may inadvertently direct an individual's attention towards or away from an item's focal content as conceptualized by the original test developers.

For the reasons above, interviews with the youth's primary caregivers may be a very helpful supplement, as they may provide information regarding the meaning of specific symptoms and shed light on how cultural factors may play a role in the expression of these emotional/behavioral problems. Of course, the information gained by adult informants needs to be weighed according to what is known from the existing research regarding informant disagreements regarding youth emotional/behavioral problems and the role that culture may play in whether a problem is viewed as worthy of clinical attention, and the preliminary findings that syndromes established with Western samples may not be similar across different Asian cultures. For the above reasons, it may also be important to assess the acculturation levels and/or ethnic identity of both the parents and youth in order to gain some additional context around the degree to which each informant may ascribe to more westernized conceptualizations of psychopathology and syndromes.

Overall, an integrative approach should be utilized for clinical assessment which combines both standard and ethnocultural assessment strategies such as the one described by Huang (1994). An ecological approach to assessment provides multiple sources of data essential to a holistic picture of the youth, and combines the evaluation of domains of a standard assessment (e.g., physical appearance, language, affect, family composition, demographics, communication patterns) as well as an ethnocultural assessment (e.g., generational status, acculturation level, ethnicity and self-concept, migration history, salience of ethnicity, history with cultural differences; Huang, 1994).

References

Achenbach, T. M. (1991). *Manual for the Child Behavior Checklist/4-18 and 1991 profile*. Burlington, VT: Department of Psychiatry, University of Vermont.

Achenbach, T. M. (1995). Empirically based assessment and taxonomy: Applications to clinical research. *Psychological Assessment, 7*(3), 261–274.

Achenbach, T. M., McConaughy, S. H., & Howell, C. T. (1987). Child/adolescent behavioral and emotional problems: Implications of cross-informant correlations for situational specificity. *Psychological Bulletin, 101*, 213–232.

American Psychiatric Association. (2000). *Diagnostic and statistical manual of mental disorders* (4th ed., text rev.). Washington, DC: Author.

Arnold, B. R., & Matus, Y. E. (2000). *Test translation and cultural equivalence methodologies for use with diverse populations. Handbook of multicultural mental health: Assessment and treatment of diverse populations* (pp. 121–136). New York, NY: Academic Press.

Bannai, H., & Cohen, D. A. (1985). The passive-methodical image of Asian Pacific Islander students in the school system. *Sociology and Social Research, 70*(1), 79–81.

Chang, D. F., & Sue, S. (2003). The effects of race and problem type on teachers' assessments of student behavior. *Journal of Consulting and Clinical Psychology, 71*, 235–242.

Chao, R. K. (1994). Beyond parental control and authoritarian parenting style: Understanding Chinese parenting through the cultural notion of training. *Child Development, 65*(4), 1111–1119.

Chao, R. K. (2000). Extending research on the consequences of parenting style for Chinese Americans and European Americans. *Child Development, 6*, 1832–1843.

Doi, T. (1989). The concept of amae and its psychoanalytic implications. *International Review of Psychoanalysis, 16*, 349–354.

Dusek, J. B., & Joseph, G. (1983). The bases of teacher expectancies: A meta-analysis. *Journal of Educational Psychology, 75*, 327–346.

Emde, R. N. (1992). Amae, intimacy, and the early moral self. *Infant Mental Health Journal, 13*, 34–42.

Gee, C. B. (2004). Assessment of anxiety and depression in Asian American youth. *Journal of Clinical Child and Adolescent Psychology, 33*, 269–271.

Gryn, T., & Gambino, C. (2012). The foreign born from Asia: 2011. *American Community Survey Briefs*. Retrieved from http://www.census.gov/prod/2012pubs/acsbr11-06.pdf.

Hoeffel, E. M., Rastogi, S., Kim, M. O., & Shahid, H. (2012). The Asian population: 2010. *2010 Census Briefs*. Retrieved from http://www.census.gov/prod/cen2010/briefs/c2010br-11.pdf

Huang, L. N. (1994). An integrative approach to clinical assessment and intervention with Asian-American adolescents. *Journal of Clinical Child Psychology, 23*(1), 21–31.

Huang, L. N. (1997). Asian American adolescents. In E. Lee (Ed.), *Working with Asian Americans: A guide for clinicians* (pp. 175–195). New York, NY: The Guilford Press.

Kinzie, J. D., Manson, S. M., Vinh, D. T., Tolan, N. T., Anh, B., & Pho, T. N. (1982). Development and validation of a Vietnamese-language depression rating scale. *American Journal of Psychiatry, 139*, 1276–1281.

Lau, A. S., Garland, A. F., Yeh, M., McCabe, K. M., Wood, P. A., & Hough, R. L. (2004). Race/ethnicity and inter-informant agreement in assessing adolescent psychopathology. *Journal of Emotional and Behavioral Disorders, 12*, 145–156.

Le, C. N. (2013). The model minority image. *Asian-nation: The Landscape of Asian America*. Retrieved from http://www.asian-nation.org/model-minority.shtml

Lee, J., Lei, A., & Sue, S. (2001). The current state of mental health research on Asian Americans. *Journal of Human Behavior in the Social Environment, 3*, 159–178.

Li, H., & Seidman, L. (2010). Engaging Asian American youth and their families in quality mental health services. *Asian Journal of Psychiatry, 3*, 169–172.

Marsella, A. J., & Kameoka, V. A. (1989). Ethnocultural issues in the assessment of psychopathology. In S. Wetzler (Ed.), *Measuring mental illness in psychometric assessment for clinicians* (pp. 231–256). Washington, DC: American Psychiatric Association.

Mizuta, I., Zahn-Waxler, C., Cole, P., & Hiruma, N. (1996). A cross-cultural study of preschoolers' attachment: Security and sensitivity in Japanese and U.S. dyads. *International Journal of Behavioral Development, 19*, 141–159.

Paniagua, F. A. (2000). Culture-bound syndromes, cultural variations, and psychopathology. In I. Cuellar & F. A. Paniagua (Eds.), *Handbook of multicultural mental health: Assessment and treatment of diverse populations* (pp. 139–169). San Diego, CA: Academic.

Rothbaum, F., Weisz, J., Pott, M., Miyake, K., & Morelli, G. (2000). Attachment and culture: Security in the United States and Japan. *American Psychologist, 55*, 1093–1104.

Schneider, B., & Lee, Y. (1990). A model for academic success: The school and home environment of Asian student. *Anthropology and Education Quarterly, 21*, 358–377.

Schoen, C., Davis, K., Collins, K. S., Greenberg, L., Roches, C. D., & Abrams, M. (1997). The commonwealth fund survey of the health of adolescent girls. Retrieved from http://www.commonwealthfund.org/~/media/Files/Publications/Fund%20Report/1997/Nov/The%20Commonwealth%20Fund%20Survey%20of%20the%20Health%20of%20Adolescent%20Girls/Schoen_adolescentgirls%20pdf.pdf

Su, L., Wang, K., Fan, F., Su, Y., & Gao, X. (2008). Reliability and validity of the screen for child anxiety related emotional disorders (SCARED) in Chinese children. *Journal of Anxiety Disorders, 22*(4), 612.

Szapocznik, J., & Truss, C. (1978). Intergenerational sources of role conflict in Cuban mothers. In M. Montiel (Ed.), *Hispanic families: Critical issues for policy and programs in human service*. Washington, DC: National Coalition of Hispanic Mental Health and Human Services Organizations.

U.S. Department of Health and Human Services. (2001). *Mental health: Culture, race, ethnicity, supplement to mental health: Report of the surgeon general*. Washington, DC: Department of Health and Human Services.

Weisz, J. R., McCarty, C. A., Eastman, K. L., Chaiyasit, W., & Suwanlert, S. (1997). Developmental psychopathology and culture: Ten lessons from Thailand. In S. Luthar, J. Burack, D. Cicchetti, & J. Weisz (Eds.), *Developmental psychopathology: Perspectives on adjustment, risk, and disorder* (pp. 568–592). New York, NY: Cambridge University Press.

Weisz, J. R., Suwanlert, S., Chaiyasit, W., Weiss, B., Walter, B. R., & Anderson, W. W. (1988). Thai and American perspectives on over-and undercontrolled child behavior problems: Exploring the threshold model among parents, teachers, and psychologists. *Journal of Consulting and Clinical Psychology, 56*(4), 601–609.

Weisz, J. R., Weiss, B., Suwanlert, S., & Chaiyasit, W. (2003). Syndromal structure of psychopathology in children of Thailand and the United States. *Journal of Consulting and Clinical Psychology, 71*(2), 375–385.

Assessment of Childhood Behavioral Disorders

24

Judy Ho, Natalia Moss, and May Yeh

Introduction

The purpose of this chapter is to provide an overview of some of the common assessment measures for emotional/behavioral problems, and to review whether they have been tested for use with Asian-American youth samples. When psychometric data is lacking for Asian-American groups in the extant literature, we discuss psychometric studies undertaken in Asian countries. Some measures for which psychometric data are available only for Asian populations are also highlighted. Asian-American youths in the USA are quite diverse, consisting of immigrants and first generation individuals who may ascribe more to the values of their country of origin, as well as those youth whose families have been in the USA for several generations and/or those who have adopted a strong affiliation to the mainstream American culture. In comparison, their counterparts who reside in Asian countries may more readily behave in accordance with the values of the indigenous culture. Although the two populations are quite different, learning about how the instrument operates with samples from Asian countries might represent an important step towards understanding how these assessment tools might work for their Asian-American counterparts, particularly those who report a higher cultural affiliation to their indigenous cultures. In addition, such information may help inform the selection of assessment tools and interpretation of results. Finally, we conclude with recommendations of how to utilize these measures and provide suggestions for future research to improve the utility of behavioral assessments for Asian-American youth.

J. Ho, Ph.D. (✉)
Pepperdine University Graduate School of Education and Psychology, 6100 Center Drive, Los Angeles, CA 90045, USA
e-mail: judy.ho@pepperdine.edu

N. Moss
Department of Psychology, MSC03 2220, 1 University of New Mexico, Albuquerque, NM 87131, USA

M. Yeh, Ph.D.
Department of Psychology, College of Sciences, San Diego State University, 6363 Alvarado Court, Ste. 103/10, San Diego, CA 92120-4913, USA
e-mail: myeh@mail.sdsu.edu

Overview of the Organization of Assessments

The following sections will be organized by the types of rating scales in the current youth behavioral assessment literature: (1) Global impairment scales, (2) Domain-specific scales, and (3) Symptom-specific scales (Park, Lee, & Schachar, 2011). Global impairment scales enable the rating of a child on a single scale of functioning. Domain-specific impairment scales provide scores for one or several domains of functioning. Finally, symptom-specific impairment scales measure the degree of disability associated with a specific symptom or diagnosis (Park et al., 2011).

L.T. Benuto et al. (eds.), *Guide to Psychological Assessment with Asians*,
DOI 10.1007/978-1-4939-0796-0_24, © Springer Science+Business Media New York 2014

Global Impairment Scales

The Children's Global Assessment Scale (CGAS)

The Children's Global Assessment Scale (CGAS: Shaffer et al., 1983) assesses general functioning in youth aged 1–16 on a scale from 1 to 100, with scores ranging from 1 to 40 (normal), 41–60 (slight disability), 61–80 (moderate disability), and 81–100 (serious disability). Test–retest reliability reliability was assessed by having five distinct raters conduct a new CGAS on the same 19 participants 6 months later. All but one rater was found to be consistent over time (ICC = 0.87, 0.92, 0.93, 0.95, and 0.69; Shaffer et al., 1983). In this study a modest correlation was found between CGAS and the Conners' Ten Item Abbreviated Parent Checklist. However, these two instruments are different in that the CGAS is a global measure rated by clinicians while Conners' Checklist is a syndrome-specific measure rated by parents. The authors also investigated the discriminant validity for the CGAS between inpatients and outpatients. The mean CGAS score for outpatients was 65.4 (SD = 14.8) and for inpatients 46.0 (SD = 19.0), which was significant at the $p < 0.001$ level. To date, the CGAS has not been specifically validated with Asian-American populations in the USA, and no psychometric studies have been undertaken in Asian countries.

Child and Adolescent Functional Assessment Scale (CAFAS)

The Child and Adolescent Functional Assessment Scale (CAFAS: Hodges, 2000a; 2000b) assesses emotional behavioral, and psychological problems in youth. Information is collected during a routine interview and the clinician then selects items that best describe the youth's problematic behaviors, strengths and goals on eight domains: (1) at home, (2) at school, (3) in the community, (4) behavior towards others, (5) moods/emotions, (6) self-harm, (7) substance use, and (8) thinking (which assessing irrationality). A total score and subscale scores are calculated with higher scores indicating greater impairment in functioning. The CAFAS has been used to evaluate Evidence Based Treatments and interventions in the community. Results indicate that the CAFAS is able to discriminate between youth in various levels of treatment (e.g., inpatient vs. outpatient; Hodges & Wong, 1996), different living situations (e.g., home, foster care, inpatient; Hodges, Doucette-Gates, & Liao, 1999), and with varying levels of severity and comorbidity of psychological diagnoses (Ezpeleta, Granero, de la Osa, Domenech, & Bonilla, 2006; Hodges et al., 1999). Previous studies have shown the CAFAS to be sensitive to the degree and rate of change over time. For example, in an investigation conducted at Fort Bragg, a statistically significant reduction in impairment was observed from intake to 6 months and intake to 12 months, with large to moderate effect sizes (Hodges, 1999; Hodges & Wong, 1996; Hodges, Wong, & Latessa, 1998). Additionally, the CAFAS has been shown to be a reliable indicator of youth's psychological functioning in a variety of settings, cultural contexts, and among youth with diverse backgrounds (e.g., in mental health facilities, schools, foster care, youth and adolescent justice system, etc.). The CAFAS has not been specifically validated on Asian-American or Asian populations.

The Child and Adolescent Functioning Impairment Scale (CAFIS)

The Child and Adolescent Functioning Impairment Scale (CAFIS) is a symptom-specific rating scale that assesses the most severe level of dysfunction in the youth within the past month and has established preliminary reliability and validity for the diagnosis of youth with ADHD in Korea. It utilizes a Likert Scale (0 indicating no impairment to 4 indicating severe impairment), includes both the CAFIS-parent and CAFIS-teacher forms, and has been used to measure functional impairment in Korean children and adolescents. The scales were developed in the Korean language, and developed based on the collection of items from widely used, validated scales measuring global impairment in youth with the addition of open-ended questions. The CAFIS-parent consists of 14 items and has four factors: (1) family relationship; (2) teacher relationship; (3) peer relationship; and (4) academic achievement. The CAFIS-teacher form consists of ten items and has three factors: (1) peer relationship; (2) teacher relationship; and (3) academic achievement.

The CAFIS was examined for its reliability and validity in a sample of 114 youth (72 children diagnosed with ADHD using the DSM-IV criteria, and 42 children who did not meet DSM-IV criteria for ADHD) aged 6–14 years who had visited the department of psychiatry at Soonchunhyang University Bucheon Hospital for the assessment of inattention, hyperactivity, and impulsivity. Factor structures of the CAFIS-parent and CAFIS-teacher were confirmed in this sample (Variance accounted for in four factors of CAFIS-parent = 64 %; variance accounted for by three factors of CAFIS-teacher = 66 %). The internal consistency of both scales was satisfactory, with Cronbach's alpha ranging from 0.71 to 0.90 for the CAFIS-parent and from 0.74 to 0.90 for the CAFIS-teacher. The test–retest reliability coefficients of the CAFIS-parent subscales were between $r = 0.71$ and $r = 0.86$, and between $r = 0.81$ and $r = 0.89$ for the CAFIS-teacher subscales. Convergent validity was demonstrated by significant correlations between the subscale scores of the CAFIS-parent and the CAFIS-teacher to the Children's Global Assessment Scale (C-GAS: Shaffer et al., 1983). Discriminant validity was confirmed by analyzing the mean subscale scores of the CAFIS-parent and CAFIS-teacher forms between the ADHD and non-ADHD youth subsamples. All subscales of the CAFIS-parent and CAFIS-teacher forms of the ADHD group were significantly higher than the control group. Receiver Operating Characteristic (ROC) analyses were calculated to assess the sensitivity and specificity for the CAFIS subscales with clinician diagnosis of ADHD as the gold standard. Results demonstrated that for all subscales on both forms, areas under the curve (AUCs), which is a measure of overall accuracy (Sackett, Haynes, Tugwell, & Guyatt, 1985), were significant. The optimal cutoff score of the CAFIS-parent form was a total score of 7 (sensitivity: 0.75, specificity: 0.83), 3 for the family relationship subscale (sensitivity: 0.60; specificity: 0.74), 1 for the teacher relationship subscale (sensitivity: 0.61; specificity: 0.76), 1 for the peer relationship subscale (sensitivity: 0.64; specificity: 0.67), and 3 for the academic achievement subscale (sensitivity: 0.63; specificity: 0.79). In the CAFIS-teacher form, optimal cutoff scores were 6 for total score (sensitivity: 0.68; specificity: 0.69), 1 for the teacher relationship subscale (sensitivity: 0.54; specificity: 0.72), 3 for the peer relationship subscale (sensitivity: 0.63; specificity: 0.67), and 3 for the academic achievement subscale (sensitivity: 0.58; specificity: 0.79; Park et al., 2011). There are several limitations to this measure. The CAFIS is not able to distinguish among psychiatric symptoms other than ADHD symptoms, it has limited generalizability as nationally representative normative data in Korea has not yet been collected and no evidence exists for how this measure might perform for Korean Americans, and the impact of comorbid diagnoses on ratings of youth functional impairment is unknown as it was not directly assessed.

Domain-Specific Scales

The Achenbach Scales

The Achenbach Scales (Achenbach, 1991; Achenbach & Rescorla, 2001) are a collection of comparable questionnaires designed for different respondents (parents, teachers, and youth) used to assess child emotional and behavioral problems and competencies. The Child Behavior Checklist for ages 6–18 (CBCL 8/6–18) is a parent-report questionnaire composed of 113 items based on a 3-point Likert scale [0 = Not true (as far as you know), 1 = Somewhat or Sometimes True, 2 = Very True or Often True]. The Teacher's Report Form for ages 6–18 (TRF) is a teacher-report questionnaire composed of 113 items based on a 3-point Likert scale [0 = Not true (as far as you know), 1 = Somewhat or Sometimes

True, 2 = Very True or Often True]. The Youth Self-Report (YSR) (Achenbach, 1991; Achenbach & Rescorla, 2001) is a reliable and valid self-report measure for ages 11–18 (YSR/11–18) composed of 112-item form based on a 3-point Likert scale [0 = Not true, 1 = Somewhat or Sometimes True, 2 = Very True or Often True]. The CBCL/6–18, TRF, and YSR scales are based on factor analysis of the following Empirically based syndrome scales: Anxious/Depressed, Withdrawn/Depressed, Somatic Complaints, Social Problems, Thought Problems, Attention Problems, Rule-Breaking Behavior, and Aggressive Behavior. Internalizing problems are measured through the Anxious/Depressed, Withdrawn/Depressed, and Somatic Complaints scales, Externalizing Problems consist of Rule-Breaking Behavior, and Aggressive Behavior scales. Reports are scored using age- and gender-normed national comparisons. The three components of the CBCL measure have well-established reliability (mean *r* test–retest for CBCL and TRF = 0.90) and construct validity (Achenbach & Rescorla, 2001). Normative data was obtained from parents of 1,300 children who were proportionate to the general US population with respect to race and socioeconomic status (Achenbach, 1991). CBCL and TRF scales correlate with corresponding Conners' Parent Rating Scale-Revised and Teacher Rating Scale-Revised (Conners, Sitarenios, Parker, & Epstein, 1998) ranging from 0.71 to 0.85. In this study of 2,200 participants ranging in age from 3 to 17 years, 84 % were European American, 5 % were African-American, 4 % were Hispanic, and 7 % were designated as Other. Correlations between CBCL scales and the Behavior Assessment System for Children (BASC: Reynolds & Kamphaus, 2004) ranged from 0.38 to 0.89. Correlations between BASC and CBCL Internalizing, Externalizing, and Total Problems scales ranged from 0.74 to 0.89.

A confirmatory factor analysis using robust weighted least squares estimation of the CBCL was conducted in a sample of 516 girls adopted from China aged 6–15.7 years (average age = 8.2, SD = 1.9). Results suggested that the fit of the 8-factor model was good (root-mean-square error of approximation = 0.047). Support was found for the second order factor structure of Internalizing and Externalizing Problems which further provide evidence of the factorial validity of the scores from the CBCL in Chinese girls. Comparisons of average scores for the Internalizing scale, Externalizing scale, and Total Problems scale revealed mostly small differences between the sample of adopted Chinese girls and the normative samples reported by Achenbach and Rescorla (2001), and the pattern of syndrome correlations and factor loadings was consistent with Achenbach and Rescorla's (2001) model. Internal reliability for the Chinese sample were lower (ranged from 0.57 to 0.93 on all scales) than those reported by Achenbach and Rescorla (2001) (ranged from 0.89 to 0.97 on all scales), with the lowest reliabilities reported on Somatic Complaints (0.57), Thought Problems (0.61), and Rule-Breaking Behavior (0.61). These results suggest that reliability may not be an intrinsic property of the questionnaire but may fluctuate as a function of sample characteristics and testing conditions (Thompson & Vacha-Haase, 2000).

Liu, Cheng, and Leung (2011) examined the cross-cultural factor validity of the CBCL/1.5–5 and C-TRF to a community sample of 876 Mainland Chinese preschoolers (462 males) aged 4–5 years (average age = 66.6 months, SD = 5). Parents and teachers were asked to assess the children with the Chinese language version of the CBCL/1.5–5 and C-TRF which was translated and back-translated, then finalized by a team of expert child psychologists to ensure equivalence of the translation. Confirmatory factor analysis confirmed the seven-syndrome and two-higher-order-broadband-problem factor structure as reported by Achenbach and Rescorla (2001) with a US sample. The six-syndrome and two-higher-order-broadband-problem factor structure of the C-TRF was also confirmed in this Mainland Chinese sample. These findings support the factorial validity of the parent and teacher report, and suggest that the US-derived taxonomy is appropriate for assessing Chinese preschool children for psychopathology. In the CBCL/1.5–5, significant difference between Chinese and US samples confirm prior findings that Chinese and

Asian youth experiencing more internalizing symptoms and Western children experience more externalizing symptoms (Liu et al., 2001; Yang, Soong, Chiang, & Chen, 2000). On the C-TRF, teachers also reported fewer externalizing problems for Chinese preschoolers compared to teacher reports in Western countries, but no significant differences were found for the report of internalizing problems for Chinese preschoolers compared to teacher reports in Western countries. It may be that Chinese teachers are less able to detect covert internalizing problems than parents because of their relatively less frequent interactions with students (Yang et al., 2000). Ratings of Total Problems by either parents or teachers are mostly similar between Chinese and US samples, with boys scoring significantly higher than girls on all externalizing symptom scales across both parent and teacher report. No gender differences were found on the internalizing symptoms on either the parent or teacher report. Finally agreement between parents' and teachers' ratings was relatively low ($r=0.18$) compared to the US sample ($r=0.40$). These findings corroborate other studies of standardized assessments of psychopathology in Chinese youth samples which have reported ranges of $r=0.07$ to $r=0.36$ (Deng, Liu, & Roosa, 2004; Ho et al., 1996). Future research should continue to employ confirmatory factor analyses and reliability analyses with additional samples of Chinese American children to test the generality of present findings. Additionally, a further examination of the factor structure of the CBCL is needed to evaluate how the scores correlate with other measures (e.g., strength-based) in Chinese American youth.

Confirmatory factor analyses were performed on the YSR on a sample of 30,243 youths 11–18 years old from 23 societies to test the generalizability of an 8-syndrome taxonomy model for youth psychopathology (Ivanova et al., 2007). Three societies represented Asian samples: (1) Hong Kong, $N=1{,}593$ (53 % male), aged 12–18 years (average age = 14.7) (Leung et al., 2006); (2) Japan, $N=2{,}542$ (48 % males), aged 11–15 years (average age 13.1) (Kuramoto et al., 2002); and (3) Korea, $N=3{,}211$ (39 % males), aged 12–17 years (average age = 14.8) (Oh et al., 1997). The 8-syndrome taxonomic model met criteria for good fit to the data from each of the 23 societies, which corroborated the findings for the CBCL and TRF as reported by Achenbach and Rescorla (2001). Specifically, for Hong Kong, the root-mean-square error of approximation (RMSEA) was 0.043, with a comparative fit index (CFI) of = 0.845. For Japan, RMSEA = 0.037 and CFI = 0.856; and for Korea, RMSEA = 0.038, CFI = 0.863, indicating acceptable to good model fit.

Another study utilized a sample of 100 adolescents in Southern India who had been exposed to traumatic life events to revise, translate, and explore the construct validity of the Post-traumatic Stress Disorder Scale of the CBCL in Tamil (Russell, Subramanian, & Russell, 2005). Revision of the content of the scale was completed by three psychiatrists and one psychologist who assigned each of the 113 CBCL items to one of the three DSM-IV-TR symptom categories for PTSD, which resulted in 13 final items for the Post-traumatic Stress Disorder Scale. Translation of the CBCL was achieved through independent forward–backward translations by experts who were knowledgeable of both languages in order to ensure semantic convergence of the English and Tamil version of the instrument. Exploratory factor analysis results suggested three underlying factors, and the ROC analysis threshold score of 0.5 was determined to be an effective screening score for individuals who have experienced trauma.

A study was designed to provide standardized norms for the Japanese version of Child Behavior Checklist/4–18 (CBCL/4–18) and to examine the scale's reliability and validity (Itani et al., 2001) in a sample of 5, 159 parents of children aged 4–15 years. Within the full community-based sample, 432 parents had children who received consultation from or visited medical institutions and consulting agencies, thus approximating a clinical subsample. Based on the standardization process of the original CBCL as reported by Achenbach and Rescorla (2001), *T*-scores were calculated for eight Syndrome Scales, two broad-band scales (Internalizing and Externalizing), and the total score. High internal consistency was confirmed in seven syndrome scales with the exception for Thought Problems which yielded a lower than adequate Cronbach's alpha coefficient ($r < 0.70$). Construct validity was confirmed through high correlations with scores on the Rutter's Questionnaires for parents. Cutoff criteria for normal, borderline, and clinical ranges were established (Itani et al., 2001).

A study investigated interrater agreement between Japanese parents and teachers regarding the emotional/behavioral problems of 316 youth (141 males) 6–12 years old (average age = 9.4, SD = 1.7) in Japan (Satake, Yishida, Yamashita, Kinukawa, & Takagishi, 2003). Comparison of average scores did not yield significant differences from the Japanese published standardization data (Itani et al., 2001) on internalizing scale, externalizing scale, and total problems. Parent–teacher agreement was examined through three indices; mean scores, correlations, and D scores (generalized distance between item profile). Parent–teacher correlations were in the low to medium range (Pearson's correlation = 0.13, $p < 0.05$ for internalizing scale; Pearson's correlation = 0.30, $p < 0.001$ for externalizing and total problems scales). Greater parent–teacher agreement occurred on the externalizing scale ($z = 1.87$, effect size $q = 0.21$, $p < 0.05$) and total problems scale ($z = 1.86$, effect size $q = 0.21$, $p < 0.05$) for boys than girl with small effect sizes. Results suggest that Japanese parents and teachers assess youth problems differently, namely, with parents indicating more serious problems (significantly higher average scores), similar to findings in Western countries (Touliatos & Lindholm, 1981). This was also observed in Thailand (Weisz et al., 1989) and China (Weine, Phillips, & Achenbach, 1995) but not in Taiwan (Yang et al., 2000). Results suggest that there may be greater contrasts between home and school settings in developing countries than in developed countries (Weine et al., 1995). In a study by Weisz, Weiss, Suwanlert, and Chaiyasit (2003) findings suggested that certain child psychopathology syndromes may not match up very well when comparing markedly different cultures. For example, comparing syndromes for Thai children with those obtained for US children by Achenbach and Edelbrock (1983) and Achenbach (1991), they observed mixed findings. Seven of 41 specific narrowband syndrome comparisons (17 %) met Landis and Koch's (1977) thresholds for substantial to almost perfect agreement (i.e., kappas ranging from 0.61 to 1.00), and 23 of the 41 comparisons (56 %) showed only slight to fair agreement, with kappas ranging from 0.00 to 0.40. Similarly, Weisz et al. (1988) found Thai and American caregivers and teachers made similar judgments about patterns of child behavior, yet they appeared to view the behavior from different perspectives. Thai adults expressed less concern than Americans (e.g., they were much more confident than Americans that problem behavior would improve). In the studies with the Japanese language version of the scale, substantial sample attrition, small sample size, and limited geographical area for participant recruitment preclude generalization of findings to the national population (Satake et al., 2003). Future studies that utilize large sample sizes with participants from various regions in Japan would be helpful.

A study conducted with a Korean community-based sample of 46 subjects (33 boys) examined the clinical utility of the CBCL in identifying children with attention-deficit hyperactivity disorder (ADHD) (Kim et al., 2005). Thirty-three subjects were diagnosed as having ADHD utilizing a T-score of 60 on the Attention Problems scale of the CBCL, a cutoff which resulted in a reasonable level of sensitivity (0.727) or positive predictive value (0.750) in the diagnosis. This corroborates previous findings that a T-score of 60 was associated with the optimal level of diagnostic discrimination in psychiatric samples in Western countries (Biederman et al., 1993; Steingard, Biederman, Doyle, & Sprich-Buckmister, 1992). Future studies are needed to establish national norms in Korea and to examine the clinical utility of the Achenbach scales with Asian-American groups in the USA.

Eyberg Child Behavior Inventory (ECBI)

The Eyberg Child Behavior Inventory (ECBI) (Boggs, Eyberg, & Reynolds, 1990) is comprised of 36 items designed to measure the parent's perception of their children aged 2–16 years. The measure produces a "problem score" which measures the frequency of disruptive behaviors and an "intensity score" which is the sum of the participants' intensity of behavior ratings on a 7-point scale. More specifically, the measures assess whether the behavior is currently occurring (i.e., yes or no), and severity (i.e., never, seldom, sometimes, often, and always) of disruptive behaviors in home and school settings, using parent and/or teacher report. The assessment was normed on a sample of 159 children (87 % White, 11 % Black, and 2 % Other) mostly from lower to middle class families who were referred for evaluation at a university psychology clinic. Norms for chronically ill children and other special populations were reported. The ECBI Intensity and Problem scales demonstrate high internal consistency, significant test–retest reliability, and significant interrater reliability, as well as convergent, concurrent, and discriminant validity (Boggs et al., 1990). The correlation between the ECBI Intensity scale (IS) and Problem scale (PS) for the total sample was 0.74. Concurrent validity was established through significant correlations with both the Internalizing and Externalizing scales of the CBCL (Boggs et al., 1990). Discriminant validity was established by differentiating between the behavior problem treatment groups from the learning disability and no treatment groups, and the learning disability group from the no treatment group (Boggs et al., 1990).

Leung, Sanders, Leung, Mak, and Lau (2003) examined test–retest reliability with 91 parents attending Maternal and Child Health Centers (MCHC; $n = 74$) and Child Assessment Centers (CAC; $n = 17$) with children 3–7 years who were referred because of child behavior problems. The youth and caregiver participants had been living in Hong Kong for a minimum of 12 consecutive months. Of the youth participants, there were 25 females and 44 males attending kindergarten or elementary school. Test–retest reliability estimated at pre- and post-intervention were 0.88 and 0.94 (problem), and 0.91 and 0.95 (intensity). The mean pre-intervention scores of the Triple P Positive Parenting Program intervention group and waitlist groups were in the elevated range on the ECBI (intensity > 127 or problem > 11).

Vineland Adaptive Behavior Scales-Survey (VABS-II)

The Vineland Adaptive Behavior Scales-Survey (VABS-II) Form (Sparrow, Balla, & Cicchetti, 1984) aids in clarifying diagnosis of intellectual and developmental disabilities of youth through a semi-structured interview with a primary caregiver. The instrument assesses five areas of adaptive behavior including: Communication (receptive, expressive, and written language), Daily Living Skills (self-care, contribution to a household, and community involvement), Socialization (interpersonal relationships, leisure activities, and play activities), Motor Skills (fine and gross motor abilities), and Maladaptive Behavior (an optional scale that assesses problematic behaviors that interfere with functioning). The Composite Scale is made up of the first three scales, and the Total Scale comprises the four required scales. Each item is scored on the basis of whether the behavior never occurs (0 points), occurs sometimes or partially (1 point), or is usually exhibited (2 points; Oakland & Houchins, 1985). Additionally it is possible to translate single scale, composite, and total scores into age-equivalent scores. The median split-half reliability coefficients are 0.94 for the composite score and range between 0.83 and 0.90 for the specific domains, demonstrating acceptable internal consistency. The assessment was administered to 484 participants in a 1-month span, demonstrating acceptable test–retest stability through a reliability index of 0.88 for the composite score and reliability indices between 0.81 and 0.86 for the domain scores. Interrater reliability was demonstrated with two distinct interviewers assessing 160 participants within a 2-week interval. The coefficients for the VABS were 0.74 for the composite and ranged 0.62 and 0.78 for the domains. The lower coefficient (0.62) was demonstrated on the Socialization domain. The measure demonstrated construct validity through an increase in raw scores at successive age groups while criterion related validity was assessed through correlations between the VABS and the ABIC (0.58), AAMD Adaptive Behavior Scale (0.40–0.70), Kaufman Assessments Battery for Children (K-ABC) Achievement Scale (0.52), K-ABC Mental Processing Composite (0.32), and the Peabody Picture Vocabulary Test-Revised (0.28) (Oakland & Houchins, 1985).

Tombokan-Runtukahu and Nitko (1992) investigated whether this measure could be successfully adapted to the Indonesian population. The translation phase applied both an ethnographic translation procedure (Brislin, 1983; Hulin, Drasgow, & Parsons, 1983) and an empirical tryout. Each of the 252 items of the survey was translated from English to Bahasa Indonesian and back-translated to English. The correlation coefficients between the scores on the English version and the back-translation of each subtest ranged from 0.926 (Maladaptive Behavior) to 0.995 (Daily Living Skills), which were deemed satisfactory. Tittle's (1982) guidelines were followed to review the translated items for fairness. Twenty-five item translations were judged inadequate by the panel and were rewritten with the help of an Indonesian language teacher. Four items were eliminated because they were inappropriate to the Indonesian context and equivalent cultural behaviors could not be substituted easily, and three items were modified to incorporate Indonesian-equivalent content. The resulting set of 245 items was moved forward to the validation phase.

Forty-three children with mental retardation were matched on the basis of age, gender, and SES with 43 children of normal intelligence. Internal consistency was examined by analyzing the parent-based ratings after pooling the two groups of children. The coefficient alphas were 0.98, 0.98, 0.96, and 0.99 for Communication, Daily Living Skills, Socialization, and Composite, respectively, suggesting high internal consistency. Examination of the frequency distributions of the two groups of children showed statistically significant differences in the mean scores of the two groups, with children of normal intelligence scoring higher. These differences were replicated with both teachers' and parents' ratings. This finding provides support for the interpretation that IVABS is capable of distinguishing between children with various degrees of development in adaptive behavior and of distinguishing between children with mental retardation and those with normal intelligence in this Indonesian sample. Although the sample at each age level was small, there is a general tendency for the Indonesian data to support the contention that the IVABS appears to follow an incremental development pattern similar to that found with the VABS in the USA. The procedures developed and used in this study also serve as a model to operationalizing the domain of adaptive behavior in new cultural contexts.

A study was conducted by Goldberg, Dill, Shin, and Nhan (2009) to examine the adaptation of the Vineland Adaptive Behavior Scale to the Vietnamese culture (VVABS). The Vineland was translated into Vietnamese and was evaluated for cultural relevance and semantic equivalence by three bilingual Vietnamese clinicians. The participants in the study were 120 Vietnamese mothers of preschool-age children (3–6 years of age) who were enrolled in kindergarten programs in Hue City, Vietnam. The mean age of the children was 4.9 ($SD = 1.1$) with a range of 3–6 years with 75 males and 44 females. The mean age of the mothers was 33.4 ($SD = 5.2$) with a range of 23–51 years. Coefficient alpha was used to assess internal consistency for the 11 sub-domains of the VABS. Internal consistency of the VVABS sub-domains were shown to be high with the exception of receptive communication. Construct validity was assessed through a correlation matrix for the 11 sub-domains which were statistically significant (all $ps < 0.001$) and ranged from 0.39 to 0.84. The VVABS was found to successfully discriminate between disabled and non-disabled children. In another study that adapted the VABS through empirical testing for the Vietnamese population, the researchers adapted items to fit the cultural context, and made necessary adjustments to test and administration procedures (i.e., deleting items that could not be successfully translated or adapted; Goldberg et al., 2009). However, further exploration of this method of adaptation is needed in order for cross-cultural adaptation of other psychological constructs to be empirically tested for reliability and validity.

Social Skills Rating System (SSRS)

The Social Skills Rating System (SSRS; Gresham & Elliott, 1990) is a psychometrically sound (Demaray, Ruffalo, Carlson, & Busse, 1995), nationally standardized, norm-referenced, social skills assessment for 3–18-year-old children. Informants rate the frequency of children's prosocial behaviors on a 3-point Likert scale (0 = never, 1 = Sometimes, and 2 = Very Often). Examples of social skills include the display of prosocial behaviors such as sharing, initiating interactions with others, and management of interpersonal conflicts such as controlling one's temper. There are three versions of the SSRS to gather data from different respondents: The SSRS-P (parent), SSRS-T (teacher), and SSRS-S (student). Effect size estimates presented by Renk and Phares (2004) in their meta-analysis of 74 studies showed an average parent–teacher correlation of 0.38, a mean self–teacher correlation of 0.25, and a mean self–parent correlation of 0.21. The teacher form (SSRS-T) includes three subscales (ten items each): (a) social skills (e.g., invites others to join in activities), which is divided into the subscales, cooperation, assertion, and self-control; (b) problem behaviors (e.g., argues with others), with the subscales of hyperactivity, internalizing, and externalizing; and (c) academic competence (e.g., "In reading, how does this child compare with other students?"). The SSRS-P and SSRS-S includes four subscales (ten items each): cooperation, assertion, empathy, and self-control. Sample items include: (a) e.g., "I make friends easily" (assertion), (b) "I do my homework on time" (cooperation), (c) "I listen to adults when they are talking with me" (empathy), and (d) "I ignore other children when they tease or call me names" (self-control). For each of the forms, cutoff points are provided to assign children's scores for each subscale (as well as their Total Social Skills score) into three categories: below-average (below one standard deviation of the mean), average (within one standard deviation of the mean), and above-average (above one standard deviation of the mean). In the national normative sample, the percentage of children in the below-average, average, and above-average categories are 16, 68, and 16 % for both parent and teacher ratings.

A study was conducted with 869 girls residing in the USA and adopted from China utilizing the SSRS-P (parent sample = 869) and SSRS-T forms (teacher sample = 611; Tan & Camras, 2011). Average age of adoption was 15.6 months (SD = 13.9) and average current youth age was 6.9 years (SD = 2.9). Adoptive mother's average age was 44.2 (SD = 6.1) years and the adoptive father's average age was 45.3 (SD = 7.3) years. Internal consistency was good for both the SSRS-P and SSRS-T subscales, ranging from 0.67 (the Responsibility subscale on the SSRS-P) to 0.93 (the scale of Academic Competence on SSRS-T). The adopted Chinese girls in all three age-groups (preschool-age, elementary-age, and secondary age) scored similar to or higher than same-age girls from the US normative sample on both parent and teacher rating. For 10 of the 15 comparisons on parent ratings and 11 of the 14 comparisons on teacher ratings, the adopted Chinese girls outperformed the normative US sample, which may be explained by examining characteristics of Chinese adopted children which includes more favorable prenatal experiences compared to the US sample (Tan, Marfo, & Dedrick, 2010) and possibly easier temperament associated with Chinese youth (Kagan & Fox, 2006). Investigators propose that temperamental qualities may put adopted Chinese children at a relative advantage. For example, Kagan, Kearsley, and Zelazo (1978) suggest that Chinese children may have easier temperaments than Caucasian children serving as a protective factor. Parent–teacher agreement for youth social behaviors was significant but modest in magnitude, similar to existing literature on parent–teacher agreement on non-adopted children's behaviors (see meta-analysis by Achenbach, McConaughy, & Howell, 1987). This sample was limited to adopted Chinese girls and findings might not reflect Chinese American children as a whole.

Further research needs to be conducted to examine the psychometric properties of this scale in other Asian-American samples in the USA.

The Strengths and Difficulties Questionnaire (SDQ)

Strengths and Difficulties Questionnaire (SDQ; Goodman, 1997) is a brief behavioral screening questionnaire for 3–16 year old children. The SDQ includes 25 items on psychological attributes: emotional symptoms (five items), conduct problems (five items), hyperactivity/inattention (five items), peer relationship problems (five items), and prosocial behavior (five items), that are administered to parents. All forms rate items on a 3-point scale (not true, somewhat true, and certainly true). In a recent study (Janssens & Deboutte, 2009), internal consistency was adequate (0.72 for parent SDQ, and 0.75 for teacher SDQ, 0.62 for youth SDQ), interrater reliability was adequate, and the concurrent validity of the SDQ was established through significant correlations with the Achenbach System of Empirically Based Assessment (ASEBA) scores and with the Child Behavior Checklist (CBCL) scores.

The psychometric properties of the SDQ have not been explicitly examined in any Asian-American samples, but there are several studies that have examined translations of the SDQ internationally. Du, Kou, and Coghill (2008) established normative data and examined the reliability and validity of a Chinese translation of the SDQ (parent, teacher, and youth self-report versions). Parent and teacher data were used for 1,965 subjects and self-report data for 690 subjects from Shanghai. Students ranged in age from 3 to 17 years. In this study, the SDQ was translated into Chinese and back-translated into English by academic staff at the Center for Clinical Trials and Epidemiological Research at the Chinese University of Hong Kong. Principle components analysis indicated a partial agreement with the original five-factored subscale structure. However, this appears to hold more strongly for the Prosocial Behavior, Hyperactivity–Inattention, and Emotional Symptoms subscales than for Conduct Problems and Peer Problems. Internal reliability for subscales were generally adequate (range 0.30–0.83) with only parent and teacher Hyperactivity–Inattention and teacher Prosocial Behavior subscales having an alpha <0.7. Mellor, Wong, and Xu (2011) examined 752 school-aged children (320 males) with an average age of 8.7 years (SD = 1.69) in China. Internal reliability coefficients ranged from 0.25 to 0.71, and were lower than what is usually considered to be adequate (0.70; Cicchetti, 1994), particularly for the Conduct and Peer Problem subscales. Similarly, in another study with Chinese preschool children in Hong Kong (Leung et al., 2003) internal consistency coefficients also ranged from 0.41 to 0.77, which are lower than what is usually considered to be adequate. In yet another study with 457 Chinese preschool children in Hong Kong (230 males) aged 4 and 5 years old, Cronbach's alphas for the SDQ subscales were 0.59 (emotional problems), 0.52 (conduct problems), 0.73 (Hyperactivity), 0.46 (peer relationship problems), 0.69 (prosocial behavior), and 0.77 (total problem behavior) (Leung, Lo, & Leung, 2012), again, lower than what is usually considered to be adequate. These findings are also consistent with large studies in Australia (Mellor, 2004), China (Du et al., 2008), and Japan (Matsuishi et al., 2008). Interrater correlations were low to moderate (range 0.23–0.49), and correlations among parents and teachers were found to be higher for the younger children (3–10 years) than for the older children (11–17 years) (Du et al., 2008). In another study, interrater reliability was again in the low to moderate range (range 0.40–0.79). With regard to interrater reliability, interparent agreement is higher for externalizing problems than emotional problems regardless of the gender of the target child. For both boys and girls, mother and father correlations were strongest for total difficulties and the combined Externalizing Problems subscale, whereas the lowest correlations were for emotional symptoms (Mellor et al., 2011).

Convergent validity was demonstrated by significant correlations between the parent-completed SDQ and the Parent Symptoms Questionnaire (PSQ). Discriminant validity was established by effectively distinguishing between 47 subjects from the normative sample with 47 age and gender matched ADHD outpatient participants using ROC curves. Total difficulty scores cutoffs were calculated with the intention of placing approximately 10 % of the sample with the most extreme scores as "abnormal," the next 10 % as "borderline" and the remaining 80 % in the "normal." About 85 % of the subjects were placed in the "normal" range and 7.5 % in the "abnormal" and "borderline" ranges.

Findings regarding the Chinese language version need to be replicated in other Chinese samples, including those from rural rather than urban settings. Du and colleagues (2008) observed possible differences in the way the Chinese interpret the questions relating to Conduct and Peer Problems. Further investigation should be made to clarify this issue and assess whether particular items should be altered or removed from the Chinese version.

Matsuishi and colleagues (2008) attempted to establish community-based normative data for the Japanese language version of the SDQ (Goodman, 1997). Because translated versions can yield different results, Matsuishi et al. (2008) established national norms rather than applying the recommended score bandings and cutoffs established for the English version SDQ. The impact of age and gender on the SDQ parent form was assessed in addition to evaluating the structure, and homogeneity of the Japanese scales. Following these steps, culturally informed score bandings were proposed for normal, borderline, and clinical ranges, and were defined for the total score as well as for each of the five subscales of the SDQ. In this study, investigators assessed 2,899 Japanese children (1,463 males) aged 4–12 years. Parents were asked to complete the extended version of the SDQ (Goodman, 1999) which supplements the 25 core items with an overall rating of whether their child has emotional or behavioral problems. The proposed factor structure of the 25 SDQ items was verified through an exploratory factor analysis with varimax rotation. The results illustrated that the pattern of main loadings replicated the original SDQ subscales. Cronbach's alpha of the total difficulties score (comprising of 20 items) was 0.77, which suggests adequate internal consistency. For the total difficulties score, the clinical range (defining approximately 10 % of community cases with the highest scores) for the Japanese sample included total difficulties ratings of 16 or more points, whereas the British normative data suggested a slightly higher cutoff requiring a total score of at least 17. Overall, the obtained findings were consistent with previous work investigating the psychometric properties of the SDQ in other countries including Sweden (Smedje, Broman, Hetta, & von Knorring, 1999), Germany (Klasen et al., 2000), the Netherlands (Van Widenfelt, Goedhart, Treffers, & Goodman, 2003), and Australia (Hawes, Hawes, & Dadds, 2004). The investigators noted concerns with comparing results across international studies because they use different study methods, children of different ages, and were performed in different eras. Further investigation is needed to establish national norms and to assess whether these results may be generalized for use as part of clinical screening programs, in pediatric neurology clinics, and in child psychiatric research settings for Japanese youth (Matsuishi et al., 2008).

Clinical Interview Schedule-Revised (CIS)

The Clinical Interview Schedule-Revised (CIS-R) (Lewis, Pelosi, Araya, & Dunn, 1992) is a structured diagnostic instrument designed for use by a variety of trained interviewers in assessing minor psychiatric needs in the community, general hospital, occupational and primary care research in a standardized way. The CIS-R was developed from the Clinical Interview Schedule (CIS), which was designed specifically for use by clinically experienced interviewers (i.e., psychiatrists). In Britain, the CIS-R instrument was validated in a community setting by comparing it with the Schedule for Clinical Assessment in Neuropsychiatry (SCAN), a semi-structured instrument. The participants this study ranged in age from 16 to 64 years. Results evidenced overall specificity of the CIS-R instrument to be good, but sensitivity was shown to be poor (Lewis et al., 1992). Interrater agreement ranged from 0.7 to 0.9. Concordance of diagnoses by the two instruments was in the poor to very poor range demonstrated by low kappas.

In a study by Subramaniam, Krishnaswamy, Jemain, Hamid, and Patel (2006), the investigators describe the psychometrics of the Malay version of the CIS-R. The CIS-R questionnaire was translated into Malay and back translated into English. Next, the original questionnaire and the back-translated questionnaire were compared for meanings and necessary corrections were made to the Malay version with the help of a language teacher. Interrater reliability was established for raters who were medical student in this study. Participants included 59 psychiatric inpatients, outpatients, relatives and other visitors who were there at the National University of Malaysia Hospital (33 clinical cases and 26 control cases). The sample included 51 % Malays, 29 % Chinese and 20 % Indians. The overall sensitivity, specificity, positive predictive value, and negative predictive value for the instrument were calculated. The Malay version of CIS-R showed 100 % sensitivity and 96.15 % specificity at a cutoff score of 9.

National Institute of Mental Health Diagnostic Interview Schedule for Children (NIMH DISC-IV)

The Diagnostic Interview Schedule for Children (DISC) is a structured diagnostic instrument designed for use by non-clinicians. Several versions have been produced with the most recent being the National Institute of Mental Health Diagnostic Interview Schedule for Children (NIMH DISC-IV). The NIMH DISC-IV is equipped to assess over 30 mental health disorders in children and adolescents. There are parent and youth versions of this instrument. The parent form is for caregivers of youth ranging in age from 6 to 17 years while the youth form is for children and adolescents aged 9 to 17 years. Preliminary reliability and acceptability results of the NIMH DISC-IV in a clinical sample of 84 parents and 82 children (aged 4–17 years) drawn from outpatient child and adolescent psychiatric clinics at three sites. Sixty percent of this sample was African-American and/or Hispanic. Despite its greater length and complexity, the NIMH DISC-IV was shown to compare favorably with earlier versions.

Doi, Roberts, Takeuchi, and Suzuki (2001) published a multiethnic comparison of adolescent major depression in a school-based study in the USA and Japan. Subjects were participants in the Teen Life Changes Survey conducted in 1994 where questionnaires were collected from 5,496 students in grades 6–8 in a Houston, TX school district, and 504 students in grades 7–9 in a public junior high school in Maebashi, Japan. Surveys were administered in English only in the US sample and in Japanese only in the Japanese sample. The Japanese version of the NIMH DISC-IV was developed through the process of various translation stages including translating the original version from English into Japanese, then the translated Japanese version was back-translated, and finally, both versions were examined by different bilinguals. The preliminary Japanese version was pretested for word meanings, and content on each item among Japanese junior high school students who were not involved in the study. The authors then reviewed the results and the final Japanese version for use in this study was created. Prevalence rates in this study were highest for Mexican-American students followed by African-American students, then Anglo-American students, and the lowest rate of major depressions was found in the Japanese student population. After sociodemographic adjustments were made, ethnicity was not found to be significantly associated with adolescent major depression, although father's level of education and family financial status were statistically significant.

In Ho et al. (2005), authors report on the development of the Chinese version of DISC-IV and examine its test–retest reliability. Participants included 78 Chinese parents and 79 youths (mean age = 13) attending child psychiatric clinics. Participants were interviewed at two time points about 22 days apart using the Chinese DISC-IV. All participants were Cantonese speaking.

The initial translation from English to Chinese was completed by a bilingual-speaking Chinese teacher. The authors reviewed this version and made semantic adjustments to better fit psychiatric content. The modified version was then tested in the clinics. Following this phase, revisions were made to improve semantic equivalence once again. Finally, an independent translator (blind to the first translation process) back-translated the revised version into English. The kappa coefficients in this study were good to excellent for obsessive compulsive disorder (OCD) for both youth and parent participants, major depressive disorder (MDD) for parent participants, and attention deficit hyperactivity disorder (ADHD) for parent participants. Kappa coefficients were fair for anxiety disorder (i.e., generalized anxiety disorder, separation anxiety disorder, panic disorder, agoraphobia, social phobia, and specific phobia) for parent participants, fair for oppositional defiant disorder (ODD) in both youth and parent participants, and fair MDD for youth participants. Kappa coefficients were found to be poor for anxiety disorder and poor for ADHD in the youth participants. Overall, parent informants had better test–retest reliability than youth informants, and the Chinese DISC-IV had comparable test–retest reliability with the original English version.

In a study evaluating the reliability and validity of the Korean version of the DISC-IV, Cho et al. (2007) interviewed 91 children and adolescents in an outpatient clinic at the Seoul National University, and the community. Of these participants, 44 were selected for an evaluation of test–retest reliability. Results indicated kappa values ranging from 0.25 to 0.40 in the clinical sample and 0.65–1.00 in the community sample showing good reliability and validity for the DISC-IV in the Korean youth.

Symptom-Specific Scales

Conners' 3rd Edition (Conners 3)

The Conners' 3rd Edition (Conners 3) (Conners, 2008) is a measure designed for assessing attention deficit hyperactivity disorder (ADHD) and common comorbid problems/disorders (e.g., oppositional defiant disorder, and conduct disorder) in children and adolescents. The measure has three forms: parent and teacher forms for children and adolescents 6–18 years old and self-report measure for youth aged 8–18 years. For each version (parent, teacher, and self-report), full-length and short versions are available. The Conners 3 contains multiple scales including, content scales (Inattention, Hyperactivity/Impulsivity, Learning Problems/Executive Functioning, Aggression, Peer Relations, and Family Relations), DSM-IV-TR Symptom Scales (ADHD Inattentive, ADHD Hyperactive-Impulsive, ADHD Combined, Conduct Disorder, and Oppositional Defiant Disorder), and validity scales (Positive Impression, Negative Impression, and an Inconsistency Index). All test items are scored on a 4-point Likert-type scale (0 = not at all, 1 = just a little true, 2 = pretty much true, and 3 = very much true) with higher scores indicating a greater number and/or frequency of concerns.

Normative data on the Conners 3 includes 1,200 parents, 1,200 teachers, and 1,000 self-report raters who were matched on the 2000 US Census information on ethnicity/race, gender, and parent education level (Conners, 2008). The Conners 3 reliability was assessed by Gallant (2007, 2008) where internal consistency was measured using Cronbach's alpha. Mean alphas for the Content scales were parent = 0.91, teacher = 0.94, and self-report = 0.88, respectively. Mean reliability coefficients for the DSM-IV-TR Symptom scales were parent = 0.90, teacher = 0.90, and self-report = 0.85. For the validity scales, Cronbach's alphas were parent = 0.90, teacher = 0.72, and self-report = 0.56. For test–retest reliability, two separate administrations of the test were given between 2- and 4-week intervals. Mean correlation coefficients for Content scales were parent = 0.85, teacher = 0.94, and self-report = 0.88, and for the DSM-IV-TR Symptom scales, the correlation scores were parent = 0.89, teacher = 0.90, and self-report = 0.85. Interrater reliability was assessed using correlation scores, and moderate to strong levels of rater agreement were found across all scales, indicating high levels of consistency between parent–parent and/or teacher–teacher ratings of youth participants. Mean Content scale correlations were parent=0.81, and teacher=0.73; and DSM-IV-TR Symptom scale scores were parent=0.84 and teacher=0.70. An exploratory factor analysis utilizing both the general and clinical samples indicated that the general factor structure of the three forms remained consistent across demographic groups (Kao & Thomas, 2010). A confirmatory factor analyses indicated the teacher model was slightly lower than the parent models but both were adequately fit. Informant correlations were significant showing high consistency between various raters of the same youth. The mean parent-to-teacher rating was 0.60 (range=0.52–0.67), the mean parent-to-youth correlation was 0.56 (range=0.49–0.62), and the mean teacher-to-youth correlation was 0.48 (range=0.43–0.56) (Conners, 2008). Convergent and divergent validity was determined by comparing Conners 3 scores with scores from the Behavior Assessment System for Children, Second Edition, the Conners' Rating Scales-Revised, the Achenbach System of Empirically Based Assessment, and the Behavior Rating Inventory of Executive Functioning (Kao & Thomas, 2010). Overall, correlations indicated the constructs converged and diverged in the expected directions (Kao & Thomas, 2010). To date, the Conners 3 has not been specifically validated in Asian-American populations in the USA, and no psychometric studies have been undertaken in Asian countries.

Depression Self-Rating Scale for Children (DSRSC)

The Depression Self-Rating Scale for Children (DSRSC) is an 18-item self-report measure for children and adolescents (Birleson, 1981) that has been used in a range of cross-cultural contexts. Items are presented as statements, e.g., "I sleep very well" and measure symptoms over the past week. Responses are a 0=mostly, 1=sometimes, 2=never, with higher scores indicating more severe depression (maximum score=36 points). Cronbach's alpha with a sample of psychiatric inpatients was 0.90, and the split-half correlation was 0.85, suggesting high internal reliability. Eighty-one of the psychiatric inpatients also rated their symptoms using the Beck depression inventory (BDI), and the scores were highly correlated suggesting convergent validity ($r=0.79$, $p<0.01$; Birleson, 1981).

A study was conducted to establish standardized norms of the DSRSC in Chinese urban youth and to examine the scale's reliability and validity (Su, Wang, Zhu, Luo, & Yang, 2003) in a sample of 1,943 subjects (968 males) from 14 cities of China with an average age of 11 years (SD=2). Test–retest reliability coefficients, split-half reliability coefficients, and Cronbach alpha coefficients ranged from 0.53 to 0.73, indicating acceptable reliability. Significant correlations were found between DSRSC total score, the depressive symptoms subscale of the CBCL, and the Piers-Harris Children's Self-concept Scale, suggesting good convergent validity. The scores of children with the depressive disorders as determined by the DSRSC were significantly higher than that of nondepressed children, suggesting discriminant validity. Results demonstrate that the Chinese language version of the DSRSC is may be utilized to assess depressive symptoms in Chinese urban children.

The 18-item version of the DSRSC was utilized to assess depressive symptoms over the past week on a 3-point scale in a school-based cross-sectional survey of junior high schools in Bengby city of Anhui Province in China (Cao et al., 2011). The sample consisted of 5,003 adolescents (2,606 males) aged 11–16 years (average age=13.2 years, SD=1). Test–retest reliability, split-half, and Cronbach's alphas in this sample ranged from 0.53 to 0.73. The clinically significant cutoff utilized in this sample was a score of 15 (with possible scores ranging from 0 to 36).

A Japanese language version of the DSRSC was prepared by Murata, Shimizu, Mori, and Oshima (1996) utilizing the translation/back-translation technique. The internal consistency of the Japanese language DSRSC was examined by administering the measure to 456 students ranging from elementary school second-graders to students in the second year of middle school.

Cronbach's alpha was 0.77, suggesting adequate internal consistency (Murata et al., 1996). The test–retest reliability of the Japanese language version of the DSRC was tested on 65 elementary school students (35 third-graders and 30 fourth-graders) twice at an interval of 2 weeks. The correlation coefficients for the administrations were 0.55 for the third-graders and 0.79 for the fourth-graders ($p<0.001$) (Murata et al., 1996). Convergent validity was established between the Japanese language DSRSC and the Japanese language version of the Child Depression Inventory (CDI) to 62 third-graders and fourth-graders ($r=0.71$). The Japanese language DSRSC has also demonstrated utility for distinguishing between depressed and nondepressed youth in 99 patients (aged 7–14 years) as diagnosed by an outpatient psychiatrist, suggesting discriminant validity. The mean score was 19.3 for the group with depression ($n-36$) and 10.7 for the group without depression ($n=63$) ($t=7.49$, $p<0.001$). The cutoff score determined from the ROC curve was 16 points (sensitivity 75 %, specificity 88.9 %) (Murata et al., 1996).

The Japanese language DSRSC was utilized in a sample of 2, 453 elementary and middle school children (1,114 males) ranging from 6 to 15 years old (average age = 8.76 years, SD = 5.68) in two medium-sized cities in Japan to assess the prevalence of depressive symptoms in youth in the general community population (Denda, Kako, Kitagawa, & Koyama, 2006). Cronbach's alpha in this sample was 0.84, suggesting good internal consistency. Subjects with DSRSC scores above the 15 point cutoff as utilized by Birleson, Hudson, Buchanan, and Wolff (1987) constituted the depressed group (14.9 % of the sample). Average DSRSC score was 8.15 in the total sample (SD = 5.14), 8.47 (SD = 5.22) for boys and 8.98 (SD = 5.99) for girls, but this gender score difference was nonsignificant. The average score in the total sample was similar to the average score obtained by Murata et al. (1996) (average score = 9.08, SD = 4.87) in a sample of 395 subjects ranging from second to sixth grade (ages 7–12). DSRSC score increased significantly with each year of age (average score for elementary school students = 7.97, SD = 5.02; average score for middle school students = 11.10, SD = 6.73). Further studies including the screening and psychiatric evaluation of nonclinical populations using the DSRSC are needed to generalize the use of this measure for other populations including Japanese Americans in the USA.

Beck Depression Inventory (BDI-II)

The Beck Depression Inventory-II (BDI-II) consists of 21 items assessing various emotional, neurovegetative, cognitive, and somatic symptoms of depression experienced over the previous 2 weeks rated on a four-point scale (BDI; Beck, Steer, & Garbin, 1988). The BDI-II was developed to measure depression in adolescents and adults from 13 to 80 years. The summation of all items yields a total score with specific ranges indicating levels of severity (0–9 indicates no depression, 10–16 indicates mild depression, 17–29 indicates moderate depression, and 30–63 indicates severe depression). The alpha coefficient of the BDI-II was 0.92 indicating high internal consistency (Beck, Stanley, & Zebb, 1996) with a replication study corroborating these findings (Steer & Clark, 1997). The correlation between the BDI-II and the BAI was 0.56 ($p<0.001$) for 160 outpatients, comparable to the correlation of 0.60 reported by Beck et al. (1996) for 297 of their outpatients (Steer & Clark, 1997).

The Chinese version of the BDI-II (BDI-II-C) was translated by the Chinese Behavioral Science Corporation in the year 2000 and has been used to diagnose the severity of depression as indicated through self-report of nonclinical populations in Taiwan. Wu and Chang (2008) explored the BDI-II-C with a focus on dimensionality, appropriateness of item difficulty, and category functioning for nonclinical adolescents. Participants were 2,095 (925 males) 10th to 12th grade senior high school students in Taiwan ranging from 14 to 18 years old with an average age of 16.75 years old (SD = 1.7). The average BDI-II-C total score was 12.90 (SD = 8.64). All 21 items produced mean square statistics within an acceptable range (0.60–1.40) except for Item 10 (crying) and Item 21 (interest in sex), which may be explained by cultural variations in the expression of depressive symptoms. Findings also suggest that item difficulty overall is inappropriate for differentiating differences in depressive symptoms for nonclinical community samples because items do not target individuals with low levels of depression. Further, people who endorse cognitive-affective symptoms are more apt to appear more depressed with respect to their BDI-II score than those with somatic symptoms as reported on the BDI-II, which may warrant further study concerning the construct validity of the BDI-II in Chinese and other international samples. Yeung et al. (2002) noted limitations that may be useful considerations in assessing Asian-Americans in future studies. The researchers found an overall reluctance of participants to self-report their symptoms, which makes for difficulty in assessing the psychometric properties of the BDI-II in screening for depression among Asian-Americans in primary care. For future depression screening among Asian-Americans in primary care, it may be necessary to develop a briefer screening scale to improve participation rate. It was also noted that often times Asian-Americans tend to avoid mental health services because of their fear and rejection of mental health disorders. Future efforts should focus on providing easier access to mental health services for Asian-Americans in an effort to decrease cultural barriers to the treatment of depressive symptoms.

Children's Depression Rating Scale-Revised (CDRS-R)

The Children's Depression Rating Scale-Revised (CDRS-R) aids in diagnosing and monitoring depression in youth aged 6–12 years (Mayes, Bernstein, Haley, Kennard, & Emslie, 2010). It is administered as a 15–20 min semi-structured interview. The interviewer rates, on a 7-point scale, 17 symptom areas including: impaired school-work, difficulty having fun, social withdrawal, appetite disturbance, sleep disturbance, excessive fatigue, physical complaints, irritability, excessive guilt, low self-esteem, depressed feelings, suicidal ideation, excessive weeping, depressed facial affect, listless speech, and hypoactivity. A recent study (Mayes et al., 2010) sought to evaluate the reliability and validity of the CDRS-R in adolescents aged 7–18 years. Adolescent participants were seen at three visits (screening, baseline, and exit). Internal consistency for the CDRS-R was good at all three visits, and total score was highly correlated with global severity ($r=0.87$, 0.80, and 0.93; $p<0.01$). Only the exit CDRS-R score was significantly correlated with global functioning (Children's Global Assessment Scale; $r=-0.77$; $p<0.01$) suggesting some convergent validity. Reductions on the CDRS-R total score were highly correlated with improvement scores at exit (Clinical Global Impressions–Improvement; $r=-0.83$; $p<0.01$). The results of this study demonstrate good reliability and validity of the CDRS for use with adolescents with depression (Mayes et al., 2010).

The reliability and the validity of the CDRS-R was examined with 181 adolescents (106 males) ranging from 14 to 17 years old (average age = 15.3, SD = 0.4) from three schools in Southern India. The six factor structure explained 60.6 % of the variance. Cronbach's alpha for the scale was 0.76 suggesting adequate internal consistency. The interrater reliability between pediatrician and clinical psychologist respondents was found to be good (ICC = 0.73) and test–retest reliability was found to be high (ICC = 0.98). Convergent validity between the total CDRS-R score and total Beck's Depression Inventory (BDI) score was high ($r=0.71$, $p<0.001$). Divergent validity was examined by correlating total CDRS-R score with total Impact of Events scale (IES) score which measures posttraumatic stress ($r=0.28$, $p>0.05$). There was moderate concordance with the reference standard of ICD-10 diagnosis (45.5 %) in identifying depression with this scale. The average CDRS score was 27.5 (SD = 8.3) in this sample with a range of 17–54. A cutoff score of 30 (sensitivity = 83 %, specificity = 84 %; Area Under Curve (AUC) in ROC = 87 %) in CDRS-R is suggested for diagnosing depression.

These results suggest that the CDRS-R demonstrates good reliability and validity for use with adolescents in India, but several limitations are noted. First, the researchers are unable to assert whether or not their results can be generalized to the general Indian pediatric population as the study was based in a school population. Second, the researchers found a low prevalence of depression which may have limited the power and stability of the sensitivity analyses. Third, this study utilized convenience sampling to improve participation, resulting in an overrepresentation of male participants. Finally, additional studies are needed to produce national norms of this instrument in India and to test its utility with Indian Americans in the USA.

Screen for Child Anxiety Related Emotional Disorders (SCARED)

The Screen for Child Anxiety Related Emotional Disorders (SCARED) was developed by Birmaher et al. (1997) for the screening of DSM-IV childhood anxiety disorders. It is a 41-item self-report measure designed to screen for DSM-IV anxiety disorders. The SCARED includes five scales: somatic/panic (13 items), generalized anxiety (9 items), separation anxiety (8 items), social phobia (7 items), and school phobia (4 items). The participants rate the items of each factor on a 3-point scale (0 = not true or hardly ever true, 1 = sometimes true, and 2 = true or often true). The SCARED total score is derived by adding the responses, with scores ranging from 0 to 82. Exploratory factor analysis of the SCARED revealed five factors that parallel the DSM-IV classification of anxiety disorders: panic/somatic, generalized anxiety, separation anxiety, social phobia, and school phobia. Birmaher et al. (1999) added three items reflecting social phobia to the original version in a replication study, resulting in a 41-item self-report questionnaire. The psychometric properties of this screening instrument have been examined in clinical, community, and primary care settings in primarily Caucasian samples in Western countries, and was found to be reliable in regard to internal consistency, test–retest reliability (Birmaher et al., 1997, 1999; Boyd, Ginsburg, Lambert, Cooley, & Campbell, 2003; Essau, Muris, & Ederer, 2002; Hale, Raaijmakers, Muris, & Meeus, 2005; Muris, Merckelbach, Schmidt, & Mayer, 1999), and parent–child agreement (Birmaher et al., 1997; Muris et al., 1999; Wren, Bridge, & Birmaher, 2004). The convergent validity of the SCARED was supported because of its significant correlations with other measures for childhood anxiety disorders including the Revised Children's Manifest Anxiety Scale (Boyd et al., 2003; Muris et al., 1998) and the Spence Children's Anxiety Scale (Essau et al., 2002). Evidence has also accumulated for the good discriminant validity of the SCARED both between anxiety and other clinical disorders, and among different anxiety disorders (Birmaher et al., 1997, 1999).

The reliability and the validity of the 41-item SCARED was examined in a large community sample of school children in China which consisted of 1,559 youth (49.6 % males) aged 8–16 years (average age = 11.8, SD = 2.1) (Su, Wang, Fan, Su, & Gao, 2008). The Chinese language version was created utilizing the translation/back-translation method. Females had significantly higher anxiety scores on the total anxiety, separation anxiety, and social phobia scales which corroborate previous studies (Hale et al., 2005). Consistent with existing literature, children had higher scores on separation anxiety than adolescents (Birmaher et al., 1997). This study also supported previous findings of SCARED's high internal consistency especially for total score (0.89; subscale alpha ranges 0.43–0.77) and moderate test–retest reliability (2-week and 12-week Pearson correlations 0.61 and 0.57 for total score; Intraclass correlation coefficients (ICCs) = 0.57 and 0.50 for total score). The SCARED total score was significantly correlated with the internalizing factor of the child behavior checklist (0.41), suggesting convergent validity. Further, the SCARED total score was also found to correlate significantly better with the internalizing than with the externalizing scale on the CBCL, demonstrating evidence for good divergent validity (Su et al., 2008). Discriminant validity was supported as the SCARED total score and the five subscale scores significantly differentiated youth with anxiety disorders from youth with ADHD. It also significantly discriminated between anxious and depressed children on the total score and panic, somatic, separation anxiety, and social phobia subscales. Consistent with Birmaher and colleagues (1999) a cutoff point of 25 on the Chinese language version of the SCARED yielded optimal sensitivity (79 %) and specificity (82 %). Results suggested that the Chinese language version of the SCARED has appropriate psychometric properties and is a clinically useful instrument to screen for DSM-IV anxiety disorders in Chinese youth.

The 41-item SCARED(Birmaher et al., 1999) was utilized to assess anxiety symptoms over the past week on a 3-point scale in a school-based cross-sectional survey of junior high schools in Bengby city of Anhui Province in China (Cao et al., 2011). The sample consisted of 5,003 adolescents (2,606 males) aged 11–16 years (average age = 13.2 years, SD = 1). The clinically significant cutoff utilized in this sample was a score of 23.

Su and colleagues (2008) found some areas that should be considered when adapting this instrument for Chinese youth. For example, Item 9 (people tell me I look nervous) did not load on any of the factors, which may be explained by the indirectness of Chinese culture. In Chinese culture, people tend to rely on indirect, more complex methods of communication like indefinite comments while Westerners tend to adopt direct and simple methods. Additionally, the study had a relatively small sample of children and findings need to be replicated in larger and more representative samples in order to establish national norms. Future studies also need to include larger samples of children with various anxiety disorders and other psychopathologies to further evaluate the usefulness of the SCARED in clinical populations. Finally, the utility of this instrument as well as the original English instrument should be examined in Asian-American samples in the USA.

The Penn State Worry Questionnaire for Children (PSWQ-C)

The Penn State Worry Questionnaire for Children (PSWQ-C) was developed by Chorpita and colleagues (Chorpita, Tracey, Brown, Collica, & Barlow, 1997). It consists of 14 items with a 4-point scale: 0 = not at all, 1 = sometimes, 2 = frequently, 3 = always, with a range of 0–42 points (higher score indicates higher worry tendencies). The instrument showed good concurrent and discriminative validities, internal consistency, and test–retest reliability for children and youth aged 6–18 years (Chorpita et al., 1997). In another validation study (Muris, Meesters, & Gobel, 2001), the authors recommended discarding the three reverse-scored questions and utilizing an 11-item questionnaire due to problems with factor loadings of these items.

The reliability and validity of a Korean language version of the PSWQ-C (PSWQ-CK) was investigated in a study with 973 elementary school children (aged 8–12 years, average age = 10.6, SD = 1.1). The PSWQ-CK is a 14-item questionnaire with a 4-point scale: 0 = not at all, 1 = sometimes, 2 = frequently, 3 = always, with a range of 0–42 points (higher score indicates higher worry tendencies). The authors utilized the translation guidelines recommended by Guillemin, Bombardier, and Beaton (1993) and Beaton, Bombardier, Guillemin, and Ferraz (2000). The average PSWQ-CK score for all participants was 14.49 (SD = 8.06). There was no significant difference in terms of gender, and sixth graders scored significantly higher than fourth or fifth graders ($p < 0.05$). Internal consistency was high (Cronbach's alpha = 0.90), and when the three reverse items were removed, Cronbach's alpha improved to 0.91. Test–retest reliability (three weeks apart) was high ($r = 0.83$, $p < 0.001$), suggesting test stability. Convergent validity was established by comparing the results of the PSWQ-CK (both the 14-item version and the 11-item version with the three reverse-scored items removed) to the RCMAS. *Z*-test for the comparison of dependent correlations revealed that the 14-item PSWQ-CK had excellent correlation in the worry/oversensitivity subscales of RCMAS ($p < 0.01$), while the 11-item version of the PSWQ-CK demonstrated lower but significant correlation with the RCMAS subscales. The factor load and item-total correlations of the three revised-scored items was greater than that found in either the Chorpita et al. (1997) or Muris et al.

(2001) validation studies. In this study, the three reverse-scored items demonstrated an influence on the instrument's validity and were recommended by the researchers to be included in the survey. The researchers propose a linguistic structure difference between English and Korean to be accountable for the discrepancy. Unlike in English, the verb comes at the end of the sentence in Korean. Therefore, the positive or negative word also comes at the end with the result that students may be giving more attention to the last part of the sentence. In addition, more studies are needed to examine the reliability and validity of PSWQ-CK for youths and to assess the contents of children's worry in Korea. The PSWQ-CK necessitates further validation in Korean in order to establish national norms and to replicate factor structure findings of this study. Further, both the original PSWQ-C (in English) and the PSWQ-CK needs to be investigated for its utility with Korean Americans in the USA.

Childhood Autism Rating Scale (CARS)

The Childhood Autism Rating Scale (CARS) is a behavioral rating scale developed as an aid in diagnosing and describing the severity of autism in children aged two years and above. The CARS contains 15 items addressing the following areas of functioning: Relating to People; Imitation; Emotional Response; Body Use; Object Use; Adaptation to Change; Visual Response; Taste, Smell, and Touch Response and Use; Fear or Nervousness; Verbal Communication; Nonverbal Communication; Activity Level; Level of Consistency of Intellectual Responses; and General Impressions. The Childhood Autism Rating Scale (CARS; Schopler, Van Bourgondien, Wellman, & Love, 2010) is one of the most widely used instruments to evaluate the degree of autism in developmentally disabled children through clinical observation by a trained rater. The CARS consists of 15 items involving definitions of autism by Rutter and by Ritvo and Freeman. Each item is rated on a 4-point scale and the total CARS score ranges from 15 to 60. The CARS has demonstrated good internal consistency, interrater reliability, and validity. The overall interrater reliability estimate for the CARS was 0.84. Mesibov et al. recommended that cutoffs of CARS for diagnosing autism be 30 in children and 27 in adolescents. The overall interrater reliability estimate for the CARS was 0.84. In using this cutoff value 87 % of individuals were correctly identified in the sample as autistic or not autistic. Using the total raw score alone, identification of those with or without an autism diagnosis resulted in a sensitivity value of 0.88 and a specificity value of 0.86 (Schopler et al., 2010).

Kurita, Miyake, and Katsuno (1989) developed a Japanese language version of the CARS (CARS-TV) and demonstrated its reliability and validity with 167 developmentally disabled Japanese children under 16 years of age. Cronbach's alpha was 0.87 suggesting good internal reliability of the scale. The interrater reliability for each of the 15 subscales based on a subsample of 128 children was moderate and ranged from 0.43 to 0.77 with an average of 0.62. In the full sample ($N=167$), the total CARS-TV score demonstrated a good level of taxonomic validity on DSM-III diagnostic groups. Further, total CARS-TV score discriminated infantile autism and other pervasive developmental disorders from mental retardation without an additional diagnosis of pervasive developmental disorder.

Another study was conducted to evaluate the cutoffs and sensitivity/specificity of the Childhood Autism Rating Scale—Tokyo Version (CARS-TV) with 430 children (357 males) with Pervasive Developmental Disorders (PDD) ranging from 25 to 294 months old (average age = 80.8 months, SD = 46.4) and 75 children (26 males) ranging from 37 to 352 months old with mental retardation without a history of PDD (average age = 80.5 months, SD = 50.1) living in Tokyo (Tachimori, Osada, & Kurita, 2003). The CARS-TV total score was compared among these children who were classified into four DSM-IV diagnostic groups: (1) 212 (180 males) with autistic disorder, (2) 31 (24 male) with Asperger's Disorder, (3) 6 (5 males) with

Childhood Disintegrative Disorder (CDD), and (4) 181 (149 male) with PDD not otherwise specified (PDDNOS). Values of Cronbach's alpha were 0.91 for the PDD group and 0.89 for the non-PDD mental retardation (MR) group, and 0.93 for both groups combined, suggesting good internal consistency for both subsamples. The CARS-TV total score was significantly higher in PDD (mean = 30.1, SD = 4.5) than in non-PDD MR (mean = 22.9, SD = 3.3), $t(503) = 13.7$, $p < 0.0001$. The cutoff to distinguish PDD from non-PDD MR was 25.5/26, with sensitivity, specificity, positive predictive value and negative predictive value of 0.86, 0.83, 0.97, and 0.50, respectively. In addition, the CARS-TV total score differed significantly among the four DSM-IV subgroups, with CDD and AD subgroups being significantly higher than both PDDNOS and Asperger's disorder, and with the PDDNOS subgroup CARS total score being significantly higher than Asperger's disorder. No significant difference was found between CDD and AD. The cutoff to distinguish AD from PDDNOS was 30/30.5, with sensitivity, specificity, positive predictive value and negative predictive value of 0.71, 0.75, 0.77, and 0.69, respectively. Results suggest that the CARS-TV may have clinical utility for differentiating between PDD and non-PDD MR and between AD and PDDNOS.

To assess whether the CARS-TV can differentiate between high-functioning atypical autism (HAA) with IQ $\geq$ 70 and childhood autism (HCA), 74 children and young adults (63 males) aged 2–23 years (average age 6.6, SD = 0.5 years) with either a classification HAA (53 children, 45 males, average age = 6 years, SD = 0.5 years, range 2–23 years) or HCA (21 children, 18 males, average age = 8.2 years, SD = 1.1 years, range 3–18 years) were examined. On the CARS-TV with IQ and total CARS-TV score controlled for, the HAA children were significantly less abnormal than the HCA children on two items of the CARS-TV, specifically, relationship with people and general impressions. In addition, affect reports tended to be significantly milder in HAA than HCA, and anxiety reaction was significantly more abnormal in HAA than HCA. These findings suggest that the CARS-TV may be useful to clinically distinguish between HAA and HCA youth.

In looking at several studies which assess the use of the CARS-TV with Japanese children some limitations need to be addressed in future research. First, findings need to be verified by longitudinal studies as autistic symptoms change over time (Kanai et al., 2004; Tachimori et al., 2003). Findings also need verification with a clear criterion for high-functioning autism in larger sample sizes. Finally, cutoff scores for pervasive developmental disorders need replication in varied populations within Japan (Kanai et al., 2004; Tachimori et al., 2003) as well as with Japanese Americans in the USA.

Recommendations

Many of the assessments discussed in this chapter are still in early stages of test validation, and most of the surveys have been validated with international samples with Asian youth but not yet explicitly examined for their psychometric properties with different Asian-American youth residing in the USA. Thus, caution is needed when utilizing and interpreting the results of these surveys for Asian-American youth. One issue that is important to consider is whether it would be more appropriate to utilize the norms of the general US population which often does not contain Asian-American groups (or at least not a substantial proportion of Asian-Americans) in the validation sample, or if it would be more appropriate to utilize the norms for the specific cultural group established in another country. Another consideration is whether or not it is appropriate to apply Asian-American norms established in the USA to a specific cultural group (e.g., Chinese Americans, Vietnamese Americans, East Indian Americans), and many validation studies do not include the collection of factors such as immigrant status, years in the USA, primary language, and acculturation status that may help aid the clinician or researcher in determination which norms to utilize as a comparison. To assist in the decision making process, it may be helpful to supplement the implementation of the survey instrument with data from structured and semi-structured interviews and surveys that measure acculturation or ethnic identity. These methods of evaluation allow the clinician to ask the youth and his or her parent questions about the youth's participation and affiliation with the mainstream American culture and the ethnic culture of origin. Armed with this information, the clinician may be able to make a more informed decision regarding which normative sample would be most relevant for the interpretation of the youth's survey results.

In addition, it may be helpful to address in a follow-up interview with the youth certain responses on the survey instrument when there is a question of whether or not there is equivalence across cultures on specific items. This is particularly important when there are known or suspected differences in symptom expression on specific domains of functioning or culture-bound syndromes that approximate certain diagnostic categories for a specific cultural group. For example, there may be differences in how traits like extraversion and agreeableness are viewed in different Asian cultures. Some Asian cultural groups may value agreeableness more highly than some Americans, as agreeableness may reflect collectivistic ideals. Extraversion may or may not be desired as a personal quality if some Asian groups interpret it as synonymous with being boisterous or as a quality that goes against values of humility and stoicism which are prevalent in several Asian cultures. These differences, if they exist, may be more salient for Asian-Americans who are recent immigrants versus those who are second or third generation residents in the USA.

Finally, more research on the psychometric properties for existing behavioral assessments needs to be undertaken to establish norms, cutoffs, and reliability and validity in specific Asian-American populations in the USA. Most of the assessments in this chapter have validated the original versions of the surveys or the translated versions of the surveys in other countries, but no data to date has been produced for their ethnic counterparts in the USA. This research should be undertaken with specific Asian-American samples instead of grouping these heterogeneous youth into one overall sample in validation studies whenever possible to ensure applicability. In addition, within these specific ethnic samples, other factors that will likely play a significant role in the youths' interpretation of and responses to the survey items such as acculturation level, generational status, and ethnic identity should also be examined via cohort or block designs.

References

Achenbach, T. M. (1991). *Manual for the child behavior checklist/4-18 and 1991 profile*. Burlington, VT: Department of Psychiatry, University of Vermont.

Achenbach, T. M., & Edelbrock, C. S. (1983). *Manual for the child behavior checklist and revised child behavior profile*. Burlington, VT: University of Vermont.

Achenbach, T. M., McConaughy, S. H., & Howell, C. T. (1987). Child/adolescent behavioral and emotional problems: Implications of cross-informant correlations for situational specificity. *Psychological Bulletin, 101*, 213–232.

Achenbach, T. M., & Rescorla, L. (2001). *Manual for the ASEBA school-age forms & profiles: An integrated system of multi-informant assessment*. Burlington, VT: University of Vermont.

Beaton, D. E., Bombardier, C., Guillemin, F., & Ferraz, M. B. (2000). Guidelines for the process of cross-cultural adaptation of self-report measures. *Spine, 25*(24), 3186–3191.

Beck, J. G., Stanley, M. A., & Zebb, B. J. (1996). Characteristics of generalized anxiety disorder in older adults: A descriptive study. *Behaviour Research and Therapy, 34*(3), 225–234.

Beck, A. T., Steer, R. A., & Garbin, M. G. (1988). Psychometric properties of the Beck Depression Inventory: Twenty-five years of evaluation. *Clinical Psychology Review, 8*, 77–100.

Biederman, J., Faraone, S. V., Doyle, A., Lehman, B. K., Kraus, I., Perrin, J., et al. (1993). Convergence of the child behavior checklist with structured interview-based psychiatric diagnoses of ADHD children with and without comorbidity. *Journal of Child Psychology and Psychiatry, 34*(7), 1241–1251.

Birleson, P. (1981). The validity of depressive disorder in childhood and the development of a self-rating scale: A research report. *Journal of Child Psychology and Psychiatry, 22*, 73–88.

Birleson, P., Hudson, I., Buchanan, D. G., & Wolff, S. (1987). Clinical evaluation of a self-rating scale for depressive disorder in childhood (Depression Self-Rating Scale). *Journal of Child Psychology and Psychiatry, 28*(1), 43–60.

Birmaher, B., Brent, D. A., Chiappetta, L., Bridge, J., Monga, S., & Baugher, M. (1999). Psychometric properties of the screen for child anxiety related emotional disorders (SCARED): A replication study. *Journal of the American Academy of Child and Adolescent Psychiatry, 38*, 1230–1236.

Birmaher, B., Khetarpal, S., Brent, D., Cully, M., Balach, L., Kaufman, J., et al. (1997). The screen for child anxiety related emotional disorders (SCARED): Scale construction and psychometric characteristics. *Journal of the American Academy of Child and Adolescent Psychiatry, 36*(4), 545–553.

Boggs, S. R., Eyberg, S., & Reynolds, L. A. (1990). Concurrent validity of the Eyberg child behavior inventory. *Journal of Clinical Child Psychology, 19*(1), 75–78.

Boyd, R. C., Ginsburg, G. S., Lambert, S. F., Cooley, M. R., & Campbell, K. D. M. (2003). Screen for child anxiety related emotional disorders (SCARED): Psychometric properties in an African American parochial high school sample. *Journal of the American Academy of Child and Adolescent Psychiatry, 42*, 1188–1196.

Brislin, R. W. (1983). Cross-cultural research in psychology. *Annual Review in Psychology, 34*, 363–400.

Cao, H., Qian, Q., Weng, T., Yuan, C., Sun, Y., Wang, H., et al. (2011). Screen time, physical activity and mental health among urban adolescents in China. *Preventive Medicine, 53*, 316–320.

Cho, S. C., Kim, B. N., Kim, J. W., Kim, H. W., Choi, H. J., Jung, S. W., … Han, S. H. (2007). The reliability and validity of diagnostic interview schedule for children version IV-Korean version (DISC-IV). *Journal of the Korean Academy of Child and Adolescent Psychiatry, 18*(2), 138–144.

Chorpita, B. F., Tracey, S. A., Brown, T. A., Collica, T. J., & Barlow, D. H. (1997). Assessment of worry in children and adolescents: An Adaptation of the Penn State Worry Questionnaire. *Behaviour Research and Therapy, 35*(6), 569–581.

Cicchetti, D. V. (1994). Guidelines, criteria, and rules of thumb for evaluating normed and standardized assessment instruments in psychology. *Psychological Assessment, 6*, 284–290. doi:10.1037/1040-3590.6.4.284.

Conners, C. (2008). *Conners 3rd edition: Manual*. North Tonawanda, NY: Multi-Health Systems.

Conners, C., Sitarenios, G., Parker, J. A., & Epstein, J. N. (1998). The revised Conners' Parent Rating Scale (CPRS-R): Factor structure, reliability, and criterion validity. *Journal of Abnormal Child Psychology, 26*, 257–268.

Demaray, M. K., Ruffalo, S. L., Carlson, J., & Busse, R. T. (1995). Social skills assessment: A comparative evaluation of six published rating scales. *School Psychology Review, 24*, 649–671.

Denda, K., Kako, Y., Kitagawa, N., & Koyama, T. (2006). Assessment of depressive symptoms in Japanese school children and adolescents using the Birleson Depression Self-Rating Scale. *International Journal of Psychiatry in Medicine, 36*, 231–241.

Deng, S., Liu, X., & Roosa, M. (2004). Agreement between parent and teacher reports on behavioral problems among Chinese children. *Journal of Developmental and Behavioral Pediatrics, 25*(6), 407–414.

Doi, Y., Roberts, R. E., Takeuchi, K., & Suzuki, S. (2001). Multiethnic comparison of adolescent major depression based on the DSM—IV criteria in a U.S.–Japan study. *Journal of the American Academy of Child and Adolescent Psychiatry, 40*(11), 1308–1315. doi:10.1097/00004583-200111000-00011.

Du, Y., Kou, J., & Coghill, D. (2008). The validity, reliability, and normative scores of the parent, teacher, and self report versions of the Strengths and Difficulties Questionnaire in China. *Child and Adolescent Psychiatry and Mental Health, 2*, 1–15.

Essau, C. A., Muris, P., & Ederer, E. M. (2002). Reliability and validity of the Spence children's anxiety scale and the screen for child anxiety related emotional disorders in German children. *Journal of Behavior Therapy and Experimental Psychiatry, 33*, 1–18.

Ezpeleta, L., Granero, R., de la Osa, N., Domenech, J. M., & Bonilla, A. B. (2006). Assessment of functional impairment in Spanish children. *Applied Psychology: An International Review, 55*(1), 130–143.

Gallant, S. (2007, August). *Psychometric properties of the Conners 3*. Poster presented at the annual meeting of the American Psychological Association, Los Angeles, CA.

Gallant, S. (2008, February). *Conners 3: Psychometric properties and practical applications*. Annual meeting of the National Association of School Psychologists, New Orleans, LA

Goldberg, M. R., Dill, C. A., Shin, J. Y., & Nhan, N. V. (2009). Reliability and validity of the Vietnamese Vineland Adaptive Behavior Scales with preschool-age children. *Research in Developmental Disabilities, 30*(3), 592–602.

Goodman, R. (1997). The Strengths and Difficulties Questionnaire: A research note. *Journal of Child Psychology and Psychiatry, 38*, 581–586.

Goodman, R. (1999). The extended version of the Strength and Difficulties Questionnaire as a guide to child psychiatric caseness and consequent burden. *Journal of Child Psychology and Psychiatry, 40*, 791–799.

Gresham, F. M., & Elliott, S. N. (1990). *Social skills rating system: Preschool, elementary level*. Circle Pines, MN: American Guidance Service.

Guillemin, F., Bombardier, C., & Beaton, D. (1993). Cross-cultural adaptation of health-related quality of life measures: Literature review and proposed guidelines. *Journal of Clinical Epidemiology, 46*, 1417–1432.

Hale, W. W., Raaijmakers, Q., Muris, P., & Meeus, W. (2005). Psychometric properties of the screen for child anxiety related emotional disorders (SCARED) in the generalized adolescent population. *Journal of the*

American Academy of Child and Adolescent Psychiatry, 44, 283–290.

Hawes, D., Hawes, D. J., & Dadds, M. R. (2004). Australian data and psychometric properties of the Strengths and Difficulties Questionnaire. *Australian and New Zealand Journal of Psychiatry, 38*, 644–651.

Ho, T., Leung, P., Lee, C., Tang, C., Hung, S., Kwong, S., … Shaffer, D. (2005). Test-retest reliability of the Chinese version of the Diagnostic Interview Schedule for Children-Version 4 (DISC-IV). *Journal of Child Psychology and Psychiatry, 46*(10), 1135–1138.

Ho, T., Leung, P., Luk, E., Taylor, E., Bacon-Shone, J., & Mak, F. (1996). Establishing the constructs of childhood behavioral disturbances in a Chinese population: A questionnaire study. *Journal of Abnormal Child Psychology, 24*(4), 417–431.

Hodges, K. (1999). Child and adolescent functional assessment scale (CAFAS). In M. E. Maruish (Ed.), *The use of psychological testing for treatment planning and outcome assessment* (pp. 631–664). Mahwah, NJ: Lawrence Erlbaum Associates.

Hodges, K. (2000a). *Child and adolescent functional assessment scale*. Ypsilanti, MI: Eastern Michigan University.

Hodges, K. (2000b). *Child and adolescent functional assessment scale self-training manual*. Ypsilanti, MI: Eastern Michigan University.

Hodges, K., Doucette-Gates, A., & Liao, Q. (1999). The relationship between the Child and Adolescent Functional Assessment Scale (CAFAS) and indicators of functioning. *Journal of Child and Family Studies, 8*(1), 109–122.

Hodges, K., & Wong, M. M. (1996). Psychometric characteristics of a multidimensional measure to assess impairment: The child and adolescent functional assessment scale. *Journal of Child and Family Studies, 5*(4), 445–467.

Hodges, K., Wong, M. M., & Latessa, M. (1998). Use of the Child and Adolescent Functional Assessment Scale (CAFAS) as an outcome measure in clinical settings. *The Journal of Behavioral Health Services & Research, 25*(3), 325–336.

Hulin, C. L., Drasgow, F., & Parsons, C. K. (1983). *Item response theory: Application to psychological measurement*. Homewood, IL: Dow Jones-Irwin.

Itani, T., Kanbayashi, Y., Nakata, Y., Kita, M., Fujii, H., Kuramoto, H., et al. (2001). Standardization of the Japanese version of the Child Behavior Checklist/4–18. *Journal of Child Psychiatry Neurology (Japanese), 41*, 243–252.

Ivanova, M. Y., Achenbach, T. M., Rescorla, L. A., Dumenci, L., Almqvist, F., Bilenberg, N., … Verhulst, F. C. (2007). The generalizability of the youth self-report syndrome structure in 23 societies. *Journal of Consulting and Clinical Psychology, 75*(5), 729

Janssens, A., & Deboutte, D. (2009). Screening for psychopathology in child welfare: The Strengths and Difficulties Questionnaire (SDQ) compared with the Achenbach System of Empirically Based Assessment (ASEBA). *European Child & Adolescent Psychiatry, 18*(11), 691–700. doi:10.1007/s00787-009-0030-y.

Kagan, J., & Fox, N. A. (2006). Biology, culture, and temperamental biases. In N. Eisenberg, W. Damon, & R. M. Lerner (Eds.), *Handbook of child psychology: Vol. 3, Social, emotional, and personality development* (6th ed., pp. 167–225). Hoboken, NJ: John Wiley & Sons.

Kagan, J., Kearsley, R. B., & Zelazo, P. R. (1978). *Infancy: Its place in human development*. Cambridge, MA: Harvard University Press.

Kanai, C., Koyama, T., Kato, S., Miyamoto, Y., Osada, H., & Kurita, H. (2004). Comparison of high-functioning atypical autism and childhood autism by Childhood Autism Rating Scale—Tokyo Version. *Psychiatry and Clinical Neurosciences, 58*, 217–221.

Kao, G. S., & Thomas, H. M. (2010). Test review: C. Keith Conners Conners 3rd Edition Toronto, Ontario, Canada—Multi-Health Systems, 2008. *Journal of Psychoeducational Assessment, 28*(6), 598–602.

Kim, J. W., Park, K. H., Cheon, K. A., Kim, B. N., Cho, S. C., & Hong, K. (2005). The child behavior checklist together with the ADHD rating scale can diagnose ADHD in Korean community-based samples. *Canadian Journal of Psychiatry, 50*(12), 802.

Klasen, H., Woerner, W., Wolke, D., Meyer, R., Overmeyer, S., Kaschnitz, W., … Goodman, R. (2000). Comparing the German versions of the strengths and difficulties questionnaire (SDQ-Deu) and the child behavior checklist. *European Child & Adolescent Psychiatry, 9*(4), 271–276.

Kuramoto, H., Kanbayashi, Y., Nakata, Y., Fukui, T., Mukai, T., & Negishi, Y. (2002). Standardization of the Japanese version of the Youth Self-Report (YSR). *Japanese Journal of Child and Adolescent Psychiatry, 43*, 17–32.

Kurita, H., Miyake, Y., & Katsuno, J. (1989). Reliability and validity of the Childhood Autism Rating Scale—Tokyo Version (CARS-TV). *Journal of Autism and Developmental Disorders, 19*, 389–396.

Landis, J. R., & Koch, G. G. (1977). An application of hierarchical kappa-type statistics in the assessment of majority agreement among multiple observers. *Biometrics, 33*, 363–374.

Leung, P. W., Kwong, S. L., Tang, C. P., Ho, T. P., Hung, S. F., Lee, C. C., … Liu, W. S. (2006). Test–retest reliability and criterion validity of the Chinese version of CBCL, TRF, and YSR. *Journal of Child Psychology and Psychiatry, 47*(9), 970–973.

Leung, C., Lo, S. K., & Leung, S. S. L. (2012). Validation of a questionnaire on behavior academic competence among Chinese preschool children. *Research in Developmental Disabilities, 33*, 1581–1593.

Leung, C., Sanders, M. R., Leung, S., Mak, R., & Lau, J. (2003). An outcome evaluation of the implementation of the triple p-positive parenting program in Hong Kong. *Family Process, 42*, 531–544.

Lewis, G., Pelosi, A. J., Araya, R., & Dunn, G. (1992). Measuring psychiatric disorder in the community: A standardized assessment for use by lay interviewers. *Psychological Medicine, 22*(2), 465–486.

Liu, J., Cheng, H., & Leung, P. W. (2011). The application of the Preschool Child Behavior Checklist and the Caregiver–Teacher Report form to mainland Chinese children: Syndrome structure, gender differences, country effects, and inter-informant agreement. *Journal of Abnormal Child Psychology, 39*(2), 251–264.

Liu, X., Sun, Z., Neiderhiser, J. M., Uchiyama, M., Okawa, M., & Rogan, W. (2001). Behavioral and emotional problems in Chinese adolescents: Parent and teacher reports. *Journal of the American Academy of Child and Adolescent Psychiatry, 40*(7), 828.

Matsuishi, T., Nagano, M., Araki, Y., Tanaka, Y., Iwasaki, M., Yamashita, Y., … Kakuma, T. (2008). Scale properties of the Japanese version of the Strengths and Difficulties Questionnaire (SDQ): A study of infant and school children in community samples. *Brain and Development, 30*(6), 410–415.

Mayes, T. L., Bernstein, I. H., Haley, C. L., Kennard, B. D., & Emslie, G. J. (2010). Psychometric properties of the Children's Depression Rating Scale–Revised in adolescents. *Journal of Child and Adolescent Psychopharmacology, 20*(6), 513–516. doi:10.1089/cap.2010.0063.

Mellor, D. (2004). Furthering the use of the Strengths and Difficulties Questionnaire: Reliability with younger child respondents. *Psychological Assessment, 16*, 396–401.

Mellor, D., Wong, J., & Xu, X. (2011). Interparent agreement on the strengths and difficulties questionnaire: A Chinese study. *Journal of Clinical Child & Adolescent Psychology, 40*(6), 890–896.

Murata, T., Shimizu, A., Mori, Y., & Oshima, S. (1996). Childhood depressive state in the school situation: Consideration from the Birleson's Scale. *The Japanese Journal of Psychiatry, 1*, 131–138.

Muris, P., Meesters, C., & Gobel, M. (2001). Reliability, validity, and normative data of the Penn State Worry Questionnaire in 8–12 year old children. *Journal of Behavioral Therapy and Experimental Psychiatry, 32*, 63–72.

Muris, P., Merckelbach, H., Mayer, B., van Brakel, A., Thissen, S., Moulaert, V., et al. (1998). The screen for child anxiety related emotional disorders (SCARED) and traditional childhood anxiety measures. *Journal of Behavior Therapy and Experimental Psychiatry, 29*(4), 327–339.

Muris, P., Merckelbach, H., Schmidt, H., & Mayer, B. (1999). The revised version of the screen for child anxiety related emotional disorders (SCARED-R): Factor structure in normal children. *Personality and Individual Differences, 26*, 99–112.

Oakland, T., & Houchins, S. (1985). A review of the Vineland Adaptive Behavior Scales, survey form. *Journal of Counseling & Development, 63*(9), 585–586.

Oh, K. J., Hong, K. E., & Lee, H. R. (1997). Korean-Youth Self Report (K-YSR). Seoul, Korea: Jungang Aptitude Research Center.

Park, J. H., Lee, S. I., & Schachar, R. J. (2011). Reliability and validity of the child and adolescent functioning impairment scale in children with attention-deficit/hyperactivity disorder. *Psychiatry Investigation, 8*(2), 113–122.

Renk, K., & Phares, V. (2004). Cross-informant ratings of social competence in children and adolescents. *Clinical Psychology Review, 24*, 239–254.

Reynolds, C., & Kamphaus, R. (2004). *Behavioral assessment system for children* (2nd ed.). Minneapolis, MN: Pearson Assessments.

Russell, S., Subramanian, B., & Russell, P. S. S. (2005). Revision and validation of Child Behavior Checklist—Post-traumatic Stress Disorder Scale in Tamil. *International Journal of Disaster Medicine, 1*(4), 41–44.

Sackett, D. L., Haynes, R. B., Tugwell, P., & Guyatt, G. H. (1985). *Clinical epidemiology: A basic science for clinical medicine*. Boston, MA: Little Brown and Company.

Satake, H., Yishida, K., Yamashita, H., Kinukawa, N., & Takagishi, T. (2003). Agreement between parent and teachers on behavioral/emotional problems in Japanese school children using the Child Behavior Checklist. *Child Psychiatry and Human Development, 34*, 111–126.

Schopler, E., Van Bourgondien, M. E., Wellman, G. J., & Love, S. R. (2010). *Childhood autism rating scale* (2nd ed.). Los Angeles, CA: Western Psychological Services.

Shaffer, D., Gould, M. S., Brasic, J., Ambrosini, P., Fisher, P., Bird, H., et al. (1983). A children's global assessment scale (CGAS). *Archives of General psychiatry, 40*(11), 1228.

Smedje, H., Broman, J. E., Hetta, J., & von Knorring, A. L. (1999). Psychometric properties of a Swedish version of the "Strengths and Difficulties Questionnaire". *European Child and Adolescent Psychiatry, 8*, 63–70.

Sparrow, S. S., Balla, D. A., & Cicchetti, D. V. (1984). *Vineland adaptive behavior scales: Interview edition, expanded form manual*. Circle Pines, MN: American Guidance Service.

Steer, R. A., & Clark, D. A. (1997). Psychometric characteristics of the Beck Depression Inventory–II with college students. *Measurement and Evaluation in Counseling and Development, 30*, 128–136.

Steingard, R., Biederman, J., Doyle, A., & Sprich-Buckminster, S. (1992). Psychiatric comorbidity in attention deficit disorder: Impact on the interpretation of Child Behavior Checklist results. *Journal of the American Academy of Child and Adolescent Psychiatry, 31*, 449–454.

Su, L., Wang, K., Fan, F., Su, Y., & Gao, X. (2008). Reliability and validity of the screen for child anxiety related emotional disorders (SCARED) in Chinese children. *Journal of Anxiety Disorders, 22*(4), 612.

Su, L., Wang, K., Zhu, Y., Luo, X., & Yang, Z. (2003). Norm of the depression self-rating scale for children in Chinese urban children. *Chinese Mental Health Journal, 17*(8), 547–549.

Subramaniam, K., Krishnaswamy, S., Jemain, A. A., Hamid, A., & Patel, V. (2006). The Clinical Interview Schedule-Revised (CIS-R)–Malay version, clinical validation. *The Malaysian Journal of Medical Sciences: MJMS, 13*(1), 58.

Tachimori, H. T., Osada, H., & Kurita, H. (2003). The Childhood Autism Rating Scale—Tokyo version for screening pervasive developmental disorders. *Psychiatry and Clinical Neurosciences, 57*, 113–118.

Tan, T. X., & Camras, L. A. (2011). Social skills of adopted Chinese girls at home and in school: Parent and teacher ratings. *Children and Youth Services Review, 33*, 1813–1821.

Tan, T. X., Marfo, K., & Dedrick, R. F. (2010). Early developmental and psychosocial risks and longitudinal behavioral adjustment outcomes for preschool-age girls adopted from China. *Journal of Applied Developmental Psychology, 31*, 306–314.

Thompson, B., & Vacha-Haase, T. (2000). Psychometrics is datametrics: The test is not reliable. *Educational and Psychological Measurement, 60*, 174–195.

Tittle, C. K. (1982). Use of judgmental methods in item bias studies. In R. A. Berk (Ed.), *Handbook of methods for detecting test bias* (pp. 31–63). Baltimore, MD: The Johns Hopkins University Press.

Tombokan-Runtukahu, J., & Nitko, A. (1992). Translation, cultural adjustment, and validation of a measure of adaptive behavior. *Research in Developmental Disabilities, 13*(5), 481–501.

Touliatos, J., & Lindholm, B. W. (1981). Congruence of parents' and teachers' ratings of children's behavior problems. *Journal of Abnormal Child Psychology, 9*(3), 347–354.

Van Widenfelt, B. M., Goedhart, A. W., Treffers, P. D., & Goodman, R. (2003). Dutch version of the Strength and Difficulties Questionnaire (SDQ). *European Child and Adolescent Psychiatry, 13*, 3–10.

Weine, A. M., Phillips, J. S., & Achenbach, T. M. (1995). Behavioral and emotional problems among Chinese and American children: Parent and teacher reports for ages 6 to 13. *Journal of Abnormal Child Psychology, 23*(5), 619–639.

Weisz, J. R., Suwanlert, S., Chaiyasit, W., Weiss, B., Achenbach, T. M., & Trevathan, D. (1989). Epidemiology of behavioral and emotional problems among Thai and American children: Teacher reports for ages 6–11. *Journal of Child Psychology and Psychiatry, 30*(3), 471–484.

Weisz, J. R., Suwanlert, S., Chaiyasit, W., Weiss, B., Walter, B. R., & Anderson, W. W. (1988). Thai and American perspectives on over-and undercontrolled child behavior problems: Exploring the threshold model among parents, teachers, and psychologists. *Journal of Consulting and Clinical Psychology, 56*(4), 601–609.

Weisz, J. R., Weiss, B., Suwanlert, S., & Chaiyasit, W. (2003). Syndromal structure of psychopathology in children of Thailand and the United States. *Journal of Consulting and Clinical Psychology, 71*(2), 375–385.

Wren, F. J., Bridge, J. A., & Birmaher, B. (2004). Screening for childhood anxiety symptoms in primary care: Integrating child and parent reports. *Journal of the American Academy of Child and Adolescent Psychiatry, 43*, 1364–1371.

Wu, P.-C., & Chang, L. (2008). Psychometric properties of the Chinese version of the Beck Depression Inventory-II using the Rasch Model. *Measurement and Evaluation in Counseling and Development, 41*, 13–31.

Yang, H. J., Soong, W., Chiang, C., & Chen, W. (2000). Competence and behavioral/emotional problems among Taiwanese adolescents as reported by parents and teachers. *Journal of the American Academy of Child and Adolescent Psychiatry, 39*, 232–239.

Yeung, A., Howarth, S., Chan, R., Sonawalla, S., Nierenberg, A. A., & Fava, M. (2002). Use of the Chinese version of the Beck Depression Inventory for screening depression in primary care. *The Journal of Nervous and Mental Disease, 190*(2), 94–99.

25 School-Based Assessment with Asian Children and Adolescents

Chieh Li and Zhengzheng Wang

The previous chapters have presented cross-cultural considerations in psychological assessment with Asian-Americans, including discussion on specific ethnic groups, diagnoses and instruments. This chapter explores how to apply these cross-cultural considerations to school-based assessment with Asian-American or Asian immigrant (A-A/I) children and adolescents. Within the wide range of school-based assessment, the chapter focuses on its essence—evaluation for special education based on the IDEA (Individuals with Disabilities Education Act, 2004) criteria. The chapter begins with specific cultural considerations of the assessment context including school and home cultures, followed by the IDEA requirement of nondiscriminatory evaluation and implications for professionals involved in the school-based evaluation, especially school psychologists. Then, we will analyze culturally and linguistically appropriate assessment of commonly identified disability categories defined by IDEA, including specific learning disability, speech/language impairment, autism, developmental delay, and intellectual disability. We will also discuss cultural considerations for using the RTI (response to intervention) model, an alternative approach that is becoming more popular in school-based assessment, in determining the need for special education.

Consideration of the Assessment Context

Considering the School Context

To conduct culturally sensitive school-based assessment of A-A/I children, it is crucial to understand the school context and how it affects A-A/I children from a sociocultural perspective. The school context includes the general school climate, the relationships between administrators and teachers, among teachers, among students, between teachers and students, between teachers and parents, and teachers' attitudes toward A-A/I children and parents. It also includes the racial/cultural composition of the teachers and students, the curriculum, and the training of the teachers.

Consideration of the school culture also includes a sociohistorical perspective. Historically, American schools were overwhelmingly influenced by European cultures. For generations, the standard academic curriculum has been dominated by Euro-centric perspectives. It neglected the involvement of racial/cultural minorities (Bull, Fruehling, & Chattergy, 1992) in the development of American society and civilization. As standard school subjects and

C. Li, Ed.D., NCSP (✉)
School Psychology Program, Department of Counseling & Applied Educational Psychology, Northeastern University, 404 International Village, 360 Huntington Ave,, Boston, MA 02115, USA
e-mail: c.li@neu.edu

Z. Wang, M.S., NCSP
Bilingual School Psychologist, Des Moines Public Schools, Des Moines, IA, USA
e-mail: sophiawzz@gmail.com

L.T. Benuto et al. (eds.), *Guide to Psychological Assessment with Asians*,
DOI 10.1007/978-1-4939-0796-0_25, © Springer Science+Business Media New York 2014

methods reflect the European perspective, A-A/I students, especially recent immigrants, usually face a dual task in order to succeed in school: They must master not only particular skills and subject matters but also unfamiliar styles and expectations of inquiry, expression, and behavior. The way that curriculum is taught disadvantages A-A/I students, just as Bull et al. (1992) described for African-American children. The majority of the school personnel are from middle-class white backgrounds. They tend to use their own cultural values and norms to judge students' and parents' behaviors, often causing misinterpretations of culturally different behaviors to happen (Li & Vazquez-Nuttall, 2009; Ni & Li, 2013).

Considering the Home Context

The home context includes family economic status, community influence, social support, immigration reasons and history, parents' acculturation levels, children's acculturation levels, parent–child differences in acculturation levels, intensity of cultural conflicts inside and outside the family, level of acculturation stress, and coping strategies. It is also important to know parents' views of school, school experiences in the home country, views of the presenting problems, goals for their children, and ways to address the suspected disability that is being evaluated.

Considering Impacts of Different Expectations from Home and School on Children

Asian parents, like the school personnel, also use their own cultural values and norms to judge their somewhat Americanized children (Li & Vazquez-Nuttall, 2009). As a result, A-A/I students often encounter culturally contradictory expectations from home and school. Usually, the schools expect the students to follow mainstream cultural values and norms while parents expect them to follow their ethnic cultural values and norms. For example, Xiaohu, a 7-year-old recent immigrant boy used to call his older brother "Gege" (哥哥, the Chinese word "big brother") at home. He finds his peers call their older siblings by their first names at school. He wants to be like everyone else. So he begins to call his older brother by his first name. However, calling someone older than oneself by the first name is considered disrespectful in the Chinese culture. Thus, his mother criticizes him for being disrespectful. Xiaohu feels very confused, because when he tries to fit in with peers he upsets his parents, and when he follows his parents' teachings, he gets teased by peers and corrected by his teacher. Unfortunately, both parents and teachers see a problem in Xiaohu because they all perceive that his behaviors fail to meet their differing cultural standards. Thus, when reviewing school records and interviewing teachers and parents for an evaluation of social-emotional functioning, adjustment or behavioral concerns, evaluators should critically examine whether the A-A/I child is labeled as deviate or pathological due to cultural differences between school and home. For instance, in an interview, when a teacher or a parent judges an A-A/I child as disrespectful, the evaluator should ask for examples. If lacking eye contact (seen by the teachers) or calling older siblings by their first names (seen by the parents) are among the examples, then caution against the mistake of viewing cultural differences as deviance may be warranted.

With the aforementioned considerations of the school and home contexts and sociocultural issues, we shall review the IDEA (Individuals with Disabilities Education Act, 2004) regulations and their implications to school-based assessment.

IDEA and Its Requirement of Nondiscriminatory Evaluation

IDEA regulates various aspects of special education and serves as an essential reference for all professionals involved in an evaluation of suspected learning, intellectual, or other disabilities. The current IDEA website (http://idea.ed.gov/explore/home) of the Office of Special Education Programs (OSEP) of the US Department of Education states:

> The Individuals with Disabilities Education Act (IDEA) is a law ensuring services to children with disabilities throughout the nation. IDEA governs how states and public agencies provide early intervention, special education and related services to more than 6.5 million eligible infants, toddlers, children and youth with disabilities.

IDEA defines 13 categories of disabilities that qualify for special education, including autism, developmental delay, emotional disturbance, hearing impairment, intellectual disability, other health impairment, specific learning disability, and speech or language impairment. (Definitions of the categories will be discussed in the following sections.) IDEA also sets standards for the evaluation process, including requirements of nondiscriminatory evaluation for culturally and linguistically diverse children. Nondiscriminatory evaluation refers to a collection of approaches, each designed to systematically reduce bias within a broader framework (Ortiz, 2008). IDEA (2004, http://idea.ed.gov) mandates "procedures to ensure that testing and evaluation materials and procedures utilized for the purposes of evaluation and placement of children with disabilities for services under this title will be selected and administered so as not to be racially or culturally discriminatory. Such materials or procedures shall be provided and administered in the child's native language or mode of communication, unless it clearly is not feasible to do so, and no single procedure shall be the sole criterion for determining an appropriate educational program for a child". In addition, IDEA specifies that the disabilities should not be primarily the result of environmental, cultural, or economic disadvantage.

Furthermore, IDEA requires that the determination of a child's disability be made by the child's parents and a group of qualified professionals, which must include the child's regular teacher and at least one person qualified to conduct individual diagnostic examinations of children, such as a school psychologist, speech-language pathologist, or remedial reading teacher. In a school system that has adopted the RTI (response to intervention) model, a school-based assessment will be conducted to test any suspected disability underlying the low performance of a student, if the student still does not make progress at an adequate rate after several research-based interventions have been implemented, and progress monitored with fidelity checks.

Challenge to Evaluators

IDEA provides a legal protection of the civil right to education for all individuals with disabilities from all cultural and linguistic backgrounds. Ideally all evaluations could meet the expectations of IDEA; however, currently school psychologists and educators are at considerable risk of violating the IDEA requirement of racially/culturally nondiscriminatory evaluation of culturally and linguistically diverse students. This is due to multiple factors, including the strong influence of the traditional medical model that tends to look for deficits within the individual, the serious shortage of culturally valid assessment tools, and the lack of nondiscriminatory assessment training. There are serious psychometric issues when using the current standardized tests with A-A/I students due to sampling issues and lack of consideration of different levels of English language proficiency (Vazquez-Nuttall et al., 2007). As a result, using such standard tests with A-A/I students, especially English language learners, often results in various degrees of discriminatory outcomes. Risks of unintentional discriminatory evaluation of A-A/I students still exist when using the RTI model because of the dearth of culturally validated interventions for racial/cultural minorities (Muñoz & Mendelson, 2005), issues with multicultural competencies of school staff, and fidelity of implementations of the interventions.

For nondiscriminatory evaluation, IDEA mandates that assessment materials and procedures be provided and administered in the child's native language or mode of communication, unless it clearly is not feasible to do so. When assessing A-A/I students whose dominant language is not English, this requirement of IDEA is often achieved through testing with interpreters due to the cultural and linguistic diversity among Asians and the lack of bilingual evaluators from the diverse linguistic backgrounds of Asia. Using interpreters in testing and interviews also requires systematic and multicultural consideration. See Chap. 8 for the complexity and professional standards for using interpreters.

Best Practices for Racially or Culturally Nondiscriminatory Assessment?

In the current context, a practitioner could take the following rudimentary steps for racially or culturally nondiscriminatory assessment: (A) when working with A-A/I students, seek improvement on one's own multicultural awareness, knowledge and skills in the Asian-American cultures. (B) When reviewing previous assessment information in a student record, examine whether the student was assessed in a culturally fair manner and how consistent the assessment is with the nondiscriminatory mandates of the IDEA. (C) When conducting a psychoeducational evaluation (a) use assessment instruments with well-established validity and reliability for use with members of the population tested, (b) acknowledge the impact of second language learning (in practice, determine the student's English Language proficiency via dual language assessment prior to selecting the assessment method) and culture differences on the cognitive and socio-emotional development of individuals, and (c) recognize the limitations of standardized tests and the ramifications of using such tests in the assessment of culturally and linguistically diverse children (NASP, 2000) if standardized tests are administered.

In terms of manageable operations for nondiscriminatory assessment for A-A/I students, current guiding frameworks for assessing culturally and linguistically diverse students may serve as references. For example, the Stage Model for Nondiscriminatory Assessment of culturally diverse children (Ortiz, 2008) provides a systematic framework and step-by-step procedure for conducting cognitive and academic assessments of bilingual students. For a decision-making and interpretive framework, the Multidimensional Assessment Model for Bilingual Individuals (MAMBI) (Ortiz & Ochoa, 2005) provides a simplified integration matrix of the major variables to determine the modality (native language, English, nonverbal, or bilingual) of assessment that would likely yield the most valid results. For analyzing cultural and linguistic loadings in standardized cognitive tests, the Culture-Language Test Classifications (C-LTC) (Ortiz & Dynda, 2005) introduces a matrix to map the cultural loadings (the extent to which a subtest contains or requires knowledge of culturally bound content) and degree of linguistic demand (the amount of receptive or expressive language ability necessary to respond to or complete a task). Hopefully, these references could enrich practitioners' repertoire of nondiscriminatory-assessment strategies.

With the above overarching issues and strategies in mind, we shall discuss cultural and linguistic considerations for determining specific disabilities defined by IDEA in the next section.

Identifying Asian-American Students for Disabilities by IDEA Criteria

In this section we shall explore culturally and linguistically appropriate assessment of A-A/I students with suspected disabilities defined by IDEA. The focus is on the disabilities that are most commonly encountered in school such as learning disability, speech/language impairment, autism, developmental delay, and intellectual disability. For assessment of other commonly encountered disabilities, such as emotional disturbance and attention deficit and hyperactivity disorder, please refer to specific chapters related to these domains.

Specific Learning Disability

IDEA Section 300.8(c)(10) states:

> (i) General. Specific learning disability means a disorder in one or more of the basic psychological processes involved in understanding or in using language, spoken or written, that may manifest itself in the imperfect ability to listen, think, speak, read, write, spell, or to do mathematical calculations, including conditions such as perceptual disabilities, brain injury, minimal brain dysfunction, dyslexia, and developmental aphasia.
> (ii) Disorders not included. Specific learning disability does not include learning problems that are primarily the result of visual, hearing, or motor disabilities, of mental retardation, of emotional disturbance, or of environmental, cultural, or economic disadvantage.

In IDEA Section 300.309, the evaluation criteria of learning disability are further specified. It points out explicitly that learning disability does not include learning problems that are primarily the result of limited English proficiency. It also requires the multidisciplinary evaluation group to ensure that academic underachievement in a child suspected of having a specific learning disability is not due to lack of appropriate instruction in or exposure to English.

Based on the above definition and nondiscriminatory evaluation guidelines, to substantiate learning disability for special education, evaluators need to provide both evidence of cognitive processing deficit/s that affect the child's learning and evidence to exclude primary causes of environmental, cultural, language, and economic disadvantages, inappropriate instruction, visual, hearing or motor disabilities, intellectual disability, and emotional disturbance. As to how to establish these evidences for Asian-American students, current literature (Vazquez-Nuttall et al., 2007) suggests that multiple aspects of the child's context should be considered. Based on the literature and our own experiences, we recommend the following procedures:

(A) Inquiring (a) who made the referral for an evaluation of suspected learning disability and for what reason; (b) whether the learning difficulty is related to English language proficiency; (c) if so, whether the student's teachers are cognizant of the process of second language acquisition and its implications for student learning in the classroom (Cummins, 1984); (d) whether the child has received appropriate instruction; (e) what formal and informal interventions have been tried for how long, and what were the child's responses to the interventions; and (f) whether parents/caregivers and teachers share the same concern about the child.

(B) Collecting comprehensive background information on the child, including (a) developmental history, school history; (b) functioning at home and school, including relationships with family members, peers and teachers; (c) mental and physical health including visual, hearing and motor functioning; (d) cultural and linguistic information of the child and family, such as culture of origin, birth place, immigration, languages spoken by the child and parents at home; and (e) environmental and socioeconomic conditions at home.

The information is collected from multiple sources, including a careful review of the school record, and interviews with the child, parents/caretakers, and teachers.

Attaining the information from A and B will (1) inform us about the appropriateness of the referral and (2) address the IDEA exclusionary clauses of environmental, cultural, language, and economic disadvantages, of visual, hearing, or motor disabilities, and of inappropriate instruction.

(C) Gauging English and native language proficiency and acculturation level.

When assessing A-A/I students, especially before testing with nationally standardized norm-referenced instruments, gauge English and native language proficiency and acculturation level first. Research on the testing of diverse individuals has identified these two factors as major influences on performance (Cummins, 1984). English and native language proficiency can be decided by language proficiency tests. Acculturation level can be assessed by Asian-American acculturation scales (see the chapter on assessment of acculturation for more information).

Attaining information on language proficiency and acculturation will inform the selection of assessment procedures and instruments, because the less age-appropriate the individual is in the language of the test, the more likely that the test results will be a measure of language proficiency rather than ability. Similarly, the less acculturated an individual is, the less that test results reflect ability than they do level of acculturation (Ortiz & Ochoa, 2005). The information on language proficiency and acculturation will also help address the IDEA exclusionary clause of linguistic and cultural disadvantages.

(D) Addressing the IDEA exclusionary clause of intellectual disability.

To address this clause, usually an assessment of cognitive ability is conducted. However, due to multiple factors, it is very challenging to achieve a nondiscriminatory assessment of cognitive ability of an A-A/I student whose English is not yet proficient. First of all, it is very difficult to find psychometrically sound assessment tools for A-A/I children and adolescents, because most nationally standardized tests use "nationally representative" samples, which often refers to proportional representation based upon US census data. The proportion of Asians in the United States is very low compared to other groups; therefore, the number of A-A/Is in the standardization samples is often quite small. For instance, the Leiter-R includes only 55 A-A/Is in comparison to 1,138 Caucasians (Kurasaki, Okazaki, & Sue, 2002; Roid & Miller, 1997). Furthermore, most studies on cognitive testing instruments with multicultural students lack information on A-A/I children and adolescents. Therefore, the scarcity of normative information on Asian-Americans contributes to the shortage of psychometrically sound data for the use of standardized tests with this population.

In the context of extreme shortage of culturally validated cognitive and psychological tests for bilingual A-A/I, school psychologists often have to search for less culturally and linguistically loaded tools for fairer assessment of A-A/I students. Nonverbal tests are commonly used as less culturally loaded tools. It should be noted that nonverbal tests are only language-reduced, not language free (Ortiz, 2002). Some tests designed to be nonverbal actually contain content that is highly culturally bound (Braden & Athanasiou, 2005).

The only verbal intelligence test currently available in other languages for A-A/I students is the Bilingual Verbal Ability Tests-Normative Update (BVAT-NU) that measure the bilingual verbal ability, or "the unique combination of cognitive/academic language abilities possessed by bilingual individuals in English and another language" (Cummins, Munoz-Sandoval, Alvarado, & Ruef, 1998). The BVAT-NU consists of three subtests from the Woodcock-Johnson-R Tests of Cognitive Ability: Picture Vocabulary, Oral Vocabulary, and Verbal Analogies. The BVAT-NU has been translated into Chinese (two forms), Hindi, Hmong, Japanese, Korean, and Vietnamese. However, caution should be made when using it with English language learners because the test is not standardized for them (Blatchley & Lau, 2010).

It is often tempting to select an older version of a test when it is the only version available in the native language of the child. However, it should be noted that such practice creates a problem of comparing a given student's performance on a test against an outdated norm (Okazaki & Sue, 2000; Yee, 1997). In addition, the existing literature does not endorse such practice and make clear statements against such practice. Sattler (2008) has discussed the limitations with using an interpreter to translate test items. Lopez and Romero (1988) made comments in their study after reviewing the practice of translating test items during a cognitive testing that this practice fails to meet the *Standards for Educational and Psychological Testing's* mandate to establish the reliability and validity of test translation before its use.

In summary, when selecting and interpreting cognitive tests, evaluators are strongly recommended to take all the above issues into consideration in addition to the challenges and general guidelines for nondiscriminatory assessment that are discussed earlier. For more extensive discussion of cognitive assessment with A-A/I, please see the chapter on IQ testing.

(E) Addressing the IDEA exclusionary clause of inappropriate instruction.

To ensure the academic underachievement in the referred student is not due to lack of appropriate instruction, IDEA 300.309 requires (1) data to demonstrate that prior to, or as a part of, the referral process, the child was provided appropriate instruction in regular education settings, delivered by qualified personnel; and (2) Data-based documentation of repeated assessments of achievement at reasonable intervals, reflecting formal assessment of student progress during instruction, which was provided to the child's parents.

These evaluation criteria are crucial in the determination of learning disability, especially in the RTI model. A typical practice of evaluation implementing these criteria in the school is that the referred student's teacher provides the evaluation team the student's academic records and information on strengths and delays, intervention methods, length and intensity of the intervention, and progress monitoring data. The intervention must target the area in which the student is lacking the knowledge and skills.

If the student is an English language learner (ELL) and the teacher perceives him/her to be lacking in their academic progress, we should examine standards to which the student is compared. If the progress rate of an ELL student from an immigrant family is compared to that of a native speaker of English, the comparison should be questioned. The rationale behind the questioning is that, typically, it takes an ELL 3–5 years to develop proficient academic language skills (Cummins, 1984). In some cases, teachers may suspect learning disability for Asian ELLs because of low phonological awareness/decoding skills, which may be simply due to the lack of formal education in these skills. A critical question to ask is whether the child is instructed appropriately, for example, to what extent the student understands the instruction in English and whether the instruction is addressing the student's needs.

(F) Addressing the IDEA exclusionary clause of emotional disturbance.

To address this criterion, first, an evaluator could review the information from the referral source, school records, and interviews with the child, parents/caretakers, and teachers.

If there is no concern about socio-emotional functioning from any source, no formal assessment in this area will be warranted. If there are concerns, an assessment of socio-emotional functioning should be conducted. See the section on "Considering Impacts of Different Expectations from Home and School on Children" at the beginning of this chapter and chapters on assessing mood disorders, anxiety, personality disorders, and psychosis for recommendations for nondiscriminatory assessment of socio-emotional functioning.

Speech or Language Impairment

According to IDEA Section 300.8(c)(11), speech or language impairment means a communication disorder such as stuttering, impaired articulation, a language impairment, or a voice impairment that *adversely affects* a child's educational performance. The exclusionary clauses (except inappropriate instruction) in the definition of learning disability also apply to speech or language impairment. So do the procedures to address the clauses and cultural considerations in the assessment process. However, four issues specific to the assessment of speech or language impairment should be noted:

(A) A student's language ability in another language should be considered. For example, a child who has speech problems in English but not in Chinese should not be labeled as speech impaired. S/he does not need special education, but training in speech for English as a second language learner instead.

(B) When evaluating language impairment, home language, primary language, and acculturation factors should be considered. If a child's home language is not English, s/he is not likely to have the same opportunity to learn and practice English as his/her peers from English-speaking families. Therefore, his/her English language "delay" in comparison to his/her peers is likely to reflect a lack of opportunity rather than ability. See section on "Autism" for further discussion on cultural issues of assessing language impairment.

(C) Some common speech or grammatical errors in English among East Asian ELLs are related to the language differences between the native language and English. Asian languages such as Chinese and Japanese have different phonemes from the English language which can be confusing to children who learn two languages at the same time. For instance, it is not uncommon for a Chinese or Japanese to have difficulties in discriminating the sound of "r" and "l." Furthermore, this difficulty does not impact the communication in Chinese or Japanese as much as in English. Another example is the sound "th," for which many Chinese or Japanese people have great challenge with. The 'th' sound is usually substituted with the sound "z." Mispronunciation of the short "*e*" and "*a*" sounds are also commonplace among Chinese ELLs, because the Chinese language does not have these vowels. So is the confusion of *he* and *she* in oral communication, as the Chinese characters for *he* (他) and *she* (她) both pronounce as *ta* although their written forms are different. Thus, Asian ELL students' low English proficiency should be ruled out as the primary reason before identifying them as having speech/language impairment.

(D) Selective Mutism should not be considered as speech or language impairment.

Autism

IDEA Sec. 300.8(c)(1)(i) defines Autism as a "developmental disability significantly affecting verbal and nonverbal communication and social interaction, generally evident before age 3, that adversely affects a child's educational performance. Other characteristics often associated with autism are engagement in repetitive activities and stereotyped movements, resistance to environmental change or change in daily routines, and unusual responses to sensory experiences. The term autism does not apply if the child's educational performance is adversely affected primarily because the child has an emotional disturbance".

The cultural considerations and nondiscriminatory assessment methods discussed earlier for evaluating learning disability and speech or language impairment are also applicable to the evaluation of autism. In addition, it should be noted that Asian/Pacific children (0.13 %; U.S. Census Bureau, 2000) identified under the category of Autism in IDEA is disproportionally high compared to Caucasian children (0.09 %). Four possible reasons were proposed to explain the high rate of identified Asian/Pacific children: language, social skills, behavior repertoire, and culture difference (Dyches, Wilder, Sudweeks, Obiakor, & Algozzine, 2004). Based on the literature, we propose the following actions to address these concerns:

(A) When assessing the communication skills of A-A/I children, several factors should be considered: (a) the language spoken at home; (b) years spent in English-speaking schools or daycare, especially for children under the age of 3; they might have only been exposed to their home language; and (c) any potential acute or chronic stressors associated with the process of immigration that can negatively impact the child's verbal communication abilities (Sattler, 2008). Any language-based instruments in English may not be appropriate to assess young A-A/I children who have not been exposed to English.

(B) When observing a young child's social interaction, the presence of a familiar family member of the child is recommended, because observations of a child's behavior at school, where the environment may be stressful (different language, rules, and expectations, etc.) to the child, may not be a valid reflection of the child's true social skill repertoire. Furthermore, immigrant children may have experienced traumatic events in their home countries and in the process of relocating to the USA. They may experience anxiety and depression which can hinder their normal social interaction outside their home environment (Sattler, 2008).

(C) Regarding behavior repertoire, Dyches et al. (2004) stated that evidence indicates that multicultural students have more difficulty with the academic and behavioral customs of the school culture than do students from the dominant culture.

(D) When interviewing parents of A-A/I children, their job factor should be kept in mind. Some parents may not have much time with their children every day due to their overwhelming job schedules. As a result, they may not be able to provide the most accurate picture if their children's social behaviors. The instruments used to identify autism may not be appropriate with A-A/I children because of possible cultural bias in the questions and norms. For instance, among Asian families, children are taught not to make direct eye contact with adults as a way to show respect (Klein & Chen, 2000); however, limited eye contact making is one of the behaviors characterized by Autism.

Developmental Delay

According to IDEA Section 300.111(b), for children from birth to age 3 (under IDEA Part C) and children from ages 3 through 9 (under IDEA Part B), the term developmental delay, as defined by each State, means a delay in one or more of the following areas: physical development; cognitive development; communication; social or emotional development; or adaptive behavioral development.

In addition to the cultural considerations discussed in earlier sections, research on cultural differences in *developmental milestones* should be noted when assessing an A-A/I child for suspected developmental delay. For example, Eveleth and Tanner (1990) found (from X-rays) a faster rate for Black and White children in average bone growth than in East Asian children. Chinese and Vietnamese immigrant parents have noticed cultural differences between their children and mainstream American children in the development of communication, daily living, and motor skills (Li, Lee, Waldron, & Wang, 2005). See next section for details.

Intellectual Disability

According to IDEA *Section 300.8(c)(6)*, intellectual disability (called mental retardation in IDEA) means significantly subaverage general intellectual functioning, existing concurrently with deficits in adaptive behavior and manifested during the developmental period, that adversely affect a child's educational performance. The exclusionary clauses (except mental retardation) in learning disability, procedures to address the exclusionary clauses and cultural considerations in the assessment process also apply to the evaluation of intellectual disability. Of the two defining components—intellectual and adaptive functioning—in intellectual disability, intellectual functioning has been discussed at length early in this chapter and the chapter on IQ testing. This section will explore cultural issues and nondiscriminatory assessment of adaptive functioning.

Adaptive functioning is often assessed by semi-structured interviews and adaptive behavioral scales. Usually parents/caretakers serve as informants. For a fair assessment of A-A/I children, specific consideration of Asian cultures should be given to both the informants and the adaptive behavioral scales. Regarding informants, members from the extended family in Asian cultures often participate in child rearing (Nguyen, 2002). Sometimes, older siblings and grandparents may know a child better than the parents. Thus, when choosing an informant, the examiner should inquire as to who knows the child the best and obtain the parental or legal guardian's permission to interview that individual.

It is important to inquire what language/s the caretakers speak, what culture/s they come from, and how acculturated they are. Such information would help us to understand the cultural and linguistic influences on the child and the cultural lens that the caregivers bring to the assessment of the child's adaptive behavior. We should also consider the family's socioeconomic and acculturation levels as that may provide information about the child's exposure to different life tasks.

When using the available adaptive scales with A-A/I children, we should always keep in mind that adaptive behaviors are culturally defined. When norm-referenced adaptive measures have been translated, this does not ensure that the items are culturally relevant or appropriate for Asian-Americans. For instance, Li et al. (2005) conducted a review of cultural biases of the items in the *Vineland Adaptive Behavior Scales-II** (*Vineland-II*) (a widely used adaptive scale), with Chinese and Vietnamese immigrant parents. They found that, although the content of the *Vineland-II* has significantly improved from its previous version in regard to sensitivity for the culturally diverse populations, there are still 15 out of the 433 items of the Vineland II that may be culturally biased against Asian immigrants. The following section highlights the review of the 15 items and cultural adjustment ideas for them by Li et al. (2005).

Communication Domain: *Expressive language.* Item #18, regarding understanding sayings that are not meant to be taken literally (for example, "Hit the road"), is considered culturally biased, because children growing up in bilingual families often do not have exposure to idiomatic English terms to the extent of their peers growing up in English-only-speaking families. For this item, understanding idiomatic sayings in the child's native language should also be credited.

Items #32, using present tense verbs ending in "ing" #36, using regular past tense verbs, and #50, using irregular plurals correctly (e.g., children.) are considered culturally inappropriate, because these grammatical rules in English do not have equivalents in some Asian languages (e.g., Chinese, Vietnamese, or Japanese). Thus, for children who are English-language learners, items related to the forming of plurals or verb tenses may need to take into consideration the child's proficiency in his or her native language when interpreting responses.

Daily Living Skills: *Personal.* Item #7, sucking from straw (for 1-year-old), is considered culturally inappropriate because straws are not usually used in East Asian households. Bottles are more frequently used. Therefore, "sucks from bottle" should also be accepted as an alternative for this population.

Daily Living Skills: *Community.* Items 41–44 [#41. Managing own money (for example, pays most or all of own expenses); #42. Having full-time job for 1 year; #43. Budgeting for monthly expenses; #44. Having and using personal credit card responsibly (for example, does not exceed credit limit, pays on time)] for ages 16+ reflect cultural biases because 16–18-year-old students of East Asian descent, particularly those from the middle class, typically are not expected to earn or manage money. Parents prefer their children to focus on school so working to earn money on their own is often discouraged. Parents believe that a more suitable age for Items 41–44 for this population would be over the age of 18. Due to such child rearing differences, an excellent A-A/I high school student may score extremely poor on Items 41–44. Alternatives for these items may be the things that are valued in Asian-American cultures, e.g., managing time effectively, taking care of younger siblings, and respecting and/or taking care of elders.

Socialization: *Interpersonal.* Items #37, going on group dates, and #38, going on single dates (for ages 9+), are not considered culturally appropriate, because traditional East Asian parents (e.g., Chinese, Vietnamese, Japanese) usually discourage their school age children from dating to ensure focus on school and are often unaware if their teenagers are in fact dating.

Socialization: *Coping.* Items #4, chewing with mouth closed (for ages 4–5 and above), and #14, refraining from talking with food in mouth (for ages 5–7 and above), are considered culturally inappropriate because talking with food in the mouth, although not encouraged, is not considered impolite in the Chinese and Vietnamese cultures. In fact, family members talk the most during meals. Chinese parents consider item #5, saying "please" when asking for something (for ages 5–7 and above), as culturally biased because the word "please" is not used as frequently in the traditional Chinese culture as in that of the USA.

Maladaptive Domain. Item #13, not maintaining eye contact when speaking or spoken to, is culturally inappropriate for East Asians, because children are brought up to show respect by looking down and by not making eye contact when talking to adults or authorities. Therefore, it is recommended that this item be removed for bilingual East Asians.

Motor Domain. Items #36 (catching beach ball sized ball from at least 6 ft way with both hands) and #39 (catching tennis or baseball sized ball from at least 10 ft way, moving to catch it if necessary) need special attention, because not every East Asian immigrant is familiar with a beach ball, tennis, or baseball. When administering these terms, we need to check with parents/caretakers and make sure that children are familiar with these objects. Item #40 (riding bicycle with no training wheels without falling, for age 4+ years) assumes a child has a bicycle and a safe environment to ride it. Unfortunately, not every child has such opportunities. Thus, we recommend adding similar motor activities as alternatives, e.g., riding scooter, roller skates.

From a broader perspective, due to multiple issues surrounding intelligence tests, an accurate adaptive behavior assessment becomes a crucial component in comprehensive evaluations for intellectual and other disabilities, such as autism and developmental delay, for A-A/Is. As to age appropriate behaviors, one should consider the child rearing practices in varying ethnic groups. First, the cultural value of collectivism and interdependence between parents and children (Rutledge, 1992) may affect a child's score on the adaptive scales that reflects the value of independence. Second, young A-A/I children such as Chinese and Vietnamese are generally more sheltered (Do, 2002; Liu & Li, 1998). They are less independent in the daily living aspect when compared to peers from Euro-American cultural groups. Thus, they are prone to score lower on the Vineland-II. The Chinese and Vietnamese parents suggest that when considering items of daily living skills, one should add 1–2 years to the expected age marked on the Vineland-II when assessing A-A/I children. Some parents also recommend that 1–2 years be added to certain expressive items (e.g., identifying upper and lower case letters) under the communication domain if the child did not have day care or preschool exposure. However, the aforementioned cultural characteristics may vary with other factors such as acculturation level.

Cultural Considerations When Evaluating RTI for Asian-American/Immigrant Students

Compared to the traditional medical model of assessment discussed in the previous sections, the RTI (response to intervention) model is considered fairer to culturally and linguistically diverse students because it is driven by the child's response to intervention; it is more scientifically based; and it has more progress monitoring with formative evaluation and measurement precision (Reschly, 2005). However, these advantages of RTI can be diminished if the students have not received culturally responsive, appropriate and quality interventions, or, if the evaluation of the RTI is not conducted in a culturally sensitive manner. For instance, there is not enough attention focused on the role of classroom teachers in RTI implementation (Klingner & Edwards, 2006). School personnel tend to quickly attribute a child's difficulties to internal deficits or the home environment rather than systematically examining whether the child has received adequate interventions.

In addition to the issues with fidelity of implementations, lack of information on cultural validity of evidence-based interventions for racial/cultural minorities (Muñoz & Mendelson, 2005; Sue & Zane, 2006), including Asian-Americans, presents another challenge to the practice of culturally nondiscriminatory evaluation of response to intervention with Asian-Americans. Currently, the complex dimensions of acculturation and English language proficiency are still not well addressed in evaluative research on intervention strategies. For instance, of the few efficacy studies of the popular intervention "solution-focused brief therapy" with culturally diverse populations, none of them provides information on the levels of acculturation and English language proficiency of the samples (Li & Wong, 2007).

To counter the barriers discussed above when assessing an A-A/I student using a RTI model, an initial action should be to guard against the tendency of a quick attribution of a child's difficulties in school to internal deficits or family problems. We should examine systematically whether the child has received adequate interventions in all tiers of the RTI model in reference of Klingner and Edwards (2006) cultural considerations. That is, in the first tier, examine if there is a trend for low performance among ELL students and if the students have received culturally responsive and quality education. This includes if the student is taught at his/her instructional level, if the teacher's teaching style matches the student's learning style and if the support from school and home are adequate. If not, we need to solve these problems first. In the second tier, examine if the intensive academic or socio-emotional support is based on appropriate assessment results, if the method is culturally appropriate and effective for the student, and if it is delivered by a well-trained person. If not, these issues should be addressed before making a referral for a student to receive comprehensive evaluation for special education (Li & Vazquez-Nuttall, 2009).

Summary

This chapter presented challenges and strategies for conducting nondiscriminatory school-based assessment of A-A/I children and adolescents. The chapter focused on evaluation for special education based on the IDEA (2004) criteria, including specific cultural and linguistic considerations for assessment of several disability categories defined by IDEA. The overarching cultural considerations are (a) the ecological context of the child including school and home cultures, (b) the cognitive and socio-emotional impacts of acculturation on children and their families, (c) impacts of different expectations from home and school on children, (d) English and native language proficiency, (e) impacts of second language learning on cognitive and academic performance, and (f) cultural validity of the assessment tools. In addition, we should guard against the mistakes of viewing cultural differences as deviance and the tendency to attribute a child's difficulties in school to internal deficiencies or family problems. In summary, to conduct culturally competent assessments of A-A/I students for special education, we need to be mindful of Asian-American cultures as well as the IDEA requirements. We should constantly seek improvement on our own multicultural awareness, knowledge, and skills.

Acknowledgment The authors want to thank Angela Cai for reviewing and editing this chapter.

References

Blatchley, L. A., & Lau, M. Y. (2010). Culturally competent assessment of English language learners for special education services. *National Association of School Psychologists Communiqué, 38*(7), 27–29.

Braden, J. P., & Athanasiou, M. S. (2005). A comparative review of nonverbal measures of intelligence. In D. P. Flanagan & P. L. Harrison (Eds.), *Contemporary intellectual assessment: Theories, tests, and issues* (pp. 557–577). New York, NY: Guilford Press.

Bull, B. L., Fruehling, R. T., & Chattergy, V. (1992). *The ethics of multicultural and bilingual education*. New York, NY: Teachers College Press.

Cummins, J. (1984). *Bilingualism and special education: Issues in assessment and pedagogy*. San Diego, CA: College-Hill.

Cummins, J., Munoz-Sandoval, A. F., Alvarado, G., & Ruef, M. L. (1998). *Bilingual Verbal Ability Test (BVAT)*. Ithaca, IL: Riverside.

Do, P. V. (2002). *Between two cultures: Struggles of Vietnamese American adolescents. Paper presented at the National History Honor Society Conference*. College Park, MD: University of Maryland.

Dyches, T. T., Wilder, L. K., Sudweeks, R. R., Obiakor, F. E., & Algozzine, B. (2004). Multicultural issues in autism. *Journal of Autism and Developmental Disorders, 34*(2), 211–222. doi:10.1023/B:JADD.0000022611.80478.73.

Eveleth, P. B., & Tanner, J. M. (1990). *Worldwide variation in human growth* (2nd ed.). Cambridge, England: Cambridge University Press.

Klein, M. D., & Chen, D. (2000). *Working with children from culturally diverse backgrounds* (pp. 109–110). Stamford, CT: Cengage Learning.

Klingner, J. K., & Edwards, P. A. (2006). Cultural considerations with response to intervention models. *Reading Research Quarterly, 41*(1), 108–117. doi:10.1598/RRQ.41.1.6.

Kurasaki, K. S., Okazaki, S., & Sue, S. (2002). *Asian American mental health: Assessment theories and methods*. New York, NY: Kluwer Academic/Plenum Publishers.

Li, C., Lee, V., Waldron, S., & Wang, X. A. (2005, August). *Using Vineland-II with culturally diverse populations*. Research paper presented at annual National Convention of American Psychological Association, Washington, DC.

Li, C., & Vazquez-Nuttall, E. (2009). School consultants as agents of social justice for multicultural children and families. *Journal of Educational and Psychological Consultation, 19*(1(Special issue)), 26–44. doi:10.1080/10474410802462769.

Li, C., & Wong, F. (2007, March). *Is solution-focused brief therapy culturally appropriate for Asian counselees?* Research paper presented at National Convention of School Psychologists, New York, NY.

Liu, T., & Li, C. (1998). Psychoeducational interventions with Southeast Asian students: An ecological approach. *Special Services in the Schools, 13*(1/2), 129–148. doi:10.1300/J008v13n01_09.

Lopez, S., & Romero, A. (1988). Assessing the intellectual functioning of Spanish-speaking adults: Comparison of the EIWA and the WAIS. *Professional Psychology: Research and Practice, 19(3)*, 263–270. Retrieved from http://www.apa.org/pubs/journals/pro/index.aspx

Muñoz, R. F., & Mendelson, T. (2005). Toward evidence-based interventions for diverse populations: The San Francisco General Hospital prevention and treatment manuals. *Journal of Consulting and Clinical Psychology, 73*(5), 790–799. Retrieved from http://www.apa.org/pubs/journals/ccp/index.aspx

National Association of School Psychologists. (2000). *Professional conduct manual: Principles for professional ethics*. Bethesda, MD: Author.

Nguyen T. H. (2002). Vietnam: Cultural background for ESL/EFL teachers. *The Review of Vietnamese Studies, 2*(1), 1–6. Retrieved from http://www.hmongstudies.com/VietnameseStudiesCenterFrontPage.html

Ni, H., & Li, C. (2013). Cultural differences in teachers' narrative evaluations of students in non-academic areas: A study of school report cards of students from four ethnic backgrounds. *International Journal of Quantitative Research in Education, 1*(2), 123–146. http://www.inderscience.com/offer.php?id=56464.

Okazaki, S., & Sue, S. (2000). Implications of test revisions for assessment with Asian Americans. *Psychological Assessment, 12*(3), 272–280. Retrieved from http://www.apa.org/pubs/journals/pas/index.aspx

Ortiz, S. O. (2002). Best practices in nondiscriminatory assessment. In A. Thomas & J. Grimes (Eds.), *Best practices in school psychology IV* (pp. 1321–1336). Washington, DC: National Association of School Psychologists.

Ortiz, S. O. (2008). Best practices in nondiscriminatory assessment. In A. Thomas & J. Grimes (Eds.), *Best practices in school psychology V* (pp. 666–678). Bethesda, MD: National Association of School Psychologists.

Ortiz, S. O., & Dynda, A. M. (2005). Use of intelligence test with culturally and linguistically *diverse* populations. In D. P. Flanagan & P. L. Harrison (Eds.), *Contemporary intellectual assessment* (pp. 545–556). New York, NY: The Guilford Press.

Ortiz, S. O., & Ochoa, S. H. (2005). Conceptual measurement and methodological issues in cognitive assessment of culturally and linguistically diverse individuals. In R. Rhodes, S. H. Ochoa, & S. O. Ortiz (Eds.), *Assessing culturally and linguistically diverse students: A practical guide* (pp. 153–167). New York, NY: Guilford.

Reschly, D. (2005). *Child outcomes and RTI in the future of school psychology*. Paper presented at the annual conference of the National Association of School Psychologists, Atlanta, GA.

Roid, G. H., & Miller, L. J. (1997). *Leiter International performance scale—Revised.* Wood Dale, IL: Stoelting.

Rutledge, P. (1992). *The Vietnamese experience in America*. Bloomington, IN: Indiana University Press.

Sattler, J. M. (2008). *Assessment of children: Cognitive foundation. Chapter 5* (pp. 140–141). San Diego, CA: Jerome M. Sattler.

Sue, S., & Zane, N. (2006). Ethnic minority populations have been neglected by evidence-based practices. In J. C. Norcross, L. E. Beutler, & R. F. Levant (Eds.), *Evidence-based practices in mental health: Debate and dialogue on the fundamental questions* (pp. 329–337). Washington, DC: American Psychological Association.

U.S. Census Bureau. (2000). *Demographic profiles: 100-percent and sample data*. Retrieved from https://www.census.gov/census2000/demoprofiles.html.

U.S. Department of Education. (2004). *Individuals with Disabilities Education Act (IDEA).* Retrieved from Office of Special Education Programs' (OSEP's) IDEA website. http://idea.ed.gov

Vazquez-Nuttall, E., Li, C., Dynda, A. M., Ortiz, S. O., Armengol, C., Walton, J., et al. (2007). Cognitive assessment of culturally and linguistically diverse students. In G. B. Esquivel, E. C. Lopez, & S. Nahari (Eds.), *Handbook on multicultural school psychology* (pp. 265–289). Mahwah, NJ: Erlbaum.

Yee, J. (1997). Psychological testing of monolingual Asian American clients. In E. Lee (Ed.), *Working with Asian Americans: A guide for clinicians* (pp. 364–387). New York, NY: Guilford.

26 Neuropsychological Assessment of Asian-American Children and Adolescents

Nicholas S. Thaler, Daniel N. Allen, and James G. Scott

Pediatric neuropsychologists routinely assess children's cognitive, emotional, and behavioral functioning. Common referral questions include making differential diagnoses of neurodevelopmental disorders such as autism and learning disability, identifying the effects of diseases that impact the central nervous system such as tumors, sickle cell anemia, and cancer, identifying the efficacy of treatments through change in neuropsychological functioning over time, determining the impact that neuropsychological deficits have on functional outcomes, and assessing the possible impact of emotional and psychiatric disorders on cognitive functioning. Neuropsychological assessment of children differs from neuropsychological assessment of adults in a number of important ways. Children's brains develop rapidly, requiring neuropsychologists to pay careful attention normal maturational changes that occur over childhood and through adolescence. There is also increased plasticity during critical periods of growth, which may impact the severity and course of acquired brain insults (Broman & Fletcher, 1999). Within the testing setting, performance may be widely variable as attention, effort, and interest wax and wanes. Regarding effort, children are just as capable as adults at underperforming or overexaggerating symptoms (Blaskewitz, Merten, & Kathmann, 2008), though the motivations for such behaviors may be less tangible and related to issues of rapport, anxiety, or boredom. Neuropsychologists must also be mindful of environmental factors that may impact children, including rapidly changing and increasing demands placed on children within their school, home, and social settings, and must work closely with pediatricians, school psychologists, parents, and teachers in developing feasible and effective treatment plans (Bernstein & Waber, 1990). Treatment planning should incorporate appropriate academic and behavioral interventions that may not be as relevant for adult cases, while adult issues including medicolegal recommendations, adjustments for quality of life, and psychological interventions remain just as crucial.

As of 2010, an estimated 3.3 million individuals under the age of 18 were identified as Asian-American, representing a sizable and

N.S. Thaler, Ph.D. (✉)
Department of Psychiatry and Biobehavioral Sciences, Los Angeles Semel Institute for Neuroscience and Human Behavior, University of California, 760 Westwood Plaza, Los Angeles, CA 90024, USA
e-mail: nick.thaler@gmail.com

D.N. Allen, Ph.D.
Department of Psychology, University of Nevada, 4505 S. Maryland Pkwy, Box 455030, Las Vegas, NV 89154-5030, USA
e-mail: daniel.allen@unlv.edu

J.G. Scott, Ph.D.
Department of Psychiatry and Behavioral Sciences, University of Oklahoma Health Sciences Center, 920 S. L. Young Blvd. WP 3440, Oklahoma City, OK 73104, USA
e-mail: jim-scott@ouhsc.edu

L.T. Benuto et al. (eds.), *Guide to Psychological Assessment with Asians*,
DOI 10.1007/978-1-4939-0796-0_26, © Springer Science+Business Media New York 2014

growing demographic within the USA (U.S. Census Bureau, 2010). Following the proportion of Asian-Americans within each ethnicity described in Chap. 1, the majority of these children are Chinese and American Indian, followed by Filipino, Vietnamese, Korean, Japanese, and then other ethnicities including Pakistani, Cambodian, and Laotian, as well as ethnic groups such as Hmong. It is important to recognize that these groups represent a diverse array of cultures, customs, and lifestyles, and acculturation levels vary widely within the USA, although some general recommendations may be offered within a pediatric neuropsychology setting (see Table 26.1).

The clinical interview is integral to neuropsychological assessment, and here we provide general recommendations when interviewing Asian-American children and their families. Many traditional Asian cultures place an emphasis on hierarchies and the importance of deference by children to adults. This deference is behaviorally expressed through limited eye contact, restrained emotions, and little initiation of social interaction (Yee, Huang, & Lew, 1998). Neuropsychologists working with Asian-American children should consider the possibility of culturally restrained behavior and shyness in such children that may not be as common in Euro-American children. This deference is also expressed through the value placed upon behaving in a socially desirable manner. For example, children who do not fully understand or comprehend test instructions may be more reluctant to disclose any confusion in fear of upsetting the examiner, who would likely be perceived as an authority figure. Asian-American children may also be less inclined to disclose personal problems while also maintaining an agreeable demeanor. Caution should be used when asking such children leading questions, as they may simply agree with the examiner to avoid conflict. At the same time, many Asian families place value on avoiding familial shame (Yeh & Yeh, 2002), so children may be reluctant to reveal information that may shed a perceived poor light on their families.

Table 26.1 General recommendations while assessing Asian-American children

General testing/assessment considerations
Environment
Separation anxiety
Child's perception toward testing
Why they are being tested?
How are results to be used?
Stigma of being singled out for testing
Response to gender of examiner
Cultural influences
Behavioral influences
Deference
Shyness
Willingness to perform at full effort
Exposure to race/culture of examiner
Language influences
Fluency in assessment language
Bilingualism
Language at home—generationally
Acculturation
Historical—first, second, third generation
Family history of educational and occupational assimilation
Cultural perspective of illness and Western medicine
Cultural information on collaborative sources of information

When interviewing family of the patient, it is important to ascertain how family members perceive the neuropsychological assessment and mental health in general. In addition, clinicians should determine if there are cultural factors involved in how parents describe their children's functioning. Some Asian-American parents may prefer a culturally traditional parenting style that is characterized by value for conformity, respect, and deference to authority and personal restraint in public settings. This may influence how they describe their children's academic performance, externalizing and internalizing behaviors, and overall mental health (Yeh & Yeh, 2002). Parents might underreport certain symptoms or circumstances while focusing on others that conflict with more "traditional" Asian cultural values, such as interpersonal harmony and respectful indirect communication styles. For example, a parent may focus on a child's perceived misbehavior within the home and her poor grades, while minimizing current family conflict that might be contributing to the distress. Psychologists must also be aware of cultural variations in disciplining children. Some Asian cultures, including Chinese, Korean, Cambodian, and Vietnamese, traditionally espouse corporal punishment (Yeh & Yeh, 2002). Shaming behaviors such as name-calling or harsh criticisms may also be a method of correction in some households. As these practices can potentially be considered emotional or physical abuse by Western standards, psychologists are encouraged to consult with outside cultural experts when faced with ambiguous situations.

The culturally oriented issue of shame predominates several Asian cultures, and parents may indoctrinate their children to avoid shaming themselves or their families. This issue is complicated by the stigma many Asian cultures have towards mental illness, which is considered a shameful topic and therefore one to avoid discussing or dwelling on. When evaluating Asian-American children, it is therefore critical to assess the child and family's level of acculturation towards Western medicine and Western mental health, and distinguish culturally oriented deference, shyness, passivity from clinically significant phenomena. Within a cultural context, it is important to be aware of the impact that this culturally influenced behavior may have on test response and be aware of the different influence this may have on various assessment issues (e.g., direct questions versus open-ended questions, or reluctance to offer elaboration when inquired).

There remains the stereotype of the "model minority" myth in Asian-Americans, which may bias both examiners and patients during the neuropsychological assessment (Wong, 2000). The most likely bias would be the expectation that Asian-American children academically excel, and therefore would similarly excel within the testing environment. This myth is harmful for a number of reasons. While it is true that some Asian-American groups enjoy a quality of living and SES equivalent or surpassing that of Euro-Americans multiple environmental factors including generational cohort, region of birth, and level of acculturation and proficiency in the English language play a substantial role in whether a specific child will truly be an "ideal" testing patient. First or second-generation immigrants from less developing nations may face similar challenges as minorities from other ethnic rural communities. Even children raised in academically driven environments may prove reluctant examinees, due to anxiety of failure. For example, children may avoid guessing or elaborating on answers they are not definitively confident about and may prefer a deferential "I don't know" to a response that may appear haphazard or self-aggrandizing (Yeh & Yeh, 2002). In line with this, assessment measures that provide direct feedback during performance (e.g., Wisconsin Card Sorting Test) may influence later test performance in either a positive or negative direction depending on how initial performance was judged. Children with high expectations of themselves may be quicker to give up rather than face the stress of negative feedback.

There are also considerations for cross-cultural application in the interpretation of neuropsychological test results. Neuropsychological assessment relies on two general comparison methods: normative comparison standards and individual comparison standards. Normative comparisons involve the comparison of an individual's performance to general standards expected by all healthy members of the human species (e.g., language development), and to population averages on specific tests. Population comparisons rely on distribution curves that represent functioning of a known population. The biggest cross-cultural limitation of population comparisons is that individuals outside the normed population may not be able to be accurately compared to that population. Given that most neuropsychological measures were normed on samples of Euro-Americans, or stratified to represent the US Census population data at a particular point of time, these norms do not satisfy the criteria to obtained normative performance for minority immigrants. A second more general limitation of population normative comparisons is it only provides an individual's percentile of relative performance. For children with acquired neurological disorders, where some decline in cognitive function is expected as a result of brain injury, comparisons to a normative sample are not informative. For example, an Asian-American child who sustained a traumatic brain injury may score below the 9th percentile on a cognitive test, which is considered abnormal within a normal curve. However, this score may have little to do with the effects of the brain injury, but rather may reflect natural level of premorbid functioning, an underestimate relating to language proficiency or other acculturation factors, or another organic determinant. Alternatively, a performance at the 50th percentile in such a child, which indicates average performance, may actually represent a decline in functioning if premorbid ability was at the 95th percentile. Such questions regarding decline resulting from brain injury cannot adequately be answered solely based on normative comparisons.

Limitations of normative comparisons can in part be addressed by providing norms developed for a specific ethnic group. However, there are few neuropsychological measures normed for Asian-American populations, fewer for specific Asian-American ethnic groups or generational cohorts, and even fewer that are based on pediatric populations. Until such norms are provided, it is recommended that neuropsychologists interpret normative comparisons with great caution when working with Asian-American children. Determining the level of acculturation can help mitigate this concern as test scores for children who are highly acculturated may be more comparable Euro-American normative samples, although even for these children the role of ethnic differences on test performance remains unclear.

A second method of comparison is the individual comparison standard, which allows for the direct comparison of current functioning with that of premorbid functioning. This method ties directly to the deficit measurement approach that is a hallmark of neuropsychological assessment. Unfortunately, test data that would definitively establish premorbid functioning are often unavailable, and so neuropsychologists must therefore rely on historical records (e.g., report cards), medical records, behavioral observations, and if possible, child and guardian-reports and interviews. There are also regression based methods to statistically estimate premorbid cognitive ability that are based on demographic data such as sex, SES, and years of education (Schoenberg, Lange, Saklofske, Suarez, & Brickell, 2008), although these are obtained through a population standard and face similar limitations as normative comparison methods when the population is of different ethnicity than the child being evaluated. In addition, demographically corrected norms can reduce sensitivity toward any actual neurological dysfunction if inappropriately used. Finally neuropsychologists often rely on tests that are less sensitive to brain injury to determine premorbid levels of functions. These tests often involve language abilities (discussed later in this chapter), such as the Vocabulary and Information subtests from the Wechsler Intelligence Scales. However, obvious bias may be introduced into these estimates of premorbid ability estimates for children who are not proficient in English. Based on these considerations, we recommend that neuropsychologists use on normative and individual comparison standards with Asian-American children, but be aware of the potential impact that culture may have on test scores and interpret results accordingly.

The remainder of this chapter reviews the routine neuropsychological domains assessed in a pediatric evaluation with a particular focus on administration methods of common neuropsychological measures. Though the competent clinician may be familiar with several of the tasks and the constructs they assess, the chapter also integrates how performance may be affected within the context of various Asian cultures, with general recommendations provided. As mentioned, few neuropsychological outcome studies are available for Asian-American children, although an overview of some available findings is present in Table 26.2.

Table 26.2 Neuropsychological studies with Asian-American children

Stated construct	Study	Measures	Population	Comments
Selective attention, attentional control, sustained attention	Chan, Wang, Ye, Leung, and Mok (2008)	Test of Every Day Attention (TEA-Ch)	232 Mandarin and Cantonese-speaking Chinese children	Factor structure identical to that of the original TEA-Ch; discriminates children with ADHD from controls
Short-term attention and processing speed	Lee, Yuen, and Chan, (2002)	Digit Span, Symbol Digit Modalities Test, Stroop Color/ Word, Trail Making Test	341 Cantonese-speaking Chinese adolescents	Norms provided for adolescents living in Hong Kong; applicability of norms outside is questionable
Attention	Deng, Liu, Wei, Chan, and Das (2011)	Das–Naglieri Cognitive Assessment System (D-N CAS) Attention Factor	567 Mandarin-speaking Chinese children	Factor structure similar to that of the original Das–Naglieri; discriminates children with ADHD and LD from controls
Selective attention	Morooka et al. (2012)	Stroop Color/Word	108 Japanese children	Stroop task using hiragana characters valid assessment of selective attention that is distinct from response inhibition
Sustained attention	Boivin, Chounramany, Giordani, Xaisida, and Choulamountry (1996)	Test of Variables of Attention (TOVA)	46 Laotian children (24 urban, 22 rural)	TOVA measures a distinct construct (sustained attention) that predicts performance on IQ and visual-spatial abilities
Visual-spatial skills	Tamaoka, Saklofske, & Ide, 1993	Naglieri's Matrix Analogies test—Short Form	451 Japanese children	Psychometric properties of test consistent with Western version; Japanese children outperformed their North American peers
Visual-spatial skills	Jensen & Whang, 1993	Progressive Matrices	167 English-speaking Chinese American children	When compared to 585 Euro-American children, the Chinese American children had a 5-point advantage
Visual-spatial skills	Lin, Su, Guo, and Wuang (2012)	Hooper Visual Organization Test (HVOT)	900 Mandarin-speaking Taiwanese children	Modified Chinese version of the HVOT demonstrates strong psychometric properties including discriminant validity with a separate clinical sample

(continued)

Table 26.2 (continued)

Stated construct	Study	Measures	Population	Comments
Motor skills, tactile discrimination; spatial learning	Boivin, Ryan, Aldridge, and Giordani (2011)	Tactual Performance Test (TPT) (standardized version and modified version with unfamiliar shapes)	23 Laotian-speaking Laotian children	Euro-American, Laotian, and Senegalese children demonstrated a similar transfer of learning effect unaffected by familiarity to shapes
Executive functions	Shuai, Chan, and Wang (2011)	Various	500 Chinese children	Children with ADHD demonstrated expected deficits on EF measures compared to controls.

IQ

Intellectual assessment remains a routine part of the neuropsychological evaluation. Subtests within batteries can be aggregated into theoretical IQ domains, or separately analyzed to measure their underlying neurocognitive constructs. A detailed review of IQ batteries for Asian-American adults and children is provided in Chap. 10.

Attention/Concentration

Attention is a multicomponent construct conceived as the ability to concentrate on relevant cues while avoiding interference from distractors. Theoretical models of attention exist and generally agree that attention can be divided into distinct components mediated by different brain networks. These components generally include bottom-up and top-down processes that are labeled various terms, such as "short-term/alerting," "sustaining," and "executive control" (Mirsky, Anthony, Duncan, Ahearn, & Kellam, 1991; Reynolds & Voress, 2007), which appear to cross-culturally generalize to Eastern cultures (Chan, Lai, & Robertson, 2006). Executive control tasks are discussed in more detail under the "executive functioning" section. In a similar fashion, although working memory tasks are at times subsumed under attentional or memory domains, these are discussed in more detail under the "executive functioning" section. Therefore, only simple and sustained attention tasks are reviewed in this section to distinguish them from more complex constructs that are nonetheless included within attentional models.

Simple short-term attention is assessed clinically vis-à-vis various span tasks contained within cognitive batteries such as the Test of Memory and Learning—Second Edition (TOMAL-2; Reynolds & Voress, 2007) and the Wechsler Intelligence Scale for Children—Fourth Edition (WISC-IV; Wechsler, 2003). In their most basic forms, a number or letter string is read to the participant, who must immediately recall the information back to the examiner. Both phonetic and visual variations exist across various batteries. Sustained attention is distinct from simple attention in that it is typically assessed with continuous performance paradigms such as the Conner's Continuous Performance Test—Second Edition (CPT-II) and the Test of Variables of Attention (TOVA; Greenberg, Kindschi, Dupuy, & Hughes, 2008). In these paradigms, individuals must sit before a computer screen for a prolonged time period and respond only to choice stimuli while ignoring distractors.

Attention/concentration is routinely assessed during a pediatric neuropsychological evaluation. Children often present with attentional disturbances that interfere with academic and behavioral functioning. Attention deficit/hyperactivity disorder (ADHD) remains a common diagnosis for such children when medical or emotional factors are ruled out, and is a congenital neurological disturbance impacting frontostriatal networks including the basal ganglia and prefrontal cortex (Bush, Valera, & Seidman, 2005). ADHD is diagnosed through behavioral observations and rating forms, as neuropsychological tests do not always converge with behavioral ratings of attention and impulsivity (Barney et al., 2011). However, neuropsychological testing can inform relative strengths and weaknesses in the child that predicts current and future functioning, in turn aiding in short and long-term treatment planning (Lambek et al., 2010). There is also support that different clinical disorders differentially affect attentional domains; for example, ADHD may preferentially affect sustained attention while acquired brain damage first impacts executive control with sustained attention a secondary domain (Thaler, Allen, Park, McMurray, & Mayfield, 2010). Along with ADHD and brain injury, neuropsychological testing can also assess for cognitive deficits resulting from childhood diseases known to affect the central nervous system, such as sickle cell anemia, cancer, and prenatal drug and alcohol exposure. Similarly, neuropsychological evaluations may provide invaluable information regarding cognitive deficits associated with various learning disorders which commonly co-occur with ADHD (Wu, Anderson, & Castiello, 2002).

It is well established that language proficiency directly impacts digit span tasks, which typically consist of verbal stimuli that are orally presented and require the immediate recall in a specific language. This is primarily because the phonological loop is temporality limited in its storage capacity, and variations in phonemes and pronunciation impacts raw performance (Baddeley, Thomson, & Buchanan, 1975). Therefore, Asian languages with shorter digit pronunciations (e.g., Mandarin, Hokkien), as recently demonstrated (Chan & Elliott, 2011), would be expected to have superior performance compared to those with longer pronunciations (Malay, Thai). Although this may not always impact performance when English is the primary language, bilingual children adept at quickly translating numbers may have an advantage on span and simple arithmetic tasks when their native language has fewer loads on the phonological store.

Some additional considerations should be mentioned. There are several culturally influenced behaviors present in some Asian-American children that can potentially impact attention tasks. Children who have high degrees of shame and/or self-consciousness may underperform on the CPT in an attempt to avoid commissions; conversely, some East Asian children may actually be more successful on such tasks based on behavioral learning environments that emphasize the importance of sustaining attention over long periods of time (Clarke-Stewart, Lee, Allhusen, Kim, & McDowell, 2006) . In addition and outside of neuropsychological measures, parental perceptions of attention and hyperactivity may be culturally weighed and affect parent-report scores. See Table 26.2 for a sample of studies examining relevant studies with East Asian children. In general, it appears that neuropsychological attentional measures have construct validity outside of Western populations, though further studies are required to confirm this among non-Chinese-speaking populations.

Processing Speed

A separate but related neuropsychological domain is cognitive processing speed, or the ability to quickly respond to stimuli efficiently and with automaticity. While processing speed is psychometrically and theoretically a distinct construct from attention, children who cannot sustain their attention often display processing speed impairments. For example, there is increasing evidence that a sluggish cognitive tempo is a neuropsychological marker for children with ADHD-Predominantly Inattentive Type (Nikolas & Nigg, 2012; Thaler, Bello, & Etcoff, 2013). Impaired processing speed is also a typical result of general cognitive impairment relating to neurodevelopmental and acquired neurological disorders, and so is a useful indicator of subtle cognitive deficits. This domain is routinely assessed within cognitive batteries (e.g., WISC-IV), as well as standalone measures such as the Trail Making Test (TMT; Army Individual Test Army Individual Test Battery, 1944) the Symbol Digit Modalities Test (SDMT; Smith, 1982), and the Stroop Color/Word Test, and other measures that typically involve simple cancellation, coding, and sequencing tasks.

Cross-cultural cognitive psychology studies also suggest that Eastern and Western children process information differently. This may be related to differences in acquiring attentional strategies from an early age that are directly due to sociocultural factors. Eastern cultures generally deemphasize the self while Western, particularly US culture, emphasizes independence and personal achievement (Duffy & Kitayama, 2010). There is some evidence this may impact performance on visual processing speed tasks, with US children outperforming Eastern children on certain stimuli, and vice versa on other stimuli (Kuwabara & Smith, 2012). This may be because some East Asian children focus on perfectionism and therefore may trade speed for accuracy on timed processing speed tasks, while at the same time demonstrating stronger sustained attention abilities due behavioral learning in their classroom environment. Academic achievement may also influence performance on some fluency tests. For example, a study comparing Chinese American to Euro-American children found the Chinese American group retrieved well-learned mathematical abilities more accurately, perhaps due to a culture emphasis on quantitative achievement (Jensen & Whang, 1994). Although it remains uncertain how these studies may broadly translate into neuropsychological testing, it does highlight the importance of considering the potential influence across measures for different cultures, even when language is not involved.

Memory and Learning

Memory and learning are integral parts of the neuropsychological assessment and are often disrupted in neurological disorders. Like attention, memory is a multi-system construct. It generally is understood that adequate attentional ability is required to succeed on memory tasks, forming a hierarchical relationship between the two constructs. Memory is classically split into verbal and nonverbal dichotomies, though neuropsychologists also assess and distinguish short-term/immediate memory from long-term/delayed memory, and there are other distinctions such as semantic versus episodic memory, and declarative and implicit memory processes. A related construct is learning, or the acquisition rate of new material. Memory for information lasting more than a few seconds is encoded in medial temporal lobe structures, before eventually consolidating and diffusing throughout the cortex (Townsend, Richmond, Vogel-Farley, & Thomas, 2010). There is evidence that memory components differentially mature (Gathercole, 1999), with verbal memory developing particularly quickly during the school-age years, perhaps due to semantic learning strategy acquisition (Schneider, Knopf, & Sodian, 2009; Thaler et al., 2013). These differential developmental changes in memory components are also related underlying neural developmental which progresses at uneven rates in various brain regions through development (Goldstein et al., 2014). The school-age years are particularly critical for verbal memory development, which has implications cross-culturally. Children raised in backgrounds with a strong emphasis on education, as is present in many East Asian cultures, may have an advantage to verbal memory tasks, while those raised in rural environments may be at a disadvantage. It may therefore be that educational factors play a stronger role in memory performance than they do in attention/concentration and processing speed performance.

Memory is clinically assessed with specific batteries such as the TOMAL-2 and the Wide Range Assessment of Memory and Learning—Second Edition (WRAML-2; Sheslow & Adams, 2003). Such batteries are comprehensive, with subtests designed to capture distinct memory components. Typically, list-learning and semantic story recall tasks and nonverbal tasks are included in some format. Given the multi-method format and lengthy administration time of these batteries, similar cross-cultural challenges such as communication and rapport faced in longer IQ batteries may be present with memory batteries (see Chap. 10). Briefer memory measures, such as the list-learning California Verbal Learning Test—Children's Edition (CVLT-C; Delis, Kramer, Kaplan, & Ober, 1994) and the delayed trial of the visuoconstructional Rey–Osterrieth Complex Figure Test (ROCFT) are also available as alternative options. It should be noted that delayed memory as assessed in the neuropsychological evaluation is typically no longer than a 20–30 min delay, given the necessity and inconvenience of multiple administrations otherwise, and so is distinct from the traditional "long-term memory" for past semantic and autobiographical events. However, delayed memory assessment is nonetheless a necessary counterpart to immediate memory assessment to ascertain rate of information decay and memory performance that is less reliant on attentional processes.

Verbal memory tests are contingent on language proficiency and so bilingual or nonnative-speaking children can underperform. Verbal test content may be inherently biased towards Westernized cultures; for example, the CVLT-C's items were selected based on their use and semantic relatedness in the English language (Miller, Petrie, Bigler, & Adams, 2004), which may invalidate their generalizability for children from non-westernized cultures. Direct translation does not always adequately address this matter, as item familiarity within a culture may still bias performance (Lim et al., 2009), though normed alternative measures such as the Hong Kong List-Learning Test (HKLLT; Chan & Kwok, 1999) are viable options when available. Visual tests are not exempt from language bias, as nonverbal communicatory factors are still culturally bound and may affect performance (Flanagan, Ortiz, & Alfonso, 2007). Also, some visual stimuli themselves have strong cultural bias, including pictures portraying famous individuals or depicting scenes from Western cultures. This bias may be at least partially addressed by using tests with visual stimuli that do not have any inherent meaning (abstract figures or shapes) although cultural differences in visual-spatial processing may still impact performance on these types of tests. Some memory batteries (e.g., TOMAL-2; NEPSY-II, Korkman, Kirk, & Kemp, 2007), have been normed on a representative national sample consisting of various ethnicities. However, Asian-Americans are a minority of these samples, which although is an accurate reflection of the US demographic limits information on test performance among distinct generational cohorts or clinical populations.

Recognition memory tasks are an important part of memory assessment. Recognition is distinct from recall as it requires only a familiarity with the target stimuli rather than successful retrieval of it and may dissociate from free recall performance in some clinical disorders (Hanley & Davies, 1997). These tasks usually involve a forced-choice paradigm, which can be problematic for children who are anxious about performing accurately. Such children may be reluctant to guess at all, and even with gentle prompting might finally respond with a random answer to avoid a perceived risk of irritating the examiner. This can be all the more complex when measures provide direct feedback, as observed on some effort measures (e.g., Test of Memory Malingering; TOMM) and the Word Selective Reminding subtest in the TOMAL-2. Examiners should attempt to ascertain the degree to which such responding is random and discontinue the trial and attempt to regain rapport before resuming assessment.

Cognitive psychology studies suggest that as with attention/concentration, there are cross-cultural influences to memory performance within an experimental laboratory. There is evidence that Euro-American children recall more autobiographical details when recounting a story than Chinese or Korean children, although objective story recall performance was equivalent (Han, Leichtman, & Wang, 1998). There is also evidence that Japanese children outperform Euro-American children on visual memory, which may be related to a general visual-spatial advantage in certain Asian cultures (Flaherty & Connolly, 1996). It remains uncertain if these cognitive studies can be applied to neuropsychological assessment, though such studies are warranted. Of significant note, there at this time is a lack of psychometric studies examining common neuropsychological batteries (e.g., WRAML-2, TOMAL-2, CVLT-C) among pediatric Asian populations.

Visual-Spatial Functioning

Visual-spatial skills are automatic processes that allow for the perception and integration of visual stimuli for adaptive functioning. These skills are highly dependent on the parietal lobe although several cortical and subcortical networks, including the visual cortex, inferior temporal cortex, and right superior temporal sulcus are involved (Scott & Schoenberg, 2011a). Visuoconstructional skills involve both visual-spatial functioning and motor functioning and are often assessed concurrently with visual-spatial skills during the neuropsychological evaluation. These constructs are useful in informing neuropsychologists about relative visual-spatial strengths compared to verbal/language abilities, as well as localizing lesions following encephalitic insult. Simple bedside assessment tools such as clock drawing, tests and hemi/quadrant field tests are useful as brief and qualitative measures of visual agnosia and motor apraxia. Psychometrically standardized options are also available, including selected WISC-IV subtests (e.g., Block Design), the ROCFT, the Beery-Buktenica Developmental Test of Visual-Motor Integration (VMI; Beery & Beery, 2004), Benton Judgment of Line Orientation (Benton, Hamsher, Varney, & Spreen, 1983), and the Hooper Visual Organization Test (HVOT; Hooper, 1958). Visual-spatial skills are integral for children's abilities across academic tasks (e.g., arithmetic), and involved in other aspects of functioning such as artistic talent and athleticism.

Visual-spatial tests are appealing for cross-cultural applications given their de-emphasis on language abilities. However, there is evidence that education and acculturation can still affect performance on such tests (Wong, 2000). Tests with complex and multistep instructions, such as the WISC-IV Block Design subtest, may be vulnerable to issues relating to examiner–examinee communication and rapport. Of interest, there is a hypothesis that Asian societies that require children to engage in prolonged orthography skills (e.g., Chinese pictograms) may have an advantage in developing early visual processing skills which in turn results in a favorable bias for Japanese and Chinese children on visual and visual-spatial tests (Salkind, Kojima, & Zelniker, 1978), although there is conflicting evidence on this phenomenon (Flaherty & Connolly, 1996).

Table 26.2 summarizes available studies on visual-spatial measures for pediatric Asian populations. As seen in the table, efforts have been made to validate several common neuropsychological measures among several populations. There is preliminary support for cross-cultural reliability and validity within a specific population (e.g., HVOT). Although there is also some evidence of a visual-spatial advantage for some Chinese and Japanese children when compared to Euro-American peers, these results most likely reflect general academic achievement and motivational factors rather than a unique neurodevelopmental profile with these populations (Flaherty & Connolly, 1996).

Although not a visual-spatial test in the traditional sense, special mention should be made for the Tactual Performance Test (TPT; Reitan & Wolfson, 1992; Boll, 1981). This is a unique tactual-spatial motor test in which participants are blindfolded throughout administration, thereby removing any visual component. TPT performance requires numerous abilities including spatial organization, kinesthesis, and manual dexterity among others and is sensitive to lateralized impairment (Jarvis & Barth, 1984). This measure is notable for having cross-cultural studies with rural African and Laotian children (Boivin, Giordani, & Bornefeld, 1995; Boivin et al., 2011), and has been demonstrated to be useful with these populations (see Table 26.2). The studies by Boivin and colleagues are also useful models on which to base future cross-cultural studies for specific neuropsychological tests.

Motor Functioning

Motor functioning is routinely assessed through classical neurological-based approaches that involve standard species-wide normative reference information and a neuropsychological-based approach assessing quantitative differences in motor speed, dexterity, and strength (Scott, 2011). The neurological approach typically is not used by neuropsychologists, though available data can be incorporated with quantitative neuropsychological methods to provide a cohesive clinical presentation of motor functioning. Motor functions involve cerebellar, frontal, and parietal structures and neuropsychological assessment can inform on both generalized and lateralized impairments associated with these regions. Common administrative tools include the Finger Oscillation Test (FOT; Reitan, 1955), the Grooved Pegboard Test (GPT; Klove, 1963), and the Grip Strength Test (GS; Reitan & Wolfson, 1993) which respectively assess motor speed, fine motor dexterity, and upper motor strength.

Caution is encouraged when comparing motor scores to general population norms, as several factors aside from neurological insult can produce abnormal scores. In older individuals, peripheral nervous system damage, arthritis, or other age-related changes can interfere with performance, while natural developmental variability can impact scores with children and adolescents. The latter issue may lead to the substantial variability present across normative data samples for youth (Baron, 2004). In addition, there is evidence that environmental factors such as SES might influence motor performance (Leckliter & Forster, 1994). Thus impaired scores should only be interpreted in conjunction with clinical history, correlation with physical skill level and in conjunction with consistency across performance and cerebral laterality.

Unfortunately, there is little data available regarding specific motor norms with Asian-American children. Given the criticisms of available norms in general, and considering possible physical and cultural differences of Asian-American youth, population norms may not be the most clinically valid method of assessing motor deficits in this population. Uniformly standardized pediatric batteries that include motor subtests are also available (e.g., NEPSY-II), though cross-cultural and clinical research on these subtests are lacking at this time. The individual comparison standard may therefore yield the most clinically relevant data, as each child serves as his or her own control and consistent right-left score differences can be useful in identifying or supporting suspected lateralized brain damage.

Language

The assessment of language functioning is a crucial aspect of the neuropsychological evaluation, and is particularly of import within cross-cultural contexts. Language is generally lateralized to the left hemisphere, though there is substantial evidence that bilingualism, right-to-left written language, and prosodic speech influences language diffusion across both hemispheres (Fox, 1991; Lin, 2005; Peng & Wang, 2011). Neuropsychologists distinguish *receptive* language from *expressive* language disturbances. Both functions are lateralized in the left hemisphere, even for most individuals who are left hand dominant (Szaflarski et al., 2012). Expressive language is associated with Broca's area in the posterior inferior frontal gyrus while receptive language is associated with Wernicke's area in the posterior section of the superior temporal gyrus. Lesions to these areas lead to classical presentations of Broca's and Wernicke's aphasia respectively. Lesions to brain regions outside these central language areas also distinct aphasias referred to as transcortical aphasias, such as transcortical sensory, transcortical motor, conduction, and anomic aphasias (for a detailed review, see Scott & Schoenberg, 2011b). While aphasias by definition occur as a result of an acquired lesion in an individual who had previously developed normal language ability, language disorders that are neurodevelopmental in nature can be further demarcated as oral (dysphasia, communication disorder, developmental language disorder), and written (dyslexia, reading disability) which signify the nature of language impairment.

Neuropsychology language measures generally differentiate between expressive and receptive abilities, and assess for crystallized vocabulary knowledge, confrontational naming, verbal phonemic and semantic fluency, and written and oral comprehension. Appropriate tests for children include the Vocabulary subtest of the WISC-IV, selected subtests from the Woodcock-Johnson Tests of Achievement—Third Edition (WJ-III; McGrew & Woodcock, 2001) and NEPSY-II, the Boston Naming Test (BNT; Kaplan, Goodglass, & Weintraub, 1983), and the Controlled Oral Word Association Task (COWAT; Benton, 1967). As might be expected, performance on these measures is influenced by degree of proficiency in the test language, with higher scores demonstrated on English tests in Asian populations who speak English as a first language on both crystallized and fluency tests, as well as in child populations who think primarily in the English language rather than parental native language (Beech & Keys, 1997; Boone, Victor, Wen, Razani, & Pontón, 2007).

Proficiency in the English language is likely the most significant moderator of language test scores, and certain tests that assess crystallized fund of language abilities (e.g., vocabulary and reading tests) may serve primarily as measures of this proficiency. Delays in language acquisition may be primarily due to environmental factors such as the dominant language spoken within the home, and neuropsychologists ruling out a neurodevelopmental cause for language delays should take care to obtain a detailed individual and familial language history. It is our recommendation that clinicians should measure crystallized language abilities, such as reading proficiency, in Asian-American children and, ruling out organic or psychiatric contributions, use these scores as estimates of language proficiency which then should be weighed in while assessing the performance of other tests. Unfortunately, to date there remains no psychometric method of controlling for base language proficiency in estimating test scores in adults or children.

An additional consideration is the expressive component many language tests involve. Many measures incorporate querying when a response is not adequate for full credit but sufficient enough to warrant further prompting. Querying may not be as an effective strategy for Asian-American children, who may be reserved or shy and unwilling to provide additional information. Such children may respond with the ubiquitous "I don't know" rather than attempt to further elaborate on their responses, and examiners should determine if such a reply is valid or simply stated in lieu of an actual response. In addition, verbal fluency tests are similar to processing speed tests in that rapid responding is a requirement for successful performance. As with processing speed measures, Asian-American children may be more prone to sacrifice speed for accuracy. When combined with the stressors of bilingualism and/or English as a second language, this can lead to underestimations of actual fluency abilities. Of interest, letter fluency appears more influenced by English proficiency than semantic fluency (Luo, Luk, & Bialystok, 2010).

Executive Functions

"Executive functions" represent a broad array of cognitive functions that are extensively mediated by the prefrontal lobes. The prefrontal lobes are at the anterior section of the frontal lobes and are subdivided into the dorsolateral prefrontal cortex (DLPFC), orbitofrontal/ventromedial cortex (OFC), and medial frontal/anterior cingulate cortex (ACC) (Scott & Schoenberg, 2011c). Neuropsychological studies have investigated the multidimensional nature of executive functions with mixed findings in regard to the actual dissociable components that compose this construct. Early lesion studies were among the first to recognize the concept of "executive functions" by observing marked cognitive, emotional, and behavioral changes in individuals with prefrontal injuries (Nauta, 1971). Subsequent neuroimaging studies have implicated the DLPFC in cognitive skills including planning, decision-making, verbal fluency, working memory, set-shifting, and abstract thinking while the OFC was linked to social and affective functioning and behavioral self-regulatory skills (Stuss, 2007), providing evidence of "cognitive" and "social-affective" executive functioning components.

The frontal lobes are one of the last brain regions to fully mature, and so executive functions are continuously developing and changing in pediatric populations. There are several tests and batteries available that are designed to assess executive functioning, including the Comprehensive Trail Making Test (CTMT; Reynolds, 2002, the Delis-Kaplan Executive Function System (D-KEFS; Delis, Kaplan, & Kramer, 2001), the NEPSY-II (Korkman et al., 2007), among others. Although many of these tests have demonstrated criterion validity for distinguishing clinical groups from controls, their cross-cultural application remains uncertain. There is evidence that executive function constructs are impaired similar to Euro-Americans in Chinese pediatric clinical populations including ADHD (Shuai et al., 2011) and autistic spectrum disorders (Chan, Sze, Han, & Cheung, 2012), but actual norms are currently unavailable.

Executive functions encompass higher-order cognition and reasoning including social interactions and judgments. As might be expected, these are at least in part underpinned by key cultural processes. Asian cultures, which often emphasize academics and rote learning, may affect executive functioning development in young children. For example, there is consistent evidence that Chinese and Korean preschoolers exhibit superior inhibitory control skills over their Western counterparts (Oh & Lewis, 2008; Sabbagh, Xu, Carlson, Moses, & Lee, 2006). One explanation for this is cultural, in that teachers in these cultures often employ traditional Confucian beliefs in collective responsibility and individual self-control (Kwon, 2004). There is also evidence that bilingualism confers benefits in executive control for young children (Carlson & Meltzoff, 2008). Interestingly, studies found comparable performance between Asian and Western preschoolers on switching attention, working memory, and theory of mind, suggesting that executive function constructs are differentially affected across cultures.

Case Study

Ji-yoon is a 15-year-old left-handed Korean American girl in the tenth grade. She was referred for a neuropsychological reevaluation after her last report card, in which she received a C+ in geometry. Her parents were concerned about her academic performance and sought a possible learning disability diagnosis and modifications to her IEP. Notably Ji-yoon had a medulloblastoma tumor located on her left hemisphere that was resected when she was 20 months of age. She had a VP shunt implanted when she was 3 years of age to relieve intracranial pressure, and since then the tumor has gone into remission with no further complications. She had seen a school psychologist when she was 12 years of age who observed marked impairments in her visual-spatial abilities, processing speed, and working memory, with comparative sparing in language abilities. She was placed on an IEP that allowed her extra time on tests and separate testing environments, and was doing well academically until the last semester.

Ji-yoon presented as a well-groomed young lady of below average height and weight. Eye contact was limited and she proved to be a reluctant historian who only answered in brief one or two-word replies. Her mother was more verbose and expressed her pride previous in Ji-yoon academic achievements, lauded her daughter's circle of close friends, and expressed great concern about her future college aspirations if her grades do not improve. Neither Ji-yoon nor her mother endorsed any significant emotional problems. The neuropsychologist learned that Ji-yoon was born in California and immigrated with her parents to Tulsa, Oklahoma after her father received a promotion. She grew up speaking Korean and English, with Korean primarily spoken within the home. Based on her English fluency, a standard battery was administered.

Results from the battery confirmed motor performance was within normal limits with no unilateral impairment. Ji-yoon's vocabulary and information subtest scores were within normal limits, while her phonemic and semantic fluency were below average. Ji-yoon's immediate and delayed memory was consistently in the low average to average range across visual and verbal modality tasks, while her processing speed and working memory were moderately impaired. She also had moderate to severe impairment on measures of visual-spatial functions. She had an average verbal comprehension index score and a well below average perceptual reasoning index score. Academically, she met grade level expectations on basic tasks of reading, math calculation, and written expression, though she failed her geometry items. Her executive functions were variable, with above average performance on abstract verbal reasoning and moderately impaired performance on timed problem-solving tasks. Behaviorally, Ji-yoon was observed to be somewhat passive and withdrawn, though she was compliant with all requests and appeared to comprehend test instructions adequately. Affect was restricted. Effort was deemed to be adequate, and she approached all tests methodically. She did not volunteer much information to the examiner and rapport was never fully established during the session. Notably, when testing was completed she folded her hands in her lap and silently waited while the examiner put away the tests.

The neuropsychologist concluded from the test scores, clinical history, and behavioral observations that Ji-yoon continues to exhibit visual-spatial delays, which appear to have been likely compromised by the development of language abilities in her right hemisphere. This conclusion was tentatively made based on Ji-yoon's intact language processes, her handedness, and the young age at which she had the tumor. This crowding effect of normal right hemispheric abilities can occur when encephalitic insults incur at an early age (Satz, Strauss, Hunter, & Wada, 1994) and appear to have affected this patient. On the positive side, this patient appeared to have met academic milestones appropriately up until she started taking geometry classes, which include a significant visual-spatial component. Cultural issues may be most pertinent with regard to her poor performance on timed tasks, which appear related to her passive and careful approach towards testing. As such, the fact that the neuropsychologist qualified her for slowed processing speed scores may have been biased by this observation, though it is evident from her previous evaluation and her poor working memory scores that there is evidence of diffuse cognitive impairment, likely a result of the general complications caused by her tumor. Appropriate academic adjustments to Ji-yoon's IEP were made. In addition, the neuropsychologist reported that there was no substantial evidence of emotional problems, but cautioned that Ji-yoon appeared withdrawn and somewhat depressed during the assessment, and may have underreported any symptoms. No recommendations for therapy were given, but the neuropsychologist encouraged Ji-yoon's mother to contact him if there appeared to be any signs of emotional problems for proper referrals.

This case illustrates how a neuropsychological battery can cross-culturally be applied and informs on current and prospective academic functioning after a neurological insult. Ji-yoon's scores generally were valid and her English proficiency appeared to not bias her verbal abilities, which indeed surpassed her visual-spatial scores. There was a possibility of a bias in her processing speed due to the patient's careful approach toward testing, though the neuropsychologist concluded that this was likely organic in origin based on her previous evaluation, other evidence of neurocognitive impairment, and medical history. Although no emotional problems were reported by the child or her mother, the neuropsychologist noted Ji-yoon's behavior during testing, as he was uncertain if her withdrawal was related to shyness or deference, which may be present in some Asian-American youth, or was actual depression that may or may not have a neurological etiology. Such concerns could be further assessed using cultural sensitive measure of depression (see Chap. 12). If depression was in fact present, then appropriate interventions such as psychotherapy or pharmacotherapy might be recommended.

Summary and General Recommendations

The available literature on neuropsychological assessment for Asian-American children is sparse, but generally confirms that the neurocognitive constructs routinely assessed during the neuropsychological evaluation does generalize and vary in similar patterns as observed with Euro-American children. Therefore, clinicians can conceptualize their impressions and reports within the same framework of cognitive constructs as used in typical evaluations. Preliminary research suggests that the constructs themselves are influenced by cultural background. Language is perhaps the most obvious domain, but all appear impacted to varying degrees. Regardless, neuropsychological tests are highly verbal, whether because of item content or test instructions, and are therefore impacted by how fluent and confident children are in their language abilities. There is also evidence that cultural values can influence children's behavior and affect performance on sustained attention, processing speed, response inhibition tasks. The neuropsychologist who saw Ji-yoon was mindful of this, but concluded that based on her consistent low performance on processing speed that coincided with previous scores, neurological rather than cultural factors affected her processing speed scores. Exposure to complex orthographic symbols from an early age may affect visual memory and visual-spatial skills, though this has not been fully supported. Future research might further examine cross-cultural influences on cognitive domains themselves, along with providing basic test norms that assist in clinical application. Additional research is also required to establish if the localization of specific abilities to specific brain regions observed with Euro-American children cross-culturally generalizes to Asian-American children. While there is growing neuroimaging evidence that cultural background can influence this in the experimental laboratory (Goh et al., 2010; Jenkins, Yang, Goh, Hong, & Park, 2010), it is unknown whether this translates to a functionally meaningful difference in clinical neuropsychology.

The most pertinent recommendations are those that apply to all cross-cultural and minority groups, such as factoring in language proficiency, degree of acculturation, and environmental factors such as education and parents' SES prior to drawing any formal conclusions regarding the meaning of test scores or making any formal recommendations. Secondary to these are recommendations that often apply to some, though not all, Asian-American cultures. These include an awareness of the tight bond typical to many families, concerns of personal and family shame associated with mental illness, which can include cognitive impairment, and deferential and withdrawn behavior in Asian-American children, as observed with Ji-yoon. Children from countries that are particularly familiar with Western standards of living and educational systems, such as Japan and Korea, may do well on standard performance-based neuropsychological tests. However, country of origin is not a sufficient method to estimate an individual's expect performance, particularly in large and heterogeneous nations such as China and India. Other children may be refugees or offspring of such, and have limited to no exposure to Westernized educational systems and thus underperform on neurocognitive tests. When evaluating such patients, the issue of cultural competency and familiarity with the individual's background becomes all the more crucial.

Pediatric neuropsychologists are therefore urged to be as informed as possible when working with an Asian-American child. We encourage the clinician to obtain familiarity with the child's culture as well as familial background and relevant cultural and historical factors that might influence the child's parents, as well as individual qualities of the patient including premorbid functioning and language proficiency. With a growing number of neuropsychologists from diverse backgrounds, there may also be the option to specialize in working with specific minority populations. Also, the DSM-IV includes helpful information regarding cultural formulation in psychiatric diagnosis, which also has relevance in psychological evaluation as many common elements exist.

As it is unlikely that the clinician will have normative data appropriate for any one patient's cultural background, we do encourage the use of standard neuropsychological tests while assessing pediatric Asian-American patients. However, an emphasis should be placed on multi-method models of assessment that evaluate the same construct in different ways, and include comprehensive standardized batteries that allow for intra-subtest comparisons. These will assist in ascertaining relative levels of performance independent of a normative population. Test scores can still be useful when relying on Western norms, but only within the context of the child's background. Written reports should qualify any uncertainties or limitations to test administration, and impressions should be sensitive and appropriate to the patient's culture and family expectations. These recommendations will assist in ensuring cultural competency while working with Asian-American children.

References

Army Individual Test Battery. (1944). *Manual of directions and scoring*. Washington, DC: War Department, Adjutant, General's Office.

Baddeley, A. D., Thomson, N., & Buchanan, M. (1975). Word-length and the structure of short-term memory. *Journal of Verbal Learning and Verbal Behaviour, 14*, 575–589.

Barney, S. J., Allen, D. N., Thaler, N. S., Park, B. S., Strauss, G. P., & Mayfield, J. (2011). Neuropsychological and behavioral measures of attention assess different constructs in children with traumatic brain injury. *The Clinical Neuropsychologist, 25*(7), 1145–1157.

Baron, I. S. (2004). *Neuropsychological evaluation of the child*. New York, NY: Oxford University Press.

Beech, J. R., & Keys, A. (1997). Reading, vocabulary and language preference in 7- to 8-year-old bilingual Asian children. *British Journal of Educational Psychology, 67*(4), 405–414. doi:10.1111/j.2044-8279.1997.tb01254.x.

Beery, K. E., & Beery, N. A. (2004). *The Beery-Buktenica developmental test of visual-motor integration: Administration, scoring, and teaching manual* (5th ed.). Minneapolis, MN: NCS Pearson.

Benton, A. L. (1967). Problems of test construction in the field of aphasia. *Cortex, 3*, 32–58.

Benton, A. L., Hamsher, K., Varney, N. R., & Spreen, O. (1983). *Contributions to neuropsychological assessment*. New York, NY: Oxford University Press.

Bernstein, J. H., & Waber, D. P. (1990). Developmental neuropsychological assessment: The systemic approach. *Neuromethods, 17*, 311–371.

Blaskewitz, N., Merten, T., & Kathmann, N. (2008). Performance of children on symptom validity tests: TOMM, MSVT, and FIT. *Archives of Clinical Neuropsychology, 23*(4), 379–391.

Boivin, M. J., Chounramany, C., Giordani, B., Xaisida, S., & Choulamountry, L. (1996). Validating a cognitive ability testing protocol with Lao children for community development applications. *Neuropsychology, 10*(4), 588–599.

Boivin, M. J., Giordani, B., & Bornefeld, B. (1995). Use of the Tactual Performance Test for cognitive ability testing with African children. *Neuropsychology, 9*(3), 409–417.

Boivin, M. J., Ryan, K. A., Aldridge, K. A., & Giordani, B. (2011). Transfer-of-learning effect with the Tactual Performance Test using familiar and unfamiliar shapes with American, Lao, and Senegalese children. *Developmental Neuropsychology, 36*(5), 552–565.

Boll, T. J. (1981). The Halstead-Reitan neuropsychology battery. In S. B. Filskov & T. J. Boll (Eds.), *Handbook of clinical neuropsychology* (pp. 577–607). New York, NY: Wiley.

Boone, K., Victor, T. L., Wen, J., Razani, J., & Pontón, M. (2007). The association between neuropsychological scores and ethnicity, language, and acculturation variables in a large patient population. *Archives of Clinical Neuropsychology, 22*(3), 355–365. doi:10.1016/j.acn.2007.01.010.

Broman, S., & Fletcher, J. (Eds.). (1999). *The changing nervous system: Neurobehavioral consequences of early brain disorders*. New York, NY: Oxford University Press.

Bush, G., Valera, E. M., & Seidman, L. J. (2005). Functional neuroimaging of attention-deficit/hyperactivity disorder: A review and suggested future directions. *Biological Psychiatry, 57*(11), 1273–1284.

Carlson, S. M., & Meltzoff, A. N. (2008). Bilingual experience and executive functioning in young children. *Developmental Science, 11*(2), 282–298.

Chan, M. E., & Elliott, J. M. (2011). Cross-linguistic differences in digit memory span. *Australian Psychologist, 46*(1), 25–30.

Chan, A., & Kwok, I. (1999). *The Hong Kong list learning test. Manual and preliminary norm*. Hong Kong: CUHK, Department of Psychology.

Chan, R. K., Lai, M. K., & Robertson, I. H. (2006). Latent structure of the Test of Everyday Attention in a non-clinical Chinese sample. *Archives of Clinical Neuropsychology, 21*(5), 477–485.

Chan, A. S., Sze, S. L., Han, Y. M., & Cheung, M. C. (2012). A Chan dietary intervention enhances executive functions and anterior cingulate activity in autism spectrum disorders: A randomized controlled trial. *Evidence-Based Complementary and Alternative Medicine, 2012*, 11.

Chan, R. K., Wang, L., Ye, J., Leung, W. Y., & Mok, M. K. (2008). A psychometric study of the Test of Everyday Attention for children in the Chinese setting. *Archives of Clinical Neuropsychology, 23*(4), 455–466.

Clarke-Stewart, K., Lee, Y., Allhusen, V. D., Kim, M., & McDowell, D. J. (2006). Observed differences between early childhood programs in the U.S. and Korea: Reflections of 'developmentally appropriate practices' in two cultural contexts. *Journal of Applied Developmental Psychology, 27*(5), 427–443. doi:10.1016/j.appdev.2006.06.006.

Delis, D. C., Kaplan, E., & Kramer, J. H. (2001). *The Delis-Kaplan executive function system: Technical manual.* San Antonio, TX: The Psychological Corporation.

Delis, D. C., Kramer, J. H., Kaplan, E., & Ober, B. A. (1994). *California verbal learning test—Children's version.* San Antonio, TX: Psychological Corporation.

Deng, C., Liu, M., Wei, W., Chan, R. K., & Das, J. P. (2011). Latent factor structure of the das-naglieri cognitive assessment system: A confirmatory factor analysis in a Chinese setting. *Research in Developmental Disabilities, 32*(5), 1988–1997.

Duffy, S., & Kitayama, S. (2010). Cultural modes of seeing through cultural modes of being: Cultural influences on visual attention. In E. Balcetis & G. Lassiter (Eds.), *Social psychology of visual perception* (pp. 51–75). New York, NY: Psychology Press.

Flaherty, M., & Connolly, M. (1996). Visual memory skills in Japanese and Caucasians. *Perceptual and Motor Skills, 82*(3), 1319–1329.

Flanagan, D. P., Ortiz, S. O., & Alfonso, V. C. (2007). *Essentials of cross-battery assessment* (2nd ed.). Hoboken, NJ: John Wiley & Sons.

Fox, D. (1991). Neuropsychology, achievement, and Asian-American culture: Is relative functionalism oriented times three? *American Psychologist, 46*(8), 877–878. doi:10.1037/0003-066X.46.8.877.

Gathercole, S. E. (1999). Cognitive approaches to the development of short-term memory. *Trends in Cognitive Sciences, 3*(11), 410–419. doi:10.1016/S1364-6613(99)01388-1.

Goh, J. S., Leshikar, E. D., Sutton, B. P., Tan, J., Sim, S. Y., Hebrank, A. C., et al. (2010). Culture differences in neural processing of faces and houses in the ventral visual cortex. *Social Cognitive and Affective Neuroscience, 5*(2–3), 227–235. doi:10.1093/scan/nsq060.

Goldstein, G., Allen, D. N., Thaler, N. S., Luther, J. F., Panchalingam, K., & Pettegrew, J. W. (2014). Developmental aspects and neurobiological correlates of working and associative memory. *Neuropsychology.*

Greenberg, L. M., Kindschi, C. L., Dupuy, T. R., & Hughes, S. J. (2008). *TOVA clinical manual.* Los Alamitos, CA: TOVA Company.

Han, J., Leichtman, M. D., & Wang, Q. (1998). Autobiographical memory in Korean, Chinese, and American children. *Developmental Psychology, 34*(4), 701–713.

Hanley, J., & Davies, A. M. (1997). Impaired recall and preserved recognition. In A. J. Parkin (Ed.), *Case studies in the neuropsychology of memory* (pp. 111–126). Hove, England/Erlbaum, UK: Psychology Press/Taylor & Francis.

Hooper, H. E. (1958). *The Hooper visual organization test manual.* Los Angeles, CA: Western Psychological Services.

Jarvis, P. E., & Barth, J. T. (1984). *Halstead-Reitan test battery: An interpretive guide.* Odessa, FL: Psychological Assessment Resources.

Jenkins, L. J., Yang, Y., Goh, J., Hong, Y., & Park, D. C. (2010). Cultural differences in the lateral occipital complex while viewing incongruent scenes. *Social Cognitive And Affective Neuroscience, 5*(2–3), 236–241. doi:10.1093/scan/nsp056.

Jensen, A. R., & Whang, P. A. (1993). Reaction times and intelligence: A comparison of Chinese-American and Anglo-American children. *Journal of Biosocial Science, 25*(3), 397–410.

Jensen, A. R., & Whang, P. A. (1994). Speed of accessing arithmetic facts in long-term memory: A comparison of Chinese-American and Anglo-American children. *Contemporary Educational Psychology, 19*(1), 1–12.

Kaplan, E. F., Goodglass, H., & Weintraub, S. (1983). *The Boston naming test.* Philadelphia, PA: Lea & Febiger.

Klove, H. (1963). Clinical neuropsychology. In F. M. Forster (Ed.), *The medical clinics of North America.* New York, NY: Saunders.

Korkman, M., Kirk, U., & Kemp, S. (2007). *NEPSY-II: A developmental neuropsychological assessment.* San Antonio, TX: The Psychological Corporation.

Kuwabara, M., & Smith, L. B. (2012). Cross-cultural differences in cognitive development: Attention to relations and objects. *Journal of Experimental Child Psychology, 113*(1), 20–35. doi:10.1016/j.jecp.2012.04.009.

Kwon, Y. (2004). Early childhood education in Korea: Discrepancy between national kindergarten curriculum and practices. *Educational Review, 56*(3), 297–312. doi:10.1080/0013191042000201208.

Lambek, R., Tannock, R., Dalsgaard, S., Trillingsgaard, A., Damm, D., & Thomsen, P. (2010). Validating neuropsychological subtypes of ADHD: How do children with and without an executive function deficit differ? *Journal of Child Psychology and Psychiatry, 51*(8), 895–904.

Leckliter, I. N., & Forster, A. A. (1994). The Halstead-Reitan neuropsychological test battery for older children: A need for a new standardization. *Developmental Neuropsychology, 10*, 455–471.

Lee, T. C., Yuen, K. L., & Chan, C. H. (2002). Normative data for neuropsychological measures of fluency, attention, and memory measures for Hong Kong Chinese. *Journal of Clinical and Experimental Neuropsychology, 24*(5), 615–632.

Lim, Y., Prang, K., Cysique, L., Pietrzak, R. H., Snyder, P. J., & Maruff, P. (2009). A method for cross-cultural adaptation of a verbal memory assessment. *Behavior Research Methods, Instruments, & Computers, 41*(4), 1190–1200.

Lin, Y., Chen, W., Liao, K., Yeh, T., Wu, Z., & Ho, L. (2005). Hemispheric balance in coding speech and non-speech sounds in Chinese participants. *Neuroreport: For Rapid Communication of Neuroscience Research, 16*(5), 469–473.

Lin, Y. H., Su, C. Y., Guo, W. Y., & Wuang, Y. P. (2012). Psychometric validation and normative data of a second Chinese version of the Hooper Visual Organization

Test in children. *Research in Developmental Disabilities, 33*(6), 1919–1927.

Luo, L., Luk, G., & Bialystok, E. (2010). Effect of language proficiency and executive control on verbal fluency performance in bilinguals. *Cognition, 114*(1), 29–41. doi:10.1016/j.cognition.2009.08.014.

McGrew, K. S., & Woodcock, R. W. (2001). *Woodcock-Johnson III technical manual*. Itasca, IL: Riverside.

Miller, M. J., Petrie, J., Bigler, E. D., & Adams, W. V. (2004). Comprehensive assessment of child and adolescent memory: The wide range assessment of memory and learning, the test of memory and learning, and the California verbal learning test-children's version. In G. Goldstein, S. R. Beers, & M. Hersen (Eds.), *Comprehensive handbook of psychological assessment* (Intellectual and neuropsychological assessment, Vol. 1, pp. 237–261). Hoboken, NJ: John Wiley & Sons.

Mirsky, A. F., Anthony, B. J., Duncan, C. C., Ahearn, M. B., & Kellam, S. G. (1991). Analysis of the elements of attention: A neuropsychological approach. *Neuropsychology Review, 2*(2), 109–145.

Morooka, T., Ogino, T., Takeuchi, A., Hanafusa, K., Oka, M., & Ohtsuka, Y. (2012). Relationships between the Color-Word Matching Stroop Task and the Go/NoGo Task: Toward multifaceted assessment of attention and inhibition abilities of children. *Acta Medica Okayama, 66*(5), 377–386.

Nauta, W. J. (1971). The problem of the frontal lobe: A reinterpretation. *Journal of Psychiatric Research, 8*(3), 167–187.

Nikolas, M. A., & Nigg, J. T. (2012). Neuropsychological performance and attention-deficit hyperactivity disorder subtypes and symptom dimensions. *Neuropsychology, 27*(1), 107–120. doi:10.1037/a0030685.

Oh, S., & Lewis, C. (2008). Korean preschoolers' advanced inhibitory control and its relation to other executive skills and mental state understanding. *Child Development, 79*(1), 80–99. doi:10.1111/j.1467-8624.2007.01112.x.

Peng, G., & Wang, W. Y. (2011). Hemisphere lateralization is influenced by bilingual status and composition of words. *Neuropsychologia, 49*(7), 1981–1986.

Reitan, R. M. (1955). *Manual for administration of neuropsychological test batteries for adults and children*. Indianapolis, IN: Indiana University Medical Center.

Reitan, R. M., & Wolfson, D. (1992). *Neuropsychological evaluation of older children*. Tucson, AZ: Neuropsychology Press.

Reitan, R. M., & Wolfson, D. (1993). *The Halstead-Reitan Neuropsychological Test Battery: Theory and clinical interpretation* (2nd ed.). Tucson, AZ: Neuropsychology Press.

Reynolds, C. R. (2002). *Comprehensive Trail Making Test (CTMT)*. Austin, TX: PRO-ED.

Reynolds, C. R., & Voress, J. K. (2007). *Test of memory and learning. Examiner's manual*. Austin, TX: Pro-Ed.

Sabbagh, M. A., Xu, F., Carlson, S. M., Moses, L. J., & Lee, K. (2006). The development of executive functioning and theory of Mind: A comparison of Chinese and U.S. preschoolers. *Psychological Science, 17*(1), 74–81. doi:10.1111/j.1467-9280.2005.01667.x.

Salkind, N. J., Kojima, H., & Zelniker, T. (1978). Cognitive tempo in American, Japanese, and Israeli children. *Child Development, 49*(4), 1024–1027.

Satz, P., Strauss, E., Hunter, M., & Wada, J. (1994). Re-examination of the crowding hypothesis: Effects of age of onset. *Neuropsychology, 8*(2), 255–262. doi:10.1037/0894-4105.8.2.255.

Schneider, W., Knopf, M., & Sodian, B. (2009). Verbal memory development from early childhood to early adulthood. In W. Schneider & M. Bullock (Eds.), *Human development from early childhood to early adulthood: Findings from a 20 year longitudinal study* (pp. 63–90). New York, NY: Psychology Press.

Schoenberg, M. R., Lange, R. T., Saklofske, D. H., Suarez, M., & Brickell, T. A. (2008). Validation of the Child Premorbid Intelligence Estimate method to predict premorbid Wechsler Intelligence Scale for Children-Fourth Edition Full Scale IQ among children with brain injury. *Psychological Assessment, 20*(4), 377–384. doi:10.1037/a0014010.

Scott, J. G. (2011). Components of the neuropsychological evaluation. In M. R. Schoenberg & J. G. Scott (Eds.), *The little black book of neuropsychology: A syndrome-based approach* (pp. 127–137). New York, NY: Springer Science+Business Media. doi:10.1007/978-0-387-76978-3_4.

Scott, J. G., & Schoenberg, M. R. (Eds.) (2011a). Deficits in visuospatial/visuoconstructional skills and motor praxis. *The Little Black Book of neuropsychology* (pp. 201–218). Springer, New York.

Scott, J. G., & Schoenberg, M. R. (Eds.) (2011b). Language problems and assessment: The aphasic patient. The Little Black book of neuropsychology (pp. 159–178). Springer, New York.

Scott, J. G., & Schoenberg, M. R. (2011). Frontal lobe/executive functioning. In M. R. Schoenberg & J. G. Scott (Eds.), *The little black book of neuropsychology: A syndrome-based approach* (pp. 219–248). New York, NY: Springer Science+Business Media. doi:10.1007/978-0-387-76978-3_10.

Sheslow, D., & Adams, W. (2003). *Wide range assessment of memory and learning* (2nd ed.). Lutz, FL: Psychological Assessment Resources.

Shuai, L., Chan, R. K., & Wang, Y. (2011). Executive function profile of Chinese boys with attention-deficit hyperactivity disorder: Different subtypes and comorbidity. *Archives of Clinical Neuropsychology, 26*(2), 120–132. doi:10.1093/arclin/acq101.

Smith, A. (1982). *Symbol digit modalities test—Revised*. Los Angeles, CA: Western Psychological Services.

Stuss, D. T. (2007). New approaches to prefrontal lobe testing. In B. L. Miller & J. L. Cummings (Eds.), *The human frontal lobes: Functions and disorders* (2nd ed., pp. 292–305). New York, NY: Guilford Press.

Szaflarski, J. P., Rajagopal, A., Altaye, M., Byars, A. W., Jacola, L., Schmithorst, V. J., & … Holland, S. K. (2012). Left-handedness and language lateralization in children. *Brain Research, 1433*, 85–97. doi:10.1016/j.brainres.2011.11.026

Tamaoka, K., Saklofske, D. H., & Ide, M. (1993). The non-verbal reasoning ability of Japanese children measured by Naglieri's (1985) Matrix Analogies Test—Short form. *Psychologia: An International Journal of Psychology in the Orient, 36*(1), 53–60.

Thaler, N. S., Allen, D. N., Park, B. S., McMurray, J. C., & Mayfield, J. (2010). Attention processing abnormalities in children with traumatic brain injury and attention-deficit/hyperactivity disorder: Differential impairment of component processes. *Journal of Clinical and Experimental Neuropsychology, 32*(9), 929–936.

Thaler, N. S., Bello, D. T., & Etcoff, L. M. (2013). WISC-IV profiles are associated with differences in symptomatology and outcome in children with ADHD. *Journal of Attention Disorders, 17*, 291–301.

Thaler, N. S., Goldstein, G., Pettegrew, J. W., Luther, J. F., Reynolds, C. R., & Allen, D. N. (2013). Developmental aspects of working and associative memory. *Archives of Clinical Neuropsychology, 28*, 348–355.

Townsend, E. L., Richmond, J. L., Vogel-Farley, V. K., & Thomas, K. (2010). Medial temporal lobe memory in childhood: Developmental transitions. *Developmental Science, 13*(5), 738–751.

U.S. Census Bureau. (2010). *Current population survey, annual social and economic supplement*. Retrieved April 15, 2014, from http://www.census.gov/2010census/data/

Wechsler, D. (2003). *Wechsler intelligence scale for children* (4th ed.). San Antonio, TX: Psychological Corporation.

Wong, T. M. (2000). Neuropsychological assessment and intervention with Asian Americans. In E. Fletcher-Janzen, T. L. Strickland, & C. R. Reynolds (Eds.), *Handbook of cross-cultural neuropsychology* (pp. 43–53). Dordrecht, Netherlands: Kluwer Academic Publishers.

Wu, K. K., Anderson, V., & Castiello, U. (2002). Neuropsychological evaluation of deficits in executive functioning for ADHD children with or without learning disabilities. *Developmental Neuropsychology, 22*(2), 501–531. doi:10.1207/S15326942DN2202_5.

Yee, B. K., Huang, L. N., & Lew, A. (1998). Families: Life-span socialization in a cultural context. In L. C. Lee & N. S. Zane (Eds.), *Handbook of Asian American psychology* (pp. 83–135). Thousand Oaks: Sage.

Yeh, M., & Yeh, J. (2002). The clinical assessment of Asian American children. In K. S. Kurasaki, S. Okazaki, & S. Sue (Eds.), *Asian American mental health: Assessment theories and methods* (pp. 233–249). New York, NY: Kluwer Academic/Plenum.

Neuropsychological Assessment with Asian American Clients

27

Brian D. Leany, Lorraine T. Benuto, and Nicholas S. Thaler

A comprehensive neuropsychological evaluation can differentiate neurodevelopmental disorders and identify cognitive impairment due to a direct cerebral insult or progressive disease. It also allows for the development of treatment recommendations and prognoses. While the specific cultural considerations for variability within specific neurocognitive domains and behavioral sequelae are discussed herein, there is an established homogeny of known neurological organizational similarities (e.g., the function of the cerebellum in motor functioning; the role of the frontal lobes in executive functioning and decision making: Siedlecki et al., 2010). Despite this homogeny, between ethnic neurological differences do exist. For example, differences in processing semantic versus functional relationships have been observed between East Asians and American participants (Gutchess, Hedden, Ketay, Aron, & Gabrieli, 2010; Gutchess, Welsh, Boduroĝlu, & Park, 2006) suggesting specific cultural underpinnings for neurological functioning. There is also an emerging cultural neuroscience literature that has identified interactions between culture and underpinning neurobiological processes which influence the brain and behavior in meaningful ways (Chiao, 2009).

In the following sections, an overview of assessment for various neuropsychological domains is reviewed, and available research specific to Asian Americans is presented. Although not abundant in the extant literature, research that discusses the appropriateness and utility of linguistic or cultural adaptations for existing standardized tests is also discussed. This is largely due to researchers (e.g., Chan, Shum, & Cheung, 2003) who indigenously developed tests (e.g., a test designed from the ground up in the country of origin rather than an adaptation of a Western derived measure) that they demonstrated were better than adaptations of existing measures. These same researchers further noted that functional performance (in particular a hypothetical, functional shopping task), which is not uncommon to comprehensive neuropsychological assessment, demonstrated differences in performance that appeared

B.D. Leany, Ph.D. (✉)
Lake's Crossing Center: Maximum Security Facility for Forensic Mental Health Services, 500 Galletti Way, Sparks, NV 89504, USA

Northcentral University, Graduate School Faculty, 10000 E University Drive, Prescott Valley, AZ 86314, USA
e-mail: leanyb@gmail.com

L.T. Benuto
Administrative Faculty, Department of Psychology MS0296, University of Nevada, Reno, NV 89557, USA

Northcentral University, Graduate School Faculty, 10000 E University Drive, Prescott Valley, AZ 86314, USA
e-mail: dr.benuto@gmail.com

N.S. Thaler, Ph.D.
Department of Psychiatry and Biobehavioral Sciences, Los Angeles Semel Institute for Neuroscience and Human Behavior, University of California, 760 Westwood Plaza, Los Angeles, CA 90024, USA
e-mail: nick.thaler@gmail.com

L.T. Benuto et al. (eds.), *Guide to Psychological Assessment with Asians*,
DOI 10.1007/978-1-4939-0796-0_27, © Springer Science+Business Media New York 2014

to be greatly influenced by social norms, suggesting that because a shopping task that is a common occurrence in Western cultures is not a valid functional measure and translates poorly to Eastern cultures (Chan et al., 2003).

It is important to note that all clinicians will inevitably be challenged with referrals for individuals who are not well represented (if represented at all) in the normative data of traditional standardized assessments. This scenario creates a circumstance where the clinician must weigh the desire to provide beneficial services to the client against the ethical standards for assessment, which are not typically at odds (Ethical Standards for the Appropriate use of Assessments; Standard 9 and Principal A; for the most current information related to ethics, including 2010 language changes please see www.apa.org/ethics/code/index.aspx). This challenge is exacerbated in rural settings where available providers are sparse. A consistent finding across measures is the influence of acculturation and (with some exceptions that are specifically identified in this chapter) education, with higher acculturation and more years of education resulting in performance that better approximates the normative sample (Blair & Qian, 1998). As long as the clinician adheres to best practices and professional guidelines, a quality neuropsychological assessment can be provided.

General Considerations for the Neuropsychological Assessment of the Asian American Client

A benefit of the comprehensive neuropsychological assessment is the inherent inclusion of a multi-domain assessment that includes not only verbal tasks, but also nonverbal and motor coordination tasks that would appear at face value to be culturally neutral. Purportedly this should allow the neuropsychologist to make a global as well as comparative appraisal across domains. Although these motor and nonverbal tasks do not contain the cultural bias of language and Western U.S. factual knowledge, researchers identified some culture-specific differences for nonverbal tasks (Boone, Victor, Wen, Razani, & Pontón, 2007; Flaherty & Connolly, 1996; Flanagan, Ortiz, & Alfonso, 2013; Salkind et al., 1978; Wong et al., 2000). Therefore our first general consideration is that the clinician must not assume that nonverbal and motor coordination tasks are culturally neutral.

Additional considerations for cross-cultural assessment are efficiency (cost) and availability (that could come from the client, managed care, or the professional) that do not always allow for a comprehensive neuropsychological test battery such as the Halstead–Reitan. Thus, this chapter includes discussions of fixed batteries of assessment as well as flexible options and common, domain-specific measures that can be used independently and within an as needed paradigm allowed by the flexible battery approach.

Finally, when a clinician encounters an individual who is not appropriately represented by traditional standardization samples there is increased risk in obtaining inaccurate data. While culturally salient measures for Asian Americans are not as prolific as the development of assessments and normative data for Hispanic clients (for a review of psychological assessment of Hispanics please see Benuto, 2013), there are some current efforts to create new measures and adapt existing measures (through linguistic adaptation and/or collecting new normative data) for this population (e.g., The Korean version of the CVLT, the Keio Version of the WCST and data collected on individual tests for the Consortium to Establish a Registry for Alzheimer's Dementia). However, such efforts remain limited and the literature on their psychometric properties and clinical use are sparse. When neither a specific measure nor appropriate normative data are available, recommendations are provided that can aid the clinician in making an informed and ethical decision related to the evaluation and interpretation of the test scores.

Executive Functioning

Executive functioning tasks are designed to test an individual's ability to interpret, coordinate, and integrate brain processes (Lezak, 2004). This composite includes several higher-order functions that are to be mediated primarily by the prefrontal cortex. Such functions are behaviorally assessed by assessments that require patients to plan ahead, inhibit inappropriate responses, solve complex problems, demonstrate abstract reasoning, shift behavior when required, and use working memory (Lezak, 2004). While there is research specific to Asian Americans available, it is limited, and sometimes atypical, as compared to patterns of performance differences we have seen between Asian Americans and the existing normative data thus far.

For example, a test like the Wisconsin Card Sorting Task (WCST, Grant & Berg, 1948; Heaton, Chelune, Talley, Kay, & Curtiss, 2003) is designed to assesses functioning by creating a high cognitive demand on the participant to respond to the presentation of novel stimuli as well as an ambiguous rule-set, with nothing more than a correct or incorrect acknowledgment to their immediate choice. This test is sensitive to impairment of functioning within the prefrontal cortex (Sullivan et al., 1993). We identified a single study for a modified version of the WCST (Keio Version, Abe et al., 2004), but this study is likely of little value for the majority of clinicians, because it was specific to Japanese older adults in Japan, and presented research findings available only in Japanese (Abe et al., 2004).

Another example of an executive functioning test, the traditional Trail Making Test (TMT), is a two-part task (Trails A and Trails B) that assesses timed attention, mental flexibility sequencing, and nonverbal processing speed (Corrigan & Hinkeldey, 1987; Gaudino, Geisler, & Squires, 1995; Lezak, 2004; Reitan & Wolfson, 1958). In a more thorough exploration of the association between neuropsychological scores and ethnicity, language, and acculturation variables, Boone and colleagues (2007) included Trails A as part of a larger neuropsychological assessment battery. Differences between ethnic groups were identified between Caucasians and African Americans but no such differences were identified between Asians and Caucasians, African Americans, or Hispanics. The same was true for English-speaking participants vs. English-as-a-second-language participants. Conversely Spreen and Strauss (1998) found that Asian individuals took longer to complete Part A of the Trail Making Test than their Caucasian peers even when educational differences were accounted for. With regard to Trails B, Lu and Bigler (2000) demonstrated that Chinese English-as-a-second-language participants performed markedly worse on Trails B. This is of particular interest because, while this sample was small, the participants were younger in age and highly educated (described as graduate or postgraduate students). Thus even when participants are highly educated and are younger in age, impaired performance does not suggest neurological impairment and should be considered as a comprehensive assessment of the domain. Based on these findings, we recommend that normative data should *not* be the primary method of reference in identifying neurocognitive compromise in Asian nationals, particularly when they are not fluent in English. Practitioners may elect to use the Chinese version of the TMT when appropriate. Lu and Bigler also recommended that the Chinese version may be appropriate for other Asian nationals familiar with Chinese characters. However, in situations in which the clinician is unfamiliar with the task, the TMT should be interpreted with caution and corroborating evidence from other measures should be weighed into interpreting low standardized scores.

There is also evidence of differential performance for the Stroop color word interference task (Golden, 1978) with researchers suggesting a simplistic adaptation of this test is not sufficient. For example, Korean individuals have greater difficulty discriminating green and blue (Fisher, Freed, & Corkin, 1990; Golden & Freshwater, 2002). Moreover, Doan and Swerdlow (1999) found that Vietnamese individuals demonstrated a positive correlation between age and performance for a Vietnamese Language Stroop task when compared to the English Language Stroop task. While the degraded performance corresponding with increasing age on the English version was reportedly expected, the improved performance with increasing age for the Vietnamese version suggests that the measures are not truly equivalent and that there are possibly other cultural factors at play. There are linguistic adaptations for the color word Stroop task (e.g., the Korean Color Word Stroop Task; K-CWST) and the CERAD contains protocols for neuropsychological assessment that includes various translations of the Color Word Stroop Task. Therefore linguistically adapted measures of this test should be used when practical.

When assessing more complex tasks of visuospatial memory and learning. The tower of London (TOLDX; Culbertson & Zillmer, 1998; a modified task of the original Tower of London developed by Shallice, 1982) is designed to assess more complex tasks of visuospatial memory and learning. Specifically, it is designed to assess areas of executive control related to planning that also correlates well with tasks of continuous performance. Research for Asian Americans on this task appears to be limited to those studies that include Asian Americans in the research sample (e.g., Riccio, Wolfe, Romine, Davis, & Sullivan, 2004), without specific discussion of relevant cultural or ethnic differences. Thus, culturally specific normative data is absent.

Digit Span is a common measure of working memory that is incorporated into a number of cognitive assessments (e.g., MMSE, WAIS, WMS, and the RBANS). Language is an important consideration when adapting traditional tests like the Digit Span because of the varying linguistic differences for numbers among different languages. When assessing Asian Americans, there is a great deal of variability in the complexity (e.g., the word length) with languages that use short numeric representations performing better than those that use longer numeric representations (Chan & Elliot, 2011). Put simply, differential linguistic performance has been demonstrated for tasks that involve recall where number of syllables varies across languages. Vietnamese- and Chinese-speaking individuals score higher on digit span than English and Spanish speakers (Dick, Teng, Kempler, Davis, & Taussig, 2002). Of note, Mandarin Chinese speakers perform significantly better than English speakers. This is believed to be due to the linguistic brevity of digits in Mandarin. Most notable was that the forward span performance for the worst performing participants was better than the average performance of the English-speaking participants (Chen, Cowell, Varley, & Wang, 2009). When administered, English language proficiency should be considered and if the test is administered in the person's native language the results of the test should be interpreted in light of performance on other neurocognitive tasks. For example, if the patient's performance on backwards digit span is incongruent with performance on nonverbal tasks of executive functioning (e.g., WCST) the results may be attributable to sociocultural factors such as language.

Delis–Kaplan executive function system. The Delis–Kaplan executive function system (D-KEFS; Delis, Kaplan, & Kramer, 2001) is a battery of assessments designed to examine various aspects of higher-order executive functioning. This assessment system is valuable in that it corresponds with the most recent version of the California Verbal Learning Test (CVLT-II, a verbal learning and memory task discussed in more detail below) and assesses a broad range of neuropsychological abilities that are thought to be mediated by executive processes including inhibition, cognitive flexibility, verbal fluency, and sorting. The D-KEFS was also conceived as a process-oriented test in which behavioral observations factor in as much as quantifiable test data in interpreting results. The test authors endeavored to produce process scores that allow such behavioral observations that might influence test performance to be standardized and compared with normative samples. However, this measure does not contain normative data for educational attainment. There is limited research for Asian Americans, but what research exists is of great importance. Researchers have identified differential cognitive impairment between pediatric and adult cases of Moyamoya Disease. Weinberg and colleagues (2011) described this neurological disease as one that is disproportionately found in Asian individuals, and has a profound impact on the brain, but one that is readily treatable through surgery. These researchers identified that while children demonstrate FSIQ in the mildly retarded range (FSIQ$<$70), adults tend to demonstrate less impairment in IQ and greater impairment in executive functioning. Where assessment of IQ fails to identify a serious, but treatable neurological disorder, the DKEFS succeeds by identifying marked deficits in specific areas of executive functioning (as identified by Design Fluency Test, the Letter and Category Fluency Tests, and the Trail-Making Test Part B of the DKEFS). Thus, while not a specific appraisal of the performance of the DKEFS in Asian Americans per se or an identification of the specific sensitivity of the Trail-Making subtest, this study demonstrates the clinical utility of this assessment system for Asian Americans.

Recommendations for executive functioning. There is a great deal of data demonstrating variability in performance (often in unexpected ways) on tasks of executive functioning for Asian American ethnic and cultural groups. This variability is of primary importance for this domain and the unexpected nature of it (i.e., positive correlation for education and performance on some tasks, but an inverse relationship on others) suggests that there are either some sociocultural factors or perhaps a genetic factor (such as a seeming lack of color saliency between the colors Blue and Green for Koreans on the Stroop Task) beyond age and education that may result in differential performance for executive functions. Thus, for executive functioning tasks specifically, one needs to be aware of the aforementioned extant literature and attempt to collect additional collateral information from its subcomponents before making interpretations of sparing or impairment. For example, although there may be deficits suggested by poor performance on a color word Stroop task, non-impaired performance on a trails task would suggest that the Stroop impairment potentially may be a cultural rather than a cognitive deficit. Thus an assessment of executive functioning should include the use of:

- Appropriately normed and translated versions of the Stroop (e.g., the Korean CWST).
- DKEFS tasks (Design Fluency, Letter and Category Fluency, and Trail-Making Part B).
- Trail-Making Tests can be used, but one should use caution, especially given that even highly educated and young individuals have demonstrated impaired performance on this task, without true cognitive impairment.
- Digit Span Tests can be used, but the clinician should be aware that Asian Americans may demonstrate better performance when compared to their English speaking and Western counterparts.
- Translated versions of the WCST exist (e.g., the Keio Version), but even translated measures should be interpreted with caution, as the sample is limited to a specific subset of participants (older Japanese).

Visuospatial Processing

Visuospatial processing tasks have long been identified as a behavioral indicator of neurocognitive problems. In fact Benton, Sivian, Hamsher, Varney, and Spreen (1994, p. 53) reported documented observations for this relationship dating back to the latter half of the nineteenth century, and further provided a compendium of historical, empirical data for the identification of the lateralized nature of visuospatial abilities (primarily occurring in the right hemisphere). Thus, these tasks not only provide us with a measure of a specific neurocognitive ability, but allow us to develop well-supported hypotheses about the possible nature of the injury (e.g., location and extent of the insult). There are a great number of visuospatial tasks that are found both in measures of intellectual assessment and in neuropsychological batteries. Some of these common measures are discussed below.

The Rey–Osterrieth test (ROCFT; for a complete description of the test and scoring see Duley et al., 1993) is a classic neuropsychological assessment of visuospatial processing. With regard to Asian Americans, Boone and Colleagues (2007) demonstrated that there is discrepancy in performance among racial and ethnic groups for the copy condition, with ESL individuals performing better on ROCFT copy condition (when compared to native English speakers) than on verbal tasks; a post hoc analysis of these differences revealed that Asian Americans performed better than African Americans. Thus, the authors suggest that ROCFT copy performance may overestimate cognitive abilities, and extrapolating from this comment, one could infer that there is a potential of failing to identify impaired performance in Asian Americans. When using this test with Asian populations the clinician should be aware of the increased possibility of a false negative.

A visuospatial processing test that is relatively well researched for Asian individuals is Clock Drawing. There are several versions of clock drawing tests (CDT), with the general idea being that time is a construct so universal, and omnipresent, that an individual should be able to create a novel drawing of a clock, with a specified time. While researchers (Royall, Cordes, & Polk, 1998) have criticized the lack of uniformity for objective evaluation of clock drawing, a CDT is part of the CERAD protocol (described in more detail below), and includes relevant cut scores. Of importance for Asian Americans, researchers (Borson & Brush, 1999) assessed a range of multiethnic, foreign born, elders ($n=295$) with just under half reporting speaking a language other than English (Spanish or some form of Chinese, Korean, or Filipino dialects). Unique to this study was the overrepresentation of Asian American-Pacific Islanders ($n=139$). While not as specific as other screens for dementia, the authors found the CDT to have greater sensitivity than the Mini-Mental Status Exam (MMSE) or the CASI (Cognitive Abilities Screening Instrument), and also reported that the CDT was less likely to be discontinued or unscorable than the aforementioned screens. In an effort to standardize the scoring and evaluative process, Royall and colleagues (1998) created the CLOX task. The drawing tests included in the CLOX are multiple administration (CLOX1 and CLOX2) clock drawing tasks that assess executive functioning by having the individual draw a nondescript (beyond the time; CLOX1) clock and then a condition where the individual is asked to copy the administrators' clock drawing (CLOX2). Research with Chinese Singaporeans suggests that the CLOX has good sensitivity and specificity (above 75 % for all conditions of disease and drawing task) and for differentiating Alzheimer's Dementia from Vascular Dementia (84 % and 85 % respectively). The researchers adjusted for age, education, stage of dementia, and MMSE scores, and identified significantly ($p=0.0002$) different mean scores for CLOX1 (8.1 as compared to 5.5). Thus the CLOX task is a good measure for identifying cognitive impairment for Asian Americans and for differentiating the type of dementia (e.g., differentiating Alzheimer's dementia from a vascular dementia).

Visuospatial tasks can also assess judgment and comparison of visual stimuli. The Benton judgment of line orientation test (BJLOT; Benton, Varney, & Hamsher, 1978; Benton et al., 1983, 1994) presents an individual with two stimuli lines of varying or equal lengths, and asks them to identify the lines based on a response set, which consists of an arch of equidistant parallel lines of equal length, numbered 1–11. Benton and colleagues (1994) described the development of this test as a tool to identify and localize brain injury or disease in the right hemisphere of the brain. A benefit of this test is its compact size (approximately that of a small notepad) and the brief time needed for administration. This test has been used to accurately localize the insult to the right hemisphere with the majority of the cases involving a vascular problem or cancer. Thus this is an untimed and language independent task, which is used to identify very region-specific impairments. It is unfortunate that ethnic and culture-specific normative data are not available, but given its limited language requirements this test could be used to collect collateral information for making intra-individual decisions about visuospatial impairment.

A general concern when assessing cognitive functioning, in particular with those with language impairment, is the potential impact of impaired language abilities on nonverbal problem-solving tasks. When directly studying the impact of language on nonverbal problem-solving abilities, Baldo et al. (2005) found no impact in patients with aphasia, suggesting the spared ability of visuospatial problem solving. However, it should be noted that there was no description of race or ethnicity for these participants, and the performance could be an overestimate for individuals with impaired language. This is particularly true when you consider findings that show little reliance on language by Asian Americans for problem-solving tasks.

Summary and recommendations for visual processing tasks. The available research relevant to Asian Americans for this domain suggests that visual processing tasks can overestimate general cognitive abilities in Asian Americans (e.g., the ROCFT). Further research is needed with Asian Americans on tests designed to specifically assess cognitive impairment even in the presence of aphasic disorders (such as the BJLOT). Of note, block design, a task found on many IQ measures, and designed to assess constructional praxis, lacked any extant data relevant to Asian Americans. Thus for the domain of Visuospatial Processing, only the CDT have empirical data available for Asian American ethnic and cultural groups. However, data for the other assessment measures can be used to provide a broader base of information for intra-individual comparisons to determine sparing and impairment. Thus recommendations include the following:

- Use of a CDT.
- Use of the ROCFT with the knowledge that this test has overestimated abilities in Asian Americans.
- Use of tests that are traditionally used even with aphasic patients (e.g., the BJLOT) does not have extant data for Asian Americans.

Learning and Memory

Learning and memory as a domain assesses the acquisition and retention of information. It is a process that requires the coordination of multiple domains (including attention, concentration, and executive functioning tasks) and is often assessed in terms of verbal and nonverbal tasks. Common memory batteries used to assess memory function are the Wechsler Memory Scales (WMS-IV; Wechsler, 2008), the WRAML (-2; Sheslow & Adams, 2003), and the TOMAL-2 (Reynolds & Voress, 2007). These batteries all yield scales for discrete domains of memory performance.

The authors for each of the above batteries utilized complex sampling strategies in an effort to include representative samples of the population as a whole for their normative sample, which includes a small, but statistically representative group identified as Asian American. However, specific research relevant to Asian Americans for these tests is lacking. Of note, research into the impact of age and education (for the overall standardization sample) suggests that for the WMS-IV, there continues to be a correlation among these variables (Brooks, Holdnack, & Iverson, 2011). Thus one could theorize that the frequently observed impact of these variables for previously discussed measures of neurocognitive performance (including the WMS-III) is likely to be similar for the newer WMS-IV, with age and education predicting better performance even when considering culture-specific factors. Boone and colleagues (2007) examined memory performance using verbal and nonverbal tasks of the WMS-R and WMS-III. Of note, when comparing performance across ethnic groups of varying linguistic abilities (including a broad sample of English-as-a-second-language participants with a subset of Asian ethnic groups), they found no differences among ethnic group or linguistic ability in performance. Similarly, Walker and colleagues (2010) also found few differences in performance, when comparing groups of varying linguistic and educational background (native or foreign born parent(s) and English or non-English education) for a brain injured group of Australians. This study found only significant differences on the first logical memory task of the WMS, but equivocal performance on the second, for nonnative, non-English educated, individuals. The authors posited that this difference suggested the possibility of culturally salient differences for the first logical memory task, but also provided a caveat that the sample size for the nonnative, non-English educated group was small. Researchers (Hoelzle, Nelson, & Smith, 2011) have identified that the WMS-IV is a better measure of the discrete domains of auditory attention and memory as well as visual attention and memory. A principle components analysis revealed that these factors are much cleaner and more distinct than the previous unitary dimension measured by the WMS-III. Further these investigators suggest that the visual memory component is free from the verbal overlap found in the WMS-III tasks (e.g., memory for faces) and thus is a purer measure of nonverbal attention and memory. Specific recommendations are provided below.

Verbal learning and memory. We previously discussed systems of assessment that provide general measures of learning and memory such as the WMS, WRAML, and TOMAL that provide both a global measure and discreet domain scores. In addition to these systems we have domain-specific measures designed explicitly to assess learning and memory of verbal information specifically. The majority of these tasks are based on list-learning paradigms that include some measure of learning over multiple trials, interference, delayed recall, and recognition. Examples of these tasks include the California Verbal Learning Test (CVLT; Delis, Kramer, Kaplan, & Ober, 1987), the Hopkins Verbal Learning Test (HVLT-R; Brandt & Benedict, 2001), and the Rey Auditory Learning Test (Rey AVLT; Schmidt, 1996).

These tests all follow a similar pattern of administration that consists of presenting word lists over multiple trials, with immediate and delayed recall tasks as well as free and cued recall trials. There are various Verbal Learning and Memory tests designed to assess these same processes that exist in both English and the various languages of the Asian Panethnic group, e.g., the Hong Kong List-Learning Test (HKLLT; Chan & Kwok, 1999) and the Korean-CVLT (K-CVLT; Kim & Kang, 1999). The Korean-CVLT is a culturally relevant equivalent to the CVLT and Kim and Kang conducted a factor analysis of their measure. They identified six factors for their measure (identified as general verbal learning, response discrimination, retroactive interference, proactive interference, serial position effect, and learning rate), which suggest that the K-CVLT is a good measure of verbal learning and memory. Additionally, the authors suggested that when compared to K-CVLT performance, the standard deviations for the CVLT were inflated (suggested as a result of a CVLT standardization sample that includes individuals with a mean education attainment higher than would be expected in the population). Although the authors had a robust sample (357 psychiatrically healthy individuals) of participants based on census data, the sample and census data were indigenous to Korea, thus limiting the utility of this assessment for Korean populations.

Of these measures only the HVLT (Vanderploeg et al., 2000) found no relationship among age, education, and performance, suggesting that it is one of the few measures that is not influenced by these demographic variables. However, because the sample included few (0.05) Asian Americans, we cannot rule out the influence of these variables on scores for Asian American individuals particularly given data from other domains of assessment that shows an influence of age and education (e.g., Boone et al., 2007).

Similar to the aforementioned tasks, the Rey AVLT includes repeated presentation of a list as well as an interfering list, but also includes process scores that look at inhibition, subject organization, retention, and encoding compared to retrieval. Of note the author reports normative information for demographic variables including cultural and ethnic norms (Rey, 1964; Schmidt, 1996). A nice feature of the Rey AVLT is its ability to detect feigned impairment, with demonstrated sensitivity and specificity in research that included a heterogeneous mix of patients, patients with suspect performance, and unimpaired, student controls (Boone, Lu, & Wen, 2005). There exists an adaptation within the Rey–Kim memory test that includes a Korean version of the Rey AVLT, often found in literature as the KAVLT, with country-specific normative data. It also appears that there is an attempt underway to directly translate the test into Japanese (Cromer, Krishna, Nguyen, Acquadro, & Fuller, 2013), but this research is in the very early stage with little reported beyond a conclusion that the direct translation "preserved the intent and integrity" of the existing measure. Thus, when available list-learning measures should be utilized, and when this is not possible, an assessment measure such as the HVLT that has demonstrated a lack of influence based on age and educational factors should be utilized.

Summary and recommendations for assessing verbal learning and memory. Verbal tasks are, on face value, going to be influenced by factors such as proficiency, acculturation, and years of education. Many assessment batteries (e.g., the WRAML and the TOMAL) included Asian Americans in their normative sample, but do not directly assess culture or ethnic variables. Further, there is little information specific to tests of verbal learning and memory that allows us to identify specific recommendations for these tasks. The little information we have for the K-CVLT suggests that there may be some overestimation of abilities for Korean populations, which highlights that even when performance is identified as adequate, considerations for intra-individual differences and premorbid functioning must be made in making a final determination about levels or patterns of performance. When possible, the evaluator should present a list-learning test that is in the individual's native or preferred language such as the KVLT. However, when this is not possible, the clinician may wish to use a measure that is reportedly not influenced by demographic factors of age and education (e.g., the HVLT), with the caveat that the normative sample of Asian Americans was relatively small. Thus one can use (respective of the client):

- The Korean CVLT
- The Korean translation of the RAVLT (K-AVLT)
- Hong Kong List-Learning Test (HKLLT)
- Hopkins Verbal Learning Test (HVLT; when unable to utilize a translated version)

Discussion of Batteries and Systems of Assessment

Neuropsychological assessment can be conducted using a fixed battery such as the Halstead–Reitan as well as a flexible administration, either through a formal system of assessment that is designed to be administered in a flexible fashion or through the selection of subtests of other assessment systems (such as tests from the Halstead–Reitan) or stand-alone measures (such as the complex figure task, although many of these stand-alone measures and even subtests have been incorporated into flexible battery systems, for example trail making tasks). Flexible administrations may be preceded by a screen or a clinical interview as well as the collection of collateral information. However, the screening approach is more likely to occur in rural settings or impoverished communities where neuropsychologists and/or funds are limited. An overview of tasks common to both fixed and flexible batteries as well as a discussion on the full batteries themselves follows below.

Halstead–Reitan Neuropsychological Battery (HRNB; Reitan & Wolfson, 1985)

The HRNB remains a standard fixed battery designed to assess cognitive impairment stemming from possible organic sources. Originally developed to assist in pinpointing specific lesions, its original purpose has been supplanted by modern neuroimaging techniques. Despite this, the HRNB still allows clinicians to ascertain the degree to which an organic insult impacts cognition and behavior, and assesses several broad domains that overlap with those discussed above, including motor functions and cognitive flexibility, as well as basic tactile and auditory sensory functions. While there are extended norms available for African Americans, no such normative data exists for Asian Americans. However, some of the subtests of this battery have been tested independently with Asian Americans.

The Seoul Neuropsychological Screening Battery (SNSB; Kang & Na, 2003)

There are neuropsychological test batteries available for specific ethnic and cultural groups of Asian Americans (in this case Korean populations).

The SNSB is one such example, and is described by its authors as assessing the traditional domains of language, visuospatial abilities, as well as attention, memory, and executive functioning that are common in most neuropsychological evaluations. The battery has been adapted to include a dementia-specific screen (SNSB-D; Ahn et al., 2010) that has good overall convergent validity with the MMSE ($r = 0.876$), as well as moderate to good convergent validity for the General Cognitive Functioning score and the subdomains of the SNSB-D (attention $r = 0.629$, language and related function $r = 0.848$, visuospatial function $r = 0.779$, memory $r = 0.945$, frontal/executive function $r = 0.919$). Further, the SNSB-D was able to differentiate among a sample of Korean patients with Mild Cognitive Impairment, Koreans with Alzheimer's Dementia, and Normal Controls, with a high degree of test-retest reliability (0.960 for Normal Controls, 0.999 for Mild Cognitive Impairment, and 0.918 for Alzheimer's Dementia). With the exception of a subtest used to measure frontal lobe/executive functioning ($p < 0.072$), the discriminant validity of this measure is good (being able to discriminate normal controls from cognitively impaired individuals). Specifically, the remaining subtests were able to differentiate between those participants with MCI vs. AD vs. normal controls ($p < 0.001$). Despite the apparent strong psychometric properties of this measure, it was developed and designed for use in Korea. Thus, it presents several challenges for the clinician who is not fluent in Korean and who practices in the United States. It was introduced here mainly to support the initial assertion that there are universal constructs across cultures as evidenced by the inclusion of the aforementioned domains of neuropsychological functioning.

Consortium to Establish a Registry for Alzheimer's Dementia (CERAD; http://cerad.mc.duke.edu/)

While the CERAD is not a neuropsychological battery per se or even an assessment instrument, it serves as a repository and center for research and information for assessment practices (e.g., behavioral assessments, neuropathological assessment, family history), including the provision of a standard neuropsychological assessment protocol to assess common neurocognitive domains. Their stated impetus for this project was a National Institute on Aging (NIA) funded project to standardize assessment for Alzheimer's disease. The result has been the identification of standardized, psychometrically sound, assessment instruments to serve this goal. As a result of the consortium, this project has spawned subsequent follow-up research of these instruments among a broad range of cultures. Additionally, many of these individual measures have been translated into multiple languages and assessed for the relevant samples (for information related to the CERAD please see http://cerad.mc.duke.edu/).

The CERAD protocol for neuropsychological assessment of Alzheimer's disease is not a newly designed assessment battery or measure, but rather includes a number of measures found in traditional neuropsychological assessment designed to assess neurocognitive domains, and includes the following measures: Verbal Fluency, Boston Naming Test, Mini-mental State Exam, Word List Memory, Constructional Praxis, Word List Recall, Word List Recognition, and Recall of Constructional Praxis. Because many of these tests are part of larger existing batteries or independent tests themselves, they will be discussed within their relative context, and research specific to the CERAD will be referenced within those sections.

Repeatable Battery for the Assessment of Neuropsychological Status (RBANS: Randolph, Tierney, Mohr, & Chase, 1998)

The RBANS, while technically a screening instrument, is a brief battery delineated into traditional domains of cognitive functioning (e.g., verbal abilities, visuospatial abilities, attention and concentration, memory). The RBANS was initially designed as an assessment of dementia and is a relatively brief (typically 30 minutes or less) appraisal of neuropsychological impairment.

Additionally, while not a true comprehensive neuropsychological test battery, the author (Randolph, Tierney, Mohr, & Chase, 1998) suggested that it is a good screening tool for non-neuropsychologists who suspect neurocognitive impairment. The publishers indicate that the measure has been translated into over 30 languages, including Korean and Japanese. An additional benefit of this screening instrument is that it was designed with the intent of multiple administrations (utilizing parallel forms), which can be beneficial when measuring decline or assessing for the benefits of rehabilitative therapy. Unfortunately, there is limited data specific to Asian Americans for the RBANS, and within what little research exists, many studies are conducted outside of the United States. Additionally, while the RBANS includes traditional indices of neurocognitive domains, researchers (Schmitt et al., 2010) conducting a factor analysis for the RBANS and a subsequent validation of these factors suggest that the RBANS measures primarily two factors: one consisting of memory and the second factor of visuospatial/construction. Cheng and colleagues (2001) found that a Chinese version of the RBANS, administered in Shanghai, had factors similar to the original RBANS. One caveat for the RBANS should be made specific to inpatient psychiatric patients. King and colleagues (2010) found that only the total score was relevant for this population, and thus differentiating verbal and nonverbal performance in an inpatient psychiatric population might not be possible with this test.

Neuropsychological Assessment Battery (NAB; White & Stern, 2003)

The NAB contains a screening component that allows the battery to be administered as a fixed or a flexible battery, and like the Repeatable Battery for the Assessment of Neuropsychological Status (RBANS; Randolph, Tierney, Mohr, & Chase, 1998) has alternative forms available. In addition to the screening module, it contains individual modules to assess verbal performance, nonverbal performance, attention, executive functioning, and memory. The author utilized a standardization sample of 1,400 participants. While the measure does not report specific data for Asian Americans, the authors included census-matched norms for a group of 950 participants with matching based on age, education, and ethnicity. The NAB screening module has good psychometric properties and demonstrates convergent validity with the Modified Mini-Mental Status Exam ($r=0.46$) and the RBANS ($r=0.65$) which holds true even for the assessments of the full battery relative to existing measures for various neurological insults (e.g., dementia, HIV, ADHD; White & Stern, 2003). Given that the normative sample was matched to the census use of the NAB with the Asian American client who is proficient in English should be appropriate.

Research has confirmed that the RBANS is heavily influenced by SES factors, with those of older age and less educational attainment performing the poorest (Duff et al., 2003; Green et al., 2008; Sahadevan, Tan, Tan, & Tan, 1997). These findings have been replicated outside of the United States with Chinese elders in Singapore (Lee, Collinson, Feng, & Ng, 2012; May-Li, Collinson, Lei, & Tze-Pin, 2010), and while both groups of researchers found a great deal more heterogeneity for individuals with less than 6 years of education, May-Li and colleagues reported that semantic fluency and picture naming remained uninfluenced by these variables. Additionally, these authors administered the battery across multiple languages and with the exception of English-speaking participants found no effect for language on performance. Perhaps specific to the sample studied, Lee and colleagues (2012) identified atypical findings, and suggested that educational attainment was found to be of greater importance at a younger age, with poorer performance for older adults having greater educational attainment when they were compared to their peer with less education (Lee et al., 2012).

Recommendations for Systems of Assessment

The use of a particular style or approach to assessment is a matter of professional experience and theoretical orientation as well as answering the referral question. Thus, the recommendations here suggest that the clinician not alter their approach to assessment based solely on the fact that they are assessing a member of a minority cultural group, but rather consider the empirical information presented throughout this chapter in structuring their assessment and making conclusions as well as recommendations. Some of the batteries identified above include Asian Americans in the normative sample or have research for their individual subtests that are specific to Asian Americans (e.g., Digit Span, Trails, Complex Figure Drawing). Other tests have actual translations specific to Asian languages (e.g., Chinese, Korean). Further, the clinicians should continue to review for themselves extant literature related to the selection of these measures, in particular when utilizing measures where results are mixed or atypical.

Summary and Recommendations

The challenge of assessment of Asian American clients is multifaceted. Beyond the limited number of individuals in the U.S. population, there is a diversity of language that creates an additional challenge that is not present for some other minority groups (e.g., Hispanics). Thus while several psychological assessment measures have been created and adapted in Spanish, the same is not true for Hindi, Hmong, Japanese, Korean, Mandarin, etc. Further, the availability of clinicians, in particular neuropsychologists fluent in these languages, is even less likely, and presents a challenge even when translated measures are available. On a positive note, several of the systems of assessment discussed in the latter section of this chapter engaged in purposeful efforts to include a representative normative sample, to include Asian Americans, and available literature for neuropsychological assessments created indigenously (e.g., the SNSB) demonstrate the generalization of neurocognitive domains across cultural and ethnic groups. Thus, those individuals that are more acculturated to U.S. culture, with more years of U.S. education as well as English language abilities, are more likely to demonstrate performance that can be evaluated based on those measures' existing normative data. Conversely, those with less language fluency and education as well as those with a lesser degree of acculturation must rely on a strategy that evaluates intra-individual differences (such as changes in occupational and functional performance) including domain discrepant performance that considers multiple informant sources (e.g., a single impaired result for executive functioning is not sufficient or necessarily indicative of impairment for the domain).

For discreet domains there are specific differences that suggest sociocultural influences such as language, visuospatial abilities, and functional exposure (e.g., shopping tasks) exist that may impact performance. Examples of this can be seen in the differential performance (purportedly due to an insensitivity in some color differentiation, even within the larger panethnic category of Asian Americans) on the color word Stroop task and the overestimation of abilities that can occur with the ROCFT as well as digit span tasks. Nonverbal memory tasks, such as those found on the WMS, have previously shown fewer differences (Boone and colleagues) and the WMS-IV has been identified as a test with more discrete constructs (Hoelzle et al., 2011), and thus while research is not currently available specific to Asian Americans, will hopefully yield an even better measure of nonverbal memory performance. We suggest that the WMS-III nonverbal memory tests be utilized for Asian Americans, and recommend that the clinician continue to monitor for emerging research related to the WMS-IV. Further, specific tasks such as the clock drawing tasks have good normative data and application for Asian American clients, independent of acculturation, language, and education.

Language is a very salient factor in the assessment of the Asian American client. As previously discussed, those with increased fluency and years of English language use (as well as more years of Western education) should perform more approximate to the normative sample, in particular those that included Asian Americans (such as the WRAML and the TOMAL). There are learning and memory tasks specific to Asian American ethnic and cultural groups (e.g., the KVLT) as well as translated neuropsychological screening batteries (e.g., the Chinese version of the RBANS), and when possible, those tests should be utilized. However, when not practical or possible, the clinician may have to rely on an interpreter and utilize intra-individual data to make determinations of sparing and/or impairment. Further, when English is not the primary or even secondary language, consideration for the use of an interpreter may be warranted. Judd and colleagues (2009) make recommendations that suggest that the use of an appropriately trained interpreter will provide a better assessment, but one should avoid using family members and utilize interpreters that are trained at least at a medical level, and when testing is involved, a conversation between the interpreter and the clinician should happen in advance of test administration.

In sum, the existing batteries, in particular those with normative data that includes Asian Americans (such as the WMS-III and WMS-IV, as well as the RBANS and NABS), should provide adequate information for interpretation when English language fluency, acculturation, and education are high. Challenges increase as these factors decrease, and specific considerations for each domain have been described above. For those less acculturated, less English proficient (or even ESL), and lesser educated, a greater emphasis should be placed on collecting collateral data and utilizing intra-individual comparisons for diagnostic decisions and subsequent prognosis as well as treatment recommendations. However, the constructs that neuropsychologists rely on (e.g., memory, verbal and nonverbal abilities, executive functioning) appear stable across cultures and can be applied in making the aforementioned decisions and recommendations. It is hoped that future research and test development continue to yield data specific to ethnic and cultural considerations for Asian Americans, and clinicians should be diligent in seeking out this research as it becomes available.

References

Abe, M., Suzuki, K., Okada, K., Miura, R., Fujii, T., Etsurou, M., et al. (2004). Normative data on tests for frontal lobe functions: Trail Making Test, Verbal Fluency Wisconsin Card Sorting Test (Keio Version). *Nō to Shinkei, 56*, 567–574.

Ahn, H. J., Chin, J., Park, A., Lee, B. H., Suh, M. K., Seo, S. W., et al. (2010). Seoul Neuropsychological Screening Battery-dementia version (SNSB-D): A useful tool for assessing and monitoring cognitive impairments in dementia patients. *Journal of Korean Medical Science, 25*, 1071–1076.

Baldo, J. V., Dronkers, N. F., Wilkins, D., Ludy, C., Raskina, P., & Kima, J. (2005). Is problem solving dependent on language? *Brain and Language, 92*, 240–250.

Benton, A. L., Hamsher, K. D., Varney, N. R., & Spreen, O. (1983). *Judgment of line orientation*. New York, NY: Oxford University Press.

Benton, A. L., Sivian, A. B., Hamsher, K. D., Varney, N. R., & Spreen, O. (1994). *Contributions to neuropsychological assessment* (2nd ed.). New York, NY: Oxford University Press.

Benton, A. L., Varney, N. R., & Hamsher, K. D. (1978). Visuospatial judgment. A clinical test. *Archives of Neurology, 35*(6), 364–367.

Benuto, L. T. (2013). *Guide to Psychological Assessment with Hispanics*. Springer.

Blair, S. L., & Qian, Z. (1998).Family and Asian students' educational performance a consideration of diversity. *Journal of Family Issues, 19*(4), 355–374.

Boone, K. B., Lu, P., & Wen, J. (2005). Comparison of various RAVLT scores in the detection of noncredible memory performance. *Archives of Clinical Neuropsychology, 20*, 301–319.

Boone, K. B., Victor, T. L., Wen, J., Razani, J., & Pontón, M. (2007). The association between neuropsychological scores and ethnicity, language, and acculturation variables in a large patient population. *Archives of Clinical Neuropsychology, 22*(3), 355–365.

Borson, S., & Brush, M. (1999). The Clock Drawing Test: Utility for dementia detection in multiethnic elders. *Journals of Gerontology Series A: Biological Sciences & Medical Sciences, 54A*(11), M534.

Brandt, J., & Benedict, R. (2001). *Hopkins verbal learning test-revised*. Lutz, FL: Psychological Assessment Resources.

Brooks, B. L., Holdnack, J. A., & Iverson, G. L. (2011). Advanced clinical interpretation of the WAIS-IV and WMS-IV: Prevalence of low scores varies by level of intelligence and years of education. *Assessment, 18*(2), 156–167.

Chan, A. S., & Kwok, I. (1999). *Hong Kong list learning test*. Hong Kong: The Chinese University of Hong Kong.

Chan, A. S., Shum, D., & Cheung, R. Y. (2003). Recent development of cognitive and neuropsychological assessment in Asian countries. *Psychological Assessment, 15*(3), 257.

Chan, M. E., & Elliott, J. M. (2011). Cross-linguistic differences in digit memory span. *Australian Psychologist, 46*(1), 25–30.

Chen, Z. Y., Cowell, P. E., Varley, R., & Wang, Y. C. (2009). A cross-language study of verbal and visuospatial working memory span. *Journal of Clinical & Experimental Neuropsychology, 31*(4), 385–391.

Cheng, Y., Wu, W. Y., Wang, J. Q., Feng, W., Wu, X., & Li, C. B. (2011). Reliability and validity of the repeatable battery for the assessment of neuropsychological status in community-dwelling elderly. *Archives of Medical Science, 7*, 850–857. doi:10.5114/aoms.2011.25561.aoms.2011.25561.

Chiao, J. Y. (Ed.). (2009). *Cultural neuroscience: Cultural influences on brain function. Progress in Brain Research*. Oxford: Elsevier Press.

Corrigan, J. D., & Hinkeldey, M. S. (1987). Relationships between parts A and B of the trail making test. *Journal of Clinical Psychology, 43*(4), 402–409.

Cromer, J., Krishna, V., Nguyen, A., Acquadro, C., & Fuller, D. S. (2013). Cross-cultural adaptation of a research version of the Rey auditory verbal learning test (RAVLT) into Japanese. *Value in Health, 16*(3), A42.

Culbertson, W. C., & Zillmer, E. A. (1998). The construct validity of the Tower of London DX as a measure of the executive functioning of ADHD children. *Assessment, 5*(3), 215–226.

Delis, D. C., Kaplan, E., & Kramer, J. H. (2001). *Delis-Kaplan executive function system (D-KEFS)*. San Antonio, TX: Psychological Corporation.

Delis, D. C., Kramer, J. H., Kaplan, E., & Ober, B. A. (1987). *The California verbal learning test*. New York, NY: Psychological Corporation.

Dick, M. B., Teng, E. L., Kempler, D., Davis, D. S., & Taussig, I. M. (2002). The cross-cultural neuropsychological test battery (CCNB): Effects of age, education, ethnicity, and cognitive status on performance. In F. R. Ferraro (Ed.), *Minority and cross-cultural aspects of neuropsychological assessment* (pp. 17–41). Lisse, The Netherlands: Swets & Zeitlinger.

Doan, W., & Swerdlow, N. (1999). Preliminary findings with a new Vietnamese Stroop Test. *Perceptual and Motor Skills, 89*, 173–182.

Duff, K., Patton, D., Schoenberg, M. R., Mold, J., Scott, J. G., & Adams, R. L. (2003). Age- and education-corrected independent normative data for the RBANS in a community dwelling elderly sample. *The Clinical Neuropsychologist, 17*(3), 351–366.

Duley, J. F., Wilkins, J., Hamby, S., Hopkins, D., Burwell, R., & Barry, N. (1993). Explicit scoring criteria for the Rey-Osterrieth and Taylor complex figures. *The Clinical Neuropsychologist, 7*(1), 29–38.

Fisher, L. M., Freed, D. M., & Corkin, S. (1990). Stroop Color-Word Test performance in patients with Alzheimer's disease. *Journal of Clinical and Experimental Neuropsychology, 12*, 745–758.

Flaherty, M., & Connolly, M. (1996). Visual memory skills in Japanese and Caucasians. *Perceptual and motor skills, 82*(3c), 1319–1329.

Flanagan, D. P., Ortiz, S. O., & Alfonso, V. C. (2013). *Essentials of cross-battery assessment* (Vol. 84). New York, NY: John Wiley & Sons.

Gaudino, E. A., Geisler, M. W., & Squires, N. K. (1995). Construct-validity in the trail making test—What makes Part B harder? *Journal of Clinical and Experimental Neuropsychology, 17*, 529–535.

Golden, C. J. (1978). *Stroop color and word test: A manual for clinical and experimental uses*. Chicago, IL: Stoelting.

Golden, C. J., & Freshwater, S. M. (2002). *The Stroop Color and Word Test: A manual for clinical and experimental uses*. Chicago, IL: Stoelting.

Grant, D. A., & Berg, E. (1948). A behavioral analysis of degree of reinforcement and ease of shifting to new responses in a Weigl-type card-sorting problem. *Journal of experimental psychology, 38*(4), 404.

Green, A., Garrick, T., Sheedy, D., Blake, H., Shores, A., & Harper, C. (2008). Repeatable battery for the assessment of neuropsychological status (RBANS): Preliminary Australian normative data. *Australian Journal of Psychology, 60*(2), 72–79.

Gutchess, A. H., Hedden, T., Ketay, S., Aron, A., & Gabrieli, J. D. E. (2010). Neural differences in the processing of semantic relationships across cultures. *Social Cognitive and Affective Neuroscience, 5*, 254–263.

Gutchess, A. H., Welsh, R. C., Boduroĝlu, A., & Park, D. C. (2006). Cultural differences in neural function associated with object processing. *Cognitive, Affective, & Behavioral Neuroscience, 6*(2), 102–109. doi:10.3758/CABN.6.2.102.

Heaton, R. K., Chelune, G. J., Talley, J. L., Kay, G. G., & Curtiss, G. (2003). *Computerised Wisconsin Card Sort Task Version 4 (WCST)*. Odessa, FL: Psychological Assessment Resources.

Hoelzle, J. B., Nelson, N. W., & Smith, C. A. (2011). Comparison of Wechsler Memory Scale-Fourth Edition (WMS-IV) and Third Edition (WMS-III) dimensional structures: Improved ability to evaluate auditory and visual constructs. *Journal of Clinical & Experimental Neuropsychology, 33*(3), 283–291. doi:10.1080/13803395.2010.511603.

Judd, T., Capetillo, D., Carrión-Baralt, J, Mármol, L. M., Miguel-Mentes, L. S., Puente, A. E., … Valdes, J. (2009). Professional Considerations for Improving the Neuropsychological Evaluation of Hispanics: A National Academy of Neuropsychology Education Paper, *Archives of Clinical Neuropsychology, 24*, 127–135.

Kang, Y., & Na, D. L. (2003). *Seoul neuropsychological screening battery*. Incheon, Korea: Human Brain Research & Consulting.

Kim, J. K., & Kang, Y. (1999). Brief report normative study of the Korean-California Verbal Learning Test (K-CVLT). *The Clinical Neuropsychologist, 13*(3), 365–369.

King, L. C., Bailie, J. M., Kinney, D. I., & Nitch, S. R. (2010). Is the repeatable battery for the assessment of neuropsychological status factor structure appropriate for inpatient psychiatry? An exploratory and higher-order analysis. *Archives of Clinical Neuropsychology, 27*(7), 756–765.

Lee, C. Y., Collinson, S. L., Feng, L., & Ng, T. (2012). Preliminary normative neuropsychological data for an elderly Chinese population. *Clinical Neuropsychologist, 26*(2), 321–334. doi:10.1080/13854046.2011.652180.

Lezak, M. D. (Ed.). (2004). *Neuropsychological assessment*. Oxford university press.

Lu, L., & Bigler, E. D. (2000). Performance on original and a Chinese Version of Trail Making Test part B: A normative bilingual sample. *Applied Neuropsychology, 7*(4), 243–246.

May-Li, L., Collinson, S., Lei, F., & Tze-Pin, N. (2010). Cross-cultural application of the repeatable battery for the assessment of neuropsychological status (RBANS): Performances of elderly Chinese Singaporeans. *Clinical Neuropsychologist, 24*(5), 811–826. doi:10.1080/13854046.2010.490789.

Randolph, C., Tierney, M. C., Mohr, E., & Chase, T. N. (1998). The repeatable battery for the assessment of neuropsychological status (RBANS): preliminary clinical validity. *Journal of Clinical and Experimental Neuropsychology, 20*(3), 310–319.

Reitan, R. M., & Wolfson, D. (1985). The Halstead–Reitan Neuropsychological Battery: Theory and clinical interpretation. Tucson, AZ: Neuropsychology Press.

Rey, A. (1964). *L'examen clinique en psychologic*. Paris: Presses Universitaires de France.

Reynolds, C. R., & Voress, J. (2007). *Test of memory and learning (TOMAL-2)*. Austin, TX: PRO-ED.

Riccio, C. A., Wolfe, M. E., Romine, C., Davis, B., & Sullivan, J. R. (2004). The Tower of London and neuropsychological assessment of ADHD in adults. *Archives of Clinical Neuropsychology, 19*(5), 661–671. doi:10.1016/j.acn.2003.09.001.

Royall, D. R., Cordes, J. A., & Polk, M. (1998). CLOX: An executive clock drawing task. *Journal of Neurosurgery, Neurology and Psychiatry, 64*, 588–594.

Sahadevan, S., Tan, N. J., Tan, T., & Tan, S. (1997). Cognitive testing of elderly Chinese people in Singapore: Influence of education and age on normative scores. *Age and Ageing, 26*(6), 481–486.

Schmitt, A. L., Livingston, R. B., Smernoff, E. N., Reese, E. M., Hafer, D. G., & Harris, J. B. (2010). Factor analysis of the Repeatable Battery for the Assessment of Neuropsychological Status (RBANS) in a large sample of patients suspected of dementia. *Applied Neuropsychology, 17*(1), 8–17. doi:10.1080/09084280903297719.

Schmidt, M. (1996). *Rey auditory verbal learning test: A handbook*. Los Angeles, CA: Western Psychological Services.

Shallice, T. (1982). Specific impairments of planning. Philosophical Transactions of the Royal Society of London, B; *Biological Sciences, 298*(1089), 199–209.

Sheslow, D., & Adams, W. (2003). *Wide range assessment of memory and learning* (2nd ed.). Lutz, FL: Psychological Assessment Resources.

Siedlecki, K. L., Manly, J. J., Brickman, A. M., Schupf, N., Tang, M., & Stern, Y. (2010). Do neuropsychological tests have the same meaning in Spanish speakers as they do in English speakers?. *Neuropsychology, 24*(3), 402–411. doi:10.1037/a0017515.

Spreen, O., & Strauss, E. (1998). *A compendium of neuropsychological tests: Administration, norms and commentary* (2nd ed.). New York, NY: Oxford University Press.

Sullivan, E. V., Mathalon, D. H., Zipursky, R. B., Kersteen-Tucker, Z., Knight, R. T., & Pfefferbaum, A. (1993). Factors of the Wisconsin card sorting test as a test of dorsolateral pre-frontal cortical function in schizophrenia and alcoholism. *Psychiatry Research, 46*, 175–199.

Vanderploeg, R. D., Schinka, J. A., Jones, T., Small, B. J., Graves, A. B., & Mortimer, J. A. (2000). Elderly norms for the Hopkins Verbal Learning Test-revised. *The Clinical Neuropsychologist, 14*(3), 318–324.

Walker, A. J., Batchelor, J., Shores, E., & Jones, M. (2010). Effects of cultural background on WAIS-III and WMS-III performances after moderate-severe traumatic brain injury. *Australian Psychologist, 45*(2), 112–122. doi:10.1080/00050060903428210.

Wechsler, D. (2008). *Wechsler Adult Intelligence Scale: Technical and interpretive manual* (4th ed.). San Antonio, TX: Pearson.

Weinberg, D. G., Rahme, R. J., Aoun, S. G., Hunt Batjer, H., & Bendok, B. R. (2011). Moyamoya disease: Functional and neurocognitive outcomes in the pediatric and adult populations. *Journal of Neurosurgery, 30*(6), E21.

White, T., & Stern, R. A. (2003). *Psychometric and technical manual of the neuropsychological assessment battery*. Lutz, FL: Psychological Assessment Resources.

Wong, T. M., Strickland, T. L., Fletcher-Janzen, E., Ardila, A., & Reynolds, C. R. (2000). Theoretical and practical issues in the neuropsychological assessment and treatment of culturally dissimilar patients. In Handbook of cross-cultural neuropsychology (pp. 3–18). Springer US.

Assessing Risk, Recidivism, and Dangerousness in Asians

28

Lorraine T. Benuto, Brian D. Leany, Nicholas S. Thaler, and Amy Yonesawa

Assessing Risk, Recidivism, and Dangerousness with Asian Americans

The assessment of risk (including both violent and sexual), recidivism, and dangerousness in adults involves predicting the probability of an initial offense or a subsequent offence (typically criminal reoffending) either sexual or otherwise (e.g., violence and other criminal behavior; Cirlugea, Benuto, & Leany, 2013). Risk factors when assessed can be deemed as static (i.e., variables that cannot be changed) or dynamic (variables that can be changed; Palmer & Hollin, 2007). There has been considerable discussion about the accuracy of actuarial/statistical and clinical predictions. Actuarial predictions are based on empirically validated relationships between client data and the condition to be predicted whereas clinical predictions are based on a clinician's intuition, experience, and knowledge (Dawes, Faust, & Meehl, 1989). Generally, experts agree that the use of clinical judgment results in poor predictive validity (Borum, 1996; Elbogen, 2002; Litwack, 2001; Quinsey, Harris, Rice, & Cromier, 1998) while actuarial statistical methods provide more predictive value as demonstrated by several studies (e.g., Steadman et al., 1998).

For example, the MacArthur Violence Risk Assessment Study (Steadman et al., 1998) was conducted to develop an actuarial violence risk assessment "tool" for use with a clinical population. The researchers collected data from 1,136 male and female patients who were recently discharged from acute psychiatric inpatient facilities (it is important to note that the experimental group did have psychiatric conditions). Data was collected via an interview to gather information on demographic and historical factors, a structured clinical interview using the DSM-III-R checklist confirming the participants'

L.T. Benuto, Ph.D. (✉)
Administrative Faculty, Department of Psychology MS0296, University of Nevada, Reno, NV 89557, USA

Northcentral University, Graduate School Faculty, 10000 E University Drive, Prescott Valley, AZ 86314A, USA
e-mail: dr.benuto@gmail.com

B.D. Leany, Ph.D.
Lake's Crossing Center: Maximum Security Facility for Forensic Mental Health Services, 500 Galletti Way, Sparks, NV 89504, USA

Northcentral University, Graduate School Faculty, 10000 E University Drive, Prescott Valley, AZ 86314, USA
e-mail: leanyb@gmail.com

N.S. Thaler, Ph.D.
Department of Psychiatry and Biobehavioral Sciences, Los Angeles Semel Institute for Neuroscience and Human Behavior, University of California, 760 Westwood Plaza, Los Angeles, CA 90024, USA
e-mail: nick.thaler@gmail.com

A. Yonesawa, J.D.
HPL Law Firm, 330 E Charleston Blvd #100, Las Vegas, NV 89104, USA
e-mail: ayonesawa@gmail.com

L.T. Benuto et al. (eds.), *Guide to Psychological Assessment with Asians*,
DOI 10.1007/978-1-4939-0796-0_28, © Springer Science+Business Media New York 2014

Table 28.1 Risk Factors Identified in the MacArthur Violence Risk Assessment Study (Monahan, 2002)

Risk factor	Finding
Gender	Men were found to use substances (alcohol or street drugs) and less likely to have been compliant with psychotropic medication, prior to committing violence. Women were found to be more likely to target family members and to be violent at home.
Prior violence and criminality	Prior violence and criminality are strongly related to the post-discharge violent behavior of psychiatric patients.
Childhood experiences and violence	Child physical abuse was associated with post-discharge violence as were certain parental behaviors (e.g., having parents who have excessive alcohol and drug use).
Neighborhood context	Violence by persons with mental disorders appears to be related to the high-crime neighborhoods in which they typically reside.
Diagnosis	The presence of a co-occurring diagnosis of substance abuse or dependence was associated with violence. However, a diagnosis of schizophrenia was associated with lower rates of violence than a diagnosis of depression or of bipolar disorder, but higher rates of violence than the community comparison (control) group.
Psychopathy	Antisocial behavior as measured by the Hare PCL:SV predicted violence.
Delusions	While the presence of delusions did not predict higher rates of violence among recently discharged psychiatric patients non-delusional suspiciousness was linked with subsequent violence
Hallucinations	While command hallucinations did not elevate violence risk in and of themselves, if the voices commanded violent acts, the probability of the violent acts being committed over the subsequent year was significantly increased.
Violent thoughts	Patients who reported violent thoughts during hospitalization were more likely to engage in violent acts.
Anger	Patients who obtained a high score on an anger scale while hospitalized were twice as likely as those with low anger scores to engage in violent acts after discharge.

diagnoses, and supplemental material from the patients' records. Community violence was measured upon initial discharge, 20 weeks after discharge, and 1 year post-discharge (Monahan, 2002). In addition to the psychiatric outpatient sample, the authors used a comparison group comprised of 519 individuals residing in the same neighborhoods as the discharged patients (Steadman et al., 1998). Results identified several risk factors related to violence (Monahan, 2002) and these are outlined in Table 28.1. Since this study was published an abundance of research has emerged on various risk assessment measures.

Notably, Hanson and Morton-Bourgon (2009) conducted a meta-analysis including 118 distinct samples from 16 countries to examine the effect sizes of actuarial measures. They found that for the prediction of sexual recidivism, the best supported measures were the STATIC-99, Static–2002 (Hanson & Thornton, 2003), the MnSOST–R (Epperson et al., 2000), the Risk Matrix–2000 (Thornton et al., 2003), and adding the items from the SVR–20 (Boer, Wilson, Gauthier, & Hart, 1997). For the prediction of violent (including sexual) recidivism, the best supported measures were the Violence Risk Appraisal Guide (VRAG; Quinsey, Harris, Rice, & Cormier, 2006), the SORAG (Quinsey et al., 2006), the Risk Matrix—Combined (Thornton et al., 2003), the Statistical Index of Recidivism (SIR; Bonta, Harman, Hann, & Cormier, 1996), and the LSI–R and variants (Andrews et al., 2004). The measures identified as "best-supported" measures by Hanson and Morton-Bourgon for which there was relevant and recent (i.e., publications from the last 5 years) research are discussed below and other measures that are commonly used in the field are also reviewed. A description of the measures that predict sexual recidivism and relevant research to Asian populations is summarized in Table 28.2; Table 28.3 provides a similar summary for the prediction of violent reoffense.

Table 28.2 Summary of measures and relevant research for sexually based offenses

Measure	Description of the measure	Research with Asian participants
MnSOST	The Minnesota Sex Offender Screening Tool (MnSOST) is composed of 21 survey items addressing sexual and nonsexual offense history, substance abuse history, and treatment compliance among extrafamilial sex offenders. The revised MnSOST (the MnSOST-R) includes 16 items, 12 of which reflect historical data and four pertain to institutional information (Barbaree, Seto, Langton, & Peacock, 2001).	Ralston and Epperson (2013) included a small number of Asian American juvenile participants. Ethnic differences were not discussed.
PCL-R	The Hare Psychopathy Checklist (PCL-R) is a 20-item self-report measure designed to assess psychopathy. Factor studies generally agree that the measure comprises two factors including "aggressive narcissism" and "socially deviant lifestyle" (Hare, 1991). Consensus on the PCL-R is that it is a strong predictor of violence and recidivism in inmates and its factor structure generalizes across ethnicities and nationalities (Hemphill, Hare, & Wong, 1998; Salekin, Rogers, & Sewell, 1996; Sullivan et al., 1996).	Hare and colleagues (2000) examined the PCL-R's psychometric properties in a sample of inmates incarcerated in the United Kingdom. A small number (6 %) of Asians were included in the sample and no ethnic differences were identified.
STATIC-(s)	The STATIC-99 is a 10-item self-report checklist that asks adult male offenders about their history of sexual and nonsexual violence, number of convictions, and victims. Scores on the STATIC-99 place individuals in one of four risk categories ranging from low to high, and are only used to measure long-term risk potential, rather than aid in treatment planning or evaluating treatment effects. Variants of the STATIC-99 include the STATIC-99R, 2002, and 2002R with the STATIC-2002 offering the highest predictive accuracy (Babchishin, Hanson, & Helmus, 2012).	Långström (2004) found that the STATIC-99 failed to significantly predict recidivism among the African Asian offenders in a Swedish national sample. It is unclear if these results are generalizable to other Asian populations.
SVR–20	Boer et al.'s (1997) Sexual Violence Risk-20 (SVR-20) is designed to assess the risk of sexual violence by selecting 20 factors, divided into three main sections: (a) psychological adjustment—sexual deviation, victim of child abuse, cognitive impairment, suicidal/homicidal ideation, relationship/employment problems, previous offence history (nonsexual violent, nonviolent), psychopathy, substance use problems, and past supervision failure; (b) sexual offending—high-density offences, multiple offences, physical harm to victims, use of weapon, escalation, and cognitive distortions; and (c) future plans—whether the offender lacks realistic plans and has negative attitudes toward instruction.	No relevant research was identified.
SORAG	The Sex Offender Risk Appraisal Guide (SORAG) consists of 14 items and includes the administration of the PCL-R; scores range from 27 to 51 (Seto, 2005).	No relevant research was identified.
RRASOR	The Rapid Risk Assessment for Sexual Offense Recidivism (RRASOR) contains four items: number of prior charges or convictions for sexual offenses, age upon release from prison or anticipated opportunity to reoffend in the community, any male victims, and any unrelated victims (Hanson, 1997). Total scores can range from 0 to 6 (Seto, 2005)	No relevant research was identified.

Table 28.3 Summary of measures and relevant research for violent offenses

Measure	Description of the measure	Research with Asian participants
HCR-20	The Historical Clinical Risk Management-20 (HCR-20) consists of 20 (rating scale) items that are scored 0, 1, or 2, and scores are added to yield a total score with a range of 0–40, with higher scores indicating a higher risk of violence (Webster et al., 1997).	Fujii and colleagues (2005) examined ethnic differences in assessment of violence risk among psychiatric inpatients by using the HCR-20. Findings provide preliminary support for the cross-cultural validity of the HCR-20 while at the same time identifying unique ethnic differences in prediction of violence risk among psychiatric inpatients. Moreover, a few researchers (e.g., Desmarais et al., 2012 [$n=3$]; Gray et al., 2011 [$n=24$]; Dolan & Blattner, 2010 [$n=8$]) have included some Asian participants in their samples. In the U.K., Snowden and colleagues (2010) included 44 (4 %) participants who were of Asian origin in their study and found good support for both the VRAG and the HCR-20.
SIR	Statistical Index of Recidivism	
LSI-R	The Level of Service Inventory (LSI; Andrews & Bonta, 1995) is a 54-item instrument in which trained raters score each risk/need item as present (1) or absent (0) on the basis of a file review and an interview with the offender.	The LSI is a widely used researched measure. However, specific research examining the performance of Asian participants on this measure is absent. In fact, over the last 5 years very few researchers reported Asian participants in their sample. Of those researchers who did report Asian participants in their samples (e.g., Walters & Schlauch, 2008 [$n=0.1$]; Manchack et al., 2009 [$n=40$]; Palmer & Hollin, 2007 [$n=8$]; Ferguson, Ogloff, & Thomson, 2009 [$n=16$]) did so for studies conducted in the United States, England, and Australia.
VRAG	The VRAG includes 12 risk variables (psychopathy, a personality disorder diagnosis, early parental separation, early school difficulties, early onset of offending, history of alcohol abuse, no marital history, conditional release failure, nonviolent offending history, and injury to a victim: Quinsey et al. 1998).	Substantial international research has demonstrated the VRAG to have predictive accuracy regarding violence and criminal recidivism (Kröner, Stadtland, Eidt, & Nedopil, 2007) although few researchers reported Asians as participants in their study samples (Mills et al., 2007 [$n=4$]; Smee & Bowers, 2008 [$n=1$]; Snowden et al., 2007 [$n=24$]; Snowden et al., 2010 [$n=44$]).

Special Considerations for Risk Assessment with Asian Populations

While experts have noted that Asians are more likely to be involved in gangs than Euro-Americans (although less likely than African Americans or Hispanics) Asians commit an estimated 25 % fewer violent crimes than Euro-Americans in the United States (New Century Foundation, 2005). Despite the lower prevalence of crime compared to Euro-Americans among this population, they are not exempt from research or discussion on recidivism. There are indictors that recidivism assessors may evaluate this group in a different manner than how they might evaluate other ethnic groups. Specifically, Hudson and Bramhall (2005) asserted that in terms of static factors Asian offenders appear less "at risk of reoffending" than Euro-American offenders despite the fact that Asian offenders tend to have a greater presence of dynamic factors (although they offer an ample discussion on potential biases in assessment practices in favor of Euro-American offenders).

Research specific to crime statistics and recidivism aside, a review of the extant literature revealed substantial research on the topic of attitudes toward violence among Asian Americans. Generally speaking, experts discussed cultural differences in violence. For example, Hall and colleagues (2000, 2005) discussed sexual aggression in individualistic cultures vs. sexual aggression in collectivistic cultures. Hall et al. concluded that interpersonal variables may serve as risk or protective factors for sexual aggression;

specifically "loss of face" (i.e., source of shame) was determined to be a protective factor against sexual aggression in the Asian American samples studied. Researchers also examined Asian attitudes toward rape and the prevailing finding has been that Asian Americans tend be more tolerant of rape myths than their non-Asian counterparts (e.g., Kennedy & Gorzalka, 2002; Koo, Stephens, Lindgren, & George, 2012; Lee, Pomeroy, Yoo, & Rheinboldt, 2005). The link between attitudes and risk assessment is not concrete. Nonetheless, we felt it was worth acknowledging identified ethnic differences in aggression and attitudes toward aggression as possibly relevant constructs.

Unique to this chapter is the issue of language. Because the majority of the measures reviewed in this chapter are measures that the clinician can complete with a clinical interview and record review, it is not necessary that the measures in question be available in a plethora of languages. In fact, as long as the clinician can read and write in English and communicate with the client (either because the clinician and client share the same language or via the use of a translator), translated risk assessment measures are not typically necessary. Nonetheless, as discussed above there are cultural factors that theoretically should be considered. In the following section empirical research on risk assessment with Asian populations is discussed.

Research Specific to Risk Assessment with Asian Populations

Research on the assessment of risk with Asian American populations is scarce. Nonetheless, of the research that does exist, we can deduce that using actuarial of predicting aggression is a reasonable approach and actuarial correlates may very well translate cross-culturally. For example, Lee and Egan (2013) specifically examined whether or not correlates of aggression in Western male offenders were effective at predicting aggression in female inmates at a prison in Singapore. They found that just as personality, impulsivity, and psychopathy were predictive of aggression in Western male offenders, they were also predictive of aggression in female offenders from Southeast Asia. As indicated above, these findings suggest that actuarial predictors of aggression hold up cross-culturally.

Because the goal of this book is to provide information on psychological assessment practices with Asians residing in the United States or other similar countries where English is spoken and there is an Asian population (e.g., Canada, Australia, England) we mostly restricted our search to measures with applicability to this population (i.e., individuals of Asian origin residing in an country where English was the primary language). Within this context, the majority of research examining ethnic differences on risk assessments is largely limited to an examination of ethnic differences among Hispanics, African Americans, and Caucasians. In our review of the literature, we noted that some researchers included an "other" category, but most typically it was not specified who was categorized as "other." In sum, in the majority of the literature we reviewed, ethnic composition of the samples was either not included (this was most frequently the case) or Asians were not listed as an ethnic category. Tables 28.2 and 28.3 both reflect the minimal inclusion (where ethnicity was reported) of Asian samples in research on recidivism.

In identifying relevant research to include in this chapter, the first search strategy was to identify research whereby the purpose was to examine ethnic differences in recidivism. A search of relevant databases (i.e., PsycINFO, PsycArticles) using the search terms "Asian" and recidivism yielded only nine peer-reviewed publications, several of which offered statistics on Asians' involvement of crime and rates of recidivism, theoretical discussions on why Asians are involved in crime (e.g., Wolf & Hartney, 2005); other related factors associated with risk (e.g., substance use: Stoolmiller & Blechman, 2005); and several that were not relevant to the topic at hand. The second search strategy was to examine recent research (i.e., from the last 5 years) on "best-supported" recidivism measures and determine the extent to which Asians have been included as research participants in research on our measures of interest. Results from the latter search strategy are summarized in Tables 28.2 and 28.3. In these tables it is very evident that even when Asians have been included as research participants their inclusion has been fairly minimal. Results from the former search strategy are summarized below.

Chu, Ng, Fong, and Teoh (2012). Chu and colleagues (2012) compared the predictive validity of three youth risk assessment measures (i.e., the Estimate of Risk of Adolescent Sexual Offense Recidivism [ERASOR], the Juvenile Sex Offender Assessment Protocol-II [J-SOAP-II], and the Youth Level of Service/Case Management Inventory [YLS/CMI]) for sexual and nonviolent recidivism in a sample of 104 male adolescents who sexually offended within a Singaporean context. While all of the measures (i.e., the ERASOR overall clinical rating and total score, the J-SOAP-II total score, as well as the YLS/CMI) significantly predicted nonsexual recidivism and time to nonsexual reoffense for this sample of youth who sexually offended, the authors concluded that the ERASOR is best suited for assessing youth who sexually offended in a non-Western context and the J-SOAP-II and the YLS/CMI have limited utility for such a purpose. While the generalizability of these results to a U.S. context could be arguably questionable, given the limited research in general on Asian populations in a U.S. context, these findings offer a starting point for researchers to follow-up and assess these measures with Asian populations in the United States. In the interim the ERASOR seems like a reasonable option when it is necessary to assess Asian youth.

Fujii, Tokioka, Lichton, and Hishinuma (2005). Fujii and colleagues (2005) conducted one of the few studies that offer an ethnic comparison on a measure used to assess recidivism (the Historical Clinical Risk Management-20 [HCR-20]) in the United States with Asian samples. They administered the HCR-20 to a sample of 169 psychiatric inpatients including Asian Americans ($n=51$), Euro-Americans ($n=46$), and Native Hawaiians ($n=38$). Fujii et al. identified differences in scores on individual HCR-20 items were found (i.e., young age at first incident of violence, psychopathy, early maladjustment, personality disorder, and past supervision failure) as well as differences in the total HCR-20 score. Specifically, Asian Americans scored lower (less risk) than Euro-Americans and Native Hawaiians. Finally, different patterns of predictor variables for each ethnic group were also identified (i.e., impulsivity was a salient factor for the Asian American group; young age at first incident of violence was a salient factor for the Euro-American group; and young age at first incident of violence, relationship instability, and risk-management plans' lacking feasibility were salient predictors for the Native Hawaiian group). These results suggest that with a few caveats, the HCR-20 can be appropriately used with Asian populations in the United States. In keeping with Webster and colleagues' (1997) original intentions, these factors should be considered when planning interventions to manage risk, and not necessarily as a predictor of violence or reoffending.

Loza, Neo, Shahinfar, and Loza-Fanous (2005). Loza et al. (2005) compared the scores of 91 female offenders incarcerated in Pennsylvania to the scores of 183 female offenders incarcerated in a Singapore correctional system on the Self-Appraisal Questionnaire (SAQ; a 72-item self-report measure designed to predict violent and nonviolent recidivism among adult male criminal offenders). Significant differences between the scores of African American and Asian offenders and the responses of the Euro-American offenders were not observed. Moreover, results indicated that the SAQ has sound psychometric properties, with acceptable reliability and concurrent and predictive validity for assessing violent and nonviolent recidivism; thus this measure is appropriate for use with at least some Asian populations. While the generalizability of these results to a U.S. context could be arguably questionable, given the limited research in general on Asian populations in a U.S. context, this finding offers a starting point for researchers to follow-up and assess these measures with Asian populations in the United States. In the interim the SAQ seems like a reasonable option when it is necessary to assess Asian female offenders.

Långström (2004). Långström (2004) examined the predictive validity across ethnic groups for the RRASOR and the STATIC–99 among adult male sex offenders released from prison in Sweden between 1993 and 1997. Långström found that the STATIC–99 predicted recidivism among Nordic and non-Nordic Europeans but failed to significantly predict recidivism among the African Asian offenders in a Swedish national sample. Långström did note that the extent to which the differences in predictive accuracy are due to missing records or to real social-cultural differences remains to be explored. Moreover, in Långström's description of the sample it was unclear who was categorized as "African Asian"; this combined with the study being conducted in Sweden makes it difficult to determine the generalizability of his findings to a U.S. context.

Summary and Recommendations

As illustrated both in the research described above and the literature summarized in Tables 28.2 and 28.3, Asian participants have been largely excluded from research on measures that assess for recidivism. Of the research that has been conducted, results suggest that the utilization of actuarial risk factors can assist in accurately predicting risk. Therefore, clinicians are encouraged to use multiple avenues for assessment and to consider that despite the limited research that is available there, research that contradicts the use of the measures with Asian offenders is essentially absent. Future research should be conducted on these measures with individuals of Asian origin in the United States so that more specific guidelines can be developed.

References

Andrews, D. A., & Bonta, J. (1995). *The LSI-R: Level of service inventory–Revised.* Toronto, Ontario: Multi-Health Systems.

Babchishin, K. M., Hanson, R., & Helmus, L. (2012). Even highly correlated measures can add incrementally to predicting recidivism among sex offenders. *Assessment, 19*(4), 442–461. doi:10.1177/1073191112458312.

Barbaree, H. E., Seto, M., Langton, C. M., & Peacock, E. J. (2001). Evaluating the predictive accuracy of six risk assessment instruments for adult sex offenders. *Criminal Justice and Behavior, 28*, 490–521.

Boer, D. P., Wilson, R. J., Gauthier, C. M., & Hart, S. D. (1997). *Manual for the sexual violence risk-20.* Vancouver, British Columbia: The Mental Health, Law and Policy Institute and the Simon Fraser University.

Bonta, J., Harman, W. G., Hann, R. G., & Cormier, R. B. (1996). The prediction of recidivism among federally sentenced offenders: A re-validation of the SIR scale. *Canadian Journal of Criminology, 38*(1), 61–79.

Borum, R. (1996). Improving the clinical practice of violence risk assessment: Technology, guidelines, and training. *American Psychologist, 51*(9), 945–956.

Chu, C., Ng, K., Fong, J., & Teoh, J. (2012). Assessing youth who sexually offended: The predictive validity of the ERASOR, J-SOAP-II, and YLS/CMI in a non-Western context. *Sexual Abuse: Journal of Research and Treatment, 24*(2), 153–174.

Cirlugea, O., Benuto, L., & Leany, B. (2013). Assessing risk, recidivism, and dangerousness in Hispanics. In L. Benuto (Ed.), *Guide to psychological assessment with Hispanics*. New York, NY: Springer.

Dawes, R. M., Faust, D., & Meehl, P. E. (1989). Clinical versus actuarial judgment. *Science, 243*(4899), 1668–1674.

Desmarais, S. L., Nicholls, T. L., Wilson, C. M., & Brink, J. (2012). Using dynamic risk and protective factors to predict inpatient aggression: Reliability and validity of START assessments. *Psychological Assessment, 24*(3), 685–700. doi:10.1037/a0026668.

Dolan, M., & Blattner, R. (2010). The utility of the Historical Clinical Risk -20 Scale as a predictor of outcomes in decisions to transfer patients from high to lower levels of security-A UK perspective. *BMC Psychiatry, 10.* doi:10.1186/1471-244X-10-76.

Elbogen, E. B. (2002). The process of violence risk assessment: A review of descriptive research. *Aggression and Violent Behavior, 7*(6), 591–604. doi:10.1016/S1359-1789(01)00051-9.

Epperson, D. L., Kaul, J. D., Huot, S. J., Hesselton, D., Alexander, W., & Goldman, R. (November 2000). *Cross-validation of the Minnesota sex offender screening tool—Revised.* Paper presented at the 19th annual research and treatment conference of the Association for the Treatment of Sexual Abusers, San Diego, CA.

Ferguson, M., Ogloff, J. R. P., & Thomson, L. (2009). Predicting recidivism by mentally disordered offenders using the LSI-R:SV. *Criminal Justice and Behavior, 36*, 5–20.

Fujii, D. M., Tokioka, A. B., Lichton, A. I., & Hishinuma, E. (2005). Ethnic differences in prediction of violence risk with the HCR-20 among psychiatric inpatients. *Psychiatric Services, 56*(6), 711–716. doi:10.1176/appi.ps.56.6.711.

Gray, N. S., Taylor, J., & Snowden, R. J. (2011). Predicting violence using structured professional judgment in patients with different mental and behavioral disorders.

Psychiatry Research, 187(1–2), 248–253. doi:10.1016/j.psychres.2010.10.011.

Hall, G., Sue, S., Narang, D. S., & Lilly, R. S. (2000). Culture-specific models of men's sexual aggression: Intra- and interpersonal determinants. *Cultural Diversity and Ethnic Minority Psychology, 6*(3), 252–268. doi:10.1037/1099-9809.6.3.252.

Hall, G., Teten, A. L., DeGarmo, D. S., Sue, S., & Stephens, K. A. (2005). Ethnicity, culture, and sexual aggression: Risk and protective factors. *Journal of Consulting and Clinical Psychology, 73*(5), 830–840.

Hanson, R. K. (1997). *The development of a brief actuarial risk scale for sexual offense recidivism. (User Report 97-04).* Ottawa: Department of the Solicitor General of Canada.

Hanson, R., & Morton-Bourgon, K. E. (2009). The accuracy of recidivism risk assessments for sexual offenders: A meta-analysis of 118 prediction studies. *Psychological Assessment, 21*(1), 1–21. doi:10.1037/a0014421.

Hanson, R. K., & Thornton, D. (2003). *Notes on the development of Static-2002. (Corrections Research User Report No. 2003-01).* Ottawa: Department of the Solicitor General of Canada.

Hare, R. D. (1991). *Manual for the psychopathy checklist-revised.* Toronto: Multi Health Systems.

Hare, R. D., Clark, D., Grann, M., & Thornton, D. (2000). Psychopathy and the predictive validity of the PCL-R: An international perspective. *Behavioral Sciences & The Law, 18*(5), 623–645.

Hemphill, J. F., Hare, R. D., & Wong, S. (1998). Psychopathy and recidivism: A review. *Legal and Criminological Psychology, 3*, 141–172.

Hudson, B., & Bramhall, G. (2005). Assessing the 'Other': Constructions of 'Asianness' in risk assessments by probation officers. *British Journal of Criminology, 45*(5), 721–740. doi:10.1093/bjc/azi002.

Kennedy, M., & Gorzalka, B. B. (2002). Asian and non-Asian attitudes toward rape, sexual harassment, and sexuality. *Sex Roles, 46*(7–8), 227–238. doi:10.1023/A:1020145815129.

Koo, K. H., Stephens, K. A., Lindgren, K. P., & George, W. H. (2012). Misogyny, acculturation, and ethnic identity: Relation to rape-supportive attitudes in Asian American college men. *Archives of Sexual Behavior, 41*(4), 1005–1014. doi:10.1007/s10508-011-9729-1.

Kröner, C., Stadtland, C., Eidt, M., & Nedopil, N. (2007). The validity of the Violence Risk Appraisal Guide (VRAG) in predicting criminal recidivism. *Criminal Behaviour and Mental Health, 17*(2), 89–100. doi:10.1002/cbm.644.

Långström, N. (2004). Accuracy of actuarial procedures for assessment of sexual offender recidivism risk may vary across ethnicity. *Sexual Abuse: Journal of Research and Treatment, 16*(2), 107–120. doi:10.1177/107906320401600202.

Lee, V., & Egan, V. (2013). Predictors of aggression in Southeast Asian female prisoners. *Personality and Individual Differences, 54*(1), 113–117. doi:10.1016/j.paid.2012.08.024.

Lee, J., Pomeroy, E. C., Yoo, S., & Rheinboldt, K. T. (2005). Attitudes toward rape: A comparison between Asian and Caucasian College Students. *Violence Against Women, 11*(2), 177–196. doi:10.1177/1077801204271663.

Litwack, T. R. (2001). Actuarial versus clinical assessments of dangerousness. *Psychology, Public Policy, and Law, 7*(2), 409–443. doi:10.1037/1076-8971.7.2.409.

Loza, W., Neo, L., Shahinfar, A., & Loza-Fanous, A. (2005). Cross-validation of the Self-Appraisal Questionnaire: A tool for assessing violent and nonviolent recidivism with female offenders. *International Journal of Offender Therapy and Comparative Criminology, 49*(5), 547–560. doi:10.1177/0306624X04273433.

Manchak, S. M., Skeem, J. L., Douglas, K. S., & Siranosian, M. (2009). Does gender moderate the predictive utility of the Level of Service Inventory–Revised (LSI-R) for serious violent offenders? *Criminal Justice and Behavior, 36*, 425–442.

Mills, J. F., Kroner, D. G., & Hemmati, T. (2007). The validity of violence risk estimates: An issue of item performance. *Psychological Services, 4*(1), 1–12. doi:10.1037/1541-1559.4.1.1.

Monahan, J. (2002). The MacArthur studies of violence risk. *Criminal Behaviour & Mental Health, 12S*, 67.

New Century Foundation. (2005). The color of crime. Retrieved from: http://www.colorofcrime.com/colorofcrime2005.pdf

Palmer, E. J., & Hollin, C. R. (2007). The level of service inventory-revised with English women prisoners: A needs and reconviction analysis. *Criminal Justice and Behavior, 34*(8), 971–984. doi:10.1177/0093854807300819.

Quinsey, V. L., Harris, G. T., Rice, M. E., & Cormier, C. A. (2006). Actuarial prediction of violence. In J. C. Campbell (Ed.), *Violent offenders: Appraising and managing risk* (2nd ed., pp. 155–196). Washington, DC: American Psychological Association. doi:10.1037/11367-008.

Quinsey, V. L., Harris, G. T., Rice, M. E., & Cromier, C. A. (1998). *Violent offenders: Appraising and managing risk.* Washington, DC: American Psychological Association.

Ralston, C. A., & Epperson, D. L. (2013). Predictive validity of adult risk assessment tools with juveniles who offended sexually. *Psychological Assessment, 25*(3), 905–916. doi:10.1037/a0032683.

Salekin, R. T., Rogers, R., & Sewell, K. W. (1996). A review and meta-analysis of the Psychopathy Checklist and Psychopathy Checklist—Revised: Predictive validity of dangerousness. *Clinical Psychology: Science and Practice, 3*, 203–215.

Seto, M. C. (2005). Is more better? Combining actuarial risk scales to predict recidivism among adult sex offenders. *Psychological Assessment, 17*(2), 156–167. doi:10.1037/1040-3590.17.2.156.

Smee, J., & Bowers, T. G. (2008). A comparative test of clinical judgment versus actuarial prediction of future violence. *Journal of Police and Criminal Psychology, 23*(1), 1–7. doi:10.1007/s11896-008-9014-y.

Snowden, R. J., Gray, N. S., Taylor, J., & MacCulloch, M. J. (2007). Actuarial prediction of violent recidivism in mentally disordered offenders. *Psychological Medicine: A Journal of Research in Psychiatry and the Allied Sciences, 37*(11), 1539–1549. doi:10.1017/S0033291707000876.

Snowden, R. J., Gray, N. S., & Taylor, J. (2010). Risk assessment for future violence in individuals from an ethnic minority group. *The International Journal of Forensic Mental Health, 9*(2), 118–123. doi:10.1080/14999013.2010.501845.

Steadman, H. J., Mulvey, E. P., Monahan, J., Robbins, P., Appelbaum, P. S., Grisso, T., … Silver, E. (1998). Violence by people discharged from acute psychiatric inpatient facilities and by others in the same neighborhoods. *Archives of General Psychiatry, 55*(5), 393–401. doi:10.1001/archpsyc.55.5.393

Stoolmiller, M., & Blechman, E. A. (2005). Substance use is a robust predictor of adolescent recidivism. *Criminal Justice and Behavior, 32*(3), 302–328. doi:10.1177/0093854804274372.

Thornton, D., Mann, R., Webster, S., Blud, L., Travers, R., Friendship, C., et al. (2003). Distinguishing and combining risks for sexual and violent recidivism. In R. A. Prentky, E. S. Janus, & M. C. Seto (Eds.), *Understanding and managing sexually coercive behavior* (Vol. 989, pp. 225–235). New York, NY: Annals of the New York Academy of Sciences.

Walters, G. D., & Schlauch, C. (2008). The psychological inventory of criminal thinking styles and level of service inventory-revised: Screening version as predictors of official and self-reported disciplinary infractions. *Law and Human Behavior, 32*(5), 454–462. doi:10.1007/s10979-007-9117-5.

Webster, C. D., Douglas, K. S., Eaves, D., et al. (1997). *HCR-20: Assessing risk for violence, Version 2.* Vancouver, Canada: Simon Fraser University.

Wolf, A. M., & Hartney, C. (2005). A portrait of detained youth in the State of Hawaii. *Crime & Delinquency, 51*(2), 180–191. doi:10.1177/0011128704273929.

Forensic Assessment with the Asian American Client

29

Brian D. Leany and Lorraine T. Benuto

Forensic psychology is the application of psychological practices within the scope of the legal system. Forensic psychologists are called upon to provide their professional opinion on issues of competency, capacity, and diagnostic clarification for clients. Psychologists also provide recommendations pertaining to clients' amenability to treatment, appropriate interventions, and the impact of serious mental illness on functioning. These recommendations in turn assist in facilitating a court-related decision in regard to issues involving custody, liability, and in some cases a person's mental status.

The extant literature on cultural considerations for forensic practice with Asian Americans is generally lacking. However, general cultural considerations are discussed at length throughout this book. One possible explanation for the limited information specific to forensics could be a relatively low incarceration rate for Asian Americans. Specifically data from 1990/2000 through May 2013 from the Federal Bureau of Prisons revealed that only 1.6 % of their population identify as Asian American (http://www.bop.gov/news/quick.jsp#2). Given the broad nature of this field and the limited amount of empirical research on Asian Americans in the forensic setting, this chapter serves as a brief overview for the various domains covered in greater detail in other chapters, with expansion provided for their unique applications in the forensic setting.

It is important to note here at the outset that the overarching goal of this book is to provide evidence-based assessment recommendations on specific measures. As noted above, research on Asian Americans and assessment measures used in legal contexts is sorely lacking. Thus where direct recommendations based on empirical evaluations of specific measures could not be made (due to an absence of empirical literature), a theoretical position was taken. Specifically, Asian cultural values were considered in light of the construct being assessed. While in general we recommend that clinicians and researchers avoid making recommendations based on anthropological assertions that have not been empirically investigated, for measures that have high face validity this may be a reasonable approach to take when empirical data is absent.

B.D. Leany, Ph.D. (✉)
Lake's Crossing Center: Maximum Security Facility for Forensic Mental Health Services,
500 Galletti Way, Sparks, NV 89504, USA

Northcentral University, Graduate School Faculty,
10000 E University Drive, Prescott Valley,
AZ 86314, USA
e-mail: leanyb@gmail.com

L.T. Benuto, Ph.D.
Administrative Faculty, Department of Psychology
MS0296, University of Nevada, Reno, NV 89557, USA

Northcentral University, Graduate School Faculty,
10000 E University Drive, Prescott Valley,
AZ 86314, USA
e-mail: dr.benuto@gmail.com

L.T. Benuto et al. (eds.), *Guide to Psychological Assessment with Asians*,
DOI 10.1007/978-1-4939-0796-0_29, © Springer Science+Business Media New York 2014

Child Custody Evaluations

Given an overarching goal of providing a valid and reliable approach to child custody evaluations, Tolle and O'Donohue (2012) proposed a model that compares promotive factors to egregious factors. Promotive factors are considered conducive to the child and his or her well-being as well as development of the child while egregious factors are considered detrimental to the child's well-being and overall development. The factors are all factored into the evaluation with the overarching goal of joint custody so long as it is in the best interest of the child. As the name of the model suggests, many of the skills (i.e., factors) are comprised of abilities or deficits at opposing ends of a particular domain. For example, a parent's perception and expectations related to parenting are typically assessed through self-report or interview. These methods can result in the identification of either skills that are consistent with positive outcomes for children (e.g., positive parenting) or deficits and/or practices known to yield suboptimal or poor outcomes (e.g., parenting skills deficits). The disparity between Western and Asian sociocultural value systems is most evident in parenting and family relationships, and thus it is important to ensure that we appropriately discriminate problem parenting issues from behaviors that arise from ascribing to cultural value systems. Below a review of each factor that is housed within the model is provided alongside specific cultural considerations that must be taken into account with the Asian family.

Promotive Factors

Positive parenting. Positive parenting emphasizes parents identifying positive attributes of their children and an avoidance of physical punishment based on a philosophy of creating autonomy and decision-making in children (Caspi et al., 2004; Rothbaum & Weisz, 1994). Thus, in positive parenting, the goal of the parent should be to promote choices that may be more difficult, but also have more long-term benefits for the child. For the Asian American family there is value in shame and corporal punishment as it increases the socially desirable trait of conformity (Yeh & Yeh, 2002), and the notion of autonomy is distinct from the Western construct. For example, self-sufficiency is expected, though individualism is not. As a consequence, Asian American children raised in a more traditional environment are more likely to be encouraged to follow directions and not engage in independent decision-making (Yeh & Yeh, 2002). Specific normative data on how Asian parents perform on measures that assess positive parenting are absent. However, it is likely that in some situations, lower than expected scores may reflect cultural differences within the family value system rather than poor positive parenting. The clinician should therefore use supplemental nonpsychometric methods to assess how the parenting style is impacting the child. In such situations, information gleaned from the clinical interview and third-party observations may trump data obtained from self-report questionnaires.

Parental school involvement. Parental involvement at a child's school is beneficial (National Research Council [NRC], 2001; U.S. Department of Education, 2000), and thus the degree of this involvement is another identified promotive factor. The Family Involvement Questionnaire (FIQ; Fantuzzo, Tighe, & Childs, 2000) is used as an objective measure to assess parental involvement, and utilizes a 4-point rating scale to measure a child's primary caregiver's school involvement. While the measure was developed on a multicultural sample of Head Start parents, Asian Americans are not specifically described and likely fall into the "other" category that make up 11 % of the normative sample. Further, while there are a number of studies that include Asian Americans in the sample (McIntyre, 2008; Rockhill, Stoep, McCauley, & Katon, 2009), there is little information that suggests ethnic or culture-specific findings or recommendations for Asian American families. Nonetheless, minority parents (including Asian Americans) report more involvement in scholastic activities at home than at school, as compared to nonminority parents who typically have more involvement at school. Despite this, minority parents (including Asian American parents) are likely to increase parental involvement when invited to do so from teachers or the school. Moreover, economic status should be considered as lower income parents are less likely to be involved in activities at school or attend school-arranged workshops but more involved in scholastic activities at home and via alternative activities (e.g., religious activities: Mendez, Carpenter, LaForett, & Cohen, 2009). In sum, when assessing parental school involvement the clinician should factor in the extent to which the parent is involved in scholastic activities at home and also in extracurricular activities that may not be school specific.

Promotion of interpersonal development. There are several measures available to assess the status of interpersonal development including the Multidimensional Scale of Perceived Social Support (MSPSS, Zimet, Dahlem, Zimet, & Farley, 1988), the Friendship Quality Questionnaire, and the Functional Status Questionnaire (FSQ; Jette et al., 1986). Of note, the MSPSS (Zimet, Dahlem et al., 1988) has been researched specific toward Asian American participants. Using a Chinese equivalent version of the MSPSS (MMSPSS-C) for a sample of Chinese in Hong Kong, Chou (2000) found that, while it had mild to moderate construct validity with the Luben social network scale (0.41 for the Family Support factor and 0.25 for a combined factor of friends and significant others), there were two factors rather than three with the category of Friends and Significant others being combined into a single category. Based on these findings, the evaluator should be aware that the construct of interpersonal development appears to differ for Asians, with greater weight being placed on the family. Thus, the Asian parent may be more inclined to promote interpersonal development as it relates to the family and this would not necessarily be negative, provided that the child is responding appropriately to a familial emphasis. It is unclear at this time if Asian Americans would exhibit similar differences on the standard MSPSS.

Promotion of mental health. Assessment of parental promotion for mental health in children traditionally includes several self-esteem and autonomy measures as well as various parental inventories and functional assessments. As with other measures, there is limited data specific to Asian Americans. It is important however to note that Asians have been noted to not seek out mental health services (Yeh & Yeh, 2002). Currently, it is unknown whether or not this generalizes to seeking services for their children. Therefore the clinician may wish to assess the extent to which the parent seeks services for their child when needed as well as promotes positive mental health through encouraging self-esteem, engagement in positive activities, etc.

Promotion of community involvement. Research on the promotion of community involvement among Asian American families is largely absent. Nonetheless, given the emphasis the Asian culture places on the community (given the collectivistic nature of the culture; Yee, Huang, & Lew, 1998) it is reasonable to hypothesize that Asian parents will promote involvement in the community. The specifics of what constitutes community may be somewhat culturally dependent and could include religious involvement, involvement with the extended family, and perhaps the Asian cultural community (although as previously discussed, lesser importance is placed on friends and significant others; Chou, 2000). Thus, while community involvement may extend to traditional institutions like religion, for Asian Americans, the clinician should be aware that it may not include other Westernized constructs of community (e.g., social clubs).

Effective co-parenting. The Parenting Alliance Measure (PAM; Abidin & Konold, 1999) is a 20-item self-report measure developed to identify perceived alliance between parents of children less than 19 years of age. The total score for the measure is indicative of the degree to which parents see themselves to be part of a cooperative relationship when caring for their children. There are no specific investigations of the PAM, but both the initial normative sample and a subsequent follow-up factor analysis by the original authors (Konold & Abidin, 2001) included a small sample of Asian Americans (1.2 % of the overall sample; $n = 1224$). The authors did not make note of findings for ethnic or racial differences on the identified factors or total score. Given the limited available data specific to Asian Americans for this measure, it is unclear if this is a valid or reliable measure for Asian American parents. Thus, if administered the results should be evaluated against collateral information from teachers or other outside sources. The clinician should be mindful of a traditional desire to maintain social appearances and conformity and to minimize an appearance of disagreement (Yee et al., 1998; Yeh & Yeh, 2002). It may be more helpful to provide specific vignettes to asses for how each parent would resolve the conflict, and to do so with each parent independently.

Egregious Factors

Parent–child relationship. Assessment of the parent–child relationship can be accomplished through observation and the collection of information from collateral contacts, but there are specific measures designed to provide an objective evaluation of this component of the child custody evaluation. These measures include the Parental Stress Inventory (PSI), The Parent Child Relationship Inventory (PCRI; Gerard, 1994), and to a lesser extent, the Child Abuse Potential Inventory (CAPI; Milner, 1989). This latter measure is a 160-item self-report tool devised for the detection of child physical abuse. This instrument contains ten scales (seven clinical), with the primary scale being the Abuse scale. There are three validity scales to identify lying, random responding, and inconsistency in responding. While previous research has found no difference for the prediction of abuse among ethnic groups, this comparison did not include Asian American participants in the sample (Medora, Wilson, & Larson, 2001). The evaluator may wish to explore any elevations that suggest abuse, as well as attain any information to reported cases of abuse, whether founded or unfounded to either rule out maladaptive parental stress responses or identify them.

Parenting skills. As seen in other domains of child custody evaluation, objective self-report measures consider things like parenting style, expectation comparisons between parents and children and styles of discipline, as well as various other domains to identify potential deficits that would result in suboptimal or ineffective parenting. These measures include the Parental Authority Questionnaire (PAQ; Buri, 1991), the Parent Behavior Checklist (PBC; Fox, 1994), and the Parenting Sense of Competence Scale (PSOC; Gibaud-Wallson & Wandersman, 1978). These measures are all self-report measures that assess the aforementioned aspects of parenting and to our knowledge there is no research specific to Asian Americans. However, similar to the assessment of promotion for personal development and mental health, the culture of Asian Americans is one of identification with the group rather than the individual (Yee et al., 1998). Thus, self-esteem and self-confidence may be less valuable than conforming to the group and adhering to social norms, and what might be considered clinically relevant for the dominant culture may not be indicative of maladaptive parenting in Asian American parents. Here again, the clinician must be careful to not over-interpret parental views or beliefs that support a deference of children to parents and a strong hierarchical structure where children are not encouraged to engage in autonomous behavior, as these are considered culturally appropriate for many Asian American cultures (Yee et al., 1998). Thus the absence of such a belief system is a benefit to the child, but the presence of this hierarchical and authoritative structure is not necessarily an egregious factor.

Environmental instability. A specific tool designed to assess a child's environment is the Home Observation for the Measurement of the Environment (HOME; Caldwell & Bradley, 1984; Caldwell & Bradley, 2003). This tool is a measure of the number and quality of environmental interactions for a child and their family. This assessment is adapted in four different age brackets and also is available in a short form (HOME-SF) as well as for assessment of alternate care settings, such as with a family member as well as for children with disabilities. A primary benefit of this measure is that it can be administered in a single visit. As research on Asian Americans is lacking, with the exception of dangerous or blatant neglect (such as lack of shelter, food, clothing, or serious bodily injury) identification of deficiencies here should be used to make recommendations for improving the child's environment rather than as a determination of custody.

Interparental conflict. The fact that a custody evaluation is being conducted indicates that parental conflict is present. The goal for evaluation of interparental conflict within the context of a custody evaluation is to identify parental conflict that is excessive and possibly harmful to the child. To this end, two measures are frequently utilized to measure parental conflict.

The Multidimensional Assessment of Interparental Conflict (MAIC; Tschann, Flores, Pasch, & Marin, 2002) is a parent self-report measure designed to assess parental conflict in six dimensions (including frequency, intensity, child-related content, child involvement, and resolution) whereas the Children's Perception of Interparental Conflict Scale (CPIC; Grych, Seid, & Fincham, 1992) assesses the child's impression of their parents' conflict utilizing a 51-item true-false questionnaire. A review of the literature yielded few studies that included Asian Americans (usually reported as 1 % or less), and no studies that offered culture or ethnic specific recommendations. Despite the absence of normative data on these measures, it remains of utmost importance that egregious factors be thoroughly assessed as they are the most likely to cause harm to the child. Therefore, the evaluator should assess for interparental conflict, note the limited availability of the normative data for these measures, and use collateral contacts to either support or refute findings.

Parental mental health. There are a number of chapters devoted to clinical assessment of Axis I and Axis II disorders, and those specific assessments will not be discussed here. However, the presence of mental illness in a parent directly and negatively correlates with their ability to provide appropriate parenting. Of primary concern for this domain are the under-endorsement and the atypical presentation of mental health symptoms for Asian Americans (Wu & Chang, 2008; Yeung et al., 2002). Here too, the level of acculturation is an important consideration when evaluating the presence of a mental illness or personality disorder (Cuéllar & Paniagua, 2000; Stevens, Kwan, & Graybill, 1993; Tsai & Pike, 2000). If mental illness is suspected, the clinician may wish to use a structured or semi-structured interview, which is discussed in Chap. 8, to allow for additional probing rather than relying on objective assessment for these symptoms.

Summary and Recommendations for Child Custody Evaluations

Data for measures commonly used for child custody evaluations specific to Asian Americans are largely absent. Given the identifiable differences between Asian Americans and other minority groups as well as differences between Asian American parents and the dominant culture, caution should be used when utilizing these common measures of child custody and collateral contacts should be made to either support or refute findings.

Given the limited amount of data available for the measures, it would be more appropriate to discuss potential considerations for the aforementioned attitudes and behaviors rather than the specific measures. Thus, when considering promotive factors for Asian American parents, an evaluator should be cognizant that the following may be characteristic of Asian American parents: authoritative parenting; low levels of school involvement but substantial assistance with school activities at home (e.g., assistance with homework); a preference for religious activities over school activities; and a greater encouragement for acculturation (so long as there is a maintenance of respect for the culture of origin). While one would expect salient measures of impairment (such as mental retardation, severely disordered personality, and low SES) to remain as markers for poor outcomes, the less overt markers such as parental attitudes, community involvement and school involvement, as well as differential reporting of symptoms of mental illness, require further investigation and collateral support in making a determination or providing an opinion for custody. This can be accomplished by including more probative questions during interviews, as well as measures of acculturation and structured or semi-structured interviews for assessing mental illness and disorders of personality. Clinicians should always note the limited availability of the normative data for the measures administered, and use collateral contacts to either support or refute findings.

Criminal Competency

While mental health professionals are often asked to provide evaluations of competency, this construct is a legal one that is occasionally defined in statute and is ultimately determined by the court. The court often follows the recommendations made by the mental health professional; the expert mental health professional provides a discussion regarding an individual's capacity for a specific legal construct (Grisso, 2003; Melton, Petrila, Poythress, & Slobogin, 2007). This is because individuals are assumed to be competent unless the court determines otherwise. Additionally, the construct of competency is not all encompassing. This means that a finding of incompetence for one domain does not mean the individual can be considered incompetent for other domains. In fact, individual states have begun to delineate the various competencies in statute. The fact that competency is a legal construct also means that there is even less consistency for the psychological construct definition than we traditionally find for other psychological constructs. Instead the guiding principle for defining the construct is based upon the legal definition of competency for the state or municipality within which it is being conducted and relevant case law (Grisso, 2003; Melton et al., 2007; Roesch, Zapf, Golding, & Skeem, 1999).

Further, with regard to cultural considerations, there is a great deal of variability among the sociopolitical systems within which the Asian American cultures originate. Not all of these cultures function within a legal system that is both adversarial or one that assumes innocence to which the western U.S. culture ascribes. Thus, while there are a wide range of competency-related abilities where an assessment could be requested (for an expansive listing and description see Melton et al., 2007), few assessments exist to measure all possible iterations for this expanding scope of competencies, and all necessarily measure only the U.S. constructs of competency. Because all of these measures lack research specific for Asian Americans, they are summarized here as to the general process of administration and an identification of the unique components of each.

Measures of Criminal Competency

There are several measures available for the assessment of criminal competency, and each attempts to yield some semblance of an objective evaluation for the construct of competency. Adaptations have been made for use with unique populations such as individuals with mental retardation. However, there is negligible research available that is specific to the assessment of criminal competency for Asian American populations. As stated at the outset, what little information exists comes in the form of individuals who identify as Asian American in the normative sample of the respective measures or in the various participant samples of experimental paradigms for these measures that make no indication of differences specific to Asian American participants. In fact, when one embarks on a literature search using the term "Asian American assessment of criminal competency" several thousand items are identified, and while this initially may elicit hope, a cursory glance is enough to show that there is less than a handful that actually specifically discuss Asian Americans as a specific group of interest. Finally, because of the high stakes of forensic assessment, in particular criminal competency, a more conservative approach is warranted. While competency measures attempt to standardize the process and create an actuarial rather than subjective evaluation of competency, Grisso (2003) reminded us that these measures serve as a part of the process and not the determinate criteria for evaluating competency. In other words, the forensic domain is as stringent as other mental health settings (and some argue it is necessarily more stringent; APA, 2012; Grisso, 2003; Melton et al., 2007) and we would not diagnose an individual with schizophrenia or bipolar disorder based on responses to a single measure. Therefore we should not expect to do so for psycho-legal constructs like capacity, competency, or criminal responsibility. Finally, the measures of competency generally utilize some form of interview, or in the case of the CAST-MR for mental retardation, a combination of multiple-choice responses, and open-ended questions. Due to the lack of extant literature for specific data related to Asian Americans these tools are merely listed here and include the following:

- MacArthur Competency Assessment Tool—Criminal Adjudication (MacCAT-CA; Poythress et al., 1999)
- Evaluation of Competency to Stand Trial—Revised (ECST-R; Rogers, Tillbrook, & Sewell, 2004)
- Competency to Stand Trial Assessment Instrument (CSTAI; McGary, 1973)
- Georgia Court Competency Test (GCCT; Wildman et al., 1978)
- Fitness Interview Test—Revised (FIT-R; Roesch, Zapf, & Eaves, 2006)
- Competence Assessment for Standing Trial for Defendants with Mental Retardation (CAST-MR; Everington & Luckasson, 1992)

Recommendations for criminal competency. The measures listed above are those that are commonly used in practice (Archer, Buffington-Vollum, Stredny, & Handel, 2006), but there is little extant literature that discusses cultural or ethnic considerations specific to these measures for Asian Americans. Thus, consistent with recommendations in other domains with limited representative normative data, it is suggested that each step of the process incorporate cultural considerations including test selection, administration in the client's primary or preferred language, and that obtaining appropriate collateral information. We emphasize that it is important to acquire not just quantitative information (such as years of education or occupational attainment) but also qualitative information (such as level of acculturation and community participation) in an effort to either support or refute a finding (Hicks, 2004; Wong & Fujii, 2004). Thus, for highly educated and well-acculturated Asian Americans, existing standardized assessments, such as the MacCAT, FIT-R, CAST-MR, etc., would be appropriate for assessing competency. However, for lesser-acculturated Asian Americans with limited linguistic abilities, one could attempt to utilize an interpreter, but may have to rely more on assessment of related domains, such as IQ and functional abilities. Finally, and most importantly, especially in light of the lack of research for Asian Americans on measures of criminal competency, the evaluator has an ethical obligation to include a discussion of these limitations in their findings.

Capacity

Forensic assessment in civil litigation includes a spectrum of domains. It can be a singular ability including capacity to consent to research; engage in contracts or make wills; to make treatment-related decisions, parent, etc. However, assessments in the civil litigation can also require an assessor to recommend a broader denial of civil rights (including institutionalization) based on a more general appraisal of dangerousness and/or grave disability (Grisso, 2003; Melton et al., 2007). The majority of these assessments all share common domains that consist primarily of an appraisal of intellectual/cognitive abilities, mental health, and personality with some measure of functional performance for the specific domain of interest (Grisso, 2003). The comprehensive capacity evaluation, similar to a competency evaluation, also includes a psychosocial history. For example, a testamentary capacity evaluation would likely include intellectual assessment to include a brief or full intellectual capacity evaluation, an achievement measure, and a functional assessment of the constructs of testamentary knowledge. Melton and colleagues (2007) suggested that to assess testamentary knowledge, interview questions that relate to the individual's knowledge of the reason for a will; what constitutes property; the consequences of distributing property (e.g., will others have use of an object or to what extent will the inheritance of an object impact an individual); and those who may or should expect an inheritance (e.g., an assessment of why or why not an individual was included in the will, such as a significant caretaking role or close familial relationship) should be included.

The assessment of a domain like intellect may involve simply a mental status evaluation to screen for sensory and cognitive deficits before moving on to the domain of interest, or it could consist of a formal assessment of IQ (for considerations specific to the assessment of IQ) and/or specific assessment of mental health symptoms (e.g., a semi-structured interview like the SCID). The principles of forensic assessment of capacity differ from competency primarily based upon the functional domain (e.g., parenting skills for parental capacity, financial or contract-related functional abilities as they relate to testamentary capacity). Given the level of specificity in this domain there is even less empirical information specific to assessment of the individual capacities for Asian Americans, and the scope of the discussion for how to construct an assessment for these various capacities is beyond the bounds of a single chapter. Thus, it is recommended that for assessments of specific capacities for Asian Americans, one refer to a forensic assessment text (such as that of Melton et al., 2007), and utilize the recommendations for cultural adaptations discussed in the relevant chapters of this text (for example referring to the chapter on structured or semi-structured interviews when an interview is included as part of the assessment).

A key consideration when conducting an assessment of capacity is the atypical presentation for symptoms of mental illness (discussed elsewhere in this chapter as well as specific chapters in this text; for example a greater endorsement for somatic symptoms of anxiety; Gordon & Teachman, 2008) as well as the general desire for social conformity. Thus, for Asian Americans, there tends to be a general lack of acknowledgement for socially atypical thoughts or behaviors like symptoms of mental illness as well as a general deference to authority (Yeh & Yeh, 2002).

Mental Injury

Civil litigation for mental injury differs from the criminal aspects of competency, criminal responsibility, and risk assessments. It is distinct because the individual who is being assessed is seeking compensation for a mental or cognitive disorder that they believe was incurred as the result of the action(s) of another. This means that the evaluator is tasked with identifying the injury, the etiology of the injury, the severity of the injury, and the prognosis for the injury. These are all necessary components in a civil tort related to *Extreme Emotional Distress* (EED), a legal construct. The challenge for the evaluator is reconciling a historically difficult task of quantifying psychological constructs with the legal constructs necessary for civil litigation related to EED.

General Legal Construct for Mental Injury

While allegations of mental injury are addressed in the civil courts, the case can arise out of occurrences from both civil and criminal incidents. For example, Posttraumatic Stress Disorder (PTSD) can result from a near drowning in an unsupervised swimming pool (civil), as well as from an attempted homicide or sexual assault (criminal). These examples also illustrate a further delineation between negligence (simply not covering your pool) and intentional infliction (assault). Civil tort law is again a setting where traditional constructs of psychological assessment must be applied to forensic constructs that are not always convergent (Gerbasi, 2004); in order to win a case for mental injury, the injured party must demonstrate that the defendant engaged in behavior that was so extreme or outrageous it led to the mental injury. Thus sticking with our example, demonstrating that it would be outrageous (perhaps because your HOA has rules that require a pool cover or perhaps ordinances that dictate a pool cover, that leaving your pool uncovered was extreme or outrageous behavior). The forensic psychologist must, for this referral question, find a means to find concordance for psychological constructs of mental illness and legal constructs such as extreme (which at least allows for some statistical interpretation based on a normal distribution curve) and outrageous as well as the all-important constructs of clinically significant with the preponderance of the evidence. Specifically, psychologists can be of help in defining the nature of the injury, liability, nonfinancial loss, past financial losses, future fiscal losses, future financial costs, and mental capacity and also in explaining how the person has been affected by the injury (Benuto, Leany, & Cirlugea, 2013).

Normative Standard vs. Self-Standard

Typically two types of comparisons can be made when assessing for damages as they relate to personal injury—the normative standard and the self-standard (Lanham & Misukanis, 1999). Lanham and Misukanis discussed how when using the normative standard of comparison a client's test scores are compared to the scores of a group of people with similar demographic factors. The goal of the normative standard is to examine the client's functioning as it relates to a normative group. Conversely with the self-standard of comparison, the client's post-injury performance is assessed relative to their pre-injury functioning. To utilize the self-standard of comparison, a record review should be conducted including reviewing mental health records, medical records, work and school records, etc. (Witt & Weitz, 2007).

Using the self-standard of comparison could be useful with Asian American clients as it makes use of the client's "baseline" functioning prior to the injury. Thus, despite that Asian clients have been documented to underreport symptoms (Yeh & Yeh, 2002) or to endorse more somatic complaints (Gordon & Teachman, 2008), with the self-standard this would be somewhat irrelevant as the evaluator would be looking at changes from pre- to post-injury. Conversely the normative standard does call for some additional culture-specific caveats.

There are no standard measures for the assessment of mental injury. However, these injuries typically result from both physical and mental stimuli and can include, but are not limited to, generally anxiety-based disorders, mood disorders, traumatic brain injury (TBI), and adjustment disorders (Melton et al., 2007). With regard to these and the normative self-standard it is important that the evaluator keep in mind that Asian Americans may endorse more somatic complaints rather than cognitive ones (Gordon & Teachman, 2008); many of the Asian cultures have specific anxiety disorders that some argue are a culture-specific presentation of an anxiety disorder that could be diagnosed within a Westernized taxonomy (Hinton et al., 2001; Lin, 1983). Consistent with this, Asian Americans report a lower prevalence of actual anxiety disorders (Asnaani, Richey, Dimaite, Hinton, & Hofmans, 2010) and depression (Takeuchi et al., 1998; Takeuchi, Hong, Gile, & Alegría, 2007) than the general U.S. population and may be more likely to endorse somatic complaints (Mak & Zane, 2004). Put simply, if an Asian client presents with a personal injury it is important to keep in mind that their injury may indeed be substantial even when resulting symptomology is not extraordinarily high as the baseline for Asian Americans and the display of symptomology is lower than that of the general population.

Summary of Mental Injury Assessment

Because the specific assessments of the constructs that are typically assessed in a personal injury evaluation (e.g., neuropsychological insult, anxiety, depression) are discussed extensively elsewhere in this text, specific measures were not discussed here. Nonetheless, there are concrete cultural considerations that should be made when assessing mental injury for Asian Americans. First, there are a number of traditional measures that can objectively quantify the possible mental disorders resulting from EED including various measures of depression and anxiety. There are two standards for assessing for damages as they relate to personal injury—the normative standard and the self-standard (Lanham & Misukanis, 1999). While the latter compares the client's post-injury status to pre-injury status (calling for less cultural accommodations), when using the normative standard the evaluator should keep in mind norms that are specific to the Asian population. Lastly, the use of collateral contacts with the measures discussed in the chapters on anxiety, depression, and neuropsychological assessment can be effectively used to determine the emotional impact of an injury on the Asian client.

Summary

The paradox between the high stakes nature of forensic assessment and the relative dearth of information specific to forensic assessment of Asian Americans is an issue. There is clearly greater information available for discreet components of the overall assessment. For example, there is a good deal of research specific to Asian Americans, related to intellectual and cognitive assessment as well as specific mental health constructs like PTSD and depression. However there is less (or no) empirical data for the more consequential constructs of competency, criminal responsibility, and risk assessment.

Hicks (2004) provided a review of the responsibilities of a forensic evaluator with regard to cultural competency and makes recommendations that specifically address the importance and weight of an expert's testimony in the courtroom, as well as highlights areas of bias. These recommendations are not specific to Asian Americans, but should be reviewed by any evaluator working with nondominant culture populations. Hicks (2004) provided sound recommendations specific to the forensic setting that mirror recommendations for other domains such as general clinical practice and neuropsychological assessment that are specifically aimed at providing services to Asian Americans (Wong & Fujii, 2004). These include providing services either bilingually or in the preferred language of the individual being assessed, using assessments that have been appropriately validated with the specific population being assessed, as well as the seeking of consultation and frank, open identification and discussion of possible biases with other professionals. Finally, many of the above sections include a discussion of the familial and cultural values for Asian American families that are inconsistent with those of Western cultures. Consideration of acculturation and those specific cultural attitudes toward parenting, extra-familial relationships, and mental health must be considered and discussed in forensic evaluations.

References

Abidin, R. R., & Konold, T. R. (1999). *Parenting alliance measure*. Odessa, FL: Psychological Assessment Resources.

American Psychological Association. (2012). Specialty guidelines for forensic psychology. *American Psychologist, 68*(1), 7–19. doi:10.1037/a0029889.

Archer, R. P., Buffington-Vollum, J. K., Stredny, R. V., & Handel, R. W. (2006). A survey of psychological test use patterns among forensic psychologists. *Journal of Personality Assessment, 87*(1), 84–94.

Asnaani, A., Richey, A., Dimaite, R., Hinton, E. E., & Hofmans, S. G. (2010). A cross-ethnic comparison of lifetime prevalence rates of anxiety disorders. *Journal of Nervous Mental Disorders, 198*, 551–555.

Benuto, L. T., Leany, B. D., & Cirlugea, O. (2013). Forensic assessment with the Hispanic client. In L. T. Benuto (Ed.), *Guide to psychological assessment with Hispanics* (pp. 389–411). New York, NY: Springer.

Buri, J. R. (1991). Parental authority questionnaire. *Journal of Personality Assessment, 57*(1), 110–119.

Caldwell, B. M., & Bradley, R. H. (1984). *Home observation for measurement of the environment*. Little Rock: University of Arkansas at Little Rock.

Caldwell, B. M., & Bradley, R. H. (2003). *Home observation for measurement of the environment: Administration manual*. Tempe, AZ: Family & Human Dynamics Research Institute, Arizona State University.

Caspi, A., Moffitt, T. E., Morgan, J, Taylor A., Arseneault L., Tully L., … Polo-Tomas, M. (2004). Maternal expressed emotion predicts children's antisocial behavior problems: Using monozygotic-twin differences to identify environmental effects on behavioral development. *Developmental Psychology, 40*(2), 149–161.

Chou, K. L. (2000). Assessing Chinese adolescents' social support: The multidimensional scale of perceived social support. *Personality and Individual Differences, 28*(2), 299–307. http://dx.doi.org/10.1016/S0191-8869(99)00098-7

Cuéllar, I., & Paniagua, F. A. (2000). *Handbook of multicultural mental health*. San Diego, CA: Academic Press.

Everington, C., & Luckasson, R. (1992). *The competence assessment for standing trial for defendants with mental retardation (CAST-MR)*. Worthington, OH: IDS.

Fantuzzo, J., Tighe, E., & Childs, S. (2000). Family involvement questionnaire: A multivariate assessment of family participation in early childhood education. *Journal of Educational Psychology, 92*(2), 367.

Fox, R. A. (1994). *Parent behavior checklist manual*. Austin, TX: ProEd.

Gerard, A. B. (1994). *Parent-child relationship inventory*. Los Angeles, CA: Western Psychological Services.

Gerbasi, J. B. (2004). Forensic assessment in personal injury litigation. In R. I. Simon, L. H. Gold, & R. I. Simon (Eds.), *The American Psychiatric Publishing textbook of forensic psychiatry* (pp. 231–261). Arlington, VA: American Psychiatric Publishing.

Gibaud-Wallston, J., & Wandersman, L. P. (1978). *Development and utility of the parenting sense of competence scale*. Paper presented at the meeting of the American Psychological Association, Toronto.

Gordon, T. L., & Teachman, B. A. (2008). Ethnic group differences in affective, behavioral, and cognitive markers of anxiety. *Journal of Cross-Cultural Psychology, 39*(4), 424–446.

Grisso, T. (2003). *Evaluating competencies: Forensic assessments and instruments* (2nd ed.). New York, NY: Kluwer Academic/Plenum.

Grych, J. H., Seid, M., & Fincham, F. D. (1992). Assessing marital conflict from the child's perspective: The children's perception of interparental conflict scale. *Child Development, 63*(3), 558–572.

Hicks, J. W. (2004). Ethnicity, race, and forensic psychiatry: Are we color-blind? *Journal of American Academy Psychiatry Law, 32*, 21–33.

Hinton, D. E., Chau, H., Nguyen, L., Nguyen, M., Pham, T., Quinn, S., et al. (2001). Panic disorder among Vietnamese refugees attending a psychiatric clinic: Prevalence and subtypes. *General Hospital Psychiatry, 23*, 337–344.

Jette, A. M., Davies, A. R., Cleary, P. D., Calkins, D. R., Rubenstein, L. V., Fink, A., … Delbanco, T. L. (1986). The functional status questionnaire. *Journal of General Internal Medicine, 1*(3), 143–149.

Konold, T. R., & Abidin, R. R. (2001). Parenting alliance: A multifactor perspective. *Assessment, 9*(1), 47–65.

Lanham, R. A., & Misukanis, T. (1999). Estimating premorbid intelligence: Determining change in cognition following brain injury. *Brain Injury Source, 3*(3), 42–43.

Lin, K. M. (1983). Hwa-Byung: A Korean culture-bound syndrome. *American Journal of Psychiatry, 140*(1), 105–107.

Mak, W. W. S., & Zane, N. W. S. (2004). The phenomenon of somatization among community Chinese Americans. *Social Psychiatry & Psychiatric Epidemiology, 39*, 967–974. doi:10.1007/s00127-004-0827-4.

McGarry, A. L. (1973). *Competency to stand trial and mental illness*. Washington, DC: U.S. Government Printing Office.

McIntyre, L. L. (2008). Parent training for young children with developmental disabilities: Randomized controlled trial. *American Journal on Mental Retardation, 113*(5), 356–368.

Medora, N. P., Wilson, S., & Larson, J. H. (2001). Attitudes toward parenting strategies, potential for child abuse, and parental satisfaction of ethnically diverse low-income US mothers. *The Journal of Social Psychology, 141*(3), 335–348.

Melton, G. B., Petrila, J., Poythress, N. G., & Slobogin, C. (Eds.). (2007). *Psychological evaluations for the courts: A handbook for mental health professionals and lawyers* (3rd ed.). New York, NY: The Guilford Press.

Mendez, J. L., Carpenter, J. L., LaForett, D. R., & Cohen, J. S. (2009). Parental engagement and barriers to participation in a community-based preventive intervention. *American Journal of Community Psychology, 44*(1–2), 1–14.

Milner, J. S. (1989). Additional cross-validation of the child abuse potential inventory. *Psychological Assessment, 1*(3), 219.

National Research Council. (2001). *Eager to learn: Educating our preschoolers*. Washington, DC: National Academy Press.

Poythress, N., Nicholson, R., Otto, R. K., Edens, J. F., Bonnie, R. J., Monahan, J., et al. (1999). *The MacArthur competence assessment tool–criminal adjudication: Professional manual*. Odessa, FL: Psychological Assessment Resources.

Roesch, R., Zapf, P. A., & Eaves, D. (2006). *Fitness interview test—Revised: A structured interview for assessing competency to stand trial*. Sarasota, FL: Professional Resource Press.

Roesch, R., Zapf, P. A., Golding, S. L., & Skeem, J. L. (1999). Defining and assessing competency to stand trial. In A. K. Hess, I. B. Weiner, A. K. Hess, & I. B. Weiner (Eds.), *The handbook of forensic psychology* (2nd ed., pp. 327–349). Hoboken, NJ: John Wiley & Sons.

Rockhill, C. M., Stoep, A. V., McCauley, E., & Katon, W. J. (2009). Social competence and social support as mediators between comorbid depressive and conduct problems and functional outcomes in middle school students. *Journal of Adolescence, 32*(3), 535–553.

Rogers, R., Tillbrook, C. E., & Sewell, K. W. (2004). *Evaluation of competency to stand trial-revised (ECST-R)*. Odessa, FL: Psychological Assessment Resources.

Rothbaum, F., & Weisz, J. R. (1994). Parental caregiving and child externalizing behavior in nonclinical samples: A meta-analysis. *Psychological Bulletin, 116*(1), 55–74.

Stevens, M. J., Kwan, K., & Graybill, D. F. (1993). Comparison of MMPI-2 scores of foreign Chinese and Caucasian-American students. *Journal of Clinical Psychology, 49*(1), 23–27.

Takeuchi, D. T., Chung, R. C. Y., Lin, K. M., Shen, H., Kurasaki, K., Chun, C. A., et al. (1998). Lifetime and twelve-month prevalence rates of major depressive episodes and dysthymia among Chinese Americans in Los Angeles. *American Journal of Psychiatry, 155*(10), 1407–1414.

Takeuchi, D. T., Hong, S., Gile, K., & Alegría, M. (2007). Developmental contexts and mental disorders among Asian Americans. *Research in Human Development, 4*, 49–69.

Tolle, L. W., & O'Donohue, W. (2012). *Improving the quality of child custody evaluations: A systematic model*. New York, NY: Springer.

Tsai, D. C., & Pike, P. L. (2000). Effects of acculturation on the MMPI-2 scores of Asian American students. *Journal of Personality Assessment, 74*(2), 216–230.

Tschann, J. M., Flores, E., Marin, B. V., Pasch, L. A., Baisch, E. M., & Wibbelsman, C. J. (2002). Interparental conflict and risk behaviors among Mexican American adolescents: A cognitive-emotional model. *Journal of Abnormal Child Psychology, 30*(4), 373–385.

U.S. Department of Education. (2000, September). Strategic plan, 2001–2005. Washington, DC: Author.

Wildman, R. W., Batchelor, E. S., Thompson, L., Nelson, F. R., Moore, J. T., Patterson, M. E., & deLaosa, M. (1978). *The Georgia court competency test: An attempt to develop a rapid, quantitative measure of fitness for trial* (Unpublished manuscript). Milledgeville, GA: Forensic Services Division, Central State Hospital.

Witt, P. H., & Weitz, S. E. (2007). Personal injury evaluations in motor vehicle accident cases. *Journal of Psychiatry & Law, 35*(1), 3–24.

Wong, T. M., & Fujii, D. E. (2004). Neuropsychological assessment with Asian-Americans: Demographic factors, culture diversity, and practical guidelines. *Applied Neuropsychology, 11*, 23–36.

Wu, P.-C., & Chang, L. (2008). Psychometric properties of the Chinese version of the Beck Depression Inventory-II using the Rasch Model. *Measurement and Evaluation in Counseling and Development, 41*, 13–31.

Yee, B. W., Huang, L. N., & Lew, A. (1998). Life-span socialization in a cultural context. In L. C. Lee & N. W. S. Zane (Eds.), *Handbook of Asian American psychology* (pp. 83–135). Thousand Oaks, CA: Sage.

Yeh, M., & Yeh, J. (2002). The clinical assessment of Asian American children. In K. S. Kurasaki, S. Okazaki, & S. Sue (Eds.), *Asian American mental health: Assessment theories and methods* (pp. 233–249). New York, NY: Kluwer Academic/Plenum.

Yeung, A., Howarth, S., Chan, R., Sonawalla, S., Nierenberg, A. A., & Fava, M. (2002). Use of the Chinese version of the Beck Depression Inventory for screening depression in primary care. *The Journal of Nervous and Mental Disease, 190*(2), 94–99.

Zimet, G. D., Dahlem, N. W., Zimet, S. G., & Farley, G. K. (1988). The multidimensional scale of perceived social support. *Journal of Personality Assessment, 52*(1), 30–41.

Index

L.T. Benuto et al. (eds.), *Guide to Psychological Assessment with Asians*,
DOI 10.1007/978-1-4939-0796-0, © Springer Science+Business Media New York 2014

MIX
Papier aus verantwortungsvollen Quellen
Paper from responsible sources
FSC® C105338

If you have any concerns about our products,
you can contact us on
ProductSafety@springernature.com

In case Publisher is established outside the EU,
the EU authorized representative is:
Springer Nature Customer Service Center GmbH
Europaplatz 3, 69115 Heidelberg, Germany

Printed by Libri Plureos GmbH
in Hamburg, Germany